Biology Today
Second Edition

Biology Today
Second Edition

Academic Adviser and Principal Author
David Kirk *Washington University*

Editor and Rewriter
Cecie Starr *Del Mar, California*

CRM
RANDOM HOUSE

Biology Today Second Edition Book Team

Cecie Starr *Publisher, Editor, and Rewriter*
Jackie Estrada *Copy-Editing Department
    Manager and Coeditor*
Susan Harter *Associate Editor*
Donald Fujimoto *Art Director*
Cynthia Bassett *Designer*
Kurt Kolbe *Assistant Designer*
Shelagh Dalton Tennyson *Photographic Editor
    and Permissions Editor*
Victoria Self *Production Supervisor*
Roger Romito *Product Development Manager*
Gretchen Gines *Book Team Coordinator*

Second Edition
9 8 7 6 5 4 3 2 1

Library of Congress Catalog Card Number: 74–21782
ISBN: 0-394-31093-4
Manufactured in the United States of America

Overview of Chapter Sequence

Contents

Section III
The Unity of Life

Section IV
The Continuity of Life

Biology Today
Second Edition

Section I

The Study of Life

What is life? What is this property we share with all other organisms—a property that sets us apart from what we perceive as nonliving things in the world around us? In coming to understand why there is no simple answer to this question, we will be joining those who have asked the question before. We, too, will be studying the phenomenon of life at levels ranging from the interactions of molecules to the interactions of organisms of many varied types within the biosphere. At each such level of complexity, we will find part of the answer, and once we have explored all the various levels, we will have acquired some insight into a story of magnificent dimensions. But before we seek out these cumulative answers to the greater question, we must know what sort of questions may be profitably asked at each level. What kinds of questions have others asked? How have others decided whether a question is meaningful or not? What have they accepted as satisfactory answers? And how have they decided whether an answer is, in fact, acceptable? In short, we will find it useful to examine at the outset of our journey the principles that have guided others in their search and to know how those principles have been derived.

Chapter 1

Defining the Characteristics of Life

Where in the continuum of history does modern biology begin? The beliefs of the past thread inextricably into the understandings of the present, and we continue to draw upon the accumulation of human experience that has carried us to our current perspectives in this field of inquiry.

Biology (bī ol′ ə jē), n. *the science of life or living matter in all its forms and phenomena.*
(The Random House Dictionary of the English Language)

Those of us who are in the habit of pulling a dictionary off the shelf when we encounter a word we do not fully understand often find ourselves trapped into looking up a definition of the definition. Sometimes the search is exasperating, particularly when, having looked up definitions of all the additional words that must be understood in order to understand the first definition, we suddenly realize we have lost sight of what it was we had originally hoped to define.

The word "biology" is like that. Look it up in any dictionary and you find a definition similar to the one given above. But such a definition of "biology" is deceptively simple. Consider the problem in formulating even something as essential to the definition as the dividing line between living and nonliving systems. Although it may be impossible to define precisely why one thing is considered alive and something else is not, we all have an inherent awareness that some kind of difference is involved. Is it found in the composition of living and nonliving things? In their structure? In their behavior, perhaps? These and many other related questions have been asked throughout the span of human existence, and the answers have changed considerably with the passing of time. But it is only recently that we have come to the realization that a sharp dividing line between living and nonliving systems may not even exist. That we have arrived at this understanding, however, does not necessarily mean that the issue is closed. A look at the history leading up to this understanding will show why. It shows us that the extent to which answers can be formulated is limited by the prevailing knowledge and observations of the time—whether that time be today or centuries past.

IS LIFE GENERATED SPONTANEOUSLY FROM NONLIVING MATTER?

From the time of the early Greek philosophers through the seventeenth century, many educated people believed that living organisms are generated spontaneously and continuously from nonliving matter. They saw frogs and insects emerging from the mud after a spring rain; they watched worms and maggots crawling out of decaying meat; and surely that was proof enough for their belief. Spontaneous generation was a "fact of life" supported by centuries of common awareness and thus known to be "true." Adher-

ents to this idea suggested that the boundary between the living and the nonliving must therefore be subtle and readily crossed.

Then, in 1668, a series of brilliant experiments challenged this widespread belief. Francesco Redi, whose work is still cited as an example of careful scientific investigation, showed that worms arise in decaying meat only if adult insects lay their eggs in the meat *(Interleaf 1.1)*. Soon, other researchers showed that aphids, fleas, lice, and the larvae in plant galls are produced only from eggs laid by adult animals.

For a short time the theory of spontaneous generation of living creatures was discredited. Then, in 1676, Antony van Leeuwenhoek peered at a drop of water through a microscope he had devised, and he discovered an amazing world

(text continues on page 6)

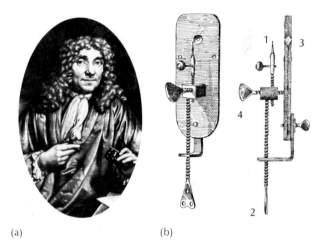

(a)   (b)

Figure 1.2   (a) Antony van Leeuwenhoek and (b) one of the microscopes he constructed. The sample to be examined was placed on the apparatus at (1), brought into position vertically by turning the lower screw (2), and moved toward or away from the lens (3) by turning the shorter screw (4). Lenses were known in ancient times and were used by Arabian mathematicians; lenses were being constructed in Europe in the thirteenth century. Galileo, in the beginning of the seventeenth century, made the earliest biological observation with the first true microscope when he examined the compound eye of an insect. Later, Johann Kepler and Christian Huygens would work out the optical properties of the "Galilean microscope." But in 1676 Leeuwenhoek added an entirely new dimension to the science of microscopy when he peered through a microscope of his own making and caught a glimpse of a bacterium. Not until the nineteenth century would microscopes be improved enough to provide additional information about these organisms.

Interleaf 1.1

Francesco Redi's Experiments on Spontaneous Generation of Insects: A Model of Scientific Procedure

Francesco Redi (1626–1698) of Italy was a distinguished scholar, philologist, physician, and poet, as well as a naturalist of wide interests. As a scientist, he is best known for a series of experiments that showed conclusively that maggots are not spontaneously generated in decaying meat. In 1668, scientists had little understanding of either the importance of experimentation or the manner in which experiments are carried out. Redi's work is significant not only because of his conclusions but because he designed his experiments so carefully that there could be little doubt his conclusions were correct. The following quotations from Redi's report are taken from a translation by Bigelow.

Redi began with a simple observation to test the belief that "the putrescence of a dead body, or the filth of any sort of decayed matter engenders worms." He obtained three dead snakes ("the kind called eels of Aesculapius") and put them in an open box to decay. "Not long afterwards I saw that they were covered with worms of a conical shape and apparently without legs. These worms were intent on devouring the meat, increasing meanwhile in size, and from day to day I observed that they likewise increased in number;

but, although of the same shape, they differed in size, having been born on different days."

After they had consumed all the meat, leaving only the bones, the worms disappeared; apparently they had escaped from the box. To discover what happened to them, Redi repeated the experiment, this time carefully sealing all holes through which the worms might escape. After three days, when the decaying meat became covered with worms, Redi noted this time that there were two different kinds of worms. Although they were alike in form, one kind was large and white and the other kind was smaller and pink. When the meat was gone, the worms tried to escape from the box but were unable to do so. "On the nineteenth day of the same month some of the worms ceased all movements, as if they were asleep, and appeared to shrink and gradually to assume a shape like an egg. On the twentieth day all the worms had assumed the egg shape, and had taken on a golden white color, turning to red, which in some darkened, becoming almost black. At this point the red, as well as the black ones, changed from soft to hard, resembling somewhat those chrysalides formed by caterpillars, silkworms, and similar insects."

Redi separated the red and black egg-shape objects and put them in glass vessels sealed with paper. After eight days, each of the red objects broke open, "and from each came forth a fly of gray color, torpid and dull, misshapen as if half finished, with closed wings; but after a few minutes they commenced to unfold and to expand in exact proportion to the tiny body, which also in the meantime had acquired symmetry in all its parts. Then the whole creature, as if made anew, having lost its gray color, took on a most brilliant and vivid green; and the whole body had expanded and grown so that it seemed incredible that it could ever have been contained in the small shell." The black objects broke open after fourteen days "to produce certain large black flies striped with white, having a hairy abdomen, of the kind that we see daily buzzing about butcher stalls."

Redi concluded that the worms had to be the immature forms of flies and he "began to believe that all worms found in meat were derived directly from the droppings of flies, and not from the putrefaction of the meat." He remembered seeing both the green and the large black flies hovering over the meat before the worms appeared. To test this new hypothesis, Redi set up another experiment, for "Belief would be vain without the confirmation of experiment."

He prepared four large, wide-mouthed flasks, each containing a different kind of meat: snake, fish, eel, and milk-fed veal. Each of the flasks was carefully closed and sealed. Then Redi prepared an identical set of flasks, but he left this set open. Within a few days the meat in the open flasks became covered with worms, and flies were seen freely entering and leaving the open flasks. However, "in the closed flasks I did not see a worm, though many days had passed since the dead flesh had been put in them. Outside on the paper cover there was now and then a deposit, or a maggot that eagerly sought some crevice by which to enter and obtain nourishment. Meanwhile the different things placed in the flasks had become putrid . . ."

This experiment is notable because it represents one of the earliest examples of the deliberate use of a *control group* in a biological experiment. Redi prepared two identical sets of flasks. One set was open and the other was sealed. By using various kinds of meat, he was able to test the effect of another variable. He found that the appearance of worms occurred only in open flasks but was not dependent on the kind of meat used. Redi repeated his experiment many times, using different kinds of vessels and different kinds of meat and keeping the vessels under different weather conditions at different seasons of the year. He even tried burying pieces of meat underground. *The results were always consistent with his hypothesis.* Worms appeared in decaying meat only if adult flies were able to place their droppings on the meat. He even tried using dead maggots and flies as the meat in the flasks, and he observed the same results.

Although these experiments might seem to offer indisputable evidence that worms cannot arise in dead flesh of any kind unless flies are allowed to make deposits in the flesh, Redi recognized another possible interpretation of his observations. In every case, the sealing of the meat to prevent the entry of flies had also prevented the free entry and circulation of air. It could be argued that only the lack of fresh air kept maggots from arising spontaneously in the sealed meat samples.

Therefore, Redi set up another experiment. He put samples of meat and fish in a large vase covered tightly with a fine veil through which air could circulate but with holes too small for the passage of flies. He put the vase inside a framework covered with the same kind of netting. "I never saw any worms in the meat, though many were to be seen moving about on the net-covered frame. These, attracted by the odor of the meat, succeeded at last in penetrating the fine meshes and would have entered the vase had I not speedily removed them."

Redi's report is a model of good scientific procedure in several respects. Not only were his experiments cleverly designed to provide unambiguous tests of his hypotheses, he described exactly what he did and what results he observed and he separated his interpretations and beliefs from the factual accounting of the experiments. Science has been built upon this sort of reporting. Each investigator is expected to describe his work and observations meticulously, without letting his own ideas or beliefs color the facts. Others may disagree with his interpretations, but their own theories must be consistent with his experimental observations.

populated with tiny organisms. He examined other drops of broth and water and found that they all were teeming with life forms—with microorganisms that eventually would become known as bacteria, yeasts, and protozoans. They were so much smaller and simpler in appearance than other known organisms that their spontaneous generation seemed quite plausible. Although Leeuwenhoek himself believed that microorganisms were distributed by air- and water-borne ''seeds,'' others regarded microorganisms as products of spontaneous generation. The controversy that had been settled so definitely by Redi's experiments started all over again.

For two centuries, controversy raged over whether these microorganisms arose spontaneously where life had not existed before. Some experimenters found that filtering, boiling, or chemically treating the samples of broth or water would rid them of live microorganisms. But in some experiments new microorganisms often appeared in spite of the most thorough attempts to prevent contamination of the sample by living microorganisms.

Finally, in the early nineteenth century, Lazzaro Spallanzani and Theodor Schwann showed that organisms do not appear in a broth that has been heated to the temperature of boiling water for nearly an hour, *if* all air reaching the broth has been similarly heated. Proponents of spontaneous generation could argue only that the heated air was somehow damaged and inadequate for the support of life. Schwann countered this argument by showing that heated air is suitable for breathing.

In 1861 Louis Pasteur finally put to rest the question of whether life could arise spontaneously under the conditions that now exist on our planet. By using a simple filtration technique, Pasteur first demonstrated that the surrounding air abounds with living microorganisms. He then boiled broth to destroy preexisting microorganisms in it and showed that it did not generate new microorganisms (in other words, ferment) if he removed airborne particles by filtering the air coming in contact with the broth.

Perhaps Pasteur's most crucial experiment was one in which he placed fermentable substances in flasks and then drew the neck of each flask out into a long, narrow S shape. Air could enter and leave the flask through the narrow opening, but any particles in the air were likely to be trapped on the walls of the long, curving neck. The flasks and their contents were heated to the temperature of boiling water for some time, then left sitting in still air. No fermentation was observed in the flasks. However, if the necks were broken so that atmospheric dust and other small

Figure 1.3 Lazzaro Spallanzani, one of the investigators whose experiments contradicted the theory of spontaneous generation, which for centuries was the rallying point for investigators who believed that living organisms arise spontaneously from nonliving matter.

Figure 1.4 Louis Pasteur, whose experiments resolved the debates over the nature of fermentation and decay by proving conclusively that even microorganisms cannot arise spontaneously. Pasteur became interested in microorganisms as a result of his work on such practical problems as the souring of milk and the making of wine. He isolated the substance that produces lactic acid in the souring of milk; the substance turned out to be a mass of bacteria. He then turned to the study of the alcoholic fermentation of sugar as it occurs in the process of wine making. He found that the fermentation depends on the presence of certain yeasts or molds that live on the skins of ripened grapes.

Pasteur's study of the defects of some wines convinced him that a number of different organisms, including some kinds of bacteria, participate in the fermentation process and that these organisms must be present in the proper proportions if a good wine is to be formed. Through further experiments (discussed in the text) he then confirmed that both fermentation and decay are the results of activity carried out by microorganisms that reach foods and dead flesh largely in the form of tiny airborne "germs." The legacy Pasteur left the world was enormous. It ranged from the definitive studies on spontaneous generation discussed here to a process for preventing the souring of milk, as well as what has been (until recently) the only effective treatment for rabies. Both of these processes still bear his name, as one of mankind's small tributes to his genius.

particles could enter with the air, the contents began to ferment within a few hours and microorganisms soon abounded in the liquid. Although this experiment did not immediately convince all the proponents of spontaneous generation that they were wrong, it did carry great weight with the majority of the scientific community. Within twenty years after the publication of Pasteur's work, the idea of spontaneous generation had essentially been abandoned.

By the end of the nineteenth century there was general agreement that life cannot arise from the nonliving under conditions that now exist upon our planet. The dictum "All life from preexisting life" became the dogma of modern biology, from which no reasonable man could be expected to dissent.

A "VITAL FORCE" IS PROPOSED AS THE SECRET OF LIFE

Even as the line of inquiry around the notion of spontaneous generation was evolving, another line of investigation was being made into the nature of the substance of life and nonlife. From ancient times, living and nonliving matter had been thought to differ only in the proportions of what were considered the four basic elements: earth, air, fire, and water. By the eighteenth century, this notion began to change drastically when experiments began to reveal the true nature and number of the elements that are the basic building blocks of matter. Yet the fact remained that all the elements found in living matter were also found in nonliving matter. Indeed, Antoine Lavoisier gave strong evidence for the essential similarity of the chemistry of the living and the nonliving. In a classic set of experiments, he showed that animals "burned" simple foodstuffs to produce exactly the *same* products and the *same* amount of heat that he himself produced by burning those substances in a test tube.

By the early nineteenth century it was firmly established that living things are composed largely of four elements found also in nonliving matter: carbon, hydrogen, oxygen, and nitrogen. (Other elements were found in living things but none were unique to them.) Reinforced as it was by the downfall of the concept of spontaneous generation, this knowledge pointed to a seeming paradox—life arises only from the living, yet it is composed of exactly the same elements found in abundance in the nonliving. What, then, does life inherit from prior life that cannot be obtained from the nonliving? The explanation that seemed to be the most logical actually had been expressed, in various forms, for many centuries. According to this explanation, the difference would not be detectable as a unique set of chemical elements because the difference was considered to be nonmaterial. A separate force—a "vital force"—was said to exist in living things and could be obtained only from something already possessing it. That is why life derives only from life.

This "vital force" was given apparent chemical reality by the observations and inferences of the nineteenth-century chemists. While acknowledging that living matter is composed of elements found also in the nonliving, these chemists were confronted with certain anomalies in the behavior of those substances. For example, the substances that make up the earth, the sea, and the atmosphere are relatively *stable*. Water can be frozen to become ice or boiled to become vapor, but it always can be returned to its original liquid form by reversing the procedure that changed it. Metals, salts, and other minerals also can be melted, even vaporized, but they will recrystallize into their original form when they are cooled. In contrast, most of the substances making up living organisms are very *unstable*. When materials such as wood and sugar are heated, they char and burn. These two processes are not readily reversible; the ashes and smoke that result cannot be restored to the original material by cooling or by any simple chemical process.

It was because of this difference in behavior that early-nineteenth-century chemists suggested that the substances derived from living organisms be called **organic** and that all other substances be called **inorganic.** They assumed that only living organisms have the power to create "organic" matter. What could this power be? They felt it was the "vital force" that can be imparted to matter only by another living thing. Such a view became a central feature of the concept known as **vitalism.**

MECHANISTS CHALLENGE THE VITALISTIC VIEW

Even while the notion of vitalism was being developed, however, it received a damaging blow from an unexpected quarter. In 1828 a German chemist, Friedrich Wöhler, was studying the *inorganic* substance ammonium cyanate. Wöhler analyzed the crystals that are produced when this substance is heated. He was startled to find that the crystals were urea, the major solid component of mammalian urine and a substance definitely considered to be *organic.*

Stimulated by Wöhler's accomplishment, other chemists attempted to create organic substances from inorganic materials. Reports of their successes soon began to accumulate. By the late 1850s, Pierre Berthelot had succeeded in producing such organic substances as alcohols, methane, acetylene, and benzene from inorganic chemicals. Clearly, at least the simpler organic substances could be produced without the addition of a "vital force."

Vitalism, however, was not completely discredited by the accomplishments of the organic chemists. Many biologists still felt that the more complex organic substances that play important roles in living systems could not be synthesized outside a living organism. Scientific opinion split into two camps. Many continued to attribute to life a force (or property) not found in nonliving matter. At the same time, others took the position that the "vital force" was just a mask for ignorance. They held that life could ultimately be explained in terms of chemical and physical laws common to both the living and the nonliving. Using an analogy that had relevance during the machine age of Western society, they often spoke of living systems as being merely highly complex mechanical systems; hence adherents to this view were called **mechanists.**

A modified form of mechanism has become the predominant approach, primarily because it has proved to be so successful. During this century particularly, the amazing discoveries that physicists and chemists have made concerning the structure and behavior of matter have had profound implications for the biological sciences. Insights at the atomic and molecular levels have been applied rapidly

(a)

(b)

to the study of cells in an era that has come to be known as the golden age of molecular biology. The scientific, moral, and ethical consequences of the ensuing penetration into the fundamental secrets of life itself will be with not only the scientist but the whole of society for some time to come.

For example, consider the fact that complex organic molecules are even now being created in the laboratory. Biochemists have recently succeeded in synthesizing one of the complex protein molecules that plays an active chemical role in living organisms. Others have succeeded in synthesizing a gene, which is one tiny part of the complex molecule that carries hereditary information in a living organism. It may be many years before further confirmation of the mechanistic view is obtained through the complete synthesis of a simple living creature from inorganic materials, but few biologists today doubt that such a synthesis is ultimately possible.

IS THE WHOLE NO GREATER THAN THE SUM OF ITS PARTS?

There is a dilemma in the minds of many modern biologists that in a real sense is the present-day equivalent of the argument between mechanism and vitalism. In its modern dress it is known as reductionism versus holism. **Reductionism** implies that life ultimately can be understood in terms of the chemistry and physics of its smallest component parts. **Holism** implies that not all the properties of a living system are exhibited by its parts, because as soon as a living system is dissected it loses many of its properties. Therefore, no amount of analysis of the parts can lead to a complete understanding of the whole.

For many biologists, however, the newer form of the argument is considered to be as outmoded as its predecessor, for these seemingly conflicting viewpoints can be incorporated into one unifying principle. Simply stated, *not all of the properties of the whole are determined by the properties of the parts; some emerge from the precise way in which the parts are organized.* This is the principle of **emergent properties.**

The following example will illustrate what this principle means. Cellulose and amylose (a form of starch), two of the substances produced by living organisms, have very different properties. Cellulose is a tough, fibrous material that provides structural strength in plants. Although it is for most organisms completely indigestible and of no nutritional value, it is the chief constituent of such useful products as wood, cotton, hemp, and paper. Amylose, on the other hand, has little structural strength; it is powdery and is soluble in water. But amylose *is* digestible by animals; moreover, it plays a major role in the storage of excess food in plant and animal cells.

If you were to take the strict reductionist approach, you could treat samples of cellulose and amylose with strong acid to break them into their component parts. Having done this, you would find that both are entirely composed of the same, simpler substance, the sugar glucose. But if you were then to take other analytical approaches, you would find that the differences between cellulose and amylose are attributable to the form in which their glucose "subunits" are joined together. You would discover that glucose exists in two forms, which are rapidly and continuously converted from one to the other when the substance is placed in a water solution. At the molecular level, one form is distinguishable from the other only in the position of the hydroxyl group (symbolized by —OH) attached to the carbon atom (symbolized by C) designated "1" on the glucose ring structure:

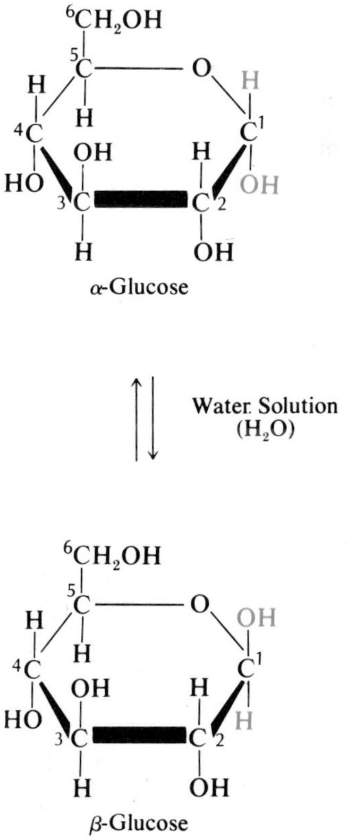

α-Glucose

Water Solution
(H_2O)

β-Glucose

Figure 1.5 Friedrich Wöhler (a) and Pierre Berthelot (b), who in separate experiments converted inorganic matter into organic matter and thereby challenged the explanation that living systems differ from the nonliving because they alone contain a "vital force."

(For now, you need not understand all the implications of these diagrams. The important thing is to note the differences between the two structures.) If the hydroxyl group projects ''below'' the plane of the ring structure, the glucose is called α; if the hydroxyl group projects ''above'' it, then the glucose is called β.

Now, individual units of glucose are often combined to form structures called polymers. The oxygen (O) on carbon 1 is the atom by which the glucose units are joined in both cellulose and amylose. They can be linked together initially in either the α or β configuration, but once they are polymerized the $\alpha \rightleftharpoons \beta$ transformation can no longer occur. When a cell joins α-glucose units, the polymer is amylose, a form of starch:

Poly-α-Glucose = Amylose

When a cell joins β-glucose units, the polymer is cellulose, which is a *very* different substance:

Poly-β-Glucose = Cellulose

From the standpoint of ''pure'' reductionism, it might be predicted that by breaking cellulose and starch into their component parts—that is, into glucose molecules—and studying their properties, you should be able to understand the properties of each substance. The holist would point out, however, that when you break cellulose and starch into their component parts you lose the very properties you are attempting to understand. Both polymers break down into glucose solutions with identical proportions of α and β glucose, so what could be gained by studying glucose if it cannot reveal the differences between cellulose and starch?

Resolution of the conflict between reductionism and holism comes with the recognition on both sides that often the argument is intellectually invalid. Even though the properties of the individual parts of a living system establish limits on the properties of the whole, the precise properties of the whole are determined by the way in which the parts are arranged. The comparison between cellulose and amylose thus exemplifies the property of emergence—*units can behave very differently when they are arranged differently.*

One more example will serve to reinforce the principle of emergence at a higher level of biological organization. The fertilized egg of an animal normally develops into a well-integrated adult. But if the egg is centrifuged in the laboratory, lighter molecules and particles are forced to migrate to one end of the egg and heavier molecules and particles are forced to migrate to the opposite end. When this is done to the fertilized eggs of certain animals, the embryos develop abnormally. Most of the types of cells and tissues normally seen during development appear, but they appear in layers organized from the ''light'' to the ''heavy'' end. Because the normal interrelationships among parts have been disrupted, the embryo cannot develop into a functioning adult. In this experiment the composition of the fertilized egg was not changed, but the organization changed considerably. As a result of the different patterns of organization, entirely different properties emerged.

Expressed in terms of the principle of emergence, the details of *organization* of the parts play a key role in determining what the properties of the whole living system will be, for certain properties of the parts are revealed *only* when they are organized in a particular way.

Prevailing theory now deals not only with the parts of systems but with the relationships among them. At each level of organization—beginning with the elementary particles and moving through atoms, molecules, cells, tissues, organisms, and even populations and ecosystems—new relationships are created and new properties emerge.

Given this insight, the challenge facing modern biologists is threefold. First, they must work to elucidate the properties of the parts of living systems at all levels of organization. Second, they must work to identify the organizational relationships that result in the emergence of new properties at each level. And finally, they must account for, in physical and chemical terms, the precise pattern of organization that does occur.

PERSPECTIVE

This chapter began by asking how we distinguish between living and nonliving systems. Any one of a number of questions into the nature of life could have served the same purpose—specifically, to show that behind almost every biological principle may lie a history of observation, experimentation, theory, and debate. This one line of history shows that what seems to be a safe generalization may turn out to be a faulty interpretation of the available evidence. What seems today to be a minor exception to some general rule may prove tomorrow to be the key to a critical new principle.

SUGGESTED READINGS

ASIMOV, ISAAC. *A Short History of Biology.* Garden City, N.Y.: Natural History Press, 1964. As the title suggests, this readable and entertaining book has the advantage of brevity.

GABRIEL, MORDECAI L., and SEYMOUR FOGEL (eds.). *Great Experiments in Biology.* Englewood Cliffs, N.J.: Prentice-Hall, 1955. A collection of some of the most significant writings from Redi, Leeuwenhoek, Spallanzani, Pasteur, and others. Readings relevant to other chapters are also included.

GARDNER, ELDON J. *History of Biology.* 3rd ed. Minneapolis: Burgess, 1972. Students interested in a more comprehensive account of biology and biologists of the past will find this fascinating reading.

Chapter 2

In Search of
Biological Principles

Our knowledge of life is an interconnected web of experiences and perceptions—stretching out fragilely at times, and at other times converging into junctures of great insight. This book presents many seemingly isolated conceptual and experimental threads; this chapter traces out the nature of the web itself—the assemblage of all those separate threads into the functioning whole we call "biology."

In a sense, all our different ways of looking at things are lenses. They focus our thoughts not on isolated observations but on how different observations fit together. Observations, as they stand alone, are not very useful. It is only when we assemble them into an intellectual framework that we gain greater understanding. These frameworks go under such names as "philosophical guidelines," "theories," "principles," even "physical laws" when we become complacent about their seeming immutability. Regardless of what names we give them, they are an essential part of our search for knowledge. Without them, each of us would have to start all over again in the attempt to make sense out of the world.

It is important to remember, however, that intellectual frameworks are only as good as the observations on which they are based. They have no meaning of their own; they are not in themselves "ultimate truths." Often the point is reached where an observation is made that simply cannot be forced into an existing framework. Then a choice must be made: Should the observation be discarded, or the framework? Unfortunately, many new perceptions are put aside or lost because observations that are inconsistent with an existing picture are sometimes discounted. This is a human failing, and difficult to avoid. But some of the greatest advances in human understanding have involved acceptance of and explanations for precisely those observations that did not fit in where we thought they ought to.

The purpose of this chapter is twofold: It will show how principles develop and change in the field of biology, and it will outline some of the major principles that currently guide biological thought. These principles will occur again and again throughout this book, and they are summarized here as an overview of the intellectual framework for this book. They are absolutely essential to any broad discussion of biology: without them, we would be forced to contend with an enormous random heap of biological observations and "facts." But it is also important to keep in mind that, as essential as biological principles may be, and as firmly as they may be stated in this chapter, they are only as valid as the observations they have tied together. They may change drastically as we generate principles capable of encompassing future perceptions of biological phenomena.

SCIENCE PROGRESSES BY REVOLUTION AND BY ACCRETION

Inquiry into the nature of life has never reached the point where biologists would, without squirming, distill their observations into "universal laws" as chemists and physicists have done. Perhaps their caution derives from the nature of the objects they study. Living things do not hold still for analysis, they often do not behave the same in the laboratory as they do in the natural state, and they never remain precisely the same even for a brief span of time. Nevertheless, biologists generally do subscribe to certain broad, biological principles. And, like scientists in any other field, they occasionally must give up those principles as new ones are formulated.

One generation after another, biologists have built a foundation of observations, methods, and concepts. Their efforts have been the legacy of each new generation, who in their turn add new observations, new methods, and new concepts to it and thereby broaden the base itself or one of the levels of understanding it supports. That biologists should work to strengthen, extend, and preserve the validity of what has already been done is traditional, and it is a guide for much productive research (Figure 2.2). From time to time a person of unusual ability and insight—a Darwin, Pasteur, or Madame Curie—appears on the scene and helps us attain a new level of understanding, but even such "giants" of science must have starting points, theories, or foundations.

Thomas Kuhn calls such a foundation of scientific values, techniques, and beliefs to which there often is a shared commitment a **paradigm.** A paradigm often is used

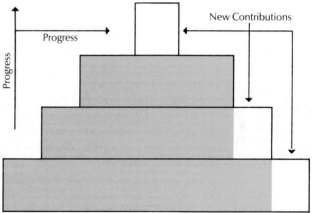

The Pyramid of Established Knowledge

Figure 2.2 A traditional model of science. In this model, we have a broad foundation of facts and theories established by past generations of scholars and philosophers. Upon this solid foundation other layers have been built; each higher layer is less broad than that on which it rests. The goal of each scientific researcher is to broaden and solidify the base or one of the levels of understanding that it supports. From time to time a "giant" of science appears on the scene whose greater insight allows erection of a new level on the pyramid of knowledge; a higher platform from which all of us may view the truth.

as a common approach to research, with new methods, observations, and concepts being added to it on the basis of a pervasive acceptance of its validity and utility. There is a danger, however, that further research may be implicitly channeled so that it adds only to the precision and scope of those observations and concepts already supportive of the paradigm. In other words, because the paradigm itself is usually not challenged, the questions asked and the problems solved are to some extent preselected. Questions and problems that seem incidental to the predictive power of the paradigm often are cast aside as distractions in the way of progress. Scientists who are tightly bound by existing paradigms and the ideas that support them are the most susceptible to such restriction.

But every now and then someone emerges who asks the distracting questions and who looks for other answers—and shows us broader paths to progress. Claude Bernard, a distinguished nineteenth-century biologist, put it this way: "... when we have put forward an idea or a theory in science, our object must not be to preserve it by seeking everything that may support it and setting aside everything that may weaken it. On the contrary, we ought to examine with the greatest care the facts which apparently would overthrow it, because real progress always consists in exchanging an old theory which includes fewer facts for a new one which includes more ... we must change [our ideas] when they have served their purpose, as we change a blunt lancet that we have used long enough.

"The ideas and theories of our predecessors must be preserved only in so far as they represent the present state of science, but they are obviously destined to change, unless we admit that science is to make no further progress. . . . As truths in the experimental sciences . . . are only relative, these sciences can move forward only by revolution and by recasting old truths in a new scientific form."

An implication of Bernard's philosophy is that major progress in science often occurs not so much by accretion (by adding bit by bit to an established body of knowledge) as by intellectual revolution. He advocated testing the predictions of our starting points or theories and, when confronted with anomalous data, discarding or changing our ideas. The result is progress by "revolutionary" change in our way of looking at nature or at a particular biological problem.

This suggests a model for some aspects of science that in many ways is the inverse of the one shown in Figure 2.2. In this case, a slender pillar of observation and theory (our "starting point") supports ever-broadening levels of inference and interpretation (Figure 2.3). The ways in which we synthesize those levels of inference and interpretation are determined by our broad views of nature—our starting points or paradigms. But often new observations or experi-

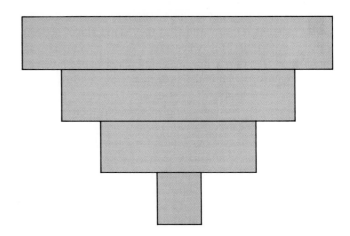

Figure 2.3 An inverse pyramid model of science. According to one model, science can be viewed as an inverse pyramid. A superstructure of inference and interpretation rests on a narrow base of fact (data) and theory. Any weakening of the base or imbalance may topple the whole inverse pyramid.

ments lead to an extension of one of the upper levels that the paradigm no longer can support. The structure then must fall because of the inadequacy of the base. This leads us not only to a modification of the paradigm but also to a resynthesis of the superstructure in a more balanced form, which encompasses both the older observations and the new. As Claude Bernard perceived, this process can be revolutionary, rather than accretionary.

If we could look inside the various layers of inference and interpretation in such a model, we would see that they consist of subsets of the whole system. Within each level, smaller inverse pyramids of starting points and levels of inference occur (Figure 2.4). Thus, in biology there are problems of different magnitudes, involving paradigms of a general or a more restricted applicability. The more broadly encompassing paradigms—those viewpoints from which the largest and most diverse blocks of biological information may be related in orderly fashion—are sometimes called "principles" of biology. Thus, in Chapter 1, the principle of emergent properties was described as a contemporary alternative to the vitalism, mechanism, strict reductionism, and holism paradigms. Thus, seemingly incontrovertible paradigms may, in time, give ground to others that seem better to encompass the available evidence. In Chapter 1 we also followed historical shifts in the usefulness and acceptance of the spontaneous generation paradigm. And Chapter 3 shows how the principle of evolution supplanted the principle of the immutability of

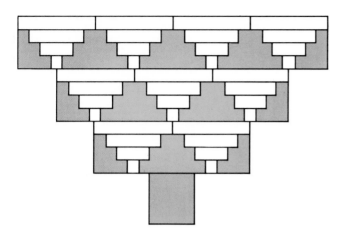

Figure 2.4 Internal organization of the inverse-pyramid model. Each layer of the system may be envisioned as containing many smaller inverse pyramids of fact-theory and inference-interpretation.

species when it became clear that organisms can and do change.

Is the search for biological understanding *accretionary*, then—a bit by bit addition to an established foundation of knowledge? Or is it *revolutionary*—a testing of the predictive powers of established theories and a tossing out and replacement of the ones that fail the test? It is both. In the words of Kuhn, ". . . a new theory, however special its range of application, is seldom or never just an increment to what is already known. Its assimilation requires the reconstruction of prior theory and the re-evaluation of prior fact, an intrinsically revolutionary process that is seldom completed by a single man and never overnight." Accretion provides a substantial amount of observation and theory that can be subjected to testing and evaluation. And revolution, when it occurs, provides a new theory that is the focus for accretion in a new direction.

THE RISE AND FALL OF PARADIGMS IN BIOLOGY

A consideration of some of Bernard's specific contributions to biology will illustrate how paradigms may be supplanted by others of more widespread applicability. When, in the early 1840s, Bernard started work on his doctoral thesis, a firmly entrenched paradigm was there to guide his thinking: ". . . the vegetable kingdom alone had the power of creating the individual compounds that the animal kingdom is supposed to destroy." Thus sugar was regarded

as "the respiratory nutriment" obtained by animals exclusively from foods and destroyed in their body. Bernard's research "problem" was to identify the organ in which the sugar disappeared. But his measurements of sugar levels in the blood of animals and some of their organs were contrary to the predictions that he could make within the confines of the existing paradigm. He observed that an animal maintains its blood sugar level even when sugar is removed from its diet and that an organ within the animal—the liver—is capable of synthesizing sugar. The "only plants synthesize" paradigm had to be abandoned.

As Bernard later reflected, "As a result of the experiments . . . I was not indeed led to find an organ for destroying sugar, but, on the contrary, I discovered an organ for making it, and I found that all animal blood contains sugar even when they do not eat it. *So I noted a new fact, unforeseen in theory, which men had not noticed, doubtless because they were under the influence of contrary theories which they had too confidently accepted.*" [italics added]

But the research that led to the breakdown of one paradigm led directly to formation of another paradigm of a very different sort. It has expanded our understanding far more than the "only plants synthesize" paradigm ever could have. Over a period of time, Bernard perceived that a vertebrate organism carefully regulates its blood sugar so that it is maintained at a relatively constant level despite marked variation in the availability of sugar from the diet. He also discovered that many other blood constituents are regulated, as is body temperature.

The generalization Bernard drew from such observations is that *the living cells of an organism exist in a carefully regulated internal environment that is much more stable than the fluctuating external environment surrounding the whole organism.* An organism survives, he concluded, only as long as it maintains the relative constancy and fitness of the internal environment. This process of maintaining constancy was later termed *homeostasis* by the physiologist Walter B. Cannon. (Loosely, the term means "staying the same.") The concept of homeostasis has become one of the most useful and pervasive principles in biology, and Bernard's contributions to its development rank him as one of the giants of biological history.

It has been determined that homeostatic regulatory processes always involve negative feedback systems. As shown in Figure 2.5, through these systems every deviation from the normal condition triggers some response having the opposite effect as the original deviation. For instance, mammals normally maintain about 0.1 percent sugar in the blood plasma. An increase in blood sugar to a higher level, as after a carbohydrate meal, stimulates removal of the sugar from the blood by triggering the synthesis of sugar-

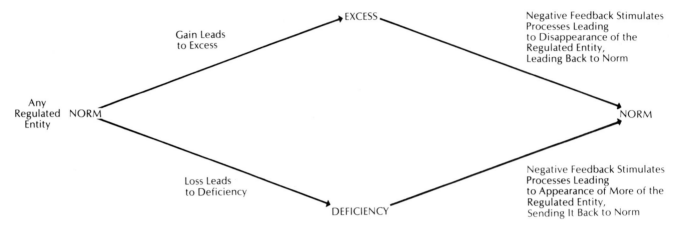

storing compounds in the liver. A drop in blood sugar triggers the breakdown of these same compounds, which thereby releases sugar into the blood once again.

Negative feedback systems are at work in environments *outside* an organism as well as inside. In a stable ecological community, for example, the balance between numbers of plants, plant eaters, and animal eaters is thought to be maintained by similar homeostatic negative feedback controls. The principle of homeostasis, as it applies at the level of the biosphere, is popularly referred to as the "balance of nature." One indication of the current importance of the concept of homeostasis is the fact that most biologists believe we do not adequately understand *any* process until we know how it is regulated. As you will read in Section V, the principle of homeostasis has provided impetus and direction in the search for regulatory mechanisms.

Having looked at one example of the way paradigms can evolve into an organizing principle, let us now turn to consider other current principles that are widely accepted.

THERE ARE LEVELS OF ORGANIZATION IN NATURE

The preceding discussion might be taken to mean that a given set of observations is pertinent to only one paradigm. This is not always the case. Paradigms often have overlapping application in that they may provide different ways of looking at the same thing.

For example, even though Bernard's study of liver function destroyed a paradigm concerning the metabolism of sugar in living systems, his observations supported the reductionist paradigm. Reductionism implies that *function in a whole system may be understood in terms of the functioning of its parts.* Thus, the animal physiologist takes this approach when he believes that the function of an animal can be understood, to a large extent, in terms of the functioning of its component organs. He may even study isolated organs, believing that a knowledge of their various physiological states can lead to an understanding of function in the intact organism.

The reductionist paradigm is not restricted in application to organ physiology. Examination of any aspect of the living world—whether it be the nature of cooperation within a beehive or the self-reproduction of a single cell—reveals that everything has a number of interrelated component parts. In fact, biologists now recognize several separate levels of organization within the living world, as shown in Figure 2.6.

Having read Chapter 1, you know already that the hierarchy of organizational levels in this figure may also be viewed as a scheme for describing the new properties that emerge at each level when parts are organized to form a whole living system. It is almost always possible to observe properties in an organized system that are not readily observable in its separate, unorganized components. This principle of emergent properties permeates all of modern biology.

Part of being able to "think biologically" is being able to move up and down the organizational scale, looking at phenomena at one level and considering their sources at a lower level—and their significance for some higher level of organization.

AT THE ATOMIC LEVEL, THE SAME LAWS GOVERN THE LIVING AND NONLIVING

In taking the reductionist approach, many biologists have analyzed in detail the composition of living things at the level of atomic organization. They have shown conclusively that there is no difference between living and nonliving systems at this level: All the kinds of atoms found in living things occur in nonliving things as well. Any differences between the two do not arise because of any unique kinds of component atoms.

It was often suggested in the past that if there is no difference in the *kinds* of atoms, there must be a difference in the *behavior* of atoms to account for the properties of living things. Indeed, the hope of finding fundamental "laws" unique to living things attracted large numbers of brilliant physicists and chemists to the study of biology in

Figure 2.5 A generalized model of homeostasis. For a regulated entity, a departure from the norm triggers processes that lead to a reversal of the trend. The result is that the entity is returned to the norm. This response is called negative feedback.

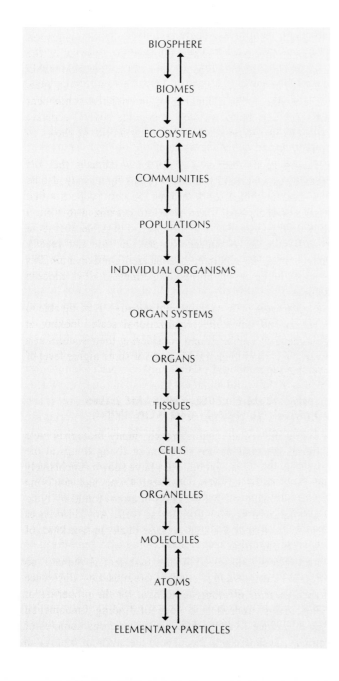

the aftermath of World War II. The expectation has all but vanished. So far it has not been possible to detect any way in which the atoms of life behave in fundamentally different ways from similar atoms in the nonliving world.

One reason a difference was expected at the atomic level is that life seemed to violate a universal law. According to the laws of thermodynamics (Chapter 12), all systems in the universe tend to run down by becoming increasingly disorganized and randomized. This trend toward randomization is true of every star and of every other system in the nonliving world. Yet living things have shown a tendency toward *increased* order and degree of organization. But we now know that the difference is illusory. The reason that life does not appear to be running down is that life continuously feeds on energy from the sun, which *is* following the universal trend and will burn out some 5 billion years hence. *A continual input of energy is required by all living things in order to maintain and increase order.* Energy from the sun is trapped first by plants in the process of photosynthesis (Chapter 15). All other living creatures depend on a constant share of this energy (Chapter 14), which they obtain by eating plants or plant products.

Once this influx of energy ceases for any organism, the universal trend sets in and disorganization follows as surely as it does for any other system in the universe, revealing with finality the common foundation of the living and the nonliving.

PROPERTIES OF LIFE BEGIN TO EMERGE AT THE MOLECULAR AND CELLULAR LEVELS

As we move up the hierarchical scale to the level of molecules (which are units of matter formed by the union of atoms), we do find a significant difference between life and nonlife. The atoms of living things are held together by the same kind of bonds that hold nonliving things together, but they are assembled into much more complex molecules of more precise structure. And these more complex structures result in more complex properties—the properties of life.

But why should there be more complex molecules in the

Figure 2.6 (left) The hierarchy of organization in nature. In the reductionist view, each level may be understood in terms of the structure and function of the levels subsumed under it; in other words, the whole may be explained in terms of its parts. According to the principle of emergent properties, each level, as a consequence of its organization, exhibits some emergent properties not evident at lower levels; the whole is more than the sum of its parts. (For simple organisms, the cell and the individual are one and the same. The tissue, organ, and organ-system levels apply only to higher plants and animals.)

living world? Again the answer is organization. The molecules of life are packaged into highly organized, self-enclosed units called cells. And within each cell is a complete set of molecules that act as templates. In other words, they are capable of recreating, in precise detail, all of the complex molecules present in the cell. This capacity for self-reproduction is a characteristic that is unique to living things. But as discussed in Chapter 17, it is not the property of any one molecule. Each molecule of the cell is capable, under certain conditions, of carrying out some of its activities in isolation from the cell. *But the capacity of the molecules to integrate their activities and reproduce emerges only when cellular organization is maintained and only as long as there is a constant influx of energy.*

The properties of a living cell, therefore, are inseparable from the organization of the cell. Indeed, the presence of what we call life within the cell demands specific organization. If a cell is squashed, it dies.

THERE ALWAYS IS RELATIONSHIP BETWEEN ORGANIZATIONAL STRUCTURE AND FUNCTION

All atoms are made of the same kinds of subatomic particles; they differ from one another only when there are differences in number and arrangement of their component parts. One molecule may have the very same number and kinds of atoms as another molecule, but it will differ from the other molecule if its atoms are arranged differently. One cell may be composed of practically the same kind of molecules that compose another cell, but it will differ from the other cell if its molecules are arranged differently. And despite their content of basically similar cells, multicellular structures will differ from one another if their cells are arranged differently. At every level of biological organization, then, structure and function are inseparable.

For teaching purposes an instructor might say, "This is the structure, and now let us consider the function." But it should be remembered that in the living world the two are inseparable. Structure implies function, and function springs from structure.

Generally, to the extent that two biological structures are similar, similarity of function is implied. And to the extent that they differ in fundamental structure, some difference in function may be expected. If two structures seem to be different in function but similar in structure, it is probably because the wrong level of organization is being examined to detect the structural difference. Two bees that look identical may behave quite differently if one is isolated and the other is in an active hive; organization at a higher level affects function of the units of lower level. Similarly, two isolated cells that look identical but behave in different ways usually can be found to differ in structure at the submicroscopic or molecular level.

BOTH UNITY AND DIVERSITY EXIST AT EACH LEVEL OF ORGANIZATION

As the preceding discussion implies, at every level of biological organization we find two qualities of life that at first appear to be contradictory: unity and diversity.

There is unity in the kinds of atoms and molecules present in all living things. There is unity in the organizational plan for the molecules of life: they are always packaged in basically similar ways as self-perpetuating cells. There is unity in the chemical reactions that cells perform to extract energy from their environment in order to maintain their integrity. Microscopic organisms and human beings, for example, use basically the same methods of energy extraction. There is unity in the way all cells perpetuate themselves. There is unity in the way cells and organisms pass on hereditary information to their progeny to perpetuate the life form. There is unity in the structure of ecosystems—always a balance between resources, plants, plant eaters, animal eaters, and microbial-fungal decomposers.

But at all these levels there is diversity as well. *To overemphasize either the unity of life or its diversity is to lose sight of the most elegant aspect of living things.* The molecules found in a bacterium and in a human skin cell are amazingly similar in general types but remarkably dissimilar in detail. Those two cell types possess hundreds of protein molecules that are basically similar and that carry out virtually identical reactions. But at the atomic level, each of these molecules is different in fine detail in the two cells. Similarly, although the basic organizational plan and many of the molecules are identical in the cells of human heart and lungs and gut and muscle, there is enormous diversity in fine detail that leads to diversity of function. At every level we find that fundamentally similar structures and processes differ enormously in their fine details. The diversity superimposed on the unity of a basic plan is most obvious in the world about us. In a walk through the woods in spring we see a profusion of diverse grasses, trees, and wildflowers, all growing at once. All these life forms are built according to the same plan, but they differ enormously in the details of their appearance.

Indeed, the study of diversity and its causes has engaged man from earliest times. The diversity of organisms was much more apparent to early naturalists than was the unity in living systems, and this extensive diversity has been viewed in several different ways. First, it has been of interest to describe, name, and catalog it in some form of information storage and retrieval system, a *taxonomy*. A good start was made in the time of Aristotle, and giant leaps of progress were made in the time of Linnaeus. Nineteenth-century taxonomists became increasingly systematic, in that they attempted to understand natural relationships rather

Figure 2.7 Stages in the life cycle of a monarch butterfly. As the adult insect emerges from the chrysalis it differs so substantially from the caterpillar that originally formed the chrysalis that the two are scarcely recognizable as related life forms. Cells that are only subtly different from those of the caterpillar are arranged with minor modifications into tissues, and those tissues take on very different foldings and enlargements to form organs such as wings and mouth parts, legs and antennae. As a result a wholly distinct organism emerges that now plays an altogether changed role both in the population of monarchs and in the community in which the monarchs live. Yet throughout the cycle an individuality present in the fertilized egg acts to tie the stages one to another. This unity, this individuality, clearly lies at a level below the level of the changing cells. The challenge is to understand the diversity in terms of the underlying unity.

than just describe and name. But the task of describing and systematizing the organisms on earth is far from complete. Taxonomy-systematics remains a very active and productive field of contemporary biology. Section II of this book may be regarded as providing an ''interim report.'' It paints the broad picture, but there still is much to be learned about the diversity of life.

There is another way to view diversity, and it has been a guiding paradigm for many biologists. An adult bullfrog is a whole animal. It is a biological whole at the ninth level from the bottom of Figure 2.6. That bullfrog had its origin as an egg, a biological whole at the fifth level on our chart. The adult frog may be viewed as the end product of its development. We can understand that frog as a biological whole in terms of the stages and processes involved in its development. An adult chicken or human being also is a biological whole, and so is a tree. Each of these organisms must start as a single cell at the fifth level and *develop* into a ninth-level individual. Thus, biological diversity can be understood in terms of different patterns of growth and development, some aspects of which will be treated in Sections II, IV, and VIII.

Of course, to focus only on the developmental period between egg and adult is to look at only part of the picture. From the time of its conception, every organism continually changes. There is no static stage. It grows, develops, reproduces, ages, and dies in some regular sequence. *Each*

species has its own characteristic life cycle—its own relationship with time. To appreciate fully the diversity of organisms, we not only must describe and classify them, we must also obtain detailed understanding of their life cycles and natural histories.

The inseparable twin principles of unity and diversity at one time posed a major riddle for those inquiring into the nature of life. Why should there be so many grossly different kinds of organisms if all life forms show much fundamental unity at lower levels of organization? In order to give even partial answers to this question, biologists have had to be concerned not only with development of life on the time scale of individual plant and animal life cycles but also on the geologic time scale of earth history (Section II).

EVOLUTION IS THE COMMON SOURCE OF UNITY AND DIVERSITY

In what is the broadest unifying principle of biology, we now see that *diversity of life forms is the result of divergent evolution from a common ancestor.* All life forms—from the bristlecone pine to the sulfur-bottom whale—share common mechanisms for extracting energy from the environment because all life forms evolved from an ancestor that used those mechanisms. Because no cell can survive without a constant flow of energy, only those cells survived in which this ancient plan was perpetuated. True, somewhere along the way, certain forms acquired a handful of additional molecules that enabled them to use sunlight to initiate the flow of energy (Chapter 15). But as unique as this capacity is, it is only a slight modification and addition to the ancient pathways; it is not a completely new innovation.

All organisms share a common means of passing on hereditary information, because each one received its hereditary information in a direct, unbroken line from that ancient ancestor to all. But as this information was passed on from generation to generation, it was slowly modified—not in its fundamental substance but only in its details—so that different progeny received slightly different versions of the common plan. The versions that did not work were lost when their carriers failed to survive and reproduce. But the versions that, in particular environments, worked as well as or better than the original version were perpetuated. In this manner, differences began to accumulate. Thus, as the "fixity of species" paradigm gave way to one of "evolution" a revolutionary change in our conception of biological diversity occurred. We can now conceive of environments of species as actually shaping the diversification of organisms through time (Section VII). The view emerges that no particular kind of organism, including man, is permanent or unchanging. Each kind of organism is continually "tuned" by evolution to its place, or "niche," in the ecological system. It is the variety of niches that has led to the great diversity of organisms. As ecological conditions have changed in the past, organisms also have changed, and so they will in the future.

When the theory of evolution was developed more than a century ago, the hereditary, cellular, and molecular mechanisms that might underlie such a process were unknown. Today we know that these mechanisms support the picture of an evolutionary process that builds diversity while retaining unity. *The principle of evolution is reinforced by analysis at all levels of organization in nature.* That is why the principle of evolution is the major unifying theme of this textbook.

But given that change is possible, why should change have led to *so much* diversity? Why did evolutionary forces perpetuate anything but the most successful life style?

COMMUNITY STABILITY DEPENDS ON BOTH COMPLEXITY AND DIVERSITY

Any kind of organism living in isolation from other organisms becomes its own executioner, regardless of how rich its environment may have been at the outset of its existence. As it lives, grows, and reproduces, that organism uses up the resources in the environment that it needs to sustain the flow of energy through its cells. It also produces a variety of waste products that pollute and thereby change the environment that nurtured it.

It is diversity that provides stability to communities of organisms, to ecosystems, and to the biosphere as a whole. There is not a single species of organism on earth that could exist for long in the absence of other kinds of organisms. Any such species, isolated in the world at large, would have no more chance of surviving than a yeast culture in a barrel of grape juice: Just as the yeast culture grows, uses up the available sugars, and drowns in its own waste alcohol, so any species would exhaust its resources and be poisoned by its own wastes.

The key to life on earth *is* diversity. What one organism needs, others produce. And the first, in turn, produces resources that yet other species consume. *It is the diversity of needs and products that causes the continuous cycling of the essential elements of life throughout the biosphere.* Plants incorporate carbon dioxide into organic compounds, but they could not do so if there were none. At the same time, they renew the supply of free oxygen in our atmosphere. Microorganisms and animals—and plants, too—respire organic compounds, using free oxygen and returning carbon dioxide to the air. Rabbits eat grass, but are eaten by foxes. Predation by foxes limits the rabbit population, which prevents the grass from being entirely consumed. But the number of available rabbits limits the fox population, and the animals fertilize the field with their excrement and with the decay of their bodies. Every ecological system depends for its stability upon a complex web of resource consumption and production interactions by its members. In any ecological community, no two species have exactly the same combination of needs and products. Each is different, and the very existence of the community *depends* upon this complex diversity.

Thus diversity arose through evolution not as a result of passive change but as a result of positive forces selecting and perpetuating novel life forms that would exploit a previously unexploited resource. Only when the resources of the community of life were kept recycling could a stable community be established.

WE ARE PART OF NATURE

This brings us to the last viewpoint or paradigm to be discussed in this chapter. We might call it the "we are part of nature" paradigm. For centuries we have behaved as if we were outside observers of nature, rather than part of the system. We have regarded the land and the plants and animals on it as being "put there" *for our use,* as the seas were for fishing, forests for cutting, fossil fuels for burning—indeed, we have regarded all natural resources as being there for our exploitation. So, we plowed the land, decimated the whales, killed the sardines, cut the forests, wasted the fuel, and so on, as if we were above nature and would not be held ecologically accountable, as was the yeast culture in that figurative wine barrel. This view is no longer tenable.

The human population has become so large that it is now dramatically apparent that we are a *part of,* rather than observers and users of, nature—and a very influential part indeed. Everything we do on a large scale affects the entire biosphere. The earth is our barrel, and the biosphere our grape juice! *If we exhaust the resources we need and poison the biosphere with our wastes, human life as we know it will cease to exist.* That is the message of environmental biologists and others who now call for an adequate code of ethics governing man's relationships with the land, waters, and other aspects of the ecosystem.

Ethics constitute moral limitations upon the exercise of expediency in attainment of any desired goal. By defining the limits of social and antisocial human behavior, ethics exercise strong controls over most aspects of our behavior. Conscience (our sense of right and wrong) guides human activities in fields of human relations, law, politics, and business, as well as in family and social affairs. In those areas where human conscience may occasionally default, we guard against activities detrimental to the general welfare by legislation, backed by law enforcement agencies and judicial systems. In all of these personal and public matters (relationships among people), ethical considerations should clearly outweigh economic or material ones.

Ethical environmentalists believe that misuse of the land and waste of natural resources by industry are as morally indefensible as genocide. The farmer who ignores erosion, the cattleman who overgrazes his range, the lumberman who clear-cuts without reforestation, the industrialist who pollutes, and all others who despoil natural resources may each gain temporary economic advantage. They are ethically wrong in so doing, however, even if they own title to the land they are exploiting, for they are stealing from their own children and are taking away that which is irreplaceable.

Conversely, those practices that protect the land, its fertility, and its supportable resources are ethically defensible whether they are immediately profitable or not. Protection of the land includes measures in behalf of the ecological communities of mature plants and animals that mean so much to its stability. These communities are our resources, for each species has its place in nature whether or not we can shoot it, eat it, or sell it. In the final analysis, ethical limitations on the exploitation of the environment are as essential to our general welfare as are the moral aspects of human interrelationships. That is the vital message in the last chapter of this book. *But to develop a rational and ethical approach to defining our place in the natural world requires an understanding of the nature of life at its many different levels.* That is the function of the rest of this book.

SUGGESTED READINGS

BERNARD, CLAUDE. *An Introduction to the Study of Experimental Medicine.* Henry C. Greene (tr.). New York: Dover, 1957 (originally published, 1865). This discourse on scientific method contains the author's accounts of some of his best experiments.

GROBSTEIN, CLIFFORD. *The Strategy of Life.* San Francisco: W. H. Freeman, 1965. Using a somewhat different viewpoint, the author approaches some of the same problems considered in this chapter. Interesting reading.

KUHN, THOMAS. *The Structure of Scientific Revolutions.* 2nd ed. Chicago: University of Chicago Press, 1970. The best available analysis of the respective roles of revolutionary and accretionary progress in science. Kuhn's orientation is historical and philosophical.

Section II
The Diversity of Life

Microorganisms, plants, fungi, animals—why do the lands and seas of the earth teem with untold millions of varieties of living things? This question is fundamental to the organization of this book; indeed, the question is basic to all of biology. The answer lies in the nature of the evolutionary process. When we examine a few representatives from the endless array of life forms, we begin to perceive that diversity of structural organization does not exist for its own sake. Underlying each structure is an adaptive function that somehow helps an organism survive in a specific environment. This relationship gives clues about the way unique structures have gradually arisen from older, more fundamental ones under the pressure of an ever-changing environment. And every successful modification of one life form has provided a stimulus for further change in others, for each modification represents a danger to be met or an opportunity to be exploited in the web of life. All organisms alive today are momentary travelers in this evolutionary journey through time. Some bear little direct resemblance to their primordial ancestors, for in complex environments, complex changes have been essential for survival. But other organisms seem little changed, for in environments where simplicity is successful there is no advantage to becoming complex. This, then, is one answer to the question of diversity: Evolution does not necessarily reflect a selection for size, complexity, or elegance—the only criterion has been survival.

Chapter 3

The Variety of Living Things

In the beginning there was a simple need to identify and know about all the world's creatures. Who would have suspected that over the centuries this manifestation of human curiosity would culminate in a theory that would send tremors through the whole of Western civilization?

Living in the remote tropical forests of the Philippines are a native people, the Pinatubo, whose existence is particularly dependent upon their direct perceptions of the natural environment. These people are able to identify and to describe the habits and behavior of an impressive number of the plants and animals found there. The bat named *tididin,* they will tell you, can be found on dry palm leaves, whereas the *dikidik* lives on the underside of wild banana leaves, the *litlit* in bamboo clumps, the *kilumboy* in tree cavities, the *konanaba* in dark thickets. In this manner they will not only identify fifteen species of bats, which they have classified on the basis of physical similarities and differences, they will also describe the habits of those creatures in relation to the plants with which they are significantly linked.

The biologist R. B. Fox noted that if you ask the Pinatubo the name of a plant and if they are not certain of its identification, they will taste its fruit, smell its leaves, break apart and examine its stalk, comment on where it is growing, and only then will they announce whether or not they know what it is. Because the Pinatubo pay such close attention to their surroundings, they can easily give names for at least 450 plants, 75 birds, and most of the insects, fish, snakes, and mammals found there—even 20 species of ants and 45 types of fungi.

Is such interest among "primitive" peoples inspired, as an early cynic once said, by nothing more than the rumblings of their stomachs? If that were so, as Claude Lévi-Strauss has pointedly remarked, then the primitive could just as easily reproach the civilized for being totally governed by organic or economic needs and for suffering from unbalanced interests. The primitive focus on the plants and animals in their surroundings; the civilized focus on brands of packaged foods and wine lists, on makes and years of automobiles. Regardless of interests, however, there is in both cases a characteristically human pursuit of knowledge and a classification of that which is considered important. No matter where we live, no matter who we are, we as a species function by making connections and distinctions between different things, by discovering and imposing some semblance of order upon the enormous diversity of our surroundings.

Each connection, each distinction made, becomes part of a symbolic code, a **taxonomy,** that helps classify the natural world so that it is intelligible to all members of a culture. The classifications of the Pinatubo represent a folk taxonomy that helps them reduce the local environment to manageable terms. Similarly unique and well-developed systems of classification have evolved over time among all peoples throughout the world. But what taxonomy is available to the individual who wishes to apply his intellect not to a local environment but to the whole of nature?

Consider the fact that biologists have already identified about one and one-half million different species throughout the world. Consider next that they study and name for the first time several thousand additional species each year. With all this work they still have probably identified only 10 or 15 percent of all the species now in existence. Indeed, many species are becoming extinct before they can be named, as is happening in the wake of technological advance through the forests of South America. As impressive as this array of diversity is in our present world, it is even more staggering when we consider all the diverse life forms that have ever existed in the history of our planet. Perhaps less than 1 percent have survived to the present day. What classificatory framework could possibly be imposed on a biological world of such magnitude?

DIVERSITY IS NOT EASILY DEFINABLE

From the time of Aristotle there have been many attempts to classify the natural world. Then, as now, there was a desire to identify precisely the organisms found in one's local environment, to group them on the basis of habitat, and to distinguish one group from another on the basis of similarities and differences in appearance. Thus, all organisms were first divided into two great realms, or "kingdoms," of life: the immobile plants and the mobile animals. Then they were grouped according to physical appearance. The cat, the lion, the panther, and the leopard, for example, were grouped apart from the dog, the wolf, and the jackal.

As a consequence of this interest, taxonomies proliferated with more or less logic—and usually less. For example, sixteenth-century botanists managed to get by with a "system" that involved drawing an illustration and writing a brief description of each and every plant they sought to identify. Then, during the age of exploration, ships—and naturalists—were sent all over the world, and each new land they visited contained a bewildering array of plants and animals. The sheer numbers of new plants and animals waiting to be cataloged soon overwhelmed the naturalists of the time. Thomas Moufet's classification of grasshoppers and locusts, taken from his *Theatre of Insects* (1590), gives us a glimpse of the embarrassing state of their art:

Some are green, some black, some blue. Some fly with one pair of wings, others with more; those that have no wings they leap, those that cannot either fly or leap, they walk; some have longer shanks, some shorter. Some there are that sing, others are silent. And as there are many kinds of them in nature, so their names were almost infinite, which through the neglect of Naturalists are grown out of use. Now all Locusts are either winged or without wings. Of the winged some are more common and ordinary, some more rare; of the common sort, we have seen six kinds all green, and the lesser of many colours.

MAN
VIVIPAROUS QUADRUPEDS
Mammals
CETE
Whales
OVIPARA
Reptiles, Birds, Amphibians & Fish
MALACIA
Cephalopods
MALACOSTRACA
Crustaceans
ENTOMA
Other Arthropods
OSTRACODERMA
Other Molluscs

ZOOPHYTA

ACALEPHAE
Jelly Fish

TETHYA
Ascidians
HOLOTHURIA
Echinoderms
SPONGIAE
Sponges

HIGHER PLANTS

LOWER PLANTS

INANIMATE MATTER

Figure 3.2   Aristotle's Scala Naturae, *or "ladder of life." Although Aristotle never attained the evolutionary point of view, his later investigations had him moving in that direction. He saw nature as moving gradually from the inanimate to the animate, from lifeless things to plant to animal. He perceived that the kingdom of plants and the kingdom of animals were not rigidly defined but were bounded by "beings in-between." His ladder of life is in a sense prototypic of modern classification schemes.*

The first of the bigger, hath as it were a grass cowle or hood which covers the head, neck and almost half the body; the wings come from the neck underneath, of a greenish colour, speckled with a few small spots, the back green, the belly dusk coloured, the tail or stem at the end blackish; it hath a great mouth, and strong big teeth, excellently made . . .

Investigators such as Moufet clearly had difficulty in communicating with one another. The problem became progressively worse over the next two centuries with increasing discoveries of new life forms in the Americas, in Africa, and in Asia. Complicating the picture even further was the development of the microscope and the consequent discovery of a whole new world teeming with still more organisms. The stage was set for widespread and rapid acceptance of a good system of classification and naming of species.

LINNAEUS CONSTRUCTS A FRAMEWORK FOR IMMUTABLE SPECIES

Drawing on the works of earlier naturalists such as Kaspar Bauhin, Joachim Jung, John Ray, and Joseph Pitton de Tournefort, the Swedish naturalist Carolus Linnaeus finally developed a workable system for assigning names to

individual kinds of organisms. In his *Systema Naturae* (1735), Linnaeus succeeded in placing every known plant and animal in an unambiguous slot. An organism was first identified by placing it in the largest of his categories, a class; then in the next largest category, called an order; then in a genus (a Greek word translating into "birth," or "stock"); and finally in a species (a particular variety within a given stock).

Instead of the confusing definitions exemplified by Moufet's scheme for grasshoppers and locusts, Linnaeus assigned a two-word designation in Latin (the scholarly language of the time) to each organism, signifying its genus and its species. The generic name for human beings, for example, became *Homo* and the species name, *sapiens*. Translated into English, *Homo sapiens* becomes "man, the reasoner." It happens that the only existing species of human beings is *Homo sapiens*. But other genera contain many existing species. The genus of dogs, for example, contains such species as *Canis familiaris* (the domesticated dog), *Canis lupus* (the wolf), and *Canis latrans* (the coyote). Some genera, such as the fruit fly *Drosophila*, encompass a thousand or more individual species. Although modern biologists have repeatedly revised Linnaeus' classifications and have discarded many of his criteria for grouping organisms into categories, his **binomial system** is still the standard means of designation for organisms throughout the world.

Even though Linnaeus' taxonomy was a practical way of cataloging the diverse forms of life, it shed little light on the interrelationships of the life forms themselves. In fact, as a conceptual framework it represented little more than a pigeonholing of the limited perceptions of his time. For instance, Linnaeus tended to group together plants that had the same number of reproductive structures in each flower, but the plants so grouped often bore little resemblance to one another. Today, biologists would say that he often grouped together species that were not related. To biologists in Linnaeus' time, the question of "relatedness" would have been meaningless, for they generally viewed each species of plant and each species of animal as a fixed unit

Figure 3.3 Carolus Linnaeus, dressed in collector's gear for an exploratory journey through Lapland, northern Sweden, and Norway. Like the names of the plants and animals he classified, Linnaeus' name succumbed to Latinization: his Swedish name by birth was Carl von Linné.

By the mid-seventeenth century, however, much of Western society took the eloquent words of Genesis literally—so literally, in fact, that Archbishop James Ussher interpreted them to mean that the world and all life were created within six days in the year 4004 B.C. Later, toward the end of the eighteenth century, naturalists would begin to accumulate the fossils of a variety of unfamiliar creatures. What were these extinct forms? Could they be part of an evolving sequence of life out of the dim past? If the time of creation had been as recent as 4004 B.C., then a vast continuum of life evolving from life seemed unlikely. Some suggested the fossils signified only that the Biblical Flood had changed the original order of living things. They argued that animals such as the dinosaurs obviously perished because they were too large to fit in Noah's Ark. Fossils of creatures that in some ways resembled living things were interpreted as prototypic models rejected during the act of creation and cast aside while they were still inorganic clay or stone.

These latter explanations highlight some of the extremes that later antievolutionary thinking would eventually reach. But certain established principles of faith were so fundamental to Western society that it would take a monumental accumulation of evidence before divergent views would be tolerated. In 1760 the accumulation of evidence for evolving life was about to begin in earnest. Its harbinger was a French natural philosopher known by the name Georges Louis Leclerc, Comte de Buffon.

BUFFON QUESTIONS THE NOTION OF IMMUTABLE SPECIES

Buffon did not start out as an evolutionist. But in the course of his experimental work he perceived the conceptual inadequacies of Linnaeus' taxonomy in conveying an understanding of the order of nature. Eventually he came to question the whole notion of the immutability of species. In his *Histoire Naturelle des Animaux,* he asked: If all mammals are the result of separate, special acts of creation, why do they all have identical limb parts? If all mammals were created with different modes of locomotion in mind,

because it had descended, without significant change, from original members that had been created independently and simultaneously in the Garden of Eden. Species, in short, were considered in Linnaeus' time to be immutable; they had not changed and never would.

It was not that the idea of evolving life had yet to be conceived. In the sixth century B.C. the Greek philosopher Thales, having studied the teeming life forms in the Aegean Sea, concluded that all living things had evolved out of water. Anaximander, and later Empedocles, viewed the world in evolutionary terms and pointed out that living creatures could change in response to their environment. Indeed, many early Fathers of the Church, including Saint Augustine, expressed philosophies that could be interpreted as an evolutionary view.

Figure 3.4   (a) George Louis Leclerc, Comte de Buffon. Deeply impressed by Isaac Newton's demonstration of basic laws that govern the physical world, Buffon became convinced that all parts of the living world must be interrelated in some fundamental fashion. For that reason he viewed all taxonomies (particularly the Linnean system) with skepticism, for he perceived that they did not reflect the general order of nature. Much of his work focused on finding the element that is universal to all living things. (b) Jean Baptiste Pierre Antoine de Monet, Chevalier de Lamarck, who was greatly influenced by Buffon's concepts. A botanist-turned-zoologist, Lamarck was forever proposing ideas that seemed eccentric to his peers. With all his reputation for eccentricity, however, Lamarck reached three important conclusions in his work: first, that species change in a changing environment; second, that there is a unity underlying the diversity of species; and third, that species develop progressively. Although his ideas on the mechanism of change turned out to be implausible, he was, in fact, one of the first to develop a complete theory of evolution.

why were they not created with different limb parts designed specifically for their intended way of life? Why, for instance, do pigs have, in addition to their two toes on each foot, two other toes that dangle uselessly above the ground? Perhaps, Buffon suggested, the pig has useless toes because it inherited them, after its form had changed, from some primitive ancestor for which lateral toes *had* been functional. Generalizing from this line of reasoning, he suggested that perhaps all mammals are related by virtue of being members of a single ancient family of mammals; perhaps, over time, members of that family had become modified (within the boundaries of some ancient mammalian plan) to meet the demands of different kinds of existence in different habitats.

Buffon drew some interesting comparisons between Old World and New World animals based on the observations of naturalists who were taking part in explorations around the world. He found it difficult to believe that species had been dispersed from a single Garden of Eden. Most likely they had originated at a number of "centers of creation" throughout the world, for there simply were too many geographic barriers against dispersion from a single center. There are no tigers in Brazil, for example, even though

conditions in that country are ideal for supporting them. Thus, tigers must have originated at some center of creation outside Brazil, with geographic barriers keeping them near their point of origin. *The origin of species, as a class of events, had to be spread out in space.*

Even though he had thought long and deeply about the nature of species, Buffon could not—or would not, because of the generally hostile reception of his ideas—go on to speculate about the fundamental question that his thoughts had raised: By what *mechanism* could a separate and distinct species change over time from its original stock? It was his student, Jean Baptiste Pierre Antoine de Monet, Chevalier de Lamarck, who proposed the first detailed explanation for the process of change. In so doing, Lamarck arrived at an entirely different view of the relationships among mammals.

LAMARCK PROPOSES A MECHANISM FOR EVOLUTION

In undertaking his own classification of animals, Lamarck had come to the conclusion that all animals fit into a scheme of progression that began with the simplest creature and culminated in man, the most complex. Lamarck believed in the spontaneous generation of simple organisms from inorganic matter (Chapter 1). From this simple beginning, he argued, the organization of a plant or an animal increased through environmental effects on the motions of its vital fluids; any gains in organization were conserved and passed on to offspring. He argued, for example, that the application of heat accelerates the vital motions in plants; therefore, variations in temperature around the world would affect plant development around the world. He further argued that, in responding to changes in their environment, animals use the organs and characteristics best suited to their new surroundings, thereby accelerating the vital fluids associated with those organs and characteristics and assuring their further development. The organs and characteristics least adaptive would no longer be stimulated by vital fluids. They would fall into disuse and wither away. In this manner plants and animals would gradually acquire special characteristics that could be passed on by an individual species to its offspring—and that is how diverse life forms could evolve.

This Lamarckian doctrine is called the theory of **inheritance of acquired characteristics.** The notion had been a common one since the time of the Greek philosophers, but for Lamarck it was simply a special part of his general thesis that *action of vital forces on living bodies can produce permanent developments in organizational complexity that can then be passed on to offspring.*

Now Buffon essentially had proposed a theory of **common descent,** whereby the common characteristics shared by the various organisms that are grouped together are inherited from a common ancestor. In contrast, the Lamarckian theory would suggest that similar organisms could be descendants of different ancestral organisms that had experienced similar environmental histories. For example, although Lamarck saw all mammals as descending from reptiles, he claimed that they are not descendants of the *same* species of reptile. The only reason that mammals have certain characteristics in common, he said, is that they have independently achieved the same general level of complex organization.

In retrospect, it is not so much a question of which of these two investigators was on the correct course of inquiry; the point of interest here is in the general focus of their thinking. Even though many of Buffon's as well as Lamarck's contemporaries were frowning on the evolutionary ideas being generated, the intellectual climate of the eighteenth century clearly was beginning to change. And with the new winds rising from the realms of geologic and geographic explorations, the torrent of evolutionary thought was about to break through the constraints of traditional belief.

GEOLOGY AND THE EMERGING EVOLUTIONARY VIEWS

It might be supposed that the ever-increasing number of unusual fossil forms unearthed in the early gropings of the infant science of geology might have had the immediate effect of inclining biologists of the early nineteenth century to an evolutionary point of view, but this was not the case. Their first reaction was to attempt to modify existing theories regarding the fixity of species to accommodate the new data. An example of this may be seen in the work of Georges Cuvier, who was a contemporary of Lamarck and a man of immense intellectual accomplishments. He was a

Figure 3.5 Lamarck's notion of the "inheritance of acquired characteristics." Taking as an example the giraffe, Lamarck would propose the following mechanism for its evolutionary development. A primitive antelopelike animal that fed on tree leaves ate all the leaves within easy reach, and it had to keep stretching its neck and its legs in order to reach higher and higher leaves. In so doing, the animal stimulated the "vital fluids" in its neck and legs, which caused these parts to grow longer. The longer legs and neck thus acquired would be passed on to its leaf-eating offspring and slowly but surely, the animal would evolve into a giraffe.

superb anatomist and paleontologist and devoted much of his energy to the description of the succession of animal fossils in the rocks of the Paris Basin. On the basis of his work Cuvier felt that he could recognize several distinct periods or intervals in the history of the earth. Each of these intervals was characterized by the presence of different kinds of animals, often in great variety. The earliest interval was characterized by the absence of life, the next by an array of apparently aquatic animals, followed by a period when amphibianlike forms were the most complex animals present. The amphibian interval was followed by a period of reptilian dominance; still younger rocks contained a record of rather unusual and bizarre mammals; and finally, the remains of familiar plants and animals were found in the very youngest rocks studied. Cuvier could see no evidence of a smooth transition between each of these periods—each appeared to give way abruptly to the next. Using the Biblical Flood as a model, he erected a theory known as *catastrophism.* Cuvier postulated that each of these intervals in earth history had been separated from the others by great natural catastrophes, of which the flood described in Genesis was only the latest example. The small number of survivors of each catastrophe, augmented perhaps by newly created forms, then repopulated the earth, with the animal types of each succeeding period being somewhat more advanced in their level of organization. So great was Cuvier's intellectual reputation and social standing that his views on the catastrophic nature of earth history dominated the scientific world of the early nineteenth century, far overshadowing the views of evolutionary theorists such as Lamarck. Even as Cuvier was at the apex of his influence, however, the evidence that would topple the theory of catastrophism was slowly accumulating.

As early as 1795 the English geologist James Hutton proposed that the sediments of ancient rock strata were accumulated in the same manner as were contemporary sediments deposited in the modern world. Hutton's concept, known as **uniformitarianism,** was in direct contrast to the catastrophic model of Cuvier. Hutton believed that the processes involved in the formation of ancient strata were essentially the same ones that operate in the contemporary world—the slow erosion of uplifted areas such as hills and mountains by the action of wind and water. The eroded sediments would be carried to lakes and oceans by streams and rivers to gradually accumulate new layers of sediment that would eventually harden into rock.

Still another line of evidence was developed by William Smith, an English engineer involved in canal construction. Since the amount of time and effort required to excavate a canal depended in part on the type of rock encountered in the course of construction, Smith attempted to develop a system for cataloging the rocks of southern England so that they could be recognized in the field. Most of the rocks were sedimentary and contained various types of fossils, so Smith began studying the fossil contents of the various rock layers in the hope that the fossils could serve as a guide to the identification of specific rock strata. He discovered that the fossil remains became increasingly less like the animals of the modern world as he examined older and older rocks and, indeed, that the fossil assemblages of each rock layer were sufficiently unique to characterize or identify that layer. But Smith's careful work uncovered an additional fact. Although the total fossil content at each level was different, the individual kinds of fossils did not appear and disappear suddenly from one layer to the next but appeared to be gradually derived from preexisting types and, in turn, gradually merged into still other similar types in still younger rocks. These observations were inconsistent with a catastrophic view of earth history.

Hutton's uniformitarianism and Smith's observations on the nature of fossil successions were ably synthesized into the first comprehensive treatment of earth history in Charles Lyell's three-volume work, *Principles of Geology,* published between 1830 and 1833. In this work Lyell suggested that the origin and extinction of species occurred slowly and continually throughout the world, with no clumping of events in time and no crowding in space. He saw changes in the landscape—mountain formation, erosion, and so on—as a continual process extended through long periods of time. The earth of Charles Lyell was an incredibly ancient stage upon which different forms of plants and animals had played out their lives and died, with each line of descent changing with the slow passage of time.

These and other ideas of Lyell influenced, among others, Charles Darwin and Alfred Wallace, whose paths were destined to cross. Although neither accepted all of the many ideas Lyell had advanced, both became consumed with the desire to test his notions about the spatial and temporal distribution of species. With diligence and with observations based on a great deal of traveling, each set out, unknown to the other, to do just that.

NATURAL SELECTION IS PROPOSED AS A MECHANISM FOR THE EVOLUTION OF SPECIES

The mountain of evidence for the evolutionary view of the diversity of life culminated in a remarkable theory that was presented to the prestigious Linnean Society on July 1, 1858, a date that was to be a major turning point in the history of biological thought. On that day the geologist Lyell and the botanist Joseph Hooker gave the Darwin-Wallace lecture, which consisted of four parts: a letter from Lyell and Hooker stating the circumstances leading up to the presentation of papers by both Darwin and Wallace; excerpts from an unpublished manuscript that Darwin had begun writing in 1839; a letter Darwin had written to Asa Gray of Boston, in which he outlined his views; and a paper that Wallace wrote in 1858 and sent to Darwin for his evaluation. Although Wallace had written his paper without knowledge of Darwin's manuscript (Figure 3.6), amazingly enough they ended up with remarkably similar arguments that evolution occurs by means of natural selection.

Darwin's view of evolution was shaped by a five-year voyage around the world in which, as the ship's naturalist, he visited several little-known areas. In traveling along the coast of South America, for example, he observed systematic changes in species from north to south. He collected many fossils and saw how they related to existing species in the same area. In visiting islands such as the Galápagos (Figure 3.7), he noted that isolation seemed to foster diversity. Upon his return to England in 1837, Darwin began to sift through his findings and to prepare them for publication, a task that was to take him many years.

In 1838, much of his thinking came under the influence of an essay published earlier by Thomas Robert Malthus, an English clergyman, mathematician, and economist. In his *Essay on the Principle of Population* (published in 1798—anonymously at first, given the general reception to new ideas during the aftermath of the French Revolution), Malthus argued that every population outgrows its food supply, and eventually starvation (and, in the case of human beings, disease and war) prunes it back. Populations, he stated, have the capacity to increase geometrically, whereas food increases at best only arithmetically.

Darwin was struck particularly by a phrase that Malthus had coined—"the struggle for existence." During his voyage to the Galápagos, Darwin had been impressed by the remarkable variety of finches that existed on those tiny, remote islands. At least fourteen different species could be identified by (among other features) differences in the size and shape of their beaks. Although all fourteen of these species were found *only* on the Galápagos, they all resembled a species of finch found in mainland South America. Darwin speculated that all fourteen species were descendants of the mainland species and that during their long isolation on the islands they had undergone differentiation. Taking his cue from Malthus, he concluded that the differentiation in beaks was a result of differentiation in the method of obtaining food and that competition for food would act as an impetus for change (Figure 3.8).

Like Darwin, Wallace journeyed around the world as a naturalist. Five years in South America and eight years in the Malay Peninsula provided him with a background of observations as extensive as those of Darwin. Indeed, several of his short papers written during his stay in Malaya came to the attention of Darwin, who wrote to Wallace and gave him enthusiastic support for his work. One day in February 1858, Wallace recalled an essay he had read many years before—the essay by Malthus. Clearly, as Malthus had said, many more animals were born than ever survived. Why did some die, and not others? The answer was that the best-suited animals lived: The strongest escaped disease, the fleetest of foot escaped predators. In his words, "Then it suddenly flashed upon me that this self-acting process would necessarily improve the race, because in every generation the inferior would inevitably be killed off and the superior would remain—that is, *the fittest would survive*."

The theory of evolution by natural selection, as formulated by Darwin and Wallace, consists of two parts. First, it presents sound evidence for the evolutionary view that species do change. Second, it proposes **natural selection** as the mechanism for change, which means that *those variants of a species best suited to a particular environment have a*

(a) (b)

Figure 3.6   Charles Darwin (a) devoted many years to collecting evidence for and working out the details of his theory of evolution through natural selection. Whereas Darwin had been carefully documenting his ideas, Alfred Russell Wallace (b) wrote his out in two days. He sent his paper to Darwin for critical review. Darwin was stunned by the parallels in their conclusions and at once circulated the paper among his colleagues, who suggested that the two naturalists collaborate in a joint presentation of the theory to the Linnean Society. One year later, in 1859, Darwin's magnum opus, On the Origin of Species by Means of Natural Selection, or the Preservation of Favoured Races in the Struggle of Life, *was published.*

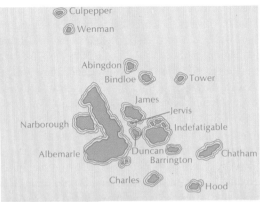

Figure 3.7 H. M. S. Beagle. *In 1831 the* Beagle *sailed from England to South America as part of a continuing survey of the continental coastlines. Darwin went as a naturalist, without salary, with meager equipment, and with his working space confined to the narrow end of the chart room. Later he would say that the need for order imposed by his limited working quarters was remarkably effective training in self-discipline. Darwin left England with strictly Biblical views of the creation and nature of species. As he was about to board the* Beagle, *however, one of his former teachers presented him with a copy of the first volume of Lyell's* Principles of Geology. *He read it with enormous interest, and it played a critical role in the reshaping of his ideas during the five-year voyage.*

The various isolated oceanic islands Darwin visited also figured prominently in his evolutionary ideas. The most influential were the Galápagos, a small volcanic archipelago 600 miles west of the coast of Ecuador named after the incredible numbers of tortoises (galapago in Spanish) that populated them. Darwin was amazed by the diverse array of plants and animals found only there and thought it surprising that the life forms did not more closely resemble those on the nearby South American continent.

selective advantage over other members of the species, and they will be the ones more likely to survive and reproduce.

The logic of the Darwin-Wallace theory can be summarized as follows:

First, Variation exists among individual members of a species, and some of these differences are inherited.

Second, In each generation, every species produces more offspring than survive to reproductive age. Those individuals that do survive and breed determine the nature of the next generation.

Third, The individuals with variations best adapted for survival in the particular environment contribute proportionately more offspring to the next generation.

Fourth, Over long periods of time this process of differential survival and reproduction will lead to divergence between organisms in different environments. Ultimately this leads to the development of separate species.

Echoing Buffon's earlier suggestion, Darwin and Wallace proposed, on the basis of these observations, that all species *share* certain characteristics because all are descended from a single ancestral species. The *differences* among species—and this was the momentous conclusion Darwin and Wallace had reached—are the result of natural selection, which has brought about gradual changes in the

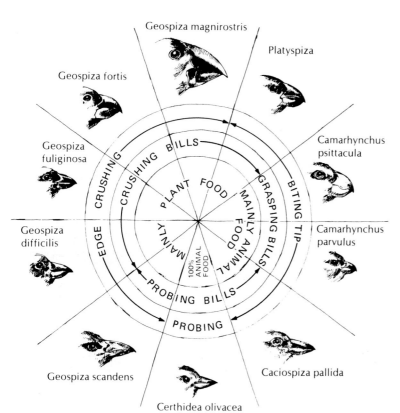

Geospiza magnirostris

Platyspiza

Geospiza fortis

Camarhynchus psittacula

Geospiza fuliginosa

CRUSHING BILLS
CRUSHING
CRUSHING
GRASPING BILLS
BITING TIP
MAINLY PLANT FOOD
MAINLY ANIMAL FOOD
EDGE
MAINLY ANIMAL
100% ANIMAL FOOD
PROBING BILLS
PROBING

Camarhynchus parvulus

Geospiza difficilis

Geospiza scandens

Caciospiza pallida

Certhidea olivacea

Figure 3.8 Darwin's finches, which exist only on the Galápagos Islands. The species from which all these divergent forms apparently descended exists in South America, which is about 600 miles away. Shortly after the ancestral species was introduced to the Galápagos it must have multiplied rapidly, for the finch had no natural predators there. In fact it did not even have to compete with other birds: it was the only permanent species of bird in the archipelago. Soon, however, the population outstripped the food supply. Those variant individuals whose beaks were better equipped, by virtue of size and shape, for eating tougher or larger seeds or insects were able to take advantage of as-yet untapped food supplies. Over the course of time, the descendants of the variant forms would come to exploit distinct parts of, or niches in, the environment. This process is called adaptive radiation. *The ancestral line did not undergo similar divergence on the South American continent because the niches were already occupied by other birds.*

many lines of descent that have at various points in time diverged, or branched away, from the common ancestral line. This, basically, is the concept of **divergence.** The fossils unearthed from clearly defined layers of sedimentary rock attest to this gradual change: the deeper the stratum, the older and less highly developed the fossil.

One of the arguments immediately raised in opposition to the Darwin-Wallace theory was that the variation observed in nature surely would not be enough to give rise to new species. It was pointed out that domesticated plants and animals were consciously selected by man, generation after generation, until their appearance was greatly different from that of their wild ancestors, but when returned to the wild they quickly reverted. Wallace countered by pointing out that this argument was faulty. In such cases, the only variations that had been selected for had been the ones most useful to man. In fact, the traits in animals that man had sought to improve by selective breeding (such as a gentle disposition) often proved to be deleterious under natural conditions. For example, if racehorses were turned loose in the wilderness, many would rapidly succumb to predators or to exposure to the elements. Their progeny would be successful only to the extent that ancestral hereditary traits necessary for survival in the wild state reappeared, and there would indeed be a rapid reversal of selection. But this

rapid disappearance of traits that had been selected for by man and that were of negative value in the wild is not an adequate basis for asserting that *all* variation occurring in the wild is just as temporary.

Although Darwin and Wallace reached remarkably similar conclusions, their emphases were different. Wallace was concerned with ecological factors such as the carrying capacity of the environment and the nature of limiting factors—one of which obviously was the amount of food available. Accordingly, he emphasized the importance of competition for resources as a prime mechanism by which natural selection might be expected to work. Darwin did not deny the importance of such considerations, but he pointed out that success in getting food and other essentials would have little impact on the future of the species unless it were coupled with reproductive success. *Which* members of a generation leave behind offspring when they die determines the nature of the ensuing generation. Following this line of reasoning, Darwin separated sexual selection from all other forms of selection and gave it special consideration as a potent factor in the evolution of species.

Even though Darwin overemphasized the importance of sexual selection, he properly focused attention on differential reproductive success as one of the main components of natural selection. Modern evolutionary theory tends to strike a balance between Wallace's emphasis on the importance of success in competing for limiting factors and Darwin's emphasis on reproductive success as criteria for the action of natural selection.

Although the process of evolution is not yet fully understood, there seems to be little doubt today that natural selection can account for the production of new species. Since the time of Darwin and Wallace, the theory has been increasingly refined, primarily as a result of the explosive growth of the science of genetics, which deals with the mechanisms of hereditary variations and with the nature of the units of heredity. These are subjects that will be dealt with in progressively greater detail in later chapters.

EVOLUTIONARY VIEWS HAVE PROFOUNDLY INFLUENCED CLASSIFICATION SCHEMES

One of the most sweeping and unifying effects of evolutionary thought relates to the manner in which we think about and classify the diverse life forms existing all around us. Today, biologists work continually to organize and arrange their systems of classification in order to reflect the degree of relatedness of different life forms. When they group organisms together, they attempt to determine whether the grouping is a natural one that reflects common ancestry rather than an artificial one based merely on superficial resemblances. Their ultimate goal is to devise a scheme of classification that accurately reflects patterns of evolutionary development—in effect, a **phylogenetic classification** that accurately places all species somewhere in a single, highly branched tree of life.

Modern Views of the Species Concept

When species were viewed as uniquely created, immutable groupings, the definition of species was straightforward. Now that we have come to view life in an evolutionary framework, a universally applicable definition is made enormously more difficult, if not impossible. Perhaps the most meaningful concept is that a **species** is a group of organisms acting as a unit of evolutionary change. In other words, *organisms belong in the same species only if a hereditary variation in one individual potentially can be transmitted to the offspring of all organisms in that species.* Organisms that are effectively and completely isolated from one another by geologic or behavioral barriers that prohibit even occasional interbreeding probably should not be considered members of the same species, no matter how much they resemble each other, because they will be unable to share future variations.

In many cases this concept of the species is impossible to apply in the field. Within "species" one can clearly

MR. BERGH TO THE RESCUE.

THE DEFRAUDED GORILLA. "*That Man* wants to claim my Pedigree. He says he is one of my Descendants."

Mr. BERGH. "Now, Mr. DARWIN, how could you insult him so?"

Figure 3.9 Darwinian theory outraged many people inside and outside science. Fundamentalists (those who interpret the Bible literally) were particularly furious over the implication that humankind might be descended from a primitive apelike ancestor. But many competent biologists rallied around Darwin. One of the key turning points for the evolutionists came when the biologist Thomas Henry Huxley engaged in a debate with Bishop Samuel Wilberforce, an orator so skilled that he was dubbed "Soapy Sam." After a round of argument, Wilberforce turned to his solemn opponent and asked whether it was through his grandfather or his grandmother that Huxley claimed his descent from a monkey. While the audience roared its approval, Huxley slowly rose to his feet and is said to have replied: "If, then, the question is put to me, would I rather have a miserable ape for a grandfather, or a man highly endowed by nature and possessing great means and influence, and yet who employs those faculties and that influence for the mere purpose of introducing ridicule into a grave scientific discussion—I unhesitatingly affirm my preference for the ape" Not only did his rejoinder shatter Wilberforce's posture, it helped turn public opinion into, if not acceptance, at least tolerance for the evolutionist's right to express his views.

identify **populations,** which are related organisms living and interbreeding in a relatively localized area and thereby forming a common pool of hereditary variation. Are two (or three, or four) such populations members of the same species? If it is possible to demonstrate that hereditary variation can and does flow from one to the other (by occasional migration, by mutual interbreeding with geographically intermediate populations, and so on), then they should be considered members of the same species. When such information is lacking—as it often is—a judgment is called for. Such judgments on whether to ''split'' or to ''group'' are constantly subject to revision as more information becomes available. Whenever possible, such judgments should be based on a laboratory test: Will members of two populations interbreed to form fertile offspring when forcibly brought together in the laboratory? Although such tests can sometimes be used to demonstrate reproductive incompatibility, they cannot be used to demonstrate that the two groups in the wild are behaving as members of a single species.

The vagueness of species boundaries is in one sense frustrating, but it is also further evidence of the exciting nature of life. Species are not dead insects on pins, or pickled fish; they are living organisms in a real world constantly undergoing change and thus defying our desire to pigeonhole them. To the extent that we force an arbitrary definition upon the word ''species,'' we lose sight of reality.

Modern Views of the Larger Taxonomic Groupings

Ideally, at the species level we take our cues from the breeding behavior of organisms. But the higher categories of classification are not reflected in any such behavioral interactions, even in principle. Instead, they are based on *inferred* relationships. Examination of several species often reveals certain structural similarities among them even though their behavior sets them apart as separate species. It is on the basis of these similarities that different species are grouped into a **genus.**

The categories above genus reflect current thinking of how a particular species relates to all other species. Hopefully this categorization of relationships parallels actual evolutionary developments. Following Linnaeus' original scheme, related genera (plural of ''genus'') are placed in the same **family,** related families in the same **order,** related orders in the same **class,** related classes in the same **phylum** and related phyla (plural of ''phylum'') in the same **kingdom.** Table 3.1 and Figure 3.10 illustrate the manner in which this scheme may be used to classify an animal (the sulfur-bottom whale) and a plant (the bristlecone pine). The efficiency of this scheme is impressive: By listing eight to ten increasingly general categories, or **taxa,** to which we believe a particular organism belongs, we can summarize much of our current understandings of that organism and its relationship to all others.

But what is a ''kingdom''? Early investigators thought that the most natural division was one between the immobile plants, which gather nutrients through their roots, and the mobile, food-ingesting animals; hence the kingdoms **Plantae** and **Animalia.** But a few years after Darwin and Wallace presented their theory of evolution, various investigators began to suggest that some single-celled organisms could be regarded as neither plant nor animal. They grouped these unicellular organisms into a separate kingdom, **Protista** (meaning ''the very first''). In some schemes, the simpler multicellular organisms, such as fungi and algae, were included in this third kingdom. Throughout the early twentieth century, however, many biologists continued to think only in terms of two kingdoms—plant and animal—with some uncertainties about the classification of simpler organisms. In evolutionary terms, this method of classification implied that plant and animal lines diverged very early in time.

As more was learned about the evolution of microorganisms and simple multicellular organisms, the ranking of Protista as a separate kingdom became increasingly popular. But even as the three-kingdom system came into common use, evidence was accumulating that other major divisions were required. Investigations were showing that single-celled organisms are characterized by very different kinds of cell structure. Bacteria and blue-green algae are organisms that lack a cell nucleus—the control center in cellular reproduction—and are different from other cells in many other important ways. The distinction being made between these organisms and all others reflected fundamental and extensive differences in cellular organization.

Additional studies of fungi revealed that these organisms depend on a supply of organic molecules in their environments, as animals do, yet they feed by absorbing substances through cell walls, molecule by molecule, much as plants do. Fungi are so unique that it is unreasonable to group them with the Protista, yet it may be that they represent an independent line of evolution that diverged from plants and animals early in the history of life.

On the basis of the most recent thoughts on evolutionary relationships, Robert Whittaker in 1969 proposed a five-kingdom system. In his view, Protista include a variety of diverging lines of evolution, all composed of single-celled organisms. **Monera** (which, owing to a poor translation from Latin, merely means ''single'') are the simplest known organisms. Since the nineteenth century, they have been presumed to be similar to the early organisms from which the other kingdoms evolved. **Fungi** are grouped into

Table 3.1
Partial Classification Scheme of the World's Oldest Plant and the World's Largest Animal

Taxonomic Rank	Bristlecone Pine	Blue Whale (Sulfur-Bottom Whale)
Kingdom	Plantae: multicellular plant; autotroph; cells with chloroplasts, well-developed vacuoles, and cellulose cell walls	Animalia: multicellular animal; heterotroph; cells with well-developed centrioles and ingesting organelles
Phylum	Tracheophyta: plants that have well-developed vascular tissues	Chordata: animals with a stiff, rodlike notochord; dorsal, tubular nerve cord; gill slits in pharynx
Sub-phylum	Spermopsida: seed plants	Vertebrata: animals with a spinal column of segmented vertebrae
Class	Coniferae: cone-bearing plants with needlelike leaves	Mammalia: animals with body hair; mammary glands
Subclass		Eutheria: female members carry developing offspring (nourished by placenta)
Order		Cetacea: marine mammals with fishlike, almost hairless bodies; forelimbs paddlelike; hind limbs absent; tail with flattened, horizontal lobes
Family	Pinaceae: spirally arranged leaves and cone scales; ovuliferous cone scales and bracts distinct	Balaenopteridae: upper jaw provided with a series of horny plates (''whalebone'') suspended from outer part of palate; pair of nostrils on top of head; throat and chest with longitudinal grooves
Genus	*Pinus:* long needles clustered singly or in groups of two, three, or five at the tips of short shoots	*Sibbaldus:* dorsal fin small and located far back
Species	*Pinus longaeva:* needles in groups of five, each with a single resin duct; cones buff to gray-brown with a stiff bristle on each cone scale	*Sibbaldus musculus:* throat and chest with about 90 furrows; length to about 105 feet, weight to about 140 tons; underside yellowish; upper side slate gray or bluish gray

a separate kingdom, and plants and animals are considered evolutionary lines of multicellular organisms that have developed from single-celled organisms. Plants, fungi, and animals are considered equally important groups of organisms that have, among many differences, three distinct modes of acquiring nutrients: *photosynthesis, absorption,* and *ingestion,* respectively (Figure 3.11).

Whittaker's system appears to be gaining increasing favor among biologists. It is the framework used in all subsequent chapters in this book and in the Appendix, which is a partial taxonomy included as a reference source. Further revisions of kingdoms may result as more is learned about the early evolution of life. Whatever revisions are accepted, however, it should be emphasized that systems of classification represent categories superimposed on nature by the human mind in its search for order. For that reason you should learn to expect that they will fit nature somewhat imperfectly. Any taxonomy is no more and no less than a

means of summarizing existing knowledge about the complex world we live in.

PERSPECTIVE

With a world populated by countless individual organisms, there is little hope of understanding the whole of nature unless we impose a system of classification, a taxonomy, upon it. All taxonomies devised in the past, and even those that exist today, may have enjoyed a period when they were considered the ''last word'' in our understanding of organisms and of the relationships between them. All have been characteristically transient: Not only is there a continual discovery of new organisms, there is a continual discovery of new interrelationships in the natural scheme of things that man-made schemes have not taken into account. Early taxonomies, such as that of Linnaeus, were based on the assumption that all the diverse kinds of organisms, or species, were immutable. Later schemes took into account

Figure 3.10   The sulfur-bottom whale, the largest animal that has ever existed in the history of the earth, and the bristlecone pine, the oldest known living organism. Some of these pines are at the very least 4,000 years old.

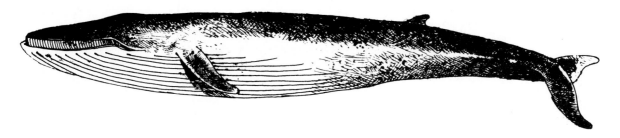

the evidence from geology and geography that the origin and evolution of species is an ongoing temporal and spatial process—in short, that species evolve all the time all over the world. Darwin and Wallace held that the mechanism underlying this evolution is natural selection, with those variants of a species best suited to a given environment being more likely to survive and reproduce. The modern theory of evolution still holds that environmental conditions select for alterations in species. It also emphasizes that the *process* of evolutionary change occurs through reproduction, with the units of heredity of those organisms that are more successful in reproduction becoming more widely represented in local populations. Often the boundaries between such local populations are determined not by environmental or physical factors but by barriers against interbreeding.

As a result of evolutionary thought, today's taxonomies ideally are phylogenetic in nature, in that biologists have been revising them to reflect patterns of evolutionary development. Linnaeus' original categories of class, order, genus, and then species are still used as units of classification. However, modern taxonomists construct those categories not merely on the basis of similarities in appearance and behavior but also on the basis of probable evolutionary divergence.

Threading through this historical account of the development of evolutionary and taxonomic theory is an important point concerning the process of science. Although you may often hear of "Darwin's theory of evolution," it should be clear that where the theoretical precedents of others end and an original theory begins is impossible to define. However fanciful or suppressed it may have been, centuries of evolutionary thought preceded Darwin's own. The remarkable contribution of Darwin and Wallace to this continuum of thought was that they identified a simple mechanism by which evolution occurs, and they backed up their theory of

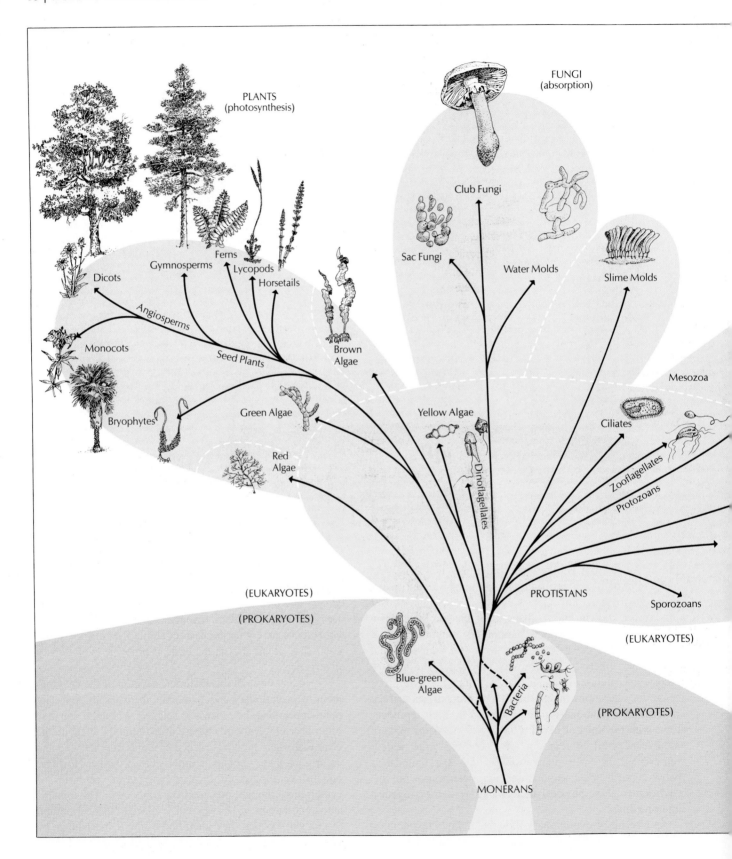

PLANTS
(photosynthesis)

FUNGI
(absorption)

Club Fungi

Sac Fungi

Water Molds

Slime Molds

Dicots

Gymnosperms

Ferns

Lycopods

Horsetails

Angiosperms

Monocots

Seed Plants

Brown
Algae

Mesozoa

Yellow Algae

Ciliates

Bryophytes

Green Algae

Dinoflagellates

Zooflagellates

Protozoans

Red
Algae

Sporozoans

(EUKARYOTES)

PROTISTANS

(EUKARYOTES)

(PROKARYOTES)

Blue-green
Algae

Bacteria

(PROKARYOTES)

MONERANS

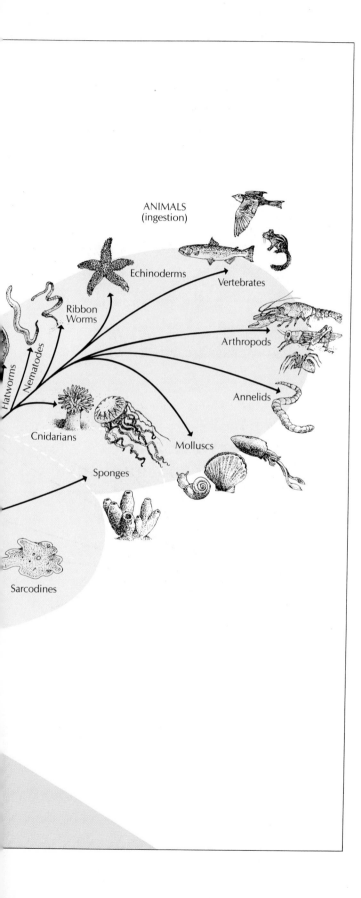

ANIMALS
(ingestion)

Echinoderms

Vertebrates

Ribbon
Worms

Arthropods

Nematodes

Flatworms

Annelids

Cnidarians

Molluscs

Sponges

Sarcodines

Figure 3.11 The Whittaker five-kingdom system of classification. (Further details of the scheme are provided in the Appendix.) In this scheme four of the kingdoms are reasonably well defined. The kingdom Monera includes all those organisms that lack true nuclei in their cells: the prokaryotes. The organisms in the other four kingdoms possess nuclei and are therefore called eukaryotes. The three "higher" kingdoms—plants, fungi, and animals—share the property of being multicellular but differ in their modes of nutrition. The remaining kingdom, Protista, includes all of the organisms not fitting into one of the other categories. Thus it is a grabbag of forms. Many protistans are less closely related to one another than to certain members of other kingdoms. This makes the boundaries between kingdoms difficult to define. In addition, each of the higher kingdoms includes a group of organisms (here set off by dotted lines) that differ so substantially from all other members of the kingdom that some feel they should not be included. (One author recently suggested that in order to circumvent such problems, nineteen kingdoms of organisms should be recognized.) What is important is not the location of the boundaries but the flow of evolutionary relationships here indicated by diverging arrows. For while the boundaries are man–made, relationships exist between groups that are both real and natural.

its existence with impressively sound scientific data. But the issue has not ended with their work. The concept of natural selection boils down to the simple fact that organisms survive. But why do they survive? Are some characteristics more important to survival than others? Answers to these and other questions about the nature of heredity would trigger one revolution after another in biological thought.

SUGGESTED READINGS

DARWIN, CHARLES. *The Voyage of the Beagle.* New York: Dutton, 1957. The journal Darwin kept of his researches into the natural history and geology of the lands he visited during the voyage of H.M.S. *Beagle.*

IRVINE, WILLIAM. *Apes, Angels, and Victorians.* New York: McGraw-Hill, 1972. An absorbing account of the lives and times of Charles Darwin and Thomas Henry Huxley.

SINGER, CHARLES. *A History of Biology to About the Year 1900.* New York: Abelard-Schuman, 1962. A glimpse into the lives and thoughts of the naturalists and biologists who shaped the early years of the science.

SOLBRIG, OTTO T. *Evolution and Systematics.* New York: Macmillan, 1966. The author outlines a framework for the appreciation of the variety of living things and explores relationships between evolution and systematics.

Chapter 4

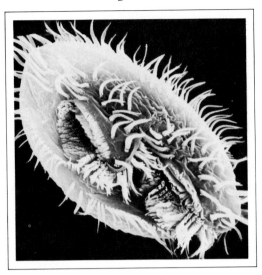

Prokaryotic and
Eukaryotic Microorganisms

Dividing Oxytricha, *into thee and thee*
I'm glad that with your fissioned mouth
You are not after me

In the diffuse, bright light of dawn a golden eagle rises from its mountain eyrie, circling slowly until it is far above the earth, where it scans the valley below for the first stirrings of life. As light spills down the mountains to the west a rabbit emerges from its burrow, alternately motionless and moving toward some succulent vegetation. It is injured—although it escaped a predator the day before, one of its legs did not, and it limps unevenly across the valley floor. The solitary bird turning in the air above the earth sees the erratic movement and plunges silently downward; it strikes true with outstretched talons. Within the hour, its belly filled, the bird is back in its nest, preening its feathers with its hooked beak and settling down to wait out another day.

This is one small, inevitable part of a timeless drama, yet we are drawn to it with the peculiar fascination of knowing that even as we are spectators we, too, are participants in the greater story. Whatever fanciful poetry is spun about a spider and its web, the spider is deadly in its production of a net to catch a wayward insect; however much we catch our breath at the spectacle of a cheetah running flat out across the African savanna, the cheetah is running down a potential meal; whatever splendid euphemisms we apply to our own forms of sustenance—prime rib, crown roast, brisket—we in our civilized manner are predators of the first rank. We and all organisms on earth are locked in one way or another into the drama of predation. At some time in the remote past there was enough space, light, and nourishment to encourage free proliferation of simple forms of life throughout the warm primordial seas. But as the numbers of organisms increased, new selective pressures went to work on those simple forms of life, and predation was one of the most significant of these pressures. A major clue to the question of diversification is found in the ingenious responses of hunters and the hunted.

Far beneath the level of human vision is a world of organisms not much more complex than those earliest forms of life. This is the teeming world of the monerans and the protistans, the simplest organisms that any classification scheme must take into account. There beneath the microscope we see them locked in the same struggle for existence, with predatory creatures engulfing others or gobbling up simple creatures smaller (and occasionally larger) than themselves. Is there, in this world, a model for the greater story? Is it possible to extrapolate from it the evolutionary sequence that all life followed? The early record may be buried forever, despite the tantalizing bits of evidence we have of the beginnings of the progression. But in the monerans and the protistans are diverse structures and behaviors that may be echoes of the past. And in taking as our point of departure these simplest of organisms we can spin a fascinating—if speculative—tale of how the whole struggle might have come about.

Insight into the evolutionary trend toward structural and functional diversity begins with understanding of the one unifying characteristic common to all organisms that have ever existed on earth. The underlying unity of life is attested to by the fact that *all organisms are made of cells.* An organism may be nothing more than a single cell, living by itself or in a cluster with other cells, or it may be made up of organized groups of millions upon millions of interdependent cells. Regardless of whether it is a whole organism or simply part of one, the cell is a fundamental unit of life.

Some cells are so small they are at the limits of the resolving power of a light microscope; at the other extreme are such large reproductive cells as the ostrich egg. Regardless of size, however, all cells share certain characteristics. For example, all cells are bounded by a membrane, and they all contain subcellular structures of various sorts within that membrane. Certain chemical substances—proteins, nucleic acids, lipids, and polysaccharides—are always present in them. And all cells are dynamic entities. Each one extracts energy from the environment and, in the process, discards waste products into the environment. Each changes constantly, replenishes itself constantly, and at some stage in its history grows and participates in reproduction of its kind. It is true that different cellular structures have evolved for carrying out these functions. But even with all the subtle and profound variations in structure that have occurred through evolutionary time, *cells have remained the basic unit of life for all organisms.*

The variations on their common heritage begin to emerge when the simplest organisms, the monerans and the protistans, are compared with more complex life forms. Some of these organisms (the mycoplasmas) are so small they can pass through filters capable of retaining bacteria; others are larger than a baseball. With few exceptions, however, *each moneran and each protistan is a single cell that can exist by itself in its environment.* Although some of these single-celled organisms may cluster into a colony with other members of their species, generally each can grow, live, and reproduce as an independent unit. A plant cell or an animal cell does not do this; it exists as part of an organized pattern of interconnected cells that depend on the functioning of the others for survival.

But there are significant variations between the simple organisms grouped into the kingdom Monera and those found in the kingdom Protista. The monerans differ from the protistans—indeed, from all other organisms—because they do not have a true nucleus. A **nucleus** is a distinctly bounded area that houses molecules of deoxyribonucleic

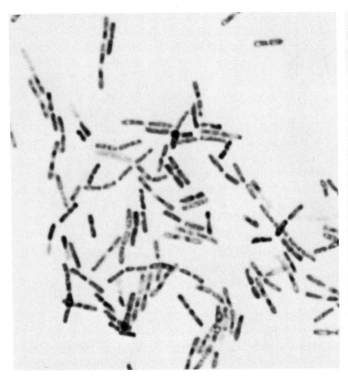

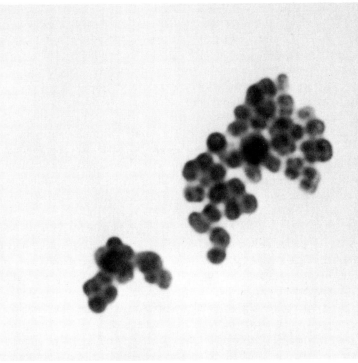

(Photograph courtesy Carolina Biological Supply Company)

acid (DNA), which contain all the hereditary information a cell needs to reproduce itself. Because all members of the kingdom Monera lack a nucleus, they are called **prokaryotic**—a word combining the Latin *pro-* (meaning "before") and the Greek *karyon* (meaning "kernel," or "nucleus"). All other organisms are called **eukaryotic,** from the Greek *eu-* (meaning "good" or "true"). In prokaryotes, the hereditary material is clustered somewhat into certain areas but it is not confined within a nuclear membrane, as it is in eukaryotes.

The basic similarities shared by cells imply that all organisms in all five kingdoms descended from a single ancestral cell line. However, the cells of protistans, plants, fungi, and animals are eukaryotic, so it seems plausible that these four kinds of organisms are descendants from a common eukaryotic ancestor that diverged from the ancient cell line. But the prokaryotic monerans are so structurally unique they may have never evolved much beyond the form of the primordial cell that gave rise to all of life.

THE SIMPLE PROKARYOTES MAY APPROXIMATE THE EARLIEST FORMS OF LIFE

Grouped into the kingdom Monera are two major kinds of microorganisms, the bacteria and the blue-green algae. At the boundaries of this kingdom are the mycoplasmas—the smallest known organisms that still display cellular characteristics—and a variety of other small groups that cannot be classified by any present schemes. Another group of microscopic biological entities, the viruses, does not fit readily into the kingdom Monera—or into any other kingdom, for that matter. These paradoxical entities, which generally are smaller than the mycoplasmas, dwell in the twilight zone between living and nonliving and have defied attempts to pigeonhole them in any evolutionary framework.

Bacteria: Diverse Solutions to the Problem of Obtaining Energy

Even though they are fairly well known organisms, **bacteria** are microorganisms barely large enough to be seen with a light microscope. The reason they have received so much attention is that they exert a significant effect on the environment. Bacteria are the fearsome agents of many of the major epidemics of human disease that have swept through the world, and if that were not enough, various species of bacteria manage to spoil food, turn milk sour, attack clothing and even buildings, and corrode metal pipes. As destructive as members of this phylum can be, however, life as we know it could not exist without bacterial activity. By bringing about the degradation of dead plant and animal bodies, for example, bacteria play a crucial role in soil formation and, beyond that, in the cycling of nitrogen and carbon through the biosphere. As another example, many bacteria live in the intestinal tracts of animals, where they synthesize essential vitamins. In looking over the whole spectrum of bacterial activity, it is obvious that the beneficial effects of bacteria far outweigh the deleterious, even from the narrow perspective of human beings.

What does the name "bacteria" signify? In the 1800s a

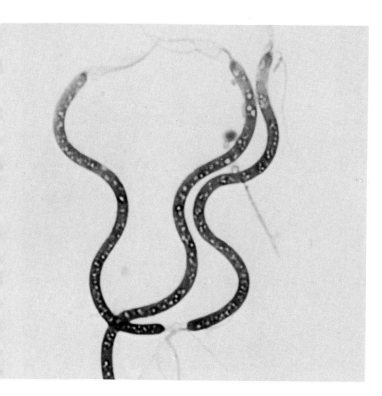

Figure 4.2 (left) The three basic types of bacteria and the colonial arrangements in which they may be found. The rodlike bacilli divide in one plane only, so they form chainlike colonies. Some spherical cocci also divide in only one plane and also form chains. But other cocci may take on different arrangements. Some divide alternately in two planes at right angles to one another, thereby creating small sheets of cells; others divide in three planes and form cubes of cells. Still others follow no characteristic pattern of division, and the resulting cells cluster at random. The spiral-shaped bacteria divide transversely, or crosswise, but rarely remain attached after division is completed.

Taxonomists at one time considered these cell arrangements to be useful for classifying bacteria, but today they know that variations in the environment of a type of bacteria will cause variations in colonial form.

French researcher, Casimir Davaine, examined microscopically the blood of cattle dying from a disease called anthrax. He discovered that certain rodlike organisms were always present in the blood of animals afflicted with the disease and that the numbers of those organisms increased proportionally with the advancement of the disease. These organisms he called *bacteridia*, after the Greek *bakteria* (meaning "rod" or "staff"). Since that time other forms of bacteria have been identified, and today taxonomists divide them into three broad groups on the basis of their shape: the rodlike **bacilli,** the spherical **cocci,** and the spiral or helical **spirilla** (Figure 4.2).

Often when bacterial cells reproduce, the new cells that are formed remain clustered together in colonies. The shape of such clusters is determined by the plane in which the cells divide. Figure 4.2 illustrates the various arrangements of bacterial colonies that are associated with two of the three basic shapes of parent cells. In all cases the colonies so formed are simply clusters of individual organisms of common descent. *Members of a bacterial colony do not integrate their activities with one another.*

The basic structural characteristics of a "typical" bacterial cell are depicted in Figure 4.3. This bacterium has a cell membrane that is surrounded by a cell wall. (In some species, the cell wall is enveloped in a protective sheath, or capsule.) The matter confined within the cell membrane, the **cytoplasm,** contains various subcellular structures, or **organelles.** The hereditary material, which consists of filaments of DNA, is clustered in a nuclear area but is not

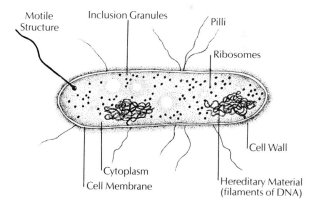

Figure 4.3 (above) Structure of a "typical" bacterial cell. As you read further in this book you will see that there is no such thing as a "typical" cell; the best approximation that can be drawn is a static representation of certain basic characteristics of a constantly changing organism. For that reason, consider this and all similar diagrams of cells to be somewhat like a single frame in a feature-length motion picture. The cast of characters basically stays the same, with some entering and some leaving the picture, but the story moves on from birth to death and each moment is unlike, yet reminiscent of, stories that have gone before.

enclosed in a nuclear membrane. However, the DNA does appear to be attached to the membrane surrounding the cell. The cytoplasm contains many **ribosomes,** which are structures composed of proteins and ribonucleic acid (RNA). They are often clustered into polyribosomes, which are sites where proteins are synthesized.

Bacteria usually reproduce through a process of division called **binary fission,** which is illustrated in Figure 4.4. Binary fission is the most common means of reproduction in prokaryotes. A cell simply grows larger for a time, then divides across its midsection into two equal daughter cells. The daughter cells then repeat this process of growth and division. The DNA of a bacterium is a single, continuous circular molecule that is attached to the outer membrane of the cell. Before the onset of division, the DNA molecule replicates itself and the two daughter molecules are attached to the membrane at separate but adjacent sites. As the bacterium continues growing, new membrane is added between the two DNA attachment sites so that they grow away from each other. Eventually, enough new membrane and cell wall material are added in the midsection of the parent cell that it can cleave into two cells, each with its own DNA molecule.

Some bacteria reproduce by **budding,** a process in which a small protuberance appears on the parent cell, enlarges, breaks off, grows a whiplike "tail," and swims away. During the budding cycle, the hereditary material doubles and then divides, and one part then migrates into the newly forming bud.

Spore formation (Figure 4.5) is characteristic of only certain species of bacteria. It is not a reproductive process; it is a kind of dormancy in which the vital parts of the cell are preserved until favorable conditions are restored, whereupon the spore germinates to give rise to a new bacterial cell, which once again resumes growth and division.

In 1947 Edward Tatum and his student Joshua Lederberg discovered that under certain conditions some species of bacteria engage in a form of reproduction called **conjugation.** Bacterial conjugation resembles sexual reproduction in higher life forms, but it also differs from it in substantial ways. As Figure 4.6 illustrates, a fine bridge forms between the mating cells, and one cell uses this bridge to "donate" a piece of its DNA to the recipient cell. In some cases, the newly donated piece becomes inserted in place of an equivalent piece that was originally present in the circular DNA molecule. As a result of this form of **genetic recombination,** a new individual is produced that possesses a combination of hereditary traits formerly possessed by separate individuals. The new combination may be better or less suited for survival; natural selection will now decide. Despite the selective advantage it offers, conjugation in bacteria occurs irregularly and erratically.

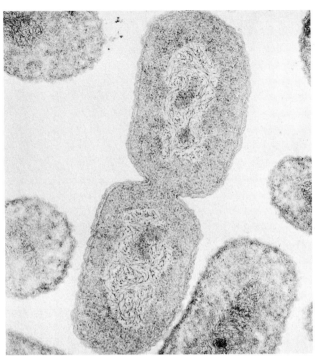

(magnification x48,300)

Figure 4.4   Binary fission in bacterial cells. Bacteria divide with startling rapidity. The time between cell divisions can be as short as twenty minutes. If nutrients and space were available for continued division at the twenty-minute intervals observed in laboratory cultures, a single bacterium could produce offspring of a mass greater than the mass of the earth in less than two days!

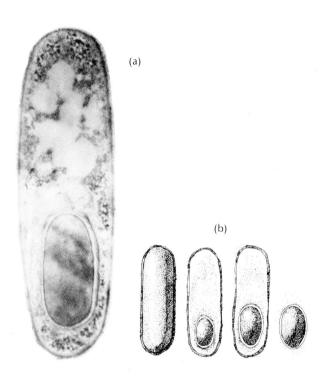

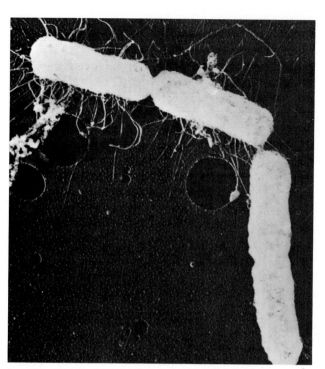

(magnification x49,000)

Figure 4.5 (a) Electron micrograph of a sporulating bacillus. The spore is the large, dark oval at one end of the cell; it is surrounded by a visible spore coat. (b) Under unfavorable conditions, a spore coat forms around the hereditary material of some species of bacteria. Once the coat has formed, the remaining portion of the cell disintegrates.

Whereas bacterial cells are killed almost instantly at a temperature of 100°C, spores can withstand that temperature for hours if they are living in a slightly alkaline solution. The existence of temperature-resistant spores played an important role in the controversy over spontaneous generation (Chapter 1). Those investigators who happened to use slightly acidic boiling water to sterilize their equipment and nutrients unwittingly prevented the recurrence of bacterial growth. Others who happened to use slightly alkaline solutions did not completely destroy the spores, and bacteria formed again—seemingly by spontaneous generation.

Exposure to a higher temperature—about 120°C for a few minutes—destroys most bacterial spores. Water cannot be heated to such a temperature at normal atmospheric pressure, but medical and laboratory equipment can be sterilized effectively in a pressurized device called an autoclave, a laboratory "pressure cooker" in which water boils at about 120°C or higher.

Figure 4.6 Conjugation in the bacterium Escherichia coli, as seen with the aid of an electron microscope. In this primitive type of sexual reproduction, a bit of hereditary information is transferred from a donor cell to a recipient cell, which may then incorporate this piece of information into its chromosome; the result is a cell that possesses hereditary information from two different parent cells.

As you will read later in this chapter, conjugation resembles the sexual processes of eukaryotic organisms in that it results in a recombination of hereditary material. But there are fundamental differences between conjugation and sex.

There are 15,000 known species of bacteria. Of interest to evolutionary theories concerning early life on earth are the bacteria that obtain energy by producing their own carbon-containing compounds from carbon dioxide; these are the **autotrophic bacteria,** the "self-feeders." Some use light as a source of energy for their autotrophic activities, just as plants do, and they are called *photoautotrophic,* or *photosynthetic,* bacteria. They capture solar energy by using their own form of chlorophyll, which is slightly different from the form used by blue-green algae and plants. In addition, there are *chemosynthetic* bacteria, which are autotrophic organisms that derive energy by degrading compounds such as ammonia and hydrogen sulfide.

Far more common than autotrophic bacteria are **heterotrophic bacteria.** Heterotrophs cannot produce their own organic molecules. Instead, they extract energy from autotrophs or other heterotrophs by breaking down the organic molecules produced by these organisms. There are two types of heterotrophic bacteria: the *aerobic* forms, which use oxygen to obtain energy, and the *anaerobic* forms, which are able to live in the absence of free oxygen. In fact, many forms of anaerobic bacteria are killed when they are exposed to oxygen, and they must obtain energy through a variety of less efficient processes known as anaerobic fermentation (Chapter 14). Among the most important heterotrophic bacteria are the ones that combine nitrogen from the atmosphere with organic compounds. These nitrogen-fixing bacteria are abundant in soil and are associated with the roots of plants such as peas and beans. Ultimately, all life forms depend on these bacteria for organic nitrogen, which is needed in protein synthesis.

Perhaps the most impressive thing that can be said about bacteria is that different species have developed an enormous range of solutions to the problem of finding energy. Some exist on petroleum, for example, and others can even degrade certain man-made plastics as a source of energy. Throughout the living world, bacteria are found in an astonishing variety of places as specialists in exploiting various aspects of the environment.

The Specialized Approach of the Blue-Green Algae

The prokaryotic microorganisms named **blue-green algae** are bacterialike organisms found throughout the world in warm moist soil, in sea water, and in fresh water—even in such aqueous extremes as hot springs and arctic pools. Blue-green algae have become specialized as photosynthetic organisms. Like the photosynthetic bacteria from which they may be derived, the blue-green algae take in water and the carbon dioxide found in their aqueous environment and then use light energy from the sun as a "trigger" to synthesize simple sugars. From these sugars, along with

(magnification x6,800)

simple mineral salts, they produce all the other materials required for their life processes. In this photosynthetic process, oxygen on which much of life depends is released as a by-product into the atmosphere. The type of chlorophyll molecule that the blue-green algae use to trap light energy differs from the type used by photosynthetic bacteria; in fact, it resembles the type found in the true algae and higher plants. For that reason the blue-green algae are thought to be some form of bridge between bacteria and true plants.

As in the bacterial cell, the DNA of a blue-green algal cell is localized in a nuclear area, but there is no nuclear membrane surrounding it (Figure 4.7). The cell itself is surrounded by a wall containing cellulose. In many species, the outer portion of the cell wall becomes covered with a slimy substance, which sometimes is present in a thick layer. This slime layer apparently protects each cell from drying out and helps keep the colony intact.

Like most bacteria, blue-green algae divide only through binary fission. Some species form filaments in which a number of cells are joined together end to end (Figure 4.8). In a few species the filaments twist and slowly glide about, but the mechanisms by which this movement occurs are not known.

The bacteria and the blue-green algae are similar in many ways. The cytoplasm in both cases lacks the characteristic membrane-bound compartments found in eukaryotic cytoplasm. Compared with eukaryotic cells, their cytoplasm is far more resistant to damage from heating, desiccation, and chemicals. In addition, the cell walls of both bacteria and blue-green algae contain complex molecules known as mucopeptides, which are not found in cell walls of other kinds of organisms. The blue-green algae are more closely related to bacteria than they are to the other algae. In fact, if it were not for the long-standing usage of their current

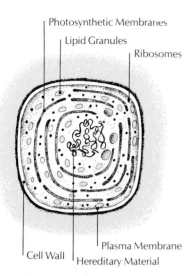

Photosynthetic Membranes
Lipid Granules
Ribosomes

Cell Wall
Plasma Membrane
Hereditary Material

Figure 4.7   Electron micrograph and structural diagram of Anabaena, *a "typical" blue-green alga. The hereditary material, composed of filaments of DNA, is localized in a nuclear region but is not bounded by a nuclear membrane.*

All of the 1,500 or so known species of blue-green algae are photosynthetic. They contain a green pigment (chlorophyll a) and a blue pigment (phycocyanin). Many species do contain additional pigments of various colors, but none contains other forms of chlorophyll. The pigments are arranged on infoldings of the membrane, which makes the algal cell interior appear to be more highly structured than the bacterial cell interior.

(a)

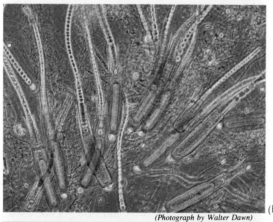

(Photograph by Walter Dawn)

(b)

(c)

Figure 4.8   Species of blue-green algae. (a) Large colonies of blue-green algae often form scumlike masses on the surface of polluted ponds and lakes. (b) Filaments of a blue-green alga of the genus Gloeotrichia. *(c) Filaments of the blue-green alga* Anabaena.

name, calling them "blue-green bacteria" would seem to be a better reflection of their true character.

Mycoplasmas: A Parasitic Mode of Survival

The smallest known cells are the **mycoplasmas,** a diverse array of aerobic and anaerobic organisms tentatively grouped together under this generic name simply because all of them lack a rigid cell wall. Essentially, mycoplasmas are nonmotile units of cytoplasm enclosed in a slightly stiffened membrane that performs some of the stabilizing functions of a cell wall. Most mycoplasmas are **obligate parasites** of animals, in that they do not grow outside the controlled environment of the organism that is their host. However, they can be grown in a suitably enriched liquid culture medium, where they take the form of irregular branchlike structures. On a solid culture medium they look like miniature fried eggs.

These organisms are about one-tenth the diameter of most bacteria. The thirty known species range in diameter from 0.1 to 0.25 micrometer. (A micrometer, which is abbreviated as μm, is one-millionth of a meter in length.) One of the smallest species was studied by Harold Morowitz and Mark Tourtellotte in 1962. They reported that it forms simple, spherical bodies of about 0.1-micrometer diameter, but during its life cycle of a few days it becomes larger and forms a cell of about 1-micrometer diameter. The large cell may divide to form other large cells, or it may develop small bodies within itself and then release them into the environment (Figure 4.9).

If organisms exist that are smaller than the mycoplasmas, they have escaped detection. Because all cell membranes are about 0.01 micrometer (or 10 nanometers) in thickness, the smallest sphere they could possibly form would be about 0.025 micrometer across. But in order to contain all the protein molecules needed for minimal cell functioning, the sphere would have to be at least 0.04 micrometer across. That would be a little less than one-half the size of the smallest known mycoplasma. *If organisms smaller and simpler than mycoplasmas do exist, they cannot be patterned on the fundamental unit of life, the cell.*

Viruses: Primitive Life or Derived From Life?

Every cell—even the simplest mycoplasma—has both DNA and RNA, ribosomes, thousands of complex organic compounds, and an outer cell wall or membrane that regulates the entry and exit of water, salts, foods, gases, and other substances essential to its survival. In contrast, a **virus** is a tiny package of hereditary information—a stripped-down structure usually containing only one kind of nucleic acid (either DNA or RNA) and a protein coat. As such, it is considered to be an incomplete biological entity.

Nevertheless, the virus has gone one step further than the mycoplasma, for it carries out its parasitic activities not in an animal but in a single cell. When it is not attached to a host cell, a virus is inert; it is no more alive than the material in a bottle of organic chemicals on a laboratory shelf. When the hereditary material of a virus invades a cell, however, it takes over the machinery of the cell and

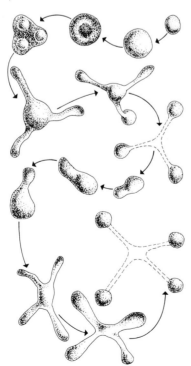

Figure 4.9 Known sequence of division during the life cycle of a mycoplasma, in which large cells may divide to form small bodies. During this cycle the cells enlarge into spherical and armlike filaments in which DNA replication takes place. Each replication center attracts cell membrane material. Following simple fission, these regions become the basis of further growth and reproduction.

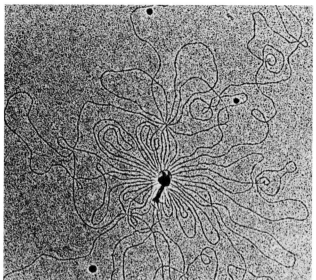

(magnification x20,500)

Figure 4.10 Virus that attacks the bacterium Escherichia coli; *it is called the T2 bacteriophage. This electron micrograph clearly shows long strands of DNA, which have been released from the viral body by a technique called osmotic shocking. Many thousands of bacteriophages can fit comfortably inside a small bacterial cell. Cells of nearly every type of organism are susceptible to attack from some kind of virus.*

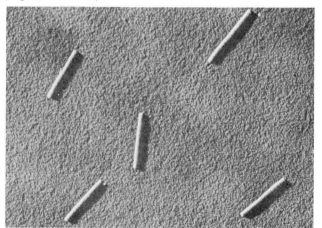

(magnification x49,500)

Figure 4.11 Tobacco mosaic virus particles. Most viruses are spherical, but some are rodlike, bricklike, cubic, or irregular in shape. They vary in size from the polio virus (0.01-micrometer diameter), which is equivalent to the thickness of a cell membrane, to certain disease-inducing viruses (about 0.5-micrometer diameter). This range in size overlaps somewhat with that of the mycoplasmas, the smallest known cells.

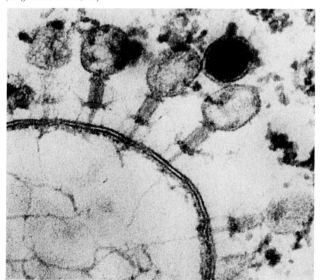

(magnification x153,000)

Figure 4.12 T4 bacteriophages attacking a bacterium Escherichia coli. *The bacteriophage protein coat remains an empty "ghost," attached to the cell wall after it has discharged its hereditary material into its host.*

The protein of the virus serves two major functions. First, it protects the viral nucleic acid from certain enzymes that would destroy bare nucleic acid molecules. Second, by showing a specific affinity for the surfaces of certain kinds of host cells, the protein permits the virus to attach itself only to appropriate cells within which it can reproduce. In other words, the protein determines the host range of the virus.

The simplicity and specificity of a virus make it a remarkable research tool for molecular biologists. It can be regarded as a naturally occurring hypodermic that can inject nucleic acid into a particular kind of cell. Used in this way, viruses have revealed a great deal of information about the hereditary mechanisms of cells.

"directs" it to produce new virus particles instead of carrying out cellular processes. In some cases this takeover results in the death of the cell, which is ruptured as the newly made virus particles grow, fill the cell, and eventually cause it to burst. The particles then make their escape into the environment.

Because viruses are unable to replicate without relying on the nutrients and mechanisms found only in a living cell, it seems unlikely that they existed as primitive systems before the appearance of cells. That is why viruses appear to be relative latecomers in the evolutionary story despite the simplicity of their structure. Many biologists believe that viruses evolved from cells that first became parasites on other kinds of cells and then eventually lost most of their own cytoplasmic machinery. It is common for parasitic organisms living off the labors of a host organism to lose all their original structures and functions except those required for infection and reproduction. Apparently, a selective advantage is bestowed on a parasitic organism that does not perform tasks its host is capable of performing for it.

EUKARYOTES ARE FAR MORE COMPLEX THAN PROKARYOTES

As we move in our discussion from prokaryotic to eukaryotic organisms we cross one of the most significant dividing lines in the living world. Prokaryotes as a group employ an enormous variety of chemical processes in extracting energy from the environment, yet each one is relatively simple in structure and behavior. Eukaryotes as a group seem to be less specific in the way they obtain energy; for example, no eukaryote can extract energy from petroleum or hydrogen sulfide, as certain bacteria can. But in eukaryotes there is much more diversity in the way energy is put to use in developing and maintaining complex structures. These structures in turn expand the opportunities for more complex behaviors.

Eukaryotic Membranes and the Separation of Function

In prokaryotic bacteria, the cell membrane is a vital part of many processes. The ribosomes attached to the membrane are sites where proteins are produced. The processes for obtaining energy from the environment occur on the membrane. The hereditary material of the cell is attached to the membrane and, during cell division, is replicated on it. In blue-green algae, the cell membrane is highly modified and infolded to form layer after layer of double membrane on which the reactions of photosynthesis occur. Essentially, however, in all prokaryotes these functions occur on the same membrane surface and within the same chamber, in which all of the enclosed molecules are free to move about.

In contrast, eukaryotic membranes are not merely surfaces upon which reactions occur. They also are the structures by which the components of one reaction system are segregated from the components of another. In an evolutionary sense, this segregation is immensely important: *With eukaryotic membranes, multiple chambers are created in which activities can be isolated from one another and independently controlled.* The details of structure and function of these chambers (organelles) will be discussed later, particularly in Chapters 13 through 15. For now, the discussion will focus only on those evolutionary aspects of structure and function that are essential to understanding the fundamental difference between prokaryotic and eukaryotic organisms.

Figure 4.13 compares one of the most complex prokaryotes, *Anabaena,* with one of the simpler eukaryotes, *Euglena.* The membrane-bound nucleus clearly visible in the euglena immediately sets it apart from the prokaryotic organism. This double membrane, or **nuclear envelope,** is riddled with pores. The structure and function of these intricate passageways are not yet fully understood, but they are known to regulate precisely the chemical communication between the contents of the nucleus and the surrounding cytoplasm.

The fact that the hereditary material of an organism such as *Euglena* is now enclosed in a nuclear envelope can be interpreted as an outcome of evolutionary pressures on the simpler, ancestral forms of that organism to become more complex. Whatever those pressures were—and shortly we will make some educated guesses as to what they might have been—*at some point in the past, certain organisms developed a reproductive mechanism more efficient than binary fission.* The mechanism and the associated structures that evolved with it would provide those organisms with an evolutionary advantage that would assure survival of all the generations to follow.

Mitosis, Meiosis, and the Sex Cycle in Eukaryotic Evolution

When any cell reproduces itself, it must provide each of its daughter cells with an exact copy of its hereditary material. A cell that fails to get a complete copy from its parent will in all probability lack the instructions for the performance of one or more essential life processes and will be doomed. As you read earlier, the hereditary information for prokaryotes is transmitted in a straightforward way: *All the hereditary instructions in a prokaryote are carried in a single, large, circular molecule of DNA that is attached at some point to the cell membrane.* How this molecule is replicated and separated during the division process is shown in Figure 4.14. In present-day prokaryotes, the capacity of the cell to handle hereditary material in this way is pressed toward what appears to be an upper limit. The following paragraph will explain why this is so.

The DNA in Figure 4.14 looks like a small loop. If the

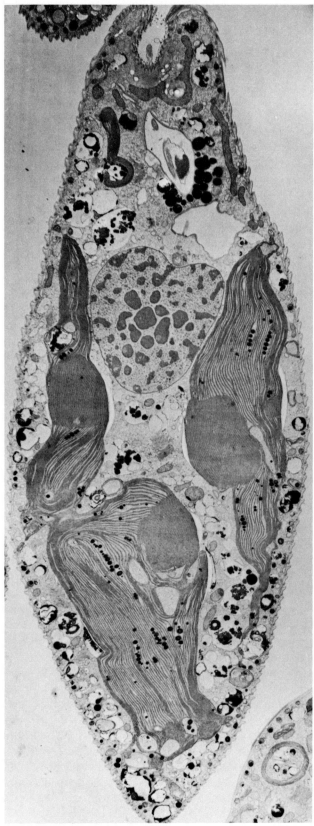

(a)

(b)

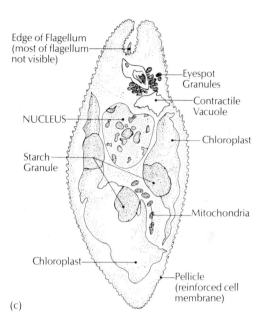

Edge of Flagellum (most of flagellum not visible)

Eyespot Granules

Contractile Vacuole

NUCLEUS

Chloroplast

Starch Granule

Mitochondria

Chloroplast

Pellicle (reinforced cell membrane)

(c)

Figure 4.13 Comparison between (a) the eukaryotic Euglena, *one of the flagellates, and (b) the prokaryotic* Anabaena, *a blue-green alga. In order to enhance the text comparison, the component parts of these organisms are shown approximately to the same scale relative to one another. (c) Sketch of* Euglena.

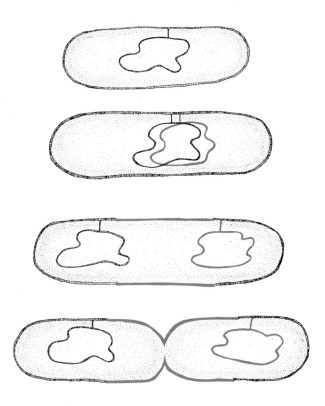

Figure 4.14 Separation of the hereditary material during division in prokaryotic cells. The hereditary material is a single circle of DNA attached to the cell membrane. Prior to cell division a second copy of the DNA molecule (red) is produced and attached to the cell membrane at an adjacent site. As the cell grows, new membrane (blue) is added between the two DNA attachment sites. Because the cell membrane grows inward and cuts the one large cell into two smaller ones, the DNA molecules end up in different daughter cells.

actual DNA molecule of *Escherichia coli* were stretched out into a perfectly round ring, however, it would have a diameter about 300 times the diameter of the cell. Clearly it must be twisted and folded into a compact structure. Given the simple process outlined in Figure 4.14, the physical problems of replicating and separating the twisted and folded DNA molecule without developing snags and tangles must be enormous. Yet all this hereditary information is required to make even a simple organism such as *E. coli*. It follows that any cell appreciably more complex than *E. coli* cannot be constructed without additional hereditary material. In evolutionary terms, this means that a more sophisticated method for handling and parceling out hereditary

instructions was an essential step in the diversification of organisms appreciably more complex than prokaryotes.

More than a billion years ago, a new process for separating hereditary information did appear and it is now used by every organism on earth other than the prokaryotes. This process, called **mitosis,** involves a system of fibers within the cell (hence the word mitosis, which comes from the Greek *mitos,* meaning "thread"). This system is known as the **spindle apparatus.** As shown in Figure 4.15, the DNA in eukaryotic cells exists in threadlike structures called **chromosomes.** Following the duplication of chromosomes, the fibers of the spindle are formed. Some of the fibers extend from pole to pole, acting like a framework on which chromosome separation can take place. Other fibers attach to the chromosomes at a specific point called the **centromere** and are involved in the movement process in which the chromosomes move to opposite poles of the spindle. (The mechanism of chromosome movement is still not known.) Then the parent cell divides. *In mitosis, each daughter cell ends up with the same number and kind of chromosomes found in the parent cell before the division process.*

The appearance of this new method for separating the hereditary material had important consequences. First, once the separation process was based on a multiple fiber system rather than a single membrane attachment site, it became possible for cells to handle more than a single DNA molecule. Cells could now begin to acquire more and more different kinds of hereditary material and faithfully parcel it out to daughter cells. (Indeed, all the millions of kinds of existing eukaryotic organisms have at least two different chromosomes, bearing different hereditary instructions. Most organisms have many different chromosomes— human beings have twenty-three, and some organisms have over a hundred.) Second, because it was no longer essential for the DNA to remain attached to the cell membrane, it could become enclosed within its own membranous chamber—within a nucleus. This isolation has had important consequences for the cell in terms of its possibilities for controlling the cellular interpretation of hereditary instructions. Finally, *the development of mitosis laid the foundations for the evolution of sexual reproduction.*

Fundamentally, **sex** is the union of two cells to give rise to a new organism. (In more complex life forms, one cell comes from the male parent and one comes from the female parent.) The organism so produced possesses inheritable traits of both cells. What are the consequences of the sexual fusion of two cells into one? Suppose we start with two parent cells, each of which contains one complete set (N) of chromosomes. We would call such cells **haploid** (which means a "single set"). After these two cells fuse, the

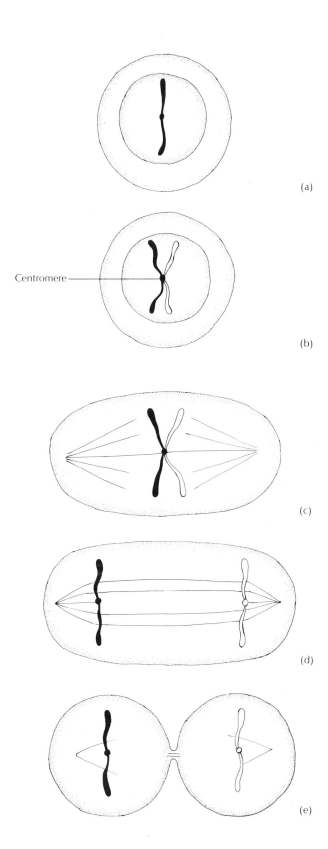

Figure 4.15 Mitosis: the process of separation of the hereditary material during cell division in eukaryotic cells. For the sake of simplicity only one chromosome is shown. But all eukaryotic organisms have at least two different kinds of chromosomes, and some have more than a hundred different kinds.

(a) DNA in eukaryotic cells exists not in circles but in threadlike structures called chromosomes. These structures are not attached to the cell membrane; they are enclosed within a nuclear membrane.

(b) Prior to cell division a copy of the chromosome is produced by a replication process similar to that which occurs in prokaryotes. The two sister chromosomes are held together by a structure called the centromere. At the time of division, the nuclear membrane temporarily disintegrates.

(c) A spindle of fibers having two poles is formed. The centromere is attached to fibers running to each of the poles.

(d) The chromosomes split; the sister chromosomes move toward opposite poles.

(e) New membrane appears, forming two cells. Each daughter cell contains a complete copy of the chromosomes of the parent cell. New nuclear membranes form.

Figure 4.16   Meiosis: the process of separating one diploid set of chromosomes into two haploid ones. In this figure, the process is sketched out in the simplest way possible. Much more is involved, as you will read in Chapter 16. For now, the point is to focus only on the implications that meiotic division holds for the evolution of eukaryotic organisms.

(a) The process of sex involves fusion of two haploid cells at syngamy (or fertilization) to form a diploid cell. (The nuclear membrane is not shown for the sake of simplicity.)

(b) The diploid cells so formed have two complete sets of chromosomes, one set from each parent cell.

(c) Prior to the onset of meiosis, each chromosome replicates but the duplicated structures remain attached at the centromere.

(d) Then, at the first meiotic division, they line up in such a way that each of the chromosomes is paired with its homolog from the other parent. Each partner is attached to a different pole of the spindles.

(e) In meiosis I, the homologues separate from each other. Each cell receives one complete set of chromosomes—some of maternal and some of paternal origin.

(f) At meiosis II, the chromosomes again line up on the spindle, but this time each duplicated chromosome becomes attached to fibers from both poles.

(g) The second meiotic division then separates halves of the previously duplicated chromosomes, producing four haploid cells from each pseudotetraploid cell that entered meiosis.

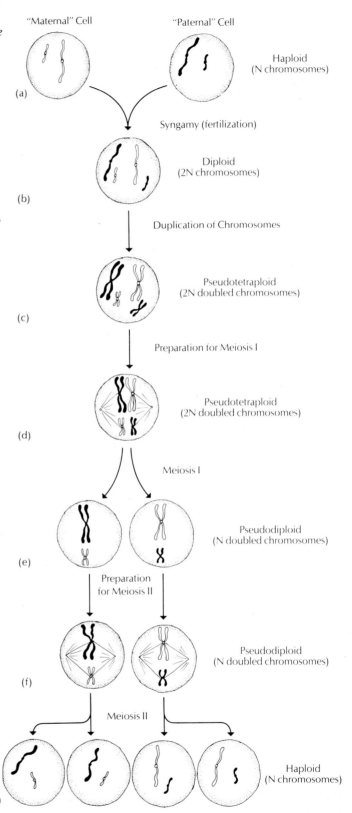

resulting cell would have two sets (2N) of chromosomes—it would be **diploid** (which means "two sets"). If two such diploid cells fused, the result would be a **tetraploid** ("four-set") cell, and so on. In just a few generations the accumulation of chromosomes per cell would reach astronomical proportions!

In prokaryotes there is no way that true sexual reproduction can occur because there is no regular mechanism for dealing with multiple chromosome sets. But in all organisms that undergo mitosis there is a mechanism for regularly achieving fusion of cells in a sexual reproductive process without doubling the chromosome number at each generation. This process occurs in two steps and is known as **meiosis** (from the Greek word meaning "reduction"), or reduction-division. The process of meiosis employs the same kind of spindle apparatus that is employed in mitosis, but the result is different. *In meiosis, each daughter cell ends up with one-half the number of chromosomes possessed by the parent cell prior to the reduction-division process.* Thus, meiosis "reduces" diploid cells to haploid (Figure 4.16).

Recall from Figure 4.15 that in mitosis, spindle fibers from opposite poles attach to opposite sides of a single centromere on a chromosome that has recently duplicated itself. Then the centromere breaks in two, permitting chromosomes that are exact copies of each other to move to opposite poles. In contrast, in the first division of meiosis the attachment of fibers is different, so a different kind of separation results. First the chromosomes line up in pairs: each kind of chromosome that originally came from the male parent lines up beside its equivalent chromosome—its **homologue**—from the female parent. Each centromere becomes attached by fibers to only one pole; in other words, the two chromosomes of a homologous pair become attached to opposite poles. Then they separate, with the maternally derived member of the pair going to one daughter cell and the paternally derived member going to the other cell.

Each chromosome pair lines up independently of all the other pairs before they separate. One daughter cell may therefore receive the maternal member of one chromosome pair, the paternal member of another, the paternal member of still another, and so on. Various combinations are possible. All chromosomes in a haploid cell can be maternal in origin, or all can be paternal, or there can be intermediate combinations of the hereditary material from both parent cells, as shown in Figure 4.16. When two such haploid cells then combine to form a new generation, many new combinations of parental chromosomes are possible. *It is this recombination of chromosomes that gives sexual reproduction its evolutionary significance.* Sexual reproduction can produce all possible combinations of parental hereditary

traits, and natural selection can then act to select the combinations best suited to the environment. A species capable of sexual reproduction has a potential survival advantage over a species incapable of it simply because of the greater probability of producing successful new combinations of traits in each new generation.

When and where does meiosis actually occur? Although all eukaryotes undergo meiosis at some point in their life cycle, in the course of evolution there has been a change in the precise time at which it occurs. Figure 4.17 shows a generalized version of the eukaryotic life cycle. In eukaryotes, meiosis alternates with **syngamy**—the fusion of haploid cells. Each alternation occurs once in each generation. Syngamy leads to the diploid phase of the life cycle, and meiosis leads to the haploid phase. In what appear to be the most primitive eukaryotes today—the flagellated protistans—meiosis occurs immediately after the fusion of two haploid cells, which means that flagellates spend almost all their life cycle in the haploid state. This pattern was probably typical of the earliest eukaryotic organisms.

In organisms of increasing complexity, there is a longer and longer delay between syngamy and meiosis. For example, in the protistans known as foraminiferans, there are two different forms of each species: a haploid and a diploid form that are basically similar in appearance except for size. When an organism spends a prolonged part of its life cycle in each of two such phases (haploid and diploid), the cycle is referred to as an **alternation of generations.** As you will read in Chapter 5, this type of cycle is also seen in plants. In some primitive algae (such as sea lettuce) even an expert cannot distinguish between the haploid and diploid phases on the basis of gross examination. However, the trend in plant evolution has been toward reduction of the haploid phase and emphasis on the diploid phase. In flowering plants, the haploid phase is reduced to a short period within the flower, just before pollination. Similarly, throughout the entire animal kingdom the haploid phase has been shortened to a minimum. In many higher animals, meiosis is not even completed in the egg until the egg has been activated by a sperm. In higher plants and animals, then, syngamy immediately follows meiosis, and the organism spends virtually all of its time in the diploid state. What advantage does the organism gain by the delay?

Through progressive emphasis on the diploid phase, higher organisms have achieved a significant advantage of sexual reproduction over more primitive forms. In a haploid organism, any change in a unit of heredity will immediately lead to a change in the individual that comes to possess it. These changes in a hereditary unit are called **mutations.** If the mutation is lethal in the environment in which it first occurs, its bearer will perish and the mutation will be lost. Now, if such a mutation occurs in a diploid organism, it

(a)

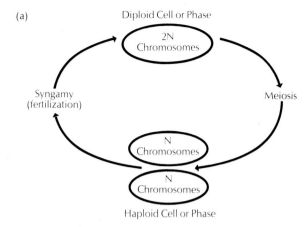

(b)

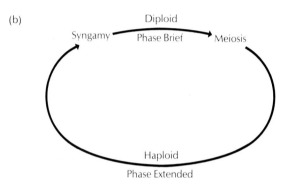

(c)

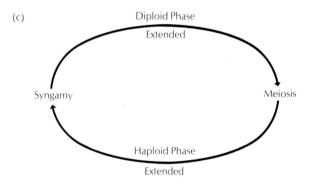

(d)

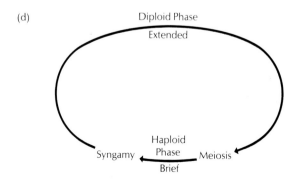

may not be sufficient to lead to death even if it is deleterious in that environment. The reason is that the normal, equivalent hereditary unit (the homologue) may act as a buffer against the effect of the mutation. However, should the environment change to one in which the effect of the mutation is advantageous, the organism has the potential for evolutionary change. *Because of the buffer it provides against deleterious mutations, the trend toward diploidy in sexual cycles has provided an increased reservoir of variation upon which evolutionary processes may act.*

In summary, tremendous reproductive advantages were bestowed on those organisms in which the nucleus first appeared. When we consider all the implications of the isolation of hereditary material from the cytoplasm, of mitosis and meiosis, and of diploidy, it is clear that the appearance of the nucleus was an evolutionary event of the first magnitude.

Mitochondria and Chloroplasts: Membrane-Bound Chambers for Energy Conversion Reactions

In all organisms, certain reactions must occur in order to convert available energy into forms of energy that can be used to do cellular work. These reactions occur on the surface membrane of all prokaryotic cells. In eukaryotic cells, many of these reactions take place in isolated, membrane-bound chambers, or organelles. Second to the nucleus, the organelle most characteristic of eukaryotes is the **mitochondrion.** Mitochrondria are clearly visible in the euglena shown in Figure 4.13. They are found in virtually all eukaryotic cells, where they convert complex carbon compounds into carbon dioxide and water. Energy is released in the process and becomes trapped in adenosine triphosphate (ATP) molecules, which can be used to provide energy for a variety of cellular processes. **Chloroplasts** are another form of membrane-bound chamber that is present in all photosynthetic eukaryotes such as *Euglena*. In these organelles, energy conversion reactions occur in which light energy from the sun is used in the production of complex carbon compounds from carbon dioxide and water.

Figure 4.17 (a) The generalized eukaryotic life cycle. (b) Flagellate-type life cycle; emphasis is on the haploid phase. (c) Alternation of generations, as seen in some protistans and lower plants. (d) Life cycle as seen in higher plants and animals; emphasis is on the diploid phase.

What is the advantage of having reactions carried out in such isolated compartments rather than on a cell membrane? The answer is found in the physical relationship between surface area and volume—a relationship that affects all sorts of biological processes as cells and organisms enlarge. The volume of a solid object increases with the cube of the average diameter. At the same time, however, the surface area increases only with the square of the average diameter. In other words, because of the **surface-to-volume relationship** of a sphere, the fraction of a cell that is in contact with its surface membrane decreases linearly as cell size increases.

The surface-to-volume ratio has severe consequences for sets of reactions in which dissolved, diffusible reactants such as sugars are transformed at the surface membrane to provide energy for cellular work. Such reactions are regulated by membrane-bound protein molecules called **enzymes.** The ratio of enzyme molecules (surface bound) to reactants (dissolved in the total cell volume) falls linearly as cell size increases. *Unless the constraint that the surface-to-volume ratio imposes on cell growth is somehow overcome, the efficiency of certain reactions essential to cell function declines with increasing cell size.*

Anabaena, which is a giant among prokaryotes in terms of cell size, represents one approach to circumventing this constraint on size. As Figure 4.13 illustrates, *Anabaena* has multiple infoldings of the cell membrane, which increases the ratio of membrane to cell volume and therefore the number of energy conversion reactions possible. But the solution is only a partial one, for the fact that all reactions are still performed on the same membrane places limits on the potential for diversification of form. Now, eukaryotic organelles such as mitochondria and chloroplasts are isolated chambers; they can actively accumulate reactants from the surrounding cytoplasm and concentrate them near their membrane-bound enzymes. In addition, to a much greater degree than *Anabaena* these organelles are characterized by layer after layer of infolded membrane. What is the functional implication of these two structural developments? As isolated, efficient energy conversion sites, eukaryotic organelles can be distributed according to the energy needs of a cell—they can, for example, be concentrated in a certain part of the cell to provide more energy for rapid movement. That these developments had evolutionary significance is seen in the phenomenal increase in the size and complexity of eukaryotic forms of life.

The Flagellum: A Mechanism for Rapid Locomotion

The eukaryotic **flagellum** (and its shorter, thinner variant, the **cilium**) is a membrane-sheathed structure for movement. The motile structure of prokaryotic bacteria has also been called a flagellum, but it actually bears little resemblance to the eukaryotic flagellum. In bacteria the motile structure is a simple, naked fiber composed of many molecules of a single protein (flagellin) that combine spontaneously into a more or less linear thread. (The mechanism by which this thread acquires the power to move is still poorly understood.) The eukaryotic flagellum is more complex and more efficient as a motile structure. Within its membranous sheath is an array of eleven fibers—nine ringed about the periphery of the flagellar shaft, or **axoneme,** and two centrally located. Because of their tubular structure, these fibers are called **microtubules.** The nine outer tubules are double in structure; they are called the **outer doublets** (Figure 4.18).

One of the most striking arguments for the basic unity of life forms is that flagella and cilia occur throughout the protistan, plant, and animal kingdoms in precisely this **9 + 2 arrangement.** Enough exceptions occur to indicate that other arrangements can be formed; for example, there are 10 + 2 and 9 + 0 arrangements. Yet the majority of cells and organisms possessing flagella or cilia have retained the apparently prototypic 9 + 2 configuration.

At the base of every flagellum and cilium is a **basal body,** which also has a unique and characteristic arrangement of microtubules. It is because of this basal body that

Figure 4.18 The eukaryotic flagellum. (a) Cross section through a flagellum, showing the 9 + 2 arrangement that is a characteristic pattern found throughout the protistan, plant, and animal kingdoms. (b) Longitudinal section through the base of a flagellum showing the basal body.

(a) 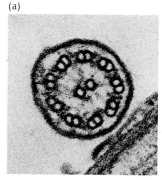   (b)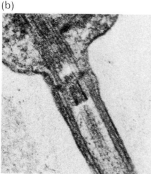

(magnification x60,000)   *(magnification x130,000)*

flagella and cilia bear a striking structural and functional relationship to the mitotic spindle. At each pole of the mitotic spindle of many eukaryotic cells is a paired structure known as a **centriole.** The centriole is not merely similar in appearance to a basal body; the two are identical. The centriole is a self-replicating structure in which a parent centriole produces a copy of itself at right angles to one end. The basal body is capable of the same kind of self-replication, but it can also arise, under certain conditions, from a centriole! The relationship between flagella and mitotic spindles is even more intriguing: The fibers of the mitotic spindle also turn out to be microtubules when examined in the electron microscope. And chemical analysis shows the proteins of both tubule types to be similar.

The functional significance of flagella and cilia will be explored further in Chapter 13. For now, the point to keep in mind is that the eukaryotic flagellum is one of the most effective structures that has evolved in organisms. Whenever this structure emerged in evolutionary time, organisms acquired the ability to move rapidly and exploit different parts of the environment.

HOW DID EUKARYOTIC ORGANELLES ORIGINATE?

From what forms did the first eukaryotes arise? Detailed analyses have led biologists to believe that eukaryotes must have diverged from a prokaryotic ancestor. But *how* did this happen? The classical theory sees the divergence as a slow process in which prokaryotes gradually became larger and more complex, eventually giving rise to organisms that would now be called eukaryotes. The problem with this theory is that neither living nor fossil representatives of intermediate forms have been found to support this view of a slow evolution of one form out of another.

An alternative explanation was proposed well over fifty years ago, but without substantiating evidence it was not taken seriously. However, evidence accumulated during the past decade has brought the theory out of the closet and into the center of a lively new controversy. According to the **symbiotic theory,** *eukaryotes may have arisen by a sudden fusion of two (or more) specialized prokaryotes that so benefited from the fusion they have sustained the relationship ever since.* The fusion mechanism might have appeared in the form of a prokaryotic organism capable of engulfing other prokaryotes as a source of food. This process of engulfment is called **endocytosis** (Figure 4.19).

Adherents to the symbiotic theory believe that an early prokaryotic organism capable of endocytosis eventually ingested another prokaryote that, for one reason or another, was resistant to digestion. This ingested but undigested prokaryote took up residence in its unwitting host and went on growing internally and dividing even as the host was

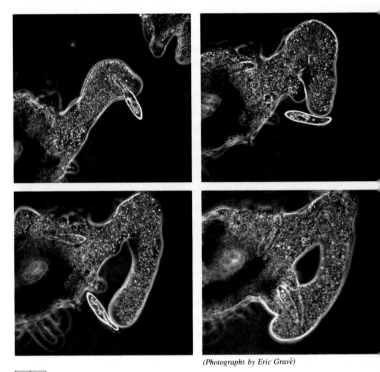

(Photographs by Eric Gravé)

(a) (b)
(c) (d)

Figure 4.19   Two paramecia succumbing to the voracious amoeba Chaos chaos *in a display of endocytosis. The paramecium in (a) has just been captured; the one in (b) and (c) is being nudged into position for capture and subsequent ingestion (d).*

growing and dividing. As the host underwent division, the enclosed resident cells divided, thus becoming part of its progeny. Eventually a mutually beneficial division of labor evolved: The internal resident took over the responsibility of certain kinds of chemical processes for which it was well adapted and, in doing so, produced essential materials for the host. The host, meanwhile, became specialized in providing the raw materials required for the chemical processes of the guest. As long as the host performed its set of functions, there would be no selective pressure upon the guest to retain the hereditary information that would enable it, too, to perform those functions. The reverse would be equally true: The host would gradually lose those elements of its own hereditary information that originally covered the processes now handled by the resident guest. Within a single cell, then, two separate hereditary systems would be acted upon differently by natural selection.

Is it possible that eukaryotes, with their distinct organelles, arose in such a manner? The symbiotic theory of eukaryotic evolution is built around some interesting albeit speculative arguments in favor of just that possibility

(Interleaf 4.1). Regardless of whether eukaryotes evolved slowly or suddenly from a prokaryotic ancestor, one thing is certain: the capacity for one organism to engulf another *did* arise at some point in the past, and from that point on the nature of the community of life was suddenly, dramatically, and fundamentally altered. As long as organisms existed by absorbing nutrients molecule by molecule from their environment, there was a simple live-and-let-live relationship. Matter was recycled through the community only when it was released from one organism as a waste product or by the process of decay after death. But once the "mouth" appeared in the community—a mouth capable of surrounding and ingesting an organism while it was still alive—the picture changed irrevocably. Natural selection previously had been acting upon the ability of organisms to cope with their chemical environment, and it now went to work on the ability of organisms to cope directly with one another as well. To those species without the mechanism for endocytosis, evolution dictated that they either find a mechanism for defense, or perish. To those species that had developed the capacity for ingestion, there was a parallel command: to find a means of circumventing each new defense, or perish.

CLUES TO THE DIVERSIFICATION OF EUKARYOTES ARE FOUND IN THE PROTISTA

According to the taxonomic scheme of Whittaker, all prokaryotic organisms are classified as monerans. If a multicellular eukaryotic organism is photosynthetic, it is called a plant; if it obtains food by absorption, it is a fungus; and if it obtains food by ingestion, it is an animal. Protistans are all the organisms in the world that do not belong anywhere else. Within the man-made boundaries of the kingdom **Protista** are one-celled algae called Protophyta, which resemble plants. Also called protistans are the hypochytrids, which resemble fungi, and the protozoans, which resemble animals.

Protistans do have size in common. With few exceptions, all are small, one-celled organisms. The exceptions include the colonial protistans, which are composed of several similar cells more or less tightly associated with one another. There is some question about whether these colonial forms should be grouped with the protistans or with some other organisms (hence the dashed lines in Figure 3.11 between the kingdom Protista and the three "higher" kingdoms). Despite the taxonomic difficulties with the boundary-straddling protistans, however, they do provide us with possible evidence linking plants, fungi, and animals to a common eukaryotic ancestor in the warm, salty seas of the past. The fossil record itself is incomplete, but by examining present-day members of this kingdom, we can speculate on the possible evolutionary pressures and responses that might have carried simple eukaryotes to the threshold of multicellular complexity that is characteristic of the next three kingdoms.

The Flagellates: Organisms at the Crossroads of Evolution

In the sea, in the lakes, in wet soil, in the digestive system, and in the blood and tissues of animals we find a fascinating array of single-celled eukaryotic organisms that move by the beating of the whiplike structure called a flagellum. They include photosynthetic producers, plant eaters (herbivores), meat eaters (carnivores), and some decomposers. Some biologists would group all these organisms into a single phylum and call them the **Mastigophora** (Greek for "whip bearers") or the **Flagellata** (Latin for the same thing). Others would subdivide them in various ways.

There are compelling reasons to believe that the earliest eukaryotes were flagellates and that they gave rise to modern protistans as well as to all the multicellular plants, animals, and fungi. According to one view, the common ancestral type became highly adapted to various ecological niches, in which certain of its descendants have existed with very little change ever since. The descendants might therefore be viewed as reminiscent of variations that may have existed between 1 billion and 500 million years ago—a critical period for which the fossil record is sparse. The danger implicit in assuming that this picture does in fact correspond to actual historical events should be apparent. None of the present life forms can be expected to be identical to their ancestral types, and many important intermediate life forms have certainly become extinct. Nevertheless, this picture does have the advantage of introducing certain contemporary forms in a way that is more coherent and understandable than current classification schemes can provide.

Consider, for example, members of the genus *Euglena*, which are flagellates of the type illustrated earlier in Figure 4.13. These flagellates possess chloroplasts and are autotrophic in light; they are capable of producing their own food by photosynthetic processes. In this sense they are plantlike. But if they find themselves in an environment rich in dissolved organic compounds—in other words, in some polluted place—they can exist simply by absorbing these compounds through their surface membrane. Under these conditions they are funguslike. These flagellates may even be capable of ingesting particulate food they find floating in their watery environment. In this case they would be animallike. If they are grown in the dark with a rich supply of nutrients and in the presence of certain drugs, they will grow and divide rapidly, but the chloroplasts inside their cell body will grow and divide at a very slow rate. Eventually some individuals will be produced by chance that contain no remnants of chloroplasts. The progeny of

(text continues on page 60)

Interleaf 4.1

Mitochondria, Chloroplasts, and the Symbiotic Theory for the Origin of Eukaryotes

At some point in evolutionary time, certain organisms began ingesting other living organisms as a convenient source of energy, and the cycling of predator and prey began. One of the most direct means of tapping this food source is endocytosis, in which one organism simply encircles another, engulfs it, and digests it—as the amoeba *Chaos chaos* is doing to the hapless paramecia shown in Figure 4.19. Did eukaryotic organelles such as mitochondria and chloroplasts arise when one prokaryote engulfed another prokaryote that could not be digested and instead entered into a symbiotic relationship with its host? There are biologists who in fact believe that the ancestors of mitochondria and chloroplasts were once free-living prokaryotic bacteria and blue-green algae. The arguments for the symbiotic origin of these organelles follow.

First, in general size and certain aspects of structure, mitochondria resemble bacteria, and chloroplasts resemble blue-green algae.

Second, bacteria and blue-green algae exist today that can grow either as free cells or as residents within eukaryotic cells.

Third, both mitochondria and chloroplasts contain DNA that physically resembles bacterial DNA— *not* the DNA of eukaryotic cells.

Moreover, both organelles possess traits that are inherited directly and independently of the hereditary instructions of the cell nucleus.

Fourth, the cell cannot produce mitochondria and chloroplasts if they are not already present. These organelles apparently arise only by division of preexisting organelles.

Fifth, both chloroplasts and mitochondria possess a complete system for synthesizing proteins. Although both depend on the rest of the cell for some proteins, they alone synthesize other essential proteins.

Sixth, all the parts of that protein-building machinery differ from the equivalent parts in the host cell that perform the same functions. And many important components of that machinery resemble their counterparts in prokaryotic cells much more closely than they do the counterparts found free in the cytoplasm of the cell.

Seventh, several substances such as antibiotics and toxins that inhibit RNA and protein synthesis in prokaryotes have identical effects in chloroplasts and in mitochondria. But these same substances have no effect on identical processes occurring in the eukaryotic cell outside the organelles. Moreover, the reverse is also found to be true. Several substances affect RNA and protein synthesis in the nucleus and cytoplasm of eukaryotic cells that have no effect on these processes either in mitochondria and chloroplasts or in prokaryotes.

Those biologists who are *opposed* to the theory of the symbiotic origin of mitochondria and chloroplasts admit that the similarities among chloroplasts, mitochondria, and the prokaryotes are real enough, but they say the similarities have been overstated:

First, there are some substantial differences in addition to the many similarities between the protein-building machinery of the organelles and the equivalent machinery of bacteria.

Second, any presumed ancestor of eukaryotes must have performed the functions that the existing mitochondrion carries out in eukaryotic cells. If that organism did not do so before it ingested the presumed ancestor to the mitochondrion, it would not have been able to survive.

Third, in order to use the symbiotic theory to explain the present diversity of chloroplasts in modern plants, three separate symbiotic events must be postulated.

Fourth, chloroplasts and mitochondria require proteins manufactured according to instructions contained in the cell nucleus. If these organelles arose symbiotically, a wholesale movement of hereditary instructions from the guest to the host would have been required. There is no precedent for such movement, nor is there any known mechanism for doing it.

Fifth, if the nucleus and other membranous or membrane-bound eukaryotic organelles arose by the isolation of functions that were once dispersed in the cell, why can't the same explanation be invoked to account for the origins of mitochondria and chloroplasts?

Sixth, the eukaryotic cell possesses two sets of protein-building machinery—one inside chloroplasts and mitochondria, and one outside them. But both kinds of systems surely must have been derived from prokaryotic ancestors. The fact that one system now bears a greater resemblance to the prokaryotic system means only that the other has changed more rapidly in the course of evolution.

Seventh, it is just as plausible to say that mitochondria and chloroplasts resulted from an infolding, rolling up, and pinching off of parts of the prokaryotic cell membrane responsible for certain processes. (Of course, such a process would be successful only if the organelle so formed also included the DNA required to synthesize certain insoluble components of the organelle membrane.)

Lynn Margulis, one of the proponents of the symbiotic theory, suggests not only that mitochondria and chloroplasts arose symbiotically but that the 9 + 2 flagellum with its basal body (and thus, in-directly, the mitotic apparatus) arose in the same way. This additional thought has been greeted with considerable skepticism. The reason is that there is not now—nor is there any record that there ever has been—a prokaryote with a motile structure sufficiently like the eukaryotic flagellum to serve as a ready-made flagellum by simple symbiosis. The argument against Margulis' runs thus: If we must postulate this complex structure arising a billion years ago, why not postulate its development directly in the primitive eukaryote rather than in some ephemeral prokaryote that subsequently became incorporated, through endocytosis, into a eukaryotic organism out looking for a meal?

The whole controversy may never be resolved with any certainty because the answers may be buried in a recordless past. Nevertheless, in their attempts to unravel the threads of the past by examining the fabric of the present, biologists interested in the symbiotic hypothesis have stimulated exciting research and have already enriched our understanding of the eukaryotic cell and its divisions of labor.

these chloroplast-free individuals will now grow normally only as long as sufficient nutrients are available in their environment. They are now heterotrophic; nourishment comes not from processes within but from the external environment. These organisms now depend utterly on the funguslike or the animallike way of life. They have become virtually indistinguishable from a naturally occurring group of protistans in the genus *Astasia* (Figure 4.20).

In what possible classificatory slot could we file both *Euglena* and *Astasia*? Clearly none exists, at least not in present schemes. But if we can at least temporarily forget about the lack of a name for such boundary-crossing eukaryotes as *Euglena*—and many more exist besides *Euglena*—then perhaps we can look at these modern-day organisms not simply as puzzles but as reflections of conditions that might have existed at some early time in the history of eukaryotic evolution.

Many biologists have asked whether the earliest eukaryotes were more like animals or more like plants. This question is still unresolved. The symbiotic theory suggests that the first eukaryotes were animallike; upon developing a permanent symbiotic relationship with ingested blue-green algae, they became plantlike. But the ease with which existing organisms such as *Euglena* can be transformed from green to colorless forms may suggest that certain animallike forms subsequently arose by simple loss of chloroplasts from plantlike ancestors. Let us turn now to examine certain green flagellates and one route of evolutionary change they have pursued.

The Green Flagellates: The Colonial Pathway to Complexity

Chlamydomonas is a single-celled green flagellate, thought by many to resemble the primitive stock from which some algae and other green plants are derived. Under favorable conditions it grows and then divides by simple fission. Normally the two daughter cells so produced separate and swim away as free organisms. Under certain environmental conditions, however, one of these motile cells may become immotile. If it does, and if it continues to divide, the daughter cells stick together in a loose, jellylike matrix. The cluster has no definite shape or arrangement: no two "colonies" of *Chlamydomonas* look exactly alike. The cells sharing the matrix apparently are oblivious to the presence of one another and apparently do not interact in any way. In fact, if environmental conditions change once more, the individual cells in the colony may develop flagella and swim their separate ways. What is the advantage of a colony so tenuously formed and so easily abandoned? It has little obvious advantage over the free cellular state other than to increase the size of the unit and thereby increase resistance to small predators.

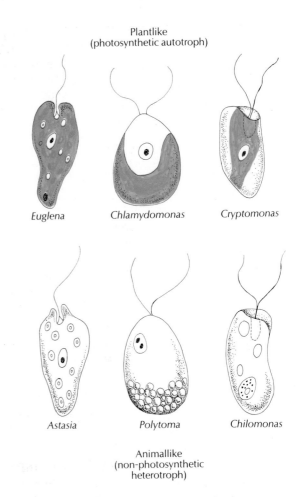

Plantlike
(photosynthetic autotroph)

Euglena *Chlamydomonas* *Cryptomonas*

Astasia *Polytoma* *Chilomonas*

Animallike
(non-photosynthetic heterotroph)

Figure 4.20 Some biologists would place Euglena *with the plants and* Astasia *with the animals. However, the fact that an* Astasia-*like organism can be produced from* Euglena *in the laboratory indicates that such a separation is arbitrary. Many additional examples of such "plant-animal" pairs of apparently related protistans exist in nature; two are depicted here. (These organisms are not drawn to the same scale, but each pair is similar in size.)*

Beginning with *Chlamydomonas*, there is a progression of types of clearly **colonial organisms.** The individual cells of these organisms resemble *Chlamydomonas* in great detail, but the aggregation of cells into colonies and the organization of these colonies is carried to increasing levels of complexity until its culmination in the genus known as *Volvox*. This progression is described in Figure 4.21.

This line of evolutionary change has carried *Volvox* to a boundary beyond which lies a selective advantage characteristic of higher plants and animals: the advantage of isolating a special group of cells for reproductive purposes. As long as every cell in a species retains the capacity for reproduction, each cell must remain relatively primitive. The reason is that no cell can become so complex and specialized that it loses the capacity for carrying out the processes of meiosis, syngamy, and the formation of a new individual. *But if the reproductive role is taken over by a small subset of cells in a multicellular organism, the rest of the cells are free to become highly specialized in form and function.* In plants, this capacity for **division of labor** led ultimately to the appearance of roots, stems, and leaves; in animals it led to the appearance of bone and muscle, blood and gut. In the *Volvox* line, however, the full advantages of this separation of **somatic** (bodily) and reproductive functions were never exploited; all the nonreproductive cells of *Volvox* are essentially indistinguishable from one another.

Interesting and illustrative as the progression from *Chlamydomonas* to *Volvox* may be, then, it appears to have been an evolutionary blind alley. Apparently there is a limit to the possible evolutionary variations on this kind of colonial theme. Volvocales, which is the name given to this series of organisms, and the genus *Volvox* represent the acme of this line of evolution in the present world. Although higher plants are not in any sense derived from *Volvox* and its close relatives, it is commonly believed that a similar process did give rise to the true algae and the higher plants. Furthermore, as you will read in Chapter 7, a similar process of colony formation and increased complexity by protistans probably gave rise to the sponges and possibly to all other animals.

The algal path to multicellularity and complexity differs from that of *Volvox* in the following way. In the *Volvox* line, daughter cells tend to adhere to one another, and the colony grows in three dimensions. Three-dimensional growth in cells is limited by the surface-to-volume ratio described earlier: As size increases, the ratio of surface to volume decreases. The *Volvox* strategy was one of keeping *all* cells on the surface in direct contact with the environment—a *Volvox* colony is simply a hollow sphere. But there are limits to the potential size and complexity of organisms structured in this way. *Volvox* appears to be near those limits, given the structural strength of the jellylike

matrix material holding the cells of Volvocales together.

The algae followed two different paths to enlargement, both of which circumvent the problem imposed by the surface-to-volume ratio and both of which are found today in the plant, fungi, and animal kingdoms. If daughter cells adhere together and the colony grows in one or two dimensions rather than in three, all the cells remain at the surface. Hence the colony can grow to much greater size without encountering problems of acquiring raw materials from, and returning wastes to, the environment. One-dimensional growth produces a threadlike organism. It is characteristic not only of some algae but also of most fungi, some animals, and even many prokaryotes (filamentous bacteria and blue-green algae). Two-dimensional growth gives rise to a sheetlike body form, which also occurs in both plants and animals.

The Golden Algae and the Diatoms: An Armor-Plated Route to Change

One line of protistans is notable because many of its members often have cell walls impregnated with silica; in effect, they live in glass houses. These protistans are the **golden algae** and the **diatoms** (Figure 4.23), grouped together as the phylum **Chrysophyta.** Certain modern golden algae, such as *Ochromonas*, do not appear to be very different from *Chlamydomonas* and its relatives. However, there are pronounced biochemical differences between the two groups. The chloroplasts of both the green and golden algae contain a number of accessory pigments in addition to chlorophyll. One group of accessory pigments common to both phyla is the carotenes (also found in carrots). In the golden algae and diatoms, the carotenes are present in much greater quantities relative to the amount of chlorophyll than is the case in the green algae and they have a characteristic golden color imparted by the carotene pigments. The end product of the photosynthetic process is also different in the two groups. The energy storage material in green algae is starch, but the chrysophytes accumulate oils.

The golden algae are not a very diverse group and are confined largely to fresh-water habitats. The diatoms, in contrast, have undergone extensive diversification and are significant components of the algal flora of virtually all aquatic habitats. The selective advantage that led to the development of the diatoms appears clear-cut: a glass house makes its resident impervious to many small and inefficient predators. In an era from 70 to 10 million years ago the diatoms must have been enormously successful: widespread deposits of diatomaceous earth are now found throughout the world. These deposits (now used by man for filtering beer, polishing jewelry, and a variety of other such enlightened pursuits) are nothing but the skeletons of countless trillions of diatoms.

(text continues on page 64)

Figure 4.21   A colonial pathway among the flagellates. The progression begins with the single-celled protistan Chlamydomonas *(a). These organisms can live independently as single cells or independently in a loose, jellylike matrix with other cells of their kind. (The cells shown in this series are actually about the same size.)*

In the genus Gonium *(b), the colony is the normal way of life. Each colony consists of 4, 8, 16, or 32 cells held together loosely in a flat, platelike jelly mass. All cells in the colony are identical, but they have no obvious functional interaction with each other. Each one retains full reproductive capacity.* Gonium *can reproduce sexually but eggs or sperm do not develop; the reproductive cells resemble the free-living* Chlamydomonas.

In the genus Pandorina *(c), the colonies are larger and more tightly organized. There are 8, 16, or 32 cells in a tightly packed sphere of jelly. As in* Gonium, *all cells retain reproductive capacity and are similar to one another—and to* Chlamydomonas.

In the genus Eudorina *(d), we see the first signs of division of labor. The colonies contain 16, 32, or 64 cells, all of which look more or less alike. In some species only cells in one-half the colony can reproduce. The cells in the other half are incapable of division once the colony has matured. The latter are capable of photosynthesis and all other bodily functions but they cannot become reproductive cells. For that reason they are called somatic cells. The reproductive cells differentiate to form sex cells that are either small, yellow, ellipsoidal, free-swimming sperm or large, round, green eggs.*

In Pleodorina *(e), the division of labor is more complete. Each colony contains 32, 64, or 128 cells of two sizes. The smaller are entirely somatic and only the larger cells can reproduce. Both sperm and egg cells are produced, as in* Eudorina.

The climax of this series is the genus Volvox *(f). A* Volvox *colony is a large, highly regular and well-integrated, well-differentiated colony. Although the number varies between different species, several thousand* Chlamydomonas*-like cells are positioned in a single layer of jelly in a colony that resembles a hollow ball. In some species of* Volvox, *all cells of the colony are interconnected by thin, cellular extensions.*

In (f), eight daughter colonies have formed from the specialized reproductive cells of the parent colony. Within the daughter colonies the specialized reproductive cells destined to form a third generation are already visible. The cross section of a Volvox *wall (g) shows intercellular connections between two adjacent somatic cells.*

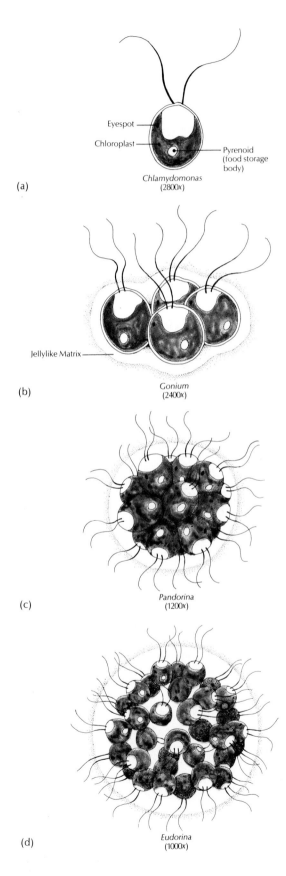

(a)

Eyespot

Chloroplast

Pyrenoid (food storage body)

Chlamydomonas
(2800x)

(b)

Jellylike Matrix

Gonium
(2400x)

(c)

Pandorina
(1200x)

(d)

Eudorina
(1000x)

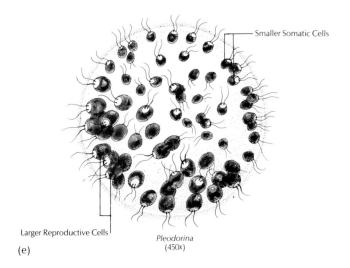

Smaller Somatic Cells

Larger Reproductive Cells

Pleodorina
(450x)

(e)

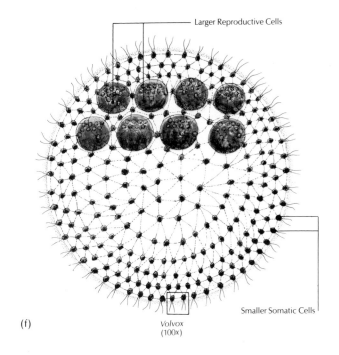

Larger Reproductive Cells

Smaller Somatic Cells

(f)

Volvox
(100x)

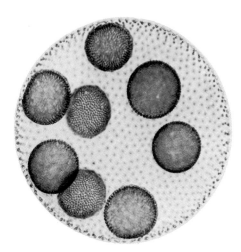

(Photograph courtesy Carolina Biological Supply Company)

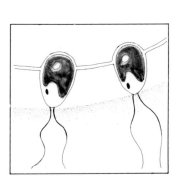

(g)

Figure 4.22 (above) In each Volvox *colony a few cells are differentiated early in the development of the colony; they become larger than the rest. These are the reproductive cells. The others are strictly somatic cells. During asexual reproduction, each reproductive cell divides to form a complete new daughter colony even while it is still enclosed in the parent colony. When the young colonies have completed the division process they escape from the parent colony, which then dies. Under some conditions, these daughter colonies can be induced to follow the sexual path of reproduction. When that occurs, the reproductive cells form eggs or sperm instead of new colonies.*

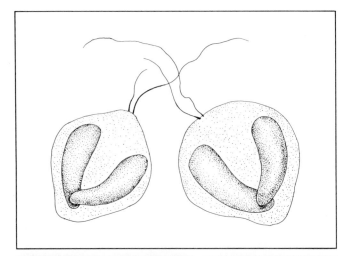

(Photograph courtesy OMIKRON)

(Photograph by Stevens from OMIKRON)

Development of protection against predators leads to a selective advantage, which leads in turn to increased numbers of the protected organisms. But a predator capable of overcoming such protective devices will itself gain a survival advantage because it will be able to prey upon the vast populations that have expanded as a result of the protection. In the oceans today, both the diatoms and the golden algae are still incredibly abundant, but abundant also are a host of efficient predatory organisms, large and small, that prey upon them. Thus the golden algae and the diatoms forge a most important link in the chain of life that exists in the seas. Not only do they serve directly and indirectly as a prime food source for many marine animals, they play a major role (as they did in the past) in producing the atmospheric oxygen on which all animal life depends. For these reasons, naturalists are becoming increasingly concerned over the extent to which humankind is escalating the pollution of the oceans. If the diatoms are lost, the consequences could be severe for all forms of life.

The Dinoflagellates: Algae of the Open Ocean

The **dinoflagellates** are a diverse group of unicellular flagellates that make up the phylum **Pyrrophyta.** The members of this phylum may be found in a variety of fresh-water habitats, but they are most characteristic of the flora of the open ocean. The motile unicells of this group bear two flagella, but the arrangement of the flagella is quite unlike that of any other group of protistans (Figure 4.24). The cells are usually slightly elliptical in outline, and both flagella originate near the middle of the cell rather than from one end. One of the flagella lies in a longitudinal groove for part of its length and trails the cell; the other wraps completely around the cell in another groove. The cells tumble and weave erratically as they swim, due to the simultaneous beating of the two flagella. The cell walls are composed of cellulose and range from relatively simple, unornamented forms to quite complex structures of interlocking plates.

The nuclear structure of the dinoflagellates is quite different from that of other eukaryotic cells. Although a true nucleus is present, the chromosomes are composed entirely of DNA with no protein. In this feature they are not unlike the chromosomes of prokaryotic forms, such as bacteria. Replication of the nuclear DNA appears to parallel the process observed in prokaryotic cells, and separation of complementary DNA strands is achieved by the attachment of the strands to different portions of the nuclear membrane. The membrane divides, and in doing so it separates the

Figure 4.23 (left) Ochromonas, *a golden alga (a). Representative diatom (b). Characteristically, the diatom shell consists of two halves fitted together like a gift box, one half overlapping the other (b). These half-shells are called frustules. When a diatom reproduces asexually, the two frustules separate during cell division. Each daughter cell forms a new frustule that fits inside the parentally derived one. Following each cell division, then, one daughter diatom will be the same size as the parent and one will be smaller. When this process of division leads to a cell of some minimum size beyond which asexual reproduction is impossible, sexual reproduction occurs and gives rise to a new, large cell ready to start the process all over again.*
Only a tiny sample of the amazing variety of form produced by different species of diatoms is shown here (c and d). As is apparent from (d), the frustules are not always circular. In some species they are triangular; in others they have complex oblong shapes. In every case, however, the two halves of the diatom fit neatly into each other.

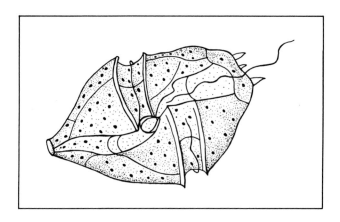

Figure 4.24 The dinoflagellate Gonyaulax. *Under certain conditions, such dinoflagellates can reproduce in great numbers, thereby turning expanses of seawater red by daylight and imparting a phosphorescent glow to it at night.*

replicated DNA strands. Study of the nuclear function in the dinoflagellates may provide insight into the derivation of the nucleus in early eukaryotes, although it is perhaps just as likely that this unusual method of handling nuclear material may be an independent path of development.

Periodic population increases in some dinoflagellate species in coastal waters are responsible for the phenomena called ''red tides.'' These algae can be present in such numbers that they actually impart a red color to the ocean waters along the coast. The particular species responsible for red tides also produce metabolic wastes that are toxic to many fish species, so that red tides are usually accompanied by extensive fish kills in the affected areas. It is felt that these sudden population increases are triggered by the availability of nutrients in the ocean waters, but all the factors that might be involved are not understood.

Amoeba and Its Kin: The Acellular Route to Complexity

A second large group of armor-plated protistans has been enormously successful in the seas, particularly in times past. These organisms are more like animals than plants. Skeletons of some of these organisms in the White Cliffs of Dover attest to their enormous abundance more than 100

(a) (b)
(c) (d)

Figure 4.25 A few representative protistans, selected to illustrate the manner in which Amoeba *and its kin might have been derived from flagellates in the ancient past.*

Oikomonas *(a) resembles many of the other flagellates in having a defined cellular shape and a flagellum, which it uses for swimming about. But it differs from the flagellates in its ability to send out projections of its body (pseudopodia, or "false feet") to surround and engulf food.*

Naegleria *(b) lacks a flagellum as long as food is plentiful; it crawls about on pseudopodia, engulfing its food as it moves. If food becomes scarce, however, it is capable of producing a flagellum, taking on the bodily shape of a flagellate, and swimming away in search of richer pastures (c).*

Amoeba *(d) never possesses a flagellum. It spends its entire life crawling about on surfaces with its pseudopodia.*

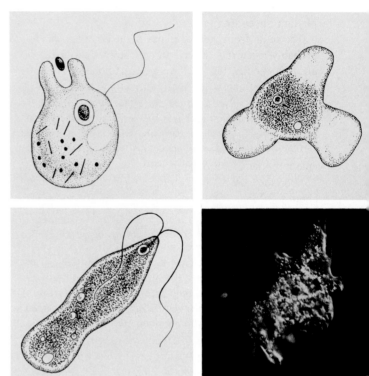

(Photograph by Eric G

(a) (b)
(c)

Figure 4.26 Heliozoan (a) and radiolarians (b and c). The radiolarians are an elaboration on the heliozoan plan. Members of this group have an intricate silica-containing skeleton, sometimes consisting of a glassy sphere-within-a-sphere-within-a-sphere of latticelike armor plates. Often the skeleton is ornamented with glassy spikes protruding symmetrically from the surface. Multiple extensions of the cell project through holes in the lattice. A single individual may have both stiffened permanent projections of the axopod type and motile temporary projections of the filopod type. Like the heliozoans, the radiolarians trap and engulf food with these appendages.

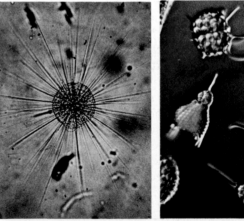

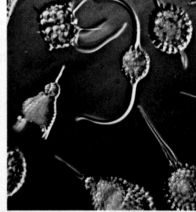

(Photograph by Eric G

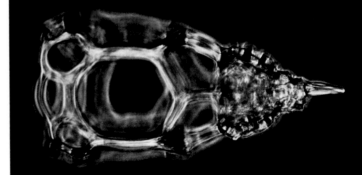

(Photograph by Eric G

million years ago. The group as a whole is classified as the phylum **Sarcodina.**

The route from the flagellates to the complex sarcodines probably occurred through an unlikely intermediate—an ancestor to the familiar *Amoeba.* Amoebas are not the primitive creatures that their formless, oozing body style might suggest. Again we can trace their probable origins by looking at certain modern protistans that may well resemble certain extinct ancestors along the way.

Most colorless modern flagellates absorb nutrients molecule by molecule through their surface membrane (as fungi do), or they use a specialized mouthlike gullet to take in chunks of food. The sarcodines as a group are characterized by the use of a variety of extensions of the body that are used to trap and engulf food particles. Amoebas send out broad, ill-defined projections of the cell, called **pseudopodia** (after the Greek term meaning "false feet"). These projections are used both for locomotion and for engulfing prey (Figure 4.19). Other sarcodines possess **filopodia** ("thread feet"), which are essentially long, slender pseudopodia that can be rapidly extended and withdrawn. Figure 4.25 depicts four forms of organisms that show progression from the typically flagellate body style to *Amoeba.* Whether this progression represents anything like the evolutionary route to the sarcodines is unclear, but it is certainly strongly suggestive.

A more complex group of sarcodines is the **Heliozoa** (Figure 4.26). These protistans have multiple projections similar to filopods, but the projections do not extend and retract. Instead, they project more or less permanently in great numbers from the surface, forming a sticky mesh that traps food. Food particles are then engulfed by small pseudopods formed on the sides of the filaments. These relatively permanent, immobile extensions are known as **axopods.** They have a structure clearly related to but different from the structure of flagella and cilia. There is a bundle of microtubules in the shaft of the axopod that often terminates next to the nucleus, deep in the interior of the cell. The more specialized heliozoans have a glassy skeletal lattice surrounding the cell, through which the axopods project.

The **Radiolaria,** which resemble heliozoans, are giants among protistans: they sometimes reach diameters of several centimeters. Despite their size and armor plating, they can remain suspended in the sea, well below the surface. They contain numerous vacuoles that apparently provide bouyancy. When these organisms die, they fall to the bottom of the sea. Their skeletons are so resistant to decay that they make up an important part of the sediment on the ocean floor. In the ocean today, radiolarians play an important role in the food chain, grazing upon microscopic plants and in turn being preyed upon by larger organisms.

The **Foraminifera** are a second group of armor-plated relatives of the amoebas; they are only indirectly related to radiolarians. These organisms have proliferated in the sea and their skeletons have been settling on the bottom of the ocean ever since they appeared many hundreds of millions of years ago. The foraminiferans can exceed the radiolarians in body size. The largest skeleton yet found measured $7^{1}/_{2}$ inches across (nearly as large as a human head). How could a single shapeless, amoebalike cell give rise to this comparatively enormous, architecturally elegant creature? There is no complete answer to this question, but there is an important clue in the fact that, like many other members of their phylum, foraminiferans are single cells by one definition only. It is more instructive to think of them as **acellular organisms,** organisms that have become extremely complex in the course of evolution but have not compartmentalized their cellular components within cell membranes.

(magnification x25)

Figure 4.27 Foraminiferans. The simplest foraminiferan looks like an amoeba that has simply enclosed itself in a tough, bubblelike organic shell reinforced with sand grains cemented into it. Other forms reinforce their shell with calcium carbonate, which they secrete, rather than with sand grains. An entire spectrum of types exists in which the organism adds chamber after chamber to itself as it grows. In the most common group of foraminiferans, the new chambers are added in a continuous three-dimensional spiral of the type seen in a snail. An opening through the preceding chambers is maintained as each new chamber is added so that the organism can inhabit all chambers at once. Each chamber is perforated with multiple holes to the exterior (hence the name Foraminifera, Latin for "hole bearer"). Through each hole a sticky filopod is projected and together these filopods make an efficient food-catching web. Other foraminiferans add chambers and enlarge in the shape of a braided or coiled rope.

The entire contents of each member in this phylum are enclosed in a single cell membrane, and if that were the only criterion they would all be considered unicellular. In many species, however, **multiple nuclei** are present. In certain large amoebalike forms, for example, the organism begins life as a simple cell with one nucleus. As it grows, the nucleus divides but the cell does not, the outcome being a mature organism that contains many nuclei. Often such cells reproduce asexually by **plasmotomy,** in which the organism simply pinches apart into two or more pieces that become separate individuals. (If such an organism is cut experimentally into as many pieces as there are nuclei, each nucleated piece will form a multinucleate individual.) In many heliozoans there is one nucleus at the base of each axopod. Similarly, multiple nuclei are often found in radiolarians, positioned symmetrically around the periphery of the ''cell,'' one next to each projection from the body wall.

Clearly the organizational themes in the phylum Sarcodina are as complex as those of many multicellular forms; its members simply lack the internal cell membranes delimiting separate cells. It might be anticipated that, for several reasons, there would be a limit to how far this body plan could be carried in the evolution of larger and more complex individuals. The radiolarians and foraminiferans surely must be pressing these limits! Hence, as successful as the radiolarians and foraminiferans are, they represent another evolutionary dead end in the narrow sense that they cannot reasonably be expected to give rise to still more complex life forms.

The Sporozoans: A Parasitic Route to Simplicity

There is a sizable group of organisms that superficially resemble the organisms grouped in the phylum Sarcodina. These are the **Sporozoa,** organisms characterized by their formation of haploid reproductive cells (called ''spores'') at one stage in their life cycle. The sporozoans are parasitic: they live within a larger organism, exploiting its machinery and products for their own benefit and contributing nothing of their own to compensate the host. Indeed, as in the case of the malaria parasite (Figure 4.28), they often produce materials that are noxious to the host.

Because parasitic forms can rely on their host to perform many essential functions for them, they characteristically tend to lose certain specialized features possessed by their ancestors; hence their evolutionary relationships to other groups are often obscure. So it is with the sporozoans. Although some of them look like an amoeba at one or more stages in their life cycle, it is not certain whether this resemblance should be taken as evidence of a direct

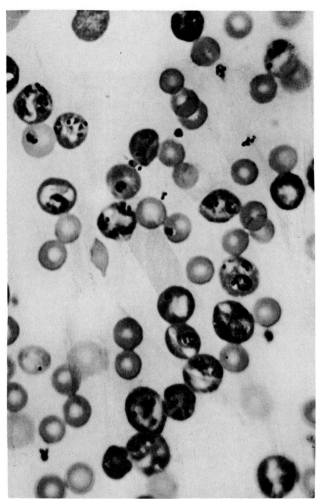

(magnification x4,000)   (Photograph by Walter Dawn)

Figure 4.28 Malarial parasites in human red blood cells. Cells introduced into the body in mosquito saliva infect circulating red blood cells, and they begin to proliferate asexually. Within forty-eight hours they cause the cell to burst, freeing them to enter uninfected cells and begin a new forty-eight-hour cycle. Each period of cell bursting is accompanied by a fever characteristic of the disease. When infected blood cells are drawn up by a second biting mosquito, they are released to reproduce sexually within the mosquito, producing more progeny that can be injected into another victim. In many tropical areas, malaria has been the leading cause of death in the human population.

relationship to Sarcodina. Indeed, it is highly likely that the organisms grouped in this category may include members of several rather unrelated groups. Their similarities may be due to nothing more than the fact that they all have become highly simplified as a result of the parasitic way of life. Regardless of their origin, the sporozoans have a significant effect on the lives of the higher animals they inhabit.

The Ciliates: The Macronuclear Route to Complexity

The most complex forms of protistans are found in the phylum **Ciliophora**—the ciliates. The characteristic feature of this group is the presence of multiple cilia, or devices derived from cilia. Once again, presently existing forms may give us a clue to phylogenetic relationships, this time between the flagellates and ciliates. Flagellates that generally appear to be primitive organisms have only one flagellum, which is used in a screwlike manner to *pull* the organism through the water. In more highly specialized flagellates, such as *Giardia* and *Macrospironympha*, multiple flagella are used as "oars" to *push* these organisms through their liquid environment. One protistan, *Opalina*, has thousands of such "oars" of the short, multiple structures we call cilia (Figure 4.29).

For years *Opalina* was classified with the ciliates; biologists now realize that, appearances to the contrary, it has many basic similarities to flagellates. It is quite likely a modern close relative of the ancient intermediates between the two groups, and it is presently classified by some biologists in a category by itself.

There are three fundamental ways in which flagellates differ from ciliates, and in all three ways *Opalina* resembles the flagellates. As Figure 4.30 shows, the ciliates evolved a unique solution to a common cellular problem. There is a limit to how much a single set of hereditary blueprints can control. If an organism is to enlarge, the number of copies of the hereditary material must be increased. *Volvox*, like all the fungi, higher plants, and animals, achieved this increase by becoming multicellular. Each cell in a *Volvox* colony has one complete set of hereditary blueprints, or its own **genome.** The heliozoans, radiolarians, and foraminiferans increased in size by becoming multinucleate. Each region of this kind of organism has its own genome, contained in the nucleus found in that region. The ciliates were able to enlarge by developing two kinds of nuclei, with a complete division of labor between them.

The ciliate **macronucleus** is entirely responsible for directing the day-to-day operations of the cell. The **micronucleus** participates in meiosis and sexual reproduction; it also gives rise to new macronuclei, which are formed by the repeated replication of hereditary material *without* cell

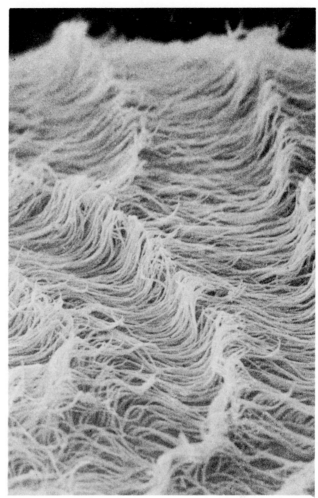

(magnification x21,300)

Figure 4.29   The multiple cilia of Opalina. *Some free-living flagellates with one or two flagella use their motile structures to* pull *themselves through the water. But organisms that live in the intestinal tract of insects and vertebrates use their multiple flagella as "oars" to* push *their way through the thick intestinal soup in which they live. Opalina, an organism found in the digestive tract of amphibians, has carried this elaboration of flagella one step further: thousands of cilia (short flagella) occur in neat rows over the entire surface of the organism.*

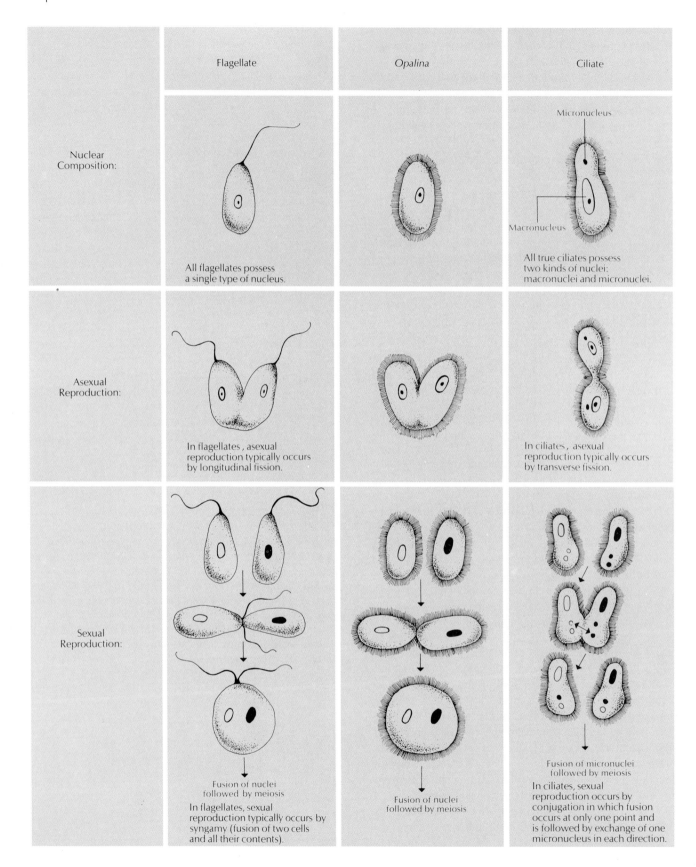

	Flagellate	*Opalina*	Ciliate
Nuclear Composition:	All flagellates possess a single type of nucleus.		Micronucleus / Macronucleus — All true ciliates possess two kinds of nuclei: macronuclei and micronuclei.
Asexual Reproduction:	In flagellates, asexual reproduction typically occurs by longitudinal fission.		In ciliates, asexual reproduction typically occurs by transverse fission.
Sexual Reproduction:	Fusion of nuclei followed by meiosis — In flagellates, sexual reproduction typically occurs by syngamy (fusion of two cells and all their contents).	Fusion of nuclei followed by meiosis	Fusion of micronuclei followed by meiosis — In ciliates, sexual reproduction occurs by conjugation in which fusion occurs at only one point and is followed by exchange of one micronucleus in each direction.

division. Thus, the macronucleus contains the same information as the micronucleus but in multiple copies—sometimes fifty or more.

When a ciliate reproduces asexually, both nuclei divide. The micronucleus divides by conventional mitosis, but the macronucleus divides by a mysterious process of **amitosis**, in which it simply is pinched into two parts that are passed on to the two daughter cells. Whether amitosis results in equal and identical daughter macronuclei is not yet known. Some ciliates are so complex that a single macronucleus will not keep the cell running. Various species contain from one to several hundred micronuclei and from one to several dozen macronuclei per cell. (For this reason, it may be more realistic to think of ciliates, like some of the sarcodines, as "acellular" rather than unicellular.)

The architectural accomplishments of the ciliates stagger the imagination. There are ciliates that possess organelles equivalent to the mouth, digestive tract, anus, nerves, muscle, skeleton, skin, and sense organs of a higher animal! In some, the body is covered with rows of cilia. Each cilium originates in a basal body, and all the basal bodies of a ciliary row are connected by a system of fibers. In addition, a network of fibers (neurofibrils), analogous to the nerve network of higher animals, appears to connect with a central motor mass in some species. It has been suggested that this interconnection pattern may be responsible for synchronization of cilia so that each cilium beats slightly out of phase with adjacent cilia. There is no doubt that cilial function is coordinated, but recent data suggest that, at least in some species, the coordination may be mediated by the cell surface and not by the neurofibril network. These organisms are extremely sensitive to tactile and chemical stimuli, and if they encounter an obstacle or noxious substance, they can instantly reverse the beat of all their cilia, back up, turn, and swim off in another direction.

Not all ciliates have their cilia arranged exclusively for such integrated swimming activity. In many species, adjacent cilia are fused side-to-side into short rows that work together in an extraordinarily strong beat directed toward the mouth, or gullet. Together these **membranelles** form a most efficient feeding structure. In other cases, many adjacent cilia are fused together inside a single membrane covering to form a strong, tapering bristlelike structure known as a **cirrus.** Such cirri are used as legs for walking about on surfaces! Both membranelles and cirri are clearly visible in the photograph of *Oxytricha* at the beginning of this chapter. The group to which *Oxytricha* belongs lacks body ciliation of the sort seen in *Paramecium*. The members of this group never swim; they spend their lives "walking" on surfaces of objects in their environment.

Many ciliates possess one of the world's most amazing weapon systems. Often thousands of fibers, or **trichocysts,** are arranged in a regular fashion so that they alternate with the cilia in ciliary rows. Each trichocyst consists of a long

Figure 4.30 (left) Comparison of the nuclear composition and the mode of reproduction of a flagellate, a ciliate, and Opalina.

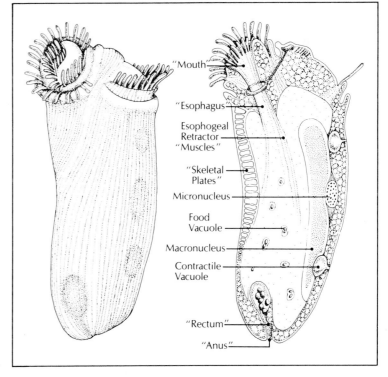

Figure 4.31 The ciliate Diplodinium.

fiber (sometimes longer than the body of the ciliate itself) coiled up in a sac and bearing a spearlike, toxin-laden tip. Upon appropriate stimulation, a barrage of trichocysts can be discharged into potential prey—or predators. They also can be discharged into a surface to serve as anchors for the organism, holding it in place while it feeds.

Beneath their surface layer, many ciliates possess contractile filaments that are analogous to (and chemically related to) the muscles of higher animals. These filaments permit the organism to change its body shape. Many ciliates and other fresh-water protistans possess one or more amazing devices known as **contractile vacuoles.** These devices function primarily to rid the organism of excess water. In a sense, they are analogous to the kidney and bladder of higher animals. Excess water picked up in various regions of the cell is conducted to a vacuole by means of a network of fine tubules in the cell. When the vacuole is filled, it does what its name suggests: it contracts and expels its contents to the exterior.

When a ciliate divides asexually, all of its highly specialized, intricate structures must be reproduced. This is accomplished through **morphogenesis**—the development of form. Morphogenesis in ciliates has been studied extensively, but it is still far from being completely understood. One thing can be said with certainty: The pattern of ciliation existing in the organism before reproduction absolutely determines the pattern that will be produced in the offspring, with no discernible involvement of nuclear information. If a "mistake" is introduced into the organization —either naturally or as the result of surgical intervention in the laboratory—the "mistake" will be perpetuated in all subsequent asexual progeny.

For example, Tracy Sonneborn and his colleagues at Indiana University have studied individual paramecia afflicted with the reversal of one or more rows of cilia; in other words, with a few rows organized (and thus beating) in the direction opposite from all other rows. Once they occur, such reversals will be inherited permanently by all asexual progeny. When such individuals are mated with normal paramecia, however, such mistakes are not transmitted. Apparently the only hereditary information controlling ciliary organization is in the ciliary row itself! This is one of the clearest examples to date of the process known as **cortical inheritance.** The extent and generality of cortical inheritance as a hereditary mechanism in the living world is still unknown.

Clearly, the variety and beauty of the ciliates alone is such that an entire biology course could be restricted to this one group and still it would cover most of the important principles of biology. Similarly, an entire course could be given on the kingdom in which they are found. But this chapter has necessarily focused on only a few groups, the purpose being only to illustrate certain evolutionary trends. The Appendix to this book does list groups not mentioned here, and it may be worth a minute to scan through its entries in order to get a better picture of the extent of this kingdom. You will in any event be returning to some of these organisms in the next five chapters, in which the evolution of plants, fungi, and animals will be explored.

PERSPECTIVE

The flagellates, the diatoms, the amoeba and its relatives, the sporozoans, the ciliates—a survey of just a few representatives of these groups can convey little more than an impression of diversity within the kingdom Protista. Beyond this level of inquiry is an astonishing number of experiments attempted in nature on a variety of evolutionary themes. But if you accept that the examples chosen here are representative of the diversification that does exist, ask yourself these questions: Is it possible to identify the cellular developments that made such diversity possible? What evolutionary pressure might have been responsible for the appearance of eukaryotes, and for their tendency to become larger and more complex? And what evolutionary developments may have provided the raw materials for the kind of diverse solutions to common problems exhibited by different groups?

As long as communities of living things consisted only of prokaryotic organisms like the blue-green algae (autotrophic producers) and the bacteria (heterotrophic decomposers subsisting on the wastes of the producers or on the remains of producer cells), there would have been no obvious selective pressure on those ancestral forms to enlarge or to develop defense strategies. When the first cell appeared that was capable of endocytosis, the whole structure of community relationships would have to change swiftly.

A tremendous selective advantage would develop for those members of the community that, by mutation and by chance, acquired heritable mechanisms of physical protection. Some would end up with heavy cell walls or shells of armor; some would develop flagella for rapid movement, and still others would grow enough in size to avoid at least the smaller predators. Regardless of the means of protection, the mere act of escaping predation ensured that some organisms would leave behind more offspring, and in so doing they would begin to predominate in the environment. At the same time, however, their one-time predators would begin to dwindle in numbers for lack of accessible prey. Now a *new* selective advantage would accrue to the predator that acquired a means of circumventing the new modes of defense. Perhaps the advantage would come from a more efficient mouth, or a still more effective means of moving about, or a more extensive set of enzymes that would facilitate digestion of previously indigestible forms. Perhaps the advantage would come when a predator adapted to the region to which the prey had escaped, or perhaps when the predator, too, enlarged in size and became capable of eating larger prey.

Regardless of the kind of change, the success of the predator could not outpace the success of the prey. If it did, both would be threatened with extinction. A stable relationship could develop only if the predator were incapable of consuming prey as fast as the prey multiplied. The outcome of such an ongoing process of offense and defense would be a rapid diversification of life forms. It seems certain, then, that the dramatic increase in size, complexity, and diversity of the life forms that evolved in the seas many millions of years ago can be attributed largely to the enormous selective pressure exerted by the first predatory cell.

Having a selective *pressure* for change is not enough, however, if a *mechanism* for heritable change does not exist. Because the hereditary blueprint (genome) of any cell basically determines the potential of that cell, a more complex blueprint would seem to be necessary before a more complex cell could be built.

As you read in this chapter, some existing prokaryotes are apparently pressing the upper limits of the size of the genome that can be passed on faithfully to daughter cells in the simple mechanism of binary fission. It is unlikely that the size or complexity of the genome (and hence the size and complexity of the cell) could ever have been increased over existing prokaryotic values without a mechanism that could effectively separate and parcel out much more hereditary information to the daughter cells. Buried in the past is the story of how such a mechanism evolved, but evolve it did and today we call it the process of mitosis. The mitotic process—whatever its origins—undoubtedly played an essential role in permitting cells to accumulate additional blueprints, which could then give rise to new and different cellular functions. Following immediately after this, the meiotic process introduced a new, rapid way of generating hereditary diversity at a quickened pace.

In short, although the "mouth" may have provided the stimulus, the mitotic apparatus provided the mechanism for increased complexity in life forms.

The problem of increasing in size is somewhat different from the problem of increasing in complexity. In growth it is not so much necessary to do a great many new things as it is to do the same things many times over. For example, a cell that increases tenfold in diameter increases a thousandfold in volume and requires a thousandfold increase in all its essential "housekeeping" molecules. There is, however, a physical limit to how rapidly a DNA molecule can function in helping to create the essential molecules of cellular structure and function. Before an organism can be produced that is large enough to perform or to escape predation, some

mechanism must be developed that will allow an increase in the number of copies of the hereditary blueprint available to each organism. The protistans have taken three different approaches to the problem.

The ciliates increased the number of copies of the genome per cell by developing a macronucleus, in which DNA is replicated over and over again even though the nucleus itself is not dividing. The outcome is an increase in the copies of available DNA—but a concurrent outcome is a nucleus too large and complex to participate in mitosis or meiosis. All ciliates therefore retain one or more micronuclei in which a diploid set of hereditary instructions is maintained for reproductive purposes only; these micronuclei play no role in the day-to-day operation of the cell.

The radiolarians are typical of many groups of protistans in which the necessary increase in the number of copies of hereditary material for each organism is achieved with multiple nuclei.

Finally, the Volvocales (*Volvox* and its relatives) followed the route to multicellularity, in which an organism is subdivided into numerous cells. It is a characteristic the Volvocales share with higher plants and animals.

All three of these routes accomplish more or less the same thing, but only in multicellularity is there sufficient flexibility to provide an evolutionary path to the large and complex eukaryotic organisms found in the higher kingdoms. You will be tracing the details of this multicellular route from the protistans to the higher kingdoms in the following chapters.

SUGGESTED READINGS

CURTIS, HELENA. *The Marvelous Animals: An Introduction to the Protozoa.* Garden City, N.Y.: Natural History Press, 1968. A good popular introduction to the protozoa, written by a skilled science writer.

DOBELL, CLIFFORD. *Antony van Leeuwenhoek and His "Little Animals."* New York: Dover, 1962 (reprint edition). A scholarly and charming account of the life and work of the discoverer of microorganisms, written by a scientist active in the field.

KLUYVER, A. J., and C. B. VAN NIEL. *The Microbe's Contribution to Biology.* Cambridge, Mass.: Harvard University Press, 1956. These brilliant essays on topics ranging from energetics to evolution were originally delivered as the John M. Prather Lectures at Harvard.

MARGULIS, LYNN. *Origin of Eukaryotic Cells.* New Haven, Conn.: Yale University Press, 1970. An outstanding textbook of microbiology.

SLEIGH, M. A. *The Biology of Protozoa.* London: Arnold, 1973. A well-illustrated, readable introduction to protozoan structure and function. Written for the nonspecialist.

Chapter 5

The Strategies of Plants

The short distance from the ocean shore to a coastal forest can be encompassed in a moment's glance. Yet it represents an incomprehensibly long journey in the movement of life from its cradle in the sea to dominance of the land. The passage of hundreds of millions of years and the accumulation of an immense number of adaptations were required for plants to bridge the gap between the modes of life illustrated here.

an it be that some sort of ancestral flagellated organism gave rise to all the world's multicellular plants? Somehow the picture of motile, plantlike things crawling up out of the primordial seas to conquer the land seems like a scene from a Hollywood thriller. Animals, of course, might have evolved this way, with their flagellated ancestors invading the terrestrial environment by retaining their ability to move about in search of the water on which they (and all of life) depend. But trees and other plants! They are rooted firmly to the earth. If confronted with a dwindling water source, they cannot pick up and move on. Animals move about; plants stay put.

And yet, it is impossible to deny that there has been a movement of immobile plants out of the water, through the coastal plains and the foothills, all the way to the high country of mountain ranges throughout the world. In some way, by strategies uniquely their own, plant forms have radiated throughout the environment. The evolution of these strategies is a remarkable story. It gives us, far more than any simple cataloging of plant forms can do, an idea of the fundamental mechanisms for survival that are shared by all the varied members of this kingdom.

THE SEXUAL PROCESS IS A KEY TO PLANT DIVERSIFICATION

Perhaps more than any other single factor, *the plasticity of reproductive strategies is the key to plant radiation and diversification.* All eukaryotic cells—plants included—reproduce sexually. In other words, meiotic division of a parent plant cell produces haploid cells, and the fusion of one of those cells with a haploid cell from another parent forms a diploid cell, or zygote. But members of the plant kingdom differ from animals, and from one another, in the length of the interval between the production and the subsequent fusion of haploid cells.

In most animals, a meiotically formed haploid cell functions directly as a sexual reproductive cell, or **gamete.** (''Gamete'' is taken from the Greek word for ''husband'' or ''wife.'') A gamete produced by a female parent cell is an **egg;** a gamete produced by a male parent cell is a **sperm.** After a sperm and an egg fuse, the diploid zygote that is formed goes through a period of growth and development. The process culminates in a mature animal—which eventually will produce new gametes by meiosis. As you shall see, most plant life cycles resemble those of animals in some respects but differ from them in others.

It may be easiest to explain these differences by starting with a generalized life cycle that applies to virtually all plants. As Figure 5.2 shows, the diploid cells of all plants undergo meiosis to produce haploid cells. But the haploid cells do not function directly as reproductive cells. They

first multiply by mitotic divisions to produce a haploid plant body. These special haploid cells are called **spores,** and the haploid body each spore creates is called a **gametophyte.** (The combining form *-phyte* simply means ''plant.'' The word ''gametophyte'' means ''gamete plant.'') The gametophyte of many simple plants can reproduce itself by various asexual processes. The gametophyte of more complex plants tends to be less pronounced, but some multicellular body is always formed. *In all plants, however, it is the gametophyte that directly produces haploid gametes by mitotic division.* The sexual fusion (syngamy) of haploid gametes then produces a diploid zygote.

Patterns of zygote development vary, depending on the plant. The various patterns possible are indicated in the upper half of Figure 5.2. For example, in certain algae, the zygote immediately undergoes meiosis to produce haploid spores, thus completing the life ''cycle.'' In other algae that encounter unfavorable environmental conditions, the zygote forms a resistant **resting spore**—a kind of dormant body. Thus meiosis and germination can be delayed until conditions become more hospitable. In more complex plants, the mitotic divisions of the zygote create an embryo and, finally, a complete diploid body called a **sporophyte** (''spore-producing plant''). Diploid sporophytes are the most conspicuous part of the earth's vegetation. Specialized cells of these sporophytes, called **spore mother cells,** eventually undergo meiosis to produce haploid spores.

In all plant life cycles, the haploid gametophyte phase always alternates with the diploid sporophyte phase. This gametophyte-sporophyte pattern is called an **alternation of generations.** *Different life cycles vary principally in their emphasis on either the gametophyte or the sporophyte phase.* The life cycles described in this chapter will be much easier to understand if this relationship is kept clearly in mind. The details of different life cycles can be viewed simply as specialized patterns that have evolved in different plants for carrying out a common reproductive sequence under varying environmental conditions. Viewed in this light, Figure 5.2 is the first step in understanding the evolutionary significance of the strategies developed in each of the plant groups.

PLANT FORMS THAT REMAINED IN THE WATERS OF THE EARTH

The term ''algae'' has been widely used in biological literature and is useful in a number of contexts, but it no longer is given any formal significance in plant classification schemes. In the broadest sense, the term would include seven phyla in three separate kingdoms. It is now known that there is at least as great a difference between the various kinds of algae as there is between certain algae and certain ''higher'' plants. The only two characteristics algal organ-

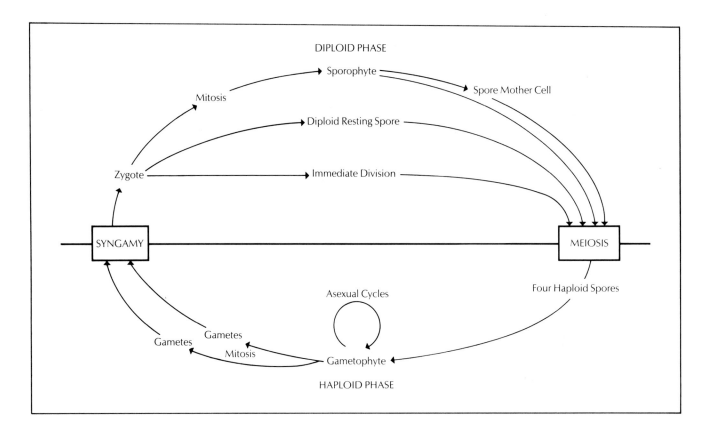

isms share with one another are the presence of chlorophyll and the general absence in their reproductive structures of the nonreproductive cells found in more complex plants. Such nonreproductive cells serve a structural role and are not directly involved in the production of gametes or spores. In contrast, the algae either lack multicellular reproductive structures, or when such structures are present all cells usually take part in gamete or spore formation.

Most algae are aquatic. They can be found in habitats that range from fresh water, to brackish water, to sea water. The aquatic forms that live attached to or at the bottom of any body of water are called **benthic algae.** The forms that live suspended in open water are called **planktonic algae.** Many fresh-water algae have a world-wide distribution. Their dispersal has probably been accomplished by migratory aquatic birds that carry algal spores from one body of water to another. Marine algae are often more limited in distribution, in part because of temperature and salinity gradients from one geographic region to another.

Terrestrial algae are somewhat less common than aquatic forms, but they can be found wherever reasonably moist soils persist for a good part of the year. Soil contains a wide variety of dormant algal cells, and active growth, even below the soil surface, may occur in some species. Certain algal species can even be found growing on ice and snow in permanent snow fields.

Algae are the foundation for all aquatic food chains. They may even be responsible for most of the photosynthesis that maintains the oxygen level in the earth's atmosphere. They are also an important factor in water pollution crises. *Algal blooms* are sudden increases in algal populations that can impart a bad taste to water supplies; they can even poison water systems. Blooms of marine algae form the destructive *red tides* (Chapter 4). In fresh water, algae respond to high nutrient levels by reaching tremendous population sizes. An algal bloom in fresh water can deplete the oxygen supply to the extent that many desirable fish species become endangered. Such population surges may be caused in part by fertilizer runoff and input of other chemicals containing high nitrogen or phosphate levels.

Seven phyla are usually included in a discussion of algae:

Cyanophyta	(blue-green algae)
Chrysophyta	(golden algae and diatoms)
Euglenophyta	(euglenoids or photosynthetic flagellates)
Pyrrophyta	(dinoflagellates)
Chlorophyta	(green algae)
Phaeophyta	(brown algae)
Rhodophyta	(red algae)

Figure 5.2   The generalized pattern of plant life cycles. All plant life cycles are characterized by an alternation of generations (alternate haploid and diploid phases). They differ primarily in the relative duration of the two phases. These differences arise largely from differences in the developmental pathway of the diploid zygote.

The first four phyla were discussed in the preceding chapter, where the blue-green algae were treated as monerans and the golden algae, diatoms, euglenoids, and dinoflagellates as protistans. Obviously the "proper" taxonomic positions for these organisms is far from clear. For example, the green algae would be considered by most botanists to include unicellular forms such as *Chlamydomonas* and related colonial forms including *Volvox*—which were treated as protistans in Chapter 4. Such inconsistencies point out the difficulties in applying a man-made system of boundaries to an evolutionary continuum of organisms. (This difficulty was alluded to in Figure 3.11 by the dashed line that separates the kingdom Protista from the other kingdoms.)

Chlorophyta: The Green Algae

The 7,000 or so members of the phylum **Chlorophyta** are found throughout the entire range of algal habitats. Essentially, the **green algae** are identical to higher plant cells in structure and biochemistry. Their characteristic green color is derived from photosynthetic pigments chlorophyll *a* and *b* found in their membrane-bound chloroplasts (Chapter 15). Other pigments are present in this group but in lesser amounts.

In the broadest sense, the form of the plant body, or **thallus,** ranges from unicellular flagellates, to filamentous

and sheetlike forms, to rather complex structures. As you read in Chapter 4, there may have been several paths that led to the development of multicellular body forms from a single cell. A thallus similar in form to the living unicellular *Chlamydomonas* is thought to be ancestral to the various present-day green algae. This view is supported somewhat by the almost universal occurrence of cells of this type in the sexual and asexual reproductive cycles of green algae. Accumulation of such cells in a three-dimensional colony such as *Volvox* is one option, but mechanical factors alone appear to limit the evolutionary possibilities of such a body form. Given the number of species that exhibit it, probably the most successful configuration has been the filamentous body form. Each long thread, or filament, of cells results from cell division along a single axis. Many algae, including common fresh-water forms such as *Ulothrix, Spirogyra,* and *Oedogonium,* have a filamentous thallus. Division of a parent cell in two axes to form a flat sheet of cells occurs less frequently in the green algae; *Ulva,* or sea lettuce, is a good example of this type of thallus. Because green algae lack differentiated support tissues, the mechanical problems of maintaining the integrity of a large sheet of cells has probably been the limiting factor on two-dimensional growth.

Sexual reproduction in green algae is marked by the alternation of haploid and diploid phases. Usually the haploid phase is dominant. The green algae are important in the evolutionary derivation of more complex plants, and for that reason several representative sexual life cycles will be described.

Perhaps the discussion ought to begin with *Chlamydomonas.* Regardless of whether it is considered a protistan or a green alga, its characteristics are such that it is a logical starting point in tracing the evolution of sexual reproduction in plants. From either point of view, part of its life cycle is representative of the most primitive sexual process—isogamy. **Isogamy** is the fusion of two haploid cells that are neither "male" nor "female"—they both simply are haploid. More complex forms of reproduction involve **anisogamy,** which is the fusion of motile reproductive cells that are different in size, and **oogamy,** in which a motile reproductive cell (sperm) from a "male" parent fuses with a nonmotile reproductive cell (egg) from a "female" parent.

The single-celled *Chlamydomonas* is a motile alga (Figure 5.3a). When environmental conditions are favorable, *Chlamydomonas* can divide by mitosis, which means it can reproduce asexually. In the sexual process, two haploid cells function directly as gametes and fuse (Figure 5.3b). Sexual reproduction is often triggered by a worsening of environmental conditions, such as a drop in temperature or a gradual drying of pools where the organisms live. First a diploid resting spore forms that is quite resistant to drying,

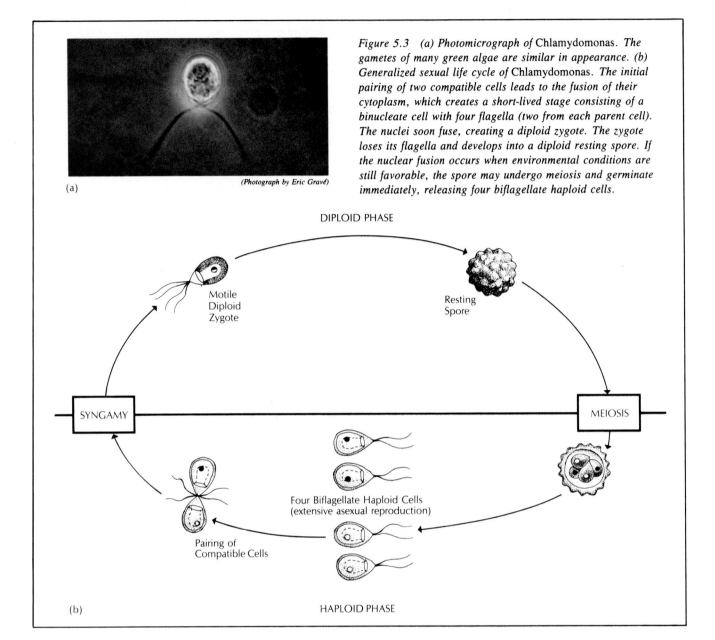

(a)

(Photograph by Eric Gravé)

Figure 5.3   (a) Photomicrograph of Chlamydomonas. *The gametes of many green algae are similar in appearance. (b) Generalized sexual life cycle of* Chlamydomonas. *The initial pairing of two compatible cells leads to the fusion of their cytoplasm, which creates a short-lived stage consisting of a binucleate cell with four flagella (two from each parent cell). The nuclei soon fuse, creating a diploid zygote. The zygote loses its flagella and develops into a diploid resting spore. If the nuclear fusion occurs when environmental conditions are still favorable, the spore may undergo meiosis and germinate immediately, releasing four biflagellate haploid cells.*

DIPLOID PHASE

Motile Diploid Zygote

Resting Spore

SYNGAMY

MEIOSIS

Four Biflagellate Haploid Cells (extensive asexual reproduction)

Pairing of Compatible Cells

(b)

HAPLOID PHASE

low temperatures, and other adverse conditions. Under such conditions, spore germination will be delayed until conditions are suitable for growth.

The sexual cycle of filamentous green algae such as *Ulothrix* (Figure 5.4) probably represents an evolutionary variation of cycles of the *Chlamydomonas* type. *Ulothrix* filaments consist of haploid cells, each of which contains a single band-shaped chloroplast. The filament is usually anchored to some substrate by a modified cell called a **holdfast.** As in the case of *Chlamydomonas,* the haploid phase is dominant, with the diploid phase restricted to a resting spore. This pattern seems to be an optimum adjustment for ensuring the success of the species. When condi-

tions are favorable, the alga reproduces asexually, populating the environment with duplicates of the organisms that apparently are well adapted to prevailing conditions. As the environment deteriorates, the onset of sexual reproduction ensures that the next generation will demonstrate a maximum range of adaptability. All of the genetic recombinations possible will be present in the small, motile cells, or **zoospores,** produced by meiosis of the resting spore.

Several green algae, such as *Oedogonium,* represent lines that have evolved to the point of oogamy. In such forms, the nonmotile egg is retained in the filament in a specialized cell called an **oogonium.** The motile gametes are analogous to sperm cells. They are smaller than the egg and are

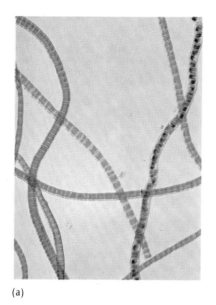

(a)

Figure 5.4 (a) Filaments of the green alga Ulothrix. *(b) The generalized life cycle of* Ulothrix. *Reproduction is mainly an asexual process. In the haploid phase the contents of cells reorganize and the cells divide mitotically. Each one forms a number of small, motile cells having four flagella. These motile cells are zoospores. They are released from a pore in the old filament cell wall, swim about briefly, and then settle down to the substrate. They then lose their flagella and divide mitotically, eventually producing a new filament.*

The sexual process is usually triggered by unfavorable environmental conditions. The sexually produced cells are biflagellate; they are virtually indistinguishable from Chlamydomonas *cells. They function as isogamous gametes. Fusion of two of these biflagellates results in a diploid zygote, which loses its flagella and develops into a resting spore. When favorable conditions return, the resting spore undergoes meiosis. Haploid zoospores are formed that settle down to form a new filament.*

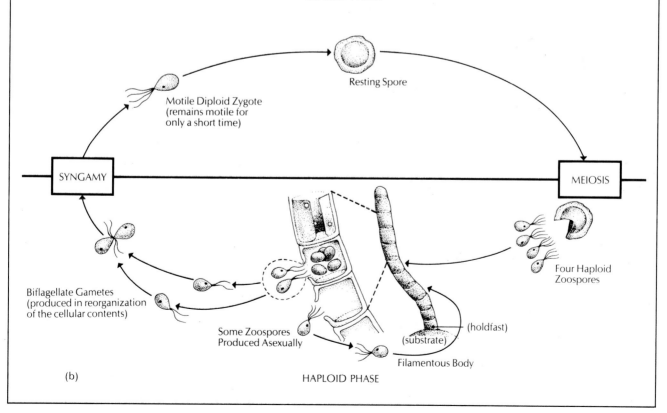

DIPLOID PHASE

Resting Spore

Motile Diploid Zygote
(remains motile for
only a short time)

SYNGAMY

MEIOSIS

Four Haploid
Zoospores

Biflagellate Gametes
(produced in reorganization
of the cellular contents)

Some Zoospores
Produced Asexually

(holdfast)

(substrate)

Filamentous Body

(b)

HAPLOID PHASE

Figure 5.5 *(a) Ulva, or sea lettuce. The haploid form of this green alga is a thin sheet of undifferentiated cells. Ulva has no roots, nor does it have stems or leaves. It is a common sight on the North American coasts, for wave action tears away at it and the plants wash up on shore. (b) Generalized life cycle of Ulva. As in Ulothrix, the haploid form reproduces asexually, with zoospores being released from individual cells. Flagellated gametes are produced in a similar way and undergo fusion. The outcome is a diploid zygote. The zygote does not undergo immediate meiosis—or even delayed meiosis. Instead, it begins a series of mitotic divisions. Eventually mitosis produces a sheet of cells that is identical to the haploid plant. Only then do cells undergo meiosis, producing haploid zoospores, which then produce a new haploid body.*

(a)

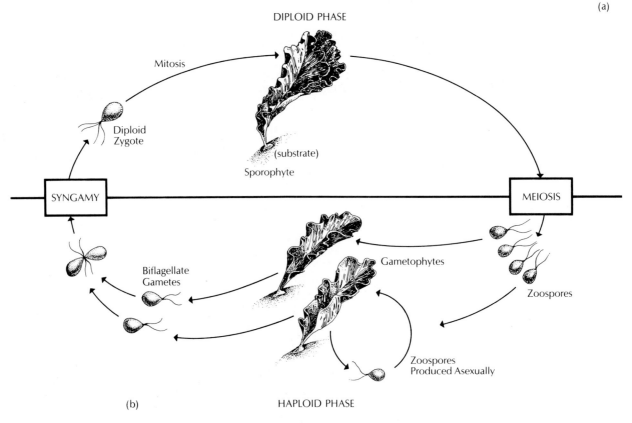

(b)

DIPLOID PHASE

Mitosis

Diploid Zygote

(substrate)

Sporophyte

SYNGAMY

MEIOSIS

Biflagellate Gametes

Gametophytes

Zoospores

Zoospores Produced Asexually

HAPLOID PHASE

produced in the filament in specialized cells called **antheridia.** The motile gametes are released into the aqueous environment, and one eventually swims through a small pore in the wall of the oogonium, where it fuses with the egg to form a zygote. The zygote is the only diploid phase in the life cycle. Eventually it germinates to form haploid zoospores. *The sexual differentiation represented by oogamy is the pattern developed in all of the more complex green plants.*

Although the life cycles of most green algae emphasize the haploid, or gametophyte, phase, some marine forms have evolved along lines in which the sporophyte becomes elaborated beyond a simple resting spore. The life cycle of *Ulva* is a case in point (Figure 5.5). In *Ulva*, there is no way to determine by simple observation whether a plant represents the diploid or the haploid phase: the sporophyte phase is essentially identical with the gametophyte phase. This pattern is quite rare among fresh-water algae.

Why do we not see more algal life cycles of the *Ulva* type? Although a definite answer cannot be given, there are some factors that may have a bearing on the question. For most green algae we can assume that the gametophyte phase is well adapted to the normal range of environmental conditions under which the plant is growing. *The sporophyte phase represents a specific mechanism for carrying the genes responsible for that adaptability through periods when plant growth is not possible.* The wide occurrence of life cycles of the *Ulothrix* type indicates the success of this strategy. Selective pressure toward elaboration of the sporophyte phase would be expected if such development would increase the potential for survival under a wide range of conditions. In the *Ulva* life cycle, the sporophyte phase appears to duplicate adaptive features of the gametophyte phase. Selection may not favor this duplication because it does not increase adaptability enough to offset the physiological cost of elaborating the sporophyte phase. Quite possibly, sporophyte elaboration is just not profitable, in an evolutionary sense, unless the pattern of sporophyte development results in new survival potential. The wider occurrence of complex diploid sporophytes in marine green algae may indicate that additional selective forces are operating in the marine environment.

Phaeophyta: The Brown Algae

There are more than a thousand species of **Phaeophyta,** or **brown algae,** and most are important parts of near-shore marine ecosystems. The group consists entirely of multicellular forms. There is speculation that the group may have been derived from a green alga ancestor, but there are profound biochemical differences between green and brown algae, and not one simple brown alga exists that might be analogous to a transition organism. Neither is this phylum a springboard toward more complex plants. True, the phylum does include some of the most complex algae (the kelps), but its biochemical pathways are quite different from those of more complex land plants, so it is unlikely that any member of this phylum gave rise to terrestrial plants.

The plant body ranges from a branched filament in the simplest forms to the quite complex structures of kelp (Figure 5.6). In kelp, cell differentiation has led to support tissues and, to a limited extent, vascular tissues for the transport of fluids. The brown, dark olive green, or even near-black colors typical of members of this group are a result of the presence of pigments called xanthophylls. These pigments supplement chlorophyll in trapping light for photosynthesis (Chapter 15).

Rhodophyta: The Red Algae

The phylum **Rhodophyta** contains approximately 4,000 species. With the exception of a small number of fresh-water forms, most **red algae** are benthic marine forms growing in near-shore and comparatively deep water habitats. The cell walls of red algae are composed of cellulose and pectin. Basically, the plant body is a branched filament, but more complex forms are composed of masses of filaments embedded in a gelatinous matrix.

The many unique features within the phylum indicate that the red algae have had a long evolutionary history, but the

Figure 5.6   Underwater view of a kelp "forest."

Figure 5.7   A red alga. The photosynthetic pigments in red algae consist primarily of chlorophyll and a complex of pigments called phycobilins. These pigments are well adapted for carrying on photosynthesis under conditions of marginal light input, specifically, in deep water where other forms of algae would not be able to survive.

nature of their relationship to other algal groups is obscure. Red algae have no flagellated cells in their sexual life cycles. A great many species are calcareous, in that the plant body accumulates calcium salts as it grows. Such calcium deposits preserve the form of the plant body long after the plant itself has died. They are in fact responsible for the comparatively good fossil record we have of the group. The lack of a parallel record for other algal groups contributes to our lack of understanding of the evolutionary relationship between the red algae and other algae.

THE CONQUEST OF THE LAND

All the organisms discussed so far are aquatic, and undoubtedly they are reminiscent of plant life that existed on earth until about 450 million years ago. The major evolutionary lines within the algae were firmly established by that time, and individual organisms were well adapted to a range of aquatic habitats. Aquatic ecosystems, particularly the plants within them, were probably as complex and finely tuned as similar systems are today. Terrestrial habitats 450 million years ago were quite another story, for life was almost entirely absent from dry land. In both composition and function, life as we know it is a phenomenon intimately linked to water. Living systems originated in an aqueous medium and it is not surprising that, even today, living systems demand water for their proper functioning. Just as an astronaut stepping onto the surface of the moon cannot

function without a spacesuit that carries a small part of his normal environment with him, so life forms leaving the water for "dry" land cannot function without adaptations for maintaining the "wet" environment.

One of the main demands on terrestrial organisms is that they must have a way of preventing evaporative water loss. In most terrestrial plants, the parts exposed to air are covered with a thin layer of a waxy substance, called **cutin,** that greatly reduces water loss. But even so, as you will read in Chapter 15, the requirements for gas exchange limit the amount of water that can be conserved. Some water is always lost, and eventually it must be replaced. Motile organisms such as animals can simply move to a source of free water and ingest it by various means. But for most terrestrial plants, the only water available is in the soil or substrate on which they are growing. Procurement of water therefore requires structures for absorbing water from the soil and a reliable system for transporting it to the aerial parts of the plant. As if these problems were not enough, photosynthesis and the production of food molecules occurs in the exposed part of green plants. Because the plant parts involved in absorption of water and precursor molecules from the soil are not exposed to sunlight, there must be some mechanism for transporting food down to them even as they send water and other molecules upward. Clearly, the transition from an aquatic to a terrestrial habitat was no simple matter.

Now, in algal life cycles, the growth and development of the gametophyte and the release and union of motile gametes require relatively large amounts of water. We might suppose that, in the transition to land, gradual evolutionary changes in the gametophyte might occur in response to selective pressures. But if we look at modern representatives of plant lineages that made the transition, we see that this development generally has not occurred. Algal gametophytes have no features that are useful for life on land. Because they are in themselves highly evolved and well adapted to an aquatic habitat, it appears likely that the evolutionary changes required for their transition to land are so profound as to be almost unachievable.

Although the evolutionary possibilities of the gametophyte may be inherently limited, the sporophyte (represented in most algal life cycles by little more than a diploid cell) would not be constrained by so vast a number of prior adaptations. *It is in the elaboration and modification of the sporophyte phase that we see the gradual building up of adaptive features that assured the development of terrestrial plants.*

Sporophyte development provided a means of entry into habitats that were essentially unoccupied. It is likely that there was fierce biotic competition in the aquatic habitats, populated as they were by a diverse assemblage of well-adapted organisms. The first plants on land faced little competition from other organisms and could undergo a rapid burst of adaptive radiation. Some of these adaptive features are highlighted in the following discussion.

Bryophyta: The Liverworts and Mosses

Of the approximately 24,000 species of organisms in the phylum **Bryophyta,** most are mosses. The gametophyte phase is prominent. The gametophyte ranges from erect, tuftlike plants in the **mosses** (Figure 5.8) to irregularly shaped, thick sheets of cells that grow parallel to the ground in the **liverworts** (Figure 5.9). The moss gametophyte consists of a central vertical strand of cells with broader, leaflike outgrowths where almost all photosynthetic activity occurs. However, these outgrowths are not considered true leaves: they lack a system for conducting water and nutrients. The central strand of cells, to which the "leaves" are attached, serves a support function but is not considered a true stem because conducting tissue is absent. The plant is attached to some substrate (usually soil) by a mass of threadlike, nonphotosynthetic cells called **rhizoids.** Like

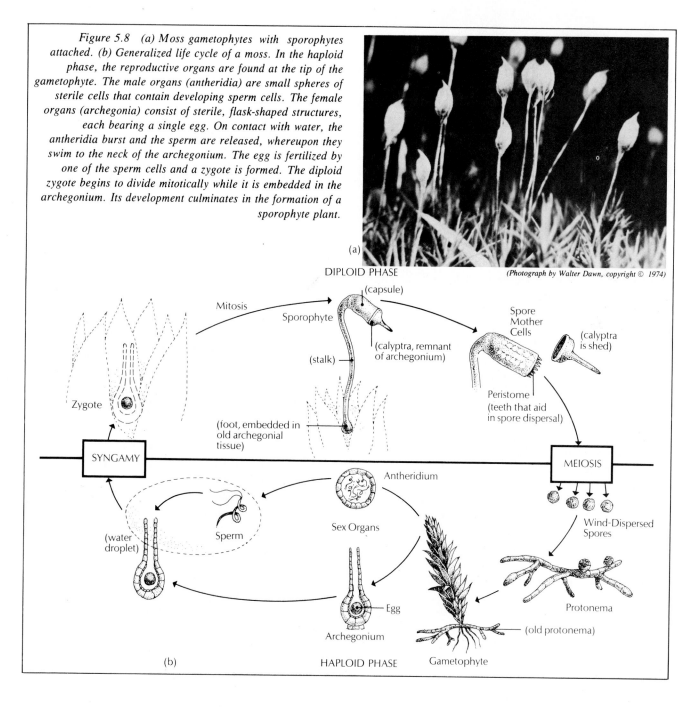

Figure 5.8 *(a) Moss gametophytes with sporophytes attached. (b) Generalized life cycle of a moss. In the haploid phase, the reproductive organs are found at the tip of the gametophyte. The male organs (antheridia) are small spheres of sterile cells that contain developing sperm cells. The female organs (archegonia) consist of sterile, flask-shaped structures, each bearing a single egg. On contact with water, the antheridia burst and the sperm are released, whereupon they swim to the neck of the archegonium. The egg is fertilized by one of the sperm cells and a zygote is formed. The diploid zygote begins to divide mitotically while it is embedded in the archegonium. Its development culminates in the formation of a sporophyte plant.*

(a)

(Photograph by Walter Dawn, copyright © 1974)

DIPLOID PHASE

Mitosis

Sporophyte

(capsule)

(calyptra, remnant of archegonium)

(stalk)

(foot, embedded in old archegonial tissue)

Zygote

Spore Mother Cells

(calyptra is shed)

Peristome (teeth that aid in spore dispersal)

SYNGAMY

MEIOSIS

Antheridium

Sperm

(water droplet)

Sex Organs

Egg

Archegonium

Gametophyte

Wind-Dispersed Spores

Protonema

(old protonema)

(b)

HAPLOID PHASE

Figure 5.9 A common liverwort, Marchantia.

the central strand and the "leaves," rhizoids lack conducting tissue and therefore are distinct from the roots of more complex land plants.

The gametophyte phase of mosses and liverworts represents the apex of gametophyte development in terrestrial plants. At best, however, this accommodation to life on land is a poor one. The "leaves" of many mosses have a layer of cutin to retard water loss, but because the plant lacks any specialized conducting system, water is carried up from the soil by **imbibition,** a mechanism similar to the moistening of a sponge placed in a shallow dish of water. This inefficient absorption mechanism severely limits the vertical growth of moss plants; the largest are just a few inches tall, and most are considerably shorter than that. Moreover, imbibition limits their range of habitats to exceptionally moist substrates. As moss leaves dry, they curl up, thereby reducing surface area and hence moisture loss. The tightly packed growth habit of the plants also reduces the rate of evaporation, but neither of these adaptations can completely compensate for the absence of a conduction system.

The sexual life cycle of a moss is outlined in Figure 5.8*b*. In the haploid phase, the transfer of motile sperm from the **antheridium** (the "male" organ) to the **archegonium** (the "female" organ) requires the presence of liquid water. This requirement places another limitation on potential adaptability. The most common transfer medium is a drop of rainwater or heavy dew deposited at the tip of the gametophyte body. In some moss species, both archegonia and antheridia are found on the same plant; in others, they are produced on separate gametophytes. In either case, the tightly packed growth habit of mosses ensures that the distance between complementary sex organs will be short.

In the diploid phase of the moss life cycle, the sporophyte that forms may be photosynthetic at first, but as it matures it loses its chlorophyll. The sporophyte itself consists of a foot, an erect stalk, and a capsule containing a number of spore mother cells, which eventually will divide meiotically to produce spores. The cap, or **calyptra,** at the tip of the capsule is actually haploid tissue torn from the archegonium during sporophyte development. Once the sporophyte matures, the cap falls away, exposing the mouth of the capsule. The mouth is equipped with a **peristome,** which is a ring of structures that help disperse the spores from the capsule when conditions are dry enough to assure that the spores can be carried by the wind. The spores themselves are thick-walled cells that are resistant to drying. Once they reach a suitable moist substrate, they germinate to form a small filament called a **protonema.** Along the length of the protonema, budlike outgrowths develop that eventually mature to form the gametophytes.

The details of the moss life cycle raise an interesting question. First, the resistant nature of the spores and the method by which they are dispersed are effective adaptations to a terrestrial environment. It is significant that both these refinements occur in the sporophyte phase of the life cycle—as they do in more complex plants. Second, the protonema that forms during the gametophyte phase is quite similar to a typical green alga filament; in fact, it could easily be mistaken for one. Is it possible, then, that the bryophytes are an evolutionary link between the aquatic green algae and the more complex terrestrial plants? The derivation of bryophytes from green algae is strongly supported by the physiological similarities between the two phyla. But transition forms linking bryophytes with complex land plants have not been found, either as fossils or as living plants. Given the lack of evidence, it is just as plausible to suppose that the phylum Bryophyta may represent an evolutionary line that has achieved only marginal success.

Tracheophyta: The Vascular Plants

Almost all land plants belong to the phylum **Tracheophyta.** The tracheophytes are characterized by a **vascular system**—an internal system for conducting water and nutrients from one part of the plant body to another. Vascular systems, which will be described in detail in Chapter 19, are the most significant feature of the sporophyte.

The vascular array serves two functions: the upward transport of water and minerals from the soil to aerial parts of the plant, and the downward transport of photosynthetically derived nutrients. The tissue system involved in upward transport is called **xylem.** The xylem also provides mechanical support for the plant. The downward transport of nutrients is accomplished by a tissue system called **phloem.** *It was the evolutionary development of xylem and* *phloem that permitted rapid development of a wide variety of plant forms adapted to a wide range of terrestrial habitats.* The diverse members of this phylum are grouped into five subphyla: Psilopsida, Lycopsida, Sphenopsida, Pteropsida, and Spermopsida.

The subphylum **Psilopsida** contains no known living representatives. Figure 5.10 is a reconstruction of the sporophyte of *Rhynia,* a genus that flourished 350 million years ago. The upright stem contained a vascular system. Because the stem was only a simple branched structure without true leaves, the stem itself must have been photosynthetic. The sporangia chambers, where spores were produced by meiosis, were borne at the tips of the branches. The plants apparently lacked well-defined roots. Part of the stem extended horizontally either at or below the soil surface, and the plant absorbed water and dissolved nutrients through numerous rhizoids. This kind of underground stem, called a **rhizome,** is quite common in vascular plants.

The evolutionary significance of the psilopsids is difficult to assess. At the same time that *Rhynia* was growing in dense, low stands in Devonian swamps, the forerunners of other vascular plants were already in existence. This fact, coupled with the existence of even earlier forms belonging to this subphylum, suggests that several vascular plant lines may have already diverged from an even more primitive psilopsid ancestor by that time. Until recently, two living genera, *Psilotum* and *Tmesipteris,* were thought to belong to this phylum, but recent research indicates they probably are related to ferns and attained their structural simplicity by a process of degeneration.

The thousand or so species of the subphylum **Lycopsida** are often referred to as the "lycopods." All have true roots, stems, and leaves. Because their leaves are small and scalelike, some members of the group are known as the "club mosses." Unlike the foliage of mosses, however, the leaves of the lycopods have a vascular system that is connected to the vascular array of the stem. The life cycle of a common lycopod, *Lycopodium,* is shown in Figure 5.11. Like all vascular plants, *Lycopodium* is characterized by a prominent sporophyte.

Lycopodium has a **homosporous life cycle;** in other words, sporangia produce only a single type of spore. It is only in the gametophyte, produced by a haploid spore, that male and female organs (antheridia and archegonia) appear. As Figure 5.11 shows, the sporangia are carried on highly modified leaves called **sporophylls** (spore-bearing leaves). Large numbers of these leaves spiral about the stem, forming a compact cone.

Other species of lycopods have **heterosporous life cycles,** in that two distinct kinds and sizes of spores are produced. The smaller **microspores** give rise only to male gametophytes; the larger **megaspores** give rise only to female gametophytes. The heterosporous condition is common among the most complex land plants. For this reason, you may wish to be certain that these distinctions are clear in your mind before reading on.

The lycopods represent one of the earliest discernible lines in the evolution of land plants. The group flourished between 345 and 280 million years ago, with many species reaching treelike proportions. Most of its modern representatives reach heights of only a few inches and are the last remnants of what was once a far more diverse group.

The subphylum **Sphenopsida,** or the "horsetails," is represented today by only a single genus, *Equisetum,* which contains twenty or so species. Like the lycopods, the horsetails are a line of great antiquity in terms of vascular plant evolution. The sporophyte phase dominates the life cycle. The sporophyte has jointed stems with whorls of leaves at each joint (Figure 5.12). Homospores are produced in cones at the tip of fertile stalks; photosynthesis is carried out in stems and in the leaves of vegetative stalks. The leaves of many of the aquatic species are much reduced in size and can easily be overlooked. Some species of *Equisetum* are an important part of the successional series of lake and pond margins in temperate areas. The group has an excellent fossil record, and the development and decline of

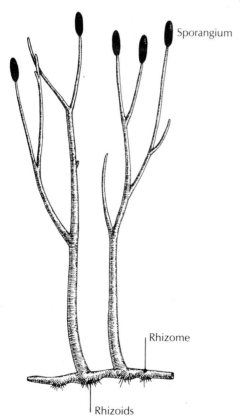

Figure 5.10 Rhynia, *a now-extinct genus of the subphylum Psilopsida, which flourished about 350 million years ago.*

Figure 5.11 (a) The "club moss" Lycopodium, which grows in temperate woodlands. (b) Generalized life cycle of Lycopodium. Spore-producing structures (sporangia) appear on the upper surface of highly modified leaves called sporophylls. Large numbers of sporophylls are arranged spirally around the stem, forming a compact cone (strobilus). Each of the spore mother cells contained in the sporophylls divides meiotically to form four haploid spores. Each spore produces a spore coat and is then shed into the air. If a spore lands on a suitable substrate, it germinates to form the gametophyte. The mature gametophyte will produce both antheridia and archegonia. Flagellated sperm cells, released from the antheridia, must be able to swim to neighboring archegonia, so some free water is required to complete fertilization. After fertilization, the new diploid zygote begins to develop. The shoot and root of the new sporophyte push out of the old gametophyte tissue, which eventually disintegrates.

(a)

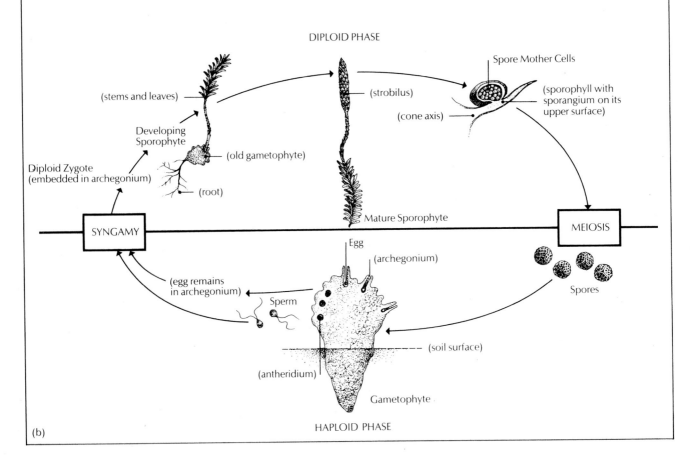

(b)

a great many lines within the subphylum can be followed with some precision.

Members of the subphylum **Pteropsida** are commonly called **ferns.** There are about 11,000 species in this subphylum, ranging from small, floating aquatic plants to the giant tree ferns of tropical forests. With their true stems, roots, and leaves, ferns generally are well adapted to terrestrial conditions. An underground stem is commonly found in ferns of temperate areas. Typically the leaves, or **fronds,** are subdivided into a number of smaller leaf parts.

The life cycle of a typical fern is shown in Figure 5.13. The conspicuous sporophyte is the fern plant with which most people are familiar. Homospores are produced in **sori,** which are clusters of sporangia on the underside of the leaves. The spores are easily carried by the wind and may travel extremely long distances. The effectiveness of such windborne spore dispersal is demonstrated by the fact that ferns are often among the earliest plants to appear in the revegetation of isolated oceanic islands following destructive events such as volcanic eruptions. Despite the well-adapted sporophyte, the gametophyte retains a pronounced dependency on water, not only to maintain its delicate structure but also for the fertilization process. Even though the sporophyte may grow in dry seasons, enough water must be present at some time during the year to permit growth and development of the gametophyte phase if the life cycle is to be completed.

Ferns apparently originated about 330 million years ago.

Figure 5.12 A horsetail, Equisetum, *which is a sphenopsid. The terminal sporangium is borne on a single elevated stalk and is surrounded by a number of vegetative stalks.*

They may represent an evolutionary line derived from the psilopsids. The peak of their diversification came during the late Paleozoic and early Mesozoic. (The terms referring to time periods in earth history are described in Figure 9.2.) Although the ferns have apparently declined in importance since that time, they are still a significant and widely distributed element in the world's land flora.

The Emergence of Seed Plants

By far, the most prominent group of contemporary tracheophytes is the subphylum **Spermopsida: the seed plants.** They are the most structurally complex of all terrestrial plants. The single unifying feature of this diverse group is the production of a specialized structure known as the seed. All seeds, regardless of the details of their development, consist of an **embryo** (a stage of development of the fertilized zygote), stored food material for early embryonic growth, and a protective seed coat. The protective coat makes seeds particularly resistant to drying, and this feature, coupled with the presence of stored food materials, permits seeds to survive through extended periods of adverse environmental conditions. *The ability to produce easily dispersed, long-lived units for propagation has apparently been an important factor in the success of the seed plants.*

Although seed production is now unique to Spermopsida, it has appeared independently in other plant lineages during earlier periods. Fossil evidence shows that early lycopods and horsetails developed the seed habit as early as the late Paleozoic, although these seed-bearing members have since become extinct. Seed production may therefore be an artificial criterion for classifying organisms, inasmuch as it represents an evolutionary strategy that has appeared in a number of lines at different times.

All seed plants have complex sporophytes with roots, stems, and leaves. All are heterosporous, and the gametophyte is so reduced in size and importance that recognizing its presence can be difficult. There are five classes in the subphylum. They are commonly called the seed ferns, the cycads, the ginkgoes, the conifers, and the flowering plants.

The **Pteridospermae,** or **seed ferns,** are now extinct, although they dominated the landscape from 345 to 280 million years ago. Its last representatives disappeared during the Mesozoic. Paleobotanists studying the forests of the Carboniferous period once referred to this timespan as the age of ferns because of the astonishing number of fossils of fernlike foliage that were discovered. Later research has shown that although ferns were present during this period, most of the fernlike foliage was actually produced by more complex heterosporous plants that produced seeds. Al-

Figure 5.13   (a),(b) Photographs of ferns in their woodland habitat. (c) Close-up view of the underside of a fern leaf, showing the developing sori. (d) Scanning electron micrograph of fern spores. (e) Generalized life cycle of a fern. The sporophyte plant produces its spores on modified, "fertile" sporangia.

The spore mother cells within the sori divide meiotically. The spores that are produced develop a thick, protective coat and are shed from the sori by a variety of specialized mechanisms. If they land on a moist substrate, they germinate and form a small, heart-shaped sheet of photosynthetic cells on the soil surface. This structure is the prothallus; it represents the gametophyte phase in ferns. The prothallus bears the sex organs—the antheridia and archegonia. The antheridia produce flagellated sperm, which require a small amount of water in order to swim to the neck of the archegonium, where they fertilize the egg. Once fertilized, the zygote is retained in the archegonium, where it begins development of root, stem, and leaves. Eventually the old archegonium is pushed aside, and it disintegrates.

(a)	(e)
(b)	
(c) (d)	

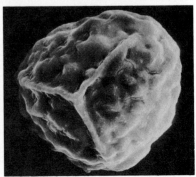

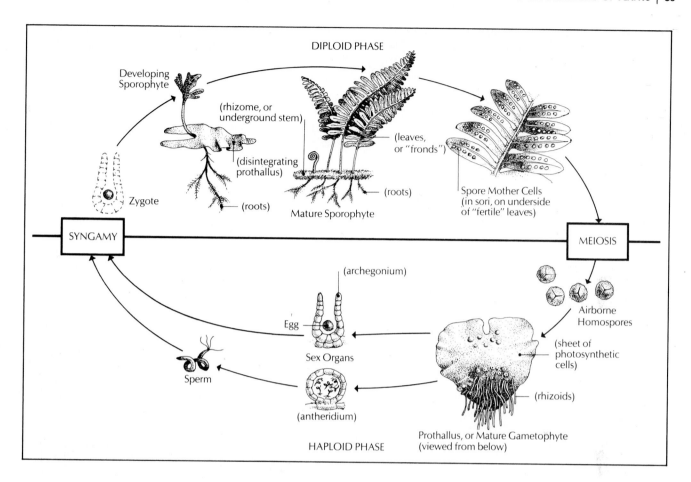

DIPLOID PHASE

Developing Sporophyte

(rhizome, or underground stem)

(disintegrating prothallus)

Zygote

(roots)

Mature Sporophyte

(leaves, or "fronds")

(roots)

Spore Mother Cells (in sori, on underside of "fertile" leaves)

SYNGAMY

MEIOSIS

(archegonium)

Egg

Sex Organs

Sperm

(antheridium)

Airborne Homospores

(sheet of photosynthetic cells)

(rhizoids)

Prothallus, or Mature Gametophyte (viewed from below)

HAPLOID PHASE

though careful research has revealed a great deal of information on the structure and reproduction of these ancient plants, there still is no clear indication whether other members of Spermopsida are related to this group.

Cycadae, or the **cycads,** are a class of nine genera and about a hundred species confined to the tropics and subtropics. Only a single genus, *Zamia* (Figure 5.14), is native to the United States. Its leaves, which are thick-textured and compound, closely resemble those of palms. The plants are heterosporous, and the spores are produced in cones. The female cones often reach considerable size, and their presence is a sure means of distinguishing these plants from palms. The cycad life cycles generally resemble those of the conifers (which will be described shortly) except that the sperm are flagellated. Although individual plants are long-lived and quite hardy, the many years required for the cones and seeds to mature results in a slow reproductive rate, which has probably hindered these plants in their competition with more advanced seed plants.

The maidenhair tree, *Ginkgo biloba,* is the only living representative of the class **Ginkgoae.** The members of this group were considerably more diverse during the Mesozoic period. As late as 25 million years ago, ginkgoes similar to the modern maidenhair tree were prevalent in temperate forests of Asia, North America, and Europe. The trees disappeared from North America between 15 and 10 million years ago and probably vanished from Europe at about the same time. Although there is some doubt whether "wild" ginkgoes are still to be found in Asia, we can be certain that the trees did survive there until historic times because it was widely planted as a temple tree in both China and Japan, where it was first noted by Western explorers. The plant, with its unusual fan-shaped leaves, is highly resistant to insects, disease, and air pollution. Because of these characteristics it has been planted as a street tree throughout the world, which virtually assures its survival even if it no longer occurs in the natural state.

The class **Coniferae** and the preceding three classes belong to a large complex known as the **gymnosperms,** or "naked seed" plants, so called because their seeds are borne on the surface of cone scales without protective tissue. Some of the conifers common to the north temperate zone are the pine, fir, spruce, larch, yew, cedar, cypress, and redwood. The conifers, with 50 genera and more than 500 species, are the most prevalent of the living gymnosperms. Their leaves are usually needlelike. The fact that

(a)

(b)

(c)

Figure 5.14   (a) Cones of the cycad Zamia. (b) A large cycad. The common name for this species, sago palm, is based on the palmlike foliage. (c) The leaves of the maidenhair tree, Ginkgo biloba, are characteristically fan-shaped.

individual leaves of most species persist for several years has given rise to their common name, the "evergreens."

The conifer life cycles are basically similar to one another. The generalized life cycle of a representative genus, *Pinus* (pine), is shown in Figure 5.15. Details of the development of the male and female gametophytes appear in Figure 5.16. Although the details of the pine life cycle seem complex, the essential plan is relatively simple. The heterosporous diploid plant produces male and female spores. The male and female gametophytes produced by these spores are greatly reduced and neither is truly self-sustaining. The male gametophyte, or **pollen grain,** is dispersed through the air. The female gametophyte is retained in the megasporangium of the female cone and is nutritionally dependent on the sporophyte. Requirements for free water in fertilization have been reduced to an absolute minimum. Moisture is furnished by the sporophyte, which is optimally adapted for obtaining water.

The de-emphasis of the haploid phase, the reduction of water requirements for completing the sexual cycle, and the evolution of an effective dispersal unit (the seed) have interacted to make the gymnosperms in general and the conifers in particular a highly successful group of plants. The conifers were a dominant part of the world's vegetation during the Mesozoic (Chapter 9), and even though they seem to have declined in importance with the rapid evolution of the flowering plants in the late Mesozoic, they are still important in tropical and temperate zones as well as in the entire forest complex of northern latitudes.

THE EVOLUTIONARY SIGNIFICANCE OF HETEROSPORY AND SEED FORMATION

What were the selective pressures in the past that led to heterospory and, eventually, to seed production? There is little doubt that the earliest land plants were homosporous. Homospory offers a selective advantage in that the close association of the male and female sexual apparatus is assured. Homospores are dispersed by winds, and if they land on a suitable substrate they will produce gametophytes that bear both types of sexual organs. It happens that most of these spores do not encounter conditions that will trigger development, and among those that do develop, many do not reach the mature gametophyte phase because of unfavorable environmental conditions. However, should favorable conditions persist long enough for the gametophyte to mature, fertilization is almost assured by the close association of complementary sex organs. This type of reproductive strategy is not as chancy as it seems. Despite the fact that homospores are dispersed by winds, many fall in the immediate vicinity of the parent plant. The very existence of the parent sporophyte at any given site implies the existence of conditions favorable for its development.

Figure 5.15   (a) The larger female cones and the smaller male cones that represent the heterosporous condition of the conifers. Both types of cones are made of sporophylls, which are spirally arranged, highly modified leaves. The sporangia on these leaves contain the spore mother cells that divide meiotically to produce the sexually differentiated spore cells.

(b) Generalized life cycle of Pinus, *a representative conifer. The adult pine tree is the mature sporophyte. Details of the sporophyte and gametophyte phases of this life cycle are shown in Figure 5.16.*

(a)

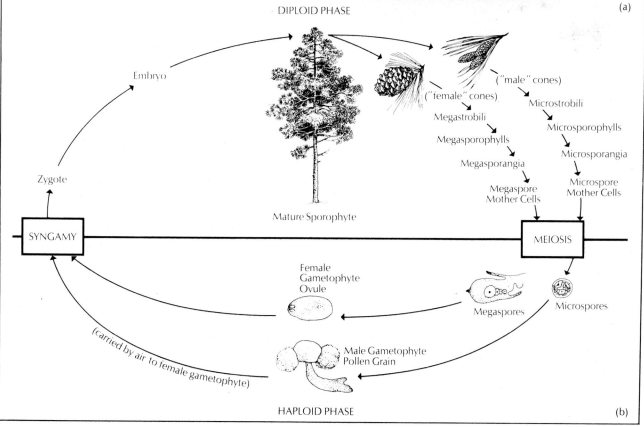

(b)

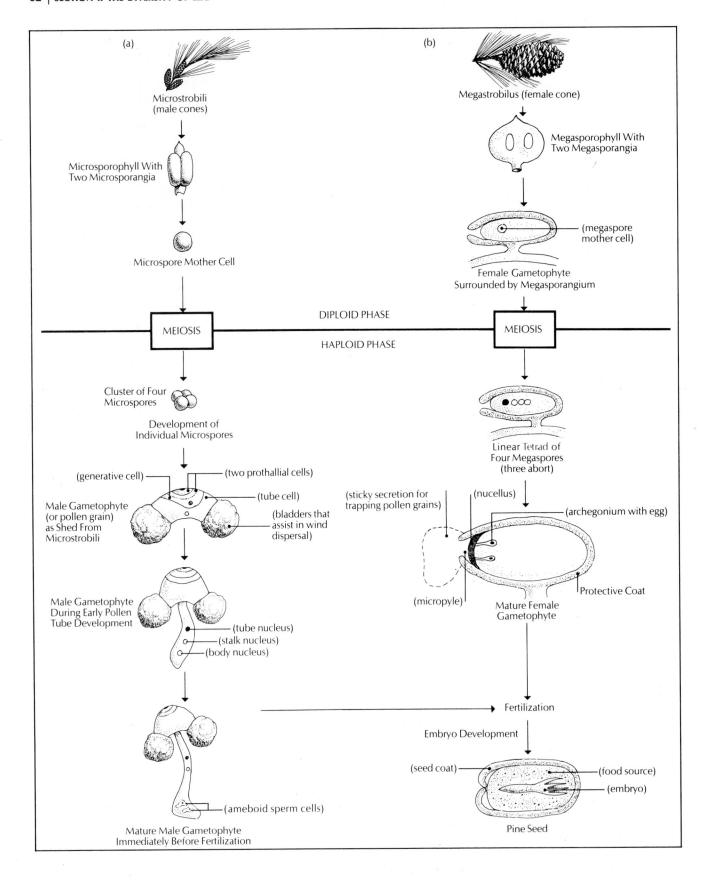

(a)

Microstrobili
(male cones)

Microsporophyll With
Two Microsporangia

Microspore Mother Cell

(b)

Megastrobilus (female cone)

Megasporophyll With
Two Megasporangia

(megaspore
mother cell)

Female Gametophyte
Surrounded by Megasporangium

DIPLOID PHASE

MEIOSIS

HAPLOID PHASE

MEIOSIS

Cluster of Four
Microspores

Development of
Individual Microspores

(generative cell)   (two prothallial cells)

(tube cell)

Male Gametophyte
(or pollen grain)
as Shed From
Microstrobili

(bladders that
assist in wind
dispersal)

Linear Tetrad of
Four Megaspores
(three abort)

(sticky secretion for
trapping pollen grains)   (nucellus)

(archegonium with egg)

Male Gametophyte
During Early Pollen
Tube Development

(tube nucleus)
(stalk nucleus)
(body nucleus)

(micropyle)   Mature Female
Gametophyte

Protective Coat

Fertilization

Embryo Development

(seed coat)   (food source)

(embryo)

(ameboid sperm cells)

Mature Male Gametophyte
Immediately Before Fertilization

Pine Seed

Figure 5.16 Details of the conifer life cycle, beginning with development of the male cones (a) and the female cones (b). In the haploid phase, the microspores develop into an extremely reduced male gametophyte called a pollen grain. A pollen grain does not have sex organs; it is merely a collection of nuclei, some of which take part directly in the sexual process. Pollen grains are shed from male cones early in the growing season and are carried by the wind to the female cones of the same or another tree. The male cones break apart soon after pollen formation.

The female cones are more durable; their individual spore-producing structures are woody cone scales. Each of these megasporophylls has two megasporangia on its upper surface, which means two female gametophytes can be formed and two seeds produced there. Four megaspores are produced in each megasporangium, but only one develops into a female gametophyte.

The female gametophyte is retained in the sporangium. It is a relatively undifferentiated mass of haploid cells with two archegonia at one end. The megasporangium wall turns into a protective coat that completely surrounds the gametophyte, except for a small opening (the micropyle). A sticky fluid secreted by a mass of sporophyte tissue (the nucellus) exudes from the opening and spreads out on the surface of the cone scale.

When the female cones are mature, their scales spread slightly, which admits pollen grains to the scale surface, where they are trapped by the sticky fluid. As the fluid dries, it contracts and draws the pollen grains through the micropyle. The pollen grains now produce a pollen tube, which grows into nucellus tissue. During its growth, each pollen grain contains three nuclei: a tube nucleus that seems to control tube growth, a stalk nucleus, and a body nucleus. When the pollen tube reaches the archegonia, the body nucleus divides to form two amoeboid sperm cells, which are released at the opening of one archegonium.

Fertilization of one of the two eggs apparently inhibits fertilization of the other. The zygote that develops into a diploid embryo is embedded in the tissue of the female gametophyte. As the embryo develops, the coating that surrounds the female gametophyte is transformed into a hard, resistant seed coat.

The mature pine seed is therefore composed of a number of tissues derived from different phases of the life cycle. The diploid seed coat comes from the preceding sporophyte generation; the embryo is diploid and represents the new sporophyte generation; and the food storage reserve is nothing more than the tissue of the haploid female gametophyte.

Spores landing close to the parent plant therefore have a reasonable chance of developing completely.

Close association of sex organs is not at all certain in heterosporous plants, which produce separate male and female gametophytes. In fact, fertilization must have been a problem in plants that were forerunners to the heterosporous condition. Unless both of its gametophytes developed close to one another, the likelihood of a sperm swimming long enough to find an egg would be narrow indeed. Perhaps this constraint was initially overcome because the dispersed male and female spores were somehow confined to a limited area. But the rarity of simple heterosporous land plants with dispersed female as well as male spores suggests this was only a partial solution, at best. *More likely it was the retention of the female spore by the sporophyte plant that conferred a whole new set of adaptive advantages over simple heterospory or homospory.*

If a sporophyte were to retain the female spore, then the female gametophyte not only would have the resources of the large megaspore during early development, it also would be able to tap nutritional reserves of the sporophyte itself. The total range of environmental variables under which the female gametophyte could develop therefore would increase considerably, for it would receive protection, water, and nutrients from the sporophyte rather than depending on chance to provide the complex series of conditions required for independent development. In that flexibility lies the selective advantage of heterospory.

Of course, the strategy of retaining the female spore also would require changes in the development of the male gametophyte. Perhaps there was a decreasing tendency for the sporophyte to shed its male spores and an increasing tendency to accomplish as much male gametophyte development as possible while the gametophyte was still associated with the sporophyte. But an association between the sporophyte and male gametophyte could never be as close and as permanent as that between the sporophyte and the female gametophyte. The reason is that one or the other gametophyte must ultimately move into close association with its counterpart if fertilization is to occur. Because female spore retention appears to have developed first, there probably was a gradual trend toward extensive development of the male gametophyte while it was associated with the sporophyte. At the same time, the whole structure of the male gametophyte must have been undergoing modifications that would allow the entire gametophyte to be shed as a pollen grain. The simultaneous development of such specialized adaptations would create a microenvironment in which final development of the male gametophyte could occur upon contact with the female gametophyte. The end result of this long series of mutual adaptations in plant function and form would be a strategy whereby gametophyte development and fertilization would be virtually assured by the resources of the sporophyte.

Once any group of plants reached this stage in the evolution of heterospory, the production of seedlike structures must have been assured. An embryo cannot develop to maturity in the female gametophyte, because the female gametophyte remains attached to the parent sporophyte body. There had to be some mechanism for dispersing and protecting the gametophyte-embryo complex. Simple dispersal would not suffice; at that point in the evolutionary development of heterosporous plants, the female gametophytes were ill-equipped for independent survival. Because the complex was already surrounded by a series of coatings derived from the megasporangium, the dispersal of a single unit containing the coatings, the gametophyte, and the embryo (a seed) was the simplest solution to the problem.

Once such structures appeared, there was further structural adaptation for improving seed function. And more effective seed dispersal mechanisms arose, not only to assure reproductive efficiency but to distribute seeds as far as possible to minimize competition among individual plants at the parent plant site.

THE FLOWER: EVOLUTIONARY FORCE AND EVOLUTIONARY PRODUCT

There are at least a quarter of a million species in the class **Angiospermae,** or **flowering plants.** They have dominated the landscape for at least 70 million years as a result of a combination of successful evolutionary strategies.

The sporophyte phase of the angiosperm life cycle is the most conspicuous; the gametophyte phase is completely dependent upon it (Figure 5.17). The reproductive structures of the sporophyte are made up of a complex series of modified leaves known as the **flower** (Figure 5.18). Two components of the flower, the *sepals* and *petals*, are sterile structures that can serve a variety of accessory functions.

The male component of the flower is the **stamen.** A typical stamen consists of a supporting *filament* and a series of chambers known as an *anther*. The anther contains the microspore mother cells from which male gametophytes are derived (Figure 5.19). The microspore mother cells divide by meiosis within the anther to produce haploid microspores, each of which develops into a male gametophyte, or pollen grain. Structurally, the pollen grains of flowering plants are even simpler than those of gymnosperms, in that only two nuclei are present at the time the pollen grain is shed from the flower. As you will read later, *one of the significant adaptations of the angiosperms has been the utilization of a wide variety of mechanisms to ensure efficient dissemination of pollen.*

The female component of the flower is a complex of structures consisting of a **pistil,** which is structurally differentiated into a *stigma* (a pollen receptacle) and a *style* (a supporting column); and an *ovary*. The nature of the fertilization process in angiosperms (Figure 5.19) is unique to the group. The male gametophyte (the pollen grain) produces two sperm nuclei. One nucleus fuses with the egg of the female gametophyte to form the zygote. The second sperm nucleus fuses with two free nuclei in the female gametophyte to form a triploid nucleus that develops into a tissue called **endosperm.** The endosperm serves as food storage tissue in many angiosperm seeds. Because there are two fusion events in the sexual cycle, one leading to zygote formation and the other to endosperm, we refer to the process as **double fertilization.** Double fertilization is a process unique to the flowering plants.

As seeds develop within the ovary, the walls of the ovary enter into a developmental sequence culminating in the structure we call a **fruit.** The ultimate form of the fruit varies widely from species to species, depending on the evolutionary strategies that have been followed to optimize seed dispersal under various environmental conditions.

The precise form of angiosperm flowers is highly varied and serves as the main basis for making taxonomic distinctions within the class. Apparently, *one of the major selective forces behind floral diversity has been the wide variety of pollinating agents available to flowering plants during their development.* Inanimate agents such as wind usually allow simplification of floral structure. For example, petals and sepals are often absent, and extensions of stamens and pistil develop so that they project into the path of the wind. The use of animals as pollinating agents has led to an incredible array of floral form, color, and odor.

The angiosperms are divided into two subclasses, the **Monocotyledoneae** and the **Dicotyledoneae.** Members of the first subclass, commonly called the "monocots," have an embryo with a single *cotyledon*, or seed leaf. The flower parts in this group occur in threes or multiples of three, and the veins of the leaves are parallel to one another. Plants such as the grasses (including such cereal crops as corn, wheat, and rice), palms, lilies, and orchids are common examples of monocots. The monocots are represented by at least 60,000 species.

The subclass Dicotyledoneae, the "dicots," contains at least 190,000 species. Two cotyledons are present in the dicot embryo. The flower parts occur in multiples of four or five, and the veins on a leaf are netted in contrast to the parallel venation of the monocots.

How did the angiosperms originate? The question has vexed botanists for the past hundred years. The fossil record consists primarily of pollen, leaves, and wood and provides little insight into the derivation and evolution of the flower. The first undeniably angiosperm forms date from 125

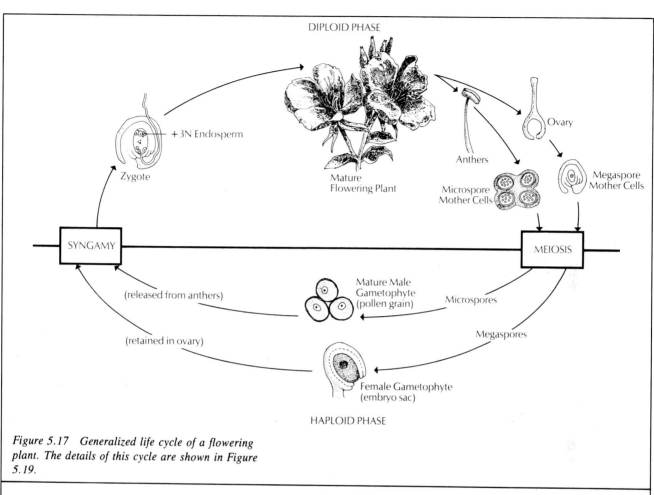

Figure 5.17   Generalized life cycle of a flowering plant. The details of this cycle are shown in Figure 5.19.

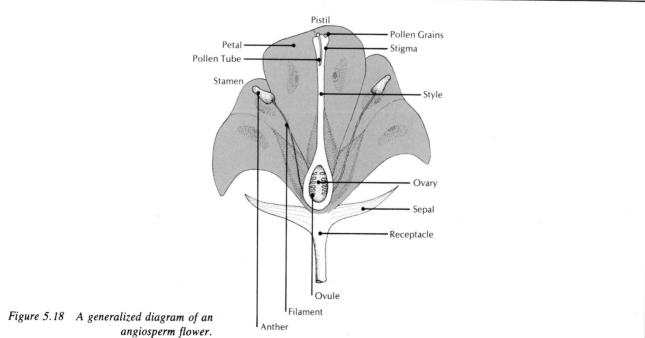

Figure 5.18   A generalized diagram of an angiosperm flower.

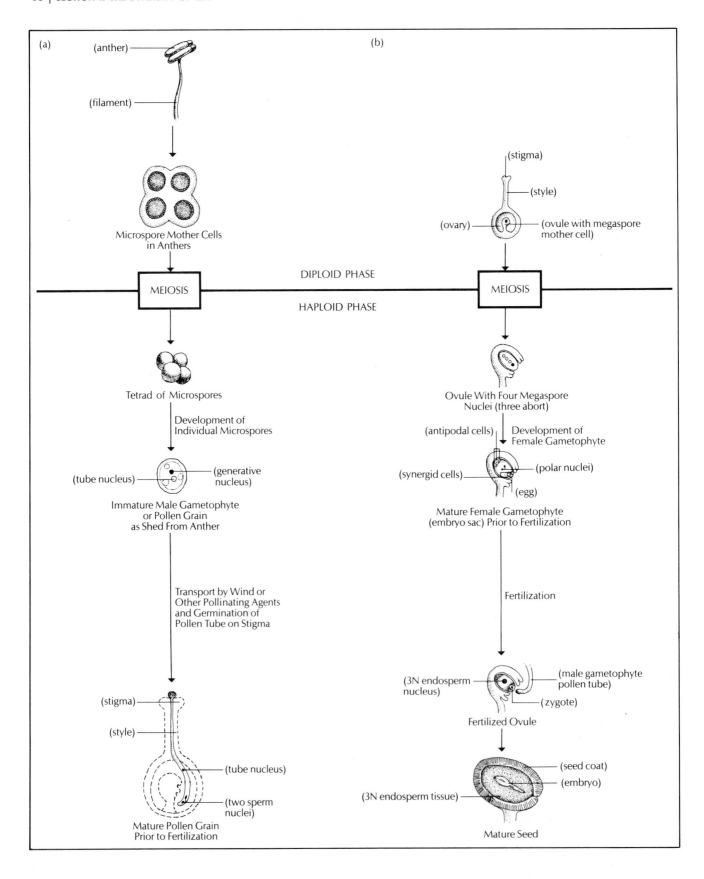

Figure 5.19   Development of the male gametophyte (a) and the female gametophyte (b) in flowering plants. In the female sporophyte, megasporangia (called ovules in flowering plants) are protected by the ovary, a structure of modified leaves that have become folded and fused at the edges. The megaspore mother cell in each ovule divides meiotically to form four haploid cells. Only one develops into an eight-celled female gametophyte (called an embryo sac). Of these eight cells, only three (the egg and two polar nuclei) function in sexual fusion.

When a pollen grain contacts a flower stigma, it forms a pollen tube that grows down into the cavity of the ovary. Its tube nucleus seems to control its growth. Its generative nucleus divides into two sperm nuclei, which enter the embryo sac and take part in double fertilization. The first fertilization is a typical fusion of a sperm nucleus and an egg to form a diploid zygote. The second involves fusion of the remaining sperm nucleus with both polar nuclei. Because the sperm and nuclei are haploid, the resulting nucleus is triploid (3N). During zygote development, the triploid nucleus divides mitotically to form a unique storage tissue, the endosperm.

The entire fertilized ovule matures into a seed that consists of a seed coat, the endosperm, and the embryo derived from the zygote. The embryo may have seed leaves (cotyledons) that serve as a food reserve during germination. Species with well-developed cotyledons often have a small amount of endosperm tissue, and vice versa.

million years ago, and by 65 million years ago the flowering plants had come to dominate the world's flora.

The prevailing opinion is that the first flowers were probably insect pollinated, with beetles being the most likely candidates. The use of animals as an essential element in the transfer of gametes is truly a unique reproductive strategy. We are so used to the role of animals, particularly insects, as pollinating agents that it is easy to overlook the evolutionary significance of the strategy. Most animals and primitive plants have motile gametes, which are themselves responsible for movement in the environment, or they have mechanisms (such as internal fertilization) for enhancing gamete transfer and minimizing the environmental variables the gamete will encounter. If we were to discover a mammal that transferred sperm to the female of the species by means of some intermediary species, we would greet such a discovery with great surprise. Yet this is precisely the process used by most flowering plants.

Once such a process becomes initiated, the selective pressures operating in the plant are enormous and complex, with a multitude of adaptive strategies as possible outcomes. Consider, for example, the problem of enticing an animal to visit a flower. Is it merely a question of having bright colors or an attractive pattern? We can be reasonably sure that insects are completely lacking in aesthetics. The inducements must be more basic than that. Two of the most fundamental forces that will prod animals into activity are sex and the search for food. Because food is an essential requirement, most flowering plants have evolved to provide some form of food for the visitor, although there are several examples in which the sex drive of insects is successfully exploited as well. The food may be nectar, edible flower parts, or even the pollen itself. The last strategy may seem to be self-defeating at first glance, but apparently the loss of an appreciable amount of pollen is justified if the pollinator is an efficient means of transferring at least some of it.

The development of food inducements is of little use to a plant species if pollinators are unable to find the food. It is here that floral form, color, and odor (as well as a number of other factors) become important as attractants. Figure 5.20 provides a sampling of the floral diversity that has emerged to signal potential pollinators.

The sexual behavior of insects has been exploited in the pollination of some orchids. **Pseudocopulation** involves a mimicry of the female of the pollinator species. The male insects, apparently mistaking the flower for a female, attempt to mate with it and in the process they transfer pollen from plant to plant (Figure 5.21). The form of the mimic may be quite striking or it may be only a rough caricature of the female insect. Given the resolving power and the limited spectral sensitivity of the compound eye of

(text continues on page 100)

Figure 5.20   A small sample of floral diversity. Flower structure, color, and odor are intimately linked to particular pollinating agents. Wind-pollinated flowers (2, 11, 15, 16, 18) are reduced, for there is no selective advantage to attracting insects. Bird-pollinated flowers (9) tend to be red to match the spectral sensitivity of the pollinator; the floral parts are fused into long tubes. Colors of insect-pollinated flowers (1) tend toward the blue end of the spectrum, often with contrasting colors to guide the insect on its approach to the flower. Fly-pollinated flowers (12, 19) attract the pollinators with an odor rather than with bright colors. Beetle pollination is characteristic of more primitive flowers with multiple, spirally arranged floral parts (3).

Many kinds of structural strategies are effective in enticing pollination. Some plants rely on colored bracts rather than elaborate petals and sepals. The flowers of the poinsettia (14) are the small yellow structures in the center, surrounded by colored leaves. Members of the family Araceeae (5, 19) have inconspicuous flowers on a fleshy axis, surrounded by a prominent bract. The "flowers" of the Compositae, (1), the most advanced dicot family, are actually composite structures where each individual petallike structure is a complete true flower (1).

(1) Tragopogon, *(2)* Cyperus *(sedge), (3)* Nelumbo *(water lily), (4)* Billbergia, *(5)* Arisaema *(jack-in-the pulpit), (6)* Passiflora *(passion flower), (7)* Coronilla, *(8)* Tigridia, *(9)* Ipomopsis, *(10)* Opuntia *(prickly pear cactus), (11)* Quercus *(oak, male flower) (12)* Stapelia, *(13)* Vaccinium *(blueberry), (14)* Poinsettia, *(15)* Acer *(maple), (16)* Betula *(birch), (17)* Lychnis, *(18)* Betula, *(19)* Amorphophallus, *(20)* Isotria *(an orchid).*

1	5	9	12	16
2	6	10	13	17 / 18 / 19
3 / 4	7 / 8	11	14 / 15	20

Figure 5.21 Sexual mimicry in orchids, which leads to pseudocopulation between flower and insect—and, in the process, the transfer of pollen from plant to plant.

an insect, the mimics manage to deceive the males enough to accomplish the task. The strategy is most effective in species that display their flowers before the female insects appear in great numbers, thus ensuring that the male insects will devote their energy to contending with flowers rather than with females. The focus of attention apparently shifts once the females do appear, but by that time pollination has been accomplished.

A great many factors influence pollination strategies, and they result in a complex network of selective forces. Some plant species are pollinated by a single insect species. Any adaptations of floral form to further attract that species can lead to a high pollination efficiency—but at the cost of increased dependency on that particular insect. Other plants, adapted to a wider range of insect pollinators, appear to balance relative pollination efficiency with the back-up capability represented by numerous potential pollinators.

Up to this point, flower structure has been treated as the result of evolving pollination strategies. Flowers, however, are more than just evolutionary products. As intricate as they may become, they are major evolutionary forces as well. *Even while flowers have responded to selective pressure and have adapted to various pollinators, the pollinators themselves respond adaptively to the presence of the flowers.* Many insect species, responding to the predictable occurrence of the food that flowers offer, have become more and more dependent on them for their own existence.

Most bees and nectar-feeding butterflies and moths are entirely dependent on nectar and pollen. Such a pattern of increasing mutual dependence and mutual adaptation is known as **coevolution.** And nowhere in the living world have coevolutionary relationships developed to the extent of those between flowering plants and their pollinating agents. The diversification of many insect groups and of the flowering plants themselves have been intimately linked for at least 50 million years. This long interaction undoubtedly contributed substantially to the rapid rise and eventual dominance of the flowering plants and the insects associated directly and indirectly·with them.

PERSPECTIVE

This introduction to modern plant groups has proceeded in a more or less orderly sequence from simple aquatic forms to complex terrestrial plants capable of existing under a wide range of environmental conditions. Along the way, there has been some speculation about how adaptations in modern species might mirror various modifications favored by natural selection during the gradual evolution of land plants. Approaching modern plant groups in this manner can indeed provide some insights into the nature of plant evolution. However, certain potential sources of bias are intrinsic to such an approach.

First, all modern plants are the end result of the same span of evolution. An exotic orchid in a tropical rain forest and a simple alga growing in a rainpool in the same forest are both living products of perhaps 3 billion years of organic evolution. The orchid is structurally complex and it evolved recently, in comparison with the alga. Hence, we usually refer to it as being more "advanced." But is such a value judgment appropriate? If there is any valid criterion at all for "success" or "fitness" of any type of organism, it is simply survival. If a strategy for survival works for an organism under a given set of biological variables, that organism will be successful in that it is able to pass its genes from generation to generation. If not, it will become extinct. In short, everything that lives in the world around us is a representative of a successful evolutionary line, regardless of structural simplicity or complexity. The alga in the tropical rainpool fills its niche extremely well—so well, in fact, that it has been doing so for hundreds of millions of years without being replaced by more "advanced" organisms.

But if structural complexity is not necessarily a requirement for biological "success," why has structural complexity appeared at all? The fact that the vegetation of the world is more diverse than an algal flora confined to pools, lakes, streams, and oceans must mean that other forces are at work. The key to the question is that there are other opportunities for plant "life styles" beyond certain types of aquatic existence. Algae are not well adapted to terrestrial conditions, yet at some point in evolutionary time, such areas were present, unpopulated, and ready for exploitation. The gradual effects of natural selection on the patterns of variations within plant lineages produced organisms with more complex structures that were better suited to the harsher conditions of terrestrial habitats. The complexity exhibited by certain organisms has been a means to an end, and not an end in itself. The end *is* survival. Complexity of organization and function is favored by selection only when it confers an additional margin of survival that compensates for the cost of the improvements. The evolution of complex plants to "out-algae the algae" would not be a successful enterprise because the added physiological cost would not yield any more functional efficiency than the algae already have. In a different habitat, however, the costs of such complexity are fully justified by the more rigorous requirements for survival. It is safe to say that no organism is more complex than it has to be in order to compete and survive in its own habitat.

If nothing else, this discussion should emphasize the interrelatedness of evolutionary developments and strategies. We cannot examine a single change, such as the sporophyte's initial retention of the female spore, without realizing that whatever the specific advantages the change offers, the plant must continue to be optimized in other areas to maintain an overall level of fitness. As a general principle, any change in one part or one function of an organism must set in motion a whole series of synchronized complementary or compensating changes in other aspects of its biology. In the final analysis, organisms succeed—or survive—not by optimizing single systems alone but by optimizing the whole system and integrating all aspects of form and function to yield a complete life cycle that is in harmony with the environment.

If solutions to the "survival equation" appear complex, it is because they are in fact complex. We have a tendency to look at a feature such as pollination as if it were in some sense pivotal, assuring great adaptive advantage to any organism that acquires the feature. Although it would be foolish to underestimate such factors, they are useful but not necessarily sufficient for survival. The various ancient lycopods, for example, developed the "advanced" feature of seed production during the Carboniferous period—and yet they became extinct. We do not know why, but it is likely that other aspects of their biology were not as refined as their mode of reproduction. Although we may never be in a position to evaluate all the selective forces and their impact on even a living species, awareness of the complexity of such an analysis may remove much of the temptation to oversimplify our picture of biological interactions in the world around us.

SUGGESTED READINGS

BAKER, HERBERT. *Plants and Civilization*. 2nd ed. Belmont, Calif.: Wadsworth, 1970. A description of the role plants have played in man's cultural development.

JENSEN, WILLIAM A., and FRANK B. SALISBURY. *Botany: An Ecological Approach*. Belmont, Calif.: Wadsworth, 1972. A highly readable, well-illustrated account of the study of plants and their interrelationships with the environment. The book gives glimpses into the scientific process as well as the challenges and frustrations of people who have helped to shape the field.

RAVEN, PETER H., and HELENA CURTIS. *Biology of Plants*. New York: Worth, 1970. A modern text on plant biology. Lengthy and detailed.

Chapter 6

The World of Fungi

The activities of fungi appear simple and commonplace—as in the case of this fancifully rotting orange. But such activities, however mundane, form a vital link in the functioning of the biosphere.

In viewing photographs taken of the earth from outer space, few of us would deny being struck by the beauty of that thin and delicate blue-white film of air and water swirling about its surface, supporting all of life. Perhaps we also feel pride and protectiveness in viewing, at last, the biosphere as a whole. But consider, now, a slowly decaying orange, artfully draped with a thin film of simple fungal organisms. Who has ever been struck by the beauty of the unpretentious fungi? Rarely are we in a position to notice that these organisms are a pervasive part of the biosphere. True, we tap into the activities of these simple organisms to bake our bread, ferment our wine, and make an array of drugs to protect us from disease. Some we eat and others we contend with as sources of disease in ourselves and our domestic plants and animals. Even so, it is easy to underestimate the overall importance of fungi, for they are barely visible against the panorama of the living world.

Plants use the energy from sunlight to accumulate both energy and matter in the form of organic substances. Both plants and animals use these stores of energy and matter, but in the process both groups produce organic wastes (including their own bodies, after death). Bacteria and fungi utilize nutritional strategies based on the absorption of such organic wastes as an energy source. This nutritional strategy is an essential element in the continuous recycling of matter in living systems. The bacteria—with their rapid growth rates in aquatic habitats—perform this vital role in the waters of our planet. But it is on land, symbolized on our ''planetary orange'' by the distribution of the green mold, that fungi are preeminent in this role. Adapted by the long process of selection for growth on virtually all organic substrates, fungi are the master scavengers in terrestrial communities. This chapter examines some of the patterns of fungal diversity and attempts to outline the many ways in which these organisms contribute to the world we live in.

THE STRATEGIES OF FUNGI

The kingdom Fungi is known to encompass 100,000 species in two phyla, and quite possibly at least as many additional species have yet to be identified. Traditionally, fungi have been considered plantlike in their biochemistry, their growth habits, and their reproductive characteristics. But in many respects they differ from plants and even from photosynthetic protistans. All fungi lack photosynthetic pigment arrays, which sets them apart from the autotrophic plants. Most fungi extract energy from their environment in a process called extracellular digestion, which sets them apart from animals that actively ingest their food. In **extracellular digestion,** a fungus secretes enzymes into the substrate on which it grows. The enzymes break down the complex molecules of the substrate into simpler molecules that are more readily absorbed through the fungal cell wall.

The strategy of extracellular digestion and absorption is quite distinct from the energy-procurement strategies of either plants or animals. Green plants can effectively synthesize their own high-energy molecules from readily available inorganic materials. And animals are capable of moving about in search of localized concentrations of organic material (usually plants or other animals). Most fungi, in contrast, have tapped into the energy-rich molecules of organic waste products and dead organisms in the sequence of food relationships within any ecosystem. So successful is this nutritional strategy that the activities of fungi and other decomposer organisms appear to be absolutely essential for the efficient recycling of inorganic resources in the biosphere.

Extracellular digestion and nutrient absorption in fungi are basically similar to the processes used by bacteria. In fact, it is possible that fungi may be descended from an ancient heterotrophic prokaryote. At the same time, many of the simpler aquatic fungi are quite similar to the green algae in structure and in sexual processes, which might mean that fungi represent a heterotrophic line evolved from a eukaryotic algal ancestor. Most botanists would at least provisionally support the second view. But the origin of the fungi may always be an enigma because the fungal complex is extremely ancient and the fossil evidence for its evolutionary lines is extremely sparse.

THE SLIME MOLDS ARE SO DIVERSE THEY MAY NOT EVEN BE RELATED TO ONE ANOTHER

There are approximately 500 highly diverse species that are grouped together in the phylum **Myxomycophyta** (the slime molds). The organisms found in the three or four classes within the phylum are grouped together only on the basis of a general similarity of form, so it is quite possible that they are not at all closely related.

Myxomycetes: The True Slime Molds

Flourishing in rotting logs, decaying leaves, and other assorted debris on forest floors are the **myxomycetes,** or **true slime molds.** (The combining form *myxo-* is from the Greek word for ''mucus,'' or ''slime''; *-mycete* is from the Greek word for ''fungus.'') The genus *Physarum,* shown in Figure 6.2, displays many of the features of this class.

The diploid phase dominates the life cycle of the true slime molds. The diploid body is a mass called a **plasmodium,** which may be from 2 to 10 centimeters long and may contain as many as several thousand nuclei. The multinucleate mass has no cellular cross walls. The entire plasmodium moves in an amoebalike fashion by the streaming of cytoplasm into pseudopodlike extensions of the plasmodial mass. In contrast to most other fungi, the slime

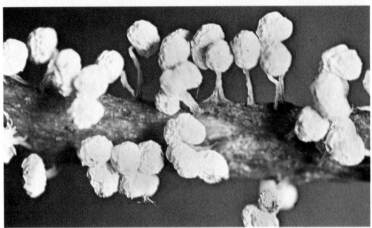

Figure 6.2   Generalized life cycle of a true slime mold, as represented by the genus Physarum. *The dominant phase of the life cycle is the multinucleate plasmodium (a). During the nonreproductive phase, the plasmodium is negatively phototrophic: it avoids the light. At the onset of reproduction it becomes positively phototrophic and moves to the surface of the substrate on which it is growing. Then a limited number of cross walls are produced, and a differentiated sporangium is formed in the "fruiting stage" (b). The sporangia consist of multinucleate cells. As indicated in (c), they produce haploid spores by meiotic division. These spores are dispersed by the wind, and if they land on a suitably moist substrate they will germinate to form flagellated gametes. Two gametes will then fuse to form a diploid zygote, which will then lose its flagella and develop into an amoeboid cell. Multiple mitotic divisions of the diploid nucleus and the production of new cytoplasm eventually result in the formation of the plasmodium.*

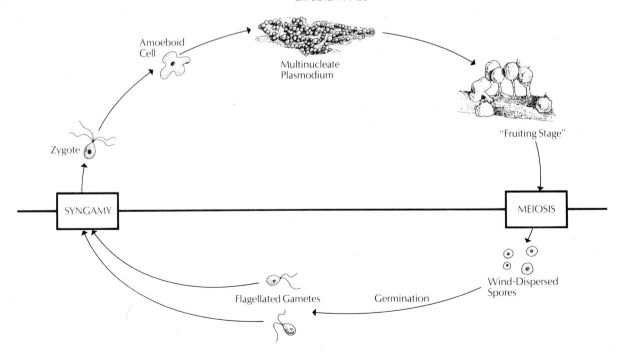

molds engulf particles of food by endocytosis (a process described in Chapter 4). When confronted with unfavorable environmental conditions, the plasmodium forms multinucleate cells with resistant cell walls. This resistant stage, called a **sclerotium,** may persist for some time until conditions are again suitable for growth and development of the plasmodium.

Acrasiae: The Cellular Slime Molds

There are eight genera and about twenty-five species in the class **Acrasiae,** and all are commonly referred to as the **cellular slime molds.** *The entire life cycle of the cellular slime molds is haploid.* Each amoeboid cell, which is produced by the germination of haploid spores, has a single nucleus. These cells lead an independent existence as long as adequate food is available. They feed by endocytosis, divide continually, and produce more amoeboid cells. When food becomes limited, the cells cluster together to form a **pseudoplasmodium.** Unlike the cells of the true plasmodium, the individual amoeboid cells of the pseudoplasmodium retain their cell membranes and their individual identity. The pseudoplasmodium eventually develops into a multicellular mass called a "slug," which shows a certain degree of coordinated activity, as described in *Interleaf 6.1.* The slug then differentiates to form a fruiting structure (a sporangium). The fruiting structure produces haploid spores, which initiate the next generation of the life cycle.

THE TRUE FUNGI INCLUDE PARASITES AS WELL AS DECOMPOSERS

Almost all organisms in the kingdom Fungi are grouped into the phylum **Eumycophyta.** These are the so-called "true fungi," and they have a tremendous effect on the biosphere. The large number of **saprophytic fungi,** which feed on dead organic material by means of extracellular digestion, are essential to the recycling of nutrients in natural ecosystems. **Parasitic fungi,** which obtain their nutrients from living host cells, can act as disease-causing organisms (pathogens) in both animals and plants. It was a parasitic fungus that brought about the virtual extinction of the American chestnut tree, a plant that once flourished in the deciduous forests of northeastern America. Another fungal species appears to be having the same effect on the American elm tree. The impact of fungal pathogens on agricultural crops can be staggering. Continuing research efforts focus on developing safe agents to control such fungal diseases as well as to develop resistant varieties of crop plants. Fungal diseases also occur in human beings and other animals. Athlete's foot and ringworm are two common examples; some less common forms have severe clinical implications.

The basic structural unit in true fungi is the fungal filament, or **hypha** (from the Greek *hyphe,* meaning "web"). Unlike most algal filaments, the hyphae of fungi lack cross walls that would partition the filament into discrete cells. In aggregate, these long, slender filaments make up a fungal body called a **mycelium.** Parasitic fungi characteristically produce extensions of the hyphae, which penetrate host cells in search of nutrients. Such a suckerlike extension is called a **haustorium** (a "drain"). Life cycles of the different classes of true fungi vary from simple to complex. We will examine only a few of the simpler cycles as appropriate to our discussion of each group.

Chytridiomycetes: The Production of Flagellated Spores and Gametes

A small class of saprophytic and parasitic fungi that occur in water and soils is the **Chytridiomycetes,** or **chytrids.** Many chytrids feed on aquatic plants. Some have only one nucleus; others form a simple multinucleate mycelium. Their cell walls are composed of chitin and cellulose. *The distinguishing characteristic of chytrids is the mitotic production of zoospores or gametes with a single flagellum.* But there is no "general" life cycle for the chytrids. Most reproduce asexually from zoospores; a rare few reproduce sexually; and individuals of one species send out slender filaments that grow toward and fuse with another individual in a process that involves migration of a nucleus from one to the other to produce a zygote.

Oomycetes: Molds and Parasites Curiously Reminiscent of Algae

Several hundred species of the *water molds* (which are largely aquatic fungi) and some terrestrial parasites such as the *white rusts* and the *downy mildews* are grouped together as **Oomycetes.** Biflagellate gametes and zoospores are produced in many aquatic forms, and in general the life cycles of many of the species are quite similar to those of some algae. *The Oomycetes, with their cell walls of cellulose and their algalike reproductive structures, provide a possible link between the higher fungi and the plant kingdom.* Notice, in Figure 6.3, the structures that are reminiscent of algal life cycles shown in Chapter 5. These structures appear in the life cycle of *Saprolegnia,* a typical water mold. Other oomycetes have a sexual cycle involving an alternation of basically similar haploid and diploid phases; still others are even more complex.

Most of the aquatic forms of the Oomycetes are saprophytic, although some are parasitic on fish and other aquatic animals. *Saprolegnia* is often found in the form of small, fuzzy masses of hyphae on dead fish or other organic material in fresh-water habitats (Figure 6.3*a*). One species within the class, *Phytophthora infestans,* which causes the late blight of potatoes, was responsible for the great Irish

(text continues on page 109)

Interleaf 6.1

Studies of Differentiation in *Dictyostelium discoideum*

The cellular slime mold *Dictyostelium discoideum* has proven useful in many kinds of studies of differentiation processes. In the laboratory, the free-living amoeboid cells of this organism can be grown in a broth medium. Thus, billions of identical healthy cells can easily be collected for biochemical study. When the cells are washed free of the medium and placed on wet filter paper, subsequent changes in development occur synchronously in all the cells. Thus, every stage in multicellular differentiation is open to convenient biochemical analysis.

Because the cells grow as individual amoebae, their genetic processes can be studied by the same powerful techniques that have proved so suitable with bacteria and other microorganisms. Amoebae can be treated with mutagenic chemicals and spread out in a dish with bacteria as food. Cells that survive under the conditions being studied grow and eat their way through the lawn of bacteria, making a clear spot, or plaque. Because each strain of amoebae forms a distinctively shaped plaque, rare mutants can easily be detected, isolated, and analyzed by noting unusual plaques and collecting cells from them. This technique has yielded mutant strains with alterations of a large variety of normal functions and differentiations.

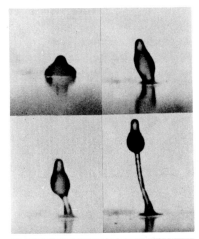

A sequence in the development of the fruiting bodies of the cellular slime mold Dictyostelium discoideum.

Almost every stage of development of *D. discoideum* raises interesting questions of cellular interactions that are similar to those found in vertebrate embryogenesis and metabolism. The first thing the individual cells must do when they are induced to develop is to get together. The cells move toward a higher concentration of a nucleotide that is derived from ATP and is known as cAMP (cyclic adenosine-3′5′-monophosphate). As a few cells happen to come together, they secrete more cAMP into the area, and additional numbers of cells are attracted toward the spot. In this way, large numbers of dispersed cells gather into a compact mass.

The alteration of amoebae that causes them to move toward higher cAMP concentration may be the first step in differentiation. In the amoeboid state, the cells normally are attracted toward some unknown substance excreted by bacteria, thus tending to move toward food. When aggregation begins, the cells cease to move toward the bacteria and begin to move toward each other along the cAMP concentration gradient. This alteration is one of the clearest examples known of a sharp biochemical switch of a nature than can be called differentiation.

After the cells have aggregated, they become mutually adhesive and remain as a single unit throughout the rest of development. The aggregate now begins to move as a worm-shaped *pseudoplasmodium*, or slug, containing up to 100,000 cells. At this stage, the front cells begin to undergo the biochemical differentiations that will transform them into stalk cells, while the posterior cells begin to differentiate into spore cells. *The proportion of prespore cells to prestalk cells is always 2:1, no matter how many cells have aggregated in the pseudoplasmodium.* (Pseudoplasmodia differing in size by more than 100-fold always achieve the same ratio.) This observation clearly points to a mechanism that allows the cells to interact throughout the organism in order to set up the correct ratio of spore to stalk cells in the final fruiting bodies. Somehow the cells at the rear must be affected by the number of cells in front of them and vice versa. The nature of this interaction is currently under intense study.

Several theories have been proposed to account for this interaction. One of the simplest theories suggests that interaction is mediated by the extracellular polysaccharide that is secreted by the cells and covers the whole organism with a layer of slime. The slime remains stationary on the supporting surface, and the cells move through it. Because the cells at the rear must follow on the slime laid down by cells at the front, the tip cells are the only ones free to control the direction of movement. Thus, the motion of thousands of previously independent cells is integrated into organismic behavior. Moreover, because the cells at the front secrete the slime and then move out of it, they are surrounded by a thinner layer of slime than are cells at the rear. It has been suggested that it is the amount of this polysaccharide coating that determines the course of differentiation. Cells at the front, surrounded by less polysaccharide, transform into stalk cells, whereas those at the rear, embedded in far more polysaccharide, transform into spore cells. This theory accounts for correct proportioning in a pseudoplasmodium containing any number of cells if the rate of movement of the pseudoplasmodium is directly proportional to its length and if the rate of slime secretion is proportional to the surface area. There is some evidence to indicate that these relationships do exist. But other

mechanisms have been proposed to explain this differentiation into two cell types and are presently being tested. The reason for the high level of interest in this problem is that parallel examples of specific cellular adhesions and cell migration leading to differentiation in various ratios occur in the embryogenesis of almost all complex organisms, but in few cases can they be studied as easily as the cellular slime molds can.

All of the biochemical steps that result in spore and stalk cell differentiation in *D. discoideum* occur after the amoebae have ceased feeding and occur without growth or division of the cells. Amino acids needed to make new proteins are derived from breakdown of old proteins. Carbohydrates for the synthesis of the slime layer and stalk polysaccharides are derived from stored glycogen and the metabolism of other molecules already in the cells. The biochemical conversions require the synthesis of many new enzymes. At present, about fifteen enzymes are known to accumulate during development, and eleven have been studied in detail. Some of these enzymes are involved in the breakdown of carbohydrates and amino acids, some catalyze steps in the synthesis of new polysaccharides, and others are formed only in spore cells, where they direct the formation of specialized polysaccharides. Although the studies of these enzymes have greatly increased understanding of the spatial and temporal pattern of differentiation, they have not led to any explanation of the nature of cell-cell interactions that cause the synthesis of these enzymes at specific times in specific cells. Nevertheless, such interactions must occur, and further studies are under way to attempt to elucidate them.

One of the clearest demonstrations of cell-cell interaction can be seen between pairs of mutant

strains. For instance, two mutant strains that fail to form pseudoplasmodia can go on to form normal fruiting bodies with well-differentiated spore and stalk cells if cells of the two strains are mixed and incubated together. Alone, neither strain undergoes the biochemical differentiations required for fruiting body formation, but together they synthesize the enzymes required for normal differentiations. This interaction appears to result from simple cross-feeding of the two cell types in which each strain produces a substance missing in the other. A slightly more complex cell-cell interaction that controls specific biochemical differentiations can be demonstrated during aggregation of normal cells. As long as both aggregation and formation of pseudoplasmodia are prevented, the synthesis of several enzymes associated with pseudoplasmodial development is inhibited in the amoebae. However, if the cells are first allowed to aggregate for eight hours and then prevented from normal pseudoplasmodium formation, the enzymes subsequently accumulate normally as they would during pseudoplasmodial differentiation. It appears that the first steps in the induction of these enzymes occur during the first eight hours and that they require intimate contact of the amoebae. This period has been called commitment and occurs long before the accumulation of mRNA for the enzymes. Experiments designed to isolate a "committer" that is transferred between the cells have not yet been successful. The interaction appears to be very subtle and may involve intracellular changes that are elicited by membrane-membrane interactions between adjacent cells rather than passage of molecules between them.

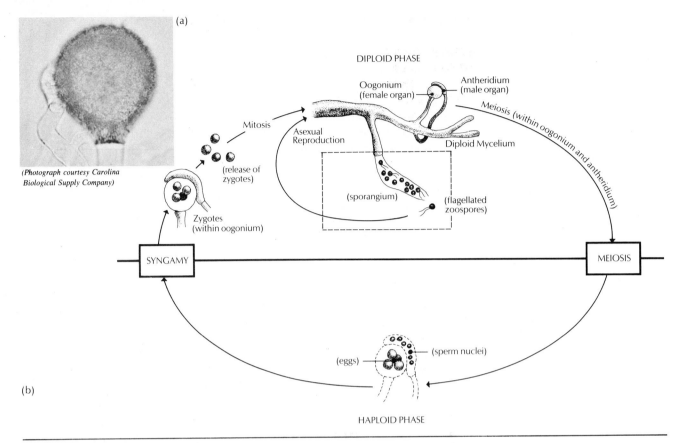

(a)

(Photograph courtesy Carolina Biological Supply Company)

(b)

DIPLOID PHASE

Oogonium (female organ)

Antheridium (male organ)

Meiosis (within oogonium and antheridium)

Mitosis

Asexual Reproduction

Diploid Mycelium

(release of zygotes)

(sporangium)

(flagellated zoospores)

Zygotes (within oogonium)

SYNGAMY

MEIOSIS

(eggs)

(sperm nuclei)

HAPLOID PHASE

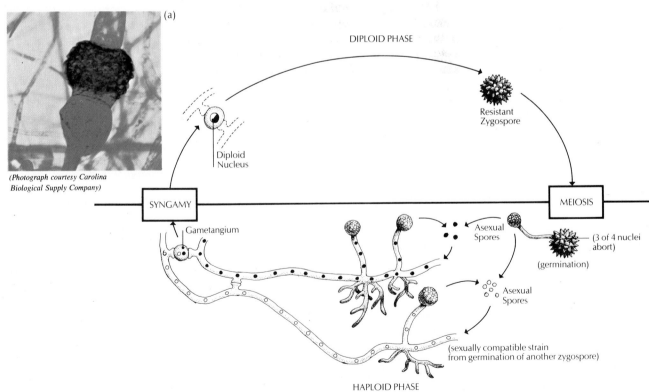

(a)

(Photograph courtesy Carolina Biological Supply Company)

DIPLOID PHASE

Resistant Zygospore

Diploid Nucleus

SYNGAMY

MEIOSIS

Gametangium

Asexual Spores

(3 of 4 nuclei abort)

(germination)

Asexual Spores

(sexually compatible strain from germination of another zygospore)

HAPLOID PHASE

Figure 6.3 The water mold Saprolegnia *(a),
a typical oomycete. (b) Life cycle of* Saprolegnia. *The
body of this fungus is made of hyphal strands with
diploid nuclei. The strands lack cross walls except
where gamete- or spore-bearing structures are
present. The diploid body can reproduce asexually by
means of flagellated zoospores. The sexual structures
consist of a spherical oogonium (egg-bearing cell) and
an elongated antheridium (where sperm nuclei are
produced). At maturity, the antheridium is in physical
contact with the oogonium, and the gametes are
produced by meiosis. The sperm nuclei penetrate the
wall of the oogonium and fertilize the eggs. The
resulting diploid zygotes are released by the eventual
breakdown of the oogonium wall. Each zygote
develops into a new diploid mycelium.*

Figure 6.4 The black bread mold Rhizopus
(a). Life cycle of Rhizopus, *in which a zygote is
formed by the fusion of two different strains of the
mold (b). Most of the life cycle is asexual.
Reproduction is accomplished by the production of
haploid spores on elevated sporangia, which
eventually disperse through the air. The black spots
on a well-developed bread mold colony represent the
spore-covered sporangia.*

*Sexual reproduction occurs when two compatible
hyphae come in contact with each other. A sexual
structure called a gametangium is formed by lateral
outgrowths from each hypha. A nucleus from each
hypha enters the gametangium and the two nuclei
fuse, forming the zygote. The wall of the gametangium
then thickens to form the resting zygospore. The
zygospore undergoes meiosis and germinates. Three of
the four nuclei that are produced abort; the remaining
nucleus develops into a new haploid hypha that will
produce asexual spores.*

famine of 1845. The rusts and mildews within this class
have a significantly detrimental effect on agricultural production in a wide variety of crops.

Zygomycetes: A Unique Form of Sexual Reproduction

Several hundred species of fungi, commonly known as
bread molds and *fly fungi,* are grouped into the class
Zygomycetes. The class is so named because a diploid
resting spore, called a **zygospore,** is characteristically
produced during the life cycle. The production of a zygospore is shown in Figure 6.4, which outlines the life cycle
of the common bread mold *Rhizopus.* The haploid hyphae
of *Rhizopus* lack cross walls. They form the cottony-
looking mycelium that was such a common embellishment
on bread before the baking industry began using chemical
preservatives.

Most zygomycetes are saprophytic (although there are
some that are parasitic on plants, animals, and even other
zygomycetes). *Pilobolus,* for example, is an interesting
saprophyte that grows on the dung of animals such as cows
and horses. The terminal sporangium (Figure 6.5) rests on a
swollen transparent structure that actually serves as a lens
system! This structure focuses light in such a way that the
sporangium is oriented toward the brightest (hence the most
open) area around the dung mass, as shown in Figure 6.5.
Sporangia are ejected from the sporangiophore by internal
water pressure. They can be propelled through the air for
many feet. The ones that land on grass or other vegetation
may be consumed by grazing animals. The spores then pass
through the animal's digestive tract and are deposited in
masses of fresh dung—where the next generation of the life
cycle begins.

Ascomycetes: A Sac for Sexual Fusion

Such diverse organisms as the *yeasts,* the green, red, and
black *molds,* the *powdery mildews,* the *cup fungi,* and the
edible *morels* and *truffles* are included in the class **Ascomycetes,** or sac fungi. There are at least 30,000 species in the
group, and it is possible that most of the 20,000 **imperfect
fungi** may also belong here. (They are so called because a
sexual phase of their life cycle has never been observed.)

Sexual fusion and meiotic division of the zygote occur in
an elongated, saclike cell called an **ascus** (Greek for
"bag," or "sac"). The ascus contains either four or eight
ascospores, which are formed by the meiotic division of the
zygote. The life cycle of a "typical" ascomycete is shown
in Figure 6.6. As shown in this figure, the ascospores are
arranged linearly. This predictable sequence follows directly from the division sequence in meiosis. For that reason the
ascomycetes—particularly the genus *Neurospora*—have
been exceptionally useful in genetic research (Chapter 16).

(text continues on page 112)

Figure 6.6   (a) Asexual conidia in an ascomycete. (b) Life cycle of a "typical" ascomycete. Individual haploid ascospores germinate to form an extensive mycelium. The mycelium is monokaryotic (which means that each division of the hyphal strand contains a single haploid nucleus). Individual mycelia have genetically determined mating types, for during meiotic division there is a segregation of chromosomes that produced the ascospores from which the hyphae were derived.

As the individual mycelia develop, they reproduce asexually by specialized spores called conidia. The conidia are little more than individual nuclei and a small bit of cytoplasm pinched off the ends of hyphal strands.

Sexual reproduction is initiated when two compatible strands come close to each other. One strand produces a spherical structure, an ascogonium, which contains a number of haploid nuclei. The ascogonium has a long, tubular extension (a trichogyne), which comes into contact with a spherical antheridium produced on a compatible strand. The antheridium also contains a number of haploid nuclei, which migrate through the tubular extension to join the nuclei in the ascogonium. The compatible nuclei pair up and a number of relatively short dikaryotic hyphal strands are produced as outgrowths from the old ascogonium. Individual "cells" of the dikaryotic hyphae are formed by the presence of cross walls. Each "cell" contains two nuclei, one from each mating type. The growing tip of each dikaryotic hypha eventually produces an asymmetric "crook cell." Each nucleus in the crook cell divides and the nuclei segregate. At the same time, cross walls form so that one nucleus of each mating type is confined to a "cell," with a pair of compatible nuclei remaining in the terminal chamber. Each member of the pair functions as a gamete.

Fusion of the nuclei to form the diploid zygote occurs in the ascus mother cell, followed by meiosis. Meiotic division leads to a linear tetrad of haploid nuclei within the developing ascus. Mitotic division follows in most ascomycete life cycles to produce a linear series of eight nuclei. The aggregation of cytoplasm and the formation of a resistant cell wall around each nucleus creates individual ascospores, which are released into the air to initiate a new cycle.

Figure 6.5 (below)   Sporangia of Pilobolus. *This drawing shows the role of sunlight in aligning the swollen transparent spore stalk toward lighted areas.*

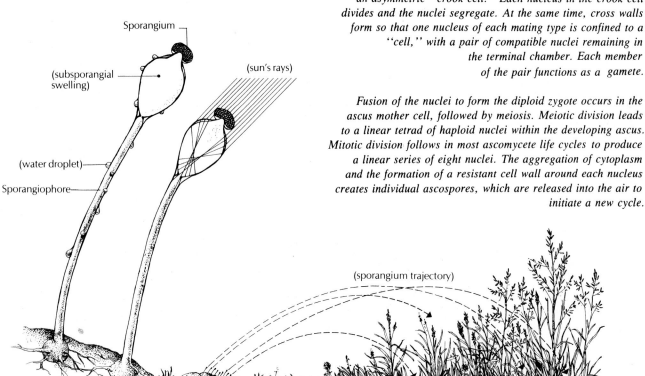

Sporangium

(subsporangial swelling)

(sun's rays)

(water droplet)

Sporangiophore

(sporangium trajectory)

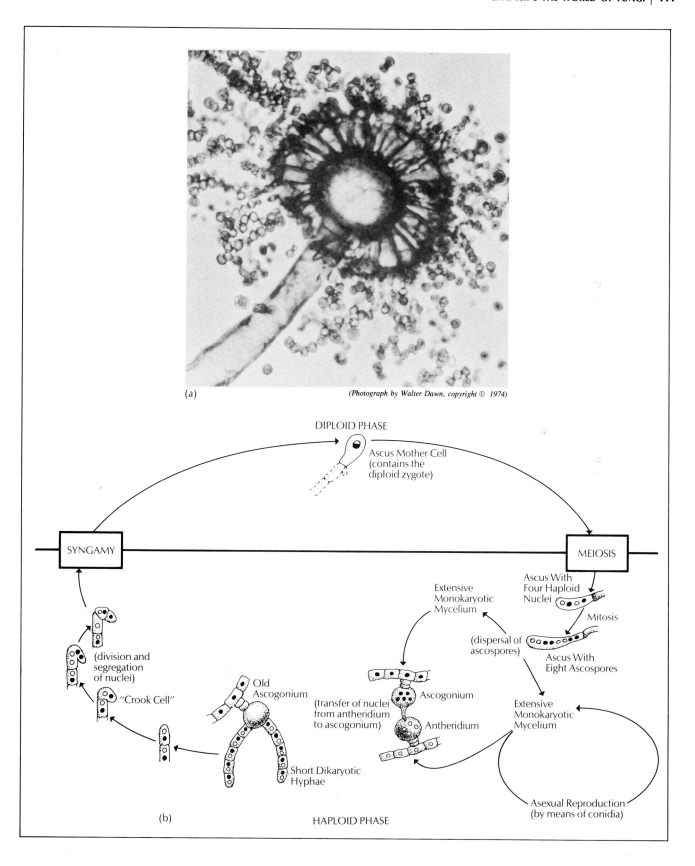

(a)

(Photograph by Walter Dawn, copyright © 1974)

DIPLOID PHASE

Ascus Mother Cell
(contains the
diploid zygote)

SYNGAMY

MEIOSIS

Ascus With
Four Haploid
Nuclei

Mitosis

Extensive
Monokaryotic
Mycelium

(dispersal of
ascospores)

Ascus With
Eight Ascospores

(division and
segregation
of nuclei)

"Crook Cell"

Old
Ascogonium

(transfer of nuclei
from antheridium
to ascogonium)

Ascogonium

Antheridium

Extensive
Monokaryotic
Mycelium

Short Dikaryotic
Hyphae

Asexual Reproduction
(by means of conidia)

(b)

HAPLOID PHASE

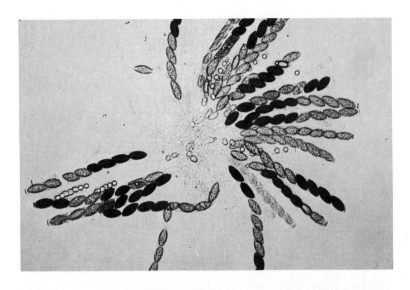

Figure 6.7   The asci and ascospores of the red bread mold Neurospora.

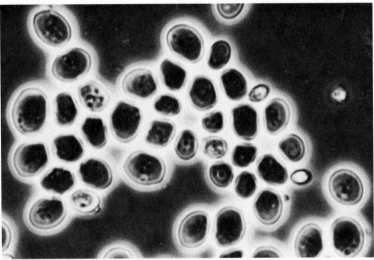

(Photograph by Walter Dawn, copyright © 1974)

Figure 6.8   Yeast cells. Yeasts are simple ascomycetes that are important in the baking and brewing industries. They are important saprophytes in natural systems.

Neurospora contains eight ascospores and has a well-developed hyphal mass (Figure 6.7). In contrast, the asci in yeasts are simple and free-floating, and they contain only four ascospores (Figure 6.8). In cup fungi (Figure 6.9), the asci are clustered into more complex fruiting structures, called **ascocarps.** (The combining form -*carp* comes from the Greek word for "fruit.") Although sexual structures serve as the basis for such classifications, *asexual reproduction by means of spores is far more common in ascomycetes.* (That is why it is so difficult to categorize individual imperfect fungi.)

The sac fungi, an extremely influential group of saprophytic and parasitic organisms in natural systems, are important even from the narrowest point of view. Yeasts are essential in the brewing and baking industries, and truffles and morels (Figure 6.10) are esteemed by gourmets. The first and still most widely used antibiotic, **penicillin,** was obtained as a metabolic product of *Penicillium notatum,* a common green mold often seen on fruits such as oranges (Figure 6.1). Although improved versions of this drug are now being synthesized, researchers are constantly screening large numbers of fungi in the search for other desirable antibiotics.

Basidiomycetes: Launching Pads for Haploid Spores

Between 25,000 and 30,000 species are grouped in the most structurally complex class of fungi, the **Basidiomycetes.** The group includes *mushrooms* (and/or *toadstools*), *smuts, rusts, jelly fungi, shelf fungi,* and *stinkhorns.* The name of the class is derived from a club-shaped structure called a **basidium,** which has small projections on its surface that are sites for haploid spore production. Most of the basidiomycetes are characterized by the formation of a complex spore-bearing structure called a **basidiocarp,** such as the one shown in Figure 6.11 for a mushroom, or the one in

Figure 6.9   The cup fungus Sarcoscypha coccinea. *The prominent, cuplike ascocarp is formed by the aggregation of many individual hyphae and is lined with many asci.*

Figure 6.10   A morel belonging to the genus Morchella. *Morels are particularly prized as food. Although their appearance may hardly be considered appetizing, many connoisseurs view them as the finest edible wild fungi. Morels are only found in the wild state, primarily in woodland habitats. All attempts to cultivate them have been unsuccessful. The mycelium can be induced to grow easily in culture, but ascocarp formation apparently does not occur under artificial conditions.*

Figure 6.12 for a shelf fungus. This structure is at least functionally analogous to the ascocarp of the more complex ascomycetes.

The life cycle of a mushroom is shown in Figure 6.11 *b*. Although the basidiocarp is the conspicuous part of the life cycle, it is produced only at certain intervals in the cycle and appears to represent a specific mechanism for spore dispersal. An extensive and long-lived hyphal mass, which proliferates beneath the surface of the soil, represents the actual growth phase of the life cycle and is called the **secondary mycelium.** (You would have to examine the soil carefully to see the interwoven network of hyphal strands.)

The pattern of growth seen in fungi such as mushrooms has a number of interesting consequences. At one time or another you may have seen a ring of mushrooms on a lawn or other open area. Such a ring (often called a *fairy ring*) is shown in Figure 6.13. Such rings are a natural consequence of the mushroom's mode of growth in open space. The

center of a ring represents the approximate point where two **primary mycelia** (short, monokaryotic hyphae) combined to form the secondary mycelium. If growth is not restricted in any particular direction, the secondary mycelium will develop a radial growth pattern, extending outward from its point of origin. When conditions are suitable for basidiocarp formation, the actual mushrooms will be formed in regions of rapid growth—at the margins of the expanding mycelium. The ring of mushrooms represents the periphery of the expanding mycelial mass. When conditions are again suitable for basidiocarp formation—weeks, months, or even a year later—the mycelium will have grown further outward and the next ring will be even larger. Eventually the ring form will be lost as the circle gets larger and larger and the periphery of the mycelium breaks down or encounters slightly different conditions that cause a differential rate of growth along the margin.

Similarly, the sudden overnight appearance of mush-

Figure 6.11   (a) A basidiocarp, the visible portion of a mushroom. Spore-bearing gills are shown on the underside. (b) Mushroom life cycle. Wind currents disperse basidiospores, which germinate into primary mycelia (monokaryotic hyphae). If two sexually compatible hyphae come together, a tubular extension forms between them that has one nucleus from each strain. The secondary mycelium now spreads through the soil, and if conditions are good, hyphal masses develop on its actively growing parts—eventually forming the basidiocarp. These hyphae are the fruiting structure (tertiary mycelium). In sexual fusion, the diploid nucleus divides meiotically into four haploid nuclei. Each nucleus is extruded with some cytoplasm through a tubelike extension (sterigma) at the basidium tip, and a resistant wall forms around it. Thus it becomes a mature basidiospore, ready to begin the cycle anew.

(a)

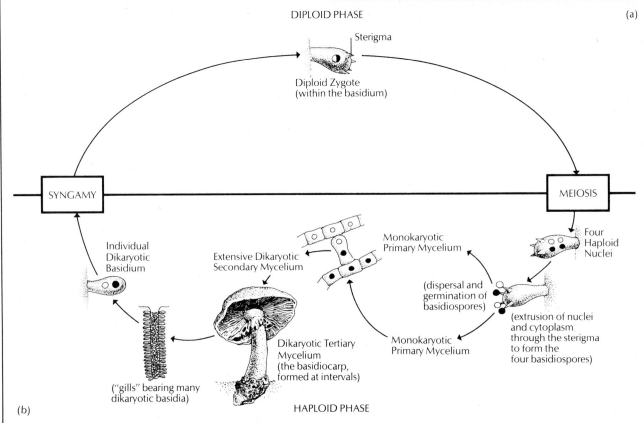

(b)

Figure 6.12   A shelf fungus growing on the bark of a tree. Although certain species of shelf fungi can rot the heartwood and sapwood of living trees, most are saprophytes on dead wood.

Figure 6.13   A fairy ring. Initiated from a single site, the secondary mycelia of these fungi grow outward in all directions through the soil.

rooms, particularly during the wet periods of late spring and early summer, is only the final stage in a longer developmental process. Immature mushrooms (called *buttons*) are preformed along the strands of the secondary mycelium below the surface of the soil. The sudden expansion of the buttons into the conspicuous basidiocarp is caused more by the rapid expansion and elongation of cells than by a rapid differentiation of the sporocarp tissue.

Although the vast majority of the Basidiomycetes are saprophytic, some forms such as the smuts and rusts are parasitic, particularly on plants. As is typical of many parasitic fungi, the life cycle of smuts and rusts is considerably more complex than that of the saprophytic forms, often involving intermediate hosts and a variety of specialized structures. The effects of smuts and rusts on crop plants (Figure 6.14) is difficult to estimate, but a figure of many millions of dollars per year in crop damage is certainly conservative.

Many mushrooms, including the common commercial mushroom *Agaricus campestris,* are valued as food delicacies, but still others are shunned because of their poisonous properties. Among the poisonous mushrooms, the genus *Amanita* (Figure 6.15) has perhaps the worst reputation. However, poisonous properties ranging from the deadly through the merely unpleasant are widely distributed through a number of groups. Indiscriminate collection of wild mushrooms, even when using a book or manual, is not a safe procedure. If you are interested in hunting wild mushrooms the safest procedure is to receive instruction in recognizing a few basic edible types and then to confine your collecting to those types. (Poison control centers in hospitals across the country do a regular business with individuals who should have confined their collecting to supermarket shelves.)

THE LICHENS ARE PART FUNGUS, PART ALGA

Although it is not a true organism, the **lichen** is usually classified within the kingdom Fungi. It is the end result of the close symbiotic association between an alga (usually a blue-green or green alga) and a fungus (usually an ascomycete). The origin and nature of the relationship is puzzling. There is little doubt that the alga obtains a certain amount of protection from the fungal component, and it appears likely that the fungus uses carbohydrates produced by the alga (Figure 6.16). The question of whether the relationship represents commensalism, mutualism, or even mild parasitism (Chapter 32) probably cannot be answered definitely, for all lichens must be assessed individually. Lichens, which are the composite product of the relationship, can survive on such formidable substrates as bare rock and under harsh environmental conditions where few other organisms can exist. It has been possible, through careful

Figure 6.14 (a) A smut growing on corn. (b) A rust growing on wheat. The most effective way of controlling the impact of smuts, rusts, and other parasitic fungi on crop plants is to produce genetically resistant crop varieties. (Rapid mutation of the fungi, however, makes this a never-ending task.)

Figure 6.15 Amanita muscaria, a saprophytic basidiomycete found in decaying plant matter. Some species of the genus Amanita are edible, but others are lethal. Because the results of an error in identification can be permanent, the entire group is best avoided.

Figure 6.16 A large, leafy form of lichen. Lichens are combinations of algae and fungi in a mutually dependent relationship. The alga provides nutrients through photosynthesis, and the fungus seems to provide moisture and a slightly acidic environment, in which the alga thrives.

laboratory techniques, to separate the algal and fungal components and to culture them separately. Experiments in recombining the two components have been less successful, although eventually we should be able to arrive at an understanding of the factors responsible for initiating and maintaining the relationship under natural conditions. Lichens can be found on most moist substrates and are important in the initial breakdown of bare rock under natural conditions. But they are generally an insignificant component of most ecosystems. One exception is the reindeer moss *(Cladonia rangiferina)*, which is an important element in arctic food chains because it is a major food source for reindeer and caribou.

PERSPECTIVE

All the diverse forms of fungi represent an interesting pattern of responses to a variety of environmental conditions. Whereas green plants have specialized in solar energy utilization, and animals in the search for relatively complex and concentrated organic materials, the saprophytic fungi have developed strategies for handling the somewhat less concentrated organic "residue" produced as by-products of other processes in living systems.

The fungi have managed to survive under terrestrial conditions without the need for structural complexity. Most of their mycelial growth occurs in local zones of moist substrate; as a result, the mycelium shows few adaptations for survival under truly dry conditions. In addition, a variety of spore-dispersing structures have effectively exploited air currents. Development of the ascocarps and basidiocarps of the higher fungi, which represent the most complex forms of structural organization, probably was favored by natural selection because they are efficient in dispersing spores.

The parasitic fungi effectively use the life-support systems of the host organism to obtain water and nutrients. In doing so, they are symbionts functionally analogous to free-living predators. Much of the specialization we see in these organisms is directed toward assuring the continued access of the parasite to the host species.

The fungi use energy from materials that normally cannot be used efficiently by more "advanced" members of the communities in which they are found. Although we are justifiably interested in fungi as agents of plant and animal disease, it is the contribution of the much larger number of saprophytic fungi in the essential flow of energy and materials that defines their most important role in most major ecosystems.

The vast store of useful genetic information contained in the present pattern of fungal diversity has barely been tapped in our tentative forays into the realm of fungi to discover useful antibiotics and fermentation products. The fields of medicine, food production, and resource utilization cannot help but prosper further as we gradually expand our understanding of the complex capabilities of these unpretentious organisms. The fact that a sizable segment of the world's population may owe their lives to the biochemical capability of a green mold on some spoiled oranges might well serve to indicate that useful information need not be packaged in a particularly spectacular fashion. The potential benefits of a developing understanding of the capabilities of fungi probably exceed anything we could imagine at the present time.

SUGGESTED READINGS

BATRA, SUZANNE W. T., and LEKH R. BATRA. "The Fungus Gardens of Insects," *Scientific American,* 217 (November 1967), 112–120. An interesting account of the importance of fungi as a food source for various insects.

BOETTCHER, HELMUTH M. *Wonder Drugs.* Einhart Kawerau (tr.). Philadelphia: Lippincott, 1964. A history of the discovery and use of antibiotics.

CHRISTENSEN, CLYDE M. *Common Fleshy Fungi.* Minneapolis: Burgess, 1965. Descriptions, keys, and photographs of common ascomycetes and basidiomycetes.

LAMB, I. M. "Lichens," *Scientific American,* 201 (October 1959), 144–156. An easy-to-read account that provides further information on these symbiotic organisms.

STONG, C. L. "How to Isolate Microorganisms That Secrete Antibiotics," *Scientific American,* 213 (November 1965), 124–130. A guide for the amateur scientist. All groups of microorganisms may be regarded as potential sources of antibiotic drugs, and the intelligent amateur has as good a chance as anyone of discovering them.

Chapter 7

The Lower Animals and Their Evolution

In the delicate, internal traceries of the flatworm are echoes of an evolutionary event of the first magnitude. When the ancestral forms of this organism first began to crawl forward over surfaces in their environment, they embarked on a journey that eventually led, through natural selection, to the development of a brain. In animals derived from those ancestral forms, the appearance of the brain changed the course of evolutionary history long before the human species emerged. At the same time, the flatworms of today, like all other simple animals, show even more fundamental links to the simpler unicellular forms that once dominated the ancient seas.

So many features are common to all organisms, particularly at the molecular and cellular levels of organization, that it is reasonable to assume they have descended from a common ancestor. If this assumption is valid, then theoretically it should be possible to determine relationships among all existing organisms, to recognize the ancestral forms from which various groups of organisms diverged, and therefore to follow these evolutionary threads back to the earliest forms of living matter. This is the goal of biologists who concern themselves with **phylogeny,** the study of the evolutionary relationships of plants and animals. Unfortunately, although progress is continually being made, the goal of phylogenetics will probably never be achieved in its entirety.

In order to understand how such studies proceed and why this somewhat pessimistic forecast has been made, let us consider for a moment a biologist trying to make sense out of the classification of land slugs. He soon realizes that not all these animals seem to be closely related. In structure, some are more similar to certain snails than to other slugs. After weighing the anatomical and embryological evidence, the biologist concludes that different groups of slugs appear to have evolved independently from several decidedly different types of snails, losing their shells in the process or at least having the shells reduced to mere reminders of things past. But when he tries to devise a comprehensive system of classification of all snails and all slugs he thinks are at least remotely related, he must make some decisions without the benefit of crucial evidence—evidence that could only be supplied by animals that are now extinct and for which fossils simply do not exist.

Because of the complete extinction of many groups and the lack of a fossil record for early forms of life, the only threads of evolution we can pick up are short scraps of relatively recent developments. There was an extremely long time span between the origin of life and the evolution of conditions favorable for the preservation of fossils. As a result, there are very few fossils from periods earlier than the Cambrian—in other words, fossils that are more than half a billion years old (Chapter 9). Nevertheless, it does appear that as far back as a billion years ago there was already a substantial variety of organisms. Algae and polyplike animals are recognizable in truly ancient deposits, and the preservation of tracks, trails, burrows, and fecal pellets suggests that some rather advanced multicellular animals, or **metazoans,** were also present. In any event, at the dawn of the Cambrian there were animals already so complex that they must have had a long and illustrious history. If the pre-Cambrian fossil record is poor, then the evolution of groups already existing at the beginning of the Cambrian clearly is going to be difficult to trace.

Why are there so few pre-Cambrian fossils? First of all, small or soft-bodied animals are not likely to be preserved after they die, especially in shallow seas where decomposers are abundant. In addition, if the seas in which life originated and had its early evolution did not contain enough of the mineral salts needed in the fossilization process, or if the water quality was otherwise unfavorable, preservation would also have been discouraged. Furthermore, during earlier phases of evolution, the dominant organisms were probably microscopic plants, herbivores feeding on the plants, and decomposers that recycled organic material. There would have been no selective pressures to encourage development of animal species with hard parts, which are more readily fossilized. Evolution of hard parts was presumably favored only after more efficient predators started to come into the picture, probably during the Cambrian period.

Another thing to remember is that during evolution of the animal kingdom, there must have been countless "trial balloons" represented by relatively few individuals. Evolution does not necessarily involve large numbers. Only after an evolutionary advance pays off will the population of a group increase sufficiently to assure a rich fossil record. And even then the characteristics of the group must be such that its members can be fossilized reasonably well.

In any case, the fact remains that few fossils are available to suggest what kinds of organisms were present during the many millions of years when most of the main lines of animals were becoming established. But *just as importantly,* biologists are still in the dark about many aspects of the structure, development, physiology, and life styles of certain organisms that are *not* extinct. It would be essential to have much more than some fossils or imprints of primitive groups in order to piece together the early evolution of the animal kingdom. Nevertheless, it is intriguing to think about the ancestors of animals living today. What possibilities for evolution were open to them? And what probable links exist between relatively advanced groups? In attempting to understand relationships that are reasonably clear, we may strengthen our knowledge of the animal kingdom as a whole. Such attempts may also lead to some productive lines of research.

WHAT STEPS LED FROM A SINGLE-CELLED ORGANISM TO A SIMPLE METAZOAN?

Assume, for the sake of discussion, that before multicellular organisms arose there must have been many kinds of plantlike and animallike unicellular organisms (similar to those described in Chapter 4), moving about with cilia and flagella and reproducing sexually. First of all, the condition of *multicellularity* would have had to arise. This condition would permit morphological and physiological specialization of different cells for varied functions. Also, there would have had to be *a system for ingesting food and eliminating indigestible residues,* although this system would call for no particular complexities beyond those seen in many simple unicellular organisms (Chapter 4). Because cells not concerned with feeding would have had to receive their share of nutritive materials, there had to be some way for these nutrients to be moved from cell to cell. Excretion of wastes would probably not have been much of a problem for a small multicellular organism living in water; the wastes could simply diffuse away. In order to move about in search of food, the animal would have needed cilia or some other mechanism for *locomotion.* There is a possibility, of course, that at least some of the simpler early organisms were sedentary and fed on whatever settled on them. *A system for integration of body activities*—not necessarily a nervous system, but a way for one cell to communicate with another and respond to stimuli—would have been essential to make locomotion efficient and to keep the animal out of trouble. Finally, there had to be a method of *reproduction.* Asexual reproduction would surely have been possible. Certain cells, or any of the cells, could break away from the mass and multiply to complete another individual. But some form of sexual reproduction would be a prerequisite for encouraging variability and thus greater success of some individuals over others.

What specific evolutionary route would have been taken by a multicellular organism that had some degree of specialization of its component cells? We do not know. But on the basis of what can be seen in the organization of certain modern colonial organisms and in the early stages in the development of modern animals, several hypotheses can be proposed. *Multicellularity may have originated a number of times and by any or all of the pathways that seem possible.* And perhaps some multicellular organisms arose in ways that biologists have not yet thought of, simply because the early stages in the evolution of cells may not be visualized correctly.

Some of the hypotheses proposed over the years that concern the origins of the metazoans are real imagination stretchers, although they are not outside the realm of possibility. Here we will discuss the ideas that seem closest to being on the right track.

If a one-celled organism were to become multinucleate, and if its cytoplasm were then to become divided into about as many membrane-bound units as there were nuclei, the result would be a multicellular organism. With specialization of some of its cells for feeding and other functions, the organism could be considered a very simple metazoan. Two engaging ideas that fit into this general line of reasoning were proposed by Jovan Hadži and by Marius Chadefaud.

Hadži's idea is depicted in Figure 7.2. It takes advantage of ciliates, which have a depression that functions as a mouth. Hadži visualized a ciliate becoming multinucleate (as some ciliates are) and then becoming subdivided into cells. The animal would then have an **epidermis** (an outer layer of cells) that would be ciliated; an inner mass functioning as digestive tissue; and some cells serving other purposes, such as reproduction. The resulting organism would be close to a very simple type of flatworm (Figure 7.2*b*). However, flatworms are already much more advanced than certain other animals such as the cnidarians (jellyfishes and polyps). And in Hadži's scheme these simpler animals would have to be *derived from* the more advanced organisms.

Chadefaud's hypothesis begins with a flagellate of the type that has a cavity **(vestibule)** within which its flagella originate (Figure 7.3). If such a flagellate were first to become multinucleate, and then multicellular, some cells could form an outer layer of cells and others could line the

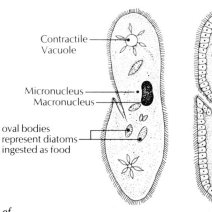
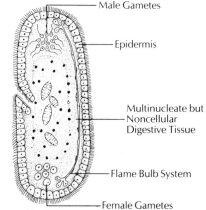

Figure 7.2   The essence of Hadži's idea of the origin of a simple flatworm from a ciliate.

Contractile Vacuole

Micronucleus
Macronucleus

oval bodies represent diatoms ingested as food

Male Gametes

Epidermis

Multinucleate but Noncellular Digestive Tissue

Flame Bulb System

Female Gametes

(a) A Ciliate

(b) A Hypothetical Simple Flatworm

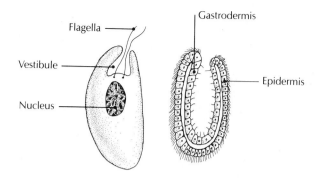

Figure 7.3   *The essence of Chadefaud's idea of the origin of a gastrulalike organism from a flagellate.*

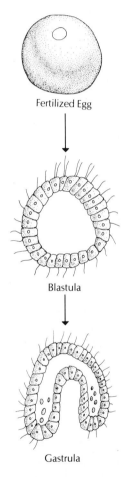

Figure 7.4   *Cross sections through the embryo of a marine animal at three early stages in its development. Similar stages are seen in the development of animals in a number of phyla. Thus, for over a century speculations on the origins of multicellular animals have centered on the development of a blastulalike or gastrulalike animal. The infolding of the blastula wall to form a gastrula gives rise to a primitive gut.*

cavity. (Such a covering or lining of any free body surface, whether it be internal or external, is called an **epithelium.**) The organism would then have a simple saclike gut and would resemble an early stage through which many animals pass in their embryonic development (Figure 7.4). In this developmental process, a fertilized egg first undergoes division to form a **blastula** (a hollow ball of cells), which eventually becomes a **gastrula** (an embryonic stage in which some cells have moved inside to form a gut). Essentially, then, Chadefaud visualized a flagellate becoming a metazoan in the form of a gastrula.

Chadefaud's idea is not popular at the present time. Hadži's idea has its adherents, but there are strong arguments against it. Although ciliates are not subdivided into multiple cells, most are complex organisms. As you read in Chapter 4, they have two kinds of nuclei and sometimes more than one nucleus of each type. The micronucleus is capable of dividing mitotically, of contributing to the formation of gamete nuclei, and of being transformed into a macronucleus. The macronucleus is active in directing the metabolism of the organism, but it does not divide mitotically (it is merely pinched in two) and it plays no role in conjugation. It does not even survive conjugation: it must be replaced by transformation of a micronucleus.

It is unlikely that ciliates are ancestral to metazoans. Ciliates could even have been derived from a group of simple metazoans. Perhaps there has been a reduction in the number of nuclei; perhaps the macronucleus is comparable to nuclei in those cells of higher animals that are no longer capable of forming reproductive cells. Conjugation between ciliates could be a vestigial form of copulation. No one knows, but it is something to think about!

A different line of reasoning about the origin of multicellularity is inspired by colonial flagellates that adhere to one another and form a blastulalike ball of cells (Figure 7.5). Conceivably, an early multicellular animal may have been of this general type, in which at least certain cells were concerned with feeding on microscopic organisms (Figure 7.6). One strange little marine animal, *Trichoplax,* was discovered in the late nineteenth century but has only recently been looked at in detail. It is actually much like a blastula that has been flattened out (Figure 7.7). It has a thin upper epidermis and a relatively thick lower epidermis, and both layers consist of cells with flagella. The lower epidermis evidently predigests small organisms externally. Gland cells among the flagellated cells are thought to secrete the digestive enzymes. When the animal humps up temporarily, a gutlike cavity may be formed on the underside. In the space between the upper and lower epidermis are some contractile cells, but how they are coordinated is not known. *Trichoplax* reproduces by fission and budding. Cells that appear to be eggs are present during its life cycle,

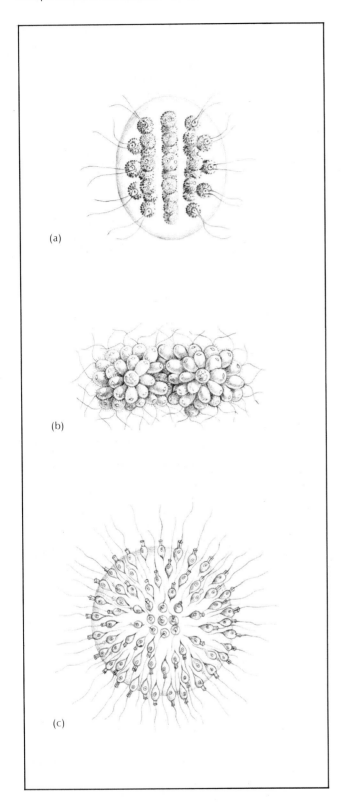

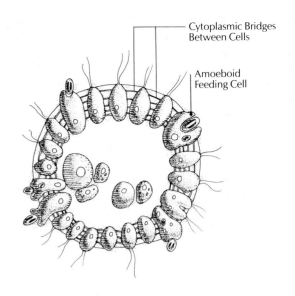

Figure 7.6   A hypothetical early metazoan, in the form of a blastula. Some cells are specialized for feeding, others for locomotion. Other functions, such as reproduction and transport of food, may be contemplated for cells in the interior. Remember, however, that this scheme is only one of many logical possibilities that could be devised.

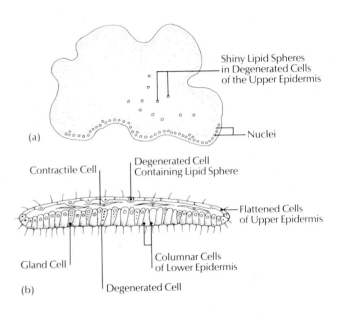

Figure 7.5   Some colonial flagellates: (a) Eudorina, Synura, and (c) Sphaeroëca.

Figure 7.7   Trichoplax, a small marine organism of uncertain affinities. Its structure is basically that of a flattened blastula, or plakula. (a) The organism as a whole is depicted as it would appear from above. (b) This section through Trichoplax shows, in a simplified way, the types of cells represented in this organism.

but formation of sperm and fertilization have not been observed. The term **plakula** has been applied to the flattened blastula type of organization shown by *Trichoplax*. This animal has figured in some speculations on phylogeny, but no one can be sure whether it is a relic related to an intermediate stage in animal evolution or whether it was derived more recently by simplification of a more advanced organism.

Another type of hypothetical early animal that might be derived from a colony of flagellates would be comparable to the gastrula stage in embryonic development, following invagination of part of the blastula wall to form a primitive **gut** (digestive cavity), as shown in Figure 7.8. The same type of organization could result if cells migrated into the interior, creating a more or less solid ball that later opened up in one region to form a mouth and a gut. Such inward migration of cells actually takes place in a stage of development of most cnidarians, giving rise to an elongated, ciliated larva called a **planula.** (A **larva** is an immature form in the life cycle of some animals. It undergoes radical transformation into the adult animal.) The theory that a planuloid organism figured prominently in the evolution of lower animals was proposed by Ludwig von Graff around the turn of the century. It still has many adherents. It is persuasive in attempting to explain the origin of bilaterally symmetrical animals, such as flatworms, as well as the radially symmetrical cnidarians. We will return to this concept later.

But perhaps the most logical thing to do now is have a look at some animals called lower invertebrates. They show, either as adults or during their development, some of the features we would expect to find in the earliest metazoans. The term **invertebrate** means ''without a backbone.'' Although many animals (including ourselves) have vertebral columns, the *vast* majority—more than 99 percent—of all animal species do not.

PHYLUM PORIFERA: THE SPONGES

Undoubtedly, the most primitive form of modern metazoans are the **sponges,** of the phylum **Porifera.** The sponges are little more than colonies of several types of cells. A sponge does not have a mouth or a digestive tract, and its cells are organized principally around a system of canals and chambers through which water circulates. Figure 7.9 is a diagram of a simple sponge that shows how members of the phylum are constructed. Notice, in this figure, that the surface of the sponge has many pores leading into canals that conduct water toward a central cavity. From this cavity, water leaves the sponge by way of an opening called the **osculum.** The central cavity is lined by small **collar cells,** or

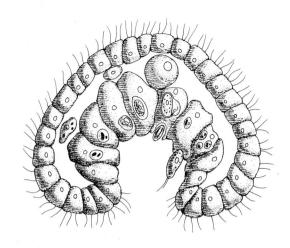

Figure 7.8   A hypothetical early metazoan, in the form of a gastrula.

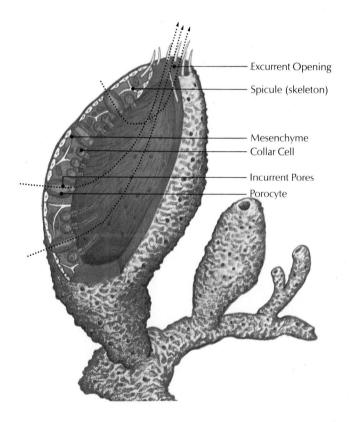

Excurrent Opening

Spicule (skeleton)

Mesenchyme
Collar Cell

Incurrent Pores

Porocyte

Figure 7.9   A very simple sponge. A portion of this drawing is cut away to show details of internal structure.

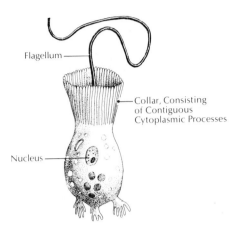

Flagellum

Collar, Consisting of Contiguous Cytoplasmic Processes

Nucleus

Figure 7.10   A collar cell of a sponge, reconstructed from electron micrographs of very thin sections.

choanocytes. These cells are rarely seen except in sponges and certain flagellates. They are characterized by a collar that surrounds the basal portion of the flagellum. The collar actually consists of a ring of fingerlike processes (Figure 7.10) that can be seen only with the aid of an electron microscope. As the flagella of the collar cells beat, they move water in the direction of the osculum and then out of the colony. If a drop of water containing some finely particulate, nontoxic substance is gently placed near the osculum, this stream of water will be strong enough to carry the substance away. All the time, of course, more water is moving into the colony through the pores. The collar cells have another important function besides that of moving water. On their sticky collars, they trap bacteria and very small particles of organic matter, and this food then becomes incorporated into vacuoles and is digested.

In this extremely simple type of sponge, the pores are actually holes in doughnut-shaped cells. These cells control the size of the pores, and contractile cells around the osculum control the size of the opening. The pores and osculum may close when the sponge is touched or when the amount of sediment in the water is increased to the point that there is danger of the colony becoming clogged. The cells that respond to a stimulus applied to the sponge undoubtedly act independently to some extent, but there is good reason to believe that one cell may somehow excite another despite the lack of an obvious nervous system. The fact that some of the cells have long processes that are applied to other cells suggests some sort of interaction.

The space between the outer covering and the layer of collar cells is largely filled with tiny skeletal elements called **spicules** (some of which may protrude to the outside) and amoebalike cells called **amoebocytes.** The spicules in the simplest sponges are made of calcium carbonate, of which

Figure 7.11   Two relatively large and complex sponges, with extensive folding of the body wall.

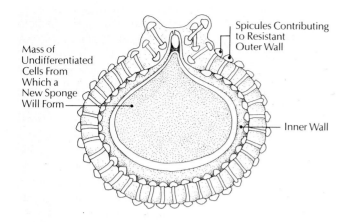

Figure 7.12   *A gemmule of a fresh-water sponge.*

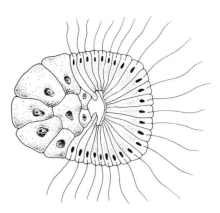

Figure 7.13   *A flagellated larval stage that occurs in the life cycle of many sponges. In similar larvae of some other sponges, all the external cells are ciliated.*

marble and limestone are also composed. The amoebocytes move about in the slightly gelatinous matrix. They play a number of roles, including secretion of spicules and transfer of food from collar cells to other cells. In some sponges, amoebocytes are involved in the formation of eggs and sperm. Collectively, the cells and materials of the middle layer of an animal are called the **mesenchyme.** In sponges, this is the layer in which the spicules and amoebocytes are concentrated.

Most sponges are organized in a somewhat more complex manner than has just been described. It is as if the body wall were highly folded. As a result, the collar cells do not line the central cavity but are situated on canals or in small chambers in the wall of the sponge. The systems of pores, canals, chambers, and central cavities interdigitate and become superficially complex. However, the basic pattern of activities in such sponges is not really different from that of a simple type.

In most sponges, especially complex types, the spicules consist of silica, a glasslike substance, rather than of calcium carbonate. There may be a considerable amount of fibrous organic material called **spongin** in the mesenchyme. The species serving since ancient times as bath sponges are some in which spongin is very abundant. After the living cells have disintegrated and the spicules are removed, the fibrous skeleton that remains is resilient and absorptive.

Any sponge, as it grows, is of necessity very plastic. It must be reorganized constantly, with some of the cells having to dedifferentiate and redifferentiate to keep up with changes in whatever part of the sponge they happen to be situated.

In general, reproduction of sponges follows three kinds of patterns. First, there can be a process of fragmentation, with subsequent reorganization leading to the development of a complete new sponge. Second, special clusters of cells released by a sponge may develop into daughter colonies. In the fresh-water sponges (of which there are relatively few kinds), these clusters, or **gemmules,** are surrounded by an impervious covering. This covering enables the living cells to withstand desiccation if the ponds in which these animals live dry up. Third, there can be sexual reproduction involving eggs and sperm, with fertilization of the egg generally followed by formation of a ciliated larva (Figure 7.13) that undergoes some odd transformations before it becomes a small sponge. As mentioned before, eggs and sperm have been reported to develop from amoebocytes, but it is certain that in some sponges, at least, the sex cells are derived from collar cells. Collar cells are also known to play an astonishing role as "middlemen" in fertilization, catching sperm that enter with sea water and transferring them to eggs awaiting fertilization. After fertilization, the eggs of sponges generally develop into ciliated larvae within the mesenchyme.

Sponges are an ancient group, and their origin is no more clear than that of other simple invertebrates. However, there are some flagellates that have the same general structure as collar cells, and some are colonial (Figure 7.5c). These organisms are called **choanoflagellates.** Possibly they are in the same line of descent, even if choanoflagellates as we know them did not give rise to sponges. It is widely believed, on the basis of many fundamental differences, that the sponges probably represent a separate evolutionary line that arose from unicellular ancestors quite independently of any of the other metazoa. In any event, the sponges almost certainly have not "paid off" in terms of evolution of other invertebrates; they seem to be a dead end. But they show us how a variety of cells, loosely organized, can function cooperatively.

PHYLUM CNIDARIA: THE POLYPS AND JELLYFISHES

Much more complex than sponges are the **cnidarians,** animals that are commonly called **polyps** and **jellyfishes.** There is a larval stage in their life cycle (the planula) that many zoologists think is reminiscent of the hypothetical multicellular ancestor of flatworms as well as of cnidarians. So regularly is the planula found in cnidarians that it may be a good idea to begin the discussion with it, then move to the structure and life cycles of a few typical members of the phylum.

The planula usually consists of an outer covering of ciliated cells and a compact inner mass of cells (Figure 7.14). The early cleavages of the fertilized egg produce a blastula. The cavity of the blastula then becomes filled with cells produced by additional divisions. The planula generally swims or crawls in only one direction. There is a simple nervous system under the epidermis, which is more concentrated at the anterior end than elsewhere. The planula has no mouth, however, and the larva must subsist on food that was stored in the egg before fertilization.

Polyps and the Gathering of Prey

In most cnidarians, the planula eventually differentiates into the type of organism called a polyp (Figure 7.15). One end (usually the anterior) of the planula settles on a firm substrate, and a mouth opens up at the opposite end. At about the same time, a cavity develops in the central mass of cells; eventually it becomes the digestive cavity. The young polyp now has an epidermis and a simple saclike gut lined by another epithelial layer called the **gastrodermis.** The organism elongates, and **tentacles** (elongated, flexible protrusions) sprout around the mouth. Viewed from the oral end, the polyp can be divided like a pie into equal quarters, or perhaps several equal sectors. This is the essence of radial symmetry, the significance of which will be discussed later.

The polyps of cnidarians are carnivores, feeding on small crustaceans and other animals. They capture food primarily with their tentacles, which are provided with complicated structures called **nematocysts,** or stinging capsules. Nematocysts are produced within specialized cells of the epidermis, and each one consists of a filament coiled up within its capsule (Figure 7.16). The filament is discharged when the trigger of the nematocyst is touched, or by a combination of being touched and chemically activated. As shown in Figure 7.17, there are three main types of nematocysts. Some act as lassos that become tangled up with the prey; some are sticky; others are barbed and penetrate the prey, injecting a paralytic toxin as they do so.

Primitive Nerve and Muscle: The Integration of Activity

Aside from the problem of quieting the prey, the cnidarian must somehow bring the prey to the mouth and swallow it. Movement must be assured by action of the contractile cells, and some sort of mechanism must exist for coordinating the activities of the tentacles, mouth, and column. A diagram of a hydra (Figure 7.18), one of the few freshwater cnidarians, will help explain how all this activity takes place.

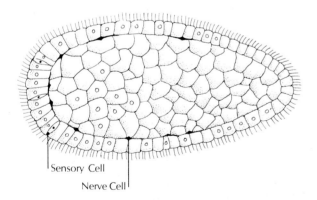

Figure 7.14 *A planula. After this organism settles on a favorable substrate, a mouth opens up (at the back end in some cnidarians, at the front end in others), and the cells of the inner mass will form the gastrodermis. In addition to the types of cells depicted here, there may be nematocyst-secreting cells in the epidermis and gland cells in both layers.*

Sensory Cell
Nerve Cell

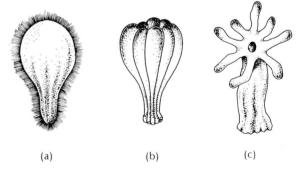

(a) (b) (c)

Figure 7.15 *Stages in the transformation of a planula into a polyp. (a) The planula is ready to settle on some substrate. (b) This is the very young attached stage, with lobulations forming where tentacles will develop. (c) A young polyp has formed, with tentacles and mouth.*

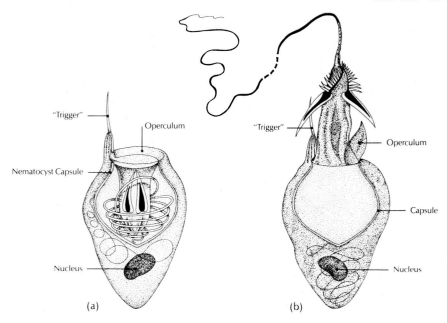

Figure 7.16 A complex nematocyst, within the cell in which it was formed. The nematocyst is shown (a) before and (b) after discharge.

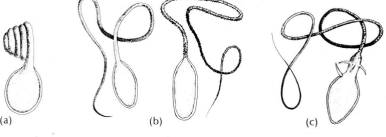

Figure 7.17 A few nematocysts, as they appear after the threads have been discharged. (a) The lasso type, (b) the sticky types, and (c) the penetrating type are illustrated.

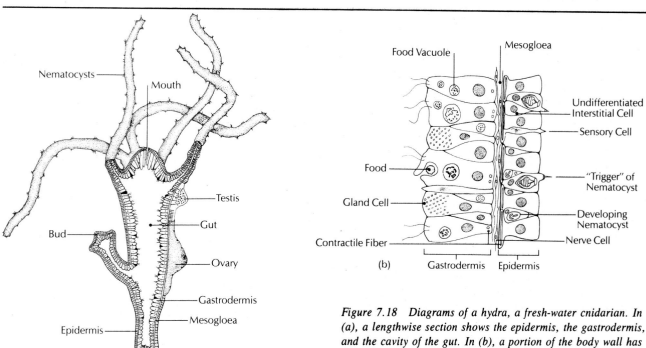

Figure 7.18 Diagrams of a hydra, a fresh-water cnidarian. In (a), a lengthwise section shows the epidermis, the gastrodermis, and the cavity of the gut. In (b), a portion of the body wall has been enlarged to show more detail.

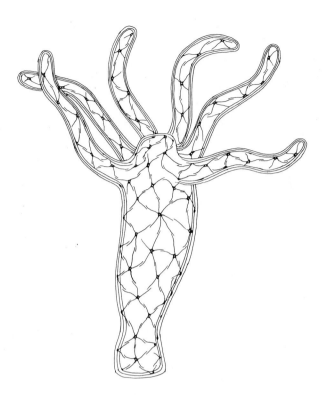

Figure 7.19 The nerve net of a hydra, which coordinates the activity of the epitheliomuscular cells.

Notice, in Figure 7.18, that the bases of some epidermal cells in a hydra are generally elongated so that they are parallel to the long axis of the column. The bases of similar cells of the gastrodermis are arranged in such a way that they collectively run in a more or less circular pattern. The bases of the cells forming these layers possess contractile filaments and can be markedly shortened or lengthened, so the cells are called **epitheliomuscular cells.**

The contractile action of the epitheliomuscular cells is most effective when the gut is filled with water and the mouth is closed. If the bases of the gastrodermal cells contract and those of the epidermis relax, the column will be lengthened. If, on the other hand, the bases of the epidermal cells contract and those of the gastrodermal cells relax, the column will be shortened. The water-filled gut acts as a kind of skeleton—a hydraulic skeleton—against which the contractile cells act. When a hydra opens its mouth, contractions drive water out of the gut cavity and the body may become quite small. If the mouth reopens while most of the epitheliomuscular cells are relaxed, cilia around the mouth can drive water back down into the gut. Contractions of the epitheliomuscular cells manipulate the tentacles in a similar manner. After nematocysts have trapped food, it is brought to the mouth and swallowed. Once the food is in

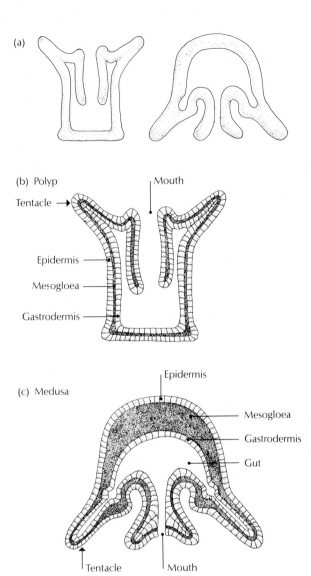

Figure 7.20   (a) Comparison of the basic organization of a polyp and a medusa, which shows how these structures are similar in basic design; (b) and (c) show how they are quite different in appearance, although even these sketches are greatly simplified. Polyps are attached to a substrate and generally have little mesenchyme. Medusae, in contrast, are typically free-swimming and have copious mesenchyme of the mesogloeal type.

the gut, enzymes secreted by certain gastrodermal cells initiate digestion. But in time, many of the cells actually take in particles, in much the same way an amoeba does. Therefore, digestion is largely intracellular.

In cnidarians, the concerted activity of the tentacles, column, and mouth during feeding is not accidental: it depends on a nervous system that coordinates the activity of the epitheliomuscular cells. In hydra and other cnidarians, the nervous system is a network without any brain or other extensive concentrations of nerve cells. This **nerve net** (Figure 7.19) is closely associated with the epithelial cells. It connects cells that receive stimuli with cells that effect movements.

Structures Characteristic of Cnidarian Life Cycles

Cnidarians, as a group, have a mesenchymal layer between the gastrodermis and the epidermis. In hydra and some other types, the mesenchyme is extremely thin. In jellyfishes, there is copious mesenchyme with the consistency of a watery jelly. The technical term for this part of a jellyfish is **mesogloea** (a word of Greek derivation, meaning "middle glue").

The body form of a jellyfish is called a **medusa.** Although the medusa and the polyp are often quite different in superficial appearance, they are basically similar in their organization (Figure 7.20). A medusa is characterized by a bell-shaped or dish-shaped body, with tentacles originating from the margin. At the bases of the tentacles, or between them, there may be light-sensitive eyespots and simple **statocysts,** which are structures concerned with equilibrium. The abundant mesogloea confers buoyancy upon the jellyfish. It also provides a resilient mass against which the contractile cells can operate to bring about movement. Contraction of the bell drives water out of the cavity beneath it, which results in jet propulsion. The mesogloea then springs back to its original shape.

Both a polyp and a medusa are generally present in the life cycles of Hydrozoa and Scyphozoa, two of the three classes of cnidarians. (In the third class, Anthozoa, there is no medusa stage.) In **Hydrozoa,** the polyp stage generally forms a branched colony in which the individuals are connected (Figure 7.21). Instead of differentiating into additional polyps, some branches become centers for the asexual production of one or more medusae. The medusae

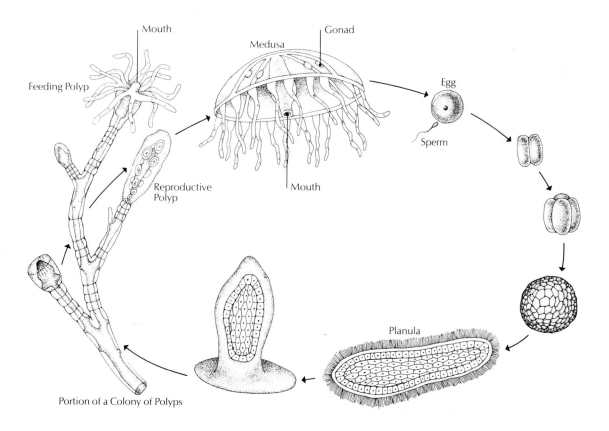

Figure 7.21 Structure and life cycle of Obelia, *a member of the class Hydrozoa.*

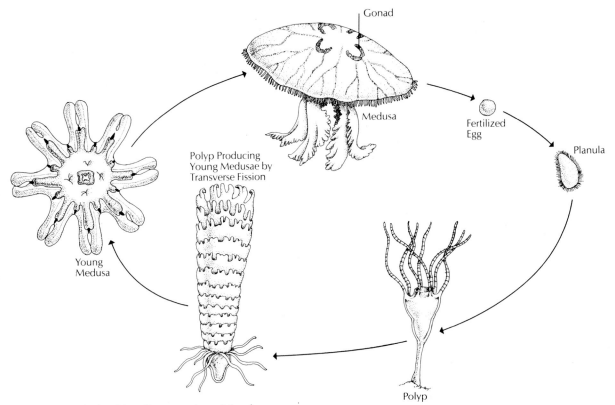

Figure 7.22   *The life cycle of* Aurelia, *a member of the class Scyphozoa.*

escape to a free-swimming existence and grow to sexual maturity.

Medusae feed on crustaceans, fish larvae, and other small organisms. As medusae approach maturity, egg- and sperm-producing centers develop in close association with the radially arranged branches of the gut, or on the stalk that bears the mouth. The gametes are usually discharged into the sea, where fertilization takes place. The fertilized eggs develop into planulae, which settle down and develop into young polyps.

In some hydrozoans, the medusae are abortive and are not released from the polyp. Usually the eggs produced by such abortive medusae also develop into planulae, which become polyps. Hydra and certain other types are exceptional in that they have no medusa stage at all. The polyp produces gametes, and the fertilized egg develops into another polyp. The development of such hydrozoans is often atypical in another respect: there is no planula larva. Asexual budding of new individuals, followed by their detachment, takes place regularly in hydra and some other members of the group. In most of the hydrozoans, however, such budding is not followed by release from the original structure. As a result, the colony grows larger.

In the **Scyphozoa,** the class to which the large jellyfishes belong, the life cycle is somewhat similar to that in

Figure 7.23   *A huge scyphozoan medusa. Notice the large lobes that originate at the edge of the mouth.*

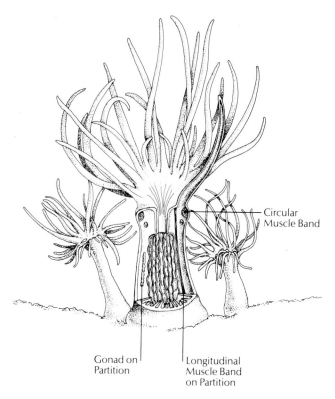

Figure 7.24 *A sea anemone, with a portion of the column cut away to show the manner in which the gut is partitioned.*

Figure 7.25 *(a) A sea anemone and (b) polyps of a colony of coral. (c) A sea pen. The branches of this featherlike colony bear numerous small polyps.*

Hydrozoa. But the emphasis in scyphozoan life cycles is on the medusa stage. There is a small, usually unbranched polyp that divides transversely into a number of lobed, saucerlike progeny, which grow into large medusae (Figure 7.22). The medusae reproduce sexually, and the planula that develops from the fertilized egg settles down to become another polyp. Some scyphozoans have no polyp stage, and the fertilized egg develops into another jellyfish. Scyphozoan medusae differ from hydrozoan medusae in several ways, but the four large lobes bordering the mouth are characteristic of most scyphozoans. These lobes may trail for some distance behind the bell when the jellyfish is swimming (Figure 7.23).

The class **Anthozoa** includes *sea anemones* and *corals* (Figures 7.24 and 7.25) and a number of other interesting allies, such as *sea pens*. Cnidarians of this group are exclusively polyps; medusae are lacking. Fertilized eggs develop into planulae, which settle on a substrate and become polyps. *A characteristic of many anthozoans is compartmentalization of the gut.* Such compartmentalization is especially characteristic of sea anemones and corals. Sea anemones are essentially solitary, although some species may form aggregations. Most corals are colonial and have calcareous external skeletons. Sea pens are colonies branched in a featherlike pattern (Figure 7.25 *c*).

PHYLUM CTENOPHORA: THE COMB JELLIES

The animals called **comb jellies** belong to the phylum **Ctenophora** (*cteno-* means "comb"; *phora* means "bearing"). There is a superficial resemblance between the jellyfishes and the comb jellies, in that both are essentially radial and both have an abundant transparent mesogloea. Like jellyfishes, the comb jellies are free-swimming. However, their swimming movements are not caused by the action of contractile cells operating against the mesogloea. A comb jelly has eight rows of comblike plates, or **ctenes,** consisting of large cilia. The beating of the cilia propels the animal slowly and steadily through the water. The mesogloea functions primarily to give form and buoyancy to the animal.

If conspicuous tentacles are present, there are only two (Figure 7.26). They originate in sheaths some distance from the mouth. These tentacles may be completely retracted, but when they are extended in a fishing posture, they may trail for some distance. *The tentacles of comb jellies are quite unlike those of cnidarians.* Comb jelly tentacles have a core of muscle, not just epitheliomuscular cells. These tentacles are distinctive in being branched on only one side. Another unique feature of comb jellies is the fact that the tentacles, and sometimes other structures, are provided with specialized sticky cells for capturing prey.

Some ctenophores that lack long tentacles either have tracts of cilia that help bring small food to the mouth or have a capacious mouth for swallowing. Some of the large-mouthed comb jellies feed to a large extent on their own relatives. The gut of these animals is heavily branched, with the canals serving to carry food to all parts of the body.

At the end opposite the mouth, there is a complex organ of balance consisting of secreted crystals resting on some sensory cilia (Figure 7.27). As the body turns, the weight of the crystals presses on certain cilia more than on others. The tentacles of comb jellies are also sensitive to touch. A simple nervous system, something like that of cnidarians, distributes impulses from sensory receptors to the effectors, such as the comb rows and muscles of the tentacles.

As in many cnidarians, the gonads are associated with branches of the gut. Generally, eggs and sperm are released into the sea, where fertilization takes place. The embryo develops directly into another comb jelly; there is nothing that resembles a polyp stage in these animals.

PHYLUM PLATYHELMINTHES: THE FLATWORMS

Moving past the simple poriferans and cnidarians in our examination of the lower animals, we come to an entirely different sort of organism—the **flatworms,** of the phylum **Platyhelminthes.** These organisms resemble the so-called higher animals in one important regard: *all flatworms are*

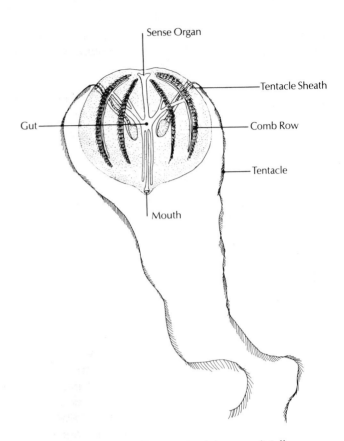

Figure 7.26   A comb jelly, an animal that superficially resembles the jellyfish but that is propelled by the action of cilia.

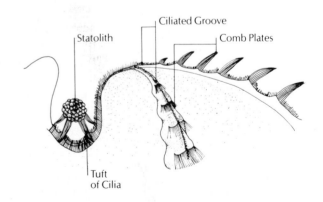

Figure 7.27   The sense organ of a comb jelly. When the animal tips to one side, the statolith presses on the tuft of cilia on that side. The pressure triggers an impulse leading to the comb plates on that side, causing them to beat faster. As a result of this action, the animal rights itself.

bilaterally symmetrical. This type of body organization has profound evolutionary significance, and for that reason it is worth taking a moment to consider its possible origin.

Bilateral Symmetry: The Origin of the Brain

If you wish to share an apple equally with a number of friends, there is no problem provided you have a sharp knife. It is possible to divide a "perfect" apple into any number of equal parts simply by making an appropriate number of equally spaced cuts, all of which pass from stem to blossom end. The apple is **radially symmetrical:** there are an infinite number of planes that will divide it into equal halves. All these planes radiate outward from the axis of symmetry defined by the stem and the blossom end.

But should you wish to divide a fish into identical portions, you would face an entirely different problem. Given a knife that is sharp enough, you can cut the fish in a plane running from head to tail and from top to bottom, separating it into right and left halves that are equivalent. But there is no other cut that would divide a fish into equal halves. Head and tail are not equivalent. Top and bottom are not equivalent. The fish has only one plane of symmetry. Because this plane divides the right side and the left side from each other, we say the fish is **bilaterally symmetrical** (*bi-,* "two"; *lateral,* "side").

How did bilateral symmetry arise, and what is its evolutionary significance? As long as an animal is attached to one spot or floats freely in the sea, there is no selective advantage to developing right and left sides—food and danger are likely to come from any direction. There must be a mouth with which to ingest food, but the animal must be ready to respond equally in all directions. *If the sense organs, nerves, and food-capturing and defensive devices of an animal are arranged radially about the mouth, then the animal is well adapted to the fixed or floating life style.*

But as soon as an animal begins to crawl forward over a surface, the selective advantages of bilateral symmetry become apparent. A crawling animal is most likely to encounter both food and danger with the end that goes forward. The probability of capturing food or escaping danger would increase if the mouth and sense organs were closer to the end that moves first. The selective advantage would become even greater if the nerve clusters required to integrate stimulus and response were also moved forward to quicken the animal's reactions. The organism that acquired such modifications as a result of genetic change would be more likely to feed well and escape danger, thereby living to reproduce and leave progeny. It would have a head—a collection of sense organs clustered about the mouth. And it would have a brain—a cluster of nerve cells for coordinating sensation and response. *When animals first began to*

creep forward with regularity, the events leading to the brain were foreshadowed.

The creeping habit also immediately established differences between **dorsal** (top) and **ventral** (bottom) sides of the organism. As an animal crawled along a surface, its ventral side would be relatively secure, but its exposed dorsal side would be subjected to selection to optimize protection or concealment. In contrast, there was no selective advantage to differentiating right from left. Because food and danger were equally likely to come from one side as the other, the animal would have an equal need to move either right or left. In short, *the only plane in which there was no evolutionary pressure to develop gross asymmetries was the lateral plane.* Little wonder, then, that the vast majority of actively moving animals are bilaterally symmetrical and that many of those that float or settle in one place are radially symmetrical.

Many zoologists have come to believe that the radially symmetrical and bilaterally symmetrical animals are related by virtue of a common planuloid ancestor. A comparison of the body plans of a planula, a cnidarian, and a simple flatworm will convey the essence of their argument (Figure 7.28). If this hypothesis is correct, *the evolution of the flatworms from a planuloid ancestor was an important step in the evolution of much of the animal kingdom, for flatworms were almost certainly in the line of descent of a number of higher phyla.*

Turbellaria: The Free-Living Flatworms

A flatworm of the type called an *acoel turbellarian* is shown in Figure 7.29. The name **Turbellaria,** given to one of the three classes of flatworms, alludes to the fact that the epidermal cilia of its members stir the water. Acoels are so called because they have no digestive cavity (the combining form *-coel* means "cavity"). Most acoels are small, about 1 millimeter or less in length. When they are young, and before their reproductive system has developed, they resemble ciliates. It is no wonder, then, that a few zoologists can visualize ciliates as being in the ancestry of flatworms. Most acoels can swim freely as well as glide on a firm surface. Much of the space beneath the epidermis is occupied by a noncellular but multinucleate mass of cytoplasm in which digestion takes place. The rest of the space is taken up primarily by the reproductive system, but there are also muscles, a variety of glands, and a simple nervous system. The majority of acoels have a distinct, brainlike concentration of nerve cells. These cells are usually associated with sensory structures in the form of a statocyst and sometimes light-sensitive eyespots. The nervous system of a few acoels is somewhat similar to that of cnidarians, a fact that has added credence to the idea that

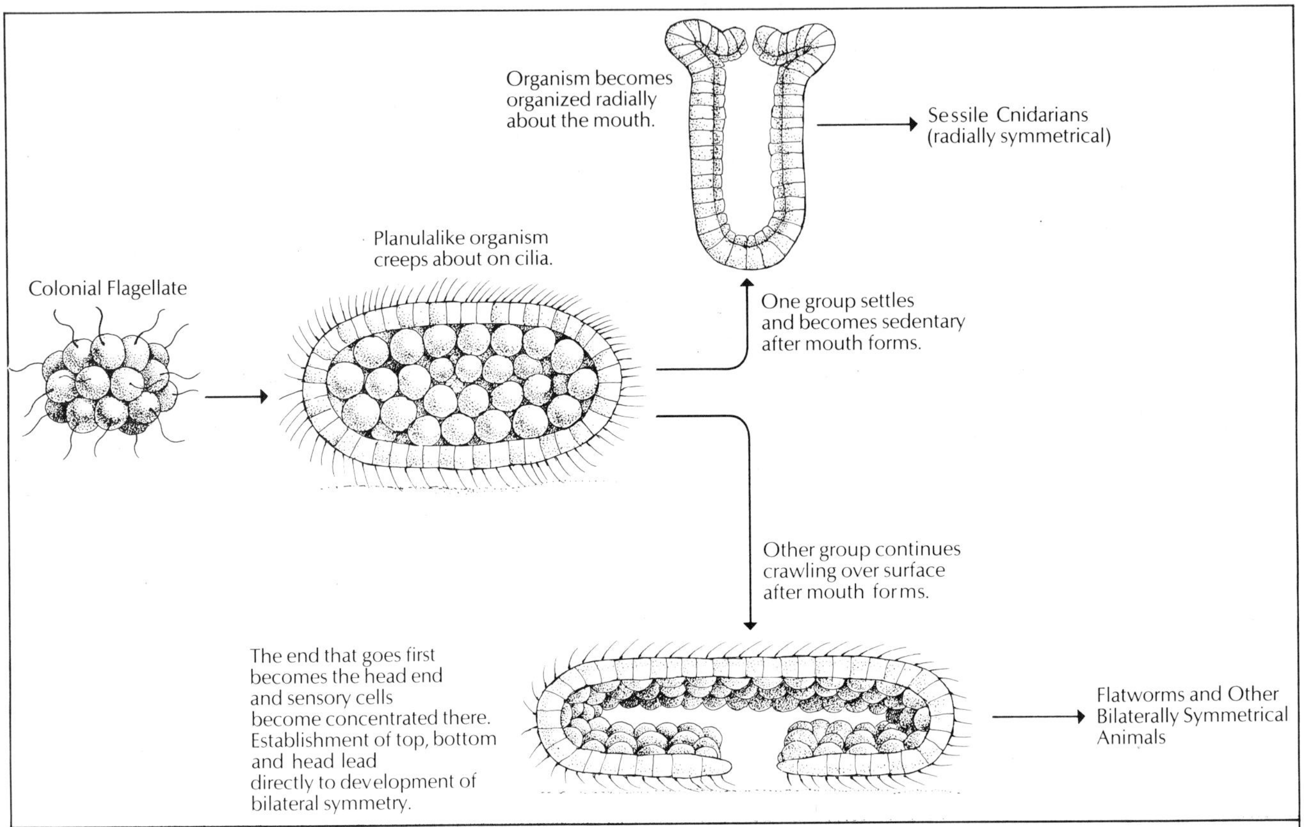

Organism becomes
organized radially
about the mouth.

→ Sessile Cnidarians
(radially symmetrical)

Colonial Flagellate

Planulalike organism
creeps about on cilia.

One group settles
and becomes sedentary
after mouth forms.

Other group continues
crawling over surface
after mouth forms.

The end that goes first
becomes the head end
and sensory cells
become concentrated there.
Establishment of top, bottom
and head lead
directly to development of
bilateral symmetry.

→ Flatworms and Other
Bilaterally Symmetrical
Animals

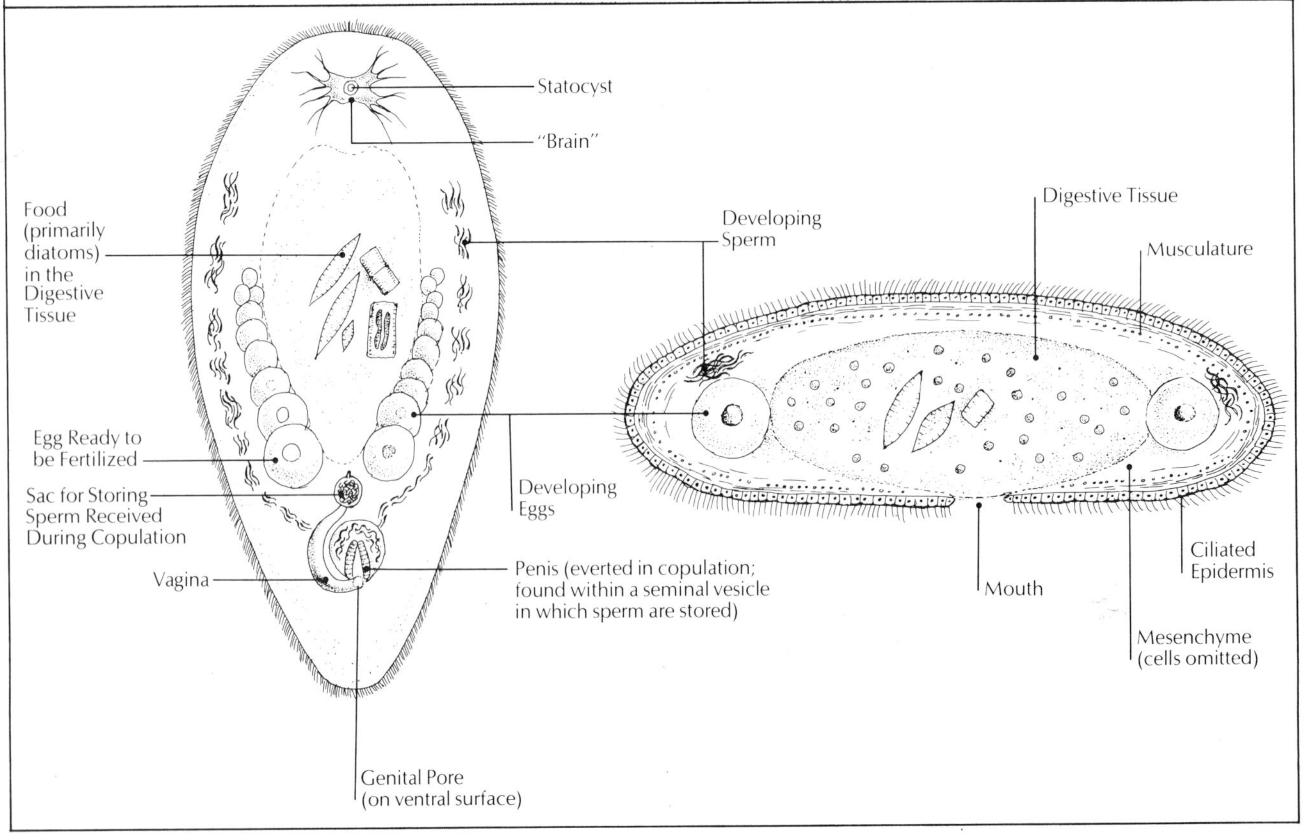

Statocyst

"Brain"

Digestive Tissue

Developing
Sperm

Musculature

Food
(primarily
diatoms)
in the
Digestive
Tissue

Egg Ready to
be Fertilized

Sac for Storing
Sperm Received
During Copulation

Vagina

Developing
Eggs

Penis (everted in copulation;
found within a seminal vesicle
in which sperm are stored)

Mouth

Ciliated
Epidermis

Mesenchyme
(cells omitted)

Genital Pore
(on ventral surface)

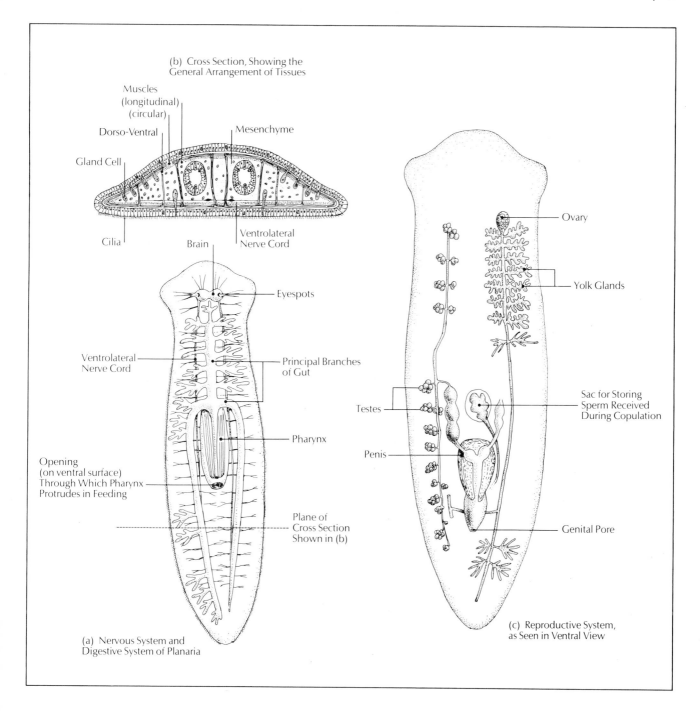

(b) Cross Section, Showing the General Arrangement of Tissues

Muscles (longitudinal) (circular)

Dorso-Ventral

Mesenchyme

Gland Cell

Cilia

Brain

Ventrolateral Nerve Cord

Eyespots

Ventrolateral Nerve Cord

Principal Branches of Gut

Pharynx

Opening (on ventral surface) Through Which Pharynx Protrudes in Feeding

Plane of Cross Section Shown in (b)

(a) Nervous System and Digestive System of Planaria

Ovary

Yolk Glands

Testes

Sac for Storing Sperm Received During Copulation

Penis

Genital Pore

(c) Reproductive System, as Seen in Ventral View

Figure 7.28 (opposite top) The planuloid hypothesis of metazoan ancestry.

Figure 7.29 (opposite bottom) An acoel turbellarian, depicted in dorsal view and in transverse section. All turbellarians produce both eggs and sperm (thus they are true hermaphrodites) but they are incapable of self-fertilization.

Figure 7.30 (above) The structure of planaria, a relatively complex turbellarian. (a) Dorsal view, showing the nervous system and the digestive system. (b) Cross section, showing the general arrangement of tissues. Reproductive organs are not shown here for the sake of clarity. (c) Ventral view of the reproductive system of planaria. For clarity, the male organs have been largely removed on the right side, and the female organs have been removed on the left side; both occur on both sides of each worm.

acoels are derived from a planuloid ancestor. In any case, there is definite **cephalization** in these simple flatworms—there is no doubt as to which end is the head end.

There are some other interesting advances that appear or become highly developed for the first time in flatworms. In the discussion of comb jellies, it was mentioned that the musculature of the tentacles of these animals consists of what may be called "real" muscle, as distinct from epitheliomuscular cells. Such a true musculature, derived from the mesenchyme, is more extensively developed in flatworms. The mesenchyme in flatworms is not a watery or gelatinous matrix with relatively few cells, as it is in cnidarians and ctenophores. It is essentially a solid mass of various tissues. *The extensive development of the true mesenchyme is significant, for it is in the mesenchyme that much of the specialization of higher animals occurs.*

In acoels, there are no complex specializations for the ingestion of food. The mouth is a simple opening on the ventral surface; it can be distended as necessary. Food consists of diatoms, ciliates, small crustaceans, and some other organisms. Food is usually pushed into the noncellular

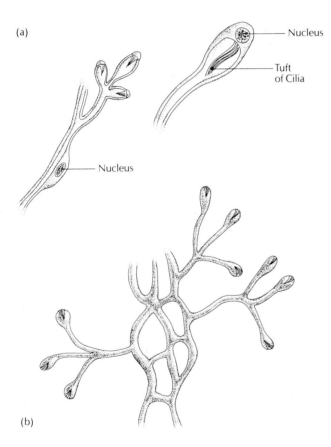

(a)

Nucleus

Tuft of Cilia

Nucleus

(b)

Figure 7.31 Flame bulbs of some turbellarian flatworms. (a) Two types of flame bulbs are depicted here. (b) Flame bulbs are shown connecting to a system of ducts.

digestive tissue during a flexing motion of the body, and it ends up in vacuoles that circulate rather freely. After digestion of a small mass has been completed, the residue is moved back to the mouth and expelled. In more advanced flatworms, however, there *is* a distinct gut that may be a simple sac or that may have two, three, or many main branches. There is also a muscular **pharynx,** for sucking in the tissues and juices of prey organisms. In some cases the pharynx can be thrust outward. *The elaboration of the pharynx raises the gut of flatworms to the level of an organ system.*

Also appearing for the first time in flatworms is an organ system for reproduction. In acoels, there are packets of cells in one region of the mesenchyme that develop into sperm. In another region are chains of cells that gradually enlarge into eggs ready for fertilization. Moreover, there is a **male copulatory complex,** consisting of a *genital pore,* a *penis,* and a *seminal vesicle* in which sperm are stored. Sometimes there is a female genital pore; sometimes it is combined with the male pore. Whether or not a separate female pore is present, sperm accumulate after copulation in a cavity near the eggs that are ripening. The eggs are apparently laid through a break in the epidermis.

The reproductive system of acoels is much more advanced than anything found in cnidarians or ctenophores. And in most other flatworms it is so complex that its evolution must have been extremely interesting. In terms of ducts, receptacles for storage of sperm before and after copulation, glands for production of yolk, and a chamber for assembling an egg shell or a cocoon to enclose several eggs, the reproductive system of flatworms is far more elaborate than that of many phyla that are more advanced in other respects!

Deep in the mesenchyme of many flatworms (especially those living in fresh water or as parasites) are large, hollowed-out cells—or branches of cells—that have tongue-like groups of cilia within their cavities. These cells are called **flame bulbs,** and their cavities connect with ducts that lead to the outside (Figure 7.31). Although the flame bulb systems are in the mesenchyme, they are of epidermal origin. Their function is that of **osmoregulation**—control of water balance. They function in much the same way as the contractile vacuoles of protozoa, removing excess water that enters the body because the salt concentration within the cells is higher than that of the external medium.

Trematoda: The Flukes

All free-living flatworms belong to the class Turbellaria. The other two classes of flatworms are parasitic, except for stages that may be encysted on vegetation or temporarily free-living and searching for a host. When external cilia are present in these groups, they are limited to certain larval types. Members of the class **Trematoda,** or **flukes,** have a two-branched digestive tract and a muscular pharynx. As adults, most of them live in various internal organs of vertebrates—the intestine, liver, lungs, bladder, and blood vessels. They feed on tissue cells and fluids, often causing structural damage. The life cycles of flukes are complex, in that they almost always involve at least two distinct hosts (Figure 7.32). Hosts in which juvenile stages develop are called **intermediate hosts;** one in which the adult develops to sexual maturity is called the **definitive host.**

During the life cycle, the egg develops into a ciliated larva called a **miracidium,** which is something like a planula. The miracidium normally escapes from the egg capsule and penetrates a snail, clam, or (rarely) a worm. It then loses its cilia and becomes transformed into a stage called a **sporocyst.** The sporocyst reproduces asexually to produce some daughter sporocysts, or else the **redia** stage (which is somewhat similar but has a short gut). A swimming stage called the **cercaria** is produced asexually by the redia or by the daughter sporocyst if there is no redia stage. The cercaria escapes from the first host and then

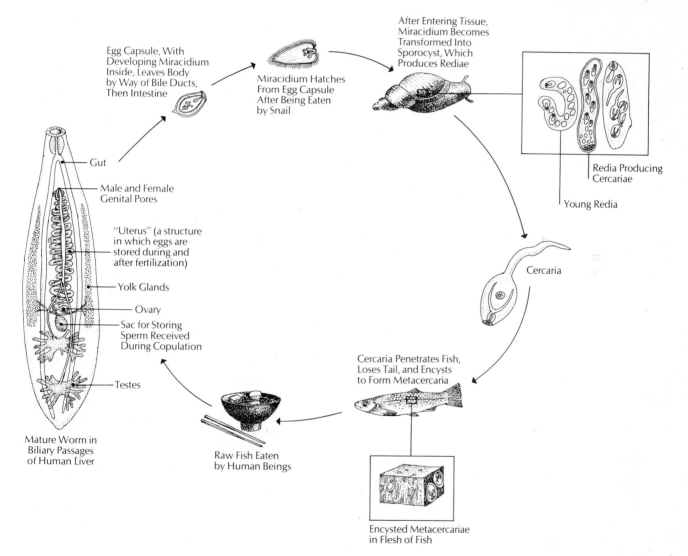

Egg Capsule, With Developing Miracidium Inside, Leaves Body by Way of Bile Ducts, Then Intestine

Miracidium Hatches From Egg Capsule After Being Eaten by Snail

After Entering Tissue, Miracidium Becomes Transformed Into Sporocyst, Which Produces Rediae

Redia Producing Cercariae

Young Redia

Gut

Male and Female Genital Pores

"Uterus" (a structure in which eggs are stored during and after fertilization)

Yolk Glands

Ovary

Sac for Storing Sperm Received During Copulation

Testes

Mature Worm in Biliary Passages of Human Liver

Raw Fish Eaten by Human Beings

Cercaria

Cercaria Penetrates Fish, Loses Tail, and Encysts to Form Metacercaria

Encysted Metacercariae in Flesh of Fish

Figure 7.32 *The Oriental liver fluke* Opisthorchis sinensis, *and its life cycle. Although this species is typical of flukes in many respects, it is unusual in that the miracidium is not released from the egg capsule until the egg is eaten by an appropriate snail. (In most flukes, the miracidium hatches and actively seeks its snail host.)*

either directly penetrates a suitable vertebrate host in which it can mature or encysts temporarily on vegetation or in some other animal. When eaten by the definitive host, it matures and the cycle is repeated.

The life cycles of flukes are masterpieces of adaptation to the ecology of the intermediate and definitive hosts. A fluke that parasitizes a bat as a definitive host will encyst in an aquatic insect larva. Thus, when the adult phase of the insect develops and takes flight, there is a good chance that it will be passed on to another bat. A fluke that parasitizes a fish-eating bird or mammal will use a fish for encystment, and one that parasitizes herbivores will encyst on vegetation

or in some small animal that is apt to be eaten along with vegetation. Another aspect of the biology of flukes that helps ensure survival is the massive number of eggs they produce. Even if only a few of the ciliated larvae reach a suitable first intermediate host, asexual reproduction builds up the numbers again, and at least some of the resulting cercariae have a chance of completing the cycle.

Cestoda: The Tapeworms

Some flatworms are specialized to the point that they lack a digestive system. They must absorb, through the epidermis, soluble nutrients from the intestines of their vertebrate

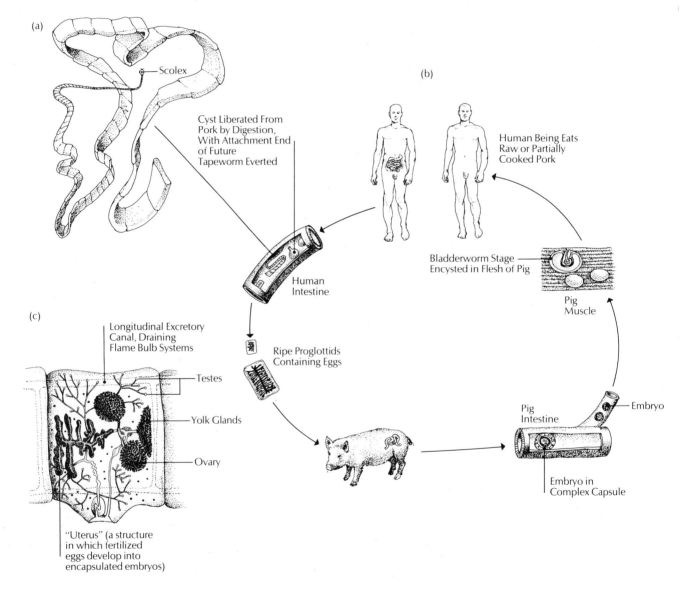

Figure 7.33 The pork tapeworm Taenia solium *(a) and its life cycle (b). Also shown is a detail of the mature proglottid, which shows the complex reproductive system of this organism (c).*

hosts. These organisms are the **tapeworms,** which belong to the class **Cestoda.** As a rule, tapeworms have no free-living larval stages, although there are some exceptions. The encapsulated embryo that develops from a fertilized egg must usually be swallowed by an intermediate host (usually an arthropod or a vertebrate) in which the larva encysts and sometimes reproduces asexually as well. When the intermediate host is eaten by an appropriate definitive host, the larvae develop into tapeworms that become attached to the intestinal wall by a specialized portion called the **scolex** (Figure 7.33). Budding results in a chain of repetitive units called **proglottids.** At maturity, each proglottid contains a complete reproductive system. Eventually, hundreds or thousands of eggs are produced. These eggs—which are often still inside proglottids that have broken away—are voided with fecal matter, and they may then infect another intermediate host.

PHYLUM NEMERTEA: THE RIBBON WORMS

A relatively small group of invertebrates with elongate and highly extensile bodies are grouped in the phylum **Nemertea**—the **ribbon worms.** These animals are found almost entirely in marine habitats. Some species may stretch to a length of many feet, but most are less than six inches in length. Ribbon worms represent a mixed bag of primitive and advanced traits. In their general organization—ciliated epidermis, cellular mesenchyme with abundant musculature, and a flame bulb system—they are much like flatworms. Their nervous system is also basically similar to that of flatworms. However, their reproductive system is extremely simple: It consists of a series of testes or ovaries that liberate gametes through pores in the epidermis.

The ribbon worms show two features characteristic of more advanced animals: a digestive tract that has both a mouth and an anus, and a system of blood vessels. An **anus** is an opening through which solid wastes of digestion are excreted. **Blood vessels** represent a system for transporting nutrients to all parts of the body as well as for efficiently transporting oxygen and wastes. The ribbon worms also have a rather astonishing structure that is unique among invertebrates: a hollow structure called the **proboscis.** The ribbon worm's proboscis lies in a closed, fluid-filled cavity above the gut (Figure 7.34). The proboscis can be turned inside out, like the finger of a glove. When the muscles

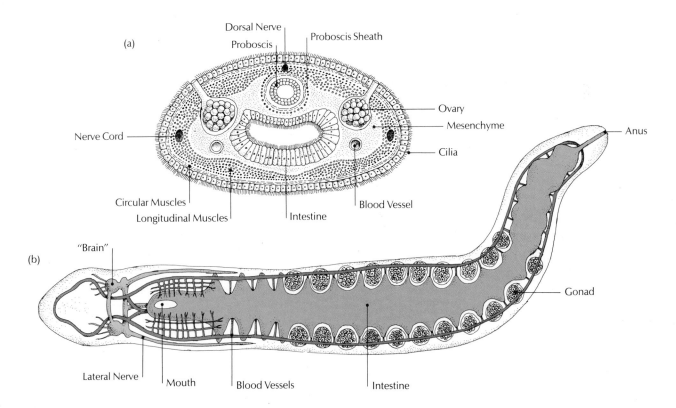

Figure 7.34 (a) General arrangement of tissues in a ribbon worm. (b) Diagram of the general structure of a ribbon worm. This is a ventral view. Only the anteriormost portions of the dorsal blood vessel and dorsal nerve can be seen.

contract around the cavity, pressure is exerted on the fluid inside. As a result, the proboscis is everted and emerges at amazing speed through a pore at the anterior tip of the body. Often the proboscis is longer than the rest of the body! In some ribbon worms, the proboscis pore opens into the mouth cavity, and in that case the proboscis is thrust out through the mouth. Prey organisms (often other worms) are trapped by sticky mucus on the proboscis or are quieted by a toxin produced by glands associated with some puncturing devices on the tip. *The proboscis not only serves to capture prey, it also helps get the prey back to the mouth.* The captured organism is generally swallowed whole, or its juices and tissues are simply sucked out. A slender retractile muscle draws the proboscis back into its sheath as the muscles around the cavity relax.

Ribbon worms are neither widespread nor diverse. Most zoologists concerned with phylogeny do not visualize them as being in the line of descent of higher groups. (However, some consider ribbon worms to be the stock from which primitive segmented worms evolved. One reason is that nemerteans have a series of gonads from which, conceivably, a series of body cavities of the type found in the segmented worms may have originated.)

In any case, the presence of an anus and therefore of a complete gut—which is characteristic of almost all higher animals—is a significant evolutionary advance. Food moves in just one direction, and indigestible wastes on their way out no longer have to be mixed with food that has just been swallowed. Furthermore, the one-way traffic provides the potential for the separation and specialization of different regions of the gut to serve different purposes. Those areas concerned with absorption of nutrients and formation of fecal pellets can be separated from those concerned with swallowing and digestion. However, in ribbon worms this sort of specialization of different regions has not occurred to any great extent. The gut, although complete, is still fairly primitive.

The system of blood vessels in ribbon worms provides the potential for development of a much larger body. No longer is enlargement restricted to two dimensions, as it is in flatworms, where all cells must be near the surface to obtain oxygen and release wastes. Some ribbon worms are rather large-bodied animals, and the circulatory system is almost certainly important to them. Respiratory pigments, comparable to hemoglobin, are present. But on the whole, the blood vessels of nemerteans are not especially efficient; there is no well-developed mechanism for keeping the blood moving in an orderly pattern.

PHYLUM NEMATODA: THE ROUNDWORMS

The most abundant group of simple animals are the **roundworms,** the members of the phylum **Nematoda.** Most of us are aware only of the nematodes that inflict damage upon

Figure 7.35   A roundworm, a member of the phylum Nematoda.

human beings, domestic animals, and plants—the hookworm, the agents of trichinosis, the forms that do extensive damage to food crops by destroying roots, and so forth. But this limited perspective gives a false picture of the importance of the group, for most nematodes live on decaying matter and are an essential link in the recycling of wastes.

It is difficult to visualize the sheer numbers of these organisms. As many as 90,000 have been counted in a single rotting apple. One teaspoonful of coastal mud was found to contain 1,074 individuals of thirty-six different species. An acre of rich farm soil may contain 5 billion nematodes! Only 10,000 species have been named so far, but it is estimated that there may be 500,000 species that are still unnamed—species that range from the poles to the tropics, from deserts to ocean depths.

Why are nematodes so successful? *The nematode body plan is relatively simple, and these animals can readily adapt to any environment rich in organic matter.* One or another species has adapted to virtually every imaginable food source. Although most live on the wastes of other organisms, a few have become parasitic. Like the nemerteans, the nematodes are built on the tube-within-a-tube plan (Figure 7.35). Some nematodes have glands in the tail region that secrete a substance that anchors the animal to the surface. The trait undoubtedly is a reflection of the sedentary nature of the earliest nematodes. Indeed, some primitive nematodes even today spend their lives anchored to one spot on the ocean floor. This sedentary life style led—as it usually does—to a body that is in some respects radially symmetrical.

Nematodes are elongated, with the complete gut terminating some distance above the posterior end of the body, so that there is a short tail. A thick, strong, and relatively impervious cuticle covers the epidermis. The large muscle cells of the body wall run lengthwise, so that nematodes can bend into C-shaped or S-shaped configurations. As a result, the worms move forward with an awkward, thrashing movement. Yet they do move forward. It is not surprising, then, that motile roundworms also show some of the features of bilateral animals. The bottom surface is marked by openings of the digestive and reproductive tracts; sides are clearly distinct from top and bottom; and so forth.

Nematodes lack a circulatory system, but in its place they have a fluid-filled body cavity between the gut and the body wall. This body cavity, called a **pseudocoel,** differs in many ways from those found in the animals to be discussed in Chapter 8. The pseudocoel is merely a remnant of the cavity of the blastula (Figure 7.4). In more complex animals, the cavity is newly formed during development, and it is lined with specialized cells and has many internal organs suspended in it. Like the complete gut, the body cavity is a structure that plays a major role in the organization of more complex animals. But the nematodes have exploited its great potential very little; in spite of their success, they are structurally rather monotonous. Their body plan has worked out well for them, and they have stuck with it.

PERSPECTIVE

It is time now to consolidate our understanding of the more significant advances in the evolution of the lower invertebrates and to review examples that illustrate some progressively more complex stages.

A sponge shows how a colony of cells operates successfully as an organism: Some cells are specialized for moving water and for feeding on minute particles; others are specialized for such functions as the formation of supporting structures. Tissues are not distinctly developed, and there is no digestive cavity or nervous system, yet the various kinds of cells are in balance and work together, so the sponge grows and reproduces successfully.

A cnidarian is adapted for capturing and digesting prey of moderate size. It has a gut, epitheliomuscular cells, tentacles provided with nematocysts, and a simple nervous system for coordinating movements. Radial symmetry is handy for an animal that does not move continuously in one direction, for the animal may react to a prey organism that contacts any sector. However, radial symmetry of cnidarians is almost certainly a secondary development. We look to the planula larva, which shows the beginnings of cephalization, as the sort of organism from which both the simplest cnidarians and the simplest turbellarians might have originated.

Success in the flatworms—at least in the free-living types—is related in part to the musculature they can use in locomotion, feeding, and copulation. But their cephalization, accompanied by bilateral symmetry, development of a brain, and a concentration of sensory structures near the brain, adapts them well to crawling and actively locating food. The success of parasitic flatworms, however, has a very different basis. It has depended on their mechanisms for feeding, the capacity to produce large numbers of offspring, and the development of life cycles tailored to the food habits of the definitive hosts.

The advent of the complete gut, as seen in ribbon worms, makes possible a one-way movement of food. It foreshadows the evolution of a gut in which efficiency is increased by specialization of regions for swallowing, digestion, absorption, and elimination. The appearance of a circulatory system is similarly important because it can provide the means of systematically moving nutrients, oxygen, and wastes—without which the development of large-bodied, highly active animals would not have been possible.

The ribbon worms clearly have two systems of great potential, although they have barely begun to exploit these potentials. It is as if selective pressures acting on this group have been met by more and more modifications of the prey-capturing proboscis to solve the problems of adaptation—to the exclusion of basic modifications of other aspects of their body plan. There is no question that the proboscis of these animals is a remarkable device adapted to a variety of different uses in different species. Hence, ribbon worms have achieved success, as measured by survival. However, they seem to represent another evolutionary dead end.

In short, although ribbon worms are probably not in the line of evolution of higher groups, their complete gut and system of blood vessels—like the body cavity of the nematodes—hint at some interesting expectations that were realized, finally, in the more complex animals to be considered in the next chapter. The evolutionary exploitation of certain generalized structures has led to an almost explosive radiation of "higher" life forms, resulting in the development of the most conspicuous and diverse groups of animals on our planet.

SUGGESTED READINGS

HARDY, ALISTER. *The Open Sea, Its Natural History: The World of Plankton.* Boston: Houghton Mifflin, 1971. One of the great students of the plankton writes about his field with charm and eloquence. Well illustrated.

RUSSELL-HUNTER, W. D. *A Biology of Lower Invertebrates.* New York: Macmillan, 1968. One of the best short introductions to the lower invertebrates, written from the standpoint of the interrelation of structure and function.

WELLS, MARTIN. *Lower Animals.* New York: McGraw-Hill, 1968. A skilled researcher in behavior and neurophysiology looks at invertebrates to see how they perceive and react to their environments.

Chapter 8

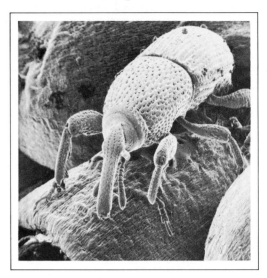

Radiation of the
More Complex Animals

*With its hardened skeletal parts and jointed
appendages, this unobtrusive insect (seen here with
the help of the scanning electron microscope)
displays the adaptive features that characterize two
extremely successful animal phyla—the arthropods
and the vertebrates.*

eaving behind the simple flatworm gliding slowly across a rock, we now enter the world of earthworms, crabs, spiders, insects, snails, slugs, octopuses, oysters, sea stars, sea urchins, fish, frogs, lizards, alligators, birds, kangaroos, cats, mice—and humankind. These are just a few of the so-called ''higher animals'' that are grouped into about twenty separate phyla. The diversity these phyla represent is staggering. Without the thread of evolutionary continuity it would be impossible to view such diversity in any kind of perspective. But that thread does exist, and by using it to weave together the evolutionary relationships among five of these phyla—the annelids, arthropods, molluscs, echinoderms, and chordates—we can try to visualize some of the common pressures different life forms have encountered in the past, and how they have changed in response to these pressures. In doing so, we can get an impression of how we and some of our contemporaries came to be.

ON THE IMPORTANCE OF BECOMING SEGMENTED

A familiar resident of garden lawns is the unobtrusive earthworm. In appearance, this member of the phylum **Annelida** is reminiscent of the nemerteans (ribbon worms) described in the preceding chapter. Annelids, too, have an anus and thus a complete gut: Food enters at one end of the body and undigested wastes leave from the other. This arrangement corresponds, as it does in nemerteans, to an elongate body with a definite head end, as well as bilateral symmetry. But a further adaptation in the annelids is a pattern of **segmentation:** Body units are repeated along the length of the organism.

If you were to slice open an earthworm as shown in Figure 8.2, you would see at once that this segmentation is not superficial. Many structures of the body, including nerves, muscles, and blood vessels, are repeated in almost every segment. But even while this generalized body plan remains constant, the parts within one or a few segments have undergone modification.

The earthworm body is not a solid mass of cells. A fluid-filled body cavity, or **coelom,** separates the gut from the body wall. Nerves, blood vessels, and other organs are suspended in this fluid-filled space. The coelom is an evolutionarily significant structure found in almost all the more complex animals. Animal groups differ in the way that the coelom is formed during development. And how large the coelom is, how it is lined, and what organs are suspended in it vary from one group to the next. Whatever the modifications, *the coelom provides a fluid-filled cradle in which sensitive internal organs may be protected from the shocks and blows of life.*

In the earthworm, the fluid-filled coelom permits the gut to grind and churn the food independently of the body wall. But its coelom is not a continuous cavity. It is a series of

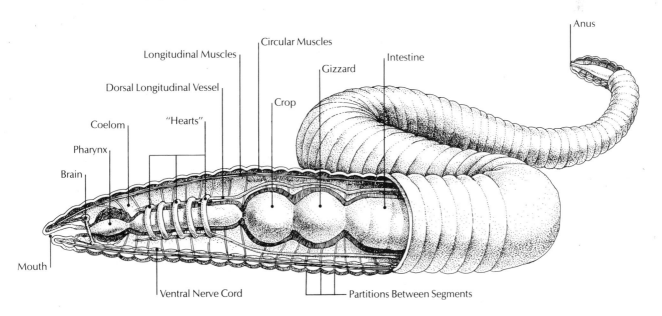

Figure 8.2 An earthworm, part of which has been sliced lengthwise to show certain internal structures. The gut is specialized into regions of food-getting, preliminary processing, digestion, absorption of nutrients, preparation of fecal pellets, and excretion.

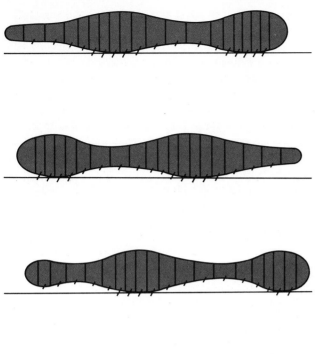

Figure 8.3   Stages in the forward progress of an earthworm. The earthworm moves forward by shortening and expanding some segments while elongating and contracting other segments. The expanded segments drive their bristlelike setae into the ground or side of the burrow. In this way they provide a firm grip to prevent backward slippage while the elongation of other segments pushes the anterior end forward.

If you have ever spaded a garden or dug for fishing worms, you know that these processes can be integrated into a surprisingly rapid forward movement. The reason an earthworm can tunnel through compact soil is that it swallows the dirt it encounters, passes it through the gut, extracts most of the organic nutrients from it, and excretes undigested sand. The soil is its food, and for an earthworm, every meal is a trip.

almost watertight compartments, partitioned off by walls between the segments. *The coelomic fluid of each cavity acts as a hydraulic skeleton against which the muscles work.* Each segment has circular muscles ringing the segment and longitudinal muscles running parallel to the long axis. When these muscles contract, the volume of the segment remains essentially the same, but its shape changes. As circular muscles contract and longitudinal ones relax, the segment becomes constricted and elongated. When the circular muscles relax and the longitudinal ones contract, the segment becomes shortened and swollen. The earthworm moves forward by shortening and expanding some segments while elongating and contracting others (Figure 8.3).

Each segment of the earthworm has a concentration of nerve cells, called a **ganglion.** A ganglion is capable of receiving stimuli and initiating nerve impulses that lead to reflex responses by muscle and other tissues. More importantly, the ganglia of the various segments are part of a continuous double nerve cord, which is connected to the large ganglia located above the gut in the head (Figure 8.2). These ganglia function as a brain, a nerve control center that coordinates the pattern of muscular contractions in the segments in response to stimuli.

Although the human nervous system is by no means derived from that of the earthworm, the parallels are

amazing—*there is organization into a brain, a nerve cord running the length of the body, serially repeated ganglia from which nerves pass outward to the periphery, and a functional integration of the whole.*

IF CIRCULATORY SYSTEMS COME, CAN LARGE BODIES BE FAR BEHIND?

The **circulatory system** of annelids is more efficient than that of nemerteans. Muscular elements are concentrated in the walls of certain lateral vessels and in the dorsal longitudinal vessel (Figure 8.2). These elements act as hearts and keep the blood flowing in one direction. The hemoglobin of the blood of the earthworm is a red, oxygen-carrying **respiratory pigment** that is similar in function to that of human blood. It picks up oxygen that has diffused across the moist skin into the underlying fine blood vessels, or **capillaries.** The system of major blood vessels is rather complex, and every part of the body is served effectively.

What is the selective advantage for an efficient circulatory system? For the answer we must return once more to the relation between predator and prey. When predation began, pressures developed for increase in body size. The larger the prey, the less likely it would be consumed. Conversely, the larger the predator, the better the chance of consuming larger prey. As you read in Chapter 4, body size can be increased by growth in one dimension. Such growth leads to a threadlike body. This route was taken by the fungi, many of the algae, and certain other life forms. Growth also can occur in two dimensions, forming a sheetlike body such as that of flatworms and several kinds of algae. In three-dimensional growth, the center of the body moves farther and farther from contact with the surrounding water. For animals, availability of oxygen is a most important consideration. There can be no cellular activity in the central part of the body unless it is supplied with oxygen.

There are three ways to circumvent this problem. The organizational plan of *Volvox* (Chapter 4) is one solution: *position cells only on the surface* so all cells are still in contact with the environment. But this solution appears an evolutionary dead end, for it prevents specialization of internal organs. Another solution is that taken by sponges and sea anemones: *bring the outside in.* Sponges can grow to a large size because they draw water in through pores in the body wall. None of the cells, even in a complex sponge, is far from the flowing stream. The large sea anemones solve the problem simply by surrounding a volume of water, which is constantly changed and kept flowing by ciliary action on the gastrodermal lining cells of the gut. Insects, as you will read shortly, are the only other major group to use the strategy of bringing the outside in. But virtually all other animals use a third strategy: *bring the inside out.* This is the function of the circulatory system: *to bring fluids from deep-lying regions to the surface, where they can exchange gases, nutrients, and wastes with the environment.*

Now, the efficiency of energy production in any animal cell depends on the availability of oxygen. In the absence of oxygen, cells are extremely restricted in the amount of energy they can produce and use in a given interval of time (Chapter 14). The protein hemoglobin has the unique capacity to combine reversibly with oxygen. What this means is that your own blood, for example, is able to carry nearly fifty times as much oxygen per unit volume as it would if there were no such oxygen-carrying pigment present. If there were no hemoglobin in your blood, your heart would have to pump fifty times as much blood every minute as it is doing now. You would need a heart fifty times as big, blood vessels that would carry fifty times as much blood past every point in your body, lungs fifty times as large, and so on. The expression ''you're all heart'' would take on new meaning, for any organism so constructed would probably be at least 90 percent heart, blood vessels, blood, and lungs! Clearly the weight of such a massive circulatory system could not be carried by a body that must devote no more than a small fraction of its mass to bone and muscle. In short, *the evolution of large, active, mobile animals could not have occurred without prior development of a circulatory system and an oxygen-carrying protein such as hemoglobin.*

But the annelid circulatory system is somewhat sluggish in carrying out its functions. In earthworms, the fluid of the coelomic cavity helps the system work. As it bathes blood vessels and tissues, the free fluid assists in the transfer of oxygen and nutrients to the cells and in the removal of waste products. Each coelomic segment also contains a pair of **nephridia,** funnel-shaped organs lined with cilia. The cilia draw fluid into the nephridium, where it passes down a duct through a pore to the exterior (Figure 8.4).

Because continuous water flow is needed to keep the coelomic fluid cleansed, and because oxygen uptake is through the skin, the earthworm is not truly terrestrial. You will never find a healthy earthworm above the earth unless there is standing water from a recent rain or a heavy dew. Thus the earthworms have not really left the water; they have just crept out into the moist banks, so to speak. Even so, they have gone farther than most annelids.

THE EXTRAORDINARY POTENTIAL OF HARD ARMOR WITH FLEXIBLE JOINTS

In the phylum **Arthropoda** there are more species than in all other animal phyla combined. About a million known species of insects account for much of the diversity of

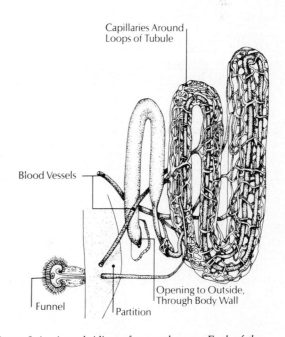

Figure 8.4 A nephridium of an earthworm. Each of the numerous paired nephridia occupies two segments. These organs remove nitrogenous wastes from both the coelom and the blood and also regulate water content. They are somewhat comparable to the tubular units of the kidneys of vertebrates.

Figure 8.5   Representative annelids. The earthworm and its nearest relatives are called Oligochaeta *because they have only a few bristles per body segment with which they push against the soil (oligo- means "few"; chaeta means "bristle"). In (a) each worm is transferring sperm to its partner in copulation.*

A larger and more diverse group are the Polychaeta, *which usually have many bristles per segment. The polychaetes are almost entirely restricted to marine environments, in which annelids developed. Some, such as the clamworm* Nereis *(b), crawl about on the bottom, tearing pieces from tough algae with their well-developed jaws; others devour small animals. Still others, such as the lugworm* Arenicola *(c), burrow in mud or sand, ingesting the substrate for the organic matter it contains or feeding on detritus. Then there are other polychaetes that build tubes. Such polychaetes usually have featherlike or filamentous outgrowths of the head region (d). The surface of the tentacles secretes a mucous film in which food of suitable size and character is trapped.*

The third major group of annelids is the Hirudinea—*the leeches (e). The leech shows a clear pattern of segmentation. A distinguishing feature of its muscular, rubbery body is a large posterior that enables the leech to remain firmly attached while the mouth and piercing jaws do their dirty work. Some leeches attack snails or other invertebrates and suck out their juices. Others attach only to vertebrates and feast on their blood.*

| (a) | (b) | (d) |
| | (c) | (e) |

arthropods. But the phylum also contains the crustaceans (crabs, lobsters, shrimp, crayfish, and a variety of less conspicuous, even if very numerous, animals), as well as the arachnids (spiders, scorpions, and their allies). The story of the arthropods is a story of evolutionary success. They have penetrated almost every environment where life is possible, and they promise to remain there for some time to come.

Certainly a large part of their success derives from their body covering. Arthropods have a hard **exoskeleton** of organic substances impregnated with materials that protect the organism from all but the most penetrating attacks. But more than this, the exoskeleton has **supple joints** that permit incredible mobility.

Despite these and other unique features, the resemblances between annelids and arthropods are numerous. These resemblances have given rise to speculation that the arthropods are derived from some ancient polychaete-like annelid stock. Interestingly enough, a group of soft-skinned, caterpillarlike worms called **Onychophora** have traits common to both annelids and arthropods. The wormlike body of an onychophoran is covered with a soft **cuticle** (outer covering). But the cuticle is lightweight enough that joints between segments or in the appendages are not present. In this sense the animal resembles many annelids. But in the shape of its claws, the nature of its body cavity, and its

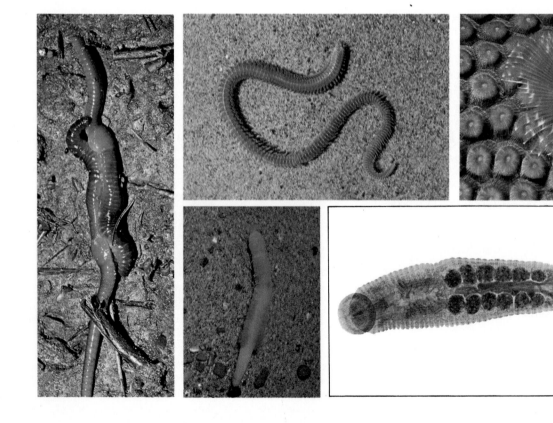

(Photograph by Walter Dawn)

circulatory system it resembles certain advanced arthropods (Figure 8.6).

Clearly, the onychophorans are not a direct link between the annelids and arthropods. But some features of onychophorans were probably present in at least certain extinct progenitors of arthropods. Somewhere in pre-Cambrian time, there may have arisen a line of annelids that had a thickened cuticle over most of each body segment; but the cuticle remained thin and flexible in regions where segments abutted. Such a body plan would improve defense without sacrificing flexibility and mobility. Now, if the same pattern of selective thickening in some regions extended to their primitive polychaete-like appendages, the stage would be set for an evolutionary change of the first magnitude.

In the annelid body plan, the musculature tends to be arranged in layers that completely encircle or run the length of the segments. This musculature leads to none-too-delicate movements of whole body segments, in which the only thing the muscles work against is the coelomic fluid. But with the thickening of the cuticle, an entirely new arrangement of musculature would be possible. Slowly, muscles would shift until they became attached to the cuticle in hard regions; they simply would cross over the soft regions or joints. *Continual selection would lead to a characteristic of today's arthropods: discrete muscles that insert into the cuticle on both sides of a joint and thus serve to bend the body at the joint.*

This pattern of musculature may have developed in the appendages, also. In that case, the emphasis would shift from gross movements of the whole body to separate movements of individual body parts. This differentiation of body regions would require a nervous system more finely tuned than that of annelids. And in fact, the nervous system of existing arthropods is almost the same as that of annelids in basic plan—but it is much more highly developed, particularly with regard to the brain.

As the capacity for independent movement of parts developed, it would not have been surprising if natural selection favored progressive differentiation of body regions and their appendages for different functions. For the most part, the dominant plan in annelids is still repetition of similar segments. *But in arthropods, particular regions of the body and the appendages arising from these regions are highly specialized for different functions.* For example, in many arthropods differentiation has led to the fusion of segments into specific body regions, such as head, thorax, and abdomen (Figure 8.7). Moreover, among primitive arthropods, each segment carried a pair of appendages. In fossilized primitive arthropods, all or most of the appendages behind the mouth were identical, but in progressively more modern forms appendages of different seg-

Figure 8.6 Peripatus, *an onychophoran that figures prominently in speculations linking annelids to arthropods at some point in evolutionary time. It has some annelid traits, including segmentally arranged ciliated nephridia and ciliated reproductive ducts. But it also has a body cavity through which blood flows, and the heart is of the sort found in arthropods. Onychophorans are carnivorous. This specimen was living under a log in a South American rain forest.*

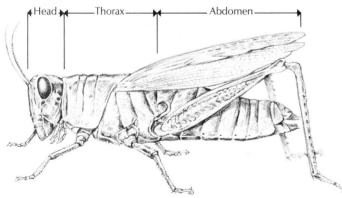

Figure 8.7 A grasshopper, a representative arthropod. The arthropods are bilaterally symmetrical, well cephalized, and segmented. Certain segments have appendages. A continuous cuticle covers the surface of the body and the appendages, forming an exoskeleton. To make movement possible, the cuticle is thinner at the joints between divisions of the body and other units.

Because of the nature of the cuticle, it must be shed periodically to permit growth. As one cuticle is molted, a new one is exposed beneath it. The new cuticle is fully formed, but it is still soft and flexible and the muscles are already attached to it. Size increase tends to occur in bursts after each molt.

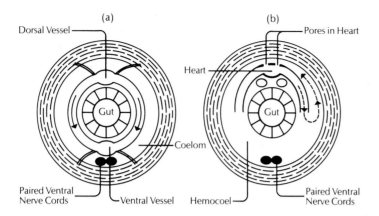

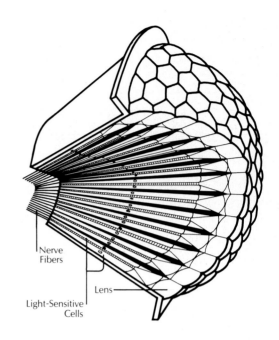

Figure 8.8   Diagrammatic comparison of the true coelom of an annelid (a) and the hemocoel of an arthropod (b).

Figure 8.9   (right) A compound eye of an insect. This sense organ consists of many separate visual units, each with its own lens and light-sensitive cell.

ments became highly specialized in different ways for specific functions. Indeed, in most types living today, the appendages of some segments are severely reduced or lost.

With the shift in the nature of the musculature, there was probably a concurrent reduction of the coelom. The coelom is the main skeletal element in annelids. But in arthropods, such turgid fluid would inhibit movement of the specialized parts. All arthropods do form annelidlike coelomic cavities during embryological development; however, these cavities are largely suppressed as development continues. Only traces of the coelom remain in adult arthropods. A different cavity, called a **hemocoel,** is present instead. Blood flows through this cavity and bathes the internal organs.

Another example of arthropod specialization is a nervous system that is much more highly developed and more centralized than that of annelids. Furthermore, the nervous system is linked to a variety of sense organs. There are both simple eyes and **compound eyes** (many separate, complete visual units side by side). Tactile sense organs and olfactory organs are often extremely well developed. Complex behavior patterns of the instinctive type are shown by many arthropods, particularly insects and spiders.

In their evolution, the arthropods have given up one of the most versatile locomotory elements found in other animals: the cilia. True, some arthropods (including insects) have typical 9 + 2 flagella on their sperm. But even though the potential for forming cilia has not been completely lost in arthropods, these animals have for the most part done away with ciliary structures.

The absence of cilia in arthropods points out the difficulty in making evolutionary generalizations. We find cilia functioning in our own respiratory and reproductive tracts, for example, and forming the basis of our sense of sight and balance. After discovering the same trend in most animal phyla, we tend to conclude that the development of cilia in the early eukaryotes played a key role in the evolution of all animals. But then we find the world's largest, most successful group of animals getting along quite well without them!

VARIATIONS ON A SUCCESSFUL THEME: A LOOK AT A FEW ARTHROPOD STRATEGIES

Early in the history of arthropods, three main lines diverged: the **Trilobita,** the **Chelicerata,** and the **Mandibulata.** The trilobites were once dominant among animals on the ocean floor, but by 500 million years ago they were rapidly declining, for reasons that are unclear. By 250 million years ago, they had disappeared entirely, leaving only their fossils to remind us of their once-great success (Figure 8.10a). Of the chelicerates that once flourished in the seas, most have become extinct (Figure 8.10b). There are only two rather small groups of marine chelicerates left—the horseshoe crabs and "sea spiders." But certain early chelicerates gave rise to the **Arachnida**—the spiders, scorpions, ticks, and mites. The arachnids are now highly successful in a wide range of habitats (Figure 8.11).

The mandibulates are now the dominant animals of marine and terrestrial habitats. They differ from chelicerates in having antennae as well as feeding appendages called

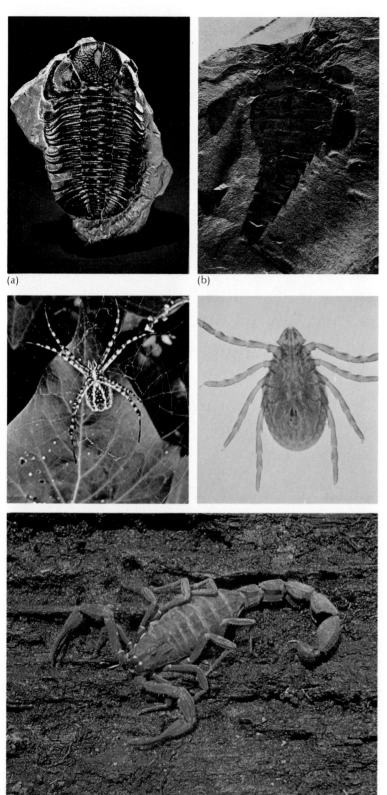

Figure 8.10 (a) A fossil of a trilobite. The trilobites were the first dominant arthropods. They ranged in size from 1 millimeter to more than 60 centimeters (2 feet). Their body segments were organized into three divisions: a head, a trunk, and a posterior region. A similar organizational plan persists in most living arthropods. The trilobites bore a pair of large, compound eyes and a pair of antennae on the head segment. Other than the antennae, all of its appendages were similar in structure and served as legs. There was one pair of legs for each body segment. Thus, up to forty pairs of legs may have been present, varying only in size. (b) A fossil of a eurypterid, an early chelicerate. This ancient group was abundant in the seas about 400 million years ago. Some species were more than 6 feet long.

Figure 8.11 Representative chelicerates. The characteristic feature of this group of arthropods is the presence of chelicerae as the first pair of head appendages. (Chelicerae are pincerlike appendages used variously for grasping, feeding, injecting poison into prey, and copulation.)

The most familiar group of chelicerates are the arachnids: the spiders (a), the ticks (b), the scorpions (c), and their kin.

The terrestrial arachnids share many of the adaptations of insects to life on land. Their hardened cuticle makes them resistant to dehydration. Like insects, they have tracheal tubes for breathing. Body segments are fused to an even greater extent in arachnids than in insects. Spiders, for example, have only two body regions: a cephalothorax (roughly comparable to a fusion of the head and thorax of the mandibulates) and an abdomen.

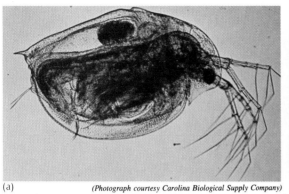

(a)   *(Photograph courtesy Carolina Biological Supply Company)*

(b)

(c)

(d)

(e)   *(Photograph by Walter Dawn)*

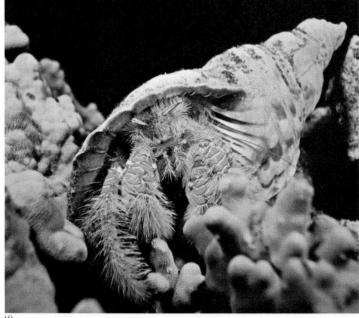

(f)

Figure 8.12   Representative crustaceans of the subphylum Mandibulata. (a) Daphnia, *the water flea. (b) The sowbug, the ubiquitous crustacean found in gardens everywhere. (c) A spiny lobster. (d) A shrimp. (e) A barnacle displaying the featherlike appendages it uses to comb microscopic food from the water. (f) A hermit crab that has taken up residence in an abandoned snail shell.*

Segments are visible in these arthropods, but adjacent segments are usually organized into three functional units: head, thorax, and abdomen. Appendages on the various segments are in most cases highly differentiated. The appendages on the first three segments distinguish the mandibulates from other arthropods and from each other. The first segment bears a pair of highly flexible sensory appendages known as antennae. All crustaceans have a second pair of antennae on the second head segment (insects do not). The third segment carries mandibles, or feeding appendages.

Eight groups of crustaceans are now recognized, but virtually all the forms that find their way into restaurants—the shrimps, crabs, lobsters, and crayfish—are members of the largest and most diverse group. All have a single, enlarged plate of the exoskeleton that covers both the head and the thorax, like a shield. This plate is called a carapace.

Dining on a lobster can be an intriguing laboratory exercise. It will give you an idea of one of the ways arthropods have exploited a simple plan: attaching discrete muscles to thickened regions of cuticle to provide armored mobility.

(a)

(b)

Figure 8.13   Other members of the subphylum Mandibulata. (a) A centipede, representing the class Chilopoda, and (b) a millipede, representing the class Diplopoda.

mandibles. The mandibulates have taken two main lines of development. The **Crustacea** (lobsters, crabs, shrimps, and a host of less tasty relatives) are central to the ecology of the sea (Figure 8.12). But the line that invaded land gave rise to the most diverse group of organisms the world has ever known—the **Insecta**—as well as the related centipedes and millipedes. Let us look at the evolutionary strategies that have made the insects our toughest competitors.

The thickened cuticle perhaps emerged in arthropod evolution as a defense structure. But the cuticle has contributed in still another way to the successful radiation of insects, for it is impervious to water. Of the approximately thirty phyla, only three—the arthropods, the molluscs, and the chordates—are truly successful on land. Other phyla have some representatives on land but they are found only in moist places. In a sense, then, they are still tied closely to water. When they are exposed to air, they rapidly lose water by evaporation, and they dry up and die. *The cuticle of many arthropods is impervious to water, so it prevents evaporative water loss: the animal can carry its water with it as it moves about on dry land.*

Once plants had invaded the land, thereby providing a food source (Chapter 9), they were joined by arthropods. Deposits about 330 million years old or older contain fossilized insects. Fossils that date to 240 million years ago demonstrate conclusively that insects had developed flight by that time.

The Development of Insect Flight

Flight has provided further impetus to the explosive radiation of insect species. A trip from one treetop to another might be a long and uncertain journey for a crawling animal. For an insect with wings, it is just a short flight. A river that prevents a crawling animal from reaching its far shore is no barrier at all for a winged insect. Once insects started to become successful on land, they penetrated a diversity of habitats in which there was very little competition from other organisms. And once they developed wings, there was very little to stop them, and eventually they came to dominate the land. Today, about half the species in the animal world are insects. Nearly a million kinds are known already, and new species are being reported every day. There may be as many species of just one genus of fruit fly as there are species of mammals!

The insect wing is not an appendage; it is an outfolding of the cuticle of the thorax region. Muscles that operate the wings are not attached directly to them. Instead, they are oriented vertically and longitudinally within the thorax. They act by changing the curvature of the dorsal plates, which results in flapping movements of the wings. The muscles powering the wings are also unique, in that they contain the most intricate and efficient mitochondria known.

Because the insect wing is not a true appendage, insects have achieved flight at a much lower evolutionary "cost" than any other group. Flying reptiles (now extinct), birds, and bats have had to sacrifice a pair of legs in order to evolve a mechanism for flight. As a result, they are often rather clumsy on land (bats are virtually immobile except when in flight). But flying insects retain six walking legs on the thorax and are fully adapted for locomotion on land—which is undoubtedly one more reason for their success.

The Development of Tracheal Systems

That insects have prospered on land is due also to their remarkable system for taking in air. Insects have a series of air-conducting tubes, called **tracheae**, that lead into the body from pores in the body wall. They branch into finer and finer tubes as they penetrate all the body tissues, ending next to virtually every cell in the body. And some of the fine tips actually penetrate the cells! Air diffuses directly through these tubes to each cell. The more active tissues, such as flight muscles, are especially well endowed with tracheal tubes.

Once again, the development of a tracheal system was possible only because of the first basic step the arthropods made away from the annelids. The tracheal tubes are lined along their entire length with cuticle that is continuous with the surface exoskeleton. Without such a stiff cuticle coat, the tracheal tubes would collapse from the pressure exerted on them by the body tissues.

But the development of the tracheal system did place one constraint on insects: it set an upper limit on potential size. Air moves through the tracheal system largely by random diffusion of air molecules. Consequently, there is a fixed physical relationship between the number of branches, the size of the main trachea, and the rate of movement of air. For each elongation or new branch that is added deeper in the body, the main tube must be enlarged to maintain the same efficiency of gas movement to the tips. There is a limit to how large these main tubes may become. They could not have a total diameter equal to or greater than the surface of the body. (If they did, there would be no room left for the insect!) From such considerations it is clear (Hollywood thrillers notwithstanding) that insects taller than houses will never evolve, given their present means of obtaining air.

Adapting Stages of Development to Different Aspects of the Environment

Insects often adapt to different parts of the environment by means of a larval stage. The larval stage frequently lasts much longer than the adult stage. An extreme example is the larvae of the periodic cicada, which may live thirteen to seventeen years underground. All the while the larvae eat voraciously and grow. When the adults finally emerge they do so in great numbers, filling the skies in an orgy of mating. Then, within a few days, they die. In some insects the larval stage and the adult stage are adapted so completely to different environments that they do not seem to be related. For example, larval mosquitoes are aquatic and form an important link in the food chains of fresh water. But adult mosquitoes are aerial, and the females demand blood in order to complete their life cycle. Similarly, caterpillars may require leaves of one particular plant on which they are born, live, grow, and transform into adults—but the adult butterflies may subsist exclusively on the nectar of an entirely different group of plants.

Figure 8.14   A small sampling of the fantastically diverse insects found in the subphylum Mandibulata. (a) A harvest ant. (b) A woolly aphid. (c) A cicada. (d) An ox beetle. (e) Ladybugs engaged in copulation. (f) A honeybee.(g) A butterfly.

(a)	(b)
(c) (d)	(f)
(e)	(g)

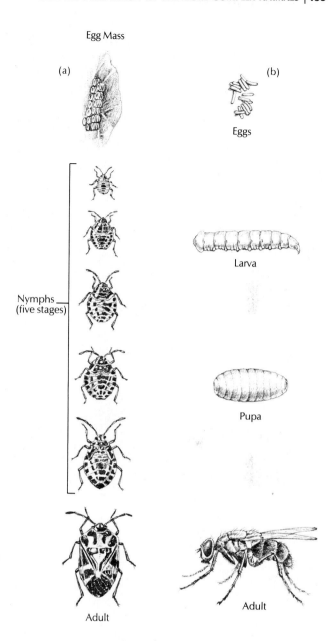

Figure 8.15   A comparison between direct development and indirect development of insects. (a) The life cycle of a cabbage bug, which is an example of direct development. (b) The life cycle of a housefly, which illustrates indirect development. The larval stage (maggot) and the pupa are completely different from the adult stage.

Coevolution between plants and insects has been going on for hundreds of millions of years. Some very interesting aspects of plant physiology and biochemistry involve adaptations to avoid being destroyed by insects. Some of the most intriguing evolutionary developments in insects are adaptations to circumvent those defenses. And some of the most intricate of all biological interrelationships involve mutual dependence of certain insects and the plants they pollinate (Chapter 5).

A FLEXIBLE BODY WALL LEADS TO FLEXIBLE BODY PLANS

There are, in evolution, no "right" or "wrong" ways by which a body plan evolves. There is only one evolutionary test: *Does it work?* Arthropods developed a thickened, hardened body wall with flexible joints. This plan assured the radiation of the most diverse and successful group the world has ever known. And yet, in terms of numbers of species and the degree of diversity, the second most successful group of animals are the molluscs—organisms that followed virtually the exact opposite evolutionary pathway taken by the arthropods!

The 100,000 or so modern species of the phylum **Mollusca** are a varied lot. They include chitons and abalones, clinging tightly to rocks. The sedentary oysters are found in this phylum, as are the slow-crawling snails and the fast-swimming octopuses and squids. Many features unite these diverse groups. But the most obvious unifying feature is their flexible body wall. *It is largely the plasticity of the molluscan body wall that has provided the impetus for diversification of body plan.* This soft, flexible wall has been readily molded and changed by natural selection, adapting different organisms to a variety of different life styles.

Figure 8.16 shows how a mollusc is divided into three body regions—a head, foot, and visceral mass (which contains most of the internal organs). This sketch is of a "hypothetical ancestral mollusc." Although few would now assert that the real ancestor of the molluscs looked anything at all like it, the sketch is useful for illustrating the basic molluscan body plan. The wall covering the visceral mass is called the **mantle.** The mantle secretes the substances needed to build the protective shell. Beneath the shell is a posterior chamber, the **mantle cavity,** which has been important in molluscan evolution. **Gills** (organs for respiration) are situated in the mantle cavity. The anus, reproductive system, and excretory system open into it. If cilia on the gills of our imaginary creature were to beat in such a way as to draw water into the mantle cavity, a stream of water would pass over the gills and then outward. The current thus formed would serve several purposes. First of all, it would act as a respiratory current, bringing oxygen-

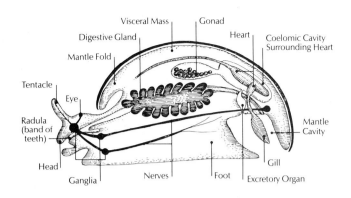

Figure 8.16   A hypothetical early mollusc. This imaginary creature is a composite of various structures found in various present-day molluscs.

bearing water over the gills and flushing away carbon dioxide. Second, it would act as an excretory current, taking away fecal matter and wastes from the kidneys. Finally, it would move the gametes (eggs and sperm) out to sea, where fertilization and development could occur.

The head region of our hypothetical mollusc shows sensory tentacles and simple eyes. The mouth, opening ventrally, is equipped with a structure called a **radula.** A radula is a band of teeth used for scraping food from rocks, tearing into plants, and even drilling holes in shells of other molluscs. The gut is provided with essential glands, and the long intestine is adapted for compacting wastes so that they will be less likely to foul the mantle cavity. The heart consists of a **ventricle** (a chamber that pumps blood out to the hemocoel) and paired **atria** (chambers that receive blood from the gills and pump it into the ventricle). The nervous system consists of a few ganglia interconnected by cordlike structures. The broad and muscular foot can cling to a hard substrate; it can also propel the body forward by waves of muscular contractions.

Structural Strategies Among Living Molluscs

Even though no living mollusc conforms exactly to the hypothetical ancestral mollusc depicted in Figure 8.16, some snails and slugs come close to it. These members of the class **Gastropoda** have a well-developed head, and the radula is usually functional. In some species, the radula is used for scraping algae off rocks; in others, it is specialized for capturing animal prey, rasping flesh, or drilling through shells. In certain predaceous gastropods, the radula consists of only a few large teeth that operate as a kind of harpoon. Gastropods generally have coiled shells, but sometimes the shell is conical or caplike. In both land slugs and sea slugs (Figure 8.17), the shell is absent or reduced.

(a)	(b)
	(c)
(d) (e)	(f)

Figure 8.17   Representative molluscs. Even this small sampling of organisms conveys the essence of the diversity that exists among members of this phylum. But this diversity has been built on a unifying structural theme: a soft, flexible body wall. (The word "mollusc" is derived from the Latin word meaning "soft.")

In some molluscs, the body wall is drawn out to form tentacles for probing the environment or for grasping food. In others, it is expanded into a broad, muscular foot that can be used for creeping over rocks or digging through the sand. But perhaps
the most versatile modification of the body wall is the mantle—a broad, flat, muscular fold. In many members of the phylum, this fold is concerned with secretion of a shell. The shell protects them from predators. But in the octopus and squid, the mantle is highly muscularized and has become one of the most efficient swimming structures in the world.

(a) An octopus and (b) a squid, two representatives of the class Cephalopoda. (c) A fresh-water snail. (d) A species of sea slug that has dorsal outgrowths that function as gills. (e) A close look inside the armored house of a scallop. Notice the light-sensitive eyes on the edge of the mantle and the numerous sensory tentacles. (f) A land slug, laying eggs.

(a)

Figure 8.18   (a) The coiled shell of a fossil cephalopod. The cephalopods have left an admirable fossil record, which documents an evolutionary trend from creeping organisms to active swimmers.
The shell is a regular feature of extinct cephalopods and is retained in modern forms such as the chambered nautilus (b). But it has been reduced to a small internal structure in other cephalopods, such as the squid and the cuttlefish. In the octopus, the shell has disappeared entirely.

(b)

The mantle cavity of most gastropods is at the anterior end, above and around the head. It usually begins to develop at the posterior end, but then a counterclockwise rotation of the visceral mass brings it forward. This type of rotation, called **torsion,** is seen in many members of the group.

Torsional movement was probably favored by natural selection because it enabled the young gastropod to pull itself back into its shell if a predator threatened. Of course, it also brought the anus and the openings from the kidneys close to the mouth, which is not the best of strategies for flushing away wastes. The problem has been solved in various ways among gastropods. In the abalone and some of its relatives, water that has passed over the gills and has picked up digestive and excretory wastes leaves the mantle cavity through holes in the shell. In some other gastropods, the gill on the side where the anus and kidney duct enter the mantle cavity has disappeared. As a result, water moves into the mantle cavity from one side, passes over the gill, then goes out on the other side, carrying wastes away with it. Then there are gastropods that have become greatly modified, often with the reduction of the mantle cavity and the loss of true gills. Most sea slugs are in this category.

As some molluscs became adapted to terrestrial environments, they lost their gills, and the mantle cavity became

converted into an air-filled lung. Many fresh-water snails have a lung, but that is because they are derived from land snails that returned to an aquatic habitat. Some of them still breathe air, but in others the lung is filled with water and functions as a gill.

Members of the class **Bivalvia**—clams, oysters, mussels, and scallops—have not invaded the land, but they are plentiful in the sea and in fresh water. The word "bivalvia" means "two valves," and it refers to the two-piece shell of these creatures. The shell once consisted of a single piece, but in the course of evolution it became separated dorsally into two portions and now there is only a hinge connecting the valves along the midline. Strong muscles can pull the two valves tightly together.

Unlike the head of a gastropod, the head of a bivalve is not in close contact with the environment, and it has neither tentacles nor eyes. The foot of these sedentary creatures is not usually constructed for crawling; instead, it is usually adapted for digging in sand or mud. In mussels, oysters, and other types that attach themselves to rock or wood, the foot is small. Bivalves do not have a radula, but their gills are usually extensively developed and concerned with trapping microscopic food (Figure 8.17). As cilia on the gills move water through the mantle cavity, small organisms, including bacteria and flagellates, are caught in

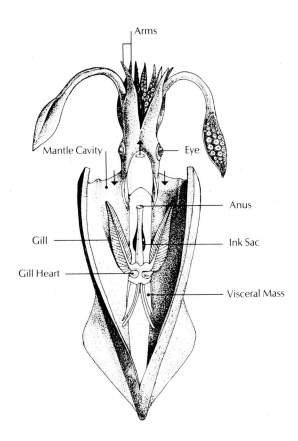

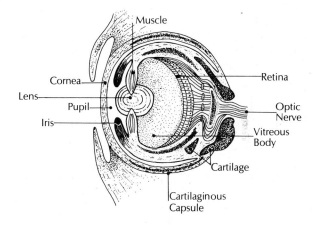

Figure 8.19 (left) A squid, partly dissected from the ventral side to show structures in the mantle cavity. The gill hearts of cephalopods such as squid are like booster pumps, increasing the pressure of blood circulating through the gills. The ink sac contains a dark pigment that can be discharged through the rectum to confuse a predator.

Figure 8.20 The eye of a squid, as seen in cross section. Compare its structure with that of the human eye (Figure 26.6).

mucus on the gills and are moved toward the mouth along special ciliary tracts.

In molluscs more than in any other group of complex animals, it is the muscular movement of the body wall that is responsible for locomotion. Consider the octopus and the squid (Figure 8.19), which are members of the class **Cephalopoda.** These marine organisms have given up the protection—and the imprisonment—of the shell and have developed a unique way to move through water. The mantle of cephalopods is highly muscularized. When it contracts, it forces water out of a tube derived from part of the foot, and the animal moves backward by jet propulsion. This adaptation has permitted cephalopods to become a highly reactive, rapidly swimming group of efficient carnivores.

Some cephalopods can change color rapidly to match the background. They do this by contracting and expanding sacs of pigment. This behavior comes in handy in the ambush of prey as well as in elusion of predators. The cephalopod mouth usually has a pair of hardened, beaklike jaws, often supplemented with glands that secrete a venom for quieting prey. Most cephalopods feed on crustaceans, other molluscs, and fish—and are in turn eaten by fish and marine mammals. The giant squid of the North Atlantic Ocean, sometimes more than sixty feet long, is eaten by sperm whales but not without making a big commotion.

Indeed, the sucker scars often observed on whales are mute testimony to titanic battles. (Sucker scars too large to have been inflicted by even the largest of the known squid keep alive the notion that monstrous cephalopods still lurk in the ocean depths.)

The cephalopod nervous system is built on the basic molluscan plan. However, it is comparatively complex. Sense organs, especially the eyes, also are highly developed. The eyes of some cephalopods (Figure 8.20) are remarkably similar to those of vertebrates, although the evolution of these two kinds of organs has been independent. But more than this, octopuses have a strong capacity to learn and to modify behavior. If primates can be considered the acme of vertebrate evolution on the basis of the development of their nervous system, then the cephalopods hold the same position among the invertebrate scheme of things.

Origins of the Molluscs

The molluscs are almost certainly related to the annelids, but the precise nature of the relationship is not clear. Many representatives of both groups have a short-lived larval stage, known as a **trochophore** (Figure 8.21). And even though there are minor differences between trochophore larvae of annelids and molluscs, the many shared similari-

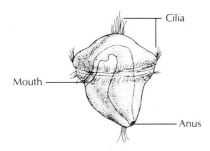

Figure 8.21   The swimming trochophore larva of a marine mollusc. A larva of the same general type occurs in the life history of many polychaete annelids.

ties point unquestionably to a common ancestor somewhere in the past. The controversy has to do with how recently the two lines diverged. Because modern molluscs show no trace of segmentation, it is often assumed that the two lines diverged from some unsegmented flatworm type of ancestor that had a trochophore larval stage. The reasoning behind this assumption is that segmentation—which has been so central in annelid and arthropod evolution—would never be suppressed by any group that came to possess it. But in 1952 *Neopilina*, a living representative of a group of molluscs previously thought to be extinct, was found in deep water off the western coast of Mexico. *Neopilina* shows signs of segmentation in its repetitive arrangement of muscles, coelomic cavities, excretory organs, gonads, and gills. Stimulated by the discovery of *Neopilina*, Donald Abbott of Stanford University has reexamined the question of molluscan origins. In his view, each typically molluscan feature may have been derived *not* by parallel evolution with the annelids from some undifferentiated flatworm ancestor, but by modification of traits found in some polychaetes. He suggests that like arthropods, *molluscs may have descended directly from annelids.*

THE POTENTIAL OF RADIAL CLEAVAGE IN EMBRYONIC DEVELOPMENT

One well-established and diverse group of higher invertebrates seems to have little in common with annelids, arthropods, and molluscs. This is the phylum **Echinodermata** (meaning "spiny-skinned" animals). The echinoderms include the sea stars (starfish), sea urchins, sea cucumbers, and brittle stars. Because all these animals have radial symmetry, they do not resemble bilaterally symmetrical chordates, the group to which we human beings belong. Yet because of certain characteristics that appear in embryonic development, it appears that the relationship between the echinoderms and chordates is somewhat closer than that between either of these groups and the annelid-arthropod-mollusc complex.

Echinoderms: Ancient Relatives of the Chordates?

During a certain period in the embryonic development of many annelids and molluscs—this period follows the four-cell stage—each cell divides obliquely to the axis that passes from its upper pole to its lower pole. This pattern is called **spiral cleavage.** In addition, from the first division onward, sister cells are not identical in their developmental potential. If one of the first four cells is removed, it may continue to divide, but it will form only a quarter of a normal embryo. Because the fate of individual cells of the early embryo is predetermined, the type of development shown by annelids and molluscs is said to be **determinate.** Moreover, when gastrulation takes place, the first opening (the blastopore) becomes the mouth—or at least the mouth forms in the same vicinity. Another opening appears later, and it becomes the anus. Because of this pattern of development, annelids and molluscs together are referred to as **protostomes** ("primary mouth").

Echinoderm development (and also the development of some chordates) typically differs from this pattern. First, cell divisions are either parallel to or at right angles to the axis running from the upper pole to the lower pole of the cell. The outcome is an early embryo in which cells are in two or more tiers, those of one tier being directly above those of another. This pattern of division is called **radial cleavage.** Second, for some period during early development, each cell retains full developmental portion. In other words, each of the first four cells can produce a complete—even if small—individual. And cells can regulate their development if neighbors are removed. The development of the echinoderm embryo is thus said to be **regulative** rather than determinate. Finally, because the anus forms at the blastopore, and the mouth develops as a

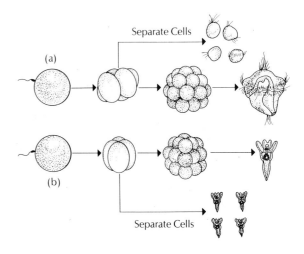

Figure 8.22   Comparison between the formation of a determinative embryo (a) and a regulative embryo (b).

(a)

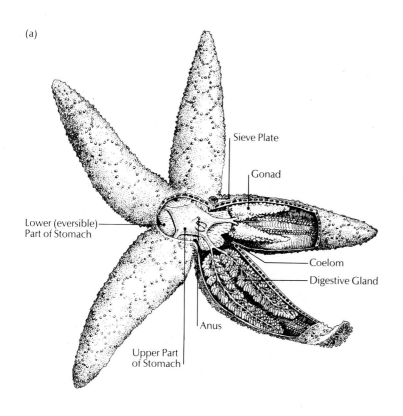

Sieve Plate

Gonad

Lower (eversible) Part of Stomach

Coelom

Digestive Gland

Anus

Upper Part of Stomach

Figure 8.23 (a) A sea star, partially dissected to show the digestive system and the gonads. (b) The main elements of the water vascular system of a sea star. Within the tissue of the arm, each tube foot expands into a bulbous swelling (the ampulla). The foot connects to a canal that runs the length of the arm and joins with a ring canal in the center of the star-shaped body. Still another canal leads from the ring canal to a calcareous sieve on the upper surface of the body. The entire system is permeated with sea water, which is filtered by the sieve and kept circulating by cilia in the canals. When the muscles of a tube foot contract, water is forced into the tube foot. Tube feet leak, of course, but water keeps coming into the system through the sieve to keep the system running.

(b)

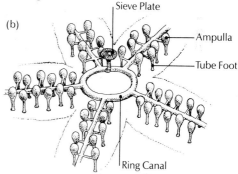

Sieve Plate

Ampulla

Tube Foot

Ring Canal

secondary opening, the echinoderms and chordates are called **deuterostomes** ("secondary mouth") to distinguish them from the protostomes.

Many believe the protostome-deuterostome separation reflects a divergence from some pre-Cambrian flatworm stocks that evolved two different patterns of embryonic development. In any case, the protostomes and deuterostomes have been on separate evolutionary pathways for more than 500 million years. Consequently, little resemblance exists between members of those two sections of the animal kingdom.

Body Plan of the Echinoderms

Most groups of echinoderms have been extinct for a long time. Five classes remain, and they differ widely in appearance. However, a look at a sea star will provide an idea of the operating principles of these groups.

The most obvious feature of a sea star is the radial pattern formed by its "arms" (Figure 8.23a). The radial symmetry of echinoderms seems to be an excellent adaptation for their largely sedentary way of life. It has evolved independently of the radial symmetry seen in cnidarians and ctenophores. Usually the symmetry is five-part, but there are sea stars with many arms. Muscles that interconnect the **ossicles** (skeletal elements) of the body wall can bend the arms slowly. But the movements of a sea star are effected largely by its fleshy **tube feet.** These projections border the groove on the underside of each arm.

The tube feet of a sea star are part of a unique water vascular system (Figure 8.23b). They can extend and swing forward, swing back, retract, and swing forward again, and that is how the animal walks lightly over the sea floor. A decentralized nervous system coordinates the activity.

In sea stars that cling to vertical rocks, the tube feet are tipped with little suction cups. Such suckers are also important in feeding. Many tube feet clinging to the shell of a clam or mussel can pull the valves slightly apart. Then the stomach of the sea star, turned inside-out for the occasion, can be inserted through the gap. Digestion of the mollusc can thus begin while it is still within its shell! Cilia on the wall of the sea star's stomach move digested material into the rest of the gut. Many sea stars simply envelop the prey with the everted stomach; some swallow the prey whole, later ejecting the indigestible residues. Mere contact with certain sea stars is enough to send some otherwise calm animals into a frenzy (Figure 8.24a).

In addition to the mouth and stomach, the digestive system of most sea stars consists of a short intestine that leads to an anus on the upper surface, and extensive digestive glands in the arms. Beneath the digestive glands are the **gonads,** which discharge the egg or sperm cells they produce through pores on the upper surface. As a rule, a

Figure 8.24 Representative echinoderms, animals that may be distantly related to the chordates. (a) A sea star, of the class Asteroides, after a meal of scallops. One scallop has managed to escape so far by swimming movements, caused by clapping its valves together.

(b) In brittle stars, of the class Ophiuroidea, the tube feet have neither suckers nor ampullae. The feet are used primarily for passing small food caught in the mucus to the mouth. The arms of brittle stars are flexible and can be used to push the animal along. They have a core of ossicles arranged much like the bones in a vertebral column.

Sea urchins (c) and (f), of the class Echinoidea, have no arms. But their five-part symmetry is evident in the way the tube feet are arranged. The tube feet are slender and numerous and are used for locomotion and attachment as well as for trapping food and passing it to the mouth. Some of the ossicles of the body wall form a tight, spherical shell; others form sharp spines that join with the shell and are surprisingly mobile. The mouth, equipped with five stout, calcareous jaws, is one of the most efficient feeding structures ever to have evolved.

(d) Sea cucumbers, of the class Holothuroidea, seem different from other classes of echinoderms. This is partly because they are elongated, with the mouth at one end and the anus at the other. It is also because they rarely have externally visible ossicles. Most sea cucumbers lie on their sides; thus, the five sets of tube feet are not equally well developed. In some burrowing types, tube feet are lacking. The tentacles around the mouth are modified tube feet that function by collecting microscopic food on their sticky surfaces. Each tentacle is thrust individually into the mouth, which then closes. As the tentacle is pulled out, food is scraped off.

The sea lilies (e) are grouped in the class Crinoidea. They are remnants of a once large group that figures prominently in the fossil record (Chapter 9). Each of the five arms of a sea lily has two main branches, which are branched again in a featherlike pattern. The tube feet are modified for knocking small particles of food down into ciliary-mucus tracts that lead to the mouth. For the most part, crinoids are sedentary, gripping rocks with some jointed, tentaclelike structures near the base. But they can swim about by graceful, fluttering movements of their arms.

(a)	(d)
(b)	(e)
(c)	(f)

fertilized egg develops into a bilaterally symmetrical larva that swims in the plankton. Eventually the larva settles and changes form (metamorphoses) to become a radially symmetrical adult. *Thus radial symmetry in echinoderms is a secondary development in a basically bilateral animal.* The metamorphosis from bilateral to radial symmetry is drastic and involves some astonishing reorganizations. Part of the left side of the larva becomes the oral surface (bottom) of the adult, and the right side becomes the upper surface. Perhaps this reorganization was favored by natural selection as the protective ossicles began to outweigh the muscular flesh and the echinoderms became sedentary. As Chapter 7 pointed out, radial symmetry is a most useful body plan for a sedentary animal.

MAJOR STEPS IN VERTEBRATE EVOLUTION

Nearly all the large, familiar animals of our environment are **vertebrates,** or organisms with backbones. Various aspects of vertebrate evolution, structure, function, and behavior are covered in later chapters of this book. For that reason, only certain key aspects of their development will be touched on here, in an attempt to identify features that account for their evolutionary success.

The Development of an Endoskeleton

Vertebrates have a coelom and a complete gut. These bilaterally symmetrical animals exhibit some traces of segmentation, especially in the branching of the nerve cord and in the arrangement of repeating skeletal elements and muscles. They possess a heart and a circulatory system. They move predominantly by the contraction of muscles that insert into hardened skeletal elements connected by flexible joints. Contraction of the muscles causes the body to flex at the joint. Appendages, when present, operate with the same kind of skeletal-muscular movements. The various classes of vertebrates are represented in the sea, on the land, and in the air. Forms that have invaded the land have a dry body covering that is rather impervious to water and thus minimizes loss by evaporation.

If all of this sounds vaguely familiar, it should, for everything said in the preceding paragraph can be applied to arthropods as well as to vertebrates. But the extensive parallels between arthropods and vertebrates are parallels only. They are not evidence of a direct relationship. Like the arthropods, the vertebrates use a combination of skeletal elements, joints, and muscles. In the struggle for survival, these characteristics have given them strength and mobility. But the vertebrates took an entirely different approach to formation of a skeleton: it is inside the body rather than on the outside. An internal skeleton, or **endoskeleton,** does not restrict growth or limit body size in the way that an exoskeleton does. That is one of the reasons why the largest animals ever to develop were vertebrates.

To visualize the development of the vertebrate skeleton, we must step back for a moment to consider the invertebrate members of the phylum **Chordata.** A feature that all members of the phylum share (and from which the name of the phylum is derived) is a tough but flexible rod of tissue lying under the nerve cord and above the gut: the **notochord.** It may disappear long before the animal reaches adulthood, but all chordates possess it at least during early developmental stages. Another feature common to chordates is a series of perforations or outpocketings of the pharynx. These are called **gill slits** or **gill pouches,** depending on whether or not they break through to the outside and become functional, permitting the flow of water from the pharynx to the exterior. In higher vertebrates, the connections to the exterior never materialize.

There are several types of simple invertebrate chordates. The **lancelets** (Figure 8.25), represented by just a few marine species, are so fishlike that they are generally thought to be close to the line of descent of fishes. They show the fundamental traits of the phylum Chordata: *a dorsal nerve cord, a notochord, a complete gut with paired gill slits in the pharyngeal region, and segmental muscles.* Lancelets live buried in rather clean sand, with just their head sticking out. Ciliary action brings water and small food organisms into the mouth, then into the pharynx,

Figure 8.25 A lancelet. This marine invertebrate is a member of the phylum Chordata. It illustrates the characteristics typical of all chordates: gill slits, a dorsal nerve cord, and a notochord.

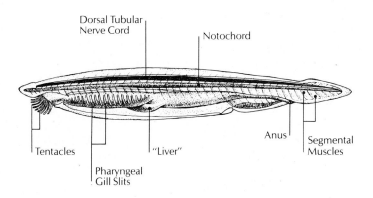

Dorsal Tubular Nerve Cord

Notochord

Tentacles

"Liver"

Anus

Segmental Muscles

Pharyngeal Gill Slits

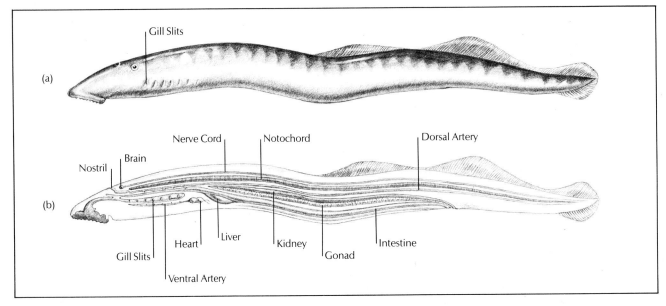

where the food gets mixed up with mucus secreted in a special tract. The food is passed into the intestine, whereas the water leaves the pharynx by way of the gill slits. *In simpler chordates, the gill slits are primarily concerned with processing water for the extraction of food; the specialization of gills for respiration is a later development.*

The oldest fossils of definite vertebrates are remains of **jawless fishes.** These marine animals almost certainly evolved from some group of nonvertebrate chordates—a group that may have had at least some of the features seen in lancelets. The spectrum of existing vertebrates still includes a few jawless fishes, such as the lampreys and the hagfishes, but they are not very close to the ancestral forms. They have a circular mouth without jaws, a series of gill slits, and a persistent notochord (Figure 8.26). They also have skeletal structures composed of a tough, organic substance known as **cartilage.** The serially arranged skeletal elements above the notochord constitute a primitive **vertebral column.** The cartilaginous skeleton of lampreys and the hagfishes also includes a cranium protecting the brain, arches supporting the tissue between the gill slits, and some other structures.

When the capacity to produce cartilage emerged in chordate evolution, it carried a potential as great as the advent of the exoskeleton in arthropods. Once the genetic and biochemical changes required to synthesize a skeletal unit had occurred, natural selection could go to work, selecting variants in which that substance was laid down in different places and in different shapes and styles.

The Varied Potential of the Vertebrate Jaw

In what was to be a major turning point in vertebrate evolution, the anteriormost gill arches evolved into a pair of jaws that could be used for swallowing and grinding food. Much of animal evolution relates directly to the structure of the mouth and its effectiveness as a food-getting device. And the vertebrate jaws eventually framed a mouth more voracious than any other mouth in the biosphere. The first vertebrates to develop jaws were a group of now-extinct armored fishes known as **placoderms.** Although their protective skeletal plating turned out to be an evolutionary flop, their fins—paired membranous appendages—were a sign of things to come. From the paired fins of the placoderms, the line runs straight to the wings of birds, the legs of the race horse, and the hands of man.

Bone: The Architectural Stuff of the Vertebrates

Descendants of the placoderms, the **bony fishes,** carried skeletal development a step further. *In the bony fishes, the cartilaginous skeleton was discarded in favor of a more rigid skeleton of bone—an altogether different material, reinforced by the deposit of mineral salts.* Because of the nature of bone, greater rigidity was acquired at very little additional cost in weight. Without the development of a bony skeleton, large land vertebrates capable of supporting their own weight never could have evolved. True bone is absent in sharks (Figure 8.27a), but it is the framework of the architecture of most vertebrates. However, its formation usually follows that of cartilage, and cartilage persists in some parts of the skeleton. Even in human beings, most of the skeleton is first built of cartilage—and then the cartilage is gradually replaced by bone.

When jaws developed, the gill slits became concerned largely with respiration—the exchange of gases between blood and sea water. *But early in the evolution of bony fishes, some of the types that appeared had lungs as well as*

Figure 8.26   External (a) and internal (b) structure of the lamprey, a jawless fish. The jawless fishes are the most primitive of the existing vertebrates. Lampreys are found in fresh water as well as in the sea, where they feed on fish by attaching themselves to the host with their circular mouth. They then proceed to rasp away the flesh.

The ancestors of lampreys and their relatives were probably mud-grubbers and may have become extinct simply because they could not compete with fishes that had evolved jaws and paired fins. The fact that lampreys developed specialized, parasitic feeding habits may be what saved them from extinction.

Figure 8.27   Representative fishes. (a) A shark, of the class Chondrichthyes. Sharks evolved from the placoderms after the appearance of bony fishes, and they still have skeletons of cartilage. (b) Lion fishes and (c) blue cromies, both of the class Osteichthyes.

Figure 8.28 Representative amphibians (a–c) and representative reptiles (d–h). The limbs of most amphibians are strong enough to function effectively on land. In a salamander (a) the limbs are adapted for crawling. In frogs (b, c) and toads, the hind limbs are adapted for jumping. Adult amphibians feed on other animals, most commonly insects, and their tongue can usually be flipped out to help capture the prey. The scaly skin of reptiles prevents loss of water and offers good protection against abrasion in a dry terrestrial environment. However, some reptiles, especially turtles and crocodiles, are largely aquatic. (e) The tokay gecko, a lizard with toes provided with pads that function in much the same way as suction cups. (d) The American alligator, a crocodilian. (f) The mangrove snake. Snakes have lost the appendages of their ancestors, and their locomotion is usually effected by backward *pressure of loops of the body against the ground. Their jaws are highly distensible, so that large prey can be swallowed whole. (g) A box tortoise, a terrestrial turtle. (h) The chameleon, an Old World lizard famed for its ability to change color to match its surroundings.*

(a)	(b)	(c)
(d)		(e)
(f)		(h)
(g)		

nasal passages opening into the mouth to provide for the passage of air. What pressures brought about these structural innovations? Although only a few modern fishes have lungs, there was a time when lungs were characteristic of many fishes. These respiratory structures surely were an adaptation for life in stagnant pools, where there was little dissolved oxygen that could be taken up through the gills. Add to such lung-bearing fishes two pairs of strong fins for supporting the body and you have the **amphibians,** vertebrates that ventured out of the water at about the same time in earth history that the insects arose. In that period, ponds and streams were alternately filling and drying up, and the capacity to move out across land would have significant survival advantage (Chapter 9). But the amphibians lacked the cuticle of the insects and were locked to the water for much of their life cycle. Even today, they characteristically hatch in the water as larvae that breathe by means of gills; only through metamorphosis do adults acquire lungs—and the capacity to live on land. Eventually, the vertebrates called **reptiles** evolved from the amphibians. With their successful adaptations of scaly, water-impervious skin and leathery eggs, the reptilian lines radiated into the drier terrestrial environments.

Having escaped from water and from dependence on gills, organisms with structures originally designed for filter feeding were modified still further. One example of the use to which these structures eventually were put is in the evolution of the middle ear of the class of vertebrates called **mammals.** When the first cartilaginous gill arch became converted into jaws, the anteriormost gill slit became modified as well. This modification is evident in modern sharks, in which the first gill slit is obviously smaller than the others and is decidedly out of line. Eventually, this gill slit became transformed, in mammals, into the middle ear. Although it is walled off from the outside by the eardrum, it is still connected to the pharynx (Figure 8.29). The three bones that transmit vibrations from the eardrum to the inner ear are derived from portions of certain gill arches. In reptiles, in fact, two of these bones are part of the hinge connecting the lower jaw to the rest of the skull. (It is the flexibility of this hinge that enables snakes to swallow animals with a body diameter larger than their own.) But as mammals evolved from reptiles, the two bones were moved up into the ear to form what we call the ''hammer'' and the ''anvil.'' (The ''stirrup,'' the third bone of the mammalian middle ear—and the only ear bone of amphibians, reptiles,

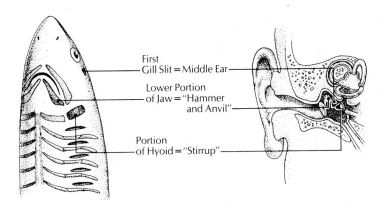

First
Gill Slit = Middle Ear

Lower Portion
of Jaw = "Hammer
and Anvil"

Portion
of Hyoid = "Stirrup"

Figure 8.29 Derivatives, in the human ear, of some structures that have a totally different form and function in the shark.

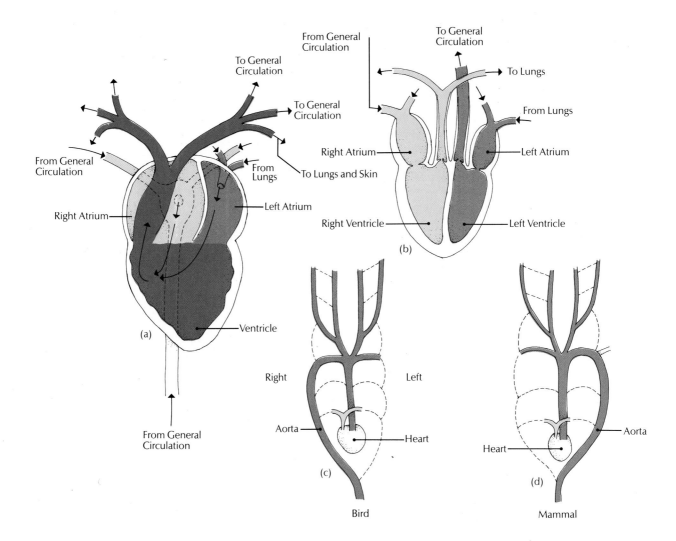

Figure 8.30 *(a) The three-chambered heart of the frog (simplified). This ventral view shows the general pattern of circulation. Highly oxygenated blood returning from the lungs goes into the left atrium. Blood returning from the general circulation goes into the right atrium; a portion of this blood has been oxygenated in the skin, but most of it is depleted of oxygen. Blood from the two atria is inevitably mixed to some extent before it is pumped away from the heart.*

(b) The four-chambered heart of birds and mammals, and diagrams showing the arteries derived from the embryonic aortic arches of birds (c) and mammals (d). All diagrams are simplified ventral views. Vessels that do not persist are indicated by broken lines. Notice especially that the part of the aorta nearest the heart has a completely different origin in birds and mammals.

Figure 8.31 *Representative birds. The feathers of birds provide insulation that helps to maintain a warm and constant body temperature. Feathers also aid in flight, provide protective coloration, and provide cues for recognition of sexes and nuptial behavior. (a) A blue-crowned pigeon. (b) An avocet, with a bill specialized for probing for food in sand. (c) A white mynah bird. (d) An emu. (e) A peacock during a courtship display.*

(a)	(b)	(c)
(d)		(e)

and birds—is derived from the second gill arch.) In one sense, then, the price of enjoying a symphony is not being able to swallow your dinner whole.

The Vertebrate Heart

Evolution seldom involves changes in only one or a few aspects of an organism. As one system changes, selective pressures on other systems change as well. As vertebrates evolved, they became air-breathing, larger, more active, more efficient in food getting, and finally warm-blooded under selective pressures for a more efficient circulatory system.

In fishes the heart has only two chambers. Blood is received in the atrium and pumped out through the ventricle to the gills, where it becomes oxygenated. The blood is then distributed to the rest of the body. In adult amphibians, the heart has three chambers (Figure 8.30). The left atrium receives blood that has just been oxygenated in the lungs, and the right atrium receives blood returning from the rest of the body. Because there is only a single ventricle, oxygenated and unoxygenated blood are mixed to some extent in this chamber. However, amphibians have a relatively low rate of metabolism, and it can be kept going as long as the blood carries a moderate amount of oxygen.

In reptiles, the heart has two atria and two ventricles, but in most forms the ventricles are not completely separate. However, the separation of oxygenated and unoxygenated blood is more nearly complete than it is in amphibians. In birds, descended from reptiles, the four-chambered heart has a complete separation of the right and left sides. Thus oxygenated blood returning from the lungs is delivered to the active tissues, which must have it for their survival.

The mammals are also descended from reptiles, but not from the same stock that gave rise to birds. Like birds,

Figure 8.32   Representative mammals. The term "mammal" refers to the mammary glands by which females of most species provide milk to their young. With two exceptions (the duckbill platypus and the spiny anteater of Australia), the young are born alive. In marsupial mammals, the young are born after a very short developmental period in the uterus. In all other mammals, there is an extended period of development within the mother, in whom the fetus is attached to and nourished by a uterine organ called a placenta. Placental mammals include such diverse creatures as the African ringed waterbuck (a), the hippopotamus (b), and the white-footed deer mouse (c). A representative marsupial mammal is the Tasmanian gray kangaroo (e). All mammals develop slowly and need the continued care of an adult parent. Although a few female mammals such as the baboon (g) have relatively few offspring, most of their infants do reach maturity and will have experienced a close mother-child relationship. Mammals have come to exploit a variety of food resources. Whereas the hippopotamus is a herbivore (plant eater), the snow leopard (d) and the sea lion (f) are carnivores (meat eaters); and still others, such as human beings, are omnivores (having diets that include plants as well as other animals).

(a)		
(b)		
(c)	(e)	(g)
(d)	(f)	

mammals have a completely four-chambered heart, but a sharp difference in ancestry is evident in the way the main artery leaving the heart originates in these two groups. In birds, this vessel is a survivor of one of the right aortic arches formed in the embryo; in mammals, it is a survivor of one from the left side. This example points out once again that two lines of organisms confronted by similar environmental demands may adapt in quite different ways to achieve the same end. There is no such thing as an arbitrary right and wrong way to adapt evolutionarily. The dictum is to adapt and leave survivors or fail to adapt and leave none.

PERSPECTIVE

This chapter and the preceding one have by no means described all the various kinds of animals that exist. Indeed, only five of the more than ten phyla of animals that possess a coelom—an important unifying feature of the so-called "higher" animals—have been brought into focus. On what basis were these phyla selected? Perhaps because they are successful. Why are they successful? Perhaps because early on they acquired body plans of great plasticity and adaptability—body plans that could be so readily modified that individuals could evolve in thousands of different, specialized ways. This chapter, then, has concentrated on the fundamental characteristics of the more versatile groups and on how those characteristics have worked as well as they have under the evolutionary test of survival.

For the annelids, success came with a segmented coelom, which provided a hydraulic skeleton against which muscles could work. Through this innovation the annelids acquired flexibility and mobility. For the arthropods, a variation on this theme was in one sense far more successful than the theme itself: thickening of the cuticle in selected regions, coupled with subtle shifts in musculature. Armored body parts and flexible joints led to the most successful body plan that has yet evolved—as measured by the degree of radiation from that plan. For the molluscs, the plan was somewhat different. A superficial look at the sedentary molluscs might cause us to overemphasize the importance of the shell. But when we consider the fast-swimming, long-ranging cephalopods we can see that probably it was the versatility of the mantle that accounts for molluscan diversification, giving rise to the shell in some and to jet propulsion in others.

For each new body plan that has evolved, certain evolutionary potentials emerge. But also emergent are certain limits imposed by the nature of the materials of life and the manner in which they are arranged. Whenever certain doors are opened, others are closed. When insects developed a tracheal system for breathing, they found the land and air waiting for exploration and colonization, but they closed the door leading back to the sea. There are relatively few marine insects, and almost all of those are at the fringes of the sea. But then there are no echinoderms in the air! Identifying the limits imposed by a particular body plan is not always an easy task, but when we are able to do so, we acquire one more clear intellectual path through the diversity of life that is so great and so different from place to place on the planet we call home.

SUGGESTED READINGS

BARRINGTON, E. J. *Invertebrate Structure and Function.* Boston: Houghton Mifflin, 1967.

GARDINER, MARY S. *The Biology of Invertebrates.* New York: McGraw-Hill, 1972.
Two modern texts dealing with invertebrates primarily from the standpoints of structure and function.

BUCHSBAUM, RALPH. *Animals Without Backbones.* Rev. ed. Chicago: University of Chicago Press, 1973. A classic elementary text on invertebrates, with many excellent photographs.

HYMAN, LIBBIE H. *The Invertebrates.* Vols. I–VI. New York: McGraw-Hill, 1940–1967. A monumental treatise, still incomplete, but the best general reference work on invertebrates in the English language. For the serious student.

RUSSELL-HUNTER, W. D. *A Biology of Higher Invertebrates.* New York: Macmillan, 1969. One of the best short introductions to the higher invertebrate groups.

THORSON, GUNNER. *Life in the Sea.* New York: McGraw-Hill, 1971. A good introduction to the natural history and ecology of marine forms by an outstanding worker in the field.

Chapter 9

Diversity Through Time

*Beneath the swirling, moisture-laden
clouds of our planet, life evolved, undergoing
recurrent patterns of abundance and extinction as
new forms appeared and disappeared through
evolutionary time. But the drama has not been
played out on a static stage. The earth itself has
changed over time, with drifting continents and
changing climates exerting profound forces on the
evolution of life.*

Beginning with the assumption that the first life form was a simple prokaryotic cell, we have so far attempted to trace from it the various lines of descent that led, eventually, to the tremendous range of diversity we see in the living world. In reconstructing these possible evolutionary lines, we have looked to the structure and function of existing organisms for clues about life in the past. But if we are to understand more clearly the forces underlying organic diversification, then we must also take into account the stage on which the evolutionary story is being played out. It is, for example, important to know that the stage itself has changed with time. We cannot, in our speculations, have organisms of the past populating a world like that of the 1970s, for the present configuration of continents, the present atmosphere and climate—and especially the present interrelated web of biotic communities—are unique in earth history. Not only must we consider the extinct organisms themselves, we must consider the conditions under which they lived.

It is also important to recognize that the length of the evolutionary drama is immense. The major rock components of our planet solidified 4.7 billion years ago; the first life forms did not appear for at least 1.5 billion years after that. Conveying the immensity of this time span is difficult, at best. Figure 9.2 is an attempt to illustrate the various abiotic and biotic events in earth history. But this figure has an extremely nonuniform scale: the past 3 million years occupy more of the page than the first $2\frac{1}{2}$ *billion* years of planetary history! Nevertheless, the scale must be compressed more and more as it goes back in time. If you were to keep everything to scale by using, say, a mere one-eighth of an inch to represent the past 5,000 years (the era of recorded human history), then you would have to use more than 10,000 pages of paper to get back to the beginning of earth history. Your evolutionary time scale would stretch about two miles away from your book—and most of the pages would be blank! This is the magnitude of the scale of events that must be kept in mind in re-creating the progression of organisms that have appeared and disappeared across the stage of evolutionary time.

THE PREBIOTIC EARTH: EVENTS LEADING TO THE ORIGIN OF LIFE

Today, understanding of early earth history is still incomplete, but it is being enriched by the findings of geochemistry, astronomy, and space exploration. According to current theories, the earth (and all other planets in our solar system) originated 4.7 billion years ago with the condensation of matter left over from the formation of the sun. As matter began to condense in the region of space destined to be the earth, it produced a localized gravitational field. The gravitational field caused still more material to be swept up from surrounding space as the preplanetary earth circled the sun. As the aggregation became larger and its gravitational field more intense, the heavier materials accumulated in the core of the developing planet. Continued accumulation and compaction soon raised the temperature of these materials to the melting point. At that stage, many gaseous substances were vented from the interior—gases that formed the first primitive atmosphere. Gradually, the planet began to cool and heat was radiated away. (There is evidence that the core of the earth is still molten, which suggests that the cooling process is lengthy indeed.)

The early atmosphere probably did not contain any free oxygen. But we are certain that it contained considerable hydrogen (the most abundant element in the universe) and varying amounts of water vapor, methane, ammonia, and other gaseous compounds in which hydrogen is an important component. Over time, much of the original hydrogen undoubtedly drifted away, leaving the atmosphere enriched with the other, heavier gases. The existence of this kind of atmosphere was the result of two factors: the size of the earth and its distance from the sun. Although such factors may seem far removed from biology, they probably were important in establishing the conditions under which life could arise. Had the evolving earth been smaller, it would have had a weaker gravitational field and much more of its early atmosphere would have drifted away into space. Because the earth was large enough to have a moderate gravitational field, it retained much of its gaseous envelope. Moreover, the earth was far enough away from the sun that its water was not kept boiling after its surface crust cooled, yet it was close enough to the sun that all its water did not freeze. *Life is based on water chemistry, and if the earth had formed outside the narrow "liquid water zone" of the solar system, life as we know it never would have come about despite the presence of all the other materials needed for its genesis.*

As the surface of the earth cooled from the molten state, the water vapor in the atmosphere began to condense and pour down. A rain began that may have lasted for millions of years, flowing over the rocks, dissolving some of their salts, and filling depressions in the earth's crust. In this way the oceans were formed—oceans that would be the cradle for life. What we infer of the sequence of events that culminated in the origin of the first cellular life forms is outlined in *Interleaf 9.1*. Although the precise timing of these events is difficult to determine, *fossils of bacterialike forms suggest that prokaryotic heterotrophs existed at least 3 billion years ago.*

THE PROTEROZOIC: PHOTOSYNTHETIC ORGANISMS CHANGE THE BIOSPHERE

The Proterozoic era (*protero-*, "very first"; *-zoic*, "life") was a vast interval encompassing nearly half the total history of the earth. It extended from the earliest appearance

(text continues on page 178)

Figure 9.2 Distribution of various biological taxa in time. The solid portion of each bar represents the known temporal distribution; the dotted areas indicate the probable existence of transitional ancestral types. Shading within each bar indicates periods when the group was particularly important in terms of dominance in the communities.

The relative geologic time scale of eras and periods has been calibrated using various radiometric dating techniques. Such dating relies on the measurement of the relative decay of radioactive isotopes contained in the rocks or other sediments.

The scale of the diagram has been distorted, in that more recent geologic periods occupy more space than do earlier periods (that were actually longer in duration). A linear scale is provided on the far right. Examination of the linear scale will indicate how little of earth history has elapsed in the evolution of most familiar plants and animals.

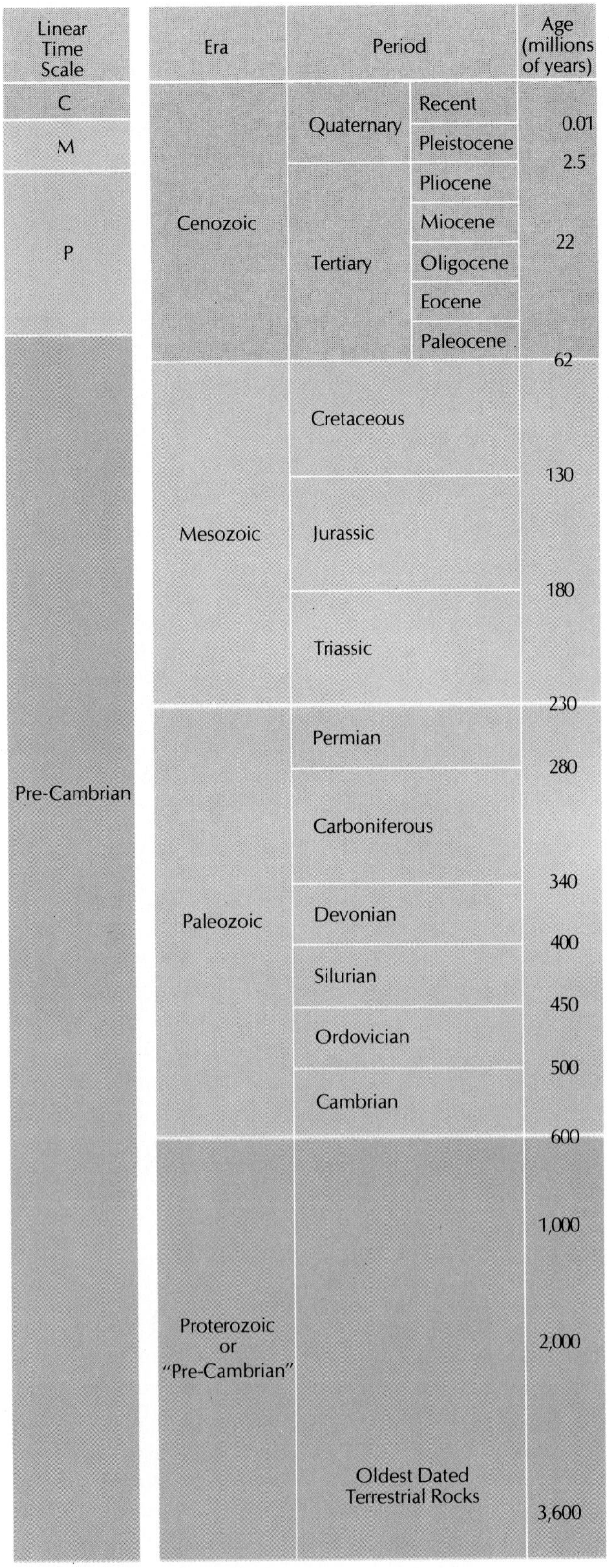

Linear Time Scale	Era	Period		Age (millions of years)
C	Cenozoic	Quaternary	Recent	0.01
M			Pleistocene	2.5
P		Tertiary	Pliocene	
			Miocene	22
			Oligocene	
			Eocene	
			Paleocene	62
	Mesozoic	Cretaceous		130
		Jurassic		180
		Triassic		230
Pre-Cambrian	Paleozoic	Permian		280
		Carboniferous		340
		Devonian		400
		Silurian		450
		Ordovician		500
		Cambrian		600
	Proterozoic or "Pre-Cambrian"			1,000
				2,000
		Oldest Dated Terrestrial Rocks		3,600

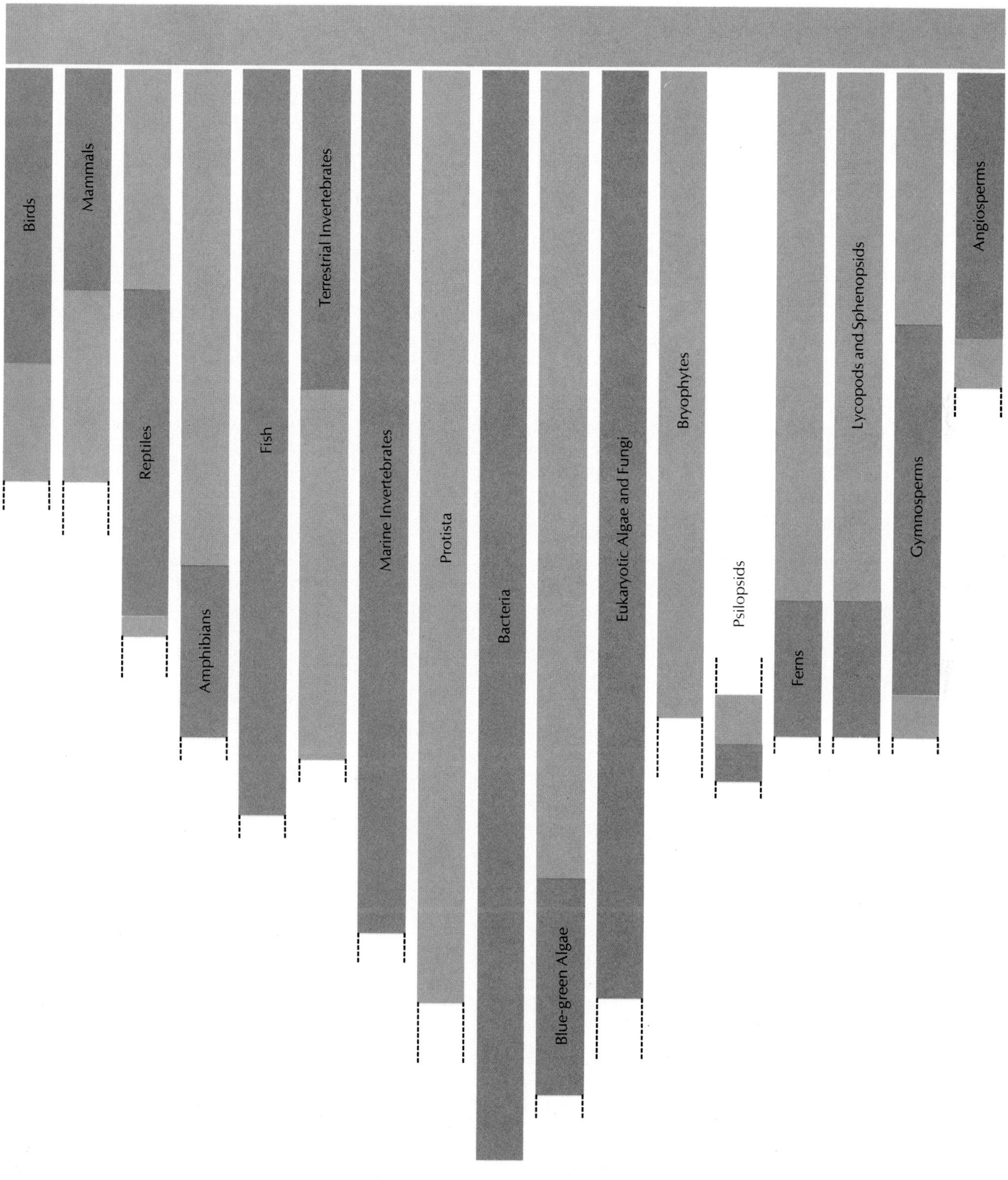

Birds

Mammals

Reptiles

Amphibians

Fish

Terrestrial Invertebrates

Marine Invertebrates

Protista

Bacteria

Blue-green Algae

Eukaryotic Algae and Fungi

Bryophytes

Psilopsids

Ferns

Lycopods and Sphenopsids

Gymnosperms

Angiosperms

Interleaf 9.1

Origins of Life

The origin of life on our planet is a mystery that has captured the imagination of biologists and nonbiologists alike. There are basically three models that offer an explanation of the phenomenon. The first is that life came into being as a result of a directed creation process. Described in innumerable ways, this concept is inherent in the religious motifs of virtually all peoples. Because the basic metaphysical assumptions and the unspecified manner in which the creation process might have been accomplished are inherently untestable, they will not be considered in this discussion.

A second model, often referred to as the concept of *panspermia*, suggests that life originated elsewhere in the universe and was transported here. The most common dispersal mechanism suggested involves the movement of dormant spores through space under the influence of light pressure. Although the interstellar movement of very small particles driven by light is quite feasible, it would require extremely long periods to complete journeys between even closely grouped stellar systems. The extreme cold of interstellar space would appear to be ideal for maintaining dormancy of such dispersal units, but the probable effects of long time periods under high vacuum and bombardment by radiation would seem to mitigate against such particles maintaining viability. Quite aside from these

physical considerations, panspermia is philosophically unsatisfying in that it merely transfers the problem of the ultimate origin of life to unreachable areas and unpredictable conditions.

The third model assumes that life evolved here on earth as a result of the gradual aggregation of molecules under the conditions present very early in our planetary history. Because this model is accepted by the vast majority of biologists, we will examine it in some detail.

To receive general acceptance, an *in situ* model for the derivation of life would have to meet three basic conditions:

1. The various inorganic constituents of living systems must have been present early in the history of the earth.

2. Environmental conditions must have been such to permit (or even promote) the kinds of chemical interactions that would result in accumulation of a variety of prebiotic building blocks.

3. Reasonable models must exist for the association of these prebiotic molecular arrays into systems that demonstrate the character of living systems.

If these three conditions can be met, we can reasonably postulate the formation of a self-replicating energy-handling molecular system. From that point natural selection and the evolutionary process we associate with life would be sufficient to "move" such systems in

the direction of currently recognizable living organisms.

The fossil record is of relatively little use in determining the earliest paths to the condition we call life, mainly because no rocks have been found that date from this period. The development and use of sophisticated analytical techniques may eventually provide useful data on the molecular phase of the development of life, but to this point much of the data presently available have been derived indirectly.

Examination of very early sedimentary rocks and the observation of the atmospheres of other planets within our solar system suggest that the earliest atmosphere of the earth consisted largely of hydrogen, methane, ammonia, molecular nitrogen, and a number of other hydrogen-rich compounds. Free oxygen was essentially absent, although oxygen bound in the form of water was common. Such an atmosphere would satisfy the first of our prebiotic requirements in that it would provide carbon, hydrogen, nitrogen, and oxygen, which are essential components of modern living systems. As water condensed in the atmosphere, it appears that rains fell continuously for millions of years, leaching rocks and providing a pool of mineral materials such as sodium, potassium, phosphates, magnesium, calcium, and other elements presently known to be important in the chemistry of modern life. Sul-

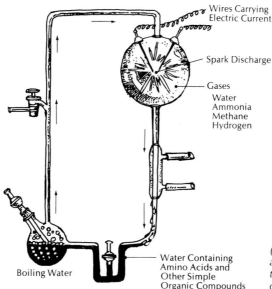

Wires Carrying Electric Current

Spark Discharge

Gases
Water
Ammonia
Methane
Hydrogen

Water Containing Amino Acids and Other Simple Organic Compounds

Boiling Water

(a) A generalized diagram of Miller's apparatus with which he demonstrated the possibility of abiotic synthesis of complex molecules.

fur, in the form of hydrogen sulfide, was also present as a result of volcanic activity. It thus appears reasonable to suppose that the various inorganic elements of which life is composed would have been richly available in the prebiotic environment.

In order to satisfy the second criterion for our model it is necessary to demonstrate that various building blocks that might lead to "living" systems could have formed under prebiotic conditions. The first definitive experiment to demonstrate the feasibility of prebiotic organic synthesis was performed by Stanley Miller in 1952. Miller's apparatus (Figure *a*) contained mixtures of materials presumed to be present in the early atmosphere—hydrogen, methane, ammonia, and water vapor. A spark discharged in the gas vessel provided an energy source analogous to that provided by lightning discharges. When the system was operated for only one week, the water in the vessel was found to contain a variety of amino acids and other organic compounds.

Since that time many experiments of this type have been run with various gas mixtures and a

variety of energy sources, including heat and ultraviolet radiation. In each case a variety of organic materials have been produced. Such experiments neither confirm the nature of the prebiotic atmosphere nor define the precise manner in which the building blocks of life did arise, but they do indicate that *prebiotic synthesis of many different essential organic materials could easily have occurred in any one of a number of atmospheric models with a variety of energy sources.* The reducing (hydrogen-rich) nature of the early atmosphere of earth is an essential element of the process, for under our present oxidizing (oxygen-rich) conditions many of the organic materials produced would break down rapidly. But under reducing conditions the molecules, once formed, would be reasonably safe from degradation and, in fact, *would exist under conditions that would favor further synthesis or polymerization under the influence of existing environmental energy.* Such molecules would gradually accumulate in the oceans and fresh water, forming a rich prebiotic "soup" where further reactions would occur.

Some concentration of the early organic products of this abiotic synthesis must have occurred. Evaporation in pools or isolated basins and adsorption of molecules on the surface of clay minerals would serve to concentrate the organic material and increase the diversity of the possible chemical interactions. It is probable that once abiotic synthesis had proceeded to a certain point, chemical energy sources promoted further synthesis. One complex molecule derived from some prebiotic experiments is adenosine triphosphate, or ATP. ATP serves today as the universal energy "currency" of living things. It seems possible that the use of ATP molecules as an energy source may well predate the origin of life itself.

Although most biologists are convinced that abiotic synthesis of rather complex molecules was an essential element in the origin of life, a consensus has yet to emerge concerning probable models for reaching our third condition: the aggregation of complex molecules into systems with the characteristics of life. Regardless of the definition one adopts for life, the ability of the system to reproduce itself

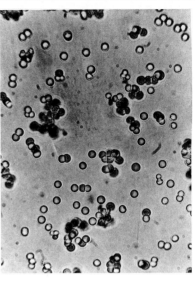

(b) Proteinoid microspheres of uniform size under low magnification. Sidney Fox and his co-workers have proposed that primitive cells could have developed from aggregates of these tiny microscopic droplets.

is obviously of critical importance. Complex chemical aggregates derived by concentration from the prebiotic "soup" certainly represented metabolism of a sort, but until such aggregates became capable of reproducing their unique chemical arrays, the development of such systems was a completely random process. Once reproduction became possible, natural selection could come into play, resulting in differential rates of reproduction. The road would then be open toward the development of still more complex systems with clear-cut strategies for survival.

A complex chemical system may compete with other systems for available materials, but without the capacity for reproduction the ascendancy of one system over the other would be a phenomenon of local interest only. In living organisms today the capacity for reproduction is achieved through the replication of nucleic acids such as DNA and RNA. The nucleic acids essentially code for the multitude of enzymes necessary for the activities of life, and the nucleic acid molecules themselves are neatly replicated (Chapters 11 and 17). The simplest systems using such mechanisms are the viruses, which consist of little more than a nucleic acid template and a protective protein coat. One theory for the origin of reproductive capacity in chemical systems, often called the theory of the *original macromolecule*, envisions the gradual abiotic synthe-

sis of a large nucleic acid molecule that eventually develops to the point at which it is capable of reproducing itself using nucleotides available in the environment— perhaps a chemical system analogous to a free-living virus.

The major difficulty with this approach is that no nucleic acid molecule is known that is truly self-replicating; all are dependent upon complex proteins (enzymes) to carry out each of the several steps required for replication. And the chance occurrence of an enzyme capable of replicating a nucleic acid molecule would be of little long-term significance unless that enzyme could also be replicated. Modern viruses achieve their ability to reproduce themselves by subverting the activities of dozens of enzymes from the complex synthetic machinery of living cells. Without such cells viruses are merely complex chemical preparations that can be stored on the laboratory shelf. The theory of the original macromolecule of nucleic acid is the most popular one, but it suffers from the lack of a mechanism to develop a protein synthesis system. Some biologists feel that other paths to complexity must have temporally preceded the nucleic acid mechanism for coding and reproducing information.

If we agree that the development of life from nonliving molecules was probably a very slow, progressive process, it would seem that an important first step would have

been the development of a self-enclosed system such that, when molecular advances occurred, the resulting molecules could be kept together rather than diffusing freely away from one another. An experimental approach, showing how such self-contained systems might arise, has led to the *molecular aggregate theory* of the origin of life. A number of workers have shown that complex chemical polymers (compounds formed of repetitive subunits) can, in water solutions, form systems that demonstrate some analogies with living cells. Sidney Fox has demonstrated that dry heating of amino acid chains can result in the formation of rather complex polypeptide chains, or proteins. If such chains are introduced into hot aqueous solutions and allowed to cool, small spherical structures called *microspheres* are formed. These microspheres, only a few micrometers in diameter (Figure *b*), consist of a double-layered protein wall and will swell or shrink as the physical and chemical conditions of the solution are changed. If sufficient proteinaceous material is present, the spheres will occasionally produce budlike outgrowths, essentially resulting in the formation of new spheres.

The Soviet chemist Aleksandr Oparin has demonstrated that various organic polymers, such as proteins, nucleic acids, and polysaccharides, will form stable droplets in water solutions (*coacervate* droplets). Fox's microspheres and Oparin's coacervate droplets are both formed as a result of rather simple physical-chemical interactions, and although neither is alive, since they do not reproduce, both show one important characteristic in common: the development of a chemical boundary layer defining an "inside" space that is buffered to some extent from the external environment. Coacervate droplets can concentrate lipids in the boundary layer, producing a layer analogous to membranes. Catalysts (enzymes) can also accumulate in such droplets, creating localized pockets where chemical reactions of certain types are facilitated.

Although ATP may have served as the principal energy source early in the evolution of life, it would certainly have begun to be used faster than it could be produced by abiotic synthesis once self-reproduction had been achieved and "life" forms began to proliferate. This would have resulted in a competitive advantage for forms that were capable of breaking down other chemical compounds in the environment and utilizing the energy thus obtained. If enzyme arrays were already attuned to the use of ATP as the energy source of "choice," the greatest advantage would accrue to forms that developed mechanisms by which the breakdown of other chemical compounds could be linked to ATP formation. Selection would eventually force further metabolic diversity as one after another the various complex molecules in the environment became ever more limited as a direct result of the earth's first population explosion. Since free oxygen was not present, the energy conversion efficiency was probably rather low, but the processes that were developing were the forerunners of the anaerobic metabolism common to life today (Chapter 14).

The development of one or more mechanisms for trapping solar energy provided certain organisms with an outside source of energy that could then be applied to the synthesis of the complex molecules on which life had come to depend. The original forms of photosynthesis probably involved the splitting of materials such as hydrogen sulfide and did not result in the release of oxygen. Development of the more efficient form of photosynthesis that involves photolysis of water and that releases oxygen began the gradual accumulation of oxygen in the atmosphere and opened the opportunity for the development of much more efficient (aerobic) mechanisms for generating energy from the complex products of photosynthesis. Long before this stage had been reached, life in a form that would be immediately recognizable had come into being.

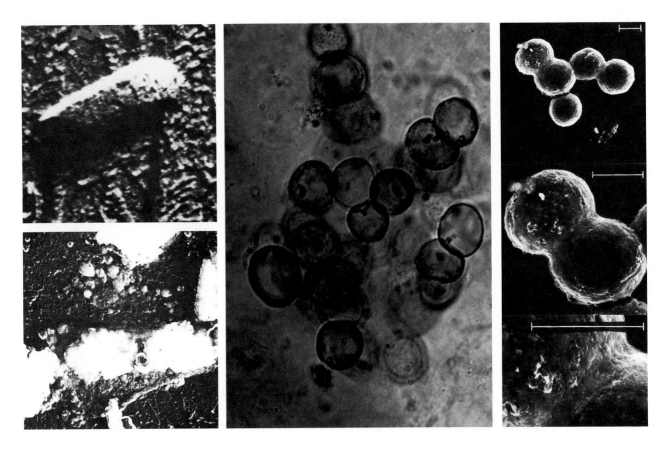

of cells through the development of the major animal phyla at the beginning of the Paleozoic. It was during this immense period that the major innovations in cell structure and function discussed in Chapters 4 and 13 developed. *There is little doubt that the first cellular organisms were prokaryotic heterotrophs, similar in form and function to many modern bacteria.* Their energy source was the "organic soup"—the rich supply of carbon-containing molecules accumulated in the oceans during the millions of years of abiotic synthesis.

But the atmosphere of the world of these early heterotrophs lacked oxygen. We know that similar kinds of organisms growing today in the absence of oxygen have relatively inefficient energy metabolism. As the first organisms proliferated in the oceans, pressure must have mounted for the selection of variant forms of organisms that could utilize the useless molecular fragments that were then building up in the environment as a result of the inefficient metabolic activities of the earliest organisms. Such strategies for handling simpler and less efficient molecules would not have been enough to avert the world's first energy crisis—the ever more rapid depletion of food molecules in the oceans. Fortunately, natural selection brought about a completely new energy-acquiring strategy.

As you will read in Section III, most of the processes by which specific molecules are broken down into simpler

parts are inherently reversible. Organisms can break down hydrogen-rich organic molecules to obtain the energy stored in chemical bonds, but the reverse is also possible. Similar molecules can be built up in order to *store* energy in chemical bonds. The key to the synthesis of energy-rich molecules is the availability of some form of environmental energy. Various chemosynthetic bacteria (Chapter 4) were probably the first living things to evolve a way of building such food molecules. They would have used various inorganic chemicals dissolved in the sea as a source of energy for building new hydrogen-rich organic molecules. These bacteria were the first autotrophs ("self-feeders"). At some point, some of these autotrophs began to use light energy from the sun to assist in breaking down molecules such as hydrogen sulfide to release the hydrogen required to form new organic compounds. The by-products they left behind—such as the world's great sulfur deposits—attest to their evolutionary success. But even the supply of hydrogen sulfide was limited in that watery world. The dramatic turning point that made life a self-sustaining permanent part of the seas came when later autotrophic forms (which probably resembled modern blue-green algae) used light energy to induce the breakdown of *water* molecules as the source of needed hydrogen. Because of the virtually unlimited supply of sunlight and water, *this photosynthetic process based on the splitting of water molecules* was

Figure 9.3 Fossils of some of the earliest known organisms. (a) Fossil of a bacterialike organism that lived 3.1 billion years ago. This fossil was taken from the Figtree Formation in South Africa. (b) Fossilized bacteria found in sedimentary rock in Canada, dating about 2 billion years before the present. (c) A fossilized clump of algal cells dating from about 900 million years before the present. These fossils were taken from the Bitter Springs Formation of Central Australia. (d) Remarkable scanning electron micrographs of a sample of the Bitter Springs algae in the process of mitotic division. Two higher magnifications of one of the dividing algal cells are also shown here. (From the collection of J. W. Schopf).

(a)		
(b)	(c)	(d)

destined to play a dominant role in subsequent evolution, for the by-product released when water molecules are split is free oxygen.

The free oxygen released into the atmosphere began to build up with the passing of time, and new opportunities unfolded for the heterotrophs. The availability of free oxygen meant that there could be different, more efficient mechanisms for extracting energy from organic molecules (Chapter 14). The earth's store of carbon compounds could now be recycled rapidly and efficiently. The recycling foreshadowed an increase in the potential rate of evolutionary change. *Without question, the availability of high-energy molecules produced by the photosynthetic autotrophs and the more efficient mechanisms developed by heterotrophs for using those molecules accelerated the adaptive radiation of multicellular life forms.*

At some time between 1.5 and 1 billion years ago, the first single-celled eukaryotes emerged. Within the comparatively brief span of the next 400 million years, progeny of those single-celled organisms evolved in various ways to give rise to most of the animal phyla we see about us today (Chapter 7). Remains from the pre-Cambrian period suggest that several groups of invertebrates were already in existence by the end of the Proterozoic, but they were not highly diverse. However, during the transition to the Cambrian period, animal diversity underwent phenomenal accelera-

tion. What were the reasons for the rapid evolutionary change? As Chapter 7 indicated, the precise answers to this question may be permanently wrapped in mystery. But we have now identified certain changes in the geographic environment that undoubtedly have significant bearing on the question.

THE EARLY PALEOZOIC: THE OCEANS TEEM WITH LIFE

Recently we have become aware that the shapes and positions of the continents have not always been as they are today. Indeed, it is now clear that through pre-Cambrian times (up to about 640 million years ago), there was only one land mass on earth—a supercontinent now called **Pangaea** (*pan-* signifies "all"; *geo-* signifies "earth"). Compared with present-day continents, Pangaea did not have an extensive shoreline (Figure 9.4a). The fossil record implies that the shoreline has always been, as it is today, the most favorable part of the ocean for animal life. But the coastline of Pangaea was relatively small, and in comparison with coastal environments that exist today, the pre-Cambrian shoreline probably held few unique environments in which specialized life forms could evolve.

However, by the dawn of the Paleozoic era, some 600 million years ago, Pangaea had broken apart in response to movements of denser material beneath the earth's surface. Four irregularly shaped continents had formed, although they were still relatively close together. Undoubtedly the rifts between these new land masses created new patterns of tides, currents, offshore water temperatures, and so forth. The increase in the extent and diversity of continental shorelines offered a rich variety of shallow marine habitats, and it seems probable that they were rapidly filled by many as-yet unspecialized marine organisms. These organisms responded to the new environments by diversifying in a multitude of ways.

Another change that had occurred by the beginning of the Cambrian surely had equally profound consequences for the community of life. By then, oxygen and carbon dioxide had accumulated in the atmosphere, thereby creating the special physical conditions that enabled organisms to deposit minerals in the surface parts of their bodies. Animals began to form hard body parts—mineralized plates, spicules, spines, and shells. In the struggle between predator and prey, development of such defensive structures undoubtedly accelerated the diversification of animals. Prey developed new defenses, and predators evolved ways around these defenses and provided the selective pressure for still better mechanisms for defense. In short, *it was in the Cambrian, at the dawn of the Paleozoic, that a profusion of organisms with hard body parts began flourishing in the waters near the edge of the land.*

During the Cambrian, animals had evolved to the point

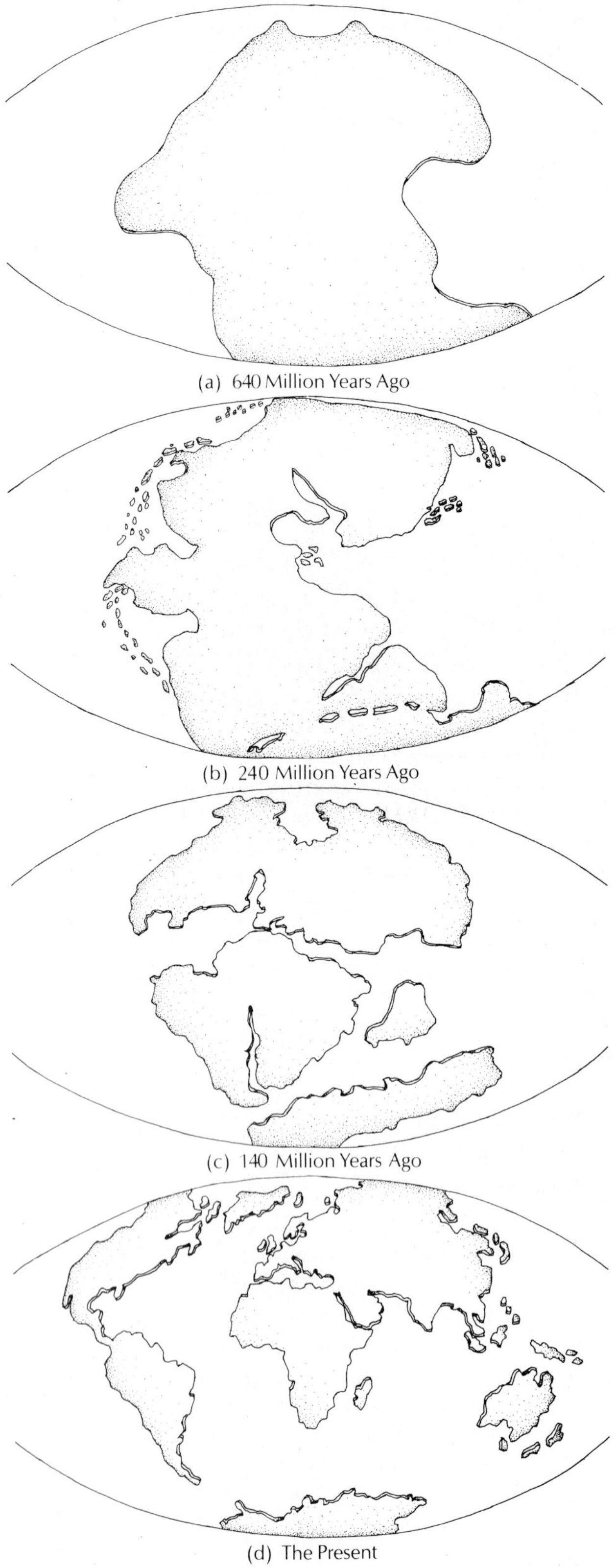

Figure 9.4 The inferred shape and distribution of continental land masses at different times in earth history. (a) The supercontinent Pangaea in the late pre-Cambrian. (b) The supercontinent of the late Permian, with its vast inland sea. (c) The land masses of the Jurassic. (d) The present configuration of continents. The recognition and documentation of this process of continental drift has provided new insight into patterns of evolution and diversification of plants and animals.

(a) 640 Million Years Ago

(b) 240 Million Years Ago

(c) 140 Million Years Ago

(d) The Present

that they employed virtually all the food-gathering strategies seen today among similar organisms. Many were plant feeders; others fed on animals that ate the plants. Some were active predators: either they concealed themselves to permit unwitting prey to come into range or they actively pursued their quarry. Still others were filter feeders, subsisting on microscopic life suspended in the water. Scavengers were also present, crawling along the bottom or burrowing in the mud in search of stray bits of organic material (Figure 9.5).

The sudden appearance of a fantastic variety of shells and other protective devices hints at intense competition. Development of mechanisms for protection, flight, concealment, offense, and defense is all to the same end: to avoid being eaten while at the same time being able to eat. Relatively efficient means of perception, such as well-developed eyes, had already evolved. The most complex organisms of the Cambrian were the trilobites, a now-extinct group of arthropods (Figure 9.5). The eye of the trilobites was essentially the same type of compound eye that would serve many of the arthropods so well throughout evolutionary history—so well, in fact, that the insects still have them.

Following the Cambrian were two periods in earth history that were witness to the rise of new groups of marine animals as well as to the diversification of others. The echinoderms first appeared during the Ordovician period, and primitive jawless fishes emerged during the Silurian (Figure 9.6). *It was from these jawless fishes that all the vertebrates ultimately would evolve.* Until the late Paleozoic, however, the radiation of life forms was confined largely to the waters of the earth. Aside from the sounds of wind and water, there was little to disturb the profound silence of the barren continents. But prokaryotic and eukaryotic algae were already clinging to moist rocks and soil surfaces, as were bacteria and perhaps some simple fungi. Along the beaches and in the mud flats of ancient seas, the burrowing worms and other invertebrates that crawled along the sea bottom were portents of life that would move onto the land.

Jellyfish Arrow Worm Sponges Glass Sponges Giant Trilobite Trilobite Snail Trilobite
Brachiopods

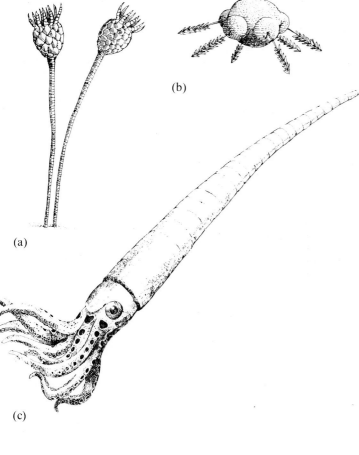

(b)

(a)

(c)

(d)

Figure 9.5 *(above) Reconstruction of a shallow-water marine community in Cambrian time. The invertebrates in such communities included sponges, jellyfishes, arrow worms, brachiopods, clams, and snails. The most complex animals were a group of arthropods called trilobites. The trilobites were predators and scavengers that crawled or burrowed along the sea bottom in search of food. They were also capable of swimming. Presumably, most algal phyla were well established by this time, with a varity of benthic and planktonic forms providing the basic energy source for the rest of the aquatic ecosystem.*

Figure 9.6 *(left) Examples of various animal groups that evolved during the Paleozoic. (a) A crinoid, or "sea lily," which is an echinoderm. The body of this filter feeder was covered by an exoskeleton made of conspicuous plates. (b) A colonial animal called a graptolite. The relationship of graptolites to other animal groups is unclear, but they became quite diverse during the Paleozoic. (c) A nautaloid cephalopod, represented in Ordovician time by a number of shelled forms. Although the first representatives of this group had straight, unornamented shells, the group would diversify tremendously into the Mesozoic, producing forms with highly ornamented and coiled shells of tremendous size. (d) An early jawless fish from the late Silurian period. The body of these fish was covered with a complex network of armored plates. A few isolated plates of this type have been found in Ordovician strata, but the first complete specimens documenting the appearance of such fish are from the Silurian.*

Nematophyton   Psilophyton   Scorpion   Millipede

Figure 9.7   An early Devonian landscape. Many of the land plants pictured here are psilopsids and ancestral sphenopsids. Arthropods (scorpions and millipedes) were the principal terrestrial animals.

THE LATE PALEOZOIC: PLANTS INVADE THE LAND

Even while invertebrates continued to diversify in the oceans, and even as the primitive jawless fishes gave way to more advanced forms, an extraordinarily rapid radiation of plants into the terrestrial environment was about to begin in the late Paleozoic. Transitional plant forms probably appeared in the late Silurian, but the first definitive remains of primitive land plants are found in rocks of Devonian age.

Figure 9.7 is a reconstruction of an early Devonian swamp. Although most of the plants were psilopsids, some may have been forerunners of the sphenopsids and lycopods (Chapter 5). There is little doubt that the earliest land plants were confined to coastal swamps and other wet regions, for their organization does not appear to have been efficient enough to allow completion of their life cycles under dry conditions. Much of the inland landscape was probably devoid of vegetation for this reason. The animals of these early communities were principally scorpions and

millipedes. *Extensive radiation of animals into the land would not occur until sufficient plant materials had evolved to support animal life.*

In less than 60 million years, toward the end of the Devonian, more complex land plants had evolved (Figure 9.8). Although the forests of the late Devonian may still have been confined to low-lying wet areas, they were quite diverse and definitely included representatives of the lycopods, sphenopsids, and ferns.

The first vertebrates to enter the late Devonian forests were fishlike amphibians such as *Ichthyostega*. (The Greek *ichthyo-* means "fish"; the Greek *stego-*, meaning "covering," is used to signify "bony plates.") These early amphibians must have been derived from the fresh-water crossopterygian ("fringed-winged") lungfishes that were abundant by then. Although Figure 9.8 depicts a wet landscape, there is indirect evidence that recurrent episodes of drought plagued the Devonian. If that is true, the lungfish in the fresh-water pools would have been under strong selective pressure as smaller pools periodically became stagnant and dried up. Any modifications of its simple bladderlike "lungs" that would enhance gas exchange would be a selective advantage in stagnant pools where low oxygen content was a recurring likelihood. And the unique

Pseudosporochnus   Lungfishes   Archaeosigillaria   Ichthyostega   Seed Fern

Figure 9.8   A late Devonian landscape showing the result of rapid evolutionary diversification from simpler land plants. Psilopsids, ferns, ancestral lycopods, and sphenopsids were present, as well as primitive conifers. Fishlike amphibians such as Ichthyostega *were the most advanced terrestrial vertebrates of the period.*

leglike fin structure of these fishes would allow some species to scramble short distances from pool to pool. Any improvements in mobility could mean the difference between survival and death. Furthermore, *compared with the fierce struggle for survival in the dwindling pools, the lack of competition on land would act as a potent selective agent for the continued evolution of amphibian types.*

The Carboniferous period followed the Devonian. Its vast coastal swamps (Figure 9.9) supported a tremendous number and variety of plants and animals. Gigantic ancestors of modern horsetails grew in great thickets; ferns ranged in size from towering trees to small herbaceous plants. Seed ferns and early conifers were also part of the forest canopy. And portions of the swamp forest sustained dense growths of young plants and trailing vines. The varied insects of the Carboniferous forests included cockroaches up to six inches or more in length and dragonflies with two-foot wingspans. The amphibians were probably confined to the wet swamps and swamp margins. But they had developed far beyond the small *Ichthyostega* of the late Devonian. The Carboniferous amphibians ranged in size from small lizardlike and froglike forms to comparative giants more than six feet long. The first reptiles were also part of the forest community.

The climate of this period has not been determined. It

may have been mild with little seasonal variation, for the trees did not produce growth rings as modern trees do when subjected to patterns of seasonal variation. The kinds of plants that grew in the low wet coastal plains are well documented, but very little can be said about the vegetation that may have been growing at higher elevations and on drier sites. *The fact that the gymnosperms were becoming well established in the Carboniferous period indicates that selection was favoring species with the ability to survive under drier conditions.*

In contrast to the fairly mild and uniform climatic conditions of the Carboniferous, the succeeding Permian period was one of extreme stress for marine as well as terrestrial communities. The continental masses, which had moved apart in the Cambrian, gradually began moving toward one another, so that by the Permian there was a supercontinent separated into two great lobes by an immense inland sea (Figure 9.4*b*). The concurrent reduction in marine habitat diversity had a profound effect on the invertebrates throughout the oceans. Many specialized types apparently became extinct; only the most generalized and versatile forms managed to survive.

The plants and animals on the continental masses did not fare much better. The almost world-wide occurrence of highly oxidized rocks in beds laid down in the Permian suggests a pattern of increasing aridity. Harsh environmental conditions drastically reduced diversity among the sphenopsids, the lycopods, and the ferns. The gymnosperms held the selective advantage, for their reproductive systems could better function under arid conditions.

The gradual desiccation had a catastrophic effect on amphibian populations: Only the best-adapted types managed to survive until the dawn of the Mesozoic. The ones that did survive carried with them a number of adaptations developed in response to increased predation, such as the presence of armor on their backs. The predators of the late Permian were almost certainly reptiles. Like the gymnosperms, the reptiles had made significant strides in adapting to drier environments. For example, they had developed a reproductive strategy that included internal fertilization and shelled eggs. They did not have to return to the water in order to breed, and as the gradual drying of the environment placed increasing stress on their amphibian competitors, the reptiles evolved rapidly. The first of the reptiles with certain mammalian skeletal features also appeared in Permian time. But it would be over 150 million years before their descendants would have any major impact on the living world. *As the Permian drew to a close, the harsh environmental conditions that had developed so abruptly had culled the plants and animals of the world's continents and had left the immediate future to two groups of organisms—the gymnosperms and the reptiles.* The ascendancy of these two groups would be one of the facts of life in the biological world for the next great era in earth history.

THE MESOZOIC: GYMNOSPERMS AND REPTILES DOMINATE THE LAND

The great inland sea that had formed two lobes in the Permian supercontinent elongated at the beginning of the Mesozoic, about 230 million years ago. The land mass split into **Gondwana,** a large southern continent, and **Laurasia,** another continent to the north. Diversity in marine habitats and therefore among marine invertebrates was still low in Triassic time. On the land, desert conditions persisted in many areas. Although there were a few lycopods, sphenopsids, pteridosperms, and ferns, the dominant plants were gymnosperms. Reptilian forms that were ancestral to modern lizards and turtles appeared in the Triassic, as did the first primitive **dinosaurs.** (The word "dinosaur" comes from the Greek words meaning "terrible lizard.") Two kinds of reptiles returned to the seas during this period (Figures 9.10 and 9.11).

The transition from the Triassic to the Jurassic period was marked by a change in the world's climate and topography. During the Jurassic, the northern continent that had been

Laurasia split into two continental masses that would become North America and Eurasia (Figure 9.4c). Although the two low-lying continental masses remained attached by a land bridge across the polar regions, the widening gap between them marked the genesis of the Atlantic Ocean. A great seaway covering much of the interior of the new North American continent would help ensure mild climatic conditions in the continental interior for the rest of the Mesozoic.

Figure 9.12 depicts a western North American landscape in the Jurassic. This was a world dominated by the dinosaurs, a diverse complex of reptiles that had evolved amazing strategies for survival. Consider the *Brontosaurus*, which was more than sixty-five feet long and weighed more than thirty tons. This reptile probably spent much of its time standing in water deep enough to support much of its weight. It had a long, sinuous neck and a small head within which was a brain of minute proportions. A close relative, *Brachiosaurus*, weighed about fifty tons and had a neck so long that the animal could have peered into a third-story window. Neither form of dinosaur had overt defenses; their amphibious existence probably was their major protection from predators.

It has been suggested that the long neck of these dinosaurs was an adaptation for life in deep water. But if you stop and think about it, the water pressure in deep bodies of water would defeat any attempt to use such a neck as a long breathing tube. Such basic physical limitations

Figure 9.10   An ichthyosaur, or "fish lizard," from the Jurassic. The close resemblance in form among the ichthyosaurs (reptiles), the sharks (fishes), and the porpoises (mammals) is an example of convergence, whereby a general similarity in form is achieved independently in different groups. Apparently the structural options are limited for animals functioning as large, free-swimming predators in the open ocean.

The ichthyosaurs were so well adapted to life in the ocean that they could not return to land in order to lay their eggs. The eggs were hatched internally in the body of the female, and the young were born alive. Unlike most live-born vertebrates, the young of the ichthyosaurs were apparently born tail first to minimize the possibility of drowning during birth. A similar pattern occurs in the modern whales and porpoises—still another example of convergence.

Figure 9.11   A plesiosaur ("near-lizard"), which, like the ichthyosaur, was a reptile that returned to the ocean. The body form of a typical plesiosaur has often been likened to what would result if you could thread a snake through the body of a turtle. The plesiosaurs were not as highly adapted to the marine environment as were the ichthyosaurs, and it is probable that they could struggle onto the land briefly in order to lay their eggs, much as marine turtles do today.

Figure 9.9   A reconstruction of a Carboniferous swamp forest. The tremendous numbers of plants in such forest communities resulted in the accumulation of vast quantities of partially decayed organic material, or peat. The ancient peat beds were later covered by other sediments. During the passage of millions of years, the heat and pressure of the overlying sediments gradually compressed the peat deposits and altered their chemical composition, transforming them into coal. The Carboniferous period was so named because of the immense coal beds that were laid down during this interval of earth history. Because North America and Europe were apparently connected as part of the same supercontinent, the swamps covering much of what is now western Europe and eastern North America bestowed particularly rich coal deposits upon those areas. The entire industrial revolution and much of our current economy has been based on the exploitation of these deposits.

Compsognathus   Allosaurus   Archaeopteryx   Stegosaurus   Rhamphorhynchus   Brontosaurus

have been overlooked in the many reconstructions showing *Brachiosaurus* strolling along in twenty or thirty feet of water. In all probability, the extension of the neck was a simple adaptation to allow these animals to feed while they stayed as far away as possible from the dangers on shore.

The dangers were very real. *Allosaurus,* one of the largest carnivores of the Jurassic, was as much as thirty-four feet long. In common with most predatory dinosaurs, it was bipedal—an adaptation that probably increased its chances of running down prey. *Allosaurus* appears to have been large and powerful enough to hunt even the largest herbivores.

What defense did foragers on land have against such predators? The herbivorous *Stegosaurus* was eighteen to twenty feet long. Its hind legs were considerably larger than its forelegs, and it probably could not run very fast. Apparently, *Stegosaurus* depended on a double row of erect bony plates along the spine to protect it from attack. The end of its tail was equipped with a number of long spikes which, when swung, may have discouraged attack from the rear. But *Stegosaurus*, with a brain smaller than a golf ball, was certainly not a bright creature even by dinosaur standards. It may have been vulnerable to as simple a strategy as being knocked over.

Some reptiles took to the air in the search for food or as a means to avoid becoming food. The small, batlike *Rhamphorhynchus* (Figure 9.12) was a member of a group of flying reptiles, the pterosaurs, that appeared in the Jurassic and evolved throughout the Mesozoic. A Jurassic fossil of *Archaeopteryx*, the first true bird, is shown in Figure 9.13. Also fighting for survival in the Jurassic environment were the first primitive mammals. These small, burrowing animals undoubtedly led a precarious existence. Although they were small enough to be ignored by the larger predatory dinosaurs, the mammals were probably of considerable dietary interest to the small agile dinosaurs such as *Compsognathus* (Figure 9.12).

At the onset of the Cretaceous, the modern bony fishes became a significant part of fresh-water and marine communities. The plesiosaurs were still present and fairly diverse, but the ichthyosaurs declined rapidly and became extinct before the close of this period. A group of predatory lizards, the mesosaurs, returned to the ocean and diversified rapidly. The first flowering plants appeared early in the Cretaceous and rapidly came to dominate the plant world. The gymnosperms were still present, but the overall landscape began to take on the appearance it would have in modern times (Figure 9.14).

The dinosaurs were still the masters of the land throughout the Cretaceous. (Mammals were also present, but they were little more than insignificant creatures scuttling through the underbrush.) Many of the largest dinosaurs (such as *Brontosaurus*) and the clumsiest (such as *Stegosaurus*) apparently had become extinct, but other major

Figure 9.12   A western North American landscape as it might have appeared in the Jurassic. The vegetation was generally similar to that of the Triassic, with large numbers of cycads, ginkgoes, and conifers. Among the new amphibian types to appear in the low-lying swamplands were the first true frogs. Familiar reptiles included lizards, turtles, and crocodiles. Ichthyosaurs and plesiosaurs continued to diversify in the marine environment, and dinosaurs dominated the land.

Keep in mind that if you were able to return to the Jurassic, you would not find these animals grouped in the manner shown here. Such peaceful associations of the hunters and the hunted do not occur today, and it is unlikely that the rules were greatly different in the Jurassic.

Figure 9.13   A fossil specimen of the first true bird—Archaeopteryx—which appeared during the Jurassic. Biologists have long suggested that birds were derived from reptiles, and Archaeopteryx is a convincing intermediate form: it has many features in common with both birds and reptiles. The legs, elongate tail, and jaws with teeth were reptilian, as were the scales that covered the legs and jaws. But most of the body was covered with feathers and the wings were moderately well developed.

lines continued to diversify. The bipedal carnivores characteristic of the Jurassic had evolved into fearsome animals by Cretaceous time (Figure 9.14). Nevertheless, as diverse and well adapted as the dinosaurs appeared to have been, every one of them became extinct at the close of the Cretaceous!

What caused this mass extinction? No one knows. Changes in climate or in vegetation, disease, predation on dinosaur eggs, and cosmic radiation have been suggested as the reason for their disappearance. The cosmic radiation hypothesis is the least tenable, for radiation levels high enough to sterilize such large animals certainly would have had a similar effect on the other reptiles, birds, and early mammals. Whatever the reasons, they must have had a fundamental effect on the ecosystems in which the animals lived in order to cause extinctions in so many diverse lines. For example, the changing nature of the vegetation in the late Cretaceous may have caused a drastic reduction in the number of herbivorous dinosaurs, particularly if those herbivores had developed an irreversible dependence on gymnosperms as a food source. A reduction in herbivore populations would result in a similar reduction in carnivore populations. Dinosaur populations, if reduced, would thus encounter greater stress from disease, egg predation, and shifts in climate. Any combination of these factors could have further reduced the populations to the point that normal breeding behavior in some species was inhibited. An extinction of one or more major herbivore species in any area would cause increased predation on remaining herbivores, resulting in still further extinctions.

Other major groups, such as the mesosaurs, plesiosaurs, and pterosaurs, also became extinct by the close of the Cretaceous. Whether the extinction mechanisms were related to those of the dinosaurs is not known. The major beneficiaries of these massive extinctions were the mammals of the late Mesozoic. The sudden vacating of innumerable niches at all levels in community structures provided the mammals with unparalleled opportunities for adaptive radiation. This sudden burst of evolutionary activity ushered in the beginning of the Age of Mammals.

THE CENOZOIC: THE DAWN OF THE FAMILIAR

During the Cretaceous period, the remains of the southern continent Gondwana separated into what would become Africa and South America; the widening gulf between these two land masses would become the South Atlantic Ocean. The great inland sea that extended across much of North America continued to lengthen, and in the late Cretaceous and the earliest epoch of the Cenozoic (the Paleocene), it essentially cut the continent in two. It was a shallow sea, and it had a moderating effect on the climate of the interior. Later in the Cenozoic the sea would gradually retreat and

Ginkgo   Dogwood   Live Oak

Ankylosaurus   Tyrannosaurus   Palmetto   Pteranodon   Magnolia   Triceratops   Fan Palms

there would be an overall cooling of the climate. But during the Paleocene and Eocene epochs, a rich mosaic of climates prevailed throughout North America and elsewhere in the world, offering essentially tropical conditions in the lowlands and quite cool conditions in mountain areas, particularly toward the north. *In combination with the extinction of the dinosaurs, the environmental diversity of the early Cenozoic triggered an explosive adaptive radiation of mammals.*

One of the major selective forces underlying mammalian diversification appears to have been the interaction between carnivores and herbivores. Any adaptation in a predator that would improve its ability to capture prey would exert a strong selective pressure for change on the prey. Any adaptation that would increase the ability of the prey to elude the predator would have a similar effect. Such predator-prey relationships served as an evolutionary prod in the Eocene. *But the significant difference from such episodes of evolutionary change was the extent to which development of the brain and learned behavior effected evolutionary change in the mammals.*

The herbivorous mammals of the succeeding Oligocene epoch were still largely forest browsers. Members of one group, the titanotheres, were eight feet tall at the shoulder. The tooth anatomy of these animals suggests they fed on soft, succulent vegetation. As the climate gradually

Figure 9.14 A reconstruction of a Cretaceous landscape in western North America. Plants were beginning to take on a modern appearance by this time, but dinosaurs still dominated the land. Crocodiles, lizards, and turtles were modern in appearance by the late Cretaceous, and the ancestors of snakes were already present. The rapidly evolving birds were generally quite modern, except that they still retained a full battery of teeth. The flying lizards had also diversified and the largest member of the group, Pteranodon, *had a wingspan that exceeded twenty-seven feet, although its body was not much larger than that of a chicken.*

Tyrannosaurus *undoubtedly was one of the world's most fearsome carnivores. It reached lengths of forty-seven feet and heights of nineteen feet, and its muscles and bones suggest a high degree of activity. Its jaws were lined with daggerlike, serrated teeth that ranged from six to twelve inches in length. The objects of this ferocious array undoubtedly were the many herbivorous dinosaurs that were the contemporaries of* Tyrannosaurus. *Some, like* Ankylosaurus, *were so heavily armored they resembled walking tanks. Others, such as* Triceratops, *had bony frills protecting their vulnerable neck. Unlike most dinosaurs,* Triceratops *and its kin may have remained near their eggs, and young animals may have been incorporated into existing herds. A group of adult* Triceratops *in a defensive circle about their young was probably sufficient to deter even* Tyrannosaurus.

changed during the Cenozoic, the kind of plants they must have depended upon became more limited; the entire group became extinct by the close of the Oligocene.

The Miocene epoch was a significant time in the development of plant and animal communities. Decreasing temperatures and increasing aridity were affecting plants and animals throughout most of western North America. (Similar events were occurring in other areas as well.) The inland sea had retreated entirely from the interior by the middle of the Miocene, and the lowering of the temperature brought about the extinction of subtropical vegetation in virtually the entire western part of the continent. Parallel to the western coastline, the Sierra Nevada mountain range was being formed. The mountain barrier was creating a "rain shadow," in that winds from the Pacific lost much of their moisture on the windward side of the mountains. The effect was a marked drop in rainfall in the interior. As rainfall decreased, the diverse temperate woodlands that had covered much of the Pacific Northwest began to become discontinuous, and many of the species they had supported became extinct. Gradually the first true grasslands formed (Figure 9.16), and by the early Pliocene virtually all of the major grasslands of the world were established. In other areas such as the southwestern United States and Mexico, the diminishing rainfall placed even more severe stress on plants and animals, and subsequent adaptations led to the first "modern" desert communities.

The restriction of forests and the spread of grasslands placed tremendous pressure on the Miocene mammals. Many of the forest browsers dwindled in numbers or disappeared entirely, and new groups appeared. The modifications required for success in the new habitat were profound. For example, unlike the tender leaves of forest species, grasses are relatively fibrous and they accumulate silica. As a result, herbivores had to develop new kinds of teeth in order to exploit the resources of the new environment. Vulnerability to predators in open country called for changes in behavior patterns (such as the formation of social organizations) and for physiological adaptations for increased speed, or concealment, or other forms of defense.

The beginning of the Pleistocene epoch marked the onset of the Ice Ages—an entirely new kind of selective pressure to which the world's plants and animals are still responding. For most of geologic time, it appears that the earth did not have polar ice caps. Although evidence suggests that some glacial activity occurred in earlier periods (for example, in the Southern Hemisphere during the Permian), the appearance of vast polar caps and continental ice sheets 3 million years ago was most unusual. What caused the profound change in environmental conditions is not known, but its effects are easy to assess. At least four times during the Pleistocene, great continental glaciers spread over much

(text continues on page 193)

Figure 9.15   A reconstruction of an Eocene landscape in western North America. The vegetation consisted of tropical or subtropical species, dominated by flowering plants. Uintatherium, a herbivore about the size of a modern rhinoceros, was the largest of the mammals. The ancestor of the modern horse was present in the Eocene; it was about the size of a large cat. A number of interesting birds lived in the Eocene forests. Diatryma, a stout, flightless bird, stood about seven feet tall. The nature of its beak implies that it was an active predator, perhaps feeding on small mammals. The existence of such predators suggests that birds as well as mammals were responding to the ecological vaccuum created by the extinction of the dinosaurs. Had birds such as Diatryma been more flexible in their behavior patterns and somewhat more rapid in their reproductive rates, it is possible that the "Age of Mammals" would have been postponed almost indefinitely in deference to an "Age of Birds."

Diceratherium

Figure 9.16   A reconstruction of a Miocene landscape in western North America. A significant development in this epoch was the emergence of grasslands. The development and spread of grasslands and even drier community types apparently was a response to a decrease in rainfall, caused by the formation of the Sierra Nevada mountain barrier along the west coast of the continent. The presence of grasslands was a significant force in the evolution of grazing animals such as the horse, the bison, the camel, and various antelopes. Later descendants of the early horses (Merychippus) and camels (Procamelus) would cross the Bering land bridge into Asia, where they would become ancestors of domesticated forms. Both horses and camels would become extinct in North America, the continent where they originated, before Homo sapiens would return with them from the Old World.

Tritemnodon   Diatryma   Eobasileus   Uintatherium

Syndyoceras

Moropus   Dinohyus   Herd of Merychippus   Procamelus   Alticamelus   Gomphoterium

Mastodon

Musk Ox

Woolly Mammoth

Saber-Toothed Tiger

Bison

of the Northern Hemisphere. (The European record indicates five glacial episodes, but the first was comparatively mild and may not have left a record in North America.) Each advance of the ice sheets had the effect of pushing various plant and animal communities southward; with each retreat of the ice, the communities migrated northward again. During the peak of each glacial advance, tremendous volumes of water were locked in the form of ice, which lowered the sea level throughout the world by more than 400 feet! Moreover, the accumulation of so much of the world's water in the form of ice caused periodic droughts far to the south. The droughts on the African plains may have been a factor in the development of a group of manlike animals that were the forerunners of *Homo sapiens*. The evolutionary story of *Homo sapiens* is treated separately in Chapter 33.

Figure 9.17 depicts some of the species of plants and animals that lived along a glacial boundary in western North America during the last major ice advance, which ended about 18,000 years ago. Most of the animals shown would soon become extinct. The time of this wave of extinction coincides with the entry of modern man into North America, which has given rise to some speculation that the human predator, to which the animals were not adapted, may have played a direct role in this mass disappearance. Certainly the human beings of the late Pleistocene were predators of the first rank. For example, alongside a hunting settlement in Czechoslovakia is a ravine filled with the carcasses of a hundred mammoths; in Solutré in central France is a mound of carcasses of thousands of horses that had been stampeded over a cliff. Whatever the extinction mechanism, many of the large mammals characteristic of the late Pleistocene had disappeared by about 9,000 years ago.

Although the "Recent" epoch is usually separated from the Pleistocene in geologic time scales, there is little basis for doing so. Each glacial advance was followed by a period of glacial retreat, in which the climate was often warmer than it is today. *There is no compelling reason to believe that the present climate is anything more than a part of another interglacial period between major ice advances.* So little time has passed since the ice began its last retreat that many plants and animals are still adjusting to the changing

Figure 9.17 A reconstruction of the landscape along the glacial boundary during the last major ice advance in western North America in the late Pleistocene. This particular glaciation began about 25,000 years ago and reached its maximum spread about 18,000 years ago. The vegetation consisted primarily of spruce, fir, aspen, and various grasses and sedges. The elephantlike mammoths and mastodons, the giant bison, the musk ox, and the saber-toothed tiger flourished during this epoch.

conditions. Quite aside from the many other biological implications of the Pleistocene, the role of its ice advances must be considered a prime factor in shaping the development of our own species.

PERSPECTIVE

As you read this brief history of life on our planet, you came across example after example of one group of organisms becoming dominant for a time, only to give way to another under changing environmental conditions. In the progression of terrestrial plants and animals, the first vertebrates were the amphibians. They flourished and diversified, only to be replaced as the dominant group by the reptiles, which in turn were replaced by the mammals. A similar progression can be seen in the progressive dominance of the psilopsid plants in the early Paleozoic, the sphenopsids, lycopods, and ferns in the late Paleozoic, the gymnosperms in the Mesozoic, and eventually the flowering plants from the Cenozoic to the present. But the replacements have not necessarily been the result of an immediate triumph of "advanced" organisms over "primitive" types. Both the reptiles and the gymnosperms appeared as early as the Carboniferous; yet they did not rise to a position of dominance until some time in the Permian. If gymnosperms and reptiles were clearly more "fit" than their fern and amphibian contemporaries, why was there a lag of almost 50 million years between their initial appearance and the beginning of their rapid diversification?

Although we may speak in generalities about the relative effects of selection on reptiles as opposed to amphibians, the fact is that selection operates on individual organisms, some of which happen to be reptiles and some of which happen to be amphibians. The reptiles first appeared in the swampy forests of the Carboniferous, which were populated with a diverse array of amphibians. The amphibians of the time required free water in which to breed, and if they were anything like the modern amphibians, they probably required moist skins in order to respire effectively. The early reptiles had developed mechanisms of internal fertilization, eggs with shells, and efficient respiratory systems, and they would appear to have had clear adaptive advantage over their amphibian contemporaries. Why, then, was there a delay in their diversification? The controlling factors were probably twofold. First, although the reproductive efficiency and independence from water are obvious advantages under dry conditions, are they superior when conditions are not dry? Does a frog in a swamp reproduce any less effectively than a lizard under the same set of conditions? The reptiles would have the advantage in a desert, but the Carboniferous was not a world of deserts. Given the widespread swampy conditions of the time, any

advantage the reptiles might have had over the amphibians would be slight indeed—if in fact they had any advantage at all. The second factor was the extent to which amphibians were well adapted to the available niches. Natural selection had been carefully tailoring various amphibians for their respective positions in the environment for more than a hundred million years. Without a great reproductive differential, and with most of the available niches already filled, diversification among the early reptiles would be a slow process indeed. Their rise to dominance, when it finally did occur, was not triggered by any innate superiority of the reptiles but rather was brought about by a change in the environment that was disadvantageous to the existing forms of amphibians. The desiccation of the Permian swamps restricted the distribution of many amphibians and opened many previously "closed" niches. Under the new, drier conditions, the reptiles had an overall advantage and rapidly began to diversify. The fact that some amphibians still occupy certain niches indicates that as long as environmental conditions have not placed them at a reproductive disadvantage, they have been able to retain a competitive position in some environments. Analogous models can be made to explain the relative success of reptiles and mammals in the Mesozoic and the Cenozoic.

New variants of existing life forms have always faced one of two situations: unexploited niches or niches that are already occupied by specialized organisms. In the first case, diversification can proceed rapidly. There are two possibilities associated with the second case. The more common situation exists when the adaptive features of the new, unspecialized organisms are not sufficient to outweigh the complex of specialized adaptations that "fit" the older group to the niches they occupy. Diversification of the unspecialized group is likely to be delayed until environmental conditions shift sufficiently to empty some of the niches. In the less common situation, a new group of organisms is overwhelmingly successful and manages to displace even well-established forms. The rapid diversification of the flowering plants appears to represent a situation of this type. It may have been caused in part by the nature of the coevolutionary relationships between the plants and their pollinating vectors—particularly animals. The incredible adaptability conferred by such coevolutionary relationships provided flowering plants with a wide range of adaptive possibilities early in their history, and diversification proceeded despite continuous competition from established conifers.

From the inception of life, organisms have been both sustained and limited by the capabilities of other organisms in the biosphere. As we examine biological history, we come to the realization that the nature of the life process to a large extent predefines the possible patterns of interaction among living things. Since the first appearance of self-replicating systems in the primordial sea, the gradual action of natural selection has brought about the movement of life into many new environments. But the essential nature of the relationships among life forms has not changed. We see new patterns of diversity arising with the passage of time, but the nature of the evolutionary process is such that a group of specialized and well-adapted organisms is not replaced by a new group because of any single factor—or even a complex of factors—in which the new group might be "superior" to the old. The conservative aspect of the diversification process may in fact be the reason why evolution appears to be revolutionary! It may well be that exploitation of new environments by an evolving group of organisms is often "easier" than the displacement of "less advanced" forms that are highly adapted to niches in the original environments. The result of such processes has been a gradual as well as a progressive increase in diversity throughout the living world.

As we look at the tremendous range of diversity in the living world and observe the intricate ways in which organisms interact, there is a natural tendency to think of the present as the culmination of the earth's long evolutionary history. But if one point is clear from this chapter, it is that there is a inevitability to change. There is no reason to think that the earth and its life forms have now ceased to change. Just how things will change is uncertain— how soon, how fast, or in what direction. Only one thing is certain: change they must, and change they will.

SUGGESTED READINGS

ANDREWS, H. N. *Ancient Plants and the World They Lived In.* Ithaca, N.Y.: Comstock, 1947. A readable and well-illustrated account of plant life through the ages.

DE CAMP, L. SPRAGUE, and CATHERINE C. DE CAMP. *The Day of the Dinosaur.* Garden City, N.Y.: Doubleday, 1968. A history of the dinosaurs, with emphasis on the trials, triumphs, and disputes of the men who hunt them.

KURTEN, BJORN. *The Age of Mammals.* New York: Columbia University Press, 1972. A thorough but nontechnical survey of the development of mammals. Nicely illustrated with line drawings and paintings of reconstructions rather than of skeletons.

LEY, WILLY. *Dragons in Amber.* New York: Viking, 1951. An entertaining description of a number of ancient plants and animals.

MARQUAND, JOSEPHINE. *Life: Its Nature, Origins, and Distribution.* New York: Norton, 1971. A provocative little book devoted to the problems involved in delineating life from nonlife and in determining the origins of life.

VALENTINE, JAMES W., and ELDRIDGE M. MOORES. "Plate Tectonics and the History of Life in the Oceans," *Scientific American,* 230 (April 1974), 80–89. An article in the influence of continental drift on invertebrate diversity throughout earth history.

Section III
The Unity of Life

If the borderline between nonlife and life was crossed only once, and if all organisms have inherited the properties of life in an unbroken line from that moment in time, might we not expect to see reflections of this common heritage in their basic organization? In fact, underlying the staggering diversity and complexity of whole organisms is a unity and simplicity at the molecular and cellular levels. Here, we see a basic similarity in the way *all* living things are put together, in the matter composing them, in their basic needs for life-sustaining matter and energy, and in the ways in which they meet those needs. But molecules and cells seem so remote from our everyday experience that their study is often approached with trepidation—sometimes with the feeling that atomistic dissection somehow detracts from the inherent poetry of life. But it is in molecules and cells that we find the beginnings of the answer to how life arose from lifeless matter—and how it sustains itself by tapping into the immense flow of universal energy.

Chapter 10

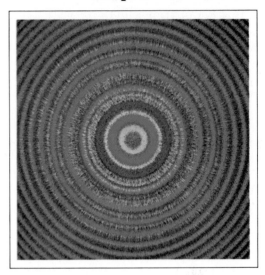

The Organization of Matter

From the organizational whole of the biosphere, to communities and populations, to individual organisms, down through cells to the molecules and the atoms that compose them—do we in reaching the atomic level arrive at last at the wellspring for all the diverse properties of life? In fact the hierarchy of organization begins at an even more fundamental level—in the world of elementary particles.

In 1772 a young Frenchman by the name of Antoine Lavoisier performed a simple experiment that turned out to be a first step toward revolutionizing our ideas concerning the nature of the universe. Lavoisier weighed a substance, burned it, and weighed the products. Surprisingly, the products weighed more than the starting substance. He repeated the experiment with a second substance and obtained a similar result. Thus he toppled a paradigm that had dominated chemistry for more than a century. According to this paradigm, when a substance burns it loses the mysterious substance "phlogiston"— which no chemist had ever isolated but every chemist believed in. This, said Lavoisier, is not the case. When a substance burns it combines with something in the air. Two years later, when an English chemist named Joseph Priestley isolated a pure substance he called "dephlogisticated air," Lavoisier correctly realized this was the substance with which other substances combine when they burn. He renamed it "oxygen" (meaning "acid former").

A hundred years earlier Robert Boyle had questioned the long-standing paradigm that only four "elements" (earth, air, fire, and water) make up the physical universe. He suggested instead that there must be *many* materials that cannot be broken down into simpler substances and, thus, should be considered elements. But it was through Antoine Lavoisier's work that Boyle's idea came to have widespread acceptance. When Lavoisier published the first truly modern chemistry textbook in 1789, he listed many substances in addition to oxygen, thirty-two of which we still agree cannot be broken down into simpler substances and therefore must be elements. His book had sweeping impact and eventually he became known as the "father of modern chemistry."

Lavoisier's work did not stop there. He went on to perform studies of profound significance for the field of biology. He first showed that living things are composed of the same elements found in the nonliving. He demonstrated that carbon, oxygen, hydrogen, and nitrogen are the principal elements of living things, and he correctly measured the proportions of these elements in what we now call sugars, proteins, and fats. He then went on to perform the most amazing experiment of all. In studying the "burning" of sugar by an animal, he found that the animal not only produced the same substances in the same amounts, it produced the same quantity of heat as when that much sugar was burned in the laboratory. From this observation, he drew a fundamentally important principle: *Living things obey the same chemical laws and perform chemical reactions that are basically the same as reactions that occur in the nonliving world.*

Letters and papers found after Lavoisier's untimely death in 1794 (Figure 10.2) indicated he had just begun this revolutionary line of biological inquiry. Although he was clearly ahead of his time, and although some of the experiments he was conducting at the time of his death would not be attempted again for decades, the die was cast. Slowly at first, and then with ever-increasing speed, biologists began to recognize not only the basic validity but also the basic utility of Lavoisier's approach to life. One after another intriguing biological question has been answered by the quantitative, analytical approach of chemistry. In fact, this work has now progressed so far that an attempt to understand and appreciate modern biology without knowing chemistry can be likened to an attempt to appreciate Göethe without knowing German. It is possible to read a translation and get the general thrust of the original work, but in-

Figure 10.2 Antoine Lavoisier being denounced in his laboratory by French revolutionists during the Reign of Terror. Lavoisier was tried, convicted, and guillotined, all within a single day. It has been said that a fervent plea for the life of this great scientist was answered by the exclamation La Republique n'a pas besoin de savants! *("The Republic has no need for scholars!") The following day his fellow countryman Joseph Lagrange remarked, "It required only a moment to sever that head and perhaps a century will not be sufficient to produce another like it."*

variably most of the stirring poetry is gone. It is at the chemical level that the most profound beauty and fundamental unity of life may be perceived.

But even setting aside the "poetry" of life, there are difficult, practical questions of daily life and public policy that increasingly cannot be answered without an understanding of chemistry. Is "the Pill" safe? Given the urgent need to produce high-yield crops for our burgeoning human population, which crop-protecting pesticides can be used without inviting ecological disaster? Can farming and industrial practices be modified to slow the pollution of streams, rivers, lakes, and oceans? Can cancer be cured with an outpouring of public taxes? Answers to such questions require either a knowledge of chemistry or acceptance of someone else's answers—without the ability to evaluate whether those answers are valid or not.

For both of the reasons just given, chemistry is an integral part of any study of the biological sciences. Should you be unfamiliar with the subject, this chapter may help you gain insight into what is now known about the chemical organization of matter.

ELEMENTS DIFFER FROM ONE ANOTHER BECAUSE THEY DIFFER IN ATOMIC STRUCTURE

Boyle's definition of an **element** is still valid: *An element is a substance that cannot be broken down into simpler substances by any known chemical reactions.* Today we recognize 92 naturally occurring elements and 13 more that nuclear chemists have synthesized in miniscule amounts. We still agree with Lavoisier's original observation that living matter is composed mainly of four elements: carbon, hydrogen, oxygen, and nitrogen. We have since learned that, in addition, substantial amounts of phosphorus, sulfur, potassium, sodium, calcium, magnesium, and iron are also found in most living things, as are trace amounts of about ten other elements (Table 10.1).

Why is it that elements cannot be broken down into simpler elements? As John Dalton deduced in 1803, an element is made up of indivisible particles called **atoms,** and *only one kind of atom is present in an element.* (Today we know that atoms can be split in extremely high-energy nuclear reactions, but in terms of all ordinary chemical reactions, Dalton's definition still holds.) In Dalton's time, atoms were thought of as solid little particles, perhaps not too different from tiny billiard balls (Figure 10.3*a*). Later, Joseph Thomson found that negatively charged particles could be removed from atoms, leaving positively charged particles behind. Perhaps, Thomson suggested, an atom was rather like a plum pudding, with negatively charged particles embedded in it like raisins which could be readily plucked out (Figure 10.3*b*). Because these negatively charged particles were already known to be carriers of

Table 10.1
Elements Found in Most Living Things

Element	Symbol
Present in large amounts:	
*Carbon	C
*Hydrogen	H
*Nitrogen	N
*Oxygen	O
Present in smaller amounts:	
Calcium	Ca
Chlorine	Cl
Iron	Fe
Magnesium	Mg
*Phosphorus	P
Potassium	K
Sodium	Na
*Sulfur	S
Present in trace amounts:	
Boron	B
Cobalt	Co
Copper	Cu
Fluorine	F
Iodine	I
Manganese	Mn
Molybdenum	Mo
Selenium	Se
Zinc	Zn

*Basic elements in the large, complex molecules of life. Hydrogen and oxygen are most abundant because all living organisms are composed primarily of water.

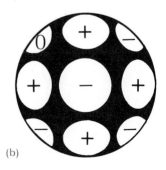

(a)

(b)

electric current, they were named **electrons,** but it was Thomson who actually demonstrated their existence as a normal constituent of atoms.

Then, in 1909, Ernest Rutherford and his colleagues aimed the high-energy particles emitted spontaneously by radioactive radium at a sheet of gold—and found that most of the particles passed through the gold as if nothing were there. But in a second experiment they determined that an even more amazing thing was happening. A few of the particles were deflected at various angles, and some even bounced straight back as if they had hit a solid, immovable object! Rutherford was "as surprised as you would have been if you had shot a 15-inch shell at a piece of tissue paper and it came back and hit you." The conclusion from this experiment was inescapable. Most of the "solid sheet" of gold atoms was "empty" space; thus most of the particles passed right through it. In addition, each gold atom must contain a very dense, solid core, or **nucleus,** where most of the mass of the atom is located. The particles that had bounced back were the ones that had encountered these nuclei. Thus the concept of the **nuclear atom** emerged: *An atom contains a dense nucleus surrounded by a relatively vast space through which electrons move.* Rutherford's measurements permit us to estimate that if a single atom were enlarged to the size of the largest football stadium, the nucleus would be like a marble suspended above the 50-yard line. And the electrons would resemble tiny flies zipping about, spending most of their time inside the stadium but occasionally making brief excursions to the outside.

Later it became clear that the nucleus itself acts as if it were composed or two primary particles: **neutrons** and **protons.** The neutrons are, as the name suggests, neutral in charge. But each proton has one unit of positive charge. *The number of protons in an element determines what its chemical properties will be.* The reason is that opposite charges attract each other. Each unit of positive charge $(+1)$ is capable of attracting one unit of negative charge (-1); in other words, one electron. This means that the number of positively charged protons in a nucleus dictates how many negatively charged electrons must be present about the nucleus in order to produce an electrically neutral atom. As you will read shortly, the number of protons also determines, indirectly, how those electrons will be distributed in space. *Because electrons are the parts of atoms that participate in chemical reactions, it is the electron distribution that determines what kinds of chemical reactions an element will engage in.*

HOW ARE ELECTRONS ARRANGED IN AN ATOM?

When the model of a nuclear atom was first proposed, there was speculation that the electrons might orbit the nucleus, much like planets orbit the sun (Figure 10.3c). Although this picture still appeals to science fiction illustrators and

(c)

Figure 10.3 Attempts to portray the nature of atoms. (a) The "billiard ball" atom of the nineteenth century. (b) Thomson's "plum pudding" atom. (c) Rutherford's nuclear atom with "planetary" electrons.

some power companies, physicists and chemists discarded it more than sixty years ago. It is not a good representation of electrons in atoms, any more than billiard balls and plum puddings are good representations.

But now that we have thrown out all the simple analogies, we are currently left with a model of an atom that bears no resemblance to familiar objects. Chemists are reasonably satisfied with it because it fits all their observations and permits them to predict chemical reactions. But the model is difficult to think about in nonmathematical terms. The problem is that, like light, *electrons seem to act as if they were particles of electric energy and, simultaneously, as if they were waves of electric energy.* Electrons resemble waves in the way they vibrate about the nucleus. But each atom is also known to have discrete numbers of electrons, and each electron is known to have discrete mass and charge. The mathematical equations describing an atom (called "wave equations" or "quantum equations") involve advanced calculus and will not be developed here, but their meaning will be summarized in the following paragraphs.

The electrons of an atom are neither rigidly positioned nor wandering about randomly with respect to the nucleus; there is always a greater probability of an electron being in certain places than in others. The word "probability" is crucial, for it tells us that the atom is currently viewed as a statistical entity. Figure 10.4 is a plot, derived from the wave equations, that shows how the probable locations of the single electron of an isolated hydrogen atom are distributed in the volume of space surrounding the nucleus. As the stippling indicates, the probability of finding the electron is highest in the area closest to the nucleus; the probability falls off with distance from the nucleus. Although there is no precise boundary beyond which the electron will never be found, a volume can be identified within which the electron will be found 90 percent of the time. Such a volume is called an **orbital** (Figure 10.4). An orbital is purely statistical in nature; that is why it is different from a planetary orbit. Because in this case the probabilities fall off equally in all directions, the shape of this orbital is spherical.

Although there are atoms with as many as 105 electrons, *there can never be more than two electrons in any orbital.* Therefore, if more than two electrons are present in an atom, they must be in orbitals other than the one shown for hydrogen in Figure 10.4.

Because there can be no more than two electrons in a given orbital, atoms with more than two electrons have a problem of "fit." The reason is that *orbitals must be separated in space as much as possible to minimize the mutual repulsion between electrons, and yet none of them can be too far from the attractive electric force of the*

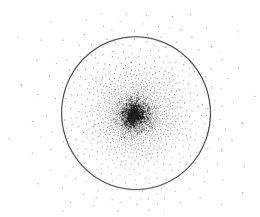

Figure 10.4   A cross section of probability distribution for the single electron of a hydrogen atom. This plot resembles what we might obtain if it were possible to take a slice through a hydrogen atom and then photograph it with a high-speed stroboscopic light flashing. With each flash, the electron would be recorded as a point. The sum of these points would be a picture like this, which would then form a sort of map showing the probability of finding the electron in some specific volume of space at various distances from the nucleus. The probability is highest near the nucleus and falls off progressively with distance from the nucleus. There is also a small probability of finding the electron at a very great distance from the nucleus, which is to say that the atom has no definite boundary. The circle drawn in this sketch indicates the volume within which the electron can be expected to be found about 90 percent of the time. Such a volume is known as the electron orbital.

All such structures may be thought of as electron charge "clouds" surrounding the nucleus. But it is important to keep in mind that in this analogy the "cloud" represents possible electron positions—not individual electrons. In more complex atoms, the orbital of electrons in the lowest energy level resembles the orbital of the hydrogen atom depicted here.

nucleus. (If they were, they would no longer be part of the atom.) The solutions to this problem are intricate indeed. Some orbitals are spherical; they are the *s* **orbitals** (Figure 10.5). More than one spherical orbital can exist in an atom, and when they do, they overlap. All the electronic orbitals of an atom overlap to a greater or lesser extent, which in effect is a compromise between the two opposing forces of repulsion among electrons and attraction of electrons toward the nucleus. There are also dumbbell-shaped *p* **orbitals** and an assortment of other kinds (Figure 10.5).

Orbitals represent distinct energy states in which electrons can exist as part of an atom. Electrons that are in orbitals close to the nucleus or of simple shape have lower

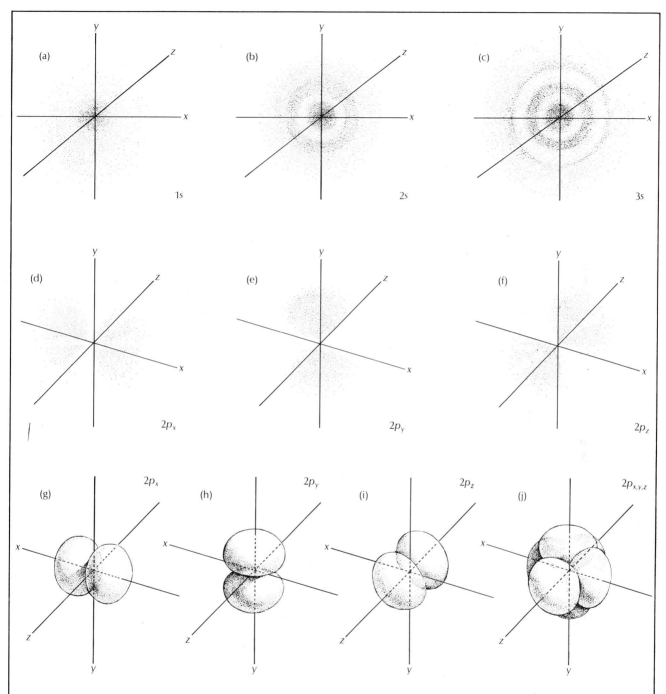

Figure 10.5   The distribution of probable locations of electrons in some of the orbitals found in biologically important atoms. The stippled figures (a–f) are similar to the one in Figure 10.4. Notice that in the 1s, 2s, and 3s orbitals (a–c), the distribution of probabilities is spherically symmetrical; in other words, lines drawn to represent the volume in which an electron spends 90 percent of its time would describe a sphere. But notice also that the organization of probabilities within the sphere becomes more complex with increasing energy levels.

The p orbitals (d–j) are not spherically symmetrical. In a p orbital, the probability of finding an electron is greatest along one of the three coordinates of space (the x, y, or z coordinates). Figures (g) through (i) show the 90 percent probability profiles of these orbitals in perspective. The three 2p orbitals are shown together in (j).

Although much more complex orbitals exist, the majority of biological reactions involve electrons in the orbitals shown here.

energy than electrons in orbitals farther away from the nucleus or of complex shape. Orbitals occur in groups having nearly the same energy. Such a group of orbitals is said to be in the same **energy level.** The number of orbitals that can occur in a given energy level is n^2, where n is the number assigned to that energy level. (The lowest energy level is number 1, the next is 2, and so on.) Thus the lowest energy level has 1^2, or one orbital (shown in Figure 10.4). Because each orbital can contain no more than two electrons, it follows that the lowest energy level can hold no more than two electrons. The second energy level may contain 2^2, or four orbitals (thus, eight electrons).

Each orbital is assigned a number that identifies the energy level to which it belongs, a letter that indicates its shape, and a subscript that indicates its orientation in space if it is not spherically symmetrical. Thus the four orbitals of the second energy level are called the $2s$, $2p_x$, $2p_y$, and $2p_z$ orbitals (Figure 10.5). The third energy level contains 3^2, or nine orbitals: one $3s$, three $3p$ (similar to, but more complex than the $2p$ orbitals) and five $3d$ orbitals (still more complex in shape). As we go to larger and larger atoms we find orbitals of more and more complex shape. (Fortunately, few of the reactions of living things involve electrons beyond the $3p$ level.) Figure 10.6 summarizes these relationships.

Unless an atom is perturbed by some outside source of energy, all of its electrons will tend to go to the lowest possible energy level. When this condition exists, the atom is said to be in the **ground state.** But if energy is supplied in the right form (light of particular wavelength, heat, electricity, and so on) electrons may absorb this energy by temporarily jumping up to a higher energy orbital. When they do, the atom is said to be in an **excited state.** *Atoms in an excited state tend to undergo reaction more readily than those in the ground state.* Because each orbital represents a discrete energy state, and because electrons can jump only from one orbital to another—no intermediate states are possible—atoms absorb energy only in discrete packets, or *quanta* (singular: quantum). If such an excited electron falls back to its ground state, it also emits energy in a discrete quantum. (This is why the study of these processes is called quantum mechanics and the equations describing electron behavior are sometimes known as quantum equations.)

HOW ARE ELECTRON CONFIGURATIONS RELATED TO CHEMICAL REACTIVITY?

There are few free atoms in nature. Most are combined with other atoms into larger units called **molecules.** For example, two oxygen atoms may combine to form molecular

(a)

Energy Level (n)	Number of Orbitals (n^2)	Maximum Number of Electrons ($2n^2$)	Types of Orbitals And Number of Each Type
1	1	2	$s(1)$
2	4	8	$s(1), p(3)$
3	9	18	$s(1), p(3), d(5)$
4	16	32	$s(1), p(3), d(5), f(7)$
5	25	50	$s(1), p(3), d(5), f(7), g(9)$
6	36	72	$s(1), p(3), d(5), f(7), g(9)^*$

*The sixth energy level (and higher energy levels) are known only in excited-state atoms. Although other kinds of orbitals are theoretically possible in the sixth energy level, they are not yet characterized.

(b)

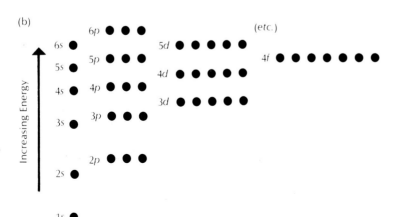

Figure 10.6 *The possible energy levels and orbitals within which the electrons of an atom may be found. In (a), a table is given of possible orbitals. Also shown is a schematic diagram (b) of relative energy of electrons in the various energy levels and types of orbitals. It is possible to draw a rather qualitative picture such as this of how the various energy levels and orbitals are related to one another, but it is not possible to make the picture exact and quantitative. The reason is that the energy of an electron in any particular orbital is influenced by all the other electrons present in the atom. Therefore, the absolute values of these energy levels are different for each element.*

oxygen, which is the form in which oxygen usually occurs in the air we breathe. But two or more *different* kinds of atoms may also join together into a molecule. Then an entirely new and different substance—a **compound**—is formed. For example, one atom of carbon joined with two atoms of oxygen forms the compound called carbon dioxide. (A substance composed of more than one kind of molecule is simply called a mixture.)

Before analyzing the basis for reactions between atoms, we need to consider briefly the shorthand notation used to symbolize atoms and molecules.

Each element (kind of atom) has been given a chemical symbol, which is an abbreviated version of its full name. You saw some of those symbols earlier, in Table 10.1. Depending on the context, the symbol can mean one of two things: it can represent either a single atom or all atoms of that element. For example, the symbol O by itself stands for the element oxygen and thus for all the atoms of oxygen in the universe. But when it is incorporated into the formula of a molecule—for example, H_2O, the formula for water—the same symbol represents a single atom of oxygen. The only time such symbols stand for more than one atom in a formula is when they are modified by a subscript. For example, in CO_2 (the formula for carbon dioxide), the 2 indicates two oxygen atoms. Similarly, an isolated formula for a molecule stands for all molecules having the same composition, everywhere in the universe. But when it is included in a chemical equation it stands for only one or a few of them. Thus H_2O means water—all the water in the world. But in the chemical equation

$$H_2O + CO_2 \longrightarrow H_2CO_3$$

the H_2O means one molecule of water (which reacts with one molecule of carbon dioxide to form one molecule of carbonic acid).

Elements do not combine randomly to form compounds; rather, they combine in regular and predictable ways. The triumph of modern chemistry and the wave-quantum picture of the atom is that it makes this regularity understandable in terms of electron orbitals. The first major step in unraveling the question of chemical reactivity was made in 1869 by the Russian chemist Dmitri Mendeleev. By that time it was known that elements combine in fixed proportions. For example, 1 gram of hydrogen always combines with 8 grams of oxygen to give 9 grams of water. By arbitrarily assigning hydrogen (the lightest element) an **atomic weight** of 1, it had been possible to assign atomic weights to all the other elements based on the proportions in which they combine with hydrogen or with each other. Now, Mendeleev observed that if all of the elements were arranged in a series, in order of increasing weight, certain chemical

properties recurred *periodically* in the list. Every eighth element in the "light" end of the list had similar properties; every eighteenth element in the "heavier" end of the list had similar properties. He arranged all the elements into a table in which elements of similar chemical properties fell in the same vertical row. This table, based on the periodic reappearance of certain chemical properties, was called a **periodic table.** Figure 10.7 is a modern version of the periodic table. It differs in only one important way from Mendeleev's table (in addition to including many elements unknown in 1869). The elements are arranged in terms of their **atomic number** (a concept unknown to Mendeleev). With the elucidation of the internal structure of the atom, *an atomic number was assigned to each element on the basis of how many protons (and therefore electrons) were present in each of its atoms.* (Thus hydrogen, with one proton, has atomic number 1; oxygen, with eight protons, has atomic

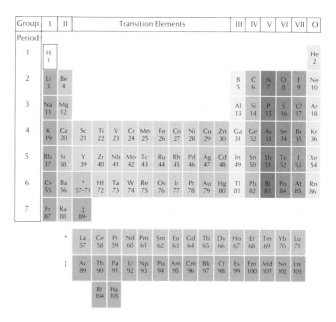

Figure 10.7 The periodic table of the elements. The number below each symbol indicates the atomic number of that element, which is the number of positively charged protons in the nucleus and the number of negatively charged electrons in orbitals outside the nucleus in each neutral atom of that element. Elements of increasing atomic number are grouped in horizontal rows. But the name for the table is derived from the fact that similar chemical properties occur with a predictable periodicity in the atoms so arranged. Here, elements with similar chemical properties are shown in boxes of the same color. It can be seen that they fall principally in vertical rows. The reason for this periodic appearance of elements with similar properties is discussed in the text.

number 8; and so on.) When these atomic numbers were used to construct the periodic table, they gave a picture of even greater regularity than the one based on atomic weights. We now know that this correspondence between atomic number and chemical properties is no mere coincidence. *The periodic recurrence of similar chemical properties in such a table is due to the periodic recurrence of similar electron configurations.*

Ionic Bonds and the Formation of Ionic Compounds

In analyzing the relationship between electronic configuration and chemical reactivity, let us first consider the elements in the vertical row designated Group O in Figure 10.7. These elements are helium (He), neon (Ne), argon (Ar), krypton (Kr), xenon (Xe), and radon (Rn). They are so unreactive that they are known as the "inert gases." Recently they have been found to be capable of forming a few chemical compounds, but they still bear the name "inert," for they are very nearly so. What they have in common is that all of their electron orbitals are full! For example, neon has atomic number 10, which means it has

ten electrons. Its $1s$, $2s$, $2p_x$, $2p_y$, and $2p_z$ orbitals have two electrons each (Figures 10.8 and 10.9). This electron configuration is apparently quite stable: Atoms possessing it have very little tendency either to gain or to lose electrons.

Next to inert neon in the periodic table is fluorine, the most reactive element of all! Its atomic number is 9, which means it is one electron short of having all its orbitals filled (Figures 10.8 and 10.10); that is why fluorine has a strong tendency to remove an electron from other atoms it happens to encounter. But a fluorine atom with ten electrons is no longer a neutral atom: it has one more electron than it has protons. It has gained a charge of -1. Any atom or group of atoms that bears such a net charge is called an **ion.**

Moving in the other direction from neon in the periodic table we come to sodium ("Na" stands for the Latin equivalent word "natrium"). Sodium has atomic number 11. Unlike fluorine, all of its second energy level orbitals are filled but it also has one lonely electron in its $3s$ orbital, which gives it a total of eleven electrons (Figure 10.10). Compared with the way it holds all its other electrons, sodium has only a weak attraction for the $3s$ electron and readily gives it up. Hence, if sodium and fluorine are mixed under appropriate conditions, they react with explosive

Element	Atomic Number	Energy Level 1	Energy Level 2				Energy Level 3			
		$1s$	$2s$	$2p_x$	$2p_y$	$2p_z$	$3s$	$3p_x$	$3p_y$	$3p_z$
Hydrogen	1	1								
Carbon	6	2	1	1	1	1				
Nitrogen	7	2	2	1	1	1				
Oxygen	8	2	2	2	1	1				
Fluorine	9	2	2	2	2	1				
Neon	10	2	2	2	2	2				
Sodium	11	2	2	2	2	2	1			
Magnesium	12	2	2	2	2	2	1	1		
Phosphorus	15	2	2	2	2	2	2	1	1	1
Sulfur	16	2	2	2	2	2	2	2	1	1
Argon	18	2	2	2	2	2	2	2	2	2

Figure 10.8 The electronic structure of some of the elements discussed in the text. Notice how electrons are added in a building-up process, beginning with the lowest energy level for each atom. Notice also that in each new energy level no s or p orbital may possess two electrons until each of them possesses at least one; this is an important rule that explains much chemical behavior. (Energy level 3 has more orbitals than are shown here; they begin to fill with electrons only after the s and p orbitals are filled.)

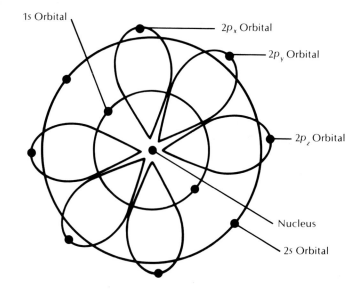

1s Orbital

2p$_x$ Orbital

2p$_y$ Orbital

2p$_z$ Orbital

Nucleus

2s Orbital

Figure 10.9   The electron configuration of the neon atom. Neon is relatively inert chemically, as are all the elements in which all of the orbitals contain their maximum of two electrons. The size of the nucleus is exaggerated, and the position of the electrons within the orbitals can never be known with the certainty that this sort of representation might suggest.

Figure 10.10 (below) Formation of ions and an ionic compound by the chemical reaction of fluorine with sodium. Fluorine has atomic number 9; it has two electrons in each orbital except the 2p$_z$ orbital, which has only one. Sodium, with atomic number 11, has two electrons in each orbital of the first and second energy levels, plus an additional electron in the 3s orbital. When these two kinds of atoms come together to form the ionic compound sodium fluoride, they are held together by the electric charges of opposite sign, which attract one kind of ion to the other. (The charges result from imbalance between the number of protons in the nucleus and the number of electrons in the orbitals.)

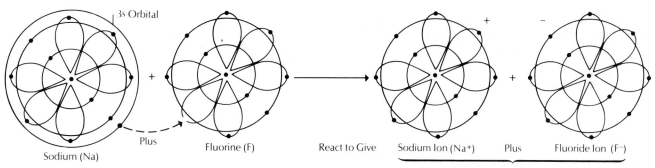

3s Orbital

Sodium (Na)   Plus   Fluorine (F)   React to Give   Sodium Ion (Na+)   Plus   Fluoride Ion (F−)

The Ionic Compound Sodium Fluoride

rapidity as sodium atoms let go of their 3s electrons and fluorine atoms take them in order to fill their 2p$_z$ orbitals. As a result of this reaction, two kinds of ions are formed: Na$^+$ and F$^-$. However, because opposite charges are attracted to each other, the sodium and the fluorine ions do not go their separate ways. They are now so strongly attracted to each other that they associate in "ion pairs" to form the compound sodium fluoride, NaF (Figure 10.10). Because these ions remain paired with each other, the compound is said to be held together by **ionic bonds.**

Although sodium readily relinquishes its outermost (3s) electron, it shows little tendency to lose any electrons from its second energy level. It takes ten times as much energy to remove a second electron from sodium as it does to remove the first. Similarly, fluorine has no perceptible tendency to gain a second electron. In both cases, they act as if they are

"satisfied" once all the orbitals in the outermost energy level are full. Like all atoms that restrict their chemical reactions to the transfer of a single electron, sodium and fluorine are said to have a bond-forming capacity, or **valence,** of 1.

More than one electron may be transferred in the reactions between other elements, however. If we move to the elements adjacent to sodium and fluorine in the periodic table, we find magnesium (Mg) and oxygen (O). Magnesium has atomic number 12: Its second energy level is filled and it has two electrons in its third energy level. Oxygen, with atomic number 8, has only one electron in each of two orbitals in its second energy level—it is two electrons short of being "satisfied." Thus, if magnesium and oxygen are brought together under appropriate conditions, magnesium donates the two electrons of its third energy level to the oxygen atom. Once the oxygen atom has accepted these two electrons, its outer orbitals are completed. Together these atoms form the compound magnesium oxide (MgO). Two electrons are transferred in this process, which means both magnesium and oxygen possess a valence of 2.

The reaction between magnesium and oxygen does not occur nearly as vigorously as the reaction between sodium and fluorine. This observation can be generalized to describe a characteristic behavior of all atoms: Any atom that must yield or gain more than one electron to complete its outer orbitals has *less* tendency to form ions than atoms that must gain or lose only a single electron. Furthermore, atoms that must gain or lose three electrons to complete their outermost orbitals have relatively *little* tendency to form ions, and atoms that must gain or lose four electrons have virtually *no* tendency to form ions.

The reason that the tendency of atoms to form ionic bonds decreases with valence is that the resulting ions would not be stable. There would be too much of an imbalance between their positive and their negative charges. This general behavior is the basis for the periodicity of chemical reactivity revealed in the periodic table: Groups I and VII are one electron away from having their outer orbitals filled and therefore are highly reactive, but as we move inward from the sides of the periodic table, we find atoms of higher valence that are less able to form ionic molecules. But these elements are not chemically unreactive. Their reactivity is simply of a different sort.

Covalent Bonds and the Formation of Covalent Compounds

The extreme opposite of an ionic bond is the kind of bond that exists in hydrogen gas. Hydrogen in the "free" state does not exist as individual atoms but as molecules composed of two hydrogen atoms (H_2). By itself, a hydrogen

atom has only one electron in the lowest energy level, which means it will react readily with another atom in an attempt to gain the other electron needed to fill that orbital. Two hydrogen atoms react not by one atom losing and the other gaining an electron, but by the two atoms coming together to *share* a pair of electrons. When the two atoms form a hydrogen molecule, they are held at a fixed distance relative to each other so that their electron orbitals overlap (Figure 10.11). This means that each orbital contains two electrons—at least part of the time. Because of these shared electrons that "satisfy" the 1s orbitals of both atoms, molecular hydrogen is much more stable (nonreactive) than free atoms of hydrogen are. A bond in which a shared pair of electrons holds two atoms at fixed distances from each other is called a **covalent bond.** And the distance between their nuclei is called the **bond length.**

Covalent bonding also exists in oxygen and nitrogen, the gases that make up air. However, the two atoms of an oxygen molecule must share two electron pairs, and the atoms of a nitrogen molecule must share three electron pairs in order to fill all their orbitals. In writing out chemical formulas, covalent bonds often are indicated by connecting the symbols of the atoms with a number of lines equal to the number of electron pairs that are being shared. Thus the three gases just described would be symbolized H—H, O=O, and N≡N.

In each of these three cases, the two atoms bound together are identical, which means the electrons are shared equally between partners. Such a bond, in which the electrons are shared equally, is called a **nonpolar covalent bond.** But different kinds of atoms also may be joined by covalent bonds in which the electrons are not shared equally. The reason is that every *kind* of atom has a different electron configuration; thus, they differ in the strength with which they attract additional electrons. In a

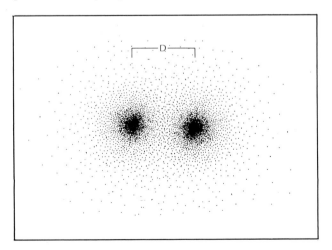

Figure 10.11 Structure of the hydrogen molecule. This structure is formed by the overlapping of the electron orbitals of two hydrogen atoms. Two electrons are thereby shared between the two atoms. Such bonding by a shared electron pair is known as a covalent bond. Two atoms involved in a covalent bond are always held at a relatively fixed and characteristic distance from one another. This distance between the two nuclei (labeled D in this drawing) is known as the bond length.

covalent bond, the atom with the greater attraction for electrons will draw the shared electrons preferentially into its orbital. Hence the molecule tends to become electrically polarized: The atom that holds the greater attraction for electrons becomes somewhat negatively charged relative to the other atom. Such bonds are called **polar covalent bonds.** Indeed, ion pair formation (discussed earlier) can be viewed as an extreme case of polar covalent bonding. Thus a spectrum of chemical bonds exists, from nonpolar covalent bonds to ion pair formation.

CARBON COMPOUNDS ARE THE STRUCTURAL BACKBONES OF THE MOLECULES OF LIFE

Because it has long been known that carbon (C) plays a unique role in the structure of living things, the study of carbon compounds has been set apart from the rest of chemistry as the field of **organic chemistry.** But this distinction should not obscure the fact that the properties and reactivities of carbon are in no way based on principles different from those governing other elements. Carbon is unique only because of its unique arrangement of electrons, which in turn derives directly from its atomic number.

Carbon has atomic number 6, which means it has two electrons in the first energy level and four electrons distributed among the four orbitals of the second energy level (Figure 10.12). Now, atoms do not readily acquire or give up as many as four electrons to form ions. What they tend to do instead is join together with other atoms by covalent bonds. Carbon, with its four electrons in the second energy level, is particularly prone to covalent bonding. Methane (CH_4) is an example of a covalent carbon compound. In methane, one carbon atom shares electrons with four hydrogen atoms. These shared electrons simultaneously complete the first-level orbitals of the four hydrogen atoms and the four second-level orbitals of the carbon atom.

Because none of the electrons escapes entirely from the sphere of influence of the nucleus with which it was originally associated, ion formation does not occur.

You might think that because a free carbon atom has two kinds of orbitals in its second energy level, two different kinds of bonds must be formed between carbon and hydrogen. But that is not the case. Every atom 'has an **electric field** about it, a region of space that is under the influence of the force of its electric charges. When a carbon atom encounters hydrogen atoms, the electric fields of the hydrogen atoms are strong enough to induce a shift in the electron orbitals of the carbon atom (Figure 10.12). When this shift is completed, it is no longer possible to distinguish between the 2s and 2p orbitals. Each one is now shaped somewhat like a teardrop, and each one is directed outward to what would be the corners of a regular tetrahedron. Because they have taken on a new configuration, they are said to be **hybrid orbitals.**

The new arrangement has important consequences for the combining of carbon with other atoms. Any atom that becomes attached to a carbon compound will do so at the "corners" of the tetrahedron (Figure 10.13). In other words, *all carbon compounds are built according to the geometric pattern dictated by the hybridization of its 2s and 2p electron orbitals.* The complex structures of living things are possible largely because of this distinctive geometry.

One effect of carbon atom geometry can be clearly seen if we consider an imaginary compound of carbon with four different atoms, W, X, Y, and Z (Figure 10.14). This compound can occur in two different structural forms having the same chemical composition. Such compounds of identical composition but different structure are called **isomers.** The particular kind of isomers shown in Figure 10.14—in which one of the structures is a mirror image of the other—is called a **stereoisomer.** One of the unique

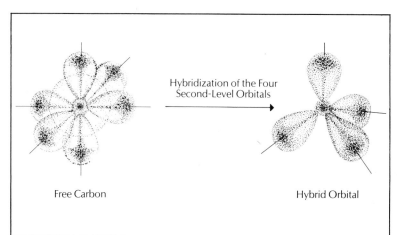

Hybridization of the Four Second-Level Orbitals

Free Carbon

Hybrid Orbital

Figure 10.12 When carbon atoms participate in the formation of covalent bonds, the electrons of the second energy level undergo a shift of location in a process known as orbital hybridization. The orbitals so produced (known as sp³ hybrid orbitals) are teardrop shaped and distributed symmetrically in space, forming a regular tetrahedron.

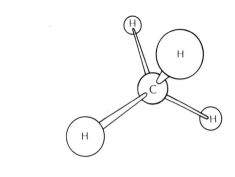

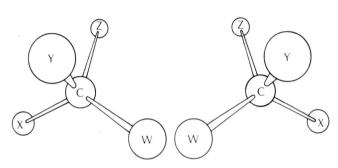

Figure 10.13 The tetrahedral structure of methane, a carbon compound. This arrangement of electron pairs minimizes the repulsion between electrons in the structure.

Figure 10.14 The effect of carbon atom geometry on the geometry of its compounds. These two imaginary molecules have the same chemical composition. But they differ in their structure: There is no way one of them can be rotated in space to be exactly like the other. They bear the same relationship to each other that your right hand bears to your left hand. In other words, they are mirror images of each other. Compounds with the same chemical composition but different structures are called isomers. Mirror-image isomers are called stereoisomers. Stereoisomers are important in living things. If a chemist were to make CXYZW in the laboratory, the result would be an equal mixture of left-handed and right-handed forms. Living cells would usually build just one of the forms.

aspects of life is that a living cell specifically produces only one stereoisomer of a possible pair. This selectivity leads to the emergence of the highly ordered, regulated structures upon which life depends.

Because of its strong tendency to form covalent bonds, carbon can combine with a wide variety of atoms, including other carbon atoms. Chains of carbon atoms can be strung together almost endlessly by covalent bonds. As Figure 10.15 shows, it is also possible for two carbon atoms to share two electron pairs, rather than just one, in a double bond ($C=C$). Double bonds are also extremely important in the chemistry of life.

Carbon can combine readily with many different elements. Because carbon, hydrogen, oxygen, and nitrogen are the most abundant elements in living things, compounds formed between them are obviously of importance. Figure 10.16 shows some of the most important groupings containing these elements. One of the things this figure points out is that oxygen, hydrogen, and nitrogen are capable of forming covalent bonds to each other as well as to carbon.

As you have probably noticed, several different kinds of notation have been used to indicate the structures of atoms and compounds. All of these notations are acceptable conventions. The reason for using different conventions at different times is because of the need to communicate different information. When we are trying to understand the

way in which carbon reacts, we need to visualize all of its electrons. But once we have moved beyond that stage, we can assume that whenever we write the letter C in a structural formula, it signifies all we have learned about the electronic structure of carbon. Similarly, as we get into more and more complex structural formulas, we can safely omit (as understood) more and more of the details that distract from rather than add to the point being made. By way of example, Figure 10.17 shows the different ways of depicting the structure of glucose, the most common sugar in living things. You will find it useful, for the subsequent chapters of this unit, to learn how to deal with these various forms of notation.

ATOMIC AND MOLECULAR WEIGHTS

Dalton's atomic theory sprang from observations he and others had made that substances react with one another in constant proportions: a given weight of element *A* combined with a given weight of element *B* always produces a fixed and predictable weight of compound *AB*. Although he suspected that elements exist in discrete units (atoms), he had no way of measuring what the weight of such small units could be. But because of the rule of constant proportions, Dalton realized that a scale of *relative* weights could be worked out. Hydrogen was known to be the lightest of all the elements. He reasoned that if the weight of a hydrogen

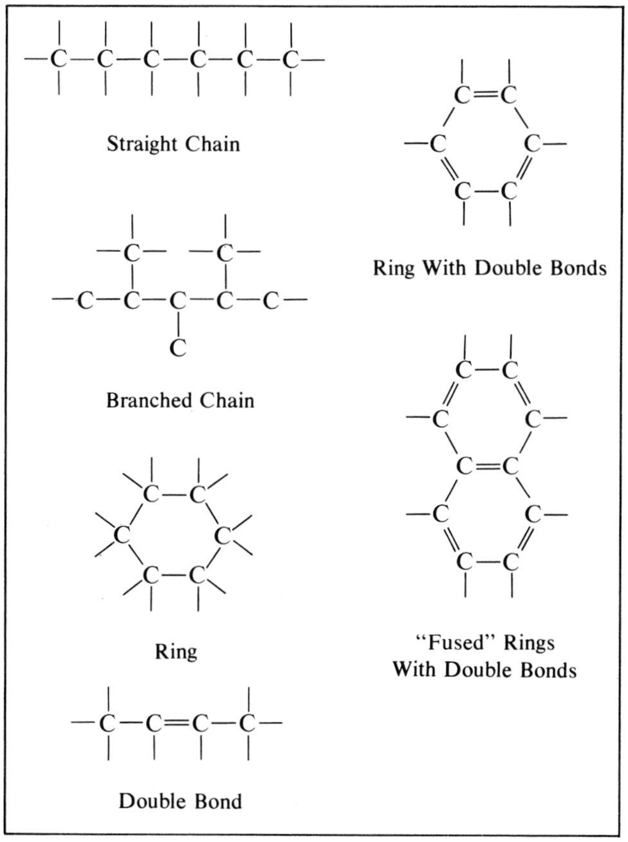

Figure 10.15 *Some carbon-carbon bonding possibilities. In all these structural formulas, the unconnected lines protruding from the carbon atoms indicate that any one of a number of elements (including more carbon atoms) may be bonded covalently to the molecule. Because the carbon atom is a tetrahedral structure, there is no such thing as a "straight chain" of carbon atoms. An unbranched chain of carbon atoms zigzags in space but is usually drawn straight simply because of the difficulty in representing a three-dimensional structure on paper.*

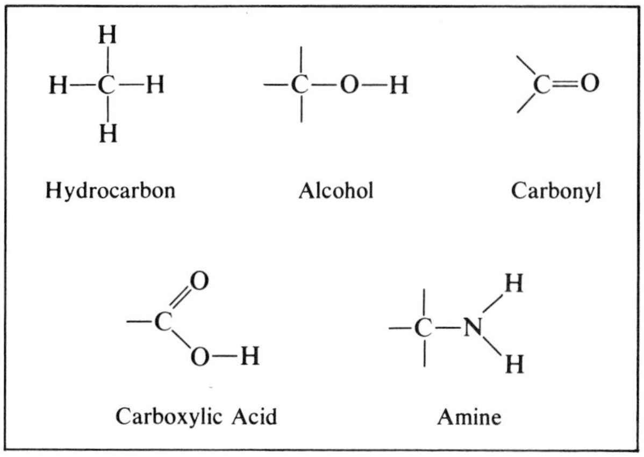

Figure 10.16 *Some important molecular groupings that contain carbon, hydrogen, oxygen, and nitrogen—the most prevalent elements in living things.*

atom were set at 1, he could determine the relative weight of another kind of atom by measuring how many grams of that element combine with 1 gram of hydrogen. (Even if some element would not combine with hydrogen, its atomic weight could be determined by studying its reactions with a third element that did combine with hydrogen and had already been assigned an atomic weight.)

The scale of atomic weights has been revised twice since Dalton's time by international agreement. For some time, oxygen was taken as the standard and was arbitrarily assigned the weight of 16 (which is approximately what it came out to with hydrogen set at 1). More recently it has been determined that the most consistent values can be obtained if carbon is used as the standard. In the current system, atomic weight is the weight of a representative atom of an element relative to the weight of the most

common form of carbon atom, which is set at exactly 12.

Molecular weight is the sum of the atomic weights of two or more elements that have combined to form a chemical compound. For example, as shown in Table 10.2, hydrogen has atomic weight 1 and oxygen has atomic weight 16. Thus water (H_2O) has a molecular weight of $(2 \times 1) + 16 = 18$. Similarly, carbon dioxide (CO_2) has a molecular weight of $12 + (2 \times 16) = 44$.

Now, because atoms and molecules are discrete units, a given weight of an element or a compound must be composed of a fixed number of atoms or molecules. In fact, 6.02×10^{23} atoms are always present in an amount of an element that is equivalent to its atomic weight in grams. Referring to Table 10.2, this means that 31 grams of phosphorus contain 6.02×10^{23} phosphorus atoms, and 127 grams of iodine contain 6.02×10^{23} iodine atoms. The value 6.02×10^{23} is called **Avogadro's number,** after the chemist who first determined its value.

Because atomic weights are additive, it follows that *a number of grams of a compound equal to the molecular weight of that compound always contains 6.02×10^{23} molecules.* Thus it follows that 150 grams of the compound sodium iodide contain 6.02×10^{23} molecules of sodium iodide. Similarly, 18 grams of water (less than an ounce) contain 6.02×10^{23} molecules of water. The magnitude of Avogadro's number is difficult to comprehend, even if you write it out with all the zeros. But if you had as many peas as there are molecules in 18 grams of water, they would cover sixty planets the size of the earth with a layer of peas about ten feet deep. (That's a lot of peas!)

An amount of an element equivalent to its atomic weight is called the gram atomic weight, or one **gram atom.** (For example, 12 grams of carbon is 1 gram atom of carbon.) *An amount of a compound equivalent to the molecular weight*

Figure 10.17 Structural formulas and a space-filling model for the simple sugar glucose. All these formulas represent the same molecule. They differ only in the manner in which they present information. Each one conveys different aspects of the same substance.

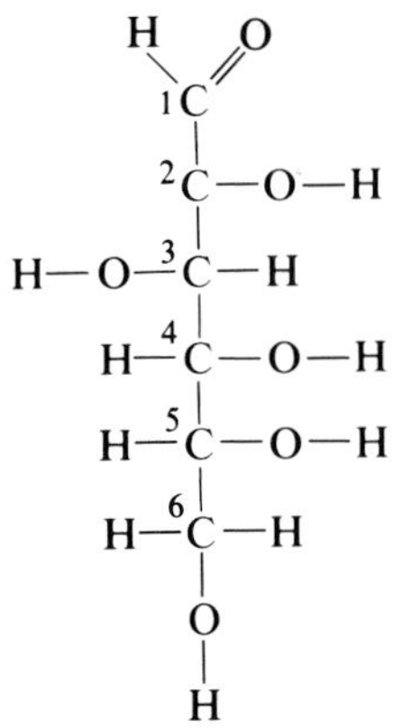

(a) "Stick" formula. In this form, the relationship between the alcoholic (—OH) groups is clear. When the molecule is arranged so that the carbon atoms are in a straight line, it can be seen that the —OH groups on carbon atoms numbered 2, 4, and 5 project to the right, and the —OH group on carbon atom 3 projects to the left.

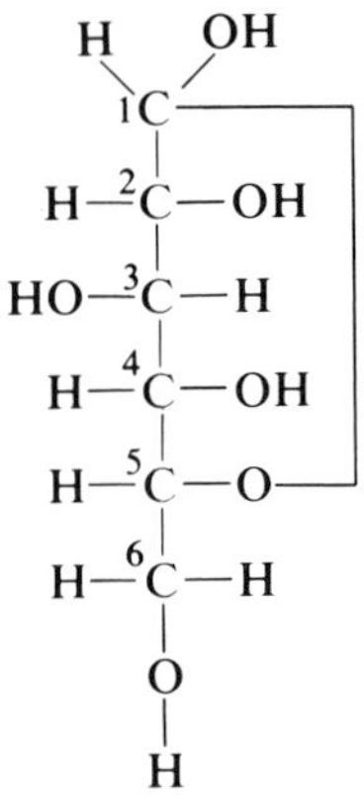

(b) Another "stick" formula, showing how glucose forms a "ring" compound by a covalent bond between carbon atom 1 and the oxygen atom attached to carbon atom 5. Glucose exists predominantly in this form, so this structural formula is a better representation than (a). Yet the long line from carbon atom 1 to 5 indicates that this formula is distorted: *all* covalent bonds are about the same length, so the actual molecule must be "bent" to bring carbon atoms 1 and 5 closer together.

Table 10.2
Approximate Atomic Weights of the Most Common Elements in the Human Body

Element	Atomic Number	Atomic Weight*
Hydrogen	1	1
Carbon	6	12
Nitrogen	7	14
Oxygen	8	16
Sodium	11	23
Magnesium	12	24
Phosphorus	15	31
Sulfur	16	32
Chlorine	17	35
Potassium	19	39
Calcium	20	40
Manganese	25	55
Iron	26	56
Copper	29	63
Zinc	30	65
Iodine	53	127

*None of the atomic weights are integral values; they have been rounded off here to the nearest whole number for simplicity. The reason the atomic weights are not whole numbers is because each value represents an average of the atomic weights of the naturally occurring isotopes of a given element. (The nature of isotopes is described in the text.) A table of precise atomic weights can be found in any chemistry book.

*in grams is the gram molecular weight, or one **mole** for short.* (Thus 18 grams of water is 1 mole of water.)

Atomic and molecular weights are useful concepts because they enable us to make quantitative inferences and predictions concerning chemical reactions. If we know the course of a reaction, we can predict how much of each component will react to produce how much product. Conversely, if we come across a reaction we do not understand, by measuring the weights of reactants and products we often can gain insight into the reaction itself.

Life originated in water, and most of the reactions of life still occur in watery solutions. That is why there must be a standardized way of talking about reactive substances that are dissolved in water. The most useful system, for most purposes, is **molarity.** A **one molar solution** (1M) of any substance is defined as 1 mole (or 1 gram molecular weight) of that substance in 1 liter of solution. (A liter is a little more than a quart.) Consider, once again, the sugar glucose, which may also be symbolized $C_6H_{12}O_6$. (This kind of notation is called a **molecular formula;** it is a "list" of the numbers of all the different kinds of atoms contained in one molecule.) Using Table 10.2 as a reference, you can calculate that the molecular weight of glucose

OH
|
H—C—H
|
C——O
H | H
| H |
C   C
HO | OH H | OH
| |
C————C
| |
H   OH

(c) "Ring" formula, which is more representative of the way the atoms in (b) are arranged in space. The bonds in the lower part of the formula are drawn with heavier lines to indicate that this part of the ring should be visualized as projecting toward the viewer, with the upper half receding away from the viewer.

(d) "Skeleton" formula. Just as it is not necessary to identify all the electrons of an atom every time the atom is portrayed, neither is it necessary to draw in all the atoms of a molecule every time the molecule is portrayed. Here, carbon atoms are assumed to occur at every corner of the ring; major repeating groups (in this case, the —OH groups) are identified by simple lines; and hydrogen atoms are assumed to be present wherever required to give carbon a valence of 4. With this kind of formula, more information can be packed into less space, and structures of greater complexity, which are built up by joining many glucose molecules together, can be drawn with much more clarity.

(e) "Space-filling" model. The other formulas shown here may tell a great deal about the nature of the glucose molecule, but they do not create an accurate picture of the molecule as it exists in three-dimensional space. Such models may be built from partial spheres made to scale so that the atoms fit together with appropriate bond angles and interatomic distances. Space-filling models sometimes make it easier to visualize how a molecule might interact with another molecule if the two should come together.

is approximately 180: $(6 \times 12) + (12 \times 1) + (6 \times 16) = 180$. If 180 grams of glucose is dissolved in enough water to bring the total volume to 1 liter, the result will be a 1 molar (1M) solution of glucose. And the 1 liter of solution will contain 6.02×10^{23} molecules of glucose.

It is difficult to imagine where the science of chemistry and, hence, the science of biology would be today if we did not have these methods of dealing with substances in a standardized, quantitative way.

ISOTOPES: NUCLEAR VARIATIONS ON AN ELEMENTAL THEME

Elements exist in multiple forms, known as **isotopes.** But if an element is a substance with fixed properties, how can it have multiple forms? The answer is found in a subatomic particle of the nucleus, the neutron. All atoms of an element always have the same number of protons, hence the same atomic number, yet they may have different numbers of neutrons. Because most of the weight of an atom is in its protons and neutrons (which are about equal in weight), variation in the number of neutrons will cause differences in the atomic weights of different isotopes of a single element. Although the protons determine electron numbers and

configurations and are therefore the most significant components of the nucleus, neutrons play a lesser role in determining the properties of the atom.

Until now, we have discussed only the most common form of hydrogen, which has one proton in the nucleus and one electron in its $1s$ orbital. But there are other isotopes of hydrogen (Figure 10.18). Two of the hydrogen isotopes are "stable"—that is, they show no tendency to break down. The third isotope, called tritium, is unstable and tends to break down; in the process, it emits an electron (which is a form of radiation). This natural breakdown process is called **radioactive decay.**

The chemistry of the three forms of hydrogen is slightly different. (But living things sometimes find even such a slight difference intolerable. The compound deuterium oxide ("heavy water") is poisonous to most organisms and cells if it replaces their "normal water" *entirely*.) Hydrogen, with its low atomic weight, is an exception in this regard; in elements heavier than hydrogen, additional neutrons have negligible effect on chemical reactivity. All the isotopes of heavier elements therefore do not have special names. They merely are distinguished by superscripts of the atomic weight of the element. Thus four

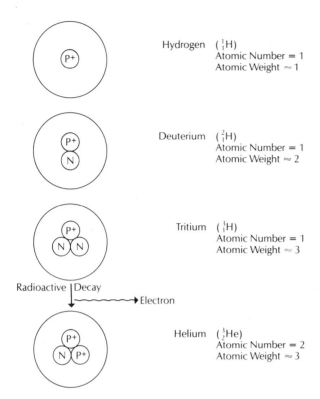

Hydrogen ($_1^1$H)
Atomic Number = 1
Atomic Weight ≈ 1

Deuterium ($_1^2$H)
Atomic Number = 1
Atomic Weight ≈ 2

Tritium ($_1^3$H)
Atomic Number = 1
Atomic Weight ≈ 3

Radioactive Decay
→ Electron

Helium ($_2^3$He)
Atomic Number = 2
Atomic Weight ≈ 3

Figure 10.18   The three isotopes of hydrogen. All have one proton and therefore have the same atomic number, but they differ in their atomic weights because of the number of neutrons present in the nucleus. (The subscript number to the left of the chemical symbol H indicates the atomic number of hydrogen; the superscript number indicates atomic weight.) Tritium is an unstable configuration, and it undergoes radioactive decay in which an electron is released from a neutron in the nucleus, which is thereby converted into a proton. The decay process thus leads to a change in the atomic number from 1 to 2: The atom changes from hydrogen to helium.

isotopes of carbon, which all have atomic number 6, are known as ^{11}C, ^{12}C, ^{13}C, and ^{14}C.

Isotopes of an element vary enormously in their abundance. For example, only 1 water molecule in 3,000 contains a deuterium atom. Tritium does not occur naturally to any significant extent; it is largely man-made in nuclear reactors. Carbon in nature is principally ^{12}C, but ^{14}C is continuously produced by the cosmic bombardment of nitrogen atoms in the upper atmosphere. Thus the atmosphere maintains constant trace amounts of the ^{14}CO$_2$ form of carbon dioxide. As long as an organism is alive, it is incorporating a constant ratio of ^{14}C and ^{12}C atoms into its body. When it dies, of course, ^{14}C uptake ceases. Now, ^{14}C is an unstable isotope, and it undergoes radioactive decay at a slow but steady pace. As a result, the ratio of ^{14}C to ^{12}C declines steadily after the death of the organism. Radioactive decay can therefore be used in the geologic dating of its remains. The less ^{14}C there is in the remains, the older they are. Because it takes 5,730 years for one-half the ^{14}C atoms in a sample of ^{14}C to decay, if we find the ^{14}C/^{12}C ratio of a fossil to be one-half that of the atmosphere, we know that the organism died about 5,730 years ago. Similarly, if it is one-fourth the ratio found in the atmosphere, we can calculate that death occurred about 11,460 years ago.

The use of radioactive isotopes is by no means restricted to the dating of natural remains. Because radioactive isotopes reveal their presence by emitting radiation as they decay, they are very easily detected even when they are present in only trace amounts. The electrons or other forms of radiation they emit can expose a sheet of photographic film, for example, and they can cause a deflection in the needle of a Geiger counter. This means that radioactive isotopes can be used to trace the fate of molecules into which they have been incorporated. A compound can be synthesized in which most of its atoms are the common, stable isotope of an element and a few are of an unstable form. Because the chemical behavior of different isotopes of an element is very nearly the same, the molecules bearing the radioactive "label" will undergo the same reactions as normal molecules. The radioactive atoms are called **tracers.** Because we can detect their presence readily, we can detect their path through a biological system, and we can infer the fate of the unlabeled molecules as well.

For example, a drug bearing a radioactive label may be administered to a patient, and at certain intervals blood and/or urine samples can be collected. By measuring the amount of radioactivity present in the samples, it is possible to determine how long the drug remains in the blood and/or when it passes into the urine. By isolating and analyzing the molecules bearing the radioactive atoms, it is possible to determine whether or not the body has chemically modified the drug.

Table 10.3 lists some of the isotopes of greatest importance in biology. As you will read in later chapters, these isotopes have been used to solve some of the basic riddles of life. You will learn how ^{3}H has been used to track chromosome replication, how ^{14}C has been used to follow the steps involved in photosynthesis, and how ^{32}P and ^{35}S were used together to demonstrate that DNA is the hereditary material. The past thirty years have often been referred to as the biological revolution. This revolution is almost entirely chemical in nature, and it is due in no small part to the ready availability and widespread use of the forms of matter called radioactive isotopes.

Table 10.3
Some Isotopes Useful in Biological Research

Radioactive Isotopes (detected by radioactive decay)

Isotope	Natural Abundance	Half-life
$^{3}_{1}H$	None	12.1 years
$^{14}_{6}C$	Trace	5,730 years
$^{24}_{11}Na$	None	15 hours
$^{32}_{15}P$	None	14.3 days
$^{35}_{16}S$	None	87.1 days
$^{36}_{17}Cl$	Trace	310,000 years
$^{42}_{19}K$	None	12.5 hours
$^{45}_{20}Ca$	None	152 days
$^{59}_{26}Fe$	None	45 days
$^{131}_{53}I$	None	8 days

Stable Isotopes (detected by the effect they cause on molecular weight of compounds in which they occur)

Isotope	Natural Abundance
$^{2}_{1}H$	0.0154%
$^{15}_{7}N$	0.365%
$^{18}_{8}O$	0.204%

PERSPECTIVE

For centuries biology has been a descriptive, qualitative science. Why, suddenly, is it moving closer to the precise, quantitative atomic and molecular arena of the physicist and the chemist? The reason is that, like everything else in the world, living things are composed of matter, and matter is composed of atoms. A comprehensive understanding of life therefore requires an understanding of the organization and behavior of those atoms. Stories about sunlight falling on a leaf will not tell you *how* photosynthesis occurs unless they also tell you about the interactions and energy transfers between particles of light and the atoms and molecules in the leaf. All the speculation about the actual unit of heredity would still be speculation without the biochemical search that ended—and in a sense began—with elucidation of the structure of the DNA molecule. All the suffering of disease-ridden human beings will not disappear by incantations, but much of it may be alleviated by the continued application of chemistry to biology at the molecular level.

If it is true that life can be studied on many levels, and if it is true that new and different properties of living things emerge at each new level, then surely the derivation of one property from another cannot be fully understood without starting at the lowest levels of organization—the atomic and molecular levels.

The points of this chapter are fairly straightforward: Atoms are composed of units of positive charge (protons), negative charge (electrons), and neutral charge (neutrons).

The properties of an atom result from the number of protons in its nucleus, because the protons determine how many electrons can circle the nucleus. And it is the number of electrons and the positions they take about the nucleus that are the keys to chemical reactions between atoms that join together into the molecules of life.

The hydrogen atom, with its single proton and single electron, has a relatively simple structure. Larger atoms are more complex in structure. Their many electrons vibrate with specific energies in specific, nonidentical regions of space called orbitals. These orbitals are organized in a regular pattern, into groups having similar energy, to form energy levels. The basis of chemical reactivity is simply the tendency for each atom to gain or lose electrons so that its outermost energy level has all its orbitals filled with their quotas of two electrons each.

If only one or two electrons must be gained or lost to "satisfy" the orbitals of the outermost energy level, atoms tend to gain or lose control of the bonding electron entirely and become ionic. But if more than two electrons must be gained or lost, atoms tend instead to seek other partners with which they can share electron pairs to satisfy the orbitals of both partners simultaneously. Such bonds are called covalent bonds. The atoms joined by covalent bonds are held at fixed distances and positions relative to one another and thus take on specific geometric relationships, which derive directly from the organization of electron orbitals in the constituent atoms.

Because of its atomic number (6) and the electron orbitals that number leads to, carbon has very little tendency to form ionic bonds. But it has an extraordinary capacity for covalent bonding. It is the diversity of covalent bonds with carbon atoms and the precise geometry of the resulting compounds that make life possible.

SUGGESTED READINGS

DICKERSON, R. E. *Chemical Principles.* 2nd ed. Menlo Park, Calif.: W. A. Benjamin, 1974. A solid treatment of basic chemistry, lucidly written with the beginning student in mind.

LINNETT, J. W. "Chemical Bonds," *Science Progress*, 60 (1972), 1. A quite readable description of the meaning of chemical bonds, at a level appropriate to the considerations of this chapter.

WHITE, EMIL H. *Chemical Background for the Biological Sciences.* 2nd ed. Englewood Cliffs, N.J.: Prentice-Hall, 1970. Probably the single best reference in chemistry for the biology student. The book provides a wealth of examples drawn from biological chemistry and a careful, readable presentation of organic chemistry.

Chapter 11

The Molecules of Life

Underlying the diversification that has occurred during the immense journey of living organisms through evolutionary time is a unity of all life forms at the biochemical level. Accept the notion of the unity of life and you accept a degree of kinship with fish and fungus, lettuce and rhinoceros, and all the assorted and seemingly unique creatures that have ever appeared on earth.

When Charles Darwin and Alfred Wallace proposed their theory of evolution by natural selection, they were greeted in more than a few quarters with cries of outrage. Particularly outrageous was the implied evolutionary relationship between man and the apes: surely man (that special creature, man) could not be kin to such hairy, low-browed creatures! But even more unpalatable was the suggestion that man might be related by common descent not only to all other animals but also to the trees and grass and teeming microorganisms in his environment. The failure to accept at once our common heritage with all other life forms is not surprising, for it is not an idea that springs easily and naturally to mind. For example, imagine yourself today (in this era of enlightenment) as a traveler through the remote countryside of Africa who, upon rounding a bend in the road, suddenly comes face to face with a rhinoceros. In that first instant of confrontation, do you imagine your reaction would be one of recognition of a long-lost kin?

Indeed, the surprising aspect of the Darwin-Wallace era is not that some objected but that so many rapidly accepted the theory. Darwin and Wallace postulated an essential unity of all life even though they had little information about the nature and organization of living matter and how much similarity or difference might actually exist between different species at more fundamental levels. Natural selection, they said, acts on heritable differences—but they did not know what the basis for inheritance might be, or how characteristics could be passed from one generation to the next, or how the process of inheritance could provide both constancy and change from one generation to the next. Answers to these questions would not come for some time. Nevertheless, the insights of Darwin and Wallace have since been validated by the work of biologists and chemists who have been probing deeper into the composition, organization, and functioning of living matter. The more that is learned about the elemental nature of an immense variety of living organisms, the more evident the essential unity of life becomes. Had Darwin and Wallace not framed a theory of common descent a hundred years ago, biologists should be driven to do so today in order to account for the implications of all the biological research that has accumulated over the past century.

This research shows clearly that, beneath surface differences, all organisms share a remarkable degree of chemical similarity at their atomic and molecular levels of organization. In addition, even though organisms derive life-sustaining energy in often highly specialized ways, they still transform similar chemical substances in quite similar ways. Even at higher levels of organization, molecules are grouped and organized in fundamentally similar ways—in threads, in sheets, in spheres—regardless of whether the organism is a pine tree, a yeast, or a rhinoceros. This similarity can be traced to the fact that the substances of all living things are composed of a very small number of general types of atoms and molecules. Each general type, however, can give rise to an almost infinite variety of specific molecules. In other words, *it is through subtle variations on a few basically simple molecular themes that life has evolved into the diversified forms we see today.*

What are the molecules that are found in all living things? In reading about a few of the more important types, you will be able to see how the properties of molecules derive from the structure and behavior of the atoms of which they are composed, and how certain characteristics of life flow from the properties of these molecules and others like them.

WITHOUT WATER MOLECULES THERE WOULD BE NO LIFE

The chemical formula for a molecule of water is H_2O—two hydrogen atoms joined with one oxygen atom. It seems simple enough, yet within that simple union is a multitude of complex properties on which all living organisms depend. Not only did life begin in water, it still cannot exist without it: All the reactions of life are in one way or another based on "water chemistry." The only organisms that have escaped from a life immersed in water to a life on land are the ones that have contrived a special way of taking and keeping their own water with them. Once you gain an understanding of the structure and behavior of water molecules, you will have gained certain fundamental insights into the chemistry of life.

How Covalent Bonds Hold a Water Molecule Together

All atoms illustrate the principle of emergent properties discussed in Chapter 1. All atoms contain the same subatomic components—protons, electrons, and neutrons—but when these components are brought together in various numbers and arrangements, entirely different properties emerge. An interesting case in point is the manner in which the properties of water derive largely from the distinctive organization of the components of the oxygen atom and, to a lesser extent, from the organization of the hydrogen atom.

Recall from Chapter 10 that the atomic number of oxygen is 8; this means that with its eight units of positive charge, or **protons,** an oxygen atom is capable of holding on to eight units of negative charge, or **electrons.** Eight electrons vibrate about its nucleus. Two of these eight electrons are in the lowest energy level in a more or less spherical orbital; this is the **1s orbital** shown in Figure 11.2*b*. Two other electrons are in the **2s orbital,** which is also spherical. The remaining four are in three dumbbell-shaped orbitals that are at right angles to one another in three planes of space.

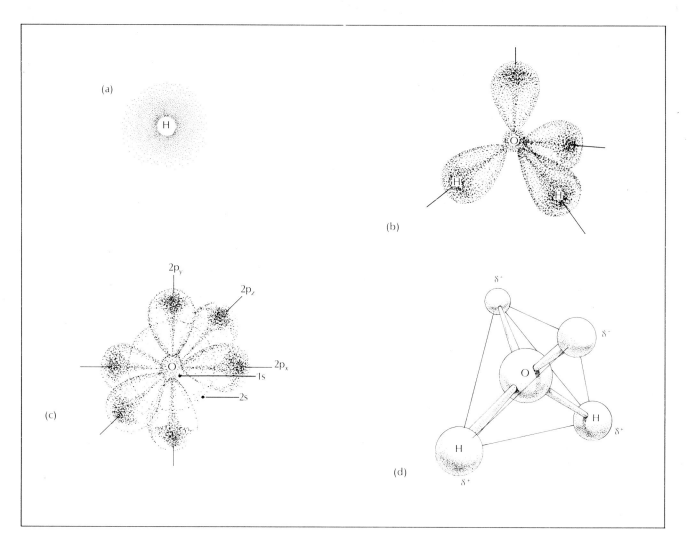

All three of these **2p orbitals** are capable of handling a pair of electrons, but only the $2p_x$ orbital is actually complete; the $2p_y$ and the $2p_z$ orbitals each contain only one electron. This means they each still have the capacity to acquire one more electron.

Now a hydrogen atom, with atomic number 1, has only one electron circling its nucleus in the $1s$ orbital even though this orbital is capable of handling a pair of electrons. That is why hydrogen can join with oxygen: The lone electrons of one kind of atom can pair up with the lone electrons of the other to fill the ''vacancies'' in each other's orbitals. Because an oxygen atom has two such vacancies, two hydrogen atoms can join with it. When that happens, the three atoms take on the distinctive shape of a water molecule, as shown in Figure 11.2c. In this molecule, the previously unpaired electrons moving about the oxygen nucleus now encompass a hydrogen nucleus in their domain as well. Similarly, the single electron of each hydrogen atom now moves around the oxygen nucleus as well as the

hydrogen nucleus. Thus, the two kinds of atoms share electrons; they are held together by a **covalent bond.**

As in many partnerships, however, the sharing is unequal. The oxygen nucleus holds a greater attraction for the electrons than the hydrogen nucleus does. For that reason the electrons being shared spend more than half their time near the oxygen nucleus. As a result, the oxygen atom takes on a partial negative charge. (On the average, the oxygen atom in a water molecule has more of the negatively charged electrons moving about it than it has positively charged protons in its nucleus.) Similarly, the hydrogen atoms take on a slight degree of positive charge. Upon reaction with hydrogen, the $2p$ and $2s$ electrons of the oxygen atom rearrange, forming the hybrid orbitals shown in Figure 11.2c. The overall result is that the water molecule takes on the form of a tetrahedron (Figure 11.2d). The hydrogen atoms, with their partial positive charges, occupy two of the apices of the tetrahedron; the other two apices represent centers of partial negative charge due to the

Figure 11.2   (a) A representation of the current concept of the organization of the hydrogen atom as described in Figure 10.4. The size of the nucleus is exaggerated here about 10,000 times relative to the size of the electron orbital. (b) A representation of the organization of the electron orbitals of an oxygen atom. (c) A representation of the organization of electrons in a molecule of water. One oxygen atom combines with two hydrogen atoms. Each hydrogen atom shares an electron pair with the oxygen atom. These shared electrons simultaneously "satisfy" the orbitals of both the oxygen and the hydrogen atoms—each contains two electrons at least part of the time. Such a pair of shared electrons forms a covalent bond. As the oxygen atom and the hydrogen atoms combine, the electrical field of the hydrogen atoms causes a shift in the distribution of the electrons about the oxygen nucleus. The s and p orbitals disappear and the electrons are now found in four teardrop-shaped orbitals. Because these new orbitals involve electrons previously found in 1s and 3p orbitals, they are called "sp³ hybrid orbitals." (This phenomenon is discussed in Chapter 10; see particularly Figure 10.12.) The sp³ hybrid orbitals are directed outward from the oxygen atom in such a way that lines connecting them would form a regular tetrahedron (a pyramid with a base and three sides). The hydrogen atoms are found at two of the four corners of the tetrahedron. The other corners are occupied merely by electrons of the oxygen atom. The electrons shared by oxygen and hydrogen are not shared equally; the oxygen atom tends to draw them into its orbitals to a greater extent than the hydrogen atom does. As a result, the hydrogen atoms tend to have a slight deficiency of electrons and thus they bear a slight positive charge, symbolized δ^+). As a corollary, of course, the oxygen atom bears a pair of partial negative charges. These partial negative charges (symbolized δ^-) are localized at the corners of the water molecule opposite the hydrogen atoms.

Thus, as shown in (d), the water molecule has the shape of a tetrahedron in which two of the corners are positively charged and two are negatively charged. It is from this structural organization that all of the strange and wonderful properties of water—upon which life is absolutely dependent—are derived!

distribution of the oxygen electrons. It is from the details of this tetrahedral structure of a water molecule that the properties of water are derived. Because the bonds between the oxygen and hydrogen atoms have one positive pole and one negative pole, they are **polar covalent bonds.** A molecule such as water, which has polar covalent bonds, is a polar compound.

How Hydrogen Bonds Affect Adjacent Water Molecules

When many water molecules come together, as they do in a drop of water, they tend to become highly ordered with respect to one another because of the polarity of each molecule. The oxygen atoms of two water molecules tend to repel each other, because of their like charge, and to attract the positively charged hydrogen atoms in a specific way. This attraction brings adjacent water molecules so close together that they nearly lose their identity. As Figure 11.3a shows, oxygen atoms that are nearest neighbors share the hydrogen atom found between them. When a hydrogen atom is shared by two adjacent molecules, the sharing is said to be a **hydrogen bond.**

Adjacent water molecules in liquid water carry this hydrogen bonding one step further. They actually "change partners." A hydrogen atom participating in a covalent bond with one oxygen atom and in a hydrogen bond with a second oxygen atom may, an instant later, be participating in a covalent bond with the second atom and in a hydrogen bond with the first. The arrangement shown in Figure 11.3a might thus change rapidly to the arrangement shown in Figure 11.3b. Such switching of partners affects more than two adjacent molecules. The reaction is propagated continuously throughout the entire water drop. *As a consequence of extensive hydrogen bonding and of "changing partners," small molecules of water are held together into a substance that has some of the properties of a very large molecule.*

Consider, for example, the molecules of a water droplet.

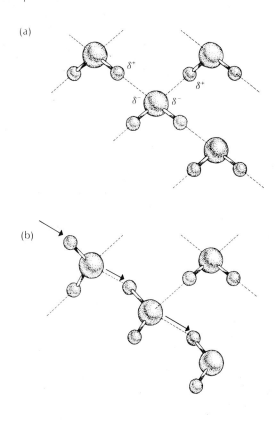

(a)

(b)

Figure 11.3 (left) Hydrogen bonding between water molecules (a). In this model, the hydrogen bonds are depicted by dashed lines. (b) Adjacent water molecules in liquid water can "change partners" instantaneously with one another, so that the reaction is propagated continuously as indicated.

Figure 11.4 (below) If any object is to penetrate the surface of free-standing water, it must first break the hydrogen bonds between molecules. The high resistance of water to penetration, or its high surface tension, is a measure of the energy required to break these bonds.

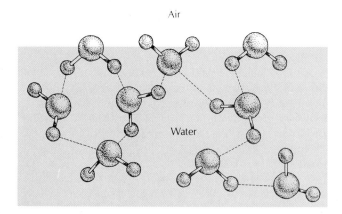

Air

Water

When a small quantity of water falls freely through the air, as it does in a raindrop, it tends to take on the shape of a nearly perfect sphere. The reason is that the surface water molecules have no chemical basis for interacting with the molecules that make up the surrounding air, but they are drawn toward the molecules in the interior of the droplet by hydrogen bonds. Similarly, the surface of free-standing water, such as that in a pond, is made up of molecules that are drawn downward by hydrogen bonds to molecules below. If any object is to penetrate the surface, it must first break some of these inward-directed hydrogen bonds (Figure 11.4). The high resistance of water to penetration, or its high **surface tension,** is a measure of the energy required to break the hydrogen bonds. It is, moreover, a property characteristic of a new level of organization that is brought about because of polar bonding. Many other properties of water can be traced directly to the polarity of its bonds.

How the High Heat Capacity of Water Affects Living Things

In the course of living and growing, cells produce enormous amounts of heat. If it were not for the capacity of the water within the cells to absorb a great deal of heat energy without increasing much in temperature, a cell would literally cook itself as it carried out the chemistry of life. Because it takes much more heat energy to raise the temperature of water than it does to raise the temperature of any other common liquid, water is said to have a **high heat capacity.**

Now, generally, the more a substance is heated, the more its molecules begin vibrating relative to each other. The incoming heat energy becomes converted into **kinetic energy**—the energy of motion. (The temperature of a substance is, in fact, a measure of the rate at which its molecules are moving relative to one another.) However, inherent in the organization of water molecules is the capacity to absorb heat without proportionally increasing the motion of whole molecules relative to one another. This capacity has to do with the process of "changing partners" between molecules. As water is heated, each hydrogen atom begins to vibrate more and more along its bond axis, which increases the frequency with which it moves between adjacent oxygen atoms. This in turn increases the changing of partners between molecules, and some of the applied heat is dissipated with each change. Because the hydrogen atoms rather than whole water molecules accomplish the conversion of the heat energy into the energy of motion, there is less rapid motion of whole water molecules than there would be with other liquid substances. In short, it is again because of the particular kind of bonds between water molecules that the degree of organization in a body of water does not change much with increasing temperature.

Given enough heat, however, water eventually can be

brought to its boiling point of 100°C. But even when the temperature does reach the boiling point, unless considerably more heat is applied water still will not boil. As you read earlier, hydrogen bonds pull the surface molecules of a body of water toward the interior. Only if enough additional heat is applied to break those bonds can the molecules at the surface be converted into steam, or vapor. When that happens, molecules break away from the surface and fly out into the air. The molecules so dispersed carry energy with them (in the form of kinetic energy) and thereby reduce the amount of energy remaining in the water left behind. In other words, a body of water is cooled when it loses molecules that bear the kinetic energy required to pass into the vapor state. The fact that it takes so much heat to vaporize each molecule of water accounts for the tremendous cooling effect of **evaporative water loss.** Many plants and animals depend on this process to dissipate the heat that they generate in the course of living or that they receive in the form of radiation from the sun.

At room temperature the organization of the water molecules is complex, but it is not perfect. Each water molecule is capable of forming hydrogen bonds with four other molecules, but it seldom does so at room temperature because there is enough thermal agitation to keep the molecules moving relative to one another. When water is cooled, however, there is a decrease in thermal agitation and the molecules become considerably more orderly and organized. At 4°C they reach the point at which they are as tightly packed as possible. Thus, water has its greatest density at 4°C. If the water is cooled still further, it becomes more highly organized but, surprisingly, it begins to expand once more. Finally, at 0°C the water molecules take on the organization shown in Figure 11.5. In this **ice crystal,** each water molecule forms four hydrogen bonds with its nearest neighbors in the four directions dictated by their characteristic bond angles. The result is a hexagonal structure peppered with "empty spaces." It is because of the openness of its lattice structure that solid water has a lower density than liquid water: In liquid water at 4°C, these spaces would be filled with other water molecules that were not completely hydrogen-bonded. And it is again because of the nature and geometry of the bonds between water molecules that this unique property emerges.

Why So Many Substances Can Be Dissolved in Water

Table salt is a compound of sodium ions and chloride ions. (An **ion** is an atom that is charged; negatively if it has gained one or more electrons, or positively if it has lost one or more electrons.) In a crystal of table salt these two types of ions alternate in a cubic array, which is a very stable arrangement (Figure 11.6). And yet, when a crystal of table salt is dropped into a spoonful of water, its stable crystalline

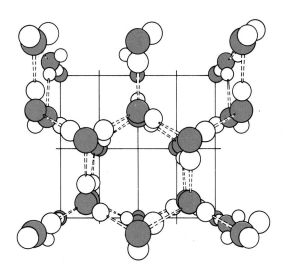

Figure 11.5 Structural model of an ice crystal. The hydrogen bonds are depicted as dashed lines. The lower density of solid water has important consequences for fresh-water organisms living in temperate climates. In lakes and ponds, the solid water formed during the changing of seasons from fall to winter floats at the top of the more dense liquid water. There it forms a crust of ice. Because water molecules cannot vibrate freely in an ice crystal, they conduct heat poorly from the underlying water to the atmosphere. Even if the surrounding air temperature drops well below the freezing point, most of the water is insulated enough by the crust of ice that it remains above the freezing point throughout the cold winter months. Without that crust, lakes and ponds could freeze solid every winter, which would be devastating to the life forms found within them. Very few other substances are known for which the liquid form is more dense than the solid form.

Figure 11.6 Packing model of sodium chloride, a cubic ionic crystal. The brown spheres represent sodium ions, and the gray spheres represent chloride ions.

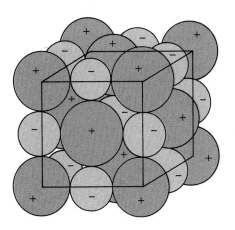

configuration breaks up—it dissolves. This happens because the salt ions have a greater attraction for the water molecules than the water molecules have for each other, and vice versa. A crystal of table salt has, on its surface, positively charged sodium ions. Each sodium ion at the surface has negatively charged chloride ions on five of its six sides. When the crystal is dropped into water, the negative (oxygen) ends of the nearby water molecules are immediately attracted to the positive charges of the sodium ions. Similarly, the positive (hydrogen) ends of the water molecules in the vicinity are attracted to the negative charges of the chloride ions. If a sodium ion breaks away from the surface of the crystal, it is immediately surrounded by a charge-oriented sphere of water molecules; the ions freshly exposed on the crystal surface then attract *their* own cloud of ordered water molecules. In this manner, the table salt rapidly dissolves as each ion is surrounded by layer upon layer of water molecules. These ordered structures, called **spheres of hydration,** are depicted in Figure 11.7.

Sugar is another substance that dissolves readily in water. The fact that a crystal of sugar dissolves when it is dropped into water suggests that sugar molecules, too, must have a greater attraction for water than they do for each other. But the kind of attraction must be different, because sugar has no ionized groups. The attraction between sugar and water is based on hydrogen bonding. The structural formula for glucose (the principal sugar in human blood) was shown in Figure 10.17. This structure has been redrawn in Figure 11.8 to emphasize the atoms that are involved in hydrogen bonding with water. Because each of the oxygen-hydrogen bonds in glucose is polar (as it is in water), each is capable of taking part in hydrogen bonding with water. *It is their tendency for ionic interactions and hydrogen bonding that makes most of the molecules of life soluble in water.*

The Difference Between Hydrophilic and Hydrophobic Substances

The solvent properties of water extend only to those substances capable of interacting directly with water by hydrogen bonding or by ionic attraction. Such substances are called **hydrophilic** (*hydro* means "water"; *philic* means "loving"). Substances lacking either polar or ionic bonds have no chemical basis for interacting with water; they are called **hydrophobic** (*phobic* means "dreading"). Recall that when polar covalent bonds hold a water molecule together, the electrons spend more time orbiting the oxygen nucleus than the hydrogen nuclei, so the electrons are shared unequally. In contrast, the kind of covalent bond that forms in hydrophobic substances is electrically neutral because the electrons are shared equally. In other words, hydrophobic substances are held together by **nonpolar covalent bonds.**

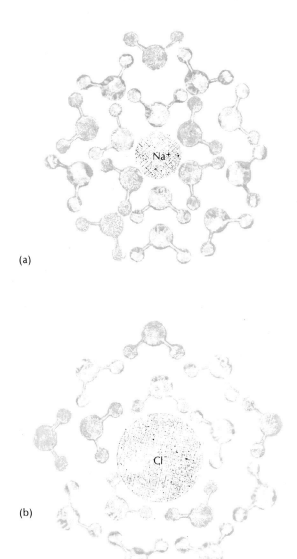

(a)

(b)

Figure 11.7 The spheres of hydration that form around (a) a sodium ion and (b) a chloride ion from a crystal of table salt that is placed in water. (These spheres are depicted in cross section.) The interaction between the water and salt has two results: The salt is dissolved, but the structure of the water is also disturbed. The water molecules taking part in such spheres of hydration are no longer available for the formation of orderly hydrogen bonds between water molecules, and they cannot participate in the formation of ice crystal lattices. That is why the oceans, with their high content of dissolved salts, are resistant to freezing.

(a)

| In Water

(b)

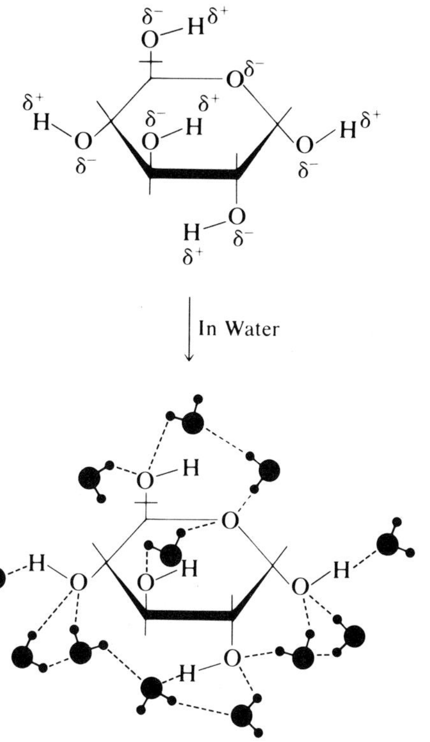

Figure 11.8 (a) Structural formula for the sugar glucose. (b) Hydrogen bonding between glucose and water.

Gasoline is a nonpolar substance. It is a mixture of related compounds referred to as ''hydrocarbons'' because they contain only hydrogen and carbon atoms. The structure of a gasoline molecule (octane) is

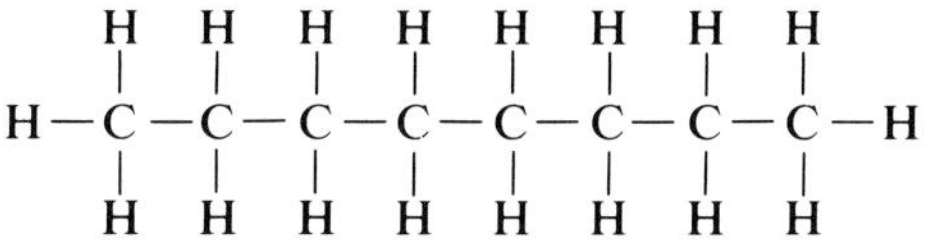

Each of the hydrogen atoms is held to a carbon atom by a nonpolar bond, so the carbon atoms and the hydrogen atoms are electrically neutral.

Now, when gasoline is stirred vigorously into a container of water, individual droplets of the gasoline become temporarily suspended in the water. Because there is no chemical basis for interaction between the water and the gasoline, there is no tendency for the mixture to become stabilized. In fact, the physical presence of the gasoline droplets decreases the number of hydrogen bonds that can be formed in the water, so there is a marked tendency for the water to ''squeeze'' the droplets of gasoline away from the interior of the suspension. Moreover, if two gasoline droplets meet, they tend to coalesce, or fuse together. When the effect of this **hydrophobic interaction** is combined

with the instability of the suspension, all of the gasoline is rapidly ''squeezed out'' to form a surface layer. Hydrophobic interaction thus enhances the possibilities for hydrogen bonding within the water and for hydrophobic bonding within the gasoline. Because the maximum number of bonds is now possible for both substances, the layering represents their most stable state of organization; it will be maintained in the absence of further stirring.

The Importance of Hydrophobic Substances in Living Things

It is possible for a polar hydrophilic group to become attached to one of the ends of a long hydrophobic molecule. When that happens, a set of interesting new properties emerges. Consider, for example, a **fatty acid** molecule, which is one of the chemical building blocks for fat.

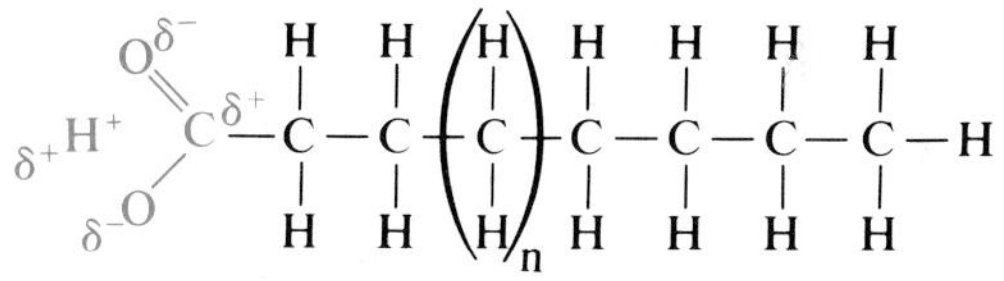

The introduction of the acid group (depicted in red) at one end of the molecule leads to a molecule with mixed properties. Because of its hydrogen-bonding potential, the acid end of the molecule interacts with and tends to be dissolved in water, but the hydrocarbon ''tail'' displays no such tendency.

When such a substance is simply dropped on water, it tends to form a surface film, as gasoline does, but the film is highly ordered. When just enough of the substance is added so that a layer one molecule thick covers the surface of the water, the structure depicted in Figure 11.9 emerges. All the molecules are lined up with their hydrophilic ''heads'' dissolved in the water (by hydrogen bonding and ionic interactions) and their hydrophobic ''tails'' sticking out and bound to each other by hydrophobic interaction. If this mixture is now stirred vigorously, droplets form. These droplets are often called **micelles.** Their cross-sectional structure often resembles the form depicted in Figure 11.10a. But these droplets differ from those of gasoline in that they will remain suspended indefinitely in the water. A stable suspension, or **emulsion,** has been formed and it represents a different state of organization. (If a tiny amount of gasoline or some other hydrophobic substance were to be added to the mixture before stirring, it would end up entirely within the interior of the micelles, where it would be held to the hydrophobic ends of the fatty acid molecules by hydrophobic bonding.)

Now, if the emulsion of water and fatty acid is created by slightly different methods, a different kind of structure forms, which in cross section has the appearance shown in Figure 11.10b. In this case the fatty acid molecules are

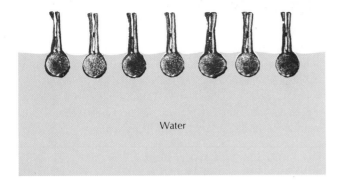

Figure 11.9 (left) A diagram of the organization of a fatty acid "monolayer" on the surface of a container of water. In such a film, which is one molecule thick, each fatty acid molecule has its polar "head" dissolved in the water and its nonpolar "tail" sticking up, away from the water.

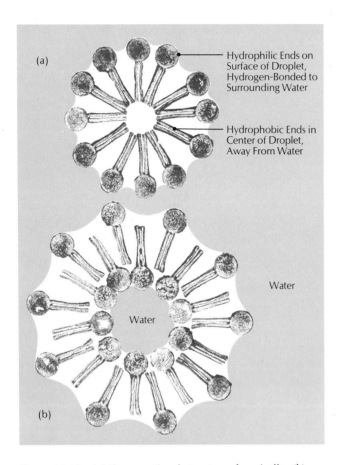

(a)

Hydrophilic Ends on Surface of Droplet, Hydrogen-Bonded to Surrounding Water

Hydrophobic Ends in Center of Droplet, Away From Water

Water

Water

(b)

Figure 11.10 (a) Cross-sectional structure of a micelle. (b) Bilayer arrangement in a micelle. The two concentric spheres are fatty acid molecules. A structure with more layers than this would not be as stable because the maximum number of possible bonds occurs in the bilayer arrangement. Nevertheless, completely nonpolar molecules such as gasoline can be dissolved in the hydrophobic region of the bilayer, which would increase the complexity of the arrangement.

organized in two concentric spheres, called a **bilayer.** The hydrophilic ends of both layers are hydrogen-bonded to water. The hydrophobic ends of both layers are held together by hydrophobic interactions. Such micelles are quite stable.

The water in the interior of the micelle diagramed in Figure 11.10*b* is thoroughly isolated from the water outside. Because the water and other polar molecules do not tend to interact with the hydrophobic parts of the bilayer, they cannot diffuse freely across this boundary. For that reason, it is possible to create a micelle in which there is a stable difference in the composition of the watery solutions inside and outside of it—for example, by adding salt to the exterior water. *It is upon simple principles related to relative water solubility of various atomic groupings that all of the membrane systems isolating and enclosing cells and parts of cells are based.*

The Capillary Action of Water

What other properties can be traced to the bonds between water molecules? Consider what happens when an end of a narrow glass tube is placed against the surface of a drop of water: The water immediately moves a certain distance up the tube. The narrower the bore of the tube, the higher the water will rise. This movement is called **capillary action.**

Figure 11.11 shows how the composition of the tube itself affects this movement of water. The hydrocarbon molecules that make up a plastic (polyethylene) tube are held together entirely by nonpolar covalent bonds, so the tube has a nonpolar hydrophobic surface. A glass tube, in contrast, has a surface studded with polar and ionized groups, which means its surface is hydrophilic. (It does not dissolve to any significant extent because the attraction of the atoms and molecules of the glass for each other exceeds their attraction to water.) *Water will rise in any tube that has a hydrophilic surface; it will not rise in tubes that are hydrophobic at the surface.*

Capillary action is due to the formation of the same kinds of ionic attractions and hydrogen bonds that account for the solubility of salt and sugar. Water molecules contacting the surface of the glass tube bond to it even as they remain

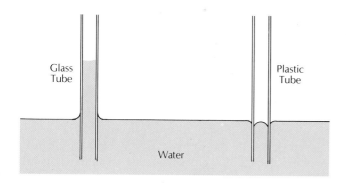

Figure 11.11 Capillary action in a glass tube, which has a hydrophilic surface, and the absence of capillary action in a plastic tube, which has a hydrophobic surface. The tubes that transport water upward through tree trunks and branches have hydrophilic surfaces. They are quite narrow and lined with an insoluble, sugarlike material that has many hydrogen bonding groups. Water molecules readily become attached to these groups; as a result, the fluid creeps upward.

bonded to nearby water molecules. As water molecules creep up the surface of the glass, making and breaking hydrogen and ionic bonds with the surface, they pull along other water molecules to which they are also attached by hydrogen bonds. How high the water can climb is determined by the bore of the tube: the greater the bore, the greater the weight of water that must be borne by the water molecules that have moved up the farthest.

Ionization of Water and pH Values

An earlier section in this chapter introduced the idea that water molecules "change partners"—that hydrogen atoms covalently bonded to one oxygen atom and hydrogen-bonded to another can switch to become hydrogen-bonded to the first and covalently bonded to the second. The shifting of hydrogen atoms is a continuous activity. But it is not sufficiently rapid or precise that all of the molecules always have the same composition. In other words, *water does not always exist in the form of a covalently bonded molecule of the composition H_2O.* At any one time, some of the molecules lack a hydrogen nucleus; they are called **hydroxyl ions** (OH^-) and they have the structure:

Meanwhile, the hydrogen nucleus is temporarily free in the form of a **hydrogen ion** (H^+) or it is attached to another water molecule to form what is known as a **hydronium ion** (H_3O^+). A hydronium ion has the structure:

(Strictly speaking, most of the time ionized hydrogen is present in water as hydronium ions, rather than as hydrogen ions. But it is more convenient at the introductory level to think of the transient hydrogen nuclei as hydrogen ions, and that is the term that will be used throughout this textbook.)

The process in which water molecules break down temporarily to form hydrogen ions and hydroxyl ions is called **ionization of water.** It is a regular and predictable process. In pure water, under normal conditions, there will be at any given time one hydrogen ion and one hydroxyl ion for every 550,000,000 water molecules. In itself this number may seem to be too small to be significant. But a drinking glass of pure water, to take one example, contains more than 10^{16} (or 10,000,000,000,000,000) hydrogen ions and an equal number of hydroxyl ions! Hydrogen ions and, to a lesser extent, hydroxyl ions play an essential role in the functioning of organisms, and an understanding of how their concentration is varied and controlled is important to the understanding of life processes.

The concentration of hydrogen ions in pure water is 10^{-7} molar ($10^{-7}M$). The concentration of hydroxyl ions is also $10^{-7}M$. Now, the concentration of hydrogen ions can be increased by adding to the pure water a substance such as hydrogen chloride (HCl), which breaks down to produce hydrogen ions but not hydroxyl ions ($HCl \rightarrow H^+ + Cl^-$). As this is done, however, some of the hydrogen ions being added react immediately with the hydroxyl ions already present, and they combine to form water molecules. As the hydrogen ion concentration rises, then, the hydroxyl ion concentration falls. If enough hydrogen chloride is added to raise the hydrogen ion concentration by tenfold (to $10^{-6}M$), the hydroxyl ion concentration will fall by tenfold (to $10^{-8}M$). Each increase in hydrogen ion concentration will be balanced by a corresponding decrease in hydroxyl ion concentration. At all times, the product of the hydrogen ion concentration and the hydroxyl ion concentration is 10^{-14} M. (For the two examples given here, $10^{-7} \times 10^{-7} = 10^{-14}$, and $10^{-6} \times 10^{-8} = 10^{-14}$.)

The concentration of the two kinds of ions always has this inverse proportionality in water solutions, so it is never necessary to specify both concentrations. One can be inferred from the other. To simplify the notation, a value called **pH** (*p*otential of *H*ydrogen) is used to express the hydrogen ion concentration in solutions:

$$pH = -\log_{10}H^+ \text{ concentration}$$

Table 11.1
pH Values for Various Solutions

Solution	pH Value
Pure gastric juice	about 0.9
Orange juice	2.6–4.4
Vinegar	3.0
Grapefruit juice	3.2
Tomato juice	4.3
Urine	4.8–7.5
Saliva	6.4–6.9
Milk	6.6–6.9
Intestinal juice	7.0–8.0
Blood	7.4–7.5
Tears	7.4
Pancreatic juice	7.5–8.0
Egg white	8.0
Sea water	8.0

Source: Adapted from Edward S. West *et al.*, *Textbook of Biochemistry*, 4th ed. (Toronto: Macmillan, 1966), p. 30.

When the concentration of hydrogen ions is 10^{-7}M, as it is in pure water, then the $\log_{10}$ of the concentration will be -7 and the pH will be 7. If the concentration of hydroxyl ions in a solution is 10^{-9}M, it follows that the pH of the solution is 5. Substances that produce hydrogen ions are called **acids,** and substances that produce hydroxyl ions or that in some way reduce the concentration of hydrogen ions are called **bases.**

A variety of the chemical reactions in living things either produce hydrogen ions as one of their products (which tends to lower the pH) or use up hydrogen ions as reactants (which tends to raise the pH). Regardless of whether the chemical reaction involves hydrogen ions as a reactant or a product, virtually all reactions are affected to some degree by the absolute concentration of hydrogen ions. *The speed with which each chemical reaction in a living organism occurs varies with changes in pH.*

Most cells of living organisms can survive only if they maintain a pH at or around 7. This means that in order to control their internal chemistry, cells must have some way of preventing wide swings in pH as hydrogen ions are produced or used up. Such control is assured by a rich array of substances known as **buffers.** A buffer is a substance that tends to remove hydrogen ions from a solution as the hydrogen ion concentration begins to rise, or to give them up to the solution as the hydrogen ion concentration begins to fall. A buffer tends to minimize the change in pH that occurs as a cell produces or uses up hydrogen ions. The most important buffers in cells are the amino acids and large molecules composed of many amino acids, which are called proteins. (As you will read later, proteins serve several other important functions as well.) The simplest amino acid is glycine. This amino acid exists in three forms, and the way it works as a buffer is shown in Figure 11.12.

Buffers cannot completely prevent changes in pH. But they can prevent the swings in pH from assuming the magnitude they otherwise would. For example, an addition of a modest amount of hydrogen chloride could change the pH of pure water from 7 to 4, which would be a change incompatible with life. But in a strongly buffered solution, the same amount of hydrogen chloride might cause the pH to change merely from 7 to 6.99!

Water as a Reactant

Water is not merely a physical medium—a solvent—in which life processes occur. It is an active ingredient in the chemical reactions of life. The more we understand **metabolism** (the chemical changes in life processes), the more we come to appreciate the fact that water is one of the most important reactants in cells. For example, one of the most critical sets of metabolic reactions is *photosynthesis*. In this process, green plants use the energy of sunlight to split water, thereby obtaining hydrogen, which is used in the synthesis of sugar from carbon dioxide. A set of reactions called *glycolysis and respiration* subsequently releases the energy stored in such sugar molecules for use by plants and animals. In these reactions, the hydrogen is removed from the sugar molecules, producing carbon dioxide as one end product. The hydrogen is combined with oxygen to form water once again. These sets of reactions are only two of many reactions in which water is directly involved.

DEHYDRATION SYNTHESIS IS THE PRINCIPAL CONSTRUCTION METHOD OF LIVING THINGS

There are many chemical reactions in which water is given off as a product. Of these, one of the most important types is the class of reactions that we will call **dehydration synthesis.** What this expression means is that larger molecules are formed (synthesized) by the hooking together of small molecules, with a concurrent removal of water molecules (dehydration). The process is summarized in Figure 11.13.

In such reactions, the building blocks, or **monomers,** may be similar, identical, or quite different molecules. The number of such monomers that bond together to yield a larger molecule, or **polymer,** may be only a very few or they may number in the hundreds or even thousands. *It is in dehydration synthesis reactions that all of the complex molecules characteristic of living things are built.* The remainder of this chapter describes four major classes of these complex molecules—the carbohydrates, lipids, proteins, and nucleic acids—and how they are linked together in dehydration synthesis reactions.

CARBOHYDRATES ARE FOOD RESERVES AND STRUCTURAL SUPPORTS FOR LIFE

Glucose is only one of many simple sugar molecules that may exist as monomers or in polymers. Its molecular formula is $C_6H_{12}O_6$. Sugar molecules, and their polymers, are called **carbohydrates.** The word means ''hydrates of carbon''; and hydrate means ''water-combined.'' In addition to glucose, several other six-carbon sugar molecules are found in living things. Fructose, for example, has the same molecular formula as glucose, but the atoms of these two substances are arranged differently, their structures are different, and their properties are therefore different. Moreover, not all sugar molecules have six carbon atoms. Ribose, an essential part of ribonucleic acid, is a five-carbon sugar molecule with the formula $C_5H_{10}O_5$. Sugar

Predominant Form at Higher pH
As pH Falls
As pH Rises
Predominant Form at pH 7
As pH Falls
As pH Rises
Predominant Form at Lower pH

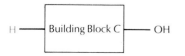

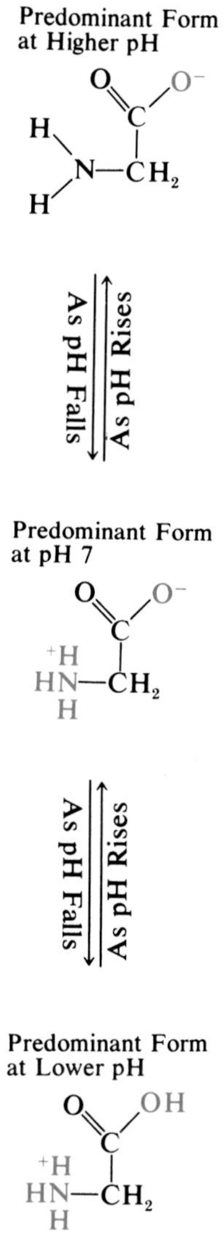

Figure 11.12 (left) The three forms of glycine, an amino acid that acts as a buffer against wide swings in pH. At or around pH 7, most of the glycine molecules bear both a negatively charged acid group (—COO^-) and a positively charged amino group (–NH_3^+). If additional hydrogen ions (H^+) are introduced into a solution containing glycine, a great many will react with the —COO^- groups to form electrically neutral (—COOH) groups. As a result, the concentration of free hydrogen ions will not rise as much as it would have if the glycine had not been present.

Now, if some other chemical process in the vicinity tends to use up hydrogen ions, their concentration will be lowered and the pH will tend to rise. The —COOH groups of glycine will in that case give up their hydrogen ions and return to the ionized —COO^- state. If the pH continues to rise after all of the glycine molecules have given up their —COOH hydrogen ions, additional hydrogen ions will be released from the amino group, thus offering further resistance to the change in pH.

Figure 11.13 (below) Diagram of a dehydration synthesis reaction. Building blocks A, B, and C may be similar, identical, or entirely different molecules. When they are synthesized into a chain of molecules, the elements of water are removed. Because the pathways by which such dehydration syntheses occur in cells are quite complex, the hydrogen and oxygen atoms may be temporarily combined with other substances rather than appearing immediately as water molecules.

H
Building Block A
OH
H
Building Block B
OH
Dehydration Synthesis
H
A
B
C
OH
plus HOH and HOH
H
Building Block C
OH

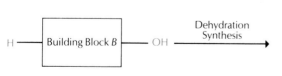

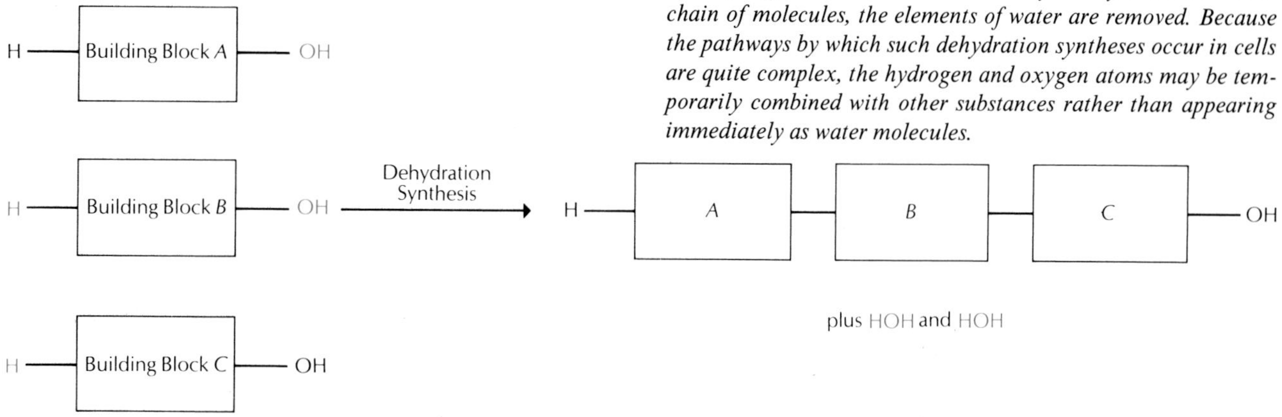

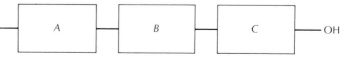

molecules containing three, four, or seven carbon atoms also exist.

Simple sugar molecules such as glucose are also known as **monosaccharides.** Some cells produce double sugar molecules, or **disaccharides,** as food storage molecules by the process of dehydration synthesis (Figure 11.14). More extensive food reserves may be produced in plants and animals, however, when dehydration synthesis reactions combine many simple sugar molecules into large, relatively insoluble polymers such as starch. The linkages in these complex sugar molecules, or **polysaccharides,** are similar to the linkages found in such simple disaccharides as lactose. But many of these more complex molecules are highly branched rather than linear (Figure 11.15). Such branching occurs when two molecules of sugar link to a third molecule through two different hydroxyl (—OH) groups. What are some of the outcomes of these different modes of attachment?

Recall, from Chapter 1, that glucose monomers linked together one way end up as amylose (a polysaccharide used for food reserves) and that the same monomers linked in a different way end up as cellulose (a polysaccharide used for

structural support rather than for food storage). In both cases, dehydration synthesis transforms these glucose monomers into polysaccharides. There is a difference between the two in terms of the manner in which their monomers are linked together (Figure 11.16). In itself, that difference is not enough to explain the gross differences in their properties. To find that explanation we must move past the level of simple, one-dimensional attachments between monomers and turn to examine three-dimensional models of the polymers they form. *Like the small molecules from which they are built, all large molecules tend to form chemical interactions, such as hydrogen bonds, with themselves and with other molecules in their environment.* The most stable—hence, the predominant—form of such a large molecule will occur when it forms the maximum number of such bonds. What happens, then, as these two large polymers curl and twist in a watery solution containing other polymers of the same type? In what shape will they come to form the greatest number of stable hydrogen bonds? Because of the difference in the angle of attachment of the glucose monomers in amylose and cellulose, the answer is different for these two kinds of polymers.

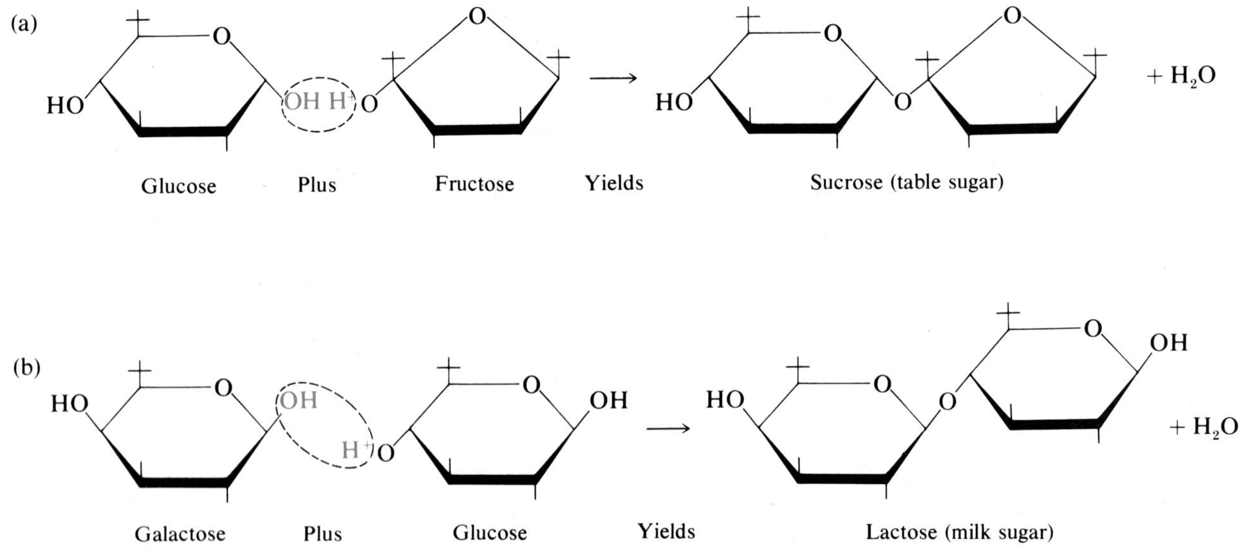

Figure 11.14 Production of disaccharides. In the example given in (a), sugar beets and sugar cane plants link one glucose molecule to one fructose molecule to form the disaccharide sucrose. When glucose is extracted from these plants and refined, it becomes the sugar we use to sweeten foods. In the milk-producing cells of animals, dehydration synthesis links glucose and galactose into the disaccharide lactose, a process that is depicted in (b). Other examples can be given. Some yeasts store food energy in the form of two glucose molecules hooked together in such a way that a disaccharide called trehalose is formed. In certain germinating seeds, two glucose molecules are linked together to form the disaccharide maltose (malt sugar). All disaccharides have the formula $C_n(H_2O)_{n-1}$.

(a)

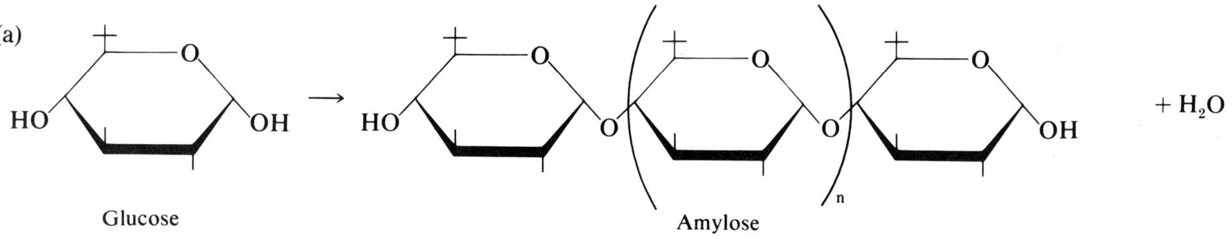

Glucose   Amylose $+ H_2O$

(b)

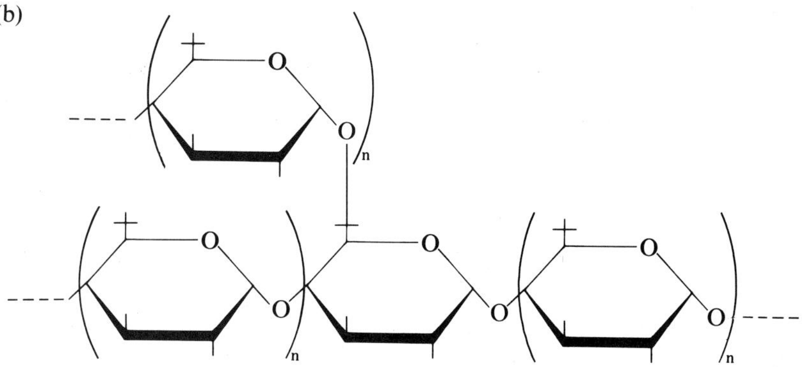

Figure 11.15   (a) The linear form of linkage of the polysaccharide amylose (n represents the fact that several dozen or several hundred glucose molecules may be linked together in such a chain), and (b) the branching pattern characteristic of some polysaccharides.

(a)

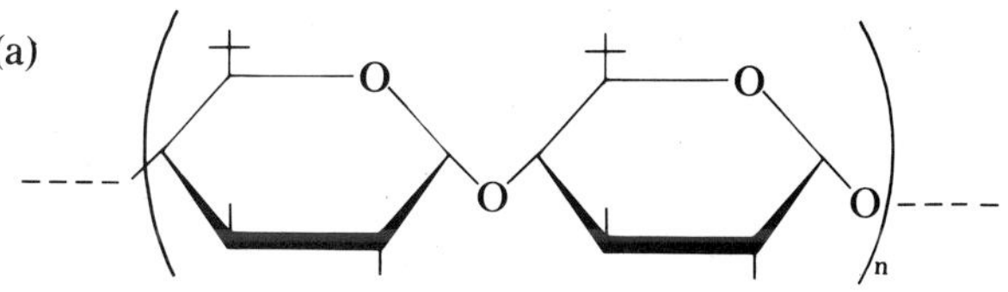

(b)

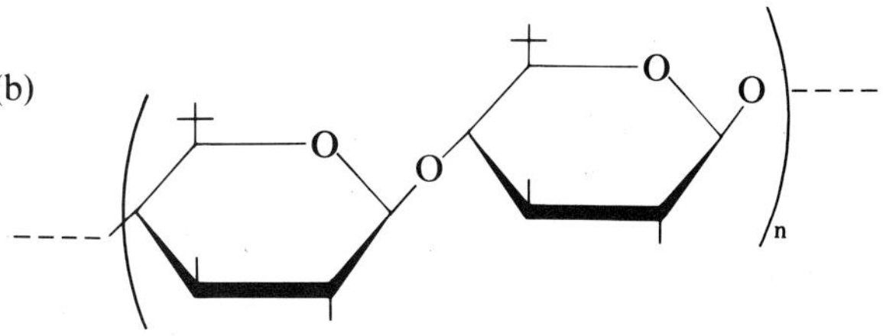

Figure 11.16   The glucose linkage in (a) amylose and in (b) cellulose.

Amylose is capable of twisting into a highly regular, coiled, chainlike structure in which the —OH groups of many of its glucose monomers come close enough to other glucose monomers in the same chain to form hydrogen bonds (Figure 11.17a). The combined strength of these bonds is enough to keep the amylose chain in this arrangement, which is called a **helix.** Not all the —OH groups of the glucose monomers are involved in stabilizing the amylose helix. Some project outward from the structure, where they are free to form hydrogen bonds with water molecules. (That is the reason why the amylose polymer dissolves in water.) This is the first example of an architectural theme you will encounter again and again in biology: *Hydrogen bonds are capable of holding a large molecule in a stable, helical shape.*

The cellulose polymer does not readily form such a helix. Instead, its unique structure permits the formation of extensive hydrogen bonds between glucose monomers in different chains of cellulose that come to lie side by side. As the first of these hydrogen bonds form, they tend to pull adjacent polymers of cellulose into more nearly perfect register, and still more bonds are formed. The whole array has the largest number of stable hydrogen bonds when each polymer is fully extended into a relatively stiff, rodlike shape surrounded on all sides by other cellulose polymers (Figure 11.17b). The number of —OH groups of their glucose monomers that become involved in such bonds is so great that few remain free to react with water. (That is why cellulose fibers have no tendency to dissolve in water.)

Amylose and cellulose are examples of **homopolymers,** which are large molecules composed of a single kind of monomer. Homopolymers are relatively rare in living organisms. **Heteropolymers**—molecules formed by dehydration synthesis reactions from one or more kinds of monomers—are much more common. If you tweak your ear or press your finger against the tip of your nose, you will feel beneath your skin a firm but flexible material known as cartilage. The unique properties of this material derive from its construction. In it is a polymer made of two kinds of modified sugar monomers that are repeated in strict succession (ABABAB... and so on). *As the number of kinds of monomers is increased in heteropolymers, the variety of emergent properties becomes enormous.* For example, complex polysaccharides (particularly the ones that become linked to proteins) are important in the process known as "recognition." Whether a grafted heart will be accepted or rejected by its recipient, whether a fish will be attacked by a sea anemone or ignored, whether a cancer cell will grow or be destroyed—all such processes are determined by precisely what kinds of complex polysaccharides are located on the surface of these biological entities.

LIPIDS ARE CHEMICAL BOUNDARIES BETWEEN THE LIVING AND THE NONLIVING

In an earlier part of this chapter, you read that two layers of fatty acid molecules surrounding a water droplet form a structure called a micelle. Although this structure in principle resembles a membrane-bound cell, the structure of the cell membrane is much more complex because of the manner in which its relatively simple parts are arranged.

Fatty acids are found in the membrane that isolates the interior of a cell from its external environment. Here they occur not as "free" fatty acids but as components of larger molecules known as **phospholipids.** Like most complex molecules of life, phospholipids are built up by dehydration synthesis from relatively simple parts (Figure 11.18).

Figure 11.17 (a) A highly schematic diagram of part of the helix formed by an amylose molecule. Here the individual glucose units are shown as beads on a long, coiled chain. The hydrogen bonds (dotted lines) between glucose monomers in adjacent turns of the helix reinforce each other and make this particular shape of the molecule exceptionally stable. The distance between successive turns of the helix is exaggerated for clarity. (b) A highly schematic diagram of part of a cellulose fiber in which adjacent polymers are hydrogen-bonded side to side with neighboring polymers. As in (a), individual glucose monomers are shown as beads, and hydrogen bonds as dotted lines.

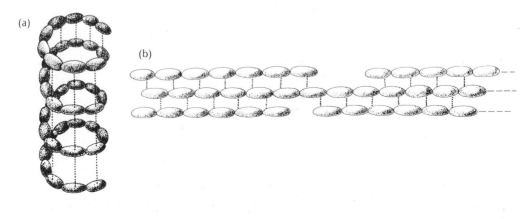

(a)

(b)

STEP 1   Formation of a Diglyceride From Two Fatty Acid Molecules
and a Molecule of Glycerin

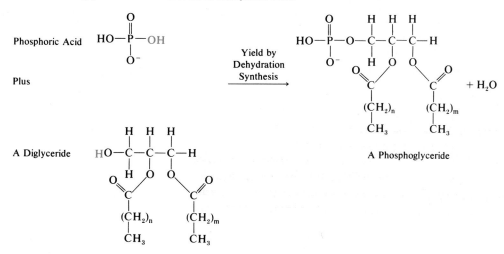

A Diglyceride

Figure 11.18   The assembly of a phospholipid. By the stepwise process depicted in this diagram, a molecule is built up that exhibits an exaggerated version of the polar-nonpolar nature of fatty acids. (The subscripts "m" and "n" indicate simply that fatty acids possessing different numbers of carbon atoms can be incorporated into a single lipid molecule.)

STEP 2   Formation of a Phosphoglyceride From a Molecule of
a Diglyceride and a Molecule of Phosphoric Acid

A Phosphoglyceride

STEP 3   Formation of a Complete Phospholipid by Addition of a
Nitrogen-Containing Base to the Phosphoglyceride

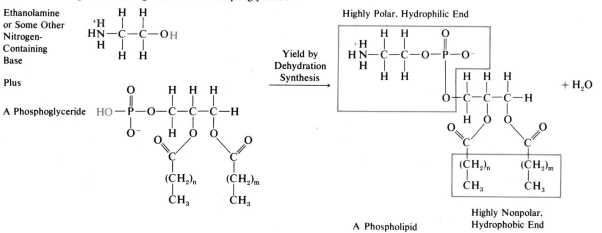

A Phospholipid

Because a wide assortment of fatty acids and nitrogen-containing bases can be assembled in various combinations, an extensive array of phospholipid molecules with differing properties is found in cell membranes. Such phospholipid molecules form micelles that are more stable than the simple micelles formed by fatty acids. These molecules are essential components of all membrane systems of all cells—not only the membranes that separate cellular contents from the environment but also the membranes inside eukaryotic cells that separate various compartments within the cell from one another. As you will see in Chapter 13, such membranes are not simple phospholipid bilayers; rather, they are complex mosaics in which other substances are dissolved spottily in the phospholipid film.

A second large group of lipids is known as the **neutral lipids.** Included in this group are the fats. They differ in structure from phospholipids in having a fatty acid attached to all three —OH groups of glycerin (Figure 11.19a). The fats often possess as many as 150 or more atoms incapable of interacting with water, but only 3 of their atoms are capable of forming hydrogen bonds. As a result they are totally insoluble in water and do not participate in micelle or membrane formation. They do, however, contain an enormous amount of potential chemical energy, and that is why fats are important storage forms of food in both plants and animals. In periods when food is scarce, fats can be converted to water-soluble forms by **hydrolysis,** in which a large molecule is split into smaller ones by the addition of water. (It is, in effect, the reverse of dehydration synthesis.) The products may then be used as food energy (Figure 11.19b).

Also included in the neutral lipids are the large, complex molecules known as **steroids.** The multiple ring structure of steroids is shown in Figure 11.20. The addition of chemical groupings at various places on this ring system can produce a diverse and important group of steroid compounds, some of which will be discussed in Chapter 22.

PROTEINS ACT AS MASTER ARCHITECTS AND CHEMISTS OF THE LIVING CELL

Through the increasingly complex linkages among the molecules of life, increasing variations in structure and function emerge. The most structurally varied molecules in living organisms are proteins. The human body contains at

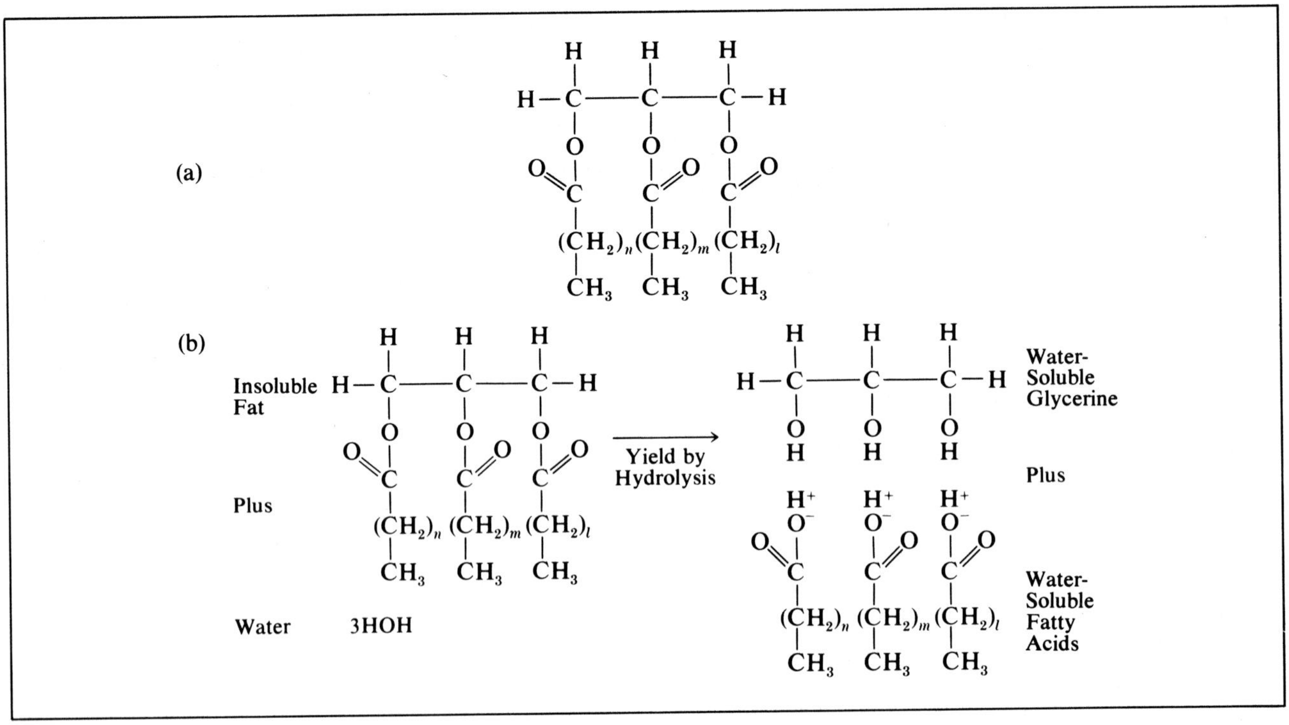

Figure 11.19 (a) Structural formula for neutral lipids. (b) Hydrolysis of insoluble fat. Many plants store energy in the form of liquid fats, or oils, which their germinating seedlings use. We, too, use various forms of these liquid fats, including cottonseed oil, linseed oil, corn oil, and peanut oil. Animals tend to store solid fats (fats with a melting temperature higher than body temperature) in periods when more food is available than is immediately required. In periods of scarce food supply these fats are converted to water-soluble forms by hydrolysis and are "burned" by the animal as an internally derived source of energy. The obesity of Western man can be attributed to the fact that modern technology has made food available to those who can afford it in excess of immediate need at all times. Thus fat is continuously stored but is seldom utilized.

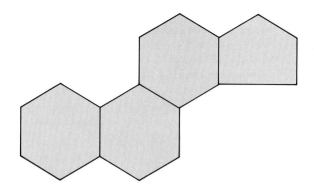

Figure 11.20 Multiple ring structure of steroids, which lends itself to the addition of chemical groupings that can produce diverse steroid compounds. One of the most abundant of the steroids is cholesterol, an important cellular component that changes the properties of cell membranes as it dissolves within the phospholipid bilayer. Both fats and cholesterol are insoluble in water, which is the reason why they tend to settle out of the bloodstream in human beings and pile up on the linings of certain blood vessels. This process can lead to narrowing and stiffening of the blood vessels, which in turn can lead to strokes or heart attacks. An important group of steroid molecules found in animals is the steroid hormones, which are modifications of the structure for cholesterol. They are produced primarily by the adrenal glands and by the gonads (ovaries and testes). Those produced by the adrenal gland are responsible for the continual regulation of such critical factors as the amount of sugar and salt in the blood. The sex hormones, on the other hand, act in a long-term way to govern the production and maintenance of all structures and functions associated with sexual reproduction.

least 10,000 different kinds of protein molecules, and the number may be much higher than that. To a large extent, the unique characteristics of many different kinds of cells are determined by the different kinds of proteins they possess. Why is a red blood cell red, and why does it carry oxygen to other cells? It contains a red protein (hemoglobin) that is not found in other cells, and this protein has the specific property of binding oxygen in an easily reversible way. Why is muscle tough and stringy, yet capable of contraction? Muscle cells contain a group of long, fibrous proteins capable of interacting with one another in specific ways so that they can slide past one another, shortening and widening the cells in the process. Why do nails, claws, hooves, horns, and hair have the properties they do? They contain a series of related tough, hornlike proteins called keratins. How does the liver function to keep the amount of sugar in the blood constant? It contains a series of proteins called enzymes that function together to store glucose when

it is plentiful in the blood and to release it when it is not. Time after time as we ask how does a cell or organism do this, or that, we find the answer returning in a familiar form: "There is a protein, and its specific structure is such that . . ." To a large extent, life is played out on the surface of protein molecules.

The Principle of Emergence as It Applies to Proteins

Nowhere in the living world is the principle of emergence more clearly demonstrated than in proteins. From only twenty or so building blocks, billions of kinds of structurally varied proteins are created. These building blocks are the **amino acids.** *It is because of the detailed way in which amino acids are arranged in different proteins that entirely different properties emerge from one kind of protein to the next.* Interestingly enough, chemical analysis of ancient fossils tells us that throughout evolutionary time there has been no detectable change in the kinds of amino acids used; change has occurred only in the detailed ways in which those amino acids have been put together. How this structural theme translates into protein function is a key to understanding how life can emerge from lifeless molecules.

The twenty or so amino acids have the basic structure shown in Figure 11.21. All contain carbon, oxygen, hydrogen, and nitrogen atoms. In all amino acids, the amino group ($-NH_3^+$) and the acid group ($-COO^-$) attach to the same carbon atom, called the **alpha carbon atom.** The differences among amino acids exist because of a difference in the size and chemical nature of their side chains, called **R groups,** which vary from nonpolar (hydrophobic) to highly polar or ionized (hydrophilic). Each amino acid is therefore restricted in the number and kinds of interactions in which it may participate, and that is why no two amino acids will behave exactly the same under the same conditions.

Figure 11.21 An amino acid. All the component amino acids of proteins are composed of carbon, oxygen, nitrogen, and hydrogen atoms and have the general structure shown here; in other words, the amino group ($-NH_3^+$) and the acid group ($-COO^-$) are always attached to the same carbon atom, called the alpha carbon atom. Amino acids differ only in the atomic groupings represented by "R." The R groups can be as simple as a single atom; they can be as complicated as two-ring structures.

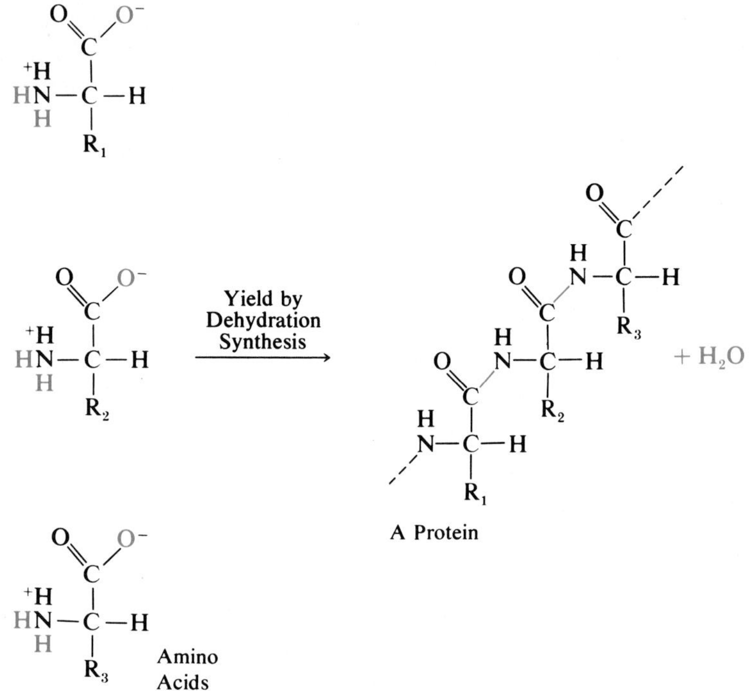

Figure 11.22   Peptide bonds joining together three amino acids into a protein. (The peptide bonds are depicted in red.) All peptide bonds form between one amino group ($-NH_3^+$) and one acid group ($-COO^-$). The bonding process is another example of dehydration synthesis, and it involves many intermediate steps not shown here.

As indicated in Figure 11.22, the linkage between two amino acids always takes place between the $-NH_3^+$ group of one and the $-COO^-$ group of the other. This particular linkage is named the **peptide bond.** When amino acids are strung together by peptide bonds, the resulting molecule is a **polypeptide chain.** Some proteins contain only one polypeptide chain; in such cases the terms "protein" and "polypeptide chain" are synonymous. But some proteins contain more than one polypeptide chain, in which case the terms obviously are not interchangeable. Hemoglobin is such a protein: it is composed of four polypeptide chains. When two or more polypeptide chains combine, the emergent properties are more complex than the properties exhibited by the single polypeptide chains.

How a Single Polypeptide Chain Assumes a Complex, Three-Dimensional Shape

Once a polypeptide chain has been formed, it initially tends to bend, twist, and curl more or less randomly. As it does so, side chains from various parts of the molecule are brought so close to one another that weak interactions or bonds sometimes occur between them. If two polar side chains come together, for example, they may form a hydrogen bond. If an acidic (negatively charged) side chain and a basic (positively charged) side chain make contact, they may form an ionic bond. When two or more nonpolar groups come together, they may undergo hydrophobic interaction (form a hydrophobic bond).

While this interaction between side chains is going on, hydrogen bonds are also being formed between the atoms that are part of the peptide linkages. (These are the atoms represented by $C=O$ and $N-H$ in Figure 11.22.) If the $C=O$ group of one peptide bond happens to come close to the $N-H$ group of a peptide bond elsewhere in the molecule, a hydrogen bond will form in the same kind of way that it does between water molecules (Figure 11.23). In many cases, the maximum number of peptide-peptide hydrogen bonds can be formed if the polypeptide chain is wound up helically, as shown in Figure 11.24. In this conformation, each peptide $C=O$ group is hydrogen-bonded to the $N-H$ group of the amino acid that is four positions away from it in the polypeptide chain. The protein shape is called an **alpha helix.**

With the exception of the peptide bond itself and one more type of bond to be discussed below, all bonds in a polypeptide chain are weak; they tend to form and to break readily. But collectively their interactions within the polypeptide chain are significant. The more weak interactions there are at any one instant, the more likely it is that the chain will be held in that shape. Then, if any one bond breaks apart, the atoms will remain close together and the same bond will re-form in exactly the same way an instant later. Thus the polypeptide chain automatically and spontaneously tends to form the specific three-dimensional shape that results in the greatest number of such bonds. Eventually, every polypeptide chain of a particular amino acid sequence takes on the same specific, complex, three-dimensional shape. Within this bonding pattern is one of the fundamental secrets of life: *The properties of proteins are*

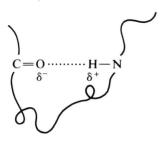

Figure 11.23   A hydrogen bond formed between two regions of a polypeptide chain. The C═O group involved in one peptide (covalent) bond is hydrogen bonded to the N—H group of a peptide bond some distance away.

Figure 11.24   Two different visualizations of the alpha helix, a common form of organization of a polypeptide chain. On the left, the polypeptide chain is represented as a simple ribbon to emphasize the helical organization. On the right, all of the atoms and bonds of the "backbone" of the polypeptide are shown. In both cases, the dashed lines represent the hydrogen bonds that stabilize the helix. Notice that the C═O group of amino acid 6 is hydrogen bonded to the N—H group of amino acid 2, whereas the N—H group of amino acid 6 is hydrogen bonded to the C═O group of amino acid 10. The properties of a polypeptide such as this would be determined by the chemical nature of the R groups projecting out of the helix.

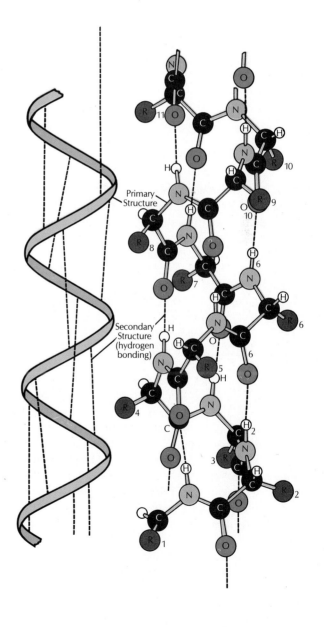

such that specifying structure in one dimension (the order of amino acids in the chain) is sufficient to specify structure in three dimensions.

It is the function of most genes in an organism to specify the exact sequence of amino acids needed to build a particular protein for a particular function. This genetically determined sequence of amino acids is called **primary (1°) structure.** Once amino acids have been assembled into a polypeptide chain, the chain may then coil helically about its own axis. This kind of coiling, called **secondary (2°) structure,** occurs only if the C═O and N—H groups of peptide bonds become hydrogen-bonded to each other. It is also possible for a polypeptide chain to bend and coil three-dimensionally in its environment. This kind of folding, called **tertiary (3°) structure,** is strongly influenced by the interactions of R groups in various parts of the polypeptide chain.

The kind and extent of secondary and tertiary structure a protein will have depends entirely on which amino acids are present, and in what order. Consider, for example, the profound effect that the presence of the amino acid **proline** often has on secondary and tertiary structures. Normally, polypeptide chains bend and twist about prior to assuming their final shape. Most of this motion is possible because an amino acid (and the rest of the chain to which it is attached by its C═O group) can rotate freely about the —N—C— bond between the nitrogen atom of its amino group and its alpha-carbon atom (Figure 11.26). Now, when proline is incorporated in a polypeptide chain (Figure 11.26*b*), rotation about the —N—C— bond is impossible because this

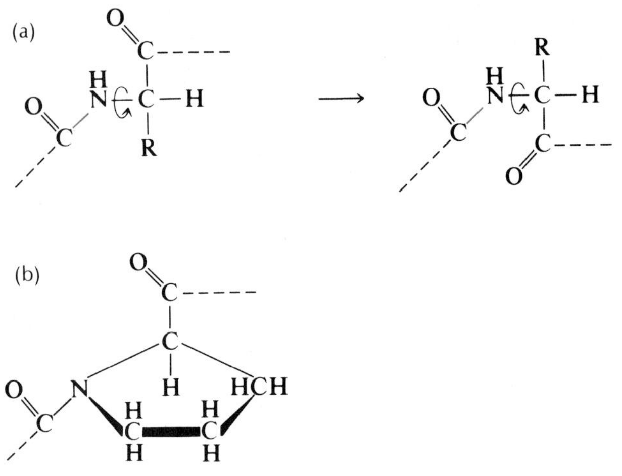

Figure 11.25 (a) The free rotation normally possible in polypeptide chains. (b) Free rotation is impossible in proline, which has an inflexible ring structure. Rotation is never possible about the peptide bonds (depicted in red).

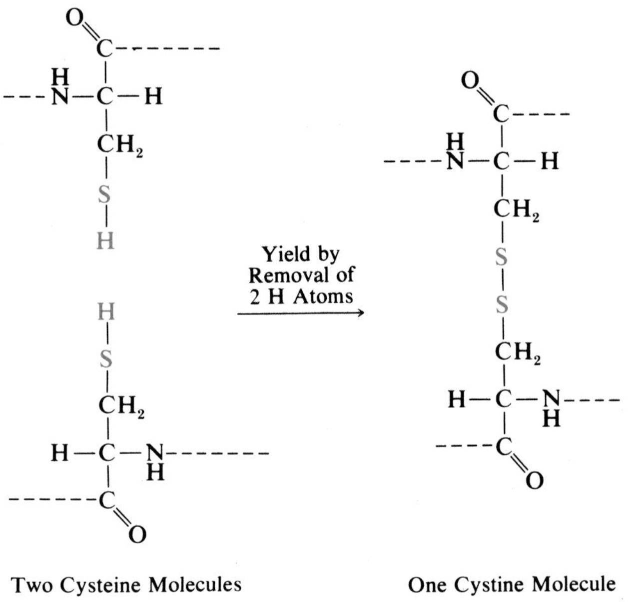

Two Cysteine Molecules   One Cystine Molecule

Figure 11.26 Formation of cystine. The dashed lines indicate the peptide bonds connecting the cysteine molecules to other amino acids in the polypeptide chain. The formation of cystine locks these two regions of the chain together.

bond is part of an inflexible ring. Wherever proline is incorporated into a chain, then, the twisting required to form an alpha helix cannot occur. (It is not that an alpha helix is always formed when proline is absent; it is simply that it cannot be formed when proline is present.) Such interruptions in the helix cause a bend, or corner, in the polypeptide chain.

Another amino acid that markedly affects protein structure is **cystine**. Strictly speaking, cystine is not an amino acid. It is a covalently bonded compound formed from two molecules of the amino acid cysteine (Figure 11.26). Cystine acts as a "spot weld," holding in a fixed relationship the two regions of a polypeptide chain that contain the cysteine molecules as part of the primary sequence. In themselves, cysteine side chains play no more of a role in determining secondary or tertiary structure than any other amino acid. But two cysteine molecules can bond together into one cystine molecule at their sulfur atoms, forming a **cystine bridge**. When that bridge is formed, the secondary and tertiary structure becomes locked into place. The result might be a loop within a single polypeptide chain; it might be a welding together of two polypeptide chains. Once welded by cystine bridges, polypeptide chains are more resistant to change in secondary and tertiary structure than they might otherwise be if their environment happens to change.

The relationship between primary, secondary, and tertiary structure, and the effect of proline and cysteine on that

relationship, is summarized in Figure 11.27. As you will read later, the exact shape of a given polypeptide may be modified by the conditions under which its bonds are formed. If conditions change in the cellular environment of the protein, new types of interactions may become possible and old ones impossible, which may give rise to a subtle change in the shape of certain proteins.

How Two or More Polypeptide Chains Combine Into a Functional Protein

It is possible for R groups that do not take part in interactions within a chain to interact with R groups on separate polypeptide chains. When that happens, the two (or more) polypeptide chains may combine to form a functional protein. Such combinations result in **quaternary (4°) structure.** Not all proteins have this structure. Two polypeptide chains join in quaternary structure only when their most stable secondary and tertiary structures leave a patch of complementary hydrophobic, ionized groups and/or hydrogen bonding on their surfaces. Such groups fit together like hand and glove.

Conservative and Nonconservative Interchanges of Amino Acids

When a gene undergoes a mutation, one amino acid in the sequence being specified may be replaced with another amino acid. How severe the consequences will be depends on two factors: Where exactly in the sequence has the

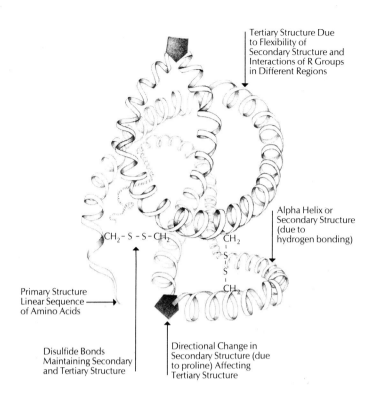

Tertiary Structure Due to Flexibility of Secondary Structure and Interactions of R Groups in Different Regions

Alpha Helix or Secondary Structure (due to hydrogen bonding)

$CH_2 - S - S - CH_2$

Primary Structure Linear Sequence of Amino Acids

Disulfide Bonds Maintaining Secondary and Tertiary Structure

Directional Change in Secondary Structure (due to proline) Affecting Tertiary Structure

Figure 11.27 A schematic diagram of the relationship between primary, secondary, and tertiary structure of a polypeptide chain. The ribbon represents the polypeptide "backbone." The coiling of the backbone is due to hydrogen bonding between peptide groups in the backbone, as shown in Figure 11.24. Notice that wherever proline (pentagons) appears, the helix bends sharply. Notice also that the disulfide bonds (formed in the conversion of two cysteine groups into one cystine molecule) result in a "spot-weld," holding the secondary and tertiary structure into place.

change occurred? And how different is the R group of the new amino acid from the R group it replaces? If the change results in replacement of one amino acid by another of the same general type (for example, acidic for acidic, basic for basic, or nonpolar for nonpolar), then the effect on the structure and function of the protein is often so subtle that it almost defies detection. Such substitutions are called **conservative interchanges.** Only if this kind of substitution occurs in a particularly critical part of the molecule will protein function be seriously affected. In contrast, if the substitution involves an amino acid of very different character (for example, an acidic side chain for a nonpolar side chain), the results in terms of structure and function are often drastic. Such substitutions are known as **nonconservative interchanges.**

A most dramatic example of a nonconservative interchange is the one that results in the human disease known as **sickle-cell anemia.** Individuals with this disease have inherited mutant genes for one of the polypeptide chains of hemoglobin, the red oxygen-carrying protein of the blood. These mutant sickle-cell genes specify the nonpolar amino acid valine at one particular place in the primary structure of hemoglobin where most human genes specify an acidic one: glutamic acid. As a result of this single change in primary structure, the hemoglobin molecules tend to stack together into long, stiff rods when exposed to certain conditions. These rods distort the cell into a "sickle" shape and puncture the cell membrane. The cells no longer are capable

of moving smoothly through the blood vessels and they pile up like logs in a log jam. Because the flow of blood through vital organs can become blocked, sickle-cell anemia can result in death.

The Evolution of Proteins Through the Accumulation of Changes in Amino Acid Sequence

Do proteins figure prominently in the evolutionary story? If we take distantly related organisms and examine one particular type of protein that serves essentially the same function in all of them, we generally find four remarkable features:

First, the proteins serving the same function in different organisms are amazingly similar in size, shape, and details of amino acid composition. The simplest explanation for this similarity would be that they are derived from a single ancestral form.

Second, at several points the proteins usually differ from one another. Usually the number of differences is inversely proportional to the degree of relatedness of the organisms that is inferred on other grounds. For example, the hemoglobin of human beings is indistinguishable from that of a gorilla, quite different from that of a mouse, and very different from that of a fish.

Third, in the great majority of cases, the points of difference fall into the category of conservative interchanges. (For example, at a point where the basic amino acid lysine is found in human hemoglobin, the basic amino acid arginine may be found in fish hemoglobin.)

Fourth, where appropriate measurements can be made, the subtle differences in function of related proteins are well suited to the organisms in which they are found. For example, proteins of cold-blooded animals function more efficiently at low temperature than proteins of warm-blooded animals do at low temperature.

Many modern studies of evolution (Section VII) concentrate on the evolution of the proteins and the genes that specify them. *It now appears to most biologists that it is the detailed structure (hence, function) of proteins that provides the variation upon which natural selection acts.* Natural selection eliminates those modifications of proteins that make the bearer less suited to a particular set of conditions, and it perpetuates those modifications that make it better suited.

THE NUCLEIC ACIDS ACT AS DRAFTSMEN AND TOOLMAKERS OF THE LIVING CELL

The "biological revolution," about which so much is written, is largely a revolution in our understanding of the chemistry and biological importance of the fourth major class of large molecules produced by dehydration synthesis: the **nucleic acids.** These molecules had long been known to be acidic substances found in the nuclei of all eukaryotic cells. But it is largely within the last two decades that we have come to appreciate the critical role of nucleic acids as the chemical agents of inheritance. Later chapters will go into the details of how nucleic acids function and of how we have come to understand these functions. Here the discussion will be limited to the simple structural plan upon which the nucleic acids themselves are built, for it is from their simple structure that the remarkable functions of nucleic acids emerge.

All Nucleic Acids Consist of Three Parts Repeated Many Times

The basic building blocks of nucleic acids, known as **nucleotides,** are somewhat more complex than those of proteins. Each nucleotide consists of three molecules that have been linked together by dehydration synthesis. One molecule is phosphoric acid, another is a sugar, and the third is a nitrogen-containing basic substance called a nitrogenous base.

Nucleotides such as the adenosine monophosphate (AMP) shown in Figure 11.28 are involved in two different and important aspects of cellular chemistry. First, as free nucleotides (more or less as depicted in this figure), they take part in the chemical reactions by which cells obtain energy from their environment and produce the materials of life. Second, when linked one to another in large nucleotide polymers, they form the nucleic acids.

When nucleotides are polymerized into nucleic acids, the

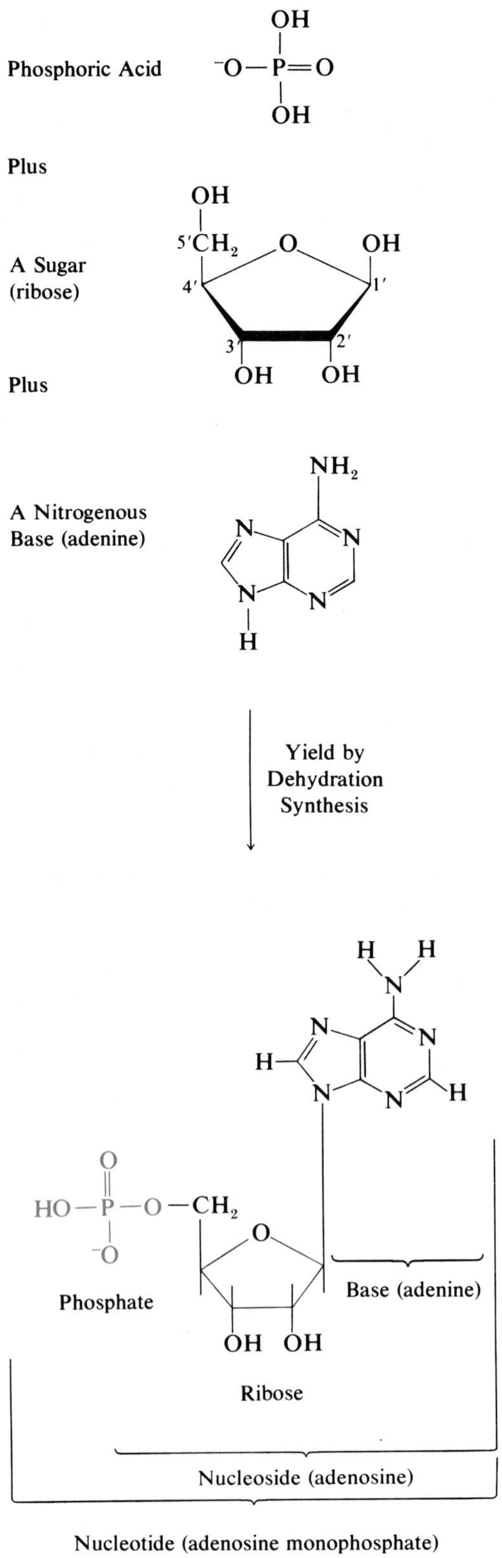

Phosphoric Acid

Plus

A Sugar (ribose)

Plus

A Nitrogenous Base (adenine)

Yield by Dehydration Synthesis

Phosphate

Base (adenine)

Ribose

Nucleoside (adenosine)

Nucleotide (adenosine monophosphate)

Figure 11.28 (left) Formation of adenosine monophosphate (AMP). Make note of the numbering of the carbon atoms of the sugar molecule, which will be referred to in later figures. When nucleotides are polymerized to form nucleic acids, one end of each chain always terminates in a 5' phosphate group; the other end always terminates in a 3' hydroxyl group, as shown in Figure 11.29.

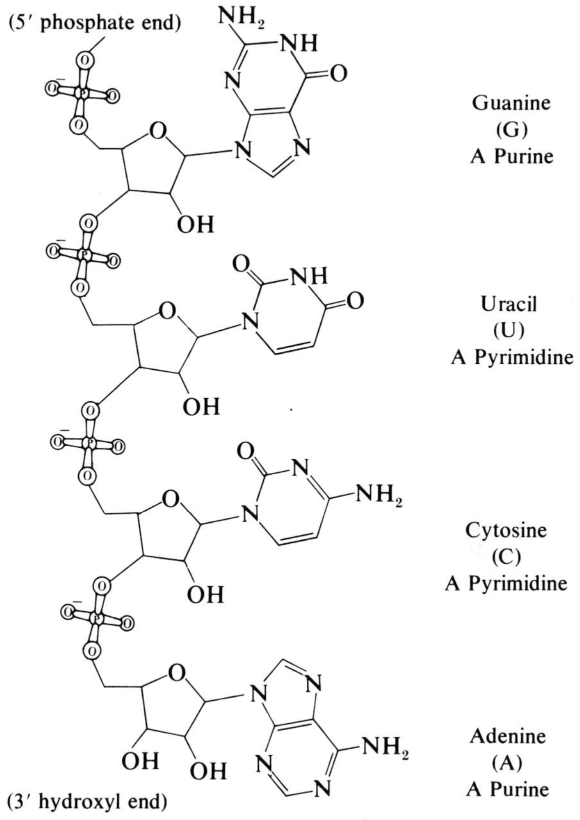

(5' phosphate end)

Guanine (G) A Purine

Uracil (U) A Pyrimidine

Cytosine (C) A Pyrimidine

Adenine (A) A Purine

(3' hydroxyl end)

Figure 11.29 (right) A short segment of a polynucleotide molecule called RNA. One of each of the nucleotide bases found in RNA is shown in this structural formula.

phosphoric acid (or phosphate) group of one nucleotide is linked to the sugar of the next. The result is a continuous string of alternating sugar and phosphate groups, called a **sugar-phosphate backbone,** from which nitrogenous bases extend along one side:

Phosphate
|
Sugar—Base 1
Phosphate
|
Sugar—Base 2
Phosphate
|
Sugar—Base 3
Phosphate
|
Sugar—Base 4

Four kinds of nitrogenous bases are found in each of the two major types of nucleic acid molecules. Two of the nitrogenous bases (adenine and guanine) are composed of two rings and are called **purines.** The other two (cytosine and uracil or thymine) contain a single ring and are called **pyrimidines.** Figure 11.29 shows what a short segment of such a molecule might look like.

RNA: A Polymer of Ribose-Containing Nucleotides

Because all four of the nucleotides shown in Figure 11.29 contain ribose as their sugar, they are called **ribonucleic acid,** or RNA. The molecules of RNA are produced by cells. They range in length from about forty to several thousand nucleotides in a single unbranched chain. The cell strictly controls the order in which the four bases occur in such a chain, and that order determines what the function of the resulting RNA molecule will be.

There are three kinds of RNA molecules, each with its own specific structural plan. These three classes of RNA molecules depend on one another as they carry out their functions in the cell. A **messenger RNA** (mRNA) molecule carries information specifying the amino acid sequence of a given protein. Its sequence of bases is, in effect, a coded version of the amino acid sequence necessary to produce a new molecule of a given kind of protein. A **transfer RNA** (tRNA) molecule plays a key role in translating this coded version into the sequence of amino acids to be produced. **Ribosomal RNA** (rRNA) molecules make up a major part of the physical structure upon which the messenger molecules and transfer molecules are brought together to achieve the decoding process. This physical structure is a ribonucleic acid body called the *ribosome,* which gives the third class of RNA molecules its name.

In short, the overall function of RNA is simple to state but of crucial importance: *RNA molecules collaborate in carrying the structural specifications for each of the proteins a cell needs and in translating those specifications into new proteins.* The details of this collaboration are treated in Chapter 17.

The DNA Molecule and the Continuity of Life

A second major type of nucleic acid found in all cells resembles RNA in that it is an unbranched polymer formed by dehydration synthesis from nucleotides. But this polymer differs from RNA in one of its bases, and all its nucleotides contain a different sugar: deoxyribose (Figure 11.30). That is why the nucleotides are called deoxyribonucleotides and the polymer is called **deoxyribonucleic acid,** or DNA.

About the middle of this century, a series of studies pointed unequivocally to DNA as *the* hereditary material of living cells and the search began to unravel the mysteries of its structure and function. It culminated in 1953 with the perceptions of two men—James Watson, who had recently completed his graduate studies at Indiana University, and Francis Crick, a graduate student at Cambridge. In their one-page paper entitled "A Structure for Deoxyribose Nucleic Acid," they proposed a structure so simple and yet so elegant that it laid the groundwork for our understanding not only of the continuity of life between generations but also of the development of life within a generation at the molecular level.

In identifying the structure of DNA, Watson and Crick did not dirty a single test tube, they did not employ a single instrument, and they did not perform a single experiment. What they brought to the problem was the sense of urgency surrounding the problem coupled with finely honed insight into the key observations made by workers who had begun the search before them. What were these key observations?

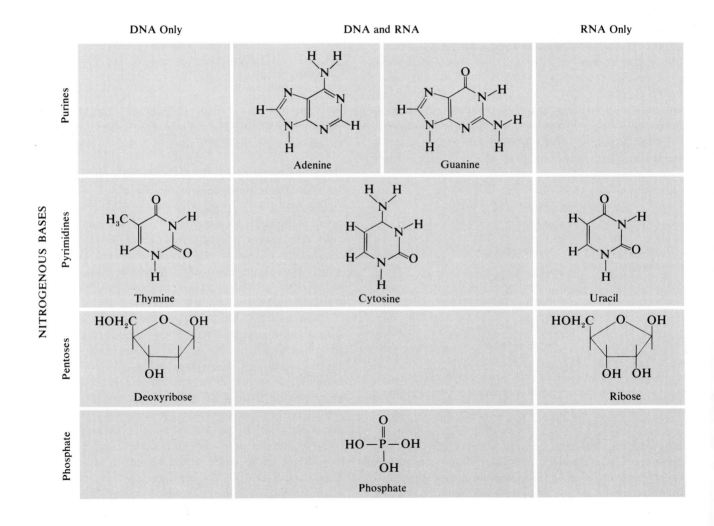

A few years earlier, the biochemist Erwin Chargaff had made a critical observation concerning the nitrogenous bases of DNA. He perceived that, although the overall composition of the DNA from different organisms varied enormously, a simple equality of parts always seemed to emerge. In any DNA molecule taken from any organism he studied, the total number of molecules of purine-type bases (A and G) was always equal to the total number of molecules of pyrimidine-type bases (C and T). In fact, within the limits of precise measurement available to him, Chargaff found that the number of molecules of adenine present in any DNA molecule was always equal to the number of molecules of thymine present, and that the number of molecules of guanine equaled the number of molecules of cytosine (A/T = G/C = 1). He found that this equality existed even though the ratio of A to G and C to T varied enormously from organism to organism.

The second set of critical observations came from the work of Rosalind Franklin, who used a process called x-ray diffraction to gain insight into the structure of DNA. Earlier, the helical nature of certain protein molecules had been discovered through x-ray diffraction techniques. Other workers, including Franklin's mentor M. H. F. Wilkins, had studied DNA with x-ray diffraction techniques, but Franklin's results were of the highest quality. She obtained strong evidence that the general form of DNA was helical. She further determined that it was long and rodlike and that it was uniformly 20 angstroms (2 nanometers) in diameter. Along that rod something was repeated every 3.4 angstroms and something else was repeated every 34 angstroms.

Watson and Crick combined these observations with information from other sources. In looking at Figure 11.30 you can see—as Watson and Crick did when looking at similar diagrams—that the two purine bases are larger (hence, bulkier) than the pyrimidine bases. This difference in size would seem to imply that the DNA molecule should be wider where it is rich in purines and narrower where it is rich in pyrimidines. Yet Franklin's work showed the diameter of the molecule is constant throughout its length. Watson and Crick concluded that the significance of the equality of purines to pyrimidines noted earlier by Chargaff was that purines were somehow paired physically to pyrimidines throughout the structure: only then would the width remain constant. But how were these pairs linked? The breakthrough came when they realized that if a molecule of adenine was oriented in a specific way with respect to a molecule of thymine, the two molecules could present to each other a pair of equally spaced atoms with the potential for hydrogen bonding (Figure 11.31*a*). Similarly, if a guanine molecule was properly oriented with a cytosine molecule, they could form three hydrogen bonds between three equally spaced atoms on each base (Figure 11.31*b*). Not only would such hydrogen bonding be highly specific, the fit of the molecules into the same structure should occur without distortion because the width of the A—T pair differed from the width of the G—C pair by less than three percent!

Watson and Crick proposed that in basic structure the DNA molecule is a pair of chains with the bases of those chains turned toward each other. Adenine on one chain

Figure 11.30 (left) Similarities and differences in the chemical structures for the ribose sugars and nucleic acid bases found in RNA and DNA molecules. Three of the nitrogenous bases found in RNA are also found in DNA. In the fourth base they differ: where uracil (U) is found in RNA, the related base thymine (T) is found in DNA.

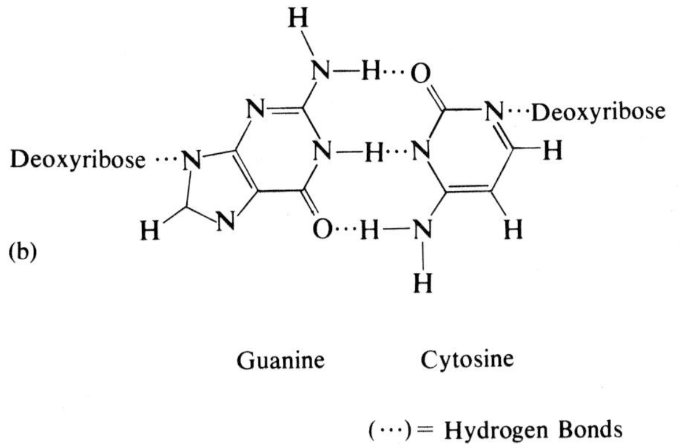

(a)

Adenine   Thymine

Figure 11.31 (a) The structural "fit" when a molecule of adenine is properly oriented with a molecule of thymine. In (b) a similar purine-pyrimidine linkage is shown: A molecule of guanine is oriented properly with a molecule of cytosine. The difference in width between these two pairings is less than 3 percent, which helps account for the known constant diameter of the DNA molecule.

(b)

Guanine   Cytosine

(···) = Hydrogen Bonds

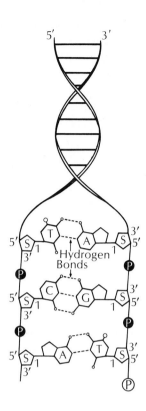

Figure 11.32 Base pairing in the DNA molecule. In addition to the base pairing, notice that the two chains of the double helix are running in opposite directions. The chain terminating on the lower left ends in a sugar (S) with a free 3' hydroxyl group, which is called the 3' end of the chain. (See Figure 11.28 for the meaning of the numbers.) The chain terminating on the lower right terminates in a phosphate group attached to the 5' carbon of the terminal sugar. (This is called the 5' end of the chain.) Both chains have the opposite kinds of termination at the other end. Thus we say one chain (on the left) is running from 5' to 3' down the page and the other chain is running from 3' to 5'. All DNA molecules have this antiparallel organization of the constituent chains.

must be hydrogen-bonded to thymine on the other chain, just as guanine on one chain must be hydrogen-bonded to cytosine on the other (Figure 11.32). This hydrogen bonding is possible only when the two chains run in opposite directions (head-to-tail, so to speak). Furthermore, all the bases can be brought into alignment only when the two chains are twisted slightly into a helix.

When a scale model was built of their proposed DNA molecule, the only twist that would work produced a base pair every 3.4 angstroms and one complete turn of the helix every 34 angstroms; and the resulting helix was 20 angstroms wide. These were the same dimensions revealed by Franklin's x-ray diffraction studies! In this configuration, all the bases end up at right angles to the major axis of the helix. Because they are in effect stacked up like pennies in a roll, stacking interactions can occur between adjacent bases in a chain, which helps stabilize the helix. In addition, all the highly charged phosphoric acid groups end up on the outside of the helix, where their charges will repel each other least and where they will be free to interact with the water of the cellular environment.

Once the structure of DNA was understood, it immediately became possible to understand its functions. As Watson and Crick pointed out, the double helix is an ideal configuration for self-replication. Consider what will happen if the two chains are separated. The only DNA base

sequence that will form a stable double helix with one of the strands is an exact replica of the strand to which it was previously paired. The general principle behind this mechanism of **self-replication** is shown in Figure 11.33. Given this mechanism, consider what will happen if a mutation is somehow introduced into a new chain that is being synthesized. The mistake will be propagated as faithfully as the original was in subsequent replications. In other words, *the structure of DNA permits not only a generally faithful reproduction mechanism, it permits the occasional introduction of change.* The mutations that do occur will persist until or unless natural selection eliminates the cell possessing the change.

The structure of DNA places absolutely no constraints on the length of a DNA molecule or on the sequence in which the bases may occur along the length of one strand. It dictates only that the other strand be complementary. Herein lies the secret of the function of the DNA molecule: *The number of distinct base sequences that can occur in a DNA molecule is virtually infinite, but each specific sequence carries a specific encoded message that RNA molecules can put into action in the form of a specific protein.*

The structure of DNA also implies the mechanism by which it can function within a cell generation to express the information it carries. In a process called **transcription,** the

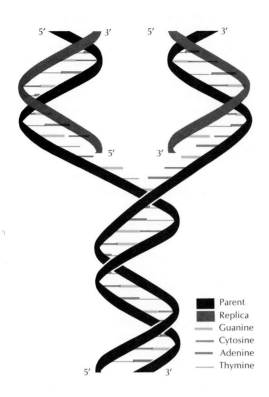

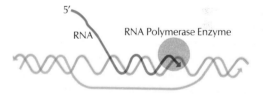

Figure 11.33   A diagram of the process of replication of the DNA molecule. The two parent strands unwind to form a "growing point." A protein enzyme called "DNA polymerase" builds a complement of each parent strand by dehydration synthesis from nucleotides. Where adenine occurs on the parent strand, DNA polymerase inserts a thymine nucleotide on the new strand; where cytosine occurs on the parent, guanine is inserted in the new strand; and so on. Thus the new strand being formed on the left is an exact replica of the parent strand on the right and vice versa. The parent strands continue unwinding as the synthesis proceeds until two complete new double helices are formed. (Details of this process will be given in Chapter 17.)

DNA molecule opens temporarily and a protein catalyst—an enzyme called **RNA polymerase**—slides along one strand of the double helix. As it slides along, it is also picking up ribonucleotide molecules from its surroundings and assembling them by dehydration synthesis into the sequence of ribonucleotides that pairs with, or is complementary to, the DNA base sequence being read (Figure 11.34). An RNA molecule formed in this way is a faithful copy of the sequence of bases carried on one strand of the hereditary material. If that RNA now functions as a messenger RNA molecule, it will code for an amino acid sequence necessary for building a certain kind of protein molecule.

As you will read in more detail later, the **translation** of a messenger RNA molecule into a protein molecule is also governed by the base-pairing rules. A messenger RNA molecule consists of a long sequence of bases that are "read" three at a time by transfer RNA molecules. Each of these three-base sequences is called a **codon,** or coding unit, that can be read only by certain kinds of transfer RNA molecules. It happens that a cell contains many kinds of transfer RNA molecules. Each specific kind carries one specific amino acid at one end and has a specific sequence of three bases—called an **anticodon**—at the other end. When a codon of messenger RNA is in the reading position

Figure 11.34   Transcription of a DNA template code to an RNA molecule. The enzyme RNA polymerase attaches to the DNA molecule and opens up a short section of the double helix for transcription. As RNA polymerase moves along one strand of the DNA template, it builds an RNA complement of the DNA strand to which it is attached, coupling ribonucleotides together by dehydration synthesis.

The base pairing rules the enzyme follows are the same as those used in making the DNA double helix, with one exception. Where adenine occurs on the DNA being copied, uracil rather than thymine is incorporated into the RNA. As synthesis proceeds, the growing RNA strand peels off the DNA, whereupon hydrogen bonds re-form the complementary DNA strands.

(After J. D. Watson, Molecular Biology of the Gene, copyright © 1970, J. D. Watson. W. A. Benjamin, Inc.)

on a ribosome, only the transfer RNA that has a complementary anticodon can read it.

In summary, there are three main functions of nucleic acids, and all three are mediated by the same kinds of specific hydrogen bonds that link the two strands of DNA together. In *replication*, each strand of a DNA double helix molecule serves as a template for the production of more DNA of complementary type. In *transcription*, a DNA strand serves as the template for the production of an RNA molecule that is complementary in sequence to itself. In *translation*, the RNA molecules cooperate to produce a protein molecule having the sequence that is called for by the original strand of DNA. Taken together, the explication of these three functions is the "central dogma" of modern molecular biology.

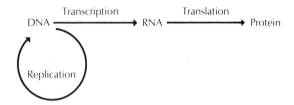

Figure 11.35 The "central dogma" of molecular biology: DNA is self-replicating, and DNA makes RNA, which makes protein.

PERSPECTIVE

At the heart of our understanding of the diversity of life is the principle of emergence as it applies to the atomic and molecular levels of organization of living things. All living systems are composed of very few kinds of basically similar atoms and molecules. But the properties of molecules derive from the structure and behavior of the atoms of which they are composed, and the increasingly varied characteristics of life flow from the properties of molecules as they are bonded in particular ways to one another and to others like them. Perhaps the most fundamental union from which increasingly subtle variations emerge is the hydrogen bond. Again and again it turns up in the progression from simple molecules such as water to the complex macromolecules of heredity.

This chapter has followed that progression by selecting a few of the most important molecules of life—water, carbohydrates, lipids, proteins, and nucleic acids—and examining how they are constructed and how they function. It is in this analysis that the principle of emergence becomes clear. All the properties of water are based on the polarity of its oxygen-to-hydrogen bonds. Because of this polarity, adjacent water molecules can combine by hydrogen bonding into a substance that has a unique set of properties. When

frozen, water acquires a lower density. When liquid, water can climb up inside tubes and tree trunks; it can absorb and dissipate large quantities of heat and can thereby help to keep cells from cooking themselves to death as they carry out the energy conversions needed to sustain life. Water can dissolve a vast array of substances that contain either charged groups or polar bonds, but it cannot interact chemically with substances that lack such polar bonds.

These latter two characteristics underlie the capacity of living systems to isolate themselves from their environment. When a charged, polar group is combined with noncharged, nonpolar groups to form a phospholipid, an important relationship with water occurs. Such molecules tend to come together in a double layer, with their polar "heads" dissolved in water and their nonpolar "tails" tucked away in the interior of the bilayer. It is on the basis of such relationships that a cell surrounds and compartmentalizes itself with phospholipid-rich membranes.

With the emergence of more complex structures comes an enormous variety of emergent properties. The macromolecules of life are constructed by dehydration synthesis reactions, in which single molecules (monomers) are synthesized into large, complex structures (polymers) and water is given off in the process. Polymers can be built either of the same kind of molecules (homopolymers) or from different kinds of molecules (heteropolymers). Some long chains of polymers are structured in a way that permits hydrogen bonding between monomers in different chains; still others often twist about their own axis, which brings certain monomers in the same chain close enough to form hydrogen bonds with each other. Such bonds hold the polymer in a stable, three-dimensional helix, which is a recurrent configuration among the more complex macromolecules.

All these variations in structure lead to variations in function. For example, from only twenty different kinds of amino acids, millions of different protein structures are constructed, each with its own specific function in an organism, whether that function is to strengthen a claw or to aid in the self-replication of DNA, or to participate in oxygen transport. How dependent function is on structure becomes clear when a gene undergoes a mutation and a wrong amino acid sequence is specified during the process by which a new protein molecule is constructed. Although some substitutions have only subtle effects, others can lead to the death of the cell or the organism. Such variations in protein structure may provide the functional variation upon which natural selection acts.

But the structures of proteins are not passed from generation to generation as such. They are passed on instead in a coded form in a special polymer known as DNA. Again, the coding properties of DNA emerge from a simple hydrogen-bonding relationship: The organic bases adenine and thymine have atoms arranged in such a way that they form stable hydrogen bonds with each other, as do the bases guanine and cytosine. In each chain of DNA, these four bases can occur in any sequence. The information carried by different pieces of DNA is simply the exact sequences of these four bases. The precision of this base pairing ensures that the same sequences are passed on from generation to generation. In a sense, then, all that each generation inherits from the preceding one is a sequence of specific hydrogen bonds between nucleic acid bases.

The information carried by DNA is put into action (in the form of proteins) by another group of polymers known as RNAs. Because they are constructed in a way that is similar to the construction of DNA, they follow the same rules of hydrogen bonding. Thus the information of heredity is not only carried in the form of hydrogen bonds, it is also put into action to produce specific proteins by means of similar hydrogen bonds.

The role of hydrogen bonds in creating the living cell does not end here. Once a protein molecule has been made, it takes on the particular and predictable three-dimensional shape specified by its amino acid sequence. To a large extent, this shape is defined and stabilized by hydrogen bonds between amino acids. Furthermore, the highly specific role that each protein plays in a living cell is a result of the highly specific tendency it has to interact with one or more of the other constituents of the cell. And these interactions, too, are mediated in large part by a specific pattern of hydrogen bonding.

You first encountered the hydrogen bond in the discussion of the unusual properties of water. By now it should be apparent that the biological importance of hydrogen bonds cannot be overstated.

SUGGESTED READINGS

CALVIN, MELVIN, and WILLIAM A. PRYOR. *Organic Chemistry of Life.* San Francisco: W. H. Freeman, 1973. An excellent compilation of articles from *Scientific American*, many of them relevant to this and succeeding chapters.

DICKERSON, RICHARD E., and IRVING GEIS. *The Structure and Action of Proteins.* New York: Harper & Row, 1970. One of the best treatments of protein structure and function, especially commendable for its clear and understandable illustrations.

ERLANDER, S. R. "The Structure of Water," *Science Journal*, 5 (1969), 60.
FLETCHER, N. H. "The Freezing of Water," *Science Progress*, 54 (1969), 227.
FRANK, HENRY S. "The Structure of Ordinary Water," *Science*, 169 (1972), 635.
These three articles are good treatments of the structure of the aqueous environment in which the drama of life is played.

KENDREW, JOHN C. "The Three-Dimensional Structure of a Protein Molecule," *Scientific American*, 205 (December 1961), 96. An early view of the anatomy of a protein molecule, as seen by a researcher who pioneered in the crystallography techniques he describes.

NASS, G. *The Molecules of Life.* New York: McGraw-Hill, 1970. A little-known but useful discussion of the role molecules play in the life of an organism, with lesser emphasis on chemical details.

WATSON, JAMES D. *The Double Helix.* New York: Atheneum Press, 1968. A highly opinionated and interesting account of Watson and Crick's elucidation of the structure of DNA, written by Watson himself.

Chapter 12

The Flow of Molecules and Energy in Living Things

From the outward streaming of the galaxies to the doubling of a tiny bacterial cell, events and processes in the universe are linked by the continuous flow of energy from one form to another and by the principles governing this flow. Once we believed ourselves to be at the center of the universe, and once we believed that the living world—with ourselves again at the center—was governed by unique laws applicable only to the flow of energy in life. But now we see that this is not so. Nowhere is our essential oneness with all things in the universe more evident than in the consideration of energy that streams from the stars, through and beyond our bodies, and in the process powering our thoughts and actions as it moves on its inexorable course through time.

Our sun is a star, one of billions of stars clustered in one of many billions of galaxies scattered in the darkness of the universe. Where the universe ends we do not know, but in attempting to decode the messages of radiation from neighboring and distant stars and galaxies we have come to suspect that it extends at least 10 billion light years in all directions, and that within those almost incomprehensibly vast boundaries galaxies are accelerating away from one another as remnants of the primordial explosion that marked the beginning of the universe. Everywhere in the universe there is a background of radiation, a lingering reminder of that cataclysmic event. And everywhere in the universe there is an outward streaming of energy that is becoming increasingly diffuse with the passing of time.

The visible light emanating from stars and galaxies is only one form of this pulsating energy; it is one small part of a spectrum of electromagnetic radiation. At the time of origin, the only forms of matter that existed were protons and electrons, which gravitational energy brought together eventually into the first stars. Over billions of years some of these stars would die out, some would explode, and some new stars would be formed from the remnants of the earlier generation. In the birth and death of stars, first the lighter elements and then the heavier elements would form. But even today, most of the matter and energy of the universe is still present in the form of hydrogen. In the continual thermonuclear reactions of stars, some of this hydrogen is being converted into the heavier elements. But at each stage of the conversion process, some of the stored energy—or potential energy—of the stars is released as light, heat, and other forms of radiant energy. As this energy travels outward it becomes increasingly diffuse. Unless it is somehow trapped and converted into other forms of energy, it is lost forever in the darkness of space.

THE LAWS OF THERMODYNAMICS GOVERN THE FLOW OF ENERGY THROUGHOUT THE UNIVERSE

Two principles underlie the immense flow of energy throughout the universe. They are so fundamental to our understanding of all physical and chemical events they are considered to be among the most important physical laws. They are known as the first and second laws of thermodynamics.

The **first law of thermodynamics** states that the amount of energy in the universe is constant. Additional energy is not being created, and none of the energy that now exists is being destroyed. One form of energy can be converted into another, but no matter how many conversions occur, and no matter how varied they are, the total amount of energy in the universe will be no more and no less than it was at the beginning of time.

The **second law of thermodynamics** states that the amount of energy that has been converted into a useless form is constantly increasing. In each energy transformation, a certain amount of the potential energy is converted into diffuse, increasingly disorganized forms that can never again be converted back into a more useful form. The extent of this disorganization of energy is called **entropy**. The second law of thermodynamics implies that the universe is slowly running down—that the cumulative energy conversions going on since the beginning of time have been gradually dissipating the potential energy of the universe. Thus the entropy content of the universe has been continuously increasing.

The decreasing *organization* of energy in any system is always accompanied by a rise in entropy; that is why entropy is often defined as a measure of the disorder, or randomness, of a system. But in living organisms there is a trend that seems to run counter to the increase of entropy in the universe: In life there is a continuous trend toward increasing order and complexity. A diatom floating about in the sea takes in simple molecules of carbon dioxide, water, and salts and combines them into such highly organized molecules as sugar and amino acids, which have higher potential energy than the molecules from which they were made. These sugar and amino acid molecules are then used in the formation of even more highly organized molecules of complex sugars, proteins, and nucleic acids, which are in their turn ordered into still more complex structures of the cell. At each stage of cell growth, then, the potential energy of the atoms and molecules in the diatom seems to increase, and the entropy seems to decrease.

Furthermore, in the history of all life on earth there has been a continuous and progressive increase in organization of living systems. Individual life forms have tended to become more complex and more highly ordered over evolutionary time. It would seem, then, that life has been bringing about a progressive decrease in entropy even as entropy is increasing everywhere else!

Over the years, many people (including some prominent scientists) have in fact concluded that life violates the second law of thermodynamics. But this is a misconception, for living things cannot be viewed as isolated systems: they, too, are part of the immense flow of energy in the universe. They appear to be unique only because they lower their own entropy by feeding on energy released in association with the rising entropy of the sun. Life on earth is a temporary holding station for a small fraction of the energy released during the inexorable decay of our sun. For example, a tiny fraction of the light energy streaming away from the sun may be intercepted on earth by a leaf. Part of this radiant energy is trapped and used in the formation of new chemical bonds between atoms; it becomes chemical potential energy. In this form it transfers from molecule to molecule, from cell to cell, from organism to organism, as it powers the reactions and builds the stuff of life. At each stage in this cycle, however, a large part of the energy originally obtained from sunlight is lost. Figure 12.2 depicts this overall flow of matter and energy in living things. This illustration makes an important point: *Although the atoms of life recycle continuously, the energy of life flows only in one direction.* If the flow of light energy to our planet were to stop suddenly, all life processes would quickly run down as all living things followed the universal trend toward an increase in entropy.

HOW DO THERMODYNAMIC PRINCIPLES APPLY TO ENERGY TRANSFERS IN LIVING SYSTEMS?

Energy transfers within living systems are accomplished through a remarkable variety of chemical changes in matter—that is, through chemical reactions. When a **chemical reaction** occurs, bonds holding together the molecules of the reactants break and new bonds form, thereby creating new molecules from the products. Energy is either released or absorbed in the process. Consider what happens, for example, when coal burns. Coal is composed primarily of carbon atoms, and when it is burned, these atoms combine with oxygen molecules in the air to form carbon dioxide. The reaction may be summarized as follows:

$$C + O_2 \rightarrow CO_2 + 94.0 \text{ kcal/mole}$$

This formula means that for each mole of carbon that is burned, one mole of carbon dioxide is created and 94.0 kilocalories of energy is released. (A kilocalorie is defined as the amount of heat required to raise the temperature of 1,000 grams of water $1°C$.) When the double bond ($O=O$) in the oxygen molecules breaks, two new double bonds form in the carbon dioxide molecule ($O=C=O$). The formation of the $C=O$ bonds releases far more energy than is consumed in the breaking of the $O=O$ bond; in other words, the products are in a lower energy state than the reactants. The energy that is released is given off as heat and light.

Each molecule has a characteristic amount of potential energy, known as its **heat content** *(H)*, or **enthalpy**. The heat released during a reaction represents the difference between the heat content of the reactants and that of the products, which is symbolized as ΔH (where Δ signifies the change in heat content H). When coal burns, the reactants have a greater heat content than the products, so ΔH for this reaction has a negative sign. A negative ΔH generally indicates the reaction is **exothermic**—in other words, it is a reaction in which heat is released. More properly, then, the reaction is written as

$$C + O_2 \rightarrow CO_2 \quad (\Delta H = -94.0 \text{ kcal/mole})$$

Figure 12.2 The flow of molecules (matter) and energy in living things. This figure illustrates three important points. First, although matter flows in a continuous cycle through the living world, energy flows in one direction. Second, energy flows from one "trophic level" (nutritional class of organisms) to the next because it is an integral part of food molecules. Third, at each level of transfer, more matter and energy is lost from life than is transferred to the next trophic level. (A ratio of 2:1 between matter and energy lost to that transferred is used in this figure. A ratio of 9:1 would be more realistic but would be difficult to represent graphically.) These three points clearly show that life does not violate the second law of thermodynamics; it, too, is contributing to the rise in entropy content of the universe.

Once a fire has been started, coal will continue to burn until all the carbon or oxygen present is consumed. But coal can be stored in the presence of oxygen for years without noticeable change. The reaction occurs only when coal is heated to a high temperature. Why is heat energy required to begin the reaction? Collision theory provides an explanation for this phenomenon.

ENERGY TRANSFERS BEGIN WITH THE COLLISION OF MOLECULES

According to the **collision theory**, chemical change occurs when the energy released in the collision between atoms and molecules is sufficient to break preexisting bonds. The amount of energy involved depends on the force of the collision, which is a function of the speed at which the atoms and molecules are moving, which in turn is a function of temperature.

For example, the chemical reaction leading to the formation of a molecule of carbon dioxide could not occur unless carbon and oxygen came together with enough physical force to break the preexisting bonds of the oxygen molecules. At a low temperature, the atoms and molecules move slowly and the energy involved in the collisions is not sufficient to break the double bond in the oxygen molecules, so chemical change does not occur. The carbon atoms and the oxygen molecules simply bounce apart. At a high temperature, however, the molecules begin to move rapidly, and collision occurs with enough energy to break the $O=O$ bond. For an instant, some sort of intermediate grouping of atoms exists that is called an **activated complex.** This activated complex has a high heat content and is unstable, and it quickly assembles into carbon dioxide molecules as the two $C=O$ bonds form with the concurrent release of energy.

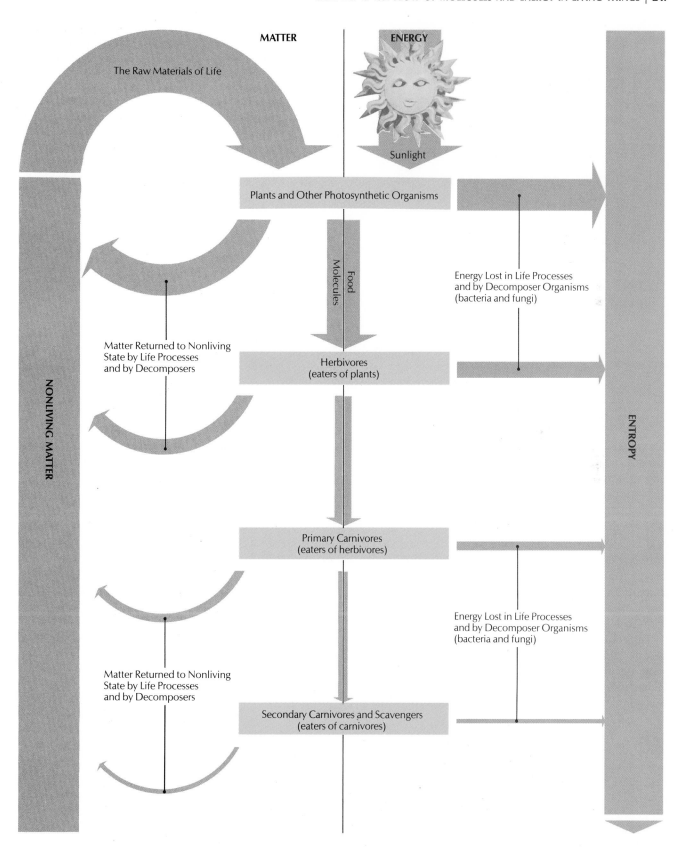

MATTER

ENERGY

The Raw Materials of Life

Sunlight

NONLIVING MATTER

Plants and Other Photosynthetic Organisms

Food Molecules

Matter Returned to Nonliving State by Life Processes and by Decomposers

Herbivores (eaters of plants)

Energy Lost in Life Processes and by Decomposer Organisms (bacteria and fungi)

Primary Carnivores (eaters of herbivores)

Matter Returned to Nonliving State by Life Processes and by Decomposers

Energy Lost in Life Processes and by Decomposer Organisms (bacteria and fungi)

Secondary Carnivores and Scavengers (eaters of carnivores)

ENTROPY

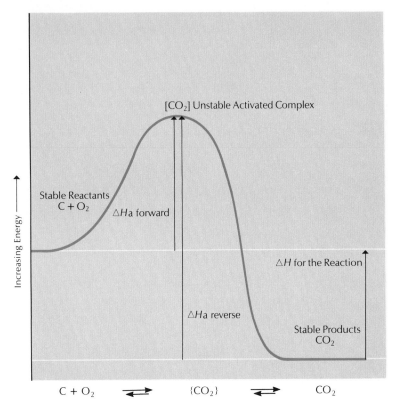

Figure 12.3 An ''energy hill'' diagram for the burning of coal in air ($\Delta H a$ = energy of activation). External energy must be applied initially so the reactants will gain enough energy ($\Delta H a_{forward}$) to reach the activated state. Once this energy is supplied (as in the form of a lighted match), it is sufficient to cause the reaction to continue until equilibrium is reached. In this case, almost all of the reactants will end up as carbon dioxide because the products have lower energy. If the reaction were run backward, the $\Delta H a_{reverse}$ would be much greater than the $\Delta H a_{forward}$.

How the various steps in this reaction fit together can be visualized by following them up and down the ''energy hill'' shown in Figure 12.3. In this analogy, the reactants (C and O_2) are ''uphill'' from the product (CO_2), so they contain a certain amount of chemical potential energy. If they ''roll downhill'' to form carbon dioxide, that energy will be released. First, however, they must overcome the barrier known as the **activation energy** ($\Delta H a$), which is the energy required to form the activated complex $\{CO_2\}$. Until external energy is applied, the molecules cannot reach the top of this hill, and none can roll down the longer slope to form carbon dioxide.

The collision theory implies that reactions proceed more rapidly at higher temperatures. Because molecules move more rapidly at elevated temperatures, they tend to collide more frequently and more of the collisions are energetic enough to pass the energy barrier of the activated complex (Figure 12.4).

Thus, once external energy is brought into the picture, the reaction begins and the energy released is sufficient to push more and more molecules up the slope and keep the reaction going spontaneously. That is why coal keeps on burning without continuous application of additional heat from an external source.

The collision theory also implies that effective collisions will occur more frequently, and reactions more rapidly, if the concentrations of reactants are increased. For example, if the amount of oxygen in the air surrounding coal were increased, the coal would burn much faster.

MOST CHEMICAL REACTIONS CAN PROCEED IN TWO DIRECTIONS

Most chemical reactions are reversible. If a molecule of product acquires enough energy during a collision with another molecule it, too, can form the activated complex, which can break apart into atoms or molecules of the original reactants. However, the energy barrier in this direction (moving from right to left in Figure 12.3) is much higher: more energy is needed for activation in the reverse reaction. This is not to say that reverse reactions are rare events: They occur continuously along with the forward reactions as long as molecules of product and reactant are present. As a reaction proceeds in the forward direction, the reactants are used up, so the frequency of collisions between reactants diminishes. At the same time, however, more product is being formed, so the frequency of collisions leading to the reverse reactions increases. A time will come when the rates of the forward and reverse reactions are exactly equal and there will be no further change that can be detected in the relative proportions of product and reactants. This counterbalanced state is called the **equilibrium point.**

Consider, for example, the chemical reaction between

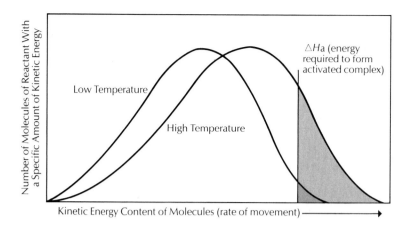

Figure 12.4 The effect of temperature on formation of an activated complex of molecules. Kinetic energy, which is a measure of how fast molecules are moving about, is a function of temperature. The higher the temperature, the faster the molecules are moving. At low temperature very few of the molecules are moving fast enough to form an activated complex when they collide. When the temperature is raised, the average rate of motion of the molecules increases. Now a much larger fraction of the molecules are moving fast enough to form an activated complex upon collision.

two substances, A and B, that leads to two products, C and D:

$$A \text{ and } B \rightleftharpoons \{AB\} \rightleftharpoons \{CD\} \rightleftharpoons C \text{ and } D$$

In this example, the two-way arrows signify that the reaction is reversible. As the reaction proceeds, the concentrations of A and B fall and the concentrations of C and D increase. As this happens, however, the rate of the forward reaction tends to slow down as a result of the decreased frequency of collision between A and B molecules, and the reverse reaction speeds up due to the increased frequency of collision between C and D molecules. When the equilibrium point is reached, both reactions are still occurring. But the reaction rates are now equal, so there is no further net change in concentration of A, B, C, or D. It does not matter whether the chemical reaction starts out in the "reverse" instead of the "forward" direction: The ratio of products to reactants will still be identical when the equilibrium point is reached (Figure 12.5).

This relationship is summarized in the expression **equilibrium constant,** which may be written as

$$K_{eq} = \frac{[C]_{eq}[D]_{eq}}{[A]_{eq}[B]_{eq}}$$

(The brackets are a convention meaning "concentration of the material enclosed herein." Thus $[C]_{eq}$ means "concentration of substance C at equilibrium." Notice that the concentrations of reactants written on the same side of the arrow in chemical equations are always *multiplied* together.)

The equilibrium constant indicates the direction in which the reaction will proceed if we start with equal quantities of A, B, C, and D. If the equilibrium constant is 1, the reaction will proceed until $[A][B] = [C][D]$, regardless of the proportions of the four substances at the outset. If the equilibrium constant is much larger than 1, then the reaction will proceed until $[C][D]$ is much larger than $[A][B]$. If it is

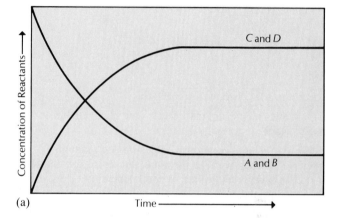

(a)

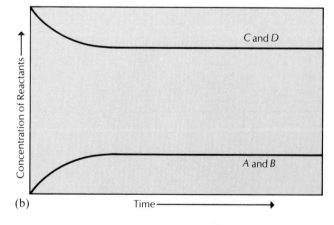

(b)

Figure 12.5 (a) The course of a reaction that begins with equal quantities of the "reactants" A and B. (b) The course of a reaction that begins with equal quantities of the "products" C and D. Regardless of whether the reaction proceeds in the forward or the reverse direction, the ratio of reactants to products is identical at the equilibrium point.

much less than 1, little *C* and *D* will have been produced from *A* and *B* at the point of equilibrium.

WHAT DETERMINES THE EQUILIBRIUM POINT IN REVERSIBLE REACTIONS?

Activation energy (the energy needed to push a reaction to the stage of an activated complex) dictates how soon the point of equilibrium will be reached. But it is the *magnitude* of the free energy change accompanying a reaction that dictates what the equilibrium point will be.

In the course of a reaction, the heat of the reaction is released in two forms: **free energy,** which is energy that can be used to do useful work; and entropy, which is useless energy that contributes to the overall progression of the universe toward disorder. This general relationship may be summarized as:

$$\Delta H = \Delta G + (T)\Delta S$$

where

ΔH is the heat change of a reaction

ΔG is the change in free energy (energy available to do useful work)

ΔS is the change in entropy (Because the randomness of matter increases with temperature, the entropy value for matter is always multiplied by the temperature *T* at which the reaction occurs.)

Figure 12.6 J. Willard Gibbs, who is often considered the most brilliant native-born American scientist (with Benjamin Franklin running a close second). The symbol G (for "free energy") honors Gibbs, who discovered the second law of thermodynamics.

Expressed another way, the change in free energy during a reaction is equal to the change in heat content less the change in entropy:

$$\Delta G = \Delta H - (T)\Delta S$$

The change in free energy determines whether a reaction will proceed in a forward direction and, if so, to what extent. How this change relates to the equilibrium constant of a reaction may be expressed in the following way:

$$\Delta G^{\circ\prime} = -RT \ell n \ K_{eq}$$

where

$\Delta G^{\circ\prime}$ is the standard free energy (It is the change in free energy per mole of reactant as carried out under standard laboratory conditions, as indicated by the degree sign. These conditions include having all of the reactants and products present in 1 molar concentrations. The prime sign indicates that the energy change is measured with the reaction taking place at a pH of 7.)

R is the gas constant (1.987 calories/degree mole)

T is the absolute temperature at which the reaction occurs

$\ell n \ K_{eq}$ is the natural logarithm of the equilibrium constant K_{eq}

The importance of this equation is that it shows *the equilibrium constant for any reaction is proportional to the free energy released by that reaction.* Therefore, if we know the value of the standard free energy for a reaction, we can predict the equilibrium point. Conversely, if we know the equilibrium point for the reaction, we can predict the standard free energy change of the reaction. This relationship is plotted in Figure 12.7.

Now, as Figure 12.7 shows, if we start from standard conditions, a reaction will proceed in the forward direction (as written) only if $\Delta G^{\circ\prime}$ is negative. Such reactions are called **exergonic.** Reactions for which $\Delta G^{\circ\prime}$ is positive are called **endergonic.** How does a cell accomplish a reaction of positive $\Delta G^{\circ\prime}$? In order to understand the answer to this question, *it is essential to understand the relationship between the free energy change under "standardized" conditions ($\Delta G^{\circ\prime}$) and the free energy change measured under "prevailing" conditions ($\Delta G^\prime$).* The free energy change associated with a reaction starting from standard conditions is a useful physical property for describing the chemical relationship between reactants and products being used in the laboratory. But in living cells, conditions are seldom (if ever) the conditions defined for $\Delta G^{\circ\prime}$. This is particularly true when we consider the concentrations of reactants and products in living cells. Because these cellular concentrations are always different from the "standard" concentrations, the measured change in free energy also

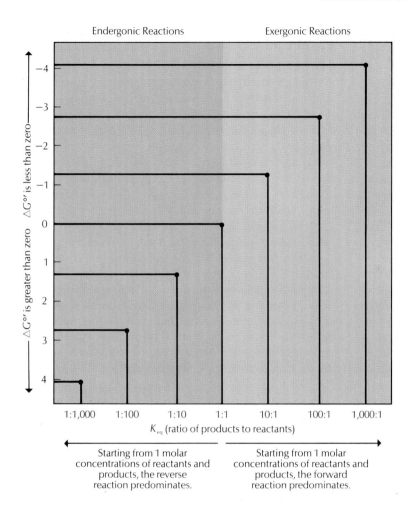

Figure 12.7   The relation between the standard free energy and the equilibrium constant in a chemical reaction. What this graph shows is that if we start with 1 molar concentrations of reactants and products (i.e., "standard conditions"), the reaction will proceed in the forward direction only if ΔG°' for the reaction is less than zero: such reactions are called exergonic. If ΔG°' is greater than zero, the reaction will proceed in the reverse direction until equilibrium is reached; such reactions are called endergonic.

differs from the standard free energy. The relationship is expressed as:

$$\Delta G' = \Delta G^{\circ\prime} + RT\ell\mathrm{n}\ \frac{[C][D]}{[A][B]}$$

where [A], [B], [C], and [D] are the actual concentrations of reactants and products in the cell at the time of measurement.

This equation means that no matter what the value of the free energy change under "standardized" conditions may be, the free energy change under "prevailing" conditions in a living cell will be negative whenever the ratio of concentrations of products to reactants is less than the equilibrium ratio, and the reaction will proceed in the forward direction. Thus, *regardless of the value of ΔG°', it is possible for a cell to perform a reaction in the forward direction as long as it maintains a ratio of products to reactants that is less than the equilibrium ratio.* We will return to a discussion of how cells maintain such ratios in a later section of this chapter, which will deal with the coupling of reactions by enzymes.

Although the free energy change for a given reaction tells

us the extent to which that reaction will occur before equilibrium is achieved, it does not tell us how rapidly the reaction will proceed toward equilibrium. The *speed* with which the reaction will occur is determined by the relationship between the energy required for activation and the kinetic energy possessed by the reactants.

Most of the molecules found in living things are quite "stable"; that is, the energy they must possess before they will react (activation energy) is high relative to their average kinetic energy at the moderate temperatures (less than 100°C) characteristic of life. Outside the living organism, then, most of the essential reactions required for life would require days, months, or even centuries to approach equilibrium. That being the case, how does an organism achieve the necessary high reaction rates for the hundreds of chemical reactions essential to maintain life?

REACTIONS OCCUR MORE RAPIDLY WHEN CATALYSTS ARE PRESENT

According to the collision theory, the rate of reaction can be accelerated if the concentrations of the reactants are increased. And in living organisms, many different mechanisms exist for concentrating reactants in some localized area, such as on a cellular membrane surface or within a membranous enclosure. This does increase the frequency of collision between appropriate molecules and leads to an increase in reaction rate. But the increases achieved by this means alone are modest. Reaction rates may be increased much further if the activation energy barrier to the reaction is lowered. For many chemical reactions, the amount of energy required to form the activated complex can be lowered by the addition of a suitable **catalyst,** a substance that lowers activation energy and thereby accelerates a reaction but is not itself consumed in the reaction.

Catalytic action is depicted in Figures 12.8 and 12.9. The presence of catalyst molecules encourages the formation of a different sequence of activated complexes that can carry out the reaction. Each of these catalytically activated complexes has a lower heat content than the activated complexes required in the uncatalyzed reaction. Although the rate of reaction along the old energy pathway is not altered, a much higher rate of reaction is made possible along the new energy pathway. Moreover, the energy barriers for the forward reaction and the reverse reaction are lowered by the same amount, which means that the effect of the catalyst on the forward reaction is balanced equally by the effect on the reverse reaction. Thus the state of equilibrium itself is a property of the molecules involved in the reactions, not of the catalyst. *A catalyst has absolutely no effect on what the equilibrium point will be; it only affects the speed with which that equilibrium point can be reached.*

ENZYMES FUNCTION AS HIGHLY SPECIALIZED CATALYSTS

All the myriad chemical reactions going on in living systems are catalyzed by complex, three-dimensional proteins called **enzymes.** Without enzymes, most of the rapidly occurring reactions in cells would not occur, to any perceptible degree, within a human lifetime. But even spontaneous reactions that proceed at a moderate rate outside the cell are accelerated tremendously by enzymes when they occur in cells. Consider, for example, the breakdown of hydrogen peroxide to form water and oxygen. This reaction occurs fairly rapidly in the absence of a catalyst: If you open a bottle of peroxide and leave it standing at room temperature, in a matter of a few weeks it will be, for all intents and purposes, pure water. If a small amount of iron is added to the peroxide as a catalyst, the rate of breakdown is increased a hundredfold. Hydrogen peroxide is lethal to cells. Because it is produced regularly as a by-product of certain reactions, cells must have an efficient means of destroying it before it destroys them. The enzyme that performs this specific function is called **catalase.** Catalase causes hydrogen peroxide to break down a *trillion* times faster than it would in the absence of a catalyst! Yet, like all other enzymes, catalase has no effect on the equilibrium ultimately established between peroxide and its products, water and oxygen.

Catalase is only one of thousands of kinds of enzymes. Yet each particular kind of enzyme catalyzes only one particular chemical reaction. Because of their specificity, enzymes are important in determining which reactions are

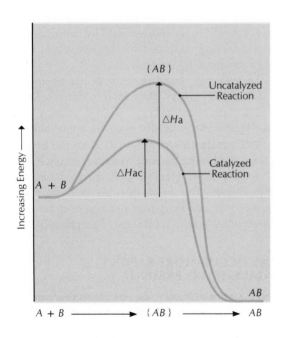

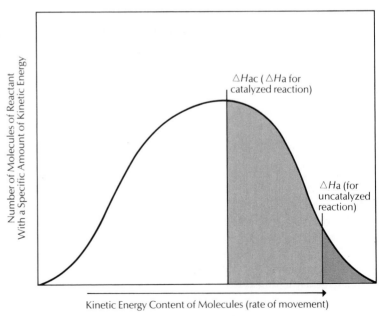

carried out in a living organism. Suppose that a certain compound can be converted spontaneously into either one of two products, A or B, and that both reactions proceed very slowly at the temperature of the living organism. Now if the reaction to form A proceeds in an uncatalyzed fashion but the reaction to form B is speeded up by the presence of a specific enzyme, then the compound in question will be converted almost entirely to B; without an enzyme catalyst, very little of A will be formed.

Now suppose, on the other hand, that a living organism can create two enzymes—one for each reaction. Suppose further that each kind of enzyme can be created only under certain conditions. Then the organism can regulate the reactions to meet varying needs for one kind of product or the other. Such enzymes are themselves created in chemical reactions that are catalyzed by still other kinds of enzymes. The information needed to direct the formation of this complex network of enzymes comes ultimately from the DNA molecules of the genes. Because genes carry information concerning which enzymes may or may not be created, and because enzymes determine which reactions may or may not occur in a cell, it is through the mediation of specific enzymes that most genes determine which heritable traits will be possessed by living beings.

Enzyme-Substrate Complexes

The following hypothetical example will illustrate how each enzyme protein in a living cell catalyzes one specific kind of reaction. An enzyme E catalyzes the reaction of two kinds of molecules, A and B, to form two different molecules, C and D:

$$A + B \underset{}{\overset{E}{\rightleftarrows}} C + D$$

In such a reaction, A and B would be called the "substrates" for the enzyme E, and C and D would be called the "products." (Because many biologically important reactions are reversible to a greater or lesser extent, it is not

always clear which molecules should be called the substrates and which the products; often the choice is arbitrary.) Enzyme E is not used up in any way in the reaction. Having catalyzed the reaction once, it is unchanged and is capable of performing the same reaction again and again. Often a single enzyme molecule will function tens of thousands of times in a single minute.

Each kind of substrate molecule shows a definite tendency to combine physically with the enzyme, forming what is called an **enzyme-substrate complex.** The chemical basis for this mutual attraction between enzyme and substrate is found in a cluster of chemical groupings on the surface of the enzyme protein. These groupings are positioned in such a way that they precisely complement the chemical groupings on the surface of the substrate. For example, if the substrate possesses a negatively charged, a hydrophobic, and an uncharged polar group on its surface, then the enzyme will normally possess a positively charged, a hydrophobic, and an uncharged polar group in a complementary orientation in space. When the two molecules come together, they will be capable of simultaneously forming an ionic interaction between the positive and negative groups, a hydrophobic interaction between the two hydrophobic groups, and a hydrogen bond between the two uncharged polar groups. *It is their multiple point-to-point complementarity that accounts for the tremendous specificity of enzymes in binding certain substrates and in catalyzing certain reactions.*

Active Sites on an Enzyme

The region on the enzyme where the substrate-binding groups are found is known as the **active site.** For the most part, the groups forming the active site are the amino acid side chains, or R groups, that become part of this region when the enzyme protein is initially synthesized and folds into its unique three-dimensional shape. In some enzymes, the active site also contains nonprotein ions or molecules that participate in the binding of substrates. If these supplemental materials are attached to the enzyme with covalent bonds they are called **prosthetic groups;** if they are held by other kinds of bonds they are called enzyme **cofactors.**

The active site is usually a pocket or groove in the protein molecule. Consequently, the enzyme surrounds the substrate on several sides when bonding occurs; in effect, the enzyme acts as a cradle for the substrate. Two substrates in the same groove or pocket in an enzyme are oriented so that the atoms about to undergo reaction are held within contact distance of one another (Figure 12.10). This arrangement contributes to the efficiency of catalytic reactions. Recall that chemical reactions involving two or more molecules are concentration-dependent because the probability of the reactants colliding increases as their concentration in-

Figure 12.8 (far left) Action of a catalyst. A catalyst lowers the energy barrier over which the reactants (A and B) must pass (ΔHac) in order to form the product AB. The catalyst does not alter the amount of energy released in the overall reaction. And it does not change the concentrations in final equilibrium. It simply speeds up the rate at which equilibrium can be reached.

Figure 12.9 (left) A catalyst functions not by increasing the average energy of molecules but by lowering the amount of energy required to form an activated complex.

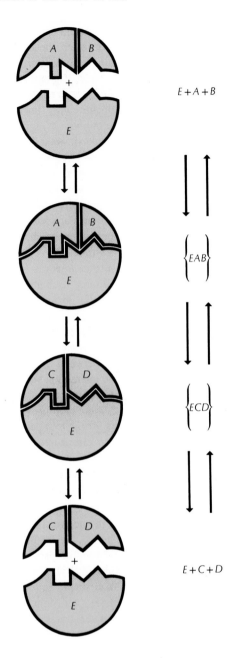

$E + A + B$

$\left\{ EAB \right\}$

$\left\{ ECD \right\}$

$E + C + D$

Figure 12.10 Highly diagrammatic, two-dimensional representation of an enzyme catalyzing the conversion of two complementary substrate molecules (A and B) into products (C and D). The enzyme molecule remains unchanged during the reaction.

creases. In binding the substrates together in the same region, an enzyme causes an enormous increase in the local concentration of reactants, which leads to an enormously increased probability of reaction. This consideration applies even in reactions where it appears that one molecule of a single substrate is split into two molecules. Such splitting reactions in cells invariably involve the participation of hydrogen ions (H^+) and hydroxyl ions (OH^-) from water. Enzymes catalyzing such reactions bind these ions in the active site within contact distance of the bond to be split. The ability of an enzyme to bring two or more reacting molecules in contact with each other is part of the reason why enzymes are such efficient catalysts.

How Induced Fit Between Enzyme and Substrate Accounts for Lowering of Activation Energy

There is a second reason for enzyme efficiency that biologists have come to regard as an important aspect of catalysis in living systems. Prior to combination, the position of the binding groups in the active site is not quite exact enough to react easily with the substrate. As the substrate approaches the active site, the complementary groups on the enzyme have to rearrange slightly to make bonding contact with the substrate molecule. The substrate in this way "induces" a fit between enzyme and substrate. This **induced fit** causes a change in the shape of the enzyme, which often can be detected by subtle physical or chemical methods. The change in shape puts the enzyme under a certain amount of tension, which is communicated to the bound substrate. The tension the enzyme exerts on the substrate tends to distort certain bonds to the degree that the electrons in the substrate are "loosened up," which makes the substrate more reactive. *We now believe it is largely the tension between enzymes and bound substrate that accounts for the lowered heat of activation.* It is this lowering of ΔHa, depicted earlier in Figure 12.9, that accounts for the existence of life as we know it.

ENZYMES COUPLE REACTIONS

A cornerstone in the chemistry of life is the ability of enzymes to link two or more reactions in such a way that the free energy released by one reaction can be used to drive a second reaction that would otherwise occur only to a limited extent. It is impossible for an enzyme to change the $\Delta G^{\circ\prime}$ (standard free energy) of a reaction (or its equilibrium constant), but there are two ways in which enzymes can facilitate reactions despite high positive values of $\Delta G^{\circ\prime}$. Both of these involve coupling of an exergonic reaction (negative $\Delta G^{\circ\prime}$) to an endergonic reaction, but the coupling occurs in two different ways.

In the first kind of coupling, the two reactions are chemically combined (into at least a two-step reaction) by a

Figure 12.11 A highly schematic model of the induced fit between an enzyme and its substrate. The hypothetical enzyme illustrated here is one that hydrolyzes the substrate A—B into its two component subunits A—H and HO—B. (a) Pockets exist on the substrate that are complementary to A and B. But the spacing between the pockets is slightly greater than the spacing between the corresponding regions of the substrate (b). Therefore, both enzyme and substrate must be distorted somewhat in order for the binding of substrate to occur (c). This results in tension on the bond joining A to B and, simultaneously, in a movement of the reactive groups of the enzyme (H and OH) toward the strained bond of the substrate. (d) The bond between A and B is broken, A and B react with the adjacent H and OH groups of the enzyme, and they are released from the substrate as products. Now the enzyme is restored to its original active state by combining with a molecule of water to replace the H and OH groups that have just reacted with the substrate.

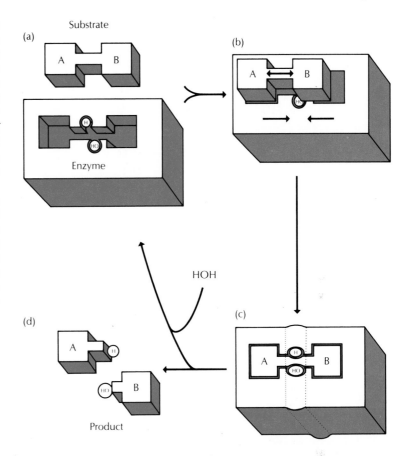

single enzyme molecule to change the nature of the reactants and the resultant products. If one half-reaction releases more free energy than the other consumes, then the combined reactions will possess a negative $\Delta G^{\circ\prime}$. The coupled reaction will proceed extensively in the forward direction.

In the second kind of coupling, an enzyme reaction of positive $\Delta G^{\circ\prime}$ is followed in a reaction sequence by an enzyme-catalyzed reaction of negative $\Delta G^{\circ\prime}$. Because the second reaction shows a strong tendency to run in the forward direction, and because it uses the products of the first reaction as its own substrates, it prevents the products of the first reaction from accumulating. Thus the ratio of products to reactants for the first reaction never reaches the equilibrium ratio. Therefore, the $\Delta G'$ (the change in free energy as opposed to standard free energy) of the first reaction becomes negative.

Let us now consider one example of each kind of coupling. (Another example of each will be given in Chapter 14, "Glycolysis and Respiration.")

High-energy phosphate compounds commonly serve as substrates in the first kind of coupled reactions. These organic compounds have phosphoric acid groups (phosphates) bonded covalently in such a way that a considerable amount of free energy is released when the phosphate group

is split off by water during hydrolysis. Phrased differently, a **high-energy phosphate bond** is one with a high free energy of hydrolysis.

Phosphoenolpyruvate and adenosine triphosphate (ATP) are two high-energy phosphate compounds (see Figures 12.12 and 12.13). For the hydrolysis of phosphoenolpyruvic acid, the standard free energy ($\Delta G^{\circ\prime}$) is -12.8 kilocalories per mole:

Phosphoenolpyruvic acid $+ H_2O \longrightarrow$

pyruvic acid $+$ phosphoric acid

($\Delta G^{\circ\prime} = -12.8$ kcal/mole)

This means that, under standard conditions, the reaction is highly exergonic and it proceeds far in the forward direction before equilibrium is reached. The hydrolysis of ATP is also a highly exergonic reaction:

ATP $+ H_2O \longrightarrow$ ADP $+$ phosphoric acid

($\Delta G^{\circ\prime} = -7.3$ kcal/mole)

where ADP is adenosine diphosphate.

Given a standard free energy of -7.3 kilocalories per mole for the hydrolysis of ATP, the equilibrium constant

(a) Adenosine Monophosphate (AMP):

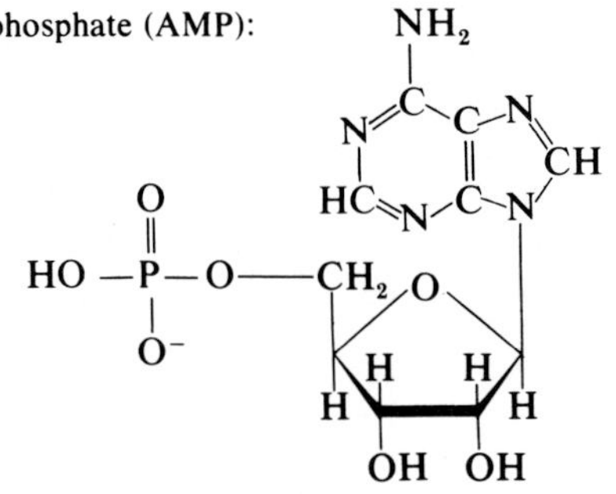

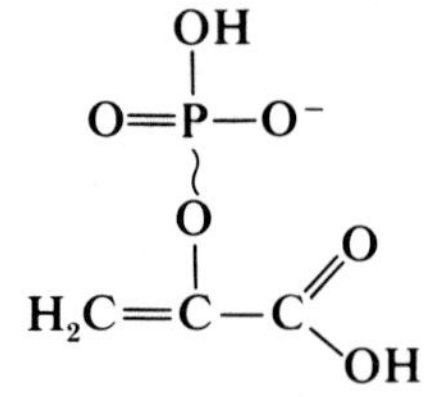

Figure 12.13 The structural formula of phosphoenolpyruvate. The high-energy phosphate bond (symbolized as ~) yields 12.8 kilocalories per mole or more of free energy upon hydrolysis.

(b) Adenosine Diphosphate (ADP):

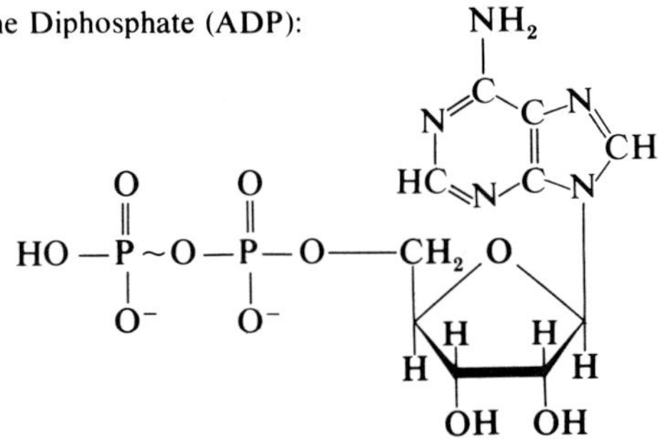

(c) Adenosine Triphosphate (ATP):

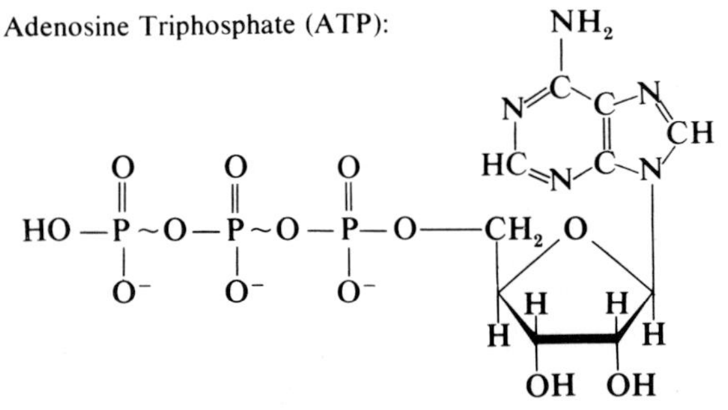

Figure 12.12 Structural formulas of three phosphate compounds involved in coupled exergonic and endergonic reactions. All are nucleotides composed of an organic base (adenine, positioned above-right in each structural formula), a sugar (ribose), and from one to three phosphoric acid molecules (phosphates). In the phosphate groups in (b) and (c), the symbol ~ represents high-energy bonds: Large amounts of energy are released when they are hydrolyzed. The third compound depicted, ATP, is an extremely prevalent carrier of energy in cells. ATP is often called the energy currency of the cell.

may be calculated to be about 1,000,000:1. This means that ATP will tend to break down in water solution until eventually there are about 1,000,000 ADP molecules for every ATP molecule remaining. That lopsided ratio clearly indicates that the production of ATP from ADP and inorganic phosphate (often symbolized as P_i) is not a reaction that can be expected to occur spontaneously to any measurable degree. Nevertheless, in all living cells molecules of ADP combine regularly with phosphate groups to yield ATP. This reaction (and any reaction that chemically combines molecules with phosphate groups) is called **phosphorylation.** In all cells, a particular enzyme couples the *hydrolysis* of phosphate from phosphoenolpyruvate (an exergonic reaction) with the *phosphorylation* of ADP (an endergonic reaction).

The free energy released when the phosphoenolpyruvic acid is hydrolyzed (-12.8 kilocalories per mole) is considerably greater than the energy required to phosphorylate ADP ($+7.3$ kilocalories per mole). When the enzyme couples the two reactions, the nature of the reactants and products is changed. Instead of releasing inorganic phosphate as such, and thus releasing all of the free energy of hydrolysis of phosphoenolpyruvic acid, the enzyme transfers the phosphate group to ADP in a two-step reaction. *When any two such reactions are coupled, the standard free energies are additive.* By adding the values of $\Delta G^{\circ\prime}$ for the individual reactions, then, we can obtain a value of $\Delta G^{\circ\prime}$ for the coupled reaction and thereby predict the equilibrium constant for the combined reactions:

$$\text{Phosphoenolpyruvate + ADP} \xrightarrow{\text{enzyme}} \text{pyruvic acid + ATP}$$

$$(\Delta G^{\circ\prime} = -12.8 + 7.3 = -5.5 \text{ kcal/mole})$$

The overall $\Delta G^{\circ\prime}$ of -5.5 kilocalories per mole tells us that the equilibrium point for this reaction will be far to the right (high ratio of products to reactants).

The ATP produced in this manner may now be used to drive a variety of other endergonic reactions in a similar way. All simple energy-requiring reactions of the cell, as well as such complex reactions as the synthesis of proteins, the contraction of muscle, and the production of light by fireflies, are driven by the free energy released in the hydrolysis of ATP. It is no exaggeration to say that *hydrolysis of ATP is the main source of energy used for powering the energy-requiring reactions in all cells.* Indeed, the prevalence of ATP as an energy carrier suggests that it must have been present in the earliest life forms.

In addition to the reactions coupling hydrolysis with phosphorylation, there are two other major ways in which ATP is synthesized from ADP. In photosynthesis (Chapter 15), light energy from the sun is used to produce ATP in a relatively direct manner. In respiration (Chapter 14), the sugars that plants have synthesized with the ATP generated by sunlight are broken down in a way that produces ATP once again.

The second form of enzyme coupling is discussed in the following section.

ENZYMES ARE ALWAYS PART OF COMPLEX METABOLIC PATHWAYS

Energy-requiring reactions in living systems are also driven by the coordinated activities of several enzymes that have been incorporated into a reaction series known as a metabolic pathway. An example of how a metabolic pathway can function to "pull" a reaction in the forward direction despite an equilibrium constant that predicts a low ratio of products to substrates can be given by considering the interconversion of three organic acids important to all living things: malic, fumaric, and aspartic acid. First, the conversion of malic to fumaric acid is catalyzed by an enzyme E_1:

$$\text{Malic acid} \underset{}{\overset{E_1}{\rightleftharpoons}} \text{fumaric acid}$$

$$(\Delta G^{\circ\prime} = +0.7 \text{ kcal/mole})$$

Because the standard free energy for this reaction is positive, starting with malic acid the reaction would be expected to proceed in the forward direction only until about 20 percent of the substrate has been converted to products. But if a second enzyme is added to the mixture that is capable of converting fumaric acid to a third compound, aspartic acid, virtually all of the malic acid will be converted first to fumaric acid, and then to aspartic acid:

$$\text{Fumaric acid} \underset{}{\overset{E_2}{\rightleftharpoons}} \text{aspartic acid}$$

$$(\Delta G^{\circ\prime} = -3.7 \text{ kcal/mole})$$

$$\text{Malic acid} \underset{}{\overset{E_1}{\rightleftharpoons}} \text{fumaric acid} \underset{}{\overset{E_2}{\rightleftharpoons}} \text{aspartic acid}$$

$$(\text{overall } \Delta G^{\circ\prime} = -3 \text{ kcal/mole})$$

The second reaction moves so strongly in the forward direction that as soon as molecules of fumaric acid appear they are quickly picked up by the second enzyme and converted to aspartic acid. Thus the first reaction never reaches equilibrium; its $\Delta G'$ therefore remains negative and the reaction continues in the forward direction. In a sense, the presence of the second enzyme "pulls" the first reaction in the forward direction. At equilibrium, then, more than 99 percent of the malic acid is converted to aspartic acid.

To generalize from this example, reactions in a living cell never occur in isolation. They are interconnected into complex networks of branching and converging pathways in which the products of one enzyme are often the substrates of one or more other enzymes. Even many reactions that appear thermodynamically unfavorable when considered in isolation can occur at high rates in living cells when they are integral parts of metabolic pathways, which prevent their products from ever reaching equilibrium concentrations.

ENZYME-CATALYZED REACTIONS CAN BE CONTROLLED AND MODIFIED

Without enzymes, most reactions of organic compounds would occur too slowly to maintain the flow of energy and matter through the web of life. Nevertheless, most enzymes are so efficient in their specific catalytic tasks that if all the enzymes of a cell were performing at once at maximum rate, there would be utter chaos. Fortunately, most enzyme-mediated reactions do not operate at the maximum rate in most cells most of the time. Cells are able to modify the rate of enzyme activity in two major ways: by controlling the amount of enzyme present and by controlling the activity of the enzyme molecules that are present. Both of these control mechanisms will be discussed in later chapters, but some of the ways in which the activity of an enzyme molecule can be regulated will be described here because it gives further insight into the nature of enzymes and the interactions between enzyme and substrate.

Effect of Substrate Concentration on Reaction Rate

Figure 12.14a depicts one of the most common ways in which the rate of an enzyme-catalyzed reaction is controlled: through the availability of substrate. There is a certain maximum rate at which a given amount of enzyme can catalyze its specific reaction. Only when the concentration of substrate is extremely high can this rate be achieved. Under conditions of high substrate concentration, the enzyme is said to be "saturated"; in other words, its active site is occupied at all times by substrate or product molecules. When that happens, further increases in substrate will have no effect on reaction rate because additional active sites are not available for action. If substrate concentration does exceed saturation levels in a cell, a further

Figure 12.14 Some of the ways in which enzyme activity is regulated in the cell.

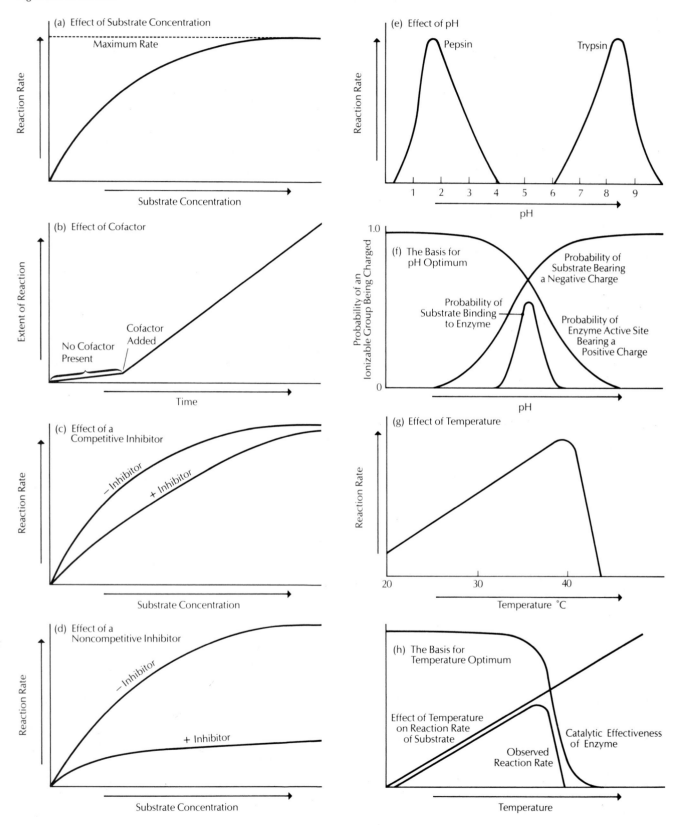

increase in the rate of reaction can be achieved only if the cell produces additional enzyme. Most enzymes are not usually saturated with substrate, however, so the rate of reaction is continuously being determined by the level of substrate that is available. At any given time, many of the molecules of enzyme are inactive simply for lack of substrate molecules upon which they can work.

Effect of Cofactors

Some enzymes require small molecules known as cofactors in order to demonstrate catalytic activity. For example, certain enzymes require specific mineral ions to complete their active site. In all the reactions that involve transfer of phosphate groups from one substrate molecule to another, the magnesium ion (Mg^{++}) is required. Its two positive charges permit the magnesium ion to act as a bridge, holding the negatively charged phosphate group to a negatively charged group in the active site of the enzyme. Figure 12.14b shows the effect that cofactor availability has on enzyme activity. Although such all-or-nothing situations are not too common, they do play important roles in some life processes. For example, a certain enzyme that mediates a muscle-contraction process requires a calcium ion (Ca^{++}). A relaxed muscle fiber is low in calcium ions; the nerve impulse that triggers contraction functions by causing calcium to flood into the muscle, which leads to activation of the previously inactive enzyme.

In addition to the metallic cofactors, a variety of small organic compounds serve as cofactors. They are given the name **coenzymes.** Their effect on activity of their corresponding enzymes is similar to that of metallic cofactors. Many cellular reactions are controlled by the availability of essential coenzymes.

Effect of Competitive and Noncompetitive Inhibitors

Some key enzymes in living cells are subject to direct and specific kinds of inhibition that control their rate of function. In **competitive inhibition** (Figure 12.14c), a molecule that is structurally similar to the substrate for a particular reaction competes for a position at the active site. Although the competitive inhibitor can be bonded to the active site, it lacks the particular structure required for the enzyme-catalyzed reaction. As a consequence, it tends to sit for a considerable period in the active site, which means that particular molecule of enzyme is not available to the substrate. The probability that an active site will be occupied by a substrate or an inhibitor is a function of their relative concentrations. Therefore, competitive inhibition can be overcome if the concentration of substrate is raised to sufficiently high levels while the inhibitor's concentration is held constant. An example of an enzyme reaction and its competitive inhibitor is shown in Figure 12.15.

Competitive inhibition probably is not an important regulatory mechanism in cells. But competitive inhibition has been a valuable tool in the analysis of the nature of active sites. It is employed by performing step-by-step modifications of substrates, then testing whether such modified substrate molecules act as competitive inhibitors. This procedure makes it possible to determine which groups are essential for binding to the enzyme, which are required to serve as substrate, and so on. Competitive inhibitors are also valuable in the field of medicine. The sulfa drugs that played such an important role in saving lives during World War II are competitive inhibitors of an enzyme that catalyzes an important step in the growth of bacteria. Today antibiotics have largely supplanted sulfa drugs. Antibiotics are substances produced primarily by fungi in a form of biological warfare against bacteria. Most antibiotics function as competitive inhibitors of certain processes essential for bacterial growth. Sulfa drugs and antibiotics such as penicillin affect enzyme reactions that occur in bacteria but not in human beings. An active area of cancer research in recent years has been, and continues to be, the search for a competitive inhibitor that will block an enzyme reaction that is essential for cancer cells but not for normal cells.

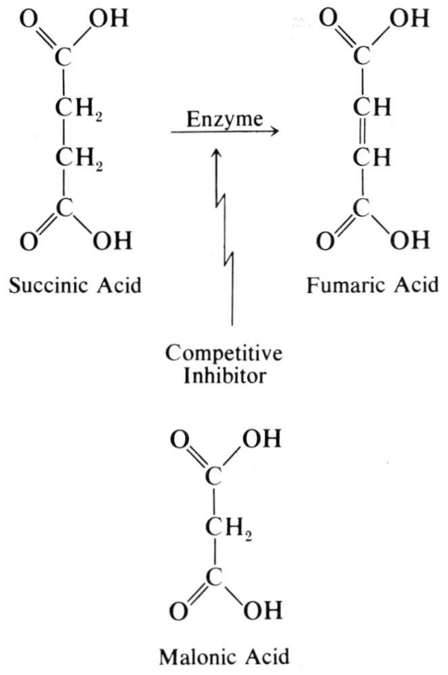

Figure 12.15 An example of an enzyme-mediated reaction and an associated competitive inhibitor in the reaction. The malonic acid structurally resembles the substrate sufficiently to combine with the active site designed for succinic acid, but it lacks the two adjacent CH₂ groups required for the reaction.

A second kind of inhibition process is shown in Figure 12.14d. **Noncompetitive inhibitors** generally bind to a site other than the active site. In doing so, they change the nature of the enzyme to the degree that its catalytic properties are lost. Because substrate molecules cannot reverse the binding of a noncompetitive inhibitor, increasing the concentration of substrate will not reverse the inhibition (compare Figure 12.14c with 12.14d). Once an enzyme molecule is combined with a noncompetitive inhibitor, it is more or less permanently poisoned.

There is a third kind of inhibition that plays a crucial role in regulating life processes. It is known as **allosteric feedback inhibition,** and it is similar in certain ways to both competitive and noncompetitive inhibition. It is one of the most important means employed by all living cells to regulate and coordinate the activities of various enzymes to meet changing conditions. Because it will be described in detail in Chapter 20, we shall defer discussion of it here.

Effect of pH

Enzyme activity can also be modified in a way that gives enzymes tremendous evolutionary plasticity. Figure 12.14e depicts the effect that changes in pH (or H^+ ion concentration) have on the activity of particular enzymes. All enzymes show this kind of profile of activity versus pH, although the peak is sometimes broader than it is in this figure. Enzymes are proteins. As you read in Chapter 11, each protein has a unique and enormously complicated three-dimensional structure that includes many ionizable groups that take part in stabilizing secondary, tertiary, and quaternary structure. It is not surprising, then, that the structure (hence the functioning) of enzymes can be modified by a change in pH. But why does enzyme activity show a sharp peak in one particular pH range? Figure 12.14f gives one example of this peak, which is referred to as **pH optimum.** In this example, the binding of substrate to enzyme requires a linkage between a negatively charged group in the active site and a positively charged group on the substrate. However, there is only a relatively narrow range of pH in which the structure of both enzyme and substrate will bear the necessary complementary charges. Below this range (in other words, when the surrounding medium is more acidic than the pH range in which that enzyme operates), the negatively charged group on the enzyme would pick up a hydrogen ion and become neutral, or incapable of binding substrate, at that site. Above this range (when the medium is more basic), the substrate would lose a hydrogen ion and become neutral in a key location required for binding to the enzyme.

Only a small number of charged groups are available for protein structure; these are the ionizable side chains (or R groups) of the five basic and acidic amino acids used to build proteins. The amazing thing is that even with this small number it is possible, through the slow accumulation of evolutionary changes, to develop proteins with a wide range of pH optima that are matched to the pH conditions in which they operate. In fact, most enzymes possess a pH optimum matched very closely to the normal pH of the region in which they function. For example, trypsin and pepsin are two digestive enzymes. They are secreted into the digestive tract of animals, where they break down the protein molecules contained in food. Pepsin is produced by (and secreted into the lumen of) the stomach, where the pH is around 2; this environment is tremendously acidic because of the hydrochloric acid that the stomach also produces. The pH optimum of pepsin activity is 2—it is matched to the environment in which it functions. Trypsin, on the other hand, is secreted into and functions in the alkaline environment of the intestine, where the pH is about 8. Trypsin also has a pH optimum suited to the environment in which it functions. Most enzymes that are active within cells have a pH optimum fairly close to the range of pH that cells normally maintain.

Effect of Temperature

Most chemical reactions tend to occur more rapidly as the temperature rises. In the case of enzyme-catalyzed reactions, however, there comes a time when further increase in temperature causes a drastic decline in reaction rate, for if any protein is heated beyond a certain point its structure changes rapidly (see Figures 12.14g and h). This loss of active protein structure is called **denaturation.** What happens is that the increased thermal agitation tears apart many of the bonds that normally hold the protein molecule in its highly organized, three-dimensional arrangement. When that arrangement is disrupted, the molecule no longer can carry out its intended function. In some cases the process can be partly or entirely reversed, but sometimes denaturation proceeds to the point that the protein loses its solubility (coagulates), and it will never regain its original properties. (That is why it is impossible to un-fry an egg.)

Most often, thermal denaturation of protein comes about when the temperature rises merely a few degrees above the highest temperature normally encountered by the organism from which the protein is derived. For example, the enzymes of cold-blooded organisms living in the Antarctic seas often are active near the freezing point of water and undergo denaturation well below what we call ''room'' temperature. In contrast, equivalent enzymes from blue-green algae found in the hot springs of Yellowstone Park show little activity at room temperature but are so resistant to thermal denaturation that they can be boiled without loss of activity! Evidently, when there is no evolutionary pressure to resist thermal denaturation, natural selection acts primarily on the active site, thus perpetuating many enzymes that function effectively only at very low temperatures. But as the temperature of the environment rises, selection acts to a greater and greater extent on regions outside the active site, favoring variants that have more extensive bonding between different regions of the molecule—and therefore are less sensitive to the disrupting effects of thermal agitation.

PERSPECTIVE

In this discussion of various aspects of chemical reactions—the free energy available to power reactions, the nonusable forms of energy that emerge when reactions take place, the enzyme activity that synchronizes and controls reaction rates—you have crossed a subtle dividing line between chemical equilibrium and the metabolism of organisms. True chemical equilibrium, the point at which no further net reaction occurs, in fact is reached only within closed systems, into which matter and energy do not continue to enter and from which they do not leave. It does not occur in living systems to any significant extent. For instance, even though some enzyme reactions in cells do have the appearance of being in equilibrium from time to time, as they do when the relative concentrations of substrate and product are those predicted by the equilibrium constant for the enzyme, the appearance is illusory. New molecules of substrate are appearing continuously as the result of other enzyme-mediated reactions, and molecules of product are being removed continuously by still other reactions.

Consider, by way of analogy, the light released in the continuing thermonuclear reactions of the sun. The light looks more or less the same today as it did yesterday, and it will look more or less the same tomorrow. But the only thing that is really the same is the process that sustains it. The atoms that feed the reactions at one instant are different from those that will feed it an instant later. The energy released in the process is different each instant also, and flows in only one direction. So it is with you. Little of your body is composed of the same atoms that composed it five years ago, and little of the ''you'' that exists today will be present five years from now, but ''you'' will retain a unique identity.

Clearly an organism or even part of one is an open system: Matter and energy flow incessantly between it and its surroundings as long as the condition called ''life'' exists. Life is not an equilibrium state; it is a quasi-steady state in which a continuous flow of molecules and energy maintains a more or less constant entity despite the ongoing change and replacement of its component parts. Studies of metabolism—the chemical changes associated with life—attempt to follow this transfer of matter and energy through the chemical pathways of a living system in a given period of time, and we have benefited immeasurably from those studies. But in focusing on metabolic processes at the molecular level, you should not lose sight of the fact that a biological system changes over time as well—from development, through the period of growth and aging, and on to eventual death. The quasi-steady state of life is time-dependent, and it moves in one direction. With its ingenious manner of extracting matter and energy from its environment, and of synchronizing and controlling the rate of their transfer through various complex metabolic pathways, a living system resists for a while the trend toward increasing entropy. The illusion of equilibrium derives from this resistance. Eventually, however, a living system runs down. It is no more and no less than a part of the flow of all matter and energy toward entropy—toward true and final equilibrium on the vast scale of the universe many billions of years hence.

SUGGESTED READINGS

BLUM, HAROLD F. *Time's Arrow and Evolution.* New York: Harper & Row, 1962. A readable account of the meaning of physical chemistry for biology.

BRONK, J. RAMSEY. *Chemical Biology.* New York: Macmillan, 1973. Does a thorough and comprehensive job of applying biochemical principles to biological problems.

CARTER, L. C. *Guide to Cellular Energetics.* San Francisco: W. H. Freeman, 1973. A programmed learning approach to cellular energetics, dealing especially with free energy, coupled reactions, and oxidation/reduction reactions.

CHRISTENSEN, HALVOR H., and RICHARD A. CELLARIUS. *Introduction to Bioenergetics: Thermodynamics for the Biologist.* Philadelphia: Saunders, 1972. A programmed learning approach to bioenergetics that makes only minimal starting assumptions and is oriented strongly toward biology.

LEHNINGER, ALBERT L. *Bioenergetics.* 2nd ed. Menlo Park, Calif.: W. A. Benjamin, 1971. A solid but readily understandable treatment of the flow of energy at the cellular level.

Chapter 13

The Cellular Basis of Life

Each cell in your body is a living thing, not merely a passive chamber for some vital force but a thing that moves, that grows, that multiplies, that requires sustenance, and that performs some essential function in the community of cells in which it lives. The scanning electron micrograph above shows a hamster cell that had been growing in a culture dish in the laboratory. At the time the micrograph was taken, the cell was raising its edge in a ruffling movement while sending out processes to sense the environment, find new "toeholds," and form new anchors so that the cell could then move on.

A cell is a fundamental unit of life . . . all living organisms are single cells or aggregates of cells . . . a cell is the smallest unit of life capable of independent reproduction.

This is the **cell theory,** a concise statement about the nature of living things. The origin of this theory lies in the work of the classical microscopists of the seventeenth century, who were the first to glimpse the world beneath the threshold of the unaided eye. Included in their ranks were Galileo, Antony van Leeuwenhoek, Nehemiah Grew, and Robert Hooke. It was Hooke who introduced the word ''cell'' into biological literature. *Cella* was a word that early Latins had used to signify a small room, or a small prison cell, or even the small chambers found in honeycomb, and in 1665 Hooke used it to signify the empty chambers of a thin section of cork he was examining microscopically. *''Cellulae''* he called them; they were the remnants of dead cells of the bark of a cork tree, although Hooke did not think of them as being ''alive'' or ''dead.'' Other microscopists examining sections of plants saw ''little bodies'' stuck together, each surrounded by what was indisputably some kind of wall, and they saw some sort of ''bladders'' as well—thin-walled structures filled with juices and obviously growing. In examining bean plants, the naturalist Grew identified a single row of these ''bladders,'' stacked perpendicularly and opening one into the other, thereby forming a continuous cavity. In the heyday of classical microscopy there eventually came recognition that one single cell could be alive; many microorganisms being identified for the first time were unicellular. Then in 1805 Lorenz Oken concluded that *all* organisms must be cells or aggregates of cells.

This progression of thought was further developed and became widely accepted as the result of the work of Matthias Schleiden and Theodor Schwann. Schleiden concluded in 1838 that all higher plants ''are aggregates of fully individualized, independent, separate beings, namely the cells themselves.'' Schwann extended Schleiden's conclusions on the basis of his own comprehensive studies of different animal tissues. In 1839, Schwann wrote that all animal tissues are composed of individual cells. He perceived that the fertilized egg from which any animal grows is a single cell surrounded by a membrane and containing a nucleus, much like the membrane and nucleus found in animal tissues. The development of an animal occurs, he said, through the creation of new cells. He concluded that animals and plants—all organisms, in fact—are composed entirely of cells and of substances produced by cells, that cells are to some extent independent living units, and that they are subordinate to the entire organism.

Within a few decades, biological observations were pieced together to yield a valid picture of the manner in which cells divide. This line of investigation was sum-

Figure 13.2 (a) Lorenz Oken, who set forth an early version of the cell theory. (b) Matthias Schleiden and (c) Theodor Schwann. The observations Schleiden and Schwann made on the nature of cells were extensive, but both were mistaken about the nature of cell division. Schwann believed new cells arose from amorphous buds pinched off the parent cell. Schleiden interpreted the nucleus (which was known to be present in all cells) as a new cell forming within the old. Although they drew few correct conclusions that had not been previously drawn, Schleiden and Schwann were both active in winning wide acceptance for the cell theory among other biologists. Hence history generally records them as the ''fathers'' of the cell theory.

marized by Rudolf Virchow in his dictum: *Omnis cellula e cellula* (''Every cell from a cell''). By the end of the nineteenth century, the cell was accepted as the smallest living unit capable of independent reproduction, and the cell theory—the distillation of a long series of observations into a core principle—was essentially completed.

THERE IS NO ''TYPICAL'' CELL, BUT CERTAIN STRUCTURES TYPICALLY ARE FOUND IN CELLS

If we were to search for representative cells displaying most of the features common to eukaryotic cells, we might select a pair such as those depicted in Figure 13.3.

(text continues on page 266)

263

Figure 13.3   Some structural features of eukaryotic cells. The drawings depict several features typically found in all plant and animal cells as well as a few that are found only in one kind or the other. Details of these structures and their functions are discussed later in the chapter.

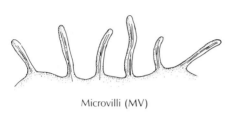

Microvilli (MV)

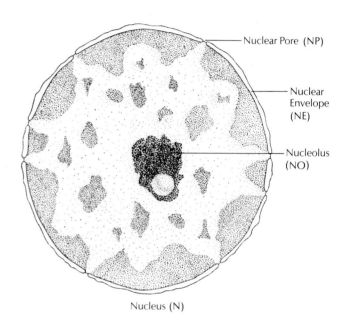

Nuclear Pore (NP)

Nuclear Envelope (NE)

Nucleolus (NO)

Nucleus (N)

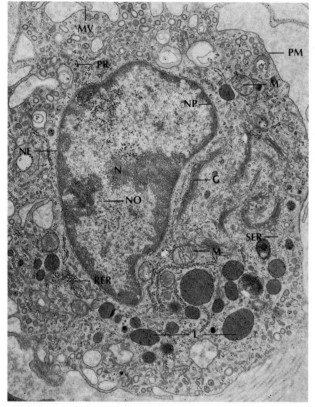

ANIMAL CELL   (magnification x 10,600)

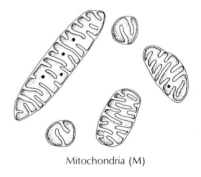

Mitochondria (M)

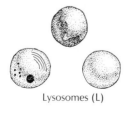

Lysosomes (L)

Rough Endoplasmic Reticulum (RER)

Plasma Membrane (PM)

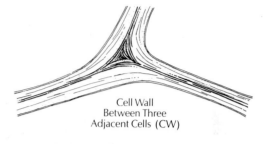

Cell Wall
Between Three
Adjacent Cells (CW)

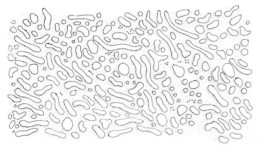

Smooth Endoplasmic
Reticulum (SER)

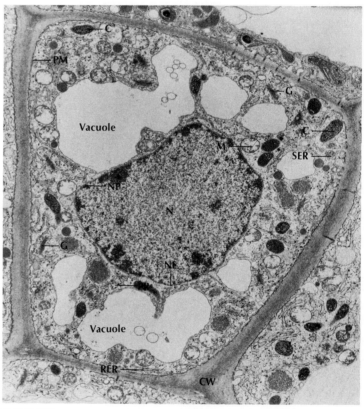

PLANT CELL

(magnification x 6,300)

Golgi
Complex (G)

Clusters of
Ribosomes (PR)

Chloroplast (C)

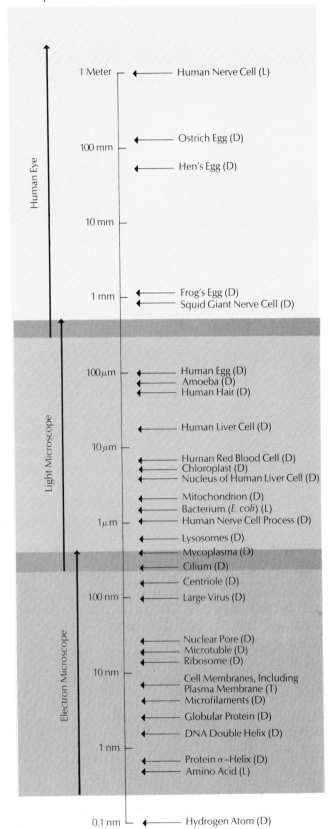

Light Microscope

Electron Microscope

1 Meter — Human Nerve Cell (L)

100 mm — Ostrich Egg (D)

— Hen's Egg (D)

10 mm

1 mm — Frog's Egg (D)
— Squid Giant Nerve Cell (D)

100 μm — Human Egg (D)
— Amoeba (D)
— Human Hair (D)

— Human Liver Cell (D)

10 μm — Human Red Blood Cell (D)
— Chloroplast (D)
— Nucleus of Human Liver Cell (D)

— Mitochondrion (D)
— Bacterium (*E. coli*) (L)
1 μm — Human Nerve Cell Process (D)

— Lysosomes (D)

— Mycoplasma (D)

— Cilium (D)

— Centriole (D)

100 nm — Large Virus (D)

— Nuclear Pore (D)
— Microtuble (D)
— Ribosome (D)

10 nm — Cell Membranes, Including Plasma Membrane (T)
— Microfilaments (D)

— Globular Protein (D)

— DNA Double Helix (D)

1 nm — Protein α–Helix (D)
— Amino Acid (L)

0.1 nm — Hydrogen Atom (D)

Figure 13.4 Approximate dimensions of some cells and cellular components. Because most of the objects listed are highly variable in size, the position of the arrows indicates only part of the size range in which such objects fall. Note particularly the lower limit resolution for the human eye, the light microscope, and the electron microscope. Letters in parentheses indicate which dimension is being listed: L = length, D = diameter, and T = thickness. [Electron microscopists conventionally have expressed dimensions in angstroms, where 10 angstroms (Å) = 1 nanometer (nm), but recent recommendations of an international commission discourage use of the angstrom unit.]

There is no such thing as a typical cell, however. Such generalizations are useful only insofar as they provide us with an idea of what parts to look for in a cell and of the role the various parts play in the functioning of the whole.

How large is a "typical" cell? A few, such as certain large single-celled organisms and the eggs of birds, can be seen with the unaided eye, but most cells can be seen only with a microscope (Figure 13.4). Even when cells are viewed with a conventional microscope, their details are indistinct or invisible. That is why early microscopists concluded (incorrectly) that all cells contain nothing more than a few granules suspended in a homogeneous substance, which they named **protoplasm.** With improvements in microscopy *(Interleaf 13.1)* and with continuing chemical investigations, we now know that the contents of cells are far from homogeneous. In fact, the complexity of cellular organization is such that it is necessary to make a distinction between **cytoplasm** (the complex *mixture* of substances and structures found in the cell, exclusive of the nucleus) and **nucleoplasm** (the complex *mixture* of substances and structures found in the nucleus). Fortunately there is a logical way of approaching this diversity in cellular structures, for certain structural patterns have recently been identified that occur over and over again within cells and from one kind of cell to the next. One of these patterns has to do with the nature of cell membranes.

A CHALLENGE TODAY IS THE ELUCIDATION OF MEMBRANE STRUCTURE AND FUNCTION

Unless a cell is severely cut or punctured, it retains most of its contents and its individual identity, often for periods of many years. And yet, many substances are being exchanged continuously between its internal and external environment. Any theory of the nature of the cell surface must explain these two facts. Some nineteenth-century biologists held that the cell surface was merely an interface like the one that exists between a water droplet and the surrounding air. Others held that some sort of invisible skin enclosed the contents: Why else would the contents flow out when the cell was punctured with a fine needle? Then, in the early part of the twentieth century, biologists observed that many oil-soluble materials enter cells more rapidly than most water-soluble materials do. The interior of a cell was known to be watery, so this observation suggested that the cell must be bounded by an oily film, or "membrane." Oil-soluble materials could dissolve more efficiently in such a membrane, which would account for their more rapid penetration into the cell.

Certain studies of red blood cells also pointed to the possibility that cells have membranes. When red blood cells were suspended in very dilute salt solutions, they became swollen by osmosis (the movement of water across a semipermeable membrane). Eventually they burst open and released the red blood protein that composed most of their interior (Figure 13.5). All that remained was a lipid-rich material, which was dubbed the "ghosts" of the red blood

cells. Could these ghosts be the cell membranes? In one classic experiment, the lipids of such a preparation of ghosts were dissolved and spread on the surface of water. Interestingly enough, if the surface layer so formed was exactly one molecule thick, the area of water covered was exactly *twice* the surface area of the red blood cells from which they were derived. A cell membrane therefore had to be composed of a lipid film two molecules thick, and the concept of a **lipid bilayer membrane** entered biological theory. It was known at the time that most of the lipid molecules of such preparations had a polar, hydrophilic head and a nonpolar hydrophobic tail (Figure 13.6), so there was general agreement on what seemed to be the most plausible arrangement of such a bilayer (Figure 13.7).

The lipid bilayer membrane concept was elaborated upon in 1935, when J. F. Danielli and H. Davson measured the surface tension of a cell membrane and found it was very different from the surface tension of an artificially constructed lipid bilayer. The difference, they proposed, could be accounted for if the surfaces of the lipid bilayer were sandwiched between two coats of protein molecules (Figure

(text continues on page 271)

Figure 13.5 Osmotic shrinking and swelling of a red blood cell. Water passes in and out of a cell continuously by diffusion (random movement of individual molecules). This process is known as osmosis. The direction of net movement of water via osmosis is determined by the relative concentration of substances inside and outside the cell.

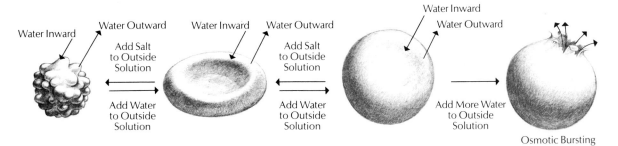

Hypertonic Conditions: When the total concentration of substances in water outside the cell *is greater than* the concentration of interior substances, more of the water on the outside is bound to the dissolved substances. In other words, less water is free to diffuse into the cell. Thus water diffuses outward faster than it diffuses inward. As a result, the cell shrinks and becomes what we call "crenated" in appearance.

Isotonic Conditions: When the total concentration of substances dissolved in the water outside the cell *is equal to* the total concentration of substances inside the cell, water diffuses inward and outward at the same rate. Thus the cell maintains its normal biconcave shape.

Hypotonic Conditions: When the total concentration of substances dissolved in the water outside the cell *is less than* the concentration inside the cell, fewer water molecules on the outside are bound to dissolved substances and more are free to diffuse into the cell. Thus water diffuses inward faster than it diffuses outward, and the cell swells up because of "osmotic pressure" (the pressure resulting from

one-way osmosis of water). If this osmotic pressure becomes greater than the strength of the cell membrane, the membrane will burst, the contents will flow out, and the empty membrane will be left behind as a mere "ghost" of its former self.

Interleaf 13.1

The Light Microscope, the Transmission Electron Microscope, and the Scanning Electron Microscope

The ability to see details of small structures is limited by the resolving power, or resolution, of optical systems. "Resolution" and "resolving power" refer to the minimum distance at which objects can be distinguished as separate things. Any two objects separated by less than that distance will blur together as a single object. The lower limit of resolution of the unaided human eye is about 200 micrometers (0.008 inch); that of a light microscope is about 200 nanometers (or 0.000008 inch)—a limit set by the nature of light.

In a **light microscope,** wavelengths of light pass through a condenser lens, which focuses them into a beam. The beam passes through the specimen being examined and is focused into an image by the objective lens. Then an eyepiece lens magnifies the image the objective lens produces. Two effects associated with the wavelike nature of light have influenced microscope lens design. "Chromatic aberration" occurs with any lens made of a single kind of glass, which brings different wavelengths of light into focus at slightly different distances past the lens. This produces annoying rings of color around each small object in the viewing field. The problem was solved by designing a lens of

two kinds of glass that have equal but opposite chromatic aberration and thereby compensate for each other. "Spherical aberration" occurs when light passing through the center of a lens is focused in a different plane from light passing through the edge. This problem was overcome by grinding lenses into certain shapes and by adding elements to them. But even with improved lens design, resolution of a light microscope is limited by "diffraction"—by the bending of light waves as they pass the edge of an object. Diffraction blurs the edge of an image so much that it becomes impossible to distinguish between two closely adjacent points. Thus it will never be possible to see anything smaller than one-half the wavelength of violet light (400 nanometers), which lies at the short wavelength end of the visible spectrum. This means the theoretical limit of resolution of the light microscope is 200 nanometers.

Greater resolution is possible with a **transmission electron microscope** because a beam of electrons has properties corresponding to wavelengths 100,000 times shorter than visible light. Because electrons also have the properties of charged particles, they can be focused with magnets. By altering

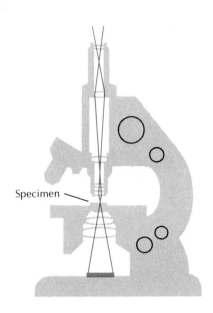

Specimen

Light Microscope
(Maximum Resolution ≈ 200 nm)

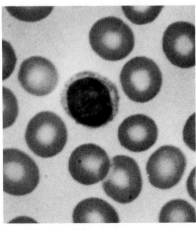

(magnification x 1800)

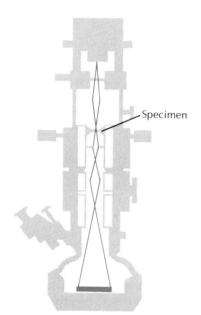

Specimen

Transmission Electron
Microscope
(Maximum Resolution ≈ 0.1-0.2 nm)

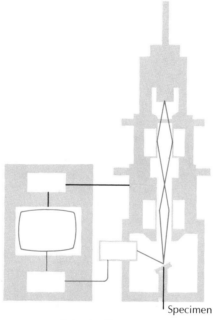

Specimen

Scanning Electron
Microscope
(Maximum Resolution ≈ 20 nm)

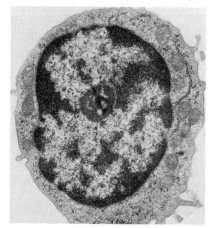

(magnification x 12,400)

(magnification x 4,500)

the strength of the magnetic field through which electrons flow, the path of the electrons can be bent to a variable extent. In an electron microscope, an electric field propels electrons from a negatively charged electrode (a cathode). Magnetic fields created by electromagnets in the instrument focus the streaming electrons onto a stained specimen. Many of the electrons pass right through the specimen. But some are absorbed or scattered by atoms of metallic stains that have been combined with certain atoms of the specimen. The electrons that do pass through are focused with electromagnets onto a screen coated with a phosphorescent material. Electrons striking the screen cause it to glow, creating a pattern of light and dark areas corresponding to areas of greater or lesser electron density in the specimen. The electrons may also be focused onto a photographic film to create a photographic image. Specimens must be extremely thin (less than 10 nanometers in thickness). Thicker specimens will so disrupt the electron beam that a uniformly dark image will result.

Specimen preparation includes fixing the material (treating it chemically to preserve its size and shape), staining it to bring out details, treating it with solvents to remove all traces of water, embedding it in plastic, and cutting thin sections from it. Sections are mounted on a fine wire screen, which is inserted into the microscope. "Electron stains" are electron-dense (or electron-scattering) materials that combine preferentially with certain atoms and molecules of biological structures. In "negative staining," a specimen is treated with a solution of electron-dense material which, upon drying, fills all the spaces between the separate particles of the specimen. This produces a negative (light) image on a dark background. In "heavy-metal shadowing," a fine film of electron-dense metal is sprayed at an angle over a specimen so that heavy deposits build up on one side of it and a transparent "shadow" is left on the other.

The "wavelength" of a typical electron beam is about 0.005 nanometer, which (in theory) should permit resolution of 0.0023 nanometer. Because of difficulties in construction and operation of magnetic lenses, however, the highest resolution now available is about 0.1 to 0.2 nanometer.

Both the light microscope (as usually employed) and the transmission electron microscope send light or electrons through a specimen. The **scanning electron microscope,** in contrast, permits photographs to be made by electrons reflected from the surface of an object. Electrons are focused into a narrow beam (about 20 nanometers in diameter), which is swept across a specimen in a sequence of linear passes. An electronic device is used to detect the electrons bouncing back from the surface at a particular angle. More electrons are returned when the beam hits the specimen directly than when it hits at an angle. Specimen composition also determines how many electrons are returned at various points of impact. Such variations are picked up by the signal detector, amplified, and replicated line by line on the face of a television tube. Because there are more scanning lines per inch of screen, scanning electron micrographs have much higher image quality than commercial television.

Specimens for the scanning electron microscope must be fixed, dehydrated, and plated with a gold alloy, which is an excellent conductor. (Unless conductivity is imparted to a specimen, the electron beam can deposit a charge on the specimen surface that will cause distortions in the final image.) In the "gold evaporation" process, specimens are placed on a metal plate and positioned in an evacuated chamber. A sheet of gold alloy is heated to its boiling point in the chamber. As atoms of the metal are evaporated, they travel outward in the vacuum chamber until they meet an object (such as the specimen) that has a temperature below their boiling point. The atoms settle on such objects and soon the specimen has a uniform gold plating a few atoms thick. Because the specimen itself does not have to transmit electrons in order to be viewed, relatively large objects can be used without sectioning, which provides great depth of field. Dramatic surface images can be obtained that appear three-dimensional. The specimen holder of the scanning scope can be tilted in any direction, permitting microscopists to examine the object from all angles and obtain otherwise impossible views.

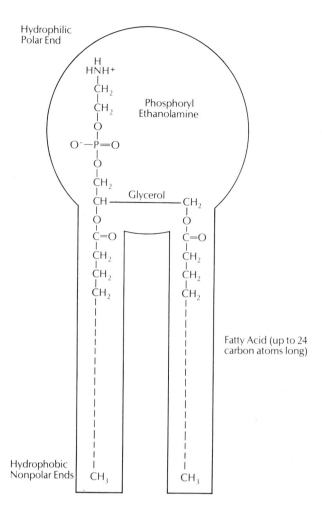

Hydrophilic
Polar End

Phosphoryl
Ethanolamine

Glycerol

Fatty Acid (up to 24
carbon atoms long)

Hydrophobic
Nonpolar Ends

Figure 13.6 (above) One kind of molecule found in red blood cell ghosts and in other membrane preparations. Of importance here are the two ionized groups, the P=O group, and the two C=O groups. All are capable of interacting with water, as described in Chapter 11.

13.8). Visual support for their proposal seemed to come from transmission electron micrographic studies, which suggested that *all* cell membranes are three layers thick (Figure 13.9). In 1959, J. David Robertson interpreted these images to mean that a lipid bilayer was sandwiched between two layers of protein. He suggested the three-layer configuration be called the **unit membrane.** The unit membrane was considered to be a continuous, homogeneous film, interrupted only occasionally by pores but otherwise completely surrounding some substance. (Such pores were never seen but they had to be inferred in order to explain the known passage of certain materials through the membrane.)

Today, many biologists believe the unit membrane concept must be modified. Results from both functional studies and structural studies based on such processes as **freeze-cleave etching** (Figure 13.10) lead to the conclusion that membranes are not homogeneous films any more than "protoplasm" is a homogeneous fluid. The exterior of a cell membrane is smooth, but stippling its interior are many granular objects that are too large to be the lipids of the proposed unit membrane configuration (Figure 13.11). These intramembranous granules must be proteins: they disappear when certain enzymes specifically capable of digesting proteins are brought into contact with them. The appearance of these proteins is regular and predictable for a given kind of cell under a given set of conditions, but it varies from one kind of cell to another and at different stages in a cell's life cycle. These observations tie in with a fact that chemists have known for some time: Although the lipid content per unit area of membrane surface is relatively constant, the amount of protein (and carbohydrate) intimately associated with membranes varies widely from one membrane to the next. In many cases the distribution of some of these proteins has been shown to be nonrandom—they occur in localized patches in the membrane. It has also been shown that such proteins are free to move laterally through the lipid bilayer in response to changing conditions in the cellular environment. Finally, the proper-

(text continues on page 274)

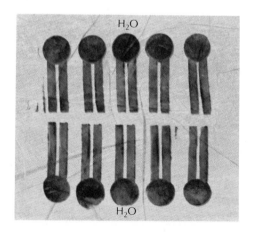

H₂O

H₂O

Figure 13.7 Proposed orientation of molecules in the lipid bilayer membrane. Nonpolar, hydrophobic point toward each other and away from the water phases (see Chapter 11).

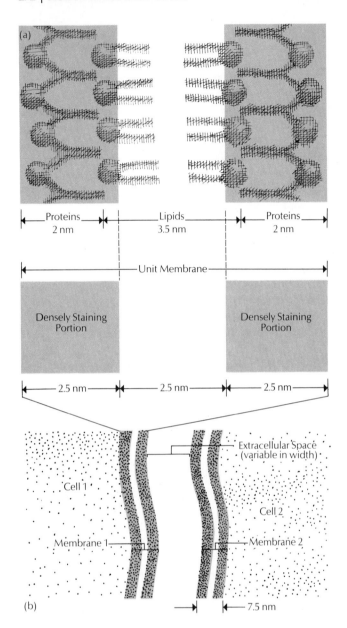

(a)

Proteins
2 nm

Lipids
3.5 nm

Proteins
2 nm

Unit Membrane

Densely Staining
Portion

Densely Staining
Portion

2.5 nm   2.5 nm   2.5 nm

Cell 1

Extracellular Space
(variable in width)

Cell 2

Membrane 1

Membrane 2

(b)

7.5 nm

Figure 13.8   (a) A diagram of the Davson-Danielli-Robertson unit membrane concept. The lipid bilayer is sandwiched between two layers of protein bound to the hydrophilic ends of the lipid molecules. (b) A representation of how unit membranes appear under the electron microscope.

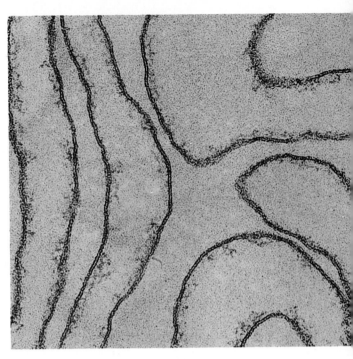

Figure 13.9   Electron micrograph showing the appearance of red blood cell ghost membranes treated with a heavy-metal stain that binds to membranes. Notice the two regular black lines separated by a thin, light line. Where membranes were cut at an oblique angle during specimen preparation, this appearance is blurred.

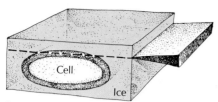

Step 1. Freeze Cleavage

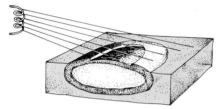

Step 2. Etching

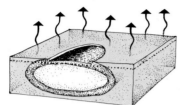

Step 3. Metal "Shadowing"

Figure 13.10 *The freeze-cleave etching technique. In Step 1, a block of ice containing a cell is struck with a sharp knife, which fractures the block. The fracture line passes above one region of the membrane and through another region. The split-off piece of ice is discarded. In Step 2, part of the ice is evaporated (etched) to reveal part of the membrane that lies below the fracture line. In Step 3, a metal (in this case, platinum) is evaporated from a hot filament in a vacuum, which results in the deposition of a layer of metal over the surface of the block containing the fractured cell. Because the filament is positioned off to one side, the metal layer is thicker on the side of the protruding object that is closest to the filament, and a metal-free ''shadow'' occurs behind the object. The process gives electron micrographs a three-dimensional appearance.*

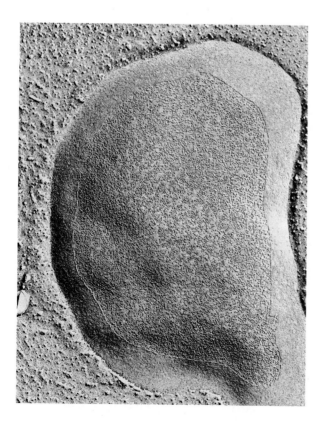

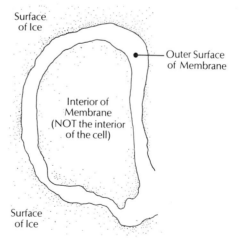

Figure 13.11 *The structure of a red blood cell membrane as revealed by freeze-cleave etching. Notice the granular appearance of the membrane interior, which presumably corresponds to the light middle line seen in cross sections (compare with Figure 13.9). This granular texture is in marked contrast to the smooth appearance of the outer membrane surface. (The rough texture of the surrounding ice is due to random imperfections in the ice crystal that occur during rapid freezing.)*

Figure 13.12   The lipid-globular-protein-mosaic model of membrane structure.

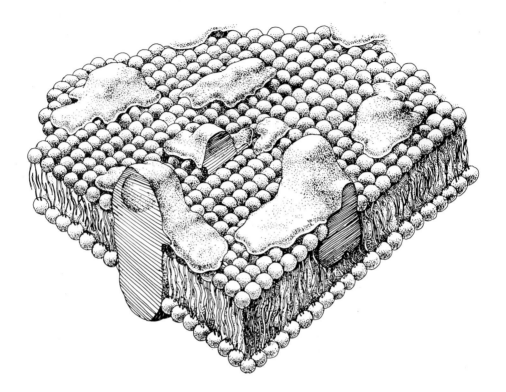

ties of cell membranes are known to vary in terms of the kinds of molecules present within them and in terms of the rate at which certain materials are transported across them.

All this evidence points to the same conclusion: Even though the basic structural plan is the same for all membranes, the presence and the organization of different kinds of protein granules in membranes is the source of the unique (as opposed to the common) membrane properties of different regions of a cell and from one kind of cell to the next. Consequently, most biologists now agree that membrane specialization is not primarily an outcome of the loose attachment of proteins to one side of a membrane or the other, as the unit membrane model would suggest. *A membrane is now thought of as a rich mosaic with many different and specialized substances embedded in its surface in a complex cell-specific, membrane-specific pattern.* Is there a model of how such a mosaic might be put together? One particular model (there are others) is shown in Figure 13.12. It is referred to as the **lipid-globular-protein-mosaic model,** and it represents an important shift in the conceptual focus of research into cellular organization: Although the unit membrane concept is still useful for conveying an idea of the essentially similar structure of all membrane systems of all cell types, still to be explained in

detail are the patterns of organization of the vast array of different protein inclusions now known to be embedded within all membranes and imparting to them their functional diversity.

THE PLASMA MEMBRANE REGULATES THE FLOW OF SUBSTANCES INTO AND OUT OF A CELL

The most important property of a surface membrane, or **plasma membrane,** is its ability to regulate the passage of substances into and out of the cell. The structure of the plasma membrane is such that the cell it encloses is neither isolated completely from nor in complete equilibrium with the environment—there is a continual but highly selective exchange of substances across the membrane boundary.

The Controlled Distribution of Ions Inside and Outside a Cell

If we measure the concentrations of certain kinds of charged substances on either side of a plasma membrane, we find predictable and substantial differences in how they are distributed. Potassium ions, for example, are usually concentrated inside a living cell, whereas sodium and chloride ions are concentrated on the outside. Figure 13.13 depicts this asymmetry for a vertebrate muscle cell. Of course, the

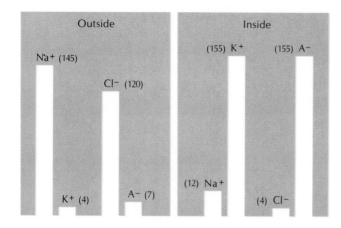

Figure 13.13 *Distribution of selected ions inside and outside a muscle cell. A⁻ is the sum of all negatively charged organic compounds such as organic acids, ATP, and proteins. Notice that the concentration of sodium (Na⁺) is more than ten times greater outside the cell, and the concentration of potassium (K⁺) is more than twenty times greater inside the cell. These differences in concentrations of various ions result in a voltage across the plasma membrane. Large amounts of cellular energy are required to maintain these differences between inside and outside concentration. In a muscle cell at rest, 10 percent of the ATP being produced by the cell is used to maintain this pattern of ion distribution.*

absolute amount of each kind of ion outside the cell varies from one environment to the next. For instance, the concentrations of sodium and chloride ions outside a unicellular organism living in the ocean are quite different from those found outside similar organisms living in freshwater lakes and streams. *Regardless of variations in the concentration of ions, the same pattern of asymmetrical distribution across a plasma membrane always occurs.*

Asymmetrical distribution of ions leads to a potential difference, or voltage, across the plasma membrane. In all living cells this difference in electric potential energy is given the special name **membrane potential,** and it can be shown to exist by a simple experiment. If a tiny electrode (less than 1 micrometer in diameter) is inserted inside a living cell and a second electrode is placed outside the cell, a voltage is measured in much the same way that it would be if the electrodes had been placed on the positively and negatively charged poles of a small battery. The interior of living cells is usually negatively charged with respect to the outside environment.

The distribution of ions between the inside and outside of a living cell is not random; it is a state of low entropy. Therefore, a cell must expend large amounts of energy to maintain the degree of order that does exist. If a cell is

poisoned in such a way that it can no longer produce energy molecules (adenosine triphosphate, or ATP), the asymmetry of ion distribution is destroyed. For example, potassium ions begin to flow out of the cell and sodium ions flow into it. And as the potassium/sodium ion (K⁺/Na⁺) ratio inside the cell falls, the membrane potential also falls. This relationship between energy metabolism and ionic composition is reciprocal: *Just as the loss of metabolism destroys membrane potential, interference with membrane potential results in a loss of energy metabolism.* In experiments that interfere directly with the K⁺/Na⁺ ratio, the membrane potential of a cell falls and life grinds to a halt as essential reactions slow down or go out of control, one by one, for lack of adequate intracellular potassium.

Forms of Transport Through the Plasma Membrane

If radioactively labeled sodium ions are added to the environment of a cell, and if the cell interior is periodically checked for the presence of these radioactive ions, we find that sodium is capable of entering the cell at a substantial rate. Potassium ions, too, are capable of moving across the plasma membrane. Because all living cells must maintain a certain K⁺/Na⁺ ratio, the potassium and sodium ions must move continuously in both directions at such a rate that no *net* change in ion concentrations results. How does the plasma membrane maintain the asymmetry?

The plasma membrane has what can be viewed (in a functional sense, at least) as **"pores."** Because of their kinetic energy, ions and molecules are constantly bouncing around inside or outside the cell and occasionally they strike the plasma membrane. If they hit a "solid" region, they simply bounce back. But they *can* pass through to the other side if they happen to hit a pore. This random, thermally induced movement of ions (and small molecules) from a region of high concentration to one of low concentration is known as **diffusion.** It is a passive event. Nevertheless, *diffusion is the basis for the continuous movement of ions and small molecules into and out of the cell, from regions of high concentration to low concentration.*

A good deal of evidence points to the existence of some kind of structures that function as pores. We know that they have effective diameters of about 0.35 nanometer, which is slightly larger than sodium ions with their spheres of hydration. We know also that less than 0.1 percent of the plasma membrane surface functions as pores—that over 99.9 percent of the cell surface is impenetrable by ions. Several models of structures with these characteristics have been proposed (Figure 13.14 lists five of them). But the nature of the "pores" themselves has not yet been established.

Many other substances besides sodium and potassium ions cross the plasma membrane, moving as continuous

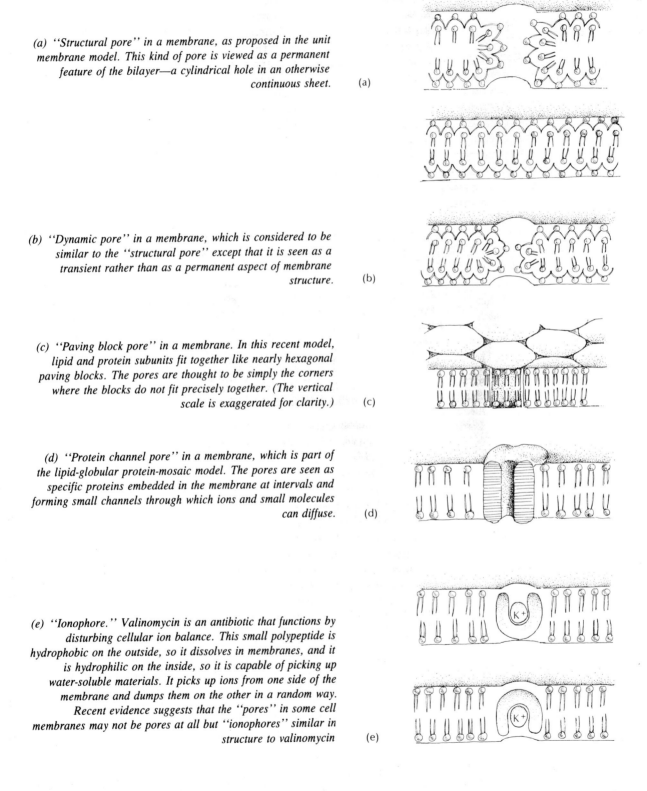

(a) "Structural pore" in a membrane, as proposed in the unit membrane model. This kind of pore is viewed as a permanent feature of the bilayer—a cylindrical hole in an otherwise continuous sheet.   (a)

(b) "Dynamic pore" in a membrane, which is considered to be similar to the "structural pore" except that it is seen as a transient rather than as a permanent aspect of membrane structure.   (b)

(c) "Paving block pore" in a membrane. In this recent model, lipid and protein subunits fit together like nearly hexagonal paving blocks. The pores are thought to be simply the corners where the blocks do not fit precisely together. (The vertical scale is exaggerated for clarity.)   (c)

(d) "Protein channel pore" in a membrane, which is part of the lipid-globular protein-mosaic model. The pores are seen as specific proteins embedded in the membrane at intervals and forming small channels through which ions and small molecules can diffuse.   (d)

(e) "Ionophore." Valinomycin is an antibiotic that functions by disturbing cellular ion balance. This small polypeptide is hydrophobic on the outside, so it dissolves in membranes, and it is hydrophilic on the inside, so it is capable of picking up water-soluble materials. It picks up ions from one side of the membrane and dumps them on the other in a random way. Recent evidence suggests that the "pores" in some cell membranes may not be pores at all but "ionophores" similar in structure to valinomycin   (e)

Figure 13.14 Several models proposed for the "pores" in plasma membranes, through which small molecules and ions are thought to diffuse across the membrane.

streams of incoming nutrients and outgoing products. Because of the size of the functional pores in the plasma membrane, gas molecules such as oxygen and carbon dioxide can readily diffuse through the membrane. Some small organic molecules such as urea (one of the main waste products of human cells) also diffuse freely through it. But larger organic molecules cannot pass through at adequate rates by diffusion. They must be transported either actively or by a process called **facilitated diffusion,** which occurs through special channels embedded in the plasma membrane. These channels are highly selective. For example, various sugar molecules of identical size might be present inside or outside the cell, but the channels somehow distinguish slight variations in structure and move certain molecules across the membrane hundreds of times faster than others. Facilitated diffusion is probably mediated by carrier molecules that are capable of combining specifically but loosely with a given substance on one side of the membrane and of rotating or shuttling it to the other. *Facilitated diffusion is not based on the input of cellular energy, so it can move a substance only from a region of higher concentration to one of lower concentration.* But it does so in a selective way, moving some molecules at a more rapid rate than others of the same size (Figure 13.15).

When a substance must be moved in the opposite direction—from a region of low concentration to one of high concentration—cellular energy must be used to counter the trend of matter to become randomized. Consider once more the flow of ions through a typical plasma membrane. The flow by diffusion is sufficient that, if the cell did nothing to reverse the flow, the disproportionate K^+/Na^+ ratio would quickly vanish. The reason the positively charged sodium ions do not accumulate in the negatively charged cell interior is that the cell actively pumps sodium ions out just as fast as new sodium ions move in. Similarly, new potassium ions are pumped in just as fast as potassium ions flow out. This is a special case of a generalized membrane function known as **active transport,** which is illustrated in Figure 13.16. *In active transport, cellular energy is used to move ions (or molecules) from areas of low concentration to areas of high concentration.* It is a process that is mediated by membrane-bound enzymes.

In this case, the mediating enzyme is known as adenosine triphosphatase (ATPase), and it is activated by sodium and potassium. ATPase is generally found in all plasma membranes. This enzyme apparently is embedded asymmetrically in the membrane in such a way that it picks up an ATP molecule and a sodium ion from the inside of the cell at the same time it picks up a potassium ion from the outside. Only when ions of both types are bound to it does the enzyme become catalytically active, triggering the hydrolysis of the ATP molecule to form a molecule of adenosine diphosphate (ADP) and a molecule of inorganic phosphate. As discussed in Chapter 12, the hydrolysis of ATP releases about 7 kilocalories of energy per mole of ATP. The energy released changes either the enzyme's shape or its position (the nature of the change is not yet known). In its new shape or position, the enzyme releases the ADP, the inorganic phosphate, and the potassium ion into the cell interior and it releases the sodium ion to the outside. The enzyme then returns to its original state, ready to repeat the reaction.

There is one more way in which cellular energy is used to counter the trend toward randomization. *Cellular energy can be used to bind or change a substance in such a way that it cannot return to the external environment of the cell.* This related energy process is called **active accumulation.** Substances vitally important to the cell may be subject to both active transport and active accumulation. Glucose, for example, apparently can be transported actively through the membrane of certain animal cells. Once inside, however, it immediately undergoes reaction with ATP on a specific enzyme, thereby becoming converted to glucose-phosphate as the ATP is converted to ADP:

$$\text{Glucose + ATP} \xrightarrow[\text{(hexokinase)}]{\text{enzyme}} \text{glucose-phosphate + ADP}$$

In this manner, the energy released in the hydrolysis of ATP is used to "trap" the glucose in the cell; unlike free glucose, the glucose-phosphate so produced cannot leave by diffusion.

So far, only the transport of individual molecules across the plasma membrane has been discussed. *But some cells are capable of transporting not only single molecules but sizable chunks of materials from their environment.* For instance, in the process of **endocytosis,** one organism encircles another, engulfs it, and digests it. This process is illustrated vividly in Figure 4.19. Similar transport processes are employed by certain cells of higher animals. For example, one of your chief lines of defense against disease is a group of white blood cells, patrolling about and engulfing and digesting bacteria that have found their way into your body. This process is known as **phagocytosis,** or "cellular eating." A similar but more widespread process is one known as **pinocytosis,** or "cellular drinking." Figure

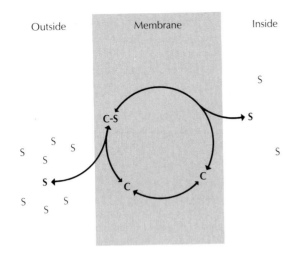

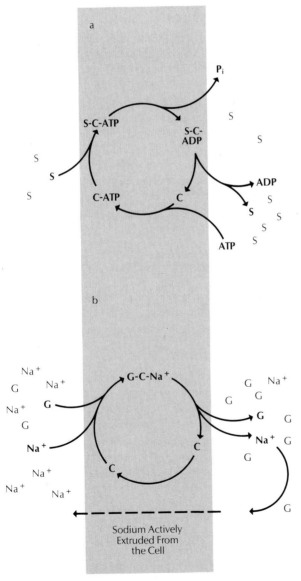

Figure 13.15 *A schematic model for facilitated diffusion. A substance (S) is shuttled across the membrane by a carrier protein molecule (C), embedded in the membrane mosaic that has a specific binding site for S. The carrier will tend to bind a molecule of S more frequently on the side of the membrane where S is in higher concentration. But when the complex breaks down, the substance S may be released on either side with equal probability. As a result, there will be net movement of S from the area of higher concentration to the area of lower concentration. But this movement will be much more rapid than if the substance S were crossing the membrane by diffusion through a pore.*

Figure 13.16 *Schematic models of two kinds of active transport. (a) Direct utilization of energy by the transport system. The carrier molecule (C) binds a molecule of ATP from the interior of the cell. This causes a change of shape or position to occur, so that C can now specifically bind a molecule of S from the outside of the membrane. Once S is bound, the ATP molecule is hydrolyzed, releasing inorganic phosphate (P_i) to the inside of the cell. This causes another change in the shape or position of the carrier protein, so that both the ADP and the substance S are now released to the interior of the cell. Because ATP is available only from the inside, and because the hydrolysis of ATP is an essentially irreversible process (high free energy of hydrolysis), the movement of S is strictly one way. Thus, as long as ATP is available, S continues to be pumped into the cell even after the concentration inside the cell has become much higher than that on the outside.*

(b) Indirect utilization of energy by the transport system. In some cells, the sugar glucose (G) is transported actively by a process that involves only the indirect expenditure of energy. In this case, the carrier molecule (C) can combine with a molecule of glucose and an ion of sodium simultaneously, but not to either alone. Because sodium is always present in much higher concentration outside the cell than inside, the complex tends to form only at the outside surface and to break down at the inside surface, releasing the glucose and sodium ion to the interior. But the sodium ion is now actively extruded from the cell by an ATP-utilizing active transport system (see text). Here, the movement of glucose resembles facilitated diffusion, but because of the asymmetric distribution of sodium, the movement is one way and glucose continues to be pumped inward even when the internal glucose concentration exceeds the external concentration.

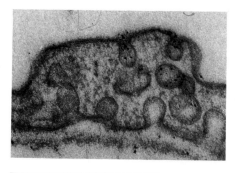

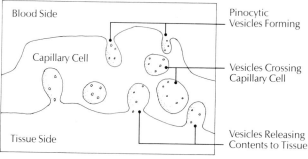

Figure 13.17   Electron micrograph of a portion of a capillary lining cell. The invaginated membranes are forming pinocytic vesicles on the blood side. The edges of these vesicles pinch off, move across the cell, fuse with the membrane on the tissue side, and then open and dump out their contents.

13.17 shows how pinocytosis is used for transferring materials across a capillary lining cell rather than into the cellular body. In many other cases, pinocytic vesicles release their contents into the cell interior. This transport mechanism was long overlooked because it is not readily detected in dead, sectioned cells prepared for conventional microscopy. But with modern techniques, new examples of pinocytic activity are frequently observed, and the mechanism is now considered to be much more important than was commonly believed a few years ago.

The Role of Surface Glycoproteins in Cellular Recognition

Whereas some proteins mediate the directional transport of materials into and out of a cell, certain other proteins in the plasma membrane mosaic function as mediators in **cellular recognition**—in the response of one cell to other cells of the same type or of different types. *The response of one cell to another apparently is triggered by a molecular complementarity of surface materials that is analogous to the complementarity of enzyme and substrate* (Chapter 12). For the most part, a protein involved in such cellular recognition

possesses a complex and uniquely patterned branched chain of specific sugar groups. These sugar-containing proteins are called **glycoproteins.**

It is through surface glycoproteins that ''male'' and ''female'' bacteria recognize each other, that two different mating types of *Paramecium* recognize each other, that mouse liver cells recognize one another as being of the same cell type but different from muscle cells, that the human body recognizes a grafted heart as being foreign and tries to reject it, and that the human body recognizes certain cells as being infected with measles virus and attacks them. A single cell may possess *many* different kinds of surface recognition glycoproteins in its plasma membrane; in effect, it may present a whole ''library'' to be ''read'' by another cell it encounters. For example, each of your white blood cells of the lymphocyte type carries, on its surface, glycoproteins that identify it as being (1) human; (2) from your blood group—A, B, AB, or O; (3) uniquely yours and different from the lymphocytes of other human beings, unless you have an identical twin; (4) a lymphocyte; (5) a lymphocyte that has (or has not) recently passed through the organ called the thymus; and (6) armed to attack one particular kind of foreign cell or substance. Other examples of cellular recognition will be examined during the course of this book.

ALL EUKARYOTIC CELLS CONTAIN MEMBRANE-BOUND CYTOPLASMIC ORGANELLES

Within the cytoplasm of all cells are several kinds of regular structural components, collectively called **organelles.** In eukaryotic cells, many of the organelles consist of or are enclosed by membranes. Most of what has been said about the structure and function of the plasma membrane applies also to these membranes: Each has a rich lipid content with some sort of bimolecular layering, each is capable of directional transport of materials, and each possesses the capacity for a certain amount of cellular recognition.

Mitochondria

Nearly all eukaryotic cells contain **mitochondria**—small, typically oval organelles surrounded by two layers of membrane. In most mitochondria the inner membrane is folded into sheets or tubules, called **cristae,** that often extend across the interior of the organelle (Figure 13.18). Enclosed by the inner membrane is the **matrix,** a complex mixture that often includes fibers, granules, and droplets.

As you will read in Chapter 14, the main activity of mitochondria is cellular respiration, the process in which the oxygen produced in photosynthesis is used to extract energy from food molecules. The energy so obtained is used to convert ADP into ATP, the energy currency of the cell. Many enzymes are required for this task. They are or-

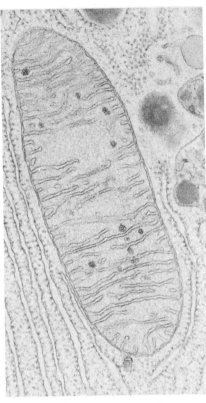

Figure 13.18 Electron micrograph of mitochondria. Most mitochondria are about 0.5 micrometer in diameter and from 0.5 to 7.0 micrometers in length. They range in number from a single mitochondrion per cell in one kind of eukaryotic alga to hundreds of thousands of mitochondria per cell in some amoebae.

(magnification x 37,200)

ganized in the matrix and inner membrane of the mitochondrion in such a manner that energy derived from food molecules can be passed from one enzyme to the next in the reaction sequence. The ability of the mitochondrion to generate ATP depends totally on the precise arrangement of certain enzymes in the mosaic of its cristae membranes. If this orderly arrangement is disturbed even slightly, the capacity to generate ATP is lost.

Mitochondria function as cellular powerhouses. Cells that demand large amounts of energy—muscle cells, for example—contain many large and complex mitochondria. Cells that have low energy needs have smaller, fewer, or simpler mitochondria. These organelles are not distributed uniformly within a cell; instead, they tend to be concentrated "where the action is." For example, mitochondria accumulate near the basal membrane of kidney tubule cells, where a great deal of energy is used in transporting substances across the plasma membrane. As discussed in Chapter 4, mitochondria contain their own deoxyribonucleic acid, their own ribosomes, and their own machinery for protein synthesis. Therefore, they are to some extent autonomous organelles within the cell body.

Plastids

Certain membranous organelles called **plastids** exist only in plant cells. Plastids are in many ways structurally similar to mitochondria. They, too, are enclosed in a two-layer membrane and are characterized by elaborate infoldings of the inner membrane layer. They also contain their own DNA and to some extent may be able to reproduce independently of the cell nucleus.

Plastids are involved in photosynthetic energy conversions and in the storage of nutrients in the cell. One kind of plastid, the colorless **leucoplast,** functions as the site for the conversion of glucose into polysaccharides, lipids, or proteins. Leucoplasts also store these products for use by the cell (Figure 13.19). That is why a potato is white: it

contains an abundance of starch-filled leucoplasts. Other plastids are rich in colored pigments and are known as **chromoplasts.** The pigments enclosed by the chromoplast membrane have a characteristic color because of the way their molecular structure responds to specific wavelengths of light. The pigment carotene, for example, absorbs blue and green light and reflects red and yellow; hence the orange appearance of the chromoplasts of carrots. The pigment chlorophyll absorbs red light and reflects green light. It is found in **chloroplasts**—chromoplasts in which photosynthesis takes place.

The outer membrane of a chloroplast is structurally similar to the plasma membrane of a cell, but the inner membrane is far more complex. Like the mitochondrial inner membrane, the inner membrane of the chloroplast is folded inward. But the primary infoldings of the membrane are, in certain regions, folded back on themselves in tightly packed membranous stacks (Figure 13.20). The pigment molecules are embedded primarily in these stacks in regularly arranged units that facilitate photosynthetic reactions. As with mitochondria, any disturbance of the orderly array of pigment and enzyme molecules in the membrane mosaic leads to loss of function. We will return to the nature of chloroplast structure and function in Chapter 15.

Small plastids exist that do not have an elaborate internal structure. They are thought to be the parent structure from

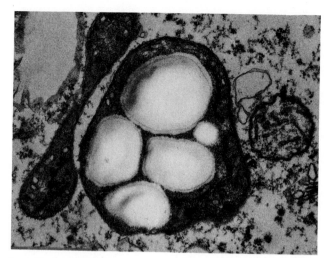

(magnification x 22,750)

Figure 13.19 Electron micrograph of a leucoplast, a structure specialized for synthesis and storage of polysaccharides.

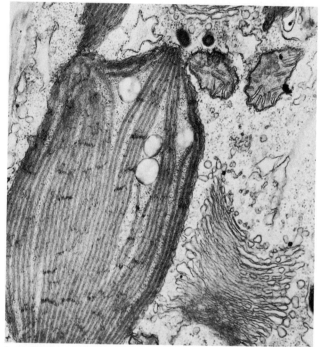

(magnification x 22,800)

Figure 13.20 Electron micrograph of a chloroplast, showing the elaborate system of infolded membranes that facilitates photosynthetic reactions. In higher plants, mosses, ferns, and some algae, chloroplasts are disk-shaped bodies about 2 to 4 micrometers in diameter and 1 micrometer or less in thickness. Other forms exist, but the internal structure of all chloroplasts functions in the same way from one form to the next.

which the different types of plastids develop. These simple **proplastids** reproduce by binary fission, as do mature chloroplasts.

The Endoplasmic Reticulum

Folded through the cytoplasm of eukaryotic cells is the **endoplasmic reticulum,** an elaborate system of membrane sheets that form tubules, vesicles, and sacs (cisterna). The membrane of the endoplasmic reticulum is structurally similar to the plasma and nuclear membranes; in fact, in some places it may be continuous with them (Figure 13.21).

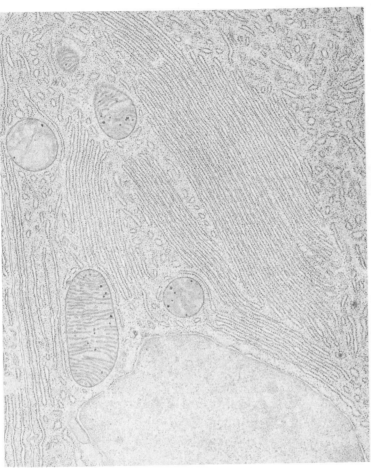

Figure 13.21 Electron micrograph of endoplasmic reticulum (ER).

(magnification x 9,400)

Some parts of the endoplasmic reticulum membranes are heavily studded with ribosomes, which appear as granules in Figure 13.22. Such a region is called the **rough endoplasmic reticulum.** As was mentioned in Chapter 11 and will be discussed in detail in Chapter 17, ribosomes function as sites for protein synthesis. Ribosomes are found in three forms in the cell. First, they may be temporarily scattered in the cytoplasm; they are not involved in protein synthesis when they are found as "free" ribosomes. Second, they may be suspended in the cytoplasm in rows, clusters, or rosettes called **polyribosomes.** They are held together in such configurations by a single molecule of messenger ribonucleic acid (mRNA) that is being translated into a protein. Finally, ribosomes may be found in polyribosomal clusters on the membrane surface of the endoplasmic reticulum, of the nucleus, and, occasionally, of other cell organelles.

Polyribosomes suspended in the cytoplasm generally are making protein to be used in the cytoplasm. Those bound to the outer surface of the nuclear membrane appear in some cases to be making proteins for use in the nucleus. But those found on the rough endoplasmic reticulum usually are making protein to be secreted from the cell for use elsewhere. Thus, *if a cell has an extensive rough endoplasmic reticulum, we can infer that the cell is a producer of large quantities of protein for export.*

Smooth endoplasmic reticulum lacks ribosomes. *Smooth endoplasmic reticulum is the site where certain lipids are synthesized and assembled for storage.* It is particularly abundant in such glands as the adrenals, the testes, and the ovaries, all of which make steroid hormones. Fractionation of the cell *(Interleaf 17.1)* shows that all the enzymes required to make steroid hormones are incorporated into smooth endoplasmic reticulum membranes. Smooth endoplasmic reticulum also participates in the production of fats for storage. The components of fats are actually produced in the mitochondrion, but membrane-bound enzymes of the smooth endoplasmic reticulum assemble the components by dehydration synthesis. The fats then accumulate in the cisterna between the reticular membranes.

The Golgi Complex

Almost all eukaryotic cells contain a **Golgi complex.** Although it varies in size and appearance from cell to cell, it

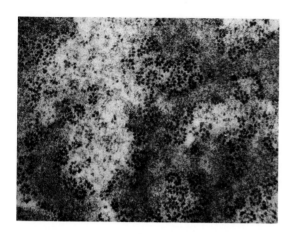

Figure 13.22 Polyribosomes on rough endoplasmic reticulum. The plane of this section is at right angles to the plane shown in Figure 13.21. The dark areas are faces of endoplasmic reticulum exposed in this section. The light areas are "free" cytoplasm adjacent to the membranes. On the endoplasmic reticulum the ribosomes are not randomly distributed but cluster into rows, circles, or whorls. All the ribosomes in one cluster (polyribosomes) are making the protein coded for by the single messenger RNA molecule to which they are bound. Different clusters may be making different kinds of proteins.

Polyribosomes must somehow be inserted into the rough endoplasmic reticulum membrane because the protein being made is fed continuously into the space, or cisterna, between two membrane layers.

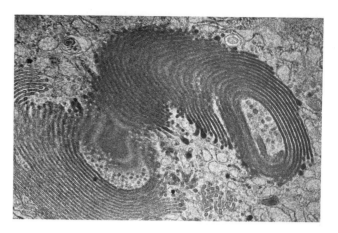

Figure 13.23 Electron micrograph of a Golgi complex, seen in cross section. The network of branching tubules (lower right) associated with the highly organized stack of vesicles indicates this example is a variant of a Golgi complex known as a dictyosome.

The Golgi complex has had a long and rocky history in the annals of cell biology. It was first discussed in the nineteenth century by Camillo Golgi. Because only one particular stain permitted its visualization, because even that particular staining method did not reveal its presence in all cells, and because it could not be seen in living cells, the structure was for over half a century discounted as being a "staining artifact." Only when electron microscopy was brought to bear on cell structure was Golgi vindicated.

most often resembles a stack of flattened membrane-bound sacs, or **vesicles** (Figure 13.23). Often several stacks appear together, with each one surrounded by a branching network of tubules. This arrangement, called a **dictyosome,** commonly occurs in plant cells that are making cell walls, but it has also been seen in some animal cells.

The Golgi complex takes part in the polymerization and secretion of carbohydrates. In plant cells, for example, the Golgi complex takes part in synthesis of cellulose and other materials of the cell wall. In animal cells, enzymes in the Golgi membrane mosaic synthesize various complex carbohydrates, including those needed to produce cartilage. Once such materials are synthesized, they accumulate inside the sacs of the Golgi complex. When the end of a sac becomes filled, it is pinched off and becomes a vesicle in the cytoplasm of the cell. The vesicle stays in the neighborhood of the Golgi complex until it coalesces with other vesicles into larger and larger bodies. Eventually the large vesicles travel to the plasma membrane, fuse with it, and dump their contents outside the cell.

The rough endoplasmic reticulum is often closely associated with the Golgi complex in the synthesis and secretion of glycoproteins. Proteins made in the rough endoplasmic reticulum accumulate in vesicles, which are pinched off the membrane. These vesicles fuse with the Golgi complex, the outcome being that the newly made proteins are dumped into the Golgi sacs. The enzymes embedded in the Golgi membrane attach carbohydrates to the proteins, and the glycoprotein product is then pinched off into vesicles and transported to the plasma membrane for secretion. In some cases, however, vesicles containing the proteins manufactured by the endoplasmic reticulum bypass the Golgi complex and fuse directly with the plasma membrane. The proteins secreted in this manner have no carbohydrate component. (Whether any proteins emerge from the Golgi complex without having carbohydrate added to them is not known, but the likelihood is not great.) The process by which vesicles formed in the endoplasmic reticulum and the Golgi complex fuse with the plasma membrane and release their contents is the reverse of endocytosis; it is called **exocytosis.**

How the vesicles traveling back and forth within a cell find and fuse only with the right membranous structure at the right time is still a mystery. Although we may postulate that each vesicle must bear some type of identifying marker in its membrane mosaic, such markers have so far defied detection.

Lysosomes

A **lysosome** is a sac of hydrolytic enzymes isolated from the cytoplasm by a single unit membrane. The enzymes vary somewhat from cell to cell, but all are typically capable of rapidly digesting at least proteins and nucleic acids—the major molecules of life. Lysosomes (Figure 13.24) have a very simple structure; in fact, they are believed to be pinched-off sacs from the Golgi complex. They were not detected until the 1950s, and they have not been identified in any plant cells.

Lysosomes are the disposal units of the cytoplasm. They fuse with, or engulf, membrane-bound organelles containing material to be disposed, thus forming what is called a *secondary lysosome.* Fragments of mitochondria, ingested food particles, microorganisms, worn out red blood cells, and other debris have been found within such structures. It is no coincidence that lysosomes are most abundant in cells that specialize as scavengers within a multicellular organism and in cells that participate in the breakdown of other cells. One example of this kind of breakdown is the absorption of the tail structure of a tadpole as it develops into a frog. As another example, when a phagocytic white blood cell encounters a marauding bacterium, it promptly engulfs it. The invader is carted off in a phagocytic vacuole to fuse with one or several lysosomes in the cell interior. The digestive enzymes of the lysosome flow over the bacterium, all the while remaining segregated from the rest of the cell by the membrane of the phagocytic vacuole. Digestion then begins. (One reason tuberculosis has traditionally been so difficult to cure is that the tuberculosis bacilli are wrapped in a waxy coat that resists penetration by the lysosomal enzymes. The bacilli can live for years inside a phagocytic cell, undigested and waiting for a chance to escape.)

Lysosomes not only dispose of the invaders and the assorted debris in a cell, they also are capable of disposing of the cell itself. If the cell in which lysosomes are found is injured or exposed to certain chemicals, the lysosome membranes break down and their hydrolytic enzymes flood into the cytoplasm, changing and destroying macromolecules and thereby hastening cell death. A number of human diseases appear to be linked to the malfunctioning of this organelle. Whether the malfunctioning of the lysosomes is a cause or a result of the disease is unclear in most cases.

Peroxisomes

Like lysosomes, **peroxisomes** are sacs of powerful enzymes separated from the cytoplasm by a membrane. They are widespread in nature, occurring in many higher plant cells, in many protistans, and in at least the kidney cells and liver cells of higher animals. All contain one or more enzymes that produce hydrogen peroxide, a highly toxic substance, as a by-product of their catalytic role in certain metabolic pathways. But these organelles also contain the enzyme catalase, which destroys hydrogen peroxide. In this way, hydrogen peroxide never leaves the sac to exert its toxic effects on the cytoplasm.

THE NUCLEUS IS THE MEMBRANE-BOUND CONTROL CENTER OF EUKARYOTIC CELLS

The distinguishing feature of a eukaryotic cell is the **nucleus**—a membrane-bound structure that isolates the cell's hereditary instructions from the cytoplasm, where those instructions must be executed. Clearly, in order to understand the functioning of eukaryotic cells it is necessary to understand not only how the heritable information is

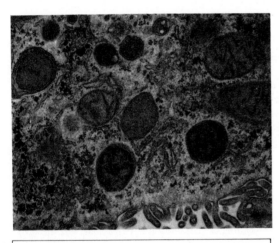

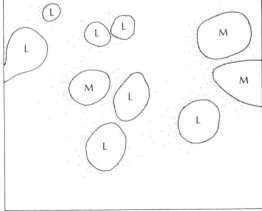

Figure 13.24 Electron micrograph and diagram of lysosomes (L = lysosomes and M = mitochondria).

organized within the nucleus but also how nucleus and cytoplasm communicate with each other to determine *which* nuclear instructions should be activated and *how* and *when* these instructions should be executed in the cytoplasm. As you will read in later chapters, biochemical studies have revealed partial insights into these aspects of cell function.

The Nuclear Envelope

The nucleus of a cell is made up of a matrix called the nucleoplasm, which is enclosed in two layers of membrane. These layers are roughly equivalent to two unit membranes, and they are separated by a space of variable width. Occurring at regular intervals over the surface of this double membrane are numerous circular structures called **annuli,** first described in 1950 and still not fully understood. Between 10 and 25 percent of the nuclear surface is devoted to these annuli. Taken together, the membranes and annuli form the **nuclear envelope.**

Annuli function as selective channels for moving materials between the nucleus and the cytoplasm (Figure 13.25). Two things are clear about the way they function: They permit passage of particles up to about 12.5 nanometers in diameter, and yet they do not permit free diffusion of small ions one-thirtieth that size! In one classic study, it was shown that annuli having diameters of about 65 nanometers would not permit the passage of particles having diameters any larger than 14.5 nanometers. Obviously, annuli are not merely open pores. Perhaps they permit the flow of materials by a form of pinocytosis; but if that is true, the membrane lacks the characteristic ''unit membrane'' appearance (both layers appear to end at the edge of an annulus) and so must be different in chemical composition from all other cell membranes. Perhaps the annular opening is guarded by an array of protein molecules capable of expanding and contracting the annuli. Whatever their construction, *annuli play an essential part in the control of cellular activities by regulating the two-way flow of materials between the nucleus and the cytoplasm.*

The Nucleolus

The **nucleolus** (Figure 13.25) is the most conspicuous feature of the nucleus of a nondividing cell. It is more or less spherical in shape and partly fibrous, partly granular in appearance. *The nucleolus is the site within the nucleus where ribosomes are made.* Although the nucleolus may be involved in other cellular activities as well, that is its primary function. Ribosomes are made of two subunits that contain RNA and protein. The nucleolus produces in one piece the RNA required for both subunits. This piece is then cut in two, trimmed, modified chemically, and combined with the specific ribosomal proteins—all within the nucleolus. It appears that the ribosomal proteins are made in the

cytoplasm and then transported to the nucleus for incorporation into the new ribosomes. Most of the substance of the nucleolus is ribosomal RNA and protein being processed.

Structure of Chromosomes, the Carriers of Hereditary Material Found in the Nucleus

Chromosomes are known to be the carriers of genes— the specific packages of DNA that ultimately control the characteristics of a cell and that control most of the day-to-day functioning of a cell. But little is known with certainty about chromosome structure. An electron micrograph of a section of an **interphase nucleus** (a nucleus of a cell that is between cell divisions) is not highly informative. All that shows up is an irregular, granular mass of variable density and, occasionally, short, fibrous pieces. We now know, from a variety of reconstructions, that a thin section of an interphase nucleus can be likened to what we would

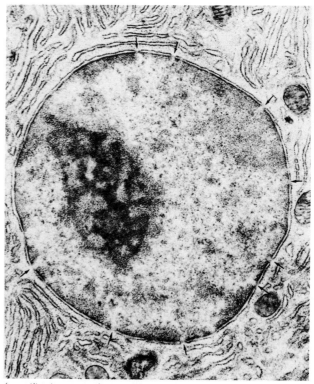

(magnification x 11,000)

Figure 13.25 Electron micrograph of a cell nucleus, showing the double nuclear membrane and its annuli. Also shown is the nucleolus. Annuli at one time were thought to be open pores, and one early report suggested that the inner nuclear membrane was continuous across them. More recent reports suggest the existence of diaphragms, fibers, or globular proteins in them.

see if we took several pieces of string, tangled them up into a ball, embedded the ball in plastic, and cut a very thin slice out of it. All that slice would show would be thousands of cut ends and, occasionally, short lengths of string. It would be exceedingly difficult to determine which cut ends originally were parts of one piece of string and which were parts of others.

This tangled ball is **chromatin**—the chromosomal material that becomes visible as distinct chromosomes during cell division. Chromatin contains DNA, RNA, histones (proteins rich in the basic amino acids lysine, arginine, and histidine), and nonhistones (proteins that are acidic in nature). In the interphase nucleus, part of the chromatin is densely packed and part of it is loosely packed and dispersed throughout the nucleoplasm. A functional difference accompanies the difference in appearance. The loosely packed chromatin (called *euchromatin*) is the part of the chromosomal material concerned with the production of RNA. The densely packed chromatin (called *heterochromatin*) is of two kinds. "Structural" heterochromatin is always inactive, no matter what kind of cell it is found in and no matter what stage in the life cycle that cell happens to be in at the time it is studied. Most likely it has something to do with the structural framework for chromosomes or for cell division. "Functional" heterochromatin, in contrast, may be found condensed and inactive in one cell at one time and expanded and active in RNA synthesis in another cell type at another time.

Whenever a cell prepares to divide, the seemingly disorganized chromatin always condenses into coiled fibers that form the chromosomes. Prior to cell division, each chromosome consists of two identical units called **chromatids.** The sister chromatids are joined together at some point along their length called the **centromere.** Such behavior is always predictable. And the numbers, sizes, and shapes of the chromosomes are always characteristic of the species being studied.

Each chromatin fiber (one per chromatid) is about 20 to 30 nanometers in diameter, and each chromatin fiber contains DNA. There is a question of "how" and "how much" DNA fits into this fiber. The DNA double helix is known to be only 2 nanometers in diameter, but the chromosomes are much thicker than this. Is there only one DNA double helix per fiber, or are there more than one? Individual DNA molecules have been isolated that are more than 150 times as long as the chromosomes from which they are derived. Clearly, then, *no matter how many strands of DNA are present in chromatin, the DNA must be extensively coiled or folded within each fiber.*

Much evidence seems to support the idea of one DNA double helix per chromatin fiber. The most persuasive evidence comes from autoradiographic studies of chromo-

Figure 13.26 Autoradiography of cells. In autoradiography, a cell is placed in a radioactive medium so that particular cellular structures can take up the radioactive molecules. The cell is then placed in contact with photographic film, which is exposed by the radiation. When the film is developed, dark silver grains appear wherever radiation has exposed the film.

These two photographs show cells that were exposed to a radioactive precursor of RNA. The cells in (a) were removed from culture and prepared for autoradiography just a few minutes after the radioactive substance had been added; all the radioactive atoms appear to be concentrated in the nucleus. The cells in (b) were treated similarly, but they were left in culture for a prolonged period after addition of the labeled precursor. Under these conditions, all the radioactive atoms appear to be concentrated in the cytoplasm. From such studies, it is possible to conclude that RNA made in the nucleus (a) is passed to the cytoplasm (b), where it accumulates.

some replication. The process of **autoradiography** is described in Figure 13.26. A population of eukaryotic cells was allowed to grow in the presence of radioactively labeled thymidine (a building block of DNA) until all the chromosomes of that population had become radioactively labeled. The cells were then transferred to a medium containing nonradioactive thymidine and allowed to continue growth. All chromosome material generated after the transfer was therefore nonradioactive.

When these cells were studied by autoradiography over several generations, a distinctive pattern of labeling was observed, as described in Figure 13.27. This pattern was exactly analogous to the pattern observed for replication of individual DNA molecules (Chapter 17). (In each generation, the two strands of DNA separate and each serves as a template for the synthesis of a new copy of the other. Thus, each new molecule consists of one "old" strand and one newly synthesized strand.) The labeling pattern observed in these studies was exactly that which would be predicted if there is only one DNA molecule per chromatid. It was much more regular than would be predicted if there were several DNA molecules per chromatid. Although some feel the question is not fully answered, it seems reasonable to make the simplest assumption consistent with present evidence: there is only one DNA molecule in each chromatid.

If we accept the possibility that only one DNA double

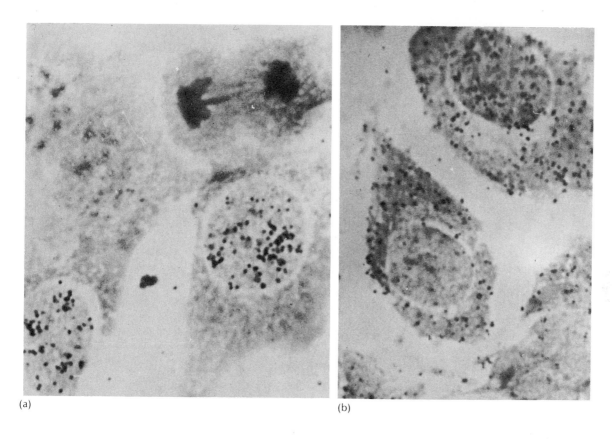

(a)

(b)

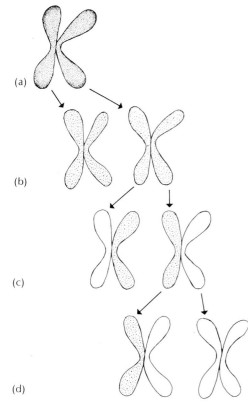

(a)

(b)

(c)

(d)

Figure 13.27 (left) Autoradiographic analysis of replication of eukaryotic cell chromosomes. Cells are grown in radioactive thymidine until all their chromosomes are radioactively labeled. Then the cells are transferred to a nonradioactive medium. After each cell generation, cell samples are removed and subjected to autoradiography (Figure 13.26). (a) This is how a chromosome appears during cell division, following growth in the radioactive medium. Silver grains above all chromatids show that radioactive precursor molecules have been incorporated in the chromosome structure. The number of silver grains is a measure of the number of radioactive atoms present.

(b) This is how chromosomes appear during cell division, following one cell generation of growth in a nonradioactive medium. All chromatids are still labeled, but the number of silver grains per chromatid has been reduced by one-half. (c) After two cell generations of growth, only one chromatid of each chromosome is labeled. The chromatids that are labeled have as many silver grains per chromatid as in the preceding generation. (d) In subsequent cell generations some chromatids remain fully labeled, but there is a progressive increase in the number of unlabeled chromatids. Taken together, these observations imply that one-half of each chromatid is conserved intact and one-half is new in each generation. This interpretation is consistent with the idea that there is only one continuous DNA double helix in each chromatid.

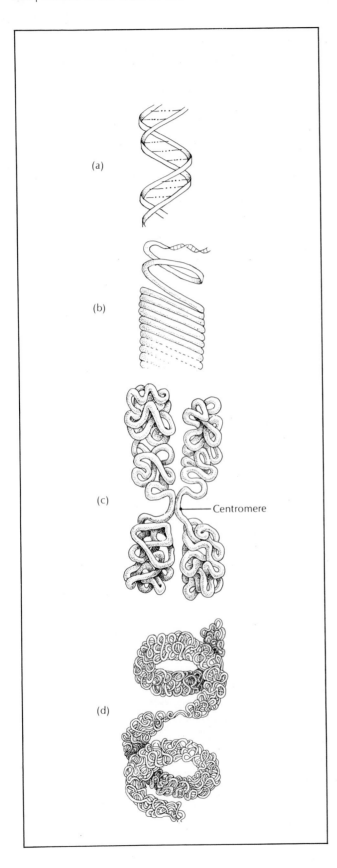

Figure 13.28   The DuPraw folded fiber model of chromosome structure. Although certain aspects of chromosome structure are not readily explained by this model, it is widely considered to be at least as plausible as any other model proposed to date. Future research may call for some minor modifications to this picture. (After Ernest DuPraw (1968), Cell and Molecular Biology, Academic Press.)

(a) First-order coiling. The Watson-Crick double helix is the basic structure for all double-standard DNA (see Chapter 12). This helix is 2 nanometers in diameter.

(b) Second-order coiling. The DNA double helix is coiled into a 20–30 nanometer fiber by the histones with which it is associated in eukaryotic chromosomes.

(c) Third-order coiling or folding. The 20–30 nanometer fibers are folded or coiled up at metaphase to form chromosomes, which are visible in a light microscope. Two sister chromatids are held together at the centromere; the DNA coil runs continuously on through the centromere. (Not shown here are two granules through which spindle fibers attach to the centromere.)

(d) Fourth-order coiling. In some species, some large chromosomes show a helical structure that is obvious at metaphase of the cell division cycle. This structure represents a further coiling of the folded fibers as shown here.

helix occurs in a single chromatin fiber, we must look for an explanation of how these fibers are arranged in the chromosomes. One of the more recent suggestions comes from the cell biologist Ernest DuPraw. His **folded fiber model** of chromosome structure, depicted in Figure 13.28, is based on four different and complex degrees of coiling. What possible advantage could be gained from such a compact structure? *If the long strands of eukaryotic DNA were not somehow coiled tightly during cell division, the apparatus that parcels out the DNA in cell division might be faced with a tangled-up bundle of nuclear material that might—or might not—be sortable into the next generation of cells.*

CHROMOSOMES SEPARATE AND MOVE APART IN MITOSIS

All eukaryotic cells follow the same general cycle of activity in duplicating and dividing their nuclear material. The various periods of this cycle are shown in Figure 13.29, but their boundaries are not really this rigid. In living cells, one activity flows smoothly into the next, and the duration of each period varies from cell to cell. But the sequence of events is characteristic of all of them.

Of interest to this discussion is the period of mitosis, introduced earlier in Chapter 4. *In mitosis, one nucleus divides into two nuclei, each having the same number of chromosomes.* Mitosis is a continuous dynamic process and must be viewed in that context. But for purposes of analysis, it is convenient to subdivide it into four stages: **prophase, metaphase, anaphase,** and **telophase.** The activity going on in each of these stages is summarized in Figure 13.30. The structures that appear during these stages, and how they function in the movement and separation of chromosomes, are discussed below.

The Mitotic Spindle and How It Functions

As you will read later in this chapter, the structures and processes of chromosome movement appear increasingly to be related to other kinds of structures and processes of movement, to shape change, and to the growth of cells. Emerging as one of the most intriguing elements in this picture of cellular movement is the **mitotic spindle.**

The mitotic spindle is composed of many microtubules. Each one is about 15–25 nanometers in diameter and is composed of spherical protein subunits. Mitotic spindles contain at least two kinds of microtubules: "continuous" microtubules extend continuously from pole to pole without attaching to chromosomes; "chromosomal" microtubules extend from one pole of the spindle to a chromosome, where they are attached by a crescent-shaped granule called a **kinetechore.** Each chromosome has two kinetechores, but each kinetechore is attached at the centromere to only *one* chromatid and to microtubules from only *one* pole of the

Figure 13.29 A diagram of the cycle of growth and nuclear division of a "typical" eukaryotic cell. The total time required to complete one cycle varies widely from one cell to another and with varying environmental conditions. In the embryos of some animals there is a complete cell cycle every thirty minutes.

In adult mammals, however, the cell cycle commonly takes about twenty-four hours and never less than six hours. The periods most variable from one cell to the next are G_1 (when the cell grows but does not synthesize DNA) G_2 (when the cell grows and prepares for the onset of cell division). In rapidly dividing cells these periods may be almost nonexistent; in slowly dividing cells they may be measured in hours, or even days.

In multicellular organisms, many cells leave the cell cycle permanently as they become differentiated to perform their functions in the mature organism. For example, human nerve cells are incapable of cell division after the first year of life. Such cells spend the rest of their life in the G_1 phase.

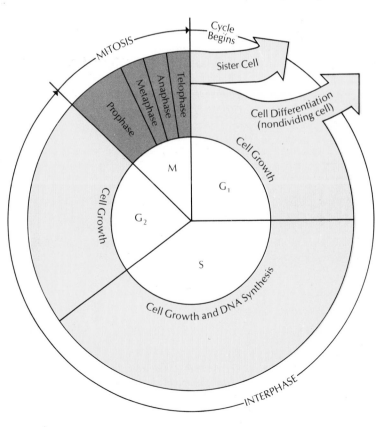

Figure 13.30 Mitosis. (a–g) Simplified drawings of the various stages of mitosis as it appears in cells of an onion root tip. (h) A photomicrograph of a section of an onion root tissue, showing cells in several stages of mitosis.

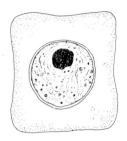

(a) Interphase. The nuclear envelope is intact, and the nucleolus is prominent. Dispersed chromatin cut in cross section gives the nucleus a granular appearance. Chromosomes are replicated during interphase.

(b) Prophase. Chromatin strands are coiling up to form visible chromosomes. The nucleolus has disappeared and the nuclear envelope is breaking down.

(c) Early metaphase. Chromosomes are fully condensed. Each consists of two chromatids connected at the centromere. Chromosomes move so that their centromeres are lined up on the equator of the cell.

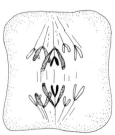

(d) Mid-metaphase. The mitotic spindle is formed and the centromere of each chromosome is attached to fibers that run to opposite poles.

(e) Anaphase. Centromeres joining sister chromatids break and sister chromatids move toward opposite poles.

(f) Telophase. Chromatids are drawn to and cluster at the two poles. A new cell plate forms at what was previously the cell equator. Spindle fragments persist as division of the cytoplasm proceeds.

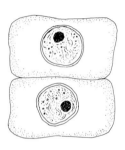

(g) Interphase. Two new daughter cells have been produced. Chromatin fibers of the chromosomes unwind, and the nuclear envelope and nucleolus are re-formed.

(h)

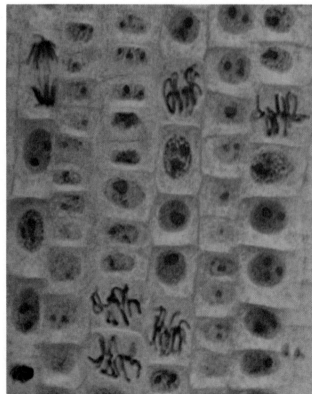

(magnification x 2,200)

spindle. *The specificity of kinetechore attachment accounts for the regularity with which sister chromatids separate and move to opposite poles at anaphase.* In 1967 a dexterous cell biologist, R. B. Nicklas, poked fine needles into a metaphase cell and cut one chromosome free of the spindle. If the chromosome was turned 180 degrees immediately after being cut loose, it quickly became attached to the pole in its *new* orientation. Nicklas concluded that each kinetechore granule attaches to microtubules extending from whichever pole falls in its "line of sight."

At metaphase, two sister chromatids are still joined at their point of attachment (the centromeres), as they have been since the chromosome replicated. All the chromosomes line up on the equator of the spindle apparatus and then, usually, there is a slight pause in the process. When the pause ends, sister chromatids no longer are joined at the centromere—they are free to separate. No one yet knows precisely how this separation is accomplished. At anaphase, the chromosomes move away from each other. There are two ways they might do this. First, the continuous microtubules might elongate, which would make the poles move apart and thereby lead to the separation of sister chromatids. Second, the chromosomal microtubules might shorten, which would draw the chromosomes toward their respective poles. (Usually both mechanisms appear to be involved in the movement of chromosomes, although in some cells primarily one or the other seems to occur.)

How do the microtubules lengthen and/or shorten during the anaphase movement of chromosomes? Severo Inoué, a cell biologist, suggests that microtubules connected to the chromatids shorten because protein subunits are progressively removed from their ends. He proposes that the microtubules passing from pole to pole lengthen at the same time as subunits are added to their ends. (It has in fact been demonstrated that microtubules generally grow when subunits found in the cytoplasm are added to one end and that they shorten when subunits are removed from one end.) But W. Brinkley believes that the microtubules do not change in length at all during chromosome movement. He suggests instead that anaphase movement occurs as a result of chromosomal microtubules and continuous microtubules sliding past one another by cross-bridges, which connect and move them in a ratchetlike manner. For technical reasons, both models are difficult to prove or disprove.

The Relationship Between the Mitotic Spindle and the Centrioles

In animal cells and most protistan cells, a pair of microtubular structures are found at each pole of the mitotic spindle. These structures are **centrioles,** which are identical with the basal bodies of cilia and flagella. A centriole is not formed by simple growth and division of a parent centriole. During the interphase period, a new centriolar body organizes in the vicinity of a preexisting centriole. The newer (and shorter) one always forms at right angles to, and at one end of, the longer, preexisting centriole (Figure 13.31).

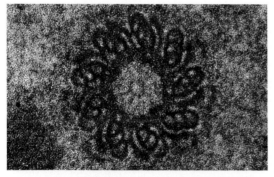

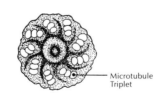

Microtubule Triplet

(a)

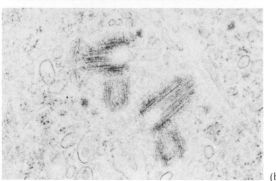

(b)

Figure 13.31 Centrioles. The micrograph in (a) and the sketch next to it show the characteristic triplet-tubule appearance of a centriole that has been cut in cross section. (b) This longitudinal section shows the L-shaped conformation in which centrioles normally are formed. The shorter member of the pair has formed beside the longer one during the most recent cell cycle.

Several lines of evidence suggest that centrioles function as organization centers for the microtubules of the mitotic apparatus. The first visible event of cell division is the separation of centrioles, which have been lying next to the nucleus. The centrioles migrate toward what will become the spindle poles, with one L-shaped pair of centrioles moving toward each pole. Second, as the centrioles migrate, spindle microtubules begin to organize about them. Third, in the completed, metaphase spindle, all the microtubules seem to originate near the centrioles, but they are not attached to them. Finally, if experimental means are used to prevent centriolar duplication, the spindle that forms in the next cell division will have only one pole instead of two, and the cell will fail to divide. If the centrioles are then allowed to duplicate normally, a new spindle will appear that is bipolar and that has a centriole pair at each pole.

Equally persuasive evidence supports the opposite conclusion—that the spindles function as organizers of the centrioles, moving them to the poles as a way of ensuring that each daughter cell receives one centriole. Most plant cells, for example, have no centrioles, but they have no problem in establishing a bipolar spindle. And if centrioles are physically manipulated out of the polar region of a forming spindle in certain cells, the spindle will continue to form normally and the cell will divide normally even as the centrioles lie passively in the cytoplasm.

Do centrioles determine the position of the spindle, then, or does the spindle determine the position of the centrioles? It may well be that there are at least two answers because there may be at least two evolutionarily divergent kinds of mitotic spindle organization centers—those in which centrioles (if present) play a passive role and those in which they play an active role.

THE CELL BODY ITSELF DIVIDES IN CYTOKINESIS

Mitosis involves extensive changes in the behavior of the nucleus. It is important to keep in mind, however, that the usual function of mitosis is to produce two cells out of one. Normally, once nuclear materials have been separated at anaphase, the cytoplasm undergoes **cytokinesis,** in which the cell divides by the production of a new membrane surface that passes through the plane occupied earlier by the equator of the spindle at metaphase. This process is evident in Figure 13.30. (There are exceptions to this process. In some protistans, in certain animals, in some algae and fungi, and in certain parts of plants, mitosis takes place regularly without completion of cytoplasmic partitioning.)

The separation of cytoplasmic organelles into daughter cells is accomplished by a variety of mechanisms. Some organelles, such as mitochondria, are more or less randomly dispersed in the cytoplasm and are segregated by chance. Other, less numerous organelles such as lysosomes tend to align around the poles of the mitotic spindle, which ensures their proper distribution. In some algae where only one chloroplast is found in the interphase cell, the organelle itself undergoes cleavage that is timed to and oriented with cell division, thereby ensuring that one organelle ends up in each daughter cell.

Cytokinesis in animal cells normally begins at late anaphase. The newly formed membrane in the equatorial region begins to constrict into a **cleavage furrow,** which divides the one cell into two. In animal cells, at least, experimental work strongly suggests it is the position of the mitotic spindle poles that determines where cleavage will occur. For one thing, if the mitotic spindle develops toward one end of the cell rather than in the middle, the cleavage furrow still passes midway between the poles, resulting in formation of one small and one large cell. For another, if an experimenter moves the spindle about in the cell during prophase or metaphase, it is the *new* position of the poles that determines the position of the cleavage furrow. (By the time anaphase movement has begun, the position of the cleavage furrow is established; movement of the spindle at this time has no effect on the plane of subsequent division.) Finally, if the number of spindle poles is modified experi-

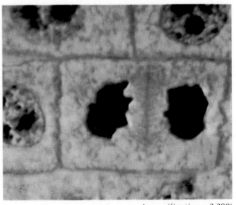

Figure 13.32 Cytokinesis in an onion root tip cell. In plants, cytokinesis is initiated by the alignment along the cell equator of vesicles derived from the Golgi complex to form the cell plate. Often, as in this photo, remnants of the mitotic spindle persist at the equator throughout this stage. Subsequent fusion of the vesicles results in formation of the two plasma membranes and the primary cell wall that divides the one cell into two.
(Photograph courtesy Carolina Biological Supply Company)

(magnification x 2,200)

mentally, the number and position of cleavage furrows is modified to match. Thus if a monopolar spindle is induced, there is no cell division. If a tripolar spindle is formed, the cell divides into three cells. And if a tetrapolar spindle is developed, the cell divides into four!

The process by which the cleavage furrow becomes established in late metaphase apparently involves a ring of microfilaments, which form under the plasma membrane in the region destined to give rise to the furrow. These microfilaments are composed of a protein similar to actin, one of the proteins of muscle. (Such microfilaments are now known to play a major role in a host of cell movements and shape changes.) At telophase, the microfilament ring appears to contract, drawing in the cell membrane. Accompanying this action is the appearance of new membrane at appropriate places, which forms a partition between the sister cells.

Because plant cells are surrounded by rigid cell walls, cleavage furrows cannot develop as they do in animal cells. In plant cells, a special structure called a **cell plate** appears along the equatorial plate of the mitotic spindle during telophase (Figure 13.32). The cell plate forms by the fusion of vesicles derived from the Golgi apparatus. When these vesicles come together, they form a new double membrane that eventually fuses with the original plasma membrane.

A VARIETY OF STRUCTURES ACCOUNTS FOR THE DIVERSE APPEARANCE OF CELLS

Life at the cellular level is characterized by diversity as well as unity, for even though all cells share certain common features, a vast array of structurally and functionally distinct cells exist. Apparently evolution has imposed few limits on the number of variations on the common cellular theme.

Intracellular Modifications

Some of the most striking variations in cell structure and function result when certain inclusions become modified. Many plant cells look quite different from protistan and animal cells because of the exaggerated size of a single central vacuole, even though that vacuole is structurally similar to the various cellular vesicles. The ability of the cell to keep such a vacuole filled with water under high pressure accounts for much of the rigidity of nonwoody plant parts, and the loss of water from such vacuoles under conditions of drought accounts for wilting.

The unique appearance of other cells results when they accumulate massive amounts of specific proteins related to specific cell function. For example, hemoglobin accounts for 95 percent of the solid matter in mammalian red blood cells, but it is not found in other cells. The cells making up the lens of a human eye consist almost entirely of transparent proteins. The storage of food reserves also brings

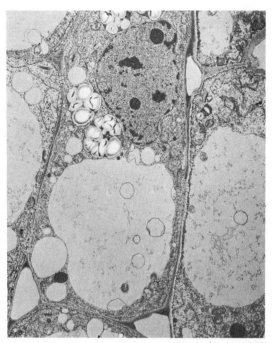

(magnification x 5,850)

Figure 13.33   Electron micrograph showing large vacuoles in a plant cell. Starch storage plastids can be seen surrounding the nucleus.

about diversity in appearance, for the accumulation of such reserves distorts cellular proportions almost beyond recognition. In animals, for example, fat is a major material for long-term storage. A piece of fatty tissue examined in the microscope looks only remotely cellular: a wispy film of cellular material surrounds each giant globule of stored fat. In plants, too, stored foods sometimes distort cells tremendously. The white face of a cut potato attests to the bloating of leucoplasts with white starch. The yolk of a hen's egg is so distorted by food reserves that if you prepared this single cell for microscopic examination and randomly began examining sections of it, you might look for days before finding anything that resembled a "typical" cell structure.

Widespread examples of intracellular modifications are the cilia and flagella, discussed at length in Section II of this book. Cilia differ from flagella only in that they are shorter and usually more numerous wherever they appear. Both are enclosed within the plasma membrane, and both cause distortion in the cell boundary. These cellular appendages occur in almost identical form in the protistan, plant, and animal kingdoms. Cilia and flagella form the basis of locomotion in such whole organisms as protistans, some algae, and in the sperm of some ferns and most animals.

Some of the smallest flatworms and the embryos and larvae of certain animals also move with cilia, but in larger

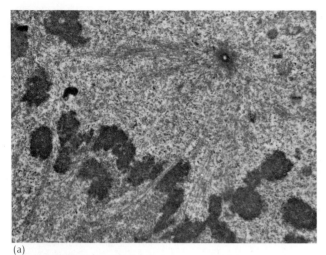

(a)

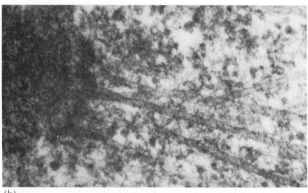

(b)

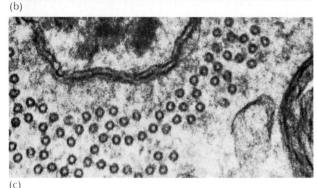

(c)

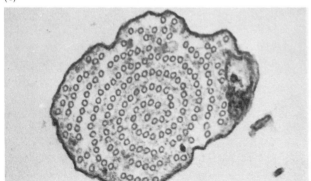

(d)   (magnification x 81,400)

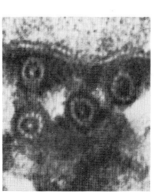

(e)   (magnification x 283,500)

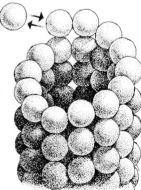

(f)

Figure 13.34 Microtubules: a recurring theme in cellular architecture.

(a) The mitotic spindle. The fibers seen radiating from the centromere at the upper right to the chromosomes below and to the left are in reality microtubules.

(b) Part of a mitotic spindle seen at higher magnification; at this magnification, the tubular nature of the spindle can be clearly seen. The centromere region of a chromosome can be seen in the upper left corner. The dark structure to which the microtubules are attached is the kinetechore.

(c) A portion of an interphase cell in which a series of microtubules have been cut in cross section and that therefore appear as rings. Such microtubular arrays function importantly in modifying and maintaining the shape of many cell types.

(d) A cross section through an axopod of a heliozoan of the species shown in Figure 4.26. Such axopods lack the typical 9 + 2 arrangement characteristic of cilia and flagella but often have a regular arrangement of their own. Cross bridges between adjacent tubules have been shown to exist and to stabilize such extensions.

(e) At higher magnification, the walls of microtubules are seen to be composed of globular subunits.

(f) Interpretation of many such electron micrographs has led to the picture of microtubular structure shown here. The globular subunits are arranged in a helix, with thirteen units per turn of the helix. This results in subunits in adjacent turns of the helix being aligned one above the other, giving the impression in some views that the tubule is composed of thirteen parallel fibers. Microtubules grow and diminish in size by addition or removal of subunits at the end.

animals muscular movement has largely supplanted ciliary action. Clams, certain worms, and a variety of lesser-known animals use cilia to collect, sort, and pass foodstuffs to their mouths. In human beings and other mammals, the cells lining the respiratory tract are studded with cilia, which beat continuously away from the lungs to maintain a constant outward flow of bacteria and other particles. They are also found in such tubular systems as the female reproductive tract and the auditory tube. Dozens of highly specialized sensory cells and organs found throughout the animal kingdom incorporate modified cilia; Figure 13.35 shows a sampling of them. Clearly, few structures in the living world have been so highly modified in evolution for so many diverse functions as cilia.

As discussed in Chapter 4, many protistan relatives of amoeba possess long, slender, microtubule-containing cellular projections of two types: axopods and filopods. The microtubules of the axopod tend to be arranged in bundles or whorls rather than in the regular 9 + 2 arrangement of cilia and flagella. The microtubules appear to be extensively cross-connected to each other, forming a stiff, immotile, relatively permanent cellular extension for trapping small food particles. Filopods, on the other hand, are more flexible and dynamic structures capable of fairly rapid extension and withdrawal. Cellular extensions somewhat reminiscent of filopods occur in a variety of motile, wandering cell types throughout the animal kingdom. But the most remarkable cellular extension is in the vertebrate nervous system, where extensions 2 meters or more in length (in the giraffe forelimb, for example) may be produced by a cell only a few micrometers in diameter. The microtubules of nerve processes have a slightly different appearance from other microtubules and have been given a special name—**neurofilaments.**

The microtubules found in cilia, in flagella, and in the long, cellular extensions of cell types ranging from protozoa to sea urchin embryos to human nerve cells are fundamentally similar to microtubules found in the mitotic spindle. Similar microtubules are also found in plant cells, where they appear to be related both to **cytoplasmic streaming** (the rapid movement and mixing of substances in the cell body), and to the orderly deposition of cellulose in the cell walls. To cite only one bit of evidence for the basic similarity of microtubules of diverse cells, J. Rosenbaum, G. Borisy, and others recently demonstrated that subunits isolated from mammalian brain neurofilaments will readily assemble on pieces of flagellum from the green alga *Chlamydomonas*, where they will extend the flagellar microtubules.

A second kind of supportive and shape-directing element in cells is a slender (4–6 nanometer diameter) fiber called a **microfilament.** There may be two kinds of microfilaments,

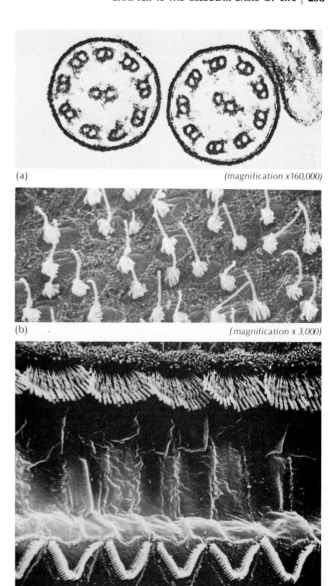

(a) *(magnification x160,000)*

(b) *(magnification x 3,000)*

(c) *(magnification x 3,300)*

Figure 13.35   Cilia. (a) A cross section through the shaft of two cilia from a clam gill, showing the characteristic 9 + 2 arrangement of microtubules. Note also the arms projecting in a counterclockwise direction from the outer doublets. These arms have been implicated in the interaction of outer doublets that leads to bending of the ciliary shaft. (b) Motion-sensing organ of the middle ear. As the head of the frog changes position, the long cilium in each bundle exerts force differentially on the short cilia around it. This action results in a nerve impulse that carries positional information to the brain. (c) The hair cells of the organ of hearing in the inner ear. When sound waves cause the fluids of the inner ear to vibrate, these modified cilia are distorted, leading to a change in the membrane potential of the hair cell and eventually to an action potential in the associated neurons. A variety of other sensory structures are built upon modified cilia (see Chapter 26).

one that passively supports cell structure and another that actively brings about transformations of cell shape. It could be, however, that they are two different expressions of the same chemical entity. Microfilaments are found in the advancing edge of an amoeba and in all other cells that move with a pseudopodial, creeping motion; they are the physical basis for the ruffling edge of the hamster cell illustrated at the beginning of this chapter. Microfilaments also tend to be found in concentric rings in areas where cellular constrictions are occurring or have occurred. They appear to be involved in movement of secretory granules in some cell types. The chemical similarity of at least some microfilaments to the muscle protein actin has been amply demonstrated.

Microfilaments help maintain the structure of **microvilli,** the fingerlike projections on the surface of some cells. Microvilli provide a means of increasing the amount of cell surface that is in contact with the environment and available for absorption of materials. In the cells pictured in Figure 13.36, the microvilli are quite numerous and have over 100 times as much surface area as a similar cell with a smooth, flat surface. Although it is not noticeable in this picture, each microvillus has a core of microfilaments running parallel to the long axis of the microvillus; at the internal end of the microvillus they come together in a packed array.

It was only a short time ago that microtubules and microfilaments were identified as generalized mediators of cell shape and movement; previously they had not been seen in electron micrographs because the fixatives commonly being used had failed to preserve them. Their identification has given us important insights into cell structure and function.

Specialized Cell Attachments That Modify Cell Shape and Functions

Figure 13.36 shows two different forms of association (tight junction and gap junction) between two adjacent intestinal cells. The occurrence of different regions with different degrees of spacing between the cells is no accident. All surface-lining cells, or **epithelial cells,** show a similar pattern of cell attachment. Many different kinds of cell-cell junctions are found in nature, but they all serve two purposes. First, in determining how much and which parts of adjacent cells are firmly connected, they mediate not only the shape of individual cells but the shape of the **tissue**—the aggregation of cells that junctions create. Second, specific cell attachments, called **junctional complexes,** govern the type and the degree of chemical communication that exists between cells. Throughout the plant and animal kingdoms, cells having certain kinds of junctional complexes are chemically coupled. Even though certain ions and molecules cannot diffuse freely from cells to the exterior, they are free to move from cell to cell through their adjacent membranes as if a boundary did not exist! (Larger molecules are prohibited from such cell-to-cell movement.)

Some cell types carry intercellular communication even further. For example, the **plasmodesmata** of plants (Figure 13.37) are but one example of cytoplasmic continuity, in which adjacent cells are not really isolated from one another but have channels that permit large molecules and even some cellular organelles to move from cell to cell. In the organizational plan of fungi, all cells are separated so incompletely that even nuclei can move from cell to cell. In vertebrates the skeletal muscle is formed from long **myotubes,** structures that contain dozens to thousands of

Figure 13.36   Electron micrograph of microvilli on two intestinal cells. The microvilli are on the surface facing the lumen of the intestine. In addition to participating in the absorption of foodstuffs, the membranes of the microvilli are studded with certain digestive enzymes involved in specific kinds of breakdown of foods. Water-soluble materials are absorbed through the membrane one by one, but at the base of two of the microvilli shown here are two droplets of fat being taken up in pinocytic vacuoles for transport through the cell in undigested form. Notice the tight junction between the two cells just below the microvilli. This membrane specialization fuses the cells of the intestinal lining together and prohibits foodstuffs from slipping between them.

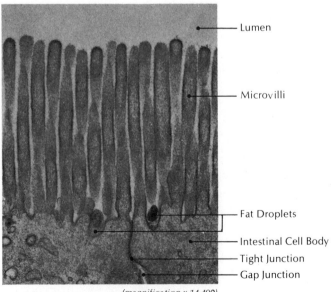

Lumen

Microvilli

Fat Droplets

Intestinal Cell Body

Tight Junction

Gap Junction

(magnification x 14,400)

"fused" cells. When the plasma membranes of these cells make contact, they stick and then break down in the contact area, resulting in the complete mixing of the cellular contents. Once the cells have fused, their nuclei never divide again. Growth occurs only by additional fusions and increases in cytoplasmic mass. The meaning of the word "cell" begins to break down with such systems. Where cytoplasmic continuity between "cells" is so extensive that clear cell boundaries do not exist, the system is called a **syncytium** (from *syn-*, meaning "together," combined with *cyto-*, meaning "cell").

Thus, in multicellular organisms, cellular contact and cooperation ranges all the way from cells that are independent agents to cells in which cooperation is so great that all cellular identity is lost. Every point along this spectrum has its consequences in terms of the resulting appearance and behavior of the cells involved.

The Effect of Extracellular Products on Cell Shape and Function

The cell theory might be taken to imply that life ends at the outer edge of the plasma membrane. Although this is true to a certain extent, *the success of the living cell and the diversity of cellular life forms has been intimately tied to the capacity of cells to secrete protective and supportive structures of nonliving material about themselves.* Much of what we see as characteristic of cells (and organisms) is dead, extracellular materials that cells produce and then secrete to their exterior (Figure 13.38). The development of form, of protective coatings, and of similar aspects of cell shape and function is based primarily on secretions of only three types of materials—minerals, carbohydrates, and

proteins. But the variations on this simple structural theme are nearly as numerous as all the kinds of organisms that exist in the natural world.

PERSPECTIVE

Omnis cellula e cellula—all cells arise from preexisting cells. With this observation, made less than a century ago, Rudolf Virchow summarized the investigations that led to the understanding that a cell is the smallest unit of life capable of independent reproduction. Since that time biologists have been attempting to explain the nature of the cell—how it is organized, what structures characteristically are part of it, how its parts function to sustain and reproduce the whole. Because of the awesomely complex diversity of cell structure and function, these are not easy tasks. In fact, it has been only with the relatively recent advent of electron microscopy, coupled with modern biochemical analysis, that biologists have begun to explore the fine structure of cells. As a result of these explorations, certain underlying cellular themes have begun to emerge, but much remains to be learned.

For example, after reading this chapter you know that the boundary between a cell and its environment is now thought to be a rich lipid-protein mosaic, studded with specific structures that function as channels for communication between cells and between a cell and its environment. You know that if you were to examine the diverse kinds of cytoplasmic organelles within eukaryotic cells, you would find again and again a similar kind of membrane involved in the directional transport of materials essential to cell functioning. Such is the underlying unity relating the surface membrane to the endoplasmic reticulum, to the plastids and

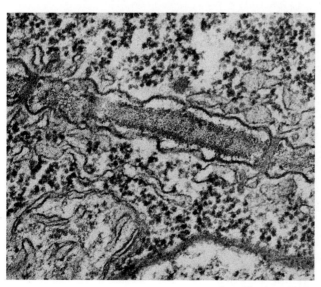

(magnification x 23,300)

Figure 13.37 Plasmodesmata. In several plant tissues, adjacent cells are incompletely separated from one another. Cytoplasmic channels that are enclosed in plasma membrane completely penetrate the cell walls, thereby maintaining the potential for flow of materials and information among neighboring cells.

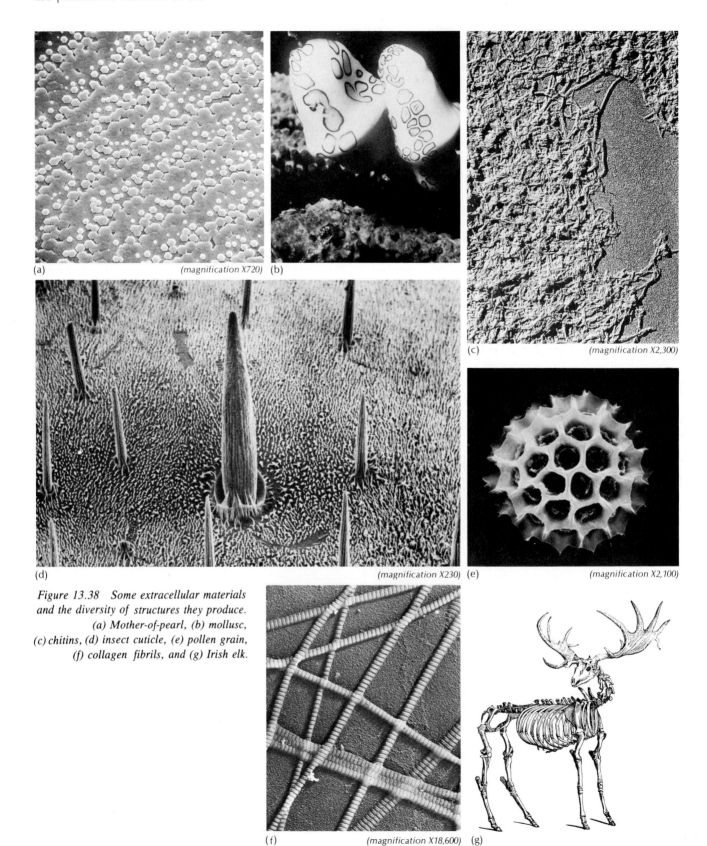

(a)　　　　　　　　　　　　*(magnification X720)*　(b)

(c)　　　　　　　　　　　　*(magnification X2,300)*

(d)　　　　　　　　　　　　*(magnification X230)*　(e)　　　　　　　*(magnification X2,100)*

Figure 13.38　Some extracellular materials and the diversity of structures they produce. (a) Mother-of-pearl, (b) mollusc, (c) chitins, (d) insect cuticle, (e) pollen grain, (f) collagen fibrils, and (g) Irish elk.

(f)　　　　　　　*(magnification X18,600)*　(g)

mitochondria, and even to the nucleus that is at once isolated from and in communication with the cytoplasm surrounding it.

But membrane structure is not the only unifying theme of cellular organization. If you examine the mitotic spindle, you see a structure composed of microtubules; a look at cilia and flagella, or cellular extensions (from the filopodia of protistans to the nerve cells of a whale) reveals a similar kind of microtubule involved in controlling shape and movement. Even the nonmotile plants use the same kinds of microtubules to control their shape and move the contents within the cell from place to place.

And yet, as intriguing as these and other similarities may be, equally important are the immense variations that exist in structure and function. On the basic mosaic membrane theme, variations arise from the unique organization of specific kinds of proteins embedded in a given membrane type. Membranes become specialized in the transport of some kinds of molecules and not others; in the engulfment, the devouring, or the drinking of nutrients; in the recognition of one kind of cell and not others; in the stockpiling of enzymes or pigments to generate energy; in the synthesis of complex molecules needed by the cell; in sweeping up the debris that, in one way or another, finds its way into the cell body. These are only a few examples of variations on a unifying theme, but they serve to emphasize an important point: *At the cellular level, the twin principles of unity and diversity emerge, and the intimate relationship between organization and function becomes clearly evident.*

Touching again on Virchow's summarization, for more than a hundred years the cell has been known to be the smallest unit of life capable of independent reproduction, and yet precisely *how* cells reproduce themselves is still, to a great extent, a mystery. Clearly the control center for cell growth and reproduction lies in the nucleus, where the master plan is encoded in DNA. But how is DNA organized into chromosomes? How is its replication initiated and controlled? How do the chromosomes coil up in preparation for division? And precisely how are the chromosomes separated by the spindle fibers? What goes on in the nucleus during division contains many enigmas. But the interphase period, during which the nucleus is chemically most active, is even less well understood. Further elucidation of nuclear organization is, to say the very least, a major challenge confronting biologists today. It is the existence of so many unanswered questions of fundamental interest that keeps cell biology the exciting field of inquiry it is today.

Inquiry into the nature of cellular processes is in a sense at the center of modern biology. It is not possible to understand heredity or behavior, development or evolution, ecology or human medicine, or any other area of biology without returning again and again to cells and their many and diverse properties.

SUGGESTED READINGS

JENSEN, WILLIAM A., and RODERIC B. PARK. *Cell Ultrastructure.* Belmont, Calif.: Wadsworth, 1967. An excellent and reasonably priced atlas of cellular structure. Excellent electron micrographs.

KENNEDY, DONALD (ed.). *The Living Cell* (1965); *From Cell to Organism* (1967); *Cellular and Organismal Biology* (1974). San Francisco: W. H. Freeman. Collections of articles that originally appeared in *Scientific American.* Most of the articles are readable firsthand accounts of cellular structure.

LENTZ, THOMAS L. *Cell Fine Structure: An Atlas of Drawings of Whole-Cell Structure.* Philadelphia: Saunders, 1971. A well-done collection of interpretative drawings of cellular structures as they appear in the electron microscope.

NOVIKOFF, A. B., and E. HOLTZMAN. *Cells and Organelles.* New York: Holt, Rinehart and Winston, 1970. An excellent, well-written account of eukaryotic organelles and cellular structure. Pleasantly readable and scientifically accurate.

PALADE, G. E. "Structure and Function at the Cellular Level," *Journal of the American Medical Association,* 198 (1968), 815. A stimulating essay on the relationship between cellular structure and function.

ROSENBERG, E. *Cell and Molecular Biology: An Appreciation.* New York: Holt, Rinehart and Winston, 1971. A pleasant presentation of cell theory in historical perspective.

SATIR, PETER. "How Cilia Move," *Scientific American,* 231 (October 1974), 44–52. Description and graphic examples of how a sliding-microtubule mechanism might operate in ciliary motility.

Chapter 14

Glycolysis and Respiration

Over eons of evolutionary time the phenomenon we call life has slowly worked out strategies for dealing with changing and changeless elements in the environment. Intricate yet precarious balances now exist between organisms and their surroundings—and between organisms themselves. The metabolic pathways of glycolysis and respiration are among the most fundamental of these strategies for maintaining conditions favorable to the continuance of life.

A billion years of chemical turbulence preceded the appearance of life on earth—a billion years of chance collisions between inorganic molecules that had become sufficiently agitated by volcanic heat, or lightning, or ultraviolet light from the sun to combine into carbon-containing organic molecules. In time these molecules accumulated in the environment, and they became the source of energy for the first life forms: heterotrophic cells. The heterotrophs fed on these energy-rich molecules, they multiplied, and undoubtedly their proliferating progeny soon began to have drastic effects on the environment. Long before the appearance of humankind, this burgeoning crowd of heterotrophs must have been giving off enough waste products to create a primordial form of air and water pollution. In addition, usable organic molecules were certainly being consumed faster than they could be replaced by chance reactions.

If life was to be more than a fleeting appearance of reproducing bits of organic matter, two things had to happen: Organic molecules had to be synthesized faster and in a more dependable way than environmental events alone could provide. And some kind of dynamic equilibrium had to develop between life forms so that the chemical wastes of one kind of organism would become the foodstuff of another, rather than being dumped into the environment and disrupting conditions favorable to survival.

Early in the history of life on earth, organisms did evolve that were capable of using various forms of available energy to transform inorganic molecules into organic compounds. These organisms were the autotrophs, the "self-feeders." In the long run, the most important of the autotrophs would be the ones that developed the ability to trap light energy from the sun and use it to trigger the synthesis of organic compounds from carbon dioxide and water molecules. In this process of *photosynthesis,* a continuous supply of organic molecules—including sugar molecules—could be produced from the supply of carbon dioxide and water found in the environment. The sugar molecules so formed could then be metabolized ("changed chemically") by heterotroph as well as autotroph, so that each organism would be supplied with the energy and the chemical building blocks necessary for its survival. But the problem of assuring continuity of life was only partially solved by photosynthesis.

Primitive organisms undoubtedly extracted energy from the sugar molecules by means of a metabolic pathway called *glycolysis.* In glycolysis, a molecule of sugar is split in half to form two molecules of a small organic acid. When this splitting occurs, part of the energy from the sugar is released in a form that can be used to do cellular work. Virtually every cell on earth still uses this energy-yielding process. Indeed, many existing cells obtain *all* their energy

from glycolysis. But for the community of early life, a "cycle" consisting only of photosynthesis and glycolysis had several shortcomings. First, glycolysis releases less than 10 percent of the energy stored in glucose by photosynthesis. Second, in high enough concentrations the products of glycolysis are toxic to cells—even to the cells that produce them. Third, the oxygen released as a by-product of photosynthesis is also toxic to many cells if its concentration exceeds certain limits. Finally, glycolysis usually does not provide for the replenishment of the carbon dioxide that is used in photosynthesis and without which photosynthesis could not continue.

Thus the appearance of photosynthesis set the stage for the development of another form of energy metabolism. In *cellular respiration,* oxygen produced as a by-product of photosynthesis is used to extract, in usable form, the energy still remaining in the organic acids produced by glycolysis; carbon dioxide is released as an end product. (Although cellular respiration depends on air, it is not to be confused with breathing, which has also been called "respiration.") With the appearance of cellular respiration, a dynamic equilibrium of life forms became possible. *Photosynthesis, glycolysis, and cellular respiration are now the major pathways of the immense cycle in which carbon atoms flow continuously through the life forms that exist on earth.* This overall cycle is sketched out in Figure 14.2. As you read about the nature and results of glycolysis and respiration, and (in the next chapter) of photosynthesis, refer back occasionally to this sketch. The details of each of these three events are complex, and it is easier to grasp the meaning of each step if you visualize where it fits into the overall strategy of energy metabolism in the community of living organisms.

Because of the complicated nature of the processes of energy metabolism, this chapter is structured to provide an initial, simplified overview of these processes, and then a more detailed analysis of the reactions involved in them.

AN OVERVIEW OF GLYCOLYSIS, THE KREBS CYCLE, AND OXIDATIVE PHOSPHORYLATION

If all the gasoline in the tank of a car were exploded at once, the car would not move forward for very long. Gasoline is a useful energy source only when a small amount at a time can be exploded, under conditions in which a good portion of the energy released can be captured in a usable form. So it is with life. If a spoonful of sugar is burned, it releases its stored chemical energy primarily in the form of heat and light. These forms of energy would not be of much use to a cell; they would do little but raise its temperature to a dangerous level. Cells perform the same overall reaction, but they do so in a series of small steps. About 30 different steps are used to convert one molecule of the sugar glucose

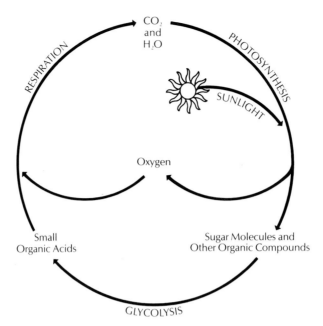

Figure 14.2   The major features of the carbon cycle. In photosynthesis, light energy from the sun is used in the conversion of carbon dioxide and water molecules into organic compounds such as sugar molecules. In glycolysis, energy trapped in the sugar molecules during photosynthesis is extracted when the molecule is split into small organic acid molecules. In respiration, the energy still remaining in the organic acid products of glycolysis is extracted, with the help of the oxygen produced as a by-product of photosynthesis, and carbon dioxide is released, thus providing raw materials for the cycle to begin anew.

The reactions of photosynthesis can be summarized as:

$$6CO_2 + 6H_2O \xrightarrow{\text{Energy (light)}} C_6H_{12}O_6 \text{ (sugar)}$$

The reactions of glycolysis plus respiration can be summarized as:

$$C_6H_{12}O_6 \xrightarrow{} 6CO_2 + 6H_2O$$
$$\text{Energy (ATP)}$$

Although carbon atoms cycle continuously through the living

world, it is important to remember that energy cannot be recycled (Chapter 12). Part of the energy gained from sunlight is used for cellular work, but part of it is also given off as nonusable forms of energy (heat and entropy) at each step in the cycle. It is only because of the continuous input of sunlight that the cycling of carbon atoms can be maintained.

In many textbooks, the term "respiration" is used to mean all the energy-yielding reactions of sugar breakdown. When used in this way, the term subsumes all the reactions discussed in this chapter. Thus, for a cell that cannot use oxygen or to which oxygen is not available, the term "anaerobic respiration" has been applied. However, respiration traditionally has referred to "the taking in of air," so to speak of anaerobic respiration is a contradiction in terms: it means "the taking in of air without air." That is why the term "cellular respiration" in this book is restricted to those reactions that can occur only in the presence of and with the utilization of air (oxygen) and "anaerobic glycolysis" is used for the energy-yielding reactions of cells lacking air or unable to use air.

to carbon dioxide and water. But because many of these reactions must be performed more than once, the total number of steps required to break down each molecule of sugar is really about 140! In nearly a third of these steps, some of the energy released from glucose becomes trapped in new molecules of adenosine triphosphate (ATP), which are produced by the addition of phosphate to adenosine diphosphate (ADP). The cell then uses these ATP molecules to maintain its membranes, to move in response to stimuli, to build new macromolecules, or to perform a vast array of other cellular activities.

The 30 different chemical reactions needed to metabolize glucose are neither spontaneous nor random events. For each reaction step there is a specific protein *enzyme*, and the enzyme structure is such that it catalyzes only that particular step of the breakdown process. Several of the reactions also require nonprotein *coenzymes* (small molecules required to help catalyze the reaction). The enzymes are arranged so that the product released by one enzyme becomes the substrate for the next. In other words, the molecules derived from glucose flow from one enzyme to the next, being modified and releasing some of their chemical energy and then moving on to the next enzyme in the series. As you read in Chapter 12, a series of sequentially active enzymes and/or the reactions they catalyze is known as a *metabolic pathway*. A single cell may contain hundreds of these

Figure 14.3   A simplified version of the glycolysis pathway, in which one sugar molecule (glucose) is split in half to form two molecules of the organic acid pyruvate. The net result for each molecule of sugar that is metabolized is the production of two ATP molecules from two ADP molecules, plus two inorganic phosphate (P_i) molecules.

In steps 1 and 3, two ATP molecules are used up in order to form sugar phosphates, which are much more reactive than plain sugar molecules. In step 4, the six-carbon (6C) sugar diphosphate is split into two different kinds of three-carbon sugar monophosphates. Step 5 interconverts these two kinds of sugar phosphates, so that both may flow through the subsequent steps.

In step 6, the sugar molecule loses hydrogen (H) to the coenzyme NAD, becomes converted to an acid and at the same time picks up a second phosphate group from the inorganic phosphate found in the cell. In step 7, one of these phosphate groups is transferred to ADP, thus regenerating an ATP molecule used up earlier. In step 10, the remaining phosphate group is transferred from the three-carbon acid to another molecule of ADP.

Steps 6 through 10 are performed twice for each sugar molecule. (That is what the "2" in front of the reactants in this figure means.)

The ATP produced in such reactions is used to transfer the chemical potential energy of glucose into the performance of cellular work. How the pyruvate and the NADH are used depends on the cell type. In cells capable of respiration, both of these molecules are fed into the respiratory pathways (Figures 14.4 and 14.6). In some yeasts growing in the absence of air, the NADH is used to convert the pyruvate to ethyl alcohol and carbon dioxide. In various other cell types, the NADH is used to convert the pyruvate to lactate.

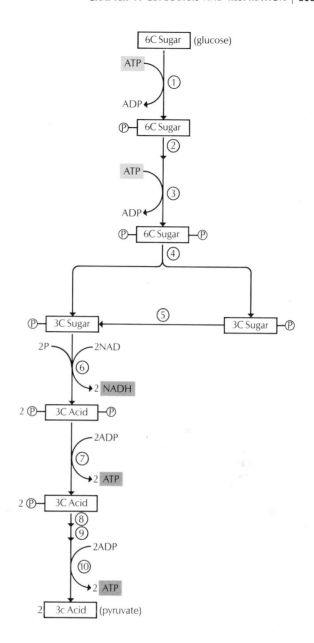

pathways. Some involve the breakdown of food molecules and others involve the synthesis of new cellular components.

The total breakdown of one molecule of glucose requires three distinct but interconnected metabolic pathways: glycolysis, the Krebs cycle, and oxidative phosphorylation. The Krebs cycle and oxidative phosphorylation pathways together constitute the process of cellular respiration.

Figure 14.3 shows the steps in **glycolysis** that split one glucose molecule in half to form two molecules of the organic acid pyruvate. "Pyruvate" is a term that is sometimes used interchangeably with "pyruvic acid," but there is a distinction made between them. The *-ate* suffix of

"pyruvate" signifies the ionized form of the molecule:

$$O\diagdown \overset{\displaystyle }{\underset{\displaystyle }{C}}\diagup OH \qquad O\diagdown \overset{\displaystyle }{\underset{\displaystyle }{C}}\diagup O^-$$

$$C=O \rightleftharpoons C=O + H^+$$

Pyruvic Acid $\quad CH_3 \qquad CH_3 \quad$ Pyruvate

Because most organic acid molecules such as pyruvic acid ionize at the pH level characteristic of cells, terms using the *-ate* ending are more appropriate and will be used throughout this discussion.

The glycolysis pathway has ten steps, catalyzed by ten different enzymes. In two of the first three steps, ATP is used to form phosphate derivatives of the sugar. It may seem strange that a pathway functioning to produce ATP uses up ATP. But one of the principal ways in which ATP is used within the cell is to facilitate cellular reactions. The phosphate groups derived from ATP are an effective means of ''loosening up'' the electrons in organic molecules, thus making otherwise unreactive molecules reactive.

In eukaryotic cells, the enzymes of glycolysis are found in the cytoplasm, but the enzymes of the two respiratory pathways are enclosed in mitochondria. Figure 14.4 traces what happens to pyruvate from the time it enters the mitochondrion. In the first respiratory pathway, the **Krebs cycle,** the carbon atoms of this organic acid are oxidized (Figure 14.5) to form carbon dioxide molecules, which are removed in a stepwise manner. Meanwhile, hydrogen (H) atoms and their associated electrons are transferred to a coenzyme, nicotinamide adenine dinucleotide (NAD) to form a reduced coenzyme, NADH. *The most important function of the Krebs cycle is the production of reduced coenzymes.* These molecules are the ones that drive the reactions of oxidative phosphorylation.

In **oxidative phosphorylation** (Figure 14.6), the electrons donated by glucose and carried by NADH are transferred from one electron carrier molecule to another. Eventually they are passed on to a molecule of oxygen, which thereby becomes converted to water. As they leave glucose, the electrons are at a high energy level. But with each transfer their energy level falls, like water falling through the power turbines of a dam. This process is called **electron transport** and the molecules that pass along the electrons are called the electron transport chain. Many of these carriers are iron-containing proteins called *cytochromes.* At three of these transfer steps, the energy given up by the electron is coupled to a reaction that results in the production of a molecule of ATP from ADP and inorganic phosphate. Thus, for each molecule of NADH produced in glycolysis and the Krebs cycle, three molecules of ATP are generated.

The electrons gained by the reduced coenzyme FADH in reaction 18 of the Krebs cycle also enter the electron

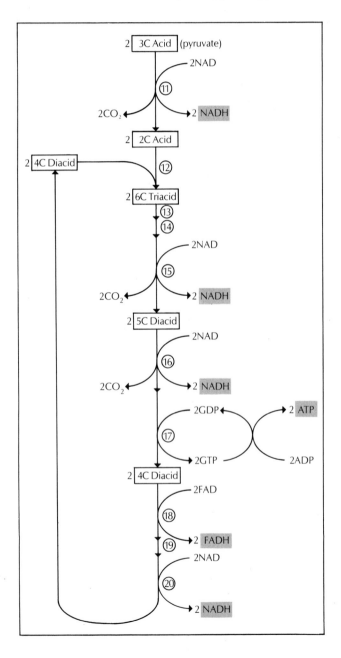

Figure 14.4 A simplified version of the Krebs cycle. In this cycle, the pyruvate produced from glucose is completely oxidized to carbon dioxide; ATP is produced and NAD is reduced to NADH in the process (Figure 14.5).
In step 11, pyruvate is split, forming a two-carbon acid. In step 12, this molecule combines with a four-carbon diacid (a compound having two acid groups), thereby forming a six-carbon compound having three acid groups. In the subsequent reactions, the carbon, oxygen, and hydrogen atoms that the pyruvate contributed are removed. Eventually the four-carbon acid, which is capable of starting the cycle over again, is re-formed.

The most important function of the Krebs cycle is the production of NADH, which is used in the oxidative phosphorylation pathway (Figure 14.6) to generate more ATP. Each molecule of NADH carries two electrons (originally part of the glucose molecule) to the electron transport chain, where they are used to generate more ATP.

Because a molecule of glucose yields two molecules of pyruvate, two turns around the Krebs cycle are required for each molecule of glucose. (That is the significance of the ''2'' in front of all reactants.)

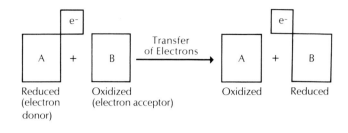

Figure 14.5 Oxidation and reduction. "Oxidation" means the removal of an electron from a molecule. In biological systems this happens most frequently when a hydrogen atom is removed, taking an electron with it. "Reduction" means the addition of an electron to a molecule. In biological systems this often happens when a hydrogen atom (with its electron) is added to a molecule. A "reduced" compound, then, has not been reduced in energy at all; in fact, it has gained energy in the form of an electron.

Neither oxidation nor reduction can occur alone. In order for one molecule to be reduced, another molecule must be oxidized. Thus, an oxidation-reduction reaction is one in which an electron (often accompanied by an H^+ ion) is passed from one molecule to another.

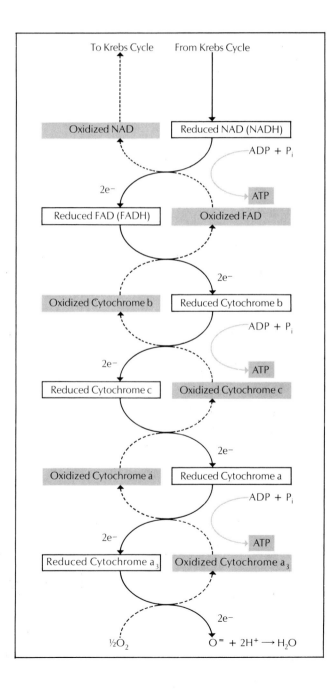

Figure 14.6 A simplified version of the oxidative phosphorylation pathway. This pathway consists of two separable sets of reactions: electron transport and phosphorylation.

Phosphorylation is described in Chapter 12. In electron transport, electrons derived from reactions of the Krebs cycle are passed in sequence from one carrier to another. Each carrier alternates between the reduced state (in which electrons are bound to them) and the oxidized state (in which electrons are not bound to them). The solid black arrows in this diagram trace the path of the electrons through this scheme. The dashed arrows show the regeneration of the oxidized carrier at each step. The final electron acceptor is oxygen. The oxygen does not recycle between oxidized and reduced forms. It is permanently reduced and combined with hydrogen ions to form water. This reaction accounts for the continuous need for oxygen by all organisms that depend on respiratory metabolism.

At each step of electron transfer, the electrons lose some of their energy. At three of the transfer steps, this lost energy is coupled to the formation of ATP from ADP and inorganic phosphate. These are the critical steps needed to extract the chemical energy from a sugar molecule in a form that can be used for cellular work.

transport chain. But these electrons bypass the first ATP-generating step, so the electrons carried by FADH generate only two molecules of ATP.

All of these ATP-yielding reactions add up to the balance sheet shown in Table 14.1, which shows that when glycolysis and respiration are both used, nineteen times as much energy is obtained per glucose molecule as when glycolysis is used alone. The overall efficiency of glycolysis and respiration is summarized in *Interleaf 14.1*. This concludes the overview of glycolysis, the Krebs cycle, and phosphorylation. These three metabolic pathways will now be explained in greater detail.

GLUCOSE MOLECULES ARE DISMANTLED ALONG THE EMBDEN-MEYERHOF PATHWAY

The sequence of reactions involved in the conversion of glucose to pyruvate is called the **Embden-Meyerhof pathway,** in honor of two men who in the 1930s identified its major steps. Figure 14.7 gives the names of all the intermediate compounds in this sequence; Figure 14.8 gives the formulas for them.

In steps 1 through 3 of the pathway, glucose is converted

Table 14.1
Products From One Molecule of Glucose in Glycolysis, in the Krebs Cycle, and in Oxidative Phosphorylation

Products	NADH	FADH	ATP
In Glycolysis:			
ATP molecules needed to start glycolysis:			−2
ATP molecules produced directly by glycolysis:			4
NADH molecules produced directly by glycolysis:	2		
In the Krebs Cycle:			
ATP molecules produced directly by the Krebs cycle:			2
NADH molecules produced by the Krebs cycle:	8		
FADH molecules produced by the Krebs cycle:		2	
In Oxidative Phosphorylation:			
ATP molecules produced for each NADH molecule from glycolysis, times the 2 NADH molecules (3 × 2):			6
ATP molecules produced for each NADH molecule from the Krebs cycle, times the 8 NADH molecules (3 × 8):			24
ATP molecules produced for each FADH molecule from the Krebs cycle, times the 2 FADH molecules (2 × 2):			4
NET ATP MOLECULES PER MOLECULE OF GLUCOSE:			38

ATP obtained directly from glycolysis:	5%
ATP obtained directly from the Krebs cycle:	5%
ATP obtained from oxidative phosphorylation:	90%

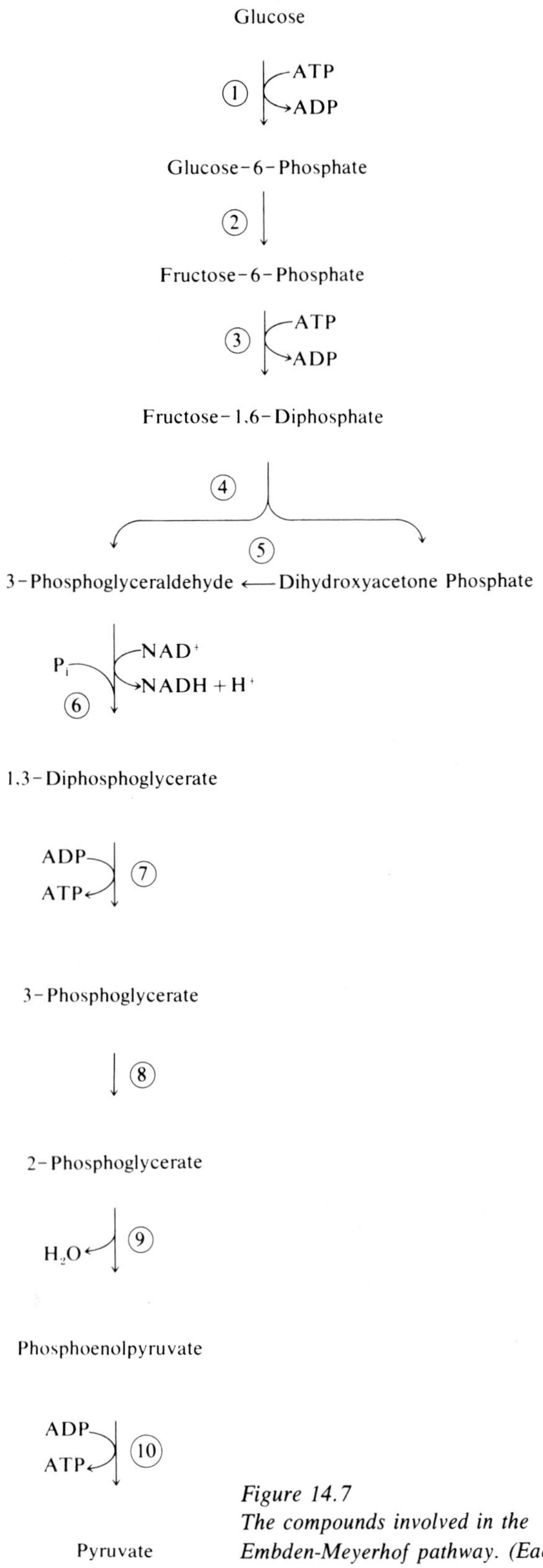

Glucose

① $\begin{array}{c}\curvearrowleft ATP \\ \searrow ADP\end{array}$

Glucose-6-Phosphate

②

Fructose-6-Phosphate

③ $\begin{array}{c}\curvearrowleft ATP \\ \searrow ADP\end{array}$

Fructose-1,6-Diphosphate

④ ⑤

3-Phosphoglyceraldehyde ⟵ Dihydroxyacetone Phosphate

P_i $\begin{array}{c}\curvearrowleft NAD^+ \\ \searrow NADH + H^+\end{array}$ ⑥

1,3-Diphosphoglycerate

ADP $\searrow$ ⑦ ATP $\swarrow$

3-Phosphoglycerate

⑧

2-Phosphoglycerate

H_2O $\swarrow$ ⑨

Phosphoenolpyruvate

ADP $\searrow$ ⑩ ATP $\swarrow$

Pyruvate

Figure 14.7
The compounds involved in the Embden-Meyerhof pathway. (Each of the reactions indicated by an arrow is catalyzed by a specific enzyme.)

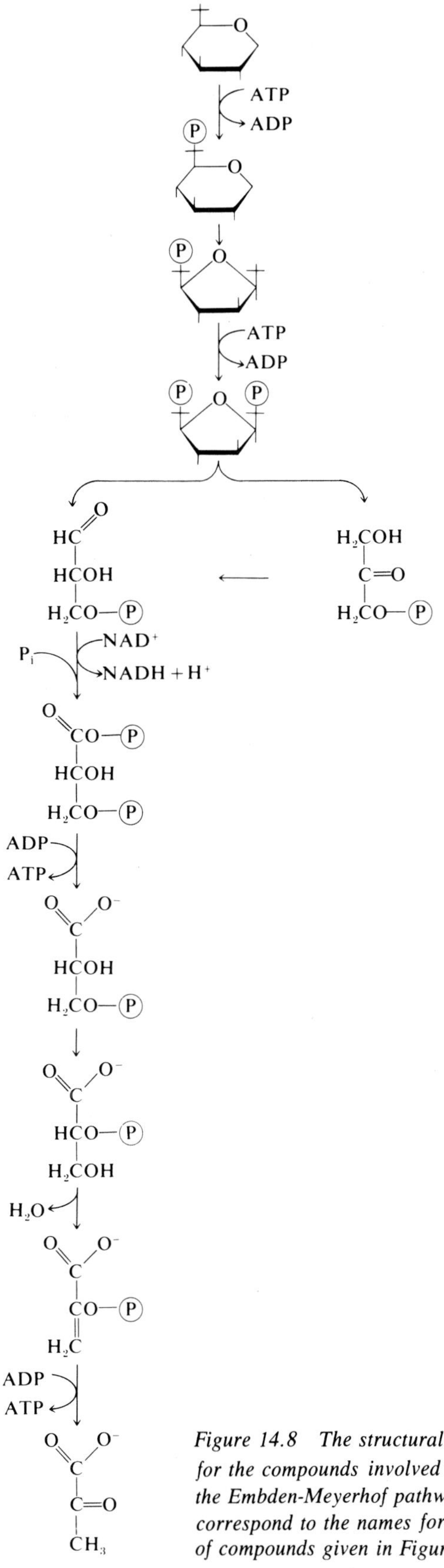

to fructose diphosphate by the addition of two phosphate groups from ATP molecules. The net result of these three steps is the conversion of the glucose molecule to a higher energy, unstable intermediate, and the conversion of two molecules of ATP to ADP. In other words, the cell has invested two ATP units of energy in order to prepare the glucose molecule for its imminent dismantling.

In step 4, the unstable six-carbon molecule is split into two three-carbon units, phosphoglyceraldehyde and dihydroxyacetone phosphate. These two compounds are interconverted in step 5.

Step 6 is the first reaction in which there is a return on the investment of energy made in steps 1 and 3: energy is now released from the substrate sugar molecule. An enzyme called phosphoglyceraldehyde dehydrogenase speeds up the reaction. It is a large enzyme containing more than 1,300 amino acids in four polypeptide chains. This enzyme catalyzes the transfer of two hydrogen atoms (with their electrons) from 3-phosphoglyceraldehyde to the coenzyme NAD^+. (The generalized form of this hydrogen-transfer reaction is shown in Figure 14.9). This hydrogen transfer to NAD^+ is always accompanied by the release of a large amount of free energy; specifically, 10.3 kilocalories per mole under standard conditions:

$$3— P —glyceraldehyde + NAD^+ \longrightarrow$$
$$3— P —glycerate + NADH + H^+$$
$$(\Delta G^{\circ\prime} = -10.3 \text{ kcal/mole})$$

where P represents the entire phosphate group

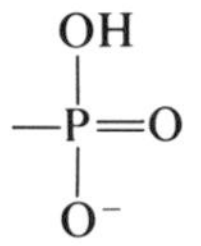

$$-\overset{OH}{\underset{O^-}{P}}=O$$

and $\Delta G^{\circ\prime}$ is the standard free energy of the reaction, as described in Chapter 12. Now, if the hydrogen atoms really were removed from phosphoglyceraldehyde in just the manner written above, the 10.3 kilocalories of energy would be lost as heat and would not be available to do useful work for the cell. But that is not how it happens. The energy released in the transfer of the hydrogen atoms is used to perform an otherwise improbable reaction:

$$3— P —glycerate + P_i \longrightarrow 1,3\text{-di-} P —glycerate$$
$$(\Delta G^{\circ\prime} = +11.8 \text{ kcal/mole})$$

The high, positive value for the standard free energy of this phosphorylation reaction indicates that the equilibrium for the reaction is far to the left (in fact, at equilibrium the ratio of reactants to products would be about a billion to one). But, as Figure 14.10 shows, the enzyme phosphoglycer-

Figure 14.8 The structural formulas for the compounds involved in the Embden-Meyerhof pathway. (These correspond to the names formulas of compounds given in Figure 14.7.)

(text continues on page 310)

Interleaf 14.1

The Efficiency of Glycolysis and Respiration

How efficiently do cells extract usable energy from the sugar molecules they "burn"? Are cells more or less efficient than the internal combustion engine, which extracts usable energy in the burning of gasoline? These seemingly simple questions are regularly posed in textbooks and by students and are regularly answered in a glib way. But it turns out that simple answers are not now and never will be available.

The amount of energy released in the complete oxidation of 1 mole of glucose can be measured easily and rather precisely:

$$1 \text{ glucose} \longrightarrow 6CO_2 + 6H_2O$$

$$(\Delta G^{\circ\prime} = -686 \text{ kcal/mole})$$

The value of 686 kilocalories per mole for the standard free energy ($\Delta G^{\circ\prime}$) of oxidation of glucose is the same regardless of the way glucose is oxidized—whether it is burned in a flame or processed in a cell. Now, as Table 14.1 indicates, when a cell oxidizes glucose it temporarily stores the usable portion of this energy in the form of 38 ATP molecules. In order to determine the efficiency of energy storage in this process, it is necessary to know how much energy can subsequently be released for the performance of cellular work when each of the 38 ATP molecules is hydrolyzed to ADP and inorganic phosphate (P_i). Recall that the standard free energy ($\Delta G^{\circ\prime}$) of hydrolysis of ATP is −7.3 kilocalories per mole:

$$ATP + H_2O \longrightarrow ADP + P_i$$

$$(\Delta G^{\circ\prime} = -7.3 \text{ kcal/mole})$$

If this value is multiplied by 38, and if the product is then divided by the amount of energy released from the glucose molecule (from which the 38 molecules of ATP are derived), it is possible to arrive at an estimate for the overall efficiency of glycolysis and respiration:

$$\frac{(-7.3)\,(38)}{-686} = \frac{277}{686} = 0.404$$

or about 40 percent efficiency. This value is considerably higher than the 25–30 percent energy conversion efficiency characteristic of most automobile engines. Nevertheless, it is an unrealistically low value for the efficiency of cellular metabolism. The reason it is too low is that the value used in this calculation for the free energy of hydrolysis of ATP is too low. Recall from Chapter 12 that a distinction must be made between free energy change under "standard" conditions ($\Delta G^{\circ\prime}$) and free energy change under prevailing cellular conditions ($\Delta G'$). For the hydrolysis of ATP, the *standard* starting conditions used to measure $\Delta G^{\circ\prime}$ are 1 molar concentrations of ATP, ADP, and inorganic phosphate; a pH of 7.0; and saturating quantities of Mg^{++} ions. But cells do not perform *any* reaction under any such (arbitrarily) chosen standard conditions: $\Delta G'$ of hydrolysis of ATP in fact varies enormously with reaction conditions. This variation arises because much of the energy required to perform the reverse reaction ($ADP^= + P_i^- \longrightarrow ATP^=$) is required just to bring together these two negatively charged ions, which tend to repel each other. Now, the strength with which ADP and inorganic phosphate repel each other depends greatly on cellular pH, the concentration of other ions in the immediate vicinity, and other factors. If we study ATP hydrolysis, changing conditions one at a time from those specified as "standard" toward those actually existing in cells, the measured value of $\Delta G'$ rises with nearly every change. Thus, if we set aside "standard" conditions for measuring ATP hydrolysis and use instead an estimated "average" or "typical" set of cellular conditions, we obtain a $\Delta G'$ for ATP hydrolysis of about -12.5 kilocalories per mole. This "*cellular* free energy" is more than 70 percent higher than the *standard* free energy figure usually used in calculations! In fact, the $\Delta G'$ of ATP hydrolysis has actually been measured in intact red blood cells, and the $\Delta G'$ was determined to be *still* higher in these cells: -13.1 kilocalories per mole!

If this last value is used to estimate the efficiency of energy metabolism, the result is surprising:

$$\frac{(-13.1)\,(38)}{-686} = \frac{498}{686} = 0.72,$$

or 72 percent efficiency!

In short, the efficiency of cellular energy metabolism varies not only from one cell type to the next, but also from time to time within a cell as conditions within the cell change. But even though a value cannot be applied that is correct in all cases, a generalization can be made. Energy metabolism in living, respiring cells is enormously more efficient than man-made energy-transforming devices such as gasoline engines.

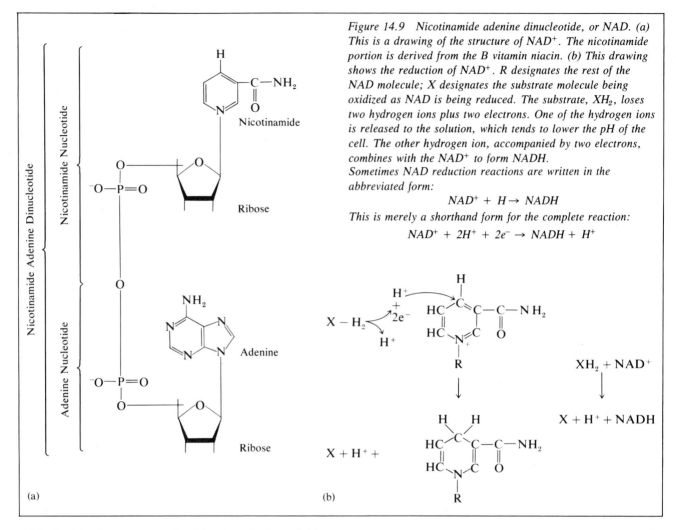

Figure 14.9 *Nicotinamide adenine dinucleotide, or NAD. (a)
This is a drawing of the structure of NAD⁺. The nicotinamide
portion is derived from the B vitamin niacin. (b) This drawing
shows the reduction of NAD⁺. R designates the rest of the
NAD molecule; X designates the substrate molecule being
oxidized as NAD is being reduced. The substrate, XH₂, loses
two hydrogen ions plus two electrons. One of the hydrogen ions
is released to the solution, which tends to lower the pH of the
cell. The other hydrogen ion, accompanied by two electrons,
combines with the NAD⁺ to form NADH.*
*Sometimes NAD reduction reactions are written in the
abbreviated form:*

$$NAD^+ + H \rightarrow NADH$$

This is merely a shorthand form for the complete reaction:

$$NAD^+ + 2H^+ + 2e^- \rightarrow NADH + H^+$$

aldehyde dehydrogenase couples this otherwise improbable phosphorylation to the previously described dehydrogenation in a two-step reaction. This is one of the two major ways. in which enzymes couple improbable reactions (of high positive $\Delta G^{\circ\prime}$) to energy-yielding reactions (of highly negative $\Delta G^{\circ\prime}$). The other major way is illustrated by the next step in the Embden-Meyerhof pathway.

Because *the standard free energies of two coupled reactions are additive*, we can readily see that the overall reaction has a small positive value:

$$3—\text{(P)}—\text{glyceraldehyde} + NAD^+ + P_i \longrightarrow$$

$$1,3\text{-di—(P)}—\text{glycerate} + NADH + H^+$$

$$(\Delta G^{\circ\prime} = -10.3 + 11.8 = +1.5 \text{ kcal/mole})$$

Thus, even in the coupled form, the equilibrium favors the reverse reaction: here the ratio of reactants to products would be about 20 to 1 at equilibrium. But, as discussed in Chapter 12, one way of making a reaction of positive $\Delta G^{\circ\prime}$ proceed continuously in the forward direction is to remove

the products of that reaction as rapidly as they are formed, so that the reaction never reaches equilibrium. That is what happens in the example given here. The diphosphoglycerate formed as the result of the above reaction is a high-energy phosphate compound. Indeed, its standard free energy of hydrolysis (−11.8 kilocalories per mole) is so much higher than that required to phosphorylate ADP (+7.3 kilocalories per mole) that it is possible for an enzyme to couple hydrolysis of diphosphoglycerate to the phosphorylation of ADP in a highly exergonic reaction:

$$1,3\text{-di—(P)}—\text{glycerate} + ADP \longrightarrow$$

$$3—\text{(P)}—\text{glycerate} + ATP$$

$$(\Delta G^{\circ\prime} = -4.5 \text{ kcal/mole})$$

The highly negative $\Delta G^{\circ\prime}$ for this reaction indicates that it tends to run strongly in the forward direction. Because the enzyme catalyzing this reaction is present in adequate quantity, in association with 3-phosphoglyceraldehyde de-

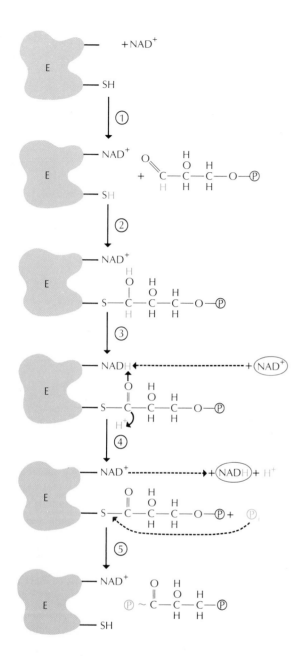

Figure 14.10   Steps in the reaction catalyzed by the enzyme phosphoglyceraldehyde dehydrogenase (depicted as E). This was the first enzyme reaction analyzed in sufficient detail to visualize how the energy provided by oxidation was actually coupled to the formation of high-energy phosphate bonds within a cell.

Step 1: Activation of the enzyme occurs by the binding of an NAD$^+$ molecule.

Step 2: 3-phosphoglyceraldehyde is now bound next to the NAD$^+$ by means of a sulfur atom on the enzyme.

Step 3: The 3-phosphoglyceraldehyde passes one of its hydrogen atoms and two of its electrons to the bound NAD$^+$, and its other hydrogen atom is released to the solution as an ion.

Step 4: The bound NADH transfers a hydrogen atom and two electrons to an unbound molecule of NAD$^+$.

Step 5: The bond between the enzyme and the 3-phosphoglycerate is split by a molecule of inorganic phosphate.

At the completion of this reaction, the 1,3-diphosphoglycerate is released from the enzyme; the energy stored in this newly formed phosphate bond is used to phosphorylate ATP in the next step of glycolysis. As the diphosphoglycerate is released, the enzyme is restored to a form capable of reacting with another molecule of 3-phosphoglyceraldehyde.

hydrogenase, the reactions are coupled. Once a molecule of 1,3-diphosphoglycerate is produced by the first enzyme, it is taken up by the second enzyme and converted to 3-phosphoglycerate. In other words, the second enzyme reaction lowers the concentration of the product that results from the first reaction, prevents the attainment of equilibrium, and thereby "pulls" the first reaction forward. The overall relationship can be summarized in this way:

3— (P) —glyceraldehyde + NAD$^+$ + P$_i$ + ADP $\longrightarrow$

3— (P) —glycerate + NADH + H$^+$ + ATP

($\Delta G^{\circ\prime} = -3.0$ kcal/mole)

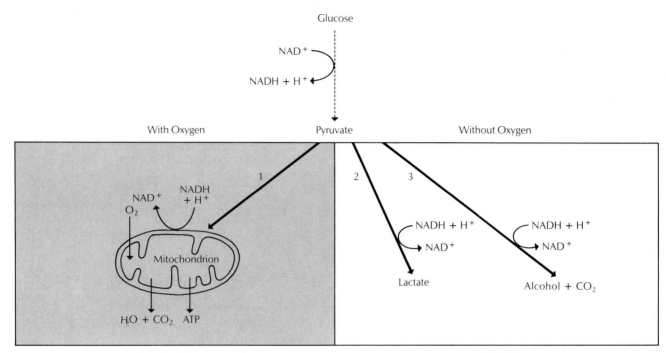

Glucose

NAD^+

$NADH + H^+$

With Oxygen   Pyruvate   Without Oxygen

1   2   3

NAD^+
O_2 $NADH + H^+$

$NADH + H^+$ $NADH + H^+$

Mitochondrion

NAD^+ NAD^+

Lactate   Alcohol + CO_2

$H_2O + CO_2$ ATP

Aerobic Pathways   Anaerobic Pathways

The negative value of the standard free energy indicates that these two reactions together tend to run strongly in the forward direction. At equilibrium, the reactants would be about 99.5 percent converted to products.

This set of reactions is a clear example of the mechanisms used for coupling energy-yielding and energy-requiring reactions. It is also one example of **substrate level phosphorylation**—the direct coupling of the oxidation of a substrate to the phosphorylation of ADP. Another substrate level phosphorylation occurs at step 10 of the Embden-Meyerhof pathway (Figure 14.7).

Alternative Metabolic Pathways the Glycolytic End Products Can Follow

What happens to the pyruvate that is produced as a result of glycolysis? It can be metabolized in one of a variety of ways, depending on cell type and on environmental conditions, as shown in Figure 14.11. Under aerobic conditions (in the presence of oxygen), cells capable of respiration pass both NADH and pyruvate to the respiratory pathways, which continue the oxidative process and the generation of ATP. But if oxygen supplies become limited or if the cell is of a kind that is incapable of respiration, the cells must resort to the more primitive pathways of **anaerobic glycolysis** (Figure 14.11). The important thing is that NAD^+ must be regenerated from NADH so that further glycolysis may occur. (The amount of such coenzymes is always limited in cells; if the NAD^+ were not regenerated, glycol-

ysis would rapidly cease for lack of a coenzyme capable of accepting hydrogen atoms in step 6 of glycolysis.)

Organisms or cells capable of using aerobic (respiratory) metabolism when oxygen is abundant, and anaerobic glycolysis when it is not, are called **facultative anaerobes.** Some organisms, however, are incapable of respiration. Usually they are primitive organisms found in mud, underground, or in other environments where oxygen is absent. Some, called **obligate anaerobes,** are killed if even traces of oxygen enter their environment.

Other Precursor Molecules That Can Take Part in Glycolysis

Glucose is the most common single sugar molecule in nature, and that is why it has been used as the example for this discussion. But as Figure 14.12 shows, the glycolytic pathway can be used to metabolize sugar molecules other than glucose. Figure 14.13 depicts a familiar process in which the atoms of two sugar molecules, fructose and glucose, travel the same Embden-Meyerhof pathway of energy extraction.

RESPIRATION: THE KREBS CYCLE PLUS OXIDATIVE PHOSPHORYLATION

As you read in the beginning of this chapter, glycolysis in itself is an inefficient form of metabolism: It releases less than 10 percent of the energy stored in glucose, it causes the build-up of toxic end products, and it usually produces

Figure 14.11 (left) Alternative pathways for metabolism of the pyruvate and NADH that are produced as a result of enzyme activity in the Embden-Meyerhof pathway. (Several other alternative pathways are known besides the most common ones shown here.)

Alternative 1: In cells capable of respiration, when air is available the pyruvate is oxidized completely to carbon dioxide and water, and a great deal of additional ATP is produced in the process. The NAD$^+$ is also regenerated by the respiratory pathway. In eukaryotic cells, respiration occurs in the mitochondrion; in bacteria, it occurs on the cell membrane. When air is lacking, however, such cells are generally capable of using alternative pathways 2 or 3.

Alternative 2: When oxygen is not available for respiration, the cells must regenerate NAD$^+$ if they are to continue to obtain energy. Under such conditions, the cell reverts to the more primitive pathway: Pyruvate is reduced to lactic acid, which regenerates NAD$^+$. (It is the lactic acid produced under such conditions that causes the cramping of overexercised muscles and the souring of milk.)

Alternative 3: Some yeasts and certain other organisms reduce the pyruvate by a slightly different pathway under anaerobic conditions. They first break the pyruvate into carbon dioxide and acetaldehyde and then use the NADH to reduce acetaldehyde to ethyl alcohol. These two products are somewhat less toxic than lactic acid. In either case the end result is the same—NAD$^+$ is regenerated so that glycolysis can continue.

Figure 14.12 (below) The entry of other forms of sugar molecules into the glycolytic pathway. All of the simple sugar molecules require a molecule of ATP for phosphorylation before they can enter the glycolytic pathway. The starches do not—they are phosphorylated by inorganic phosphates. In the short term, starch is a more efficient source of energy because one less ATP molecule is required to get things started. In the long term, however, it is not as efficient, for it takes more than one ATP molecule for each precursor glucose molecule to initially form the starch.

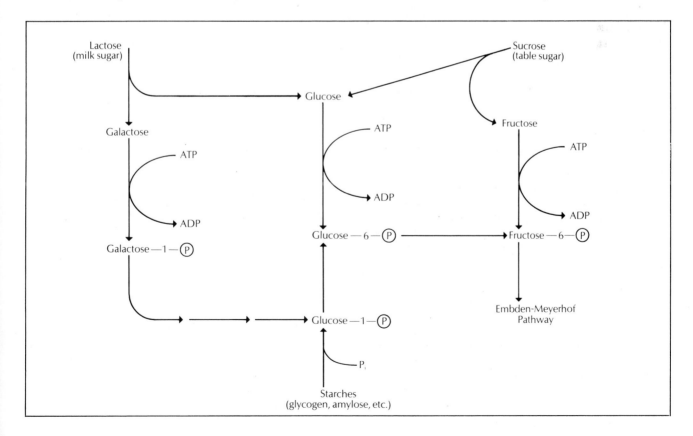

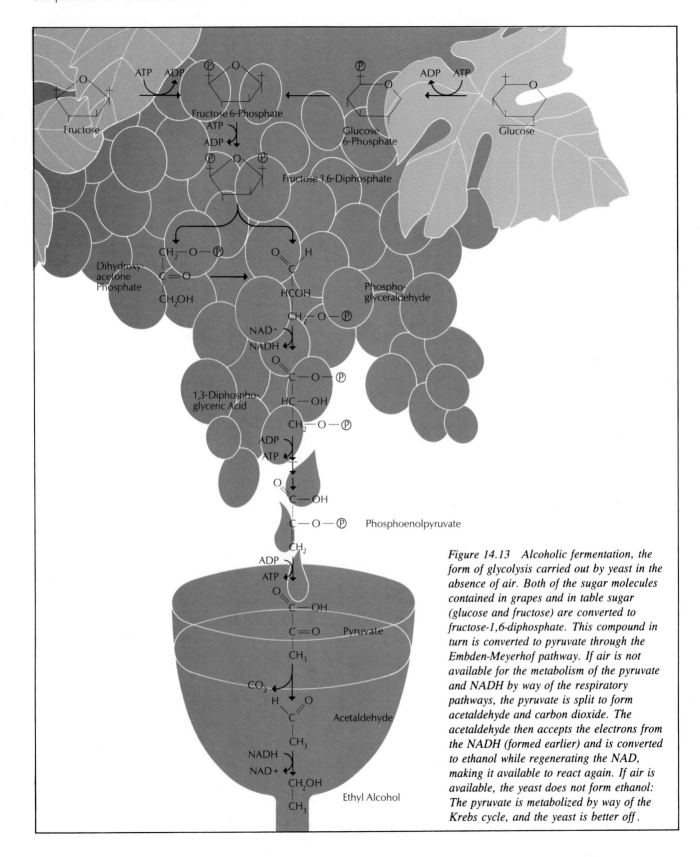

Figure 14.13 Alcoholic fermentation, the form of glycolysis carried out by yeast in the absence of air. Both of the sugar molecules contained in grapes and in table sugar (glucose and fructose) are converted to fructose-1,6-diphosphate. This compound in turn is converted to pyruvate through the Embden-Meyerhof pathway. If air is not available for the metabolism of the pyruvate and NADH by way of the respiratory pathways, the pyruvate is split to form acetaldehyde and carbon dioxide. The acetaldehyde then accepts the electrons from the NADH (formed earlier) and is converted to ethanol while regenerating the NAD, making it available to react again. If air is available, the yeast does not form ethanol: The pyruvate is metabolized by way of the Krebs cycle, and the yeast is better off.

nothing that can be used as starting material for photosynthesis. Small wonder, then, that the appearance of respiratory metabolism in evolutionary time met with such success. It is a process now used by all organisms on earth except the obligate anaerobes.

How Energy Is Released From Pyruvate and Trapped in the Form of Reduced Coenzymes

Figure 14.14 shows the reaction sequence in which the atoms of pyruvate enter respiratory metabolism. This metabolic pathway is known as the Krebs cycle. Pyruvate contains three carbon atoms. At steps 11, 15, and 16 of the reaction sequence, these atoms (or their equivalents) are transformed into three molecules of carbon dioxide, which may ultimately be used as raw material for continued photosynthesis. But there is an even more important aspect of the Krebs cycle than this. The Krebs cycle also generates molecules of reduced coenzymes: NADH and $FADH_2$. ($FADH_2$ is the reduced form of a coenzyme derived from the vitamin riboflavin.) Essentially, *respiratory metabolism has been an evolutionary success because the energy stored in reduced coenzymes can be used to generate ATP.*

The Krebs cycle is one of the fundamental pathways that has permitted life on earth to evolve into its current state and by which it continues to exist, and for that reason it is worth a closer look. This does not mean it is necessary to memorize all the names and all the structural formulas for the various compounds that take part in the cycle in order to understand it. Rather, it is possible simply to focus on the atoms involved in the cycle (paying particular attention to the ones depicted in blue and red) and visualize what is happening at each reaction arrow. Trace the carbon atoms that enter the cycle from the pyruvate—are they actually the atoms released at steps 15 and 16? How many turns of the cycle will be required before they are released as carbon dioxide? Looking at the pathway in this manner can give insights into the elegant simplicity that underlies the complex cycle of events.

How Oxidative Phosphorylation Transfers Energy to the Terminal Phosphate of ATP

Whenever NAD functions as a coenzyme in the breakdown and oxidation of glucose (Figure 14.10), it gains a hydrogen ion. More importantly, however, it also gains two electrons from the substrate molecule. These electrons still bear much of the potential energy they gained during photosynthesis. Some of this potential energy can now be released as free energy if these electrons are passed on to some other molecule that has a stronger tendency than NAD to bind such electrons.

The tendency for the electrons to flow from NAD to other electron acceptors of higher electron affinity can even be used to produce an electric voltage, as shown in Figure 14.15. This voltage is proportional to the free energy that would be released if the substances in the two vessels were to undergo direct chemical interaction. Under standardized conditions, 1 volt in such a cell is equal to a standard free energy of about -46 kilocalories per mole of reactants. Therefore, because 1.14 volts are produced by the half-cells shown in Figure 14.15a, we can conclude that if NADH interacted directly with oxygen, a free energy change of -52.4 kilocalories per mole should be obtained ($1.14 \times -46 = -52.4$):

$$NADH + H^+ + \tfrac{1}{2}O_2 \longrightarrow NAD^+ + H_2O$$
$$(\Delta G^{\circ\prime} = -52.4 \text{ kcal/mole})$$

This is a much larger energy change than is usually seen in biological reactions. Hence it should come as no surprise to find that electrons are not passed directly from NADH to oxygen in the living cell. Rather, they are transferred in a series of smaller, intermediate steps by a chain of electron acceptors. The electron-binding strengths of these acceptors span the range from that of NADH to that of oxygen. The potential energy of these electrons is thus released in a series of smaller packets. A simplified version of this electron transport scheme was shown in Figure 14.6. Figure 14.16 gives a more complete list of the electron acceptors, and also shows the change in free energy as electrons are transported through the chain.

In three sections of this electron transport chain (NADH to cytochrome b, cytochrome b to cytochrome c, and cytochrome c to cytochrome a_3), the change in free energy exceeds 10 kilocalories per mole. In each of these sections, the released energy is coupled to the phosphorylation of ADP. How the energy released from the electron during its transport might be coupled to the phosphorylation of ADP is tied intimately to the organization of the components of the respiratory pathways within the mitochondrion.

OXIDATIVE PHOSPHORYLATION REQUIRES THE STRUCTURAL INTEGRITY OF MITOCHONDRIA

At all levels of biological organization, structure and function clearly bear the most intimate interrelationship. In few cases is their essential unity more readily apparent than it is in the case of the mitochondrion. The integrity of mitochondrial structure is essential for the performance of mitochondrial function.

(text continues on page 318)

Figure 14.14 The Krebs cycle, named after Hans Krebs, the biochemist who first described most of it. Atoms about to undergo reaction in each step are depicted in blue; important by-products of the cycle are depicted in red. The position of the two carbon atoms derived from pyruvate are marked by asterisks in the citrate molecule. Because the first product of the cycle is citrate (the ionized form of citric acid), and because citric acid has three carboxylic acid groups, the cycle is sometimes called the citric acid cycle and sometimes the tricarboxylic acid (TCA) cycle.

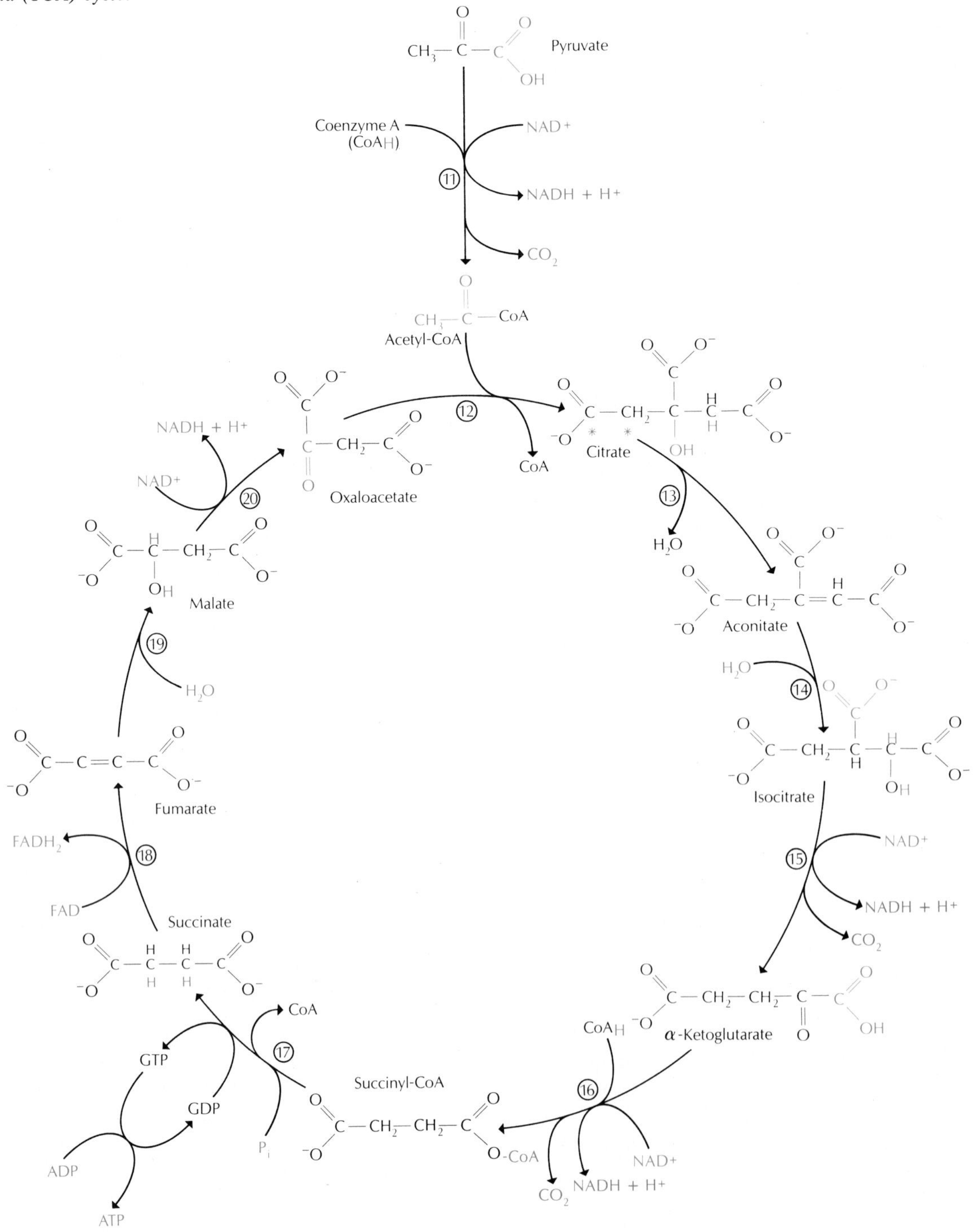

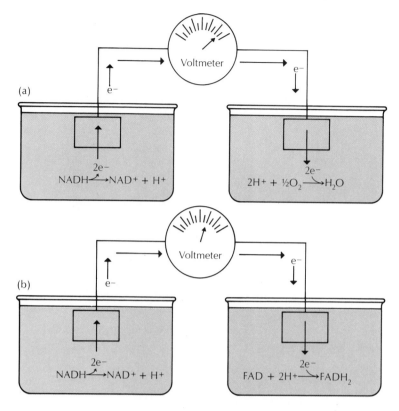

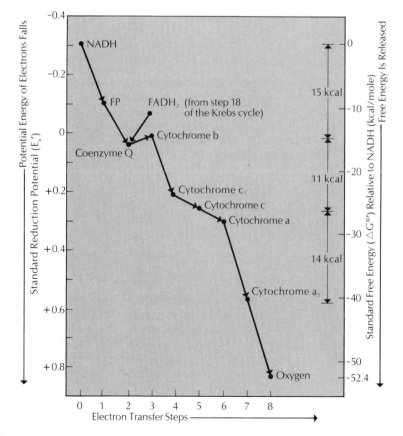

Figure 14.15 A device for measuring the tendency of electrons to flow from one chemical compound to another. Two half-cells are constructed that contain the reactants in question under defined, standardized conditions of concentration, temperature, pH, and so on. Two platinum electrodes are connected by a voltmeter and inserted into the two vessels. If the reactants in one vessel have a weaker affinity for electrons than the reactants in the other, then electrons will tend to flow out of the first solution, through the voltmeter, and into the second vessel, where they will combine with the electron acceptor. The meter will thus indicate not only the direction but also the magnitude of this tendency. The greater the difference in affinity, the greater will be the voltage between the two half-cells. Under standardized conditions, the voltage measured in (a) would be 1.14 volts, and that in (b) would be 0.26 volt.

By convention, the oxidation-reduction potential (the tendency of a molecule to give up or take on an electron) of any substance is given as the voltage produced when that substance is in one half-cell and when the other half-cell contains water and hydrogen gas to give the reaction: $H^+ + e^- \rightleftharpoons \frac{1}{2}H_2$. The voltage produced under such conditions is called the standard reduction potential, or E_o'. The standard reduction potential values of NAD, FAD, and oxygen are -0.32, -0.06, and $+0.82$ volt, respectively.

Figure 14.16 The flow of electrons through the electron transport chain. In each step but one (coenzyme Q → cytochrome b), the receptor binds electrons more strongly than the donor. This difference is reflected by the decreasing negative values or increasing positive values of the standard reduction potential. At each step, then, the electrons release some of their potential energy as free energy.

In each of these sections of the transport scheme, the energy released by the electrons is coupled to the phosphorylation of ADP, forming ATP. Thus, each pair of electrons coming from NADH yields three molecules of ATP, whereas those coming from FADH₂ yield only two molecules of ATP. (Several additional intermediates have now been identified, but they are omitted from this figure for the sake of simplicity. Further research may lead to minor modifications of this scheme without affecting the overall picture.)

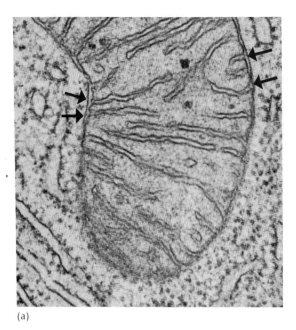

(a)

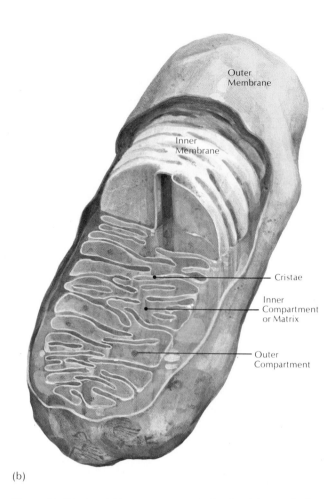

(b)

Figures 14.17 and 14.18 summarize the general features of mitochondrial structure. As you read in Chapter 13, each mitochondrion consists of two compartments formed by two layers of membranes. The inner membrane is folded deeply into cristae.

As indicated in Figure 14.18, the enzymes responsible for the Krebs cycle are dissolved in the fluid, or matrix, of the inner compartment. Thus the reduced coenzymes generated by the Krebs cycle are produced within the matrix. From there they pass their electrons to the proteins of the electron transport chains. The electron acceptors of these chains are firmly embedded in the inner membrane; they are part of its protein mosaic. These electron-accepting proteins are believed to be incorporated within the membrane in a nonrandom way: Each one is positioned between others of higher and lower affinity for electrons, which parallels their functioning in the electron transport chain shown in Figure 14.16. This organization explains the regularity with which electrons pass through the chain. For example, despite the fact that cytochrome a has a much higher affinity for electrons than flavoprotein (FP) does, NADH cannot pass its electrons directly to cytochrome a because the structure of the membrane prohibits NADH and cytochrome a from coming into direct contact. Similarly, each component of the chain can interact only with its two nearest neighbors, accepting electrons from one and passing them to the other.

Intimately associated with the electron transport chain in the membrane are a series of identical enzyme units, called **F₁ enzymes,** that extend through the thickness of the inner membrane and protrude into the matrix. The organization of F₁ enzymes can be demonstrated more clearly when fragments of mitochondria are isolated and treated with negative

Figure 14.17 (above) Gross structure of mitochondria. (a) In this electron micrograph of a section of a mitochondrion, the infolding of the inner membrane to form cristae (see arrows) is clearly visible. (b) This artist's reconstruction depicts the three-dimensional relationships between the component parts of the organelle. The space between inner and outer membranes has been exaggerated for clarity.

Figure 14.18 (right) Details of mitochondrial organization. For the sake of simplicity, some components of the electron transport chain are omitted, and the molecules are not all drawn to the same scale. In addition to the enzymes of the Krebs cycle, the matrix contains mitochondrial DNA, a complete set of the machinery required to synthesize protein (ribosomes, etc.), and enzymes involved in the degradation and synthesis of fatty acids.

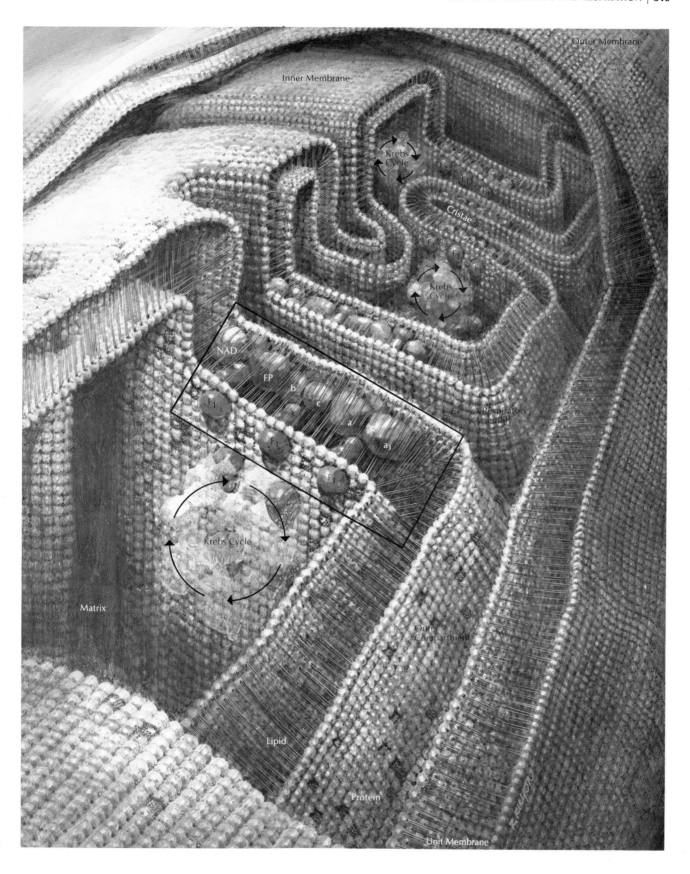

staining. As Figure 14.19 shows, the F_1 enzymes of isolated fragments protrude so much into the matrix that they look like balls on stalks. When they were first observed, each of these stalked spheres was thought to contain all of the components of oxidative phosphorylation. It is now clear that they do not. First of all, they are too small. Second, if they are selectively removed from the membrane fragments, the fragments lose the ability to metabolize ATP by any means but they retain full capacity for electron transport. Thus the F_1 units are now known to be the enzymes that somehow use the energy of electron transport to phosphorylate ADP, thereby producing ATP.

Figure 14.18 depicts the relationship between F_1 enzymes and the electron transport components that is thought to exist in the intact mitochondrion. A complex that contains one of each of the electron carriers and the associated F_1 enzymes is called a **respiratory assembly.** In the intact mitochondrion, the passage of electrons through the electron transport chain (which releases energy from the electrons in a stepwise manner) is coupled to the phosphorylation of ADP by the F_1 enzyme. *Any disruption of the organization of the membrane of a crista leads to a greater or lesser degree of uncoupling of the two processes.* In a tightly coupled mitochondrion, the passage of two electrons from NADH to oxygen results in the formation of three ATP molecules. When partial uncoupling occurs, fewer than three ATP molecules are formed. In a completely uncoupled mitochondrion, electrons flow through the electron transport chain at normal or supernormal rates but absolutely no ATP is produced.

Uncoupling is brought about not only by physical damage but by a variety of chemical substances. One of these substances, a chemical called DNP (dinitrophenol), had a short but flamboyant career as a weight-reducing pill in the 1930s. Because DNP reduced the amount of useful energy (ATP) obtained by the oxidation of foodstuffs, it prevented the accumulation of excess food in the form of fat, and/or it caused the utilization of fat reserves in order to generate enough ATP to maintain life processes. Although its effects on body weight were dramatic, it was, as can readily be imagined, deadly. A moderate overdose led to excessive uncoupling. As a result of the ensuing fatalities, the chemical was quickly removed from the market.

The hormone thyroxin, which is produced by the thyroid gland, also leads to partial uncoupling of oxidation from phosphorylation under some conditions. But it has other effects on mitochondria as well. Thus, it is a matter of controversy whether it is because of an uncoupling action of thyroxin that persons with an overactive thyroid gland tend to have a high rate of respiration and generally are underweight, while those with an underactive thyroid gland

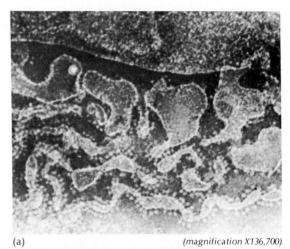

(a)   *(magnification X136,700)*

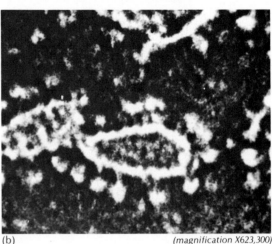

(b)   *(magnification X623,300)*

tend to have a low rate of respiration and generally are overweight.

Because subtle physical damage to the mitochondrion leads to uncoupling, it has been extremely difficult for biochemists to discern the mechanism by which coupling normally occurs. How can a process be dissected into its component steps if the process disappears as soon as dissection begins? *Interleaf 14.2* summarizes three current views of the basis for the coupling of oxidation to phosphorylation; none of the three is as yet universally accepted.

THE INNER MITOCHONDRIAL MEMBRANE ALSO REGULATES MITOCHONDRIAL COMPOSITION

In addition to its role in organizing the enzymes of oxidative phosphorylation, the inner membrane of the mitochondrion plays a crucial role in accumulating and maintaining the intermediates and cofactors taking part in mitochondrial metabolism. It is freely permeable to carbon dioxide and certain substrates, such as pyruvate. But most of the molecules undergoing reaction in the mitochondrion cannot

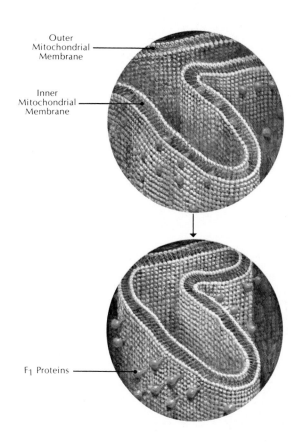

Outer Mitochondrial Membrane

Inner Mitochondrial Membrane

F₁ Proteins

Figure 14.19 The appearance of F_1 protein units on the inner surface of cristae in fragments of mitochondria isolated under conditions where the membranes are distorted. Each F_1 protein unit is now known to be an enzyme capable of generating ATP from ADP by using the energy released during the electron transport process. (a) and (b) are electron micrographs of negatively stained mitochondria membrane fragments. Under these conditions, the F_1 proteins appear as stalked spheres protruding at relatively regular intervals from the inner surface of the inner membrane. (c) This artist's reconstruction of the change in appearance of the F_1 particles as a result of the isolation procedure is based on the appearance of mitochondrial structures in electron micrographs. The upper drawing depicts a region of an intact mitochondrion; the lower drawing depicts an isolated fragment with the F_1 particles protruding from the membrane.

pass the membrane by simple diffusion. For several of these molecules, specific transport proteins exist in the inner membrane that permit **exchange diffusion,** a process in which a particular molecule is permitted to leave the inner compartment only if a "compensating" molecule is available to be simultaneously brought in to take its place.

For example, a molecule of ATP can leave the mitochondrion only if a molecule of ADP is available to take its place; the two are transported simultaneously in opposite directions by a carrier that might be analogous to a revolving door. This ATP-ADP exchange diffusion has two important consequences. First, the total concentration of adenine nucleotide in the mitochondrion is held constant. Second, the rate of ATP release from the mitochondrion is adjusted to meet the demands of the cell. Only when ATP hydrolysis has occurred elsewhere in the cell (forming ADP) will ATP flow out of the mitochondrion. The faster ATP is being used up, the faster it will flow out of the mitochondrion.

Among the other pairs of molecules transported by exchange diffusion are succinate and malate, citrate and malate, and α-ketoglutarate and malate. All four of these compounds are intermediates of the Krebs cycle (Figure 14.14). Each is also used by the cell for other purposes outside the mitochondrion; each can also be formed outside the mitochondrion by a metabolic route other than the Krebs cycle. If the cell finds itself with an excess of one of these four organic acids and a deficiency of another, a trade-off can be effected with the mitochondrion. Because all are interconvertible within the mitochondrion, the total amount of Krebs cycle intermediates within the organelle remains the same. In this way, the mitochondrion satisfies the metabolic needs of the rest of the cell while maintaining its own supply of essential metabolites at optimum levels.

THE KREBS CYCLE IS THE METABOLIC CROSSROADS OF THE CELL

The main function of the Krebs cycle in the cell may well be the respiratory breakdown of sugar molecules, but it is by

(text continues on page 326)

Interleaf 14.2

The Mechanism of Coupling in Oxidative Phosphorylation: Three Views

For more than twenty-five years biochemists (1) have known that phosphorylation of ADP is coupled to electron transport in mitochondria, (2) have been able to study the process in mitochondria free of other cellular components, and (3) have been able to uncouple the two processes at will by either physical or chemical means. Yet despite intensive work, the mechanism of coupling is still unknown. Significant progress has been made in disassembling the process and putting it back together again, but no one has yet recreated oxidative phosphorylation in the absence of a relatively intact inner mitochondrial membrane. Merely having all of the components present is not enough: the components must be properly organized into a functioning structure.

In this frustrating experimental situation, three major models for possible coupling mechanisms have been proposed. These views are called the "chemical coupling," the "chemiosmotic coupling," and the "conformational coupling" hypotheses.

The **chemical coupling hypothesis** is based on the belief that oxidative phosphorylation probably will resemble substrate-level phos-

phorylation. The kinds of reactions that are postulated to occur as electrons pass from NADH to FP are given below. A similar set of reactions is postulated to occur at two subsequent steps in the electron transport chain, with an overall yield of three ATP molecules.

Step 1. The electron carrier about to be reduced (in this case, FP) combines with some unknown intermediate, symbolized by "I":

$$FP + I \longrightarrow FP—I$$

Step 2. As this FP—I complex accepts electrons, it becomes "activated," so the bond to I becomes a high-energy bond:

$$NADH + H^+ + FP—I \longrightarrow$$
$$NAD + H_2FP{\sim}I$$

Step 3. This activated complex now undergoes reaction with a second unknown compound, "X":

$$H_2FP{\sim}I + X \longrightarrow H_2FP + X{\sim}I$$

Step 4. X~I is now split by inorganic phosphate to form a high-energy phosphate bond:

$$X{\sim}I + P_i \longrightarrow X{\sim}P + I$$

Step 5. This high-energy phosphate is now transferred to ADP:

$$X{\sim}P + ADP \longrightarrow X + ADP{\sim}P \ (ATP)$$

Thus the overall reaction is:

$$NADH + H^+ + FP + I + X \\ + P_i + ADP \longrightarrow \\ NAD^+ + H_2FP + I + X + ATP$$

Eliminating reactants that occur on both sides yields:

$$NADH + H^+ + FP + P_i + ADP \longrightarrow \\ NAD^+ + H_2FP + ATP$$

The intermediate I is presumed to be different at each phosphorylation site, whereas X is presumed to be the same for all three. In this hypothesis, uncoupling is viewed as occurring when the X~I complex breaks down without forming a high-energy phosphate bond; uncouplers are thought to accelerate this breakdown. Although the chemical coupling hypothesis can be used to explain most of the known facts about oxidative phosphorylation, it has one severe drawback. Despite intensive searches, neither I nor X has been found. Compound after compound

...sembly and Reassembly Experiments With Mitochondrial Inner Membrane Fragments

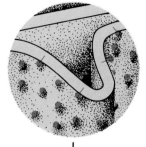

Isolated, Intact Mitochondrion

Disruption With Ultrasound

(spheres are formed from the inner membrane which, under appropriate conditions, are still capable of oxidative phosphorylation)

Extraction Followed by Centrifugation

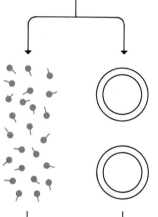

...ble fraction contains ...articles, which can ...TP but not generate it; and also, certain small molecules)

(insoluble fraction contains membrane spheres, which can carry out electron transport but not oxidative phosphorylation)

(recombine under controlled conditions)

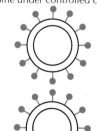

(the F₁ particles reattach to the membrane spheres and capacity for oxidative phosphorylation returns)

has been nominated as one of these intermediates but has been dropped from consideration following critical tests.

Because of the failure to find these intermediates, and because of the repeated observation that an intact mitochondrial membrane is required for phosphorylation of ADP, alternatives have been sought. One hypothesis that had been proposed previously was developed in detail by Philip Henry Mitchell and is now called either the **chemiosmotic coupling hypothesis** or the **Mitchell hypothesis.** This hypothesis begins with recognition that the phosphorylation of ATP is a case of dehydration synthesis:

$$A-O-\overset{\overset{\displaystyle O}{\|}}{\underset{\underset{\displaystyle O^-}{|}}{P}}-O-\overset{\overset{\displaystyle O}{\|}}{\underset{\underset{\displaystyle O^-}{|}}{P}}-OH \;+\; HO-\overset{\overset{\displaystyle O}{\|}}{\underset{\underset{\displaystyle O^-}{|}}{P}}-OH \longrightarrow$$

$$\text{ADP} \qquad + \qquad P_i \qquad \longrightarrow$$

$$A-O-\overset{\overset{\displaystyle O}{\|}}{\underset{\underset{\displaystyle O^-}{|}}{P}}-O-\overset{\overset{\displaystyle O}{\|}}{\underset{\underset{\displaystyle O^-}{|}}{P}}-O-\overset{\overset{\displaystyle O}{\|}}{\underset{\underset{\displaystyle O^-}{|}}{P}}-OH \;+\; H^+ \;+\; OH^-$$

$$\text{ATP} \qquad\qquad + \qquad H_2O$$

$$(\Delta G^{\circ\prime} = +7.3 \text{ kcal/mole})$$

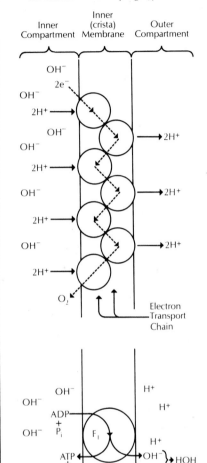

The Chemiosmotic Coupling Hypothesis

As you have read in this chapter, a reaction can move strongly to the right despite a high positive standard free energy change if a way is found to remove rapidly some of the products. Thus, if a way can be found to quickly remove the H^+ and OH^- ions, the reaction should proceed in the direction of ATP synthesis. This, according to the Mitchell hypothesis, is what happens in the mitochondrion:

First, the electron transport chain is arranged asymmetrically in the inner mitochondrial membrane, so that as a pair of electrons flows down the chain, a total of six hydrogen ions are expelled from the inner compartment to the outer compartment.

Second, this expulsion results in a rise in pH (excess of OH^- ions) on the inside and a fall in pH (excess of H^+ ions) on the outside of the inner membrane. The inner membrane is impermeable to these ions, so the gradient is maintained. As a result, there is a rise in the electric potential across the membrane (more positive on the outside and more negative on the inside).

Third, the ATPase is asymmetric in its structure and orientation in the membrane. When it combines ADP and P_i, the organization of the active site is such that the H^+ ion is preferentially released to the inside of the membrane while the OH^- ion is preferentially lost to the outside. Once released in this asymmetric manner, these ions quickly combine with their alternative types on their respective sides, forming neutral water molecules that causes a drop in the pH and potential gradient across the membrane.

Although the Mitchell hypothesis has by no means been proven cor-

rect, the following observations tend to strengthen its credibility. First, there is evidence that the components of the electron transport chain are built into the membrane in an asymmetric (zigzag) manner. NADH and cytochromes a and a_3 appear to be closer to the inner surface of the membrane, whereas cytochromes b and c appear to be closer to the outer surface. Second, the inner membrane is impermeable to hydrogen ions, but substances that uncouple oxidative phosphorylation make it "leaky" to hydrogen ions. Third, an artificially created pH gradient across the membrane results in phosphorylation of ADP in the absence of electron transport. Finally, in the absence of ADP and P_i, the energy of electron transport can be used to pump Ca^{++} ions into the mitochondrion rather than to form ADP. Under these conditions, six Ca^{++} ions enter and six H^+ ions leave the mitochondrion for each pair of electrons that flows from NADH to oxygen. Despite this evidence, the Mitchell hypothesis is not universally accepted primarily because it requires some reshuffling of the order of electron acceptors from that shown in Figure 14.16.

As a result of recent improvements in fixation techniques, it is now clear that mitochondria differ grossly in appearance, depending on whether or not they are actively involved in respiratory metabolism. This has been taken as evidence that the two phenomena are causally related and that the change in conformation of the mitochondrion (more specifically, the change in conformation of the inner or crista membrane) somehow drives the phosphorylation process. (In the presence of uncoupling agents, no change in appearance of the mitochondrion occurs despite rapid electron transport.) This **conformational coupling hypothesis** is less clearly defined, but it states that the flow of electrons leads to an "energized state" of the membrane, which then results in phosphorylation of ADP.

The observed change in shape clearly implies the passage of relatively sizable volumes of water from the inner to the outer compartment during oxidative phosphorylation (resulting in shrinking of the former and swelling of the latter compartments). It is worth noting that the Mitchell hypothesis proposes first the expulsion of hydrogen ions during electron transport, followed by the expulsion of hydroxyl ions during phosphorylation. This results in the expulsion of three water molecules for each NADH molecule oxidized, or a total of fourteen water molecules expelled for each molecule of pyruvate oxidized! This may or may not be adequate to account for the shape changes observed.

The search for I and X goes on, but most biologists doubt that the search will lead anywhere. Whether the mechanism of phosphorylation will ultimately be found to be some fusion of the mechanisms proposed by the chemiosmotic and conformational hypotheses, or some wholly new mechanism, awaits the results of future research.

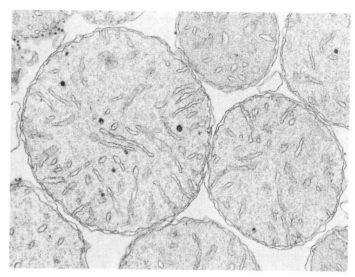

(mitochondrion in the resting state; low level of oxidative phosphorylation)

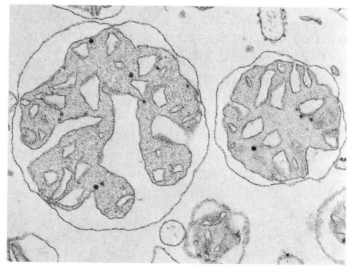

(mitochondrion of same cell under conditions where oxidative phosphorylation is occurring at a rapid rate)

no means its only function. The breakdown of other food molecules (such as fats, nucleic acids, and protein) also results in products that the Krebs cycle metabolizes into carbon dioxide and water to yield ATP by oxidative phosphorylation. But when adequate fatty acids, nucleotides, or amino acids are not available from food to meet the requirements of a cell that is engaged in the production of new lipids, nucleic acids, and protein for cell growth, the cell can generate these building blocks by starting with intermediates of the Krebs cycle (Figure 14.20).

It is in the regulation of these multiple pathways of breakdown and assembly of cell components that the exchange diffusion system of the mitochondrial inner membrane plays such an essential role. If a cell did not have sufficient Krebs cycle intermediates to maintain energy metabolism within the mitochondrion, it would be forced to fall back on the far less efficient process of glycolysis. Thus, before one intermediate of the Krebs cycle can be removed from the mitochondrion for synthesis purposes, a replacement molecule must somehow be generated from another source.

THE REACTIONS OF ENERGY METABOLISM ARE REGULATED TO MATCH THE NEEDS OF A CELL

In every living cell there are thousands of enzymes organized into hundreds of metabolic pathways. In many

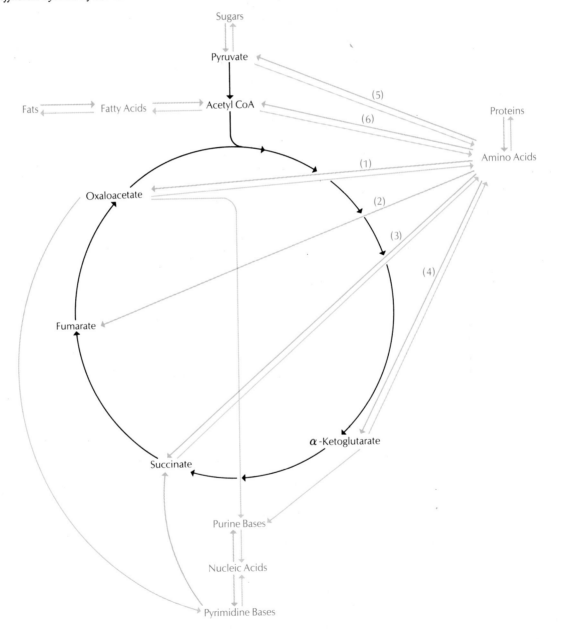

cases, these enzymes carry out opposing reactions: what one enzyme builds up, another enzyme destroys. If all these enzymes were to be functioning at once, utter chaos obviously would result. Direct observation of cells leads to the conclusion that most enzymes are performing well below their capacity most of the time in most cells; in fact, they function at a variable rate that corresponds to variable conditions. This sort of observation has led many to suggest some sort of "wisdom of the cell."

We now know in many cases that this "wisdom" has a simple yet elegant physical-chemical explanation. As a result of the tremendous survival advantage bestowed on a cell that conserves its resources, many enzymes have evolved that possess (in addition to active sites capable of binding and transforming substrates) sites that specifically bind end products of the pathways in which they participate. When such an end product is bound, the shape of the protein is changed so that it no longer binds the substrates as well; hence it functions much more slowly or not at all. This kind of enzyme is called **allosteric** (from the Latin word meaning "other shape"). A more detailed discussion of allosteric enzymes, including the molecular basis for changes in shape and catalytic efficiency, will be given in Chapter 20. For this discussion, the point to consider is merely the role such enzymes play in regulating glycolysis and respiration to match the varying needs of the cell.

Return for a moment to the Embden-Meyerhof pathway of glycolysis (Figure 14.7). Of the ten reactions involved in this pathway, the slowest is usually at step 3. Thus reaction 3, the phosphorylation of fructose-6-phosphate by the enzyme phosphofructokinase (PFKase), is said to be the **rate-limiting reaction.** Glucose cannot be converted to pyruvate at a rate faster than the rate at which PFKase carries out its reaction. Phosphofructokinase is an allosteric

Figure 14.20 The relationship between the Krebs cycle and sugar, protein, fat, and nucleic acid metabolism. The red arrows indicate breakdown reactions in which these substances are oxidized to yield, ultimately, ATP. The blue arrows indicate the synthetic reactions in which new building blocks are produced for cell growth.

The eighteen amino acids commonly found in protein are broken down by a variety of different routes. The numbers in parentheses beside the arrows in the figure indicate how many of the eighteen amino acids break down to give each of the products indicated. Some yield more than one breakdown product, and that is why the numbers do not total eighteen. This diagram clearly shows that the Krebs cycle plays a central role in the cell, regulating the flow of material between processes that tear down molecules and processes that synthesize new molecules.

enzyme. In addition to the active site that binds fructose-6-phosphate and ATP, it has a **control site** that binds either ATP or ADP (but not both at once). When ADP is bound at the control site, the enzyme is fully active, but when ATP is bound the enzyme changes shape and becomes relatively inactive; it is unable to phosphorylate fructose-6-phosphate. What this means is that the enzyme oscillates between two forms:

$$\text{Active PFKase} \underset{\text{ADP}}{\overset{\text{ATP}}{\rightleftharpoons}} \text{Inactive PFKase}$$

The probability that the control site will be occupied by ADP or ATP at any instant (hence the probability that the enzyme will be active) is a function of the relative concentrations of ADP and ATP. Therefore, if the cell is in a resting state in which ATP is not being rapidly split, the ATP/ADP ratio will be high, ATP will be bound to the control site of PFKase, the enzyme will be quite inactive, and glycolysis will proceed very slowly. If a sudden burst of activity occurs (for example, if a muscle cell contracts), ATP will be split to form ADP to power the cellular event. Thus the ATP/ADP ratio will quickly fall, ATP will be replaced by ADP in the control site of PFKase, the enzyme will become active, and glycolysis will accelerate, producing new ATP. Once the ATP/ADP ratio has been restored to resting levels, PFKase (and, consequently, glycolysis) will be shut off once more.

This homeostatic process, by which an ultimate product of a lengthy metabolic pathway regulates the rate of functioning of the pathway, is called the **feedback regulation.** It is analogous to the thermostat of a furnace, through which the heat produced by the furnace controls its own production.

PFKase is not the only enzyme of energy metabolism involved in feedback regulation, although it is the most important one in the Embden-Meyerhof glycolysis pathway. An enzyme of the Krebs cycle that is feedback regulated in some cells is isocitrate dehydrogenase, which catalyzes step 15 shown in Figure 14.14. Isocitrate dehydrogenase exists in two forms: a highly active **dimeric form** (in which two enzyme molecules are bound together) and a **monomeric form** (single-enzyme molecules). The monomers possess far less than half the catalytic activity of the dimers. The monomer-dimer interconversion is mediated by allosteric interactions with four small molecules: ATP, ADP, NADH and NAD$^+$:

$$\underset{\substack{\text{Two Monomers of} \\ \text{Isocitrate Dehydrogenase} \\ \text{(low activity)}}}{\bigcirc \; \bigcirc} \quad \underset{\text{ATP + NADH}}{\overset{\text{ADP + NAD}^+}{\rightleftharpoons}} \quad \underset{\substack{\text{One Dimer} \\ \text{(high activity)}}}{\bigcirc\!\bigcirc}$$

Because the Krebs cycle functions to cause the direct conversion of NAD[+] to NADH and the indirect conversion of ADP to ATP, this regulation obviously is of adaptive significance to the cell. When the ratio of ATP/ADP or NADH/NAD[+] is high, isocitrate dehydrogenase will fall apart into inactive monomers and the entire Krebs cycle will slow down. But a lowering of either ratio will trigger renewed Krebs cycle activity: the dimer will tend to re-form, and increased production of NADH and ATP will result.

ENERGY CHARGE DETERMINES THE ACTIVITY OF ATP-USING AND ATP-GENERATING REACTIONS

All of the relationships just discussed plus a variety of similar ones have been summarized by the biochemist D. E. Atkinson in a useful concept known as **energy charge.** In this concept, each cell is visualized as having a charge of chemical energy readily available for doing cellular work. Because this charge is stored primarily in the form of high-energy phosphate bonds, the state of energy charge of the cell can be expressed as the fraction of the total adenine nucleotides in the cell that are in the form of ATP plus ADP (as opposed to AMP). The relationship is given by:

$$\text{Energy Charge} = \frac{1}{2} \left(\frac{2[\text{ATP}] + [\text{ADP}]}{[\text{ATP}] + [\text{ADP}] + [\text{AMP}]} \right)$$

If all the adenine nucleotide were present as ATP, the charge would be equal to 1.0; if it were all present as AMP, the charge would be equal to 0.

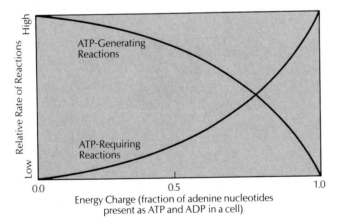

Figure 14.21 The energy charge concept. As the fraction of cellular adenine that is present as triphosphate falls, ATP-generating reactions become capable of running at higher rates. The ATP-requiring reactions run at lower rates. These tendencies cause the cell to maintain a relatively constant level of ATP (near the crossover point for the two lines in this figure) despite large changes in the rate at which energy is being used.

Now, the important aspect of the energy charge concept is that not only do ATP-utilizing and ATP-generating reactions affect the energy charge of the cell, they are affected by it. The lower the energy charge, the more rapidly ATP-generating reactions will occur and the more slowly ATP-requiring reactions will occur. As the energy charge of the cell rises, this relationship reverses, as shown in Figure 14.21. The conclusion from feedback-regulation studies is that most cells exist most of the time poised at or near the crossover point depicted in the graph in Figure 14.21. Should the energy charge of the cell temporarily move some distance from the crossover point due to some transient event, the shape of the curves is such that the cell will be brought back quickly to the balance point. In other words, because of an extensive network of feedback loops and circuits, most cells maintain a relatively constant energy charge at all times despite huge fluctuations in the rate of ATP production and use.

PERSPECTIVE

Early in the history of life on earth, heterotrophic organisms flourished in the prevailing oxygen-free environment, feeding somewhat inefficiently on the supply of organic nutrients that had been formed in the primordial seas. Eventually there came a time when this burgeoning biomass began to have severe effects on the surroundings, for nutrients were being used up rapidly and waste products were building up. Had heterotrophs continued alone on this course of environmental exploitation, life would have long ago become an experiment that failed.

But through random variation coupled with natural selection, organisms arose that were capable of generating new organic substrates by photosynthesis, releasing oxygen in the process and changing the nature of the atmosphere. This set the stage for the appearance of a third metabolic approach to life: the use of oxygen to extract additional energy from the products of photosynthesis. Because of the chemical interdependence of these ways of life, the various organisms that evolved managed to achieve dynamic equilibrium with one another. This equilibrium is still maintained today in what is known as the carbon cycle—in the flow of carbon atoms through different organisms in a continuous cycle of energy extraction, energy utilization, and the formation of new organic molecules.

There are three major stages in the carbon cycle. In *photosynthesis*, organisms trap light energy from the sun and use it to convert carbon dioxide and water molecules into energy-rich organic compounds, such as sugar molecules. Oxygen molecules are given off in the process. When these photosynthetic products are used as foodstuffs, the energy they have stored within them is extracted first in *glycolysis*, whereby each sugar molecule is split into small organic acid molecules accompanied by the production of two ATP molecules, which can be used to do cellular work. Glycolysis takes place in the cytoplasm. In *respiration*, the energy remaining in these small organic acid molecules is extracted in mitochondria; the oxygen produced by photosynthesis is used as an essential reactant. Carbon dioxide is released as a by-product—thereby providing one of the raw materials for photosynthetic organisms, which are able to begin the cycle anew.

The metabolic pathways that have evolved to achieve this dynamic equilibrium appear to be complex, but they are truly quite simple. In the pathways discussed in this chapter, only about thirty catalyzed reactions are involved. In the glycolytic pathway, each sugar molecule is split in half and the cell gains two molecules of ATP. The end products of glycolysis become the raw materials of respiration in the pathways known as the Krebs cycle and oxidative phosphorylation. In the Krebs cycle, energy is released in the form of electrons, which are used to reduce coenzymes (principally NAD^+). In oxidative phosphorylation, the reduced coenzymes pass their electrons to an assembly of electron acceptors called the electron transport chain. As electrons travel down this transport chain, the energy they release is coupled to the phosphorylation of more ADP. Under conditions where respiration follows glycolysis, 38 ATP molecules are produced for each sugar molecule that is metabolized. Thus glycolysis plus respiration yields nineteen times the useful energy yielded by glycolysis alone. The processes of respiration are dramatic examples of the interrelatedness of structure and function in living systems: If the structure of the mitochondrion is perturbed, its function is lost.

The Krebs cycle not only participates in energy release, it also is the hub of the overall metabolism of the cell. Through the Krebs cycle, the interconversion of proteins, nucleic acids, fats, and carbohydrates occurs. Yet the properties of the mitochondrial membrane assure that the mitochondrion always maintains a full supply of the Krebs cycle intermediates required to meet its first priority—which is to satisfy the energy needs of the cell.

All these processes are regulated and controlled by elegant yet simple feedback loops in which the products of energy metabolism control their own rates of production by shutting off the activity of key enzymes involved in their production. As a result, most cells maintain a full charge of energy (in the form of ATP) at all times, regardless of the level at which such energy is being used. In this way, cells are always poised for rapid response to changes in environmental conditions but are not unnecessarily degrading foodstuffs when conditions do not demand it.

Millions of years went into the evolution and refinement of all these stages of the carbon cycle. And it was not a deliberate sense of direction on the part of the first organisms that brought all of it about. Those organisms could not gather together and discuss, as we discuss, an impending curtain of pollutants in the air or a dangerous volume of the by-products of existence being dumped into the seas. Selection went to work on the first surge of life because conditions changed: By chance, organisms arose that were capable of responding differently, and by selection their success was assured.

But equilibrium is a tenuous thing, and with the passing of time selection has not become subordinate to the needs of any organism—including ourselves—despite the illusion conjured up by our agricultural machinations and other cultural inventions. We cannot be lulled into thinking that we have risen above dependency on the various links in the carbon cycle. When we unwittingly upset the chemical balance of our surroundings—by polluting the oceans, for example, thereby endangering that thin surface layer of photosynthetic marine organisms that are major participants in the carbon cycle—we are gambling with evolutionary success. If this chapter tells us anything at all, it is that the intricate and interconnected pathways of energy procurement and extraction by living organisms are not merely a pedagogical abstraction. They are an experiment in survival, worked out over eons of time and as vulnerable today as they have been through all times past.

SUGGESTED READINGS

DYSON, ROBERT D. *Cell Biology: A Molecular Approach.* Boston: Allyn & Bacon, 1974. The discussion of mitochondrial function in Part I is admirably integrated with that of chloroplast function, making the reference appropriate to both this and the next chapter.

GREEN, D. E., and J. H. YOUNG. "Energy Transduction in Membrane Systems," *American Scientist,* 59 (1971), 92. An engaging look at the questions of electron transport and phosphorylation from an eminent and provocative worker in the area.

KREBS, H. A. "The History of the Tricarboxylic Acid Cycle," *Perspectives in Biology and Medicine,* 14 (1970), 154. Recommended for a well-written firsthand account of the elucidation of a major metabolic pathway, by a grand old master of science.

KREBS, H. A. "The Citric Acid Cycle," and Lipmann, F., "Development of the Acetylation Problem: A Personal Account," in *Nobel Lectures, Physiology or Medicine,* 1942–62. Amsterdam: Elsevier, 1964. Firsthand accounts of Krebs' and Lipmann's contributions to respiratory metabolism, as told in their Nobel Prize lectures of 1953.

VAN NIEL, C. B. "Lipmann's Concept of the Metabolic Generation and Utilization of Phosphate Bond Energy: A Historical Appreciation," in N. O. Kaplan and E. P. Kennedy (eds.), *Current Aspects of Biochemical Energetics.* New York: Academic Press, 1966, p. 9. The original formulation of high-energy phosphate bonds.

Chapter 15

Photosynthesis

In the waters of the earth, on the plains, the deserts, the mountain ranges—wherever there is sufficient water and air and light there also are the photosynthetic organisms, clinging tenaciously to their place in the sun. It is with no casual interest that we wish them success: each of these organisms, large and small, uses light energy from the sun to transform carbon dioxide and water into sugar and oxygen. Each year they collectively produce more than 150 billion tons of sugar molecules on which we and every other living thing directly or indirectly feed.

Every cell, every tissue, every organism depends, ultimately, on the flow of light energy from the sun. This energy is first trapped by photosynthetic organisms—primarily plants—where it is converted to useful chemical energy for cellular work. These organisms use some of the chemical energy immediately for cell maintenance and growth. They also store some of it in the form of sugar molecules. In that act of storage they create a stable energy source, which is tapped by animals that feed on the photosynthesizers—and on one another in chains of predator and prey. Even the monerans and the fungi tap into this energy flow, feeding as they do on the waste products and remains of plants and animals. So stable is this form of energy that it can be stored over eons of time and still be used, as we use coal and oil—reservoirs of energy derived photosynthetically millions of years ago.

AN OVERVIEW OF PHOTOSYNTHESIS

As you have read in earlier chapters, the process of photosynthesis involves the use of light energy to convert carbon dioxide and water into sugar and other organic compounds. Often this process is summarized by the formula:

$$6CO_2 + 6H_2O \xrightarrow[\text{chlorophyll}]{\text{light}} C_6H_{12}O_6 + 6O_2$$

Now, this formula suggests that light somehow causes a direct reaction between CO_2 and H_2O. *This is not the case.* As first recognized by the biochemist Robert Hill, under certain experimental conditions the overall process can be shown to occur in two stages of reactions. In one stage, water is split to yield hydrogen ions, oxygen gas, and two electrons. Hill's experiments showed that, as long as some substance is provided to accept the released electrons, then the splitting of water will occur continuously in the light—even if carbon dioxide is not present!

Because the splitting of water is driven by light energy, the first stage of photosynthesis is called the *light reactions of photosynthesis.* The products of the light reactions are then used to produce sugar from carbon dioxide. Because these reactions do not involve the direct participation of light, they are called the *dark reactions of photosynthesis.* Details of the dark reactions most commonly used to "fix" carbon dioxide (convert it from the free gas into a solid organic compound) and produce sugar were provided largely by the work of Melvin Calvin, Andrew Benson, and their associates. Thus, these reactions are now referred to as the Calvin-Benson cycle.

In the light reactions, electrons derived from water are "excited" (raised to higher energy levels) in two steps, called photosystems I and II. In both steps, the green pigment substance chlorophyll is the agent that absorbs light energy and uses it to excite the electrons. At the end of the first step, the excited electrons pass down an electron transport chain containing cytochrome molecules similar to the ones taking part in respiration (Chapter 14). As the electrons pass down this chain, they give up part of the energy they have just gained from sunlight. The energy they lose is used to generate adenosine triphosphate (ATP) in a manner analogous to the production of ATP in mitochondria. *ATP is one of two important products of the light reactions.*

In the second step of the light reactions, the electrons are excited further—to still higher energy levels—by chlorophyll and sunlight. Once again these electrons enter an electron transport chain and lose part of their newly gained energy. This time, however, ATP is not generated. Instead the electrons are united, at the end of the transport chain, with the coenzyme nicotinamide adenine dinucleotide phosphate (NADP$^+$). The outcome is the reduced coenzyme NADPH. *The reduced coenzyme NADPH is the second important product of the light reaction.*

In the Calvin-Benson cycle of dark reactions, the ATP and NADPH produced by the light reactions are used to produce sugar from carbon dioxide. In a cycle made up of about twenty different reactions, sugar (glucose) is produced, and all of the reactants other than ATP and NADPH are regenerated, ready to "fix" more CO_2.

Let us go back now to the details of the photosynthetic process, beginning with the organization of the organelle in which photosynthesis occurs.

CHLOROPLASTS RESEMBLE MITOCHONDRIA IN FORM AND FUNCTION

All eukaryotic organisms (including the photosynthesizers) contain mitochondria, the structures in which respiration occurs. But only photosynthetic organisms contain **chloroplasts**—the complex, membrane-rich structures in which the highly ordered chemical interactions of photosynthesis take place. In outward appearance, at least, chloroplasts seem to be as diverse as cells. A single cup-shaped chloroplast occupies nearly half the volume of some flagellated, unicellular organisms. Long, helical ribbons of chloroplast twist through certain filamentous algae. The chloroplasts in many algae assume such elaborate shapes as stars and perforated sheets. Dozens of small, football-shaped chloroplasts may be found in a single cell of a flowering plant. But such differences are superficial: internally, all chloroplasts are organized to function in essentially the same way. Their basic organization is illustrated in Figures 15.2 through 15.5.

Like the mitochondrion, the chloroplast is always bounded by a double layer of membrane, and the inner

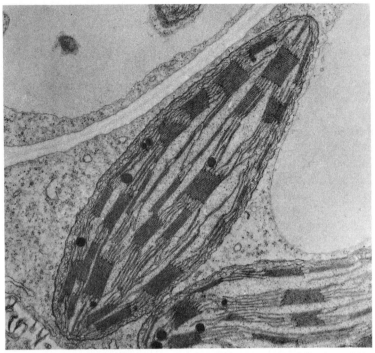

(a)

(magnification x 40,000)

Figure 15.2 (a) Electron micrograph and (b) corresponding diagram of a chloroplast in cross section. Notice that the stroma membranes are continuous with the thylakoid disks. (c) The stroma contains dissolved salts, enzymes, ribosomes involved in chloroplast protein synthesis, the chloroplast DNA, and the more widely spaced stroma membranes.

Aside from obvious similarities in membrane structure, chloroplasts resemble mitochondria in having a complete genetic system that is separate and unique from the nuclear genetic system of the cells in which they occur. The complete roles of these organellar genetic systems are not yet known in detail, but it is clear that the construction of a chloroplast requires the cooperation and dovetailing of operations of the nuclear-cytoplasmic genetic system with the genetic system of the organelle.

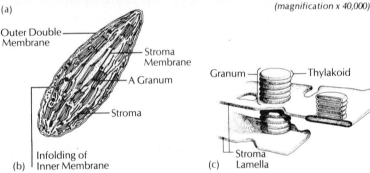

Outer Double Membrane

Stroma Membrane

A Granum

Stroma

Infolding of Inner Membrane

(b)

Granum — Thylakoid

Stroma Lamella

(c)

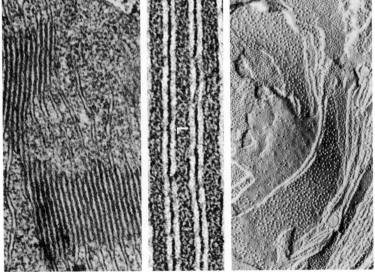

(magnification x 58,000)   (magnification x 310,500)   (magnification x 38,500)

Figure 15.3 A cross section of the chloroplast at higher magnification, showing the way that stroma membranes fold and stack to form the many thylakoid disks of a single granum.

Figure 15.4 A cross section of a granum at still higher magnification, showing the regular, ordered structure of the thylakoid disks.

Figure 15.5 An electron micrograph of a freeze-cleaved and etched granum. Starting at lower left, the plane of cleavage has passed through successively deeper membranes. The larger granules exposed by certain fracture planes are thought to be the quantosomes—the organized pigments and enzymes of the photosynthetic reactions. Other granules are thought to include the electron transport assemblies involved in photosynthetic phosphorylation.

membrane is always infolded into the complex matrix of the chloroplast body, called the **stroma.** However, the folds of the chloroplast inner membrane are much more complex than the relatively simple folds of the mitochondrial cristae. The primary infoldings are known as **stroma membranes.** In certain regions these membranes fold back on themselves, producing a parallel array of flattened sacs that looks like a stack of coins. Such a folded and stacked structure is called a **granum;** it is connected to other grana in the chloroplast by the stroma membranes. (Flattened membranous sacs in parallel arrangement are called **lamellae,** not only in the chloroplast but wherever they occur. Hence, the chloroplast contains two distinct kinds of lamellae: stroma lamellae and grana lamellae.)

A single sac of a granum, together with the material it encloses, is called a **thylakoid disk.** The material within a thylakoid disk contains the pigment molecules, enzymes, and electron carriers that are involved in trapping and using light energy. How these components are arranged is not known with any certainty, but freeze-cleavage studies would seem to support the suggestion that the pigments and enzymes are organized in the grana membranes into compact structural entities called **quantosomes** (Figure 15.5). Even though dissection of chloroplasts and analysis of their

membranous structures is proceeding on several fronts, understanding of their detailed organization is far from complete. What is clear is that, like mitochondria, normal chloroplast functioning depends on the structural integrity of its complex membranes.

CHLOROPHYLL IS THE PRIMARY ENERGY CONVERTER OF THE CHLOROPLAST

Within the internal membrane systems of the chloroplast there may be more than one kind of **pigment** (a substance capable of absorbing light). But as Figure 15.6 indicates, in the energy conversions of photosynthesis the green pigment **chlorophyll** is the most important of them. Like all pigments, chlorophyll appears to be a certain color because it absorbs only certain wavelengths of light, and either transmits or reflects others. To see why it does this, we must first consider the nature of light itself.

All light travels in vibrating packets of energy called **photons** (after the Greek *photo-,* meaning "light"). The different colors of the visible spectrum exist because the vibrations of each kind of photon have a characteristic spacing, or **wavelength,** as they travel through space. The shorter the wavelength, the more rapid the vibration. Depending on the structure of the atoms and molecules that

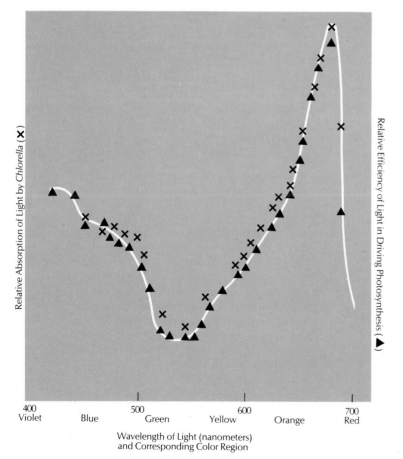

Figure 15.6 Comparison of the absorption spectrum and the action spectrum for the unicellular alga Chlorella. *The photosynthetic efficiency of light of different wavelengths (action spectrum) exactly parallels the relative absorption of light of those wavelengths (absorption spectrum) by the alga. Because the absorption spectrum for this organism can be shown to be due principally to the chlorophyll within it, this comparison strongly suggests that chlorophyll plays a key role in photosynthesis.*

happen to intercept photons of light, these vibrations may cause certain energetic interactions between the photons and the molecules. If the electrons of a molecule are appropriately organized, they may be capable of absorbing the vibrational energy of photons of particular wavelengths. The energy so gained by the electrons is known as **excitation energy,** for the electrons are now at a more energetic (or excited) state.

Now, a chlorophyll molecule has a complex, multiple ring structure with many alternating single and double bonds (Figure 15.7). Because of these alternating bonds, the electrons of its atoms are free to move rapidly back and forth *(resonate)* between adjacent atoms of the ring structure. When light of certain wavelengths strikes a chlorophyll molecule, it causes the electrons to resonate more rapidly. Because the photons of red and blue light are particularly effective in exciting these electrons, red and blue light are readily absorbed by chlorophyll molecules. (Photons of green light are not effective in exciting electrons of chlorophyll; as a result, they are reflected by the chlorophyll molecules. That is why leaves look green to us.) Once a chlorophyll molecule absorbs this light energy, its electrons begin to oscillate more rapidly. This excitation energy can now be passed from molecule to molecule of chlorophyll because of the way they are packed together in the thylakoid disks.

The most common form of chlorophyll is called **chlorophyll *a*** (Figure 15.7). When it is purified and dissolved in an appropriate solvent in a test tube, it readily absorbs light of a wavelength of 663 nanometers (red-orange light). When these same molecules are present in chloroplasts, however, their absorption properties are not the same. The reason is that *other* molecules in the chloroplast membranes interact with chlorophyll *a* molecules and modify their electronic structure to the degree that most of the molecules become more efficient in absorbing light of wavelengths ranging from 670 to 680 nanometers. In other words, their absorption peaks are shifted toward the red end of the spectrum.

The details of the observed spectral changes vary both within a single plant and between plants. But in all cases, refined chemical and spectral analyses reveal the existence of two very specialized forms of chlorophyll *a*. The absorption peaks of these forms are shifted more than those of the chlorophyll molecules around them. One of these forms has been known for some time. Its absorption peak lies at a wavelength of 700 nanometers, hence its name **P700.** The other form was identified more recently. Its absorption peak occurs at a wavelength of 680 nanometers, and it is called **P680.** It is not because of inherent structural differences that P680 and P700 are unique; both are molecules of chlorophyll *a*. Their uniqueness derives from their association with particular nonchlorophyll molecules

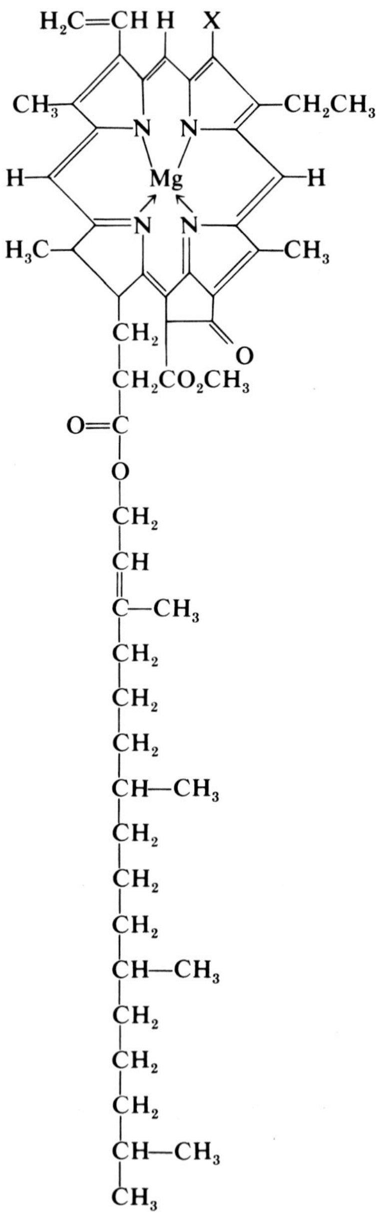

Figure 15.7 The generalized structural formula of chlorophyll. Most photosynthetic cells contain two chemical forms of chlorophyll. One form, chlorophyll a, is always present in all cells except photosynthetic bacterial cells. In this form, the X in the formula represents a methyl (—CH₃) group. In higher plants, chlorophyll b is also present. This form has a —CHO group at the X position. In various algae, diatoms, and other organisms, chlorophyll b is replaced by one of the related compounds chlorophyll c or d. Photosynthetic bacteria possess none of these forms. Instead they have their own variant of chlorophyll a, known as bacteriochlorophyll, which is probably the most primitive of the existing chlorophyll molecules.

(a)

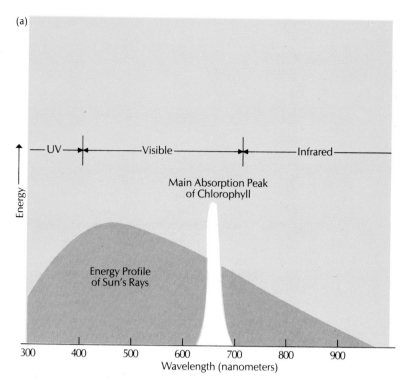

Figure 15.8 The role of accessory pigments in increasing photosynthetic efficiency. As shown in (a), the main absorption peak of chlorophyll traps only a small portion of the energy reaching the earth in the form of sunlight. In many plants, accessory pigments that are intimately associated with chlorophyll absorb other wavelengths of light. The absorption spectra of two kinds of accessory pigments are compared with the spectrum for chlorophyll in (b). These two pigments differ structurally from chlorophyll, but they resemble it in having a complex system of alternating single and double bonds between atoms. It is believed that they pass on to adjacent chlorophyll molecules the excitation energy they gain from the capture of light energy.

(b)

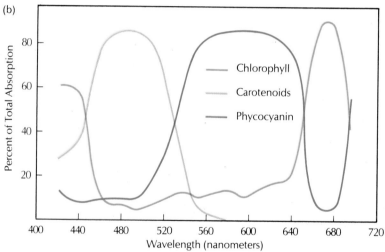

in the thylakoid disks. P680 and P700 make up less than 1 percent of the chlorophyll but they play a crucial role in photosynthesis: *Although all chlorophyll molecules can absorb light energy and thereby raise the energy levels of their electrons, only P680 and P700 can release excited electrons to react with nonchlorophyll electron acceptors.*

It is now believed that, with the exception of P680 and P700, all the chlorophyll molecules in the chloroplast act like antennas—absorbing light energy, becoming excited, transferring their excitation energy to their nearest neighbors, which pass it on in their turn until that energy eventually reaches a so-called reaction center, in which a P680 or P700 molecule is located. As Figure 15.8 indicates, in some plant cells other pigment molecules also participate in this antennalike behavior. These accessory pigments include the orange **carotenoids,** the blue **phycocyanins,** and the red **phycoerythrins.** They absorb light of wavelengths that chlorophyll does not absorb and they pass their excitation energy on to neighboring chlorophyll molecules.

THE ENERGY CONVERSIONS TRIGGERED BY LIGHT ENERGY PRODUCE ATP AND NADH

The principal organic products of photosynthesis are sugar molecules:

$$6CO_2 + 12H_2O + \text{light} \longrightarrow C_6H_{12}O_6 + 6H_2O + 6O_2$$

This simple scheme does not call attention to the most important thing that is going on: *Light energy activates electrons in the chlorophyll molecules and those electrons, originally gained from the oxygen atoms of water, are passed to the carbon atom of carbon dioxide.* In other words, in photosynthesis oxygen atoms are oxidized and carbon atoms are reduced. How the electron transfer occurs can be seen more clearly by examining what is happening on either side of the reaction arrow in the above formula. First, consider what happens to a pair of water molecules that serve as starting substances:

$$2H^+O^=H^+ \longrightarrow 4H^+ + O_2° + 4e^-$$

Each of the two oxygen atoms, which starts out with a valence of −2 (symbolized by $O^=$), loses two electrons to form gaseous oxygen, with a valence of zero ($O_2°$). On the other side of the reaction arrow, these four electrons ultimately are passed on to the carbon atom of a carbon dioxide molecule, which thereby acquires the ability to react with two of the hydrogen ions (H^+). The remaining hydrogen ions react with the displaced oxygen atom of the carbon dioxide to form a *new* molecule of water. Thus,

$$CO_2 + 4e^- + 4H^+ \longrightarrow (CH_2O) + H_2O$$

Now, this flow of electrons from oxygen to carbon atoms runs counter to their natural tendency, because the oxygen atoms have a much higher affinity for electrons than carbon atoms do. If we could construct a battery in which these two parts of the reaction occurred in two half-cells (as discussed in Figure 14.15), we would find that the electrons tend to flow from carbon to oxygen with a considerable release of energy. In fact, the energy released when electrons flow from carbon to oxygen is the energy used to produce ATP in respiration, as discussed in Chapter 14.

In order to reverse the flow of electrons, energy must be supplied to drive the electrons "uphill." To phrase this

differently: Because oxygen has a relatively high affinity for electrons, electrons bound to oxygen are in a relatively stable, low-energy state. The carbon atom of carbon dioxide will not combine with electrons unless they have a relatively high energy content. Therefore, energy must be used to raise the electrons removed from oxygen to the energy level at which they will combine with the carbon atoms.

The energy of one photon is not enough to make an electron react with carbon dioxide. Each electron removed from water must be excited twice in order to be raised to an energy level sufficient for reaction. These two steps take place in two chlorophyll-laden complexes called **photosystem II** and **photosystem I.** (These systems were named in the order of their discovery. Unfortunately, this is not the order in which they function.) The initiation of both of these steps depends on light energy from the sun; hence they are called the **light reactions.** As Figure 15.9 shows, each photosystem involves a special set of pigment molecules and special electron acceptors (called "Q" and "Z" at the time they were first identified because no one knew exactly what they were). Each set of components appears to be grouped in the membranes of the chloroplast in a highly organized unit.

Recent fractionation studies of chloroplasts tend to support the idea that the photosynthetic pigments occur in tightly clustered units of interacting molecules. If chloroplasts isolated from leaves are treated with certain detergents, their membranes dissolve partially, freeing (but leaving intact) the complexes of pigments and other molecules that normally occur together in their membranes. In a centrifuge (*Interleaf 17.1*), two *different* chlorophyll-bearing complexes can be isolated from such preparations. One complex contains 1 molecule of the chlorophyll P680, about 200 other molecules of chlorophyll *a,* and about 50 molecules of carotenoid pigments; it corresponds to photosystem II. The other complex contains 1 molecule of the chlorophyll P700, about 200 other molecules of chlorophyll *a,* and roughly an equal number of molecules of chlorophyll *b;* it corresponds to photosystem I. These pigment-containing complexes are thought to be organized in the granules called quantosomes (Figure 15.5). Further analysis of such pigment complexes may lead to increased understanding of the organization and functioning of these all-important structures.

How Electrons Excited in Photosystem II Are Derived From Water and Used to Generate ATP

When the chlorophyll and carotenoid molecules of photosystem II absorb light, their electrons become excited. The excitation energy is passed from molecule to molecule by a complex process thought to be analogous to the flow of

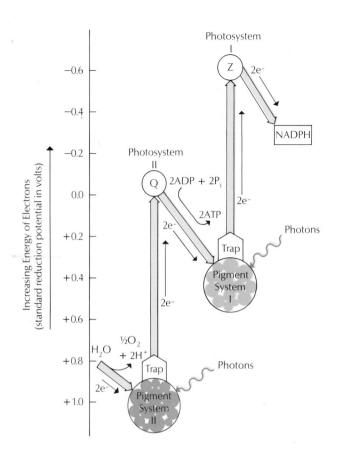

Increasing Energy of Electrons
(standard reduction potential in volts)

−0.6
−0.4
−0.2
0.0
+0.2
+0.4
+0.6
+0.8
+1.0

Photosystem
I

Z   2e⁻

NADPH

Photosystem
II

Q   2ADP + 2P$_i$

2ATP

2e⁻

Trap

Pigment
System
I

Photons

2e⁻

2e⁻

H$_2$O

½O$_2$
+ 2H⁺

Trap

Photons

2e⁻

Pigment
System
II

Figure 15.9 The two-stage process in photosynthesis whereby light energy is used to raise the energy level of electrons removed from water molecules. Each stage has its own special set of pigment molecules (pigment system II and pigment system I respectively) and its own special electron acceptors (Q and Z respectively). As indicated in this figure, electrons are probably passed through these two stages two at a time. Thus, electrons first pass through photosystem II and then pass through photosystem I.

The description of the major chemical events associated with these light-dependent reactions came from D.I. Arnon and his associates. In their research, they demonstrated that illumination of a suspension of isolated chloroplasts results in the formation of ATP from ADP and inorganic phosphates.

energy in certain semiconductors found in transistor radios. This energy arrives almost instantaneously at a reaction center, where it is absorbed by the P680 chlorophyll. If a P680 molecule becomes sufficiently excited, one of its electrons gains enough energy to leave the molecule completely. Once it is released it is passed to the electron acceptor molecule designated Q in Figure 15.9. The loss of an electron leaves a vacancy in the P680 molecule. This vacancy is filled by an electron removed from water.

Electrons are removed from water by a manganese-requiring enzymatic process known as **photolysis** (splitting by light). P680 is known to be the ultimate acceptor of electrons released from the water in this process. But the actual process by which electrons are removed from water molecules—one of the most important steps in photosynthesis—has until recently been shrouded in mystery. However, recent work by Bessel Kok and Pierre Joliot has shown that the splitting of water and the production of oxygen are intimately coupled to the activation of the chlorophyll electrons by light. The enzyme has four possible states of electric charge. As each photon enters photosystem II, an electron is lost from P680 and is replaced by an electron from the enzyme, raising it to a different state. When four charges have been transferred from the enzyme to the

reaction center, the enzyme reaches its catalytically active state. Water is split, oxygen is produced, and four electrons are released to replace the charges previously removed from the enzyme. The enzyme returns to the inactive state, ready for the cycle to begin again.

In many photosynthetic bacteria, compounds other than water serve as the source of electrons. For example, the so-called sulfur bacteria (Figure 15.10) use hydrogen sulfide (H$_2$S) instead of water as a source of electrons and produce elemental sulfur (S) instead of oxygen (O$_2$) as a by-product. Water-dependent, oxygen-evolving photosynthesis is now thought to be a relatively recent photosynthetic pathway. The use of other compounds is undoubtedly representative of the more primitive condition.

For the electron acceptor molecule Q, electrons are thought to move two at a time through an electron transport chain (Figure 15.11). This chain is analogous to the transport chain described in Chapter 14 for the oxidative phosphorylation in mitochondria. The destination point for these electrons is the reaction center of photosystem I, where they will combine with the P700 molecule.

At each transfer from one electron carrier to the next, the electrons lose part of their excitation energy. And some of the energy they give up as they tumble down the transport

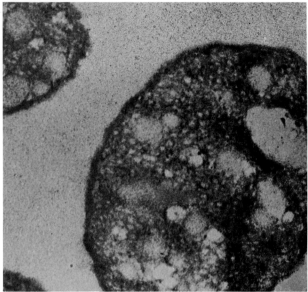

[magnification 72,000]

Figure 15.10 Electron micrograph of a thin section of cells of the purple sulfur bacterium Chromatium, *strain D. Deposits of elemental sulfur that are by-products of photosynthesis in this organism can be seen throughout the cells. The world's great sulfur deposits are thought to represent the sulfur produced by vast numbers of this type of organism.*

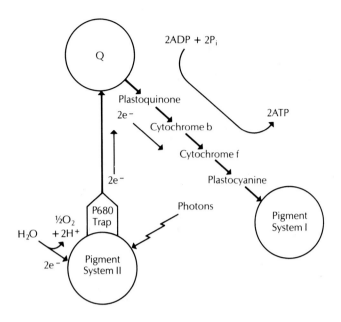

Figure 15.11 The electron transport chain linking photosystem II to photosystem I. Somehow, along this chain, the energy given up by the electrons being transferred from one carrier to the next is coupled to the phosphorylation of ADP. The complete chain of electron carriers has not yet been identified. Electrons are known to be passed from Q to plastoquinone and then to a molecule of cytochrome b (which is similar to the cytochrome b molecule found in the respiratory chain). Eventually the electrons reach another molecule, cytochrome f (which is chemically similar to cytochrome c in the respiratory chain). From cytochrome f the electrons pass to a molecule called plastocyanine and then to the P700 chlorophyll in pigment system I. The nature of the electron acceptors interposed between the cytochromes b and f is not known, but additional carriers are thought to be involved.

chain is coupled to the phosphorylation of ADP. It is now generally believed that two ADP molecules are phosphorylated for each pair of electrons transported from electron acceptor Q to photosystem I. But the actual coupling mechanism in the phosphorylation process has yet to be unraveled. It may be similar to the mechanism in mitochondrial respiration *(Interleaf 14.2);* in both cases it depends on the integrity of the membrane in which the electron carriers and the phosphorylation enzymes are embedded.

Photosystem I: How Electrons Derived From Photosystem II Are Used to Generate NADH

The initial events in photosystem I resemble those in photosystem II. In photosystem I, pigment molecules absorb light energy from the sun and their electrons are boosted to higher energy levels. This excitation energy is shuttled from molecule to molecule until it reaches the reaction center of photosystem I and is absorbed by the P700 chlorophyll. If the excitation energy is great enough, a single electron will leave the chlorophyll molecule and will be passed on to the electron acceptor long identified as Z. This electron acceptor is now known to be a flavoprotein (an enzyme that contains a flavin coenzyme related to the vitamin riboflavin). Because flavoprotein passes the elec-

trons on to ferrodoxin, it is now called ferrodoxin-reducing substance, or FRS. As electrons leave P700, an electron vacancy is created in this molecule, which becomes filled by electrons flowing down the electron transport chain from photosystem II.

The high-energy electrons gained by the flavoprotein are passed to a ferrodoxin molecule, which is the next component of the short electron transport chain associated with photosystem I (Figure 15.12). From ferrodoxin the electrons are transferred to another flavoprotein. Here they are used to reduce the coenzyme nicotinamide adenine dinucleotide phosphate ($NADP^+$), which is present in the chloroplast matrix. This coenzyme is identical to the coenzyme NAD^+ except for the occurrence of an additional phosphate group as part of its structure (Figure 15.13). When a molecule of $NADP^+$ gains a pair of electrons, it becomes

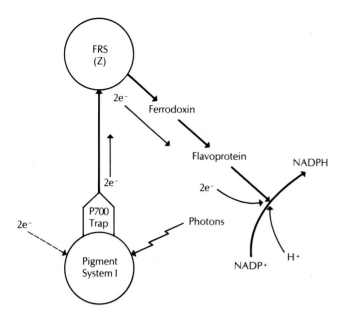

Figure 15.12 *The electron transport chain in the second half of the light reactions of photosynthesis. At the end of this chain, electrons combine with the coenzyme NADP⁺, which is present in the chloroplast. As NADP⁺ is reduced in this way, it also combines with one of the hydrogen ions released in the splitting of water at the beginning of the photosynthesis process, which yields NADPH.*

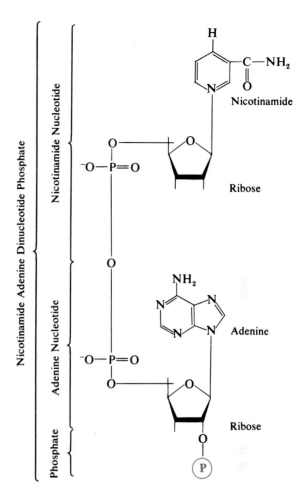

Figure 15.13 *Nicotinamide adenine dinucleotide phosphate, or NADP⁺. This coenzyme differs from NAD⁺ (shown earlier in Figure 14.9) only by the addition of a phosphate group, designated ⓟ. The NAD⁺ and NADP⁺ are reduced in identical ways, but enzymes capable of reducing one of them will not accept the other. Thus the cell maintains two separate pools of NAD coenzymes for quite different pathways. This permits independent regulation of the various pathways.*

capable of combining with one of the hydrogen ions released in the first step of the photosynthetic pathway. This union results in the formation of a molecule of NADPH.

It is the ATP produced in the first electron transport chain and the NADPH and the additional H^+ produced in the second that are used to reduce carbon dioxide to form carbohydrates.

Cyclic Photophosphorylation: An Alternative Pathway Mediated by Photosystem I

The transfer of electrons from water to NADP⁺ in the reactions just described is noncyclic: the electrons flow continuously in one direction. That is why phosphorylation of ADP associated with these reactions is called **noncyclic photophosphorylation.** But all chloroplasts are capable of a second kind of photophosphorylation, which can occur in the absence of an electron donor (such as water) or an electron acceptor (such as NADP⁺). Because this alternative route is based on the recycling of electrons through photosystem I, it is called **cyclic photophosphorylation.** In the living cell, cyclic photophosphorylation probably plays a minor role as long as sufficient carbon dioxide is available to complete the reactions of photosynthesis. But if carbon dioxide becomes limiting, cyclic photophosphorylation pro-

vides a mechanism whereby the cell can continue to generate ATP for the performance of other work.

Figure 15.14 outlines the pathway of cyclic electron flow and the accompanying phosphorylation. The fact that electrons do recycle continuously in this pathway means it is not possible to collect them with an electron acceptor and determine how many ATP molecules are formed with each pair of electrons that takes part in the cyclic electron flow. Moreover, because noncyclic electron flow always occurs to a greater or lesser extent along with the noncyclic light reactions, it has not been possible to measure accurately how many ADP molecules are phosphorylated per pair of

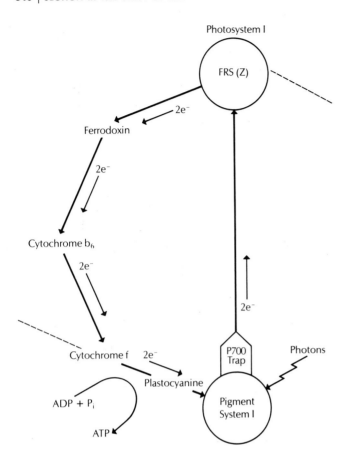

Photosystem I

FRS (Z)

Ferrodoxin

2e⁻

Cytochrome b₆

2e⁻

Cytochrome f   2e⁻

Plastocyanine

ADP + P_i

ATP

P700 Trap   Photons

Pigment System I

2e⁻

2e⁻

Figure 15.14 Cyclic photophosphorylation. The cyclic electron flow and cyclic photophosphorylation depicted here accompany the noncyclic processes of the light reactions (Figures 15.11 and 15.12). Cytochrome b₆ apparently takes part only in this cyclic pathway, whereas all the other components are also involved in the noncyclic photosynthetic light reactions.

electrons flowing through the noncyclic pathway. Hence the value of two ATP molecules shown in Figure 15.11 is just a guess. Many botanists suggest there may only be one.

THE DARK REACTIONS OF PHOTOSYNTHESIS LEAD TO THE STORAGE OF ENERGY

The production of NADPH and ATP requires light; hence these reactions are called the light reactions of photosynthesis. But the formation of sugar from carbon dioxide does not require light directly: it requires only the products of the light reaction. That is why the reactions in which sugar is actually formed are called the **dark reactions** of photosynthesis. The dark reactions can occur in sunlight but they do not require it. Indeed, in a natural setting with continuous illumination by sunlight, the light and dark reactions occur continuously and simultaneously in a plant. But if, in a laboratory situation, the light is supplied in brief flashes only, the light reactions occur while the light is on and the dark reactions occur for a brief period after it goes off.

Because of the interdependency of the light and dark reactions, the rate of photosynthesis is proportional to the intensity of the light source only up to a point (Figure 15.15). In dim light, the overall rate of photosynthesis is determined by the rate at which the products of the

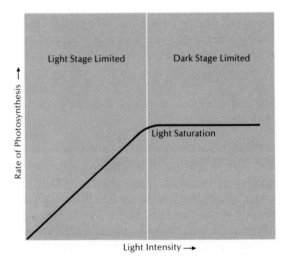

Figure 15.15 Light saturation in photosynthesis. The rate of photosynthesis is proportional to light intensity but only up to a saturation point. At that point the rate remains constant despite further increases in light intensity.

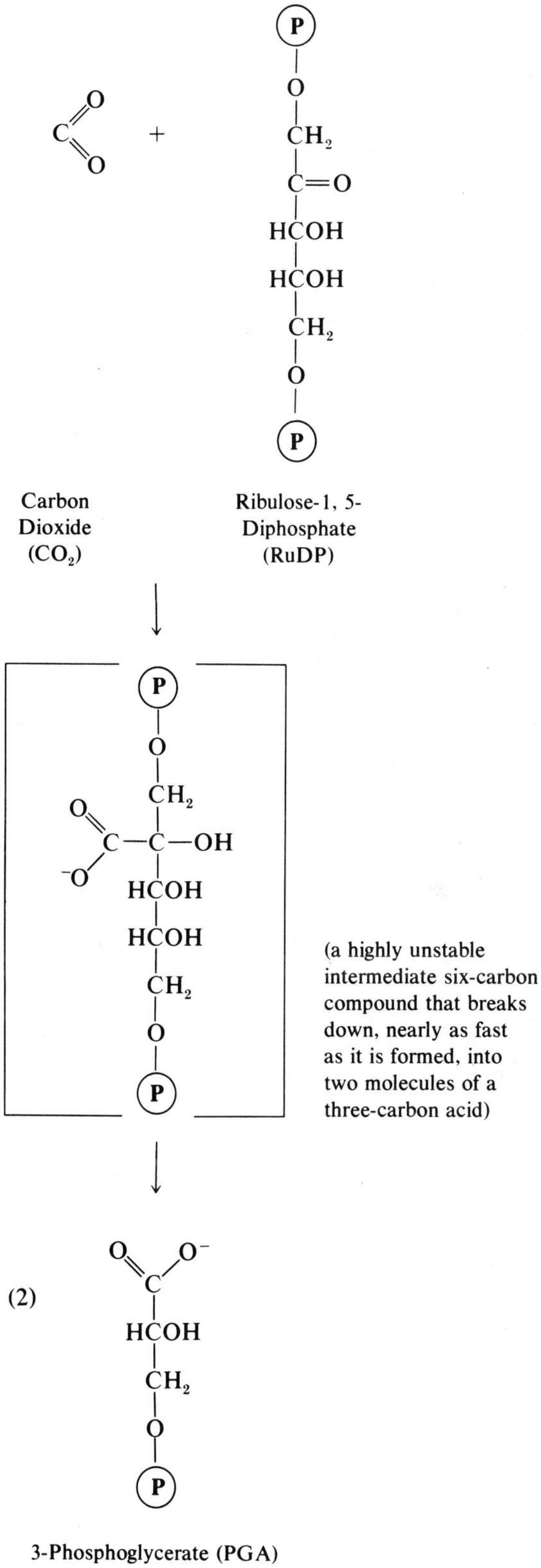

Figure 15.16   Carbon dioxide fixation: the first photosynthetic dark reaction. The "2" in parentheses indicates that two molecules of PGA are formed.

light-dependent step are made available. But as the light intensity is increased, a point is reached where these products are being made available as fast as they can possibly be used in the dark reactions. Further increases in light intensity do not cause further increase in the rate of photosynthesis and, as F. F. Blackman correctly inferred in 1905, it is now limited by the rate at which the dark reactions are occurring, and this rate cannot be increased simply by providing more light.

There are many ways in which a plant uses the NADPH and ATP produced by the light reactions. The discussion that follows focuses on only one pathway by which materials are produced for cell growth and maintenance. Not only is this pathway the best known and best understood, it is probably the most important in a quantitative sense.

The Fixation of Carbon Dioxide

The first task of the dark reactions is **carbon dioxide fixation:** the incorporation of carbon dioxide into a nongaseous, organic compound. This step does not require the direct participation of the products of the light reaction. It involves the reaction of one molecule of carbon dioxide with one molecule of ribulose 1,5-diphosphate (RuDP), which is a phosphorylated five-carbon sugar. The resulting six-carbon compound is unstable and breaks down to form two molecules of 3-phosphoglycerate, a three-carbon organic acid, which (in discussions of photosynthesis) is often abbreviated PGA. As Figure 15.16 shows, PGA is the first product released and the first one that is accumulated to any appreciable extent. The enzyme that catalyzes the reaction between RuDP and carbon dioxide has the rather burdensome name ribulose diphosphate carboxy dismutase (often called "the dismutase" for short). The dismutase appears to be incorporated into the inner membrane of the chloroplast, along with the components of the light reactions. It is a large, complex enzyme that is, as enzymes go, rather sluggish and inefficient *(Interleaf 15.1)*. Yet it catalyzes an absolutely crucial reaction. What the dismutase lacks in catalytic efficiency, it makes up for in quantity: it is the most abundant protein in the chloroplast. Even though the chloroplast has dozens of enzymes capable of performing dozens of different reactions (only a few are discussed here), the dismutase constitutes as much as 15 percent of the protein in the chloroplast!

(text continues on page 344)

Carbon Dioxide (CO_2)

Ribulose-1, 5-Diphosphate (RuDP)

(a highly unstable intermediate six-carbon compound that breaks down, nearly as fast as it is formed, into two molecules of a three-carbon acid)

(2)

3-Phosphoglycerate (PGA)

Interleaf 15.1

Why a Lush Expanse of Bluegrass in Spring Becomes a Motley Crabgrass Patch in Summer

The production of sugars and other organic compounds in plants begins with fixation of carbon dioxide by the enzyme ribulose diphosphate carboxy dismutase, a notoriously inefficient enzyme. For one thing, it picks up the carbon dioxide molecules used in photosynthesis only if their concentration approaches 300 parts per million parts of air (or 300 ppm). If the concentration of carbon dioxide falls below 50 ppm, photosynthesis stops. The plant survives only because it resorts to the respiratory pathways which use up sugars and generate carbon dioxide.

Now, plants pick up carbon dioxide from the air through *stomata,* or openings in the leaf surface (Figure *a*). Stomatal pores can be opened and closed by changes in the shape of the guard cells surrounding the pore. When the stomata are open, carbon dioxide diffuses in. As it does so, however, water vapor also diffuses out. This is what is known as *transpiration.* Only a fraction of the water absorbed by a plant's roots is used as a photosynthetic reactant: most of it evaporates through the stomata. When stomata are completely closed, loss of water by transpiration is almost nonexistent. At the same time, however, adequate carbon dioxide is not available for

(a) A stoma (plural, "stomata") in the surface of a leaf. The stomatal pore is surrounded by two specialized cells known as guard cells. By changing shape the guard cells can open and close the pore and thus regulate flow of gases into and out of the leaf. Because the surface of the rest of the leaf is covered with a waxy cuticle, gases diffuse into and out of the leaf only through such stomata.

photosynthesis: Because uptake of carbon dioxide and loss of water are linked, every plant has a characteristic value known as the "photosynthetic water use efficiency."

For a plant growing in a wet area or during a rainy season of the year, photosynthetic water use efficiency is of little consequence. But as the days become hotter and drier, it becomes an important factor in the plant's economy. If stomata are opened, precious water is lost; if they are closed, photosynthesis halts for lack of carbon dioxide.

More than a hundred different genera of plants in ten distinct families have developed the same way to circumvent the water/carbon dioxide dilemma. They are all known as "C4 plants" because the first compound formed as a result of carbon dioxide fixation in these plants is a four-carbon acid rather than the three-carbon acid formed in conventional plants, or "C3 plants." Very closely related species in the same genus may be of the C3 and C4 type.

In C4 plants, carbon dioxide fixation occurs in cells that are in contact with surface air by way of the stomata. The reaction they use is one that is found in plants and animals but is not usually associated with photosynthesis: the formation of oxaloacetate (an intermediate of the Krebs cycle) from phosphoenolpyruvate (an intermediate of the Embden-Meyerhof pathway):

CO_2
(carbon dioxide)
+
CH_2
(P)—O—C
$-O$ O
(phosphoenolpyruvate, or PEP)

↓

O^- O
C
CH_2
$O=C$
$-O$ O
(oxaloacetate)
+
P_i
(inorganic phosphate)

This reaction is catalyzed by the enzyme PEP carboxylase, which is present in most cells. PEP carboxylase is one mechanism used to replace Krebs cycle intermediates when one of them is being used for synthesis (Chapter 14).

Now, these four-carbon acids do not enter photosynthetic reactions directly. Instead, they are passed to adjacent cells active in conventional photosynthesis. Here the four-carbon acids are broken down again to form carbon dioxide plus pyruvate. The pyruvate then returns to the cells that are fixing atmospheric carbon dioxide while the newly released carbon dioxide is now taken into the Calvin-Benson cycle by the dismutase in the usual manner. This cycle is diagramed in Figure (b). Because this cycle requires hydrolysis of one ATP molecule for every molecule of carbon dioxide that undergoes fixation, how can it possibly provide a selective advantage to the plant? The answer lies in the water use efficiency of this pathway as opposed to the conventional C3 pathway.

Because PEP carboxylase has a *much* higher affinity for carbon dioxide than the dismutase does, it can operate with much lower concentrations of carbon dioxide! Thus the stomata need not be open very wide to keep carbon dioxide levels high enough to keep PEP carboxylase running at full speed. The rest of the cycle then serves to "pump" carbon dioxide into the cell where it is taken up into the Calvin-Benson cycle.

Under conditions of ready water availability and/or low light intensity, the ATP required to phosphorylate the pyruvate makes the C4 system unjustifiably costly to a cell. But under conditions in which water is the limiting factor, light intensity is usually high enough to make ATP abundant by means of photosynthetic phosphorylation. Then, considering the water loss

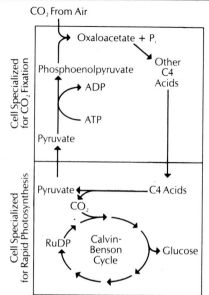

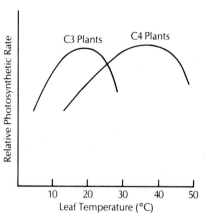

(b) The pathway of carbon dioxide fixation in C4 plants. A cell in contact with surface air fixes carbon dioxide by forming oxaloacetate. This compound is transformed into a related C4 acid, which is transferred to another cell specialized for photosynthesis. Here the C4 acid is broken down to pyruvate and carbon dioxide. The carbon dioxide enters the usual photosynthetic pathway while the pyruvate returns to the carbon-dioxide-fixing cell. Before it can pick up another molecule of carbon dioxide, the pyruvate must be rephosphorylated at the expense of ATP.

(c) Comparison of photosynthetic rates as a function of temperature in C3 and C4 plants under a fixed level of illumination. C3 plants tend to reach maximum photosynthetic rate at relatively cool temperatures, then to decrease photosynthetic rate if leaf temperature rises above this value. C4 plants are less efficient at lower temperatures, but their efficiency increases at higher temperatures.

that is prevented, the cost (in the form of the extra ATP) is worthwhile. Thus, the C3 plant is at an energetic advantage under cool, wet conditions but the C4 plant surpasses it in efficiency as the weather becomes hot and dry. As indicated in Figure (c), a C3 plant tends to slow its photosynthetic rate as temperature rises, while a related C4 plant increases photosynthetic rate with increases in temperature over a much wider temperature range.

Bluegrass happens to be a C3 plant, and crabgrass, a C4 plant. In the heat of summer, the bluegrass

closes its stomata and resorts to respiratory metabolism, while the crabgrass thrives photosynthetically.

Not only are most desert plants of the C4 type, so are several agricultural crops that thrive in hot, moderately dry conditions—such as sugar cane, corn, sorghum, and sunflowers. Attempts are now under way to convert some C3 plants of agricultural importance to the C4 way of life by selective breeding.

The Reduction of 3-Phosphoglycerate and the Formation of Glucose

In the next stage of the dark reactions, the PGA produced by the dismutase is first converted to fructose phosphate and then to glucose in a series of steps that are, essentially, the reverse of the first seven steps of the Embden-Meyerhof glycolysis pathway (Figure 15.17). In this pathway, however, the enzyme that reduces 1,3-diphosphoglycerate to form 3-phosphoglyceraldehyde differs from the comparable enzyme in glycolysis because it requires NADPH rather than NADH. It is in the phosphorylation and subsequent reduction of PGA to yield 3-phosphoglyceraldehyde that the ATP, NADPH, and H^+ produced by the light reactions come into play: *When ATP and NADPH concentrations are high relative to ADP and $NADP^+$ concentrations, the reaction series will run in the forward direction.*

Two additional reactions assist in keeping this reaction series running in the forward direction by using up products of earlier reactions before they can reach equilibrium concentrations. These are the two reactions in which inorganic phosphate is released (first from fructose diphosphate and then from glucose phosphate). Both these reactions are highly exergonic (high negative $\Delta G^{\circ\prime}$) and tend to "pull" the reaction series toward glucose production. The glucose produced in these reactions is either exported to nonphotosynthetic cells or is rapidly converted to one storage form or another. It never accumulates as free glucose to any great extent in the photosynthetically active cell.

Sugar Conversions in the Regeneration of Ribulose 1,5-Diphosphate

The final task of this set of dark reactions is to provide a continuous source of RuDP that the dismutase can use as a carbon dioxide acceptor. Without RuDP, carbon dioxide fixation, and hence all the dark reactions, cannot occur. This task is accomplished through a rather complex-looking series of sugar interconversions. All of these reactions are summarized in Figure 15.18. As with the Krebs cycle of

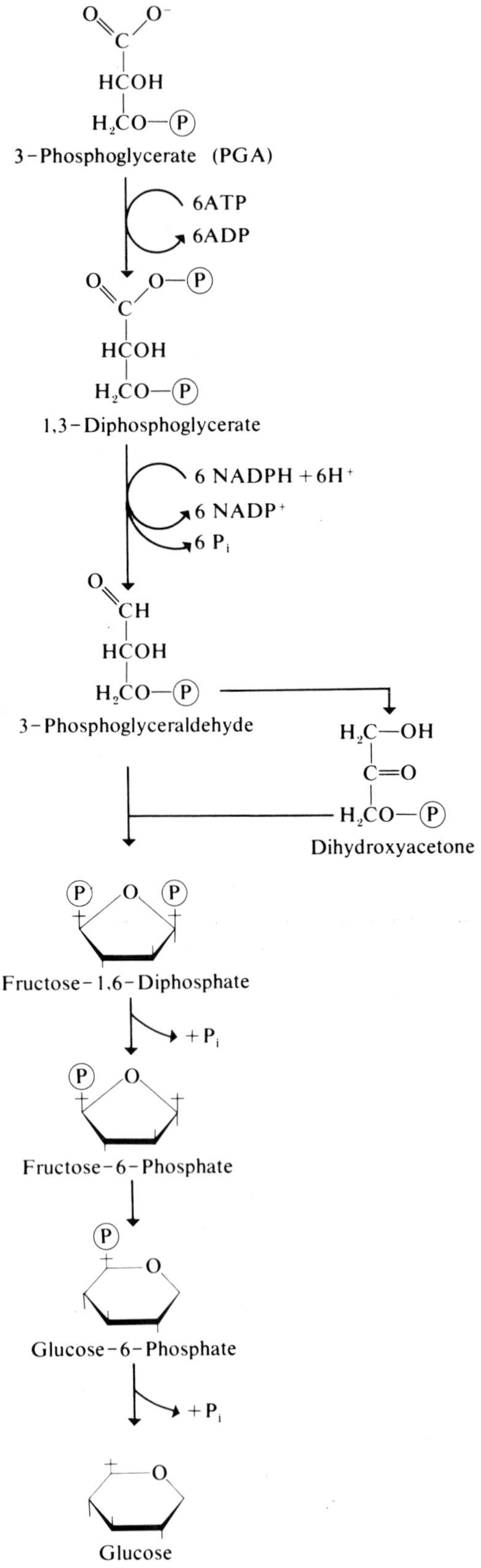

Figure 15.17 The first portion of the Calvin-Benson cycle. Here the ATP and NADPH produced in the light reactions are used first to phosphorylate and then to reduce the PGA formed as a result of carbon dioxide fixation. Essentially this part of the cycle involves a reverse of part of the glycolytic pathway to produce fructose diphosphate. Some of this fructose diphosphate is used to form glucose for storage; the rest enters the second portion of the cycle in order to take part in the regeneration of RuDP. The three-carbon sugars used in the second portion of the cycle are also produced by the first three to four steps shown here. (Compare this figure with the glycolytic pathway shown in Figure 14.7).

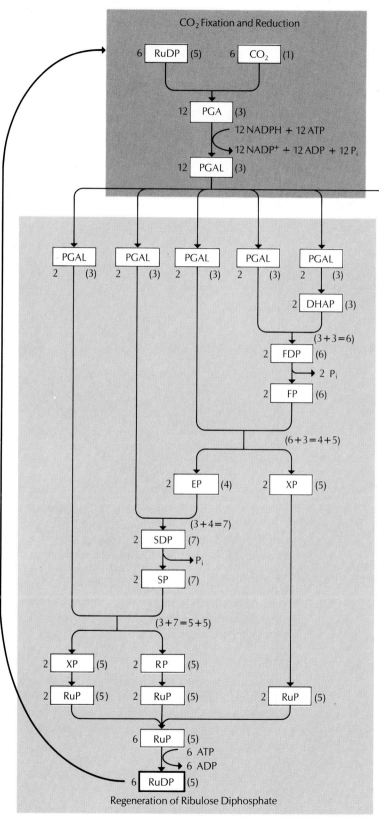

Figure 15.18 The dark reactions of photosynthesis. Although these reactions occur continuously in an interdependent way, it is convenient to think of them in three blocks as shown here. First, carbon dioxide is fixed and reduced, using the products of the dark reactions. The result is the formation of twelve molecules of PGAL for every six molecules of carbon dioxide fixed. Then two of these PGAL molecules are condensed to form, ultimately, a new molecule of glucose. The remaining ten PGAL molecules are then rearranged to replace the six molecules of RuDP used in the carbon dioxide fixation step.

The interconversions of the sugar-phosphates to re-form the RuDP are far less formidable than they appear. The numbers of carbon atoms present in each of the reacting sugars are given in parentheses. Thus it can be seen that all that is involved is a series of fusions and rearrangement of sugars of various sizes.

The three-carbon sugars involved in the pathway are phosphoglyceraldehyde (PGAL) and dihydroxy acetone phosphate (DHAP). The four-carbon sugar is called erythrose phosphate (EP). The five-carbon sugars are ribulose phosphate (RuP), diphosphate (RuDP), ribose phosphate (RP), and xylulose phosphate (XP). The six-carbon sugars are fructose phosphate (FP) and diphosphate (FDP). The seven-carbon sugars are sedoheptulose phosphate (SP) and diphosphate (SDP).

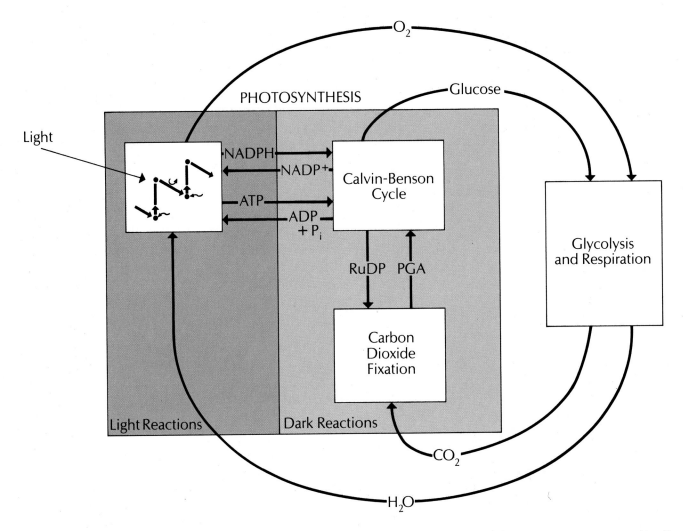

Figure 15.19 Summary of photosynthesis and the carbon cycle.

respiratory metabolism, it is not necessary to memorize all of the names of the intermediates and the reactions in order to appreciate the elegance of this essential pathway of life. In a mere handful of reactions, the chloroplast not only converts carbon dioxide to glucose (something that would take a chemist years to perform, at best), it regenerates its own substance to keep the wheels of life turning.

PERSPECTIVE

Life originally functioned by using molecules produced by random chemical interactions in the environment. Today it is utterly dependent on the molecules, such as sugar, that are produced by the highly ordered chemical interactions of photosynthesis:

$$6CO_2 + 12H_2O + light \longrightarrow C_6H_{12}O_6 + 6H_2O + 6O_2$$

This equation looks simple enough, but many of the steps it summarizes remain mysteries. One thing has been clear for some time: Photosynthesis occurs in special cytoplasmic organelles called chloroplasts, and it occurs in two separable but interrelated stages—those that require light and those that require some unstable products of the light-dependent stage. The two processes that make up the light reactions are completed in less than a hundredth of a second. In each of these sequential reactions, light energy (photons) is captured by intricately organized systems of pigment molecules, of which chlorophyll is the most important. The concentration of this energy activates electrons of specialized chlorophyll molecules (P680 and P700), sending them to energy levels that are high enough to permit their escape from the grip of the chlorophyll. And escape they do—to special electron acceptor molecules that transfer them to electron transport chains. As the electrons tumble down these chains, they give off some of the energy they gained during their excitation. In one of the transport chains, this "lost" energy is used to produce ATP. In the other chain the electrons are used directly to produce the reduced coenzyme NADPH.

The ATP and NADPH so produced are the molecules that are used to drive the dark reactions of photosynthesis, in which carbon dioxide is fixed and reduced to form carbohydrates. The carbon atom obtained from carbon dioxide is carried through a series of intermediate compounds in a reaction sequence known as the Calvin-Benson cycle. It begins with the union of carbon dioxide and a five-carbon sugar, ribulose 1,5-diphosphate (RuDP), to form an extremely unstable compound that promptly falls apart into two molecules of the three-carbon compound, 3-phosphoglycerate (PGA). PGA is then phosphorylated by ATP and reduced by NADPH to form the three-carbon sugar, 3-phosphoglyceraldehyde. Some of this compound can then be converted into a more stable form of sugar for chemical storage, but most of it must be used in the regeneration of RuDP to begin the cycle all over again.

The Calvin-Benson cycle is not the only way ATP and NADPH are used. It is not even the only pathway through which carbon dioxide can be converted to useful organic compounds—it is one of several constructive pathways. Nevertheless, it is of central importance in that it provides a form of sugar (glucose) that can be used for at least three essential purposes. Glucose can be used as a source of energy for nonphotosynthetic cells within the plant body. It can be used also as a structural element to permit growth of the plant—recall that cell walls of plants are reinforced primarily with the glucose polymer cellulose. Finally, glucose can be stored in the form of starch during periods of high photosynthetic activity as a reserve for use during periods of low photosynthetic activity—for maintaining the cell during the night and in periods of drought or cold, and

for providing energy for the development of seeds. It is because of this accumulation of such food reserves that plant life has become the richest energy source for life on earth.

SUGGESTED READINGS

BASSHAM, J. A., "Photosynthetic Carbon Metabolism," and ARNON, D. I., "The Light Reactions of Photosynthesis," in *Proceedings of the National Academy of Science*, 68 (1971), 2877 and 2883. Originally presented as contributions to the Photosynthetic Bicentennial Symposium sponsored in 1971 by the National Academy of Science, these two papers are excellent reviews of the two major aspects of photosynthesis, written by two of the guiding lights in the field.

BASSHAM, JAMES A. "The Control of Photosynthetic Carbon Metabolism," *Science*, 172 (1971), 526. An up-to-date account of the path and regulation of carbon metabolism during photosynthesis, written as a review article by a prominent worker in the field.

BIDWELL, R. G. S. *Plant Physiology*. New York: Macmillan, 1974. Chapter 7 is recommended for a plant physiologist's view of photosynthesis, including a brief discussion of environmental factors affecting photosynthesis.

LEVINE, R. P. "The Mechanism of Photosynthesis," *Scientific American*, 221 (December 1969), 58. A readable account of the involvement of light in photosynthesis. Recommended for its accuracy and the quality of its illustrations.

NASH, L. K. "Plants and the Atmosphere," in James B. Conant (ed.), *Harvard Case Histories in Experimental Science*, vol. 2. Cambridge, Mass.: Harvard University Press, 1957. The words of the original investigators are used to present the early work on photosynthesis in its historical context.

Section IV

The Continuity of Life

In the preceding sections of this book, we examined first the diversity of life and then its underlying molecular and cellular unity. The question now becomes: How is unity maintained and yet formed into diversity through time? Somehow, an organism that reproduces itself must perpetuate the essential characteristics of its kind. Yet somehow, the very mechanism that conserves those essential features must also allow for gradual change. What aspect of life allows for both constancy and change—and does so simultaneously? The answers to this paradox are astonishing in their simplicity. It is at the molecular level that this part of the story begins.

Chapter 16

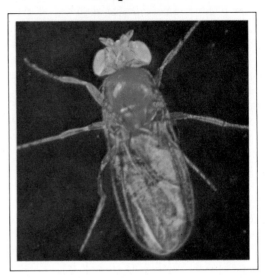

The Units of Heredity

How many of us have experienced irritation as we reached for a piece of fruit only to have a cloud of tiny fruit flies take to the air? But where, we might ask, would the science of heredity be if a man by the name of Thomas Hunt Morgan had chosen some organism other than the tiny fruit fly with which to test his ideas of heredity? Mendel, Morgan, Beadle, Lederberg—our expanded understanding of heredity can be traced in large part to a few men who chose the right organism at the right time and asked the right questions about it.

We all accept without a second thought that in most characteristics, offspring resemble their natural parents. Cows, for example, have never been known to give birth to creatures that look like chickens, nor chickens to creatures that look like cows. But if it is obvious that the characteristics of offspring are inherited, then it must be just as obvious that the physical bridge between generations is narrow indeed: It takes very little substance from parents to create a new individual in their image.

Until the middle of the nineteenth century, heredity was thought to be a direct transfer of bodily characteristics of one parent to a newly forming individual, and then a subsequent blending with bodily characteristics of the other parent. A new individual, then, would have features that were a blend of parental features, and certainly it would not be different in a feature that was identical in both parents. But if this assumption were true, how, for example, could two red-flowered plants produce an individual with white flowers? How could two people with brown eyes have a child with green eyes? *The fact remained that the hereditary mechanism somehow allows for change even as it provides constancy from one generation to the next.* But it would not be until after the work of Gregor Mendel in the mid-1860s that the pieces of the puzzle would begin to fall in place.

GREGOR MENDEL IDENTIFIES THE NATURE OF HEREDITY MECHANISMS

Gregor Johann Mendel is often pictured as an obscure monk who stumbled onto the nature of heredity mechanisms while puttering in his garden between morning and evening prayers. But a careful look at his life and works leads to an entirely different picture. Mendel was an alert, practical man of science whose entrance into the monastery was as much a part of his academic training as it was a response to a devout calling. Furthermore, his observations on heredity in plants were neither casual nor out of the mainstream of his life. He grew up on a farm near his birthplace in Silesia (then part of Austria), and throughout his life he was actively concerned with crop improvements. He won several awards for developing new varieties of fruits and vegetables and was a founding member of the Moravian and Silesian Agricultural Society. During his training in science and mathematics at the University of Vienna, he not only developed the statistical skills that would characterize his later work, he became influenced by Franz Unger, a botany professor who came under attack for suggesting (eight years before the Darwin-Wallace paper) that species are not fixed and that the diversity of the plant kingdom had arisen through natural processes. Within months following his training at the university, Mendel established thirty-four

"pure" strains of peas in his garden in anticipation of some kind of hybridization experiments. Seven years later he would present to the Brünn Society for the Study of Natural Science a paper in which he would describe the results of intensive cross-breeding of his plants.

Essentially, *Mendel selected plants that differed in a single heritable feature, or trait, and then he followed the results of crossing those plants and their progeny for several generations.* The strains he used differed in seven traits:

Seed shape: round versus irregular and wrinkled seeds.

Seed color: yellow versus green seeds.

Plant pigmentation: plants with pigmentation in flowers, stems, and seed coats versus those with unpigmented flowers and seed coats.

Pod shape: round and inflated versus constricted and wrinkled pods.

Pod color: green versus yellow pods.

Flower position: axial flowers (along the stem) versus terminal flowers (at the top only).

Height: tall plants (six to seven feet) versus short plants (nine to eighteen inches).

For each pair of opposed traits, Mendel obtained two strains that differed *only* in those traits and "bred true." For example, he obtained a group of plants with round seeds that, when crossed with each other, produced progeny with round seeds only. Similarly, plants with wrinkled seeds produced only progeny with wrinkled seeds when crossed with each other, and so on.

The Monohybrid Crosses

Mendel began by cross-pollinating plants from each pair of strains that differed in a single trait. For example, he dusted flowers of plants from the round-seed strain with pollen from plants of the wrinkled-seed strain. Wrinkled-seed plants, in turn, were fertilized with pollen from round-seed plants. Similar cross-fertilizations were performed for each pair of pure-breeding strains. In this and all subsequent experiments, Mendel found that in such cross-fertilizations the *direction* of the cross did not affect the outcome. In other words, the results did not depend on which was the male and which was the female parent—either way, the results were the same. He concluded that *the hereditary contributions of a male and a female parent are equal and equivalent.*

Further description of Mendel's experiments will be easier if we use terminology developed long after his paper was published. The original parental generation is designated the P_1 **generation;** the offspring of P_1 make up the F_1 **generation** (or "first filial generation"); the offspring of F_1 are the F_2 **generation;** and so on.

Table 16.1
Ratios of Traits in F$_2$ Generations of Mendel's Seven Crossing Experiments

Dominant Trait	Occurrence in F$_2$ Generation	Recessive Trait	Occurrence in F$_2$ Generation	Ratio
Round seed	5,474	Wrinkled seed	1,850	2.96:1
Yellow seed contents	6,022	Green seed contents	2,001	3.01:1
Pigmented seed coats	705	Unpigmented seed coats	224	3.15:1
Inflated pods	882	Constricted pods	299	2.95:1
Green pods	428	Yellow pods	152	2.82:1
Axial flowers	651	Terminal flowers	207	3.14:1
Long stems	787	Short stems	277	2.84:1

Source: Hugo Iltis, *Life of Mendel* (New York: Hafner, 1966).

After collecting the seeds produced from cross-fertilization of the P$_1$ generation plants, Mendel planted the seeds and recorded the traits of the resulting adult plants. He called the F$_1$ plants **hybrids.** (A cross-fertilization between parents that differ in only one trait is a **monohybrid cross.**) The F$_2$ generation in each case was produced by self-fertilization of the F$_1$ plants.

The traits of the P$_1$ plants did *not* blend to give intermediate characters in the F$_1$ generation. For each of the seven monohybrid crosses, all members of the F$_1$ generation resembled only one of the two parental types. Mendel called the character that had prevailed in the F$_1$ generation the **dominant** trait; he called the one that disappeared the **recessive** trait. For example, in a cross between plants with yellow seeds and those with green seeds, all the F$_1$ plants produced only yellow seeds: Yellow was dominant and green was recessive.

But following self-fertilization, the F$_1$ generation plants gave rise to F$_2$ plants in which the recessive trait reappeared! Traits that disappeared and then resurfaced had been observed before, but all earlier attempts to find out what was going on had ended in frustration. Mendel went a step further: He *counted* the individuals with dominant and recessive traits. In the cross between plants with yellow seeds and green seeds, for example, he counted 8,023 peas in the F$_2$ generation. Of those peas, 6,022 were yellow and 2,001 were green. His mathematically trained mind could not miss the fact that this ratio was almost 3 to 1. Moreover, *all* of his monohybrid crosses gave ratios of nearly 3:1 between dominant and recessive traits in the F$_2$ generation (Table 16.1).

In his explanation of these results, Mendel introduced symbols such as *A* and *a* to represent dominant and recessive traits, respectively. His introduction of symbols is significant, for it suggested that individuals inherit discrete factors that "stand for" the trait rather than inheriting the trait itself. Each plant, he suggested, inherits two hereditary factors—one from each parent—for each trait. The plant then passes on *one* of those factors in each reproductive cell (ovule or pollen grain) during pollination. Assuming that pollination of an ovule is a random process, then such a mechanism would account for the results he observed (Figures 16.2 and 16.3).

Now, if dominant and recessive traits *were* segregated and recombined in this manner, then Mendel's hypothesis would predict specific outcomes for the following series of test crosses.

First, if the F$_1$ hybrid were back-crossed to the pure-breeding *recessive* parental strain, the dominant and recessive traits in the F$_2$ generation should show up in a 1:1 ratio ($Aa \times aa \longrightarrow \frac{1}{2}Aa + \frac{1}{2}aa$).

Second, if the F$_1$ hybrid were back-crossed to the pure-breeding *dominant* parent, the recessive trait should not show up at all in the F$_2$ generation ($Aa \times AA \longrightarrow$ no individuals *aa*).

Third, if each member of the F$_2$ generation were *self-fertilized,* the plants showing the recessive trait should "breed true" (in other words, produce plants in which only the recessive trait is expressed). But the plants showing the dominant trait should fall into two groups. One-third should give offspring with *only* the dominant character ($AA \times AA \longrightarrow AA$); the remaining two-thirds should resemble the F$_1$ generation. The result would be a 3:1 ratio of progeny expressing the dominant trait as opposed to those occasionally expressing the recessive trait.

Mendel performed these test crosses for all seven of his monohybrid crosses. In each case the results were consistent with the predictions derived from his hypothesis.

The Dihybrid Cross

Mendel next crossed strains differing in two traits. (A cross-fertilization between parents that differ in two traits is a **dihybrid cross.**) For example, he crossed a strain with round, yellow seeds with a strain producing green, wrinkled

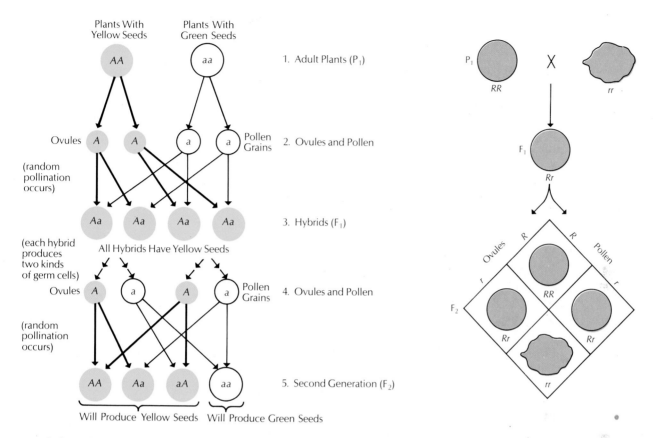

Plants With Yellow Seeds
Plants With Green Seeds

AA   *aa*   1. Adult Plants (P₁)

Ovules   *A*   *A*   *a*   *a*   Pollen Grains   2. Ovules and Pollen

(random pollination occurs)

Aa   *Aa*   *Aa*   *Aa*   3. Hybrids (F₁)

All Hybrids Have Yellow Seeds

(each hybrid produces two kinds of germ cells)

Ovules   *A*   *a*   *A*   *a*   Pollen Grains   4. Ovules and Pollen

(random pollination occurs)

AA   *Aa*   *aA*   *aa*   5. Second Generation (F₂)

Will Produce Yellow Seeds   Will Produce Green Seeds

seeds in order to determine how the two characters interacted in inheritance. Because the round seeds and yellow seeds were dominant traits, the F_1 generation plants would be expected to produce only round, yellow seeds. But would the F_2 generation plants produce only round, yellow seeds and wrinkled, green seeds? (That would suggest that the two factors responsible for the traits were somehow linked together and traveling together in the production of ovules and pollen.) Or would the F_2 generation plants produce some round, green seeds and some wrinkled, yellow seeds? (If that happened, it would suggest that the factors were *not* linked but had segregated into ovules and pollen independently of each other.)

For all seven traits that Mendel studied, the results suggested that such independent segregation of factors had occurred. In other words, *in every dihybrid cross, all four possible combinations of traits were observed in the F_2 generation.* In fact, the four possible combinations of traits always turned up in the F_2 generation in approximately the ratio of 9:3:3:1. Mendel recognized this ratio as the product of the ratios obtained when the two characters were examined separately: $(3:1)(3:1) = 9:3:3:1$. Figure 16.4 shows how such independent segregation of hereditary factors into pollen and ovules would give rise to a 9:3:3:1 ratio in the F_2 progeny. This pattern of segregation further

Figure 16.2 (above (left) Mendel's explanation of the results of the monohybrid cross between plants with yellow seeds and with green seeds:

(1) Adult plants contain two factors for seed color.

(2) Ovules and pollen grains contain one factor each.

(3) All members of the first generation have one factor of each kind, but only the dominant factor will be expressed.

(4) During self-fertilization of the hybrids, all combinations of factors will be formed by random fertilization. (The gametes of only two of the four F_1 hybrids are shown, for the sake of simplicity.)

(5) As a result, three-fourths of the plants produced by the second generation will express the dominant trait, and one-fourth will express the recessive trait.

Figure 16.3 (above) Mendel's hypothesis shown in more modern form in a monohybrid cross between round (RR) and wrinkled (rr) seed strains. The types of ovules produced by the F_1 plants are displayed on one side of the square; the types of pollen produced are displayed on the other. Then, by filling in the boxes, it is possible to predict in what ratio traits will be seen in the progeny, assuming random pollination. This type of diagram is known as a Punnett square, in honor of the man who first suggested its use.

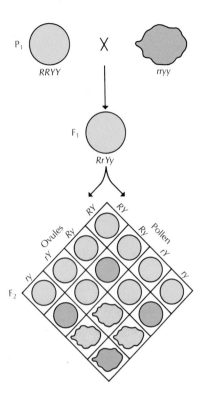

Figure 16.4 A representation of one of Mendel's dihybrid crosses. If we assume that factors controlling seed shape sort independently from the factors controlling seed color during the production of reproductive cells, four kinds of ovules and four kinds of pollen grains should be produced by the F₁ plants. Then if these four kinds of pollen fertilize the ovules randomly, sixteen combinations should result, as shown in the diagram. But because yellow and round traits are dominant, green and wrinkled seeds will be formed only in those combinations that lack a factor for a dominant trait. And in fact that is what Mendel observed:

In the F₂ generation, four kinds of plants were produced in the specific proportions 9:3:3:1. Nine had round, yellow seeds; three had round, green seeds; three had wrinkled, yellow seeds; and one had wrinkled, green seeds.

Crosses involving more than two independently assorting factor pairs can be diagrammed in the same way, but such diagrams rapidly become more complex. With three pairs of factors, the predicted ratio of distinguishable kinds of individuals in the F₂ generation is 27:9:9:9:3:3:3:1. With four-factor pairs, there are sixteen possible kinds of individuals, and with five-factor pairs, the number of possible kinds is thirty-two. With only twenty-three different, independently assorting pairs of factors, the offspring of a cross between multihybrid individuals could be of about 8 million different observable types! It is easy to see why Mendel was impressed with the ability of his concept of simple hereditary factors to account for the variability in nature.

supported the basic hypothesis of what is now called the Mendelian theory of inheritance:

1. *The traits of an individual are determined by discrete factors.*

2. *Each individual has a double dose of hereditary factors (which can be either the same or different).*

3. *These factors are inherited, one from each parent. They retain their identity throughout the life cycle. One may dominate the other in expression, they segregate at gametogenesis, and they assort independently.*

Reactions to Mendel's Paper

Mendel did not live to take part in modern genetics. In his own lifetime, no one showed even the slightest interest in his work, which was a bitter disappointment to the man. His paper was discussed at two evening meetings of the Brünn Society for the Study of Natural Science, but no one understood the significance of his conclusions. In a letter written the next year, Mendel commented sadly: "As was only to be expected, I encountered very various views, but, so far as I know, no one undertook a repetition of the experiments."

A number of scientists must have read Mendel's paper, but they may not have been impressed with it for several reasons. First, no agreement existed over the details of animal and plant reproduction. (Darwin, for example, believed that more than one pollen grain was required for a single fertilization in plants.) Second, anyone glancing at the title of Mendel's paper and then skimming over its contents could easily get the impression the conclusions applied only to pea plants. (Mendel did discuss the results of some crosses among bean plants, which generally supported his results with peas. However, the beans also presented some new phenomena that Mendel had tentatively explained by making further assumptions about the combined effects of *several* factors influencing the same trait.) Third, mathematics—however elementary—was seldom used in discussions of plant breeding. Naturalists would have been baffled by the formulas, and those scientists who could have followed Mendel's mathematical arguments were unlikely to bother reading an article on pea hybrids. Fourth, there were no immediate follow-up articles on his research, much less a book. When Mendel finally wrote another article in 1870, the news was bad. In experiments with hawkweed (*Hieracium*), he found that *both* the F₁ and the F₂ generations of a hybrid cross showed only the dominant trait. The recessive trait failed to reappear in later generations—which seemed to support older theories of blending inheritance rather than Mendel's theory of discrete hereditary factors. It is now known that hawkweed usually reproduces asexually, and that many of Mendel's supposed crosses of hawkweed plants were not crosses at all.

MENDEL'S WORK IS REDISCOVERED

Around 1900, Mendel's work was rediscovered independently by three men—Hugo DeVries, Carl Correns, and Erich Tschermak. Just before publication of their own papers, each one realized that he had been scooped thirty-four years earlier. DeVries had worked with flower shape and color in fifteen different species of plants and in each case found a 3:1 ratio in the F_2 generation. Both Correns and Tschermak had made some of Mendel's exact observations on the same strains of peas. Thus, a number of Mendel's experiments had been independently confirmed by two different investigators.

The timing of this rediscovery was no chance affair. In the forty intervening years, a series of fundamental shifts in biological theory had triggered a general search for principles governing the inheritance of single traits. As you read in Chapter 13, by 1900 the cell theory was generally established, the nature and role of male and female sex cells in syngamy had been clarified, and nuclear fusion had been identified as the crucial event in syngamy. In several different theories, subunits were assumed to exist within the cell nucleus, and in some theories the submicroscopic particles were said to be involved in the transmission of hereditary characters. Many biologists were aware of the central role of chromosomes in cell division, and some had speculated that the chromosomes might be involved in heredity. Furthermore, unlike the plant breeders of Mendel's day, the biologists studying heredity at the turn of the century were ready to accept mathematical and statistical concepts. In short, Mendelian theory was compatible with the basic biological paradigms of the early 1900s.

Within a decade, there were more than 200 reports of breeding studies of a variety of plants and animals, and most of the results were compatible with Mendel's theory. A specialized vocabulary sprung up with these studies. The symbols P_1, F_1, and F_2 began to be used. The word **gene** was introduced to signify the hereditary "factors" themselves. (The word was taken from the late Latin *genealogia*, which signified "the tracing of descent." The word **genetics** was also introduced in this era to signify the scientific study of heredity.) The words **genotype** and **phenotype** were coined to distinguish genetic constitution and genetic expression, respectively.

In the vocabulary of the day, the Mendelian theory of inheritance was rephrased in this manner: *Each trait is determined, in a given individual, by two discrete genes that are inherited, one from each parent.* The fact that there could be different forms of the same trait (yellow versus green seed color, for example) implied the existence of *alternative forms of genes.* Such alternative forms of a gene for a single trait were called **allelomorphs** (meaning "other forms"); later the word was shortened to **alleles.** If the two alleles for a given trait were identical (yellow versus yellow

Figure 16.5 Gregor Johann Mendel. Mendel was certainly not the first person to cross plants, nor was he the first hybridizer trying to discover the mechanism of inheritance. But no one before him had studied large numbers of single-trait crosses with the intention of developing a general theory that would describe the statistical distribution of single traits among successive hybrid generations.

The core of Mendel's thinking was the assumption that the hereditary factors present in a hybrid are not irreversibly blended together: they can reappear separately in the next generation. But it is not clear what first led him to this assumption. Obviously, he had cultivated his peas for some years before he began his intensive experiments. And the strains of pea plants he selected were the best assortment he could have possibly chosen: Many years earlier, others had reported the results of crosses between several of these strains—and Mendel was known to have kept abreast of the scientific literature.

Furthermore, there is agreement that most of his experimental results simply are too good to be true. The close fit between his recorded results and the frequencies expected from theoretical calculations is extremely improbable. Duplications of Mendel's experiments and modern statistical analysis both show that it is highly unlikely that he could have observed results so close to his expectations.

This evidence does not necessarily imply deliberate dishonesty; the improbably close fit is more likely due to unconscious bias in scoring the plants or to termination of counts when ratios were close to the predicted number. In any case, it appears that many if not all of the experiments were performed to confirm his hunches about what the patterns of inheritance must be.

seed color, for example), then an individual was said to be **homozygous** for that trait. If the two alleles were different, the individual was said to be **heterozygous** for that trait.

Genetics quickly became one of the most active fields of biology. But soon after the rediscovery of Mendel's work it became obvious that there were exceptions to his "rule" of dominance. First one and then many heterozygotes were noted that were intermediate between the two parent homozygotes. For example, in certain species a cross between red- and white-flowered plants gave rise to an F_1 generation of entirely pink flowers, and the subsequent F_2 generation plants expressed red, pink, and white flowers in a 1:2:1 ratio. Thus the concept of dominance was dropped as a *necessary* part of the Mendelian theory, for this work proved there somehow could be incomplete dominance—or **codominance**—of genes, in which both alleles are expressed more or less equally in a heterozygote.

More bothersome yet were traits that simply did not yield to simple Mendelian analysis. We now know that some of these characters, such as height in human beings, are complex cases in which a trait is under the control of many independently segregating genes. Other kinds of complex interactions of genes have now been elucidated, but some exceptions to the simple Mendelian scheme have not yet been explained.

In the early days of genetics, perhaps the most provocative exceptions to Mendel's theory were those in which independent segregation of genes was not observed. In such cases it was observed that in a dihybrid cross, the F_2 generation contained only individuals of the original parental types instead of the four theoretically possible combinations Mendel always observed. In some cases, genes apparently were "linked" to each other and did not sort out independently. What was the physical basis for this behavior? Why did each organism possess several sets of genes that appeared to be linked to each other—but not to the organism's other genes?

STUDIES OF THE CHROMOSOMAL BASIS OF HEREDITY BEGIN

Of all the changes occurring between 1866 and 1900, none was more influential in assuring the rapid acceptance and growth of Mendelian genetics than the study of chromosomes and their behavior in dividing cells. *With the convergence of genetics and cell biology, the physical nature of the hereditary material would be identified, and the chemistry and dynamic mechanisms of the gene would begin to be understood.*

The Behavior of Chromosomes in Dividing Cells

In 1882 Walther Flemming watched cells divide rapidly in growing salamander larvae. As he did so, he noticed the threads of deep-staining material of the nucleus were splitting longitudinally. This division process he called "mitosis," after the Greek word for "thread" (Chapter 13). The following year, Carl van Beneden, who was studying a parasitic worm of horses, observed the same process. Not only did he find that the split threads were identical to one another down to the finest detail he could observe, he found that the two daughter cells formed by mitosis received identical sets of these threads. These "threads" would later be called chromosomes ("colored bodies").

Van Beneden made a second discovery of major importance. Whereas the egg and sperm cells of this worm each contained *two* chromosomes, after fertilization each cell of the dividing egg contained *four*. He suggested that the sperm and the egg each contribute a single (**haploid**) set of chromosomes; the cells of the embryo and the adult therefore would contain two sets and would be **diploid**. In 1887 August Weismann predicted that a special division must occur at some point in the development of sperm and eggs, thereby reducing the number of chromosomes by half. That same year, Flemming confirmed Weismann's prediction when he observed two unusual divisions occurring in quick succession. These two divisions are now called **meiosis I** and **meiosis II**. They are described in detail in *Interleaf 16.1*.

W. S. Sutton in 1903 pointed to the compatibility of chromosome behavior with the Mendelian scheme. Mendel's "factors," he suggested, were carried on Flemming's "threads." Direct substantiation of this concept was not an easy task, to say the least, and how it was finally accomplished is one of the more interesting stories of biological inquiry. The first lead came from an analysis of sex determination.

The Chromosomal Basis of Sex

Before the turn of the century, the biologist Herman Henking had been watching male insect cells undergo meiosis as they prepared for sperm formation. And he observed, beneath the microscope, a strange-looking chromatin body. Whereas the normal-looking chromosomes occurred in pairs that divided equally between daughter cells in meiosis, the strange body (which he called "X" because he didn't know whether it was a chromosome) went to one daughter cell; the other daughter cell did not receive an equivalent structure. In 1902, Clarence E. McClung suggested that the **X chromosome** was the sex-determining chromosome. *In all species, it is the X chromosome that directs development of a fertilized zygote into a male or female individual.*

Soon afterward, Edmund B. Wilson showed that in such insects the female has *two* X chromosomes and that each egg it produces contains *one* X chromosome. Whether or not an egg formed a female offspring depended on whether or not it was fertilized by a sperm that carried an X chromosome. If it was, the egg would have two X chromosomes. But if it was fertilized by a sperm lacking an X chromosome, then the egg formed a male offspring. In other insect species, Wilson discovered that, in addition to the X chromosome, the male carried a smaller one, which he called the **Y chromosome.** Thus, sex determination in those species depended on whether the fertilizing sperm carried the large (X) or the small (Y) sex chromosome.

Sex determination is now known to follow a similar pattern in many animal groups. *The most prevalent sex-determining pattern in animals is XX = female and XY or X alone = male.* But in some groups such as butterflies, birds, amphibians, and certain fishes, it is the male—not the female—that has two X chromosomes. In these groups it is the female that has a single X chromosome and either a Y or no second chromosome. The eggs it produces are of two different types; the sperm are of a single type.

Sex-Linked Genes: The Accommodating Fruit Fly

For many, Mendelian genetics was looked upon as providing an adequate explanation for heredity and evolution. But the whole idea was unthinkable to the embryologist Thomas Hunt Morgan. Until 1910 he was openly hostile to the whole Mendelian viewpoint. In fact, he entered genetics to prove that evolution occurred not by slow accumulation of subtle changes, as Darwin suggested, but by sudden changes—or **mutations**—to wholly different forms.

Morgan chose the common fruit fly *Drosophila melanogaster* for his studies. These little flies thrive on a diet of mashed fruit and yeast; they can be kept by the hundreds in half-pint milk bottles. And they require only about twelve days to reach maturity—which means they yield some thirty generations a year for genetic studies. Morgan subjected his flies to heat, cold, x-rays, radioactivity, and a variety of chemicals in an attempt to induce massive changes in them. But for a considerable time, changes were not observed. Then, in 1910, a male fly with white eyes appeared in a bottle that had contained only the **wild-type** (normal) red-eyed flies. Morgan was certain the white-eyed male was a mutation.

He bred the male to a virgin, red-eyed female. All the F_1 progeny had red eyes. When the F_1 progeny were interbred, some of *their* offspring had white eyes, which was consistent with a Mendelian interpretation that the gene for white eyes was recessive. But in the F_2 generation, all the white-eyed flies were males! At first Morgan interpreted this outcome to mean that white eyes could not be expressed in females. But when he bred a white-eyed male to an F_1 generation female, both males and females with white eyes were produced. Morgan concluded that the white-eyed

character had failed to appear in female progeny in the original F_2 generation because it was somehow linked to sex-determining factors. In fact, his results were consistent with the assumption that the eye color gene is actually carried on the X chromosome (Figure 16.6). *When a trait is controlled by a gene carried on the X chromosome, it is now said to be sex-linked.*

It was the parallelism between the behavior of the white-eye allele through generations and the behavior of the sex chromosomes that drove Morgan (a) to accept the existence of Mendelian genes and (b) to postulate that genes are carried on chromosomes. Virtually overnight, his laboratory at Columbia University became the most productive Mendelian genetics laboratory in history. By focusing the search on subtle rather than massive mutations, Morgan suddenly began to see them with regularity. By year's end, he had discovered forty mutants in his fruit fly stocks—all of which fit Mendelian models and several of which had sex-linked mutations.

Morgan's work quickly attracted a small but dedicated group of students to his laboratory: Alfred Sturtevant, Calvin Bridges, and Hermann Muller. By 1915 they had identified and studied nearly a hundred mutant traits. In performing dihybrid crosses, they soon found that all the genes being studied fell into four groups. In the crosses that brought together genes of two different groups, all four possible combinations of traits turned up in the F_2 generation in a 9:3:3:1 ratio. Just as Mendel would have predicted, the genes had assorted independently. But when a dihybrid cross was made between two genes from *within* a group, the results were markedly different. Most of the F_2 progeny had the same combination of traits as one of the two original parents. The other two possible combinations were always relatively rare. *It was as if genes within a group were physically linked together and could not assort randomly.* All genes within a class that failed to assort randomly were said to be in the same **linkage group.**

Now, all the genes in *one* of the linkage groups were also sex-linked. Thus it was reasonable to suppose that all genes in this linkage group were carried on the X chromosome. (To this day, very few genes on the Y chromosome are known.) Of the three remaining linkage groups, two were large—they included many known genes—and one was small. The haploid chromosome set of *Drosophila* was known by then to consist of only four structures: the sex chromosomes and three **autosomes** (a term used to signify any other kind of chromosome). Two of the autosomes were large, but the other was extremely small (Figure 16.8). Clearly there was a correspondence between linkage groups and chromosomes.

Although all the known fruit fly mutations could be divided into these four linkage groups, there were certain

(text continues on page 359)

Interleaf 16.1

Meiosis:
An Evolutionary
Scrambler

Meiosis is central to biological evolution. It serves as a mechanism for reducing the chromosome number of cells by one-half. As you read in Chapter 4, because of meiosis the chromosome number of a species remains constant rather than doubling, and quadrupling, and so on when two reproductive cells join together in sexual fusion. In effect, meiosis and syngamy (fertilization) are evolutionary "scramblers," recombining hereditary traits within a species in a limitless variety of new ways. Two events, which occur simultaneously in meiosis, give rise to this increase in diversity. These events are the separation of homologous chromosome pairs, and chromosomal crossing over.

In meiosis I, each pair of homologous chromosomes (one from the maternal and one from the paternal parent) is separated. One chromosome of each pair ends up in one of two daughter cells. Whether all or some or none of the maternally derived homologues end up in one daughter cell as opposed to the other is an entirely random

1. *After the last mitotic division that occurred and before the onset of meiosis, a reproductive cell, like all somatic cells, is diploid. It contains the number of chromosomes that is characteristic of the species. Here, only two pairs are shown, for simplicity. One member of each pair came from the maternal parent (red) and the other (black) came from the paternal parent.*

2. *Just before meiosis begins, the quantity of DNA in the nucleus is doubled. When the chromosomes condense (fold in such a way as to become visible entities) for the beginning of meiosis, they are visibly double; each chromosome consists of two chromatids joined at the centromere. The cell is said to be pseudotetraploid.*

3. *In prophase of meiosis I, the maternally derived and paternally derived members of each homologous pair of chromosomes line up along their length in a process called synapsis. The four chromatids of a pair of chromosomes form a tetrad.*

4. *Subsequently, adjacent chromatids of maternal and paternal chromosomes cross over at a point of contact called a chiasma, or at several chiasmata. At metaphase of meiosis I, the chromosome pairs line up on the equator of the division spindle. Each chromosome becomes attached, at the centromere, to fibers from only one pole of the spindle. As chromosomes move apart at anaphase, centromeres do not split. But homologous chromosomes, having exchanged parts, separate from one another at the chiasmata.*

5. *By telophase of meiosis I, two pseudodiploid daughter cells are formed. Each has a haploid number of chromosomes. But each chromosome is still double: One of its chromatids has and the other has not participated in crossing over and recombination. Meiosis I is completed.*

6. *Meiosis II follows rapidly. In metaphase of meiosis II, each chromosome is connected to both poles at the centromere. Anaphase of meiosis II resembles mitotic anaphase, in that the centromeres split, which permits sister chromatids to move to opposite poles.*

7. *By telophase of meiosis II, four haploid cells are produced for each pseudotetraploid cell that entered into meiosis I. Potentially, at least, all four cells are genetically different.*

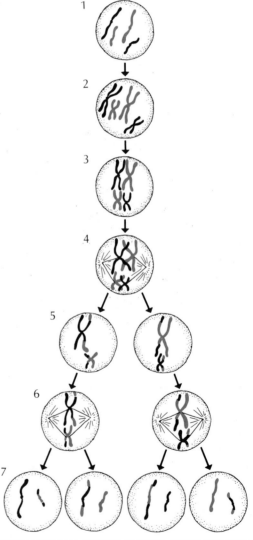

CHROMOSOMAL CROSSING OVER, RECOMBINATION, AND SEPARATIONS IN MEIOSIS I AND MEIOSIS II.

process; the same is true for the paternally derived homologues. What this means is that all sorts of combinations of traits are possible.

For example, an organism such as a male *Drosophila*, with only four chromosome pairs, can produce 2^4, or 16, different combinations. Because fertilization is also a random process, an organism with four chromosome pairs can produce $2^4 \times 2^4$, or 256, kinds of fertilized eggs on this basis alone. A human male and female, each with 46 chromosomes, theoretically could produce $2^{23} \times 2^{23}$, or more than 70,000,000,000,000, different kinds of offspring on this basis alone!

But even this staggering figure in no way reflects the true potential diversity that meiosis and syngamy offer. *Because chromosomal crossing usually occurs during meiosis I, parts between homologous chromosomes are regularly exchanged!* Thus the number of different sex cells that can be formed—and, in turn, the number of different progeny that can be produced by a single mating pair—is inestimably higher than 70,000,000,000,000! (Little wonder that siblings never look exactly alike unless they are identical twins, derived from the splitting of a single fertilized egg.)

The timing of meiosis in the development of sex cells varies from one species to the next. And it is usually different in the two sexes of a single animal species as well.

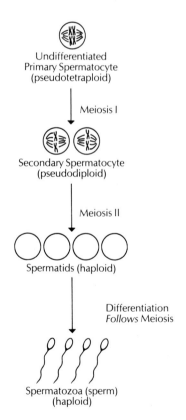

Undifferentiated
Primary Spermatocyte
(pseudotetraploid)

Meiosis I

Secondary Spermatocyte
(pseudodiploid)

Meiosis II

Spermatids (haploid)

Differentiation
Follows Meiosis

Spermatozoa (sperm)
(haploid)

THE TIMING OF MEIOSIS
IN MALE ANIMALS

Undifferentiated
Oogonium
(pseudotetraploid)

Growth and differentiation *precede* meiosis, occurring in a prolonged meiosis I prophase that may last more than forty years in human females.

Primary Oocyte
(pseudotetraploid)

Meiosis I occurs at one end of the cell, resulting in daughter cells vastly different in size.

In some species neither meiosis I nor meiosis II occurs until after fertilization. In others, meiosis I occurs before and meiosis II occurs after fertilization. In still others, both divisions are completed prior to fertilization.

Secondary Oocyte
and First Polar Body
(pseudodiploid)

Meiosis II occurs in both the oocyte and the polar body.

Following meiosis II, the polar bodies degenerate.

Ovum (egg) and
Three Polar Bodies
(haploid)

THE TIMING OF MEIOSIS
IN FEMALE ANIMALS

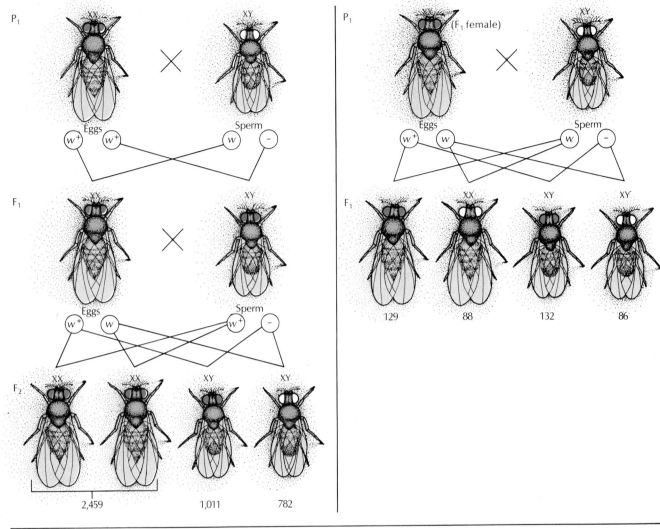

(a)   (b)   (c)   (d)

Figure 16.6 (left) A diagram of Morgan's observations and interpretations of his white-eye experiments with the fruit fly. Morgan and his students introduced a system of notation in which the "mutant" (in this case, "white-eye") allele is symbolized by the first letter (or letters) of that trait. If the mutant is recessive to the wild-type allele, the letter is lowercase; if dominant, it is uppercase. The wild-type allele is indicated by the same system of abbreviation, but it is given a superscript plus (+). In more recent work, the plus sign alone indicates the wild type. Thus w^+/w stands for an individual that is heterozygous for the white allele, and $^+/w$ indicates the same thing. The minus symbol (−) indicates the Y chromosome, which does not bear genes that are equivalent to the X chromosome. Thus, $w^+/^-$ indicates a male carrying a wild-type gene for eye color on the X chromosome, plus a Y chromosome.

Half the males in the original F_2 generation of these experiments were white-eyed because they had only a single X chromosome; if that chromosome carried the white allele, the eyes would be white. White-eyed females could arise only when a white-eyed male was crossed with a female that was a carrier (heterozygote) of the white allele.

The number below the last generation in the two experiments shown is the number of flies that Morgan actually observed. Notice the low number of white-eyed flies in both cases. These low numbers were later shown to be due to the fact that the w *gene is semilethal; it reduces viability of embryos when it is present in the homozygous state.*

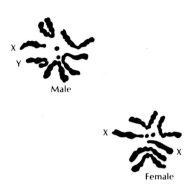

Figure 16.8 The appearance of the diploid chromosome sets (known as karyotypes) of male and female Drosophila. *Notice the difference in appearance of the X and Y chromosomes and the pair of tiny (dotlike) autosomes.*

Figure 16.7 (left) Thomas Hunt Morgan (a) and his students. Two of those students, Alfred Sturtevant (b) and Calvin Bridges (c), began working with Morgan while they were undergraduates; the third, Hermann Muller (d), was a graduate student who had been working with Edmund Wilson in the same department. Muller left the laboratory shortly after finishing his doctoral work, but Sturtevant and Bridges stayed on after receiving their doctoral degrees, forming a collaboration that was to last a lifetime and that would become one of the most productive in the history of biology.

irregularities within each group that remained puzzling at first. Certain pairs of genes appeared to be very *tightly linked*—they never assorted independently in a dihybrid cross. (Virtually all the F_2 progeny of such crosses had the same combination of alleles as one of the two P_1 parents.) Other pairs of genes in the same linkage group appeared to be *loosely linked*—they assorted almost as independently as if they had belonged to separate linkage groups. These relationships are shown in Figure 16.9. If two genes fell into one linkage group because they were carried on the same physical structure—the same chromosome—how could they show *any* degree of independent assortment? Why didn't all genes on the same chromosome remain *completely* linked at all times? What was the basis for the process of **genetic recombination**—the process whereby genes that acted as if they were on the same chromosome in one generation acted as if they were on separate chromosomes in a subsequent generation? Were the chromosomes breaking up and rearranging at some point in the development of the eggs?

As is often the case in science, these anomalous results were indicative of something important about the nature of the system. Analysis of these results was not only destined to open up a whole new field of genetic research, it was to provide insight into a basic evolutionary mechanism.

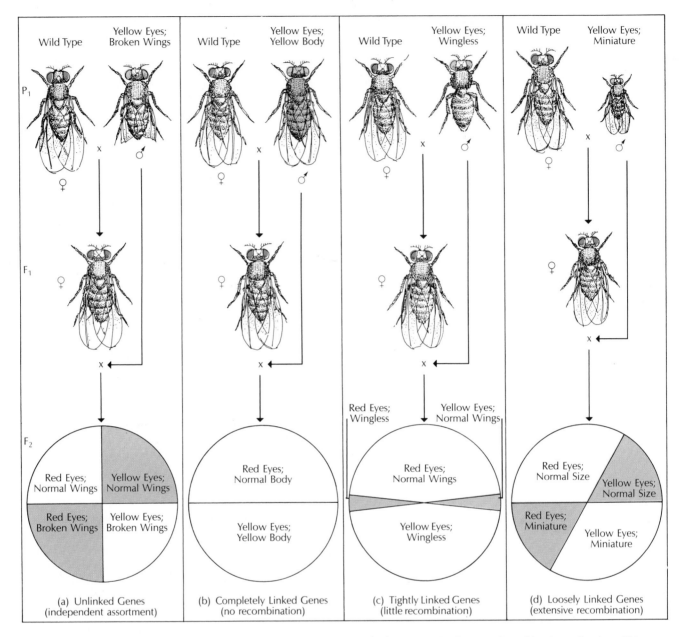

(a) Unlinked Genes
(independent assortment)

(b) Completely Linked Genes
(no recombination)

(c) Tightly Linked Genes
(little recombination)

(d) Loosely Linked Genes
(extensive recombination)

Figure 16.9 Linkage relationships among genes. In these hypothetical crosses, each male parent is homozygous (possesses identical alleles) for the two recessive traits involved in the cross. The F₁ female is homozygous for the wild-type alleles of these genes. To simplify analysis, a heterozygous female of the F₁ generation is back-crossed to the homozygous recessive male.

If the genes show independent assortment, the F₂ generation should have a 1:1:1:1 ratio of the four possible combinations of traits, as in (a).

If the two genes are completely linked, the F₁ female will produce only two kinds of eggs: those containing both wild-type genes and those containing both mutant genes. In such a case,

only the two original parental combinations of traits will be seen in the F₂ generation, as in (b).

In most such crosses, however, Morgan and his associates found that dihybrid crosses involving two genes within a linkage group gave results intermediate between the two extremes, as in (c) and (d). There was some deviation from Mendel's rule of independent assortment. The deviation was greater in crosses involving certain gene pairs (c) than in others (d).

CHROMOSOMAL CROSSING OVER AND GENE MAPPING

Resolution of the questions raised by the puzzling behavior of gene pairs within a single linkage group came with the realization that *homologous chromosomes exchange parts during meiosis.* The cell biologist F. A. Janssens had observed that just before the first meiotic division, homologous chromosomes paired up along their lengths. Then they became attached at one point. Janssens called this point of attachment between homologous chromosomes a **chiasma** (plural: **chiasmata**). When the chromosomes separated again, it was apparent to Janssens that the chromosomes had exchanged equivalent segments from the point of chiasma formation on. This process of chiasma formation and reciprocal exchange of parts between homologous chromosomes came to be known as **crossing over.** It was seen in every female *Drosophila* cell about to enter meiosis.

Upon reading Janssen's description of this process, Morgan realized at once that such crossing over was likely to provide the answer to the linkage riddle. In discussing the process with Sturtevant, he suggested that it is crossing over that prevents complete linkage in genes. And if that were true, *the degree of linkage might be an indication of the relative distances between genes.* He reasoned that the farther apart two genes are on the chromosome, the more likely it is that a chiasma will form between them. Mutant alleles that were previously on separate chromosomes then could be recombined in a single chromosome, or vice versa (Figure 16.10). Thus genes that were close together on a chromosome would appear to be tightly linked; those that were far apart on the chromosome would appear to be loosely linked.

Sturtevant realized that if Morgan's assumptions were correct, it should be possible to draw a map of the locations of genes on a chromosome, showing the order of their occurrence and the correct distances relative to one another. Using existing data on the degree of linkage observed in dihybrid crosses, he sat down that evening and drew the world's first chromosome map, locating each of five sex-linked genes in its relative position, or **locus,** on the X chromosome *(Interleaf 16.2).* A chromosome map that is based only on the degree of linkage between gene pairs is known as a **linkage map.** The map he drew is little modified as of today, except that dozens of other genes have been added to it.

Subsequent work showed that it was always possible to draw an unambiguous linear map. No branches or circles were required to fit all the genes into a map that was consistent with cross-breeding data. Thus the concept was strengthened that *genes are arranged in linear series on chromosomes,* somewhat like beads on strings.

Recombination of genes by crossing over occurs with
(text continues on page 364)

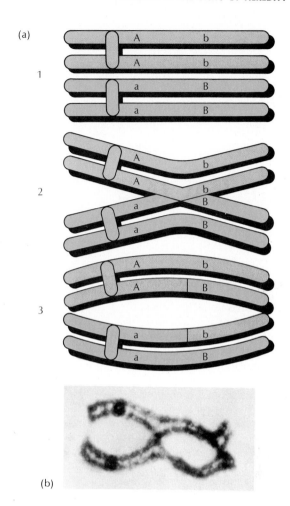

(a)

(b)

Figure 16.10 (a) Schematic model of a chromosome crossover that results in genetic recombination and (b) micrograph showing crossover. (1) Two homologous chromosomes (each composed of two chromatids) line up. (2) The adjacent chromatids (one from each chromosome) form a chiasma. Both chromatids break in this region and the fragments so formed are exchanged. (3) After crossing over is completed, two new chromatids are formed. They possess novel combinations of the genes on opposite sides of the crossover point. The process by which such novel combinations of genes are created is known as recombination.

When these chromatids separate from each other in meiosis (one chromatid into each egg or sperm cell), four different kinds of gametes will be produced. Thus, the result of crossing over will be detected by the appearance of offspring bearing the new combinations of traits. At the time Sturtevant drew his first map, it was not known how many strands were involved in crossing over. It has now been shown in a variety of organisms that the pattern shown here (crossing over between two non-sister strands at the four-strand stage) is the usual one.

Interleaf 16.2

Chromosomal Crossing Over and Gene Mapping

In constructing his first maps of the X chromosome of *Drosophila*, Alfred Sturtevant made two assumptions. First, he assumed that the absence of complete linkage between two genes is due to recombination of chromosome parts during chromosomal crossing over. Second, he assumed it is possible for crossing over to happen with equal likelihood at any point along the length of a chromosome. If these assumptions are valid, then the frequency of recombination between any two genes may be considered a measure of the distance between those genes. Said another way, *the farther apart two genes are, the greater the probability that crossing over will occur in the span between them.*

Consider a hypothetical chromosome bearing the genes *A, B,* and *C.* If crossovers occur more often in the span between genes *A* and *B* than they do in the span between genes *A* and *C,* then we must conclude that *A* and *B* must be farther apart than *A* and *C.* But this answer does not tell us *where* gene *C* falls relative to *A.* There are two possible arrangements: *C   A   B* or *A   C   B.* To determine the right order, it is necessary to observe the number of crossovers that occur between genes *B* and *C* relative to the number occurring be-

tween *B* and *A.* The order would be *CAB* if more crossovers occurred in the span between *B* and *C;* it would be *ACB* if the converse were true. In short, crossover frequency can be used to determine the order of genes on the chromosome. But, in addition, *if crossover frequency is proportional to distance, it can be used to determine relative distance between the genes.*

The measure of distance used is the percentage of the offspring that exhibit the results of crossing over. For example, suppose that when two mutant genes are passed along to offspring, 5 percent of these offspring have a combination of traits that could have arisen only as the result of a crossover in the chromosome during meiosis. The genes would be separated by 5 "map units."

Straightforward breeding procedures are used to obtain crossover data. A female is used that is heterozygous for the two genes in question. Prior work will have established whether the two recessive alleles the female bears are on the same chromosome (which would mean they both came from a single homozygous parent) or are on opposite chromosomes (which would mean each recessive allele came from a different parent). The male

must be homozygous for the recessive alleles of both genes. An example of such a cross would be (ab/a^+b^+) ♀ × (ab/ab) ♂. If the genes being studied are sex-linked, the male must bear the recessive gene on its single X chromosome: $ab/(-)$.

In the absence of crossing over, all the progeny of such a cross will have either the wild-type phenotype for both traits or the mutant phenotype for both traits. Progeny that have the wild-type phenotype for one trait and the mutant phenotype for the other must have a chromosome that resulted from crossing over:

It follows that, by determining the percentage of offspring with one—but not both—mutant characters, we can determine the percentage of crossing over between the genes in question. This percentage in turn equals the map distance between the two genes.

Table 16.A lists the data Sturtevant used to create his first map. Sturtevant's first step was to locate the *w*, *v*, and *m* genes on a map representing the X chromosome.

Table 16.A
Crossover Frequencies for Sex-Linked Gene Pairs

Genes Concerned	Crossover Frequency (percent)
w and *v*	29.7
w and *m*	33.7
w and *r*	45.2
w and *y*	1.0
v and *m*	3.0
v and *r*	26.9
v and *y*	32.2
m and *y*	35.5

Source: Adapted from A. H. Sturtevant, *Journal of Experimental Zoology,* 14 (1913), 43–59.

Gene *v* was clearly between *w* and *m,* but it was much closer to *m* (Figure a). In the second step, he added gene *r* to the right—clearly "outside" the other three and farther from *w* than from *v.* (Data for *m* and *r* were not available.) The remaining step was to place gene *y.* Because the frequency of crossing over between *w* and *y* was low, *y* must be close to *w.* Now, by examining crossover data for the span between these two adjacent genes and between genes *v* and *m,* it appeared that *y* was farther away than *w* from both of them. Thus *y* had to be "outside" gene *w.* Later work showed that this map order was correct.

In setting the scale for the map, Sturtevant had to determine the length of chromosome between two distant genes. That distance, he deduced, would be represented

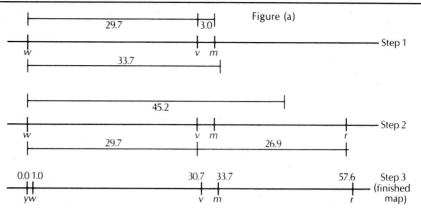

Figure (a)

more precisely by the sum of the distances from intermediate genes than by the distance (as measured by crossover frequency) between the two distant genes. In other words, he assumed (correctly) that crossover frequencies measured over short distances would be more reliable than those measured over long distances. He reasoned that if two genes are far enough apart, more than one crossover event might occur between them during meiosis. Such *double crossovers* would be detected only if the female were heterozygous for a third gene interposed between the crossover points:

$$a^+ \quad a$$
$$b^+ \quad b$$
$$c^+ \quad c$$

↓

$$a^+ \quad a$$
$$b^+ \quad b$$
$$c^+ \quad c$$

↓

$$a^+ \quad a$$
$$b \quad b^+$$
$$c^+ \quad c$$

Thus crossover distance between *a* and *c* should be more accurately determined by summing their individual crossover distances from *b* than by estimating it directly.

Sturtevant tested the hypothesis of double crossover by using a *three-point cross.* The female had one X chromosome bearing mutant alleles for three genes—"singed" bristles (*sn*), miniature wings (*m*), and fused wing veins (*fu*)—and one X chromosome bearing the three wild-type alleles of those genes. The male carried the recessive genes on its X chromosome. Of the progeny obtained, 66 percent received chromosomes in which no crossover had occurred in the region of these three genes (sn m fu or sn^+ m^+ fu^+). Of the remaining progeny, 31 percent had phenotypes that required a single crossover (such as sn^+ m fu). But 3 percent had phenotypes that could have resulted only if they received chromosomes derived as a result of a double crossover (sn m^+ fu or sn^+ m fu^+).

Because Sturtevant had known the gene order before he performed the three-point cross, he was able to confirm that double crossovers could occur. Such a three-point cross is still used to establish gene order and map relationship. The double crossover group is always the most rare, and the gene that is moved by a double crossover is obviously between the other two genes on the chromosome.

Similar mapping techniques have now been applied to a wide variety of organisms, including bacteria and their viruses.

extremely high frequency—at least one crossover per chromosome per generation in most species. It requires cellular energy and risks genetic disaster if crossing over is imperfectly executed. What evolutionary advantage does chromosomal crossing over provide that makes it so widely maintained despite the risk?

Crossing over permits a much greater range of genetic diversity than would otherwise be possible; it provides a greater reservoir of gene combinations from which natural selection can select the most adaptive complexes. New mutations are not permanently trapped in the chromosome in which by chance they first occur. As a result of crossing over, they can be tested in a variety of homologous chromosomes that have accumulations of other mutations. Then, if a combination of mutated genes occurs that works well together in a particular environment, selection can act to perpetuate that combination. It will do so even as that combination is still being tested for further improvement by further recombination.

In 1916, Bridges made a discovery that put the chromosomal theory of heredity almost beyond doubt. He noticed that a vermilion-eyed female *Drosophila* occasionally occurred in the offspring of a cross between vermilion-eyed females and red-eyed males. Because the allele for vermilion eyes is a sex-linked recessive gene, a vermilion-eyed female must have two X chromosomes bearing the mutant gene. Yet, in this cross, the male could not contribute an X chromosome with a mutant gene; its red eyes indicated that it had the wild-type gene on its X chromosome.

Bridges guessed that these two alleles might occur if the X chromosomes of the maternal fly failed to separate during meiosis. In this way, an egg would receive a pair of X chromosomes, each carrying the mutant allele for vermilion eyes. If this egg were then fertilized by a sperm carrying a Y chromosome, the resulting zygote would have the abnormal genotype $vv(-)$ and would have vermilion eyes. When Bridges examined the cells of the unexpected vermilion-eyed females, he found exactly what he had predicted: two X chromosomes and a Y chromosome. His experiment provided dramatic and convincing support for the theory that genes are carried on chromosomes.

Still further evidence came when Bridges was studying certain *Drosophila* and observed a phenomenon known as **pseudodominance,** whereby a gene that is known to be recessive in all other cases acts as if it were dominant! Bridges postulated that the corresponding wild-type gene must be missing altogether from the homologous chromosome in such flies. Later, the salivary glands of *Drosophila* larvae were found to contain "giant" chromosomes in which regular and extremely detailed banding patterns could be seen (Figure 16.11). When the chromosomes of flies showing pseudodominance were examined microscop-

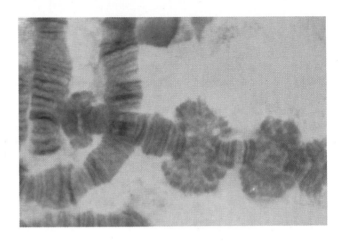

Figure 16.11 Photomicrograph depicting the giant salivary-gland-cell chromosomes of Drosophila. *Notice the distinct banding. In fruit flies that show pseudodominance, a small number of these are always missing in one particular region of one particular chromosome. Such deletions in the normal banding pattern signify the absence of genes. Chromosomes such as this are seen in several fly tissues that are composed of giant cells. In these tissues, the cells grow continuously without dividing. As the cells grow, the chromosomes replicate but fail to separate from each other as they normally do in mitosis. Thus a chromosome such as this one may consist of 1,024, 2,048 or even 4,096 chromosomes packed side-by-side so that regularities in their structures reinforce one another. The presence of these giant chromosomes is one reason why Morgan's choice of the fruit fly for an experimental organism was fortunate. (As someone once said, "God created* Drosophila *for Thomas Hunt Morgan and his students.")*

Figure 16.12 (right) The linkage map (a) compared with the cytological map (b) of a short segment of one Drosophila *chromosome. The lines connecting the two maps represent specific deletions that were observed.*

Although the order of the genes on the two maps is identical, the spacing is not. This is because one of the assumptions made by Morgan and Sturtevant was false. They assumed that the probability of chiasma formation was uniform along the chromosome. It is not. It is lower in regions where the genes appear to be jammed together on the linkage map.

ically, it was found that *a small number of bands was always missing in one particular region of one particular chromosome;* they had what was known as a **deletion.** The missing gene must normally be located in the region where the deletion was observed. Subsequently, flies showing pseudodominance for other genes were examined. They, too, lacked bands but in other specific regions.

It soon became possible to draw a wholly new kind of genetic map based on physically examining the chromosomes of fruit flies known to be lacking specific genes. This kind of map, based on cytology (the microscopic examination of cells) is called a **cytological map.** The fact that the linkage map and the cytological map were in all details completely parallel (Figure 16.12) proved beyond doubt that genes were entities physically carried on chromosomes.

Morgan—who had begun his career in genetics as an opponent of the Mendelists—became one of the outstanding proponents of a modified, chromosomal version of Mendelian genetics. He and his colleagues became the recognized leaders of genetic research and theory.

CHROMOSOMAL ABNORMALITIES

The extra X chromosome in some vermilion-eyed *Drosophila* females was not the only chromosomal abnormality that Bridges discovered. If some eggs received an extra X chromosome during meiosis, it might be equally possible for an egg to develop with no sex chromosome. Fertilization of the egg by a sperm with an X chromosome would produce a zygote with a single unpaired X chromosome. Bridges found this condition in certain male flies that produce immotile sperm and thus do not reproduce. Apparently, the Y chromosome plays some role in the normal development of sperm. Fertilization of an egg without a sex chromosome by a sperm with a Y chromosome would produce a zygote with an unpaired Y chromosome. Bridges was unable to locate any flies with this condition, so he concluded that such zygotes die at a very early stage of development. Apparently, this condition is a lethal chromosomal abnormality. A fourth possibility would involve fertilization of an egg with two X chromosomes by a sperm with a third X chromosome. Bridges found cells containing

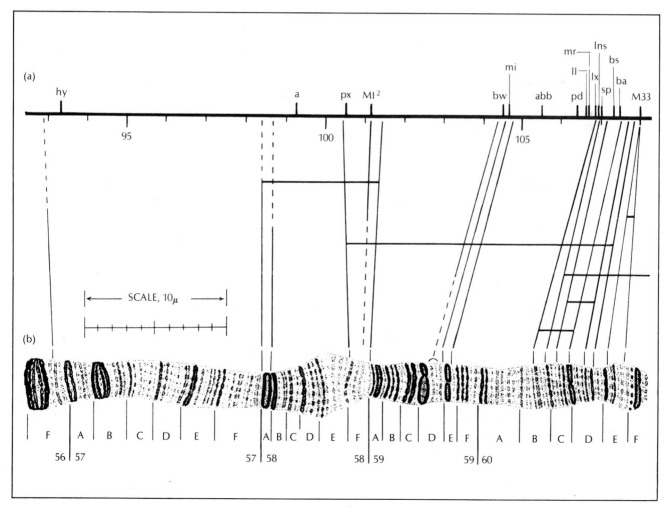

Normal Autosomes

A1   A2   A3

B4-B5

C6-C12

D13-D15

E16   E17   E18

F19-F20

G21-G22

Abnormal Autosomes

Down's Syndrome

G21   G22

Sex Chromosomes

Normal

Female   Male

Abnormalities

Female With Turner's Syndrome

Male With Kleinfelter's Syndrome

XX   X

Y

X

XX

Y

three X chromosomes in certain female flies that die before reaching maturity.

The absence of one chromosome is now called **monosomy.** The presence of an extra chromosome is called **trisomy.** Such chromosomal abnormalities occur in human beings (Figure 16.13). The general term for the absence or duplication of part of the normal diploid chromosome set is **aneuploidy.** In most cases of aneuploidy in animals, the zygote fails to develop into an adult. In cases where adulthood is reached, the aneuploid individual is usually unable to reproduce. Thus, aneuploidy is seldom transmitted from one generation to the next. In some plants, a number of varieties with extra copies of particular chromosomes do exist, and the aneuploid condition may be passed along to offspring.

The presence of one or more complete extra sets of chromosomes is called **polyploidy.** Cells with three complete sets of chromosomes are called *triploid,* those with four sets are called *tetraploid,* and so on. Because polyploidy interferes with normal pairing of homologous chromosomes during meiosis, polyploids are characterized by extremely low fertility.

Polyploidy in plants often results in exaggeration of certain traits of the flowers or of the fruit—for example, the size and number of petals or the fleshiness and sugar content of the fruit. Because such traits may be prized by farmers or gardeners, many domesticated plants are polyploid mutants. Many of these mutants (particularly triploids) do not reproduce effectively by sexual means but must be reproduced through grafting or slipping techniques. Those polyploid species that can reproduce sexually pass the polyploid condition along to their descendants. Polyploids are usually not viable in animals.

Some hybrid plant species are formed by a combination of complete chromosome sets from the two parental species. For example, suppose that one species has the diploid set of chromosomes *AABBCC* and a fairly similar species has a different set, *XXYYZZ.* In most cases, fusion of an *ABC* gamete from one species with an *XYZ* gamete from the other will produce a sterile hybrid with chromosomes *ABCXYZ.* Because the homologous chromosomes do not pair properly during meiosis, the gametes of the hybrid will have incomplete chromosome sets and will be inviable. If each species becomes tetraploid and thus produces diploid gametes, the fusion of an *AABBCC* gamete with an *XXYYZZ* gamete can produce a zygote with a complete diploid set of chromosomes: *AABBCCXXYYZZ.* This hybrid can produce gametes with full chromosome sets because all of its chromosomes have homologous pairs. Furthermore, the hybrid will produce relatively infertile triploid zygotes if it crosses with one of the parental species. Thus the hybrid becomes reproductively isolated and is apt to evolve rapidly into a species having traits quite different from those of the parental species. It appears that this process has been of great importance in the evolution of new plant species.

INDUCED MUTATIONS

The extreme rarity of naturally occurring mutations hampered the genetic research in Morgan's laboratory. Hundreds of thousands of flies were examined in order to find a few hundred mutant genes. Muller reasoned that most mutations involve only a single gene. For that reason, he needed to attack the chromosome with some agent that would affect only a tiny part of its length. High-energy radiation seemed to be the only thing that could accomplish

Figure 16.13 The normal human diploid chromosome set (or karyotype) and some abnormalities. To display the karyotype of an individual, the chromosomes of one dividing blood cell are photographed (hence they are doubled, ready for mitosis). In order to facilitate analysis, the individual chromosomes are then cut out of the photograph and grouped on the basis of size, as shown here.

Absence of a chromosome or presence of an extra one leads to aberrant development. In Turner's syndrome, sexual development is retarded and sterility results. From the fact that an XO fruit fly is a sterile male but an XO human being is a female, it can be deduced that the detailed mechanism of sex determination is different in the two groups. The human male with Kleinfelter's syndrome is sterile and usually develops some female characteristics in addition to being mentally retarded. Down's syndrome is the most common cause of what was once called mongolian idiocy. Most cases of trisomy in human beings result in highly abnormal embryonic or fetal development, and most are lethal.

the necessary microscopic damage. In 1927 he subjected a group of *Drosophila* to a dose of x-rays so strong that some of the flies became sterile. He then crossed the remaining fertile flies with wild-type flies. When the offspring matured, Muller found more mutants than he could have hoped for. Comparison with a control group of untreated flies showed that the radiation had increased the mutation rate by 150-fold. (Recall that Morgan started out by using x-rays, among other agents, in an attempt to induce mutations. Why he was unsuccessful is not altogether clear.) But a large number of the new mutant genes proved to be lethal. Some were **dominant lethals,** in that they brought about a decreased reproduction rate of the treated flies. Others were **recessive lethals,** in that the heterozygous first-generation flies matured but the genes proved fatal to their offspring that were homozygous for the mutant allele.

Many of the mutant traits already known were produced among the irradiated flies as well as a number of new mutant traits—splotched wings, sex-combless, and so on. But in addition to these mutations that appeared to involve a single gene—now called **point mutations**—a variety of changes in chromosome structure were also observed. Under the microscope, many cases of chromosome breakage, inversion of segments, and **translocations** (exchange of parts between nonhomologous chromosomes) could be seen. Chromosome mapping confirmed that known genes had assumed a new location as a result of such chromosomal rearrangements.

Other investigators soon discovered that x-rays are equally effective in producing mutations in other organisms. Because large numbers of mutations could now be produced, the nature of mutations and the nature of the gene itself could be studied far more easily. And perhaps of most importance, *the fact that radiation produces mutations provided an explanation of the source of naturally occurring mutations.* Cosmic rays, ultraviolet light, and natural radioactivity provide a constant source of low-level radiation that strikes all organisms. The natural radiation accounts at least partially for the natural appearance of mutations at a low rate in all organisms. Mutations provide the variability of traits that can be reassorted to provide a variety of phenotypes within a population. And this variety makes possible evolution through natural selection.

HOW DOES GENOTYPE CONTROL PHENOTYPE?

The success of the Morgan group was such that for twenty years they (and everyone they attracted to the field) singlemindedly pursued two basic questions: How are genes arranged on chromosomes, and how do they behave between generations? They did not concern themselves with the nature of genes, or how genotype becomes expressed as phenotype. It was not that they were unaware of these interesting issues. It was simply that they considered such issues irrelevant to their research interest. In fact, it was pointed out with some pride during this period that the questions they did pose could be answered without any consideration of the chemical nature of a gene or how genes work. By 1930, however, there was growing uneasiness among newcomers to genetics that the more fundamental considerations could no longer be brushed aside.

In 1931, Morgan's group (which was now at the California Institute of Technology) welcomed George Beadle, a Nebraska farm boy who had just received his degree from Cornell University in corn genetics and who was originally interested in the mechanism of crossing over. By 1935, with Morgan's encouragement and in collaboration with the embryologist Boris Ephrussi, Beadle was analyzing gene action.

Beadle and Ephrussi chose *Drosophila* eye color genes for investigation. They proceeded by implanting the eye-forming region of one fruit fly larva into the body cavity of another. They knew that when the eye developed in the host, an eye would develop in the body cavity, also. They discovered that the color of the eye that formed in the cavity was determined partly by the genotype of the host and partly by the genotype of the implanted eye tissue. Apparently, eye pigmentation depended on substances produced outside the eye and then transformed into pigment within the eye. If eye disks from flies with the cinnabar (*cn*) eye-color mutation were placed in hosts with the vermilion (*v*) mutation, the cinnabar coloration developed. But if vermilion eye disks were implanted in cinnabar mutant hosts, they developed wild-type pigmentation! Apparently the cinnabar fly produced something that permitted the vermilion eye to produce normal pigment. But the reverse was not true. To explain these results, Beadle and Ephrussi postulated that the wild-type equivalents of the two genes (v^+ and cn^+) acted to produce enzymes, and that the enzymes functioned as follows:

$$v^+ \text{ Gene} \longrightarrow v^+ \text{ Enzyme}$$

Substrate

$$v^+ \text{ Substance}$$

$$cn^+ \text{ Gene} \longrightarrow cn^+ \text{ Enzyme}$$

$$cn^+ \text{ Substance}$$

Brown Pigment

The vermilion mutant apparently lacked the enzyme required to make the v^+ substance. But in the cinnabar host, this substance was available and could be converted to brown pigment by the implanted vermilion eye. The cinnabar fly, however, lacked the enzyme required to convert v^+ substance to cn^+ substance. Hence it *never* made the brown pigment required for wild-type eye color. Although Beadle and Ephrussi did not express their ideas in generalized terms, they were developing the idea that genes function by way of the production of enzymes.

In 1936 Beadle moved to Stanford University and gained a new collaborator, the biochemist Edward Tatum. For four years they struggled with further analysis of eye pigmentation in *Drosophila,* without notable success. Then, one day in 1940, while Tatum was lecturing to a genetics class and Beadle was sitting in the back of the room, it dawned on Beadle that just because *Drosophila* had been an ideal

(a)

(b)

Figure 16.14 (a) George Beadle, Nobel Prize-winning geneticist. Beadle is known for his work on Neurospora crassa, *which led to the one gene–one enzyme hypothesis. (b) Edward Tatum, who was Beadle's collaborator in this research.*

Figure 16.15 (right) (a) The perithecium, or sexual fruiting body, of Neurospora crassa. *(b) This photograph shows the asci just being released from a perithecium. Each ascus contains eight ascospores (some have been broken in the photographed sample). Because the ascospores are lined up in the order they are formed during meiosis (c), it is possible to dissect them out of the ascus one at a time, grow them separately, and analyze when during meiosis and where in the chromosomes crossing over occurs.*

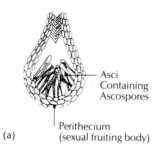

Asci
Containing
Ascospores

Perithecium
(sexual fruiting body)

(a)

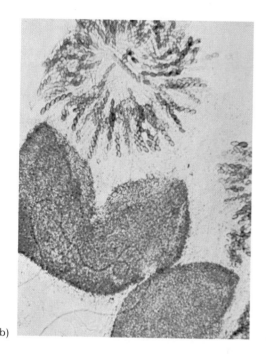

(b)

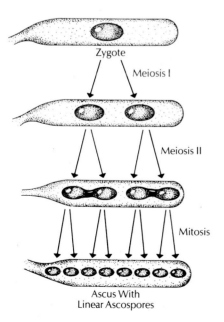

Zygote

Meiosis I

Meiosis II

Mitosis

(c)

Ascus With
Linear Ascospores

organism for studying chromosome mechanics, it clearly was not the best organism for studying gene action. Beadle reasoned they should switch to the red bread mold, *Neurospora crassa* (Figure 16.15), which he had been hearing about and observing for twelve years.

The advantage this organism offered was its nutritional simplicity. All it requires from the exterior for growth and reproduction is a medium containing sugar, salts, and the vitamin biotin. Because *Neurospora* cells contain all the other vitamins, amino acids, and other molecules known in other life forms, they must be capable under normal conditions of synthesizing all these entities. Now, if it were possible to select mutants that require an additional nutrient for growth, it should be possible to examine which step is defective in the synthesis of that nutrient. Instead of taking phenotypically determined genetic mutations and looking for their biochemical basis, Beadle and Tatum would start with reactions for which the biochemistry was known and look for genetic mutations that modified the biochemistry!

Beadle's expressed hope at the outset was to demonstrate there is a one-to-one correspondence between genes and enzymes. Success came within a matter of weeks: mutant *Neurospora* were found that required one or another additional nutrient for growth to occur. As word spread, fruit fly bottles began to move aside to make room for *Neurospora* tubes in many genetics laboratories. In case after case, it turned out that a mutant form that required an additional nutrient had a defect in one (and only one) of the enzymes in the pathway by which that nutrient was normally synthesized (Figure 16.16).

On the basis of such results, Beadle and Tatum developed the **one gene–one enzyme concept.** This phrase implied that it was the function of a gene to specify the properties of an enzyme.

It turned out that Beadle and Tatum were not the first to propose such a role for genes. In 1909 the brilliant biochemist Archibald Garrod showed that a human disease, "alkaptonuria," occurs when the body fails to break down the amino acids phenylalanine and tyrosine when they are present in excessive amounts. He determined that one specific step in the breakdown process did not take place in afflicted patients. As a result, an intermediate compound built up in the body and eventually caused brain damage. Garrod studied several such diseases and called them "inborn errors of metabolism." Genes, he concluded, were normally supposed to produce enzymes essential for bodily processes; mutations of genes led to defective enzymes and faulty metabolism. Unfortunately, Garrod (like Mendel) was a generation before his time. The chemical nature of enzymes was not known then and would not be known for one and one-half decades. Although Garrod's work was referred to intermittently over the years, his influence was

Class of Mutants	Growth On:				Reaction Blocked
	Minimal	Ornithine	Citrulline	Arginine	
1	−	+	+	+	1
2	−	−	+	+	2
3	−	−	−	+	3

(a)

(b)

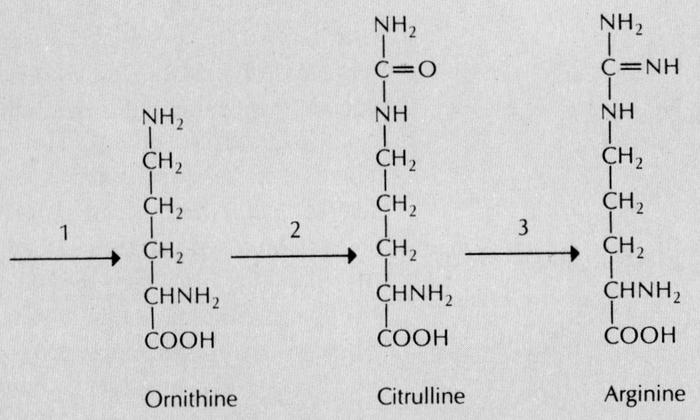

Ornithine   Citrulline   Arginine

(c)

Figure 16.16 The findings of Adrian Srb and Norman Horowitz, who analyzed x-ray induced Neurospora mutants that required the amino acid arginine for growth. Conventional genetic analysis showed the organisms were mutants of seven different genes. On the basis of what they would use as a source of arginine, these mutants fell into three groups (a). Group 1 contained mutants of four genes; those strains would grow if arginine, citrulline, or ornithine were present. Group 2 involved mutants of two genes and grew on either arginine or citrulline, but not ornithine. Group 3 contained mutants of a single gene and had an absolute requirement for arginine; citrulline and ornithine would not substitute.

From these data, three conclusions were drawn. The first was that arginine is normally synthesized by the following enzyme-catalyzed reaction pathway: simpler cellular compounds → ornithine → citrulline → arginine (b).

The second conclusion was that each group of mutants had enzymatic deficiencies at a corresponding conversion step, shown in (b). Group 3 apparently lacked an enzyme capable of converting citrulline to arginine and therefore could not grow on either of the precursors. Group 2, however, was able to carry out that conversion and thus could grow on citrulline. But apparently it was deficient in an enzyme required to produce citrulline from ornithine. Group 1 mutants apparently were blocked at steps leading to ornithine but could convert either ornithine or citrulline to arginine.

The third conclusion was that, if Beadle and Tatum were correct in their one gene–one enzyme concept, there must be a total of seven enzymes involved in the pathway: four leading to ornithine, two required to go from ornithine to citrulline, and one to convert citrulline to arginine (c). Later biochemical studies confirmed the existence of these enzymes and reinforced the Beadle-Tatum concept.

minimal. Even Beadle made no mention of Garrod or his work in the 1939 genetics textbook he coauthored with Sturtevant.

Although the one gene–one enzyme concept was not immediately and universally accepted, over the years its basic validity became inescapable. However, it later became known that some enzymes contain two or more polypeptide chains that are the products of separate genes. So the concept was modified to the **one gene–one polypeptide chain concept.**

PERSPECTIVE

The history of genetics is intimately connected with the story of particular men who chose the right organism to study: Mendel with the pea, Morgan with the fruit fly, Beadle with *Neurospora.* Had Mendel and his rediscoverers chosen hawkweed first, the history of genetics might have been very different. Yet the importance of genetics has been the generality of its principles. Mendel's generalizations apply to every other organism—including hawkweed and bacteria—yet discovered. The secret of the model organisms is not that they have a unique hereditary system but that their life style makes them particularly amenable for asking particular questions in experimentally simple ways. Nothing yet studied is better suited than fruit flies are (and few are as well suited) to showing that genes are arranged linearly on chromosomes. Yet once that generalization is made for fruit flies, we can find ways of testing whether it is true of other organisms. Crossing over would never have been discovered by studying viruses had it not already been known in the fruit fly. Yet understanding of how it works in fruit flies is now coming from analysis of viruses. Nothing has contributed more to our sense of life's unity than the analysis of heredity.

The hereditary mechanisms discovered by Mendel and those who followed him provide insight into how evolutionary changes must have occurred. Each living system is tuned at once to maintaining constancy while testing innovations. The chromosomes reproduce themselves faithfully at every cell division and perpetuate the necessary genes to provide the necessary enzymes to make life possible. But mutation can and does occur, to yield a product with a change of function. If deleterious, it will be quickly lost. If the mutation is not deleterious, it will be maintained, but it will be recombined in new ways with each new generation by crossing over and reduction-division in meiosis, followed by fusion with a new set of genes at fertilization. Neither so conservative that it prevents change nor so liberal that it fails to protect existing strengths the genetic system in combination with selection is continuously testing for new and more adaptive complexes of genes while continuing to maintain complexes that are successful.

The one gene–one enzyme concept gave rise to the next major focus of genetics: the analysis of gene structure and function at the molecular level. This is the topic of Chapter 17. As with previous stages in the development of genetic theory, a new organism was to come under the spotlight as approaches changed. This time the organism was the intestinal bacterium *Escherichia coli.* It was Edward Tatum and his student Joshua Lederberg who would show that *E. coli* was a suitable organism for genetic research. Together they would initiate one of several lines of research that would converge in the explosive scientific development now known as the biological revolution. It is ironic but not unusual in science that molecular genetics would spring from the one gene–one enzyme concept and then go on to show the inadequacy of the concept by demonstrating the existence of genes that function in ways other than defining the structure of an enzyme. These are the control genes, and they are a topic of Chapter 20.

SUGGESTED READINGS

BEADLE, G. W., "Genes and Chemical Reactions in Neurospora," and Tatum, E. L., "A Case History in Biological Research," in *Nobel Lectures, Physiology or Medicine,* 1942–1962. Amsterdam: Elsevier, 1964. Highly personal accounts of Beadles's and Tatum's work in genes and enzymes.

PETERS, JAMES A. (ed.). *Classic Papers in Genetics.* Englewood Cliffs, N.J.: Prentice-Hall, 1959. An excellent compendium of original research papers, each a classic contribution to the field. Not easy reading, but recommended for the determined student.

STERN, CURT, and EVA R. SHERWOOD (eds.). *The Origin of Genetics: A Mendel Source Book.* San Francisco: W. H. Freeman, 1966. Mendel's original papers, translated into English and annotated by the editors. A fascinating insight into the origins of Mendelian genetics.

STURTEVANT, ALFRED H. *A History of Genetics.* New York: Harper & Row, 1965. A delightfully readable account of genetics from Mendel's peas to modern molecules, as told by one whose career has spanned much of the history about which he writes.

SWANSON, C. P., T. MERZ, and W. J. YOUNG. *Cytogenetics.* Englewood Cliffs, N.J.: Prentice-Hall, 1967. A competent and comprehensive introduction to cytogenetics. Although detailed and technical, it is of value to anyone especially interested in this area of genetics.

Chapter 17

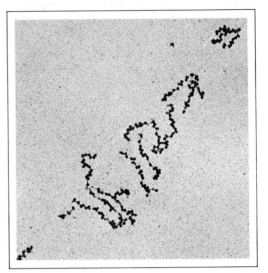

Genes in Action

DNA makes RNA makes protein. This simple concept, often termed the central dogma of modern biology, summarizes the results of thousands of experiments performed in hundreds of laboratories around the world in the past two decades. But here, in this electron micrograph, we see this central process of life frozen in time. The long, slender fiber represents the genetic material of a bacterium—its DNA. Spun out from the DNA are even more tenuous strands of RNA in the process of being copied from the DNA. Before their birth has been completed, these RNA messages have become studded with ribosomes. And these ribosomes have begun to translate the coded message of the gene, forming the vital proteins that will put the genes into action in the cell.

In 1928 Fred Griffith, a British medical officer, reported the astonishing outcome of a simple experiment. He was studying what was then a fearsome killer: *Diplococcus pneumoniae,* the pathogenic bacterium that causes pneumonia. Normally these bacteria are encased in a carbohydrate coat, but Griffith had isolated a strain in which it was absent. Without that protective coat, bacteria were quickly destroyed by the defense systems of mice into which they were injected; they could not cause the disease. Griffith then mixed the live, harmless strain with pathogenic bacteria that had been killed by the application of heat. He injected the mixture into live mice—which promptly contracted a fatal infection. At the time the mice died, their blood was swarming with live, capsule-forming, pathogenic bacteria! It was highly improbable that the dead pathogens in the injection had been brought back to life. More likely, the dead pathogens had somehow transformed the harmless bacteria. Furthermore, through subsequent tests Griffith found that the transformed bacteria passed on the capsule-forming trait to all their progeny. Capsule formation clearly was a heritable trait—and the transformation of harmless strains into deadly ones involved some sort of genetic change.

The implications of Griffith's experiments were particularly intriguing to an American bacteriologist, Oswald Avery, and his associates. For ten years they worked to identify the "transforming principle" that had brought about the change. Then in 1944 Avery, together with Colin MacLeod and Maclyn McCarty, cautiously announced they had purified the transforming principle. It was "largely, if not exclusively, composed of DNA." When pure DNA extracted from virulent pneumococci was added to harmless strains of pneumococci, deadly strains resulted. Furthermore, the activity of the transforming principle could be destroyed by the digestive enzyme that specifically degrades DNA but *not* by enzymes that digest proteins. This demonstration of the relationship between a heritable factor (a gene) and a DNA molecule was met with almost universal apathy. For the most part, those who did react said they did not believe it.

Two prejudices hampered acceptance of this work. First of all, because bacteria do not have a nucleus or visible chromosomes and because they do not undergo meiosis and syngamy, few would believe the genetic system of these simple microorganisms could be like that of more complex organisms. Second, although eukaryotic chromosomes possess both DNA and protein, there was near-universal belief that it must be the protein that carries the genetic information. There was not a scrap of direct evidence to support this idea, but it was nevertheless firmly entrenched. Nearly a decade would pass before the scientific community would give it up.

BACTERIA AND THEIR VIRUSES HAVE A GENETIC SYSTEM

In 1946 Joshua Lederberg discovered conjugation in the bacterium *Escherichia coli* (Chapter 4). He identified two different strains, one with a "fertility factor" (F^+) and one without it (F^-). When F^+ and F^- bacteria were brought together, they attached to each other in the manner shown earlier in Figure 4.6. At the end of the conjugation process, all the F^- bacteria had been converted to F^+ strains. A few also gained certain heritable traits of the F^+ donor (such as the capacity to grow on a certain sugar or to form a particular amino acid). The original F^+ strain never gained heritable traits from the F^- strain; the transfer of information was strictly one-way. Later, a strain was identified that could transfer genes about 10,000 times more efficiently than the original F^+ strain. The new donor strain was called **Hfr** (*H*igh *f*requency *r*ecombination).

Experiments with the Hfr strain showed that bacteria resemble higher organisms in an important way: *Bacterial genes are carried in a linear array.* When conjugation was allowed to run to completion, all the Hfr genes were donated to F^- recipients. But when a conjugating pair was separated mechanically before conjugation was complete, some genes had been transferred with high frequency and others had not been transferred at all. By interrupting the process at different intervals, it was possible to show that there was a linear series in which certain genes were predictably transferred early—and certain others were transferred only later. It was as if the genetic information was on a chain that was being threaded slowly through the bridge between the Hfr donor and the F^- recipient. When conjugation was stopped prematurely, the chain broke off. The part of the chain already in the F^- bacterium would remain there, but the rest would not be transferred. The order of transfer was so regular that an **interrupted mating map** of the gene order could be determined, in which map distance from the origin was measured in minutes required to transfer a certain gene from Hfr to F^-.

Eventually several different Hfr strains were identified. All behaved similarly, in that they passed genes to the bacterium F^- in a regular, predictable order. But the order was not the same for any two Hfr strains! The starting places varied, and sometimes the order of gene transfer made by one strain was the exact opposite of that made by another strain. When all the different interrupted mating maps were put together, they pointed to the same thing: *The genes of E. coli are arranged in a circle.* As Figure 17.2 shows, the Hfr factor determines the point at which the circle will be broken; it also determines the direction in which a copy will be produced and passed to the F^- strain.

While the implications of bacterial conjugation were being mulled over, Norton Zinder and Lederberg dis-

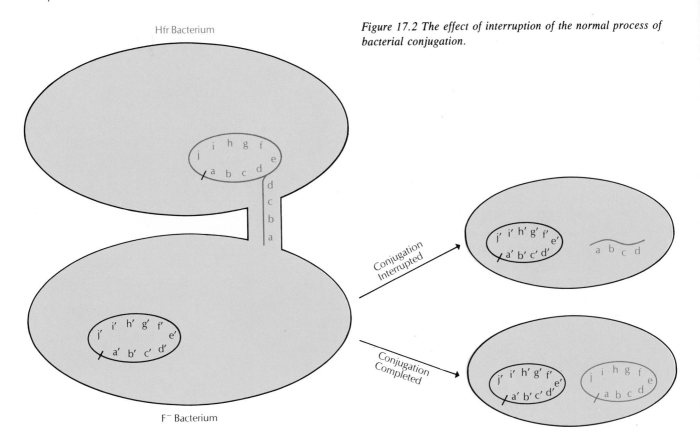

Figure 17.2 The effect of interruption of the normal process of bacterial conjugation.

covered an entirely different process of genetic exchange between bacteria, which is now called **transduction.** In transduction, a **bacteriophage** (a bacterial virus, often simply called "phage") infects a bacterium and starts to proliferate. In certain cases it picks up a piece of genetic information from the bacterium as it does so. When the original host cell dies, bacteriophage are released that are capable of infecting other cells. But now they will introduce into the second host cell the bacterial genes picked up from the first (Figure 17.3).

In their first experiment on transduction, Zinder and Lederberg showed that bacteria growing on one side of a filter (through which bacteria could not pass) could nevertheless pick up one or more genes from bacteria on the other side of the filter. Considering the small size of the bacteriophage, the amount of genetic information that could be transferred at any one time would have to be extremely small. Now, if two genes were **co-transduced** (transferred at once between bacteria by a single bacteriophage), then that would imply they must have been very close together in the original gene sequence. Because the probability of two genes being co-transduced would be inversely proportional to the distance between them, Zinder and Lederberg reasoned that a **co-transduction map** of gene order could be developed. Later, mapping of genes by co-transduction and

interrupted mating were shown to yield similar results.

During this period, others began to prove that bacteriophage have a simple genetic system. In 1930, Frank Macfarlane Burnet had shown that certain bacteriophage properties, such as host range, are heritable. (The term "host range" refers to the range of bacterial strains a bacteriophage will or will not infect.) Late in the 1930s, Max Delbrück, Alfred Hershey, and Salvador Luria began working in earnest on the genetics of bacteriophage (Figure 17.4). It was Delbrück and Hershey who in 1945 made a most important observation: If two genetically different bacteriophage were permitted to attack the same host cell, then during the time of infection they underwent genetic recombination. When the infected cell burst open, all possible combinations of the traits shown by the parental bacteriophage could be found among the progeny. *Genetic recombination in bacteriophage was therefore similar to genetic recombination in all "higher" organisms—but it occurred despite the absence of meiosis and syngamy!*

DNA HAS THE PROPERTIES REQUIRED OF THE GENETIC MATERIAL

Just three years after Mendel had published his studies of pea heredity, Johann Friedrich Miescher discovered what is now called deoxyribonucleic acid (DNA). A complex of

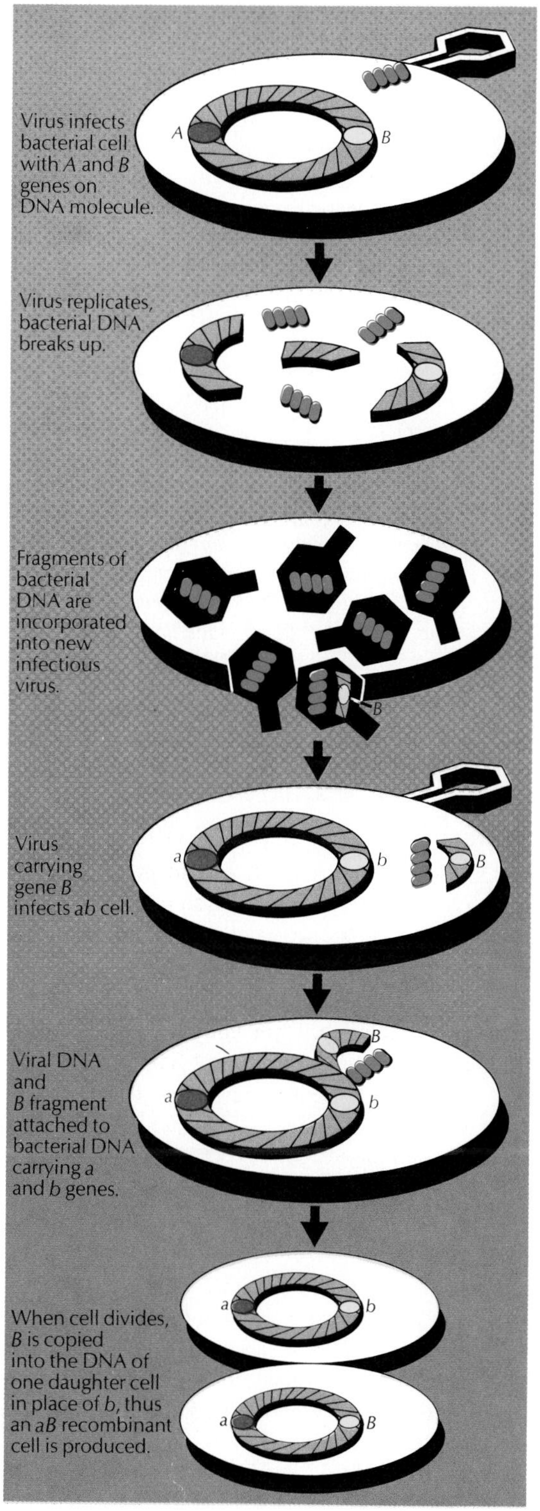
Virus infects bacterial cell with A and B genes on DNA molecule.
A
B
Virus replicates, bacterial DNA breaks up.
Fragments of bacterial DNA are incorporated into new infectious virus.
B
Virus carrying gene B infects ab cell.
a
b
B
Viral DNA and B fragment attached to bacterial DNA carrying a and b genes.
B
a
b
When cell divides, B is copied into the DNA of one daughter cell in place of b, thus an aB recombinant cell is produced.
a
b
a
B

Figure 17.3 The process of transduction by a bacteriophage.

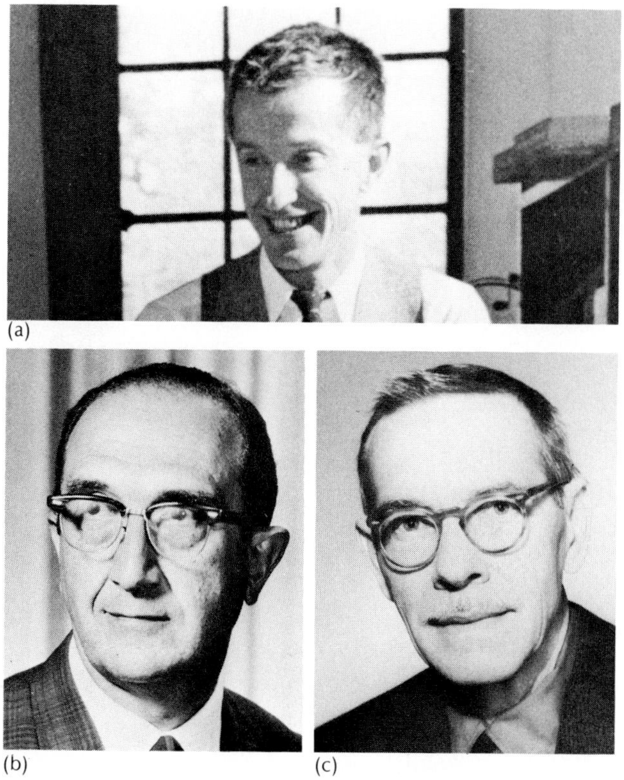
(a)
(b)
(c)

Figure 17.4 The founders of the "Phage Group": researchers into the genetics of bacteriophage. (a) Max Delbrück, (b) Alfred Hershey, and (c) Salvador Luria. This group would ultimately affect the course of genetics in a most dramatic way. But at first they worked in isolation from the mainstream of genetics, and by 1947 they had attracted only five other scientists to the first formal meeting of the Phage Group.

nucleic acid and protein, he said, is the main constituent of the nucleus of eukaryotic cells. About fifty years after that, a technique would be devised for selectively staining the DNA material in the nucleus, so that by the time the chromosomal theory of inheritance was developed, nuclear DNA was known to be located in the chromosomes. However, for the next four decades the *protein* part of the chromosomes was assumed to be the carrier of genetic information. Proteins (particularly enzymes) were found to be diverse substances capable of executing a broad array of biological functions. In contrast, *the nucleic acid DNA was amazingly similar from species to species.* It contained only four bases (adenine, thymine, guanine, and cytosine), which were always present in roughly equal proportions. Indeed, DNA was once thought to be a polymer in which the four bases alternated, one after the other, in a regular

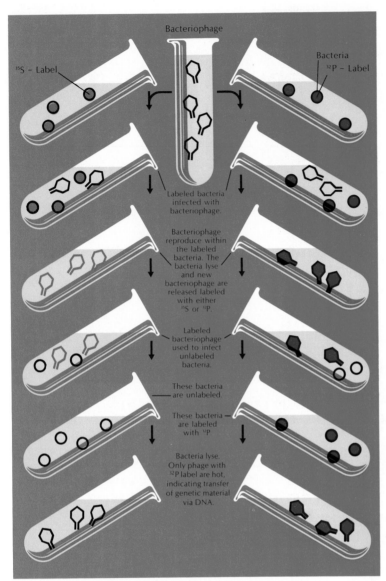

Bacteriophage

³⁵S – Label

Bacteria
³²P – Label

Labeled bacteria
infected with
bacteriophage.

Bacteriophage
reproduce within
the labeled
bacteria. The
bacteria lyse
and new
bacteriophage are
released labeled
with either
³⁵S or ³²P.

Labeled
bacteriophage
used to infect
unlabeled
bacteria.

These bacteria
are unlabeled.

These bacteria
are labeled
with ³²P.

Bacteria lyse.
Only phage with
³²P label are hot,
indicating transfer
of genetic material
via DNA.

Figure 17.5 (left) The Hershey-Chase experiment that provided compelling evidence that DNA is the carrier of hereditary information.

Figure 17.6 (right) Model (a) and electron micrograph (b) of a T-even bacteriophage. This strain belongs to a family of viruses that infect the bacterium Escherichia coli. *The strains were identified in the order of their discovery as T1, T2, T3, and so on; the T-even strains (T2, T4, and T6) are all closely related.*

A typical bacteriophage has a large, polygonal head composed of protein and housing a tightly coiled DNA molecule. At the base of the head is a protein collar with a tail assembly attached. The intricate tail consists of a sheath of 144 contractile protein subunits wrapped around a hollow protein core. The top of the core-sheath complex is attached to the collar region. The bottom is attached to a flat, hexagonal end plate that has six spikes protruding from it. Extending from these spikes are long, kinked tail fibers made up of several proteins.

This elaborate structure acts as a microsyringe to inject viral DNA through the tough polysaccharide cell wall of a bacterium. When a bacteriophage bumps into a host cell (bacteriophage have no means of moving about themselves) that has appropriate protein receptor sites on its surface, the bacteriophage tail fibers "recognize" the sites and attach themselves by weak, noncovalent bonds to the surface.

Although the attachment process is reversible, what immediately follows is not. An enzyme produced by the attached bacteriophage digests a small part of the cell wall, creating a hole in it. The contractile sheath of the tail then contracts, the head of the bacteriophage collapses, and the DNA contents of the head are extruded through the tail into the cytoplasm of the host. Only the viral DNA and a small amount of its internal protein enter the bacterial cell. Most of the bacteriophage protein remains as a "ghost" on the outer surface (Figure 4.12).

and monotonous procession. How could such a uniform substance carry genetic information?

In 1948 André Boivin and Colette and Roger Vendrely made a critical observation that would help solve the riddle. In each sample of various tissues taken from a bull, they had counted nuclei and had measured the DNA content. With one exception, all the tissues had the same DNA content per nucleus. The exception was sperm nuclei—which had only half as much DNA as other cell types! Now, unlike all other tissues of the bull, sperm were known to be haploid rather than diploid. These results were consistent with the idea that hereditary instructions are carried in DNA. The following year Alfred Mirsky and Hans Ris extended this observation to many other organisms. Although the amount of DNA per nucleus was shown to vary enormously between species, it was constant within a species—except for the sex cells. The

next year Hewson Swift made observations that led him to the conclusion that *cells double their DNA content during preparation for either mitosis or meiosis.*

Between 1949 and 1950, Erwin Chargaff and his coworkers reexamined the chemical composition of DNA from various sources. Each species was shown to have a fixed molar ratio of the four bases (adenine, thymine, guanine, and cytosine) in its DNA, and the ratio was found

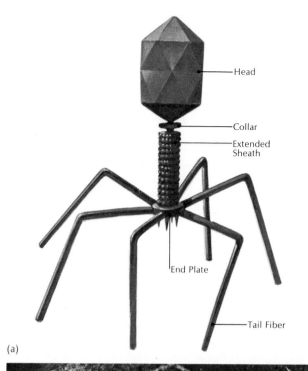

Head

Collar

Extended
Sheath

End Plate

Tail Fiber

(a)

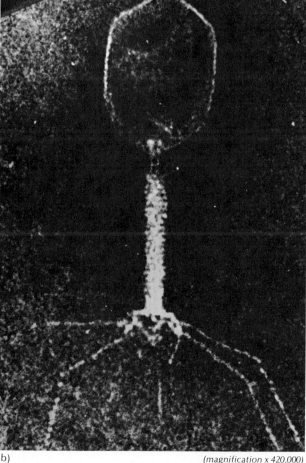

(b)

(magnification x 420,000)

to be different from one species to the next. Thus, the base ratio of the DNA seemed to be a stable characteristic of species. Through such studies, the sequence of nucleotides along a DNA molecule began to be perceived as variable, rather than a regular repeat—and the variability from one species to the next was thought to somehow correspond to the heritable characteristics of species.

DNA IS THE HEREDITARY MATERIAL

In 1952, Hershey had been working on bacteriophage for well over a decade. By then it was well established that bacteriophage consisted almost exclusively of two kinds of molecules: DNA and protein. It was also known that DNA contained phosphorus but no sulfur—and that protein contained sulfur but usually no phosphorus. Hershey and one of his colleagues, Martha Chase, devised an experiment around these facts. Their results would convince biologists that DNA is the carrier of hereditary information.

They grew one set of bacteriophage in the presence of radioactive phosphorus (^{32}P), which labeled the DNA. They grew another set in the presence of radioactive sulfur (^{35}S), which labeled the protein. The bacteriophage so labeled were used to infect unlabeled bacteria. After the onset of the infection process, each of the cultures was put in a blender and churned briefly, like a milkshake. The churning action was enough to remove any bacteriophage particles that were loosely attached to the outside of the bacteria but it was not enough to break any bacteria or to release bacteriophage that had penetrated to the interior of bacterial cells. The culture was then centrifuged (*Interleaf 17.1*) under conditions that would cause bacteria and their contents to settle to the bottom of the tube and form a pellet even as free bacteriophage remained suspended in the liquid phase. The supernatant fluid and the pellet were assayed for ^{32}P and ^{35}S. Most of the ^{35}S (hence, most of the bacteriophage protein) turned up in the fluid phase—but most of the ^{32}P (hence, most of the DNA) turned up in the pellet. The bacteriophage DNA had penetrated the bacteria, but the protein had not (Figure 17.5).

The bacteria were then returned to culture medium. The infection followed a normal course, resulting in death and disruption of the bacteria. A new generation of bacteriophage was released that contained a sizable amount of the ^{32}P—but these bacteriophage contained *none* of the ^{35}S from the parental strain!

The meaning of these results was inescapable. First, only the DNA of the phage entered the bacterium during infection. The protein portion remained loosely attached to the exterior, where it could be removed in the blender. Second, removal of the bacteriophage protein from the infected cells did not affect the course of the infection. Third, bacteri-

(text continues on page 380)

Interleaf 17.1

How to Use the Centrifuge for Analyzing Cell Components

If you tie a rock to a string and rotate it above your head, the rock will exert a pull on the string. If you let go of the string, the rock will fly outward in a straight line away from you. The heavier the rock, the longer the string, or the faster you rotate it, the more tension the rock will exert on the string and the farther it will fly when released. The effects of this force are used to advantage in the *centrifuge,* a device that rotates specimens at high speed and thereby separates their component parts for analysis.

The force acting to drive a rapidly rotating specimen outward from the center of rotation is known as *centrifugal force.* It is measured in Gs, where 1 G is equivalent to the gravitational force acting to draw objects toward the center of the earth.

Now, objects of different weights—such as cell components—move outward with different speeds when they are subjected to the same centrifugal force. In such *differential centrifugation,* cells are broken apart and their components are dispersed in a buffered salt solution to yield a *homogenate.* The homogenate is then centrifuged at moderate speed to drive the largest particles toward the bottom of the tube, where they form a *pellet.* The overlying fluid, known as the *supernatant fluid,* is poured off, transferred to a fresh centrifuge tube, and recentrifuged at higher speed to cause the next largest particles to form a pellet. This process is repeated with increasing centrifugal force to segregate cell components into a series of pellets, which may then be resuspended and analyzed. In this way, nuclei, nucleoli, cilia, peroxisomes, and other organelles of various cell types have been isolated.

Now, if differential centrifugation is modified so that acceleration is *not* linked with distance traveled, specimens can be separated in still other ways. Consider what happens when the density (weight per unit volume) of the fluid in the centrifuge tube is increased. When all other things are equal, the greater the density of the surrounding fluid, the more slowly a particle will travel in a centrifugal field. When a centrifuge tube has been filled in such a way that the fluid density ranges from low at the top to high at the bottom, particles move at uniform speed throughout the length of the rotating tube. As they get farther from the center of rotation, the centrifugal force becomes greater and tends to drive them faster. But the density of the fluid becomes greater also, and tends to slow the particles. These opposing forces balance each other, and particles move with essentially uniform speed along the length of the tube; particles of similar size travel together in a group.

Sucrose (table sugar) is commonly used to produce a density gradient. The tube is prepared so that the concentration of sucrose varies from top to bottom. The sample to be analyzed is layered at the top of the tube. The speed and duration of centrifugation are adjusted so that the particles (or molecules) eventually are spread throughout the tube, although none have reached the bottom. Then the tube contents are carefully removed, layer by layer, and the contents of each region are analyzed. Because different components are segregated in different regions of the tube, the process is called *zonal centrifugation.*

A CENTRIFUGE AT REST

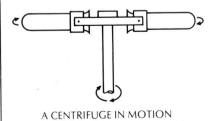

A CENTRIFUGE IN MOTION

Table 17.A
Segregation of Cellular Components in a Typical Centrifugation Process

Fraction	Principal Cellular Components Present
2,000 G pellet	Unbroken cells and nuclei
15,000 G pellet	Mitochondria
40,000 G pellet	Lysosomes, etc.
100,000 G pellet	Endoplasmic reticulum and ribosomes
100,000 G supernatant fluid	Soluble, nonparticulate components of the cell, including many enzymes

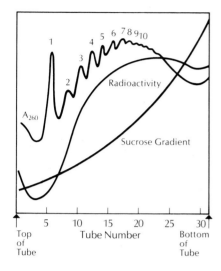

SUCROSE DENSITY GRADIENT ANALYSIS

A sucrose density gradient analysis of the protein-synthesizing components of embryonic chicken cells growing in culture flasks. The cells were exposed briefly to a solution containing radioactive amino acids, then they were homogenized. The ribosomal fraction (isolated by fractional centrifugation) was suspended once more and applied to a sucrose gradient tube.

Following centrifugation, the tube contents were carefully pumped out of the tube and sent through a spectrophotometer, which measured the absorption of light of wavelength 260 nanometers (A_{260}). (Absorption at that particular wavelength is a measure of nucleic acid concentration.) Successive volumes of the tube contents were then caught in separate tubes, and the radioactivity of each fraction was determined.

Microscopic examination of the sample that gave the peak reading designated "1" showed it consisted predominantly of free single ribosomes. Later peaks contained polyribosomes (polysomes); successive peaks contained increasing numbers of ribosome per polysome as indicated.

Because the level of radioactivity per unit of nucleic acid (A_{260}) is low in the region of free ribosomes and increases with increasing size of the polysomes, it can be concluded that most protein synthesis was occurring on large polysomes and that free ribosomes were inactive in protein synthesis at the time the cells were broken apart.

There is still another method of centrifugation. If the gradient in the tube is constructed so that particles end up in a region where their own density exceeds the density of the medium, they will "float" toward the top of the tube despite the centrifugal force. (The same thing happens when you try to submerge a cork: It pops to the top of the water despite the force of gravity. This tendency to float in a medium of higher density is known as buoyancy.) Thus, when various substances are centrifuged in this kind of density gradient, each one will move toward the bottom of the tube *only* until it reaches the point in the gradient where the density of the surrounding medium is identical to its own density. Because each substance is found in the tube region where the density is identical to its own, the method is called *isopycnic centrifugation* (*iso-* means "same," and *pycnic* means "density").

Zonal centrifugation separates molecules and particles primarily on the basis of size and is relatively insensitive to composition of the particles. In contrast, isopycnic centrifugation separates molecules and particles primarily on the basis of composition (all molecules of the same chemical composition have about the same density). It is relatively insensitive to differences in size. The density of the medium in which a particular substance comes to rest defines the buoyant density of that substance.

It turns out that different molecules of fundamental interest in biology have different buoyant densities owing to their differences in molecular composition and structure. Protein molecules have a buoyant density of about 1.3 grams per milliliter. Carbohydrate molecules have densities around 1.6; DNA molecules, around 1.7; and RNA molecules, around 2.0 grams per milliliter. It is possible to make a concentration gradient of certain salts, such as cesium chloride, that spans all these densities; hence it is possible to separate protein from RNA and DNA in a cesium chloride gradient.

But much more subtle differences can be detected by isopycnic centrifugation. DNA rich in guanine and cytosine is more dense than DNA rich in adenine and thymine. Therefore, DNA molecules of different base compositions may be separated from one another. For example, mitochondrial DNA has been separated from nuclear DNA, and genes bearing the code for making ribosomes have been separated from all other genes. Double-stranded DNA may also be separated from unpaired strands of DNA, because the two forms differ in density. Even molecules containing heavy isotopes (Chapter 10) may be separated from those containing only naturally abundant isotopes.

All the centrifugal methods just described are performed in an instrument known as a *preparative ultracentrifuge*. Other kinds of analyses can be performed in an *analytical ultracentrifuge*. In this device, a small sample is placed in a transparent chamber that is rotated at high speed past a camera lens. A photographic record is made of the velocity with which a substance moves under controlled conditions in a centrifugal field. From this record it is possible to determine the *sedimentation coefficient* of the substance, which is a function of the size, composition, and shape of the substance as well as of the controlled conditions. Sedimentation coefficients are expressed in S units in honor of Theodor Svedberg, the inventor of the instrument. It is upon differences in S values of the components to be separated that all centrifugal methods (except isopycnic centrifugation) depend.

(a)

(b)

Figure 17.7   James Watson (a) and Francis Crick (b), who in 1953 presented a model of the molecular structure of deoxyribonucleic acic that led to an explanation of the mechanism whereby genetic material might be duplicated. Watson first began working with Crick in 1951 at the Cavendish Laboratory of Cambridge University. Amidst piles of old books in a shack often referred to as "The Hut," the two biologists began constructing a three-dimensional model of DNA, using wire, colored beads, rods and clamps, and pieces of sheet metal. They worked to develop a representation that would be consistent with all known information about DNA. Using Erwin Chargaff's data on DNA composition and Maurice Wilkins' and Rosalind Franklin's x-ray diffraction results (Chapter 11), supplemented by data and theories from other investigators, Watson and Crick were able to develop such a model. In 1962 Watson and Crick shared the Nobel Prize with Maurice Wilkins in recognition of their landmark contribution to our understanding of genetics.

ophage DNA was passed intact between generations. But the protein was new with each new generation. In short, *it was the DNA of the bacteriophage, and not the protein, that carried the hereditary information.*

The Hershey-Chase experiment was not as clear-cut as the earlier experiments of Avery. For example, not *all* the ^{32}P stayed with the bacteria, not *all* the ^{35}S was removed in the blender, and only about 25 percent of the ^{32}P was passed on to the progeny. Nevertheless, it was dramatic corroboration of Avery's results. Until the Hershey-Chase experiment was performed, the Avery experiment was not accepted. But had the Avery experiment not been done, the Hershey-Chase experiment would not have been as readily accepted.

Overnight the focus of interest shifted to DNA. The following year there would be a one-page paper by James Watson and Francis Crick, entitled "A Structure for Deoxyribose Nucleic Acids" (Chapter 11). Their double helix model for the DNA molecule would become an intellectual turning point of the first magnitude in the continuing search for hereditary mechanisms.

REPLICATION OF DNA OCCURS BY BASE PAIRING

In one of the classic understatements of biological literature, Watson and Crick wrote: "It has not escaped our notice that the specific pairing we have postulated immediately suggests a possible copying mechanism for the genetic material." *Adenine pairs only with thymine, and guanine with cytosine; therefore, each of the two strands of*

a DNA double helix molecule could, upon separation, serve as a "template" for the synthesis of two new, complementary molecules that were exact replicas of the original molecule (Figure 17.8). The implication of the Watson-Crick proposal was that the process of replication should be **semiconservative,** with one-half the parent molecule conserved in each of two daughter molecules. Experiments performed in 1957 by Matthew Meselson and Franklin Stahl were compatible with this hypothesis (Figure 17.9). Similar semiconservative replication of DNA has now been observed with respect to viral DNA and the chromosomes of eukaryotic cells.

It might be useful at this point to mention that the term "chromosome" was first applied to structures observed in nuclei of eukaryotes. These large, complex structures contain RNA and a variety of histone and nonhistone proteins, in addition to the DNA (Chapter 13). In contrast, the naked, circular DNA molecules of bacteria and viruses lack chromosomal proteins of the eukaryotic type. For that reason, alternative names have been suggested for these prokaryotic structures—for example, "genophore" ("bearer of genes") or "chromoneme" ("colored thread") as opposed to chromosome ("colored body"). However, there is not yet any widespread agreement on such terminology.

Starting Points for DNA Replication

Insight into one aspect of the self-replication process came from the work of John Cairns, who grew bacterial cells in radioactive thymidine (the nucleotide containing the base

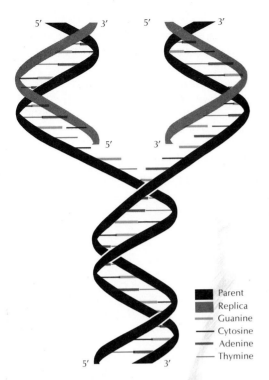

Figure 17.8 *A representation of the DNA double helix molecule in the process of self-replication.*

Parent
Replica
Guanine
Cytosine
Adenine
Thymine

Figure 17.9 The Meselson-Stahl experiment demonstrating the semiconservative replication of DNA. Meselson and Stahl first established that bacteria grown in the heavy isotope of nitrogen (^{15}N) contained DNA that was sufficiently more dense than normal DNA that the two could be separated easily by isopycnic centrifugation (see Interleaf 17.1). Then they showed that when cells containing this heavy DNA were transferred to and grown in a medium containing the normal (light) isotope of nitrogen (^{14}N), the cells produced DNA that was intermediate in density between the light and heavy types.

This result was compatible with the concept that each strand of the original DNA serves as a template for the synthesis of a new, complementary strand of DNA.

In subsequent generations, the amount of DNA of hybrid density remained constant, but it was diluted by the accumulation of increasing amounts of light DNA. This result, too, was consistent with a model in which both light and heavy strands of DNA were acting as templates for synthesis of new, light, complementary strands.

From James D. Watson, Molecular Biology of the Gene *(First Edition), copyright © 1965 by J. D. Watson; W. A. Benjamin, Inc., New York and Amsterdam.*

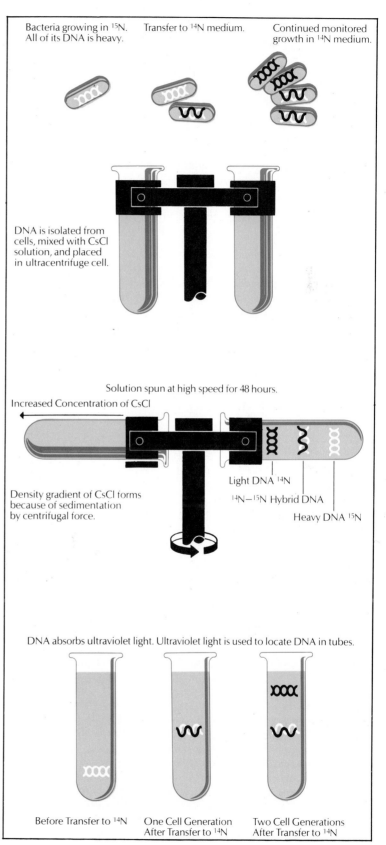

Bacteria growing in ^{15}N. All of its DNA is heavy.

Transfer to ^{14}N medium.

Continued monitored growth in ^{14}N medium.

DNA is isolated from cells, mixed with CsCl solution, and placed in ultracentrifuge cell.

Solution spun at high speed for 48 hours.

Increased Concentration of CsCl

Density gradient of CsCl forms because of sedimentation by centrifugal force.

Light DNA ^{14}N

$^{14}N-^{15}N$ Hybrid DNA

Heavy DNA ^{15}N

DNA absorbs ultraviolet light. Ultraviolet light is used to locate DNA in tubes.

Before Transfer to ^{14}N

One Cell Generation After Transfer to ^{14}N

Two Cell Generations After Transfer to ^{14}N

thymine). Cairns used autoradiography (Figure 13.27) to examine the DNA molecules released from these cells. He found that every replicating DNA molecule consisted of three partial circles that were fused at two points (Figure 17.10). The result was consistent with a view that the circular DNA double helix opens in one region, allowing the two sister strands to be replicated even as the circle otherwise remains intact.

The replication of bacterial DNA is always initiated at a specific point on the circular molecule. Thus, DNA in the process of replication always duplicates genes in a specific order. Genes near the **initiation point** are present in two copies per cell before genes more distant from the initiation point. At first, this observation was taken to mean that bacterial DNA is replicated in one direction only, with synthesis proceeding around the circle until it reaches the termination point immediately adjacent to the initiation point. However, autoradiographic evidence now suggests that *DNA may be replicated in both directions from the initiation point.* As shown in Figure 17.11, each initiation point may be accompanied by two growth points rather than just one.

Eukaryotic chromosomes are not circular. Their DNA appears to be linear, extending through the entire chromosome as one unbroken molecule. They are not, however, replicated in one continuous process from a single point on

Figure 17.10 Autoradiograph of an E. coli *DNA molecule undergoing replication. The DNA was labeled with ³H-thymidine for two generations of DNA replication before being released from the cell. The same structure is drawn as a diagram at the upper right. It is divided into three sections (A, B, and C) that arise at two forks (X and Y). Section A represents the unreplicated portion of the molecule; B and C are the two replicated loops. (Because the two DNA strands are twisted about each other in a double helix, they cannot be resolved in the actual autoradiograph.)*

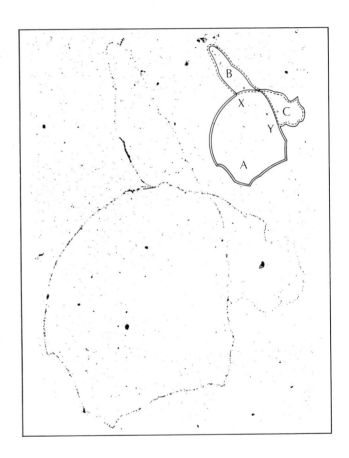

Figure 17.11 Bidirectional replication of DNA. At the time DNA synthesis was initiated in a synchronized population of E. coli, *a DNA precursor with a low level of radioactivity was present. After a few minutes, precursor of a much higher level of radioactivity was introduced. A few minutes later, the cells were broken apart, and their DNA was stretched out on a surface and coated with photographic emulsion in preparation for autoradiography.*

In this autoradiograph, three tracks of silver grains are present, revealing the presence of three E. coli *chromosomes. In each track, a region of low grain density in the midsection is bracketed by regions of high grain density on the end sections. This pattern suggests that the center region was being synthesized when the radioactivity of the precursor was low and that growth occurred in both directions at the time when the level of radioactivity was increased. These data would seem to suggest that a chromosome, such as that shown in Figure 17.10, grows at both branch points.*

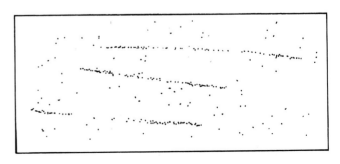

each chromosome. Instead, *replication of eukaryotic DNA starts more or less simultaneously at many specific initiation points on the chromosome.* A unit of replicating eukaryotic DNA, from the specific initiation point to the termination point, is known as a **replicon.** Some eukaryotic chromosomes are estimated to contain several thousand replicons! As with prokaryotic DNA, detailed autoradiographic analysis of replicating eukaryotic chromosomes suggests the replication proceeds in both directions from each initiation point.

Attachment of Nucleotides to Growing Chains of DNA

As you read in Chapter 11, the two strands of a DNA double helix run in opposite (antiparallel) directions. One runs from 5' to 3' and the other runs from 3' to 5' (Figure 11.33). But if both are synthesized from the same branch point, the growing end of one must have a free 3' hydroxyl (—OH) group and the growing end of the other must have a 5' phosphate group. To add more nucleotides directly to two such chains either would require that one enzyme carry out two very different reactions or it would require two different enzymes. Now, many enzymes, isolated from many different sources, are capable of joining deoxyribonucleotides to form DNA. Arthur Kornberg isolated and characterized the first of these enzymes, which are called **DNA polymerases.** All have one thing in common: They catalyze the addition of nucleotides to the —OH group at the 3' end of a DNA chain (Figure 17.12). But the long, intense search for an enzyme capable of adding nucleotides to the 5' end has been unrewarding, and most biochemists now are convinced that no such enzyme exists.

Figure 17.12   A generalized reaction for DNA polymerase. The enzyme is capable of adding only 5' triphosphates to the 3' end of the growing chain. Thus the short stretches of DNA assembled by DNA polymerase always grow in the same direction.

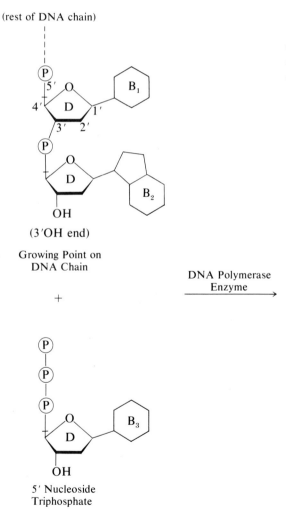

(rest of DNA chain)

(3'OH end)

Growing Point on
DNA Chain

+

5' Nucleoside
Triphosphate

DNA Polymerase
Enzyme
⟶

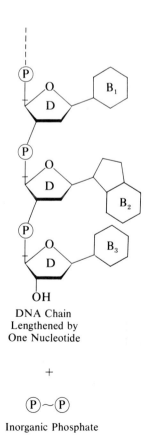

DNA Chain
Lengthened by
One Nucleotide

+

P~P

Inorganic Phosphate

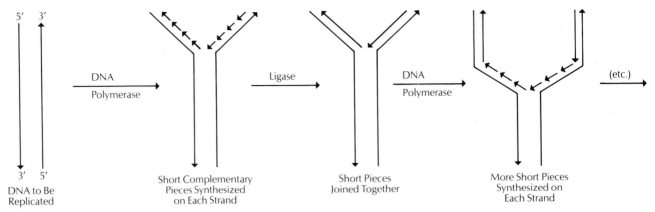

Figure 17.13   Okazaki's discovery concerning the mechanism of DNA replication.

How, then, are nucleotides attached to the 5′ end of a growing chain? The answer seems to have been found with the demonstration by Reiji Okazaki that *DNA polymerase does not attach nucleotides directly to the end of growing DNA chains!* Okazaki subjected cells very briefly to radioactive nucleotides so that only the most recently synthesized DNA was labeled. Upon breaking the cell, Okazaki determined that this newly synthesized DNA existed in extremely short pieces held in place by hydrogen bonds to the parent strands. A second enzyme, known as **ligase** (or the "linking enzyme"), subsequently joined the short pieces together and to the end of the growing strand. Thus, although the two strands grow in the same direction in an overall sense, for very brief periods they grow in opposite directions (Figure 17.13).

Replication is not a simple task. An *E. coli* cell, for example, can undergo binary fission twenty minutes after it has been created from a similar fission. In that brief time span its DNA must be faithfully replicated. First, the two strands of the DNA molecule must separate from each other. Because they are intertwined in a helical coil, they must be untwisted. To untwist the 360,000 turns of the *E. coli* DNA molecule within a few minutes must require an astounding rate of rotation. As they are whipping around, the two strands cannot tear apart; if they do, the hereditary sequence will be lost. As difficult as it is to visualize the process, it gets worse when we recall that the circular DNA molecule of *E. coli* is much longer than the cell itself. It is precisely folded and packed in the cell—which means it must unfold and refold as synthesis proceeds and the strands rotate at high speed! Furthermore, if each DNA strand is to build a complementary strand, there must be 3.6 million nucleotide pairs of precisely the right kinds available in the cellular environment. Within another few minutes, the 7.2 million precursor molecules must be

moved to their proper locations, fitted into place, and joined together to form new double strands. How this incredible process is synchronized and completed within a mere twenty minutes is, at the present, anybody's guess.

Mechanisms for Repairing the Replicated Molecules

There is a group of enzymes that function continuously to monitor the DNA molecules for damage or for replication mistakes and to repair the damage. For example, ultraviolet light causes adjacent thymine bases to become covalently bonded to one another, forming what is known as a thymine-thymine dimer. Certain **repair enzymes** act in concert to recognize the presence of such dimers and cut out the affected portion of the DNA strand, throw it away, replace it with a new section of correct sequence—and then seal the mend! Without these enzymes life could not exist: damage would accumulate progressively and the DNA (hence the cell) would cease to function.

But the repair enzymes can detect only whether or not a region of DNA has the usual overall structure; they cannot determine what the proper sequence is. As a result, *repair enzymes sometimes perpetuate errors rather than correct them.* For example, adenine should always pair with thymine. But if "by mistake" guanine is inserted opposite adenine in the growing chain, the DNA double helix will be distorted by the mismatch. The repair enzymes will detect the error, but they cannot "recognize" which strand is wrong and therefore which one should be repaired. If the enzymes excise the guanine and replace it with thymine, they will reverse the error. If they instead replace the adenine with cytosine, the helix will no longer be distorted (the G—C pair has the same dimensions as the A—T pair) and the error will seem to be corrected. But in terms of the survival of the cell, the difference between the two repairs can be crucial. The first represents a restoration of the status quo, which has been tested by natural selection and found to work; the second results in a mutation of the base sequence, which may or may not work. Indeed, if the change occurred in a region of an essential gene, the consequences might be disastrous for the cell. Yet it is upon such usually fatal but occasionally beneficial enzymatic errors that evolution is based. To understand the connection between change in the base pair sequence of a DNA molecule and evolutionary change, it is necessary to understand how genes determine the nature of the characters upon which selection acts.

THE PRINCIPLE OF COLINEARITY AND THE GENETIC CODE

How do genes determine the traits of an organism? Alexander Dounce, in 1952, suggested what now seems obvious: *The linear sequence of bases in DNA determines the linear sequence of amino acids in a protein.* This insight came to be known as the **principle of colinearity** of gene and protein. Charles Yanofsky and his co-workers proved its validity. They mapped a large number of mutations that affected the activity of one particular enzyme in *E. coli*. They found that each mutation caused a change in one particular amino acid at one specific site in the enzyme. *The order of the mutations on the genetic map was exactly parallel to the order of the corresponding amino acid changes in the protein.*

But *how* does DNA sequence determine an amino acid sequence? Dounce further proposed that each sequence of three nucleotides formed a code word that stands for a particular amino acid. In making a protein, the cell somehow read this **genetic code** and assembled amino acids in the order called for by the corresponding gene.

A gene of bacteriophage T4 of *E. coli* provided the first detailed insight into the nature of the genetic code. The **rII gene,** first studied by Seymour Benzer, turned out to be ideally suited for analysis of structure within a gene. Bacteriophage with a wild-type rII gene can grow in either B or K strains of *E. coli*, but bacteriophage with a mutant rII gene cannot grow in strain K. Now, two different kinds of rII mutant bacteriophage can be used to infect B strain bacteria simultaneously. While reproducing in the B cells, the bacteriophage undergo genetic recombination. In the rare case in which crossing over and recombination occur within the rII gene (between the mutations carried by the two strains), one of the two recombinants picks up both mutations, whereas the other loses both mutations and is restored to the wild type.

After they run their infection cycle, kill their hosts, and release vast numbers of progeny, the progeny can be added to a culture of K strain bacteria. The only ones that grow in the K cells are the rare individuals that carried the wild-type rII genes as a result of recombination; bacteriophage still bearing mutant rII genes would not grow. Thus, the rare recombinants can be rapidly selected from a vast population of nonrecombinants. In fact, one recombinant can be detected in the midst of a hundred million nonrecombinant, mutant siblings. In a single day, then, it is possible to study recombination between mutations that were so close together they would not have been found to recombine in a lifetime of breeding and counting organisms such as fruit flies. (Recall, from Chapter 16, that the frequency of recombination falls as the distance between two genetic regions falls.) By 1961 Benzer had studied several thousand natural and chemically induced mutations of the rII gene and had determined their relative positions within the gene itself.

That same year Crick, Sydney Brenner, and their colleagues at Cambridge University became interested in the class of rII mutants that are induced by the drug proflavin. These mutants have properties that differ from those induced with other chemical mutagens. Crick guessed that whereas most mutagens cause a change of base pair sequence in the DNA (such as switching an A/T pair to a G/C pair), proflavin often causes the **insertion** of an additional nucleotide into a chain.

If bacteriophage carrying a proflavin-induced rII mutant were grown in B cells, they produced a few extremely rare individuals capable of growing in K cells. Such mutants acted as if they had reverted, or **back-mutated,** to the wild type. But their growth on B cells was now somewhat abnormal, which implied they were not identical to wild-type T4 bacteriophage.

By recombination with wild-type bacteriophage, it was possible to show that these individuals carried two rII mutations that were extremely close together: the original proflavin-induced mutation and a new mutation that somehow compensated for it. Separately, both prevented growth in K cells; together, they permitted it. Because the original mutation was thought to be due to an insertion of an additional base, it was suggested that the compensating mutation was a **deletion** of a nearby base. Such a deletion would restore the gene to its original length. The key observation was that three insertion mutations in the same bacteriophage resulted in a phenotype very similar to the wild type. Similarly, bacteriophage with three deletion mutations could grow in K cells, like the wild type. From such observations, Crick deciphered the genetic code:

1. *Three nucleotides in a DNA molecule code for one amino acid in the corresponding protein.*

2. *The genetic code itself is read from a fixed starting point.*

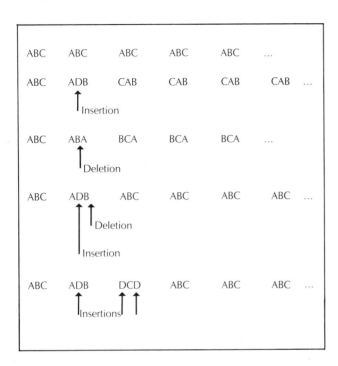

Figure 17.14 Crick's interpretation of the data from analysis of insertion and deletion mutations of the rII gene of bacteriophage T4.

3. *The nucleotides are read three at a time in a non-overlapping manner.* Such nucleotide triplets that code for an amino acid are called **codons** (or coding units). Given a nonoverlapping code, every insertion of an additional base causes misreading of all codons beyond that point. But an insertion followed by a deletion causes misreading only between the sites of the two mutations; outside that region, the correct triplets are read. Similarly, three insertions cause misreading only in the region between the first and last mutations (Figure 17.14).

4. *Most of the sixty-four possible nucleotide triplets stand for an amino acid.* The observation behind this statement is that most insertion-deletion base pairs give rise to a phenotype similar to the wild type.

5. *A few of the sixty-four possible codons are "nonsense," in that they do not code for any amino acid.* A few insertion-deletion base pairs do not compensate for each other; therefore, some triplets cannot be translated as an amino acid to be inserted in the protein.

6. *The genetic code is degenerate in the sense that two or more different codons must represent a single amino acid.* There are approximately sixty codons that make sense—but there are only twenty amino acids.

Once the general features of the genetic code were determined, the search was on to discover which particular nucleotide triplets are codons for which amino acids. A great deal had already been learned about the nature of protein synthesis (Chapter 11). By then it was known that a DNA molecule codes for proteins not directly but through a messenger RNA (mRNA) molecule of complementary sequence. It was known that the mRNA was decoded on particles called ribosomes and that the decoders were transfer RNA (tRNA) molecules having a specific amino acid on one end and a nucleotide triplet complementary to the corresponding codon on the mRNA. This knowledge was put to use in a series of experiments.

In the first experiments, synthetic RNA *homopolymers* were used as messenger molecules in which identical nucleotides were strung together. These homopolymers were then fed to ribosomes. The products the ribosomes made told the meaning of the triplet containing that one kind of nucleotide. For example, when polyuridylic acid (. . . UUUUUU . . .) was used, the resulting polymer contained only phenylalanine. Therefore, UUU had to be a codon for phenylalanine. But only four codons could be assigned by this method.

Next, synthetic RNA *copolymers* were employed, in which two nucleotides were repeated in random sequence. Then copolymers of three nucleotides were employed. Through such studies it was possible to say, for example, that at least one of the codons specifying arginine must contain C, A, and G. But was the codon CAG, or ACG, or CGA, or GAC, or . . . ?

The breakthrough came with the work of Marshall Nirenberg. Rather than looking for all the steps of protein synthesis to occur, he simply asked: If ribosomes are provided with a "messenger" only three nucleotides long,

FIRST LETTER	SECOND LETTER				THIRD LETTER
	U	C	A	G	
U	PHENYLALANINE	SERINE	TYROSINE	CYSTEINE	U
U	PHENYLALANINE	SERINE	TYROSINE	CYSTEINE	C
U	LEUCINE	SERINE	STOP	STOP	A
U	LEUCINE	SERINE	STOP	TRYPTOPHAN	G
C	LEUCINE	PROLINE	HISTIDINE	ARGININE	U
C	LEUCINE	PROLINE	HISTIDINE	ARGININE	C
C	LEUCINE	PROLINE	GLUTAMINE	ARGININE	A
C	LEUCINE	PROLINE	GLUTAMINE	ARGININE	G
A	ISOLEUCINE	THREONINE	ASPARAGINE	SERINE	U
A	ISOLEUCINE	THREONINE	ASPARAGINE	SERINE	C
A	ISOLEUCINE	THREONINE	LYSINE	ARGININE	A
A	START—MET	THREONINE	LYSINE	ARGININE	G
G	VALINE	ALANINE	ASPARTIC ACID	GLYCINE	U
G	VALINE	ALANINE	ASPARTIC ACID	GLYCINE	C
G	VALINE	ALANINE	GLUTAMIC ACID	GLYCINE	A
G	VALINE	ALANINE	GLUTAMIC ACID	GLYCINE	G

Figure 17.15 The genetic code: the amino acids represented by each of the sixty-four possible base triplets in an mRNA molecule.

Amino acids of similar chemical nature are shown in the same color. No two amino acids have precisely the same properties. But a mutation that causes one amino acid in a protein to be replaced by another of the same color group usually does not drastically change the properties of the resulting protein. In contrast, a mutation that substitutes an amino acid from another color group may have dire consequences. Hence the former are called conservative interchanges and the latter are called nonconservative interchanges.
Notice the clustering of amino acids of similar type. Such

clustering means that a sizable proportion of all single base changes results in a conservative mutation. Indeed, many single base changes cause no change in an amino acid.
AUG is called the initiation codon. It inserts methionine (MET) or formyl methionine (fMET) at the beginning of each chain. Three codons exist that do not represent any amino acid. These codons—UAA, UAG, and UGA—are called ''nonsense'' or ''termination'' codons: They signal the end of a gene and cause the finished protein molecule to be released from the ribosome.

and of defined sequence, which labeled amino acid–tRNAs will they bind? It is on the basis of **tRNA binding assays** that most of the coding assignments in Figure 17.15 were derived. Later on, Ghobind Khorana developed ways of synthesizing longer and longer polynucleotides of completely defined sequence. When these polymers were used in a protein synthesizing system, they yielded peptides of the predicted sequence.

Dramatic evidence for the ''universality'' of the genetic code came when mRNA was first extracted from rabbit cells active in making hemoglobin. The mRNA was added to ribosomes, enzymes, and tRNA molecules of *E. coli*. The

bacterial protein-synthesizing system read the rabbit mRNA exactly as the rabbit cells would have—and it produced hemoglobin polypeptide chains that were indistinguishable from those circulating in the blood of the donor rabbit! The ''universality'' of the code has now been extended to encompass every other organism studied. *All organisms use the same set of codons to specify the same amino acids.* This is not surprising, for an evolutionary change in the meaning of one codon would change the amino acid sequence of every protein in the cell whose genes contained that codon. In the evolutionary sense, the probability that any such wholesale revision could succeed is virtually zero.

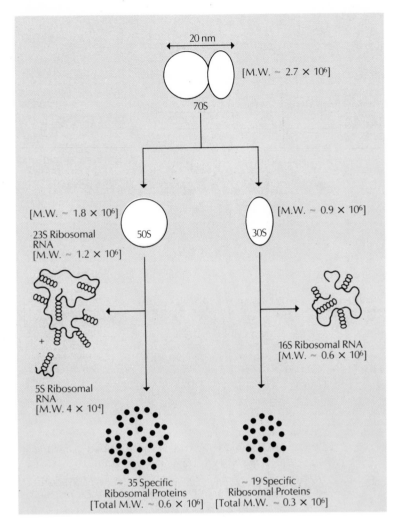

Figure 17.16 The composition of ribosomes. Each ribosome is about 20 nanometers in diameter and is composed of two subunits. These subunits, and the RNA molecules they contain, are usually named in terms of how fast they move in a centrifuge, where the measure is in Svedberg (S) units (see Interleaf 17.1). S values are not additive; they are proportional to molecular weight in a nonlinear way. One 70S ribosome, for example, is composed of a 50S and a 30S subunit. The 50S subunit is composed of two pieces of RNA (one large 23S molecule and one small 5S molecule) and about thirty-five different kinds of ribosomal proteins. The 30S subunit is composed of a 16S piece of RNA and twenty-one kinds of proteins, all of which are different from the proteins of the large subunit.

Although ribosomes can be reassembled in a functional form from their sixty or so component parts, we have no clear picture of how they fit together or what the function is of most parts. The sizes given here are for bacterial ribosomes. Ribosomes in the cytoplasm of eukaryotic cells are larger in nearly all respects, but otherwise they are quite similar.

After J. D. Watson, Molecular Biology of the Gene, copyright © 1970, J. D. Watson. W. A. Benjamin, Inc.

Let us now consider the details of the mechanism by which the genetic code is put into action by means of the coordinated activities of the three classes of RNA.

MESSENGER RNA IS THE GENE-SPECIFIC COMPONENT OF PROTEIN SYNTHESIS

Ribosomes (Figure 17.16) are particles rich in RNA. It is upon the ribosomes that proteins are synthesized. Ribosomal RNA molecules were once thought to be the bearers of gene-specific information, coding for protein structure. But it is now clear that the ribosomes can take part in the synthesis of *any* protein—even one never found in the organism from which the ribosomes are derived. Which protein they make depends entirely on what molecule of mRNA they are combined with. By means of **nucleic acid hybridization** (*Interleaf 17.2*), it has been established that each mRNA molecule bears a base sequence that is complementary to that of a particular stretch of the DNA from which it was produced. And each mRNA molecule is known to carry all the information needed to make a specific protein. Thus, mRNA acts as the agent of the gene, putting its instructions into action.

The enzyme responsible for making an RNA complement of a gene is called **RNA polymerase.** *In the cell, the RNA polymerase functions to make an RNA molecule complementary to one (and only one) strand of the DNA double helix. Which strand will the enzyme copy?* That is determined by a site on the enzyme called a **promotor region.** It has a specific chemical affinity for a nucleotide sequence that occurs at the beginning of each section to be read. Once it attaches to the promotor, the enzyme rolls down the adjacent stretch of DNA, selecting nucleotides that will hydrogen-bond by base-pairing rules to the DNA chain (Figure 17.17). This process is called **transcription,** and the mRNA molecule so produced is sometimes called a **transcript.**

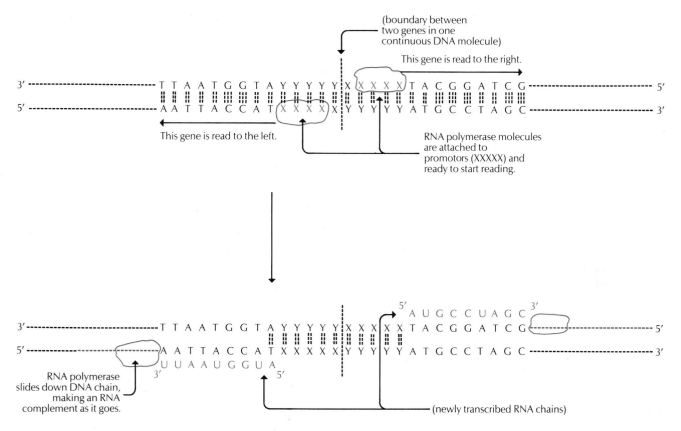

Figure 17.17 Hypothetical DNA segment containing parts of two genes transcribed in opposite directions from adjacent starting points (promotors). Here, Xs mark promotor regions. Different promotors have similar but not identical sequences.

Because the complement of the promotor region has a different chemical nature (symbolized by Ys), RNA polymerase does not attach to it. Thus there is no tendency for both strands to be transcribed. The promotor region itself is not transcribed.

Although only one strand of DNA is read in any region of the chromosome in order to produce an mRNA molecule, the strand that is read need not be the same in different regions. In the lambda (λ) bacteriophage of *E. coli,* some genes are read in one direction from one strand, and adjacent genes are read in the opposite direction, from the opposite strand (Figure 17.17). As with DNA, the RNA chains always grow by addition of 5′ triphosphates to the 3′ —OH group of the growing chain. How a cell determines which of the many possible mRNA molecules (hence which protein) should be made at any given time is described in Chapter 20.

TRANSFER RNA READS THE CODE CARRIED BY MESSENGER RNA

Whereas mRNA is protein-specific, tRNA is amino acid-specific: *Each kind of tRNA molecule can combine co-valently with only one kind of amino acid.* For each kind of amino acid, there is at least one (and sometimes several) kind of tRNA molecule in each cell.

In 1965, Robert Holley of Cornell University worked out the nucleotide sequence of a tRNA molecule. Since then, the complete sequence has been worked out for several kinds of tRNA. The structures of the tRNA molecules shown in Figure 17.19 emphasize a recurring biological theme: unity with diversity. All are basically the same because their basic role is the same: aiding in the translation of the genetic code. But they differ because each has unique features that enable it to combine with a specific amino acid and then assure that the amino acid is inserted precisely where it is called for in each protein.

Like mRNA, the tRNA and rRNA molecules are formed by transcription from specific sequences of DNA. But unlike mRNA, they are not subsequently translated into proteins. Instead, they participate in the synthesis of proteins. Let us now examine how all the parts of the

(text continues on page 394)

Interleaf 17.2

Nucleic Acid Annealing and Hybridization: Insights Into Gene Organization and Function

Through hydrogen bonds, A pairs with T and G with C in a DNA molecule. Each hydrogen bond is extremely weak. But when a long sequence of bases on the two strands of DNA show point-to-point complementarity, the many weak bonds combine to produce a structure that is stable enough to assure the continuity of hereditary instructions. The weakness of individual bonds, together with their cumulative strength, underlies the capacity of the double helix to open and close like a zipper. And this capacity in turn underlies the transcription and replication of DNA.

NUCLEIC ACID ANNEALING

The nature of hydrogen bonding in the DNA molecule forms the basis for one of the most potent methods yet devised for analyzing nucleic acids. In *nucleic acid annealing,* a DNA double helix structure is completely destroyed, and then samples of its nucleic acids (which have been broken into short pieces) are brought together under conditions in which a double helix can be re-formed. Now, a stable double helix can be formed only if two strands have a relatively long and complementary sequence of bases. *Thus the amount of double helix that is formed in such an experiment is a measure of the degree of complementarity existing between the nucleic acids in the sample.*

What are some of the ways in which the double helix can be broken and re-formed? When DNA is isolated from a sample of cells in an intact, double-stranded form and then dissolved, the solution absorbs a certain amount of ultraviolet light of 260-nanometer wavelength. But when the solution is heated slowly, the amount of light absorbed undergoes a marked increase over a certain temperature range (Figure *a*). The increase in absorbance occurs as the double helix falls apart to form two single-stranded molecules. The helix "melts." Repeated analysis shows that under the same testing conditions, a sample of DNA from the same source always melts at the same temperature. But samples of DNA from different species melt at somewhat different temperatures. Thus the temperature at which the DNA undergoes a transition from the double-stranded to the single-stranded state is a species-specific property of each DNA sample. The melting temperature (T_m) is a func-

tion of the guanine and cytosine content of the DNA. The higher the G and C content, the higher the melting temperature (Figure *a*).

Now, when a sample of DNA that has been melted is cooled rapidly, its absorbance remains high. A double helix does not re-form. But when it is returned to the melting temperature and cooled very slowly, the absorbance value falls once more. How much the absorbance value falls is a measure of how much of the double helix is restored. The process of double helix re-formation from a solution containing only one kind of nucleic acid is called *reannealing*. If reannealing is complete (that is, if every piece of DNA finds the complementary strand and re-forms a double helix), the absorbance will return to its precise starting value. Now, if the matching of complementary bases was complete and perfect, it should be possible to repeat the melting curve precisely. If matching was imperfect, the melting temperature will be lower than originally. A 1 percent mismatching will cause about a 1 degree fall in the observed melting temperature. Thus the T_m curve can be used to determine the precision of reannealing.

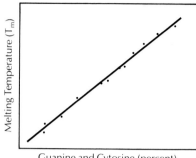

(a) A DNA melting curve.

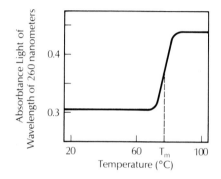

(b) The relationship between base composition and melting temperature.

Other methods can be used to detect double helix re-formation and to isolate single-stranded from double-stranded molecules. For example, certain filters made from plastic disks with extremely fine pores will hold back single-stranded DNA while permitting double-stranded molecules to pass through. As another example, single-stranded DNA may be attached chemically to some surface, and if it is then exposed to a solution of single-stranded DNA under conditions that permit double helix formation, the amount of DNA removed from solution will be a measure of the sequence complementarity of the two samples. In addition, double-stranded and single-stranded molecules may be separated by isopycnic centrifuga-

tion because single-stranded DNA has lower buoyancy than double-stranded DNA of the same composition. Finally, under certain conditions, double-stranded nucleic acid molecules will stick to particles of a mineral called hydroxyapatite, whereas single-stranded molecules will not stick.

NUCLEIC ACID HYBRIDIZATION
A DNA helix will form not only from molecules originally derived from the same double helix; it also will form between *any* two molecules of complementary base sequence. If single-stranded molecules are derived from two different sources, a "hybrid" double helix may be formed—if they are related molecules. Measuring double-helix formation between molecules of two different sources is called *nucleic acid hybridization.*

In hybridization studies, one of the nucleic acid samples is usually present in large amounts; the other is present in trace amounts but bears a radioactive label. Once a helix has formed, double-stranded molecules are isolated. The amount of radioactive label found in the isolated double-stranded molecules is a relative measure of the relatedness of the two nucleic acids. The probability that two randomly selected nucleic acid molecules ten nucleotides long will have a complementary base sequence is only one in a million! The probability that two molecules a hundred nucleotides long will have a complementary sequence as a result of sheer chance is 1 in 10,000,000,000,000,000,000, 000,000,000,000,000,000,000,000, 000,000,000,000,000,000! Therefore, if two molecules have sufficient complementarity to form a hybrid molecule, the argument is strong that the complementary base sequence is the result of a biological relationship, not mere chance.

A method called *DNA-DNA hybridization* has been used to measure the degree of relatedness between the DNA of two different organisms. It has been found that evolutionary relationships established on the basis of other criteria are reflected in the degree of hybrid formation that occurs between their DNA molecules.

In *RNA-DNA hybridization,* RNA molecules can be mixed with DNA. If the DNA contains sequences complementary to the RNA, a hybrid double helix containing one strand of DNA and one of RNA may be formed. RNA-DNA hybridization was used to prove that the RNA made in a bacterial cell immediately after infection and associated with bacterial ribosomes was made from the bacteriophage DNA. It formed hybrids with bacteriophage DNA but not with bacterial DNA. RNA-DNA hybridization is the most potent tool yet devised for analyzing the synthesis of mRNA.

RNA-DNA hybridization is also used to count the number of genes coding for a specific kind of RNA. For example, if excessive ribosomal RNA is added to a sample of DNA, only the sequences complementary to (coding for) ribosomal DNA will form RNA-DNA hybrids. The fraction of the total DNA capable of forming such hybrids is a direct measure of the fraction of DNA coding for rRNA. From this fraction, it is a simple matter to calculate how many ribosomal genes there are per cell. In prokaryotes the number turns out to be less than a dozen, but in eukaryotes, each cell is found to have many hundreds (or thousands) of ribosomal genes.

Because double-stranded molecules can be separated from single-stranded ones, hybridization can be used to isolate genes! This technique has been used to isolate the ribosomal genes, using

RNA-DNA hybridization. But it has also been used to isolate genes coding for specific mRNA molecules, using DNA-DNA hybridization. In this case, DNA molecules from two viruses have been used. The viruses were preselected either because they had only one gene in common or because they shared all *but* one gene. This kind of fishing expedition, in which specific genes are pulled out of a complex mixture by hybridization, has just begun, but it promises to yield important information.

Perhaps the biggest surprise to emerge from studies of the type described here came from studies of the reannealing of DNA isolated from eukaryotic nuclei. The formation of a double-stranded molecule from two single-stranded ones takes but an instant, once the two complementary strands collide in such a way that a few complementary bases make contact. The helix zips up rapidly as each set of hydrogen bonds brings neighboring nucleotides into register to form still more hydrogen bonds, and so forth. *The time-consuming step is the initial collision of the two complementary strands in register.* Now, if all the genes of an organism are present only once per haploid cell—or twice per diploid cell—they all ought to have equal probability of collision between complementary strands. Therefore, they should all reanneal at the same rate. But when DNA from the nucleus of a eukaryotic cell is reannealed, some parts of the DNA always anneal much more rapidly than others! The reason: *In every diploid eukaryotic nucleus, most DNA sequences (genes) are present in only two copies per cell, but others are repeated several thousand times and still others may be present as many as a million times.* Therefore, when the total DNA of the cell is isolated and subjected to reannealing condi-

tions, the unique genes spend a million times as long bumping about in the solution looking for their partners as the most highly repetitive sequences do. Figure (c) shows a breakdown of the DNA of a mouse cell in terms of percentages of the total DNA found in each repetition class. Each species has its own characteristic pattern of repetitive DNA that is the same in all members of the species. This pattern of repetition is a part of the evolutionary endowment of the species.

What is the meaning of the three classes of DNA? The unique sequences, we can now say, contain most—if not all—of the genes studied by classical geneticists. Isolated mRNA molecules coding for known proteins (such as hemoglobin) hybridize to genes in the unique class. In mice, the most highly repeated DNA sequences are not genes at all. Studies of RNA-DNA hybridization fail to detect any RNA (made under any

conditions) that is complementary to the DNA. All of this highly repetitive DNA is located at the centromere regions of chromosomes (equal amounts at the centromere region of each chromosome). Hence, the suggestion is that this kind of DNA somehow functions in the behavior of chromosomes during mitosis and meiosis. The class of intermediate frequency is a puzzle and a challenge. Ribosomal genes are in this class (as mentioned above, they are repeated many hundred or thousand times per cell), but they account for only a tiny fraction of total DNA in it. The only other genes now known to be in this class are those coding for histones. So far, the remainder of this fraction of intermediate repetitiveness is speculative. Most speculations center on a role for this DNA in the control of the expression of unique genes in eukaryotic cells. Some of these speculations will be discussed in Chapter 20.

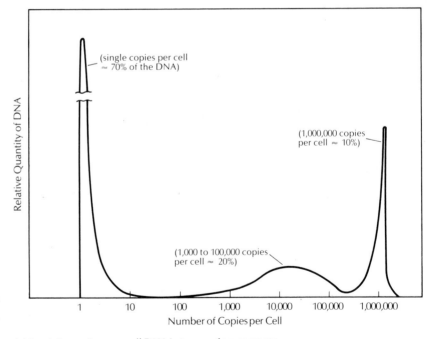

(c) Breakdown of mouse cell DNA in terms of percentages found in different frequencies per cell.

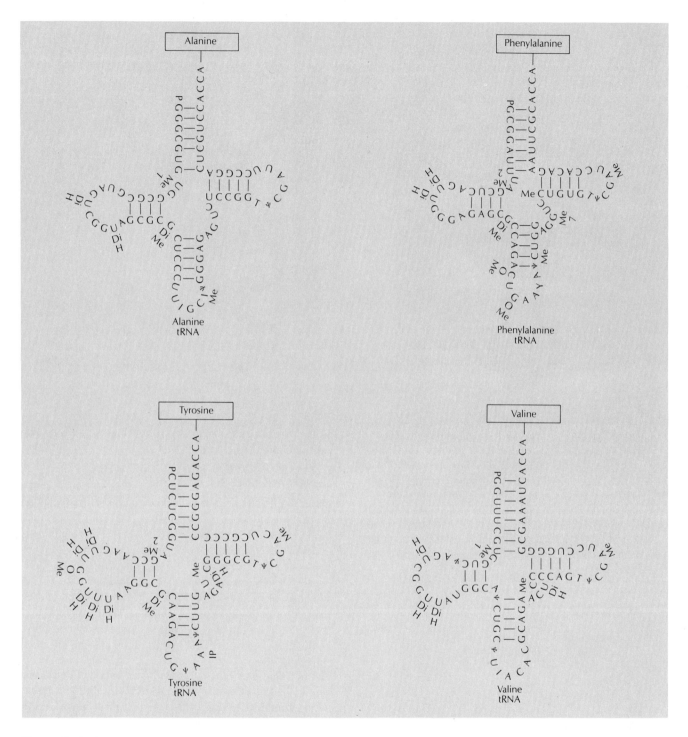

Figure 17.18 The nucleotide sequences of four representative kinds of tRNA molecules. Notice the common features. Each has a CCA sequence at the end where the amino acid is attached. Each has four regions of complementary nucleotides that permit base pairing. Such base pairing results in the "cloverleaf" conformation, with three loops and one stem. Each has an assortment of unusual bases (I, MeI, MeG, di-

MeG, and so on) not found in other kinds of RNA molecules. The loop opposite the amino acid stem bears on its tip the three nucleotides that recognize the codon in mRNA for the amino acid they bear. This triplet sequence is the anticodon. A three-dimensional model of the structure of tRNA is shown in Figure 17.19.

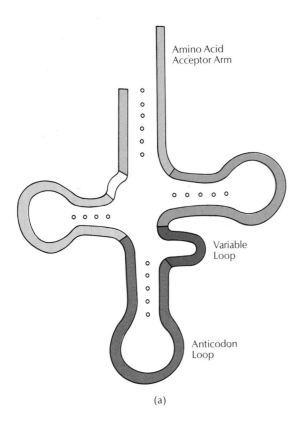

Amino Acid
Acceptor Arm

Variable
Loop

Anticodon
Loop

(a)

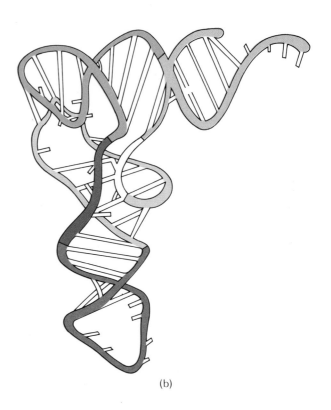

(b)

Figure 17.19 The three-dimensional structure of tRNA. The "cloverleaf" two-dimensional structure of tRNA shown in Figure 17.18 is repeated in (a) to help show how the molecule folds to take on its three-dimensional structure, as shown in (b). The variable loop (purple) may be an important feature that aids the amino acid–tRNA synthetases in distinguishing between different tRNA molecules. The dots in (a) and the rungs in (b) indicate hydrogen bonds between complementary base pairs that form double-helical regions in each of the four arms and thereby stabilize the structure.

protein-synthesizing machinery fit together to translate the genetic code into action.

ENZYMES PROVIDE THE LINK BETWEEN GENOTYPE AND PHENOTYPE

The DNA double helix has the potential for self-replication. But the potential can be realized only through the action of the enzyme DNA polymerase. DNA has the potential to code for mRNA, but this potential is realized only through the action of the enzyme RNA polymerase. The three classes of RNA have the potential to collaborate in the synthesis of proteins of defined sequence; this potential is realized only through the action of a series of enzymes that catalyze the various steps of protein synthesis. We will now consider the steps involved in translation and the enzymes catalyzing them.

The translation of gene into protein can only be as accurate as the joining of amino acids to tRNA molecules. If the wrong combinations occur, the proteins will not have the sequence specified by the gene. The coupling process is, indeed, highly precise. It is carried out in the cytoplasm of a cell by a family of twenty enzymes known as the **amino acyl–tRNA synthetases.** *Each synthetase enzyme is specific for one of the twenty amino acids and, simultaneously, for the tRNA molecules carrying the anticodons for that amino acid.* The mismatches they make are so infrequent they are virtually undetectable, despite the apparent overall similarity of the various tRNA molecules.

Both the tRNA molecules and the synthetases are remarkably similar among all organisms. Obviously, there has been strong evolutionary selection preventing marked change, for any organism that regularly linked the wrong amino acid to a tRNA molecule or read the wrong codon with it would change every protein simultaneously and drastically.

The coupling of an amino acid to a tRNA molecule occurs in two steps, and the same enzyme catalyzes both steps. First, the amino acid is "activated" by reaction with ATP to form a highly reactive complex. The acid group of the amino acid is linked to the phosphate group of AMP. Two phosphate groups are released in a form known as pyrophosphate:

Second, the amino acid is transferred to the adenine at the end of the tRNA molecule:

The ATP loses two phosphate groups in the reaction and two phosphorylations are required to restore it.

The Three Stages of the Translation Process: Initiation, Elongation, and Termination

A protein, like any good short story, must have a beginning, a middle, and an end. Three different sets of reactions are needed to construct these three parts of the protein, and a different set of enzymes catalyzes each set of reactions. The overall process of protein synthesis is called **translation.** Because the beginning of a chain is the most complex step, translation is most easily understood if we start in the middle, with the process known as *peptide chain elongation.* Then we will consider what happens when the chain is finished—the process of *chain termination and release.* Finally, we will consider how each beginning occurs in the process of *chain initiation.*

There are six reaction steps that are repeated over and over again in **peptide chain elongation.** As shown in Figure 17.20, these reaction steps require the participation of four enzymes. First, the amino acid to be added next to the chain binds to the ribosome in the form of an amino acid–tRNA complex. Second, the peptide bond is formed, transferring the growing peptide to the tRNA that has just arrived at the site. Third, the tRNA that passed on the peptide chain is released. Fourth, both the peptide–tRNA complex and the messenger RNA move down a "notch" on the ribosome, thus preparing the ribosome for the addition of the next amino acid. Fifth, the enzyme that is responsible for binding an amino acid–tRNA complex to the ribosome is restored to its active state. Finally, this enzyme binds to the appropriate amino acid–tRNA complex to prepare the entire system for the next round of elongation.

Two of these steps (1 and 4) involve the hydrolysis of a high-energy phosphate bond. When we add these bonds to the two bonds involved in formation of the amino acid–tRNA complex, we find that *the formation of one peptide bond requires hydrolysis of four high-energy phosphate bonds.* Using a free energy of hydrolysis ($\Delta G'$) of −10 kilocalories per mole for each phosphate bond—which is clearly too low for most cells—we find that the energy expended to form one peptide bond is at least 40 kilocalories per mole. Now, when the peptide bond so formed is itself hydrolyzed, its free energy of hydrolysis is only about −5 kilocalories per mole. Thus it takes at least 40 kilocalories of free energy to form a bond with a free energy of hydrolysis of only 5 kilocalories. We can conclude that protein synthesis has, at best, an efficiency of about 5/40, or 12.5 percent. (With all things considered, such as the "cost" of making the RNA molecules, the efficiency may be as low as 5 percent!) This is extraordinarily inefficient, in comparison with such life processes as respiration and photosynthesis. But it is the cost of precision. When we consider the central importance of making proteins of

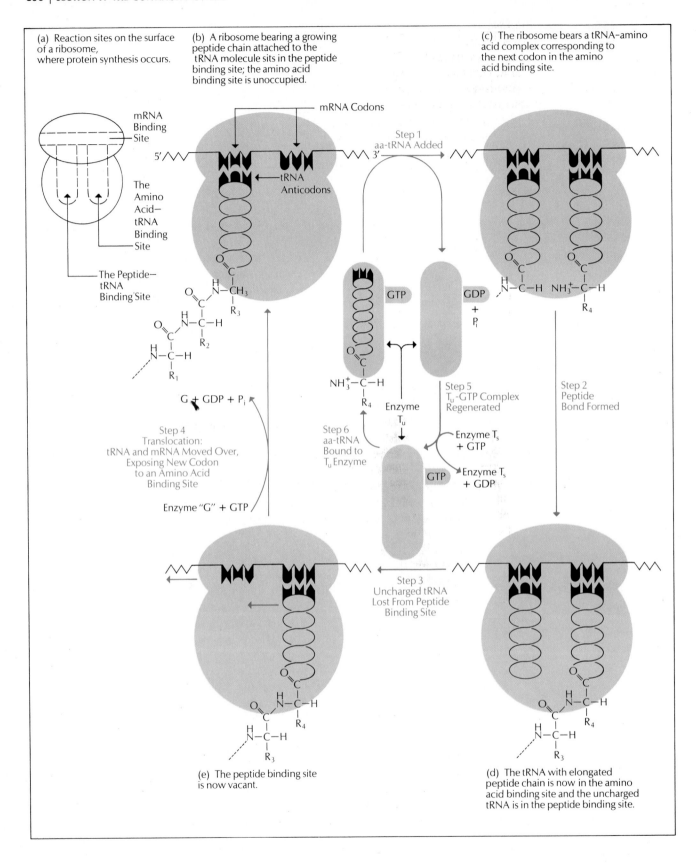

(a) Reaction sites on the surface of a ribosome, where protein synthesis occurs.

(b) A ribosome bearing a growing peptide chain attached to the tRNA molecule sits in the peptide binding site; the amino acid binding site is unoccupied.

(c) The ribosome bears a tRNA–amino acid complex corresponding to the next codon in the amino acid binding site.

mRNA Binding Site

The Amino Acid– tRNA Binding Site

The Peptide– tRNA Binding Site

mRNA Codons

tRNA Anticodons

Step 1 aa-tRNA Added

Step 2 Peptide Bond Formed

Step 5 T_u-GTP Complex Regenerated

Step 6 aa-tRNA Bound to T_u Enzyme

Enzyme T_u

Enzyme T_s + GTP

Enzyme T_s + GDP

Step 4 Translocation: tRNA and mRNA Moved Over, Exposing New Codon to an Amino Acid Binding Site

Enzyme "G" + GTP

G + GDP + P_i

Step 3 Uncharged tRNA Lost From Peptide Binding Site

(e) The peptide binding site is now vacant.

(d) The tRNA with elongated peptide chain is now in the amino acid binding site and the uncharged tRNA is in the peptide binding site.

Figure 17.20 The reactions of peptide chain elongation. (a) This sketch shows the reactive sites on the ribosome surface. A ribosome upon which proteins are being built holds its two subunits in this stable complex. The mRNA is bound only to the small subunit. Together the large and small subunits form two parallel tRNA binding sites that differ in chemical properties. One is the peptide-tRNA binding site and the other is the amino acid–tRNA binding site.

(b) The three key nucleotides at the anticodon end of the tRNA molecule are hydrogen-bonded to complementary bases of the mRNA codons; thus these ends lie on the surface of the small subunit. The ends bearing the amino acids lie on the surface of the large subunit.

On a ribosome that has just finished adding one amino acid to the growing chain, we find the tRNA bearing the polypeptide lying in the peptide binding site. The next codon of the mRNA to be translated lies immediately adjacent in the amino acid binding site, which is prepared to accept the next tRNA–amino acid complex.

Step 1 of the reaction sequence, whereby the tRNA–amino acid complex is bound to the vacant amino acid site, is catalyzed by an enzyme called T_u. This enzyme forms a complex with one amino acyl–tRNA (aa-tRNA) molecule and one GTP molecule. (GTP is analogous to ATP; guanine is present instead of adenine.) As the aa-tRNA is bound, the GTP is split into GDP and inorganic phosphate.

Step 2 is the central reaction of protein synthesis. It is catalyzed by the enzyme peptide synthetase, which is an integral component of the ribosome. It lies right below and between the amino acid ends of the two binding sites. The instant both tRNA molecules (with their respective charges) are in place, this enzyme functions to form the peptide bond. This reaction results in the transfer of the growing chain to the tRNA in the amino acid site.

Step 3 appears to require no enzyme. Its job done, the un-charged tRNA simply pops off.

Step 4, translocation, is the most mysterious. It is as if the enzyme G picks up the mRNA and the tRNA peptide chains and moves them down a notch while keeping them hooked together with tenuous hydrogen bonds. In the process, another high-energy phosphate bond is split. When step 4 is finished, a new codon lies above the now-vacant amino acid binding site and the ribosome is ready for another go-around.

In step 5, an enzyme called T_s reactivates the enzyme called T_u by replacing its bound GDP with a new molecule of GTP.

In step 6, an amino acid–tRNA molecule corresponding to the next codon to be translated is bound to the enzyme T_u. The entire system is now ready to repeat the cycle again, lengthening the peptide chain by one more amino acid.

predictable structure and function, it is a small price to pay.

The process of chain elongation continues along the mRNA molecule, one codon at a time, until it reaches the end of the message (which is not necessarily the end of the molecule). What signals the end of the message and calls for chain termination from the ribosomal machinery? As Figure 17.15 showed, it is a codon for which no complementary tRNA exists—a codon that does not specify an amino acid. The three nucleotide triplets that do not code for amino acids (UAA, UAG, and UGA) are widely known as *nonsense codons*. But they are "nonsense" only in that they do not imply a particular amino acid, as the other sixty-one nucleotide triplets do. Any one of them can lead to chain termination; hence, **termination codons** is a more accurate description. Sometimes two termination codons will occur in sequence at the end of a message, as if to reinforce the STOP signal.

When a termination codon is reached, an enzyme called "R" (for "Release") binds to the ribosome. It reads the STOP codon and clips the finished protein molecule from the tRNA to which it has been bound. Then the finished protein, the tRNA, and the R enzyme pop off the ribosome.

What is the fate of the mRNA–ribosome complex? If the mRNA molecule contained a sequence specifying only a single polypeptide chain, then the mRNA separates from the ribosome at this stage. But some mRNA molecules contain the information required to make two or more related protein chains; the stop signal for one is followed closely by the start signal for the next. In such cases the mRNA may remain bound to the small ribosomal subunit, ready to start the next protein chain.

In any case, the complete ribosome that has just finished making one protein chain cannot participate immediately and directly in the synthesis of a new one. Instead, the large and small subunits must be separated before initiation of a new chain can begin. An enzyme exists that leads to this separation. Having separated, the subunits are capable of participating in a new round of activity, which involves re-forming a complex between a large and a small subunit.

In chain initiation, everything depends on starting in the right place. This stage of the translation process involves several steps and requires participation of three *initiation enzymes* (Figure 17.21).

Like chain termination, the process of chain initiation involves specific codons. *Reading of the genetic code must always proceed from a fixed starting point.* If it did not, the chances are two out of three that every codon would be misread. The START signal for every protein yet examined in either prokaryotes or eukaryotes is one of two nucleotide triplets: either AUG or (more rarely) GUG. These triplets are called **initiation codons.** In bacteria, both can be

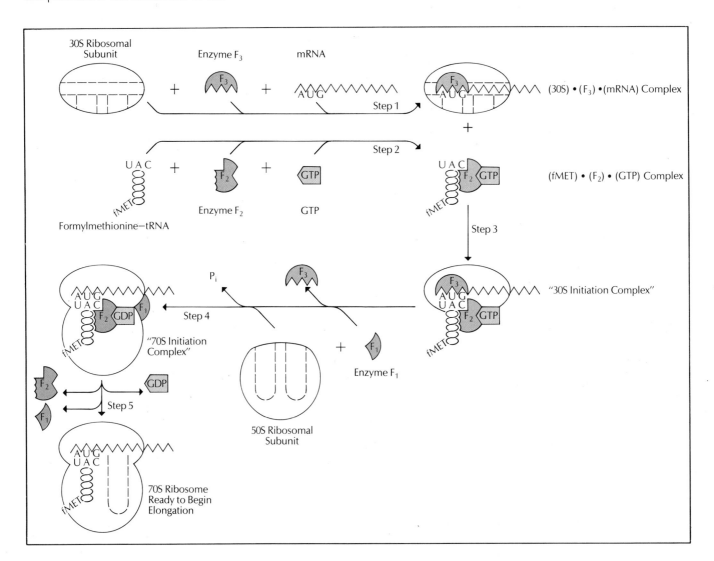

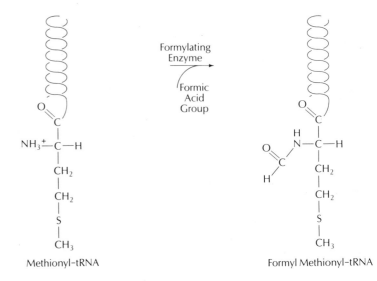

Figure 17.21 The reactions of peptide chain initiation. The function of the initiation reactions is to assure that the proper starting point on the message is selected as the ribosome is assembled and combined with mRNA and tRNA. All subsequent codons will then be read properly. The participation of three enzymes is required to achieve this kind of precision.

In step 1, an enzyme called F_3 brings the mRNA molecule and the small (30S) ribosomal subunit together in such a way that the initiation codon (AUG) lies directly above the peptide-tRNA binding site of this subunit.

In step 2, the enzyme F_2 combines with the initiation tRNA (formyl methionine–tRNA, see Figure 17.22) and a molecule of GTP.

In step 3, the complexes formed in the first two steps come together in such a way that the tRNA anticodon is aligned with and hydrogen-bonded to the initiation codon.

In step 4, the enzyme F_1 (required to bind the large ribosomal subunit) is added. As the enzyme F_1 enters, the enzyme F_3 leaves, its job completed. Now the large (50S) subunit may be bound to complete assembly of the ribosome; as it is bound, the GTP molecule is hydrolyzed, releasing inorganic phosphate.

In step 5, the enzymes F_1 and F_2 leave the ribosome, as does the GDP. Now the ribosome, the message, and the tRNA are properly aligned so that the reactions of elongation can begin.

Figure 17.22 Formation of the substituted amino acid–tRNA complex used to initiate protein synthesis in prokaryotes. Notice that when the formic acid group is coupled to the amino group, it neutralizes the charge of the group and forms a bond resembling a peptide bond. This similarity is significant, because chain initiation requires that the first amino acyl–tRNA complex sit in the peptide binding site usually occupied by a peptide-tRNA complex rather than an amino acid–tRNA complex. The absence of a charged amino group and the presence of a peptidelike grouping apparently is enough to adapt this molecule to the peptide-tRNA site.

"read" by only one kind of tRNA when they occur at the beginning of an mRNA sequence (Figure 17.22). This tRNA bears a modified amino acid, formyl methionine (a methionine to which a formic acid group has been added to cover up the amino acid group).

The reason an amino acid derivative like formyl methionine is used as the initiator of a peptide chain appears at first to be straightforward. In order to start a chain, two amino acid–tRNA complexes must be bound at once. That means one must be bound in the peptide binding site, which is specialized to hold a peptide-tRNA complex rather than an amino acid–tRNA complex. Addition of a formyl group (formylation) to the amino group of methionine, on the methionyl tRNA, abolishes the ionic nature of that group and gives it a chemical nature more like that of a peptide, so that it more readily fits the peptide binding site. In fact, it has been possible experimentally to initiate protein synthesis at sites other than an initiator codon by employing man-made derivatives of other amino acid–tRNA complexes that are peptides or resemble them and that will sit in the peptide binding site.

Having worked all of this out for bacteria, molecular biologists were in for a real surprise when they finally discovered the nature of the initiation mechanism used by the cytoplasmic ribosomes of eukaryotic cells. It turns out that the initiator codons are the same as they are in bacteria (AUG and GUG); the tRNA involved is of the same kind, but the methionine is not—indeed must not be—formylated! If the methionyl tRNA that initiates protein synthesis in eukaryotes is exposed to the formylating enzyme of bacteria, it can be formylated as well as the bacterial methionine tRNA can be. But once formylated, the complex loses all capacity for initiating protein synthesis on eukaryotic ribosomes! Thus eukaryotic cells have retained the initiation processes of their prokaryotic forebears in all details but one, and in this perplexing detail they have undergone a complete evolutionary turnabout.

The Translation of mRNA in a Polyribosomal Complex

An mRNA molecule is usually hundreds of nucleotides long, and each ribosome works on only six nucleotides at a time. Therefore, once one ribosome has moved past the initiation codon and before it has reached the termination codon, a second ribosome may become attached to the molecule and begin translation. Indeed, most actively synthesizing ribosomes are found in clusters, bound together by the message that is in different stages of being translated. Such clusters are known as **polyribosomes,** or **polysomes** (Figure 17.23).

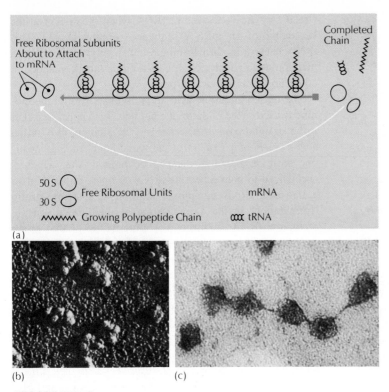

(a)

(b)   (c)

Figure 17.23 (a) How polysomes work in protein synthesis. Ribosomes are shown moving from left to right. (b, c) Electron micrographs of polysomes, showing the thin strand of mRNA connecting them.

After J. D. Watson, Molecular Biology of the Gene, copyright © 1970, J. D. Watson. W. A. Benjamin, Inc.

PERSPECTIVE

Genes, the units of heredity, are made of DNA. During reproduction, the genetic information that is common to the species and, in some respects, unique to the individual is transferred from one cell to another in molecules of DNA. That this information will be transferred faithfully from one generation to the next is assured by the simple rules of base pairing. Because A always pairs with T, and G with C, each strand of the double-stranded DNA molecule has the information needed to replicate the other. That, with the help of an enzyme, is how DNA can engage in self-replication.

The hereditary information carried by a specific DNA molecule (a gene) is simply the paired sequence of bases along the length of its double strands. The base sequence stands for a sequence of amino acids, which, when assembled, will be a specific protein. Proteins are the agents that produce the specific characteristics of a cell or an organism. Thus, the manner in which a sequence of DNA bases becomes translated into a sequence of amino acids is at the heart of the relationship between genotype and phenotype.

But DNA does not participate directly in protein synthesis. Instead, a messenger RNA molecule is synthesized on one of the double strands of DNA, thereby forming a complementary transcript of it.

Once transcription is completed, the mRNA molecule leaves the DNA molecule. The translation of the message it carries takes place on structures called ribosomes, which contain ribosomal RNA. The function of rRNA is simply to participate with proteins in the formation of the physical structure upon which new proteins will be built. Ribosomes bind mRNA. When they do, they become committed to the synthesis of the specific protein coded for by that mRNA molecule.

The act of translating the message requires a third class of RNA molecules, called transfer RNA. Many kinds of tRNA exist in a cell, but each is capable of being linked, by a specific enzyme, to only one kind of amino acid. At the end of the tRNA molecule opposite the end that carries the amino acid there is a specific sequence of three nucleotides with their bases directed outward. These three bases are capable of binding to three complementary bases on the mRNA molecule, using essentially the same base-pairing rules that are involved in synthesis of DNA and RNA.

A series of three bases in the mRNA can be bound only by a tRNA molecule that possesses a complementary sequence. The tRNA bearing that sequence will invariably be coupled to one particular kind of amino acid. It follows, then, that each series of three bases in mRNA always specifies a particular amino acid; it is a code word—a codon—representing that amino acid. The complementary bases of tRNA constitute the anticodon.

When six nucleotides in the mRNA molecule are positioned on the ribosome to which they are bound, two specific kinds of tRNA can be hydrogen-bonded to them, carrying two kinds of amino acids. These amino acids can then be linked together by a peptide bond, forming a dipeptide. The ribosome then moves down the messenger by one codon, making room for an additional tRNA with its amino acid, and so the peptide chain grows.

As the peptide chain grows, it begins to curl and fold in space as amino acids of mutual chemical affinity in different parts of the chain meet each other and interact. By the time the chain is finished, the protein has taken on its characteristic three-dimensional shape from which its unique capacities are derived.

Thus, on the ribosome the linear one-dimensional code of the gene is translated into a complex three-dimensional entity capable of executing a unique role in the life of a cell. The potential of genotype is well on its way to becoming the reality of phenotype.

All of these processes are summarized in the simple phrase, *DNA makes RNA, and RNA makes protein.* Understanding the meaning of these words not only represents insight into how genes work, it also represents profound insight into the fundamental nature of life.

DNA is the master code specifying the details of the cell's potential, inherited in a direct but slowly changing line from the primeval ancestor of us all. Its secret is its capacity for self-replication. But that is an oversimplification. DNA is not autonomous; it cannot replicate itself without assistance. Without assistance from the enzyme DNA polymerase, from the energy-generating mechanisms of the cell, and from all the enzymes required to produce and make available all of the nucleoside triphosphates required for replication, DNA is nothing more than another molecule.

RNA is the master agent of gene action, translating genetic potential into cellular reality. But by itself, RNA is also impotent. To be produced, the RNA requires the enzyme RNA polymerase. To be functional, the RNA requires a host of collaborating enzymes, a supply of all the amino acids, and a constant flow of energy from the ATP-generating systems of the cell.

But all the cellular components required to put the gene action system into a functioning state are themselves products of the gene action system! Each enzyme required for gene action is produced as a result of prior gene action. An rRNA molecule cannot take on its functional role in a ribosome until it is combined with ribosomal proteins. But where do these ribosomal proteins come from? They must be made on other ribosomes that are already functional. And where did those ribosomes obtain their proteins? As the result of functioning of earlier ribosomes—and so on.

The components of the living cell are locked in an unbroken chain stretching back through unrecorded time to the first cell that assembled, from the rich primeval soup, all the molecules required for self-perpetuation.

It is because of this great cycle of molecular in-terdependence that we find "all life from preexisting life" and "all cells from preexisting cells." It is not that a vital spirit must be passed along; it is that a battery of molecules must be passed along, none of which can be made without others having gone before.

SUGGESTED READINGS

CAINS, J., G. STENT, and J. D. WATSON (eds.). *Phage and the Origins of Molecular Biology.* Cold Spring Harbor, N.Y.: Cold Spring Harbor Laboratory, 1966. Reflections on the "interactions, folklore, and method of operation" of some of the men who shaped the field of molecular biology. A fascinating, highly personal account.

LURIA, S. E. "Molecular Biology: Past, Present, and Future," *BioScience*, 20 (1970), 1289. Luria captures much of the excitement of molecular genetics in this essay.

SRB, A. M., R. D. OWEN, and R. S. EDGAR (eds.). *Facets of Genetics.* San Francisco: W. H. Freeman, 1969. A collection of readings from *Scientific American.* Includes articles on all aspects of genetics, with particular emphasis on molecular genetics.

STENT, GUNTHER S. *Molecular Genetics: An Introductory Narrative.* San Francisco: W. H. Freeman, 1971. An excellent introduction to the whole area of molecular genetics, deftly written by one of the field's most engaging spokesmen.

WATSON, J. D. *The Molecular Biology of the Gene.* 2nd ed. Philadelphia: W. A. Benjamin, 1970. A classic in its own time, this is the best single discourse on the gene.

ZUBAY, GEOFFREY L. (ed.). *Papers in Biochemical Genetics.* 2nd ed. New York: Holt, Rinehart and Winston, 1973. An excellent collection of original papers; well worth the effort it will take an advanced undergraduate to read them.

Chapter 18

Sexual Reproduction and Development in Animals

Unless it is accompanied by successful reproduction, of what evolutionary advantage is the acquisition of greater size, or greater complexity, or any other new feature of an individual? Evolutionary success, in the end, depends on the capacity to leave progeny. With apologies to the nineteenth-century novelist Samuel Butler, we might say that a frog is, after all, merely an egg's way of producing another egg.

Dawn breaks in the summer sky and two tiny flatworms crawl aimlessly across the floor of a tidal pool. They meet; they recoil slightly. And then they begin to circle each other. Suddenly, as if on signal, they rise up against each other, curling into a ball in which the male copulatory organ of each flatworm is pressed into the female pore of the other. As they roll about, muscular spasms send sperm from each body into the other. Then, just as suddenly, the flatworms separate and crawl off in opposite directions, grazing on their simple algal pastures as they go. In less than five minutes the daily drama has been completed and a new generation has begun. For the remainder of the day those flatworms are oblivious of each other's presence. As dusk falls, each pauses in its separate wanderings, writhes, and contracts until a break forms in its skin. And the progeny conceived that morning—now rapidly dividing balls of cells—are deposited between sand grains to continue development on their own. As dawn breaks the following morning the daily cycle begins again, before yesterday's progeny have yet begun to crawl.

Everywhere in the animal kingdom the patterns of life revolve around the act of reproduction. Of course, the strategies for achieving reproductive success vary. For example, the young of many mammals are born in small numbers, only once a year, and then they are protected and defended by adults of their kind until they are almost fully grown. In contrast, the sedentary sea urchin may never contact its mate or its own offspring. But beneath its spiny skeleton it hides a body cavity dominated by gonads that produce eggs and sperm in countless millions. Upon an appropriate signal (the appearance of the first eggs in the water), sea urchins throughout a given region discharge a profusion of reproductive cells. The success of future generations is left almost entirely to chance—chance encounters between eggs and sperm and chance survival of the young, which a teeming assortment of predators find most tasty. But the sea urchin has hit upon a strategy that works nevertheless: the strategy of numbers. The quantity of eggs it produces each breeding season is so immense that if even one egg in every million escaped predation to become a reproducing adult, sea urchins would soon overpopulate the oceans!

Between the two reproductive extremes of mammals and sea urchins are many intermediate modes of reproduction that are tuned to the conditions of diverse habitats. Yet despite superficial differences in reproductive style, throughout the animal kingdom there is an underlying unity in the subsequent development of the young—a unity that undoubtedly reflects both the common heritage of all animals and a common set of problems all must circumvent. In this chapter you will read about some of the common features of embryonic development in the animal kingdom whereby a single fertilized egg gives rise to a complex adult through the process of **differentiation**—*the capacity of one cell to give rise to cells different from itself and from one another.*

Now, one of the sources of apparent differences in the development of various kinds of animals is a result of different solutions to the problem of feeding the developing young. Because a reproductive cell lacks the specialized features of the adult animal, it also lacks the means of obtaining nutrients from the environment. No cell can function without a continuous supply of nutrients; cells of a developing reproductive unit, or **embryo,** are no exception. Somehow the embryo must be provided with enough nutritional reserves to see it through **embryonic development**—*the period of development in which it lives off nutrients provided by the female parent.*

There are basically three variations on the theme of nutritional support of the embryo. First, there can be brief embryonic development with minimal food resources, followed by a juvenile stage in which the young acquire their own food to sustain growth. Second, there can be prolonged development in which the fertilized reproductive cell is sustained by a concentrated food reserve, or **yolk.** And third, there can be prolonged development within the female parent's body, sustained by the direct transfer of nutrients from the body fluid of the female parent to the embryo.

For example, marine animals such as sea urchins produce reproductive cells in vast numbers. As a result, the amount of yolk that can be included in each embryo is sparse indeed. But in such forms, development is so simple and rapid that the young are hatched and are able to fend for themselves within a day or so. Usually the young of such animals follow a course of **indirect development,** going through a free-living larval stage that differs greatly in organization from the adult form. The larvae feed, grow, and eventually **metamorphose** (change in form) to become adults.

In contrast, the embryos of birds and reptiles undergo prolonged **direct development** as shell-protected eggs. They hatch into what are essentially young adults. Typically, the eggs of these animals must be heavily laden with yolk, for they often require several weeks to reach the hatching stage. The amount of yolk present is usually correlated with the rate and duration of development. At the time of hatching, the yolk is almost entirely gone; only enough reserves are left to carry the young through the time of the first feeding. The presence of these massive food reserves places mechanical restraints on the embryo. As a result, processes basically similar to those seen in other organisms appear quite different, as you will read later.

Finally, in many groups of organisms, the reproductive

cell is packaged with only enough reserves to initiate development. But the female parent retains the developing embryo. Within the female the embryo is bathed with fluids rich in nutrients that are absorbed and used for growth. Such internal development occurs in many animal groups, but two groups of invertebrates, certain sharks, and most mammals carry the process even further. In these groups, the embryo attaches to the wall of the maternal reproductive tract, and a placenta forms. A **placenta** is an organ by which nutrients pass directly from the blood vessels of the female parent into those of the developing embryo. Because the embryo of these species must be fed from the start, placenta formation commonly takes precedence over other developmental processes. Therefore, events that occur early in the development of other animals are often delayed for hours or days in placental animals until after the placenta has been formed and is functional.

But these variations are variations in detail only. *The early stages of development of all animal species include the same three processes: fertilization, cleavage, and gastrulation.* What happens in each of these three processes is described in the next three sections. *How* certain key steps in these processes occur is a somewhat more intriguing but also a more difficult question that will be asked later on in the chapter.

FERTILIZATION ACTIVATES THE DEVELOPMENTAL PROGRAM OF THE EGG

In most species, the essence of mating behavior is to provide mechanisms for ensuring that the development and release of sperm and eggs is coordinated in time and space. The evolutionary forces driving this coordination are obvious: only those individuals of a species that are reproductively active at the same time will leave offspring. Consider a male salamander with mutated genes that cause him to arrive at the breeding pond in midsummer instead of immediately after the first warm rain of spring. It will find the pond a lonely place, and, as a consequence, it will leave precious few offspring to inherit its individualistic mating preferences.

But assuming members of a species get together at the right time in the right place, how are egg and sperm brought together? In some cnidarians, the egg-bearing female structures release a chemical attractant that actively guides the sperm through the ocean to the eggs. But the sperm of most animals swim or float randomly, colliding with eggs only by accident. Now, for many species (particularly those that produce only a few eggs at a time), that is a little too chancy. In such species—from flatworms to insects, from sharks to ourselves—the male has a specialized copulatory organ that is used to deposit sperm directly within the female reproductive tract. Thus, the likelihood of sperm encountering an egg is enormously enhanced. Such a copulatory organ is particularly useful in terrestrial habitats, where sperm would hardly be capable of fending for themselves in the open air. But it is equally advantageous in aquatic animals that have small numbers of large, yolky eggs with direct development; and it is essential in species in which development takes place within the female parent. In mammals and birds, there are social hierarchies and rituals surrounding the copulatory act, dictating who donates sperm to whom.

Regardless of how egg and sperm are brought together, the events that ensue upon their contact are quite uniform. **Fertilization** begins as the tip of a sperm cell contacts the surface of an egg (Figure 18.2). At that moment, egg and sperm cease to be members of the earlier generation; together they become a new generation. At the point of contact, plasma membranes surrounding the two cells fuse and then part, so that the contents of the two cells are suddenly enclosed in a single, continuous membrane.

Fusion of the two cells sets in motion a series of events known as **activation of the egg.** One of the earliest events is a change in the properties of the egg membrane. It begins at the point of sperm contact and radiates outward, sweeping over the entire surface in a very brief period. Often it involves the fusion of many **cortical granules** (small, membrane-enclosed vesicles) with the surface membrane so that their contents are dumped to the exterior. This so-called **cortical reaction** changes the egg surface so that its former receptivity for sperm vanishes—one sperm cell is enough!

Accompanying the visible changes in the surface are a variety of other changes. For example, most eggs become receptive to sperm without having completed meiosis; the remaining meiotic divisions are triggered almost at once by activation of the egg. Also, many eggs are metabolically inactive before fertilization, and activation leads to sudden increases in the rates of respiratory metabolism, protein synthesis, and other cellular activities. In many species, activation sets off the movement of specific kinds of inclusions within the egg to new locations, where they will play some key role in future development.

Such changes might be taken to mean that the sperm directs the early development of components of a passive egg. But surprisingly, the only truly essential role the sperm plays in development is to donate its chromosomes. In species after species, it has been shown that eggs can be artificially activated. In other words, they can be induced to begin development by many agents that simply disturb the egg surface. These agents include such nonspecific stimuli as heat, cold, strong salt solutions, very dilute salt solutions, dilute acid, and even the point of a fine needle. In nature, the activating stimulus is most commonly—but not always—a sperm. For example, in many insect species such as bees and aphids, eggs regularly develop without fertilization. Such development is known as **parthenogenesis**

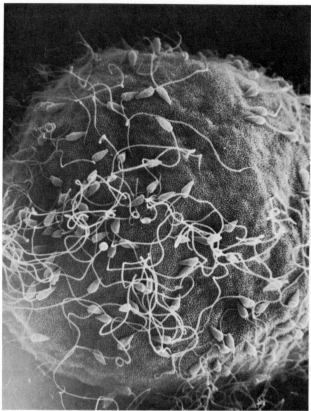

(a)

(magnification x 1,400)

Figure 18.2 Fertilization of sea urchin eggs. (a) A swarm of sperm attached to and attempting to fertilize an egg. At the instant that the first sperm fuses with the egg, it activates changes in the egg membrane that prevent additional sperm from penetrating. (b) A sperm and egg just after the moment of fusion. Sperm and egg membranes are now one; both nuclei are now in a common cytoplasm. Already the egg has been activated, resulting in elevation of the fertilization membrane from the egg surface; this is one of the changes preventing penetration by a second sperm.

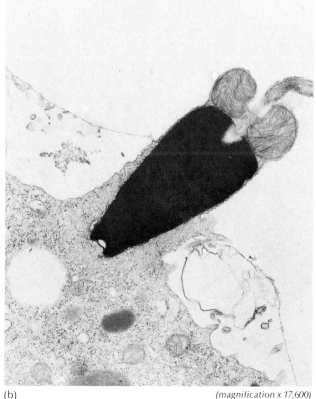

(b)

(magnification x 17,600)

("virgin birth"). Indeed, parthenogenesis is possible even in species that normally require fertilization; for example, parthenogenesis commonly occurs in one strain of turkeys. Whether the virgin-born offspring are male or female, haploid or diploid, varies from species to species. The drawback of parthenogenesis (or any other form of asexual reproduction) is that all the offspring are genetically similar to the female parent. *Sexual reproduction involves genetic recombination; therefore, it has an inherent advantage over all types of asexual reproduction and has been fostered during evolution despite the fact that eggs can develop without fertilization.*

The process of fertilization is not complete until the contents of the sperm nucleus and the egg nucleus are fused. Once that happens, the fertilized egg has become a zygote, ready to proceed with further development.

CLEAVAGE SUBDIVIDES THE EMBRYO IN PREPARATION FOR FURTHER DEVELOPMENT

Shortly after fertilization is complete, the zygote begins a series of rapid cell divisions called **cleavage** (Figure 18.3). There are many minor variations in cleavage patterns (Figure 18.4), but the basic process is always the same. As a general rule, *the less protected the egg, the faster the cell divides.* For example, the naked sea urchin egg floating in the open sea divides nearly as fast as the most prolific bacteria—one division every half-hour, in some cases. Virtually all the machinery of the cell is channeled into maintaining the rapid pace of division. Cell growth does not occur during cleavage. The cell cycle becomes restricted to only two of its normal four phases: the brief S phase of DNA synthesis and the brief M phase of cell division (Figure 13.30). Most of the energy being consumed goes into cleavage, and most of the proteins being synthesized are the ones needed to produce new nuclei, mitotic spindles, and so forth.

What does cleavage accomplish? Basically it does four things. First, *cleavage creates many small cells out of one large reproductive cell.* This cell, the egg, is usually the largest the organism produces. In frogs, for example, the

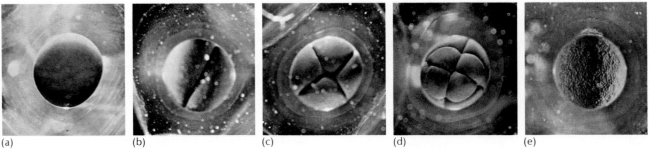

(a) (b) (c) (d) (e)

Figure 18.3 Cleavage in a frog embryo. The fertilized frog egg is suspended in a thick, jellylike coating that protects it from bacterial attack and a variety of potential predators. Many eggs cohere to form a huge mass. Shortly after the egg nucleus has completed meiosis and has fused with a sperm nucleus, cleavage begins (b). A series of rapid divisions (c and d) eventually results in the formation of a blastula (e). In the blastula, the cytoplasm of the fertilized egg has been divided up into tens of thousands of much smaller cells. A cross section through (e) would show it to be a hollow ball; and the center is a fluid-filled space. The embryo is viewed from above in all five photomicrographs.

(Photographs courtesy Carolina Biological Supply Company)

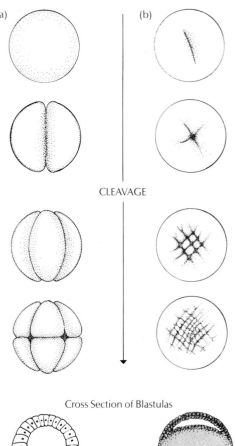

(a) (b)

CLEAVAGE

Cross Section of Blastulas

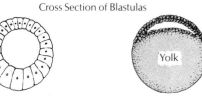

Yolk

Figure 18.4 The effect of yolk deposits on the pattern of cleavage and on the appearance of the blastula.

(a) When little yolk is present in the fertilized egg, the cleavage planes pass completely through the egg, dividing it into discrete blastomeres. Such cleavage patterns are seen in many species that undergo indirect development, such as frogs and sea urchins. Usually such development leads to the formation of a larva (a tadpole, in the case of frogs). In such species, the blastula simply is a hollow ball of cells.

(b) When much yolk is present, cleavage furrows pass only partly into the mass in a somewhat disorganized-looking way. Eventually, membrane moves out from the cleavage furrows and parallel to the surface. There it encloses all the discrete cells that lie near the surface of the yolk. As a result, the blastula that forms is flattened out over one surface of the yolk mass. The structure is usually called a blastoderm rather than a blastula, but the two are functionally equivalent. This pattern of superficial cleavage is seen in many species that undergo direct development, in which the individual hatches from the egg as essentially a young adult. Fish, birds, and reptiles fall into this category.

egg is 10,000 to 100,000 times as large as the somatic cells of the adult. Only a cell that large can carry all the food reserves the embryo needs. But a single cell cannot carry out all the developmental processes leading to a multicellular organism; through cleavage it produces the numerous small cells that can.

Second, *there is a limit to how much cytoplasm the chromosomes of a single nucleus can control, and cleavage restores the normal ratio between cytoplasmic volume and nuclear volume.* There is a limit to how fast a nucleus can make new RNA molecules, how fast those RNA molecules can be translated into protein, and so on. In most species, all somatic cells are about the same size. If the egg has a cytoplasmic/nuclear volume ratio 10,000 times the normal ratio, the nucleus could not be expected to direct its metabolic activities very well. It is not surprising, then, to find that the metabolic activities during cleavage are *not* under the control of the chromosomes in the zygote. During cleavage, preexisting enzymes and mitochondria handle glycolysis and respiration; protein synthesis takes place via ribosomes and messenger RNA molecules that were already packaged into the egg. Toward the end of the cleavage period, however, the cytoplasmic/nuclear volume ratio approaches that typical of the species. Only then do nuclei of the embryo begin to play an active role in directing cellular activities.

Third, *cleavage segregates the cytoplasmic substances that are crucial in directing the nuclear activities of the separate cells in the developing embryo.* Ultimately, differentiation of the parts of the embryo is a result of different kinds of nuclear activity. For example, in cells destined to become blood cells, the genes coding for blood proteins are read, but in other cells they are not read. Similarly, only in cells destined to become brain cells are the genes coding for brain proteins read. But which nuclei express which genes? As you will read shortly, that is determined initially by the kind of cytoplasm in which the various nuclei come to rest. No egg is a completely homogeneous sphere. To a greater or lesser extent, eggs always contain localized deposits of substances that influence development. Prior to cleavage, these substances are somewhat free to move about. But as cleavage proceeds, these substances become locked into some cells but not others; they are capable of influencing the nuclei of the cells within which they are enclosed, but not other nuclei.

Fourth, *cleavage creates a hollow sphere in which the next events of development occur.* The uncleaved zygote is rather solid in appearance. But as cleavage occurs, the cells being formed tend to adhere in some regions and not in others. They also secrete fluids from their inner surfaces. In this manner they form a hollow ball of cells—a **blas-**tula—with a fluid-filled cavity in the center. It is largely within this cavity that the crucial events of the next phase of development occur.

GASTRULATION BEGINS THE SHAPING OF THE EMBRYO

Once the blastula has been formed, the pace of cell division usually slows down dramatically. Even though there has been very little visible change in the cells other than a progressive decrease in size, the embryo has gone through an important preparatory stage. A complex individual can now be molded from these cells, beginning with the process of **gastrulation.** The most obvious features of gastrulation are a series of **morphogenetic movements** (movement of parts in such a way as to give rise to form). Cells from the exterior of the blastula move toward the interior to form a multilayered embryonic structure known as a **gastrula** (Figure 18.5). A gastrula has the beginnings of a gut, and its multiple layers will give rise to tissues and organs.

By the end of gastrulation, three discrete layers of cells are formed. The outermost layer is called the **ectoderm** (*ecto* means "outer"; *derm* means "skin"). It gives rise to the nervous system, to skin, and to skin appendages such as feathers, hair, and claws. The innermost layer is called the **endoderm** (*endo* means "inner"). It gives rise to the gut and the associated digestive organs, such as the pancreas and the liver in vertebrates. The layer of cells between the ectoderm and the endoderm is called the **mesoderm** (*meso* means "middle"). It gives rise to a variety of internal organs such as skeleton, muscle, blood, blood vessels, and heart. It is in the structures derived from the mesodermal layer that the various animal phyla differ most from one another.

Throughout cleavage and gastrulation, the developmental patterns of all animal groups show extensive similarities. But as development proceeds beyond gastrulation, differences between groups become more apparent. Figure 18.6 follows the development of a sea urchin gastrula into a free-swimming larva. Figure 18.7 follows the development of a chick embryo in its first three days of incubation. Although the end products of these two processes look quite different, they involve a series of basically similar processes. Rather than concern ourselves with the details of what structures arise where, when, and from what preexisting structures in different embryos, let us now turn to the problem of identifying the mechanisms common to all species. For the past century, the fundamental question facing developmental biology has been this: Why does a cleaving zygote give rise to a complex individual instead of just a cluster of identical cells?

(text continues on page 410)

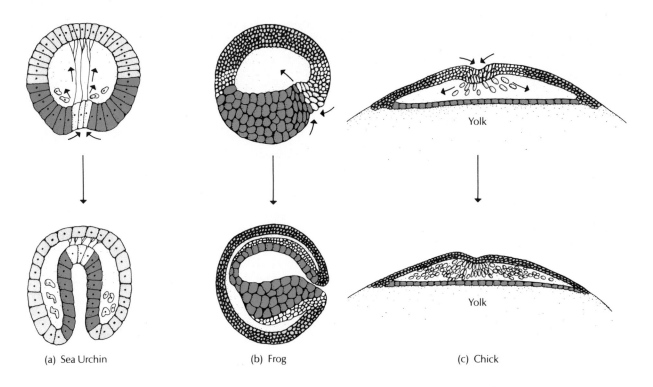

(a) Sea Urchin   (b) Frog   (c) Chick

Figure 18.5 Three patterns of gastrulation, as they would appear in cross section. The mechanisms of gastrulation vary from species to species, but the outcome is always the same: An embryonic stage forms that has three layers of cells. The ectoderm (shown in gray) gives rise to skin and nerves. The endoderm (blue) gives rise to the gut. The mesoderm (white) is the source of skeleton, muscle, and a variety of other internal organs.

Although there apparently has been strong evolutionary pressure to maintain gastrulation, there has been no such pressure to maintain a single mechanism for accomplishing the task. Most variations can be attributed to differences in yolk deposition and cleavage patterns.

In sea urchins (a), some of the cells destined to become mesoderm crawl out of the blastula wall at the time of invagination (the infolding of the blastula). They proceed to wander about the cavity. Meanwhile, cells at the point of invagination send out long filopods. The filopods attach to cells on the roof of the cavity and then contract, pulling the invaginating cells inward. The ectoderm cells flatten and cover the exterior of the gastrula. Later, a second set of mesoderm cells leaves the endoderm and joins the first set in the cavity.

In frogs, gastrulation depends on changes in the shape of cells at the blastopore (the point of invagination). As cells move around the lips of the blastopore, they become elongated in such a way that they move inward. As they do so, they exert tension on their neighbors, drawing them around the corner. After the large, yolk-rich endosperm cells have moved to the

interior, the mesoderm cells slide as a continuous sheet over the endoderm, completely surrounding it.

In chicks, cleavage occurs on just one region of the yolk, producing a blastoderm. The layer of blastoderm cells abutting the yolk becomes the endoderm, and a space forms between the endoderm and the overlying cells. During gastrulation, a depression called the "primitive streak" forms at one end of the blastoderm. Cells migrate to the primitive streak, become detached from it, and move inward one by one. Once inside they spread out, becoming the mesoderm.

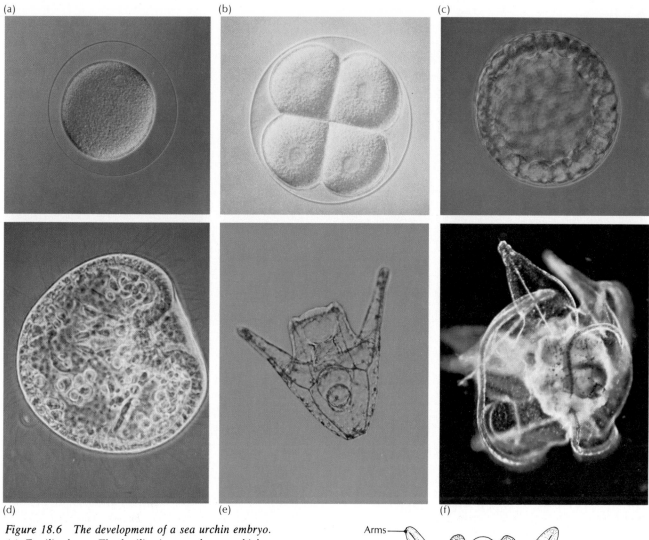

(a) (b) (c)

(d) (e) (f)

Figure 18.6   The development of a sea urchin embryo.
(a) Fertilized egg. The fertilization membrane, which prevents
penetration by a second sperm, is evident in this photograph.
(b) Four-cell stage. Notice the prominent nucleus in each cell.
(c) Early blastula. Notice the larger cells at the bottom, which
mark the region in which invagination will occur. (d) Early
gastrula. Clusters of mesenchyme cells appear above and to
either side of the invagination. The tube formed by the
invagination will become the gut, and the opening so formed
will become the mouth. (e) The pluteus larva. Compare this
photograph with the line drawing of the equivalent stage (g). In
(f), the larva is shown in the process of metamorphosing into an
adult sea urchin.

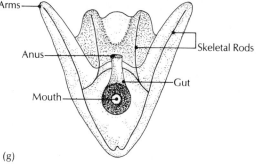

(g)

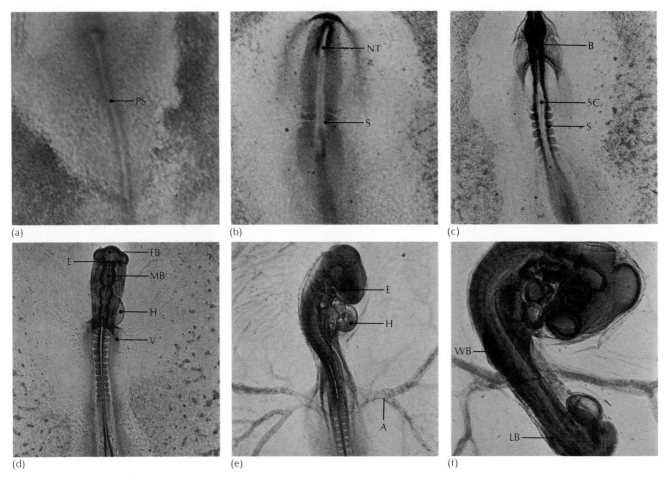

(a)   (b)   (c)

(d)   (e)   (f)

DO PERMANENT CHANGES IN CELL NUCLEI ACCOUNT FOR EMBRYONIC DEVELOPMENT?

In the late nineteenth century, August Weismann ventured that each feature of an adult is contained within the egg (and also in the sperm) in the form of a particle called a "determinant." Development occurs, he suggested, because different cell lines in the embryo lose certain determinants at each cell division while retaining others. Thus the leg cells would possess "leg determinants" but would have lost "head determinants," and so on.

If Weismann was correct, then the nucleus of a cell from a later stage of development should not be able to promote complete embryonic development of an egg. The first test of his prediction came in 1900, when Hans Spemann experimented with embryonic development in a newt. Spemann constricted a newt egg with a loop of hair, as shown in Figure 18.8. Half the zygote contained the nucleus and began cleavage; the half that lacked the nucleus did not. After several divisions, a nucleus happened to pass through the constriction. Spemann then tightened the noose, cutting the zygote in two. The half that was late in receiving a nucleus was delayed in its development, but otherwise it

was normal. Spemann concluded that the nuclei retained all their "determinants," at least for the first few divisions. Through that stage, at least, the nuclei remained **totipotent** (capable of directing all phases of development).

In 1952 Robert Briggs and Thomas King devised a way of testing later stages of development for totipotent nuclei. With fine glass needles they activated a frog egg parthenogenetically. Then they removed its nucleus. With a glass pipette drawn to a fine tip, they replaced the nucleus with a nucleus removed from a cell of a more advanced embryo. They found that when the transplanted nucleus came from a cell of a fully cleaved blastula or an early gastrula, many eggs went on to form normal adults! Thus, at least by the beginning of the gastrula stage—when tens of thousands of cells had been formed by cell division—the nuclei remained totipotent. However, when cells from increasingly advanced stages were used as nuclear donors, abnormalities began to appear in the frogs that developed from the recipient eggs. Briggs and King concluded that the developmental capacity of the nuclei changed permanently as development progressed.

John Gurdon took issue with this interpretation. In

Figure 18.7 Organ development in the first three days of life of a chick embryo. In (a), gastrulation is occurring in the region of the primitive streak (PS). In (b), the ectoderm has folded inward to form the neural tube (NT) from which brain and spinal cord will develop. The mesoderm has begun to condense alongside the neural tube to form separate body segments called somites (S). Each somite will form a vertebra and associated muscles.

In (c), the somites have become more numerous. Here the edges of the neural tube have folded over and have met in the region of the brain (B); the spinal cord region (SC) is still open.

In (d), the main regions of the brain have become clearly developed: forebrain (FB), midbrain (MB), and hindbrain (HB). The vesicles destined to form the eyes (E) are growing out of the forebrain. The heart (H) has become functional. Veins (V) from blood vessels on the surface of the yolk can be seen entering the heart.

In (e), the head has turned to the right (as it always does). Many details of the head, including the eye (E), are clearly visible. Here arteries (A) connecting the embryo to the yolk can be seen.

In (f), the beginnings of the outgrowths destined to form the limbs have appeared. The wing bud (WB) is more obvious than the leg bud (LB). The outlines of the forming vertebral column can now be seen clearly in the neck region.

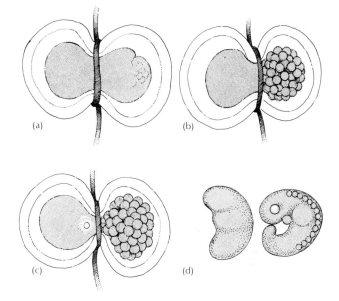

Figure 18.8 Spemann's delayed nucleation experiment. (a) An uncleaved newt egg was constricted with a loop fashioned from the fine hair of a newborn child. (b) The half that—by chance—contained the nucleus began to cleave. As cleavage progressed, however, a nucleus slipped through the noose during one cell division (c). At this point Spemann tightened the loop, cutting the embryo in two. The half receiving the nucleus at this later stage went on to form a normal embryo (d), although it was somewhat delayed in its development relative to its twin.

parallel studies on a different amphibian species, he showed that nuclei from cells of rather advanced tadpoles could be used to direct normal embryonic development. The question of irreversible change in the nucleus has been vexing, however, because of the low numbers of normal individuals Gurdon obtained in early experiments and because of lingering doubts concerning the exact nature of the donor cells in these rare cases. But resolution seems close at hand. Sally Hennen, a former student of Briggs, suggests that at least some of the imperfect development Briggs and King had observed can be attributed to technical difficulties in using advanced cell types as nuclear donors. By cooling the recipient egg and by treating the donor nucleus with a substance to prevent its breakdown, she has shown that nuclei derived from advanced developmental stages function in many cases to direct normal development. In short, *nuclei probably do not become irreversibly changed in the course of development; and any changes that do appear are probably a result, rather than a cause, of cellular differentiation.*

Furthermore, if irreversible changes in nuclei do occur, it is not by outright loss of nuclear "determinants" (genes),

as Weismann suggested. Detailed chemical studies show clearly that *all nuclei in the various cells of an adult contain the complete complement of DNA found in the zygote nucleus.* Development is not the result of loss of genes in various cell lines. True, some gene products are found in some types of cells and not others. But the reason for the difference is that *development involves controlled, differential gene expression in different cell types.* Currently much of the work in developmental biology is aimed at discovering the controls of this differential expression of genes in time and space (Chapter 20).

(text continues on page 414)

Interleaf 18.1

Intracellular Differentiation: Basis for Morphogenesis

Most body cells are asymmetrical, ordered, and spatially differentiated. And it is from the shapes of cells that body organs take their shape. Thus the process of intracellular differentiation is a key to *morphogenesis*—the development of form. Understanding how cells become regionally specialized should provide insight into how a complex organism develops from a single cell.

Many processes of intracellular differentiation are still not understood. We know something of the mechanisms whereby cells selectively attach to one another. Jack Lilien and others have isolated tissue-specific glycoproteins that cause cells of only one specific type to cohere. But why do such cells adhere to one another in some regions of their surfaces and not in others—thereby giving a specific form to the tissue they compose? And why, during development, do cells that previously were adhered suddenly and predictably separate to form a cavity? The spatial control of the adhesion process over the surface of a single cell is yet to be explained.

One interesting aspect of intracellular differentiation is the role of the cellular "skeleton" in shaping the cell. In the 1960s, new fixatives permitted better preservation of intracellular structures in tissues being prepared for elctron microscopy, and a lattice of microtubules and/or a profusion of microfilaments were seen where they had never been seen before. The ordering of these structures suggested they played a part in cellular shape and movement. Further technical breakthroughs in this area involved the discovery of reagents that selectively disassembled or inactivated the microtubules and microfilaments. A family of plant alkaloids (including colchicine) was known to prevent mitotic spindle development. It turned out that it also can prevent the assembly or cause the disassembly of cellular microtubules—but it had no effect on microfilaments. Then an antibiotic called cytochalasin was found to cause the inactivation or disassembly of microfilaments. Through use of these two reagents, microtubules and microfilaments are now known to be crucial in intracellular differentiation and in development of form.

Consider, for example, the process of *neurulation*—the folding of the ectoderm to form the neural tube from which brain and spinal cord later develop (Figure 18.7). Two types of intracellular changes can be distinguished in the process (Figure *a*). First, cells that are to form the neural tube elongate, forming the neural plate.

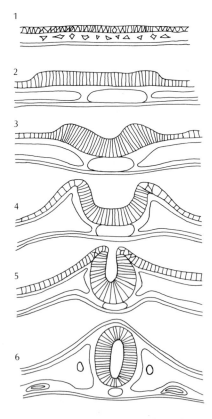

(a) Neurulation in the chick embryo. Shown are successive stages in the formation of the neural tube from undifferentiated ectoderm.

Then cells of the neural plate become wedge-shaped, thereby causing the entire plate of cells to curve. As this transformation to wedge shape occurs in more and more cells, the curvature becomes so great that it finally brings the edges of the plate together to form a tube. A simple experiment showed that the forces bringing about the curving of the neural plate are generated within the plate cells, not by pressure from adjacent cells. When a section of neural plate was cut out and then replaced in an inverted orientation, it proceeded to curl toward the center of the embryo rather than toward the exterior (Figure b).

so no neural tube forms. Electron microscopic studies of untreated neural plate show a ring of microfilaments lying just below the upper surface of the cells and attached to the cell membrane. They apparently are involved in contraction of the upper region of the cell, leading to the wedge shape (Figure c). Significantly, in a vast number of cell types, such filaments are now known to be capable of specifically interacting with myosin isolated from skeletal muscle cells and to be indistinguishable from the muscle protein actin in chemical structure. Myosin molecules, resembling the myosin found in nonstriated muscles, have

to the roof of the cavity normally, but they never contract so vagination does not occur.

In case after case where a developmental system involves changes in shape or motility of cells, microtubules and/or microfilaments have been found to be involved. In each case, the microtubule system acts like a skeleton, reinforcing the cell and maintaining its shape; and the microfilaments act like a muscular system, causing change in shape. Usually the component proteins needed to assemble the tubules or filaments are found to preexist in the cells, and morphogenesis is largely a matter of assembly rather than synthesis. But as with localized cell-cell attachments, so it is with the cytoskeleton: we as yet have no clear picture of how the positioning of morphogenetic elements within the cell is determined. Microfilaments—whether involved in changing cell shape or mediating cellular motility—are usually found to be attached to the cell membrane in regions where the cell membrane is visibly specialized on the inner surface. But how are the locations of these and other membrane specializations patterned by the cell? One of the major challenges confronting cell and developmental biologists in the coming years is to shed light on this all-important process whereby the outer membrane of a cell becomes regionally specialized on both its inner and outer surfaces. From this pattern of specializations many of the unique properties of specific cell types are derived.

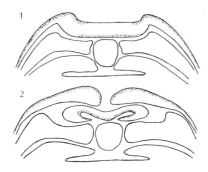

(b) When a piece of the neural plate of an amphibian (1) was cut out, turned over, and put back in place, it proceeded to form a neural tube in inverted orientation (2).

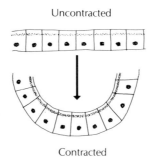

Uncontracted

Contracted

(c) The change in shape that occurs in a sheet of cells due to contraction of a band of microfilaments at one end of each cell.

If the embryo is treated with colchicine during neural plate formation, cells that have already elongated collapse, and cells that otherwise would have elongated fail to do so. Electron microscopy confirms that normally elongating cells develop numbers of microtubules parallel to the long axis of the cell, whereas in colchicine-treated embryos these microtubules are disassembled or fail to form.

In embryos treated with cytochalasin, cells elongate normally but never become wedge shaped. And the neural plate never folds,

also been isolated from such cells. The myosin may interact with the microfilaments to cause them to slide past one another, thereby resulting in contraction.

Neurulation is not the only developmental process in which microfilaments and microtubules have been implicated. Gastrulation fails to occur in sea urchin embryos treated with colchicine or cytochalasin. If colchicine is present, filopodia that normally extend across the cavity of the blastula (Figure 18.5) fail to develop. In embryos exposed to cytochalasin, filopodia are extended and attach

DO FACTORS IN EGG CYTOPLASM CONTROL DEVELOPMENT?

The fact that different genes are expressed in different cells tells us something about the *mechanism* of development, but it tells us little about *causation*. What causes different cells to express different genes? If the cause is not to be found in the nucleus, it is reasonable to look to the rest of the cell—the cytoplasm—for the answer.

The Effect of Isolation on the Fate of Individual Blastomeres

In an attempt to determine the causal relationships between developmental events, Hans Driesch attempted about eighty years ago to determine whether each cell of an embryo was preprogrammed to form a particular part of the complete organism. He induced fertilization of a sea urchin egg, and after it had divided once, he shook it until the two **blastomeres** (cells produced by cleavage) fell apart. As darkness fell the two isolated blastomeres were cleaving. As the sun rose the next morning, Driesch could hardly believe his eyes. There in the dish were two complete but miniature sea urchin embryos! He interpreted this result to mean that each cell had the "end-in-view," as he put it. In other words, each cell "knew" how a complete individual should be formed and went on to form such an individual despite the intervention of a human being. Although Driesch had a long-standing record of sound scientific work, he never fully recovered from the awesome implications of this isolated blastomere experiment. Eventually he retreated to a monastery with several of his protégés and devoted the rest of his life to mysticism.

Shortly after Driesch showed that both of the first two blastomeres of sea urchins are capable of giving rise to complete embryos, Edmund Wilson showed that the same result could *not* be obtained with snail embryos. Wilson found that only one of the first two and only one of the first four blastomeres of the egg were capable of developing into a complete snail larva. The others lacked a mesoderm layer. Furthermore, the presence or absence of mesoderm depended on the presence or absence of a particular kind of cytoplasm found in the lower hemisphere of the egg. During cleavage, this cytoplasm was passed entirely to one cell by way of a structure known as a **polar lobe** (Figure 18.9). Wilson's study of the polar lobe cytoplasm was the first to point out that *particular kinds of cytoplasmic inclusions in the egg play a crucial role in development.*

Because the results of Wilson's study were different from those of Driesch, the eggs were viewed as fundamentally different. Because the first two or four blastomeres of a sea urchin egg were equipotent and capable of forming a complete embryo, these eggs were called "regulative." In other words, they seemed to regulate their activities and

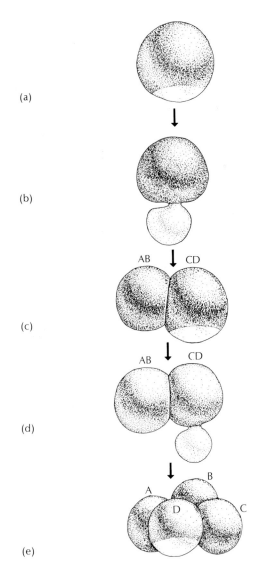

(a)

(b)

AB | CD

(c)

AB | CD

(d)

B
A | C
D

(e)

Figure 18.9 Cleavage in a snail egg. In (a) the clear polar cytoplasm can be seen at the bottom of the uncleaved zygote. As the zygote prepares for the first cleavage, a "polar lobe" forms (b). All the polar cytoplasm is drawn into the polar lobe. Following mitosis, the polar cytoplasm is drawn back into the cell to which the polar lobe was attached (c). E. B. Wilson showed that this cell (labeled CD) is capable of forming a complete embryo, while the AB cell forms a partial embryo lacking mesoderm. Prior to the second mitotic division, the polar lobe reforms (d). Thus, of the first four blastomeres produced (e), only D contains polar cytoplasm and only it is capable of forming mesoderm. Wilson also showed that if the polar lobe were snipped off at a stage comparable to (b) or (d), no mesoderm at all was formed by the embryo. This result demonstrated conclusively that the capacity of the D blastomere to produce mesoderm is somehow determined by the polar cytoplasm.

compensate for missing parts. Eggs such as those of the snail were called "mosaic" (they were said to be composed of nonidentical parts). These terms are still widely used.

However, the distinction is no longer considered valid. In a sense, the D blastomere in Figure 18.9 is regulative—it is capable of compensating for the absence of blastomeres A, B, and C and of forming parts it would not otherwise form. Furthermore, as Figure 18.10 shows, it is possible to bisect either frog or sea urchin eggs in such a way that they appear mosaic, like the snail egg! Which result you get depends *entirely* on how you perform the experiment. The only reason the sea urchin appeared to be "regulative" in the Driesch experiment was because the first cleavage furrow happened to split the important cytoplasmic inclusion equally between the first blastomeres!

Fertilized eggs have developmentally important inclusions that are localized in specific parts of the cytoplasm. In some cases, the localized inclusions are split equally between blastomeres in early cleavage and the eggs are called regulative. In others, they are split unequally between blastomeres and the eggs are called mosaic. But in both cases *the localized cytoplasmic inclusions trigger development by influencing the behavior of the nuclei with which they become associated during cleavage.*

Figure 18.10 The effect of plane of separation on subsequent development of half-embryos. A frog zygote (a and b) is heavily pigmented on its upper hemisphere but not its lower hemisphere. Shortly after fertilization and before cleavage, the pigment thins along one region of the margin between the hemispheres, forming a "gray crescent." If, after cleavage has begun, zygotes are divided so that each half receives gray crescent material, each half will develop into a complete embryo (a). But if one half is deprived of gray crescent material, it fails to develop into anything but a shapeless ball of cells (b).

Similarly, sea urchin zygotes often have visible pigments that permit the upper hemisphere to be distinguished from the lower hemisphere. If such embryos are divided (c) so that each half receives material from both hemispheres, two complete but miniature larvae are formed. But if they are divided as in (d), each half develops the structures it would normally form in early stages and neither half forms a complete embryo. Thus, in both cases the simple question "Will half an embryo produce an entire individual?" has two different answers.

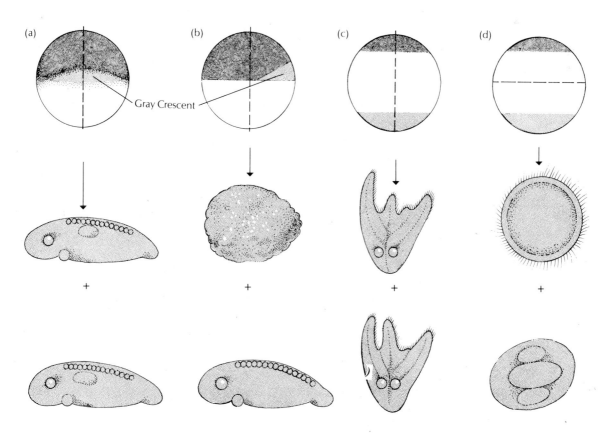

One such inclusion in the eggs of many animal species is a substance called **germ plasm.** Cells that form in a particular region of the embryo are set aside very early to form "germ cells"—eggs or sperm. If this region or the substance it contains is removed from the zygote or is otherwise destroyed, the adults that develop will be normal—except for the fact that they will be sterile.

Dennis Smith, among others, has worked with germ plasm in frogs. If frog zygotes are irradiated at the lower hemispheric pole with ultraviolet light, they grow into normal-looking adults. But upon dissection, their gonads (ovaries and testes) are found to be totally devoid of eggs and sperm. Smith showed that the most effective wavelength of light for sterilization is precisely the wavelength that is most readily absorbed by nucleic acids. The germ plasm, he suggested, is either DNA or RNA. He went on to show that cytoplasm taken from the lower hemisphere of normal zygotes and then injected into the lower hemisphere of ultraviolet-sterilized eggs would restore the complement of germ cells.

Smith has identified a dense, granular substance in the appropriate region of the zygote cytoplasm that is unlike any previously characterized organelle. He has tentatively proposed that this substance contains the "active principle." If the germ plasm of these frogs can be isolated and characterized, it will be the first major step toward understanding how such cytoplasmic factors function in determining the fate of cells during embryonic development.

How the Program for Early Development Is Laid Down in the Forming Egg

Like all other less-well-characterized but equally important inclusions in the egg, germ plasm appears to be a regulator of gene function of nuclei in the embryo. And like all such inclusions, it is itself a product of the genes of the female parent. Consider a certain mutation in the fruit fly *Drosophila melanogaster* that can block the fly's capacity to form germ plasm. Females that are homozygous for this mutation are themselves fertile. But functional germ plasm is absent in the eggs they produce. Hence, their young grow up devoid of eggs and sperm. For obvious reasons, the mutation has been called "grandchildless." Such developmental defects arising as the result of genetic lesions in the female parent are called **maternal effects.** Mutations in genes responsible for maternal effects usually have no perceptible effects on their homozygous male or female carriers other than the production of defective eggs. In most cases, the defect in the egg cannot be corrected by fertilization with a nonmutant sperm.

Literally hundreds of maternal effects are known in dozens of species. They influence a wide variety of early developmental events and processes such as positions,

rates, and planes of cleavage; various aspects of gastrulation; and the appearance of a variety of embryonic cell types. Together they lead to a conclusion that is supported by many other lines of embryological research: *Although the differential functioning of nuclei in the embryo becomes important in later stages of development, early development is largely if not completely under the control of the female parent's genes.*

One of the lines of evidence recently developed to support this conclusion came from studies of protein synthesis in young embryos. Sea urchins have been particularly useful in such studies because of the enormous numbers of eggs each female produces. The unfertilized egg of sea urchins is rather dormant, but the rate of a variety of metabolic processes (including protein synthesis) dramatically increases shortly after fertilization, and it remains at high levels throughout the cleavage period. But if an egg fragment lacking a nucleus is activated parthenogenetically, the fragment undergoes an increase in protein synthesis that is indistinguishable from the pattern of a normal, nucleated zygote (Figure 18.11). Thus the zygote nucleus plays no perceptible role in directing the synthetic events of the early developmental period. It is now clear that the unfertilized sea urchin egg (like the egg of most other species studied) contains a store of messenger RNA molecules made while the egg was developing in the mother's ovary. These messenger RNA molecules are packaged into the egg in an inactive state. They have been called **masked messengers.** Fertilization or artificial activation of the egg "unmasks" them, thereby initiating the developmental program of the species. Just how they are masked remains uncertain, despite intensive study during the past decade. But Tom Humphreys and others have shown that all the other components required for protein synthesis are present and active in the unfertilized egg. The major change following activation is the number of maternally produced messenger RNA molecules that are accessible to the protein synthetic machinery.

Perhaps the most convincing evidence that the resident nucleus plays a negligible role during early development comes from the work of Dennis Smith and his colleagues, who are working with frog eggs. They dissected mature eggs from the ovary of a hibernating female frog and then surgically removed the nucleus from such eggs. Next they treated the enucleated eggs with the hormone that the female normally produces as it prepares to spawn. The eggs sitting in a culture dish underwent all of the complex changes normally associated with the ovulation (spawning) process. More than a day after hormone treatment, these eggs underwent the same rapid and enormous increase in the rate of protein synthesis seen in eggs spawned normally. If the eggs were coated with egg jelly, they could be

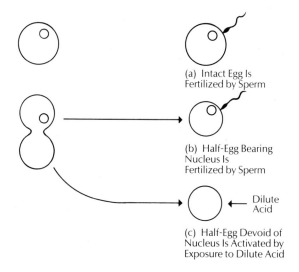

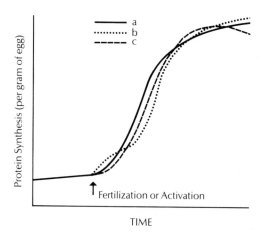

Figure 18.11 The cytoplasmic control of protein synthesis during early sea urchin development. A series of eggs were centrifuged under conditions where each egg was split in two to yield halves with nuclei and halves without. Subsequently, the enucleated halves were activated by exposure to dilute acid, whereas the nucleated halves and some untreated eggs were exposed to sperm. In all three cases, there was a rapid rise in the rate of protein synthesis; the absence of a nucleus had no effect upon this process. Eventually, of course, the enucleated egg would grind to a halt while the nucleated eggs went on developing. Eventually the nucleus comes to play a crucial role in directing protein synthesis.

activated later and would commence cleavage! Of course, development eventually ground to a halt. (Unquestionably the zygote nucleus does play a crucial role in development after the very early stages.) Nevertheless, these studies clearly point out the extent to which the events of early development are preprogrammed in the egg cytoplasm, as a result of messenger RNA and other substances produced by the maternal parent during egg development.

What is the nature of the proteins produced by these maternal messengers? Studies using radioactively labeled amino acids in both sea urchins and frogs have shown that a major portion of the proteins synthesized during this early period are **nuclear proteins**—proteins made in the cytoplasm and then accumulated in the nuclei of the cleavage cells. Although the evidence is not yet conclusive, it is tempting to suggest that these proteins may help modulate the behavior of DNA in different nuclei in order to initiate differential expression of genes in different parts of the embryo.

In any case, *it is now clear that embryonic development does not begin with fertilization—it begins in the developing egg in the ovary.* Considerable research is now being directed toward the study of **oogenesis** (the process by which eggs are made) at the cellular and molecular level. The events occurring during this period will not be easily unraveled, for they are many and complex. Oogenesis, we now know, involves the cooperative efforts of many cell types both inside and outside the ovary.

In vertebrate females, for example, yolk protein is made not in the ovary at all, but in the liver. (If a rooster is given an injection of a female sex hormone, his liver furiously begins to make and secrete yolk proteins, which build up in the bloodstream for lack of any eggs to receive them!) Arriving in the ovary by way of the blood, these yolk proteins first enter the cluster of specialized cells that feed the developing egg in every species: the **accessory cells.** The accessory cells then modify the yolk proteins chemically and actively pass them on to the **oocyte** (immature egg), where they are further modified and stored.

Yolk proteins are the chief substances but not the only ones moving between accessory cells and oocyte. There is an extensive and continuous process of flow between the cells. The oocyte is usually associated asymmetrically with the accessory cells of the ovary. (Often oocytes are attached to the ovary by only one end, like grapes on a stem.) Therefore, materials arriving from the accessory cells are deposited asymmetrically in the egg. *In many cases, it is the asymmetrical relationship between oocyte and accessory cells that leads to developmentally important asymmetries in the mature egg.*

But as important as the contributions of other cells are in the overall development of the egg, *the control of oogenesis and the execution of the most critical steps clearly are the function of the oocyte itself.* The role of the oocyte has been demonstrated experimentally by Antoine Blackler. He transplanted germ cells between embryos of two strains of frogs that differed with respect to egg size, color, and so forth. He performed the transplantation before the germ cells had begun to migrate into the developing ovaries. As a result, a female was produced in which only the germ cells differed in genetic constitution from the host. But the eggs produced by these females resembled the eggs of the germ cell donor strain rather than those of the strain in which they developed. This control by the oocyte even covered aspects known to occur largely outside the oocyte, such as yolk production! (Perhaps Samuel Butler was correct when he said a hen is merely an egg's way of making another egg.)

The most intensive and unusual activity within the developing oocyte occurs within the nucleus. Most of oogenesis occurs during the prophase of meiosis I (*Interleaf 16.1*). In human females, meiotic prophase may last forty years. During one part of this prophase, chromosomes take on a peculiar conformation that is not observed elsewhere (Figure 18.12). When they were first seen in amphibian oocytes, they were named **lampbrush chromosomes** because of the appearance of many fibers protruding from a main axis. (If they had been discovered instead in this era of electric lights they might have been termed "test-tube brush chromosomes" or "bottle brush chromosomes.") Lampbrush chromosomes apparently represent a common stage in egg development, for they have now been seen in mammalian oocytes, among many others. Each of the fibers extending from the main axis is a loop of DNA pulled out of the continuous DNA fiber of the chromosome and actively involved in RNA synthesis. Many thousands of genes are expressed during the lampbrush stage. Direct analysis of the RNA molecules made during this period and those present in the unfertilized egg lead to the conclusion that it is during this flurry of genetic activity that at least some of the messenger RNA molecules used during cleavage are made.

During the lampbrush stage, one particular region of one chromosome behaves differently from all the rest during amphibian oogenesis. This is the region where the nucleolus is normally found. Here, loops of DNA pinch off the chromosome and float freely in the nucleoplasm. They are extra copies of the DNA that codes for ribosomal RNA (Figure 18.13). A nucleolus is formed and ribosomes are rapidly made and accumulated on each of them. Thus, the typical frog cell nucleus has two nucleoli (one on each of the homologous chromosomes bearing the ribosomal genes), but the mature egg nucleus has thousands of nucleoli, each containing hundreds of ribosomal genes that produce ribosomes in countless millions. This process, whereby one specific genetic region is preferentially repli-

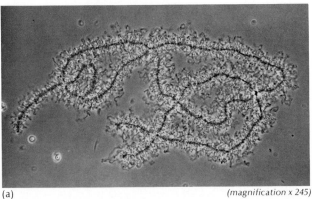

(a)   *(magnification x 245)*

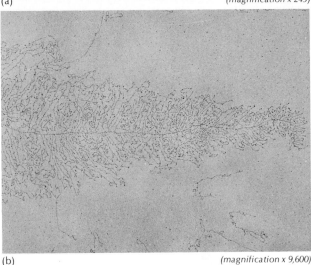

(b)   *(magnification x 9,600)*

Figure 18.12 Lampbrush chromosomes from an amphibian oocyte. (a) A light micrograph, in which hundreds of loops can be seen projecting from the main axis all along each chromosome. (b) An electron micrograph of one of these loops. The strand has been shown by enzymatic methods to be a single DNA double helix. The strands projecting from it are RNA molecules in the process of being transcribed. Each is joined to the main axis by a molecule of RNA polymerase. The point of initiation of RNA synthesis is apparently at the top, where the RNA strands are short. During the period of several weeks that the oocyte nucleus spends in the lampbrush stage, a major portion of the genetic material is transcribed and gene products accumulate in the oocyte.
(Compare with Figure 18.13.)

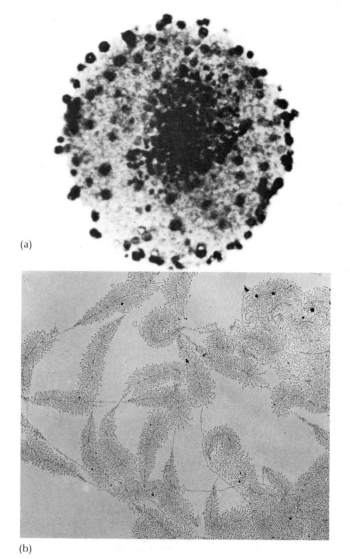

(a)

(b)

Figure 18.13   Nucleoli of an amphibian oocyte. (a) A light micrograph showing the multiple nucleoli in the periphery of the nucleus. Other cells in this species possess only two nucleoli. (b) An electron micrograph of the nucleic acid core isolated from one of the nucleoli. The continuous strands that serve as the main axis of each pine-tree-looking structure are the genes coding for ribosomal RNA. The branches are molecules of ribosomal RNA in the process of being transcribed. The bare stretches of RNA are "spacers" between the ribosomal genes that are not transcribed. By replicating the ribosomal genes so extensively, the single oocyte nucleus synthesizes in a matter of weeks a quantity of ribosomes that would otherwise take many years to produce.

cated to expand the number of copies of that region, is called **gene amplification.** The extent to which gene amplification occurs in other developmental processes is a topic of active research.

Why this frenetic activity of the ribosomal genes? The selective advantage of such a process is clear. Ribosomes are time-consuming and costly to make, in terms of ATP equivalents. Yet they are essential in the synthesis of new proteins. If an embryo can be set off on its own with a prepackaged supply of ribosomes that will see it through hatching, it will be able to initiate and maintain protein synthesis at much higher rates than would otherwise be possible. Furthermore, it will be able to pass more rapidly through the defenseless embryonic stage. But the number of ribosomal genes in one nucleus would not be enough to make that many ribosomes unless the period of oogenesis lasted many years or decades. Thus, more copies of these genes are required if such a large store of ribosomes is to be included in the egg's endowments.

Indeed, it has been shown that an amphibian egg contains just enough ribosomes to get the embryo to the hatching stage, but not beyond. Mutant embryos lacking any ribosomal genes develop normally up to the hatching stage. But then they die as a result of their inability to produce new ribosomes at the time growth normally begins.

Although we have learned much concerning the processes of oogenesis, much more is still shrouded with mystery. Further analysis of oogenesis promises to be one of the most productive areas of future embryological research.

IS THE FATE OF ALL PARTS PREDETERMINED, OR DOES DETERMINATION OCCUR CONTINUOUSLY?

It is one thing to say that at least parts of the embryo are foreshadowed in the egg. But if *all* the future parts were fixed with any degree of rigidity, the loss or malfunction of any part would lead to grave problems for the embryo. But many embryos can compensate for loss of one-half or even three-fourths of the material of the zygote. And if that is true, then not all parts of the embryo can be rigidly predetermined in the substance of the fertilized egg; some parts must arise progressively as development proceeds.

Dependent and Independent Development

It was Spemann and his students who verified the progressive nature of development by conducting grafting experiments with pigmented and unpigmented animals. Blocks of tissue can be removed from a particular region of a donor embryo and transplanted to different regions of a host embryo of the same age. Now, if a pigmented and an unpigmented species of newts are used as donor and recipient, the presence or absence of pigment in the animal that develops will signify which cells came from the graft and which came from the host.

If transplantation is done when both host and donor are in the *early* stages of gastrulation, tissues tend to develop in the manner expected for tissue in the new sites; they do not develop as they would in their normal site. For example, a piece of ectoderm removed from the region where brain normally forms and then transplanted to a site where skin normally forms develops into skin! If transplanted into other sites, this same piece of tissue is capable of forming muscle, bone, kidney, and virtually any other tissue. The tissue is said to be **pluripotent** and subject to **dependent differentiation:** Its fate depends on the environment in which it develops.

However, if tissue from the same brain-forming area is transplanted between embryos in *late* stages of the gastrulation process, the result is very different. This block of tissue develops into brain no matter where it is transplanted! Similarly, if a piece of ectoderm is taken at a late gastrula stage from a region where skin normally is formed and is transplanted to the brain-forming region, it eventually forms skin even though it becomes trapped in the interior of the brain! The capacity to form structures characteristic of the site of origin regardless of the environment is termed **independent differentiation.**

Clearly, something dramatic happens during gastrulation to restrict the developmental potentials of much of the embryo. Cells that enter gastrulation *uncommitted* as to their prospective fate become *committed* to a specific path during gastrulation. They undergo what has come to be called **determination.**

Embryonic Induction

Insight into the nature of the events occurring in gastrulation can be gained by retracing a dramatic experiment first performed by Hilde Mangold. In this experiment, transplants were taken from a region of an early gastrula called the *dorsal lip of the blastopore.* It is the region where the invagination movements of gastrulation begin. This region undergoes independent differentiation; when transplanted to a very different site in another embryo it goes on to invaginate. However, Mangold observed that when the host developed further, a whole new set of organs developed at the graft site. In fact, almost an entire additional embryo had developed. Only the anterior part of the head was missing (Figure 18.14). Because the graft was unpigmented and the host was pigmented, it was possible to determine which cells came from the graft. The notochord was of graft origin, but little else was. The brain, spinal cord, kidneys, gut, and virtually all of the twin embryo had been derived

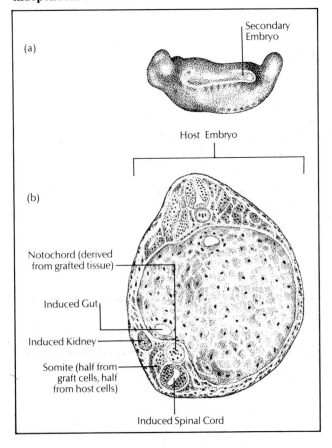

(a)

Secondary Embryo

Host Embryo

(b)

Notochord (derived from grafted tissue)

Induced Gut

Induced Kidney

Somite (half from graft cells, half from host cells)

Induced Spinal Cord

Figure 18.14 Induction of a secondary embryo by a graft of the dorsal lip of the blastopore. (a) Mangold's drawing of the external appearance of the twin embryos. The secondary embryo lies along what would otherwise have been the belly of the host; it failed to develop some head structures, but everything from the ear vesicles to the tail formed in a relatively normal manner but was slightly reduced in size. (b) This drawing of the microscopic appearance of a cross section through the trunk of the embryo reveals the role played by the graft. Because only the notochord and part of the somite (Figure 18.7) are unpigmented, only these structures came directly from the transplanted tissue. The rest of the structures are pigmented and therefore were induced as the graft acted upon host cells that normally would not have produced any of these structures.

from the host—from cells that normally would not have formed *any* of these structures. The graft had induced the formation of virtually an entire new embryo! The process by which one block of cells elicits a new path of development in another is now known as **embryonic induction.**

Subsequent work demonstrated that induction (by what Spemann came to call the "primary organizer") is not one event but a complex series of events. The first region to invaginate induces only the development of the forebrain. The next region of invaginating tissue specifically induces midbrain, the next region induces hindbrain, the next induces spinal cord, and so on.

We might now pause to ask: What is the relationship between the determination of parts by cytoplasmic inclusions of the egg and determination of parts by induction? An impressive experiment by Adam Curtis in 1960 provides a link between the two. Recall from Figure 18.10 what happens when a frog zygote is bisected in such a way that the entire gray crescent region is contained in only one half: The half with the gray crescent develops into a complete embryo and the other half does not. Curtis transplanted the **cortex** (membrane and associated cytoplasmic layer) from the gray crescent region of one uncleaved frog zygote to another (Figure 18.15). The donor zygote failed to gastrulate, but the recipient formed two blastopores—one at each

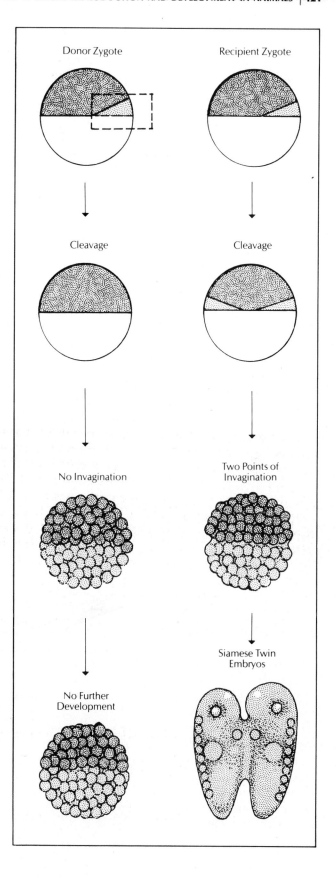

Figure 18.15 Curtis' gray crescent transplantation experiment. The region of cortex containing the gray crescent was removed from one uncleaved frog zygote and transplanted to another, opposite its original gray crescent. The wounds healed and both embryos began to cleave. When the time of gastrulation was reached, the donor embryo failed to form a blastopore and no further development occurred. But the recipient embryo underwent invagination in both regions where gray crescent had been present. The result was the formation of "Siamese twin" embryos. This experiment demonstrated the importance of the cytoplasmic components in the gray crescent region in inducing the dorsal lip of the blastopore, which in turn acts as the "primary organizer" in eliciting further embryonic development.

site where there had been gray crescent material—and went on to form twin embryos.

This experiment demonstrated that all the attributes of the dorsal lip of the blastopore arise from the localized inclusions of the egg cytoplasm that are localized in the region known as the **gray crescent.** In other words, the dorsal lip of the blastopore is "determined" *intra*cellularly by the unique substances trapped in its cells during cleavage. It goes on to cause the determination of other structures *inter*cellularly by producing substances that move out of its cells and affect neighboring cells. There presently is no reason to believe that there is any fundamental difference between the two pathways to determination. *Even the inductive events that actually occur long after the egg is released from the female are part of a continuous causal series set in motion during oogenesis.*

Not all the tissues that appear in the induced embryo are induced at once, nor are all induced by the same tissue. For example, the forebrain is induced by the invaginating tissue from the dorsal lip of the blastopore. From the forebrain, the optic vesicles—future retinas of the eyes—grow out. When the optic cups touch the skin, they induce a lens to form. Once the lens has formed, it induces the cornea to form, and so on. *The development of the eye, like the development of many other organs, proceeds by a progressive series of induction events, one after the other.* If the sequence is surgically interrupted at any point, the later stages fail to appear. Literally hundreds of such **inductive interactions** have been identified in a variety of developing systems.

How do inductive interactions occur? Johannes Holtfreter showed that the primary organizer region retains its capacity to induce even after it has been killed in any one of a variety of ways, which suggested that induction must be chemical in nature. An extensive list of substances that cause mild cellular damage have since been found that mimic one or another aspect of the function of the primary organizer. But taken together, they still fail to reveal a clear picture of the mechanism of induction at the molecular level. The significant question, it seems, is not what substances will act as inducers, but rather what specific changes these substances induce in the reacting tissue. Therefore, emphasis has largely shifted from analysis of the acting tissue to the reacting tissue.

Oscar Schotté performed an experiment that suggested what the nature of the inductive response might be expected to entail. Schotté transplanted prospective belly skin of a frog embryo to the undeveloped head region of a salamander embryo. The larval forms of these two kinds of amphibians differ in head structure. Immediately after hatching, the frog develops a sucker by which it attaches to objects for stability. Later it develops a disk of horny

structures outside the mouth which function as teeth. The salamander, in contrast, develops a pair of appendages called balancers. These appendages project from the sides of the head and are used to stabilize the newly hatched larva until its legs develop. The salamander also develops a set of true teeth within the mouth.

Schotté found that when the frog belly skin was grafted to the salamander head, it responded to the inductive stimuli emanating from the salamander and produced head structures—which it would never have done if left in place. Thus the belly skin was induced by influences in the head. But the amazing thing was that *the frog belly skin responded to the head inducers of the salamander by producing frog head parts!* As Figure 18.16 shows, it first produced the sucker and then the horny, scaly jaw typical of the frog larva—structures never found on the salamander. The reciprocal was also true: Salamander skin from the belly region formed balancers and salamander mouth parts when grafted to the frog embryo head.

These simple experiments tell us a great deal about the nature of induction. First of all, *inductive stimuli are not rigidly species-specific.* Frog skin responds to salamander inducers, and vice versa. Many other cases of induction

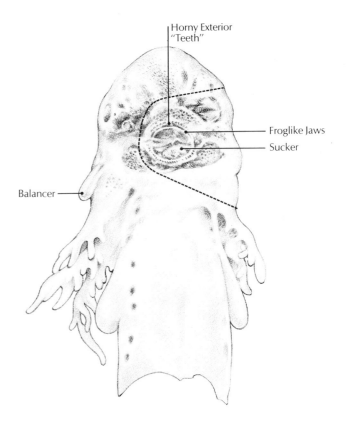

Horny Exterior "Teeth"

Froglike Jaws

Sucker

Balancer

across species lines are now known, although the relationships are not universal. Second, *the inducer is not simply a release mechanism.* In other words, the inducer does not function as a trigger that simply discharges a system that is loaded, cocked, and ready to fire. The inducer causes the reacting system to do something it normally would *never* have done. (We do not, for example, see tadpoles in the wild with head structures growing from their belly skin.) Third, *the inducer is not a detailed set of blueprints for effecting the induced response.* Had the head inducer of the salamander carried detailed information concerning what structures to make and how, the frog belly skin should have made balancers, not a sucker.

Experiments into induction focus attention on the genetic system of the responding cells and how specific parts of that genetic system are activated. When the salamander dictated: "Make head structures," the frog skin responded with the only head structures it had the genetic capacity to produce! *Thus the action of an inducer is now viewed as some kind of selective switch mechanism that activates a block of coordinated genes in the responding cells.* Accordingly, emphasis has shifted in many embryological laboratories from an analysis of induction per se to an analysis of

Figure 18.16 The response of frog belly skin to salamander head inductors. The dashed line indicates the approximate margin of the piece of frog skin that was grafted to the salamander head at an earlier stage. On the side of the head still covered by salamander skin, a normal balancer is formed; on the side covered by frog skin, none is formed. In the center, a perfectly formed mouth is present that connects flawlessly to the gut. But it is a frog mouth connected to a salamander gut! The sucker, horny jaws, and horny toothlike exterior scales are all features typical of frog larvae but never seen in salamanders.

The reciprocal experiment works in the reverse manner: Salamander belly skin grafted to the head of a frog embryo forms balancers and a typically salamander mouth (with real teeth) connected to the frog gut.

how genes may be turned on and off in developing cells, a topic that will be treated at some length in Chapter 20.

ONCE AN ORGAN HAS BEEN INDUCED, ARE ALL ITS PARTS DETERMINED?

One of the regular and striking features of embryonic development is the balance that is normally achieved. Although the size of adults may vary enormously in some species because of a combination of genetic and environmental factors, the parts are almost always coordinated into a balanced whole. One insight into how such a balance of parts may be achieved originated with the work of Ross Harrison in his studies of limb development.

Harrison removed tissue from the region of a salamander embryo that was known to be the site of formation of the foreleg. He transplanted it to another spot on the body where limbs never normally form. The site of removal healed over. Now, from what has been said so far concerning dependent and independent development, one might predict three possible outcomes. If the leg tissue had not yet become determined, the leg would be expected to form in its normal position but not on the grafted site. If the leg tissue had been determined, the leg might be expected to form at the new site but not the old. On the other hand, if the leg had been determined but the leg tissue had been incompletely transplanted, part of the leg would be expected to develop in each of the sites. Harrison obtained none of these results. A complete and *perfect leg of normal size* was produced *both* at the site of the graft *and* at the site from which the graft was removed! Tissue that normally would have given rise to a single, well-integrated organ had given rise to two such organs.

Harrison later did the reverse experiment: he removed one entire leg-forming region, or **field,** and transplanted it immediately adjacent to another leg field. Although twice as much leg-forming tissue was present in this graft site as normal, a single, normal-sized, normally proportioned leg developed. The leg-forming field was thus shown to be capable of **embryonic regulation** (compensation for missing or excess parts) in the same way that the first two blastomeres of a frog or sea urchin embryo are.

We cannot yet explain the phenomenon of embryonic fields and their capacity to regulate their performance to compensate for missing or excess parts. But they are as real and inescapable as anything in our experience. Fields with similar regulative potentials are known to exist in the formation of a whole range of embryonic structures; two eye fields brought together experimentally produce a single Cyclopean eye, for example. Since Harrison's time we have learned a great deal about the progressive development of limbs. We have come to appreciate that the development of a series of coordinated bones and muscles, nerves and blood vessels, skin and skin coverings involves an extraordinary web of reciprocal interactions of the parts as they develop. One structure is induced by another and in turn influences the development of the tissue by which it was induced. But as much as we understand of these details, we are far from possessing any clear understanding of how the limb manages to develop in an identical manner whether we reduce its starting bulk by half or double it. Explaining such processes is indeed a major challenge to the investigative skills of the biologists of the future.

PERSPECTIVE

Reproduction is the crux of life. Every existing organism is here only because its forebears managed to produce enough progeny to ensure that some would survive and continue the species. Ultimately, then, all aspects of the life cycle are important only as they affect survival of the plan of reproduction of the species. Those species whose members fail to reproduce in a single generation become extinct; it is as simple as that.

Given its position of central importance, a great deal of investigation has gone into reproductive and developmental processes, and a great deal has been learned. We know that the first step in sexual reproduction is to bring together two haploid cells produced by meiosis, thereby forming the diploid zygote from which the new organism will arise. This is called fertilization. The next step is to subdivide the single large cell of the fertilized egg, thereby producing the many smaller cells required to carry out subsequent stages of development. This process of cleavage occurs by a rapid series of cell divisions in the absence of growth. Cleavage commonly results in the formation of a hollow ball, a blastula, in which all of the cells are positioned near the surface. The next stage of development involves moving some of these cells to the interior to produce a two- or three-layered structure, a gastrula, from which development of exterior and interior structures may proceed. Gastrulation is one of the most crucial stages of development. As the embryo is reorganized into the multilayered structure, the process of laying out all the future parts of the organism in specific locations begins or accelerates.

The process by which the developmental fate of the cells in various regions is established is called determination. But determination only fixes the potential of each cell. In order to produce an organism, these different potentials of different cells must become converted to reality. The process by which cells begin to express their unique kinds of potentials, to become visibly different from one another, to accumulate particular kinds of molecules, and to take on different function is called cellular differentiation.

Simultaneous with cellular differentiation and inseparable from it is the process whereby cells of like and unlike kinds begin to change their shapes and associations with one another to form larger, multicellular structures of defined function. Those processes, through which the form of the organism begins to appear, are grouped under the term morphogenesis. Sooner or later in this process—the timing is dependent on the nutritional style of the embryo—all these processes become associated with changes in size of the whole embryo and of the parts relative to each other. In placental organisms, growth begins very early, as soon as the placenta is formed. In other eggs, overall growth cannot occur until the egg hatches and the larva or young adult begins to feed. While fertilization and gastrulation occur only once, determination and growth go on for extended periods; and cellular differentiation occurs in certain parts of the organism until the moment of death.

But as much as we know about the sequence of events in reproduction and development, the details of the underlying mechanisms have largely eluded us. We see clearly that all of the features that arise during the course of development are under genetic control. Different kinds of cells produce characteristically different groups of protein molecules—contractile proteins in muscle, digestive enzymes in gut, hemoglobin in red blood cells, and so on. Each of these proteins is coded for by a gene that is received by all cells; yet some cells express one set of genes, and some express another. Thus attention is focused on mechanisms of selectively controlling gene expression. Real progress is being made in understanding how gene expression may be controlled, as you will read in Chapter 20. And although the mechanisms utilized during development may be complex—with many kinds of control being exerted at many different levels in the gene action system—a picture is beginning to emerge concerning the web of events involved in establishing different gene products in different cells.

But there is a problem that lies beyond the synthesis of specific proteins and it provides an even greater challenge. It is the problem of morphogenesis: the organization of differentiated cells into a complex multicellular array and specific form suited to a specific function.

The legs and wings of a bird, for example, are composed of very similar cell types. Muscles contain the same proteins and function identically at the cellular level in the two limbs. The same may be said for bone, skin, and nerves. Yet understanding the difference between muscle and bone gives precious little insight into the difference between leg and wing. We can describe in detail how the different bones of the two structures develop, yet we have little insight into causation. *Why* do different shapes of bones arise in different regions? Because mutations exist that lead to misshaping of one or a few bones, we know that these morphogenetic processes are themselves controlled by genes. But illuminating how these genes act and how their expression is controlled is a major challenge for future students of embryology. The elegant advances discussed in Chapter 20 are a mere beginning. The excitement of the living organism is that the more of its secrets we come to understand, the more riddles there are to greet us.

SUGGESTED READINGS

BALINSKY, B. I. *An Introduction to Embryology.* 3rd ed. Philadelphia: Saunders, 1970. An elegant in-depth study of developmental biology.

DAVIDSON, ERIC H. *Gene Activity in Early Development.* New York: Academic Press, 1969. An extensive and detailed analysis of the relative role of maternal and zygote genomes in the control of early embryonic development. The discussion of egg organization and localization of control factors is thorough, well-documented, and extremely thought provoking. Highly recommended for the serious student of the problem.

EBERT, JAMES D., and I. M. SUSSEX. *Interacting Systems in Development.* 2nd ed. New York: Holt Rinehart and Winston, 1970. A well-organized, highly readable, non-technical account of the interactions between egg and sperm, nucleus and cytoplasm, acting and reacting tissues, and organism and environment that affect the control of development.

FLICKINGER, REED A. (ed.). *Developmental Biology.* Dubuque, Iowa: William C. Brown, 1966. This collection of readings includes modern classics by King and Briggs, Gurdon and others that will fascinate the serious student of biology.

Chapter 19

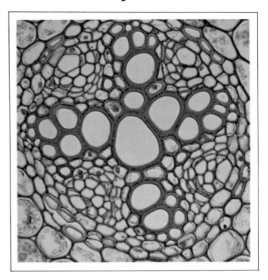

Growth and Development in Plants

Unlike animals, plants do not move rapidly in response to environmental stimuli. We therefore tend to think of them as rather passive things, physically trapped where the seed from which they grew happened to germinate. But plants are continuously in tune with their environment, sensing its critical signs of change and adapting to them. In this illustration we see vascular tissue of a plant—a key link in the integration of plant behavior as it transports both nutrients and hormones from one region of the plant to another.

The simplest plantlike forms of life are not all that different from the simplest animallike forms except when it comes to their means of nutrition—their capacity for photosynthesis. But even in the simplest multicellular forms, members of the plant and animal kingdoms begin to take on unique traits (Chapter 4). And by the time we turn to complex multicellular forms, differences are so multiplied that the basic unity underlying both kingdoms is readily apparent only at the cellular and subcellular levels of organization.

Nowhere are the differences between complex plants and animals more apparent than in their modes of development. Consider, for example, the development of a vertebrate animal and of a seed plant. In the early phases of the vertebrate life cycle, separate organs develop from undifferentiated cells. A young animal quickly forms; it has all the structures—eyes, legs, lungs, reproductive organs—that the adult will ever have. The rest of its life cycle is devoted to growth, maturation, and functioning of the adult form. Often the developmental phase is clearly separate from the adult phase.

In seed plants, development of new organs—leaves, flowers, reproductive cells—continues throughout the life cycle. Now, for some annual plants growing in the deserts, the entire life cycle must be completed in a matter of the few weeks when water is available. Accordingly, their life processes are compressed in time, so the cycle is not all that different from the life cycles of animals. At the other extreme, these processes may continue for hundreds or even thousands of years in such long-lived plants as the bristlecone pine. *But for most plants most of the time, some parts of the plant body are rapidly dividing cell masses, while other parts are in an advanced stage of development and differentiation, and still other parts are fully mature and are carrying out vital life processes.*

The pattern typical of animals is **determinate development:** The genetic make-up of the organism *determines* how many organs of each kind will be present, where they will be located, and when they will develop. The pattern typical of higher plants is **indeterminate development:** The genetic make-up establishes the *capacity* to develop specific kinds of organs, but it does not rigidly determine how many will develop, or when or where. There are exceptions, of course, as in the arrangement and number of flowers in annual plants. But generally speaking, plant development, growth, and function are not clearly separate topics for discussion. The processes are too closely integrated, and the outcome is too variable. That is why this chapter integrates discussion of these processes as much as possible. To simplify things, the emphasis is on one type of flowering plant—the **dicotyledons** (or dicots). Other kinds of plants are mentioned only to the extent that they help point out basic processes common to all the higher plants.

You already read about the reproductive structures and strategies of flowering plants in the chapter on plant diversity (Chapter 5). Here you will follow the processes from the moment of pollination through the development and functioning of mature tissues and organs. Many of these processes are under the control of plant hormones, and this aspect of plant growth and development is integrated with the discussion to some extent. But discussion of the effects of individual hormones will be covered in much more detail in Chapter 23.

CELLULAR DIFFERENTIATION BEGINS IN THE EMBRYO

The embryo of a flowering plant develops inside the adult plant in a structure called an **ovule.** As you read in Chapter 5, once a flower is pollinated, double fertilization occurs. The outcome of double fertilization is a diploid zygote and a triploid endosperm nucleus (Figure 5.17). In preparation for embryonic development, the endosperm nucleus divides rapidly and the ovule synthesizes materials to aid in endosperm formation. The zygote nucleus does nothing during this burst of activity. Once the endosperm develops around the zygote, however, the zygote nucleus begins to divide mitotically.

The First Stages of Embryonic Development

At the onset of development, the zygote becomes polarized and divides into two cells. One is called a **terminal cell;** it is small and dense with cytoplasm. The other is called a **basal cell;** it is larger and not nearly as dense. Divisions of the basal cell eventually give rise to the **suspensor**—the filament by which the developing embryo becomes suspended in the seed.

It is the terminal cell that differentiates into the embryo. The first few divisions create a spherical (or globular) embryo. Through morphogenesis and cellular differentiation, the cells in the embryo become organized into structures that will give rise to the basic organs of the adult—the shoot apical meristem, the root apical meristem, and (in the case of dicots) two **cotyledons,** which are the preformed leaves that unfold as the seed germinates. These structures are shown in Figure 19.2.

The word **meristem** means "divisible part." It refers to the cells in the growing plant that continue to divide mitotically and that give rise to new structures throughout the life cycle. The *apical meristems* are the growing tips (apices) of shoots and roots. The *lateral meristems* are positioned around the circumference of the shoots and roots. These cells are responsible for lateral growth (increase in diameter) of the roots and stems.

Dicots have two growth regions that become established during the globular stage of the embryo. These growth

Figure 19.2 A longitudinal section through a developing dicot embryo. Notice the beginnings of cellular differentiation in the region between the root apical meristem and the shoot apical meristem.

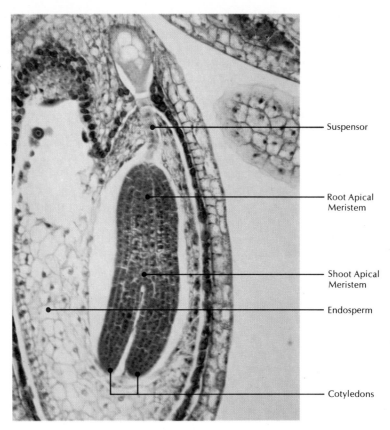

Suspensor

Root Apical Meristem

Shoot Apical Meristem

Endosperm

Cotyledons

regions will form two cotyledons. As they are formed, the two cotyledons grow upward, giving the embryo its heart-shaped appearance (Figure 19.2). But of greater long-term significance is the growth region that lies between the cotyledons; this becomes the shoot meristem from which the entire aerial portion of the plant will develop. The growing tip of the main root forms at the other (suspensor) end of the embryo.

As the embryo develops, the growing tips get pushed apart by the cells they produce. The axis between the growing tips elongates, and the embryo takes on a "torpedo shape." During this stage, cellular differentiation is readily visible among the cells that have been left behind in the central part of the embryo. These cells will give rise to the plant tissue called the **procambium** (*pro-* means "before," and *cambium* means "exchange"). The word refers to the plant tissue before it differentiates into permanent **vascular tissues,** which carry fluids through the plant.

Effect of Hormones on Early Embryonic Development

During the 1930s, there were several attempts to grow isolated embryos in tissue culture in order to see how far the embryo would develop outside the ovule. Very early embryos isolated in a liquid culture medium that contained minerals, sugars, vitamins, yeast extract, light, carbon dioxide, and oxygen did not develop. But if embryos were isolated *after* they had reached the torpedo-shaped stage, they differentiated into normal seedlings. Furthermore, embryos isolated at increasingly later stages continued normal development in increasingly simple culture mediums. What was the factor controlling early embryonic development?

Part of the answer came in 1941, when Johannes van Overbeek and his co-workers succeeded in culturing embryos in the heart-shaped stage. Their culture medium included coconut milk—the liquid endosperm of the coconut seed. The endosperm, it turns out, contains more than just nutrients: it also contains a complex mixture of hormones. Since that time, it has been shown that extracts of the endosperm from other kinds of seeds also support *in vitro* development of very young embryos. Three plant hormones are found in such extracts, and the heart-shaped embryo can now be grown in a medium containing a few simple nutrients and a balance of these three hormones. In the absence of the hormones, the embryo shows little or no growth. But an imbalanced mixture of the hormones may cause the embryo to grow into a shapeless, tumorlike mass.

Thus it is now clear that a balance of hormones normally present in the endosperm is essential for proper development of a very early plant embryo.

But the really remarkable finding of this line of experimentation was that any single cell removed from the embryo and cultured in this hormone-supplemented medium would give rise to a complete embryolike structure (an **embryoid**) and then to an entire flowering plant! The possibilities of such experiments were pursued even further by Frederick Steward at Cornell University. He showed that if a single cell isolated from the root of an adult carrot is cultured in coconut milk under carefully controlled conditions, it, too, gives rise to an embryoid (Figure 19.3). Amazingly enough, the embryoid derived from the root cell also gives rise to a complete and fertile carrot plant. Steward has gone on to show that similar methods can be applied to a variety of plants. (Even pollen grains, or "male" reproductive cells, have been cultured to produce embryoids that develop into haploid plants. These plants are considerably smaller than normal adult plants, and they flower but do not produce seeds.) When Steward found a

way to grow orchid plants from single cells, the nature of the orchid industry changed quickly. Now when a new variety of orchid is produced, it is propagated rapidly by Steward's methods.

Do such experiments mean that a single "differentiated" cell of an adult plant is capable of producing all the cells of the adult plant? Such an interpretation must be made with caution. The experiments suggest that *some* cells of the adult plant have this capacity. But in view of the indeterminate pattern of plant growth and development and the widespread existence of meristem cells, this capacity is not altogether surprising. It remains to be seen whether the same results can be obtained with an unmistakably differentiated cell of an adult. In any case, these experiments point up the fundamental difference in the origin of reproductive cells between higher plants and animals. In vertebrates and most other complex animals, the only cells capable of giving rise to an adult are the eggs. And eggs form only from cells containing germ plasm—new eggs cannot be formed from somatic cells in animals. But as you will soon read, wherever and whenever the right environmental

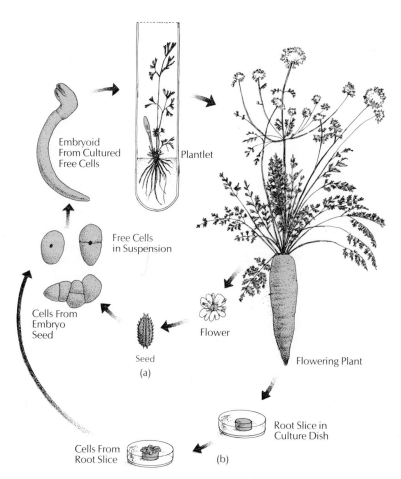

Embryoid From Cultured Free Cells

Plantlet

Free Cells in Suspension

Cells From Embryo Seed

Seed
(a)

Flower

Flowering Plant

Root Slice in Culture Dish

Cells From Root Slice
(b)

Figure 19.3 Growing carrots from single cells. As shown in (a), a seed produced by the normal flowering process is dissected to obtain the embryo. The embryo is then separated into single cells. Each cell, if grown in the right medium, develops into an embryoid (an embryolike structure). From the embryoid it develops into a complete flowering plant.

As shown in (b), single cells from the root of the carrot may also be used. A piece of carrot root is placed into a medium that causes the cells to grow into a shapeless mass. Single cells from this mass are then grown in a proper medium, and they develop into mature plants.

In both cases, growth is induced by the medium, which must contain a mixture of hormones and nutrients that duplicates the mixture present in the endosperm.

conditions prevail, new flowers (and thus new ovules) can be developed from meristem cells that would otherwise form only leaves and stems.

The Dormant Period Before the Seed Germinates

The extent to which the embryo develops within the ovule varies from species to species. *But growth, division, and most metabolic activities cease once a seed coat forms around the embryo.* The embryo is inactive while the seed is transported away from the parent plant; often it remains inactive for some time after it has come to rest. Germination of the seed represents at least in part the resumption of growth and development in the embryo.

The existence of a period of seed dormancy is advantageous to a plant growing in a region where there are marked seasonal fluctuations in growing conditions. There are clear advantages to suppressing development until the beginning of spring (or the beginning of the wet season), particularly in the case of annual plants, which must complete their life cycle in one season. But dormancy implies the need for careful control of the germination process. *Germination must be tied to specific changes in the environment—changes that reliably foretell the coming of conditions favorable for growth.*

How might such controls have evolved? Imagine a primitive plant invading a new area. Perhaps it produced seeds that germinated in response to a variety of environmental conditions. But what would happen if, through mutations, the time of germination were suppressed until a certain combination of temperature, light, and moisture was present that reliably signaled the onset of favorable growing conditions? The seed would be assured of a greater probability of reproductive success. The heritable change could be passed on to the next generation of seeds, conferring the same adaptive advantage upon them. Such mutations would be strongly fostered by natural selection. Small wonder, then, that we find the germination of most plants closely tuned to local seasonal variations. In many cases, for example, germination cannot be induced by springlike conditions unless the seed has first been exposed to a protracted period of extreme cold. This control mechanism serves to counteract any warm spells during the fall that might otherwise trigger premature germination.

Germination in most seeds involves a similar series of steps. Usually it begins when the seed absorbs water from the surroundings. The seed swells up and the seed coat bursts. An assortment of previously inactive, dehydrated enzymes in and around the endosperm now become active. The enzymes begin breaking down the food reserves of the seed, producing nutrient molecules that are passed on to the embryo. These nutrients provide the energy that reinitiates development in the embryonic cells.

Germination has been extensively studied in barley seeds. Even though the details of barley germination do not apply to all other seeds, they give us an idea of one way in which the process may be controlled. The main food stored in the endosperm of barley (and other cereal grains) is starch. Once a seed germinates, the starch is broken down by an enzyme produced by the *aleurone* (a layer of specialized cells surrounding the endosperm). But if the embryo is removed from the seed before hydration, no enzyme is produced by the aleurone, and no starch is hydrolyzed. It has now been shown that when the embryo becomes hydrated, it releases the specific hormones that stimulate the aleurone cells into action.

Some seeds that normally remain ungerminated for years will germinate rapidly if the soil is treated with hormones. Seeds that normally germinate only in the light will germinate in the dark if they are supplied with hormones. The opposite effect can be induced in seeds that normally germinate in darkness. Seed dormancy may often be controlled by the embryo itself, which delays the release of an essential hormone until all the environmental cues appear that signal the advent of favorable growth conditions.

ONCE A SEED GERMINATES, THE MERISTEMATIC TISSUES TAKE OVER DEVELOPMENT

Once a seed has germinated, the shoot apex is elevated to the surface by growth of the underlying cells. Development then becomes a function of the meristematic tissues. The aerial part of the plant develops from the apical meristem of the shoot, and the underground part develops from the apical meristem of the root.

How the Leafy Part of a Plant Develops and Functions

Leaf development is initiated at the shoot apex. On the very tip of the shoot apex is a dome-shaped structure that is sometimes called the **apical dome.** Surrounding the apical dome are **leaf primordia,** structures destined to develop into leaves. These structures are formed in a regular sequence when cells in the shoot apex divide mitotically. Depending on the species, they form singly, in pairs, or in many whorls (Figure 19.4). At any given time, the primordia are in various stages of development.

What factors trigger leaf development? And what determines the species-specific arrangement of leaves on a stem? The processes are not fully understood, but work is well under way to find the answers. In some experiments, parts of a shoot apex have been removed from a plant in order to determine how well the parts develop in isolation from the rest of the plant. For example, the shoot apex of a flowering plant was removed and placed in a nutrient medium. If a

Figure 19.4 The apical meristem of the horsetail, a sphenopsid plant (Figure 5.12). The many leaf primordia are developing around the apical dome. These primordia give rise to the whorls of leaves characteristic of sphenopsid plants. In flowering plants, the leaves are more highly developed and larger; hence, there are fewer primordia developing in the apical meristem than is characteristic of the sphenopsids.

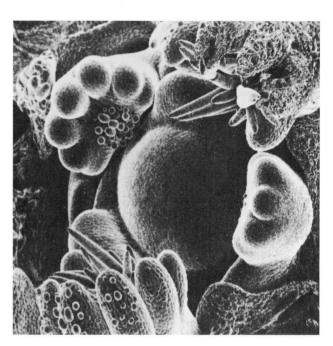

Figure 19.5 Scanning electron micrograph of the apical meristem region of a fern. The apical dome is in the center of this micrograph; it is ringed by a series of leaf primordia in various stages of development. The leaf primordium to the upper right of it shows the beginnings of development of seven leaf primordia. In the primordium to the upper left, the leaflets are in a more advanced stage of development. Just to the right of the apical dome is a primordium that has developed into little more than just a swelling. Interactions among growth regions determine the position and spacing of such primordia.

few leaf primordia were present on the excised apex, it grew in a relatively simple nutrient medium and eventually gave rise to a complete plant with roots and leaves. But if the apical dome alone was removed, growth occurred only in a much more complex medium. The implication in this case is that cellular differentiation in the apical dome may depend on cellular substances produced by the leaf primordia. And yet, in ferns and other simpler plants, the apical dome alone can grow and develop normally in a simple medium.

In other experiments, certain parts of the shoot apex itself were incised to see what effect the incision would have on development of the apical dome and the leaf primordia. For example, if the tip of the shoot apex of a flowering plant was bisected, cells along the flanks developed into new apical meristems. In this case, the implication is that the central cells of the apical dome normally inhibit the development of additional apices from flank cells.

What is clear from such experiments is this: *Most meristem cells have the potential for becoming primordia—but the apical meristem and older primordia inhibit*

the expression of this potential except at certain positions. The pattern of leaf primordium development fixes the arrangement of leaves. And this arrangement in turn determines the arrangement of leaves on a stem.

Studies of shoot apex development in ferns (Figure 19.5) gives insight into some of these interactions. If the site of an as-yet undeveloped fern leaf primordium is isolated from older primordia by a series of deep cuts in the surface, the new primordium becomes larger than normal. This simple experiment indicates that older leaf primordia normally inhibit the growth of new neighbors, perhaps by releasing some substance that diffuses just beneath the surface. Thus, new primordia can develop only when the older ones have moved far enough away. The result is a spacing of leaves along the stem as it grows. Inhibitory effects may regulate the radial development of primordia about the stem in a similar way. Given such effects, *the amount of inhibitory substance being produced by older primordia and differences in sensitivity of younger primordia to those inhibitors could largely account for diverse leaf arrangements seen in different plant species.*

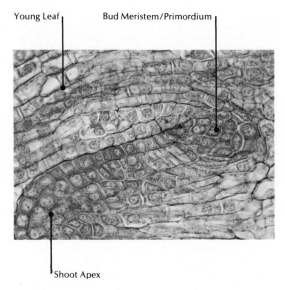

Young Leaf

Bud Meristem/Primordium

Shoot Apex

Figure 19.6 Microscopic view of a section through the apical meristem region of a flowering plant. The cluster of darkly staining cells at the juncture between the leaf primordium and the apical dome is the primordium of an axillary bud. Under certain conditions, this bud may grow out to form a new stem and leaves—resulting in a branching of the plant.

Stem Elongation

In some plant species, the length of the **internodes** (the stem between leaves) remains much the same throughout growth. But in most plants the internodes become longer, which extends the stem. Cell divisions responsible for stem elongation occur mainly in a region just below the shoot apex. This region is sometimes called the **primary elongation zone.** In at least some cases, certain hormones can stimulate the activity of these zones, causing elongation and enlargement of the plant cells. If long-stemmed plants are treated with substances that inhibit the synthesis of those hormones, they fail to develop elongated internodes.

Effect of the Main Shoot Apex on Branching

In most flowering plants, the lateral buds that develop into branches are called **axillary buds.** They grow out of the angles between the leaves and the stem. (These angles are called axils, after the Latin word for ''armpit.'') They are found in the axil of each leaf primordium. Whether axillary buds grow or not depends on still another inhibitory effect, called **apical dominance.** Apical dominance means that the main shoot apex may inhibit or prevent the growth of buds into branches. When the apex is cut away or damaged, buds along the shoot begin to grow. That is what happens when a plant is pruned back, as gardeners have known for thou-

Figure 19.8 (right) Leaf components (a) and stomata (b). Stomata are openings that permit the exchange of gases between the interior cells and the surrounding air; they also permit evaporative water loss. Usually they are found on the lower surface of leaves, although (for obvious reasons) they are present on the upper surface of floating leaves such as those of water lilies. In (c), a photomicrograph of a leaf cross section shows most of the structures depicted in the diagrams.

Figure 19.7 (below) Regulation of axillary bud outgrowth. As long as an apical bud remains in place (a), growth of lateral (axillary) buds is inhibited. But when the apical bud is removed, lateral buds develop (b), which demonstrates that the presence of the apical bud was inhibiting their development. If the apical bud is replaced by a block of agar containing the hormone auxin, the lateral buds fail to grow (c). This experiment suggests that it may be auxin, which also is produced by the apical bud, that inhibits lateral bud outgrowth.

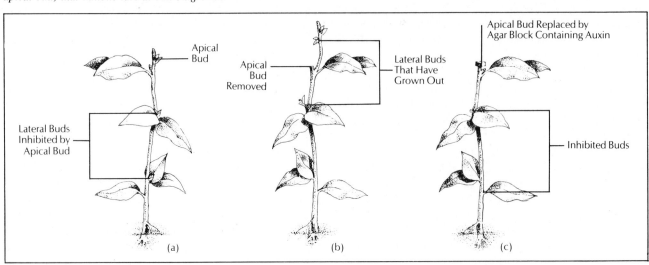

Apical Bud

Lateral Buds Inhibited by Apical Bud

(a)

Apical Bud Removed

Lateral Buds That Have Grown Out

(b)

Apical Bud Replaced by Agar Block Containing Auxin

Inhibited Buds

(c)

sands of years. But *why* it happens is only now becoming understood, and again hormones seem to be part of the reason.

When a shoot apex is cut away and certain hormones are applied to the cut surface of the shoot, lateral buds do not grow (Figure 19.7). *It appears that hormones normally secreted by the shoot apex are important in determining the branching pattern of a plant by controlling development of lateral buds on the same shoot.*

Structure and Function of Adult Leaves

Why are fully grown leaves so varied in internal and external appearance? *Variations in leaf structure represent adaptations to different environmental conditions.* Plants must be able to carry on photosynthesis, but in order to do so they must adapt to the specific environmental conditions. Some desert plants, such as cacti, have lost their leaves entirely in response to severe moisture stress; they carry on photosynthesis in their stems. In most environments, however, leaves are effective photosynthetic structures.

Regardless of details in appearance, leaves generally perform certain basic functions, so they share certain structural features. Most have outer layers of colorless cells, called the **upper epidermis** and the **lower epidermis** (Figure 19.8). A waxy coating called a **cuticle** is usually present on the outer surface of the epidermal layers. In regions where humidity is high, the cuticle is thin; in arid regions, the cuticle may be quite thick in order to help control moisture loss.

But no matter how thick the cuticle may be, there must always be some provision for gas exchange. As you read in Chapter 15, carbon dioxide is needed for photosynthesis, and oxygen is released as a by-product of that process. The movement of these gases into and out of the plant occurs through small surface openings called **stomata** (singular, **stoma,** from the Greek word for "mouth"). Specialized epidermal cells known as **guard cells** flank the stomata. Unlike other epidermal cells, guard cells are photosynthetic. The production of sugars and the resultant osmotic changes in these cells (Chapter 13) appear to govern the opening and closing of the stomata.

Now, when stomata are open, cells inside the leaf lose water through evaporation. Such water loss is called **transpiration,** and it is an important part of leaf function for at least two reasons. First, a continuous supply of dissolved nutrients is needed in photosynthesis. Water in the vascular system of a plant carries these dissolved nutrients in a steady flow that is driven (as you will read later) by the transpiration process. Second, leaves exposed to sunlight accumulate heat energy. And if it were not for the cooling

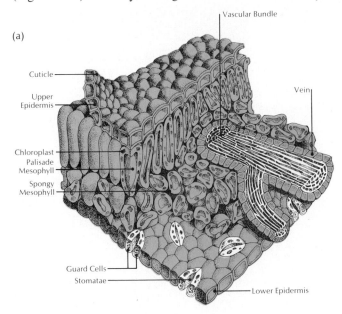

(a)

Vascular Bundle

Cuticle

Upper Epidermis

Vein

Chloroplast
Palisade Mesophyll

Spongy Mesophyll

Guard Cells

Stomatae

Lower Epidermis

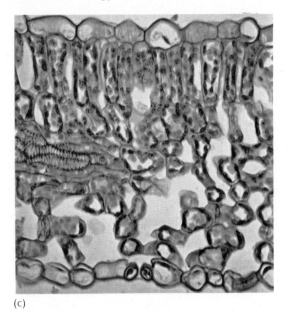

(c)

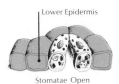

(b)

Lower Epidermis

Stomatae Open

Stomatae Closed

effect of transpiration, the photosynthetic enzyme arrays in cells would soon be disabled.

Photosynthesis occurs most actively in the **palisade layer,** which is located directly beneath the upper epidermis of a leaf. The palisade layer is made of densely packed, vertically aligned cells that contain numerous chloroplasts. The nature of the palisade layer varies, depending on how much light the plant receives. For example, plants found in habitats where there is not much sunlight have multiple palisade layers. It is true that the layer of loosely arranged cells between the palisade layer and the lower epidermis are photosynthetic also. But this layer, the **spongy mesophyll,** is apparently concerned principally with gas exchange.

CELLULAR DIFFERENTIATION ALSO LEADS TO VASCULAR TISSUES

During the development of a plant, the cells formed by mitotic division in the apical meristem gradually enlarge. Eventually they differentiate into the various tissues of the shoot. The first sign of differentiation into shoot tissues appears just behind the apical meristem: an outer layer of vacuolelike cells forms around a cylinder of more densely staining cells. A little farther down from the shoot apex, groups of densely staining cells that are elongated in the axis of the stem can be seen at positions that correspond to the leaf primordia. These are the procambium cells that differentiate into conducting, or vascular, tissues (Figure 19.9). Each region of procambium will eventually connect a new leaf primordium to the vascular system of the rest of the plant. Even farther down the shoot (Figure 19.10), the procambium cells toward the outside of the stem differentiate into the first cells of the **phloem,** the tissue that conducts nutrients and other substances from the photosynthetic tissues to the rest of the plant. The innermost procambium cells differentiate as elements of the **xylem,** the tissue that conducts water and dissolved substances from the roots to the rest of the plant. Together such a cluster of cells containing xylem, phloem, and cambium is called a **vascular bundle.**

In structure and organization, xylem and phloem are markedly different from the blood vessels of animals. The tubes of animal vascular systems have elastic and contractile walls, which assures rapid circulation of fluids. In contrast, the tubes of plant vascular systems are rigid, and the fluids move rather slowly within them. In one sense, the vascular tissues of plants and animals are similar in function: *Both move fluids from one region to another, thereby permitting the development of a large, complex body with specialized parts that interact in an integrated way.* But in another sense they are quite different: *The fluids of the animal vascular system circulate continuously, whereas in plants, the fluids travel in two separate one-way channels*

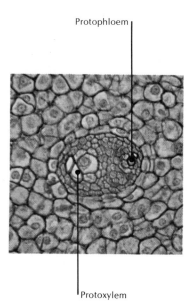

Figure 19.9 Photomicrograph of a cross section through a developing vascular bundle. The smaller cells are the procambium cells. They are elongated in the axis of the stem. From them, the xylem and phloem develop. In the specimen shown here, development has proceeded only to the stages known as the protoxylem and protophloem.

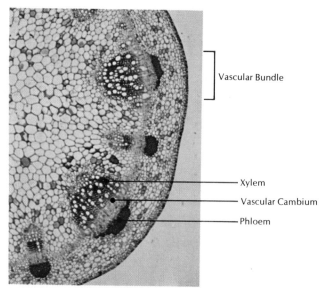

(Photograph courtesy Carolina Biological Supply Company)

Figure 19.10 Organization of vascular bundles in a dicot stem, as seen in cross section. Typically the vascular bundles are arranged in a ring near the periphery. Phloem tissue begins to form in older, more mature tissues; it then grows upward into the developing leaf primordia. Differentiation of xylem tissue begins at the level of attachment of a leaf primordium. It proceeds upward into the young primordium and downward to join the mature elements in the stem.

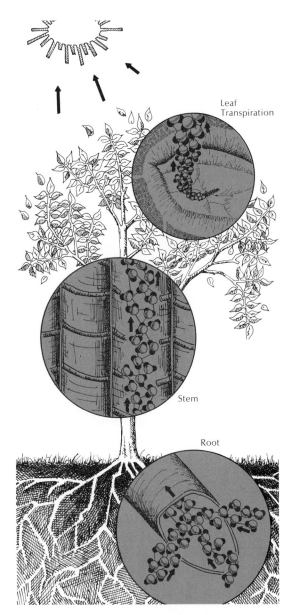

Figure 19.11 The transpiration-cohesion concept of sap flow in xylem. Water evaporates through the stomata (openings in the surfaces of leaves) in the process known as transpiration. Transpiration exerts a negative pressure on the entire column of water in the xylem below the leaf. Because of the hydrogen bonding of molecules, the column of water does not break; it is drawn up from the roots in a continuous strand, like a fine wire.

and never circulate. Just as veins and arteries in animals are constructed in quite different ways, xylem and phloem in plants are constructed differently to perform quite different functions.

How Sap Rises in Xylem

For the most part, xylem is dead tissue. It is made of specialized cells called **tracheids** and **vessel elements,** which have deposited layer upon layer of cellulose and sometimes lignin on their walls before they die. These thickened cell walls form the hollow tubes in which **sap** (water and dissolved minerals) rises from the roots to the aerial parts of the plant. They are reinforced by other thick-walled cells that form rather long, rigid, fibrous tissue before they die. Such supportive tissues composed of the thickened walls of dead cells are known as **fibers.**

The only living part of the xylem is the **parenchyma,** which are cells scattered between the vessels and fibers throughout the plant body, forming specialized structures called **rays.** Parenchyma cells are unspecialized, thin-walled cells with large vacuoles. Parenchyma cells in rays function to move nutrients through the woody stem. Parenchyma cells in nonwoody plants can serve a variety of support and storage functions.

Because xylem vessels are dead, they cannot be actively pumping the sap. Something else drives the sap to the top of the tallest trees. An early notion was that the processes by which roots take in water created enough pressure to force water up the stems. But if that were true, how would it be possible for cut flowers in a vase to continue transporting water upward, which they do? Furthermore, measurements of sap pressure in trees show that the sap in the trunk is under considerable *negative* pressure, not the positive pressure that would be expected if the sap were being pushed up from below. Sap, it appears, is pulled up from the top!

The most widely accepted theory at present is that the loss of water from the leaves through transpiration is the main driving force behind sap movement. As water is lost from leaves, more water is drawn up from below to replace it. What keeps the thin strand of water from breaking instead of rising continuously? It is the hydrogen-bonding tendency of water discussed in Chapter 11. This tendency, derived from the polar nature of the water molecules, gives water a cohesive property. Measurements show that a column of water inside a thin, airtight tube can withstand a pull of 300 pounds per square inch without breaking! This cohesiveness is more than enough to draw water up a xylem tube 370 feet long—in other words, to the top of the world's tallest redwood. This **transpiration-cohesion concept** of sap transport is diagrammed in Figure 19.11.

(Photograph courtesy Carolina Biological Supply Company)

Figure 19.12 (above) Guttation in the leaflets of a strawberry plant. The droplets of moisture that fringe the leaflets are neither rainwater nor dew. They are drops of sap being forced out the end of the xylem tubes by root pressure when the air is too humid to permit evaporation.

Figure 19.13 Organization of vascular tissue in a plant stem. The organization of xylem and phloem may appear rather similar at first glance. But these vascular tissues are fundamentally different. The vessels of xylem are hollow tubes formed by the remains of dead cells; through these tubes sap flows upward by physical forces. The transporting tubes of the phloem are composed of live sieve tube cells, which sort the materials produced by photosynthesis and transport different substances at different rates and in different directions.

Both vessel systems are reinforced by adjacent dead fiber cells, as well as by the thickened cellulose wall of the tubes proper. The cambium cells are capable of giving rise to new xylem and phloem elements under appropriate conditions.

Figure 19.14 (right) Regions of root differentiation. As regions of a root mature, the epidermis and root hairs they contain are gradually lost and are replaced by a corky, barklike layer. When that happens, the region loses its absorptive capacity. The drawings show the pattern of primary root growth. Roots of woody dicots like the stems of such plants also demonstrate secondary growth. Such secondary growth results in an increase in root diameter.

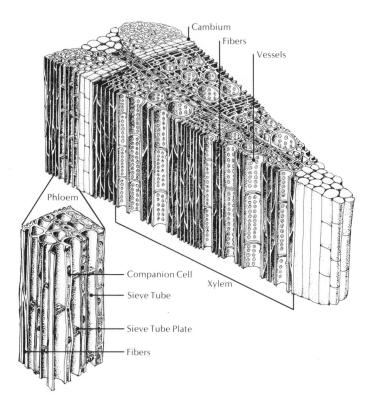

Although root pressure is not enough to account for movement of sap to the tops of even moderately tall trees, it does exist. Under extremely humid conditions, water cannot evaporate as rapidly from the leaves as it is taken in by the roots. As a result, root pressure may become great enough to force water out of the leaves of relatively short plants in a process called **guttation** (Figure 19.12).

How Phloem Distributes Nutrients

Phloem is organized differently than xylem. The main difference is that the transporting tubes of phloem are not hollow skeletons of dead cells; they are made of living cells that are joined end to end to form tubes (Figure 19.13). Although some of these cells lose their nuclei as they mature, they all retain their cytoplasm. The junctions between adjacent cells are places where selective transport of materials occurs. That is why the cells are called **sieve cells,** the tubes **sieve tubes,** and the plates **sieve plates.**

Sieve cells are one of a class of plant cells called **collenchyma,** which have moderately thickened walls and remain alive at maturity. Closely associated with the sieve cells are smaller **companion cells** that apparently take part in the transport process, perhaps by regulating the activity of sieve cells. Just how they function remains unclear. Like xylem, phloem is reinforced by a series of fiber cells and also contains parenchyma cells.

Phloem cells are quite delicate and are drastically altered by almost any mechanical attempt to observe them. That is why understanding of how they function is still rudimentary. The movement of substances in phloem is far slower than in xylem, and nutrients produced photosynthetically in the leaves move from areas of high concentration to areas of

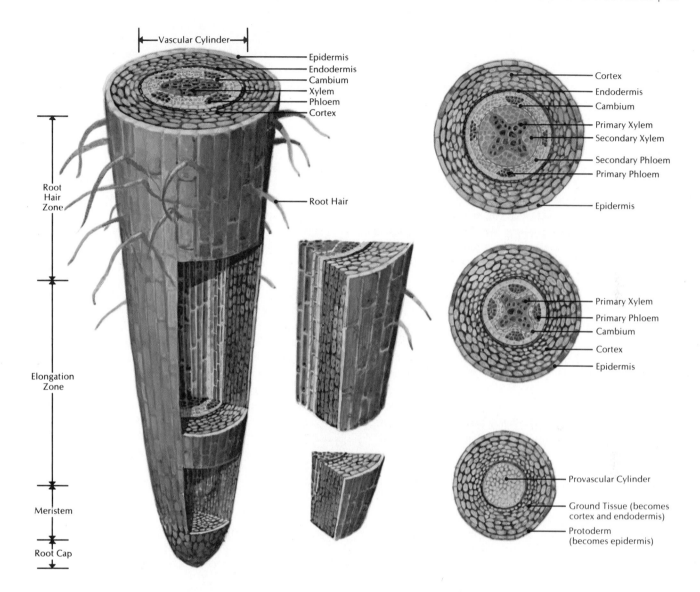

lower concentration in other parts of the plant. But studies using radioactively labeled materials show that different substances move at different rates. Moreover, the materials moving from a leaf into the main stem divide in the phloem tissue of the stem: Some moves upward through the stem, and most of it moves downward.

From such studies we know that phloem is used to transport nutrients from the upper leaves to the growing apical meristem; that it transports nutrients from lower leaves chiefly to the roots; and that it transports nutrients from intermediate leaves in both directions. Among the mechanisms that seem to be involved in transport within the phloem are simple diffusion, cytoplasmic streaming, and active transport across sieve plates. None of these mechanisms alone is enough to explain all known facts about phloem transport, but they all appear to be involved in it.

Secondary Growth in the Shoot

The patterns of meristematic activity, elongation, and differentiation that we have discussed to this point represent **primary growth.** Primary growth that results in an increase in stem length occurs in all vascular plants. Some plants, including woody dicots and conifers, demonstrate a phenomenon called **secondary growth.** Secondary growth results in a gradual increase in stem diameter caused by development of additional vascular tissue. Secondary growth is caused by the presence of a meristematic tissue called the **vascular cambium.** Vascular cambium differentiates from the procambium remaining between the xylem and phloem, and from parenchyma cells between the vascular bundles. It eventually forms a complete cylinder (a lateral meristem) around the xylem part of the stem (Figure 19.14). For the most part, the cambium cells divide in a plane parallel to the stem surface. Tissue formed on the inner side of the cambium differentiates to become xylem; tissue formed on the outer side becomes phloem.

In woody plants that survive for many years, the cambium becomes active each spring (in temperate climates) and ceases activity each fall. This periodic cambial activity is responsible for the formation of annual rings in the wood of temperate trees. Each reactivation of the cambium closely follows the outgrowth of new buds on the shoot system. It begins near the new buds and progresses along the branches and down the trunk. Hormones secreted by the growing buds seem to trigger cambium activity. If buds are removed before their growth has begun in the spring, the cambium layer remains inactive. But relatively normal activity of the cambium layer can be stimulated if a mixture of hormones is applied to the sites from which the buds were cut.

Phototropism and Geotropism

Light has a significant effect on shoot growth. Its effect was demonstrated as long ago as 1880, when Charles Darwin and his son Francis showed that seedlings illuminated on one side curve toward the light—but that they will not do so if the apical meristem is covered with an opaque cap. Such a tendency of growth toward or away from light is called **phototropism.** This growth tendency helps orient the plant in space, so that the leaves are turned in a way that will catch the most light.

Seedlings can curve toward light by means of unequal growth rates on the sides of the stem. The amount of growth is proportional to the amount of certain hormones received from the apical meristem—and the amount of hormones produced in various parts of the apical meristem is proportional to the amount of sunlight reaching those parts.

Some shoots also demonstrate **geotropism**—that is, the direction of growth or curvature is determined by gravity. Hormones produced in varying amounts by different parts of the apical meristem are also involved in geotropism. This topic is treated in greater detail in Chapter 23.

HORMONES MAY ALSO STIMULATE DIFFERENTIATION OF FLOWER PARTS

How does a plant develop flowers? The answer varies from species to species. One important factor is the length of day. In temperate regions, days are longer in the summer and shorter in the winter, and the result is seasonal flowering.

Flower production begins with transformation of the shoot apex. In many cases, increased cell division in the central apex region is one of the earliest transformations observed after the onset of flowering. Increased cell division leads to changes in the size and shape of the apex.

(Such changes vary from species to species.) The flowers may develop from flower primordia that form around the flanks of the apex; they may form through a conversion of the entire shoot apex into a floral apex, or **floral primordium,** which gives rise to the lateral appendages we call flower parts.

The eventual differentiation of flower parts seems to be the result of complex interactions of hormones or other factors that somehow alter the environment of individual cells within the floral apex. It is possible that changes in the length of day cause a hormone to be produced in the leaves and that the hormone travels to the shoot apical meristem, where it triggers the beginning of flower production.

Various experiments suggest that leaves must be present before flowering can occur and that the leaves must be exposed to certain day-length conditions. (Sensitivity to day length is not the only induction mechanism—some plant species respond to certain temperatures—but it is an example for which some experimental evidence exists.) In some cases, flowering can be induced if as little as 1 square centimeter of a single leaf is exposed to the proper day-length conditions. If the leaves are removed within a few hours after their exposure to the triggering stimulus, flowers do not form. But if they are removed after a day or two, flowers develop normally. Stems with leaves that have been exposed to triggering influences can be grafted onto other plants that have not been exposed—and the host plants will flower. These and other experiments strongly support the idea that a hormone moves from the leaves to the shoot apex to stimulate flower production. But if such a hormone exists, it has not yet been isolated or even identified. Active research is going on in this area and alternative explanations are being sought (Chapter 23).

Although many details of the flowering-induction mechanism are not known, florists have put present knowledge to commercial use. For example, by manipulating periods of darkness in their greenhouses, they make sure that all their poinsettia plants will be in full bloom for Christmas and that their Easter lilies will flower at the proper time.

THE APICAL MERISTEM OF THE ROOT CONTROLS DEVELOPMENT OF THE UNDERGROUND PART OF THE PLANT

There are two broad categories of root type. In many dicots, the root system consists of a **taproot** (main root) with lateral branches. A carrot is an extreme example of this kind of system. Some dicots (and most monocots) lack any discernible major root axis. Instead they possess a number of smaller, highly branched roots. Grasses are an example of this kind of **fibrous root system.** *As with branching of the stem, branching of a root is largely controlled by the* *number of regions of apical meristem activity as well as by apical dominance interactions.*

The apical meristem of the root is covered by a **root cap** of parenchyma cells. These cells ease the path of the root through the soil by continuously releasing enzymes that digest away organic substances in front of the growing tip. Cells on the root cap surface are worn away as the growing root pushes through the soil, but they are replaced by new cells. The replacement cells are added to the inner surface of the root cap through mitotic divisions in the apical meristem.

The apical meristem of the root controls the capacity of the root to grow downward in response to gravitational attraction in much the same way as the apical meristem of the shoot controls the phototropic and geotropic responses of the stem. If the root tip is removed, a root that has been placed horizontally in the soil will continue to grow horizontally; it will not curve downward. Apparently, the root apical meristem controls the distribution of substances that affect the growth rates of the other root cells.

Cell division and elongation occur chiefly in the region near the root apex. The hormones that stimulate stem elongation also control root elongation. But the root cells respond to much lower concentrations of hormones than the stem cells do. In fact, the concentration of hormones that stimulates stem growth may actually inhibit root growth. But the hormone concentration in the actively growing plant is always far lower in the root than it is in the stem at the same time! Both cell types are maximally stimulated by precisely the concentrations that they actually experience

under optimum growth conditions, but these concentrations may be a thousandfold different.

As in the shoot, differentiation of a central procambium core occurs near the apical meristem. Slightly farther back from the root tip, the procambium differentiates to form alternating xylem and phloem (Figure 19.14). The pattern of vascular tissues (including the number of strands of xylem) is one of the most characteristic features of the roots of a particular plant species. Figure 19.1, for example, shows the organization of xylem and phloem in a ranunculus (plant of a genus that includes the buttercups). Such patterns seem to be influenced by the root diameter and by concentrations of various hormones.

In the region right behind the zone of elongation (Figure 19.14), extensive differentiation of tissues takes place. Within the epidermal layer of most species, cells called **trichoblasts** become more densely cytoplasmic than others. The trichoblasts develop into single-celled extensions called **root hairs** (Figure 19.15). Development of this region is critical, for the root functions not only to anchor the plant in the soil but to absorb water and dissolved nutrients. And in most cases, *active water and nutrient absorption is confined to the narrow zone near the tip of the growing root where root hairs are developed on the epidermis.*

As Figure 19.16 shows, root hairs essentially are outgrowths of the epidermal cells that extend into the surrounding soil. Absorption of water and dissolved nutrients takes place principally by diffusion through the cell wall of the root hair cell, then through the walls of the cortex as far as the endodermis. **Endoderm** cells (the cell layer surrounding

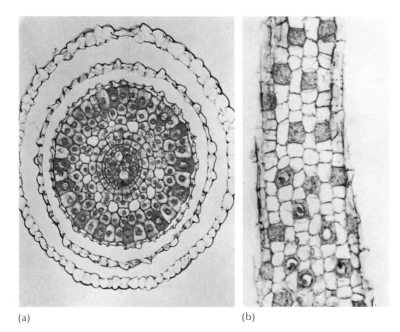

(a)   (b)

Figure 19.15 Transverse section (a) and longitudinal section (b) of a root tip. Trichoblasts, the more densely staining cells, form by unequal divisions of immature epidermal cells. Each trichoblast will develop into a root hair (Figure 19.16).

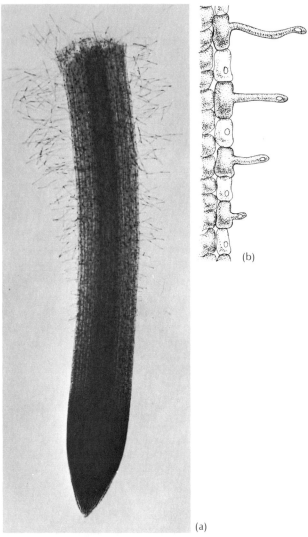

(b)

(a)

(Photograph courtesy Carolina Biological Supply Company)

Figure 19.16 Root hairs. In (a), root hairs are shown in silhouette. In (b), the manner in which root hairs grow out from trichoblast cells is shown. Root hairs provide an increase in surface area that can function in water absorption. Water, with its dissolved minerals, diffuses through cell walls of the root hair and cortex to the endodermis, which actively pumps it into the xylem. From there it rises to the top of the plant.

the vascular cylinder) apparently use cellular metabolic energy to "pump" water and dissolved minerals into the xylem. This active water transport may account for the root pressure and, in turn, for guttation (Figure 19.12).

Because many roots absorb water only behind the growing tip, they must grow continuously. That, in essence, is the plant strategy: to maintain regions of growth and development throughout the life cycle. Stems and roots are more or less continuously extended, and development of new organs is continuously initiated as a result of cell division, differentiation, elongation, and growth. Thus, although a plant is restricted in its ability to respond with rapid movements to changes in the environment, it is flexible in its capacity to shed old organs and grow new ones in response to environmental change.

PERSPECTIVE

The adaptation of an animal to its environment involves, to a large extent, changes in behavior—such as rapid movement in response to environmental stimuli. Such behavioral adjustments demand that skeletal elements, muscles, and nerves be integrated in such a way that different types of movement can be elicited rapidly. As a result, animals (the more complex ones at least) tend to have fixed numbers of body parts that early in life are developed and integrated into the whole system by a nerve network.

But escape is not an available option for a plant that is threatened by an environmental change. When the weather cools, a plant cannot seek a burrow in which to hibernate. When an insect bites a leaf, a plant cannot slap it away. Where there is no rain, a plant cannot travel to a stream for a drink. The strategy of defense is fundamentally different in the world of plants. In regions where the weather grows too cold for leaves to function efficiently, the plant resorbs some of their contents and they fall to the ground; the plant becomes dormant. Then, when conditions become favorable once more, the plant produces an entirely new set of those organs of photosynthesis and starts anew. If insects threaten its foliage, the plant lets the chewed leaves fall—and it produces a new set. If water runs out in the surface soil, it sends new root growth even deeper.

Thus the key adaptive strategy of flowering plants is developmental. It becomes possible as a way of life for a hundred- or a thousand-year-old tree only because of its built-in fountain of youth: the meristematic tissues that retain the capacity for cell division, differentiation, growth, and development of new tissue and organs throughout the life cycle. But if growth and development are always possible, what determines where, when, and how much new growth and of what type should occur? This control comes from a series of hormones, mentioned in passing in this chapter and the topic of consideration in Chapter 23. Produced in one region of the plant under specific sets of environmental conditions—temperature, light, moisture—these hormones travel through the cells and vascular tissues of the plant, eliciting the response that has been fostered, by natural selection, as an appropriate response to specific sets of conditions.

Thus, although plants lack the nervous systems characteristic of animals, they are not without means of communication. The channels provided by the vascular systems called xylem and phloem continuously maintain the flow of the vital substances of life up and down the plant body, making the division of labor between roots and shoots, leaves and meristem a smoothly running collaboration.

From our narrow (animal) perspective, the level of integration and the speed of response of plants might appear to be primitive. But it has met the test of selection: *The surface of the land is green,* despite the consumptive skills developed by the most efficient herbivores that evolution has ever produced.

SUGGESTED READINGS

BIDWELL, R. G. S. *Plant Physiology.* New York: Macmillan, 1973. An excellent and generally quite scholarly treatment of plant physiology, including an extensive, comprehensive, and well-documented discussion of plant development.

KOLLER, D. "Germination," *Scientific American,* 200 (April 1959), 75. An interesting treatment of the natural mechanisms used by many plants to keep their seeds dormant until the environmental conditions are right for germination.

RAY, P. M. *The Living Plant.* 2nd ed. New York: Holt, Rinehart and Winston, 1972. A knowledgeable and readable account of plant biology, with a distinctly functional orientation. Excellent illustrations and well-chosen references.

SALISBURY, FRANK B. "The Flowering Process," *Scientific American,* 198 (April 1958), 108. A lucid discussion of the now-classic experiments on the induction of flowering in previously vegetative plants. The paper is old, but the findings are still valid.

STEWARD, F. C. *Growth and Organization in Plants.* Reading, Mass.: Addison-Wesley, 1968. A thorough treatment of plant growth and organization.

VAN OVERBEEK, JOHANNES. "The Control of Plant Growth," *Scientific American,* (July 1968), 75. A good overview of the role of plant hormones in the regulation of growth and development, stressing the interactions between promotive and inhibitory hormones.

Section V

Integration of Life Processes

Until now, we have been considering the flow of life over evolutionary time and how there can simultaneously be constancy and long-term adjustments in genotype. In this section we will be considering short-term phenotypic adaptations of individual organisms to changes in their immediate surroundings. As conditions change, so must an organism adapt to the change if it is to survive. As the flow of nutrients from the external environment falls, the organism must bring to bear new mechanisms that somehow maintain its vital internal functions despite the impending energy crisis. If foreign matter invades the organism, mechanisms must be brought into action to combat it—again, to maintain the internal environment. If a predator threatens, action must be taken to fight it or escape from it. There is immense diversity in the external signals that trigger such life-maintaining adjustments; there is equally immense diversity in the responses given. Nevertheless, the basic mechanisms connecting stimulus and response are amazingly similar at the molecular and cellular levels. In each case a molecule exists that has been selected for because of its contribution to the species in past episodes of rapid changes. That molecule interacts with the stimulus in a precise way, causes a change in membrane properties or in the properties of the genome of the cell, and rapidly induces a change in phenotype that acts to restore the status quo.

Chapter 20

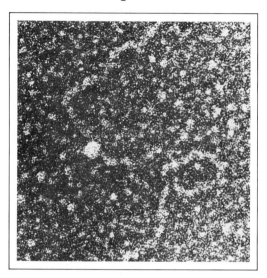

Cellular Regulation and Control

At every moment in time, every cell bears more genetic information than it can possibly use. The expression of the various potentials in that store of information must be continually regulated, for a cell cannot afford to spend energy on the performance of unneeded or counterproductive tasks. This electron micrograph shows one method of genetic regulation that is associated with prokaryotic cells—a globular protein molecule, called a repressor, sits on one specific genetic region of a DNA molecule and thereby prevents adjacent genes from being expressed.

All cells embark on their journey through time with a basically similar endowment and a similar set of problems. Each one has inherited a set of blueprints that defines its capacity to produce specific proteins for specific cellular functions. Through natural selection, each cell is assured that its particular blueprints give it the potential to deal with all the situations a cell of that species normally encounters. But what would happen if all these blueprints were expressed at once? Many of the proteins they specify are counterproductive with respect to one another. What one protein produces, another destroys. If any cell were simultaneously to possess *all* the proteins that it is genetically capable of producing, it would dizzily slide toward death as essential materials were built up by one system, only to be destroyed by another.

Underlying all life processes is control. Control exists whether the unit of life is a multicellular animal or a single cell within its gut, whether it is a complex plant or a single cell within its stalk. Control may not appear to be necessary in the case of certain substances that must be produced continuously in order for the cell to survive. But even here, the substances must be produced only at rates that are in balance with all the other processes occurring in the cell. (For example, a cell that devoted all its resources and energy to the synthesis of ribosomes would be as doomed as a cell that failed to make ribosomes altogether.) Table 20.1, which lists the kinds of substances found in a simple prokaryotic cell, barely hints at the magnitude of the problem. The levels of every one of these substances—from water to DNA—must be regulated by the cell.

Complicating the problem of control is the changing nature of the environment. Temperatures rise and fall. Day follows night, and a dry season gives way to a rainy one. Resources may be abundant one moment and in short supply the next. A metabolic pattern that is adapted to an environment in which food is plentiful may be a pattern for disaster when food is scarce. How does a cell control its chemistry in such a way that its processes are balanced under normal conditions and yet are capable of shifting when conditions change? Even more puzzling, how does a cell in a developing organism change its pattern of activities in a controlled manner to give rise to a new structure with a new function?

THE NEGATIVE FEEDBACK LOOP IS THE BASIS OF CELLULAR CONTROL

In the living cell, a series of processes grouped together under the term **homeostatic control** works to maintain an optimum internal state as conditions change. These controls, which cells have acquired over evolutionary time, have parallels in some of the ways we manipulate our local environment. Consider the way temperature is controlled in homes. If a furnace produced heat at a constant rate, day and night, summer and winter, the house would tend to be too hot part of the time and not hot enough the rest of the time. If the furnace is capable of producing enough heat to keep the house warm on the coldest nights, then some step must be taken to prevent overheating at other times. Basically, there are two ways to even things out. It is possible to control the *loss* of heat—for example, by opening the windows to increase the rate of heat loss whenever the temperature reaches a certain level. Although this solution would provide some relief, it would be extremely wasteful of resources. The more efficient way to regulate temperature is to control the *production* of heat—by shutting off the furnace whenever the temperature reaches a comfortable level. In this way, resources are used only when they are needed to meet changes in the environment. In homes with central heating, this kind of control is most commonly achieved by use of a thermostat (Figure 20.2). When a thermostat is wired to a furnace, the heat feeds back into the system through the thermostat and influences its own production—the more heat there is, the less will be produced; the less heat there is, the more will be produced. In this interaction, a regulated quantity that has departed from the norm is triggering processes that return it to the norm. This kind of interaction is called a **negative feedback loop** (Figure 2.5).

Table 20.1
Approximate Chemical Composition of a Rapidly Dividing *E. coli* Cell

Component	Number of Different Kinds	Average Molecular Weight	Approximate Number of Molecules per Cell	Percentage of Total Cell Weight
Water (H$_2$O)	1	18	40,000,000,000	70
Inorganic ions	20	40	250,000,000	1
Carbohydrates*	200	150	200,000,000	3
Amino acids*	100	120	30,000,000	0.4
Nucleotides*	200	300	12,000,000	0.4
Lipids*	50	750	25,000,000	2
Other small molecules	200	150	15,000,000	0.2
Proteins	2,000–3,000	40,000	1,000,000	15
Nucleic acids				
DNA	1	2,500,000,000	4	1
RNA				6
16s rRNA	1	500,000	30,000	
23s rRNA	1	1,000,000	30,000	
tRNA	40	25,000	400,000	
mRNA	1,000	1,000,000	1,000	

*Including precursors.

Source: James D. Watson, *Molecular Biology of the Gene*, 2nd ed. (New York: Benjamin, 1970) p. 85.

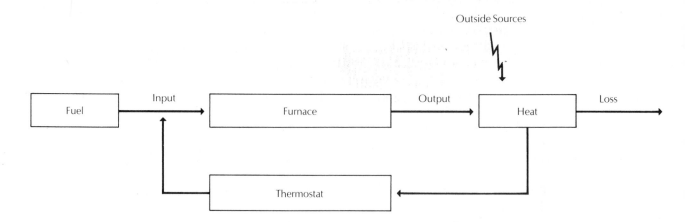

Figure 20.2   How a thermostat is used to control heat production. When the furnace is functioning, it produces heat. When the heat output by the furnace exceeds the heat loss, the temperature rises. This rise in temperature affects the temperature-sensing device in the thermostat, causing it to throw a switch that stops the input of fuel and, hence, the production of heat. When there has been enough heat loss to cause the temperature to drop, the thermostat switches on the flow of fuel, restoring heat production. Thus, by means of the thermostat, heat regulates its own production in a negative feedback loop. Over time, the amount of heat produced is balanced with the rate of heat loss to maintain a relatively constant temperature. To the extent that heat enters the system from an outside source, the furnace can function at a lower capacity to provide heat.

Figure 20.3   Generalized form of a negative feedback loop. The output of any production unit may be regulated to match the rate at which the product is needed. The key component is a sensor-switch, a unit that can measure product availability and shut off the flow of raw material into the production unit when the product has accumulated beyond some preset level. Then, when available product falls below that cutoff level, the sensor-switch turns on the flow of materials into the production unit once again.

Now, controlling heat production with a thermostat is a specific solution to a specific problem. But the negative feedback loop on which this solution is based can be generalized to any problem of control. The critical element of any negative feedback loop is the **sensor-switch mechanism,** a unit that measures product availability and controls its output (Figure 20.3). Clearly, if such negative feedback loops existed in an organism, they would bestow tremendous selective advantage on that organism. Through such mechanisms, an organism could guard its resources, using them whenever conditions demanded and reserving them whenever conditions did not require their use. It is not surprising, then, that amazing webs of negative feedback loops have evolved throughout the living world. As you will read in later chapters, some of these controls have long been known to exist in large, multicellular animals. But only recently has there been any sort of understanding of the types of controls and the nature of the sensor-switches at the cellular level—and that understanding comes primarily from studies of the bacterium *Escherichia coli.* This tiny organism is particularly well suited for analysis of homeostatic controls. As a result, we now understand how the activity and the production of many critical enzymes are

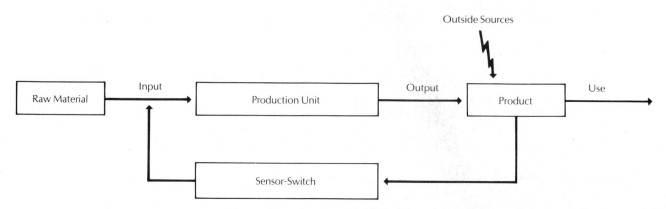

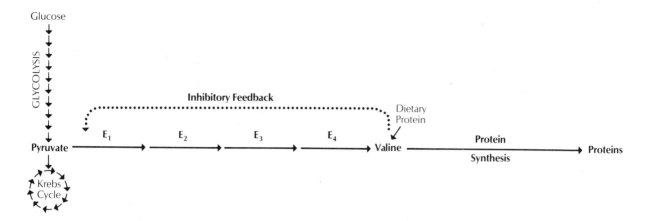

regulated by an *E. coli* cell in response to environmental changes. An extensive network of negative feedback loops is involved, and details of many of the loops are known.

END-PRODUCT INHIBITION OF KEY ENZYMES IS A FORM OF NEGATIVE FEEDBACK LOOP

Like all other life forms, *E. coli* requires twenty different kinds of amino acids to make proteins. If this organism is fed only glucose and salts, it forms all twenty amino acids from the carbon atoms of glucose. But if one amino acid—say, valine—is added to the growth medium, within a minute or less the cell stops making that particular amino acid even though it continues making all the others at a constant or accelerated pace! How is such rapid and precise control exerted? It turns out that the control mechanism is remarkably simple. Valine is an inhibitor of the enzyme that carries out the first step in its synthesis. The first enzyme of the synthetic metabolic pathway acts as the sensor-switch that converts the pathway into a feedback loop (Figure 20.4). Because the molecule that inhibits the key enzyme is the final product of the pathway, the general term for this type of control system is **end-product inhibition.**

Similar regulatory loops are now known to help regulate synthesis of the other amino acids, the nucleotides, the various coenzymes (such as NAD), and an assortment of other cellular components. *Each essential building block is an inhibitor of the enzyme that carries out the first step in its synthesis.* This kind of end-product inhibition has been observed throughout the plant and animal kingdoms as well as in prokaryotic organisms. In each case, the starting materials of such a biosynthetic pathway are materials the cell normally produces for other purposes. In the case of valine, the starting material is pyruvate, which plays a central role in energy metabolism. Other pathways use other common substances as starting points. But each such biosynthetic pathway represents a *branch* off the main

(text continues on page 448)

Figure 20.4   End-product inhibition: a negative-feedback loop. Valine is an amino acid that is an essential part of all proteins. If valine is not provided through the host's diet, E. coli synthesizes it from pyruvate that has been derived from glucose by the glycolysis pathway. A specific enzyme (E_1) catalyzes the condensation of two molecules of pyruvate. The product of this reaction undergoes three more enzyme-catalyzed reactions to form valine.

Thus, the synthesis of one molecule of valine costs the cell thirty-six molecules of ATP that otherwise would have been produced as the two pyruvate molecules were processed through the Krebs cycle. In addition, the equivalent of three ATP molecules is needed to complete the second reaction in the sequence. Thus each valine molecule costs the cell thirty-nine ATP molecules. As costly as it seems, it is a small price to pay to be able to grow in the absence of this essential amino acid. But if valine is avaliable from the exterior, the cell reaps an enormous selective advantage if it is able to turn off this drain on the intermediates of energy metabolism. In fact, if valine is provided to the E. coli culture, as soon as it penetrates the cells and reaches a concentration adequate to maintain protein synthesis it combines with enzyme E_1, making it nonfunctional.

The enzyme remains nonfunctional and the pathway fails to produce any valine as long as valine levels in the cell remain high. When, for any reason, valine levels fall again, the valine bound to enzyme E_1 falls off, the enzyme becomes active, and synthesis of valine molecules starts anew. The level of valine synthesis at all times remains exactly that needed to maintain protein synthesis—no less and no more!

Interleaf 20.1

Ecological Aspects of the Molecular Biology of *E. coli*

Biologists estimate that they are aware of about 25 percent of the specific chemical reactions occurring in the bacterium *Escherichia coli* and, in many cases, they know how the cell controls the rates of these reactions. *E. coli* has proved to be a particularly rewarding organism for these studies of homeostatic control. First of all, it is unicellular, so intracellular controls are not complicated by interactions between cells. Second, the natural history of the species has shaped it into an organism that survives rapid surges of chemical change in the environment. It lives in the mammalian intestine, where one day may bring a feast and another, famine. *E. coli* is adapted to survive when its host eats nothing but starch (or nothing at all)—and to out-compete other organisms when a meal of seeds and berries floods the intestine with all manner of nutrients.

In the laboratory, *E. coli* will grow continuously on a medium as simple as sugar, water, and a few inorganic salts. When its diet is enriched with amino acids, vitamins, and nucleosides, it responds by growing faster—reaching the point where a full generation requires a mere twenty minutes. To maintain this sort of flexibility it must be capable of making many kinds of molecules for itself but not waste time doing so if such molecules are provided from the outside; it must possess homeostatic controls. Finally, it has a genetic system that is readily analyzed by means of conjugation and transduction (Chapter 17), which has permitted study of the genetic basis for many of its control systems. Because of these attractive properties, *E. coli* has become the most studied organism on our planet.

E. coli and its ancestors have probably occupied the same kind of environment for 100 million years. Given the large numbers of *E. coli* in each intestinal tract, and given this organism's short generation time relative to the host, there have been perhaps 10^{30} times as many *E. coli* as mammals. Each of these cells has been subject to selective pressures of the environment. It is therefore safe to assume that they are by now optimally adapted to their environment.

When dividing once an hour or so in the laboratory, *E. coli* channels its energies efficiently into growth and division. In contrast, when it is reproducing only once a day—as it often does—it would almost seem that it squanders away its resources. For example, when *E. coli* is grown in the laboratory under conditions where it divides only once a day, it contains nearly a third as many ribosomes as a cell dividing once an hour. Now, regardless of the rate of growth, a cell must double its size between divisions. Thus it must make the same amount of protein between divisions regardless of growth rate. Because a single ribosome can assemble the same number of proteins per hour at any growth rate, a cell doubling once a day should require only 1/24 as many ribosomes as a cell dividing once per hour. Because in fact it has about 1/3 as many ribosomes as the more rapidly growing cell, it seems to possess more than seven times as many ribosomes as it needs. Ribosomes are large and complex structures to build and they are an expensive investment in terms of materials and energy. Therefore, it is surprising to find that slowly growing cells would have such an apparent excess of ribosomes. These extra ribosomes represent about 10 percent of the dry weight of the cell. Every time the cell divides, it must devote 10 percent of its raw materials and energy toward the production of these extra ribosomes. Clearly, *E. coli* cells that did not make the extra ribosomes would be able to divide 10 percent more rapidly under the same culture conditions; they would soon outgrow the cells containing the extra ribosomes.

What has prevented this adaptation from occurring in nature during the 100 million years that *E. coli* has been around? Its environment provides the probable answer. When the host eats, *E. coli* cells are suddenly presented with food for which each cell must rapidly compete. Each cell then tries to take in as many nutrients and grow as quickly as possible. Under these circumstances, the rate at which it can grow is limited by the availability of the protein synthetic machinery—*primarily ribosomes.* A cell with excess ribosomes can immediately begin to make protein more rapidly. In contrast, a cell that does not contain excess ribosomes would have to take the time to make more ribosomes before it could begin to synthesize protein at a faster rate.

Consider what would happen if it were possible to create an *E. coli* cell that had no excess ribosomes. If it were placed in a medium with a normal *E. coli* cell (one that contains a sevenfold excess) and then suddenly given unlimited food, calculations show that the normal cell will have divided before the other even starts to grow significantly faster. Between meals, of course, the cell that was not "burdened"

with excess ribosomes would grow about 10 percent faster. But with every meal provided by the host, the normal cell will gain a 100 percent advantage! The host need provide it with a meal only once every nine days for the normal cell to have a 10 percent selective advantage. Therefore, *E. coli* cells with extra ribosomes are not inefficient but are "wise" indeed.

The transport systems of *E. coli* provide another example of how laboratory studies of an organism often must be correlated with its natural environment in order to be fully understood. If *E. coli* cells in a test tube are grown on lactose in concentrations that occur in the intestine, the growth rate is limited by the rate at which lactose enters the cell, *not* by the rate at which it is metabolized. Why, then, did *E. coli* not evolve a more efficient transport system for lactose? The answer is found in the nature of the intestinal environment. Intestinal contents are about as viscous as lightweight motor oil. In such material, the rate of diffusion of lactose is about 100 times slower than it is in water. In fact, it is so slow that the cell is able to transport lactose inside as fast as the lactose can diffuse through the intestinal slosh to the cell. Therefore, the cellular growth rate is limited

not by lactose transport from the cell surface to the interior but by how fast lactose can actually move through the intestinal contents! Obviously, improvements in the efficiency of the transport system in the intestine would not increase the growth rate and would have no selective advantage.

In short, an organism must be studied in relation to its natural environment if we are to appreciate its biochemistry. True, what we observe at the molecular level may be viewed simply as chemical building blocks assembled in complex ways. But *E. coli* is not a "device" for satisfying the research needs of a molecular biologist; it is a living organism that has adapted for survival.

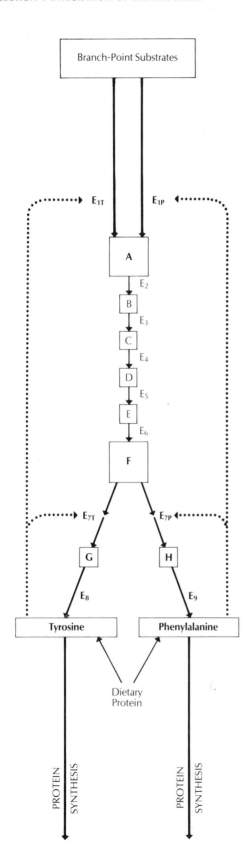

Figure 20.5 End-product inhibition by tyrosine and phenylalanine. Phenylalanine and tyrosine are similar amino acids. Thus, they are synthesized from the same starting materials by pathways in which seven of the eight intermediate compounds are identical.

If tyrosine, when freely available, were to shut off the branch-point enzyme completely, phenylalanine synthesis would stop, and vice versa. It turns out that in this case E. coli *possesses two different enzymes (coded for by two distinct genes) that catalyze the same reaction—the branch-point reaction. One of these enzymes (E_{1T}) is subject to inhibition by tyrosine and is insensitive to phenylalanine. The other enzyme (E_{1P}) is inhibited by phenylalanine but not tyrosine. Thus, if only one of these amino acids is supplied, only one of the branch-point enzymes is inhibited and the flow of cellular metabolites into the pathway is reduced.*

Now, a molecule of the intermediate F bears no marks of how it entered the pathway, and if all enzymes subsequent to F in the pathway are functional, both tyrosine and phenylalanine would be produced. But here, as the two pathways diverge, we find another point of feedback inhibition. Tyrosine blocks the enzyme leading into its side branch, whereas phenylalanine blocks only the other branch. If a control engineer had been asked to design a logical and efficient switching network to regulate two processes that shared a common pathway, he could not have designed a more elegant system than has evolved here!

metabolic route. Because the first enzyme in the pathway determines whether the branch functions, this enzyme is called the **branch-point enzyme.** *In nearly every case it is the strategically located branch-point enzyme that is subject to end-product inhibition.* In principle, valine synthesis could be blocked at any of the four reaction steps. But if the second reaction were blocked instead of the first, pyruvate would continue to be removed from the pathway of energy metabolism, the cell would continue to pay nearly the full cost of valine synthesis, and an unusable intermediate would accumulate in the cell. It is only by blockage of the branch-point enzyme that selective advantage of feedback inhibition can be fully realized, and it is at the branch point that such inhibitions are observed!

The synthesis of valine occurs by a short, simple pathway, and it is readily understood. However, some biosynthetic pathways are more complex and are themselves branched. In such cases, the feedback loops appear more

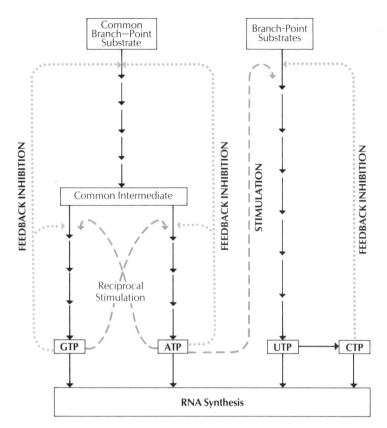

Figure 20.6   Controls balancing the synthesis of nucleotides required for RNA synthesis. Four nucleoside triphosphates are required in rather equal concentrations in order to synthesize RNA: GTP, ATP, UTP, and CTP. The pathways leading to production of these four molecules are under the sort of end-product feedback inhibition of branch-point enzymes already described. In addition, there is reciprocal stimulation of the synthesis of one pathway by the product of another. GTP stimulates ATP production, and ATP in turn stimulates the production of GTP, UTP, and CTP. As a result, the cell maintains a balanced ratio of the four nucleoside triphosphates.

complex. But they are still only variations on the simple theme. Figure 20.5 depicts such a pathway. This scheme involves one main pathway (with a main branch point) that subsequently branches internally to form two different end products. Each end product feeds back to inhibit entry into the main branch by one-half and also inhibit completely the entry into its own side branch!

Even more complicated schemes exist, but all lead to the same end—the precise control of cellular chemistry to match precisely the metabolic "needs" of the cell. For example, the amino acid glutamine plays a critical role in the cell. It is produced from the related amino acid glutamate and ammonia by the enzyme glutamine synthetase. The amino group added to glutamate to form glutamine is subsequently used as a donor of amino groups in several biosynthetic pathways, such as the synthesis of other amino acids, nucleotides, and so on. Thus, in a very real sense, glutamine synthetase is a branch-point enzyme

for all these other metabolic pathways. It should come as no surprise, then, that eight different substances—each the product of a particular pathway involving transfer of the amino group from glutamine—are feedback inhibitors of glutamine synthetase in *E. coli!* Each of these end products is capable of only partial inhibition of glutamine synthetase; only when all the products are present at once is glutamine synthetase shut off completely.

Metabolic pathways do not exist for their own sake, nor do they stand in isolation in the cell. They are themselves integrated into the larger schemes of cellular growth and reproduction. For example, in order to synthesize RNA, a cell must have the four nucleoside triphosphates (ATP, GTP, CTP, and UTP) in roughly equal concentrations. But all four of these triphosphates are relatively unstable and are readily degraded. Hence, the cell must balance the levels of all four and not let any one accumulate excessively. As Figure 20.6 illustrates, this task is achieved by a web of feedback interactions in which a nucleoside triphosphate serves not only to suppress its own synthesis by negative feedback but also to stimulate synthesis of the others.

FEEDBACK REGULATORS FUNCTION BY MODIFYING ENZYME SHAPE

By what mechanism does the end product of each metabolic pathway inhibit the branch-point enzyme? Is it possible that each end product so resembles the substrate of the corresponding branch-point enzyme that it acts as a competitive inhibitor, competing for space on the active site of the enzyme? That theory has been tested and found wrong. Not one case of end-product inhibition has yet been found to act in this manner. Instead, *the enzyme being feedback-regulated is known to possess two separate sites: an active site to which the substrate binds and a control site to which the feedback regulator binds.* The regulator affects enzyme activity by changing the shape of the active site when it binds to the control site. The general term for such effects is **allosteric regulation** (*allo*, "other"; *steric*, "space").

How does allosteric regulation occur? The branch-point enzymes regulated by negative feedback have a common feature in addition to their capacity to be regulated by end products. All are large, complex proteins made of more than one polypeptide chain having more than one active site and more than one control site. In such enzymes, the binding of substrate to one active site facilitates the binding of substrate to the other(s). Similarly, the binding of inhibitor to one control site facilitates the binding of inhibitor to the other(s).

Figure 20.7 summarizes the current interpretation of how the binding of substrate and inhibitor controls the activity of allosterically regulated enzymes. The basic principle is that each enzyme subunit is capable of rapidly interconverting between two different states, or **conformations.** In one state, a subunit binds the substrate, does not bind the inhibitor, and interacts strongly with another subunit of the same shape. In the other state, all these properties are shifted. As a result, the substrate tends to induce a concerted shift of the enzyme subunits to the active state and the inhibitor tends to do the opposite. In the ensuing "tug of war," the inhibitor has two inherent advantages. First, while substrate molecules undergo rapid enzymatic conversion by the enzyme and are rapidly released as products, the inhibitor molecules are not transformed in any way by the enzyme. Thus, they tend to form a more stable complex. Second, recall that the starting material of each biosynthetic pathway (the substrate of the branch-point enzyme) is always a molecule involved in other metabolic pathways in the cell. As a result, its concentration tends to remain fixed at some moderately low level. But if the feedback inhibitor is a nutrient suddenly provided by the host animal, its

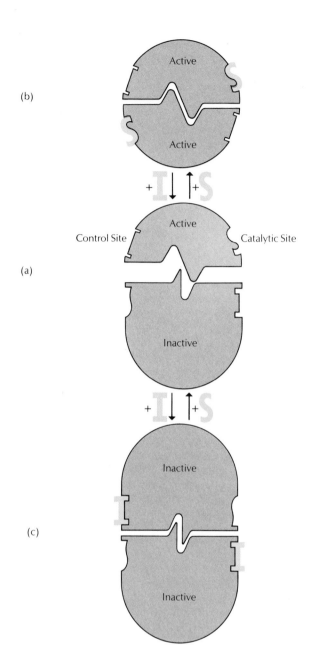

(b)

(a)

Control Site   Catalytic Site

(c)

Figure 20.7   Shape changes induced in an allosteric enzyme by substrate and feedback inhibitor. The subunits (polypeptide chains) of the enzyme are capable of alternating rapidly between two slightly different shapes, as shown in (a). In one state the catalytic site forms a pocket complementary in size and shape to the substrate (S); hence it can bind substrate and is catalytically active. In this state, the control site is distorted and will not bind the inhibitor (I). When a shift to the second state occurs, both binding sites change shape. Now the inhibitor can be bound but the substrate cannot be; the enzyme is in a catalytically inactive form. The contact surfaces between subunits also change contour during a change from one state to the other. Hence, two subunits can interact strongly with each other only when they are both in the same state.

Now, if substrate is added to the enzyme, it will bind to an enzyme unit that happens to be in the active state. In so binding, it will temporarily stabilize that subunit in the active state. Because of the mutual interaction between subunits in the same state, a subunit held in the active form by substrate will act as a trap, drawing an additional subunit into that state. Now a subunit lacking a bound substrate molecule will be temporarily stabilized in the active state where substrate can be readily bound. Thus the binding of the first molecule facilities the binding of a second. Substrate molecules cooperate in activating the enzyme!

The reverse is also true. If the feedback inhibitor is now added, it will bind to any subunits that happen to be in the inactive state and by an analogous process will form a trap, drawing an additional subunit into the inactive state. The inhibitor molecules will also show cooperative binding. The ratio of active to inactive subunits will thus be some complex function of the ratio of substrate to inhibitor, but if sufficient inhibitor (end product) is present, the enzyme will be almost entirely in the inactive form, and flow of substrate through the pathway will not occur.

concentration may rise to high levels. Thus, the pull of the substrate tends to be constant and that of the inhibitor to be variable in the "tug of war" between them. Like substrates, stimulators of allosteric enzymes (as shown in Figure 20.6) function by binding to and stabilizing active subunits. Taken together, these controls function to keep the enzymes of protein and RNA synthesis supplied with just the quantity of building blocks they require for optimal functioning.

CONTROL OF ENZYME SYNTHESIS IS ALSO USED TO CONTROL CELLULAR METABOLISM

Feedback inhibition of enzyme activity gives a cell a significant advantage in terms of energy efficiency. But the synthesis of the enzymes themselves involves a sizable expenditure of energy—at least four ATP molecules per peptide bond formed (Chapter 17). Thus an even greater energy saving should accrue to a cell that simply fails to produce an enzyme that is not needed, in comparison to a cell that makes an enzyme only to keep it continuously inoperative. This saving in energy should be possible in the case of synthetic enzymes that are not needed when a rich supply of nutrients becomes available to the cell. It should also be possible in the case of enzymes that are required only infrequently to break down foodstuffs that appear sporadically in the diet.

Consider, for example, the predicament *E. coli* got itself into when it chose the mammalian gut as its ecological niche. If a bacterial species is to colonize the digestive tract of a mammal before all the growing space is filled by other life forms, it must be prepared to exist on the nutrients available in the only diet its host consumes for the first weeks or months of life: milk. But the only sugar available in substantial quantities in milk is one that is not found elsewhere: namely, lactose (milk sugar). Although lactose is a rich source of energy during the period that the host is suckling, it will never be seen in the diet again once the young animal is weaned (unless the host happens to be a human being). The dilemma is clear. If a bacterium lacks the enzymes required to metabolize lactose, it will be unable to establish itself in the gut during the suckling period. If it goes on producing those enzymes after weaning, it will be carrying so much extra baggage for the rest of the life of the host. But imagine what a selective advantage such a bacterium would have if it were able to produce the appropriate enzymes only when lactose became available!

In the late 1930s and 1940s, André Lwoff at the Pasteur Institute in Paris found that *E. coli* has just that capacity with regard to several nutrient sugars, including lactose. He observed that cells grown in the absence of lactose lacked any detectable lactose-metabolizing enzymes. But if the same cells were transferred to a new medium in which lactose replaced the sugar on which they had previously

Figure 20.8   The biologists François Jacob and Jacques Monod. André Lwoff's discovery of adaptive enzymes—enzymes that are present in cells only when they are needed for growth—laid the groundwork for the subsequent studies by Jacob and Monod that ultimately led to the operon concept and the formulation of a detailed model of the regulation of gene activity in E. coli. Their observations also provided the first indication of the existence of what is now known to be messenger RNA. The work of these three men has had an impact on the research of others that has few parallels in biological history. In recognition of their contributions, Lwoff, Jacob, and Monod were awarded the 1965 Nobel Prize in medicine and physiology.

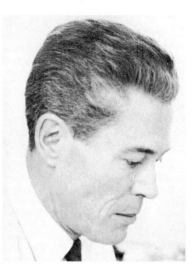

grown, it was only a matter of minutes before the appropriate enzymes appeared and the cells began growing on the lactose. Such enzymes, which are only present in cells under conditions where they are of clear adaptive value, are called **adaptive enzymes.** This term distinguishes them from the class of enzymes that are always present in the cell regardless of growth conditions. The enzymes that form part of the regular constitution of the cell are called **constitutive enzymes.**

LACTOSE METABOLISM OFFERS A MODEL FOR THE CONTROL OF GENE EXPRESSION

Around 1950, Lwoff directed the attention of two younger colleagues—Jacques Monod and Francois Jacob—toward the problem of adaptive enzymes. Over the next decade, these investigators pieced together a detailed picture of the mechanisms controlling synthesis of these adaptive enzymes, and they developed a general model for the control of gene expression. The paper they published in 1961 summarizes their observations and models. It has become the most widely cited paper in modern biology.

From their studies with *E. coli,* Jacob and Monod made the following observations and drew the following conclusions:

1. The lactose-metabolizing enzymes begin to be made almost at once when lactose is present. But their synthesis stops almost as quickly when lactose is withdrawn. Therefore, a short-lived intermediate between the gene and the protein-synthesizing machinery—a messenger molecule—must exist. (This was the first prediction of the existence of what turned out to be messenger RNA.)

2. The three enzymes involved in lactose metabolism are always made in a fixed ratio relative to one another, despite variations in the absolute rates of synthesis. Therefore, synthesis of related enzymes must be coordinated.

3. The genes for the three enzymes were found (by mapping procedures) to be right next to one another in the DNA of *E. coli*. Therefore, genes for related enzymes must be located on a single stretch of DNA that operates as a single unit. They called this coordinated group of genes an **operon.**

4. In addition to the **structural genes,** which determine the structure of the enzymes, they detected certain genes that determine when, and in what quantities, the enzymes are made. In short, **control genes** must exist.

5. When an *E. coli* cell (normally haploid) was made diploid by genetic manipulation, one of the control genes was capable of regulating the activity of the structural genes on both DNA molecules. A **regulator gene** therefore must exist that makes a chemical mediator capable of regulating more than one operon.

6. In contrast, the two remaining control genes were shown to be capable of controlling the function of only those structural genes to which they were physically attached. They had no influence over structural genes on a separate DNA molecule within the same cell. These two genes had to be exerting control over the adjacent structural genes in some direct, physical way. In other words, some control genes can influence adjacent structural genes *without* synthesis of a diffusible chemical mediator.

7. One of the two control genes that functioned in this direct manner determined whether the structural genes were "on" or "off." An **operator gene** must exist that determines whether or not the operon should be active.

8. The remaining control gene determined how fast the products of the structural genes were synthesized. Therefore, a **promotor gene** must exist that determines how fast the operon should function when it is active.

From these observations and deductions, Jacob and Monod developed the **operon model of gene control.** As Figure 20.9 shows, the central concept is that *the product of*

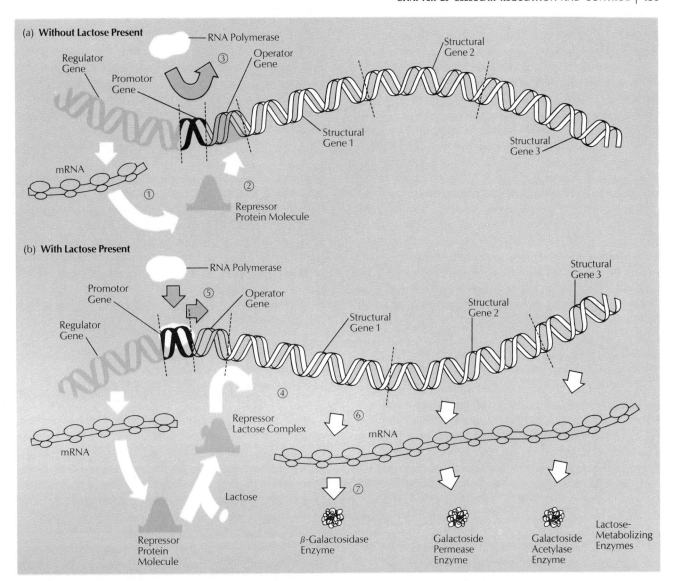

Figure 20.9 *The Jacob-Monod operon model for control of the synthesis of lactose-metabolizing enzymes.*

(1) The regulator gene produces a messenger RNA (mRNA) molecule that is translated to yield a protein called the repressor protein molecule.

(2) In the absence of lactose, this repressor molecule binds specifically to the operator gene, which lies between the promotor gene and the structural genes.

(3) The promotor gene is the site where RNA polymerase must attach to begin transcribing the mRNA molecules required to express the structural genes. But if the operator gene is occupied by the repressor protein, RNA polymerase is physically blocked from initiating the transcription; hence, no products of the structural genes are made.

(4) But when lactose appears in the cells, it combines specifically with the repressor protein and induces a change in shape (the repressor protein is an allosteric protein) such that the repressor can no longer bind to the operator.

(5) With the operator site unoccupied, the RNA polymerase enzyme can now attach to the promotor site and begin to slide down the DNA, synthesizing RNA.

(6) As a result, mRNA corresponding to the three structural genes is produced in one continuous piece.

(7) This mRNA molecule is now translated (by ribosomes and transfer RNA molecules) to form the three enzymes required before lactose can be used as an energy source. (If the operator is transcribed, it is not translated into protein.)

Once all the available lactose has been metabolized by these enzymes, the repressor protein will return to the lactose-free state, in which it will combine with the operator once again and immediately shut off transcription of the structural genes. Because the mRNA molecules are very unstable, once new messengers cease to be made, synthesis of the lactose-metabolizing enzymes will cease within minutes.

a regulator gene interacts with an operator gene to determine whether products of the structural genes will be made.

The process whereby lactose switches on the synthesis of lactose-metabolizing enzymes is known as **derepression.** In the absence of lactose, the product of the regulator gene—the *repressor protein*—combines with the operator gene and represses transcription of the lactose operon. Lactose reverses this repression; it is a *derepressor molecule.* Because transcription of the appropriate messenger RNA molecules is the event that is being regulated, this process is one of several known as **transcriptional regulation.**

In recent years, both the repressor protein and the region of DNA bearing the operator sequence have been isolated. It is clear that of all the DNA sequences in *E. coli,* the lactose repressor recognizes and binds *only* to that short stretch of nucleotides known as the lactose operator. The detailed molecular basis for this interaction is unknown as this sentence is being written—but it may well be known before this sentence appears in print!

A PROMOTOR REGION DETERMINES HOW OFTEN THE ADJACENT GENES ARE TRANSCRIBED

RNA polymerase, the enzyme that synthesizes RNA, specifically recognizes and combines with the promotor region of DNA. It cannot initiate RNA synthesis from any other region. It is known that all structural genes are linked to their own promotor genes. Because the same molecules of RNA polymerase can transcribe all genes, promotor regions must have certain common structural elements that the enzyme recognizes as meaning ''promotor site, start here.'' But RNA polymerase attaches more readily to certain promotor regions than to others. So there must also be differences in details of the structure of different promotors that are superimposed on the common structural plan.

The significance of these differences is that the more readily the RNA attaches to a given promotor region, the more frequently the adjacent structural genes will be transcribed—and, thus, the more of the corresponding proteins will be made. *The rate of production of constitutive proteins is determined mainly by the relative affinity of RNA polymerase for the corresponding promotor regions.* Certain enzymes and structural proteins are always needed by the cell, regardless of growth conditions. But they are not all needed in equal amounts. It turns out that proteins required in large amounts are coded for by structural genes that lie adjacent to promotors to which RNA polymerase attaches readily. But other proteins, required in constant but trace amounts, have promotors that RNA polymerase attaches to only infrequently.

It is easy to see why such differences exist. A cell that produced a constitutive protein either too slowly or too rapidly would be at a disadvantage compared to one that produced the protein just fast enough to keep pace with the growth of the cell. Therefore, a promotor mutation that matched the frequency of transcription to this optimum would be favored by selection, and a promotor mutation that led to either an increase or decrease in transcription rate would be selected against.

For example, the repressor protein for the lactose operon is a constitutive protein. Its promotor is such that the regulator gene is transcribed only about once per cell generation. As a result, there are less than a dozen molecules of repressor proteins per cell. This is enough to keep the lactose operon repressed and, at the same time, extremely sensitive to the presence of lactose. Mutants have been obtained that have a more efficient promotor region next to the regulator gene. These mutants produce about a hundred times as much repressor protein as normal. They have been useful for isolating the repressor protein, but they cannot compete against normal *E. coli* in a lactose medium. In a concentration of lactose that derepresses the normal cells, the mutants remain repressed and starve to death.

FEEDBACK LOOPS MAY REGULATE BOTH ACTIVITY AND SYNTHESIS OF A SINGLE ENZYME

The way synthesis of the lactose-metabolizing enzymes is regulated is a form of negative feedback. It differs from the examples of feedback inhibition discussed earlier in the same way a thermostat regulating an air conditioner differs from one regulating a furnace. The entity to be removed (heat in the case of an air-conditioning system; lactose in the case of the lactose operon) triggers the sensor-switch to initiate processes leading to its removal.

But a form of transcriptional regulation that is more directly analogous to end-product inhibition of enzyme activity also occurs. This form is known as repression. In **repression,** the end product of a biosynthetic pathway functions to repress synthesis of the enzymes of that pathway. As Figure 20.10 shows, the end product of a pathway may act simultaneously in two different kinds of negative-feedback loops. It may inhibit the branch-point enzyme, and it may repress synthesis of all the enzymes in the pathway.

While Jacob and Monod were working on lactose metabolism, others demonstrated that amino acids repress synthesis of the enzymes needed for their own production. And in several cases, the structural genes for all the enzymes needed in the synthesis of an amino acid were shown to be adjacent to one another on the DNA molecule. In their now-famous paper, Jacob and Monod proposed that the basic plan of control of repressible operons was similar to that of derepressible ones. The only difference, they as-

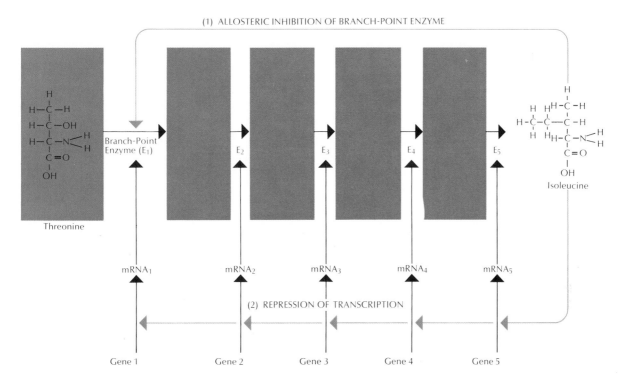

(1) ALLOSTERIC INHIBITION OF BRANCH-POINT ENZYME

Threonine

Branch-Point Enzyme (E₁)   E₂   E₃   E₄   E₅

Isoleucine

mRNA₁   mRNA₂   mRNA₃   mRNA₄   mRNA₅

(2) REPRESSION OF TRANSCRIPTION

Gene 1   Gene 2   Gene 3   Gene 4   Gene 5

Figure 20.10   Dual levels of feedback control of isoleucine synthesis. The isoleucine produced by this pathway functions (1) to inhibit the branch-point enzyme and (2) to repress transcription of the mRNA molecules required for synthesis of the five enzymes of the pathway.

serted, is that the switch operates in the opposite direction. In other words, *the regulator protein of a repressible operon cannot combine with the corresponding operator until it has first combined with the end product of the pathway being regulated.* Thus, in this case, the small molecule regulates its own metabolism by activating the corresponding repressor. Such a molecule is called a **co-repressor** (Figure 20.11). Subsequent work has strengthened the Jacob-Monod model for repressible operons, even though there has been some variation in the structural details of the different operons.

THERE ARE ALSO POSITIVE REGULATORS OF TRANSCRIPTION

There are some control aspects of the lactose operon that the model shown in Figure 20.9 simply cannot explain. Specifically, it has been known for some time that the enzymes of lactose metabolism are not synthesized if lactose is merely added to a medium already containing enough glucose to support the growth of *E. coli.* Such enzymes are made only if lactose *replaces* glucose. Now,

ecologically, this makes sense because glucose is the most widely available sugar in nature. Enzymes of glucose metabolism exist regularly in all known organisms. Therefore, if enough glucose is present to support maximum growth, it would be pointless for the cell to make the enzymes needed in the extraction of energy from lactose. In fact, it would be downright disadvantageous in terms of wasted energy and resources.

The same argument applies to the use of other sugars or any other carbon compounds as alternative sources of energy. And the same thing is observed: *E. coli* will not "switch on" synthesis of the enzymes needed in the extraction of energy from arabinose or tryptophane or any other substance as long as glucose is available. (The branch of metabolism that deals with such degradation of and release of usable energy from compounds is called **catabolism,** and the repression of such pathways in the presence of glucose is known as **catabolite repression.**)

Thus, although the presence of lactose is a necessary condition for derepression of the lactose operon, that in itself is not enough. Another substance must also be present

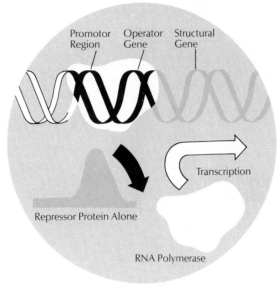

(a) Corepressor Absent

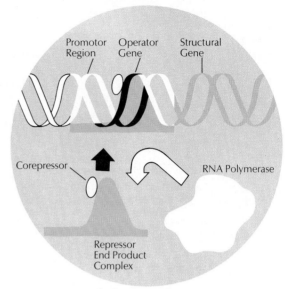

(b) Corepressor Present

Figure 20.11   Control of transcription of a repressible operon. When the corepressor (usually the end product of the pathway) is absent, as shown in (a), the repressor protein cannot bind to the operator. Therefore, the polymerase binds to the promotor, transcribes the operon, and the enzymes of the pathway are produced. When the end product of the pathway accumulates (b), it binds to the repressor and causes a change in shape such that the complex now binds to the operator. The polymerase is now blocked, and transcription and synthesis of the enzymes cease.

Although the general nature of the elements controlling all repressible and derepressible operons are similar, the selectivity of the controls comes from the specific structures of the regulator genes, their products (the repressor proteins), and the operators. Each operon has control elements of a unique structure; as a result, they take part in the control of only that operon.

to turn on the operon. Recently this substance was identified as the nucleotide cyclic adenosine-3′,5′-monophosphate, or **cAMP** (Figure 20.12). *RNA polymerase cannot attach to the promotor genes of catabolic operons in the absence of cAMP.* That is why catabolic enzymes cannot be synthesized without cAMP. As long as glucose is present, cAMP levels remain low. But when glucose levels fall, cAMP is produced. Then the RNA polymerase is activated by forming a complex with cAMP and the cyclic AMP receptor protein, known as **CRP**. In short, as Figure 20.13 shows, *cAMP basically functions to regulate the availability of glucose or some alternative energy source.* Later, in Chapter 22, you will read about how cAMP fulfills an analogous

Figure 20.12   The structural formula of cyclic adenosine-3′, 5′-monophosphate (cAMP). The term refers to the ring formed when the phosphate group is attached to the 3′ and 5′ —OH groups at the same time. This nucleotide, produced from ATP by an enzyme known as adenyl cyclase, is one of the most widespread regulators of cellular metabolism in the world. Hence the enzyme adenyl cyclase is a crucial element of control systems throughout the living world. In E. coli, adenyl cyclase is apparently inactive as long as glucose is present in the cell. When the glucose level falls, adenyl cyclase becomes active and cAMP appears. This cAMP is required for the derepression of the lactose operon and all other catabolic operons.

role in mammals, but through a very different mechanism.

In a sense, cAMP is a negative feedback element. Together with the cAMP binding protein called CRP, it functions to maintain synthesis of catabolic enzymes at only that level required to replace glucose as an energy source. But the mechanism of the cAMP-CRP complex is different from the mechanism of repressors. *A repressor is a negative regulator of transcription.* The only active role it can play is to *block* transcription of an operon; when it is missing or inactive, transcription proceeds. *But the cAMP-CRP complex acts as a positive regulator of transcription.* It functions actively to *facilitate* transcription of an operon. If it is missing or inactive, transcription of certain genes is impossible.

Unforeseen in Jacob and Monod's scheme was the fact that certain operons under negative feedback control *lack* repressor proteins! In such cases, the product of the regulator gene is, like the cAMP-CRP complex, a positive control element needed for the functioning of the RNA polymerase! The arabinose operon (Figure 20.14) is an example of such a control system. (Arabinose is a five-carbon sugar that *E. coli* can use as an energy source if its supply of glucose fails.) When arabinose is added, it apparently binds to the product of the arabinose regulatory gene. This complex, plus the cAMP-CRP complex, is needed to initiate transcription of the arabinose operon because RNA polymerase cannot attach to the promotor region of the arabinose operon in the absence of an arabinose-regulator protein complex. *It now appears that many more operons in bacteria are under positive control than are under negative control.* The differences between the three kinds of negative feedback transcriptional controls that have been discussed are summarized in Table 20.2.

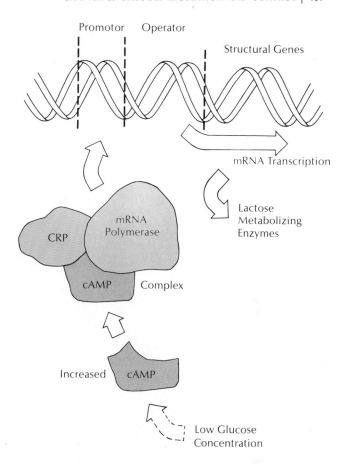

Figure 20.13 *The role of cAMP as a mediator of lactose operon derepression. When the glucose level falls, cAMP appears and binds to the cAMP binding protein known as CRP. Together they form a complex with the RNA polymerase, making it possible for the RNA polymerase to attach to the promotor region of operons (such as the lactose operon) that code for catabolic enzymes.*

Table 20.2
Three Kinds of Negative Feedback Transcriptional Controls

Compared Characteristic	Negative Controlling Elements		Positive Controlling Elements
	Lactose	Isoleucine	Arabinose
Type of control:	Derepression	Repression	Induction
Effect of regulator protein on transcription:	Repressor	Repressor	Stimulator
Effect of small molecule on transcription:	Derepressor	Corepressor	Costimulator
Effect of regulator gene deletion:	Enzyme synthesis constitutive	Enzyme synthesis constitutive	Enzyme synthesis uninducible

Note: Although some operons have positive controlling elements and others have negative controlling elements, all are negative feedback systems in which a small molecule regulates the pathways by which it is metabolized.

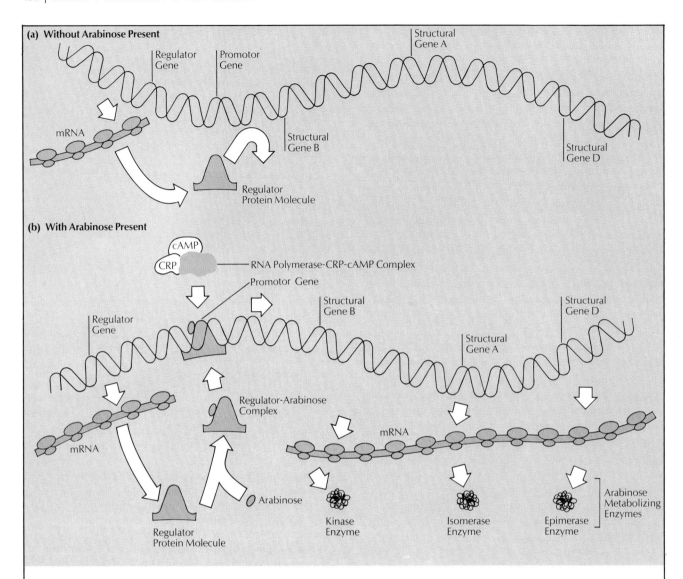

Figure 20.14 Positive control of transcription in the arabinose operon. Notice that operons with positive control lack operator genes. In the absence of arabinose (a), the regulator protein does not interact with the promotor gene or the RNA polymerase, and transcription does not occur. In the presence of arabinose (b), the regulator protein combines with the arabinose and undergoes an allosteric transformation in shape. Now it is able to combine with the promotor gene and/or the RNA polymerase-CAP-cAMP complex, and the process of transcription begins.

IF IT IS TRUE OF *E. COLI,*
IS IT ALSO TRUE OF ELEPHANTS?

With their formulation of the operon model, Jacob and Monod excited considerable interest among researchers concerned with the developmental control of multicellular plants and animals. By 1960 it was clear that cell lines differ in a multicellular organism not because they *possess* different genes but because they *express* different genes (Chapter 18). And the operon model was the first definitive example of how differential expression of genes might be controlled.

One of the strongest appeals of the operon model was its generality. Although no operon has ever been found in *E. coli* (or any other organism) that has precisely the same detailed features as the lactose operon, the general features of the operon model appear to be widely applicable in prokaryotes. In one of their early papers, Jacob and Monod proposed a series of modifications of the basic operon model that explained in theory, at least, many developmental events in more complex organisms—in eukaryotes. With tongue in cheek, they asserted that surely what is true of *E. coli* must also be true of elephants (Figure 20.15). But some accepted the basic validity of this aphorism as an article of faith; after all, were there not extensive prior demonstrations of the unity of life at the molecular level? With great optimism, many set out to apply this concept to embryonic development.

Repressible and derepressible genes bearing some parallels with *E. coli* systems have been identified in one group of eukaryotes (yeasts). But no convincing evidence has yet been found to support the validity of the operon model as a description of either the organization or the control of genes in any eukaryote. And certainly no evidence has been obtained to implicate operonlike controls as regulators of development. Perhaps such evidence never will be found. In retrospect, it appears that such optimism may have been rather ill-advised from the outset. In *prokaryotes,* the main kind of control required is homeostatic regulation that will keep the interior of the cell relatively constant despite a changing environment. In the development of complex *eukaryotes,* controls lead to progressive change in the interior of cells despite a relatively constant environment!

This is not to say that differential gene expression does not occur in eukaryotes. Indeed, it is central to their development. *But control of gene expression in eukaryotes has already been shown to involve many mechanisms that are nonexistent in* E. coli. If operator genes are ever found in flowering plants or mammals, they will compose only one of many systems functioning to control gene expression, not the only system or even the dominant one.

There are many differences between *E. coli* and elephants. But in terms of control of gene expression, perhaps none is more significant than the presence of a nuclear envelope in all eukaryotes. This envelope has the effect of separating the two major steps in gene expression—transcription and translation—in space and time.

As Figure 17.1 illustrated, in *E. coli* and other prokaryotes, transcription and translation occur simultaneously. As a messenger RNA molecule is spun off the DNA molecule by RNA polymerase, it lies in the cytoplasm, surrounded by ribosomes, transfer RNA molecules, the enzymes involved in protein synthesis, and so forth. These molecules go to work on the messenger RNA, converting it to a polysome and initiating its translation even before it is completely synthesized! There is little question that although other kinds of controls do exist in *E. coli,* the predominant control

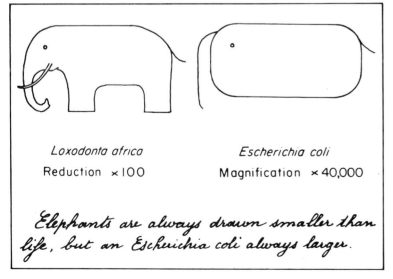

Loxodonta africa
Reduction ×100

Escherichia coli
Magnification ×40,000

Elephants are always drawn smaller than life, but an Escherichia coli always larger.

Figure 20.15

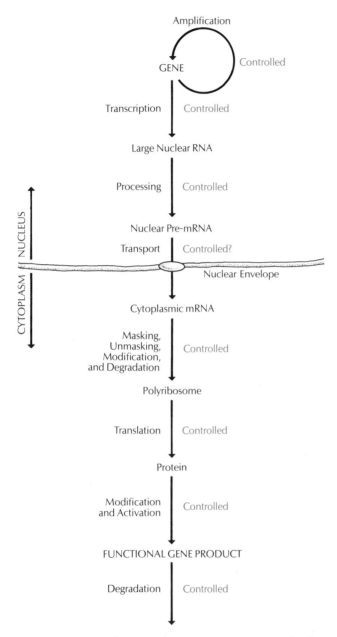

Figure 20.16 *Possible sites of control over gene expression in eukaryotic cells. Controls have actually been observed at all but one of these postulated sites. In some cases it is clear that expression of a single gene may be controlled at virtually every step from transcription onward.*

of gene expression is at the initiation of transcription. And once transcription of a gene has begun, it is only a matter of minutes before the gene is expressed and exerts its effect on the phenotype of the cell.

In eukaryotes, however, the machinery of transcription and translation lie in different compartments. In most (if not all) eukaryotic nuclei, there are neither functional ribosomes nor any of the other components required to translate a message as it is transcribed. Those components of the gene action system lie on the other side of the highly selective filter—the nuclear envelope—in the cytoplasm. As a result, there is a finite interval between the time that transcription of a molecule is completed and the time its translation can begin. Within that interval are a whole series of controls that regulate whether a gene, once transcribed, shall be expressed, and if so, when. As Figure 20.16 shows, there are additional control points after the messenger RNA molecule exits from the nucleus to the cytoplasm. Let us now briefly consider each of these levels of control and assess the role that each may play in the development and functioning of multicellular eukaryotic organisms.

GENE AMPLIFICATION IS A PRETRANSCRIPTIONAL CONTROL

Chapter 18 pointed out that, in amphibians, amplification of the ribosomal RNA genes occurs during egg development. The genes coding for ribosomal RNA are *selectively* replicated many hundredfold or thousandfold as egg development gets under way. Subsequently, each loop of ribosomal DNA is actively transcribed, and it develops into a nucleolus in which ribosomal subunits are assembled. Within a matter of a few weeks, the single nucleus is thus able to produce the number of ribosomes needed to serve the thousands of cells that will be produced by cleavage of the egg following fertilization. Without prior amplification of these genes, the synthesis of such massive quantities of ribosomes would require many years, and oogenesis would be incomplete within the lifetime of any female frog. Similar amplification of DNA has now been observed in the oocytes of other species.

But it would seem that if a mechanism exists for selectively amplifying genes, it would have been exploited more widely in nature than in just this one cell type. For that reason, there has been an intensive search for other cell types in which it might occur. Donald Brown (who, with his colleagues, provided the critical documentation for gene amplification in the amphibian oocyte) reasoned that amplification would be of greatest selective advantage in a cell line that was suddenly called upon to produce copious quantities of the product of a single gene. He investigated the silk-gland cells of the silkworm. These cells produce prodigious amounts of a single protein called silk fibroin with which—in a very short time—they wrap themselves in a cocoon. Because silk fibroin is a large protein with an unusual amino acid composition, its messenger RNA is large and of atypical base composition; hence, it could be readily isolated in pure form. Having isolated the molecule, Brown and his colleagues proceeded to apply the methods of RNA-DNA hybridization (*Interleaf 17.2*) in order to count the corresponding genes in the nuclei of the silk-gland cells. They found only two copies of this gene per nucleus—which is what they found in every other diploid cell of the species!

Similar negative results were encountered by those who used RNA-DNA hybridization to count the genes coding for the globin (protein) portion of hemoglobin in developing red blood cells. At late stages of the life cycle of red blood cells, at least 95 percent of the protein being made is globin. Yet no amplification of the genes occurs to support this massive synthesis. In other cases that have been less rigorously examined, amplification of genes coding for specific proteins has been reported, but technical considerations demand that judgment be suspended on the validity of these reports.

TRANSCRIPTIONAL CONTROLS HELP REGULATE GENE EXPRESSION IN EUKARYOTES

No gene can be expressed unless it is first transcribed. And there is strong evidence that eukaryotic cells specifically control the transcription process. Different cells predictably transcribe different genetic regions. Let us briefly examine two lines of evidence supporting this assertion and then discuss current views on how transcriptional regulation might occur in eukaryotic cells.

The giant chromosomes in certain insects often possess regions in which the normal banding pattern is disrupted by a swollen, unraveled-looking area known as a **chromosome puff** (Figure 20.17). In some regions of the chromosomes, puffs occur sporadically in all cell types. But there are other specific genetic regions in which puffs are seen only in one cell type and only at a particular time during development. Some puffs can be controlled experimentally. For example, certain regions show puffing only when the insect larva is undergoing early stages of metamorphosis. These puffs can be induced in very young larvae by injecting them with ecdysone, the hormone that triggers insect metamorphosis. In at least one case, the puff has been shown to be causally related to the subsequent appearance of a characteristic cellular protein.

Now, *chromosome puffs are sites of RNA synthesis*. If radioactive precursors are provided, radioactive RNA accumulates in the puffed regions. The evidence that this

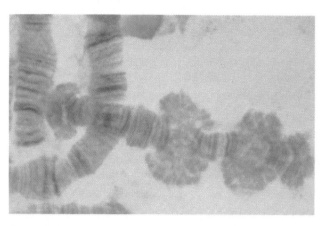

Figure 20.17 Photograph of the giant salivary gland chromosomes of Drosophila. *Notice the two chromosome puffs. The staining indicates that these regions are rich in RNA. Studies with radioactive precursors indicate that such puffs are the sites of active RNA synthesis (transcription). Some chromosome regions undergo puffing sporadically in all cell types; others are puffed only in one cell type at one stage in the life cycle.*

newly synthesized RNA is actually being made in the puffed region comes from one dramatic series of experiments. Puffs at one particular genetic region of one chromosome were manually dissected from a series of cells. The RNA extracted from these isolated puffs was shown to be capable of specifically forming an RNA-DNA hybrid with the DNA of the isolated puffs—but not with the DNA in the rest of the chromosomes! Because the puffs are sites of RNA synthesis, and because the occurrence of many puffs is clearly controlled in time and space, it follows that RNA synthesis (transcription) is controlled in a specific manner in these eukaryotes.

Analysis of temporal and spatial control of transcription in species lacking giant chromosomes has been less direct. The most persuasive evidence has been obtained by the use of DNA-RNA hybridization to compare the RNA molecules made by two different cell types. Such experiments are replete with technical problems and are difficult to interpret. Nevertheless, one generalization seems to be emerging: different cell types make different RNA molecules. *Transcription is not random but is controlled in a cell-specific, stage-specific manner.*

The conclusion from such studies is that at any one time, *most eukaryotic cells transcribe only a few percent of their genes*. And different cells transcribe different genes. How is this selectivity achieved? **Histones** (the main proteins associated with DNA in eukaryotic chromosomes) were once considered prime candidates for this task. But histones are now known to be lacking the properties required of the gene-specific regulators. There are only five kinds of histone molecules, and at least four are present in all nuclei in relatively fixed amounts. Moreover, they are quite similar from cell to cell. Histones are apparently organized on the chromosomes in a regular, repetitive way. They undoubtedly play a nonspecific role in stabilizing the DNA of the eukaryotic chromosome, and perhaps they are involved in the coiling of chromosomes prior to cell division.

In addition, histones may play a nonspecific role in repressing DNA transcription. If purified DNA is added to a test tube containing RNA polymerase and all the precursors of RNA, the DNA is transcribed indiscriminately—all regions appear to be copied. But if a sample of purified histones is added to such a mixture, it immediately forms a complex with the DNA (the many positively charged amino acids on the histone molecule interact with the negatively charged phosphate groups of the DNA). Suddenly the DNA becomes inaccessible to the RNA polymerase, and transcription of all regions slows or stops. This result has led many to suggest the following: *In the intact chromosome, histones act to keep all the genes silent until some specific molecule intervenes to loosen the DNA-histone complex in a particular region.*

Support for this hypothesis and a suggestion concerning the nature of the gene-specific molecules that open up certain genetic regions has come from further analysis of the chromosome. As discussed in Chapter 13, chromosomes (and the chromatin composing them) contain a series of nonhistone proteins as well as DNA and histone. Although the nonhistone proteins are present in smaller amounts than the histones, they are much more varied in type. They are different in various species, different in the various cells within a species, and different at various stages in the life cycle of a single cell. John Paul and Stewart Gilmour showed that if the nonhistones from one cell type were mixed with a DNA-histone complex from another cell type, and if RNA polymerase was then added, RNA was produced that was typical of the cell from which the nonhistones came! This observation has since been confirmed by others and extended to apply to nonhistones extracted from a single cell type at different stages. In short, *the regions of DNA transcribed in a test tube from any DNA-histone-nonhistone mixture appear to be the regions that were transcribed by cells from which the nonhistone proteins were derived.*

If the nonhistone proteins of the chromosomes are involved in gene-specific regulation of transcription, how do they act and how is their presence controlled? Because the nonhistone proteins tend to be acidic (because of their many negatively charged side chains), it is easier to visualize them combining with the basic histone molecules

Figure 20.18 Proposed steps in the production of mRNA in the nucleus of a eukaryotic cell. Most of the nonribosomal RNA made in the nucleus is made in large pieces that range from 1 to 100 million in molecular weight. Such RNA is called heterogeneous nuclear RNA, or HnRNA. Most molecules are then promptly modified by addition of a string of 100 to 200 adenylate residues to the 3' end prior to further processing. The average molecular weight of the HnRNA is $10–20 \times 10^6$. The average molecular weight of the pre-mRNA is 0.3×10^6; less than 5 percent of the RNA transcribed is conserved.

than with the acid DNA. But if the histones themselves are not gene-specific, how could the nonhistones impart gene-specific control if they combined directly with the histones? If they are to act in a specific way, they must be capable of recognizing specific genes. Any regulator must interact specifically with the entity it regulates. Indeed, recent studies suggest that some nonhistones are capable of binding to specific DNA sequences in a manner analogous to the regulator proteins of prokaryotes.

Where do the nonhistone nuclear proteins come from? They must themselves be the products of other genes. These genes in turn must be regulated in some manner, and so on. At first this progression seems hopelessly circular until we recall that in complex multicellular organisms, the history of the individual is, in fact, a linear progression of developmental changes. One change occurs that sets the stage for another change, and so on. Usually, if the chain of events is interrupted at any point, all subsequent changes fail to occur. Knowledge of these transcriptional controlling elements is still far from complete. But it is reasonable to expect that as we learn more, the facts gained at the molecular level will fall into place with understanding of developmental events at the cellular and organ level.

CONTROLLED PROCESSING OF RNA TRANSCRIPTS OCCURS IN THE NUCLEUS

Transcription is necessary for gene expression. But transcription does not assure expression of a gene in eukaryotes; several other levels of control exist. About 90 to 95 percent of the RNA made in any eukaryotic nucleus is degraded immediately within the nucleus; it plays no further role in the cell! The process of nuclear degradation of RNA is nonrandom. Certain select sequences are degraded, and others are chemically modified and then transported to the cytoplasm where they function.

Messenger RNA production involves a series of steps (Figure 20.18). Transcription results in long molecules (long enough to code for 10 to 100 protein molecules). Because the size range is extremely variable, and because this kind of RNA is never seen outside the nucleus, it has been called **heterogeneous nuclear RNA,** or **HnRNA.** The first step in its processing is the addition of a string of 100 to

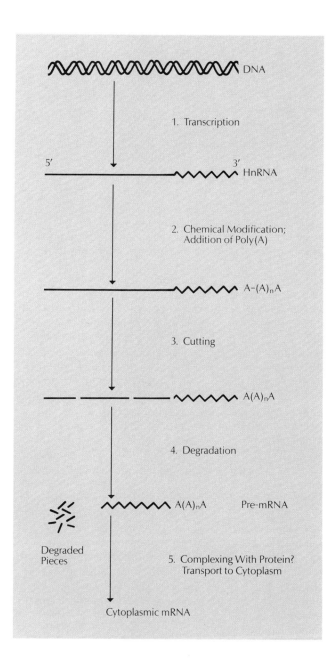

1. Transcription

5'   3' HnRNA

2. Chemical Modification;
Addition of Poly(A)

A-(A)$_n$A

3. Cutting

A(A)$_n$A

4. Degradation

A(A)$_n$A   Pre-mRNA

Degraded
Pieces

5. Complexing With Protein?
Transport to Cytoplasm

Cytoplasmic mRNA

200 adenine nucleotides to one end! The synthesis of this long **poly(A)** tail is an enzymatic reaction. In other words, it is not simply a continuation of transcription, for there are no DNA sequences coding for these tails. It is not clear what purpose such poly(A) tails serve (*Interleaf 20.2*); the best guess is that they help control gene expression by preventing subsequent degradation of molecules destined to function as messenger molecules.

In the next step in the processing of HnRNA, the molecule is rapidly cut into pieces, and most of it is immediately destroyed in the nucleus where it has just been made. Only a tiny fraction of the HnRNA lasts more than a few minutes, and that fraction manages to escape to the cytoplasm and act as messenger. This destruction within the nucleus is clearly selective. It can be shown that many sequences present in HnRNA are never found in the cytoplasm as messengers.

An important question is this: Can one molecule of HnRNA ever provide more than one molecule of messenger? In theory, the HnRNA molecule could be cut to produce more than one messenger molecule. But there is as yet no evidence for this process. In developing red blood cells, the hemoglobin messenger is originally transcribed in a long molecule of the HnRNA type. Each HnRNA molecule appears to contain only a single copy of the hemoglobin message; this section of the molecule is preserved while the rest is destroyed.

What is the nature and what is the meaning of the rest of the HnRNA molecule? One possible insight comes from the fact that much of the RNA that is transcribed and then destroyed is coded for by DNA sequences that are repeated many times. But most of the sequences that are preserved to function as messengers are coded for by DNA sequences that occur only twice per diploid cell! As discussed in *Interleaf 17.2*, every eukaryotic cell contains many families of DNA sequences that are repeated hundreds or thousands of times per diploid cell. It is now known that such sequences are not clustered in one spot. They are scattered through the chromosomes, interspersed with unique sequences that occur only once per haploid cell or twice per diploid cell. Because these redundant sequences appear to be transcribed even though their transcripts are rapidly destroyed, several investigators believe these redundant sequences have a role in controlling the transcription process. Their theories (one of which is outlined in Figure 20.19) are built on the basic assumption that redundant sequences are "start" signals for transcribing messages of related function and are not in themselves codes for proteins. Thus, once they have been transcribed, the transcripts of these regions can be destroyed while the adjacent messenger that they caused to be produced is preserved and

(text continues on page 466)

Interleaf 20.2

The Puzzle of Poly(A)

Few aspects of eukaryotic nucleic acid structure and metabolism seem easier to study than the poly(A) tails of messenger RNA and heterogeneous nuclear RNA. Yet few cellular entities have remained as mysterious.

A simple method is available for isolating poly(A)-containing molecules. A cellular extract is exposed to man-made poly(U) or poly(T) molecules that have been immobilized by attachment to some solid surface. Under conditions in which double-helix formation occurs, poly(A)-containing molecules will be bound specifically. Then, after everything else has been washed away, the poly(A)-containing molecules can be released in pure form by application of heat in order to break the hydrogen bonds between the two polymers.

Moreover, an inhibitor is available that selectively prevents poly(A) addition to RNA molecules. The inhibitor is 3'-deoxyadenosine, which lacks the 3' —OH group through which successive nucleotides are normally linked in a nucleic acid chain. Therefore, when a 3'-deoxyadenosine is added to a chain, no further groups can be added. Because of differences in the enzymes involved in linking the nucleotides, poly(A) addition to RNA is much more readily inhibited by this adenosine analogue than is the original transcription of the RNA.

Thus 3'-deoxyadenosine can be added readily to cells, and the effects of preventing poly(A) additions can easily be observed.

Certain aspects of poly(A) metabolism are now generally agreed upon. Poly(A) is added to the 3' end of HnRNA molecules in the nucleus by an enzyme other than the RNA polymerase involved in transcription. There is no poly(T) sequence in the DNA coding for the poly(A) tails. On the average, about 200 adenine nucleotides are added to each molecule. The portion of the molecule adjacent to the poly(A) tail has a better chance of surviving than more distant parts of the HnRNA during the processing of HnRNA to produce messenger RNA. New mRNA molecules in the cytoplasm also have a tail of about 200 nucleotides. But as these molecules function as messengers, the tail gradually becomes shortened by one-half or more. In many cell types, inhibition of poly(A) addition with 3'-deoxyadenosine prevents the appearance of new types of proteins that would otherwise have appeared. The existence of poly(A) tails is so widespread and regular in the plant and animal kingdoms that it is impossible to deny its functional significance in the gene action system. But *what* that function is, is a puzzle, to say the least.

Perhaps the most perplexing observation made to date is that even though all other messengers seem to possess poly(A) tails, one class of messengers—the ones that code for histones—does not. This observation is at once comforting and disturbing. It is reassuring to know that if the cell selectively adds tails to some RNA molecules but not to others, there must be some functional significance to the process. At the same time, however, whatever purpose poly(A) serves, we must explain why histone messenger RNA molecules are an exception!

Again, poly(A) is added in the nucleus and then is preferentially conserved in molecules that escape degradation and are passed to the cytoplasm. Therefore, the poly(A) tail may serve as a marker for the nuclear enzymes—identifying which sequences are to be preserved and utilized. But several observations contradict this suggestion. First, histone messages *do* escape degradation and escape the nucleus without such a marker. Second, not *all* of the poly(A) made in the nucleus and not *all* of the adjacent RNA sequences escape the degradative enzymes of the nucleus. Third—and most importantly—it has now been shown that poly(A) addition goes on in the cytoplasm *as well as* in the nucleus! In fact, it appears that from the time messenger RNA exits the nucleus it is subjected to enzymes that delete subunits from the tail and to enzymes that add adenine nucleotides back on. These two processes apparently reach equilibrium when the tail becomes about 50 to 100 nucleotides long. If poly(A) has only a nuclear function, why should enzymes exist in the cytoplasm that continue to delete from and add to the poly(A) sequence?

Two lines of experimentation suggest that presence or absence of a poly(A) tail may be important in regulating translation of the message. Isabel and Dennis Slater showed that in the cytoplasm of unfertilized sea urchin eggs, inactive messenger RNA molecules exist that lack poly(A). Upon fertilization, these molecules have a tail added and they become translated. In a parallel system, Virginia Walbot studied the role of poly(A) addition in the germination of cotton seeds. Like sea urchin embryos, cotton seeds had been known from the studies of Leon Dure to have a supply of masked messengers (Chapter 18) that became activated at one of the early steps in germination. Walbot showed that if 3'-deoxyadenosine was added to the germination medium, the two critical enzymes required for germination were not made and germination of the seeds did not occur. Inhibitors of RNA transcription had no such effect. She concluded that a poly(A) tail was required before the messengers for these two enzymes could be translated. But if poly(A) is required for translation, how are histone messenger RNA molecules translated?

Another suggestion concerning the role of poly(A) came from the observation that the mean length of the tails always tends to dwindle in the cytoplasm. It was suggested that the poly(A) tail served to protect the messenger RNA from degradative enzymes in the cytoplasm. It was once suggested that the tail served like a commuter's ticket, being shortened (punched) every time a ribosome passed over it; when all the tail was gone this might signal the end of the useful life of the molecule. Two considerations seemed to argue against the role of the tail in messenger stability. First, if a poly(A) tail is required to escape degradation, how do histone messengers escape degradation? Second, studies from Robert Perry's laboratory seemed to indicate quite clearly that the probability of messenger RNA molecules being degraded in the cytoplasm was identical for new molecules with long tails and older ones with shorter tails.

But a recent and dramatic experiment has revived the theory that poly(A) may play an important role in regulation of the life span of a messenger RNA molecule. Following the lead of John Gurdon, who had previously experimented with injections of messenger RNA into oocytes, G. Huez and G. Marbaix isolated the messenger RNA coding for hemoglobin from developing rabbit cells. They split the sample in half. From one half they removed the poly(A) tail with a specific enzyme that left the messenger molecule itself untouched. The poly(A) tail of the other sample was left intact. Then the two different samples were injected separately into toad oocytes. In the first hour they found no difference in the rate of hemoglobin production in the two batches of oocytes. But after an hour, the rate began to fall in the oocytes containing tailless messenger RNA—but it remained high for two days in oocytes injected with intact messenger RNA. The inference is that the "detailed" messenger RNA molecules were degraded more rapidly than the intact molecules. Further evidence for such a role for poly(A) comes from recent observations that all histone messengers are destroyed at one particular point in each cell cycle, whereas other messengers are not.

As this is written, poly(A) is still an enigma. Whether poly(A) will be found to have a single function or (as now seems more likely) several functions is uncertain. But many expect that when the puzzle is finally solved, we will have taken a large step forward in our understanding of how eukaryotic cells control expression of their genes in time and space.

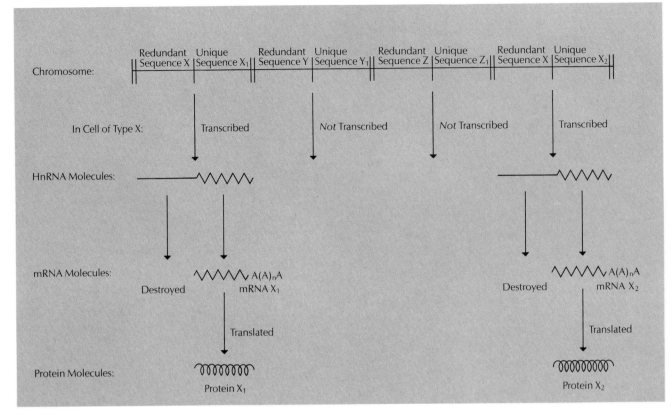

Figure 20.19 *A highly speculative model for regulation of transcription by redundant (highly repeated) sequences. In this scheme, sequences from each repetitive family are visualized as being adjacent to genes of the unique class that code for proteins needed by one particular cell type. By initiating transcription wherever a sequence of one particular type occurs, the cell would produce mRNAs and then proteins of related function. Once transcription was complete, the RNA coded by the redundant sequence would be destroyed; the adjacent messenger region of the transcript would be preserved. Much more complex models built on this general theoretical plan have been proposed.*

used. Such models have not yet been validated or invalidated. However, it seems reasonably certain that such models cannot account for *all* the selective processing that occurs in the nucleus. Some unique sequences also are destroyed.

Once all this nuclear processing is completed, the messenger molecule is passed to the cytoplasm, often (perhaps always) in association with some kind of protein. Whether transport across the nuclear envelope to the cytoplasm is controlled in a selective manner is not known. But it is clear that the process of controlling gene expression is by no means completed as the messenger exits to the cytoplasm.

TRANSLATIONAL CONTROLS REGULATE GENE EXPRESSION IN EUKARYOTES

An unfertilized sea urchin egg is capable of synthesizing proteins, but it does so at a low rate. Once the egg is fertilized or activated, the pace of protein synthesis picks up rapidly. The acceleration does not require synthesis of RNA (Chapter 18); protein synthesis occurs on messengers long since transcribed, processed, and passed to the cytoplasm. Yet despite the existence of functional ribosomes and all the other necessary ingredients of protein synthesis, these messengers were not translated at once. They were "masked" in the dormant egg and are "unmasked" as a result of fertilization. The unmasking does not occur all at once. The pattern of protein production changes predictably after fertilization, even in the absence of new RNA synthesis. Thus it appears that unmasking is not an "all or none" process but another point for selective control.

The surprise for biologists who set out to apply *E. coli* models of gene regulation to eukaryotes was that translational control exerts a strong influence on development in eukaryotes. (Translational controls are not unknown in bacteria, but they apparently play only a minor role.) *In system after system, it appears that a major means of regulating the differential expression of genes in eukaryotes is the controlled utilization of messenger RNA.* How soon will it be used? How fast? How long? All of these processes appear to be under *selective* control.

For example, in the synthesis of hemoglobin to form red blood cells, all of these processes appear to be controlled (in addition to nuclear controls over transcription and processing). In the early stage of embryonic development of a chick, the globin messenger RNA appears in the cytoplasm hours before it begins to be expressed. (*"When" is controlled.*) The rate at which the globin (protein) part of hemoglobin is synthesized is carefully balanced with the rate at which the heme (nonprotein) part is available. Heme inactivates an inhibitor that selectively inhibits globin synthesis. (*"How fast" is controlled.*) When the globin messenger RNA begins to be read, the cell contains many other messages that are also being translated. But all these other messages are destroyed in the cytoplasm of the developing cell even as the hemoglobin message is carefully preserved. As a result of this selective protection, the cell reaches the point that 95 percent of the protein being synthesized is hemoglobin. (*"How long" is controlled.*)

The molecular nature of all these translational controls is still being explored. Their existence and importance in eukaryotic cellular control is clear. The advantages of translational control are also clear. It is a way of "preprogramming" a cell so that it sits, like a loaded firearm, ready to rapidly discharge once triggered. It is, essentially, a way for the cell to plan ahead.

POSTTRANSLATIONAL CONTROLS ALSO REGULATE GENE EXPRESSION

We cannot consider a gene to be expressed until its product has become functional and begins to affect the phenotype of the cell. If all the steps leading to protein synthesis are complete and if the resultant protein is inactive, the gene is for all intents and purposes unexpressed. Certain digestive enzymes are known to be produced in an inactive form; in this way they do not attack the cells in which they are made. They only become functional when they are dumped into the digestive tract, where they become attacked by other digestive enzymes. Only after a piece of their structure has been digested do these enzymes become active. It was once thought that this situation was unique, related to the special role of these proteins. It is now clear that many proteins are made in an inactive state. For example, insulin (the hormone that controls the passage of glucose from the blood into muscle and certain other cells) is made in a form that is totally inactive. This pre-insulin molecule consists of one polypeptide chain looped back on itself. In order to become active, the loop region in the middle of the polypeptide chain must be digested away, leaving the two ends bound together in the form that functions as a hormone.

Perhaps the most dramatic case of posttranslational control of gene expression came to light through the work of David Sonneborn and others on a water mold called *Blastocladiella*. This organism spends part of its life cycle as a flagellum-bearing, motile, oval-shaped single cell incapable of growth or division. Suddenly, upon receiving an appropriate cue from the watery environment, it settles down in one spot, reels in its flagellum, rounds up, rearranges all of its intracellular organelles, synthesizes a rigid cell wall—and begins an entirely new way of life as a nonmotile, growing organism. Now the amazing thing is this: *virtually all of these transformations occur in the absence of any detectable synthesis of new proteins!* Preexisting but inactive proteins are activated; preexisting cell organelles are rearranged and many new genes of *Blastocladiella* are expressed for the first time—but all in the absence of either RNA or protein synthesis.

As dramatic as this example is, it is far from a unique case of extensive posttranslational control in the living world. For example, in many cases it has been shown that the protein subunits of microtubules and microfilaments (Chapter 13) are preformed in cells for some time *before* extensive changes occur in cell shape or cell motility. And often the changes in the cell environment that are needed to set them in motion appear to be subtle. But the effects of such controlled gene expression acting at the last possible step are often profound.

There is another form of posttranslational control over gene expression that appears to be important in eukaryotes. *This control involves rapid and selective destruction of enzymes before they can be used but after the cell has gone to all the trouble (and energy expenditure) of making them!* For example, several enzymes required for destroying particular amino acids whenever they are present in excessive numbers seem to be controlled (at least partially) by this mechanism in the vertebrate liver. The messenger RNA is produced and translated more or less continuously, but the product is *selectively* destroyed by a mechanism that is controllable. When the enzyme is needed, the rate of enzyme destruction appears to fall, and the relevant gene is "expressed." It is not known what selective advantage can possibly compensate for such a profligate expenditure of "unnecessary" energy. But as someone once said, "Life does not come as clean as we would prefer."

In summary, there are many steps between genotype and phenotype. Each step offers a point for possible regulation. And it begins to appear that in complex organisms, where control is possible, control exists.

PERSPECTIVE

The demands imposed on *E. coli* by selective forces operating in the intestinal tract are relatively simple: grow and divide. If building blocks essential for growth are lacking, make them. But if those building blocks are available from the outside, waste no time or energy on their synthesis. If unusual sugars are the only energy source provided, be prepared to use them. But if glucose is available, ignore other sugars. But above all, grow and divide. Thus maintain your place in the gut.

These demands have been met through the evolution of control circuits that are simple and logical. If amino acid X is missing in the diet, enzymes are rapidly synthesized that will produce it from simpler substances abundant in the cell. But if X appears from the outside, the picture changes. It combines at once with the first enzyme in the pathway leading to its synthesis; it elicits an allosteric change in that enzyme's shape; it distorts the active site so that it will not bind substrate—and thus it shuts off the flow of energy metabolites into the pathway. This interaction boosts the amount of energy available for other aspects of growth. At the same time, other molecules of the amino acid bind to a specific regulator protein, which changes its shape. With this change in shape, the regulator protein now binds to the corresponding operator gene and blocks RNA polymerase from reading the structural genes coding for the enzymes involved in its synthesis.

And once again there is a sizable savings in energy, which can be channeled into more rapid cellular growth. The controls over catabolic pathways are equally logical and simple. A sugar, such as lactose, can combine with its corresponding regulator protein and open up its operon for transcription. But transcription of such operons occurs if—and only if—glucose is not present in sufficient quantity to maintain rapid growth. If enough glucose is available, cyclic AMP is not, and therefore catabolic operons cannot be read. Thus the cell never synthesizes these catabolic enzymes unless the growth of the cell depends on it!

Viewing such control mechanisms in "lowly" *E. coli,* biologists optimistically set out to solve the riddles of control in the development of complex eukaryotes. If control mechanisms in *E. coli* were so logical, would mechanisms in, say, *Homo sapiens* be less so? The expressed hope was to find "the mechanism" by which differential expression of genes in time and space occurs in developing eukaryotes. But what has been found is not just a simple variation on the *E. coli* theme, nor an absence of detectable controls. Instead there is a profusion of controls! It seems that in one system or another, every step that might be controlled is controlled. And many of the controls of eukaryotic gene expression might be considered quite illogical from our *present* perspective. Ten times as much RNA is transcribed as is ever used as messenger RNA—the rest is rapidly destroyed. Some proteins are synthesized only to be actively degraded because they were not needed in the first place.

Why should these activities exist? If the nature of the gene action system is fundamentally the same in all cells, why should we not expect the control of gene action to be similar from cell to cell, also? Perhaps this assumption would have been valid if it were true that *E. coli* represents some sort of primitive, unevolved organism and that its control systems are equally primitive. *But E. coli has been living in and adapting to the mammalian intestine for perhaps a hundred billion generations.* And over the course of time it has been continuously molded by natural selection to be attuned to both the certainties and the uncertainties of its environment. Thus, its control network represents a highly specialized, highly evolved system that suits it for one particular life style—rapid and *reversible* response to changes in available nutrients. But the control problems of developing eukaryotic cells are very different. Whereas an *E. coli* cell must be prepared to respond the same way time and time again to any particular set of environmental conditions, a cell in a developing eukaryote must be capable of modifying its response to a particular signal in a manner that reflects its past history.

Confront two *E. coli* cells of the same genetic make-up with a defined environmental set of conditions and they will both respond identically, regardless of any differences in past history. But confront two metazoan cells of identical genetic composition with the same stimulus and they may respond in exactly opposite ways. For example, if a piece of jelly that contains thyroxin (the hormone that induces metamorphosis from larval to adult stage) is implanted in the brain of a frog, one brain cell will enlarge and differentiate, but the cell right beside it will atrophy and die. If a piece of back skin and a piece of tail skin from a tadpole come in contact with this same hormone in a culture dish, the back skin begins to synthesize new skin proteins with renewed vigor—but the tail skin produces nothing but the enzymes required to destroy skin proteins!

In effect, every cell in a developing eukaryote carries a road map and a watch—it has a record of where it is and what time it is. It determines its responses on the basis of where it has been and what it has previously been through. Obviously its control circuitry must be more complex than that of a cell whose survival depends not on remembering what has gone before but rather on always giving the same response when the conditions are the same.

Thus modern biologists have come face to face with a fact of life that is at once frustrating and exhilarating. In viewing multicellular eukaryotes in the "premolecular age," it appeared that control of their development was quite complex. With the elucidation of the simple control circuits of prokaryotes, it appeared that perhaps the complexity of eukaryotes was more apparent than real. *But as time goes on, it becomes increasingly clear that the complexity of multicellular plants and animals is more real than was apparent.* While initially a disappointment, this realization has given many a new appreciation of the fundamental beauty of the properties inherent in that first shapeless mass of self-reproducing matter that appeared on the earth's surface. For it now is clear that the greatest mystery of life is that it is understandable at all.

SUGGESTED READINGS

BAUTZ, E. K. F. "Regulation of RNA Synthesis," *Progress in Nucleic Acid Research and Molecular Biology*, 12 (1972), 129. A comprehensive yet engagingly written summary of transcriptional regulation by one of that rare breed of scientists who write as well as they research.

BECKWITH, JONATHAN B., and DAVID ZIPSER (eds.). *The Lactose Operon.* Cold Spring Harbor, N.Y.: Cold Spring Harbor Laboratory, 1970. A collection of papers presenting the lac operon as it stood in 1970. Formidable reading, but good for both the perspective provided and the wealth of experimental evidence.

DARNELL, JAMES E., WARREN R. JELINEK, and GEORGE R. MOLLOY. "Biogenesis of mRNA: Genetic Regulation in Mammalian Genes," *Science*, 181 (1973), 1215. A detailed yet readable account of the posttranscriptional processing of nuclear RNA to messenger RNA in mammalian systems, with emphasis on the nature of heterogeneous nuclear RNA, models for mRNA formation, and speculation on the possible significance of the ubiquitous poly(A) tracts.

JACOB, FRANÇOIS, and JACQUES MONOD. "Genetic Regulatory Mechanisms in the Synthesis of Proteins," *Journal of Molecular Biology*, 3 (1961), 318–356. The classic paper that introduced to the biological world both the concept of messenger RNA and the operon model of genetic regulation. Not easy reading in any sense, but a must for anyone really interested in the origins of much of our current thinking about regulatory mechanisms.

STEIN, GARY S., THOMAS C. SPELSBERG, and LEWIS J. KLEINSMITH. "Nonhistone Chromosomal Proteins and Gene Regulation," *Science*, 183 (1974), 817. A readable account of the possible roles that nonhistone chromosomal proteins may play in the specific regulation of gene transcription in eukaryotes, as seen by three young investigators in the field.

WATSON, JAMES D. *The Molecular Biology of the Gene.* 2nd ed. Menlo Park, Calif.: W. A. Benjamin, 1970. Truly a classic in its own time, Watson's overview of what it means to be a gene represents the single best and most inclusive reference for many of the topics of this chapter.

Chapter 21

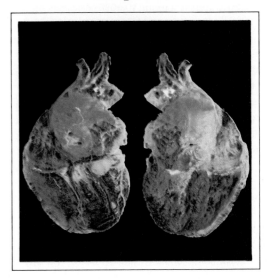

Vertebrate Regulation and Control

In proportion as we ascend the scale of living beings, the organism grows more complex, the organic units become more delicate and require a more perfected internal environment. The circulating liquids, the blood serum and the intraorganic fluids all constitute the internal environment. C. Bernard

More than a century ago, Claude Bernard perceived that the living cells of a vertebrate body are bathed in their own isolated and stable internal environment. Even when external conditions change dramatically, an organism can maintain the specific composition of this internal environment and thereby remain alive. How does it do this? A vertebrate has organs and organ systems that take part in maintaining the *milieu intérieur* described by Bernard. And to keep things in good working order, it has homeostatic feedback mechanisms of various sorts. In this chapter we will consider a few of the regulatory parts and processes of that all-time favorite organism for study—ourselves—and thereby gain some idea of how remarkably intricate regulation is for vertebrates in general.

BLOOD AND INTERSTITIAL FLUIDS MAKE UP OUR INTERNAL ENVIRONMENT

How much water is there inside a human body? Bernard approached this question in a somewhat unorthodox manner: He weighed Egyptian mummies and compared their weight with the weight of live humans of about the same size. The human body, he concluded, had to be 90 percent water. He was wrong. Today, modern (albeit less dramatic) measuring techniques include introducing radioactive water into the bloodstream and measuring the extent to which the water is diluted by the nonradioactive water of the body. Through such methods we now know that as much as 66 percent of the body is water—which is still an impressive amount!

But not all the water in the human body is found in the fluid we call the "internal environment." To prove this, we can inject a substance such as salt containing radioactive chloride ions into our bloodstream, which barely penetrates the cells. When we do so, we find the substance is diluted far less than one that can penetrate cells. Such methods indicate that nearly two-thirds of the body water is *intracellular* (inside cells), and the remaining body water is *extracellular.*

By doing one further experiment, we can "subdivide" the internal environment still further. If we inject into the bloodstream a sample of labeled blood cells (which cannot leave the blood vessels), we can determine how much of the extracellular water is **blood plasma**—the protein-containing fluid found in blood vessels. Surprisingly, perhaps, the plasma represents less than one-fifth of the extracellular water. The rest is largely a thin film lying between the blood vessels and the cells, penetrating all the tiny spaces between cells, and bathing and lubricating them. This fluid compartment is called the **interstitial fluid** (Figure 21.2). *Together, the blood plasma and the interstitial fluid make up the internal environment.*

Plasma and Interstitial Fluid Are in Equilibrium

There are major differences between intracellular and extracellular fluids (Figure 21.3), but there is relatively little difference between the interstitial fluids and the blood plasma. Except for differences in protein (and compensating differences in cations, or positively charged ions), the plasma and interstitial fluid are virtually identical. In fact, materials other than proteins are free to move between them. The main point of exchange is in the system of thin-walled blood vessels, called **capillaries,** that lie between arteries and veins throughout the body. Capillary walls are a flattened, single layer of cells. This layer is a selective filter, permitting the free passage of small molecules but preventing movement of the large protein molecules from the blood vessels. In this way, the difference in protein concentration between plasma and interstitial fluid is maintained.

Because the concentration of solids is higher in plasma than it is in interstitial fluid, it follows that the concentration of water is lower in plasma. For that reason, water molecules tend to flow down the concentration gradient from interstitial fluid to plasma. Such movement of water across a membrane from an area of high concentration to low concentration is called **osmosis.** The tendency for such

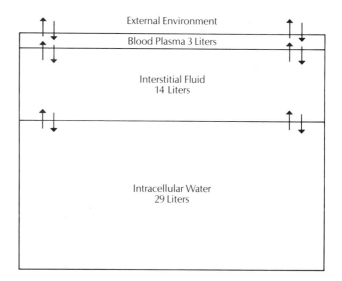

Figure 21.2 The relative volumes of the three major fluid compartments of an average 70 kilogram human being. It is by continuous, controlled exchange of materials at the interfaces between the various compartments that the intracellular compartment is maintained in a condition compatible with life.

Part of the intracellular water is suspended in the blood plasma in the form of approximately 2 liters of blood cells that travel through the circulatory system with the plasma (blood = plasma + cells). Thus, these cells are bathed directly by the plasma.

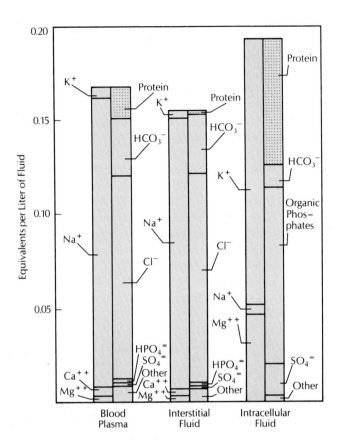

Figure 21.3 The major ionized constituents dissolved in the three main fluid compartments of the human body. The left half of each bar indicates the concentration of cations (positively charged ions); the right half indicates the concentration of balancing anions (negatively charged ions). Concentrations are given in equivalents per liter (which is molarity of ions multiplied by charge per ion) in order to demonstrate that each compartment is essentially neutral in terms of electric charge. The main difference between the plasma and the interstitial fluid is the concentration of protein.

point at which osmotic pressure *exceeds* hydrostatic pressure—and fluid flows back into the blood. Overall, then, *the equilibrium established between plasma and interstitial fluid is simply the sum of two equal but opposite movements of fluid.*

This flow results in much greater mixing of the contents of the two compartments than would occur by simple diffusion across the capillary wall as the blood goes shooting past. Nevertheless, diffusion also occurs. As a nutrient such as glucose is used up by the cells in an area, its concentration falls in the interstitial fluid. And as blood carrying higher concentrations of glucose passes by, the glucose diffuses out of the capillary (from regions of high concentration to low). Similarly, waste products that are in high concentration in the interstitial fluid will diffuse into the blood, where the concentration of these products is lower. Even so, the two-way bulk flow resulting from pressure differences along the capillary enhances such movement.

Blood Volume Is Regulated by Flow Between Interstitial Fluid and Plasma

In the tissue fluid–capillary wall–plasma system just described, any given state of overall equilibrium will be maintained only if the underlying forces of osmotic pressure and hydrostatic pressure do not change. Whenever either of these forces is altered, there will be a net flow of fluid from one compartment to the other until a new equilibrium is reached. For example, if you were to increase your blood volume by drinking a quantity of water, hydrostatic pressure will be slightly increased and osmotic pressure slightly decreased. Fluid will flow from plasma to tissue until the forces are balanced once more. Because the tissue fluid compartment is much larger than the plasma compartment, most of the added water will become tissue fluid, and the original blood volume will be restored. Similarly, blood volume is maintained during dehydration and is restored following hemorrhage by changes in hydrostatic pressure as

movement produces a measurable pressure on the membrane, which is called **osmotic pressure.** In the human body, however, *net* water movement does not regularly occur because the fluid in the capillaries is under a different kind of pressure: physical **hydrostatic pressure** created by the pumping action of the heart. The hydrostatic pressure tends to drive water out from the capillary and into the interstitial spaces. Thus, an overall dynamic equilibrium is established across the capillary wall—the outward force resulting from hydrostatic pressure exactly balances the inward force of osmotic pressure, and there is no net movement of water for the system as a whole.

But the existence of an *overall* state of equilibrium does not necessarily imply an absence of any flow in any part of the system. Quite the contrary: flow exists in localized areas of the capillary bed, and it results in bidirectional bulk fluid exchange between blood and interstitial compartments. As blood enters a capillary, the hydrostatic pressure is relatively high—higher than the osmotic pressure difference. Thus fluid is forced out of the capillary and into the tissue. This movement has two effects. First, it reduces the volume of blood somewhat and thereby diminishes the hydrostatic pressure. Second, it concentrates the plasma proteins somewhat and thereby increases the magnitude of the osmotic pressure difference between blood and tissue fluid. Consequently, as the blood flows along the capillary, it reaches a it relates to blood volume. Any drop in blood volume leads to lower hydrostatic pressure, and fluid flows from tissue to plasma until the original volume is restored. The system is homeostatic: *Any change in blood volume alters plasma-tissue fluid equilibrium in such a way that, as a new equilibrium is approached, original blood volume is restored* (Figure 21.4). This homeostatic regulation is important, but it differs from many of those we will discuss in that it operates on a strictly physical basis and derives from the interaction of two opposing physical forces.

THE CIRCULATORY SYSTEM IS ESSENTIAL IN MAINTAINING THE INTERNAL ENVIRONMENT

The constancy of the interstitial fluid that bathes and maintains the cells clearly depends on the functioning of the **circulatory system**—the heart, blood vessels, and blood (Figure 21.5). Even though the fluid exchange between plasma and interstitial fluid operates on such physical principles of diffusion and pressure gradients, this exchange system cannot operate at all unless the heart itself is functioning, creating the vital flow of blood.

The Heart Is a Self-Activated Pump

The vertebrate **heart** is a muscular organ that pumps blood through the circulatory system. All the dynamic life proc-esses of the body are linked to its pulsating activity. From the time of its emergence in the developing embryo, it must beat regularly and continuously as long as the individual is alive—more than $2\frac{1}{2}$ *billion* contractions in seventy years!

Rhythmic contraction is intrinsic to **cardiac muscle** cells (the Greek *kardia* means "heart"). If the heart of a chick embryo is removed and separated into single cells, the cells beat independently as they grow on the bottom of a culture dish! When two such cells beating at different rates come into contact, they immediately establish a common pattern and beat together. And as more and more cells are added, all of them follow the pulsating pattern established by the strongest of them—the cells that will become the **pacemaker.** *Throughout life, such functional coordination, dependency on a pacemaker, and potential autonomy from outside signals characterizes the heart.* Isolated from the body, the heart of some vertebrates will continue beating rhythmically for days if it is bathed by a suitable nutrient-rich liquid.

What accounts for the heart's remarkable properties? Like other excitable cells (nerve cells, skeletal muscle cells, and so forth), cardiac muscle cells normally have a slight excess of negative charges on the interior. Therefore, the inside of the cell membrane is negatively charged with respect to the outside; the cell membrane is *polarized*. It is a loss of polarization of the membrane (a depolarization) due to positive charges leaking in that sets off the contraction

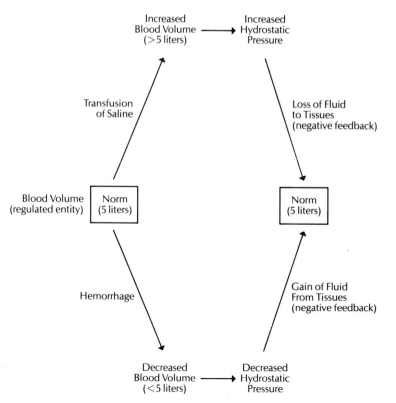

Figure 21.4 Regulation of blood volume. Such regulation is a specific example of the model of homeostasis given earlier in Figure 2.5.

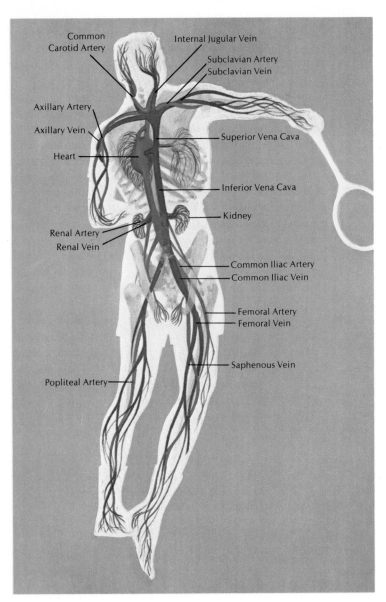

Figure 21.5 (left) The circulatory system of the human body. Capillaries are the small, thin-walled structures that form networks through which blood is brought in contact with all body elements. Nutrients and oxygen pass through capillary walls to reach nearby cells, and cellular products flow the other way into the blood, to be transported elsewhere in the body.

Figure 21.6 (right) The "syncytial" nature of cardiac muscle. Notice the intricate pattern of branching and fusion of cells. Although boundaries between cells can be seen ("intercalated disks"), the cells act as if no such boundaries exist. Hence, when one cell contracts, all cells contract.

Figure 21.7 (right) A representation of the mammalian (human) heart. Arrows show the direction of the blood flow. A = aorta; RA = right atrium; RV = right ventricle; LA = left atrium; LV = left ventricle; PA = pulmonary artery; PV = pulmonary vein; SA = sinoatrian node; AV = atrioventricular node; PF = Purkinje fibers. The numbers indicate the interval (in seconds) between activation of the sinoatrial node (pacemaker) and activation of various parts of the heart musculature.

mechanism, as described in Chapter 26. The basic contraction mechanism is the same as it is for skeletal muscles. But three unique features of cardiac muscle cells combine to give rise to the heartbeat. *First,* cardiac muscle cells do not require a nerve impulse to trigger depolarization and contraction, as skeletal muscles do. Instead, they have specialized "leaky" membranes that permit them to depolarize spontaneously—and thus to contract autonomously—after having been polarized for a given period of time. *Second,* the cells of the cardiac muscle are functionally interconnected into what acts like a syncytium (Chapter 13). In other words, changes in ion concentration in one cell are rapidly communicated to adjacent cells as if there were no boundary between them (Figure 21.6). When one cell

depolarizes, its neighbors do likewise—which accounts for the heart's coordinated contraction pattern. *Third,* after depolarization and contraction have occurred, cardiac muscle cells repolarize very slowly. All excitable cells must be repolarized after being depolarized; they are refractory (resistant) to further excitation until they are repolarized. But cardiac muscle cells have one of the slowest repolarizations known. Their prolonged refractory period assures a rhythmic pattern to the contraction. Sustained contraction of heart muscle would be fatal, of course, but properties of the cells work to prevent that from happening.

The mammalian heart is a marvel of evolutionary "engineering," and its gross organization helps to account for its effectiveness as a pump. Although it is derived from a

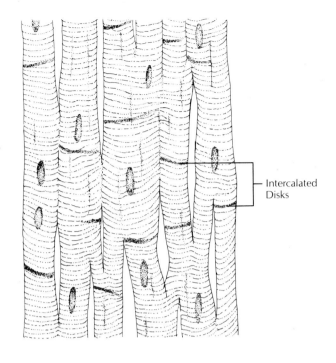

Intercalated Disks

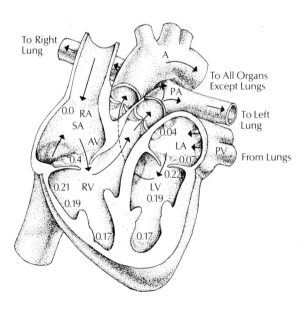

To Right Lung

A

To All Organs Except Lungs

PA

To Left Lung

0.0 RA
SA

0.04

LA

AV

0.07

PV

From Lungs

0.4

0.22

0.21 RV

0.19

LV
0.19

0.17

0.17

two-chambered tubular heart (Chapter 8), the mammalian heart actually is a double pump. The right side receives blood from the body and pumps it to the lungs; the left side receives blood from the lungs and pumps it to the body. Furthermore, it is not a linear heart like the organ from which it was derived: the mammalian heart has been partitioned into four chambers. Venous blood from the head and body enters the right receiving chamber, or **atrium.** It then enters the right pumping chamber, or **ventricle,** goes by way of pulmonary arteries to the lungs, and through pulmonary veins to the left atrium. From the left atrium, the blood enters the thick-walled, muscular left ventricle. From there it is pumped by way of the aorta to the arteries of the head and body. Backflow of blood in the heart is prevented by **atrioventricular valves** separating atria and ventricles, and by **semilunar valves** in the aorta and pulmonary artery (Figure 21.7).

Three features account for the efficiency of the mammalian heart. First, the fact that its right and left sides are separated by a partition does not mean that its two atria function separately, or that its two ventricles function separately. The two atria make up one syncytium, and the two ventricles another. Whenever any part of an atrium contracts, all atrial tissue contracts; the same goes for the ventricles. The contractions of the two syncytia are coordinated, but they are functionally separate. Second, one region of specialized cardiac tissue has a faster self-activating rhythm than any other part of the heart: the **sinoatrial node** located in the right atrium. Activity of the sinoatrial node determines beat frequency of the entire heart; thus it serves as the pacemaker mentioned earlier. Third, a special system of conducting fibers connects the atrial and ventricular syncytia. This system consists of the **atrioventricular node** and the associated **Purkinje fibers.** At the atrioventricular node, the spreading wave of activation is delayed by about 0.1 second. Then it is transmitted rapidly by the Purkinje fibers to all parts of the ventricles, which contract as a unit. Thus, contraction of the ventricles always follows the atrial contraction by about 0.1 second, and thereby enhances heart efficiency (Figure 21.8).

The heart functions as a pump in the circulatory system because its contraction puts pressure on the fluid contents of its chambers. The filling and emptying of those chambers is governed by changes of pressure within them, and the valves open and shut in response to differences in pressure across them. The cardiac cycle includes a relaxed "filling" period, called **diastole.** During diastole, blood flows from the systemic veins into the right atrium and from pulmonary veins into the left atrium; from there the blood moves on into the ventricles through open atrioventricular valves. The semilunar valves are held shut by blood pressure in the pulmonary arteries and aorta. Next, the atria contract,

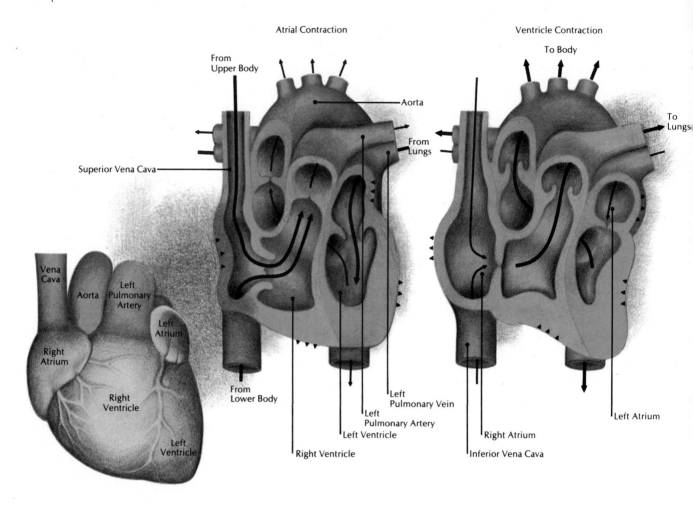

Atrial Contraction

Ventricle Contraction

From Upper Body

To Body

Aorta

From Lungs

To Lungs

Superior Vena Cava

Vena Cava

Aorta

Left Pulmonary Artery

Left Atrium

Right Atrium

Right Ventricle

Left Ventricle

From Lower Body

Right Ventricle

Left Ventricle

Left Pulmonary Artery

Left Pulmonary Vein

Right Atrium

Inferior Vena Cava

Left Atrium

forcing more blood into the ventricles. Contraction of the ventricles follows about 0.1 second later. This contraction phase of the cycle is called **systole.** Because of higher pressure in the ventricles, the atrioventricular valves snap shut, the semilunars open, and blood flows into the aorta and pulmonary arteries. As the ventricles start to relax, pressure in the arteries exceeds that in the ventricles, the semilunar valves snap shut, the atrioventriculars open, and the cycle starts all over again. When you listen through a stethoscope to a beating heart, the lubdub, lubdub . . . sounds you hear are the successive closings of the atrioventricular and semilunar valves.

Many Factors Participate in Homeostatic Regulation of Cardiac Output

Isolated from the body, a heart may continue to beat with a rhythm all its own. But that does not mean that its activity is not subject to any modulation to meet changing circumstances in the body. The volume of blood available to be pumped per stroke, the rate of contraction, and the strength of contraction can all be modified. Together these three factors determine **cardiac output:** the volume of blood pumped per minute.

An average individual (one who weighs about 70 kilograms) who is standing still has a heart rate in the range of seventy beats per minute. And on each beat, the ventricles may receive and pump about 70 milliliters of blood. This leads to a cardiac output of about 5 liters per minute in the resting state. *This means that under resting conditions, the volume of blood passing through the heart every minute is equal to the entire volume of blood in the circulatory system!* But under these conditions, the output of the heart is far from maximal. It is limited mainly by the extent to which the chambers fill during diastole. And this process in turn is limited by the rate of **venous return** (the rate at which blood returns from the body through the veins).

When you stand still, about half the blood in your body is in the nonmuscular veins. But when you do nothing more than twitch your leg muscles, the muscular contractions exert pressure on the vein walls. The contractions, working with the series of valves the veins possess (Figure 21.9),

Figure 21.8 (left)   The flow of blood through the human heart. Deoxygenated blood from the body flows through the right side of the heart and becomes oxygenated in the lungs. It then returns to the left side of the heart and is pumped to the body.

Triangles denote direction of movement of the heart walls. As the atria contract and the ventricles relax, the atrioventricular valves open and the semilunar valves close. This causes the ventricles to be filled. Then, as the ventricles contract and the atria relax, the semilunar valves open and the atrioventricular valves close. This causes the ventricles to empty and the atria to fill.

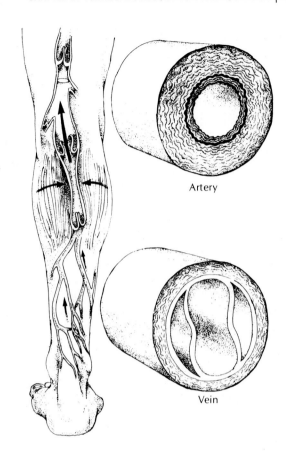

Artery

Vein

Figure 21.9 (right) Return of blood to the heart through the veins. Valves prevent the blood from flowing in the wrong direction, and muscular action serves to push the blood along. Arteries have thicker walls than do veins; they expand and contract with greater force to direct blood flow to tissues and organs.

cause a one-way flow of blood toward the heart. With increased venous return, the chambers fill more completely and *stroke volume* is increased. Thus, moderate exercise leads to increased cardiac output by simple physical means—without affecting the beat of the heart muscle. This is a feedback system in which the sensing element is the heart itself: increased return indicates increased demand, and output is increased by simple physical means. Each stroke becomes more efficient simply because the heart chambers are more completely filled.

When you exercise vigorously, a more involved feedback circuit is needed to regulate cardiac output. As long as the rate of venous return does not exceed the filling capacity of the heart (as it beats at the standard rate), pressure does not rise in the atria or the veins. But as soon as the body is exercised vigorously, blood begins to return faster than the heart can pump it, unless the beat speed is increased. This reaction causes the blood pressure to rise in the veins and right atrium. There, pressure sensors are triggered at once. They send impulses to the *medulla*, hindmost region of the brain (Chapter 25), where centers controlling heart rate are

located. The result is a change in the rate of impulses traveling from the brain to the heart. These impulses impinge on the pacemaker, changing its sensitivity. Because of the reflex triggered by rising venous pressure, the sensitivity of the pacemaker is raised and the heart beats more rapidly. The increased contraction rate leads to still further increase in cardiac output. Under vigorous exercise, both heart rate and stroke volume may be doubled, leading to a fourfold increase in cardiac output.

Under conditions where still more cardiac output is needed, the sympathetic nervous system (Chapter 25) and the adrenal medulla (Chapter 22) may both be called into play. The adrenal medulla releases the hormone epinephrine into the blood, and the sympathetic nervous system releases the related compound norepinephrine at nerve endings all over the surface of the heart. Together, these reflexes increase the forcefulness of contractions and thereby lead to more complete emptying of the heart on each stroke. It has been reported that a trained athlete, exerting short-term maximal effort, may achieve a cardiac output of 35 liters per minute! On the average, a blood cell in this case makes a circuit from the arteries, through the capillaries, back through the veins, through the right side of the heart, through the lungs, and back to the left side of the heart in about nine seconds.

Other reflex systems exist to monitor pH, oxygen and carbon dioxide levels in the blood, temperature, blood pressure in the arteries, and so on. Each of these systems feeds impulses from the receptors in blood vessel walls to the brain and elicits a reflex feedback effect on the heart, thereby changing cardiac output. And in each case, the resulting change in cardiac output tends to move the monitored parameter back toward the norm.

HOMEOSTASIS REQUIRES POINTS OF EXCHANGE WITH THE EXTERNAL ENVIRONMENT

As impressive as the speed and efficiency of the circulatory system may be, it would be of little use if the body were a closed system. Recirculating blood past tissues at a high rate would do little good if the blood returned with the same chemical composition as it had before it left. The plasma would soon be clogged with wastes and depleted of nutrients, the internal environment would lose the properties required by living cells, and the organism would die. It is only because of the existence of several exchange points

with the external environment, where wastes can be deposited and essential raw materials obtained, that the circulatory system functions to maintain the internal environment. Figure 21.10 depicts these exchange points.

Gas Exchange Occurs in the Lung

The mammalian **lung** is a much-divided sac that is central to respiration. Air passes through the *trachea,* through primary and secondary *bronchi,* and succeedingly fine *bronchioles,* which terminate in respiratory bronchioles lined with microscopic *alveoli* (Figure 21.11). The alveoli are in direct contact with pulmonary capillaries, and it is between alveoli and capillaries that gas exchange takes place. Why is it necessary to have such an elaborate subdivision of the lung sacs? Such elaboration vastly increases the respiratory surface of an organ that must fit into the relatively small space of the **thoracic cavity** (chest cavity) between the neck and the diaphragm.

Because mammalian lungs have only one passageway to the exterior, air must pass in one direction during inhalation and in the other direction during exhalation. This **tidal ventilation** of the lungs is the result of cyclic changes in the volume of the thoracic cavity, caused by contractions of the *intercostal muscles* (between the ribs) and the muscular

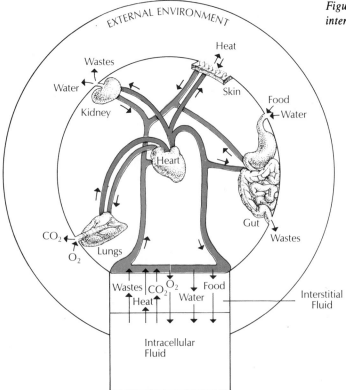

Figure 21.10 The major exchange points between internal and external environments.

Figure 21.11 The human respiratory system. General view (top); enlarged view of bronchioles terminating in the grapelike clusters of alveoli (lower left); further enlarged view of alveoli surrounded by a capillary network (lower right).

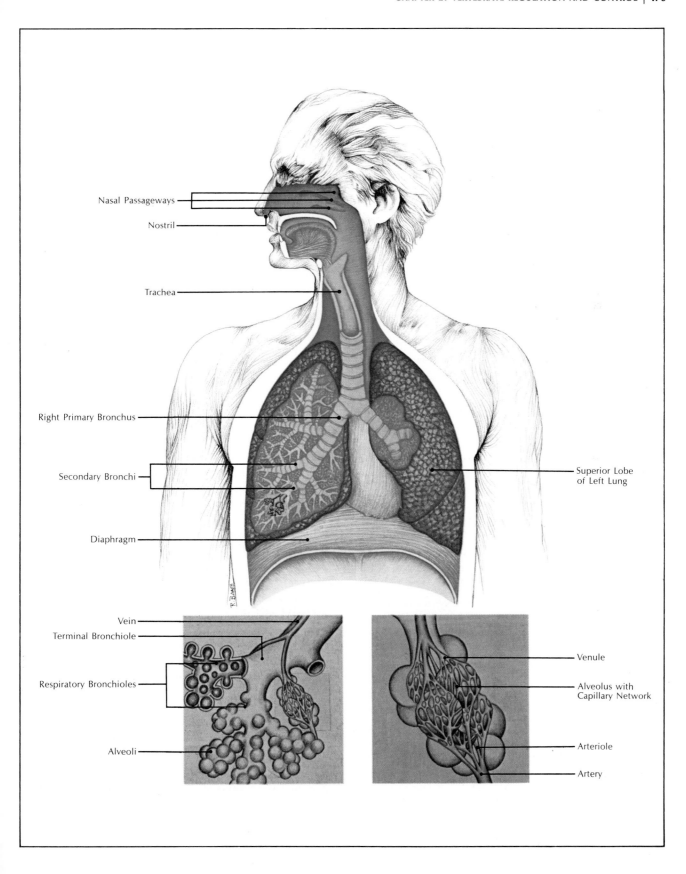

Nasal Passageways

Nostril

Trachea

Right Primary Bronchus

Secondary Bronchi

Diaphragm

Superior Lobe
of Left Lung

Vein

Terminal Bronchiole

Respiratory Bronchioles

Alveoli

Venule

Alveolus with
Capillary Network

Arteriole

Artery

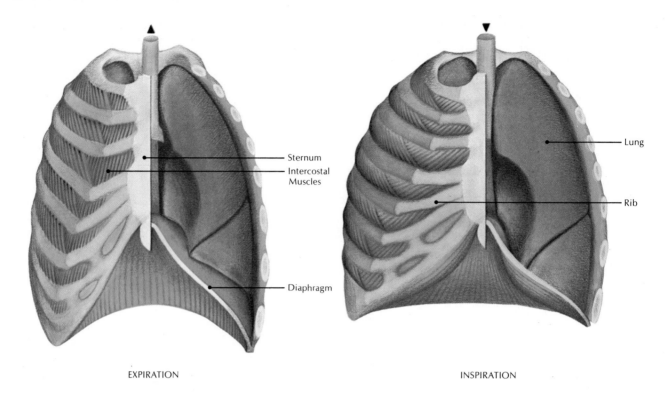

EXPIRATION   INSPIRATION

diaphragm that separates the thoracic cavity from the abdominal cavity (Figure 21.12).

A 70-kilogram human being in a resting state has a **tidal volume** of about 500 milliliters. In other words, each inhalation-exhalation cycle moves about 500 milliliters of air in and out of his body. However, there is about 3,000 milliliters of inspiratory reserve capacity and 1,100 milliliters of expiratory reserve (Figure 21.13). This gives a total **vital capacity** (maximum exchangeable volume) of about 4,600 milliliters. During exercise, some or all of the reserve capacity is used. (There is, however, a residual volume of gas that cannot be forced from the lung.)

Aside from the functional reserve of volume in the lungs, there is another reserve in the form of potential increases in ventilatory rate. During exercise, both tidal volume and rate of breathing usually increase. With a resting tidal volume of 500 milliliters and a ventilatory rate of twelve expansions per minute, the **minute respiratory volume** (volume of air exchanged per minute) would be about 6 liters. During sustained vigorous exercise, the ventilatory rate may increase to forty-five per minute and the tidal volume may at least double, to give a minute respiratory volume of more than 45 liters! During short periods of peak activity, minute respiratory volume may even be higher.

Although we can make short-term modifications to our rate and depth of breathing, ventilation is basically under the involuntary reflex control of a **respiratory center** in the medulla. This center contains neurons that stimulate the external intercostals and diaphragm during inhalation, and other neurons that activate the internal intercostals during exhalation. Stretch receptors in the lungs sense the changing state of expansion of the thoracic cavity and switch these two sets of neurons on and off in an oscillating fashion.

The concentration of certain substances in arterial blood influences the intensity of respiratory center signals to the lungs and the rate of alternation between inspiratory and expiratory impulses. Carbon dioxide level is probably the most influential factor in respiratory center activity. If this level increases above a given norm, ventilation of the lung increases and the carbon dioxide level returns toward the norm. If the level decreases, ventilation is inhibited and the concentration increases again. Oxygen concentration and pH of the blood also affect ventilatory volume, but they appear to be somewhat less important than carbon dioxide.

Oxygen and Carbon Dioxide Are Not Merely Dissolved in Blood

Before proceeding with a discussion of gas exchange between air and blood and between blood and tissue fluid, it is necessary to define the terms used to describe concentrations of gases in liquids. The pressure of a gas is usually given in terms of the height of a column of mercury that would be required to exert an equivalent pressure. At sea

Figure 21.12 Position changes in the diaphragm and rib cage during expiration and inspiration. During inhalation the external intercostals contract, raising and expanding the rib cage. At the same time, the diaphragm contracts, further enlarging the thoracic cavity. The lungs expand accordingly, and air is forced into them by atmospheric pressure. During exhalation, the external intercostals and diaphragm relax, contractions of the internal intercostals depress the rib cage, and the diaphragm returns elastically to its former shape. Pressure inside the lungs temporarily exceeds atmospheric pressure, and air leaves the lungs.

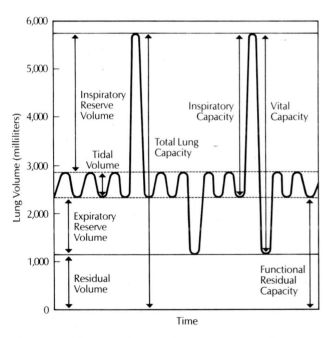

Figure 21.13 Diagram showing the respiratory excursions during normal breathing and during maximal inspiration and maximal expiration. The normal tidal volume uses little more than 10 percent of the lung's vital capacity. The remainder is a reserve that can be tapped in times of high oxygen demand.

level, our atmosphere exerts a pressure equivalent to that exerted by a column of mercury 760 millimeters high. Thus we say **atmospheric pressure** at sea level is 760 mm Hg (Hg is the chemical symbol for mercury). Because dry air is about 21 percent oxygen, and because equal volumes of all gases exert the same pressure at the same temperature, it follows that 21 percent of the atmospheric pressure is due to oxygen. Thus we may express the amount of oxygen present in sea level air as the **partial pressure of oxygen** (pO_2). It is simply $(760)(0.21) = 160$ mm Hg.

Now, if we were to expose a sample of blood plasma from which all gases had been removed to dry sea level air, oxygen molecules would begin to dissolve in the fluid. As the concentration of oxygen in the plasma increased, dissolved oxygen molecules would tend to leave the solution and return to the gas phase. Eventually, an equilibrium phase would be reached in which some oxygen molecules would be leaving the solution at the same rate others were dissolving, and there would be no further net change in dissolved oxygen concentration. We would then say that the plasma had an oxygen **tension** of 160 mm Hg. *The tension of a dissolved gas is given as the partial pressure of free gas with which it would be in equilibrium.* Now, although the plasma in this example has a tension of 160 mm Hg, it does not have the same *concentration* of oxygen as the gas phase with which it is in equilibrium. The concentration of oxygen in the gas phase is 21 percent. But because of the limited solubility of oxygen in water, the concentration in the plasma is nowhere near 21 percent. In fact, if we allowed equilibrium to be reached at the human body temperature of 38°C (solubility of gases in fluids decreases with increasing temperature), we would find that plasma with an *oxygen tension at 160 mm Hg would have an oxygen concentration of only 0.44 percent!* This is a miniscule amount.

Given the rates at which mammalian cells must be supplied with oxygen, we can quickly calculate that if oxygen were carried in the blood in simple solution, the flow rate of blood through the capillaries would have to be about fifty times the maximum rate that has ever been observed! When we calculate what would be required in terms of a larger heart, larger lungs, larger blood vessels, more blood—and so on—to achieve this kind of incredible blood flow, we can conclude that large, active, warm-blooded animals such as mammals could never have evolved in the absence of some mechanism more efficient than simple solution in the plasma for transporting oxygen.

In all vertebrates and many invertebrates, we find in the red blood cells the protein *hemoglobin,* which does the job of transporting most of the oxygen. In the human bloodstream, about 98.5 percent of the oxygen is carried by hemoglobin; only about 1.5 percent is carried in simple solution. Hemoglobin is a protein composed of four peptide

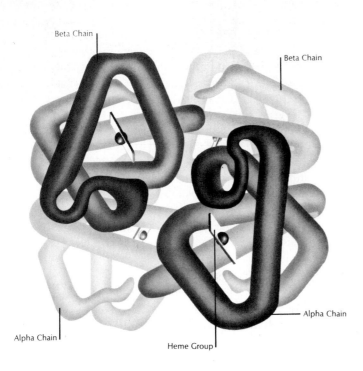

Beta Chain

Beta Chain

Alpha Chain

Alpha Chain

Heme Group

Figure 21.14 A highly schematic diagram of the organization of the hemoglobin molecule. The oxygen combines chemically with and is carried by the iron atom shown as a dark ball on the heme group. But subtle changes in the shape of the protein portions greatly affect the affinity of the iron atom for an oxygen molecule.

chains, two of a type called *alpha* and two of a type called *beta* (Figure 21.14). Each peptide chain bears an iron-containing nonprotein component called **heme,** which is capable of binding one molecule of oxygen in a reversible manner. Thus one hemoglobin molecule with its four hemes is capable of carrying four oxygen molecules.

When we add oxygen to a solution of hemoglobin and measure the amount that becomes bound to hemoglobin, we discover a curious phenomenon. At low oxygen tension, the hemoglobin combines with oxygen rather poorly. But if we double the pO_2, the amount of oxygen bound is more than doubled! This phenomenon is termed **cooperative binding:** The molecules ''cooperate'' to increase the affinity of the hemoglobin for oxygen (Figure 21.15). When the first oxygen molecule is bound, the affinity of the hemoglobin for oxygen rises. The reason is that each of the peptide chains may exist in two different shapes; the affinity for oxygen is markedly different between the two. The first oxygen is taken up slowly because all four peptide chains of each molecule are in the low-oxygen-affinity shape. But when oxygen becomes bound to the first heme, that peptide chain shifts to the oxygen-binding shape and is held there by the oxygen. The shape change in one chain increases the likelihood that adjacent chains within the molecule will shift also, because the number of peptide-peptide interactions is greatest when adjacent chains have the same shape. And as

soon as a second chain does shift, its affinity for oxygen rises dramatically.

What is the outcome of cooperative binding of oxygen? It makes hemoglobin far more effective in taking up and releasing oxygen than it would be if the binding curve were not S-shaped. As you will read shortly, both the pO_2 and the pCO_2 in the area affect the extent of oxygen binding or its release by hemoglobin. For the moment, however, consider how the pO_2 in the body affects oxygen binding by hemoglobin.

The pO_2 of dry atmospheric air is 160mm Hg. But by the time air reaches the alveoli of the lungs, it becomes saturated with water vapor and diluted by the unexpired air in the lungs, which is rich in carbon dioxide. As a result, the pO_2 in the alveoli normally is only about 100mm Hg. This is enough to saturate the hemoglobin with oxygen (Figure 21.15). (In evolutionary terms, this means that there has been no selective pressure favoring the development of mechanisms that would empty the lungs more completely. Even if the lungs were totally emptied and refilled on every breath—so that the pO_2 approached that of atmospheric air—the amount of oxygen picked up by the hemoglobin would be insignificant.)

When the blood reaches the tissues in the periphery of the body, the oxygen tension is reduced because oxygen has been used in cellular respiration (Chapter 14). An average value for the oxygen tension in the interstitial fluid of a resting individual is about 40mm Hg. By referring again to Figure 21.15, we can see that at this pO_2, the hemoglobin will give up about one-fourth of its oxygen. It has been calculated that if hemoglobin did not show cooperative oxygen binding, it would give up only about 3 to 5 percent of its oxygen at a pO_2 of 40mm Hg! *Thus, the cooperative binding curve results in a fivefold to eightfold increase in the amount of oxygen that can be delivered to the tissues by the hemoglobin molecule.*

Still, a release of only 25 percent of the oxygen seems quite inefficient. What happens to the remaining 75 percent? It serves largely as a reservoir, which may be tapped by tissues whenever they are called upon for extra effort. When a muscle is exercised vigorously, two changes occur. The increased rate of cellular respiration means that the muscle cells rapidly take up and use the oxygen of the interstitial fluid; thus the pO_2 in the area may fall from the normal value of about 40mm Hg to as low as 15mm Hg. At the same time, the carbon dioxide released from these rapidly metabolizing cells may raise the carbon dioxide of the interstitial fluid from its resting value of about 46mm Hg to as much as 60mm Hg. These two changes affect the release of oxygen from the blood arriving from the heart. As

Figure 21.16 shows, a rise in pCO_2 shifts the oxygen-binding curve of hemoglobin to the right, so that the hemoglobin gives up more oxygen at any given oxygen tension. This *rise* in pCO_2, combined with the *fall* in pO_2 in the interstitial fluid of the exercising tissue, means that each hemoglobin molecule discharges about 85 percent of its oxygen—not the 25 percent observed for the resting state. In other words, *in times of activity the hemoglobin molecule is capable of discharging more than three times as much oxygen per transit, so the cardiac output needed during exercise is three times lower than it is during the rest state.* Cardiac output may thus rise by as much as fivefold during vigorous exercise. When this is coupled with a greater than threefold increase in efficiency of oxygen release, the result is about a fifteenfold increase in oxygen delivery to the tissues per minute. Such an increase could not be accomplished by increased cardiac output alone.

How the blood transports carbon dioxide is another important aspect of this discussion. Is carbon dioxide dissolved in the plasma, or is it carried by hemoglobin? Carbon dioxide is more soluble in plasma than oxygen is, but its solubility is not enough to account for any more than 10 percent of the carbon dioxide transported. Carbon dioxide can bind to hemoglobin (to certain amino groups on

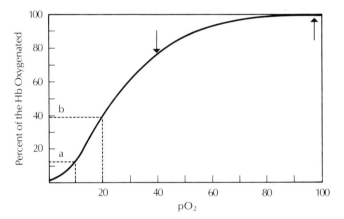

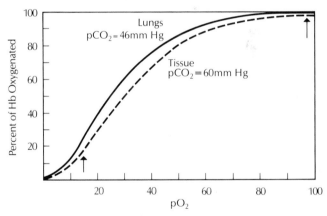

Figure 21.15 Oxygen binding curve of hemoglobin (Hb). Note the shape of the curve. At a partial pressure of oxygen (pO_2) of 10 percent, only 12 percent of the Hb is in the oxygenated form (a). But when the pO_2 is doubled, the percent Hb oxygenated rises over threefold to about 38 percent (b). This is what is known as cooperative binding. The first bound oxygen raises the affinity of the Hb molecule for additional oxygen molecules.

The arrows indicate the average pO_2 observed in the lungs (left arrow) and tissues (right arrow) of a resting individual. Thus it can be seen that hemoglobin becomes fully oxygenated in the lungs and discharges about one-fourth of its oxygen to the tissues under resting conditions.

Figure 21.16 The effect of exercise on oxygen uptake and release by hemoglobin. Despite intensive exercise, there is little change in the gas concentrations in the lungs (due to marked increases in minute respiratory volume). Thus hemoglobin continues to be fully oxygenated in the lungs (upper arrow). When the blood reaches the tissues, however, the elevated pCO_2 and lowered pO_2 combine to cause the hemoglobin to discharge most of its oxygen (lower arrow). Thus a single blood cell may deliver three times as much oxygen as it would to the resting tissue.

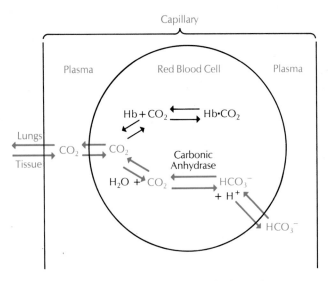

Figure 21.17 Carbon dioxide transport and release. In metabolizing tissues, the pCO_2 is higher in the interstitial fluid than in the plasma. Thus it diffuses into the blood vessel and then into the red blood cells. Here, a small proportion of the CO_2 may bind to hemoglobin, but most is converted to bicarbonate by the enzyme carbonic anhydrase. Most of the bicarbonate then leaves the cell and travels to the lungs, dissolved in the plasma. Because of the lower pCO_2 in the lungs, the CO_2 still dissolved in the blood diffuses outward, lowering the CO_2 tension in plasma and blood cells. Therefore all the reactions are pulled toward the left.

the polypeptide chains rather than to the heme iron where oxygen is carried), but this reaction does not account for any more than 20 percent or so of the amount transported. Most of the carbon dioxide that the tissues pick up is immediately converted by the blood to the highly soluble bicarbonate ion (HCO_3^-), and it is transported in that form. The bicarbonate ion is produced by the enzyme carbonic anhydrase, which exists in red blood cells:

$$CO_2 + H_2O \underset{\text{Anhydrase}}{\overset{\text{Carbonic}}{\rightleftharpoons}} HCO_3^- + H^+$$

Figure 21.17 summarizes these reactions. Although most of the gas is transported in some way other than simple solution, it is the *diffusion* of this dissolved gas that determines the extent to which the other transport mechanisms are formed or broken down. Under normal resting conditions, the blood yields 10 percent or less of its carbon dioxide to the air in the lungs (just as hemoglobin gives up only a fourth of its oxygen to resting tissues). But during strenuous exercise, changes in tissue pCO_2 levels and other factors may combine to increase efficiency of carbon dioxide transport as much as sixfold.

In each physiological aspect of the respiratory and circulatory system, then, the same theme is repeated. Under resting conditions, the system operates with relatively low efficiency. But the system reserves the capacity to increase the efficiency of the transport and exchange process when intracellular conditions demand. The signals eliciting this increased performance are few and simple—changes in concentrations of oxygen, carbon dioxide, changes in the volume of blood returning to the heart, and so on. But the responses range from simple physical events preprogrammed into the molecules (such as the increased dissociation of oxygen from hemoglobin) to complex neural reflex

arcs involving the control centers in the brain. Together the pieces fall into one coordinated feedback loop that adjusts supply to the momentary demands of the body.

ENERGY ENTERS THE HUMAN BODY THROUGH THE GUT

Without food molecules to oxidize, a ready supply of oxygen would be of little value to the system just described. To see how these molecules enter the human body, let us turn our attention to a different exchange point between internal and external environment: the gut.

An adult animal typically maintains a constant body weight over long periods even though food is regularly supplied to it. The obese animal and the obese human being are clearly exceptional cases in the evolutionary history of life. An increase in body weight is an inevitable consequence if energy (food) intake exceeds energy expenditure by even a small amount over a prolonged period. Therefore, the relative constancy of body weight in the mature animal implies a homeostatic control mechanism that carefully regulates food intake to energy expenditure. We recognize this phenomenon in ourselves in the contrasting sensations of hunger and satiation. Vigorous exercise or exposure to cold (both of which increase energy expenditure) normally lead to compensating increases in the amount of food consumed (if food is freely available). In contrast, organisms from sea anemones to humans tend to withdraw from food after having just completed a meal. The food item that would have elicited a flow of saliva or a vigorous feeding reaction just before a meal may elicit revulsion immediately after a heavy meal. There are many components to hunger and satiation. Studies in experimental animals show that many separate elements normally act in concert in controlling food intake but some of them can be dissected by careful experimental design.

One of the main factors controlling hunger is the level of glucose circulating in the blood. Manipulations that tend to elevate blood glucose suppress feeding behavior and food intake; manipulations that lower blood glucose levels stimulate feeding behavior. The cells that detect blood glucose levels and control hunger have been thought to reside in the brain region called the hypothalamus (Chapter 25). Certain chemical analogs of glucose appear to bind specifically to cells in this region and make them insensitive to glucose, resulting in overeating and obesity. But the control circuitry may be more complex than this observation implies. Rats that have these specific regions of the hypothalamus destroyed surgically begin overeating as soon as they recover from the anesthesia, and they gain weight as much as twenty-five to fifty times faster than do control rats given the same access to food. But the striking thing is that despite continual overeating, the blood glucose levels of the operated rats are much lower than those of the control rats! And the operated rats with the lowest blood sugar levels eat the most. This outcome has led to the suggestion that perhaps the hypothalamus is somehow involved—in a way we do not yet understand—in regulating blood sugar levels rather than in responding to them. This would imply that the glucose detectors regulating feeding behavior are in another, as-yet undiscovered anatomical location.

But factors other than blood glucose levels and a balance between energy intake and energy expenditure clearly are involved in regulating hunger and feeding behavior. If experimental adult rats or dogs are given an unlimited quantity of a standardized diet, they will rather quickly come to adjust their daily intake to the level that will maintain constant body weight. But if a nondigestible, nonusable "filler" is added to the diet (such as cellulose powder), the rats will go on eating the same bulk of food for a time and begin to lose weight. If the dilution of the food does not exceed about 25 percent, the rats will eventually compensate by eating more; they thereby restore and then maintain their original body weight. If the filler is now removed, they tend to overeat for a time and gain weight, until a new compensation sets in. *These results show clearly that in addition to short-term controls regulating the presence or absence of hunger, there are long-term controls regulating the amount of food to be consumed per meal when food is regularly available.* The nature of these long-term controls is not certain, but they appear to be learned behavioral responses involving higher brain centers than the short-term controls do.

One of the more amazing observations made in this respect is the existence of *specific hungers.* If a normal rat is given a choice between plain food and salty food or plain water and salty water, it will strongly avoid the salt. But if the adrenal gland is removed surgically, the hormone responsible for controlling sodium levels in the blood is lost and the body becomes depleted of salt. Such a rat now prefers to eat the salty food or drink the salt water. Taste plays an important part in this control process. The taste buds of the adrenal-ectomized (hence salt deficient) rat are fifteen times as sensitive to salt as those of a normal rat. It will prefer to drink salt solution that is so dilute a normal rat cannot detect any saltiness—and that is, in fact, too dilute to have any significant effect on the animal's salt deficiency! If the nerves leading from the taste buds to the brain are cut, the rat is no longer capable of selecting food or drink on the basis of its salt content.

But salt is not the only substance for which selective feeding occurs. If young rats are given free access to a variety of foods that each contain certain essential nutrients and lack others, they select foods in proportions that give a balanced diet and that lead to optimum growth rate. Similarly, children who know nothing of nutrition and are given unsupervised access to a cafeteria line may gorge on calorie-rich, nutrient-poor foods for a short time. But eventually they will settle down to a balanced diet. Furthermore, a rat given a choice of foods that lack adequate B vitamins will select a diet low in carbohydrate and high in fat. The significance is that certain of the B vitamins are required for the utilization of carbohydrate, but they are not required as much in a fat-rich diet!

Thus we see the feeding process in its true evolutionary perspective—not as a drive for meat and potatoes, but as a component in a complex feedback circuit designed to maintain the internal environment and to provide cells with the essential sources of energy, amino acids, vitamins, and so on that they need to maintain life processes. Therefore, let us take a brief look at the specialized region of the external environment—the gut—where food is broken down to the nutrients required by cells.

Digestive Functions Are Under Complex Controls

Digestion of foods requires integrated activities of several specialized regions of the long, linear tube known as the **gastrointestinal tract,** as well as accessory organs such as the **pancreas** and **liver** (Figure 21.18). Integration of these processes involves a variety of mechanical and chemical signals, a complex of neural and hormonal communications between parts, and a resulting predictable pattern of muscular and secretory responses. As examples of the integrated digestive processes, let us examine the elements controlling secretion of the digestive juices of the stomach (the *gastric juices*) and the passage of partially digested food from stomach to intestine.

Three kinds of glands exist in the stomach wall. They produce three products: *pepsin* (a protein-degrading enzyme), *hydrochloric acid* (required in order for pepsin to be

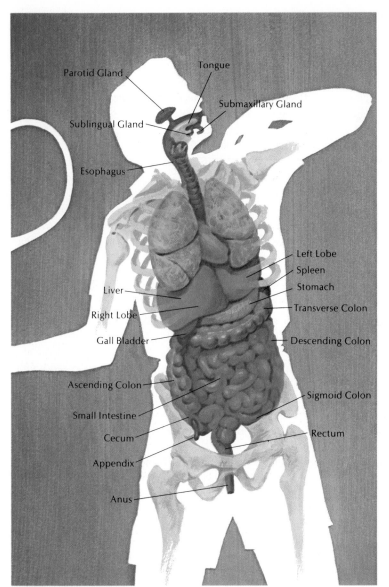

Figure 21.18 The human digestive system. The mouth region is specialized for taking in food, physically disintegrating it, and initiating its chemical processing. From the mouth, the food moves through the esophagus to the stomach, which in mammals is a muscular saclike organ that can be closed at both ends by sphincters (rings of muscle). Muscle contractions in the stomach wall churn and squeeze the food, thoroughly mixing it with mucus, hydrochloric acid, and digestive enzymes secreted by cells and glands in the stomach lining. Subsequently, the food is forced into the small intestine.

The short segment of small intestine closest to the stomach is known as the duodenum. Here, secretions from the pancreas and liver enter the gut. In addition to enzymes, pancreatic juices contain sodium bicarbonate, which neutralizes the acid passed down from the stomach and makes the contents of the intestine rather alkaline. Within the long, coiled tube of the small intestine, digestion is completed and the resulting small organic molecules are absorbed into the cells that line the tube.

The major part of the large intestine, the colon, is a corrugated tube with a smooth lining. The colon serves primarily to remove excess water from undigested material. It houses large numbers of bacteria, principally the species Escherichia coli, which synthesize significant amounts of certain vitamins that are subsequently absorbed by the colon and used by the body. At the end of the large intestine is a short section, the rectum, where undigested waste material is stored until eliminated from the body through the anus.

enzymatically active), and *mucus* (required to protect the stomach wall from attack by the acid and pepsin). All three kinds of glands must be activated more or less in parallel if food is to be digested efficiently without also digesting the stomach. In his now-famous studies of dog behavior, in which he discovered the phenomenon of the conditioned response (Chapter 27), Ivan Pavlov demonstrated that gastric secretion begins with the tasting of savory foods. In humans as well, no gastric secretion occurs unless the flavor of the food in the mouth elicits a positive response. Thus it is called ''appetite juice'' (hence the function of hors d'oeuvres before meals). Because this stimulation of gastric secretion has been shown to be a complex neural reflex involving the participation of the brain, it is called the **cephalic phase** of gastric secretion.

Once food enters the stomach, a second phase of stimulation occurs: the **gastric phase.** This phase has two components. Mechanical distention of the stomach wall can increase secretion as a direct result of pressure on the glands. (This is probably of little significance because even large meals cause little distention of the stomach.) But in addition, certain specific foods stimulate gastric secretion chemically. Meat extracts (soup), milk, and partially digested foods of many sorts have this effect. In response to such foods or many food breakdown products, cells in one particular region of the stomach release a hormonelike substance known as *gastrin* into the blood; gastrin stimulates secretion of the digestive juices by all regions of the stomach. Gastrin release continues and maintains the flow of digestive juices as long as any incompletely digested food remains in the stomach.

Finally, there is an **intestinal phase** of control over gastric secretion; it was also discovered by Pavlov. Certain regions of the intestine produce a hormone similar (or identical) to gastrin in response to the same kinds of foods and food breakdown products that cause its release from stomach cells. But an inhibitory influence of the intestine is probably more important than stimulation by gastrin. If fat is placed in the intestine, it stimulates the release into the blood of a different regulator substance (called *enterogastrone*) that *inhibits* secretion of digestive juices in the stomach. Fat takes longer to digest than most other foodstuffs (because of the difficulty of bringing water-borne enzymes into intimate contact with the fat molecules). Hence it is significant that the presence of fat in the intestine elicits a signal that feeds back to the stomach and says in essence, "Slow down."

In addition to all of these effects of agents within the digestive tract, the secretions of gastric juices are under control of the parasympathetic nervous system and are therefore subject to extensive modulation by emotions in humans. Many quick but intense emotional reactions—such as rage—tend to suppress secretion of gastric juices. But prolonged, low-level emotions such as tension, apprehension, and anxiety tend to stimulate gastric secretion, even in the absence of food in the gut. These emotions tend to stimulate the flow of acid and pepsin, but they stimulate mucus production much less. Thus they play an important part in development of ulcers.

What determines when food will pass from stomach to intestine? It was once thought that the circular muscle at the juncture between stomach and intestine determined the timing of such flow by simply opening and closing. In fact, this muscular ring was given the colorful name of the *pylorus*—which is the Greek word for "keeper of the gate." But modern studies show that the pylorus is relaxed (open) most of the time and that, even so, food flows out of the stomach irregularly. Movement of food requires a simultaneous relaxation of both the pylorus and the adjacent region of intestine (the *duodenum*) at the same time that the pyloric end of the stomach contracts. This creates a pressure differential that sends food into the intestine. Contraction of the pylorus now comes into play to prevent backflow as the duodenum undergoes the rhythmic contractions known as **peristalsis** (Figure 21.19) to move the newly received food somewhat farther down the gut. Thus the pylorus acts principally as a one-way gut—to prevent backflow, or *regurgitation,* from intestine to stomach.

What controls this coordinated relaxation of the pylorus and duodenum and contraction of the pyloric end of the stomach that constitutes the *stomach emptying* response? Once again, many factors are involved. Among them are

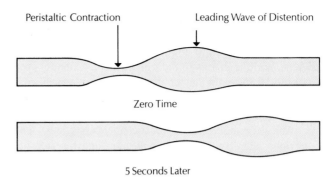

Figure 21.19 Peristalsis in the intestine. A wave of relaxation of circular muscles sweeps slowly down the intestine, followed immediately by a wave of contraction. Together these result in movement of the intestinal contents.

the *acidity of stomach contents.* Acid in the pyloric end of the stomach stimulates the stomach emptying response and dilute alkali suppresses it. Thus when acid secretion and mixing of the meal have been sufficiently prolonged to achieve a certain low pH value in the contents, emptying is promoted. In contrast, acid in the duodenum suppresses the stomach emptying response and stimulates duodenal peristalsis. This duodenal response prevents the stomach from emptying more than a little at a time. Another control is the *fluidity of stomach contents.* Water, soup, and so forth pass through the stomach rapidly, but large particles remain behind. Mechanical stimulation of the stomach wall inhibits the emptying response. Thus chunky foods tend to be held in the stomach until they are rather thoroughly broken down and liquified. A third control is *solute concentration of the gastric contents.* A concentrated salt or sugar solution passes into the intestine more slowly than a dilute one. Thus food tends to be held back until it is diluted sufficiently by gastric secretions. (This is one reason why a glass of water will often relieve an overfull feeling.) A fourth control is the *quantity and consistency of duodenal contents.* Acid in the duodenum inhibits stomach emptying. But, to an only slightly lesser extent, so does a salt solution. And mechanical stimulation of the intestinal wall (as by chunks of food that have escaped the stomach) intensifies this inhibition of stomach emptying. Such inhibition of stomach emptying occurs by neural reflex—cutting nerves abolishes it. A fifth control has to do with *fat in the intestine.* The hormonelike substance enterogasterone that inhibits gastric secretion also inhibits stomach emptying. Finally, another factor controlling the stomach emptying response is *emotional state.* In humans, the same emotional reactions that tend to stimulate gastric secretion (fear, anger, and so forth) stimulate gastric emptying; those that suppress gastric secretion (anxiety, apprehension, and so on) suppress gastric emptying.

If we continued this kind of analysis down the intestinal tract, thereby determining how such processes as secretion of digestive juices into the intestine by the liver, the pancreas, and the glands in the wall of the intestine, or the motility of various regions of the intestine are controlled, we would find most events fall under a similarly complex but integrated, multicomponent system of feedback controls. And we would find that most elements of control are of obvious adaptive significance in adjusting the rate of digestive processing to the physical and chemical attributes of the meal at hand.

Most Digestion and Absorption of Nutrients Occurs in the Small Intestine

When food enters the intestine, it is in a relatively liquified state. Digestion of proteins and carbohydrates has begun but is far from complete, and virtually no absorption of nutrients has yet occurred. Secretions of alkaline fluids from the pancreas, pancreatic digestive enzymes, fat-solubilizing detergents from the liver, and digestive enzymes from multitudinous glands in the lining of the intestine (Figure 21.20) all serve to dilute the food mass and initiate final digestion. These secretory products are all thoroughly mixed with the food by a process of *segmentation movements* of the intestinal wall (Figure 21.21).

The whole thrust of digestion is recycling: to break down nutrient-rich but unusable materials from the bodies of consumed organisms into the usable small molecules needed to build and maintain the cells of the consumer. The DNA of a steer (present in a hamburger) contains all the building blocks required to construct new genetic material in a growing child, but obviously steer genes cannot be absorbed intact and incorporated into the child's cell nuclei any more than the whole muscles of the steer could be used directly. Each food component must be broken down into the only chemical entities that are identical in consumer and consumed—the basic building blocks. The process whereby large molecules are broken down into their reusable building blocks is analogous in the case of the three major categories of macromolecules (proteins, carbohydrates, and nucleic acids). The general process catalyzed by the digestive enzymes is hydrolysis (splitting by water), which is in a sense the reverse of dehydration synthesis (Chapter 11). It can be symbolized as:

$$A \bullet B \bullet C + HOH \rightarrow A—H + HO—B—H + HOC$$

Three categories of enzymes take part in breaking down each class of macromolecules. The first are *endohydrolases* that attack the macromolecules at internal positions in the polymer and break it into many pieces of intermediate size. These are supplemented in their action by *exohydrolases*,

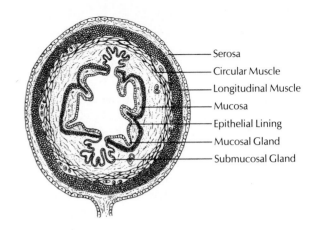

Figure 21.20 Typical cross section of the small intestine.

Serosa
Circular Muscle
Longitudinal Muscle
Mucosa
Epithelial Lining
Mucosal Gland
Submucosal Gland

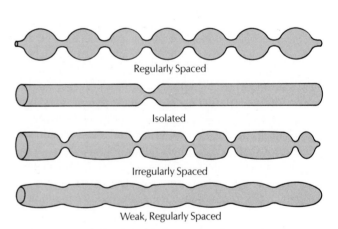

Regularly Spaced

Isolated

Irregularly Spaced

Weak, Regularly Spaced

Figure 21.21 Segmentation movements of the small intestine. In segmentation, rings of muscle contract simultaneously at more or less regularly spaced intervals down the gut. A few seconds later these muscle bands relax while others, intermediate in position, contract. These segmentation movements do not result in forward propulsion of the food mass as peristalsis does. But they achieve very efficient mixing and churning of the food mass with the digestive juices.

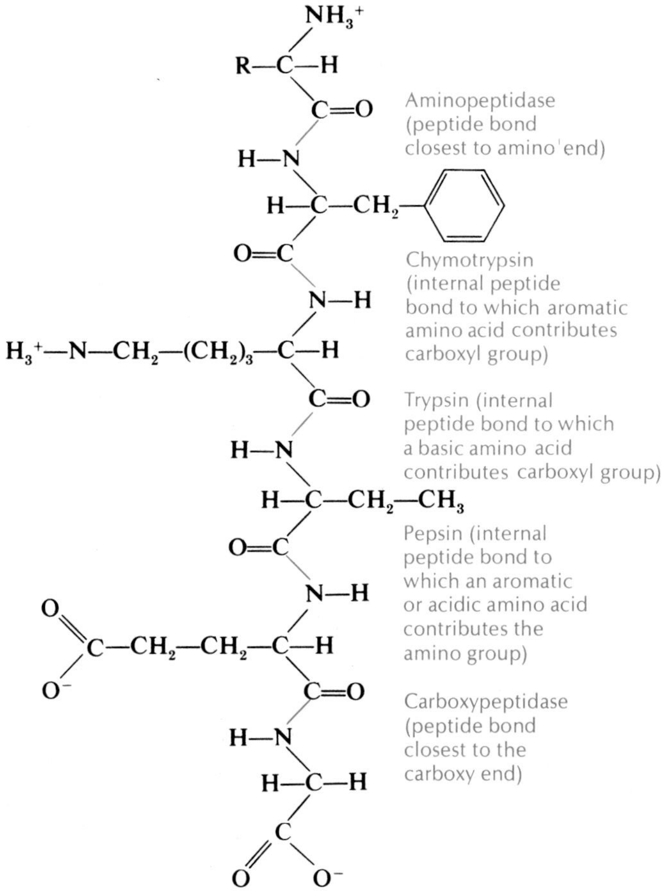

Figure 21.22 Action of some proteolytic enzymes in digesting proteins. The endoproteases (chymotrypsin, trypsin, and pepsin, plus others not shown here) break the protein into fragments by hydrolyzing peptide bonds adjacent to specific amino acids in the interior of the molecule. Thus trypsin, acting alone, will break a protein into as many pieces as there are basic amino acids in the sequence. The digestive process is then completed by the exoproteases (carboxypeptidase and amino peptidase) that chew in from the ends of the fragments, removing one amino acid at a time, regardless of the nature of the amino acids.

which remove successive terminal building blocks (amino acids, sugars, or nucleotides) from one or the other end of the pieces. Figure 21.22 depicts how these two categories of *proteases* (enzymes that digest proteins) cooperate to degrade a protein to amino acids. Similar hydrolytic patterns are exhibited by the *carbohydrases* (enzymes that digest complex carbohydrates to simple sugars) and *nucleases* (enzymes that degrade nucleic acids). The third category includes such hydrolytic enzymes as dipeptidases and disaccharidases which, as the names imply, hydrolyze dipeptides and disaccharides into their component two amino acids or two sugar molecules, respectively.

As digestion proceeds and simple sugars, free amino acids, and so forth are released, these end products of digestion (along with the vitamins and inorganic salts of the foodstuffs) are absorbed by the epithelial lining cells of the intestine and passed on to adjacent blood vessels. From there they are carried off to the rest of the body. (The subsequent processing and storage of these absorbed nutrients is controlled largely by hormones and is therefore discussed in Chapter 22.) The uptake of most of the digestion products is an active transport process involving

energy expenditure at the membrane of the lining cells. Extensive outfolding of the intestinal walls in the form of *villi* and microscopic outfolding of the membranes on the surface of the villi, to form *microvilli*, serves to increase the absorptive surface of the intestine enormously (Figure 21.23). As the nutrients are actively absorbed from the food mass, it becomes more and more dilute. As a consequence, water is absorbed from the intestinal contents by osmosis. This is an impressively effective process. Of the approximately 1 liter of saliva, 1 liter of pancreatic juices, 700 milliliters of bile from the liver, and 3 liters of intestinal secretions that an average adult human produces each day—plus the several liters per day in food and drink—all but about a half liter is usually absorbed in the small intestine and most of the rest is absorbed in the large intestine!

The only foodstuff that is absorbed before digestion is completed is fat. Some breakdown of fats to fatty acids and glycerol does occur as the result of intestinal lipolytic (lipid-splitting) enzymes called *lipases*. The fatty acids so produced then act as detergents, causing suspension of the fat in the watery environment of the intestine in the form of

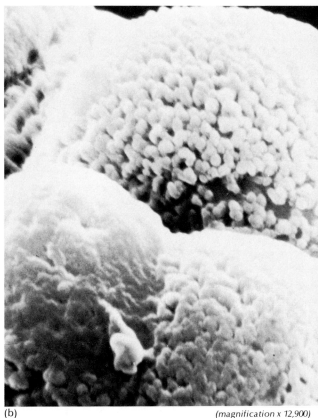

(a)   (magnification x 215) (b)   (magnification x 12,900)

tiny droplets. Each droplet consists of a sphere of fat surrounded by a layer of fatty acids that are oriented with their nonpolar tails dissolved in the fat and their acidic, polar heads dissolved in the surrounding water (Chapter 11). Such droplets are then taken up by the intestinal lining cells through endocytosis and passed on into the blood and lymph vessels that drain the intestine. Upon arrival at fatty tissues in other regions of the body, the process of lipolysis is carried to completion, and new fat molecules are synthesized for storage.

The lumen of the gut is a specialized region of external environment folded into the interior of the animal during its development. It is the more or less continuous flow of energy (in the form of food molecules) from this region of the external environment to our internal environment that postpones our descent into disorder. Thus these digestive processes are of central importance to the maintenance of the internal environment.

THE KIDNEYS DISPOSE OF ORGANIC WASTES AND REGULATE SALT CONTENT OF BODY FLUIDS

To maintain life-sustaining internal conditions, an organism not only must obtain energy-rich organic nutrients, it must also regulate its internal content of inorganic salts and dispose of the waste products of metabolism. In these two aspects of homeostatic control, still another point of exchange between internal and external environment is dominant: the kidneys.

Land animals, including ourselves, must obtain water by drinking and eating. Because excess salts are frequently included in food, excretory systems are specialized for elimination of salts and retention of water. In many land animals, salts and water are also lost through the body surface by sweating.

Much of the food that affluent humans eat (meat, dairy products, eggs, and so forth) is rich in proteins. As noted above, ingested proteins are hydrolized into amino acids, which are absorbed into the blood. Some of these amino acids are reused by cells in synthesizing needed proteins and other molecules, but another part of this supply is further broken down as a source of chemical energy. The first step in the metabolism of an amino acid is the removal of amino groups. The amino groups are converted into ammonia during this process of ''deamination.''

Ammonia is toxic to animals if it accumulates in high concentrations. Ammonia does not diffuse readily into the air, as does waste carbon dioxide. Only dilute ammonia

Figure 21.23 Scanning electron micrographs of the small intestine. (a) A low-power view showing the outfoldings of the intestinal wall to form villi. (b) A higher magnification shows that each of the cells on the villus is covered with a series of very fine projections called microvilli. (Figure 13.36 shows such microvilli in longitudinal section.) Because of such extensive folding of the surface on both the macro and the micro scale, the total surface area for absorption in the intestine is well over a hundred times what would exist if the wall were a simple flat membrane.

solutions can be tolerated in the internal environment. In mammals, instead of being accumulated, ammonia is combined with carbon dioxide in a multistep reaction to form

$$urea\ (H_2N-\overset{\overset{\displaystyle O}{\|}}{C}-NH_2),$$

a substance that can be tolerated in concentrations substantially higher than that of ammonia alone but that still must be disposed of.

In vertebrates it is the kidney that adjusts the concentrations of various salt ions and water in the blood. In addition, the kidney helps to regulate blood concentration of glucose and excretes nitrogenous wastes such as urea and creatinine, a substance formed as a waste product of muscular activity. Useless materials that find their way into the organism across the intestinal or respiratory epithelia are also excreted by the kidney. These functions are accomplished by a combination of three processes: *ultrafiltration* of blood, *reabsorption* from the filtrate of materials required by the organism, and specific *secretion* of certain materials directly into the filtrate.

The kidney is essentially a collection of many thousands of similar small units called *nephrons* (Figure 21.24). Each nephron consists of a network of blood capillaries and a *renal tubule.* The wall of the renal tubule is made up of a single layer of epithelial cells. In the outer part of the kidney, the *renal cortex,* each tubule originates from a cup-shaped structure, called *Bowman's capsule,* which surrounds a network of capillaries. A narrow, twisting portion of the tubule (the proximal convoluted tubule) extends from the capsule to a straighter *loop of Henle,* which loops into the inner portion, or medulla, of the kidney and returns to the cortex, where it leads into another narrow, twisted segment of tubule (the **distal convoluted tubule**). Each tubule joins with other tubules to form a larger **collecting tubule,** which leads back through the medulla to the **renal pelvis** in the center of the kidney (Figure 21.24).

The cluster of capillaries within the cup of Bowman's capsule is called the *glomerulus.* Blood flows into the glomerulus from a branch of the arterial system serving the kidney, and blood flows out of the glomerular capillaries into a smaller arteriole that leads to a second capillary network surrounding the proximal and distal convoluted tubules and the loop of Henle. From this network, blood collects into the veins leading from the kidney back toward the heart.

Blood filtration takes place in the glomerulus. Because the exit from the glomerular capillaries is smaller than the entrance, considerable blood pressure is built up in these capillaries. Under this high pressure, about one-fifth of the fluid portion of blood is forced through the capillary walls into Bowman's capsule, leaving only blood cells, plasma proteins, and fluid within the capillaries. The ultrafiltrate in the kidney tubule at this stage then contains the same concentration of small molecules as the incoming plasma, including nutrients and salts in addition to waste products. (The human kidneys filter the blood at such a rapid rate that a volume of blood equivalent to the total contents of the circulatory system passes through the Bowman's capsules about every twenty-five minutes.)

The filtrate moves through the renal tubule, where it comes back into proximity with the blood from which it was filtered. Cells lining the proximal and distal convoluted tubules are specialized for carrying on active transport of particular substances. They pump glucose, amino acids, and some ions out of the tubule fluid; these materials then diffuse back into the blood. The high concentration of dissolved materials in blood creates an osmotic pressure that forces water out of the tubule and back into the blood. A few substances, creatinine and hydrogen ions, for example, are actively transported by the tubule cells in the opposite direction (from blood to tubule fluid).

Each region of the tubule processes a different group of substances. Glucose and amino acids are returned to blood from the proximal convoluted tubule, whereas ions move back into the blood in all parts of the tubule. Under normal

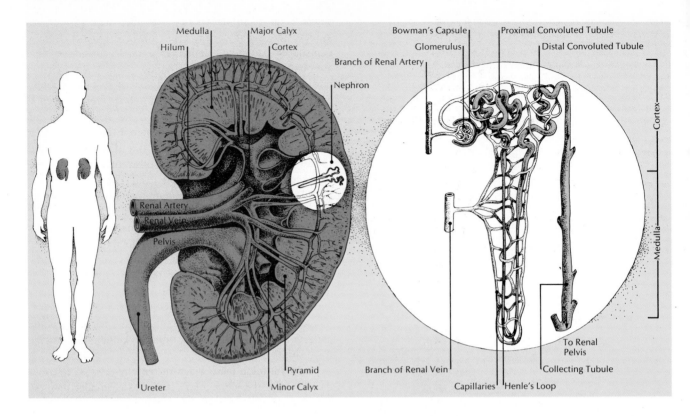

Figure 21.24 The major organ of the human excretory system is the kidney. Three processes, including filtration, reabsorption, and secretion, enable this organ to remove wastes from the blood and simultaneously conserve the useful components of the blood.

conditions, all glucose is returned to the blood, whereas the amount of ions left in the tubule fluid is variable and depends on the physiological needs of the organism. Sufficient amounts of each ion are actively transported back to the blood to restore the normal homeostatic concentration of each substance in the circulatory fluid. The urine that leaves the collecting duct represents about 1 percent of the volume of fluid that entered the Bowman's capsule.

Urine formation is subject to controls that tend to adjust the urine volume and concentration to counteract changes in the internal environment. These controls are based on two types of information—blood pressure and osmotic concentration of body fluids. When arterial pressure increases, the pressure in the glomerulus rises, forcing more blood through the filter and resulting in an increase in the volume of urine. A corresponding decrease in blood volume reduces the blood pressure and the system returns to normal. Thus, long-term regulation of blood volume and pressure is facilitated by this simple homeostatic system.

The osmotic concentration of body fluids is monitored by

sensory receptors in the brain. When the receptors are exposed to an increased concentration of solutes in the fluid that bathes them, they tend to shrink. Osmotic shrinkage excites these receptors and starts a chain of events in the brain that results in the release of a hormone from the posterior pituitary gland. This antidiuretic hormone (ADH) increases the permeability to water of cells lining the collecting tubules in the kidney. The result is an increase in the amount of water returned to blood and the excretion of a smaller volume of more concentrated urine. An increase in the amount of water returned to blood decreases the osmotic concentration of body fluids, again tending to restore normal conditions. Two common substances affect these control mechanisms. Caffeine, found in coffee, stimulates the arteries to contract, raising the blood pressure and producing an increased flow of urine. Alcohol inhibits a component of the system that maintains a steady level of antidiuretic hormone. When the secretion of ADH is cut down, less water is removed from the urine and the volume of urine increases.

PERSPECTIVE

An organism is like a city; like New York, St. Louis, or San Francisco. It gives the appearance of completeness. A city contains everything people need. There is food in the markets and restaurants; there are sanitation and sewage systems that accept wastes; there is lumber, plaster, and pipe to repair and build; and there is a network of transportation arteries for distribution of goods. The systems are coordinated by networks of wires.

An organism is a city on a smaller scale. It contains everything cells need. There is glucose and oxygen, and convenient places to dump carbon dioxide and urea. Amino acids and nucleotides replace lumber and plaster in the system. And an organism is coordinated by neuronal and chemical regulators.

Thus, with everything present that is needed, the city or the organism can be continuously active. Activity never ceases; an organism or a city is *dynamic.* But the appearance of completeness is illusory, for neither one can be considered a closed system. Materials must enter and leave at rates commensurate with need. Otherwise, function of the system is seriously impaired (do you remember the last "garbage strike" in New York?). Raw materials must constantly enter and waste products be removed, and each system has points of exchange where this is accomplished.

The life and health of a vertebrate organism depend on the individual's ability to maintain the constancy and adequacy of its internal environment—to maintain its apparent completeness. The constancy of this internal environment is maintained by means of finely tuned homeostatic systems. But the capacity to maintain these systems within the "steady state" is absolutely dependent upon an efficient transport system and effective points of exchange between internal and external environments.

SUGGESTED READINGS

ADOLPH, E. E. *Origins of Physiological Regulations.* New York: Academic Press, 1968. This book deals with development or ontogeny of physiological regulation in vertebrates. The excellent organization and straightforward language make each chapter fascinating to read.

CANNON, WALTER B. *The Wisdom of the Body.* New York: Norton, 1963 (originally published, 1939). No one, except perhaps Claude Bernard (Chapter 2), contributed more to the theory of homeostasis than Walter B. Cannon. His views on that subject are of more than historical interest.

GUYTON, ARTHUR C. *Textbook of Medical Physiology.* Philadelphia: Saunders, 1971. This professionally oriented textbook is less encyclopedic and more easily read than most. It is suggested that students read the preface before using this advanced physiology book.

SMITH, HOMER W. *From Fish to Philosopher.* Garden City, N.Y.: Doubleday, 1961. A delightfully written evolutionary history of the vertebrate internal environment, with emphasis on comparative physiology of kidney function. Readers who find this interesting may also wish to read Smith's *Kamongo.*

SNIVELY, W. D., with J. THUERBACH. *The Sea of Life.* New York: McKay, 1969. Deals with the composition, function, evolution, and regulation of the internal fluid, and also touches on some medical problems.

Chapter 22

Hormonal Integration in Animals

If an animal is to be more than a collection of independently functioning cells, the cells must communicate with one another. One system for such communication is the network of endocrine glands and the hormones they produce. Sensing changes in the internal environment, the glands respond by releasing their hormones, which then effect appropriate changes in cells elsewhere in the body. Such systems integrate behavior of many kinds, from regular patterns of feeding to the cyclic patterns of reproduction and care of the young.

nderlying all of life is controlled chemistry. Even free-living individual cells have an extensive network of control systems that adjust the chemical activity as environmental conditions change. But with multicellularity there comes a demand for controls of a much more complex nature. A division of labor between cells—the ultimate advantage of multicellularity—demands a system in which the needs of one region can be rapidly communicated to the cells responsible for meeting those needs. Furthermore, there must be ways in which competing needs of different regions may be weighed and priorities quickly established before a response is selected. And these internal communications and controls must be continuously subject to modification by external events, for an internal response that is appropriate at one instant might well be disastrous if conditions suddenly change.

Consider an animal that has just eaten a meal. Its digestive tract assumes high priority: Blood vessels to the gut are wide open, flooding its cells with oxygen and thereby permitting the gut muscles to churn actively and the cells to digest and absorb nutrients quickly. As fast as nutrients are absorbed, the blood carts them off for immediate use or for storage. Blood vessels leading to the brain and muscles are partially closed down during this digestive and absorptive activity, and the animal becomes drowsy. But what happens if a predator suddenly appears? Blood vessels to the gut close down at once even as those to the brain and muscles are thrown wide open. Cells throughout the body that have been actively engaged in storing food instantly reverse their chemistry and begin to tear down the newly made storage molecules, pouring sugar and fatty acids back into the blood. Muscles of the gut go limp; skeletal muscles spring into action to power the reactions of fight or flight. Only when (and if) danger passes do all these responses reverse, and digestion of the meal once more becomes the focus of body activity.

Dominating such selective controls in animals are the nervous system and the endocrine system, which are both tuned in to external and internal stimuli. Because they are so complex, these systems must be treated in more than one chapter. We will focus on the endocrine system here, but the interconnected and coordinated activities of both systems make any such separation of their functions arbitrary and it is important to keep this in mind.

The **endocrine system** comprises a series of specialized cells that produce and secrete chemical messengers that are called hormones. An animal **hormone** is a chemical substance produced in cells in one part of the body and released in small amounts into the blood; upon reaching its specific sites of action it functions to regulate rates of reactions in the responding cells. (This definition is worded so as to specifically exclude many substances that possess one or more of the listed attributes, such as neurotransmitters, food molecules, digestive enzymes, and so forth.) Usually, but not always, the cells producing a hormone are clustered into discrete organs known as **endocrine glands.** Such a gland may produce a single hormone, or it may contain two or more different types of cells that produce unique hormones of unique function.

REMOVAL OF AN ENDOCRINE GLAND GIVES INSIGHT INTO ITS FUNCTION

Diabetes is a disease caused by insufficiency of a certain hormone. A generation or two ago it was fatal. It still cannot be cured, yet even people who develop it as children may now live relatively normal lives. It is worthwhile to review how this change came about, for the way we learned how to treat diabetes serves as a model for the way all endocrine functions have been and are being studied.

Nearly ninety years ago it was observed that when a dog's pancreas was removed, the dog developed symptoms similar to human diabetes. It drank and urinated excessively, and the urine contained sugar—which is symptomatic of an abnormally high concentration of sugar in the blood. If the blood sugar level rose too high, the dogs lapsed into unconsciousness and died. Because of certain technical difficulties, nearly forty years passed before it was demonstrated that an extract of pancreas tissue was capable of preventing or reversing these diabetic symptoms. Shortly thereafter, the active substance of such pancreas extracts was isolated, purified, and crystallized. It became known as **insulin.** Many years later, insulin was the first protein for which the complete sequence of amino acids was established. Still more recently, insulin has become one of the first proteins to be made in the laboratory from its constituent amino acids. The synthetic insulin proved to be fully effective in reversing the effects of diabetes. This synthesis completed the proof that insulin is a hormone produced by the pancreas and involved in the regulation of blood sugar.

Five steps were crucial in this analysis. The first was *removal* of the gland and identification of the symptoms resulting from its absence. The second was *replacement* by an extract of the gland—thereby demonstrating that deficiency symptoms are caused by absence of a chemical substance produced by the gland. The third step was *isolation* of the chemical substance (hormone); the fourth was its *chemical characterization*; and the fifth, its *synthesis* from simpler substances.

Ideally, all five of these steps should be performed to prove that a substance should be added to the list of recognized hormones. But the last two or three steps are often difficult, and usually major advances in knowledge and application of that knowledge have been made long before the chemical identity of the hormone has been established. (For example, countless thousands of lives were saved by insulin injections long before the structure of insulin was known in detail.) As a result of such removal and replacement studies, several organs of the vertebrate body have been clearly identified as endocrine glands and several others are suspected to serve endocrine functions. The locations of most of these organs in the human body are shown in Figure 22.2. Because relatively little change in endocrine organs has occurred during vertebrate evolution, the comparable organs would be found in roughly the same relative position in all vertebrates. A list of the major vertebrate hormones, along with data on their nature, origin, target organs, and functions, is given in Table 22.1. Rather than attempting to catalog the roles of all the hormones mentioned in this table, we may select a single control problem involving participation of several hormones—say, control of the level of glucose in the blood. We may then use that problem to ask: How do hormones work? The question may be posed at several different levels. How do hormones function at the level of the whole organism? What changes do they elicit in the cells they affect? How do they act at the molecular level?

REGULATION OF BLOOD SUGAR LEVEL: HOW HORMONES ACT IN FEEDBACK LOOPS

A typical vertebrate experiences alternate periods of eating and fasting. During the period of eating and immediately thereafter, food is available in far greater amounts than the

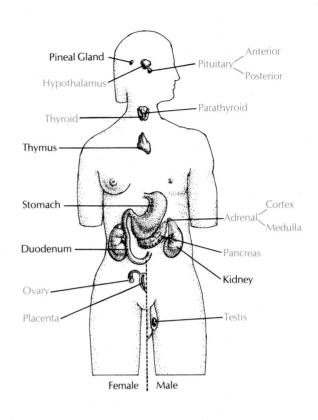

Figure 22.2 The locations of the human endocrine glands. Those labeled in red are uniformly recognized as endocrine glands. Those labeled in black are ones for which one or more endocrine functions have been suggested by experimental work but that, for one reason or another, are not usually included in a listing of endocrine glands.

Table 22.1
Major Endocrine Glands and Their Main Hormones

Gland	Hormone	Chemical Nature	Principal Target Sites	Principal Effects
Adrenal cortex	Glucocorticoids (e.g., hydrocortisone)	Steroids	Many cell types	Promote synthesis of sugar, breakdown of proteins
	Mineralocorticoids (e.g., aldosterone)	Steroids	Kidney	Promote retention of Na^+ and loss of K^+ in urine
Adrenal medulla	Epinephrine and norepinephrine	Modified amino acids	Liver	Promotes glycogen breakdown and sugar synthesis
			Adipose tissue	Promotes fat breakdown
			Heart	Increases heart output
			Blood vessels	Constricts some, dilates others
Hypothalamus	Releasing factors	Peptides	Anterior pituitary	Cause secretion of corresponding pituitary hormones
	Oxytocin	Peptide	Mammary glands	Causes release of milk
			Uterus	Causes rhythmic contractions

	Vasopressin (ADH)	Peptide	Kidney	Promotes reabsorption of water
Ovary	Estrogen	Steroid	Reproductive tract and body generally	Causes development of female characteristics
			Uterus	Causes cyclic preparation for pregnancy
	Progesterone	Steroid	Uterus	Causes development for and maintenance of pregnancy
Pancreas	Insulin	Protein	Muscle, liver, and adipose tissue	Promotes processes leading to lowering of blood sugar
	Glucagon	Protein	Liver and adipose tissue	Promotes processes leading to rise in blood sugar
Parathyroid	Parathyroid hormone	Protein	Bone, gut, and kidney; other cells	Elevates level of calcium in blood, lowers level of phosphate
Pituitary (anterior)	Adrenocorticotropic hormone (ACTH)	Protein	Adrenal cortex	Promotes synthesis and release of glucocorticoids
	Growth-stimulating hormone (GSH)	Protein	Bone and muscle	Promotes protein synthesis and growth
	Follicle-stimulating hormone (FSH)	Protein	Ovary	Promotes development of follicle and secretion of estrogen
			Testis	Promotes sperm formation
	Luteinizing hormone (LH)	Protein	Ovary	Promotes development of corpus luteum and secretion of progesterone
			Testis	Promotes secretion of testosterone
	Prolactin	Protein	Mammary gland	Initiates milk production
	Thyroid-stimulating hormone (TSH)	Protein	Thyroid gland	Stimulates production and release of thyroxin
	Melanophore-stimulating hormone (MSH)	Protein	Skin	Modifies skin pigmentation
Pituitary (posterior)	Oxytocin and vasopressin	(see hypothalamus)		
Placenta	Chorionic gonadotropin (CG)	Protein	Ovary	Has some effects similar to both FSH and LH
	Placental lactogen	Protein	Ovary	Has effects similar to LH
			Mammary gland	Has effects similar to prolactin
Testis	Testosterone	Steroid	Reproductive tract and body generally	Development of male characteristics
Thyroid	Thyroxin	Modified amino acid	Most cell types	Regulates rate of cell's energy metabolism
	Thyrocalcitonin	Protein	Bone, kidney, and other cells	Lowers blood calcium and phosphate

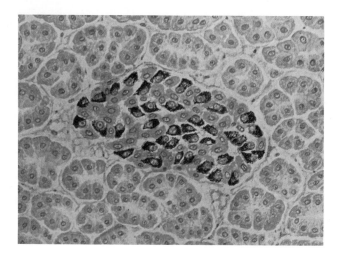

body requires to satisfy immediate energy needs. But within two hours or so after completing a meal, the nutrients entering the body from the digestive tract fall below the levels required to power the activity of the moment. Thus, even the well-fed, affluent members of Western society who never experience true hunger and never let anything interfere with their regular intake of food spend most of their lives—perhaps three-fourths of each day—in the state of fasting. But for most human beings in the world and for most in the history of the species—as well as most other animals—the fasting state is even more common and more prolonged.

Consider the effect of fluctuations in the supply of blood sugar to the brain. The brain is an extremely sensitive organ and requires a continuous supply of blood sugar (glucose), but it is unable to tolerate either excesses or deficiencies. If the glucose level of the blood rises too high or falls too low for a prolonged period, unconsciousness and serious brain damage may result. Not surprisingly, there has been strong selective pressure to develop systems that will maintain blood glucose level within rather narrow limits despite marked fluctuations in its availability from food intake. As a result, in a normal individual the level of blood glucose seldom rises above 160 milligrams per 100 milliliters of blood plasma when glucose is being rapidly absorbed from the gut. Furthermore, it usually does not fall below about 60 milligrams per 100 milliliters during prolonged fasting. How is this careful regulation achieved? By looking at only a few of the body components involved, we can arrive at a satisfactory answer.

Insulin Stimulates the Uptake of Nutrients by Cells

As food is digested and absorbed, the level of glucose (like that of amino acids, fats, and fatty acids) increases in the blood. The glucose reaching the pancreas has two effects on cells of specialized regions of the pancreas known as the **Islets of Langerhans** (Figure 22.3). The **β islet cells**, which produce insulin, are stimulated by the rise in blood glucose and begin to release their hormone. Meanwhile, the adjacent **α islet cells**, which produce **glucagon** (a hormone that acts antagonistically to insulin) are inhibited and their rate of secretion falls.

The insulin released from the β cells is now transported throughout the body in the blood, affecting a wide number of cell types in various ways. One of the key organs involved in regulating blood sugar level is the liver. Insulin stimulates the metabolism of glucose by liver cells. As a result, the rate at which glucose is oxidized is increased slightly. But oxidation accounts for only a small portion of the glucose taken up by the liver cells. The energy obtained when part of the glucose is oxidized is used to convert the rest of the glucose to the storage form, **glycogen** (a kind of starch). After a single meal the liver can store enough glucose in this way to supply the body's need for glucose for about eight hours. The elevated insulin level acts similarly on skeletal muscle cells to increase utilization and storage of glucose. But in contrast with liver cells (which are always permeable to glucose) muscle cells respond to insulin by becoming more permeable to glucose, thereby greatly increasing the rate at which they remove glucose from the blood.

Perhaps the most important aspect of the role of insulin during this period is the way it acts on the fatty tissues of the body (the so-called **adipose** tissue). First of all, insulin modifies the adipose cells so that they become more active in breaking down, taking up, and storing fats that have been absorbed from the meal. (These stored fats will be of importance in the regulation of blood glucose during the fasting period.) In addition, insulin stimulates the conver-

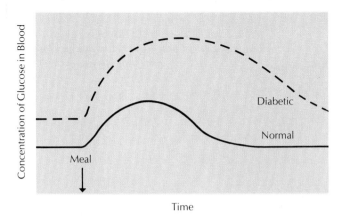

Figure 22.4 Glucose clearance in normal and diabetic individuals following similar meals. The effect of insulin inadequacy can be seen clearly: Blood levels of glucose rise much higher and fall much more slowly in the diabetic. This difference can be abolished by a combination of dietary changes and insulin administration.

sion of glucose to fat by the adipose cells; much more energy is stored in 1 gram of fat than in 1 gram of starch. (Insulin stimulates similar fat synthesis and storage by liver cells, although they normally store much less fat than the adipose tissue does.) The combined effects of insulin on glucose uptake and on metabolism in adipose tissue, muscle, liver, and other cells result in rapid *clearance* of glucose from the blood, as shown in Figure 22.4. In the absence of insulin, the glucose level rises much higher and falls much more slowly. Thus, glucose regulates its own blood level in a negative feedback loop in which insulin plays the key role (Figure 22.5).

Finally, insulin modifies the handling of amino acids derived from the meal. It stimulates the uptake of amino acids and the synthesis of protein by liver, muscle, and

Figure 22.5 The negative feedback loop initiated by a rise in blood glucose. Elevated blood glucose initiates a series of processes that result in lowering of blood glucose levels.

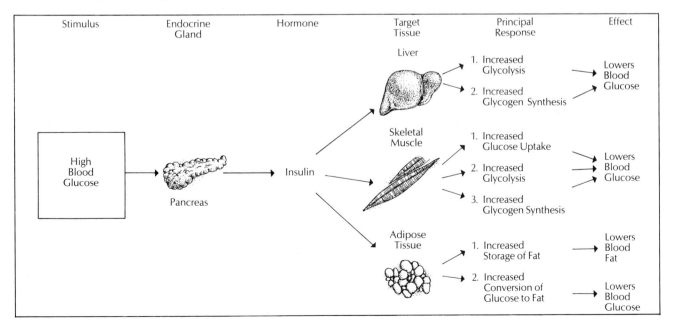

certain other cells. But any protein that is to be synthesized must be made quickly, for insulin also stimulates the conversion of excess amino acids to glucose (which is then stored as glycogen) or to fatty acids (which are then stored as fat).

In this time period, then, insulin has sweeping effects on many cell types. But the central nervous system is totally unaffected by insulin. Brain cells take up and utilize glucose in precisely the same manner whether insulin is present or not. Thus, although insulin function is essential for normal brain function, it acts only indirectly, by preventing the brain from being flooded with glucose.

During Fasting, Several Factors Combine to Cause Release of Stored Nutrients

About two hours after eating, the flow of glucose from the intestinal tract slows down, so the amount of sugar in the blood begins to fall. But even though the uptake of glucose from the gut soon stops, the blood level does not continue to fall. It sinks to about 70 milligrams per 100 milliliters of blood plasma but no lower, even if fasting is maintained for many hours.

As glucose levels begin to fall, the stimulation of insulin secretion also falls, so the level of insulin in the blood falls. (The capacity of *all* hormones to regulate bodily activity demands that they be subject to regular and rapid destruction. Otherwise they would accumulate in the blood and cause chaos. Thus, all hormones are unstable and exert their effects only during the time that they are being actively secreted into the blood.) As a result of falling insulin levels, the muscles become relatively impermeable to glucose and hence decrease their glucose uptake. Synthesis of glycogen and fat is no longer stimulated in any of the tissues. As fasting continues and the glucose level falls toward its minimum value, the inhibitory action of glucose on the α islet cells of the pancreas diminishes. These cells now begin to secrete glucagon. And the medulla of the adrenal gland begins to secrete **epinephrine** (adrenalin).

Both epinephrine and glucagon act on the liver to reverse the actions stimulated earlier by insulin. Now, instead of

Figure 22.7 The negative feedback loop initiated by a fall in blood glucose level. The falling glucose level activates a series of processes that in turn increase the amount of glucose in the blood.

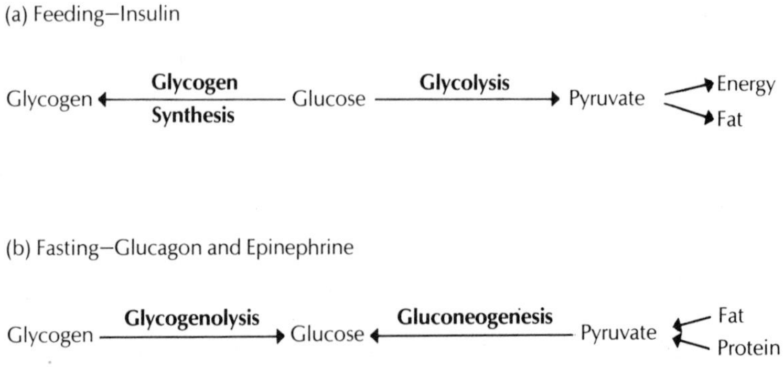

synthesizing glycogen, the liver is stimulated to break glycogen down to form glucose, which is released into the blood. This process, called **glycogenolysis** (splitting of glycogen), is diagramed in Figure 22.6. In early stages of fasting, glycogenolysis by the liver accounts for most of the glucose that flows into the blood from the liver. But progressively, a new process supplements the flow of glucose. Whereas insulin stimulated glycolysis (glucose breakdown), glucagon and epinephrine now stimulate the reverse process: **gluconeogenesis**, the synthesis of new sugar molecules from fats and amino acids.

As in the case of insulin, epinephrine (and, in some species, glucagon as well) has perhaps its most important effect on adipose tissue. Whereas insulin stimulated fat synthesis and storage, epinephrine now stimulates **lipolysis** (splitting of fat) in the adipose cells. Lipolysis does not increase the availability of glucose directly, but it contributes indirectly in two important ways. First, it provides an alternative energy source for most of the cells in the body. The brain can utilize only glucose as an energy source, so continuous availability of glucose is of obvious importance. But other cells are not so restricted; most cells can use fatty acids as a source of energy. And when glucose level is moderately low and fatty acid levels are high in the blood, most cells burn the fatty acids preferentially. This has the effect of "sparing" the glucose—reserving it for brain cells that demand it. Second, the products of fat breakdown (both the fatty acids and the glycerin) can now be used by the liver to synthesize new glucose molecules by

Figure 22.6 Pathways of glucose storage and mobilization during feeding and fasting. When glucose is entering the body faster than it is being used, two processes are stimulated by insulin to cause storage: glycogen synthesis and glycolysis. The latter causes the atoms of glucose to be stored as fat. But during fasting the reverse processes are stimulated by glucagon and epinephrine. Both glycogenolysis and gluconeogenesis increase the amount of glucose available for use by the brain.

(a) Feeding—Insulin

Glycogen ← Glycogen Synthesis — Glucose — Glycolysis → Pyruvate → Energy / Fat

(b) Fasting—Glucagon and Epinephrine

Glycogen — Glycogenolysis → Glucose ← Gluconeogenesis — Pyruvate ← Fat / Protein

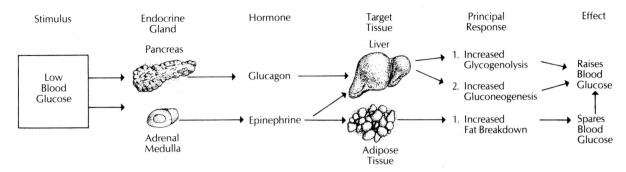

gluconeogenesis. Thus we see that glucose regulates its own level during fasting by means of a different negative feedback loop in which glucagon and epinephrine play key roles, as shown in Figure 22.7.

And what of the muscles during the fasting stage? As long as the individual is relatively sedentary, the muscles are neither using nor supplying blood glucose to any great extent. The low insulin levels present during fasting make the muscles relatively impermeable to glucose, so they do not remove it from the blood. But muscle glycogen is not mobilized for use by other tissues, either. It is retained in the cells as a local energy source. Thus when muscles are called upon to contract, they utilize their stored glycogen as the principal fuel and thereby spare blood glucose. If *vigorous* exercise is called for during fasting, however, the muscles produce a *potentiator* of insulin action. The potentiator interacts with the small amount of insulin that is present in the blood to increase the permeability of the muscle cells to glucose, thereby permitting them to momentarily supplement their food reserves with blood glucose. (For this reason diabetics require less insulin when they are exercising than when they are sedentary.)

If a fight-or-flight reaction is called for, two sources rapidly increase the supply of epinephrine (and the related compound norepinephrine): the nerve endings of the sympathetic nervous system and the adrenal medulla (which itself is activated by the sympathetic system). This slow of epinephrine and norepinephrine has marked effects on the activity of the gut, the behavior of blood vessels, and so on, and—more relevant to our present discussion—it causes further stimulation of glycogenolysis and gluconeogenesis by the liver and lipolysis by adipose cells. As a result, glucose and fatty acid levels rise and supply the necessary energy for the fight-or-flight reaction.

If the epinephrine level in the blood remains elevated for a long time, as it would in the case of a prolonged period of fear, hunger, or cold, an additional endocrine pathway is brought into play to produce a new source of blood glucose. This complex pathway involves the *sequential* release and activity of three other hormones: corticotropin **r**eleasing **f**actor (**CRF**) from the hypothalamus, **a**drenocorticotropic

hormone (**ACTH**) from the pituitary, and **hydrocortisone** from the adrenal cortex (Figure 22.8). Hydrocortisone causes further stimulation of gluconeogenesis in the liver. In particular it speeds up the rate at which body proteins are converted to glucose that can be used as an energy source. This is a drastic step, but one that often spells the difference between survival and death for the organism. The direct effects of epinephrine on the liver occur within seconds and reach maximum in minutes once the adrenal medulla is stimulated to action by the sympathetic nervous system. But the indirect effects of epinephrine on the liver—mediated through the hypothalamus, pituitary, and adrenal cortex—require many minutes of stimulation to be initiated and reach maximal effectiveness only after an hour or more has passed. Thus this pathway is definitely a reserve system called into play only in cases of emergency created by severe and prolonged stress.

The final link in the complex of feedback loops involved in regulating blood sugar is in the hypothalamus. A cluster of cells here play an important part in regulating the food-seeking behavior (appetite) of the animal; they have been called the "appestat." In a manner not yet clearly understood, blood glucose levels (as well as blood levels of fatty acids) modify the activity of this center. High blood glucose appears to decrease appetite and food-seeking behavior, whereas prolonged low blood glucose levels lead to increased appetite and food-seeking. The intake of food then reverses all the processes of glucose and fat metabolism as described earlier.

Let us now examine in detail how these changes in glucose metabolism are brought about during alternate periods of eating and fasting.

HORMONES MODIFY GLUCOSE METABOLISM IN THE LIVER BY AFFECTING KEY ENZYMES

In a formal sense, the synthesis of glycogen and its breakdown are reverse reactions, as are glycolysis and gluconeogenesis. But these reverse reactions are not catalyzed by precisely the same enzymes. If we examine the pathways of glucose metabolism in liver cells (Figure 22.9),

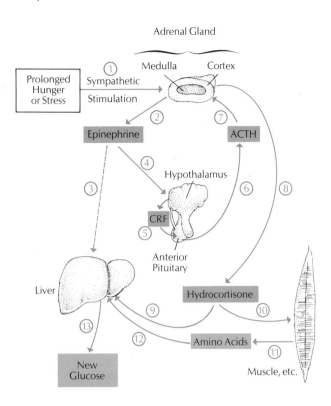

Figure 22.8 The role of hydrocortisone in elevating blood glucose under conditions of severe stress. Prolonged fear, hunger, cold, or other stress leads to prolonged stimulation of the adrenal medulla by the sympathetic nervous system (1). This leads to prolonged and elevated secretion of epinephrine (2). The epinephrine continues to have its rapid, direct effect on the liver (3), as diagramed in Figure 22.7, but in addition it eventually stimulates the hypothalamus (4). The hypothalamus secretes corticotropin releasing factor (CRF) directly into blood vessels leading to the anterior pituitary (5). The CRF causes certain cells in the pituitary to secrete adrenocorticotrophic hormone, or ACTH (6). The ACTH stimulates the adrenal cortex (7) to release hydrocortisone (8). The hydrocortisone has many effects, but two are of major significance: It stimulates the processes of amino acid uptake and gluconeogenesis by the liver (9), and it inhibits amino acid uptake and protein synthesis by muscle and other tissues without affecting the normal processes of protein breakdown (10). As a result, there is a net loss of amino acids from these tissues (11). These amino acids are now taken up by the liver (12) and converted to glucose (13).

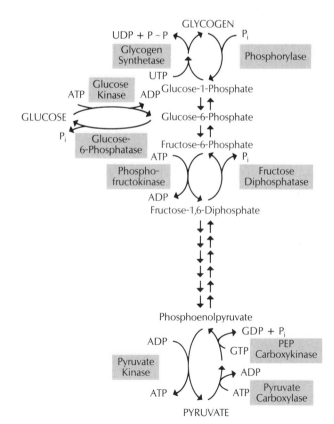

Figure 22.9 Points of control of glucose metabolism in liver cells. Most of the reactions of glucose metabolism are readily reversible. These are indicated here by small parallel black arrows. But at four key points there are reactions involving phosphate transfers that are accompanied by sufficiently large changes in free energy that they are essentially irreversible. At these four points alternate enzymes exist: one that catalyzes the energetically favorable forward reaction and one that catalyzes the reverse reaction by coupling it to the hydrolysis of a high-energy bond of a nucleoside triphosphate. The enzyme reactions shown in red are those involved in glucose utilization and are all stimulated by insulin. The enzymes shown in blue are those required for glycogenolysis and gluconeogenesis; they are all stimulated by glucagon and epinephrine.

we find that most of the reactions involve such small changes in free energy that they are readily reversible. *But at four critical points there is a phosphate transfer that involves such a large release of free energy that the reaction is essentially irreversible.* These reactions can be reversed only by coupling them to the hydrolysis of an additional high-energy phosphate bond (Chapter 12). Such coupling requires a different enzyme, because the substrates are now different. It produces a situation in which the modified reverse reaction releases so much free energy that it, too, is essentially irreversible. Thus, we have the same overall reaction catalyzed in opposite directions by two different enzymes, and involving two quite different reaction mechanisms—both of which are essentially irreversible!

Now, if both the enzymes involved in catalyzing opposing reactions were present in highly active form at all times in the cell, we would have what has been termed a "futile cycle." That is to say, one enzyme would catalyze the simpler, energetically favorable step to produce its product, then the other enzyme would immediately reverse the reaction and use up a high-energy phosphate bond in the process. We would be right back where we started, except for having lost one ATP molecule (or the equivalent). But this does not happen, because the two opposing enzymes are not normally present at maximum concentration and activity at the same time. *The hormones that regulate blood glucose levels in the organism do so by regulating both the amounts of and the activity of the enzymes involved in these four critical steps.*

Thus, in the presence of high levels in insulin the enzymes involved in glycolysis and glycogen synthesis are maximally active, whereas the enzymes for gluconeogenesis and glycogenolysis are relatively inactive. When glycogenolysis is initiated, glycogen synthesis virtually comes to a halt. And when glycolysis is stimulated, gluconeogenesis stops.

The insight into how this differential control of enzyme activity is mediated began to develop in the late 1950s and early 1960s. And as is often the case in a study of life, research into this area had far greater implications than those involved in it could ever have dreamed at the time! Let us now review how we came to understand the molecular mechanism whereby hormones regulate glucose metabolism in the liver.

Glucagon and Epinephrine Act by Raising Cyclic AMP Levels in the Cell

By the mid 1950s, **phosphorylase**, the enzyme that catalyzes glycogen breakdown, was known to figure importantly in the response of liver to the hormones glucagon and epinephrine. Phosphorylase exists in an active and an inactive form, and glucagon and epinephrine were known to

be somehow involved in the activation of the phosphorylase molecules. It was also known that there was an enzyme required for the activation of phosphorylase, but this activating enzyme was also found to exist in both an active and an inactive form.

In 1958 E. W. Sutherland and T. W. Rall reported the results of a critical experiment. They isolated and then combined the inactive form of phosphorylase and the inactive form of the phosphorylase-activating enzyme. When glucagon and/or epinephrine were added to the enzyme mixture, nothing happened. Phosphorylase did not become activated. But, if a membrane-rich fraction of liver cells was exposed to either glucagon or epinephrine (in the presence of ATP), a small molecule was formed that had unique properties. When this small molecule was added to the mixture of inactive phosphorylase and inactive activating enzyme, phosphorylase became converted to the active form and began splitting glycogen at a high rate!

This molecule was quickly identified as **cyclic adenosine-3′5′-monophosphate**, or **cAMP** (Figure 22.10). It was clear that cAMP provided the link between the mechanism of action of these hormones at the molecular level and the effects they exerted at the cellular level. The membrane fraction that had produced the cAMP was shown to contain an enzyme, **adenyl cyclase**, capable of forming cAMP from ATP (releasing inorganic pyrophosphate as the other product). In the membrane mosaic the adenyl cyclase is tightly associated with *receptor molecules* capable of binding glucagon or epinephrine; *binding of hormone apparently*

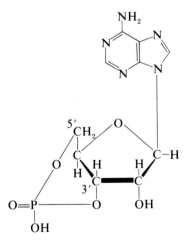

Figure 22.10 The structural formula of cyclic adenosine-3′,5′-monophosphate (cAMP). The term refers to the ring formed when the phosphate group is attached to the 3′ and 5′ —OH groups at the same time.

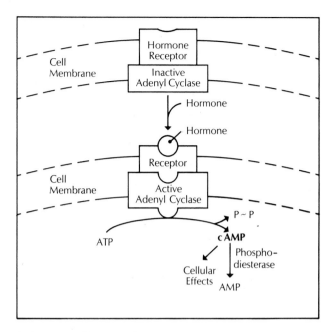

Figure 22.11 Hormone mediated activation of adenyl cyclase. As hormone binds to its receptor in the membrane mosaic, it apparently induces a change in the shape of the receptor; this change is communicated to the adjacent adenyl cyclase and activates its enzymatic site, causing the formation of cAMP. The cAMP now causes several effects in the cell. The enzyme phosphodiesterase converts cAMP to the noncyclic form (AMP). Thus, as long as adenyl cyclase is active, cAMP levels remain elevated but constant, and as soon as the hormone activation ceases cAMP levels fall rapidly.

induces an allosteric change of shape in the adjacent adenyl cyclase molecule and makes it catalytically active. (This scheme is presented in Figure 22.11.) The observations made on this test-tube system have been amply verified for intact liver cells: Glucagon or epinephrine causes a rapid rise in cAMP production, which reaches maximum within a few seconds after hormone addition.

The capacity for rapid and reversible modification of cellular activity by cAMP depends on the presence of a second enzyme that destroys cAMP—**phosphodiesterase.** When epinephrine, for example, affects the cell, the level of cAMP rises rapidly but then remains at a fixed, elevated level as long as epinephrine is present. As fast as new molecules of cAMP are made, older ones are destroyed to maintain this constant but elevated level. As soon as epinephrine disappears, the cAMP level falls again, because of the continued action of phosphodiesterase, and the cell immediately returns to its prestimulated state. In this way the cell responds very rapidly in both directions.

Now we know how cAMP is activated. But how does it cause activation of phosphorylase? It turns out that the active form of phosphorylase (which can degrade glycogen) differs from the inactive form by the presence of a covalently bound phosphate group. Thus the enzyme that activates phosphorylase does so by adding a phosphate group to it. This activating enzyme is but one of a variety of enzymes now known that have this function. They are called **protein kinases**—enzymes that couple phosphate groups to specific proteins. *The principal, if not the only mechanism, by which cAMP affects metabolism of eukaryotic cells is as a stimulator of protein kinases.* Now, the different effects that cAMP has are due to two considerations: which enzymes

Figure 22.12 The mechanism whereby cAMP causes a shift from glycogen synthesis to glycogen breakdown. (a) In the absence of cAMP the protein kinases are inactive and the protein phosphatases are active. As a result, both glycogen synthetase and phosphorylase are in the dephosphorylated form. In this form glycogen synthetase is active but phosphorylase is inactive. Hence glycogen is accumulated.

(b) When cAMP appears, it binds to protein kinase I and activates it. The active protein kinase I now has two effects. It phosphorylates glycogen synthetase and thereby inactivates it. Second, it phosphorylates protein kinase II and activates it. Protein kinase II now adds a phosphate to, and activates, the enzyme phosphorylase. At the same time that the kinases are activated, protein phosphatase is inactivated (probably by being phosphorylated by a protein kinase). As long as the kinases are active and the phosphatase is inactive, both enzymes of glycogen metabolism are kept in the phosphorylated form and glycogen is broken down.

are substrates for the protein kinases that cAMP activates, and whether these enzymes are turned off by the process of phosphorylation. As Figure 22.12 shows, activation of a single protein kinase leads, in the liver cell, to *turning on* the enzymes of glycogen breakdown and *turning off* the enzymes of glycogen synthesis. Similar effects are seen with regard to the enzymes of glycolysis and gluconeogenesis: cAMP turns on the enzymes of gluconeogenesis and turns off those of glycolysis. *Thus epinephrine and glucagon turn the glucose metabolism of the cell clear around by exerting a single primary effect: activating adenyl cyclase.*

The way in which insulin reverses the effects of glucagon and epinephrine is less clearcut. It is clear that *insulin acts to lower cAMP levels in liver cells;* it might achieve this result by stimulating the activity of phosphodiesterase (the enzyme that degrades cAMP). But definitive evidence for such a mechanism of insulin action is lacking. Although additional modes of action of insulin on the liver have been suggested, it appears that the fall in cAMP levels induced by insulin may be sufficient to explain its stimulation of glucose oxidation and storage.

So far we have discussed only the short-term effects of these hormones on the activity of preexisting enzymes of glucose metabolism. But these same hormones—glucagon, epinephrine, and insulin—also exert long-term effects on

glucose metabolism by regulating the rate of accumulation of these same key enzymes in the cell. All the enzymes of the liver are continuously "turning over"; that is, they are continuously being made and degraded at some particular rate or rates. Glucagon, epinephrine, and insulin appear to stimulate the *net* synthesis of the enzymes whose activity they also regulate. The demonstration that cAMP is involved in the phosphorylation of nuclear proteins has led some to speculate that this may be the way in which these three hormones regulate amounts of the various enzymes being synthesized. That is, it has been suggested that a rise in cAMP in the liver might result in phosphorylation of specific nuclear proteins and this in turn might modify which genes are read and which enzymes are synthesized. But so far this is pure speculation. In short, then, it is clear that hormones affecting glucose metabolism in the liver cause increased accumulation of the enzymes they activate. What is not clear is the mechanism by which they cause such accumulation.

Cyclic AMP Plays a Part in Many Other Hormonal Effects

Although, as mentioned above, cAMP effects were discovered in an analysis of liver metabolism, it quickly became obvious that the role of cAMP is not restricted to the liver. Epinephrine was shown to elevate cAMP levels in

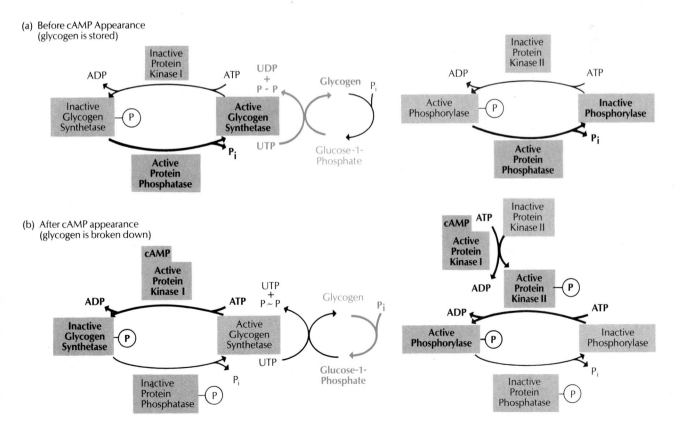

(a) Before cAMP Appearance (glycogen is stored)

(b) After cAMP appearance (glycogen is broken down)

adipose tissues within seconds. Subsequently, it was shown that a derivative of cAMP mimics the effect of epinephrine on adipose tissue, resulting in activation of the enzyme responsible for breaking down fat to release fatty acids. Similarly, epinephrine was shown to elevate cAMP levels dramatically in heart muscle within two seconds; this rise apparently mediates the epinephrine effect of increasing the forcefulness of the heartbeat. Thus we see that three quite different kinds of cellular effects can be mediated in three different cell types by a single hormone acting by a single mechanism! *The response obtained in a given cell depends on the molecules within the cell that are affected by an elevated level of cAMP.*

But the role of cAMP is by no means restricted to epinephrine and glucagon effects. For example, the stimulation by ACTH of hydrocortisone production and release by adrenal cortex (Figure 22.8) is now known to be mediated by cAMP. And a similar mechanism has now been implicated in a variety of other hormone effects (Table 22.2). This system of control obviously has tremendous versatility. By varying the nature of the receptor present in the adenyl cyclase complex in the membrane, a cell could potentially make the cAMP system responsive to almost any extracellular mediator. And by varying the nature of the molecules inside the cell that respond to cAMP (or to a cAMP-activated protein kinase) a cell could achieve virtually any kind of modification of behavior.

Little wonder, then, that at one time it was suggested that perhaps cAMP might be the *universal* mediator of hormonal effects. This prediction appears now to have been overly optimistic. *Many hormones appear to function in other ways.* Yet it is certainly not exaggerating to say that cAMP

Table 22.2

Some Physiological Changes Reputed to Be Mediated by Either an Increase or Decrease in cAMP Concentration

Hormonal Effects in Vertebrates	Nonhormonal Effects in Vertebrates	Effects in Nonvertebrate Organisms
1. Effects of epinephrine and glucagon on the liver: increased glycogenolysis and gluconeogenesis.	1. Relaxation of gut muscle by sympathetic nervous system.	1. Secretion by insect salivary glands in response to specific stimuli.
2. Effects of epinephrine, glucagon, and ACTH on adipose tissues: increased lipolysis.	2. All inhibitory postsynaptic potentials in the sympathetic nervous system.	2. Activation of protein kinases in every animal phylum examined.
3. Effects of epinephrine and norepinephrine on the heart: increased force and rate of beating, increased glucogenolysis.	3. Inhibition of cerebellar Purkinje cells by input from adrenergic nerves.	3. Aggregation and morphogenesis in cellular slime molds.
4. Effects of insulin on the liver: increased storage and utilization of glucose.	4. Membrane potential change in photoreceptor cells of retina following light-induced isomerization of retinal.	4. Spore formation in various unicellular eukaryotes.
5. Effects of insulin on adipose tissue: increased storage of fat.	5. Direct response of pineal gland to light (through the skull).	5. Formation of eukaryotic flagellum (*Chlamydomonas*).
6. Effects of the various hypothalamic releasing factors (CRF, TRF, and so on) on the anterior pituitary: specific release of the corresponding pituitary hormone (ACTH, TSH, and so on).	6. Effects of certain tranquilizers on the central nervous system.	6. Formation of prokaryotic flagellum and pilli (*Caulobacter*).
7. Effects of ACTH on adrenal cortex: increased synthesis and release of hydrocortisone.	7. Many other CNS effects.	7. Derepression of enzymes of catabolic metabolism in *E. coli* and other bacteria.
8. Effects of thyroid stimulating hormone on the thyroid: increased thyroxin release.	8. Aggregation and functioning of platelets in blood clotting.	
9. Effects of parathyroid hormone on bone: increased release of calcium to blood.	9. A variety of responses in immune cells following stimulation by antigen or other immune cells.	
10. Effects of parathyroid hormone on kidney: increased excretion of phosphate.	10. Control of cell division in many types of cells–normal and cancerous.	
11. Effects of antidiuretic hormone on kidney tubules, bladder, gills, skin, and so on in different species: uptake of water and loss of salts.		
12. Effects of luteinizing hormone on corpus luteum of ovary: progesterone secretion.		
13. Effects of gastrin on the stomach: secretion of HCl.		
14. Effects of melanocyte stimulating hormone on skin: darkening.		

is one of the most widespread and important elements of cellular control in the living world. And by no means is its function restricted to the mediation of hormonal effects. As we saw in Chapter 20, it plays a crucial role in transcriptional regulation in bacteria. It is vitally important in the life cycle of the cellular slime molds, for it is the chemical attractant that draws individual vegetative cells together to form the multicellular reproductive structure (Interleaf 6.1). Protein kinases that are activated by cAMP have been found in organisms as diverse as ciliates, sponges, jellyfish, nematodes, annelids, clams, squid, lobsters, sea stars, and chordates. Cyclic forms of other nucleoside monophosphates have also been found recently to participate in cellular control.

Having looked closely at one system of hormonal integration and control, and having examined how hormones may function at levels from the molecular to the organismic, let us now return for a broader look at a range of endocrine glands and the ways in which their functions are integrated.

THE HYPOTHALAMUS AND PITUITARY TIE THE ENDOCRINE SYSTEM TO THE NERVOUS SYSTEM

Nowhere is the structural and functional connection between nerves and endocrine cells more clearly demonstrated than at the base of the vertebrate brain where the hypothalamus and the pituitary sit side by side (Figure 22.13).

The Posterior Pituitary Is an Extension of the Hypothalamus

The posterior pituitary is little more than an extension of the hypothalamus, the region of the brain thought to control the autonomic nervous system (Chapter 26). Two hormones are released into the bloodstream from the posterior lobe: *vasopressin* (also known as *antidiuretic hormone*, or ADH)

and oxytocin (Figure 22.14). But the site of synthesis of these hormones is not in the pituitary. Rather, they are made in specialized clusters of neurons in the hypothalamus (Figure 22.13). Granules containing these hormones are then passed down the axons of the synthesizing cells and are stored in the nerve terminals that surround blood vessels in the pituitary. Stimulation of the cells in the hypothalamus then causes release of the hormones from the nerve terminals into the nearby blood vessels (in a process analogous to release of neurotransmitter substances by conventional neurons). Such cells—nervelike in origin, structure, and function but secreting their effector substances into the circulatory system rather than into synaptic contacts with the target cells—are called **neurosecretory cells.** A structure such as the posterior pituitary is called a **neurohemal** (nerve-blood) organ. Neurosecretory cells and neurohemal organs abound in invertebrates, whereas endocrine glands of the type more common in vertebrates are not found. Thus neurosecretion appears to be the original type of endocrine function.

Vasopressin was so named because injection of posterior pituitary extracts causes constriction of blood vessels and a sharp rise in blood pressure: however, with the levels of the hormone normally present in the blood it is doubtful that it plays any such role. Rather, the hormone acts on the kidney, where it stimulates reabsorption of water from the urine, thereby concentrating the urine. If a salt solution is injected slowly into the carotid artery (leading to the brain), the level of salt in the blood reaching the brain is increased, while the concentration of salt in the body as a whole is scarcely affected. But within two minutes the volume of urine being put out by the kidney drops sharply, while the concentration of salts in the urine rises. From such observations the following pathway has been worked out. Certain cells in the brain constantly monitor the concentration of

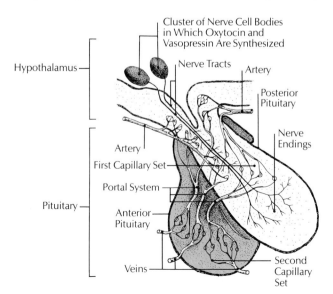

Figure 22.13 The organization of hypothalamus and pituitary gland. The posterior lobe of the pituitary gland is actually an extension of the hypothalamus region of the brain. The hormones (oxytocin and vasopressin) released from the posterior pituitary are made in nerve cells in the hypothalamus and travel down nerve tracts to nerve endings adjacent to blood vessels in the posterior pituitary. The anterior lobe (shown in yellow) is separate in origin from the hypothalamus and is functionally linked to it by blood vessels. Arteries entering the hypothalamus branch into capillary beds in the hypothalamus and in the stalk of the posterior pituitary, where they pick up any releasing factors being secreted by the hypothalamus. These capillaries then come together to form a system of portal vessels that travel to the anterior pituitary before branching to form a second capillary bed. Here the releasing factors diffuse out of the vessels to affect the pituitary cells, and hormones secreted by the pituitary are picked up to be transported through the body.

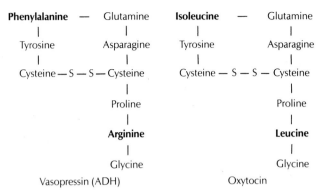

Phenylalanine	—	Glutamine
Tyrosine		Asparagine
Cysteine — S — S — Cysteine		
	Proline	
	Arginine	
	Glycine	
Vasopressin (ADH)		

Isoleucine	—	Glutamine
Tyrosine		Asparagine
Cysteine — S — S — Cysteine		
	Proline	
	Leucine	
	Glycine	
	Oxytocin	

Figure 22.14 Structures of the two posterior pituitary hormones of mammals. Each consists of nine amino acids held (by the disulfide bonds between cysteine groups) in a sort of figure 9 shape. The relationship between them is clear, but the differences in amino acids (shown in boldface) result in different target cells and totally different functions.

dissolved material in the blood; increases in blood concentration trigger signals that impinge on the hypothalamus, resulting in increased release of ADH from the nerve endings in the pituitary. The ADH travels to the kidney, where its prime target is the distal part of the kidney tubule (where substances are reabsorbed from urine just before it is excreted to the bladder, as described in Chapter 21). The ADH binds to the surface of the kidney tubule cells, causing a rise in intracellular cAMP: this cAMP, by an unknown mechanism, stimulates the reabsorption of water, pumping it from urine back to the blood.

Modifications of ADH production and sensitivity play a large part in adaptation of animals to various environments. In fish, where much of the control of blood salt concentrations occurs in the gills, the gills are sensitive to ADH. In frogs, where much exchange occurs via the skin, skin cells respond to ADH by increasing water uptake. One secret of the camel's success in the desert is the exquisite sensitivity of the kidney tubules to ADH. Other desert animals and certain hibernating animals similarly show adaptive modifications of ADH production and/or effect.

The release of the other hormone of the posterior pituitary, oxytocin, is even more obviously tied to neural stimuli. During coitus, stimulation of the external genitalia of the female initiates a reflex circuit leading to release of oxytocin, which then causes the uterine contractions associated with orgasm. Similarly, oxytocin is involved in the uterine contractions associated with the birth process. But the principal function of oxytocin is in the release of milk. Many hormones are involved in the development, maintenance, and function of the mammary glands, but it is oxytocin that causes the milk finally to be released from the cells in which it is stored. The principal route of stimulation of oxytocin release usually begins with stimulation of the nipples, but the response can also be conditioned so that it is elicited by other stimuli regularly associated with stimulation of the nipples. For example, the family cow may begin to drip milk when the milking stool is brought into the barn, and the human mother may begin to release milk in response to a cry of hunger from her infant. The release of milk appears to be the one function controlled by the

posterior pituitary that cannot be assumed by other systems if the pituitary and hypothalamic cells are nonfunctional. Other mechanisms exist to control kidney function, uterine contraction, and so forth, but no alternate route for milk release appears to exist.

The Hypothalamus and Anterior Pituitary Participate in Feedback Control of Other Glands

Functionally, the anterior pituitary is the most complex endocrine organ; with its seven known hormones (and an assortment of suspected additional ones), it participates importantly in regulation of many body processes. One of these hormones, **growth hormone**, has widespread effects, as the name suggests. Deficiency or excess of growth hormone can lead to dwarfism or gigantism, for example. But five of the anterior pituitary hormones have other endocrine glands as their targets and figure importantly in the functioning of these glands. Hence, there was once a widespread tendency to call the anterior pituitary the "master gland." But this name implies far more autonomy for the pituitary than it deserves. Secretion of each of these pituitary hormones is under control of a corresponding

Figure 22.15 Feedback circuits regulating the blood levels of thyroxin and hydrocortisone. A region within the hypothalamus produces a hormone called thyrotropin releasing factor (TRF). When released, the TRF travels through the portal vessels to the pituitary and stimulates cells of the anterior pituitary to release thyroid-stimulating hormone (TSH). This TSH activates the adenyl cyclase of the thyroid gland, resulting in a rise of cAMP and, ultimately, in the release of thyroxin. This thyroxin, on reaching the brain, inhibits the release of both TRF and TSH. When thyroxin levels begin to fall, the inhibition is released and a new round of secretion occurs. The feedback circuit involved in regulating hydrocortisone levels is similar, except that hydrocortisone exerts most of its feedback control at the level of the hypothalamus and has much less effect on the pituitary cells directly.

hormone (a so-called releasing factor) produced and secreted by the hypothalamus.

The relationship between anterior pituitary and hypothalamus is different from that seen in the case of the posterior pituitary (Figure 22.13). The anterior pituitary is not derived from nervous tissue and is not connected to the hypothalamus by axons as the posterior lobe is. Instead, the coupling is via the blood. Most (in humans, *all*) of the blood supplying the anterior lobe first passes through the capillaries of the hypothalamus. Hence, when releasing factors are secreted by the hypothalamic neurosecretory cells, they diffuse into the blood and are passed immediately to the anterior lobe.

But what controls the hypothalamus? Being, as it is, a part of the central nervous system, many of the functions of the hypothalamus, including secretion of releasing factors, are under a certain amount of neuronal control (as discussed in Chapter 26). But in addition, the neurosecretory cells are sensitive to a variety of chemical stimuli in the blood. Among the most important of these chemical regulators of the hypothalamus are the hormones whose secretions are controlled by hypothalamus and pituitary! Thus negative feedback loops occur in which hormones control their own production by affecting the secretory activity of hypothalamus and pituitary (Figure 22.15). This, then, gives us a picture of the role of hypothalamus and pituitary gland: *They are key links in several carefully balanced negative feedback circuits that maintain the homeostatic control of body metabolism.*

THE MENSTRUAL CYCLE: A PITUITARY FEEDBACK LOOP WITH BUILT-IN TIME DELAYS

Any negative feedback loop tends to be an oscillating process. For example, by the time a room thermostat turns off the furnace the temperature has risen slightly above the desired level. Then the temperature will fall slightly below the desired level before the furnace is turned on again (Figure 22.16). The magnitude of the oscillations in the system and the time period required to complete a cycle will depend on two factors: the rate at which the controlled entity is produced and the sensitivity of the sensor-switch. Most hormonal feedback loops are constructed such that the oscillations are both rapid and small. But the **menstrual cycle** of the human female is an interesting example of the way that natural selection may build in low rates of hormone production and relatively insensitive sensor-switches to result in a cyclic phenomenon involving long time delays and wide swings in hormone production.

The function of the cyclic events of the menstrual cycle is to prepare the lining of the uterine wall—the endometrium—once each month to receive an embryo. If a fertilized egg is not received, much of the endometrium is sloughed off and the cycle is initiated once again. Because the production of the hormones involved in preparing the uterus depends on the production and release of an egg, the two processes are coupled in time so that the uterus is in optimum condition for pregnancy whenever an embryo is formed.

There are two hormones produced by the hypothalamus, two produced by the pituitary gland, and two produced by the ovary that participate in this feedback cycle. The pituitary hormones are both called **gonadotropins** (stimulators of the gonads, or reproductive organs). Secretion of each of the gonadotropins is under control of a corresponding releasing factor produced by the hypothalamus. And secretion of the releasing factors is under feedback control of the two ovarian hormones. The details of the feedback circuit are described in Figure 22.17.

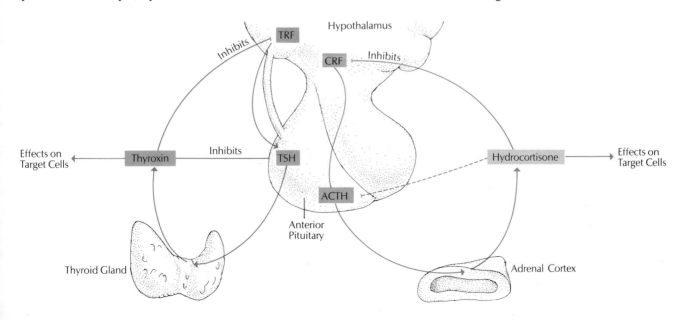

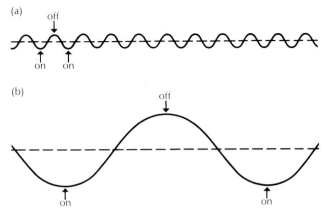

Figure 22.16 Oscillations in a negative feedback system. The sensor-switch turns on production, and the amount of the controlled entity begins to increase. Eventually the sensor-switch detects the elevated level and turns production off once more. How wide the swings will be and how long a cycle will take depend on the rate at which the controlled entity is produced and the sensitivity of the sensor-switch. The fluctuations may be a series of brief ripples, as in (a), or of widely spearated peaks and valleys, as in (b).

There are two main reasons why this feedback loop takes twenty-eight days to complete. The first is that the production of the feedback inhibitor (progesterone) does not begin at once when the gonadotropins commence to flow. It requires a sequence of developmental events to produce the active endocrine structure, the corpus luteum. But the second, and critical, aspect is that when progesterone concentration does eventually reach a sufficient level to turn off the hypothalamus, the latter stays turned off for about a week! If, as is the case in most hormone feedback loops, the hypothalamus stayed off only until the progesterone level *began* to fall, a menstrual cycle would not be possible. For if gonadotropin levels began to rise again as progesterone began to fall, the corpus luteum would still be present and receptive to stimulation. Thus we would establish a rapid oscillation of progesterone levels analogous to Figure 22.16*a* rather than the pattern shown in Figure 22.16*b*. What is the reason for this sluggish behavior of the hypothalamus? Why does it not produce a new round of secretion until the corpus luteum has degenerated and is therefore unresponsive? It appears from studies with laboratory animals that the secret lies in the hypothalamus: It undergoes sex-specific modification during its embryonic development that somehow builds in this all-important time lag.

The male also produces releasing factors, FSH, LH, and—as a result of gonadotropin action—a steroid sex hormone, **testosterone.** And testosterone, like progesterone, feeds back to inhibit the hypothalamus. But it does so in a more conventional manner, resulting in rapid, small fluctuations in testosterone levels, not the wide, slow oscillations observed in female sex hormones. It turns out that the difference resides in the hypothalamus, not in the difference between testosterone and progesterone. If a female experimental animal is exposed to testosterone during a critical stage of embryonic development, the hypothalamus develops with the male pattern of reactivity. When she reaches sexual maturity, the first cycle of ovarian activity is initiated properly but it does not terminate properly. The corpus luteum develops, produces progesterone, and turns the hypothalamic secretions off. But as

progesterone levels subsequently start to fall, the hypothalamus is reactivated at once, causing a release of gonadotropins and maintenance and continued stimulation of the corpus luteum. Thus a new cycle of egg maturation cannot be initiated and the animal is permanently infertile!

The periodic maturation and release of eggs demands the built-in delay system of the hypothalamus. Modifications of the sexual cycle in different species depend in large part on differences in the time lags built into the hypothalamus and the existence of nonhormonal factors that regulate the timing of secretion of gonadotropin releasing factors by the hypothalamic cells. In animals that breed but once a year, the hypothalamus cannot be turned back on until seasonal clues (such as day length) trigger neuronal signals to the hypothalamus that release it from inhibition. In other cases, such as the rabbit, the stimulation of the female reproductive tract by the act of coitus is required to activate the hypothalamus (Chapter 26). But in all cases the result is the same: Rather than being held in a state of constant readiness, the uterine wall is prepared for pregnancy only at the time that conception is possible.

One feature of the reproductive cycle that is found in all mammals other than primates is the existence of an estrus period (commonly known as "heat"). Only during estrus—when the ovary is prepared to release one or more eggs—is the female receptive to coitus. The progressive loss of this restricted period of receptivity in female primates, and its total absence in humans, has been suggested as one of the factors leading to the establishment of the human family (Chapter 33).

STEROID HORMONES APPEAR TO ACT WITHIN THE CELL RATHER THAN AT THE CELL MEMBRANE

As was pointed out earlier in the chapter, widespread as the role of cAMP may be in hormone action, not all hormones appear to follow the cAMP model. The steroid hormones, including the sex hormones, are prime examples. Whereas most hormones that work through activating adenyl cyclase appear to exert their effect at the cell membrane (without entering the cell), it appears that most steroid hormones

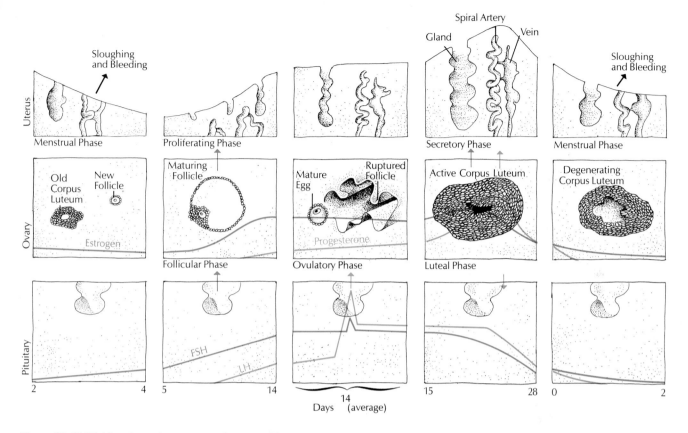

Figure 22.17 Highly schematic summary of events of human menstrual cycle.

Traditionally the cycle is timed from the onset of menstrual bleeding. During this period, levels of estrogen and progesterone are low. As a result, the hypothalamus secretes FSH releasing factor, causing the pituitary to secrete FSH. This FSH stimulates a follicle—containing an immature egg—in the ovary to begin to enlarge and mature (follicular phase of the ovarian cycle). The cells of the follicle secrete estrogen, which initiates proliferation of cells in the uterine endometrium and development of glands and blood vessels (proliferative phase of uterine cycle). During this phase the pituitary begins to secrete increasing levels of LH, which causes the follicle to begin producing low levels of progesterone.

At about fourteen days there is a sudden, brief increase in FSH release and a much larger, but equally brief, increase in the release of LH from the pituitary. (This increase is thought to be due to the sensitivity of the pituitary to some specific low level of progesterone in the blood.) The FSH and LH cause the wall of the follicle to weaken, thus permitting the now-mature egg to be released. This process is known as ovulation (ovulatory phase of the ovarian cycle).

With the egg ovulated and the level of LH now elevated, the follicle cells proliferate rapidly. The follicle is transformed into the corpus luteum, which begins to secrete increasing amounts of progesterone in addition to estrogen (the luteal phase of the ovarian cycle).

Together these hormones cause further development of the endometrium. The uterine glands become active in secreting materials into the uterus, preparing the surface to receive the fertilized egg (secretory phase of the uterine cycle).

But as the progesterone level of the blood continues to rise, it reaches the point where it inhibits the activity of hypothalamus and pituitary. Thus release of FSH and LH falls. In the absence of FSH and LH, the corpus luteum cannot be maintained. Hence it ceases releasing estrogen and progesterone. In the absence of estrogen the spiral arteries of the endometrium collapse, diminishing the blood supply. Tissues become necrotic and eventually the process of sloughing and loss of blood sets in (menstrual phase of the uterine cycle.) As a result of the low levels of progesterone and estrogen, the hypothalamus and pituitary are eventually released from inhibition and begin the cycle anew.

If the egg is fertilized, it attaches to the uterine wall before the high progesterone levels have turned off the pituitary. Cells of the developing placenta of the embryo begin at once to produce an LH-like hormone. But the placenta differs from the pituitary in one important regard: it cannot be feedback-inhibited by progesterone. Hence it maintains the corpus luteum (and, indirectly, the uterine lining) despite continued high progesterone levels.

must enter the target cell to exert their effects. Analysis of target cells has revealed the presence of intracellular receptor proteins that bind the corresponding hormones rather firmly. For example, uterine cells contain an estrogen-binding protein in the cytoplasm. Upon binding estrogen, this protein appears to move to the nucleus and undergo changes in size as well as in certain other properties (Figure 22.18).

Now, in most cases one of the results of steroid hormone action on target cells is an increase in RNA and protein synthesis. It is therefore tempting to suggest that the hormone-receptor complex is acting directly as a specific regulator of gene expression. Unfortunately, however, it has not yet been possible to demonstrate that this is so. One problem is that we are still largely in the dark about the precise mechanisms of gene control in the nuclei of eukaryotic cells (Chapter 20). The second is that, unfortunately, in many cases the problem cannot yet be analyzed outside the living animal. If the uterus, for example, is isolated from an experimental animal and is exposed to estrogen in a culture vessel, the estrogen is taken up, binds to the receptor protein, moves to the nucleus, and the complex is transformed there as in the living animal. But nothing else happens. Although the uterus can be maintained outside the animal for several days in a healthy state, conditions have not yet been found in which it will respond to estrogen in a characteristic manner.

Most other steroid hormone target tissues show the same refractoriness to stimulation in isolation, but several exceptions exist. For example, lines of cells derived from liver tumors can be grown in the laboratory, and they retain the capacity to respond in certain ways to hydrocortisone as the intact liver does. Similarly, certain embryonic tissues that depend on hydrocortisone for their normal development can be shown to respond to the hormone when grown in isolation. Analysis of such systems has given us extensive insight into the *effects* of hormone action in terms of synthesis of various nucleic acid and protein molecules. But, unfortunately, such studies have not yet yielded definitive insight into the connection between hormone binding and the ultimate responses of the cells.

HORMONES MEDIATE DEVELOPMENT AS WELL AS HOMEOSTASIS

As has been implied in our discussion, hormones are involved in development of differentiated cell structure as well as in homeostatic maintenance of cell functions. The sex hormones, for example, are required for initial development of the structures of the reproductive tract as well as for their function in the adult. In the case of certain fish and amphibians, addition of sex hormones to the water in which the embryos are grown will result in sex reversal. In other words, embryos that are of one sex in terms of chromosomes can be caused to develop into functional adults of the opposite sex. We are just beginning to realize the extent to which hormones play a part in many other aspects of normal development of the embryo.

But perhaps the most dramatic examples of the developmental roles of hormones are in species with indirect development—that is, in species that pass through a juvenile stage, known as a *larva*, before metamorphosing into adults (Chapter 18). The process of metamorphosis is—in cases that have been studied—under hormonal control. The simplest case is in amphibians such as frogs. Here the hormone thyroxin (the hormone that regulates the overall metabolic rate of virtually all cells in all vertebrates) is the agent that induces metamorphosis. Injection of thyroxin into immature tadpoles causes them to metamorphose into tiny but perfectly formed adults. This metamorphosis involves an astonishing number of changes. Tail, gills, and larval mouth structures must be resorbed. Legs must grow out and be innervated, a tongue must form, the gut must be transformed from one adapted to a herbivorous diet to one suited for the new carnivorous way of life. A whole variety of proteins and enzymes must be modified or replaced to adapt to the whole new way of life. And all these changes are initiated by a single hormone that functions in adult animals simply to control the general metabolic activity of the cells.

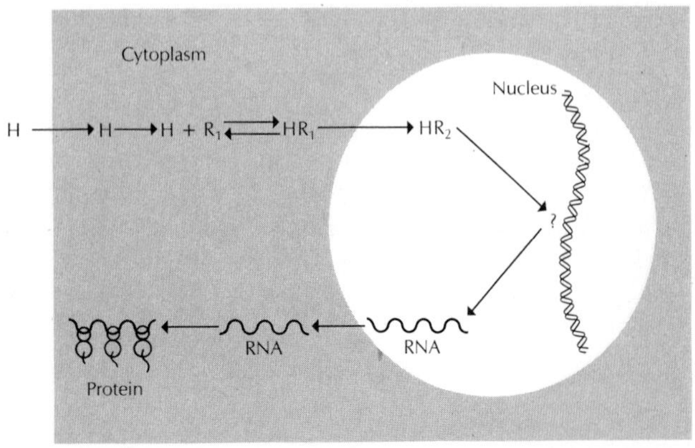

Figure 22.18 A schematic outline of the proposed mechanism of steroid hormone action. The hormone (H) enters the cell and binds with receptor protein (R_1) in the cytoplasm. The complex now moves to the nucleus where the receptor becomes modified (R_2). Ultimately the cell responds to hormone presence by making additional molecules of RNA and protein. The unanswered but critical question is: How is the formation of a hormone-receptor complex linked to the ultimate response of the cell?

Furthermore, it has been shown that all these diverse effects are exerted by the hormone directly on the responding cells. If two nerve cells are exposed to high levels of thyroxin, one will grow and develop new connections while the other will degenerate. This is one of the clearest examples of the fact that, as the result of natural selection, a single hormone can come to have a wide range of effects on different target cells. The response of the different cells clearly depends on the hormone-sensitive molecules they contain and not on any information contained in the hormone molecule itself.

PERSPECTIVE

In order to understand fully the significance of a hormone such as epinephrine in the living world, we must think in terms of atoms, molecules, metabolic pathways, genetic control systems, organelles, cells, tissues, organs, organ systems, organisms, populations, species, communities, and, finally, the flow of all of these levels through evolutionary time.

As far as we know, epinephrine has only one kind of direct effect—one mechanism of action. Atoms of this simple molecule interact with the atoms of a specific receptor protein on the surfaces of certain kinds of cells, in the way substrates interact with enzymes. This interaction causes a subtle shift in the atoms of the receptor, thus modifying its interaction with the enzyme adenyl cyclase to which it is bound in the membrane mosaic. Corresponding atomic shifts in the adenyl cyclase occur, causing it to become active in production of cyclic AMP. But from this simple interaction of epinephrine with its receptors and the resultant rise in cAMP within certain cells, what a diversity of results can be achieved, depending upon the cell types involved and the molecules they contain that are responsive to cAMP!

Muscle cells all over the body respond, but in opposite directions. Those in the heart respond by contracting more strongly, those in the walls of blood vessels leading to brain and skeletal muscle relax, those in blood vessels of the gut contract, while those in the wall of the gut itself relax. And suddenly, from one cause acting on many separate cells of the same tissue type (muscle) in several different organs, four organ systems—the circulatory, nervous, digestive, and skeletal-muscular—undergo a sudden change in functional state.

Meanwhile, cells in tissues other than muscle respond directly to epinephrine as well, and as changes in cAMP occur in the liver, gluconeogenesis and glycogenolysis are speeded up; in adipose tissue lipolysis is stimulated and in the hypothalamus the secretions ultimately leading to hydrocortisone release begin.

But when we describe the way in which epinephrine and cAMP bring about these effects in terms of activation of phosphorylating enzymes, modification of whole metabolic pathways, and changes in cell behavior, we have just begun to understand the role of epinephrine. To truly understand its meaning, we must view the animal not on the operating table of an endocrinology laboratory but in the situations in which these responses all evolved—in the natural environment. When we see the situations in nature that trigger such a flow of epinephrine from the adrenal gland, and when we observe how the behavior of the animal is changed as a result, our appreciation of the cellular and molecular details is enhanced. We find that this hormonal change (and all the others associated with it) is elicited by a wide array of circumstances that may mean life or death for the individual: absence of food, appearance of a predator, challenge by another member of the species (over space, food, or mate), appearance of a potential mate, and so on. And we see that in most cases such hormonal stimulation is followed by a shift in behavior that increases the individual's chance of surviving and of leaving progeny.

But (as we shall also see in Chapters 29 and 32) the impact of adrenal gland activity extends beyond the individual and its adaptation to the challenges of the moment—it affects the entire population of which the individual is a component. Adrenal gland activity regulates the population's prospects for success as a group in evolutionary time, for the continued stimulation of the adrenal gland that results from population pressures (and from the resulting conflicts over space and food) feeds back to lower reproductive success of the individuals. The population is thus kept within the limits that the environment can sustain. In few places in the panorama of life is the integral relationship between events at the many levels of biological organization more apparent than in the role of the animal endocrine system.

SUGGESTED READINGS

CORNER, GEORGE W. *Anatomist at Large.* New York: Basic Books, 1958. The autobiography and selected essays of the endocrinologist who contributed most to our knowledge of hormonal regulation of mammalian reproduction.

LE BARON, RUTHANN. *Hormones: A Delicate Balance.* New York: Pegasus, 1972. This highly readable book emphasizes a historical approach to our understanding of vertebrate endocrine glands and their secretions. Requires little technical background.

SAWIN, CLARK T. *Hormones: Endocrine Physiology.* Boston: Little, Brown, 1969. This book goes beyond the usual gland-by-gland, hormone-by-hormone treatment of the subject found in so many endocrinology textbooks and includes chapters on such interesting subjects as the endocrinology of reproduction, the hormonal control of daily energy supply, and the control of body fats and obesity.

Chapter 23

Hormonal Integration
in Plants

Plants, like animals, possess hormones involved in intercellular communication. But there are fundamental differences in the roles of hormones in these two groups of organisms, and these differences are related to patterns of development. In plants, most hormones regulate the growth and development of parts rather than the function of fully developed parts. Although plant hormones may be manipulated to cause bizarre growth (as they have done in these radishes), in the natural state, hormones function to maintain a balanced pattern of growth between roots and shoots, stems and leaves that is in tune with environmental conditions.

If we were to take a walk through a forest, it would not be difficult to find signs of intense activity. In the soil and in the litter of the forest floor, insects and other invertebrates would be darting about. Here and there we would come across such animals as frogs, snakes, mice, and birds. All these organisms would be variously engaged in food gathering, predation, social interaction, and reproduction. Compared with such animated characters, the plants of the forest would appear to be nothing more than a passive backdrop. But our impression of botanical inactivity would derive from our own fast-paced way of looking at the world around us. As Chapter 19 has already pointed out, plants go through a definite and precisely controlled pattern of growth and development—a pattern that begins with the germination of a seed or spore and continues (in most plants) throughout the life span of the individual. Such growth and development depends on delicately timed interactions of cell division, cell elongation, and tissue differentiation, which ultimately lead to the "adult" form of the plant. In addition to these activities, plants respond to their environment in ways that are as carefully worked out as any response seen in the animal world. Animals, for example, will orient themselves in space in such a way that they function properly. Despite the fact that plants are anchored to one place, they, too, orient themselves in the way that will best enhance their functioning. Stems and leaves are directed upward into the air toward the light; roots are directed down through the soil toward water and nutrients. Moreover, plants will change the orientation of their stems and leaves to take fullest advantage of available light; and if moisture is limited, they will send roots toward those parts of the soil that contain the most water. Tendrils and stems of climbing plants will wrap around a tree trunk or some other upright plant as they seek patches of sunlight beneath the forest canopy. In some species, leaves drop in response to changing seasons; and fruit ripens and drops from the parent when it becomes mature.

What are the mainsprings underlying the multitude of activities involved in plant growth and development—and survival? These activities are triggered, regulated, or controlled by a relatively small number of chemical messengers called **plant hormones,** which are substances formed in one part of the plant and transported to another part, where they act. In this chapter, we will examine the role of hormones in the biology of complex plants.

IDENTIFYING THE SUBSTANCES THAT CONTROL PLANT GROWTH

As you read in Chapter 19, the first indication that chemical messengers might exist in plants came with Charles and Francis Darwin's study of **phototropism** (movement in

response to light). In working with plants of the grass family, they found that a seedling illuminated from one side curves toward the light as it grows—unless its extreme tip is covered with an opaque cap. Because the curved zone was well below the tip, they concluded that some sort of "influence" moves from the tip to the parts below. Later, in 1911, the Danish botanist Peter Boysen-Jensen demonstrated that a seedling still curves toward the light even if its tip is cut off and stuck back on again with gelatin (Figure 23.2). Whatever the "influence" was, it was capable of diffusing across the cut through the gelatin. Subsequently, a Hungarian researcher, Arpad Paál, showed that some substance exists that accelerates ordinary, noncurving stem growth in the part of the seedling beneath the tip. Clearly the "influence" that the Darwins discussed had to be a growth-promoting chemical substance.

In their experiments, Boysen-Jensen and Paál used the **coleoptile,** or first shoot, of the oat (*Avena sativa*). The oat coleoptile has since become the standard subject for studies of this sort. It consists of a hollow sheath, six to seven cells thick, that surrounds the tightly rolled-up first leaves and protects them as the shoot pushes up through the soil. The tip of the coleoptile is a domelike structure that is solid for a length of about 0.3 millimeter from the top. Vascular bundles run up the sides of the coleoptile to the lower part of this solid tip. In most experiments, the "tips" removed

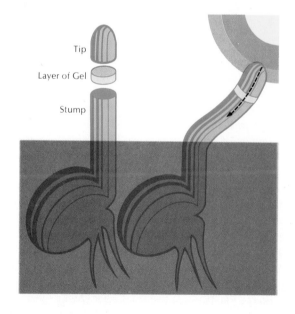

Figure 23.2   Boysen-Jensen's test for the growth substance in plants. This experiment showed that an oat seedling coleoptile will still curve toward the light if its tip is cut off and a gelatin layer is placed between the tip and the stump. This evidence strongly suggested that the substance influencing growth can diffuse across the cut through the gelatin.

Tip

Layer of Gel

Stump

from coleoptiles consist of considerably more than the tiny solid caps.

After Paál's work, there were several attempts to extract the growth substance from ground-up coleoptile tips or from other plant parts. Paul Stark devised a clever test for detecting its presence. He mixed the plant part to be tested for growth substance with melted agar, then cooled it and cut it into small blocks. Next he decapitated coleoptiles and partially pulled out the leaves inside, leaving a small piece of leaf as support. He then applied each agar block to one side of a decapitated coleoptile, resting it against the remaining piece of leaf. He reasoned that if the agar contained growth substance, the side of the coleoptile touching it should elongate more than the other side; in other words, the coleoptile would curve away from the agar block. Unfortunately, none of his coleoptiles curved in any direction.

Nevertheless, Stark was on the right track, and several years later other researchers put his test method to good use. Elizabeth Seubert mixed substances derived from malt extract and human saliva with the agar, and the coleoptiles curved. Frits Went found that intact, living coleoptile tips placed on agar blocks for a few hours would secrete the growth substance into the blocks. When positioned against coleoptiles as in Stark's test, the blocks produced curved coleoptiles. Went demonstrated that the angle of curvature (measured after the agar block had been applied for a standard time) is proportional to the number of coleoptile tips that had been placed on the agar block and to the time they remained there. Thus, Stark's test became a way of quantitatively measuring the amount of growth substance.

Of Went's many experiments with the plant growth substance, one was particularly illuminating. Earlier, the Russian botanist Nikolai Cholodny had suggested that both phototropism and **geotropism** (movement in response to gravity) in plant shoots and roots are caused by unequal distribution of growth substance. In his view, *the effects of light or gravity cause more growth substance to accumulate in one side of a root or shoot tip than in the other.* As the growth substance moves away from the tip, said Cholodny, more growth is stimulated on one side of the root or shoot than on the other side, and that is what causes curvature. Cholodny worked mostly with roots and he obtained some indirect evidence to support his view, but Went confirmed it directly. As Figure 23.3 shows, Went illuminated coleoptiles from one side and then cut off their tips. He placed the tips on the line between two small agar blocks separated by a razor blade, so that the previously illuminated side of the tip was over one block and the previously shaded side was over the other block. The two blocks were then applied to decapitated test plants, which were then allowed to grow in the dark. The block that had received growth substance from the shaded side of the tip produced a curvature of 16

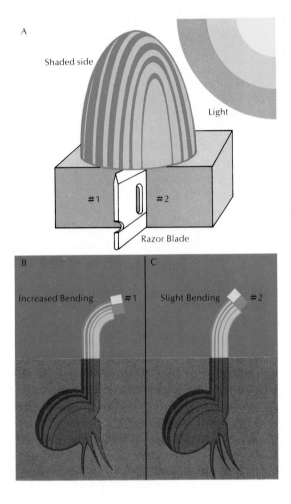

Figure 23.3   Went's experiment on the interaction between light and the growth substance in plants. In this experiment, an excised coleoptile tip that had been exposed on one side to a source of light was placed on two agar blocks separated by a razor blade (a). Growth substance from the tip was secreted into each of the blocks, which were then placed in contact with decapitated test plants (b and c). The block that had received growth substance from the shaded side of the tip caused the test plant to curve twice as much (16 degrees) as the plant with growth substance from the lighted side (6 degrees). Thus, light was shown to have an inhibiting effect on the amount of growth substance that is released by the tip or that is redistributed by the tip tissues.

degrees; the block with growth substance from the illuminated side produced a curvature of 6 degrees. In other words, the shaded side of the tip produced more than twice as much growth substance as the other side. (H. E. Dolk used similar methods to study the mechanism of geotropism, although in his studies he laid the tips horizontally so that growth substance was collected from upper and lower sides. The block in contact with the lower side produced about twice as much curvature as that in contact with the upper side.)

In all these studies, the amount of growth substance in coleoptile tips was so negligible that the substance could not be identified chemically. Eventually, however, rich sources of growth substance were found in human urine and in yeast as well as in cultures of the fungus *Rhizopus suinus*. The growth substance extracted from all three sources turned out to be indole-3-acetic acid, or **IAA.** Biochemists had already characterized this substance, although they had not suspected its role in plant growth.

Many closely related growth compounds have since been identified in plant extracts and have been called **auxins.** All seem to owe their activity as growth substances to the ability of the plant to convert them into indole-3-acetic acid (Table 23.1). A number of additional auxins have been synthesized that are similar in general structure to IAA. The structural formulas for the major natural auxins and three of the most active synthetic auxins (NAA, 2,4-D, and TCBA) are shown in Figure 23.4.

Gibberellins: Plant Hormones That Stimulate Stem Elongation

While the auxins were being identified, E. Kurosawa, a Japanese agricultural officer working in Taiwan, was studying a disease that causes rice plants to turn yellow and to grow excessively tall. After isolating the fungus *Gibberella fujikuroi* from diseased plants, he found that healthy plants treated with a medium in which the fungus has grown developed the disease symptoms—even though the fungus itself was not transmitted to the plants. Apparently the symptoms were caused by some substance that the fungus had secreted into the medium. Chemical work in Japan led to the isolation of an extract that was named (appropriately) **gibberellin A,** or **GA.** In 1956 John MacMillan in England isolated a pure compound (gibberellic acid) from the gibberellin A extract. The compound not only produced the disease symptoms in rice, it caused excessive stem elongation in a variety of other plants.

Subsequent chemical studies led to the identification of a family of closely related compounds that have similar biological effects and varying degrees of activity. On the whole, GA_7 has the highest activity—more than triple that of the original compound, which is now called GA_3. The structural formulas for these two compounds are shown in Figure 23.5*a* and *b*.

At first, biologists assumed they had discovered an interesting substance that acts as a "plant drug," with effects on plants as unnatural as those of caffeine or opium

Table 23.1
Naturally Occurring Derivatives and Precursors of Indole-3-Acetic Acid (IAA)

Derivative	Plant Source	Process of Conversion to IAA	System Responsible
Indole-3-acetonitrile	Cabbage, Brussels sprouts	Hydrolysis	Nitrilase enzyme (mustard plants, cereal leaves)
Indole-3-acetaldehyde	Several seedlings grown in the dark	Oxidation or dehydrogenation	Aldehyde dehydrogenase (milk, bacteria, and so on)
Ethyl indole-3-acetate	Apples (may be artifact of using ethanol)	Hydrolysis	Esterase
Indole-3-pyruvic acid	Corn seeds (certain cultivated varieties)	Oxidative decarboxylation requires one-half O_2 and evolves CO_2	Spontaneous in warm alkaline solution
N-(3-indolyl) aspartic acid	Pea seedlings treated with IAA	Hydrolysis to IAA and aspartic acid	Heating with alkali
Indole-3-acetyl-mesoinositol and its arabinoside	Corn (certain varieties, each occurring in two modifications)	Hydrolysis	Spontaneous but hastened by acid or alkali
Tryptamine	Leaves	Oxidative deamination to indole-3-acetaldehyde	Monoamine oxidase
Tryptophan	All plant proteins	Oxidative deamination, or transamination to indole-3-pyruvic acid followed by oxidation	Not certain that conversion occurs in higher plants free from bacteria
Gluco-brassicin	Cabbage family	Hydrolysis liberating indole-3-acetonitrile with sulfate and glucose	Myrosinase

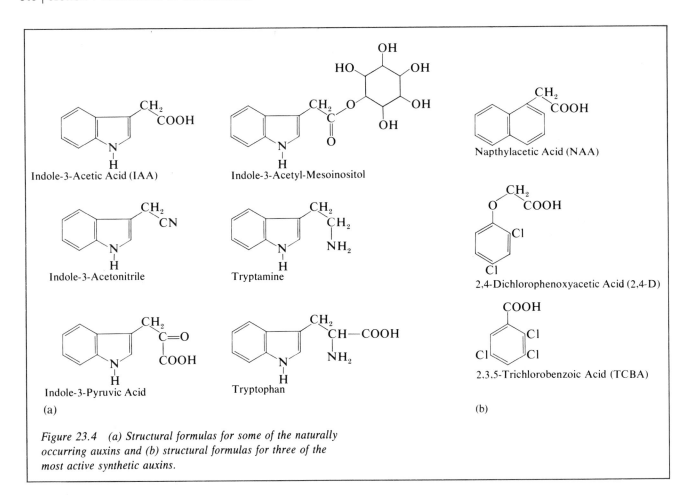

Figure 23.4 (a) Structural formulas for some of the naturally occurring auxins and (b) structural formulas for three of the most active synthetic auxins.

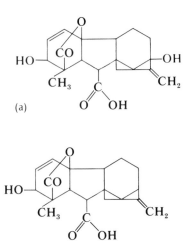

Figure 23.5 (a) Structural formula for gibberellin GA_3 and (b) for gibberellin GA_7. A separate class of plant hormones, the twenty or so known gibberellins cause stem elongation. For example, some dwarf varieties of corn (c) become almost indistinguishable from naturally tall forms after treatment with gibberellins.

on human beings. But experiments pointed to an entirely different role for gibberellins. Gibberellins were shown to have their greatest elongating effect on the stems of dwarf plants. After treatment with gibberellins, dwarf varieties of peas grew as tall as the naturally tall varieties. Some dwarf varieties of corn became almost indistinguishable from the naturally tall forms after treatment with gibberellins (Figure 23.5c). Such experiments suggested that the dwarf varieties were naturally deficient in gibberellin. Botanists began to suspect that gibberellins, like auxins, are natural plant hormones.

Their suspicions were confirmed when gibberellins turned up in natural plants. These substances were found in the seeds of a long and straggly desert gourd, *Echinocystis*, and later in many other seeds and in bamboo shoots. Chemically, the natural plant gibberellins were found to be members of the same group of compounds as the substances produced by *Gibberella fujikuroi*. In fact, more than one-third of the twenty or so gibberellins that were isolated from the fungus subsequently were found in plants. Thus, the gibberellins came to be acknowledged as a second class of plant hormones, chemically and biologically distinct from the auxins. But instead of the single natural auxin IAA, there are about thirty-five known (closely related) gibberellins.

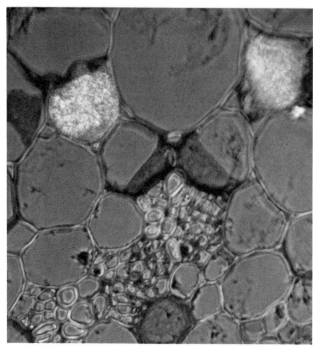

(Photograph by Walter Dawn)

Figure 23.6   Tobacco pith cells. Cultures of these cells were used in experiments that led to the discovery of the bud-forming substance, kinetin.

Cytokinins: Plant Hormones That Control Differentiation

The discovery of still another class of plant hormones followed from the discovery of auxins. The sought-after goal of getting bits of plant tissue to grow in a test tube was finally achieved when minute amounts of IAA or synthetic auxins were added to the nutrient medium. Many kinds of plant cells and tissues have since been grown in culture with dramatic results.

Soon botanists were studying the effects of various additions to tissue-culture media. They found that cultures of tobacco pith cells (Figure 23.6) normally produced masses of parenchyma tissue—but that addition of adenosine and its phosphate to the medium caused an increase in bud formation. Further experiments revealed that yeast extract is effective, and yeast nucleic acid is better still, for inducing bud formation. Because different samples of yeast nucleic acid extract varied in their effectiveness, Folke Skoog and his colleagues at the University of Wisconsin examined some of these samples chemically. The bud-forming activity was traced to a simple constituent, the previously unknown compound 6-furfurylamino-purine, or **kinetin** (Figure 23.7a).

As in the case of gibberellin, kinetin was first considered to be simply a substance extracted from other organisms

that happened to affect the growth pattern of plants. But evidence of a kinetinlike substance in plants was soon obtained, for numerous plant extracts were shown to produce similar effects on tissue cultures. Particularly effective extracts were obtained from unripe corn and young fruit in general. Preliminary studies pointed to a purine— probably an adenine derivative—as the active factor, and researchers in many laboratories set out to isolate and identify the active compound. The search culminated in 1964 with the isolation of **zeatin** (Figure 23.7b), by Letham and his associates in New Zealand, from unripe corn. This compound resembles kinetin except for the difference in the side chains on the purine ring. Later, a bacterium that causes development of multiple buds in plants was found to produce a compound identical to zeatin except for the absence of the —OH group. This family of plant hormones became known as the **cytokinins** (Figure 23.8).

Other Plant Hormones

Certainly there are other compounds that control plant growth and development. A hormone, however, is a substance formed in one part of an organism and transported to another part where it functions. Some substances are growth regulators but they are not readily transported; therefore, they are not called hormones. Probably the many **phenolic**

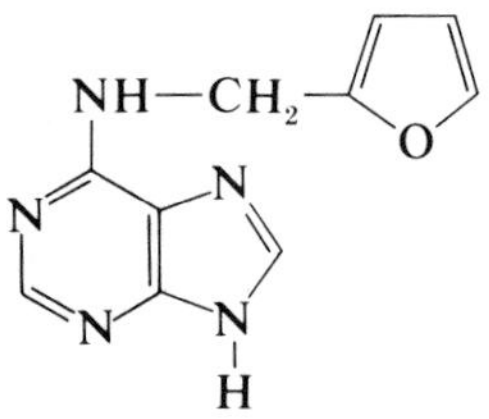

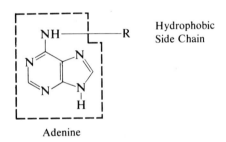

(a)

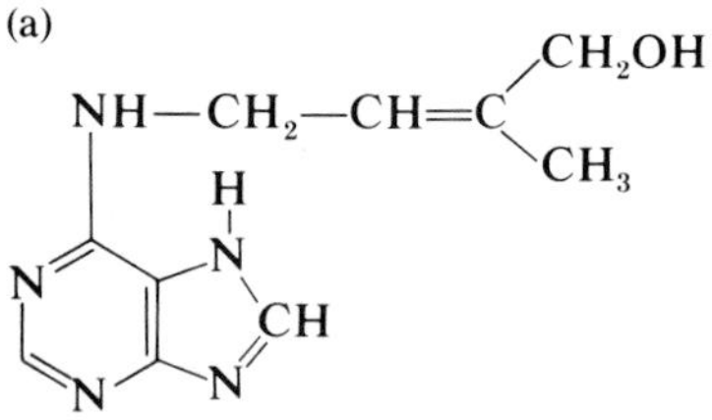

(b)

Figure 23.7 Structural formulas for the compounds (a) kinetin and (b) zeatin.

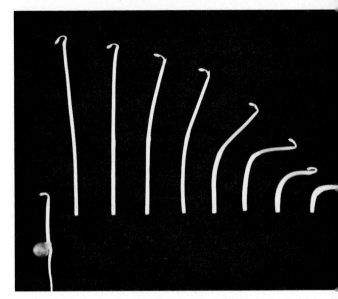

Figure 23.9 Etioliated pea seedlings showing the effects of various concentrations of ethylene on growth during a forty-eight-hour treatment period. The seedling at the far left shows the size of the plants at the beginning of the experiment. The seedling second from the left shows the amount of growth attained during the forty-eight hours by the untreated control. Remaining seedlings, from left to right, were treated with 10, 20, 40, 80, 160, 220, 640, and 1,280 parts per billion (10^{-9}) of ethylene in a flowing stream of air.

NH
R   Hydrophobic
Side Chain

Adenine

Figure 23.8 The generalized structural formula of the class of plant hormones called cytokinins.

compounds in plants, which stimulate or inhibit the destruction of auxin by oxidizing enzymes, are such growth regulators. Phenols with two adjacent —OH groups act as inhibitors, thereby protecting the auxin. But phenols with only one —OH group accelerate auxin breakdown. Scores of phenols have been found in plants—the blue, purple, red, and some yellow pigments of flowers, fruit, and autumn leaves belong to this group.

Abscisic acid, recently isolated from cotton bolls and from dormant buds, appears to be a widespread inhibiting agent; it is not a phenol but is related to the terpenes and carotenoids. Not only does it seem to have a general growth-inhibiting effect, it also inhibits transpiration. It is produced in wilting leaves and it helps to keep the leaves from drying out by causing the stomata to close. It tends to antagonize the growth-promoting action both of auxins and of gibberellins.

The gas ethylene (C_2H_4) is in a special category. In 1901 the plant-damaging effects of coal gas were traced to its ethylene content. Orange growers at one time ripened stored oranges by heating them. Biologists demonstrated that the ripening is due to ethylene from the oil heaters used in heating the oranges. One of the damaging effects ethylene has on plants is that it stimulates leaf fall. In the presence of ethylene, the petioles of the leaf blades begin to curve downward on the stem in a characteristic way. Where does the ethylene come from? In the 1930s, it was noticed that the leaves of tomato plants droop whenever they are kept in a closed space with ripe bananas. With the development of gas chromatography techniques, which can detect less than one part of ethylene in a billion parts of air, it was possible to determine that all fruits give off ethylene during ripening—and that ripening begins when the ethylene content reaches about one part per million of the air in fruit tissues.

Ethylene is a ripening substance, but is it a hormone? Plants can be stimulated into producing ethylene when auxin is applied to many of their tissues. Because roots are particularly active ethylene producers under auxin stimulation, some biologists believe that the inhibitory effects of auxin on root and bud growth are actually caused by increased ethylene production. Therefore, ethylene may be regarded as a sort of gaseous hormone.

HORMONES CONTROL ELONGATION PROCESSES

Phototropism in coleoptiles provides the clearest example of hormonal control of elongation processes. Light appears to result in the concentration of growth hormone on the shaded side of the coleoptile tip. Similar effects can be demonstrated with the growing apices of bean, radish, or lupine seedlings. More recently, IAA labeled with ^{14}C has been applied to intact tips of seedlings, and subsequent tests show that light diverts the radioactivity to the shaded side. Thus, *there is no doubt that light from one side modifies the distribution of auxin between the two sides of a seedling tip.* The side with more auxin (the shaded side) grows more, and therefore the plant curves toward the light.

Gravity acts in a comparable way. When a seedling is laid horizontally, auxin coming from the tip is diverted downward across the tip, so that the lower side receives about two or three times as much auxin as the upper side. In the shoot, the lower side grows more, and the shoot curves upward until it regains a vertical position. In the root, the extra auxin inhibits elongation (perhaps through production of an inhibiting level of ethylene), so the root curves downward (Figure 23.10).

These tropisms show that extremely small changes in the auxin concentration cause significant changes in growth rate. Instead of the normal 50:50 auxin ratio between the two sides of a growing seedling, light or gravity produces a ratio of 67:33 or 75:25, and tropisms result. Because the shoot of a young seedling must find its way to the light, and because the root must reach the moist lower layers of the soil within the short time that the endosperm can provide food for growth, these tropisms are a matter of survival for a young plant.

The control of straight growth, or simple elongation, is more complex because both auxin and gibberellin act in the same way. *Both auxin and gibberellin cause elongation, and their effects are additive.* In the oat coleoptile, gibberellin has only a small effect; thus, when auxin is applied symmetrically, the resulting increase in growth is a function of the auxin supplied. But in peas, beans, and other plants used in experiments, gibberellin plays the major controlling role. A cabbage plant fed gibberellic acid for some weeks had to be measured with the aid of a stepladder (Figure 23.11). The effect of gibberellin is exerted on the internodes or, in monocots such as corn, mainly on the leaf sheaths. In most cases, leaves become longer, thinner, and yellower.

Control of elongation in roots is even more elusive, for here only the lowest concentrations of auxin promote growth. Auxin concentrations high enough to promote the growth of shoots only inhibit that of roots. Usually, the level of auxin produced by the root tip is slightly inhibitory, so that if the tip is cut off without removing the elongating zone immediately behind it, there may be a temporary acceleration in growth rate. In seedlings, some auxin also reaches the elongating zone from the shoot above. Isolated roots growing in a nutrient medium may show the promotion effect better than roots in complete plants, but it always is small. Gibberellins neither promote nor inhibit root growth. Thus, if any hormone is an important stimulator of root elongation, it remains to be discovered. Even the inhibiting effect of auxin may be indirect and due to its stimulation of ethylene production.

Figure 23.10 The interaction of gravity and auxin distribution. This interaction is demonstrated when a growing plant is laid horizontally (a). Auxin from the growing tip is diverted, so that the lower half of the plant has as much as three times the auxin concentration of the upper half. (b) In the area of active stem growth (1), the cells exposed to high auxin levels elongate to a greater extent than cells exposed to lower auxin levels, which causes the stem to bend upward. Roots, in contrast, are more sensitive to auxin, and the auxin levels in the lower half of the plant (2) are actually inhibitory. Thus, root elongation is greatest in the upper half of the plant, causing the root to bend downward. Plant growth orientation with respect to gravity is therefore an interaction between auxin distribution and the relative sensitivity of various target tissues.

Figure 23.11   A cabbage plant treated with gibberellic acid for some weeks showed amazing growth compared to the control plants (at left) and had to be measured with the aid of a stepladder.

HORMONES INFLUENCE CELL DIVISION

Essentially growth is enlargement, and for plants the best definition of **growth** is an irreversible increase in volume. Dry weight may increase—for instance, when an old leaf makes starch by photosynthesis—without an increase in volume. And an increase in volume may be reversible in the case of temporary swelling due to osmotic water intake. Nevertheless, many growth processes involve cell division as well, and because cells do not enlarge indefinitely, continued growth usually depends on both cell division and cell enlargement. The actions of hormones on cell division are manifold.

By adding IAA (about one part per million) to a tissue-culture medium, it is possible to stimulate the growth of plant fragments that would otherwise die after a few cell divisions. In the presence of auxin, the cells divide vigorously and repeatedly, which makes permanent tissue cultures possible. Some tissue cultures show a curious change in auxin requirements after a series of transfers from one auxin-containing medium to another. The tissue changes from firm and solid to crumbly and watery. In its new form, the tissue is able to grow without addition of auxin to the medium; in fact, its growth is now inhibited by IAA concentrations that formerly were optimal for growth. These adapted tissues resemble some kinds of tissues derived from plant tumors, which also grow without added auxin. Both tumor and adapted tissues synthesize auxin, as proved by the fact that more IAA can be extracted from these tissues than they could have accumulated from the nutrient medium. Thus, although auxin production is normally associated with meristematic tissues, some cultures derived from differentiated plant tissues apparently can

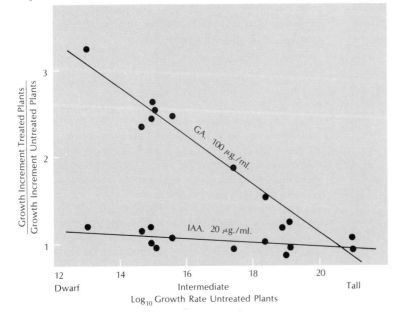

Figure 23.12   Graph illustrating the relative effects of gibberellic acid (GA) and indole acetic acid (IAA) in stimulating extensive growth of dwarf, tall, and intermediate varieties of garden peas. Stimulation of GA increases progressively from tall to dwarf varieties; the effect of IAA is relatively constant.

"recover" the capability to synthesize growth substances.

Auxin apparently affects the processes of DNA replication and chromosome doubling during interphase of the cell cycle. Auxin-treated tissues contain many polyploid cells. Cytokinins control synthesis of RNA and cytokinesis, or separation of daughter cells (hence their name). The combination of auxin and cytokinin produces the most actively growing tissue cultures and those with the most normal appearance. The first detectable effect of cytokinin on tobacco pith cells is a drastic increase in the amount of RNA in each cell. Values up to ten times the normal RNA content have been measured. A later effect is multiplication of normal diploid cells, so cytokinin apparently affects mitosis as well as RNA synthesis.

The most striking cell divisions in an intact plant occur in the cambium, where divisions form long new walls in the tangential plane. These divisions and subsequent cell enlargement cause thickening of the stem. At Oxford University in 1933, Robin Snow showed that there is no cambial activity in decapitated sunflower seedlings, but that addition of a small amount of crude auxin extract (from urine) stimulates typical cambial divisions. In later experiments, crystalline IAA has produced strong cambial activity in both herbaceous and woody plants. Cambial activity in trees begins in young twigs in the spring when buds open. It progresses along the branches and down the trunk at a rate of movement close to that determined directly for auxin. Scrapings of the cambium layer taken in the spring are rich in auxin.

Because the cambium normally produces xylem on its inner side and phloem on its outer side, it is not surprising that auxin also stimulates formation of vascular bundles. This formation is marked in tissue cultures, where many of the cells are essentially undifferentiated. A local spot of auxin or a local insertion of an actively growing bud gives rise to zones of xylem below; if sugar is added, phloem is also formed. In decapitated stems, these zones continue downward until they find their way into existing vascular bundles and join up with them. Oddly enough, however, if that vascular bundle is in connection with an active bud (an auxin source), the newly formed bundle does not fuse with it but is repelled.

A special case of xylem formation occurs when the xylem in a herbaceous stem is cut. New xylem cells gradually differentiate just above the cut and form a C-shaped strand of xylem, which finally joins into the old xylem below the cut and thus reestablishes the continuity of the conducting tissue. This process occurs only if buds or young leaves are present on the stem above the cut or if auxin is applied above the cut. The number of new xylem strands so formed is proportional to the auxin concentration. As in tissue cultures, if sugar is added, phloem strands form also. Auxin

thus acts to heal wounds in the plant body. However, the actual types of xylem elements formed appear to depend also on cytokinin.

The formation of roots on stems is a quite different process involving cell division. Roots will form spontaneously on stem cuttings of some plants, particularly if developing buds are present. Botanists long ago observed that roots tend to form directly below a bud and on the same side of the stem. Raymond Bouillenne and Went demonstrated in 1933 that extracts from rice grains can mimic the effects of the bud. Application of rice grain extract to the upper end of a cutting stimulates root formation at its base. Apparently, a root-forming hormone is produced in the buds and travels downward through the stem. Auxin moves in this fashion and is a growth stimulator, and by 1935 Kenneth Thimann and Joseph Koepfli had demonstrated that pure IAA applied to the apical end of stem cuttings stimulates root production at the base. This treatment is now used widely by nurserymen to stimulate root growth on cuttings used for plant propagation. Commercial preparations containing synthetic auxins are available for this purpose.

As you read in Chapter 19, root development in a stem begins with cell divisions in the layer of cells beneath the epidermis. Other divisions follow rapidly until a conical mass of small cells begins to push outward through the cortex. As this developing root elongates, vascular bundles form behind it and connect with the bundles of the stem. Even on green stems, the root is colorless. It grows out laterally at first and then begins to curve downward, showing a positive geotropism. Thus, differentiation has occurred; the new root shows characteristics typical of root rather than stem tissues. The mechanism that triggers this change in the tissue is not known, except that auxin serves as the initial stimulus to set the changes in motion.

HOW HORMONES ARE TRANSPORTED THROUGH PLANTS

Throughout this discussion, the terms "above" and "below" are prominent. In plants, the directions up and down, as set by gravitation, are distinct; the properties of the apex and base of the plant are quite different. A cutting can be placed upside down, but roots still form at the basal end of the cutting, although that end is now uppermost. *The apex-to-base polarity of a plant is produced by the tendency of auxin to move from plant apices, buds, or young leaves down the stem toward the base.* Auxin tends to move from the apex toward the base even when the position of the stem is altered with respect to gravitational forces (Figure 23.13), although the rate of movement steadily decreases in this position.

This movement of auxin can be demonstrated readily in a

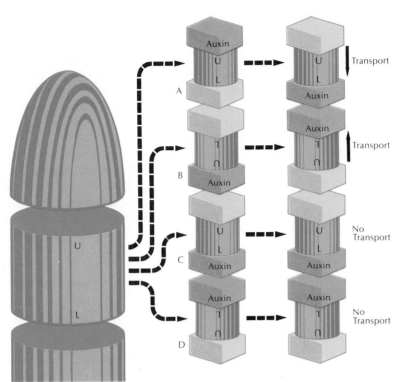

Figure 23.13 The apex-to-base polarity of auxin transport. In this experiment, a series of sections were cut from coleoptiles. In each case the original upper and lower surfaces were marked. An agar block containing auxin was then applied to one end of each section and a plain agar block to the other. Three hours later the auxin content of the various blocks was determined. As A and B show, auxin was transported from the original upper surface to the surface that originally was the lower one, whether or not the section of coleoptile was inverted during the experiment. But, as B and C show, transport did not occur in the opposite direction. This experiment shows that it is a polarity established in the cells and not the orientation with respect to gravity that determines the direction of auxin flow.

short section cut from an oat coleoptile. An agar block containing auxin is applied to the apical end and a plain agar block to the basal end. After a short time, auxin can be detected in the basal block, and within two or three hours as much as half of the auxin travels through the section to the basal block. If the blocks are reversed and the auxin is applied to the basal end, little if any auxin moves through the stem section into the apical agar block. The auxin can be detected by testing the blocks on newly decapitated coleoptiles and measuring the angle of curvature produced. These results have been confirmed by using IAA labeled with radioactive carbon and measuring the level of radioactivity in the agar blocks. The rate of auxin transport in most stem tissues held at room temperature is 10 to 12 millimeters per hour. At this rate, auxin would travel from the apex to the base of a fifty-foot tree in about two months.

The strictness of polarity varies from plant to plant. It is generally high in young cereal seedlings, but in the stems of dicotyledons such as bean and sunflower plants there is sometimes slight base-to-apex movement. If unnaturally large amounts of auxin are applied, the polarity can be overcome, but it requires 100 to 1,000 times the normal auxin concentrations.

Auxins can be used as weed killers because high concentrations of synthetic auxins poured on the soil can be taken up by the roots, as is any other dissolved substance (nitrate, for instance), and drawn up to the leaves in the transpiration stream. Tall trees sometimes can be killed in this way. On the way up through the xylem, some of the auxin diffuses laterally into the living cortex cells, where it becomes subject to polar transport, which conducts it downward again. Thus, a sort of auxin circulation can occur under artificial conditions.

Polar transport in roots is not this simple. Auxin moves from the base of the shoot down into the root—but auxin also is formed in the root tip and is transported from there into the elongating zone behind the tip. Thus, there are two polarities, neither one of which is very strict, and in the intermediate zone there is very little transport in either direction.

Cytokinin and gibberellin are not subject to such polar transport. *Gibberellin moves freely in both directions.* It can be applied to the base of a stem, or even to the roots, and causes excessive elongation in the growth zone just behind the stem apex. When applied to the terminal bud, it has the same effects. *Cytokinin is transported very poorly in living tissue.* It has been shown to move down a petiole only to the extent of 2 percent of the amount applied in twenty-four hours, which is over 100 times less than IAA. Recently, however, cytokinin has been detected in the bleeding sap that exudes when the stem of a healthy plant is cut off; this sap represents water taken in by the roots and pushed upward in the xylem by root pressure. The sap is known to contain amino acids synthesized in the roots, and the presence of cytokinin as well may help to explain why roots exert so much effect on the growth rate and greenness of shoots.

ABSCISSION AND DEFOLIATION

When leaves become old and when fruit becomes ripe, they fall off, or **abscise.** The process normally depends on special cells that are formed at the base of the petiole, where cell divisions begin to occur as the leaf or fruit gets older. Eventually, the middle lamella that holds these cell walls together begins to hydrolyze and the cells fall apart. As a result, the leaf or fruit is held only by the vascular bundle, which breaks off in the slightest wind. This entire process is inhibited by auxin. The **abscission layer** (Figure 23.14) of special cells does not form while the leaf is young and growing because the young leaf secretes a steady stream of auxin. Only when that stream wanes to a trickle and then stops does the abscission process begin. *Thus, abscission, like elongation of roots, is inhibited by auxin under normal conditions.*

Surprisingly, if the plant is provided with massive amounts of auxin, abscission is promoted. This opposite action is probably due to ethylene, which is formed in many cells under the influence of excess auxin. Thus, concentrated sprays of synthetic auxins are used to thin crops. By this process, some young fruit fall in the spring, and the ones that remain become larger.

Fruit normally falls in the spring if the plant has not been fertilized. Without developing seeds, auxin is not produced in young fruit. The June drop of apples and their fall when ripe in autumn coincides in each case with a low level of auxin production. But the picture is complicated somewhat by the fact that gibberellin also promotes abscission. This hormone seems to be present in high levels when the auxin drops, so they may work together to promote abscission. Several factors probably interact in this process.

APICAL DOMINANCE AND PLANT INTEGRATION

One aspect of plant growth that clearly depends on the interaction between two or more hormones is the influence that buds have on one another. Growing buds secrete auxin, which travels down the stem to elicit the formation of roots below. The same auxin inhibits the development of lateral buds on the stem. Thus, the growing terminal bud prevents other buds from developing. If the terminal bud is removed and auxin is applied in its place (in amounts comparable with what the bud would have produced), lateral buds remain inhibited. Before auxin was known, such inhibitions were attributed to the withdrawal of materials for growth by the developing terminal bud, which would have the effect of starving out the other buds. However, auxin applied in such a small concentration that it produces no visible growth of the stem still produces complete inhibition.

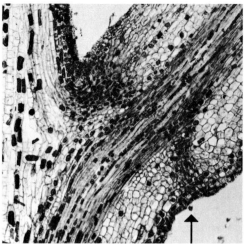

(Photograph courtesy Carolina Biological Supply Company)

Figure 23.14 *A coleus leaf showing the abscission layer at the base of the petiole (arrow). Notice the small size of the cells in the abscission layer. The formation of these cells depends on cessation of auxin flow through the tissues of the leaf petiole.*

Figure 23.15 *Effects of aerial dissemination of synthetic auxins (usually 2,4-D and 2,4,5-T in various combinations) on the forests of Vietnam. In this manner, the tropical growth such as that shown in the upper photograph was cleared to expose enemy positions during an extended period of warfare.*

The inhibiting action of the terminal bud is incomplete in some plants—larch, gingko, apple, plum, cherry trees—and as a result they form "short shoots." The lateral buds open and produce a few leaves or a flower, but the lateral shoots do not elongate more than a few millimeters. They remain short throughout the season and develop into normal, or "long," shoots only if the terminal bud is cut off. Again, the effects of the terminal bud are closely mimicked by the application of auxin.

Many theories have been proposed to explain how a growth substance inhibits a typical growth process. But it now seems possible that the effect is indirect. Under the influence of auxin, the cells in and around the node begin to produce ethylene, which seems to inhibit the small buds arising from each node. Apparently, internode tissue forms very little ethylene.

Auxin is necessary to induce growth in tissue cultures, but such cultures usually produce masses of undifferentiated tissue. When kinetin is added to the medium, the tissue produces numerous buds or nodules of differentiated tissue, which suggests that bud development and growth is favored by kinetin. A simple test system has been devised in which a piece of stem with a single node bearing a bud is floated on sugar solution. After a few days, the bud develops and elongates. But if auxin has been added to the solution, the bud remains completely inhibited. If kinetin is now added as well, this inhibition is relieved and the bud grows just as well as in the controls. About two parts of kinetin to one part of auxin are required for such complete reversal, but partial reversal can be obtained with much smaller amounts. However, too much kinetin decreases the bud growth again, so that the phenomenon evidently depends on an exact balance between the two hormones.

Cytokinin also can be applied directly to the bud and cause it to grow out. Because cytokinins are poorly transported, the application must be on the bud and not merely nearby. Auxin, on the other hand, can come from the apex many centimeters away. Applying cytokinin directly to the bud can cause outgrowth not only of the lateral bud itself but also of smaller buds at its base, so that a mass of little buds (called a witch's broom) develops. This mass closely imitates a well-known bacterial plant disease, and it has been shown that cultures of that bacterium on a nutrient medium synthesize a cytokinin. Thus, this particular condition has a rather simple explanation.

The outgrowth of a lateral bud under the influence of cytokinin has been ascribed to the formation of a functional vascular bundle leading to the bud. While the bud is inhibited, its vascular connection to the main stem is incomplete, and the units of xylem appear short and not well adapted for conduction. Kinetin causes a connection of normal xylem with long functional units within about seventy-two hours. A full understanding of hormone action in this or any other function, however, is a long way off.

HOW AUXINS ARE FORMED AND DESTROYED

Hormones that are effective in such small amounts must be destroyed rapidly; if they were not, their accumulation might cause serious abnormalities in the plant. Little is known about the destruction of cytokinin and gibberellin, but the destruction of the natural auxin IAA has been well studied. It is brought about by the enzyme **peroxidase,** so called because it normally causes peroxide (H_2O_2) to oxidize organic compounds such as phenols and ascorbic acid, which occur widely in plants. In oxidizing IAA, however, the peroxidase uses oxygen instead of peroxide; only a trace of peroxide is needed, apparently to keep the enzyme in an active form. The carbon dioxide of the IAA acid group is removed, and the products are rearranged to form a mixture in which 3-methylene-oxindole predominates (Figure 23.16). This compound is totally inactive as a

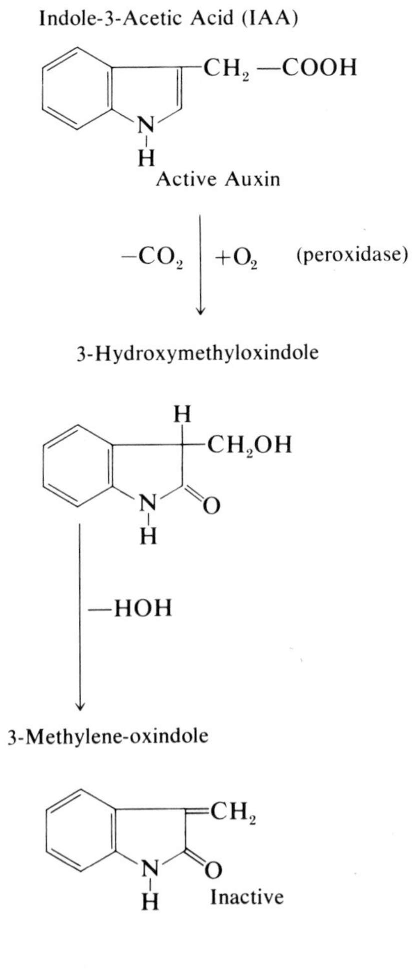

Indole-3-Acetic Acid (IAA)

$-CH_2-COOH$

N
H
Active Auxin

$-CO_2$ | $+O_2$ (peroxidase)

3-Hydroxymethyloxindole

H
$-CH_2OH$
O
N
H

$-HOH$

3-Methylene-oxindole

$=CH_2$
O
N
H
Inactive

Figure 23.16 Destruction of the natural auxin IAA.

growth hormone and may even have a very weak growth-inhibiting effect.

IAA also can be destroyed by light in the presence of certain activating pigments, such as eosin or riboflavin. Prolonged exposure to bright light is required, and the process is of doubtful biological significance. Ultraviolet light is more effective and can even cause some destruction without an activating pigment, the IAA itself absorbing the ultraviolet. Among synthetic auxins, 2,4-D is subject to a similar action of bright light in the presence of riboflavin. Its side chain is removed through oxidation, leaving 2,4-dichlorophenol.

The discovery that γ-phenylbutyric acid could suppress the auxin stimulations of growth led to the discovery of chemicals called **antiauxins.** Since then, various compounds have been found to be antiauxins. These compounds possess certain of the common structural features of auxins, but they lack at least one of the requirements of a true auxin. Thus, they apparently can compete for auxin binding sites but not fulfill its biological role.

If only one of the reaction sites is filled, then the product formed is inactive. Antiauxins could fill only one site, thus forming an inactive complex. An excess of auxin could also act as an antiauxin because two molecules could fill up the active sites of one substrate.

PERSPECTIVE

Hormones play an important role in the integration of growth and functional activities in both animals and plants. But there are substantial differences between the two groups in terms of the way hormones are produced and in the way they function. In animals, a large number of hormones are produced, usually by highly specialized secretory cells in localized glands. Most often the hormones affect mainly certain specific "target" cells. In general, these target cells then respond in a specific and rather uniform manner to the presence of that particular hormone. Plant hormones differ in several regards from this pattern. First, there are fewer kinds of hormones in plants. Second, the areas of hormone production are less clearly defined and usually involve cells that are simultaneously fulfilling other functions within the plant. Third, plant hormones seldom have specific target cells. Nearly all living parts of a plant respond in some way to some concentration of a given hormone.

Some cells respond to particular concentrations of hormone. But in other cases it is a change in hormone concentration that triggers an effect. Therefore, an important insight in understanding how plant hormones function is obviously to be gained by visualizing how concentration gradients of hormone become established, change, and affect the responding cells.

Unfortunately, the pattern of hormone concentration often becomes quite complex, for it depends on several interacting factors: the areas and rates of hormone production, the path and rates of diffusion and active transport, the rate and locations of hormone breakdown, and so forth.

These concentration patterns are not static. They change as the plant grows, as elongating stems and branches move apart the various areas of production, destruction, and response and give rise to new sites of hormone release. But the pattern of response is not static, either. At different stages of development, cells are responsive in different ways to (or to different concentrations of) a single hormone.

Furthermore, the response to one hormone is often conditioned by the concentration of a second hormone that happens to be present at the same time. In some cases, the presence of one hormone counteracts the effect of another. In other cases, two hormones reinforce each other, giving a greater than additive effect. Because the sites of production and destruction are different for different hormones, the plant at any one time has a unique array of overlapping concentration gradients.

When these localized patterns of interference and reinforcement are considered in combination with the varying sensitivities of different cells and tissues, it becomes obvious how such a relatively small handful of chemical mediators can orchestrate the development and function of so many individual instruments of life. Thus, while the course of plant evolution has resulted in a hormone network that is superficially far simpler than that of animals, it is one uniquely adapted to the indeterminate growth pattern and life style of the plants in which it is found.

SUGGESTED READINGS

BIALE, J. B. "The Ripening of Fruit," *Scientific American*, 190 (May 1954), 40–44. A general article on the ripening process.

GALSTON, ARTHUR W., and PETER J. DAVIES. *Control Mechanisms in Plant Development.* Englewood Cliffs, N.J.: Prentice-Hall, 1970. Provides an excellent discussion of each of the major plant hormones and its involvement in the regulation of development. The writing is clear, crisp, and concise.

JACOBS, WILLIAM P. "What Makes Leaves Fall?" *Scientific American*, 193 (November 1955), 82–89. A popular article on the role of auxins in leaf abcission.

LEOPOLD, A. CARL. *Auxins and Plant Growth.* Berkeley: University of California Press, 1955. A text on the action of auxins as plant growth substances.

LETHAM, DAVID S. "Cytokinins and Their Relationship to Other Phytohormones," *BioScience,* 19 (1969), 309–316. A short technical article on the role of cytokinins.

Chapter 24

Immune Responses

The immune system functions like a bulletproof vest, shielding the delicate balance of the vertebrate body from the continuous assault of potential invaders in the form of bacteria, viruses, and cancerous cells.

L

ife is the maintenance of an equilibrium that is perpetually threatened. The first great book on immunology, written in 1898 by Jules Bordet, opened with this sentence. It is still a useful way to think about immunological responses in vertebrates. Immune responses function primarily to maintain the integrity of the body, working to ensure that no foreign substances or cells enter it that could disturb the exquisitely balanced and self-correcting mechanisms of maintenance and control essential to life.

In a sense, immunity as it occurs in human beings and other vertebrates is a communications system. The chain of communication begins when foreign material enters the body, which can happen during surgical implantation of the skin or of an organ from another individual, when certain types of cancer arise, and—most frequently of all—when microorganisms invade and multiply. When the body is confronted with such an invasion, there first must be recognition that the invading material *is* foreign—that it is "not-self" as opposed to "self." Second, cells appropriate to mount a campaign that is specifically directed against the alien material must be made to multiply and become functionally active. And third, the cells or their specialized products must seek and destroy the foreign material. This three-stage process constitutes a **primary immune response.**

Immunity, however, is usually thought of in terms of the *increased* resistance that follows the first attack of an infectious disease. For example, it has been known for centuries that a person who has suffered smallpox and survived never again contracts the disease. The reason is that once a foreign substance has been dealt with successfully, the body of a vertebrate has an enlarged population of cells that can be called into action more rapidly and more effectively against any subsequent invasion by that particular substance. Such increased resistance to a second attack is called a **secondary immune response.** There are many defense systems employed by organisms of all types to counteract threats from the environment. But the vertebrate immune response differs from all these others by virtue of the two characteristics implicit in the term secondary response: *specificity* and *memory*. Exposure to smallpox virus leads to increased resistance to that virus (memory) but not to increased resistance to unrelated viruses (specificity). *It is the extraordinary specificity of the response for the agent eliciting it and the capacity for long-term, specific memory that sets apart the vertebrate immune response from all other defense mechanisms that have been evolved in other groups.*

All vertebrates are capable of mounting two quite different kinds of immune reactions in response to different kinds of environmental challenges. The more familiar is the

Figure 24.2   Bronze statue of the physician Edward Jenner inoculating a child with cowpox germs. Jenner grew up in a region of England noted for its dairy cattle. He observed that milkmaids who contracted cowpox on their hands (from contact with the cows) never contracted smallpox. After more than forty years of careful observation and study, he performed his first deliberate inoculation of cowpox material under the skin of a child. The process was so successful as a means of preventing smallpox that he soon found himself doing little else. Londoners lined up outside his door by the hundreds to be treated. The French termed the process "vaccination" (literally "encowment") to express their derision. Many years later, when Louis Pasteur developed similar immunization techniques, he termed them vaccinations, but this time as a term of respect for Jenner, whom he considered a medical genius. Many of us owe our lives to such processes, which have largely removed the threats of smallpox, diphtheria, polio, and other diseases that once were scourges of mankind.

humoral immune response, which is so named because it results in the production of specific, soluble proteins that are released into the body fluids ("humors") and that interact specifically with the foreign material. This is the reaction that is primarily responsible for defense against bacterial infections. The second kind of reaction is the one responsible for (among other things) the rejection of surgically transplanted organs. Such a response is not the result of action of the kinds of proteins characteristic of the humoral response. Instead, the blood contains specifically armed cells that directly attack the foreign cells. Hence, this kind of reaction is known as a **cellular immune response.** As you will soon perceive, these two responses share many features in addition to specificity and memory, but they also differ in certain fundamental ways.

THE HUMORAL IMMUNE RESPONSE PRODUCES SPECIFIC ANTIBODY MOLECULES

Any substance that elicits an immune response in a given animal is called an **immunogen.** Immunogens consisting of single cells or their products (for example, proteins or polysaccharides) elicit the appearance in the blood, within a few days, of sizable amounts of protein capable of specifically interacting with the immunogen. Such proteins were named **antibodies** long before their chemical nature was known. Today, all antibody molecules are known to be members of a related group of proteins known as **immunoglobulins.** (The two terms are more or less synonymous, although the term "antibody" emphasizes the specific biological role of such a molecule, whereas "immunoglobulin" emphasizes the chemical nature of the same substance.) Antibodies are the agents that mediate the humoral response.

A substance that is capable of interacting with an antibody in a specific manner is called an **antigen.** *All immunogens are antigens, but not all antigens are immunogens.* There are some antigens that can react with a specific antibody but cannot induce its formation. They are known as incomplete antigens, or **haptens.** The nature of an antigen-antibody interaction is similar to that of an enzyme-substrate interaction. The antibody contains a pattern of chemical groups on one particular region of its surface that are specifically complementary to chemical groupings on the surface of the antigen (Figure 24.3). The area of the antibody that takes part in this reaction is known as the *antigen binding site,* or *combining site.* The region of an antigen that reacts is known as an *antigenic determinant.* A hapten usually represents a single antigenic determinant in isolation. But most immunogens have at least two *kinds* of antigenic determinants. Furthermore, the strongest natural immunogens (such as bacterial cells) carry hundreds of copies of each antigenic determinant per particle. The

Figure 24.3 A highly schematic representation of an antigen-antibody reaction. An antibody molecule has two identical halves, each structured from one large and one small component. A particular antibody reacts with a particular antigen because the configuration of its combining site interlocks with that of the antigen. When the antigen and antibody make contact at the proper angle to bring the complementary patterns together, a union between antigen and antibody is formed, thus immobilizing the antigen.

specificity of the vertebrate immune response is perhaps best illustrated by the strength of the interaction possible between antigen and antibody. We tend to think of enzyme-substrate reactions as being highly specific. *But it is not unusual for an antibody to bind its specific antigen a hundred thousand times more firmly than most enzymes bind their substrates!*

Protection Is Usually an Indirect Result of Antigen-Antibody Interaction

If an antibody is directed toward the region of a virus that normally attaches to a cell in the first step of the infection process, such an antibody will inactivate the virus by preventing attachment. Similarly, an antibody directed toward a harmful substance produced by a bacterium will often destroy the toxicity of the substance upon combining with it. But the interactions are among one of the few cases in which a simple combination of antigen and antibody provides any defense whatsoever. Usually, some additional step is required beyond simple antigen-antibody interaction before the host animal achieves protection.

The most prevalent means by which antigens provide protection is based on the fact that *each antibody molecule has at least two identical antigen binding sites.* Because natural antigens also possess multiple determinants, this means that when antigen and antibody are brought together, a large, complex *lattice* is formed in which each antibody is attached to at least two antigen molecules (or cells) and each

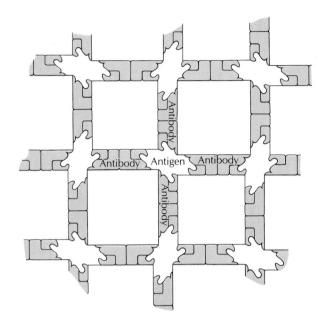

Figure 24.4   An antigen-antibody lattice. In the case represented here, each antigen molecule bears four identical antigenic determinants, and each antibody bears two identical combining sites. Because some antibody molecules bear as many as ten combining sites and some antigens bear hundreds of antigenic determinants, extremely large and complex lattices can be formed.

antigen molecule (or cell) is attached to two or more antibody molecules (Figure 24.4). If the antigen is a soluble protein, the lattice formation leads to such a large molecule that solubility is lost and an *immune precipitate* is formed. If the antigen is a cell, lattice formation causes the cells to be bound to one another by antibodies forming an *immune agglutinate* (*Interleaf 24.1*), which immobilizes the cells. In either case, the antigen is thus trapped in a large insoluble deposit where it can be readily engulfed and digested by wandering scavenger cells of the blood called **macrophages** ("big eaters"). Together, lattice formation and scavenging lead to removal of the antigen in what is called *immune clearance.* Precipitate formation and agglutination can be used by physicians and investigators to detect the presence of antibodies in a blood sample and can even be used to determine how much antibody is present.

In the case of cellular antigens such as bacteria, the antibody molecules may initiate an entirely different process that leads to destruction of the foreign cells. This is the process of **immune lysis,** in which the cells are punctured. Their contents spill out and the cells perish. Immune lysis involves the cooperation of a series of nine blood proteins that are unrelated to immunoglobulins; they are known collectively as **complement.** Thus the process is properly termed *complement-mediated immune lysis.* The complement proteins are a series of enzymes that are always present in the blood, but they are normally in an enzymatically inactive state. As outlined in Figure 24.5, a complex of antibody with a cellular antigen activates the first

(text continues on page 534)

Figure 24.5   Complement-mediated cell lysis. Complement is a series of enzymatically inactive proteins found in the blood. They react with neither antigens nor antibodies alone. But when antibody is bound to a cellular antigen, it changes shape and binds the first protein and activates it. This enzyme then acts on the next complement protein and activates it, and so on. The last step in this series of enzymatic reactions results in activation of an enzyme that has as its substrate the membrane of the cell. Thus, when activated, this enzyme digests a hole in the cell, allowing cell contents to pour out.

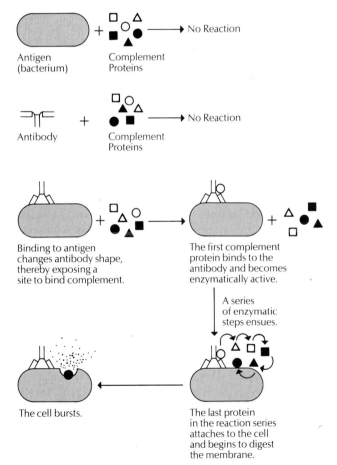

Interleaf 24.1

Human Blood Groups

Many deaths following serious injury or hemorrhaging are due to loss of blood. Why not replace the lost blood with blood from another person or from an animal? Over the ages, many physicians tried such a treatment but the results were often disastrous. In a few cases, the blood transfusion was successful and the patient recovered rapidly. In most cases, however, the patient reacted violently to the transfusion and soon died. By the end of the nineteenth century, most European nations had outlawed attempts at blood transfusion. There seemed to be no way to predict the response to the treatment.

In the laboratory, experimenters showed that *agglutination,* or clumping, of red blood cells almost always occurs when blood samples from two animal species are mixed. Similar agglutination occurs often—but not always—when blood samples from two human beings are mixed. The Austrian physician Karl Landsteiner began investigating this phenomenon in 1898. He took red cells from the blood of one person and mixed them with blood serum (the cell-free fluid portion of the blood) from another person. In some cases, the serum caused agglutination of cells; in other cases it did

not. At first, Landsteiner suspected that the blood of some persons lacks the agglutinating factor, either because of illness or because of a hereditary abnormality. To test his idea, he obtained blood samples from all the workers in his laboratory and mixed cells and serum in all possible combinations.

Landsteiner soon discovered that serum from one individual may agglutinate cells from some individuals but not from others. He was able to classify individuals into three groups, each having blood of a type that reacts in particular ways with blood from individuals of other groups. In further studies, Landsteiner found a fourth blood group.

The German bacteriologist Paul Ehrlich recognized this phenomenon as being similar to antibody-antigen reactions involved in bacterial infections. Ehrlich suggested that agglutination is caused by a "lock-and-key" fitting together of antibodies in the serum with antigens on the cells. He thought that each of Landsteiner's four types of blood contains a different set of antibodies and antigens, with agglutinating combinations possible only between certain pairs of antibodies and antigens.

Landsteiner modified Ehrlich's explanation somewhat, showing

that his observations could be explained with only two kinds of antibodies (α and β) and two kinds of antigens (A and B). A antigens combine with α antibodies, and B antigens combine with β antibodies. The blood of a person in group A contains β antibodies in the serum and A antigens on the cells, whereas that of a person in group B contains α antibodies and B antigens. A mixture of these two blood types will always produce agglutination. The blood of a person in group AB contains both A and B antigens but no antibodies. Thus, serum from AB blood can be mixed with either A or B cells without producing agglutination, but the AB cells will be agglutinated by serum from persons of either the A or the B group. The blood of persons in the fourth group (O) contains both kinds of antibodies, but there are no antigens on the cells of O blood.

It was soon demonstrated that blood types are inherited according to simple Mendelian principles (Chapter 16). The production of cell antigens is coded by a particular gene. One allele (I^A) codes for production of A antigens, and the other (I^B) codes for the production of B antigens. Thus, a person with genotype $I^A I^A$ will have type A blood, and a person with genotype

$I^B I^B$ will have type B blood. The blood of a person with genotype $I^A I^B$ contains both types of antigens and is called group AB. The existence of type O blood is due to the presence of a third allele for this gene. This allele (*i*) does not code for either kind of antigen and thus acts as a Mendelian recessive. A person of genotype *ii* has neither type of antigen on his cells and belongs to group O. These facts are summarized in Table 24.A.

Landsteiner's definition of blood groups made it possible to predict the outcome of a transfusion. The blood types of donor and recipient can be determined by simple tests with standard serum samples. It is then easy to predict whether the transfusion will cause agglutination. Soon after Landsteiner's research was published, blood transfusion became a standard and indispensable medical treatment.

Blood-group genetics is widely used in the study of racial distributions. Different populations show different proportions of the three alleles I^A, I^B, and *i*. For example, the I^B allele appears with a high frequency in Central Asia and in parts of India, but it becomes less and less frequent in populations farther and farther away from these centers. The corresponding phenotypes (type B and type AB blood) show a similar decrease in frequency in populations farther away from Central Asia and India. Among Australian aborigines, nearly 70 percent of the population is of blood type A, and the remainder is of type O; the I^B allele is entirely absent from this population. There are no sharp boundaries between population areas. Instead, the frequency of one allele rises and that of another drops as population samples are tested along any particular line.

Landsteiner continued his research on blood types for many years. He found a number of other antigen-antibody pairings that are controlled by other genes. These have less extreme effects in normal transfusions but are of importance in many special cases. Landsteiner discovered the M and N blood groups, and in later work with apes and monkeys he found the *Rh factor,* or Rh antigen, which plays an important role in certain previously unexplained birth difficulties. Women whose blood cells lack the Rh factor (Rh negative) may have children who are Rh positive if the father is Rh positive. In the first pregnancy, this factor causes no complication, but during birth, blood cells of the child enter the mother's bloodstream and initiate immunization. Then, in subsequent pregnancies, antibodies from the mother pass to the fetus, react with fetal cells, and cause major circulatory problems. It has now been found that such Rh incompatibility problems can be prevented if the mother is given an injection of antibodies to the Rh factor at the end of an incompatible pregnancy. Apparently such antibodies react with the Rh positive cells coming from the child and prevent the mother from initiating an active immune response to them.

Table 24.A
Genetics of Human Blood Groups

Genotypes	Blood Group	Red Cell Antigens	Serum Antibodies
$I^A I^A$ or $I^A i$	A	A	β
$I^B I^B$ or $I^B i$	B	B	α
$I^A I^B$	AB	A and B	(none)
ii	O	(none)	α and β

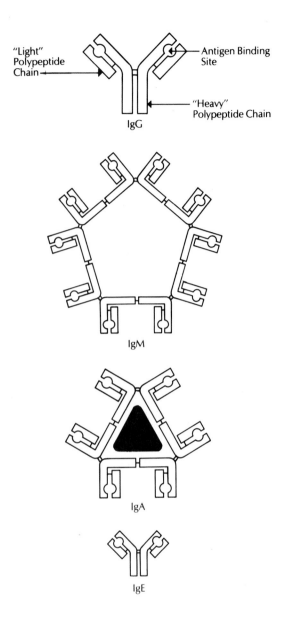

Figure 24.6   Schematic diagram of structures of four of the classes of immunoglobulins.

IgG is the most abundant immunoglobulin class in the blood. It consists of two identical heavy (large) and two identical light (small) chains, all joined together by disulfide (—S—S—) bonds. IgG is the main immunoglobulin produced in a secondary response. It is very stable and provides long-lasting protection.

IgM is more complex than IgG in structure. It contains five units that resemble IgG in that they each consist of two heavy and two light chains. But these five units are joined together by disulfide bonds to form a pentagon that has ten antigen binding sites. IgM is produced rapidly in the primary response. Because of its multiple binding sites, it is much more efficient than IgG in precipitation, agglutination, and complement-mediated lysis reactions. But it is an unstable molecule and provides only short-term protection.

IgA contains three immunoglobulin molecules in a triangle. Its unique feature is a "transport peptide" (t) that allows it to be passed across cell membranes. It is secreted in tears, saliva, mucus, milk, and so forth. Hence, it forms a first line of defense, stopping foreign agents before they can enter the body.

IgE is similar to IgG in structure but not in function. It is of no obvious advantage in fighting disease. It tends to be present in lungs, on mucous membranes of the nose and throat, and so on, where it causes symptoms of allergy in response to antigens such as pollen grains in the air.

complement protein so that it acts on and activates the next complement protein, and so on. (Actually, the reactions involved are far more complex than Figure 24.5 indicates.) The substrate for the last complement protein to be activated is the membrane of the cell with which the antibody originally acted. This enzyme digests part of the membrane, resulting in formation of a hole that permits the cell contents to rush out into the surroundings, ending the life of the cell. In the process of this series of reactions, several side products are produced that call into play certain other host defenses. Among the results of these reactions is the accumulation of macrophages and other scavenger cells in the area. These cells subsequently clean up the remains of the dead bacteria and damaged tissue. Some of the products

of the complement reaction stimulate the phagocytosis directly.

Different Classes of Immunoglobulins Play Different Roles

Primitive vertebrates (jawless fishes) have only a single basic type of immunoglobulin of rather generalized properties. But during the course of evolution, more and more variations on this original theme have appeared. As a result, in human beings there are several classes of immunoglobulins called **IgG, IgM,** and so on (Figure 24.6). They are all built upon the same basic plan: two *heavy chains* (long polypeptide chains) bound to two *light chains*. But they are modified so that they participate in different ways in the immune protection of the individual. Antibodies of all immunoglobulin classes may be produced in response to a single antigen. They differ not in terms of the kinds of antigens with which they can combine but in terms of the biological consequences that ensue from such a combination. The evolutionary diversification of the immunoglobulins has resulted in a system of protection and defense unparalleled in the living world. But in the process, a class of immunoglobulins has developed for which no adaptive significance has been clearly shown! This is the class known as **IgE**: the antibodies responsible for hay fever and other bothersome allergies. If there is any advantage to being allergic, it escapes the comprehension of most of us who are!

The greatest puzzle concerning antibodies is how each individual acquires the potential for producing so many different kinds of antigen binding sites. If a protein is injected into an animal, and if that protein differs in sequence by only *one* amino acid out of several hundred from the equivalent protein in the animal, it will elicit an antibody that clearly distinguishes between the two molecules! The list of ''foreign'' proteins to which any animal can respond must run in the millions. There are also many naturally occurring nonprotein molecules that are immunogenic. To make matters worse, a seemingly endless list of man-made molecules found nowhere in nature also act as antigens! (They are usually haptens; they become immunogenic only if they are coupled to a protein or some other carrier substance that is itself an immunogen. At least some of the antibodies produced in response to such a complex are directed exclusively toward the man-made hapten and do not react at all with the carrier.) Thus, the immune system has this potential for producing antibodies toward man-made antigens no ancestral animal had ever encountered—a capacity that has been termed ''the molecular biology of expectation.'' We cannot avoid asking: How did a system evolve that is capable of responding to environmental insults that have not yet loomed up on the evolutionary horizon? We will return to this challenging question later, but first let us review the properties of the cellular immune response.

THE CELLULAR IMMUNE RESPONSE INVOLVES SPECIFIC KILLER CELLS

Let us consider the results of a simple series of experiments in which pieces of skin are exchanged between members of three different strains of mice. A piece of skin is removed from the side of a mouse of strain A. In its place, a piece of skin from another mouse of strain A and a piece taken from a mouse of strain B are grafted side by side. Both grafts heal into place and begin to grow. But about two weeks later, the B skin begins to swell and redden, and eventually it is shed off as a dead scab. But the grafted A skin flourishes and grows. Later, a piece of skin is removed from the other side of the same mouse and is replaced in this case by three pieces of skin: one from strain A, one from strain B, and one from a third mouse of strain C. This time, before the B skin can really initiate growth, it dies and is cast off within a week or less; this time it is the C skin that grows for two weeks before it begins to swell, redden, and die. Clearly, this process has the marks of an immune response: specificity and memory. The B skin is subjected to an accelerated rejection (a secondary response) the second time around. But this secondary response is specific. It does not affect the survival of a skin graft from an unrelated mouse.

The thing that puzzled immunologists for a long time was that such a response cannot be attributed to antibodies in the blood. Sometimes antibodies are produced, but they do not appear to be the agents affecting rejection of the graft. If an animal is made immune to a bacterium, its blood serum can be injected into another animal, which imparts temporary immunity against the bacterium. This response is called *passive immunization* (to distinguish it from *active immunization*, in which an animal is exposed to an antigen directly and must make its own antibodies). But immune responsiveness to grafted organs cannot be transferred with serum from a grafted animal in a parallel manner. The first breakthrough in understanding graft rejection came with the demonstration that although specific memory of a graft cannot be transferred from animal to animal by serum, it can be transferred by certain white blood cells. This was demonstrated with a simple experiment. A mouse of strain A was grafted with B skin. As soon as rejection was complete, white blood cells were removed from this mouse and injected into a previously ungrafted strain A mouse. When this mouse now received a strain B graft, it rejected the graft in the accelerated fashion typical of a secondary response. The cells responsible for this transfer of immunity were found to be a group of tiny white blood cells called **lymphocytes.**

The lymphocytes of an animal that has rejected a graft include a population that will bind to and react directly with cells of a subsequent graft that bears the same antigens as cells of the first graft. Such lymphocytes are called *sensitized lymphocytes.* When confronted with cells bearing the antigens to which they have become sensitized, they become vigorous *killer lymphocytes.* They attach firmly to their *target cells* (the graft) apparently because they possess antibodylike molecules on their surface that specifically recognize the foreign antigens. Then, in a process that is not yet understood, they selectively kill the cells to which they are attached. But that is not all. They simultaneously release

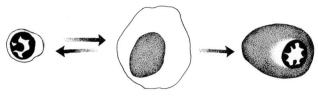

Small Lymphocyte
(information carrier)   Lymphoblast or Plasmablast   Plasma Cell
                              (intermediate)   (antibody producer)

Figure 24.7   The origin of plasma cells. Small lymphocytes act as a reservoir of potential antibody-forming cells. When stimulated by antigen, these cells enlarge to form cells known as lymphoblasts or plasmablasts ("blast" means "bud," or "sprout"). The blast cells then undergo division to form two cell types: plasma cells that become active antibody producers, and more small lymphocytes that function as "memory cells," ready to repeat the cycle upon a second exposure to antigen.

a series of substances that call in reinforcements to join the fray. One of these substances is called *transfer factor*. It causes other nonsensitized lymphocytes to become sensitized to the graft and to become killer cells. (Transfer factor is not an antibody; it is a small molecule whose mode of action is entirely mysterious.) In addition, the killer lymphocytes release a factor that stops macrophages in their tracks to keep them around for cleanup work. They appear to release another factor that whets the appetite of the macrophages and converts them into "angry macrophages," which eat any foreign particles voraciously. The killer lymphocytes also release a factor that calls in other kinds of white blood cells to the graft site to aid in the destruction of the graft. As a result of this intensive skirmish, various additional substances are released that have drastic effects on the blood vessels in the graft. Eventually blood flow in the vessels is shut off, which leads to the death of any previously unkilled cells.

It is this onslaught that the surgeon faces when he grafts a heart or kidney from one person into another. He uses hormones that inactivate or destroy lymphocytes, and he also uses antilymphocyte antibodies (directed against lymphocytes of the killer class), inhibitors of cell division that block the proliferation of killer cells, and a variety of other procedures that are grouped under the term **immune suppression.** Tragically, his best efforts are often no match for the vigor of the patient's immune response, and the grafted organ fails.

But even when immune suppression succeeds, the patient may not be safe. Often lurking in the wings is another character as deadly as graft rejection: cancer. A long-term study in Australia of the recipients of grafted kidneys showed that one-fifth of the patients whose grafted kidneys resisted rejection later contracted skin cancer; this is an incidence far in excess of the national average. Other studies show smaller increases among graft recipients, but the trend is always present.

This unfortunate response gives insight into the evolutionary origins and natural significance of the cellular immune response. Obviously, the number of animals that received grafted tissues through the course of evolutionary time must have been rather low. Surely such a highly tuned system as graft rejection did not evolve to deal with such a rare, unnatural phenomenon. An alternative hypothesis can be drawn from the increased incidence of cancer in patients who have been subjected to suppression of the cellular immune response. Most cancer cells, of whatever origin, have surface antigens different from those of the normal, noncancerous cells from which they arose. Perhaps the cellular immune response evolved because of the selective advantage of having a system of surveillance capable of detecting and destroying such modified (cancerous) cells whenever they arise. In this view, it is thought that cancerous cells arise far more often than previously suspected but that most are destroyed at once. Only the rare cancer cell that escapes immune surveillance somehow proliferates and causes trouble. It is of interest to note that cancer, like the immune response, is largely a vertebrate phenomenon.

The reactions of children with hereditary defects in their immune response provide a supplementary hypothesis about the meaning of cellular immunity. Each year, a few children are born who are genetically incapable of making antibodies but have normal cellular immunity. They are extremely susceptible to bacterial infections but, surprisingly, they have virtually normal immunity to viruses! Once measles runs its course in these children, they are immune for life. However, for children who are born with no immune response at all (cellular or humoral), the story is very different. In such infants, measles causes no rash, but it causes extensive disease symptoms of other kinds and usually leads to fatal brain damage. Now, bacteria generally multiply outside body cells. Viruses of necessity multiply inside body cells, where they are beyond the reach of antibody molecules. However, a virus-infected cell has characteristic antigens on its surface—not unlike a cancer cell. Apparently the patrolling lymphocytes of the cellular immune response detect these surface changes and mount an attack upon the infected cells and selectively destroy them along with their viral parasites. *Thus both viral infections and cancer may have provided the evolutionary driving force for the graft-rejection response that now frustrates the surgeon.*

Because of the enormous effects ability to control the cellular response would have upon alleviation of human suffering—the ability to cure cancer as well as to graft organs—research into the basic controlling elements of the cellular response is now intense.

LYMPHOCYTES MEDIATE BOTH CELLULAR AND HUMORAL IMMUNITY

Given the similarities between cellular and humoral immunity, is it possible that they spring from separate cell types? For a time it appeared so. Lymphocytes clearly are the agents of cellular immunity, but the main antibody-forming cells are larger, distinctively staining white blood cells called **plasma cells.** However, it has now been determined that plasma cells are the progeny of one kind of lymphocyte (Figure 24.7). It appears that the lymphocytes and their progeny mediate both kinds of immunity, but *there are two distinct lines of lymphocytes with very different roles in the immune system.*

Modern analysis of the origin and function of lymphocytes began with and still centers on the role of the **thymus,** a lymphocyte-rich organ in the chest (Figure 24.8). If the thymus is removed from a newborn mouse (a process called *thymectomy*), the mouse develops quite normally except for the fact that, as an adult, it is markedly deficient in immune responsiveness. It is totally unable to reject grafts that would normally be rejected. It also lacks the capacity to make antibody to certain, *but not all,* antigens. If thymus cells from a normal adult mouse of the same strain are now injected into the thymectomized animal, immune responsiveness is restored. Other experiments suggest that the thymus acts as an endocrine gland, secreting a hormone required for normal functioning of certain immune cells. In these experiments, a thymus is placed inside a diffusion chamber (a chamber that permits fluids to pass but that prevents cells from entering or leaving). When such a chamber is placed in the body cavity of the thymectomized animal, immune responsiveness is restored. Such studies have led to the identification of a population of lymphocytes that are **thymus dependent.** Thymus-dependent lymphocytes are also called T lymphocytes, or simply **T-cells.** They are derived from thymus lymphocytes, and they

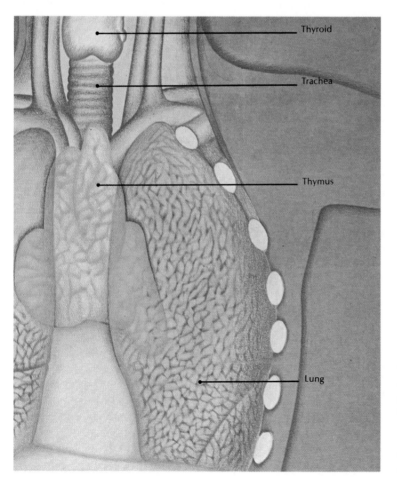

Thyroid

Trachea

Thymus

Lung

Figure 24.8   The human thymus gland. Lymphocytes produced directly by the thymus (or by the descendants of cells produced by the thymus) appear to be concerned with cell-mediated immune responses. Thymus-derived lymphocytes also play a role in antibody production but do not themselves make antibodies in significant amounts.

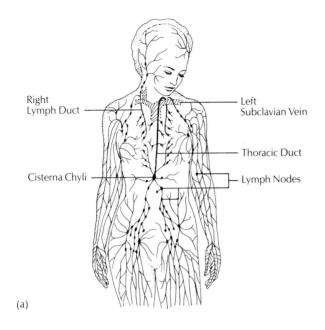

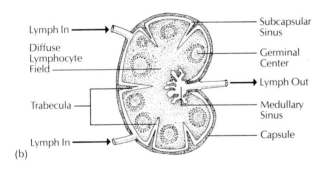

Figure 24.9 The lymphatic system. (a) Intercellular fluids pass into a branched network of fine lymph capillaries such as those shown on the extremities here. This fluid, now called lymph, flows into larger and larger vessels such as those shown here on the trunk. At the point where the largest lymph vessels join with veins, the intercellular fluids return to the bloodstream. But because of the strategic placement of lymph nodes on the major vessels, all intercellular fluids are filtered through at least one node. (b) A cross section of a lymph node. To pass from one side of a node to the other, lymph must percolate through the tightly packed cells of the node. This results in a filtering action so efficient that over 99.9 percent of all foreign particles and bacteria are removed. While the thymus-dependent lymphocytes and macrophages capable of recognizing foreign antigens and initiating a reaction are found in the diffuse field, the thymus-independent cells executing immune responses are found in germinal centers.

depend on a diffusible substance (a hormone) produced by the thymus for their maintenance and functional potency. *The thymus-dependent lymphocytes are the mediators of graft rejection—they give rise directly to killer lymphocytes.*

It can be demonstrated that T-cells somehow take part in antibody production as well. Lymphocytes are highly sensitive to x-rays. If a thymectomized animal is given a large dose of x-rays, it loses all immune responsiveness. Now if this thymectomized, irradiated animal is injected with T-cells, cellular immunity is restored, but the capacity to make antibody is not. In contrast, if such a thymectomized, irradiated animal is given an injection of lymphocytes derived from bone marrow, it regains the capacity to make antibodies to certain antigens but not others—and it still lacks any cellular immunity. Thus, it appears that bone marrow contains a population of lymphocytes quite different from those in the thymus. These cells have come to be known as B lymphocytes, or **B-cells.**

Now, if B-cells and T-cells are injected together into an irradiated, thymectomized mouse, all immune responses are restored. Thus, there is a class of antigens that will not elicit antibody formation unless both B-cells and T-cells are present. Antigens that elicit antibody formation in the absence of T-cells are called *thymus-independent antigens.* Antigens that are unable to elicit antibody unless T-cells are present in addition to B-cells are called *thymus-dependent antigens.* It has been shown that the antibodies in both cases are produced by the B-cells. *Antibody production is a B-cell function; but for response to certain antigens, T-cells play some essential role as "helper cells."*

Interaction of these two cell types occurs in **lymph nodes,** the lymphocyte-rich structures located widely throughout the body (Figure 24. 9). Lymph nodes contain both T-cells and B-cells in an arrangement designed to bring them into frequent contact. The lymph nodes also contain numerous macrophages and macrophagelike cells that immobilize antigen in the lymph nodes, where contact with both B-cells and T-cells is possible. The T-cells circulate in and out of the nodes continuously, traveling through the body, penetrating tissues, and then returning to the nodes. It is during such wanderings that T-cells detect cells bearing "non-self" antigens, and they initiate the cellular response. B-cells wander less frequently, but when they are stimulated by antigen, they give rise to plasma cells that release copious quantities of antibody.

How do B-cells and T-cells cooperate? Two theories have been developed. According to one theory, B-cells and T-cells come in physical contact by an "antigen bridge," whereupon the T-cell passes a "second signal" to the B-cell and reinforces the stimulus provided by the antigen, thereby activating the B-cell. The second theory suggests that the

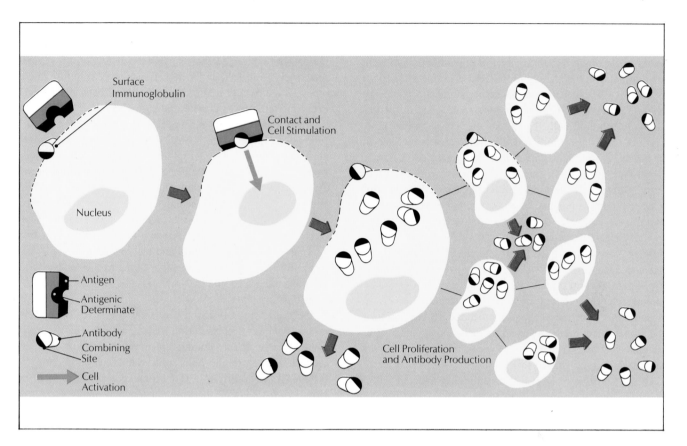

Figure 24.10 The clonal selection theory of antibody production. In this theory each potential antibody-forming cell is thought to bear on its surface a sample of the only kind of antibody it has the capacity to produce. When antigen enters the system, it combines specifically with a cell or cells bearing antibodies complementary to it. This interaction activates the cell to begin differentiating and proliferating. As a result, each cell stimulated by antigen produces a clone of similar cells, all of which produce the same antibody.

interaction of T-cells and B-cells occurs at a distance; the T-cell interacts with antigen and releases a substance capable of "turning on" a B-cell that is reacting to the same antigen. At present, both theories are supported by some findings, but other findings are not explained by either one.

ARE LYMPHOCYTES PRECOMMITTED TO RESPOND TO SPECIFIC ANTIGENS?

Because an individual can respond to a vast array of antigens, it was once considered unlikely that the capacity to form antibodies to each of them could be genetically predetermined. Instead, it was suggested that when a foreign substance enters the body it must somehow instruct the lymphocytes on what kind of antibody to make. Several theories of how antigen might provide such instructions to the lymphocytes have been proposed over the years. The most widely supported of these instructive theories suggested that one antibody differs from another only because different antigen molecules act like templates, causing a specific three-dimensional folding of the antibody molecule. This theory was tested in the following manner. An antibody preparation was treated in a way that removed all specific three-dimensional structure. When it was allowed to refold in the *absence* of antigen, it re-formed as an antibody with exactly the same antigen-binding capacity that it originally possessed. Although this experiment destroyed the instructive theory, it reinforced a concept that emerged from analysis of other proteins: three-dimensional structure (hence function) is a direct result of amino acid sequence. In the case of antibodies this means that *differences in antigen-binding capacities of different antibody molecules result from differences in amino acid sequences.*

Research Supports the Clonal Selection Theory

For this and a variety of other reasons, immunologists have come increasingly to believe in a *selective* rather than an instructive role for antigen in the immune response. In other words, antigen selects from preexisting possibilities rather than instruct cells to give rise to new potentials. The most widely held modern theories concerning antibody synthesis are variants of the theory proposed by Frank Macfarlane Burnet as a modification of an earlier suggestion made by Niels Jerne. Burnet suggested that each potential antibody-forming cell has a genetic precommitment to produce only one kind of antibody; different cells bear different commitments. Each cell, he suggested, bears on its surface a sample of the antibody it can produce. When antigen enters the system, it binds to those cells bearing antibody complementary to it and in this way stimulates them to differentiate, divide, and produce plasma cells and memory cells. Because a line of cells derived by common descent from a single ancestral cell is called a **clone,** and because antigen is viewed as *selecting* which cells should proliferate to form clones, Burnet's theory is known as the **clonal selection theory** of antibody production. Despite experiments over the years that have cast strong doubt on the clonal selection theory as an adequate explanation of the immune response, three lines of recent experimental work have added great support to it.

In the first line of research, an animal is injected with a highly radioactive antigen in a dose that would have elicited a vigorous immune response had the antigen been nonradioactive. The radioactive antigen not only fails to induce an immune response, it prevents the animal from responding to subsequent injections of nonradioactive forms of that antigen! But it has no effect on the capacity of the animal to respond to any other antigen. *Interpretation:* All the cells capable of making antibody to that antigen bound the radioactive antigen to their surfaces, whereupon they were selectively irradiated and killed. Because the response to all other antigens was unaffected, the killed cells must have been restricted in their potentials.

The second line of research is similar to the first. A sample of lymphocytes is passed over a column containing glass beads to which a particular antigenic determinant has been chemically attached. The cells exiting from the bottom of the column resemble the cells put in at the top in all but one regard: They retain the capacity to react to all antigens except the one attached to the column! *Interpretation:* The cells capable of forming antibody to the antigen on the column bound to the column and were selectively removed by it. Because responses to other antigens are unaffected, the cells bound to the column must be restricted in their potentials.

The third line of research is different but leads to an even more stringent interpretation. Lymphocytes (particularly B-cells) carry sizable amounts of immunoglobulin on their surface. If a particular antigen is added to a population of B-cells, it binds only to a few of the cells. If the antigen is large, with the same determinant repeated many times, it leads to "capping" (Figure 24.11), in which all the immunoglobulins are drawn to one end of the cell. No immunoglobulin can be detected outside the region where the bound antigen is located. *Interpretation:* Only a small percentage of the lymphocytes bind any one antigen. And

Figure 24.11 Photomicrograph of a lymphocyte that has bound antigen and has been "capped." It is surrounded by several cells that have not been capped.

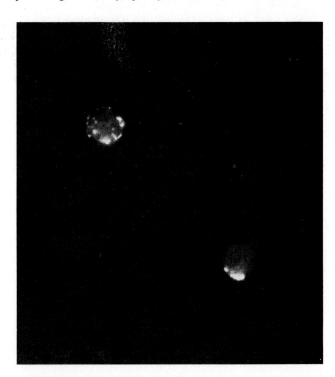

those that do, possess no immunoglobulins other than those capable of binding that particular antigen.

Taken together, these experiments lead to two conclusions. First, *in their surface membrane, B-cells bear samples of the only antibody they are capable of producing.* Second, the binding of antigen to B-cells leads to a rearrangement of these surface antibodies in the membrane mosaic. T-cells also contain specific surface immunoglobulins, although in smaller amounts than are found in B-cells. Both those who suggest T-cells act as helper cells by formation of an antigen bridge and those who believe T-cells act as helper cells by releasing a specific substance now tend to implicate the T-cell surface immunoglobulins in the T-cell/B-cell cooperative interaction. In fact, in one study, surface immunoglobulins isolated from T-cells were shown to be capable of turning on specific B-cells in the presence of antigen.

Capping of B-Cell Receptors May Be Essential for Initiating Antibody Receptors

The mechanism of "capping" B-cell immunoglobulins is probably similar to the kind of lattice formation shown in Figure 24.4. If antibody molecules that are widely scattered in the cell membrane are free to move in the membrane mosaic as they combine with antigen, they will all come together eventually; as soon as two antibody molecules attach to one antigen molecule, they are held firmly together. Thus, the individual molecules will tend to wander randomly until—and only until—they are joined to another antibody molecule by an antigen molecule to which they are both attached.

Either free T-cell antibody or antibody still attached to the T-cell surface should tend to accelerate this process. But antigens that are very large, with many repeating groups per particle, should not require participation of T-cell antibody in order to cause capping. Because of their complexity, they should be capable of causing capping of the T-cell receptors by themselves. This capability is particularly significant for the following reason. *The antigens that can stimulate B-cells in the absence of T-cells (thymus-independent antigens) are all large structures bearing multiple repeats of the same antigenic determinants.* In several experiments, antigens that are thymus-independent when presented as immunogens in a high molecular weight form have been shown to be thymus-dependent if broken up and presented to an animal in a low molecular weight form. Taken together, these observations imply that activation of a B-cell to initiate proliferation and production of antibody may occur whenever the B-cell antigen receptors (surface immunoglobulins) are all drawn to one spot on the cell surface. Direct demonstration of the importance of capping in the

activation of lymphocytes is lacking, but many find the indirect evidence quite persuasive.

THE BASIS FOR IMMUNOGLOBULIN DIVERSITY IS A GENETIC PUZZLE

Antibody molecules are a clear example of the twin principles of biological unity and diversity. A single individual is capable of producing a vast array of antibodies. All these antibodies have a certain unity in that they are built on the same basic plan of two light chains bound to two heavy chains. But they show enormous diversity in details.

As discussed earlier, there is diversity of immunoglobulin class: IgM differs from IgG and IgA in structure and function. But the diversity *within* a class is even more astounding. If a single antigen—say, a protein—is injected into a single animal, antibodies of several classes will subsequently appear in the bloodstream. If only those antibody molecules belonging to the IgG class are isolated, they are not all the same. They differ in terms of which region (determinant) they bind to on the protein. The ones that bind to the same determinant differ with respect to how firmly they bind to it, and so on. *A single antigen will elicit more kinds of antibody molecules than we yet know how to count.* These molecules will share only one common feature: all will bind specifically to some part of the immunizing antigen. And all the differences in detail among these antibodies can be attributed to differences in their amino acid sequences. Only at one level do we find homogeneity of antibodies: *One antibody-forming cell and all the cells derived from it produce only one amino acid sequence.* Thus, the heterogeneity of the antibodies found in the blood is not due to the heterogeneity of antibodies produced by a single clone of cells; rather, it is due to the fact that a single antigen stimulates the activity of many different clones, each of which produces a unique antibody sequence. (A similar generalization apparently can be made concerning lymphocytes of the cellular immune response system, although these cells produce only the antibody found in their cell membranes.)

Because of the diversity of antibodies produced in response to stimulation by a single antigen, the nature of antibody structure might still be a total mystery. But in using an "experiment of nature," immunologists have found a way to avoid sifting through the complex assortment that exists. Occasionally a single antibody-forming cell becomes cancerous. It then divides endlessly, giving rise to billions of cells—a clone far larger than is ever produced by antigenic stimulation. This form of cancer is known as a **myeloma.** Because all members of a clone of antibody-forming cells produce identical immunoglobulin molecules, the blood of myeloma patients becomes syrupy

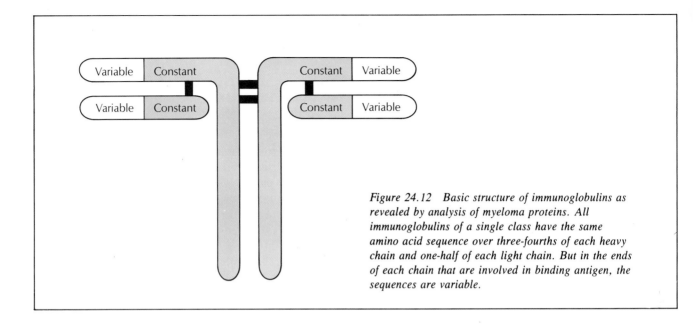

Figure 24.12 Basic structure of immunoglobulins as revealed by analysis of myeloma proteins. All immunoglobulins of a single class have the same amino acid sequence over three-fourths of each heavy chain and one-half of each light chain. But in the ends of each chain that are involved in binding antigen, the sequences are variable.

from the presence of enormous numbers of an immunoglobulin molecule of identical sequence. These immunoglobulins—known as **myeloma proteins**—can be isolated, purified, and their amino acid sequences established. The myeloma process acts as an amplifier that picks one antibody at random and amplifies it sufficiently that we can determine its structure. Hundreds of such myeloma proteins have now been isolated from the blood of human patients and mice and analyzed.

Each myeloma patient produces a single immunoglobulin sequence, but no two patients produce an identical sequence. As Figure 24.12 shows, *the differences between different myeloma proteins of the same immunoglobulin class are always restricted to the end of the molecule that binds antigen.* Each immunoglobulin polypeptide chain contains a **constant region** that is the source of unity of antibody function and a **variable region** that is the source of antibody diversity—the capacity to bind different antigens.

The question is this: How does the variability of immunoglobulin sequence arise? There are nearly as many theories proposed as there are biologists working on the problem. Two extreme views are presented in Figure 24.13. At one extreme is the **unigene hypothesis,** which suggests that each individual inherits from each parent *only one gene for each immunoglobulin class.* During development of the immune cells, this gene is visualized as undergoing rapid **somatic mutation** to give rise to many cells, each with a single but different genetic potential. At the other extreme is the **polygene hypothesis,** which suggests that each individual inherits from its parents *a separate gene corresponding to each variable region it will be capable of*

producing as an adult. (Estimates vary on how many such genes would be required, but they are all in excess of 10,000.) During development of the immune cells, each cell is visualized as undergoing **somatic restriction** in which only one immunoglobulin gene remains operative.

Neither the unigene nor the polygene hypothesis seems to be consistent with all known facts. Thus, a series of intermediate hypotheses have been developed that postulate the existence of a limited number of inherited immunoglobulin genes that undergo a limited amount of somatic diversification.

There is one point upon which all theories agree. Whatever the path by which diversity of immunoglobulins has arisen (whether in the course of evolution of the species or in the course of development of the individual), it must differ from all other evolving gene systems in one important regard. It must be essentially random. In other words, genes must be accumulated not because each has already been tested and found to have a selective advantage in permitting response to a specific environmental threat, but because natural selection has favored individuals that have developed a large library of possibilities—some of which may never be called into play. The observed ease with which animals can be caused to make antibodies to man-made antigens requires us to postulate that what natural selection is acting upon is not a sequence of individual genes but rather a mechanism for generating genetic diversity.

The solution to this riddle of the basis for immunoglobulin diversity is certainly not in. But because of the widespread belief that when the answer is finally obtained it may cause the modification of some cherished beliefs of molecu-

(a) Unigene Model

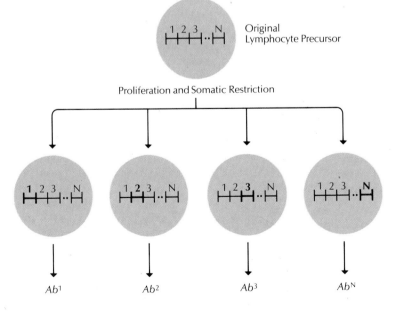

Original Lymphocyte Precursor

Somatic Mutation and Proliferation

Somatic Mutation and Proliferation

Ab^{11} Ab^{12} Ab^{21} Ab^{22}

(b) Polygene Model

Original Lymphocyte Precursor

Proliferation and Somatic Restriction

Ab^1 Ab^2 Ab^3 Ab^N

Figure 24.13   The unigene and polygene models of immunoglobulin diversification. (a) The unigene model suggests that the immunoglobulin diversity arises in the course of development of the individual. Each individual receives a single gene for each class of immunoglobulins from each parent. During development of the immune system, these genes undergo rapid somatic mutation by some specialized mechanism. As a result, different cells in the adult possess genes coding for different antibodies.

(b) In contrast, the polygene model suggests that immunoglobulin diversity arises in the course of evolution of the species. Each individual inherits genes coding for all the different kinds of antibodies it will ever be able to make. During development of the immune system, one gene gets switched on in each cell, and all others get permanently switched off. As a result, all immune cells possess the same genes, but different cells express different ones.

Neither model explains all the observed facts of immunoglobulin diversity; hence many models that are intermediate between these two extremes have been postulated.

lar genetics, the analysis of immunoglobulin diversity remains one of the most active fields of basic biological research.

THE CAPACITY TO RECOGNIZE NON-SELF IMPLIES THE CAPACITY TO RECOGNIZE SELF

The capacity to respond immunologically to non-self could not have evolved without the simultaneous capacity to ignore self antigens. An animal that regularly produced antibodies and/or killer cells directed against its own cells and cell products would be doomed. Hence **natural tolerance** (the failure to respond immunologically to self antigens) is inseparable from immune responsiveness.

How is tolerance established? Experimental analysis shows clearly that it is established developmentally, not genetically. If a foreign antigen is introduced into an animal during development of the immune cells, that antigen becomes tolerated as if it were self. (This is called **induced tolerance**.)

Burnet's original clonal selection hypothesis was developed because of the perceived need for an explanation of tolerance. He suggested that clones of cells encountering their antigens during a critical stage of development were *selectively killed*. Thus, the adult was viewed as tolerating self antigens because of an absence of "forbidden clones"—those capable of synthesizing an antibody with a sequence that will bind self antigens.

Ironically enough, in an era when Burnet's clonal selection is being raised almost to the level of an undisputed paradigm for explaining immune reactivity, his explanation of tolerance is being undermined. *Both natural and induced tolerance can be broken by a variety of techniques that "fool" the immune system.* If an otherwise-tolerated antigen is presented to an animal in chemical combination with an effective immunogen, antibodies to the "tolerated" antigen are often produced! For example, if a rabbit's own cytochrome c (Chapter 14) is chemically coupled to a foreign protein, the rabbit will make antibodies that react with its own cytochrome c. In the case of induced tolerance, the situation is even more clear. Tolerance that has been induced can quickly be broken in the adult by coupling the tolerated substance to an immunogen. When it is, the animal makes antibodies of the same type and in the same quantities as if it had never been tolerant in the first place. *Thus, evidence is lacking that tolerance involves the absence of any antibody-forming cells.*

In fact, in recent studies tolerance is often shown to involve a positive (rather than a negative) kind of reaction. In other words, some T-cells behave like active suppressors of B-cell function, which is a reverse of their usual role as helper cells. But just as there appears to be more than one way to turn *on* an antibody-forming cell, there now appears to be more than one way of turning it *off*.

The question of tolerance is not resolved. But research is accelerating. Many of the most debilitating, chronic diseases of humankind are now thought to be the result of a breakdown of natural tolerance. They are called **autoimmune** diseases. They include rheumatic heart disease, rheumatoid arthritis, lupus erythematosus, and a variety of other diseases with equally burdensome names. All are characterized by the presence of antibodies reacting with self cells and tissues, leading directly to the symptoms of the disease. A better understanding of tolerance might lead to the capacity to cure such diseases. In addition, of course, the ability to induce or break tolerance at will could change the course of transplantation surgery and cancer therapy overnight.

PERSPECTIVE

Recognition plays a central role in life—whether it is the capacity of an enzyme to recognize its substrate, of a tRNA molecule to recognize the appropriate mRNA codon, or of a bull elephant to recognize a potential mate. But in the vertebrate immune response, a mechanism of recognition has been developed that has a precision that is unexcelled in the living world.

Using this recognition system, lymphocytes patrol the vertebrate body continuously, reading every cell and molecule they find, checking it against the library of self, and reacting against those that bear an unfamiliar imprint. If the foreign substance is one that moves freely in the body (bacteria, foreign proteins, or the like) the recognition of non-self unleashes the synthesis of antibodies by B-cells, leading to immobilization of the foreign substance so that it may be engulfed and destroyed by roving scavenger cells (macrophages or the like) of the body. But if the entity recognized as non-self is embedded in the solid body tissues—if it is a cell infected by virus, a cell transformed to the cancerous state, or a graft implanted by a clever surgeon—an entirely different system of defense is unleashed. In this case, sensitized T-cells engage in cell-to-cell combat, attacking the alien directly and at the same time calling forth a system of cellular reinforcements that leads, eventually, to complete destruction and removal of the unfamiliar entity.

Many key questions of this complex system remain unanswered. How could vast potentials to respond to threats of unknown nature have evolved? How is reaction against self prevented?—and so on. But it is this very absence of basic facts that makes the immune system so fascinating to modern biologists. Resolution of these questions not only promises to enhance our appreciation of this complex biological system, it holds the promise of further alleviating human suffering in the tradition begun by Edward Jenner, when he first inoculated a child with cowpox.

SUGGESTED READINGS

BURNET, F. MACFARLANE. *Self and Not-Self: Cellular Immunology.* New York: Cambridge University Press, 1969. Provides an interesting and comprehensive account of immunology, with emphasis on the clonal selection theory that Burnet did much to develop.

KABAT, ELVIN A. *Structural Concepts in Immunology and Immunochemistry.* New York: Holt, Rinehart and Winston, 1968. Concise, quantitative, and biochemical in approach, this book is especially useful to students who appreciate the interdisciplinary nature of immunology.

MOORE, FRANCIS D. *Give and Take: The Development of Tissue Transplantation.* Garden City, N.Y.: Doubleday, 1964. This history of organ transplantation leads us into laboratories and operating rooms of some great immunologists and surgeons of our century.

ROITT, IVAN M. *Essential Immunology.* Philadelphia: Davis, 1971. This lucid textbook cuts through the complex terminology that has tended to surround ideas in immunology. It presents both the major concepts and their experimental bases in a stimulating way.

ROITT, IVAN M. (ed.). *Essays in Fundamental Immunology.* Philadelphia: Davis, 1973. Essays written in a comprehensive, timely manner by active research experts yet specifically designed to be accessible to those with a limited background in immunology.

Chapter 25

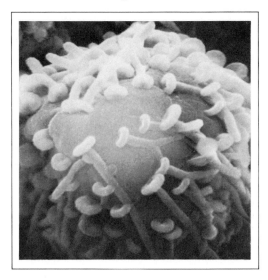

Organization of Nerves and Nervous Systems

The motile animal way of life demands rapid integration of parts. Neurons supply the network of communication channels that make such integration possible. But the neurons themselves must be integrated in function if they are to serve adaptively. As shown here, each neuron receives inputs by way of synaptic endings from many other nerve cells; while some stimulate it, others suppress it. Such varied inputs regulate the behavior of each of the components and combine them all into a harmonious unit of function.

The nervous system of an animal is one of the most amazingly complex systems in the living world. Unlike some tissues and organs, nervous tissue is not localized in a small area of the body—nerve cells radiate throughout an animal. In fact, isolating the entire nervous system for controlled study the way one might isolate the liver or heart is impossible. But in spite of this limitation, much has been learned about the function of the nervous system. Without this knowledge, many of the internal regulatory processes in animals and all of their behavior would remain mysterious. In this chapter and the next, we will review the physiology and structure of single nerve cells and integrated systems of nerve cells. Where possible, the behavioral consequences of nerve cell function will be discussed, but it is a long road to understanding how the nervous system mediates behavior. The first step along this road is the elucidation of the structure and function of the nerve cell, or **neuron.**

THE STRUCTURE OF NEURONS SUITS THEM FOR LONG-RANGE COMMUNICATION

That nerve cells are specialized for their role in information transfer over long distances is apparent even when we look at the structure of a single cell. The "typical" nerve cell consists of a globular cell body—the **soma**—and one or more radiating cytoplasmic extensions called **processes.** In some cases these processes have startling dimensions. In vertebrates, they may extend from cell bodies in the spinal cord all the way to the tips of the appendages. In humans, for example, they extend a meter or more in length; in the whale, similar cells may stretch as far as 10 meters! Even if we knew nothing else about nerve cells, we could not avoid suspecting some sort of direct communication role for cells covering such great distances.

As Figure 25.2 shows, there is really no such thing as a "typical" nerve cell. Indeed, with the exception of the soma (which always contains the nucleus), other regions of neurons are extremely difficult to characterize on the basis of structure alone. Instead, it is more useful to turn to functional information. *Neurons function to propagate signals from one point to another in the nervous system; therefore, they must have input processes and output processes.* Generally, the cytoplasmic processes that *receive* impulses are called the **dendrites.** The process that carries information *toward* the next cell is called the **axon.** (There never is more than one axonal process extending out from the soma, but some axons send off branches.) Although there are a few exceptions (Figure 25.2), a neural impulse generally travels down along a dendritic process to the soma and then out along the axon to the point of contact (usually on a dendrite) with the next cell.

NEURON FUNCTION IS LARGELY A SERIES OF MEMBRANE PHENOMENA

What began many years ago as crude measurements of "animal electricity" has by now become the highly technical analysis of neuronal function by means of membrane biophysics. This development, although revolutionary in its impact, has been marked not by major breakthroughs but rather by a steady, methodical attack on each area of ignorance. We are now able to describe systematically the essential feature of nervous tissue: the neural impulse.

Although the impulse moving along and between neurons is a unique feature of nervous tissue, its cellular origin is not unique. The neuronal properties that make such impulses possible are simply modifications of the basic properties of any cell. *The function of the cell membrane is the key to understanding the origin of the neural impulse, or* **action potential**.

As you read in Chapter 13, the intracellular environment is radically different from that immediately surrounding the cell. The total solute concentration of the cytoplasm matches that of the bathing fluid (thus preventing any net flow of water), but the chemical make-up of the two solutions is quite different. Establishing and maintaining this difference is a function of the cell membrane. The membrane acts as a *selective* barrier; it allows certain substances to pass freely but either actively or passively regulates the passage of others.

In neurons, the cell membrane is highly specialized to regulate the passage of certain metal ions common to tissue fluids. During the resting state of the cell (when no impulse activity is present), the neuronal cytoplasm is greatly enriched in potassium ions (K^+). Some cells contain at least twenty-five times the concentration of K^+ found in extracellular fluids. Conversely, resting neurons contain quite low concentrations of sodium ions (Na^+), which are the most plentiful ions in extracellular fluids. Thus, it appears that the neuronal membrane acts to accumulate K^+ while excluding Na^+.

Certain negatively charged ions (such as chloride, Cl^-) can pass through the cell membrane rather freely. But the interior of the cell contains many large molecules (such as proteins and nucleic acids) that bear a net negative charge. These large molecules are, of course, unable to pass the cell membrane. Thus, if their negative charges were not neutralized, the interior of the cell would be highly negative with respect to the exterior.

It is this reservoir of immobile, negatively charged macromolecules within the cell that causes much of the potassium actively accumulated by the membrane to be retained within the cell. Once pumped inside the cell, the K^+ ions tend to leak back out (down the concentration

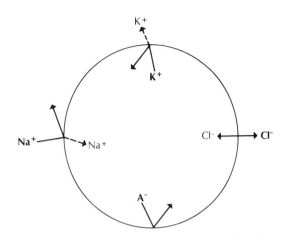

Figure 25.2 (below) Examples of neuron structure. (a) The variety of structure in neurons is so great that it is often necessary to study their physiology before the functional regions can be determined. This diagram depicts (1) an arthropod motor neuron, (2) a cnidarian nerve net cell, (3) a mammalian sensory neuron, (4) a basket cell from the mammalian cerebellum, and (5) a vertebrate retinal bipolar neuron. Notice the vastly different arrangement of processes associated with the cell body. The arrows indicate the direction of information flow from input to output. The arrow is absent for the cnidarian neuron because this type of cell both receives and transmits information in each branch.

(b) Photomicrograph of a portion of the vertebrate cerebellar cortex. The neurons appear black because they have been stained with a silver salt. There is superb delineation of cells with this staining technique; however, the procedure stains only some of the cells, so there are many more unstained (and therefore invisible) neurons in this photomicrograph than there are stained ones.

Figure 25.3 A schematic cross section of a resting nerve cell, showing the distribution of the major ions. The extracellular fluid contains high concentrations of Na^+ and Cl^-. The intracellular fluid contains low concentrations of these ions but quite high concentrations of K^+ and large negatively charged molecules such as proteins (here, designated A^-). The cell membrane permits only a small amount of Na^+ to leak into the cell. In contrast, Cl^- can pass more or less freely. K^+ diffuses out with difficulty. A^- cannot cross the membrane at all. The interior of the cell assumes a net negative charge because the tendency for K^+ to leak leaves some A^- unpaired with positive charges.

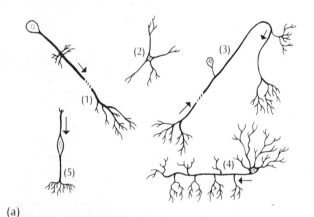

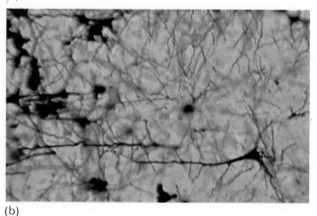

(a)

(b)

gradient). But the attraction of the negatively charged macromolecules holds them back. At some point, equilibrium is reached between the tendency for K^+ to leak out of the cell and its tendency to remain within the cell because of charge attraction. At this equilibrium point, some of the negative charges of the macromolecules remain unpaired with positive ions. As a result, the interior of the cell is somewhat negative with respect to the exterior. The electrical potential difference (measured in millivolts) resulting from this net negative charge on the interior of the cell is called the **equilibrium potential for K^+.**

If the distribution of K^+ across the neuronal membrane were the sole determinant of the cell's electrical potential, then the value of this potential should equal the K^+ equilibrium potential. For most neurons, the K^+ equilibrium potential is about -90 millivolts. But the potential measured across the membrane is in the range from -40 to -70 millivolts. This discrepancy results from charges contributed by other ions moving across the membrane. For example, despite its low permeability through the resting neuron membrane, some Na^+ does diffuse into the cell and it neutralizes some of the unpaired negative charge. Thus, it can be shown that the final **resting membrane potential** for the cell is a function of the equilibrium potential for each of the ions distributed across the membrane and their relative permeabilities (*Interleaf 25.1*).

The resting potential of a neuron is usually measured with a **microelectrode.** Simple microelectrodes are made by drawing out glass capillary tubing until it forms a tip of 1 micrometer or less in diameter and by then filling it with a salt solution. When such an electrode is inserted through the membrane of a cell, it is possible to measure the potential difference between the tip of this electrode and one placed in the medium bathing the cell (Figure 25.4). The electrode that remains outside the cell is called a *reference electrode.* Obviously, this technique cannot be used if the insertion of the electrode causes the contents of the cell to escape. But if the tip is small enough to puncture rather than tear the membrane, the membrane quickly seals around the electrode and reliable recordings can be made for several hours.

A recording from a region of a resting neuron shows that the cell maintains its internal potential within quite narrow boundaries. However, when a neural impulse passes through the cell, the electrode records a dramatic change in the membrane potential (Figure 25.5). At first, the inside of the cell gradually becomes less negative. Because the distribution of charge across the membrane of a cell at rest is said to be *polarized* (negative on the inside and positive on the outside), this gradual decrease in negativity is called a **depolarization.** At some potential level characteristic of the cell being studied, the gradual depolarization suddenly changes into an explosive depolarization. The characteristic potential at which gradual depolarization is replaced by explosive depolarization is called the **threshold potential.** Usually the threshold potential is about 20 to 40 millivolts more positive than the resting potential of the cell. As the threshold is passed, the electrode records a sharp loss of negativity and then an accumulation of excess positive charge within the cell. Next, and almost as rapidly, the cell loses this excess positive charge and begins **repolarization,** in which the cell interior returns to the negatively charged state. Often the repolarization takes the membrane potential to an even more negative value than the original resting level for a short time before the potential is restored to normal. This increase in polarization beyond the resting potential is known as **hyperpolarization.** All these changes occur every time an impulse passes down an axon; together they constitute an action potential.

How are these sweeping changes in membrane potential achieved? Because the cell interior depolarizes during the initial phase, positive charges must be added at first to neutralize and then to exceed the negative charge normally present within the cell. To accomplish this depolarization, the neuronal membrane must radically change its normal selectivity toward the only ion that is present in sufficient quantities outside the cell to be able to produce this kind of

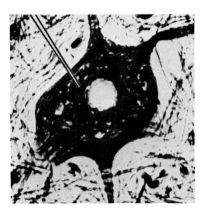

Figure 25.4 Photomicrograph of a motor neuron. Superimposed is a drawing of a microelectrode enlarged five times but shown as it would be located for intracellular recording.

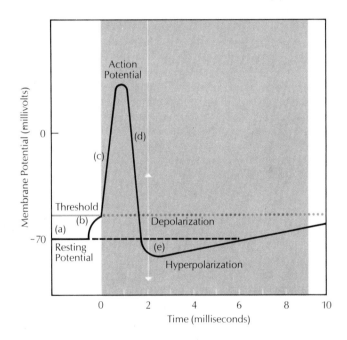

Figure 25.5 Changes in membrane potential during an action potential. This diagram represents an idealized recording from a microelectrode during an action potential. Initially (a) the cell is at a resting potential of − 70 millivolts. Then (b) a gradual depolarization begins. When the changing membrane potential crosses the threshold, the explosive depolarization begins (c). At the peak of the action potential, the cell interior is actually positive with respect to the outside. This condition is quickly reversed as repolarization (d) takes place. Then the potential actually swings below the original resting level and becomes hyperpolarized (e) before it returns to normal. The entire depolarization-repolarization event takes only 1 to 2 milliseconds (0.001 to 0.002 second).

Interleaf 25.1

Calculating the Resting Membrane Potential of Neurons

What is the relationship of ion concentrations inside and outside a cell to the resting membrane potential? And how is it determined which ions contribute most importantly? It has been shown that there is a simple relationship between the asymmetry of distribution of any one ion across a membrane and the potential difference that results. This relationship is given by an equation known as the Nernst equation:

$$E = 58mV \; \log_{10} \frac{[X]o}{[X]i}$$

This equation says that the potential across the membrane, E, will be equal to the logarithm of concentration of ion X outside (o) to its concentration inside (i) times a constant (58 millivolts).

To see how this formula is applied, let us consider a frog muscle cell. (The same approach can be used with a nerve cell or any other cell for which the appropriate values are known.) Let us calculate the potential across the frog muscle membrane due to asymmetric distribution of K^+ ion. The concentration of K^+ inside the cell is normally about 140 millimolar (140 millimolar = 0.14 molar), whereas it is only about 2.5 millimolar in the extracellular fluid. Thus, if the membrane potential for frog muscle cells were determined solely by the K^+ distribution, we could calculate that it should be −102 millivolts:

$$E_k = 58mV \; \log_{10} \frac{[K^+]o}{[K^+]i}$$

$$= 58mV \; \log_{10} \frac{2.5}{140} = -102mV$$

However, it is known from microelectrode measurements that the resting membrane potential is only −90 millivolts. The distribution of some other ion must also be contributing to this measured value. A likely candidate would be sodium ions (Na^+).

In order to fit the contributions of Na^+ into the equation, we must know not only the concentration of Na^+ inside and outside the cell but also the relative permeability of the cell membrane to Na^+ and K^+ ions. The Nernst equation must be modified as follows:

$$E = 58mV \; \log_{10} \frac{[K^+]o \; + \; b[Na^+]o}{[K^+]i \; + \; b[Na^+]i}$$

The term b is the ratio of the permeability of the cell membrane for sodium to the permeability for potassium. This can be measured by immersing a cell containing one isotope of sodium and potassium into a solution that contains a different isotope of each and measuring the rate at which the isotopes diffuse from one side to the other. For frog muscle cells, the value of b was found to be 0.013 (which means that the membrane is almost one hundred times as permeable for potassium as for sodium). The concentrations of sodium inside and outside a frog muscle cell are found to be about 9.2 and 120 millimolar, respectively. Substituting these values into the modified Nernst equation, we find that:

$$E = 58mV \; \log_{10} \frac{[K^+]o \; + \; b[Na^+]o}{[K^+]i \; + \; b[Na^+]i}$$

$$= 58mV \; \log_{10} \frac{2.5 + 0.013 \, (120)}{140 + 0.013 \, (9.2)}$$

$$= -89mV$$

The closeness of this calculated value to the measured membrane potential (−90 millivolts) is impressive. This calculated value could be improved still further by including other ions and their permeabilities, but it is clear that K^+ and Na^+ alone make the *major* contributions to the final resting membrane potential.

electrical effect—in other words, extracellular Na⁺. The exact nature of the membrane change is not yet understood, but the membrane behaves as if pores open through which Na⁺ can pass freely, moving down its concentration gradient into the cell (Figure 25.6). If this were all that happened, however, the cell would only depolarize to the Na⁺ equilibrium potential (about +60 millivolts) and remain there; the cell interior would remain positive with respect to the extracellular fluid. But this does not happen, because K⁺ "pores" now open in the membrane. Potassium then rapidly flows down its concentration gradient toward

the outside, for it is no longer retarded by intracellular negative charge. The effect of K⁺ outflow is to remove the excess positive charge from the inside of the cell and to lead to the repolarization of the cell. The repolarization depends on the closure of the Na⁺ pore at about the time the K⁺ efflux reaches its maximum. By the time the K⁺ pore closes again, the membrane has become somewhat hyperpolarized.

Although this description accounts quite nicely for the rapid excursion of the membrane potential, one problem remains. The ionic exchange has left more Na⁺ than usual inside the cell and more K⁺ on the outside. Without correcting this condition, the cell would lose its ability to generate an action potential, because the Na⁺ and K⁺ concentration gradients would be lost. The corrective measure taken by the cell is the active outward pumping of Na⁺ accompanied by the uptake of K⁺. The biochemical machinery in the membrane that performs this exchange process is called the **Na⁺/K⁺ pump** (Figure 25.7). The analogy to a mechanical pump is intentional: each ion must be pushed "uphill" in the sense that it must be moved against its concentration gradient. Movement against a gradient requires work, and work is accomplished at the expenditure of energy. (This process is described in Chapter 13.) In the neuron, as in all cells, the source of metabolic energy is ATP.

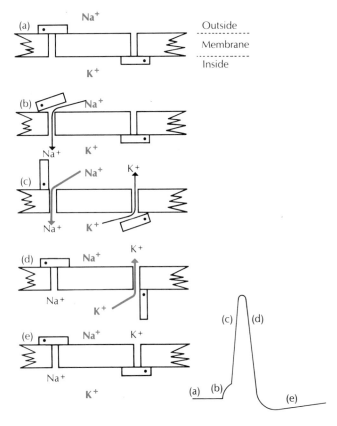

Figure 25.6 *A model to explain the phases of action potential. The neuron membrane behaves as though it contains pores through which Na⁺ and K⁺ can diffuse during the action potential. During the resting period both pores are closed (a). The gradual depolarization is brought about by a gradual opening (b) of the Na⁺ pore. At threshold, the pore opens completely (c) and Na⁺ diffuses freely into the cell. The K⁺ pore begins to open during this phase and becomes fully open just when the Na⁺ pore suddenly closes (d). The K⁺ pore then closes as well (e), and the membrane returns to very close to the normal resting potential. However, the cell now contains more sodium and less potassium than it did at rest (a). The cell cannot produce another action potential until the original distribution of ions is restored with the aid of the Na⁺/K⁺ pump (Figure 25.7).*

HOW IS AN ACTION POTENTIAL PROPAGATED ALONG A NEURON?

So far, our discussion of the action potential has concentrated on the events that occur in and around a small area of the neuronal membrane. *But the importance of the action potential is its ability to move along the membrane of the neuron and thereby carry information through the nervous system.* When physiologists first realized that the action potential is an electrical phenomenon, they assumed that neurons act like cables carrying electric currents. Indeed, the axon is a cablelike structure. It has a core of electrolyte fluid that can conduct currents, and it is surrounded by a membrane that has properties like an electrical insulator. On closer inspection, however, we see that the axon would make a poor electric cable. The resistance of the **axoplasm** (the cytoplasm within the axon) is about 100 million times greater than that of copper. In addition, the axonal membrane is an extremely leaky insulator. Thus an axon "cable" would perform far less efficiently than a well-insulated copper cable. Nevertheless, when a stimulus great enough to trigger an action potential impinges on a neuron, the action potential moves rapidly and without any decrease in magnitude along whatever distance exists between the input and the output to the next cell.

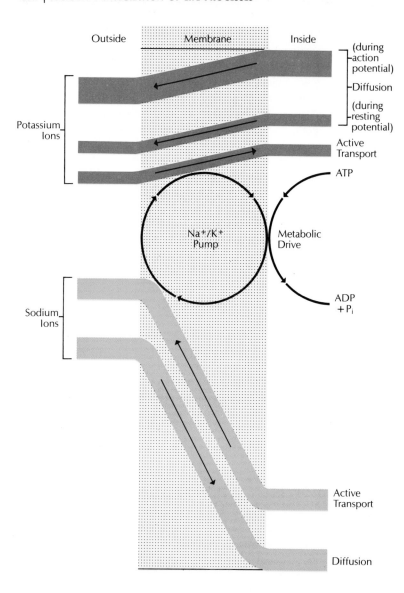

Outside   Membrane   Inside

(during action potential)

Diffusion

(during resting potential)

Active Transport

ATP

Potassium Ions

Na⁺/K⁺ Pump

Metabolic Drive

Sodium Ions

ADP + Pᵢ

Active Transport

Diffusion

Figure 25.7   Active transport of Na^+ and K^+ against their concentration gradients by the Na^+/K^+ pump. Both diffusion and transport across the membrane are shown. K^+ diffuses (leaks) out of the cell at significant rates both during the resting stage (which contributes to the membrane potential) and during the action potential.

Excessive leakage during the resting stage is retarded by the negative charges in the cell interior. But the loss of K^+ during the action potential must be reversed by action of the pump. In the case of the Na^+ ion, the diffusion occurring during the action potential is the major source of internal Na^+ to be pumped out. The steepness of the various lines in the diagram indicates the electrochemical forces that the pump must overcome. Most of the energy obtained from ATP hydrolysis is needed to pump Na^+ outward against the concentration gradient. The accumulation of K^+ is less energy requiring.

The mechanism doing the actual pumping is an enzyme called sodium- and potassium-activated ATPase (Chapter 13).

The explanation for this seemingly anomalous ability is that the action potential is not passively conducted along the axon by simple flow of electrons as it would be along a cable. It is *actively* **propagated** from one point to the next in the following manner. The depolarizing influx of Na^+ at the immediate site of the action potential causes the membrane potential in immediately adjacent regions to depolarize slowly. When this slow depolarization has pushed the membrane potential in the adjacent membrane beyond the threshold potential, the Na^+ pores open suddenly and the explosive depolarization occurs at the second site (Figures 25.5 and 25.8). This, in turn, causes a slow depolarization at a third site still farther down the neuron, and so it goes. At each sequential site along the neuron, the action potential is initiated and completed in an identical fashion as the same processes are repeated. Therefore, the

action potential moves down the neuron without any decrease in magnitude. Thus, the function of a neuron is said to be governed by the **all-or-none rule.**

The resting potential along the axon can be likened to a trail of gunpowder, with the action potential as the burning zone racing down the trail. The burning zone moves along the trail because the heat created by the fire spreads ahead and raises the temperature of adjacent gunpowder particles closer and closer to their ignition threshold temperature. Those particles just ahead of the burning zone burst into flame, and as they do they increase the temperature of those immediately ahead of them, and so on. It makes no difference whether the trail of powder is ignited by a paper match or a flame thrower; the burning zone has a constant size, moves by the same process, and advances at a constant speed. But here the analogy ends. Gunpowder cannot

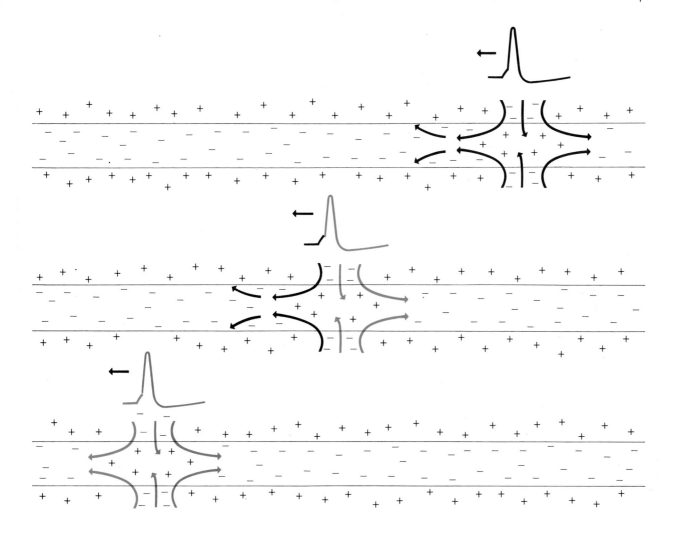

Figure 25.8   Propagation of the action potential along an axon. Propagation is the result of local circuits of current spreading through the axoplasm and surrounding fluid. Explosive depolarization at the site of the action potential causes current to spread longitudinally down the axon. This brings adjacent regions of the membrane near threshold. Explosive depolarization (an action potential) appears at the next site when the current spread from the first takes the membrane potential across the threshold. The second site then influences a third site, and so on.

regenerate itself after it has burned. *But within a few milliseconds after the passage of one action potential, the neuronal membrane is ready to propagate another.*

The velocity of impulse propagation is highly variable among different types of neurons. Velocities slower than 1 meter per second have been measured in cnidarians, whereas some mammalian neurons may show velocities greater than 100 meters per second. Several factors give rise to this variability, but certainly the most significant are differences in the cable properties of different axons. Despite their inefficiency relative to copper wires, axons do act to some extent as cables during the propagation of an action potential. This can be inferred from the observation that the action potential influences regions of membrane ahead of it to begin depolarization; the depolarization is the result of current spreading longitudinally through the axoplasm. The farther the current flows ahead of the action potential, the more rapid will be the propagation, because longer stretches of membrane are being brought near the threshold potential.

The evolutionary advantages for rapid propagation are not difficult to imagine. The ability to recognize and respond more rapidly to dangerous or advantageous situations in the environment would greatly enhance survival prospects. And it is precisely in the systems that mediate escape and prey-catching behaviors that the most rapid impulse propagation is found. But, how did high-velocity propagation develop in an inefficient axon cable? The answer requires a brief detour into the electrical properties of cables.

A good cable will conduct a pulse of current along its length without significant loss of current strength. In an ineffective cable, a current pulse will dissipate significantly in its passage. Assuming two cables are of the same length, any difference in their effectiveness will be the result of two factors: the longitudinal resistance (the more resistance, the more the current will be dissipated), and insulation (poor insulation permits some current to escape from the cable). Thus, two ways to improve an ineffective cable are to decrease its longitudinal resistance and to improve its insulation. The latter task is not too tricky. All that has to be done is to add more layers of insulating material. Although changing the longitudinal resistance seems more difficult, the solution is easy here, too. It is known from the study of electrical conducting materials that longitudinal resistance is a function of the cross-sectional area of the conductor. Thicker conductors have a lower resistance than thinner ones made of the same material. To repeat, then, an ineffective cable can be improved either by increasing its thickness or by wrapping it with more insulation.

Returning to the evolutionary problem posed by the need for rapid propagation, we can suggest two solutions: *Axons must be made thicker to reduce their longitudinal resistance; or they must be wrapped with some sort of more effective insulating material.* Both solutions emerged over the course of evolutionary time. Among the invertebrates, the need for rapid propagation has been met by the development of so-called "giant fibers," the largest axons known to exist. The largest of all is the squid giant axon, which may be a millimeter or more in diameter! (That is 1,000 times the diameter of typical axons in humans.) The giant fibers are restricted to those portions of the nervous system involved in the control of rapid muscular responses, and their propagation velocities are *much* faster than those of normal-sized axons in the same organisms.

Increased insulation is present in a wide variety of vertebrate and invertebrate nervous systems. The improved insulation has been achieved not through changes in the thickness of the axonal membrane, however, but through the wrapping of flattened accessory cells closely about the axon. The elaboration of this special relationship between accessory cells and neural cells ranges from loose, almost haphazard layering to extremely regular and highly specialized multiple wrapping.

The best example of neural insulation is found in the vertebrates. As one might expect, this modification for high-velocity propagation is largely restricted to the neurons involved in the mediation of rapid, coordinated behavioral responses. The accessory cells involved in this system are called **Schwann cells.** During development, these cells flatten and wrap around the axon many times, winding layer after layer of membrane around the axon (Figure 25.9).

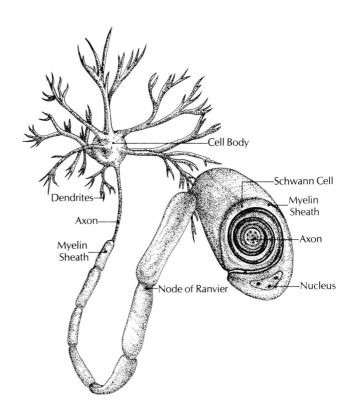

Figure 25.9   During the development of the nervous system, the Schwann cells migrate toward the axons growing from the cell bodies of specific neurons. The intriguing question of how the Schwann cells recognize the axons only of particular cells remains unanswered. Once it is close to the axon, the Schwann cell produces a large, flat cellular projection that wraps many times around the axon. In this manner a given length of axon becomes encased in a thick multiple-membrane sheath. The entire length of the axon eventually becomes encased by Schwann-cell wrapping, with each Schwann cell covering about 1 millimeter of the axon length. Interestingly, no two Schwann cells come in contact. Between the end of one wrapped segment and the beginning of the next there is always a space of about 1 micrometer of naked axonal membrane.

Each Schwann cell covers about 1 millimeter of axon; between adjacent Schwann cells about 1 micrometer of axon is left naked. The Schwann cell wrapping appears white under the microscope and is usually called the **myelin sheath.**

The result of myelination is a dramatic increase in propagation velocity. Indeed, action potential propagation *is* faster along myelinated axons than along any others so far studied—faster even than along the giant fibers. Because myelin acts as such as effective sheath, the ion flow that normally constitutes an action potential cannot occur across the axonal membrane in a region wrapped by a Schwann cell. *Only in the narrow spaces where the axonal membrane is exposed can ion flow of the sort required to produce an action potential occur.* These spaces between adjacent Schwann cells are called **nodes of Ranvier,** and the action potential ''jumps'' down the axon from one node to the next in what is called **saltatory propagation** (Figure 25.10). Such impulse conduction is extremely fast. In an unmyelinated neuron, the rapid depolarization in one region of the axon leads to slow depolarization in the immediately adjacent axon membrane. But the myelinated axon is so well insulated that a rapid depolarization at one node is immediately transmitted to the next node a millimeter away, causing it to depolarize, pass threshold, fire an action potential, and thereby depolarize the next membrane.

NEURONS ARE NOT THE ONLY CELLS IN THE NERVOUS SYSTEM

Although the neuron is the most intensively studied and best understood cellular component of nervous systems, nervous systems are not composed solely of neurons. In addition to the cells making up the various epithelial coverings of the nervous tissue, there is a major grouping of cells called glial cells—or **neuroglia.** Generally, there are many more glial cells than there are neurons within the central nervous system of most organisms.

The major roles played by glial cells are largely undefined. It appears certain that some glial cells function to provide a structural matrix within which neurons are embedded. Schwann cells aid in the propagation of neural impulses. Still other types of glia are known or suspected to serve nutritive functions for nerve cells (Figure 25.11), to act as scavengers of degenerating or damaged neurons, and to participate passively in the transfer of excitation and inhibition among groups of neurons. But even though glial cells are important, evidence suggests that the major roles in the nervous system are reserved for the neurons.

HOW DO NEURONS COMMUNICATE AND INTERACT?

Like the old saying, ''There is no such thing as *one* ant,'' it is difficult to think of a single neuron functioning autono-

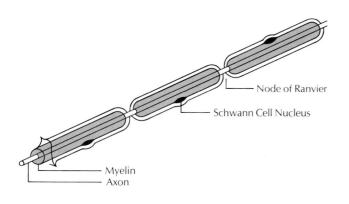

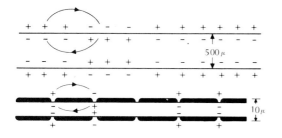

(b)

Figure 25.10   A myelinated axon. (a) Schwann cells wrap certain vertebrate axons with many membrane layers. These multiple wrappings (called myelin) serve as electric insulation and thereby greatly increase the propagation velocity of impulses on these axons. Because the Schwann cells do not overlap, there is a bare space of axon membrane every millimeter or so along the axon. The action potential jumps from one of these nodes of Ranvier to the next.

(b) This diagrammatic longitudinal section of a myelinated axon shows the local circuit for propagation in such neurons. The action potential is moving to the left. The node to the left will go over threshold next. The node to the right is still returning to normal polarization after action potential passage.

Figure 25.11 A photomicrograph of two glial cells, known as astrocytes, which may be involved in a nutritive process. The staining in this section has emphasized the astrocytes, so the surrounding neurons are not clearly visible. Each astrocyte has a process attached to the capillary running across the top. It may be that these glia take up nutrients from the blood and distribute them through their other cytoplasmic processes to the adjacent nerve cells.

mously within an organism. Ant colonies are complex, highly integrated systems with many thousands of individuals, each performing a specific function. The success of the whole depends on the fidelity with which each individual performs its task. To a considerable extent, the individual performance is in turn a product of the general state of the colony. Similarly, neurons can be viewed as both individual and interactive elements. *The function of individual neurons defines the function of the nervous system, and the function of the remainder of the nervous system determines the function of individual neurons.* Thus, as with an ant, if you find one neuron it is a sure bet there are a lot more somewhere nearby.

In this section, we will examine the interactive characteristics of neurons. We will begin with consideration of the details of synaptic processes. With this information we will be able to interpret some simple neuronal circuits and at least begin the analysis of entire systems of interacting neurons. This last undertaking will bring us very close to the limits of our interpretive ability, because when we deal with the enormously intricate nervous structures of complex organisms, we are forced to treat whole populations of neurons as if they are identical. Yet we realize that neurons are different from one another, and we cannot escape the doubt that our models are still too simple.

What Is a Synapse?

The special adaptations of neuronal structure and function that distinguish neurons from other types of cells are features associated with long-distance, high-velocity signaling. No signal being conveyed on a single neuron is of any consequence, however, unless it can be communicated to other cells.

The communication of a neuron with another cell occurs by a process called **synaptic transmission,** which takes place at a specialized structure called a **synapse.** The simplest but by no means the most common type of synapse is characterized simply by an area of extremely close contact between the membranes of two neurons. Cells having such a junction between them can be shown to be in electrical continuity with one another; depolarization of either cell leads directly to depolarization of the other. Similarly, experimentally induced hyperpolarization of one cell is reflected in the other. Apparently, modifications of membrane structure in such a junctional region produce an extremely low resistance contact between the cells. Current associated with changes in membrane potential flows from one cell to the next as if there were no boundary between them. Not surprisingly, these specialized junctions are called **electrical synapses.**

During the years when neural function was first being studied, all synapses between neurons were believed to be electrical in nature. This hypothesis seemed reasonable at the time. But we now see that it would be difficult to construct a nervous system of any complexity if each cell communicated all changes in its membrane potential to all the cells it made contact with. In a system composed entirely of electrical synapses, any change inducted by an environmental stimulus would be transmitted to all parts of the system. Thus, all stimuli would tend to merge in a blur of excitation. If stimuli received in one region are to produce a specific response, messages (action potentials) must proceed in an orderly and directional fashion through the nervous system. For orderly and directional progression of action potentials, the synapses between cells must be one-way, or **rectifying.** This means that synapses must transmit in only one direction (from cell *A* to cell *B* but not from *B* to *A*). Because electrical synapses do not distinguish the direction of current flow between cells (they are **nonrectifying**), their value in information processing is practically zero. Where they do play an important role is in fast response systems. In these systems, electrically coupled cells function in a useful manner only because they are regulated by the second type of synapse—the rectifying synapse in which communication between cells occurs by one-way flow of chemical mediators rather than by flow of current. Such a point of communication is called a **chemical synapse.**

It now appears that chemical synapses make up the vast majority of contacts among neurons and between neurons and effectors, such as muscles and glands. Because chemical synapses are rectifying, distinction must always be made between the **presynaptic** (sending) cell and **postsynaptic** (receiving) cell. At or near the tip of the axon of the presynaptic cell is a swelling that is variously referred to as a bouton, an end-foot, or simply a terminal. Part of the membrane of this specialized structure comes into close proximity with the membrane of the postsynaptic cell (Figure 25.12). The intervening space, called the **synaptic cleft,** is between 15 and 20 nanometers wide. A sending cell may synapse on any one of several different locations on the receiving cell. The functional role played by a particular synapse will depend on the location of the synapse on the postsynaptic cell. Certainly the largest number of synapses

are the **axodendritic synapses,** which are formed between presynaptic axons and postsynaptic dendrites. Also quite common are **axosomatic synapses,** in which the postsynaptic cell body receives the input from the presynaptic cell. The third general type of chemical synapse is called **axoaxonal** (Figure 25.13).

The terminal swellings of the presynaptic axons contain within their cytoplasm large numbers of small membrane-enclosed bodies called **synaptic vesicles** (Figure 25.12). These structures contain high concentrations of specific **neurotransmitters** (substances known to cause changes in the membrane potential of the postsynaptic cells).

The process of chemical synaptic transmission begins with the arrival of an action potential at the presynaptic terminal. Its arrival causes the presynaptic membrane to become depolarized. Accompanying the depolarization is an influx of calcium ions (Ca^{++}) through the presynaptic membrane. Upon calcium uptake, the synaptic vesicles fuse with the plasma membrane of the cell in the region of the synapse. A hole forms in the fused membranes and the

Figure 25.12   (a) Some general structural features of axodendritic synapses. The presynaptic terminals are button shaped and are appropriately called boutons. Within their cytoplasm are only two membranous organelles—mitochondria and synaptic vesicles. Synaptic vesicles contain the neurotransmitter chemical used at the particular synapse. Often the presynaptic membrane has thickened areas that seem to be patterned in some way, but their function is not known. Similarly, the postsynaptic membrane shows unexplained modifications. This figure also indicates another mysterious structure in some synapses—a dense material within the synaptic cleft.

(b) An electron photomicrograph showing a profile of a chemical synapse. The presynaptic terminal is on top; the postsynaptic structure is on the bottom. Mitochondria can be seen in the cytoplasm of both processes. Also evident in the presynaptic terminal are many clear, circular synaptic vesicles, approximately 40 nanometers in diameter, which contain the neurotransmitter chemical. Larger synaptic vesicles are seen in other types of neurons.

(a)

(b)

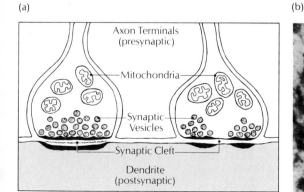

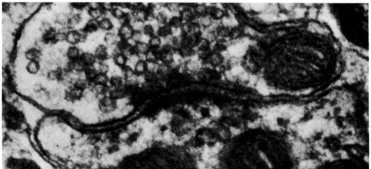

contents of the vesicle spill into the synaptic cleft and diffuse across to the postsynaptic membrane (Figure 25.14).

Once the neurotransmitter that was originally contained in the vesicles arrives at the postsynaptic membrane, it causes a change in the membrane potential of the postsynaptic cell. Thus, impulse transmission across a chemical synapse depends on diffusion of the neurotransmitter rather than a simple ''jumping'' of the action potential across the cleft, as occurs in electrical synapses. Therefore, *when compared with the transmission at electrical synapses, chemical synaptic transmission is a slow process.* Typical times required for chemical transmission range from 1 to 5 milliseconds. Most of this **synaptic delay** is the result of the time taken by presynaptic events leading to transmitter release. Once released, the transmitter diffuses across the cleft in 0.1 to 0.2 millisecond.

Here, then, we can see the rectifying character of the chemical synapse. The vesicles containing neurotransmitter are present on only one side of the synaptic cleft. Therefore, the signal proceeds clearly from presynaptic to postsynaptic cell. When the transmitter substance comes in contact with the postsynaptic membrane, it binds to a receptor molecule

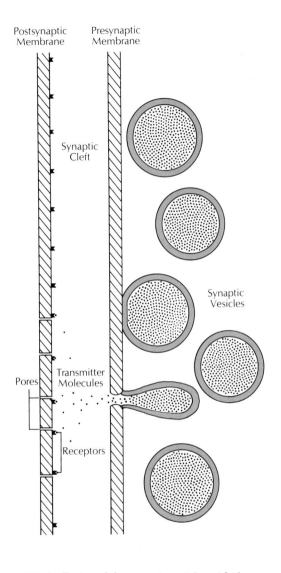

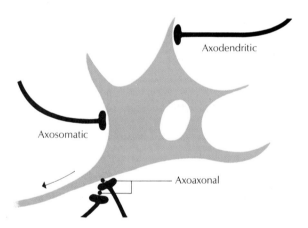

Figure 25.13 Sites of formation of synapses. Synaptic junctions may be formed between axons and any part of the postsynaptic cell. One unusual junction is a presynaptic axoaxonal synapse. Such junctions are formed by a synapse atop a synapse. The postsynaptic portion of such a synapse is the presynaptic portion of another. Undoubtedly, such an arrangement implies a role for one cell in modifying interactions between two others.

Figure 25.14 Fusion of the synaptic vesicles with the presynaptic terminal membrane in the presence of Ca⁺⁺. Once fusion occurs, the membranes break in such a way that the contents of the vesicle pass into the synaptic cleft. The neurotransmitter molecules diffuse across the cleft and activate receptors located on the surface of the postsynaptic membrane. The result is the opening of specific ion pores in the postsynaptic membrane and a consequent change in membrane potential. Controversy surrounds the question of the fate of the synaptic vesicle after it has emptied its contents. The most widely held hypothesis is that the membranes reseal and the vesicle returns to the cytoplasm to be refilled with transmitter.

in the membrane. The complex of transmitter plus receptor then causes certain ion pores in the membrane to open. The actual mechanism through which this is achieved remains a mystery; nevertheless, increased ion flux can be measured as a result of the binding of transmitter to the postsynaptic membrane. If Na^+ pores are opened, the postsynaptic cell will depolarize. This will shift the potential toward the threshold required to fire an action potential in the postsynaptic cell. This kind of change is called **excitatory postsynaptic potential,** or **EPSP.** But if K^+ pores are opened selectively, the cell will hyperpolarize. The effect of hyperpolarization is to shift the membrane potential to a more negative value and therefore away from the threshold. A hyperpolarized cell is therefore less likely than before to fire an action potential; it is considered temporarily inhibited. This kind of change is called **inhibitory postsynaptic potential,** or **IPSP.**

In short, there are actually two kinds of chemical synapses: **excitatory,** in which an action potential may be triggered, and **inhibitory,** in which an action potential is hindered (Figure 25.15).

To date, only two substances have been confirmed as being neurotransmitters, yet many other molecules are likely candidates (Figure 25.16). It is tempting to speculate that the existence of different transmitter chemicals implies different specific effects on postsynaptic cells. However, recent studies have shown that *the axonal terminals of a single cell may mediate excitation at one synapse and inhibition at another.* Because no cell has been shown to use more than one kind of transmitter at its synapses, this means that the same transmitter causes one postsynaptic cell

to depolarize and another to hyperpolarize. Therefore, we can conclude that *it is the nature of the receptor molecules on the postsynaptic membrane and not the nature of the neurotransmitter that determines whether a synaptic input will be excitatory or inhibitory.*

Each Neuron Sums Many Inputs

This discussion of excitatory and inhibitory synaptic connections between neurons might be taken to mean that a single synaptic input can cause a cell either to fire an action potential or to become incapable of firing. In some cases, particularly at axoaxonal synapses, this may be true. *Most often, however, a single synaptic input is too weak to bring about such a major change in the postsynaptic cell.* Usually the combined inputs from many synapses are required to determine whether a given cell will fire an action potential. Most neurons in complex organisms receive inputs from between 100 and 10,000 synapses. If these neurons are to act as anything other than simple relays, they must process this tremendous amount of incoming information in some manner. Several factors enter into such processing. First of all, the membrane of most neuronal dendrites is so structured that it cannot generate an action potential. Therefore, the shift in membrane potential resulting from an excitatory synaptic input on a dendrite shows up elsewhere in the cell only by means of current spreading from the point of synapse, not by a full-blown action potential. The farther away from the input the potential change is measured, the less effect will be seen, because the spreading current is dissipated through the high resistance of the cytoplasm. Similarly, an inhibitory postsynaptic potential shows de-

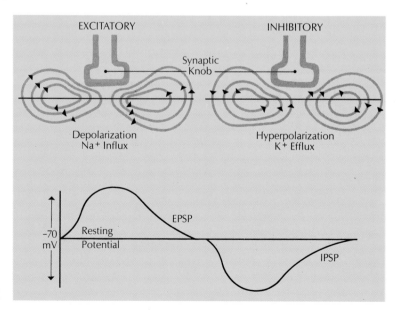

Figure 25.15 *The action of excitatory and inhibitory synapses. The current flow associated with excitatory synaptic transmission (left) depolarizes the postsynaptic membrane. The potential change in the postsynaptic cell is referred to as an excitatory postsynaptic potential (EPSP). An inhibitory synaptic event (right) results in an inhibitory postsynaptic potential (IPSP). The shapes and durations of the membrane potential change are variable and depend on many factors. Typical durations range from 1 to 10 milliseconds.*

crease in amplitude the farther it spreads along the dendrite. But at some point along the cell (sometimes at the soma; in other cells, at the beginning of the axon), the membrane becomes capable of setting off an action potential. At this point, *the sum of the small increments in membrane potential produced by the EPSPs and the IPSPs at distant dendritic synapses determines whether or not an action potential will be generated.*

This summation of positive and negative increments of membrane potential is known as **neural integration.** It is the process that underlies the analyzing and coordinating properties of the nervous system. To better visualize how such integration occurs, we must begin to look at more complex assemblages of interacting nerve cells as they are actually organized into nervous systems.

Neuronal Circuits Integrate Stimuli and Trigger Responses

Analysis of synaptic processes forms the basis for interpreting the "wiring diagrams" of nervous systems. Information from the environment enters nervous systems in the form of action potentials propagating along individual axons from sensory organs. Bundles of these sensory neurons are called **sensory nerves.** They enter the central nervous system (brain and spinal cord), where the information they bear is processed. The "products" of central neural integration and processing of sensory inputs are action potentials, which leave the central nervous system by way of axons that ultimately synapse on muscles or other effector organs. Bundles of these effector neurons are usually called **motor nerves.** Intervening between the sensory and motor neurons in the central nervous system are the **interneurons.** *Interneurons make up the bulk of most central nervous tissue; they are responsible for the intricate and subtle processing of sensory input that leads to motor output.*

The simplest types of neuronal circuits are those that underlie **monosynaptic reflex arcs.** As the name implies, these reflex circuits incorporate only one synapse between the sensory input and the motor output. The sensory impulses activate the motor neurons directly. A monosynaptic reflex circuit is particularly valuable for rapid response to a stimulus, because the only delays between the stimulus

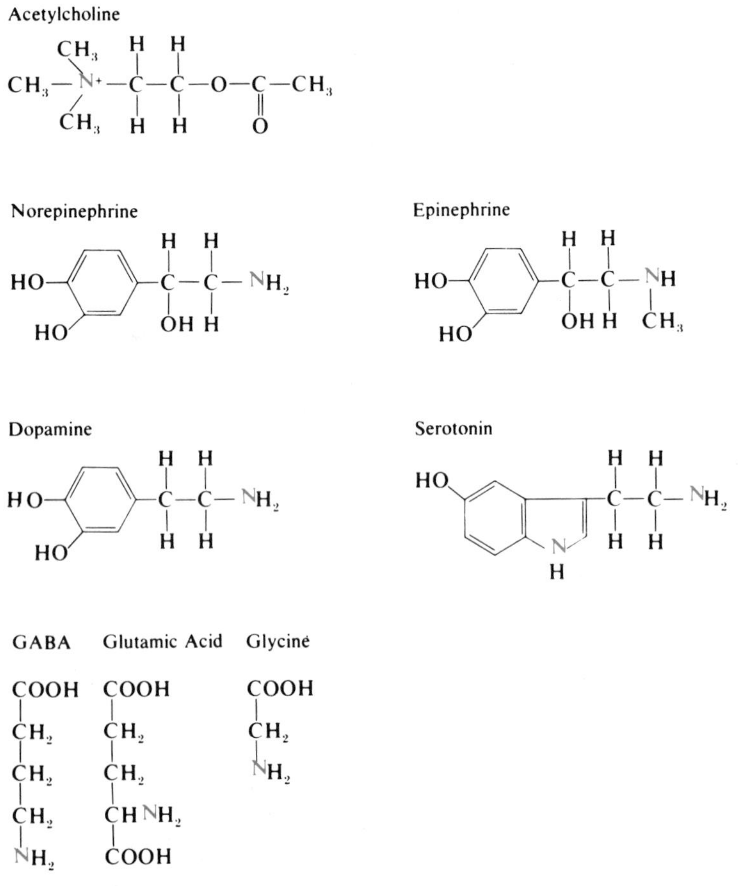

Figure 25.16 The chemical structures of confirmed (and suspected) neurotransmitters. Acetylcholine and norepinephrine meet the most rigorous criteria used in classifying neurotransmitters. Others are borderline candidates in that they meet some but not all of the criteria. Interestingly, all these molecules contain an amino group and are, with the exception of acetylcholine, closely related to amino acids (indeed, glycine and glutamic acid are common amino acids). The reasons for these common features are not clear.

and the response are imposed by the propagation velocities on the sensory and motor neurons and the delay at the single synapse. An example of such a reflex circuit in the human is the knee jerk (Figure 25.17). A firm tap just below the knee cap distorts a tendon, causing the sensory neurons in the tendon to fire action potentials. The axons of these neurons extend from the knee into the spinal cord. There, they synapse directly onto motor neurons. The axons of these motor neurons leave the spinal cord and synapse on muscles in the thigh. The response to the tap at the knee is a rapid contraction of the specific thigh muscles attached to the tendon. This contraction causes the lower leg to kick forward.

In addition to muscles that cause the lower leg to swing forward, the thigh also contains muscles that cause the opposite movement. Thus, the knee jerk is not quite so simple when the complex musculature of the thigh is considered, for neuronal integration begins to come into play even in this simple reflex. In addition to the monosynaptic excitatory reflex, there must also be control over antagonistic muscles to prevent them from blocking the forward kick. This control is accomplished by inhibition of the motor neurons leading to the antagonistic muscles. Two types of circuits that can produce the necessary simultaneous excitation and inhibition of separate groups of motor neurons have been discovered in the spinal cord (Figure 25.18). Both circuits incorporate interneurons and are therefore more complex than the monosynaptic circuit.

In one type of circuit, the axon of the *motor* neuron branches before it leaves the spinal cord. This axonal branch makes an excitatory synaptic contact with an interneuron, which in turn makes inhibitory contacts with the antagonistic motor neurons. In such a circuit, the sensory input results in a nearly simultaneous excitatory output to the thigh and inhibitory feedback on the antagonist motor neuron.

The second type of circuit acts as a "feed-forward" system. The *sensory* axon branches before the synapse with the motor neuron. One of the branches then makes an excitatory synapse with an interneuron, which (as in the other case) inhibits antagonist motor neurons. Therefore, instead of the motor neuron initiating the inhibitory signal, the incoming sensory neuron simultaneously activates the reflex response and inhibits the antagonistic response.

Despite the insight afforded by examination of simple circuits, the control and organization of behavior must be viewed as an enormously complicated process. When we stepped back from the monosynaptic reflex, we found that control of antagonistic thigh muscles had to be achieved through a slightly more complicated system. Similarly, if we take another step back we find that still other control circuits are brought into play. For example, the sensory axon might have ten branches. If each of these branches synapses with a separate interneuron, ten cells will have been influenced by the sensory input at the first stage. But each interneuron might make ten synaptic contacts as well, so that a hundred cells might be involved at the second stage. Already the wiring diagram would be complex, and it is likely that two synaptic stages would only be the beginning of a complete sensory-to-motor diagram. Thus, one must quickly give up the attempt to specify the actions at particular synapses and must begin seeking generalizations to account for the functions of nervous systems.

Organization of Neurons Into Systems Centralizes Control

Up to this point, the discussion of the structure and function of neurons has proceeded with few references to specific organisms. We should ask: Is it legitimate to speak of neurons, action potentials, synapses, and neurotransmitters as if they were essentially identical for all species, from jellyfish to man? The astonishing answer seems to be that *the fundamental properties of nervous tissue have changed in no important way through a great span of evolutionary time.* As you read in Section II, the significance of this observation appears to be that a strong selective pressure favored development of a high-speed intercellular communication method in the earliest metazoans. That so little

(text continues on page 565)

Figure 25.17 *The knee jerk reflex (patellar reflex). This reflex is initiated by a tap just below the kneecap. Sensory neurons are stimulated and send impulses to the spinal cord. Within the spinal cord the sensory axons synapse onto motor neurons, which cause contraction of the extensor muscles of the thigh.*

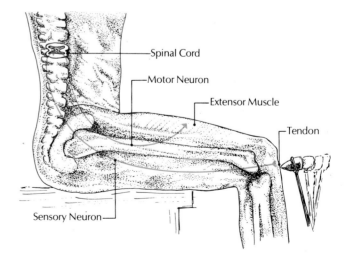

Interleaf 25.2

Neural Basis of Behavior

Neurobiology is currently progressing along several fronts. Although many problems concerned with the function of single neurons remain to be answered, enough is already known to justify beginning an analysis of the neural basis of behavior. The ultimate goal of this undertaking is to account for all behavior in terms of neurophysiological processes.

The vast number of neurons (estimated to be at least 1×10^{11}) and the bewildering complexity of their interconnections place the human brain far outside the range of detailed nueron-by-neuron analysis. Indeed, even the somewhat less complicated central nervous systems found in other vertebrates are enormous mazes from our current perspective. Thus, neurobiologists are starting this ambitious undertaking by studying the simple nervous systems in a variety of invertebrate organisms.

Among molluscs the large marine nudibranch *Tritonia diomedia* has received much attention. This "sea slug" has only 10,000 or so neurons in its CNS. Several of these cells are quite large (approaching 1 millimeter in diameter), and many are characteristically pigmented, providing a sort of color coding. Although *Tritonia* spends most of its time either motionless on the substrate or slowly grazing on algae, when it is touched by the tube feet of a predatory sea star it will begin rapid, jerky flexures of its body. These motions propel it off the substrate and through the water some distance before it settles again. This escape response is an interesting behavior because it consists of several alternating dorsal and ventral flexures of the body in response to a single brief stimulation. If this were a simple reflex arc like the human knee jerk, a single stimulus should evoke only a single response. The presence of several flexures indicates something more complicated—but what? A. O. D. Willows and his colleagues have studied the escape response at the neuronal level. These workers have found neurons serving four separate functions in the escape response. First, there are two classes of motor neurons. One stimulates muscles that cause the dorsal flexure; the other class is responsible for the ventral flexure. During the escape response, these neurons show reciprocal bursts of activity.

The dorsal flexure motor neurons show a burst of impulses, then the ventral flexure neurons are active, then the dorsal flexure cells resume activity, and so on. Because both excitatory and inhibitory postsynaptic potentials can be detected in the motor cells, it is clear that they are receiving synaptic input—but from where? Perhaps the alternating activity pattern consists of a chain of stimuli and responses. Perhaps the first flexure initiated by the sea star attack elicits a sensory feedback from the contracted muscles that acts as a stimulus for the alternate flexure, which then stimulates the third flexure, and so on. If this were true, then cutting the sensory fibers from the muscles should abolish the alternating activity. But it does not. Thus, feedback from sensory neurons in the muscles is not responsible for the alternating cycles of contraction.

One source of inhibitory synaptic input to the motor neurons derives from their antagonists. When dorsal flexure cells are active, they inhibit the ventral flexure cells, and vice versa. This reciprocal inhibition begins to explain the alternation in bursts of activity. A third class of cells completes the explanation: a group of interneurons that fire bursts of impulses whenever either class of motor neuron is active. These cells receive excitatory synaptic input from each class of motor cell and make excitatory synapses on the motor cells of the opposite class. The alternating flexure of dorsal and ventral muscles during the escape response, then, is a consequence of mutual inhibition between the antagonistic motor cells and mutual excitation via the interneurons. When the dorsal flexure neurons are triggered into activity, they simultaneously inhibit the ventral flexure neurons directly and stimulate them indirectly through the interneurons. As long as the impulse activity in the dorsal flexure cells is high, the direct inhibitory effect predominates. But as the activity begins to slow, the excitatory inputs from the interneurons become more effective until the inhibition is overcome and the ventral flexure cells begin to fire impulses, causing both ventral flexure and inhibition of the dorsal flexure neurons. But now once again, the seesaw begins to tip and the excitatory interneural pathway to the dorsal flexion cells begins to have more effect than the direct inhibition. The dorsal flexure cells take over once again. Thus the reciprocating sequence continues.

The fourth class of neurons in the CNS that play a role in this response are the cells that trigger the initial burst of activity in the dorsal flexure neurons. The trigger cells receive sensory input from the periphery. If the input is nonspecific and weak, only a few trigger cells are activated and insufficient stimulation is delivered to the dorsal flexure cells to start the escape sequence. In a sense, the trigger cells act as a committee. Only stimuli of sufficient specificity and intensity will cause enough of them to begin firing to trigger the

dorsal flexure cells. A solid majority is required for the escape response to begin.

This sort of in-depth analysis of the neural basis of a relatively simple behavioral act has provided a new dimension to our understanding of the behavior. What might have been thought to be a chain reflex of stimuli and responses mediated by feedback from the periphery is in fact a centrally generated sequence of alternating motor commands. Indeed, the autonomy of this neural circuitry from any but the initial sensory stimulus is shown by the faithful sequence of neural activities in a CNS completely isolated from the animal. An artificial electrical stimulus of appropriate intensity and frequency to the sensory fibers that excite the trigger group cells can cause the entire escape response at the neural level to be played out just as it would be in an intact animal. It is as though the impulses from the periphery signaling the presence of a dangerous predator throw the switch on a tape recorder, which plays out the prerecorded escape response.

The independence from peripheral input of this neural circuit is even more dramatically illustrated by the cessation of the motor commands in the isolated preparation after it has completed five cycles of bursting. The typical behavioral escape response in the living animal consists of five dorsal-ventral flexures of the body! How the tape recorder is shut off is not yet known, but it, too, is a central process.

Surely much of animal behavior consists of sequences in which stimulation leads to a response that in turn leads to a new kind of stimulation followed by a new response, and so on. But the analysis of the *Tritonia* escape reaction clearly demonstrates that we cannot necessarily assume this always to be true. Rather, complex behavior can be programmed in such a way that, once it is released by an environmental stimulus, it unfolds in its entirety in the absence of further environmental input. As we shall see in Chapter 27, fixed action patterns released by simple environmental stimuli figure importantly in animal interactions.

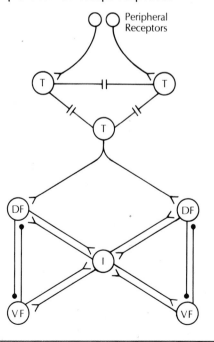

Schematic "wiring diagram" for the control of the escape response in Tritonia diomedia. Excitatory synapses are represented by ——<. Inhibitory synapses are represented by ———•. Impulses from the peripheral receptors excite the trigger cells (T). These cells make electrical synapses (——┤ ├——) with one another and excitatory synapses with the dorsal flexure motor neurons (DF). The dorsal flexure motor cells reciprocally inhibit the ventral flexure motor cells (VF). Both the DF and VF cells reciprocally excite the interneurons (I).

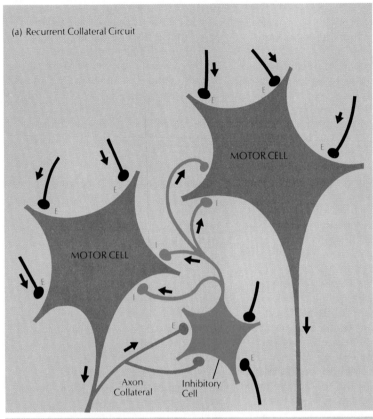

(a) Recurrent Collateral Circuit

MOTOR CELL

MOTOR CELL

Axon Collateral

Inhibitory Cell

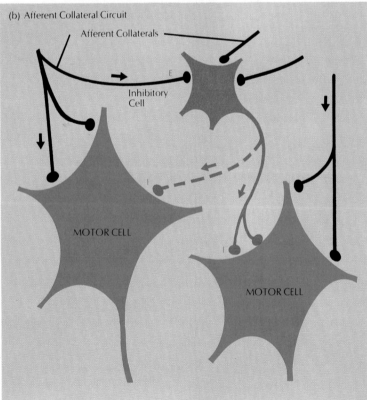

(b) Afferent Collateral Circuit

Afferent Collaterals

Inhibitory Cell

MOTOR CELL

MOTOR CELL

MOTOR CELL

Figure 25.18   Two schemes for excitation and inhibition of appropriate antagonist motor neurons. (a) In the recurrent collateral circuit the sensory neurons (black) make excitatory synapses (E) on motor neurons (red). Some motor neurons send off a recurrent axonal collateral that makes an excitatory synapse with an interneuron (blue). The interneuron makes inhibitory synapses (I) on other motor neurons. Note that the interneuron also makes inhibitory synapses on the same motor neuron that activated it. This connection prevents continued firing of the motor neuron. In the knee jerk reflex, for example, this sort of direct feedback would prevent the muscle contraction from continuing so long as to lock the leg in a fully extended position. (b) In the case of afferent collateral ''feed-forward'' circuits, the inhibitory cell is activated directly by the afferent neuron. The net effect in a knee jerk reflex would be substantially the same as with the recurrent collateral circuit.

change in neuron structure and function has occurred during what has been an otherwise turbulent evolutionary time supports the idea that the early solutions to the problems of constructing the nervous system were enough to meet intervening selective pressures with only minor modifications. In contrast, the organization of neurons into nervous systems has undergone changes that reflect changes in organization of the animal body. (Some of these differences were discussed in Chapters 7 and 8.)

Most animals that have highly differentiated, complex nervous systems are bilaterally symmetrical (Chapter 7). In such animals, several evolutionary trends in nervous system organization can be detected. First, there has been a trend toward increased **cephalization**—the concentration of many sensory organs within the head and development of the size and complexity of the brain. Second, there has been an increase in the number of interneurons. Third, there has been an increased variety of structurally different kinds of neurons and glial cells. Fourth, there has been an increase in the variety and differentiation of specialized regions within the brain. In the more complex animals, the brain has more neurons and a far more complex organization of subsystems than any other part of the nervous system.

THE VERTEBRATE NERVOUS SYSTEM: THE RIDDLE OF INFORMATION PROCESSING

Along the back of the vertebrate body, encased in bone, lies a continuous tube of nerve tissue. It is enlarged at one end and it sends off frequent branches that extend outward, making contact with all the other parts of the body.

This description of the vertebrate nervous system tells us something about its structure, but it tells us very little about the bustle of activity that occurs within this tract of cells. Somehow nerve endings sensitive to changes in light, temperature, pressure, and other cues from the environment trigger action potentials that flow into the nervous system in a continuous stream. Somehow these potentials become sorted, integrated, and processed, giving rise to new action potentials that flow outward to activate appropriate responses. The entire way of life of an animal depends on the interactions of this system.

Yet the vertebrate nervous system is so complex that it is impossible to describe all the events occurring within it during any one second in the life of an organism. Much of what goes on is totally unknown; therefore, much of what *is* known cannot yet be pieced together into a meaningful whole. What follows, then, is a riddle with many parts.

The Central Nervous System: The Main Site of Neural Integration

Traditionally, the vertebrate nervous system is divided into two parts. The neural structures encased within the skull and backbone are called the **central nervous system,** or **CNS.** All the rest—the branches coming off the central nervous system, the clusters of nerve cells lying outside the backbone, and the nerve processes stretching out through the body—has been termed the **peripheral nervous system,** or **PNS.**

Now, this distinction may be useful for certain purposes. But it is perhaps an unfortunate choice of terms, for it suggests that these are two separate systems, somehow working side by side. Nothing could be further from the truth. They are separate only in the sense that a telephone in your home is separate from the equipment in the main switching offices of the telephone company. *The central nervous system and the peripheral nervous system are parts of a functional whole; neither can work without the other.* How nerve-cell bodies and processes are organized within the various regions of the nervous system will now be discussed; in passing, some aspects of coordinated function within the parts will be considered.

The Spinal Cord: A Communication Route Between the Brain and Body

The part of the neural tube lying within the vertebral column (the backbone) is called the **spinal cord.** As shown in Figure 25.19, it is a bilaterally symmetrical structure. The organization of the spinal cord provides insight into its function. A butterfly-shaped region in its center is the site of extensive synaptic activity. It is here that axons from sensory nerves entering the cord through the dorsal root terminate. It is here that they sometimes synapse directly with dendrites of motor neurons, which have processes leading out from the ventral root to effector organs in the periphery, thus completing a single-synapse reflex arc. But more often, such sensory neurons synapse on interneurons, which in turn synapse on other interneurons or on motor neurons, completing reflex arcs of greater complexity. The region that contains all these synaptic structures, the cell bodies of interneurons and motor neurons, and their associated glial cells is called the **gray matter.**

Even though some reflex arcs are completed within a single level of the spinal cord, such activity does not go unnoticed elsewhere. Some of the sensory neuron branches synapse on interneurons running up and down the spinal cord, integrating activities at various levels of the body. And other branches terminate on neurons leading to the brain, thus keeping it informed of all the reflex behavior occurring in the spinal cord. Still other neurons descend from the brain and synapse on the motor neurons, conditioning their responsiveness or firing action potentials that lead to voluntary movements and the like. All the neuronal processes coursing up and down the spinal cord are sheathed in myelin. The glistening appearance of the myelin sheath

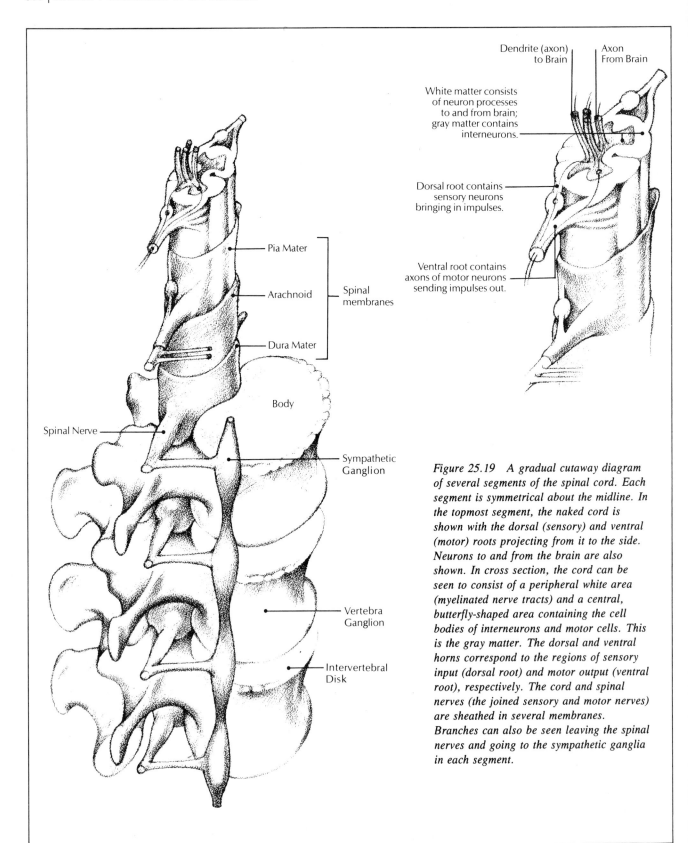

Dendrite (axon) to Brain

Axon From Brain

White matter consists of neuron processes to and from brain; gray matter contains interneurons.

Dorsal root contains sensory neurons bringing in impulses.

Ventral root contains axons of motor neurons sending impulses out.

Pia Mater

Arachnoid

Spinal membranes

Dura Mater

Body

Spinal Nerve

Sympathetic Ganglion

Vertebra Ganglion

Intervertebral Disk

Figure 25.19   A gradual cutaway diagram of several segments of the spinal cord. Each segment is symmetrical about the midline. In the topmost segment, the naked cord is shown with the dorsal (sensory) and ventral (motor) roots projecting from it to the side. Neurons to and from the brain are also shown. In cross section, the cord can be seen to consist of a peripheral white area (myelinated nerve tracts) and a central, butterfly-shaped area containing the cell bodies of interneurons and motor cells. This is the gray matter. The dorsal and ventral horns correspond to the regions of sensory input (dorsal root) and motor output (ventral root), respectively. The cord and spinal nerves (the joined sensory and motor nerves) are sheathed in several membranes. Branches can also be seen leaving the spinal nerves and going to the sympathetic ganglia in each segment.

gives the name **white matter** to the region of the cord in which such nerve tracts lie.

The Brain: Master Control Center

Cephalization has led to two kinds of functions for the brain. First of all, it plays a role similar to that just described for the spinal cord—it integrates inputs and outputs from the many complex sense organs and effector organs that were concentrated about the mouth during evolution of bilaterally symmetrical animals. But more importantly, it plays a unique role in integrating and coordinating voluntary and involuntary activities relating to

all body parts. Different aspects of this integrative behavior occur in different regions of the brain.

Figure 25.20 shows the major regions of the human brain. Let us begin with regions of the brain adjacent to the spinal cord and move to regions that are, at least during embryonic development, more and more anterior. (Because of folding that occurs during development, this linear order often is not obvious in an adult animal.)

The medulla and pons perform in the head the role that the spinal cord plays in the trunk. The **medulla** is similar to the spinal cord in both structure and function. Sensory and motor neurons serving the skin and the muscles of the head are connected to the medulla, as are neurons coming from

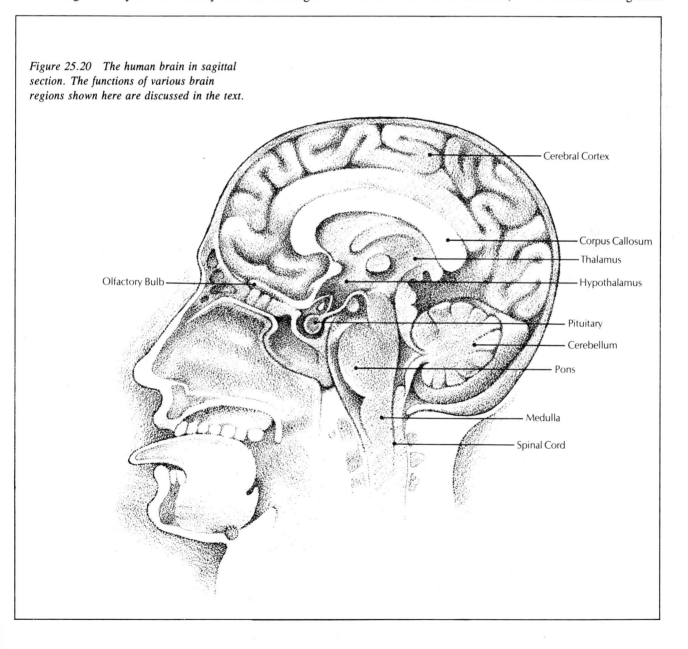

Figure 25.20   The human brain in sagittal section. The functions of various brain regions shown here are discussed in the text.

Cerebral Cortex

Corpus Callosum

Thalamus

Hypothalamus

Olfactory Bulb

Pituitary

Cerebellum

Pons

Medulla

Spinal Cord

the sensory organs of balance, taste, and hearing. In addition, the medulla controls many extremely important automatic activities—for instance, those of respiration and circulation. The **pons** is an extension of the medulla. It contains neurons that control chewing movements, salivation, and facial movements. It also contains neurons involved in hearing, respiration, and the inhibition and excitation of spinal motor neurons. Specific regions in the pons mediate the information transfer between the forebrain and the cerebellum, as well as between the cerebellum and the spinal cord.

The cerebellum integrates body movement. The **cerebellum** is a two-layered lobed structure lying above the pons. The outer layer, called the **cortex,** is gray matter. Like the gray matter in the spinal cord, it contains numerous synapses, glial cells, and neuron cell bodies. The gray matter surrounds an area of white matter. Unlike the white matter in the spinal cord, this region has many tightly packed clusters of neuron cell bodies interspersed between the nerve processes.

In simple vertebrates, the cerebellum is connected to sensory neurons coming from receptors that detect the positions of muscles. In more complex vertebrates, the cerebellar cortex is more extensively developed and is connected indirectly to *all* the sensory systems of the body. Medieval anatomists believed the cerebellum to be the seat of the soul, but modern anatomists suggest it is involved in much more mundane functions: the coordination of body movements and the maintenance of posture and equilibrium. If the cerebellum is removed, body movements become uncontrollable. The cerebellum apparently contains many feedback circuits that continuously modify behaviors on the basis of sensory information about the progress of the actions.

Recent studies indicate that the cerebellum may play even more central roles in vertebrate behavior. The cerebellum resembles the most complex part of the brain (the cerebral hemispheres, to be discussed shortly) by virtue of a cortex layer of gray matter that covers a core of white matter. The cortex of the cerebellum is characterized by **Purkinje cells** (Figure 25.21). The highly branched dendrites of these cells integrate impulses from a large region of the cortex and send impulses over their axons to relay centers in the central region of the cerebellum. Because the organization of the cerebellum is orderly and much simpler than that of the cerebral cortex, many biologists hope that its function and structure will soon be elucidated and will provide clues about the more complex organization of the cerebral cortex. Currently there are speculations that the cerebellum is also involved in the sensation of time, in visualization of continuity and position in time and space, and in modifica-

tion of learned behavior patterns to suit a wide variety of subtle changes in conditions.

The thalamus is the gateway to the cerebrum. The most obvious structural features of the **thalamus** are many tightly packed clusters of neuron cell bodies with their associated glial cells. Each cluster contains a group of cells with similar connections to other areas and hence with related functions. Neurons carrying impulses to the brain from ears and eyes enter specific regions of the thalamus, where these impulses are processed and sent on to the cerebrum. Other regions of the thalamus receive inputs from one part of the cerebrum, process the information, and send it off to other cerebral regions. Still other regions of the thalamus process information from the cerebrum and send it on to the cerebellum and medulla. This great diversity of function has earned for the thalamus the description "the great relay station of the brain."

The hypothalamus regulates many basic behavior patterns and links the nervous system to the endocrine system. The small size of the **hypothalamus** and its relatively few clusters of neuronal cell bodies belies its central role in regulating many vital processes within the body. It is an integral part of the brain, functioning in a strictly neuronal

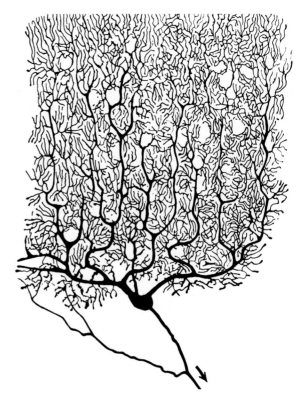

Figure 25.21 Diagram of a Purkinje cell from the human cerebellar cortex. The enormously complex dendritic structure provides for the major integrative role played by these cells.

manner to regulate many critical processes in the life-support system of the animal. Specific regions within the hypothalamus regulate body temperature, heart rate, blood pressure, and so on. Still other regions control basic drives to obtain food, water, and sex. For example, experiments show that destruction of one tiny region of the hypothalamus in rats causes insatiable hunger, almost continuous eating, and gross obesity, the outcome being rats that weigh three or four times as much as normal.

In addition, certain cells of the hypothalamus function as secretory cells, releasing quantities of specific hormones into the blood vessels that lead to the nearby **pituitary gland.** These substances cause the selective release of one or another hormone from the pituitary gland. These pituitary hormones in turn have far-reaching consequences for growth, regulation, and development of distant body parts (Chapter 22). Thus, the hypothalamus serves as the site of linkage between the body's two great systems of integration and control.

As one example of how this interaction occurs, consider the effect that mating has on a female rabbit. Stimulation of the vagina by the copulatory act triggers a flow of action potentials in the sensory neurons leading to the spinal cord. As a result of complex processing of these signals in the spinal cord and brain, certain cells of the hypothalamus are triggered to secrete a releasing hormone into the blood vessels that lead to the pituitary gland. This releasing hormone causes the pituitary gland to secrete a pair of hormones (FSH and LH, described in Chapter 22) for which the target cells are in the ovaries. The ovaries respond in two ways. Almost at once the flow of female sex hormones is increased; this begins to prepare the uterus to receive the prospective young. A few hours later, the ovary releases a series of eggs to encounter the sperm, which by now have moved up into the reproductive tract.

Many mammals release eggs spontaneously, without the need for copulation, but the hypothalamus always plays a similar role in the process. What differs is simply the mechanism by which it is triggered to secrete the key releasing hormone that initiates the process. In some species that breed only once a year, it is changes in the length of day that trigger the flow of the critical releasing substance from the hypothalamus. In the human and other species that have regular cycles of fertility, the sex hormones themselves act on the hypothalamus to modify its activity.

This variation in hypothalamic sensitivity to various kinds of input is only one example of the twin features that have characterized the nervous system in evolution: *precision* and *flexibility*. The system is "wired" to lead to precise interactions and integrated behaviors between parts.

But subtle shifts in the relative sensitivity to one input or another can occur and can be selected for if they better adapt the organism in question to its ecological niche. And this evolutionary flexibility has made all the difference. It has played a particularly important role in the evolutionary history of the brain region to be considered next: the cerebral cortex.

The cerebral cortex is the region of abstract thought in the human being. The cerebrum is the region of the brain that develops in the most anterior portion of the body. Like the cerebellum, it consists of a layer of white matter (in which many nerve-cell clusters are located) and a covering of gray matter called the **cerebral cortex.** No region of the brain has shown such dramatic change in the process of evolutionary time as the cerebral cortex. In fish, the **olfactory bulb** (the region of the cerebrum concerned with processing inputs from the organs responsible for the sense of smell) is the dominant part of the cerebrum (Figure 25.22*a*). The cortex is absent or poorly developed. As we move along the evolutionary scale through fish and reptiles to mammals, we see that the olfactory bulbs remain prominent but that the rest of the cerebrum increases relative to the rest of the brain. In primitive mammals (such as the opossum shown in Figure 25.22*d*), the cerebral cortex is quite smooth in outward appearance. But in more advanced mammals, the cortex becomes more complex, with extensive folds and wrinkles. These folds and wrinkles increase the ratio of surface area to mass.

In contrast with other mammals, primates have poorly developed olfactory bulbs, but the cerebral cortex dominates the brain cavity. The only mammals that rival the primates in the extent of cortex development are the marine mammals such as porpoises and whales; their capacity for learned behavior is correspondingly great.

How are different information-processing tasks distributed among different regions of the cerebral cortex? Surprisingly, much (but by no means all) of our knowledge about this subject has come from work directly on the brain of the conscious human! In the mid-nineteenth century, Pierre Broca, a French physician, discovered that any accident that caused damage to one specific region of the cerebral cortex leads to severe language impairment. (This area is now known as **Broca's area,** Figure 25.23.) This was the first indication that different regions of the cortex might control different human functions.

More recently, surgeons have sometimes found it essential to perform what is known as exploratory brain surgery. Most often this is done to locate a brain tumor whose presence is already established but whose exact position is unknown. Having anesthetized the skin of the scalp of the patient and carefully lifted the skull cap, the surgeon

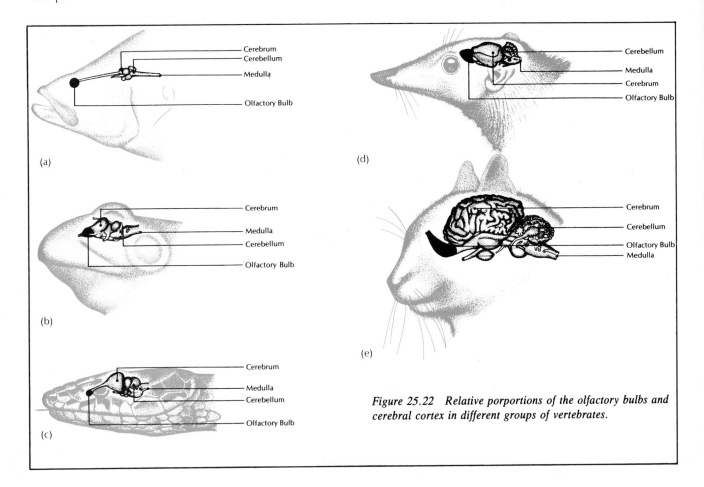

Figure 25.22   Relative porportions of the olfactory bulbs and cerebral cortex in different groups of vertebrates.

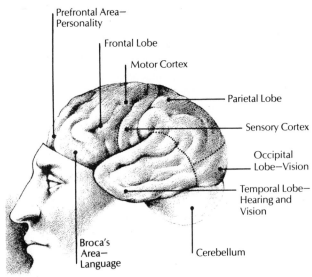

Figure 25.23   Side view of the surface of the human brain. Although certain regions of the cortex can be correlated with particular functions, many regions cannot. They are what are called "association regions" that are involved in what we think of as intelligence and consciousness.

stimulates specific regions of the brain surface electrically (with sterile electrodes) in order to detect which regions of the brain are functioning normally and which are not. Because there are no pain-sensing nerve endings in the brain, the patient (who is wide awake) feels no discomfort. However, if a stimulus is applied to a particular region of the temporal lobe of the cortex, the patient may experience complex auditory illusions. Stimulated in another region of this lobe, he may be caused to recall a rather complex series of events from the past. If the electrode is applied to a particular region of the parietal lobe, he may feel a tingling in one particular body region. Application of the electrodes to a discrete spot on the frontal lobe may cause a finger to wiggle; stimulation nearby may cause a wrist to bend.

As a result of such studies, it becomes clear that certain cerebral tasks are highly localized and that they are similar in all individuals. For example, damage to one particular region of the occipital lobe (Figure 25.23) will predictably lead to a blind spot in one particular region of the visual field. Perhaps the most well-defined regions of the cortex are those involved in receiving touch and positional information from the various regions of the body (the *sensory*

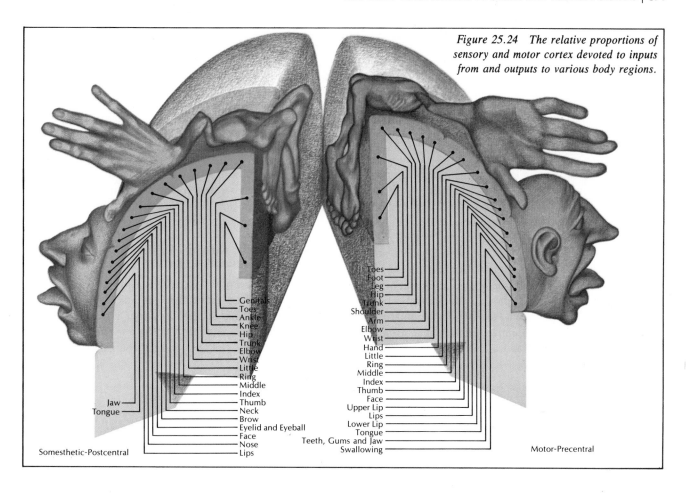

Figure 25.24 The relative proportions of sensory and motor cortex devoted to inputs from and outputs to various body regions.

Somesthetic-Postcentral

Genitals
Toes
Ankle
Knee
Hip
Trunk
Elbow
Wrist
Little
Ring
Middle
Index
Thumb
Neck
Brow
Eyelid and Eyeball
Face
Nose
Lips
Jaw
Tongue

Toes
Foot
Leg
Hip
Trunk
Shoulder
Arm
Elbow
Wrist
Hand
Little
Ring
Middle
Index
Thumb
Face
Upper Lip
Lips
Lower Lip
Tongue
Teeth, Gums and Jaw
Swallowing

Motor-Precentral

cortex) and those integrating movement of the various body parts (the *motor cortex*). These regions occur in two bands running over the surface of the cortex near the middle, as shown in Figure 25.23. The area devoted to each body region in the cortex is not proportional to the size of the part; rather, it is proportional to the complexity of the stimuli being received from that part or the complexity of the coordinated motions that part is required to play in the interaction of the individual with its environment. Thus, as can be seen from Figure 25.24, a large area of cerebral cortex is devoted to receiving and processing sensations from the external genitalia, but little motor cortex is devoted to these regions. In contrast, relatively massive areas are devoted to both sensory inputs from and motor outputs to hand and tongue, making possible the uniquely human traits of highly developed manual dexterity and speech.

In marked contrast to the precision with which these sensory and motor areas can be defined, *the processes we commonly call learning, memory, emotion, intelligence, and conscious behavior cannot be localized.* In the human, large areas of the cortex participate in these functions; these areas are called **associative cortex.** The functioning of

these areas has recently been compared to a hologram. **Holography** is a technique by which laser beams are used to create a photographic plate. When this plate is viewed with laser light, it re-creates a precise, three-dimensional image of the object that seems to be suspended in space, unconnected to the physical objects on which its existence depends. Unlike an ordinary photograph, all parts of the image are located in all regions of a holographic film. If the film is cut in half and the halves are viewed with separate lasers, they form identical images that differ from the original only in that nothing is quite as sharply defined as before. So it is with the associative areas of the cerebral cortex. Injury may occur that destroys large areas of cortex, and this may lead to a slight reduction in mental acuity, but not to loss of any specific kind of interpretive ability. Thus the attributes that we all consider so personal and that form our sense of self are clearly tied to the material substance of our cerebral cortex—but not in a manner that can be analyzed, localized, and graphed with present techniques.

The analogy to holography, while illustrative, cannot be considered to be rigorous. For example, individuals suffering extensive damage to the prefrontal region (Figure

(text continues on page 574)

25.23) often have no noticeable change in mental acuity, but they undergo such drastic changes in "personality" that their families and friends feel they no longer know them. For a time, deliberate surgical damage to the prefrontal lobe was used for treatment of certain otherwise-intractable mental disorders. Because of the lack of predictability of such procedures in some cases, considerably more discretion is now used in determining the suitability of this kind of intervention.

We are just now coming to realize that the person we call "self" is in a very real sense two individuals in constant communication. The cerebral cortex is subdivided into two halves called the **cerebral hemispheres.** Although the two halves superficially appear to be mirror images of one another, and although they start out with identical potentials, they develop very differently. As development proceeds, the left cerebral hemisphere tends more and more to suppress inputs from the left side of the body and to "concentrate" on inputs from the right side. Similarly, the right hemisphere comes to emphasize the inputs from and outputs to the left side. As a result, in the adult each half of

the body tends to be "wired" predominantly to the opposite side of the brain. In individuals that develop dominance of the right hand (right-handed individuals) the language sense comes to be located predominantly in the left hemisphere. In left-handed individuals the reverse is sometimes true. The two sides of the brain communicate continuously through several structures, the principal one being the **corpus callosum** (Figure 25.25). The implications of this connection have only recently become apparent as a result of studies of those individuals in whom it has been cut as a cure for epilepsy so severe that it resisted any other form of treatment (*Interleaf 25.3*). Clearly this connection plays a central role in the integration of behavior and personality.

The Autonomic Nervous System Regulates the Function of Internal Organs

In our discussion of the vertebrate nervous system, we have so far emphasized those elements involved in integrating processes that are, at least in principle, under voluntary control. The elements are said to constitute the **somatic nervous system.** But there is a functionally discrete group

(text continues on page 576)

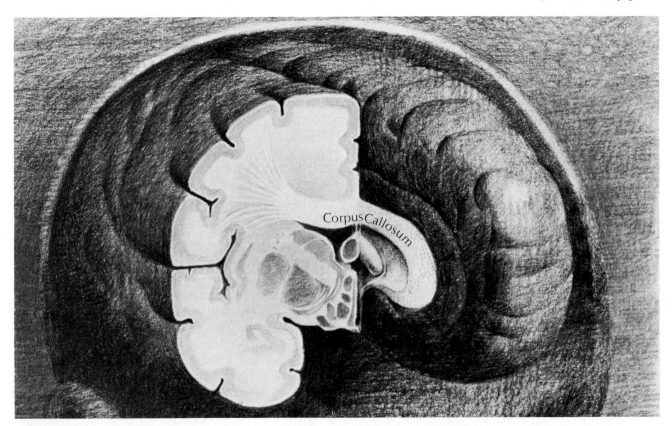

Figure 25.25 The corpus callosum. This structure constitutes the main neuronal channel by which the two cerebral hemispheres communicate.

Figure 25.26 (right) The autonomic nervous system.

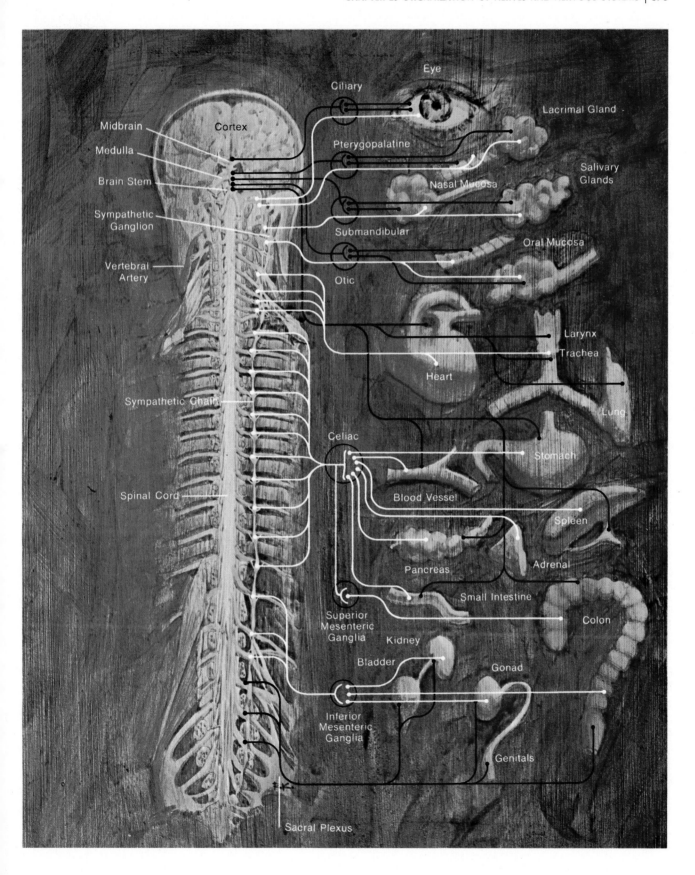

Eye
Ciliary
Lacrimal Gland
Midbrain
Cortex
Medulla
Pterygopalatine
Brain Stem
Salivary
Nasal Mucosa
Glands
Sympathetic
Ganglion
Submandibular
Oral Mucosa
Vertebral
Artery
Otic
Larynx
Trachea
Heart
Sympathetic Chain
Lung
Celiac
Stomach
Spinal Cord
Blood Vessel
Spleen
Adrenal
Pancreas
Small Intestine
Colon
Superior
Mesenteric
Ganglia
Kidney
Bladder
Gonad
Inferior
Mesenteric
Ganglia
Genitals
Sacral Plexus

Interleaf 25.3

Two Brains in One Head

Neuroanatomical and neurophysiological studies of mammalian brains have explained much about the functional interactions within these organs. But can these explanations be extrapolated to the functioning of the human brain? Although differences in brain structure and function appear at various developmental levels among the mammals, these differences appear to be largely quantitative, not radical departures from the general mammalian scheme. Now, this observation neither proves nor disproves the notion that the human brain is somehow unique. But without direct experimentation on the human brain, the most reasonable inference is that it functions in much the same way as the brains of related primates.

Assuming that the function of the human brain is, at least in principle, understandable from what is known of similar brains, can we find any evidence that thought or consciousness is specifically related to brain structure or function? Put simply, are the mind and the brain different, or are they two ways of describing the same thing? Although present knowledge makes it easy to define what we mean by the term "brain," no satisfactory definition exists thus far for consciousness, or "mind." Each of us has a clear sense of what it means to be conscious, but rigorous definition remains elusive.

A series of studies begun by Roger Sperry in the early 1960s point in tantalizing directions. Sperry and his colleagues took advantage of an opportunity to study mental processes in patients who had undergone a unique neurosurgical operation. These patients had suffered from a form of epilepsy that involves episodes of widespread disorder of the normal discharges of cerebrocortical neurons. These episodes result in severe seizures that may be fatal. In an attempt to alleviate this problem, surgeons sectioned the corpus callosum in many patients afflicted with the disease. The initial aim of the surgery was to confine the seizures to one hemisphere of the brain, thereby lessening their severity. In fact, the operation dramatically reduced the incidence of any seizure activity and thus was more successful than anticipated.

Beyond the medical benefit of this operation, however, the patient was left in a uniquely changed state. Sectioning of the corpus callosum meant there was no longer a direct neural link between the two cerebral hemispheres. Because the cerebral hemispheres are the major integrative areas of the brain, could these people be expected to function normally? Postoperative observation revealed little or no abnormality of behavior under everyday conditions. Indeed, it was only under the refined testing conditions established by Sperry that the results of this intervention became apparent.

By having patients fix their gaze on the center of a projection screen, the researchers could flash visual stimuli on either the left or right of the screen and thereby control what each hemisphere saw (words or pictures in the left visual field are transmitted to the right hemisphere, while stimuli to the right visual field are received in the left hemisphere, as shown in Figure 26.12). The patients had no difficulty reporting what was shown to them in the right visual field, but they were unable to report what happened in the left visual field. Because these subjects had experienced major neurological surgery, it seemed possible that the right half of the brain had sustained some sort of trauma, making it incapable of appropriate responses. This possibility was ruled out, however, when the experimenters requested a nonverbal response to indicate what had been shown in the left visual field: If the subject was asked to point to the stimulus object or to pick it out from a group of objects while blindfolded, he made few wrong responses. That is, provided the subject used his or her *left* hand;

the right hand was incapable of demonstrating what had been seen in the left visual field!

These and similar results have led to the conclusion that in these patients, the two halves of the brain were functioning autonomously. Correct verbal responses were elicited only when visual stimuli were presented to the right visual field, confirming earlier evidence from brain-damaged patients that speech-controlling centers commonly are located exclusively in the left hemisphere. Because cutting the corpus callosum removed the major intercommunication pathway, no verbal response was possible when the right hemisphere received a visual stimulus. Yet it is obvious that the right hemisphere was aware of visual stimuli, for it could respond nonverbally by using the left hand, over which it had principal control. Further studies using more subtle test stimuli and requiring more complicated responses have revealed that the two hemispheres differ in other respects besides the capacity for speech. Taken together, these experiments suggest that the left hemisphere is more analytical, mathematical, and literate, whereas the right hemisphere is less logical but more artistic and able to deal with spatially more complex stimuli.

Although the normal communication between the hemispheres was abolished in these patients, evidence for indirect communication was found. Patients asked to report whether a green or red light was lit were able to respond correctly only when the lights were shown in the right visual field. Responses voiced when the lights were shown in the left visual field were never more accurate than chance, because the left hemisphere was only guessing what the right might have seen. However, when the experimenters reprimanded the subjects for making

incorrect responses, there was gradual improvement. After careful observation, it became apparent that a cross-cutting system had developed between the right and left hemispheres. When the left hemisphere ventured a wrong guess as to the color seen by the right hemisphere, the patient would frown, shake his head, and then apologetically correct the response. Apparently the frown and headshake were initiated by the right hemisphere when it heard the left hemisphere respond inappropriately! The left hemisphere learned the meaning of this message and corrected its first response whenever necessary.

The studies by Sperry and his associates have thrown a dramatic new light on the organization of the human brain. It is obvious that there was extensive lateralization of brain functions in the patients they examined. That is, their hemispheres were not simply mirror images but possessed characteristic

and unique capacities. Moreover, when the brain was bisected, the two hemispheres carried on autonomously, apparently oblivious of one another. Only under conditions of necessity imposed by environmental circumstances did the two sides attempt to communicate with one another. Obviously, because these patients had been the victims of severe epilepsy before the operation, it is possible that their brains were different in some major respect from those of non-epileptics. But despite the need for cautious interpretation, it seems almost inescapable that the sectioning of the corpus callosum has produced people with two separately conscious brains.

of neural elements that is involved in regulating the functioning of internal organs such as heart, blood vessels, intestinal tract, and so forth over which little voluntary control can be exerted. This is called the **autonomic nervous system.** The autonomic system in turn consists of two subdivisions that act antagonistically; they are called the **sympathetic** and **parasympathetic** systems. Neurons from both systems enter each of the internal organs under autonomic control (Figure 25.26). But what impulses from one system effect, impulses from the other reverse. Sympathetic stimulation speeds the heartbeat, but parasympathetic stimulation slows it down. Sympathetic stimulation slows the activity of digestive organs, and parasympathetic stimulation speeds it up.

The autonomic system plays an important role in changing the whole behavior pattern of the animal in response to sudden changes in the environment: An animal that has just finished a meal sits quietly, its heart beating rather slowly, with blood vessels to muscle and brain closed down somewhat—inducing drowsiness. But blood vessels to the gut open wide and the organs of the gut churn actively. Suddenly a predator appears. Impulses from organs of sight and hearing are processed in the brain and are interpreted as threat signals that must be responded to by "fight or flight." Simultaneously, activity of the parasympathetic system is suppressed and activity of the sympathetic system is stimulated. Heart, glands, gut, and blood vessels respond as one. Heart rate speeds, blood pressure rises, blood sugar level rises, and vessels to muscle and brain open, while those leading to the gut close down and the churning of the gut comes nearly to a halt. The animal springs into action. Later, the danger past, the activity of the sympathetic system slows again, and parasympathetic activity once again makes digestion the dominant process of the moment.

PERSPECTIVE

In our review of the structure and function of neurons, we proceeded as if the differences between earthworms, squid, and humans are only matters of detail and not of fundamental importance. It is reasonable, however, to question this assumption. After all, such dissimilar organisms have developed through radically different evolutionary histories, and we might expect to find divergence even at fundamental levels. Yet the evidence suggests just the opposite—there is remarkable continuity at the basic level rather than change.

Virtually every nerve cell maintains a negative resting potential by regulating the movement of Na^+ and K^+ ions. Consequently, the action potential results from inward Na^+ movement and slightly delayed outward K^+ movement. Na^+/K^+ pumps are ubiquitous. All nervous systems appear to contain a combination of electrical and chemical synapses. Although not all suspected neurotransmitters have been found in each nervous system examined, none appears to be unique to a particular kind of organism. In every case, Ca^{++} is a requirement for release of neurotransmitter.

Evolutionary consistency is maintained at higher levels of organization as well. Easily differentiated peripheral and central nervous systems are general. Autonomic and "voluntary" systems are usually distinguishable. Aggregations of neurons serving the same or related functions in specific locations are almost always found. And, of course, cephalization is a rule from flatworms to human beings.

Thus, it seems, we must conclude that in this sense the evolution of the nervous system has been extremely conservative, and a great many generalizations from one species (or even phylum) to another are entirely justified. At present, it would be difficult to argue that any species possesses a neural function or neuroanatomical feature that represents a qualitative departure from the general pattern of neural organization.

But as we have seen in analyzing other aspects of life, superimposed on this pattern of basic unity is a rich panorama of subtle diversity. Most neurons have dendritic processes. Yes, but how many? And from how many cells does each of those dendrites receive synaptic inputs? All chemical synapses are basically the same. Yes, but will the response to an input from a particular synapse? The hypothalamus triggers the release of eggs. Yes, but what triggers the hypothalamus? Is it the season of the year, the availability of a mate, or an internal cycle of hormonal feedbacks?

It is not the diversity of fundamental units that makes life so rich and varied. Rather, it is the endless possibilities that arise from organizing similar units in subtly different ways. Thus, natural selection did not start anew in molding nervous systems to meet each new environmental challenge. Rather, it simply favored the reproductive success of those individual animals whose minor deviations from the common plan of nervous organization led to behavior that was adaptive.

But it is a long way from explaining this basic plan to understanding all aspects of the evolution of the nervous system. In moving in this chapter from single cells, to reflex arcs, to integration, to organization, and ending ultimately in a discussion of the human brain, we took several huge intellectual leaps. But can we truly say, as we view the nervous system of the flatworm, that we progressed from certain understandings through well-founded generalizations to informed speculations? Until we can speak with equal certainty about all levels of neural organization, the riddles of higher brain functions will remain unresolved.

SUGGESTED READINGS

AIDLEY, D. J. *The Physiology of Excitable Cells.* London: Cambridge University Press, 1971. The basic processes of nervous system function are presented with clarity and detail. While the book may be difficult in parts, the effort is rewarded with a more comprehensive understanding of the remarkable neural machinery.

GAZZANIGA, MICHAEL S. *The Bisected Brain.* New York: Appleton-Century-Crofts, 1970. Reviews the intriguing consequences of sectioning the corpus callosum in humans and other mammals. Fascinating reading.

SCHMITT, FRANCIS O. (ed.). *The Neurosciences.* Vols. 1 & 2: New York: Rockefeller University Press, 1970. Vol. 3: Boston: MIT Press, 1974. These volumes contain original research papers presented at interdisciplinary seminars held every three years. While many of the papers are extremely technical, these volumes represent the only single source of the most current knowledge in the rapidly advancing neurosciences.

WILLOWS, A. O. D. "Giant Brain Cells in Molluscs," *Scientific American,* 224 (February 1971), 68–75. Discusses some of the unusually favorable aspects of working with organisms having simple brains and large nerve cells.

Chapter 26

Reception and Action in the Nervous System

Without the capacity to detect change in the external and internal environment and to effect appropriate responses of glands and muscles, the nervous system would be of little adaptive significance to an animal. But various receptors do exist that sense physical and chemical aspects of the environment, thereby initiating the neural impulses that ultimately lead to a behavioral response. Here we see the antenna of a luna moth by which the male detects the presence of a female at distances of up to a mile. Females release a specific chemical into the air when they are prepared to mate. Receptor cells fringing the antenna of the male are capable of initiating a nerve impulse in response to a single molecule of the attractant.

If an organism is to live and reproduce in a constantly changing world, it must continuously monitor internal and external events and respond accordingly with changes in its position, chemical activity, and so forth. The capacity to detect and respond to various aspects of the environment is by no means restricted to complex animals. *Escherichia coli* cells will move toward a source of an essential nutrient or away from a noxious chemical; if both kinds of stimuli are present, the direction of movement depends on the relative concentrations of the two substances. If a spectrum of light is projected onto a microscope slide bearing a population of photosynthetic bacteria, the entire population will congregate at the wavelengths of light that are most effective for photosynthesis. If a plant is illuminated from one side, it grows in that direction. If a potted plant is placed on its side, its roots and shoots will adjust to the new orientation by changing the direction of subsequent growth.

In the animal kingdom, both the ability to detect and the ability to respond to properties of the environment are highly developed, because the mobile animal way of life requires constant monitoring of the environment for the presence of predator or prey, competitor or mate, and rapid, large-scale movements in response. Hence, over the course of evolutionary time natural selection has favored the development and refinement of a number of **sensory systems:** detection systems finely tuned for gathering and processing information about changes in light, chemical composition, temperature, and pressure in the environment.

In many cases, this fine tuning has made each organism sensitive to some stimuli and totally insensitive to others. And in most cases, the selective responsiveness of the species closely matches the selective stimuli of its environment. For example, many nocturnal animals are color-blind but have a highly developed sense of hearing. Certain moths are deaf to all frequencies of sound except those emitted by the hunting bats that prey on them. Most birds have a keen sense of vision but no sense of smell. Humans have a moderately refined sense of smell but simply cannot detect the aroma exuded by earthworms that attracts worm-eating snakes. Few animals other than pollinating insects can perceive ultraviolet light, and in few places other than in the flowers that those insects pollinate do we find patterns that can be discerned only by virtue of their reflection of ultraviolet light. Thus we see that the sensory systems that have evolved in animals are not merely random information-collecting devices; they are biological filters that accentuate, suppress, or distort information about the world, depending on the survival needs of the organism.

In itself, however, the gathering and processing of information is not enough. Organisms must also be equipped to respond to the things they perceive—to move quickly away from a predator or toward prey, to migrate southward when subtle environmental cues signal the oncoming winter, to challenge a competitor or court a mate. Such responses are effected through complex **motor systems**—through another set of filters that select the most appropriate response from an endless array of possible actions.

In this chapter, we will attempt to describe the nature of a few sensory systems in some detail rather than merely cataloging all the sensory systems that exist. We will examine those systems that are presently best understood. In many cases we will concentrate on vertebrate sensory systems. Human beings, from philosophers to biologists, have always been interested in the nature of their own perceptions and have wondered how faithfully those perceptions have reflected the nature of the outside world. As a result, research has concentrated on the systems most closely resembling our own, and at present these are the best understood. After discussing these sensory systems, we will turn our attention to mechanisms of response, with emphasis on the nature, functioning, and control of muscle—a uniquely animal structure that translates nerve impulses into rapid but finely regulated movement.

SENSORY SYSTEMS THAT RESPOND TO CHEMICALS

Perhaps no sense has been so fundamental in animal evolution as **chemoreception.** Simple organisms of all kinds respond to chemicals in the environment. As mentioned above, motile bacteria such as *E. coli* orient themselves with regard to chemical components of the environment, as do most protistans. In complex animals the roles of **chemoreceptors** (neurons specialized so that they are responsive to specific chemicals) are many. For example, certain leaf-eating insects have evolved a curious form of chemoreception that permits them to distinguish between edible and inedible portions of the leaf. They deposit saliva on the leaf surface, and after a moment they taste it. Just what they detect in the saliva is unknown, but as a result they subsequently chew away the soft parts of the leaf and leave the tough vascular system untouched. The result is a lacy leaf hanging on the plant with only its veins intact.

One of the most interesting adaptations of insects (about which we are just beginning to accumulate detailed information) is the use of **pheromones:** chemical substances released by one member of a species that affect the behavior of another member. *Pheromones play a role within a species analogous to the roles that hormones play within an individual.* A female moth receptive for mating releases into the night air a specific chemical from a specialized scent gland. The antennae of the male of that species (and only that species) bear thousands of tiny sensory hairs responsive to that one substance. Although the male can detect as little as a ten-billionth of a gram of the substance, his response increases with concentration over a many-thousandfold range. Thus he flies into the night, heading unerringly to the female that produced the scent.

A termite on the fringes of a colony is disturbed by a biologist who pokes it with a broom-straw. The sentinel retreats toward the center of the colony, a gland under his body secreting a chemical as he goes. The defensive members of the colony he encounters are agitated by the odor and charge outward, following the chemical trail. As long as the disturbance at the end of the trail remains, the trail becomes reinforced by others, keeping that part of the colony agitated and in a fighting mood. When the disturbance passes, so does the trail—the chemical is very short-lived in its effectiveness—and the colony returns to placidity. An ant discovers a rich source of food and returns to the colony, depositing a pheromone as it goes, providing a trail to lead others to the food source, and so on.

Pheromones are by no means restricted to insects. Scenting of landmarks plays an important role in establishment of territories by mammals of various kinds. But scents also figure importantly in mating behavior of mammals. A male mouse exposed to a receptive female in a cage previously inhabited by another male will usually display aggressive behavior rather than mating behavior. A female bred successfully by one male and then transferred to a cage in which a different male has resided will usually undergo a change in hormone secretion that causes her to terminate pregnancy and to absorb the fetuses in response to the odors left behind in the soiled litter.

In addition to chemoreceptors designed to monitor external signals, animals possess numerous chemoreceptors designed to detect changes in internal environment. These receptors figure importantly in the homeostatic regulation systems discussed in Chapters 21 and 22. For example, in the hypothalamus of mammals there exist cells that are specifically sensitive to glucose. These cells are involved in controlling the sensation of hunger and in regulating food-seeking behavior. When glucose levels of the blood are high, these chemoreceptors are triggered and feeding behavior is inhibited. Now if a chemical derivative of glucose—gold thioglucose—is injected into a rat, it combines with the specific receptors in these cells, fails to activate them as glucose does, but blocks glucose from affecting them. As a result the animal will not go out of its way to seek food but will eat continuously as long as food is available, and it will become grossly obese. Other chemoreceptors in the hypothalamus and elsewhere in the body

continuously monitor levels of salt, carbon dioxide, oxygen, and so forth and are intricately involved in the control of kidney, heart, and lung function.

But perhaps the most familiar chemoreceptors of all are those involved in tasting and smelling: those in the organs of **gustation** and **olfaction,** respectively (Figure 26.2). *The difference between taste and smell lies in the manner in which the stimuli are presented to the receptors, not in the process of detection.* Gustatory stimuli reach the chemoreceptors in physical association with food; olfactory stimuli are borne in the air or water in which the animal lives. The human tongue bears four kinds of chemoreceptors: those sensitive to the stimuli we call sweet, sour, salt, and bitter. All the other delicate and different flavors we say we taste in food, we actually smell when airborne molecules from the food diffuse up to the chemoreceptors in the rear of the nasal cavity and trigger their responses. It is still a matter of some controversy how many different kinds of chemoreceptors exist in the human nasal cavity. According to one theory, there are only seven kinds and all the varied and subtle flavors and aromas we discern result from differing proportions of these seven different receptor types being triggered. Other theories imply the situation may be more complex.

In dogs, whose sense of smell is extraordinarily acute, there may be as many as 40 million chemoreceptors per square centimeter of nasal surface (an area about the size of your little fingernail). And each of these receptors is exquisitely sensitive; a single molecule of an airborne substance may trigger a response within such a cell.

How do chemoreceptors function? There appears to be only one answer. In all chemoreceptors yet studied, presentation of the stimulus leads to depolarization of the chemosensitive cell. Apparently, the diversity of the detectors comes from the diversity of the receptor molecules embedded in the membrane mosaic of the different cells. These

Figure 26.2 The organs of gustation and olfaction in humans: the tongue and nasal cavity. The tongue seems adapted for the detection of only four tastes: salt, sweet, bitter, and sour. There is a different chemoreceptor cell responsible for each taste. These are located in specific regions, as shown. Despite the possible combinations of these four tastes, it is difficult to believe that they could provide the rich variety of flavors we recognize. In fact it appears from many studies that, outside of the primary four tastes, the tongue is not involved in the way food "tastes"; the nose does the job. As can be seen in the diagram, the olfactory bulb sends off neural processes into the mucus-lined air passage. These cells seem to have a much wider and more subtle sensitivity to chemical signals.

receptors, thought to be proteins, have specific shapes that permit each kind to interact with only one kind of chemical substance—resembling the specific interaction of an enzyme with its substrate. The result of such an interaction is probably quite similar to the excitatory effect a neurotransmitter has on a postsynaptic cell (Chapter 25). That is, it causes the sodium pores in the cell membrane to open. In a chemoreceptor (as in most sensory cells) this influx does not result in a full-blown action potential but merely a change in membrane potential. The potential change so created decreases with increasing distance from the site of stimulation. At some distance from the site of the receptor molecules, the cell forms a synapse with a second neuron. If the potential change within the receptor cell is adequate (and sometimes multiple interactions must occur at once to get a potential change of sufficient magnitude), the receptor cell may release neurotransmitter at such a synaptic site. The neurotransmitter then triggers an action potential in the second neuron, and the action potential is thereby propagated toward the central nervous system. The result of such

action potentials will, of course, depend upon the way in which they are processed within the CNS.

SENSORY SYSTEMS THAT RESPOND TO MECHANICAL STIMULI

Sensory systems also exist that monitor position of the animal in space, movement of parts, pressure of various kinds, and sound. These systems all contain **mechanoreceptor cells** that convert physical force into neural impulses. Mechanoreceptors tend to be more complex than chemoreceptors. In some cases the mechanosensitive cells themselves are structurally specialized—usually by the presence of modified cilia that create a potential change when bent. In other cases the sensory neurons are quite simple but are intimately associated with complex accessory structures, such as multilayered capsules, formed by accessory cells. In either case, application of a particular kind of force leads to distortion and depolarization of the dendrite of the sensory cell and ultimately to an action potential. Three kinds of mechanoreceptors will be used to illustrate

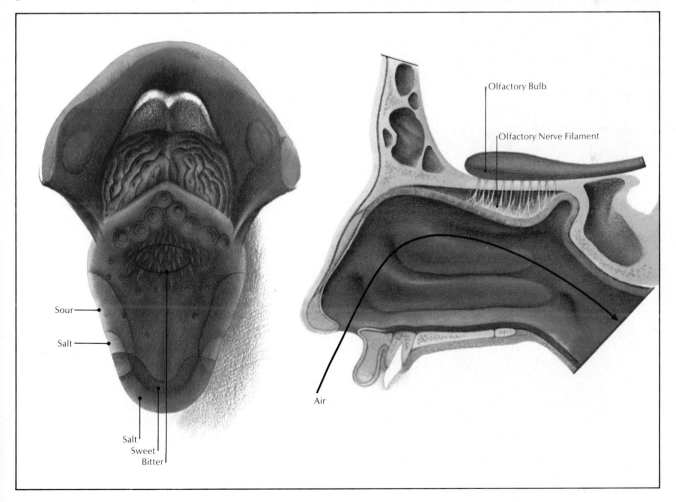

three kinds of stimuli monitored by such cells: position, pressure, and sound. A fourth type, which detects movement, will be discussed later in the chapter because its function is intimately involved with muscular contraction.

Detection of Position

Detection of position by mechanoreceptors is an essential part of an animal's control of its orientation relative to the gravitational field. Special organs called **statocysts** monitor body position and are found in nearly all animal phyla. There is considerable structural variation in statocyst organization. One type was illustrated in Figure 7.27. Another type is shown in Figure 26.3. Statocysts always have some kind of dense ball or knoblike structure, called a **statolith,** that tends to be drawn toward the center of gravity (toward the center of the earth). As the animal rotates relative to the gravitational field, the statolith stimulates different nerve endings, leading to righting behavior in the organism. A dramatic demonstration of the function of the statocyst was made in the nineteenth century when biologists replaced the statolith in a shrimp with iron filings. When a magnet was moved near the animal, the filings moved toward the magnet, signaling the shrimp that it was improperly oriented. Indeed, it was shown that the shrimp could be made to swim upside down simply by placing the magnet in the proper position!

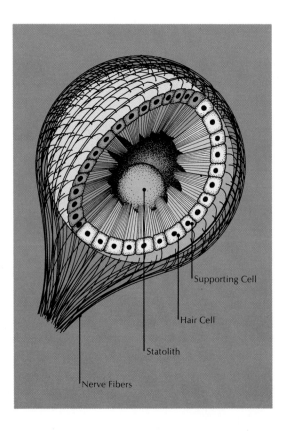

Supporting Cell

Hair Cell

Statolith

Nerve Fibers

Detection of Pressure

In mammals, a tactile sense identifies the precise location of irritating or pleasurable stimuli to the body surface. This identification is the responsibility of pressure-sensitive mechanoreceptors located in the skin. These receptors take many different forms, ranging from simple bare neuron endings to complex multilamellar structures surrounding a sensory neuron. The reasons for this variety and the stratification of each type of receptor at a particular depth in the skin are not known. One such receptor structure, the **Pacinian corpuscle,** is found in the deep layers of the skin and is known to be a highly sensitive detector of pressure. Pacinian corpuscles consist of a single sensory neuron process wrapped in layer after layer of connective tissue (Figure 26.4), which gives it the appearance of an onion about 1 millimeter long. The connective tissue sheath appears to transmit the forces of deformation of the skin directly onto the neural process, thus leading to a neural impulse. Many other forms of mechanoreceptors are found at different locations and depths in the human skin. Together these receptors produce a sense of touch that responds to the stroke of feather or the impact of a heavy object with information-rich patterns of neural impulses.

Detection of Sound

A sense of hearing is rare in the world. Only a few insects, such as crickets, locusts, cicadas, and some moths, can hear. Some spiders hear, but few other invertebrates do. Although most vertebrates have a sense of hearing, it is highly developed only in birds and mammals. In all vertebrates, however, the auditory system works upon a similar principal: mechanoreceptor cells are distorted by a vibrating liquid medium, whereupon they generate a series of neural impulses. The mechanoreceptors are sensitive only to vibrating liquid; therefore, in animals that live in air the first stage of hearing always involves using the vibrations of air to set a liquid into motion.

In order to understand how the auditory system works, let us follow the process from the entry of a sound wave through the outer ear to the generation of nerve impulses in

Figure 26.3 Schematic diagram of a statocyst receptor organ of a jellyfish. These statocysts are hollow spheres lined with hair cells. The hair cells project into the fluid-filled center of the sphere, which is occupied by a dense nodule of calcium carbonate called a statolith. If the jellyfish changes its orientation, causing the statocyst to tilt, the statolith is displaced and comes to rest on a different group of hair cells. The bending of these cells results in neural activation that signals the nerve net of the animal's new orientation. This organ therefore provides a continuous monitor for the three-dimensional position of the organism.

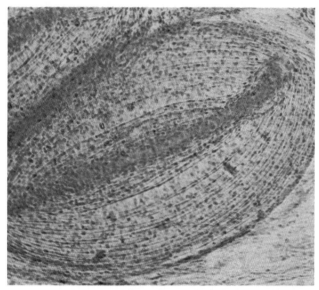

(Photograph courtesy Carolina Biological Supply Company)

Figure 26.4 Photomicrograph of a Pacinian corpuscle, shown in longitudinal section. The mechanoreceptor dendrite can be seen as the red fiber projecting across the middle of the structure. Regular layers of wrapping around the neuron are apparent in this pressure-receptor structure.

the auditory nerve, as shown in Figure 26.5. Vibrations in the ear pass down the auditory canal and strike the tympanic membrane (eardrum), causing it to vibrate. If the air vibrates with many different frequencies at once, so will the flexible eardrum, setting up many overlapping patterns of waves. Touching the other side of the eardrum is a delicate little bone known as the hammer (or *malleus*), which is linked in turn to the anvil (or *incus*) and the stirrup (or *stapes*). These three bones of the middle ear are linked and suspended in such a way that they function as a series of levers. Thus, when the eardrum moves the hammer, it in turn moves the anvil, which moves the stirrup. But as a result of the shapes of the bones and their attachment points, the vibrations of the eardrum are "geared down": The stirrup moves less far than the hammer, but it moves more forcefully. The stirrup is attached in turn to the *oval window*, a flexible membrane on the side of the snail-shaped, fluid-filled inner-ear chamber called the *cochlea*. If the cochlea were entirely rigid, the stirrup would be unable to move the incompressible fluid within. But there is a second membranous spot on the cochlea, called the round window, that can be deflected outward as the oval window is deflected inward. Thus, the vibration of the stirrup sets the fluid in the cochlea in motion, in time to the vibration of the air.

Now the chamber of the cochlea is subdivided down the middle into parallel canals by a complex membranous

(text continues on page 586)

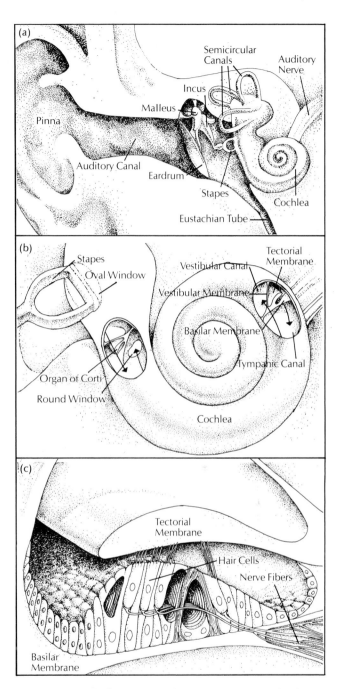

Figure 26.5 The hearing process. (a) Cross section showing the outer, middle, and inner ear. Sound waves pass through the auditory canal and are transformed into mechanical vibration by the eardrum. The three small bones amplify this motion and transmit it to the oval window of the cochlea, which is depicted in (b). The motion of the oval window sends pressure waves through the fluid in the cochlea in the directions shown by the arrows. (c) Closeup cross section of the organ of Corti, within the cochlea. Waves in the cochlear fluid cause the basilar membrane to vibrate, which in turn disturbs the hair cells, the receptor cells of hearing.

Interleaf 26.1

Behavior and Genetics

Does innate behavior exist? Few questions posed about the functioning of the nervous system have provoked as much debate as this one. One group of behavioral scientists has claimed that much behavior in most organisms is a product of genetically programmed neural wiring. Another group has asserted that little if any behavior is strictly determined by innate structures. Instead, this group believes that mature behavior develops from a dynamic interaction between an undifferentiated nervous system and a complex environment; the final behavior results from modification of neural connections and is therefore learned rather than innate. Because the existence of learning processes (whatever they might be) in neural tissues is undeniable, many have felt that the question of the existence of innate behavior is almost moot. Some sort of learning can be invoked to account for all varieties of behavioral expression. But the fact that we are able to devise a scheme to explain all behavior as learned does not prove that it is.

A group of workers associated with David Bentley of the University of California at Berkeley has provided some interesting new information that bears on this question. They have studied the neural basis of singing in crickets. Crickets produce their songs by scissoring their forewings together. Small projections of cuticle on the wings scrape past one another, causing the stiff wings to vibrate at several thousand cycles per second. This vibration produces the audible tone.

The same muscles that cause the wings to beat during flight are responsible for the more restricted movements causing song production. These muscles, which open and close the wings so that they scrape across one another, are activated by motor neurons located in the anterior two thoracic ganglia of the ventral nerve cord. Intracellular recordings from these motor neurons reveal that opener and closer muscles are alternately stimulated by one or the other of two neuron groups. When the opener muscles are being stimulated, the cells that control the closer muscles are being inhibited. Likewise, when closer muscle motor neurons are active, the opener motor neurons are inhibited. A central nervous system program appears to be responsible for this alternating sequence, because elimination of sensory input to the nervous system does not prevent the production of a normal song. The exact nature of the wiring diagram for the song-producing circuit has not yet been worked out. However, it appears that singing is triggered by interneurons located in the brain and is maintained by some sort of oscillatory interneuronal circuit in the thoracic ganglia. Here, as in several other behavioral systems studied at the neuronal level, there is remarkable autonomy of an ongoing motor command sequence from peripheral sensory feedback.

It is precisely this aspect of wholly central generation of a behavioral act that suggests its innate character. Crickets are hemimetabolous insects: They show a gradual development into adult form, with no radical metamorphic changes taking place. This makes it possible to study changes in the organization of the nervous system as the animal approaches its final molt to the adult form. In addition, the fact that crickets do not have fully developed wings and therefore cannot sing until they go through the last molt and become adults provides a sharp behavioral demarcation against which to assess the underlying neural changes. Thus, it should be possible to determine whether the neural mechanism for singing behavior develops through various stages of refinement or is encountered only in the adult insect.

Bentley and his co-workers explored this problem by studying the development of flight and singing behavior in immature wingless crickets. Comparison of flight and singing behaviors is useful because they involve the same motor neurons. These researchers found that the neuronal connections necessary to generate flying or singing are made in several steps corresponding to the developmental stages of the cricket. The circuitry becomes complete at the last preadult stage. When animals in this last preadult stage are suspended in a wind tunnel, recordings from their wing muscles reveal essentially normal patterns of contraction for flight despite absence of functional wings. Thus, the neural regulatory systems for flight are complete and functional. Yet no experimental situation will activate the singing circuitry in a normal animal at this stage. It is only after the final molt into the adult stage that male crickets begin to sing. It appears that while flight is prevented in late preadult crickets only by the absence of fully developed wings, song production is actually inhibited.

Although any argument to the contrary must encounter formidable difficulties, the case for the innate character of cricket song cannot be considered complete. What is needed is a demonstration that a characteristic song develops because of the genotype of the animal, independent of the environment. Two closely related species of cricket, *Teleogryllus commodus* and *T. oceanicus*, have song patterns that differ in several respects. Thus, if the two species could be crossed, the hybrid offspring would provide an excellent test for the contribution of genotype to the song. When the crosses were attempted, they not only produced viable offspring but the offspring were fertile, so further genetic analysis could be undertaken. The most important observation, though, was that *the F_1 hybrid males produced songs distinctly different from those produced by either of the parental species.* Moreover, the characteristic songs of the F_1 males differed from one another depending on the species of their mothers. Since a male cricket receives one X chromosome from its mother and none from its father, it is clear that cer-

tain aspects of the cricket song are specified by genes on the X chromosome.

Further genetic analysis using backcrossing to the parental species has revealed additional information about the genetic origin of the song. The offspring from backcrosses show a variety of unique song patterns, thus indicating the segregation of many genes and therefore revealing that the specification of the neural circuit is the result of the expression of many genes. In addition, detailed examination of the song patterns indicates that the backcross songs show a continuum of characteristics intermediate between the hybrid and the parent. Thus the songs vary according to the genotype of the animal.

These dramatic findings have been thoroughly supported by physiological study and environmental manipulation. The neural circuits responsible for song generation display properties unique to the genetic make-up of the individual studied. Neither the physiology nor the actual song seems sensitive to the condition of rearing. Manipulations of photoperiod, population density, and acoustical environment (including complete isolation and long-term exposure to a different song) are without effect on the genetically specified song.

In the process of providing a firm example of a genetically programmed (innate) behavior, these studies have confronted an intriguing new problem. Because the calling song of the male cricket is a means of attracting females, what would be the evolutionary consequence of a modified song? Females of both *T. commodus* and *T. oceanicus* show strong preference for the calls made by the males of their own species when they are tested with a variety of calls, including those of the hybrids. Thus, it would seem that a "chicken or

egg" situation might exist, should genetic changes appear in a natural population. Males with altered songs would fail to attract normal females. Similarly, females with altered sensory systems might not be attracted to normal males. Such a situation would forestall evolutionary changes, because genotypes involving changes in the typical calling song or the female sensory apparatus would not be reproduced. Yet, we know that two closely related species such as *T. commodus* and *T. oceanicus* have dissimilar songs. How can such a dissimilarity develop? The answer seems to be as simple as it is astonishing. Ronald Hoy tested the preference of hybrid females for the songs of both their parental species and genetically similar hybrids. *These females showed a distinct preference for hybrid songs!* This surprising finding indicates that the genetic reassortment that produced the hybrid song in the males produced just the right changes in the female sensory system to make the hybrid song more attractive than any other. Instead of an evolutionary stonewall, then, we find a remarkable process by which motor systems in the male and sensory systems in the female are altered simultaneously, thereby producing a genetically isolated group in one step.

Although the genetics of neural function, and consequently of behavior, in the cricket appear to be complicated, the results obtained so far are fascinating and prove that genetic dissection of behaviorally relevant neural circuits is feasible. A great deal remains to be learned, but these and similar studies with other species have made the first steps toward a genetics of the nervous system. Someday it may be possible to predict much of an animal's behavior simply by knowing its genotype.

partition (Figure 26.5c). Embedded in this partition is the actual organ of hearing—the **organ of Corti,** which consists of a string of mechanoreceptors positioned between two membranes. The mechanoreceptors (called hair cells) lie in the *basilar membrane*, but the tips of their modified cilia project through the fluid and contact the *tectorial membrane*. When the fluids of the cochlea vibrate, these two membranes move relative to each other and the cilia are deformed. As a result, the hair cells depolarize, release neurotransmitter, and initiate action potentials in the adjacent neurons of the auditory nerve.

How is information concerning frequency of vibration picked up and transmitted to the brain? It is *not* by the frequency with which action potentials are generated. There is no way that any neuron could transmit action potentials at the rate of 15,000 per second (a frequency of sound to which the human ear is very sensitive). Instead, the cochlea, by its unique shape and construction, transforms frequency of vibration into position of hair cell stimulation.

The oval window lies at the beginning of the *vestibular canal*, and the round window lies at the end of the *tympanic canal*. The two canals are continuous only at the tip of the spiral of the cochlea. Vibrations introduced in the fluid by the oval window must travel all the way up the vestibular canal around the corner and back down the tympanic canal to the round window. Therefore, vibrations are continuously traveling in opposite directions on opposite sides of the membrane bearing the mechanoreceptors. Because of the geometry of the cochlea, vibrations of a given frequency tend to dampen each other in one region and reinforce each other in a different region. Consequently, high-frequency vibrations cause maximum displacement of the membranes (and hence maximum stimulation of the hair cells) in the region near the oval window; low-frequency vibrations cause maximum stimulation at the inner tip of the spiral. Intermediate frequencies stimulate intermediate positions. Because each set of auditory neurons is connected to a specific brain region, inputs to different brain regions can reliably be interpreted in terms of the pitch (frequency) of the sound that elicited them.

From this discussion it follows that the shape of the cochlea determines the range of frequencies to which the ear will respond. Humans are restricted to a range of 20 to 20,000 cycles per second (usually less in adults); cats respond to sounds up to 50,000 cycles per second, and bats and porpoises respond to frequencies as high as 100,000 cycles per second.

The capacity to hear any frequency depends on the integrity of the cilia of the hair cells. If sound of excessive volume impinges on the ear, the excursions of the fluids may tear the cilia apart. This leads to irreversible loss of hearing in that frequency range. Although humans possess muscles capable of damping the movements of the stirrup in response to high-intensity sound, an extensive amount of such hearing loss resulting from destruction of the hair cells has unfortunately been introduced by modern technology—from factories and jet planes to rock and roll.

SENSORY SYSTEMS THAT RESPOND TO LIGHT

Organisms from bacteria to giant sequoias, from protistans to whales, respond to light. But the compound eyes of arthropods and the complex eyes of cephalopods and vertebrates represent the acme in the use of light to provide information from the environment.

The process of light reception is basically similar in most animals: A **photoreceptor cell** converts light into a membrane potential change by virtue of a photoreceptor pigment embedded in the membrane mosaic. But the kind and amount of information to be gained from such a potential change depends in large part on the accessory cells and structures that interact with the receptor cell and on the kinds of neuronal integration that follow upon the original potential change.

Figure 26.6 depicts a vertebrate eye. Let us follow light inward and analyze how visual perception results. The first

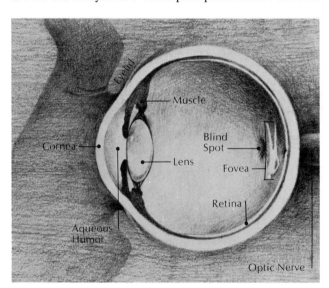

Figure 26.6   The vertebrate eye. Light enters the eye through the clear cornea. It then passes through the aqueous humor into the lens. Muscles attached to the lens can modify its shape to bring the light to focus on the retina. One region of the retina is blind because the optic nerve exits the eye at that point and there are no photoreceptor cells in that area.

Of the 360 degrees surrounding the human body, the field of most acute vision at any one time is limited to about 2 degrees. This field corresponds to the fovea, a specialized area of photoreceptors on the retina.

step is to focus the light. Unless light coming from each point on an object is made to focus on a single point on the light-sensitive portion of the eye, a blurry image will result. Light first strikes the **cornea**, a clear continuation of the *sclera*—the tough coat that surrounds the eyeball. The cornea is bowed outward to form a convex surface by the pressure of the fluid behind it—*the aqueous humor*—and thus acts as a lens to focus parallel rays of light from distant objects upon the **retina**—the light-sensitive inner surface of the eye (Figure 26.7). Light rays coming from a nearby point of light (twenty feet or less from the eye) are usually so divergent that the cornea cannot focus them on the retina. In this case the transparent *lens*, lying between the cornea and retina, is brought into play. Normally the lens is held under tension, stretched rather flat by the circular ligament that holds it in place. But contraction of the *ciliary muscle* relaxes the tension on the lens, which then bulges outward from its own inherent elasticity, and it bends the light rays further, bringing them into focus on the retina. The process by which the ciliary muscles adjust the curvature of the lens to suit the distance between the object and the eye is called **accommodation.**

Having passed through the *vitreous humor* (the clear viscous fluid that fills the main chamber of the eye and keeps it inflated), the light now falls upon the retina. The light must pass through several layers of transparent retina cells before reaching the photoreceptor cells (cells that respond to light by changing membrane potential). Let us now examine what happens when light strikes these receptor cells.

Response to Light Depends on Splitting of Visual Pigment Molecules

The photoreceptor cells of the vertebrate retina are highly modified neurons. Their most distinctive feature is the outer segment, a highly modified cilium characterized by layer after layer of membranous disks (Figure 26.8). Buried in the mosaic of these membranes are molecules known as visual pigments, which are the keys to converting light energy into a change in membrane potential. All the known visual pigments are chemically similar. Each one is made of a **retinal molecule** (a carotenoid molecule that is a derivative of vitamin A) bound to an **opsin molecule** (a protein). Different visual pigments vary only in the structure of their protein (opsin) portion.

The retinal molecule has a chain of alternating single and double bonds. For that reason it can exist in a number of slightly different isomeric forms. Rotation of atoms cannot

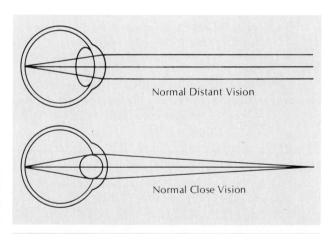

Normal Distant Vision

Normal Close Vision

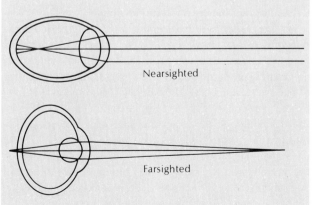

Nearsighted

Farsighted

Figure 26.7   In the normal eye the parallel rays of distant light are focused on the retina by the cornea. However, the curvature of the cornea is inadequate to focus the divergent rays of light coming from a nearby light source, so in this case the lens becomes more rounded as a result of muscular contraction and thereby focuses the rays upon the retina. In a nearsighted individual the eye is elongated, and parallel rays from distant light cannot be brought to focus on the retina without the aid of eyeglasses. In a farsighted individual the eye is so short that the diverging rays from a nearby source cannot be focused without corrective lenses.

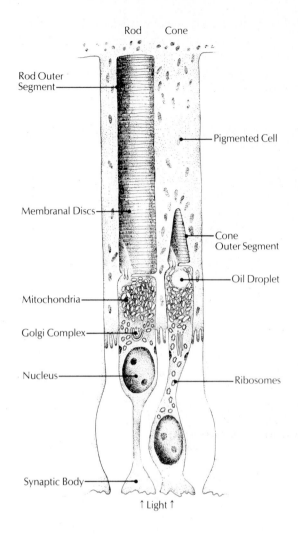

Rod   Cone

Rod Outer Segment

Membranal Discs

Mitochondria

Golgi Complex

Nucleus

Synaptic Body

↑ Light ↑

Pigmented Cell

Cone Outer Segment

Oil Droplet

Ribosomes

Figure 26.8 (left) Rod and cone photoreceptor cells from a vertebrate retina. These specialized cells have a highly compartmentalized structure. The end of the cell that is pointed toward the lens is similar to an axon (Chapter 25), with a synapse at one end of the process and the cell nucleus near the other end. In the central body of the cell is a zone containing ribosomes and a Golgi complex. The remainder of the main cell body is densely packed with mitochondria. Connected to the opposite end of the cell by a thin stalk (a modified cilium) is the outer segment, which contains a stack of hundreds of thin, membranal disks. These disks house the visual pigments.

The concentration of mitochondria below the base of the outer segment attests to the high energy requirement of maintaining the membranous disks in functional condition. Rods and cone function somewhat differently, as discussed further on in the text.

*Figure 26.9 (right) Formulas and space-filling molecular models showing the transition in the configuration of the retinal molecule when it is exposed to light. This transition from the 11-*cis *configuration to the all-*trans *configuration changes the relationship between the retinal and the opsin molecule. The all-*trans *retinal must be converted to the 11-*cis *configuration before it can associate with the opsin once again.*

occur around a double bond the way it can around a single bond. Therefore, whenever a double bond occurs within a chain of carbon atoms, two different forms (isomers) of the molecule are possible:

-----C   C----   ----C   H
       \\   /   \\   /
        C=C   and   C=C
       /   \\   /   \\
      H   H   H   C-----
          cis   *trans*

When the two parts of the carbon chain are on the "same side" of the double bond, the isomer is said to be *cis;* when they are on opposite sides, it is called *trans.* Thus, a molecule like retinal (Figure 26.9) has several possible isomers. But only one of these isomers can combine with an opsin molecule: the form in which the double bond between carbon atoms 11 and 12 is in the *cis* configuration and all the rest are *trans;* this is called the 11-*cis* isomer. When a photon of light strikes the 11-*cis* retinal molecule, it triggers

the conversion of the molecule to the all-*trans* isomeric form. When that happens, the shape of the retinal molecule no longer corresponds exactly to its opsin counterpart and they separate. The opsin molecule also changes after the retinal molecule has split away: it uncoils slightly. The retinal can subsequently be reconverted to the 11-*cis* form by an enzyme; thereupon it can recombine with the opsin.

As the retinal-opsin complex is split, the membrane potential of the photoreceptor cell changes. As we have seen in many other receptor cells, this potential change does not result in an action potential. In invertebrates the splitting of the visual pigment leads to depolarization of the cell, but in the vertebrate eye hyperpolarization results (Figure 26.10). Although the exact mechanism is not yet understood, it is assumed that in invertebrates the breakdown of the visual pigment complex causes sodium pores to open in the membrane, whereas in the vertebrate photoreceptor potassium pores are opened. The magnitude of potential change induced in the photoreceptor is proportional to the

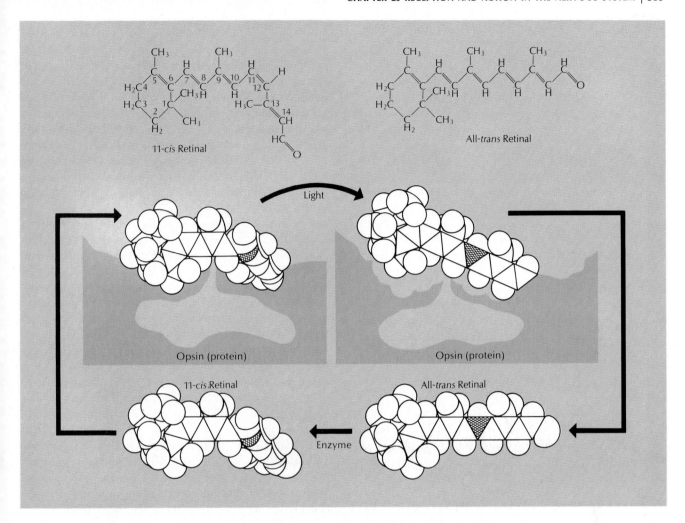

11-*cis* Retinal

All-*trans* Retinal

Light

Opsin (protein)

Opsin (protein)

11-*cis* Retinal

All-*trans* Retinal

Enzyme

intensity of the light stimulus: The more light, the more visual pigment molecules are split and the more pores are opened.

Now, as with other receptor cells, the potential change in the cell diminishes with distance from the site of permeability change. But it a potential change of sufficient magnitude reaches the synaptic end of the cell (Figure 26.8), neurotransmitter substance is released from the receptor and triggers action potentials in the postsynaptic neurons.

Processing of Visual Information Begins in the Retina

The photoreceptor cells are arranged in the outermost part of the neural retina (Figure 26.11). They synapse on *bipolar cells*. The axons of bipolar cells in turn synapse on *ganglion cells* whose axons run directly to the brain. Now if one retina cell synapsed on only one bipolar cell and it in turn synapsed on only one ganglion cell, the ganglion cell axons could carry to the brain point-by-point information concern-

ing the photoreceptor cells that had been stimulated. In a small region of the retina more or less directly behind the lens there is, in most species, a cluster of cells that are connected in essentially this manner. This is the region of maximal visual acuity, called the **fovea.**

Over most of the retina the wiring is more complex. In the outer synaptic layer a single photoreceptor may synapse upon more than one bipolar cell and in addition upon one or more *horizontal cells*. These horizontal cells connect a single photoreceptor cell to several bipolar cells and a single bipolar cell to several photoreceptor cells. Again at the inner synaptic layer three kinds of cells interact synaptically. A bipolar cell may synapse directly on one or more ganglion cells and in addition may be connected to other ganglion cells via the intermediary of *amacrine cells*. As a result, *a single ganglion cell usually receives input from several photoreceptor cells*.

What is the purpose of this complex connectivity in the retina? It diminishes the kind of visual acuity possible in the

Invertebrates

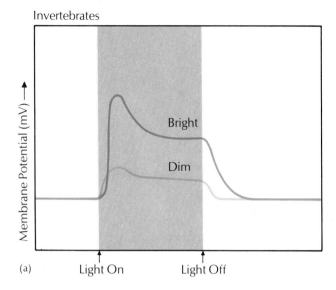

(a)

Vertebrates

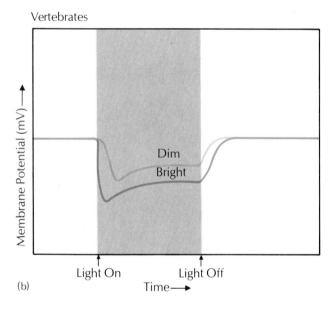

(b)

Figure 26.10 Depolarization of photoreceptor cells in invertebrates (a) and hyperpolarization of photoreceptor cells in vertebrates (b). When light falls on a photoreceptor cell, the molecular changes in visual pigments cause a change in the cell's membrane potential. Because such cells do not usually fire action potentials, the wave shape of the potential shift looks quite different from that of a typical neuron. The cell either depolarizes (invertebrates) or hyperpolarizes (vertebrates) to an extent proportional to the intensity of the light. When the light stimulus is stopped, the membrane slowly returns to the normal resting level.

fovea, where there is more nearly a one-to-one input of photoreceptors on ganglion cells. But in the tradeoff, the ganglion cell gains useful information concerning other aspects of the image. As discussed in Chapter 25, two kinds of effects can be seen in a postsynaptic cell as the result of synaptic input: excitation or inhibition. The response of a cell depends upon the sum of all the excitatory and inhibitory influences it is exposed to at any one instant. Some of the inputs to a ganglion cell are excitatory and some are inhibitory. If, in our imagination, we place a recording electrode in a single ganglion cell, we can begin to visualize how this works.

If we shine a very small beam of light on the retina, stimulating one photoreceptor cell at a time, we find for most ganglion cells not one but a cluster of receptors that, when stimulated, affect our chosen ganglion cell. Such a cluster of photoreceptors is called the *receptive field* of that ganglion cell. But not all the cells of the receptive field have the same effect. Those in the center of the field, when illuminated, cause our ganglion cell to depolarize and fire an action potential. But those on the periphery hyperpolarize, or inhibit our chosen cell! Such a ganglion cell is called an "on-center, off-surround" cell. The significance of this phenomenon becomes apparent if we consider two such ganglion cells so close together that their receptive fields overlap: the center of one receptive field is in the periphery of the other and vice versa. Now if we shine a light in the region of overlap, one cell will be excited and the other inhibited. The same thing will happen even if we shine a bright light on the center of one field and a dimmer light on the center of the other. The latter will be inhibited by the more rapid firing of the first photoreceptor, thereby enhancing contrast. Thus with such connections we have a tradeoff in which increased contrast is obtained at the expense of a slight loss in visual acuity.

Other ganglion cells have different properties with respect to their receptive fields. Some are "off" detectors. They fire only when the photoreceptors in the center of their receptive field cease receiving light. In some cases, the ganglion cell will fire an action potential only if the photoreceptors to which it is connected are stimulated in a specific order. Thus, whenever such a single ganglion cell is fired it means: "There is an object moving across the visual field from X to Y." Different motion-detecting ganglion cells are wired to detect motion in different directions and in different parts of the visual field. In some species certain ganglion cells are sensitive only to a sudden darkening of a large portion of the visual field—as would occur if a predator suddenly cast a shadow.

The visual system obviously arose for purposes other than the reading of fine type, and although extreme visual acuity is of great importance to predators that hunt by sight

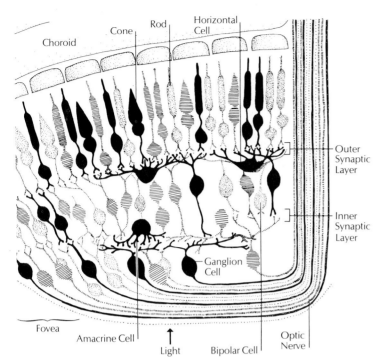

Choroid

Cone · Rod · Horizontal Cell

Outer Synaptic Layer

Inner Synaptic Layer

Ganglion Cell

Fovea · Amacrine Cell · Light · Bipolar Cell · Optic Nerve

Figure 26.11 The retina, shown in cross section near the fovea. Light must penetrate several layers of cells before it encounters the actual photoreceptors. The special acuity of the fovea may be because of the one-to-one specificity of connection between cones, bipolar cells, and ganglion cells in the area. The retinal "blind spot" can be seen at the left, where the ganglion cell axons are gathered into the optic nerve to leave the retina.

(a hawk, for example, has two large fovea in each eye and can clearly distinguish the features of a mouse from half a mile in the air), for many animals the rapid detection of movement, contrast and shadow—even if detail is lacking—has meant the difference between survival and death. Because of the intricate interconnections in the two synaptic layers of the retina, a great deal of information processing occurs before the action potentials start out the optic nerve toward the brain.

Rods and Cones Serve Different Functions

As shown in Figure 26.8, there are two kinds of photoreceptors, rods and cones, which function rather independently. At low light intensity (at night, for example) only the rod system functions. In bright light, on the other hand, only the cones ordinarily function.

The rods contain a single kind of visual pigment, called rhodopsin. It is maximally sensitive to light in the green range. Because of the occurrence of a single kind of visual pigment, rods supply no color information. But they are extraordinarily sensitive. Each cell contains about 30 million molecules of visual pigment, but under certain conditions the absorption of a single photon by one of these molecules can trigger the electrical response and the release of neurotransmitter by the whole cell. (This is not to say that such an effect leads to a *sensation* of light, though, because usually five to ten cells must be excited more or less simultaneously to lead to an awareness of light.) There are

about 100 million rods in the human eye, located primarily in the periphery of the retina.

Three kinds of cones exist in the human eye, each with a different visual pigment. One kind responds to blue, one to green, and one to red light. The 6 to 7 million cone cells are primarily concentrated in the fovea, but a few are scattered in the peripheral regions of the eye. Although cones are much less sensitive than rods, it is as a result of cone function that we are able to perceive differences in color as well as complex and detailed shapes. Color contrast is enhanced in much the same way as simple light contrast. Some ganglion cells are excited by red light in the center of their receptive field and are inhibited by green light shining on the periphery of the field. Just as any color can be reproduced by mixing red, green, and blue light, all of the subtle hues we detect are the result of the summing of the outputs of these three kinds of photoreceptor cells.

The difference in sensitivity between rods and cones points out one of the more amazing attributes of the eye—the remarkable range of light intensities over which it functions. We normally move about in environments that vary by many powers of ten in average light intensity (for example, as we step out of bright noonday sun into a dimly lit restaurant). Yet it usually takes only a matter of seconds to readjust to the extent that we can read fine print. We can continue to distinguish forms and shapes through a 100-million fold variation in light intensity! Only in extremely dim light does the switch between rods and cones play an important role in this process of **adaptation**.

Several Separate Factors Are Involved in Light and Dark Adaptation

One of the most obvious factors in adaptation is the control exerted by the iris diaphragm over the amount of light permitted to enter the eye (Figure 26.6). The iris is a ring of pigmented tissue, containing smooth muscle cells, that lies just in front of the lens. In bright light a reflex arc causes the circular muscles ringing the iris to contract, drawing the iris inward and decreasing the area of the lens illuminated. In dimmer light the circular muscles relax and radial muscles contract, opening the iris once more. Because the brain does not seem to include information about the extent to which the iris is opened or closed while processing visual stimuli, the function of the iris tends to make the observer unaware of differences in light intensity over a wide range.

A second phenomenon of adaptation comes into play at higher light intensity. Behind the retina lies a layer of heavily pigmented (black) cells. In dim light the principal function of this layer is simply to trap light that has passed through the retina and to avoid confusing reflections from the back of the eye (much as the black back of a camera absorbs light). But in bright light, these cells become amoeboid and creep down around the photoreceptor cells, partially shading them and thereby decreasing the amount of stimulation each photoreceptor receives.

But perhaps the most important aspect of adaptation lies within the photoreceptor cells themselves. If a given stimulus is applied to a photoreceptor cell and is then held constant, the rate of impulse generation drops rapidly from its original high rate. This property is not restricted to photoreceptors; it is a general function of all sensory receptors. We can generalize that *most sensory receptors are designed to be maximally sensitive to changes in stimuli*. What this means, then, is that a photoreceptor tends to be most sensitive when the background level of illumination is low and least sensitive when it is high. The basis for such adaptation of the receptors themselves is unknown. For a long time it was believed that it was due to the fact that in bright light most of the retinal was in the all-*trans* form so that there was relatively little active visual pigment. It is now known, however, that a great deal of adaptation occurs when the vast majority of the retinal is in the 11-*cis* form and is combined with opsin to form active visual pigment. Perhaps light adaptation is a result of partial depletion of transmitter. In any case, readaptation to dim light occurs rapidly as light intensity falls.

There is one important consequence of this adaptation process: you would not be able to see anything if you were truly able to stare at it! It has long been known that the eyes vibrate constantly when one tries to gaze steadily at a single point. This eye tremor was thought to be a flaw in the control system of the eye, but experiments have proved otherwise. When special optical equipment was used to compensate for eye tremor and to keep an image focused on one section of the retina, it was found that the visual sensation disappeared entirely in a few seconds! The photoreceptors adapted to unchanging light and stopped firing. Eye tremor, it turned out, is the only reason that it is possible to look at an object for any length of time; different photoreceptors are used consecutively in order to avoid adaptation of any of them to an unchanging stimulus.

Processing of Visual Information Continues in the Cerebral Cortex

The processing of visual information that begins in the retina is completed in the cerebral cortex. Axons from ganglion cells located all over the retina are brought together in the **optic nerve,** which exits through the ''blind spot'' (a small area that contains no receptors). The optic nerves meet at a crossover point called the **optic chiasma,** where each optic nerve splits. Axons from the left half of each eye go to the left side of the brain, whereas axons from the right side of each eye go to the right side. Now, because of the reversal inherent in any simple optical system, the left half of each eye receives stimuli from the right half of the visual field (Figure 26.12). Thus the outputs from the eyes are like those of nerve endings in the skin and other sensory elements: they go to the opposite side of the brain. (The left half of the brain ''sees'' objects on the right side of the midline and vice versa).

From the optic chiasma the ganglion cell axons go to the *lateral geniculate body* of the thalamus—''the great crossroads'' where they form synapses. Very little modification or processing occurs here. Instead, the visual outputs are fed, essentially unmodified, to the *visual cortex* in the occipital lobes. Here cells bearing specific kinds of information synapse at specific sites in three dimensions. Cells on the surface of the cortex are receptive to positional information; cells in the next layer receive inputs from ganglion cells that detect orientation and movement; and still deeper in the cortex are cells that respond to even more complex visual characters. It is still largely a mystery how these neural messages are combined and interpreted to yield a coherent perception of our visual environment.

MOTOR OUTPUTS: CLOSING THE CIRCLE

Sensory input and central processing, however elaborate, cannot be viewed as ends in themselves. The importance of these processes lies in their contributions to the initiation and organization of appropriate outputs. Many of the effector neurons of an organism are devoted to maintaining a favorable internal environment. It is in this realm of

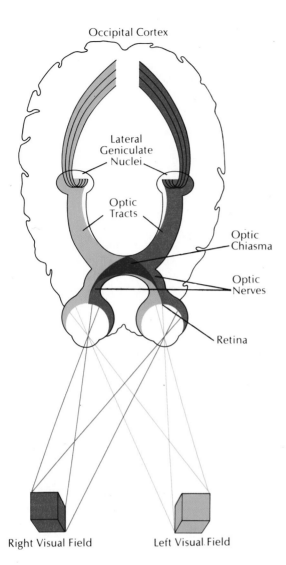

Occipital Cortex

Lateral
Geniculate
Nuclei

Optic
Tracts

Optic
Chiasma

Optic
Nerves

Retina

Right Visual Field   Left Visual Field

Figure 26.12 Pathway of the optic nerves, showing the division of the visual field by the brain. Light impulses coming from the right side of the visual field are sent into the left hemisphere; impulses from the left visual field go to the right hemisphere. The optic nerves terminate in synapses at the lateral geniculate nuclei. From there geniculate cell axons project into the occipital lobe visual cortex areas.

metabolic control that the nervous system can be considered in its proper perspective: not as a separate and mysterious inhabitant of the body but as an integral part of the living system. We saw in Chapter 25 the way in which neurons of the hypothalamus function directly as effector units by secreting releasing hormones that influence the pituitary gland. Such direct functioning of neurons as effectors via the secretion of hormones is widespread in the animal kingdom. All the hormones so secreted are polypeptides, packaged before secretion in vesicles as is the case with neurotransmitters (Chapter 25). The major difference between secretion of neurohormones and secretion of neurotransmitters by typical neurons seems to be the greater distance the former substances must travel.

Another set of effector units of general significance are the endocrine glands. An important component of the fight-or-flight response triggered by the sympathetic nervous system (discussed in Chapter 25) is stimulation of the adrenal gland to secrete adrenalin. Many such glands are under a certain amount of nervous control.

But the effector unit most uniquely animal and most characteristically involved in executing animal behavior is *muscle*. Muscles, together with the firm parts against which they pull—the skeleton—constitute the principal motor system of all animals.

Muscles Must Have Something to Pull Against

Throughout the animal kingdom there is an enormous variety of types of muscle; muscles vary in size, in shape, in the speed and force with which they function, and in a variety of other parameters, but they share the common functional characteristic of contracting when they are stimulated. In order for contraction to achieve a change in body shape that is of adaptive value for the organism, the muscles must have something to pull against. In soft-bodied invertebrates (such as sea anemones and earthworms) a fluid-filled cavity provides the "skeleton" against which the muscles work. When longitudinal muscles (running the length of the body) contract, they cause the body to shorten and become wider; when circular muscles (ringing the body) contract, they cause it to become narrower and longer. *Such antagonistic action of two opposed sets of muscles is the basic principle of muscular control of movement.* Antagonistic action of circular and longitudinal muscles against the fluid contents of the gut remains the basis for motion in the digestive systems of many types of animals.

But in arthropods and vertebrates, muscle pairs run in parallel direction across a joint between hard skeletal parts; when one muscle set contracts, the affected body part bends in one direction, and when the antagonists contract, it bends

(text continues on page 596)

Interleaf 26.2

Early Experience and the Visual System

It is a common occurrence that two or more people who have seen the same object or event will describe it in such different ways that it seems as though they had viewed wholly different things. Such variability in recounting a past situation is doubtless the result of a large number of differences between the individuals questioned. Emotional states, persistence of the memory, associations with similar situations, and language skills are a few of the possible sources of difference in recollection. However, it is rarely suggested that the observers actually saw different things at the same time, because it is assumed that the primary sensory processing was the same in each observer. Yet, can even this be taken for granted?

Information from the environment does not enter the central nervous system directly. At the sense organ it is encoded into neural impulses, which are then used in the CNS to reconstruct the external situation. The fidelity of this reconstruction process is crucial to the initiation of an appropriate response. It can be argued that the sensory system should operate, within its limitations, free from environmentally imposed bias or distortion if it is to provide the greatest possibility of adaptive responses. In the last twenty years this line of argument has been tested for the visual system.

Each ganglion cell in the retina of a vertebrate receives information in the form of a synaptic activity from photoreceptors in a limited area of the field of the ganglion cell. There are approximately 1 million ganglion cells in the human eye, so the retina is subdivided into approximately 1 million roughly circular receptive fields. Neurons in the lateral geniculate nuclei can likewise be said to have receptive fields, because they receive synaptic input from one or few ganglion cells. And, still further into the visual system, neurons in the visual cortex receiving inputs from geniculate cells have receptive fields limited to small regions of the retina. However, in the visual cortex the reconstruction of the visual world begins. The receptive fields of cortical cells can be seen to overlap to a much greater extent than those of geniculate or ganglion cells. Thus, geniculate cells must be making synapses with more than one cortical cell, thereby integrating the mosaic picture created at the ganglion cell layer.

One product of the multiple innervation of cortical cells by geniculate cells is the specific response capabilities of cortical cells. David Hubel and Torsten Wiesel of Harvard University have shown that cells in the visual cortex of cats quite specifically select for features in the visual image. For example, some cells respond only to lines or

edges oriented at a particular angle; other cells will respond only to edges moving in a particular direction, and still others may respond only to objects of a specific size or shape. Here, then, we can begin to ask our question about the autonomy of a sensory system. Will manipulations of the visual environment alter the specificities of cortical cells?

About 80 percent of the neurons in the visual cortex of cats receive synaptic input from both eyes, although usually one eye has a greater influence than the other on a given cell. With this situation it should be possible to test whether visual experience is necessary for cortical cells to become binocularly activated. Hubel and Wiesel sutured one eyelid shut in each of a group of kittens just before their eyes would normally have opened. A low level of light reached the occluded eye, but no visual patterns could be transmitted through the lid. So these experimental kittens saw visual patterns with only one eye. After several weeks, the sutures were cut and testing was begun. When the experimenters temporarily occluded the open eye with an opaque contact lens, the kittens behaved as though they could not see. More dramatically, when recordings were made from cells in the visual cortex all the cells were found to be unresponsive to light shining on the deprived eye! Because the retina and lateral geniculate areas appeared little affected by the deprivation, this experiment suggested that patterned visual information from both eyes is essential for the development of normal binocularly activated cells in the visual cortex.

Adult cats subjected to comparable periods of monocular deprivation show no evidence of behavioral or neurophysiological abnormality. It seems, then, that only in young animals is the circuitry of the visual cortex labile. Does this lability extend to other features of cortical cell function? Helmut Hirsch and D. N. Spinelli, and Horace Barlow and John Pettigrew independently arrived at an answer to this question. Both groups exposed kittens to extremely restricted visual environments. Immediately after their eyes opened, the kittens were kept in darkness except for periodic exposure to a visual environment consisting solely of either horizontal or vertical black-and-white stripes. Thus, the only visual experience any of the animals had until testing began was a stark array of black-and-white stripes. Again, after several weeks, behavioral observations revealed severe visual abnormality. Kittens exposed to horizontal stripes had no trouble negotiating obstructions that were horizontal in their visual fields; however, they seemed unable to see vertical objects! Conversely, animals with only vertical stripe experience stumbled over horizontal objects but had no difficulty with vertically oriented objects.

Apparently these kittens only possessed cells in their visual cortices that responded to lines oriented in the same way as those they had seen during the critical developmental period. Further neurophysiological examination supported this hypothesis. Cortical neurons in kittens restricted to horizontal line experience fired action potentials only when horizon-

tally arrayed lines or edges were presented in their visual fields. Similar restriction of response to vertical stimuli was found in the visual cortices of kittens exposed only to vertical visual experience. Thus, the highly restricted visual experience of these kittens produced severe limitations on their ability to reconstruct the visual world.

The significance of these findings is underlined by corollary studies that have shown that modifications of the normal neurophysiological properties of visual cortical neurons in kittens are possible only during the first three months of postnatal life. After this time, no change in the orientation, movement, or shape specificity of these neurons can be caused by visual deprivation. This implies that there is a critical period of plasticity in the primary visual integration area during early postnatal development. During this period, the fundamental discriminants of the visual world are established once and for all. It must be assumed, and there is some evidence to support this, that cats subjected to visual deprivation during the critical period are never able to develop normal visual discrimination.

Many questions remain unresolved from these studies. Among them is the role of the genome in the establishment of normal cortical connections. For example, these findings can be interpreted in either of two ways. The wiring diagram of the visual cortex may be seen as genetically programmed for normal functioning but subject to irreversible modification under restricted visual exposure. Alternatively, the cortical cells may be seen as essentially undifferentiated at first and only later taking on the characteristics imposed on them from the visual environment. Either model, however, results in the same startling conclusions: the qualitative features of

the visual world are established permanently as a consequence of early visual experience. Work with other mammals has made it clear that this conclusion is not applicable to cats alone, and similar work with primates suggests the possibility that the early development of human visual cortex may not be exempt from dramatic modification by environmental conditions. Thus, it may be that our early visual experience has determined our cortical response capabilities in such ways that each of us constructs a unique visual image even when we view the same thing!

in the other direction. Such muscles are called **skeletal muscles.**

Simple movements of the human arm provide a good example of the lever principle employed in skeletal movement. The major muscle on the front side of the upper arm (the **biceps**) is attached by a ligament to the top of the bone in the upper arm. The other end of the muscle is attached through a tough fiber called a *tendon* to the bones in the forearm. Thus, when the biceps contracts, the force is exerted against the forearm and draws it up, or flexes it (Figure 26.13). Normally, relaxation of the biceps permits the forearm to return to an extended position as it is pulled down by gravity. However, if the upper arm is held in a horizontal position, the assistance of gravity is lost and the forearm must be extended forcibly. This movement is accomplished by the **triceps** (the antagonistic muscle to the biceps). The triceps is attached in a similar way at the shoulder, but it attaches to the opposite side of the forearm. When the triceps contracts, it pulls in the direction opposite the flexion caused by the biceps and thereby extends the forearm once again.

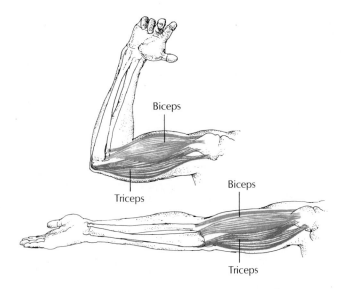

Figure 26.13 Muscle antagonism in the human upper arm. When the triceps is relaxed and the biceps contracted, the arm is flexed at the elbow. When the biceps is relaxed and the triceps contracted, the arm is extended.

Sensory Elements Within Muscles Control Movement Through Feedback Loops

The exquisitely refined gradations of muscular contractions raise a question about central control: How do the spinal cord and brain know what a muscle is doing? The answer lies in sensory elements within muscles that monitor movement and send neural impulses to the central nervous system, forming a negative feedback loop. The special, highly modified muscle cells (called **muscle spindles**) that perform this sensory function are located within each bundle of fibers in a muscle (Figure 26.14). Over most of its length, a muscle spindle looks and behaves like a normal muscle fiber. However, at or very near the middle of the fiber is a region lacking contractile elements. It is wrapped with the dendritic processes of a sensory neuron. When the muscle is at its normal resting length, the sensory neuron is quiet. When muscle becomes stretched either because of some external force or by the contraction of its antagonist, the spindle sensory neuron vigorously fires action potentials. Its axon enters the spinal cord via the dorsal root and synapses directly on the motor neuron that controls the bundle of fibers. The motor neuron then stimulates the muscle fibers to contract against the stretch and to attempt to shorten the muscle to its resting length. Because the spindle sensory neuron generates impulses in proportion to the stretch, the spindle system acts as a precise feedback circuit that maintains appropriate muscle length regardless of the load against which the muscle is working.

In addition to the automatic compensation characteristic

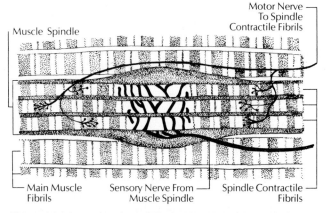

Figure 26.14 A muscle spindle. Each spindle fibril consists of two parts: a contractile region that resembles the main fibrils of the muscle (except that it is somewhat thinner) and a central region that lacks contractile elements and is wrapped by processes of a sensory neuron. When the central region of the fibril is stretched—either because of stretching of the entire muscle or because of active contraction of the spindle fibrils due to inputs from the motor neuron—the sensory nerve endings are activated. A train of nerve impulses is sent to the central nervous system and initiates a reflex that results in contraction

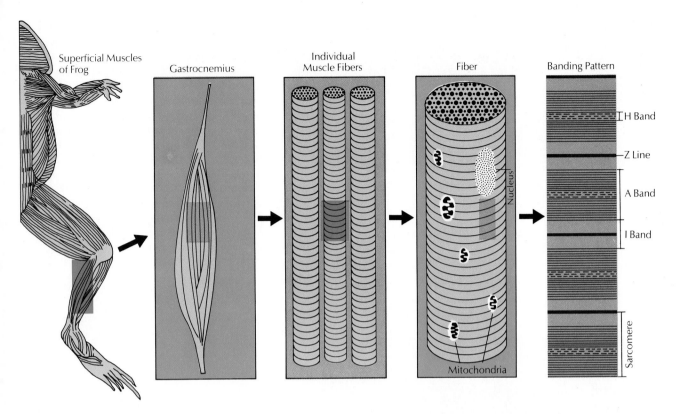

| | Superficial Muscles of Frog | Gastrocnemius | Individual Muscle Fibers | Fiber | Banding Pattern |

Figure 26.15 The internal structure of skeletal muscle tissue. This sequence of diagrams at progressively higher magnification shows that a single muscle is made up of many interacting muscle fibers (cells), which appear striated under magnification. That is, repeated patterns of light and dark bands can be seen in each fiber. The various bands have been given identifying letters that indicate certain distinguishing optical properties they possess. The region between successive Z lines is called a sarcomere; it is the functional unit of muscle contraction. The overall shortening of the muscle is the result of shortening of its many sarcomeres.

of the spindle system, there is a voluntary control element as well. Two small motor neurons controlled from the brain innervate each muscle spindle. When these neurons are active, they cause the ends of the spindle to contract. The contraction stretches the middle segment and, in a sense, "tricks" the spindle sensory neuron into firing as if the entire muscle were being stretched. The resulting reflex increases the tension in the muscle and prepares it to counteract a stretching stimulus. The preparatory function of these motor neurons can be seen in the difference between the movement of your hand when you can see someone drop a book onto it and the movement when your eyes are closed and you cannot anticipate the moment of impact. This phenomenon can also be experienced when you lift an object whose weight you have subconsciously either overestimated or underestimated.

Structure of Skeletal Muscle Provides the Key to Function

How do muscles contract? The insight to answer this question came with a careful analysis of vertebrate skeletal muscle structure. It had long been known that vertebrate skeletal muscle had a **striated** (striped) appearance when viewed with a microscope. (In fact, it is often called *striated muscle* to distinguish it from the nonstriated or *smooth muscle* found in the intestinal tract and other internal

organs.) Figure 26.15 shows that when a muscle is examined microscopically it can be seen to consist of many long cells called *muscle fibers.* Each fiber has a repeating pattern of light and dark bands that have been given identifying letters: A band, I band, Z line, and so on. The region from one Z line to the next is called a **sarcomere.** *The sarcomere is the repeating functional unit of muscular contraction.* The overall shortening observed in a muscle is simply the sum of shortening that occurs in the many sarcomeres.

For many years the significance of this banding pattern was not appreciated. It was thought that contraction of muscle was caused by contraction (folding or coiling up) of individual muscle protein molecules. But in the early 1950s

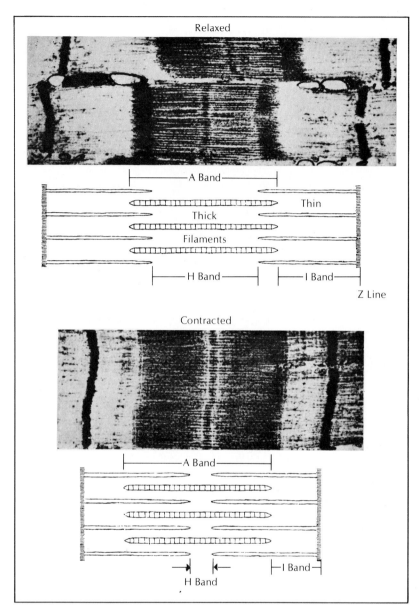

Relaxed

A Band

Thin

Thick

Filaments

H Band — I Band

Z Line

Contracted

A Band

H Band — I Band

Figure 26.16 Electron micrographs and interpretive diagrams of muscle in the relaxed and contracted state. A. F. Huxley and R. Niedergarde observed that the H band and I band decreased in length, but the A band was unchanged as the muscle contracted. H. E. Huxley and Jean Hanson provided an interpretation of these observations based on electron micrographs similar to those seen here. Their interpretation is as follows. The A band represents the length of the thick filaments. The H band represents the region where thin filaments do not overlap the thick filaments. Similarly, the I band represents the region in which thick filaments do not overlap thin filaments. Since the two areas of nonoverlap decrease during contraction, the filaments must be sliding past each other.

two research teams in England made observations that refuted this hypothesis. A. F. Huxley and R. Niedergerde observed the striation patterns during contraction of single muscle fibers with special arrangement of the light microscope designed to intensify the differences between the dark A bands and the light I bands. They found that the length of the A bands remains constant as the muscle contracts, whereas the I bands and H bands become narrower. At the same time, H. E.Huxley and Jean Hanson were studying the structure of striated muscle with the electron microscope. They observed muscles fixed in a stretched condition, at rest length, and contracted. Each of these teams drew the same conclusion from their studies: *The lengths of the filaments in striated muscle do not change during contrac-*

tion; rather, the two kinds of filaments slide past one another (Figure 26.16). Thus was born the **sliding filament hypothesis** of muscular contraction. All subsequent analysis of skeletal muscle contraction has been consistent with this hypothesis.

But *how* do the filaments slide? This has been a question more difficult to answer, but as the result of efforts of many researchers for many years, a clear picture is beginning to emerge. There are four major kinds of protein in the contractile apparatus (Figure 26.17). The thick filaments are composed of many molecules of **myosin,** a large protein shaped rather like a golf club with a long, straight, shaftlike portion and a somewhat swollen ''head'' extending from one end at an angle. These heads project from the thick

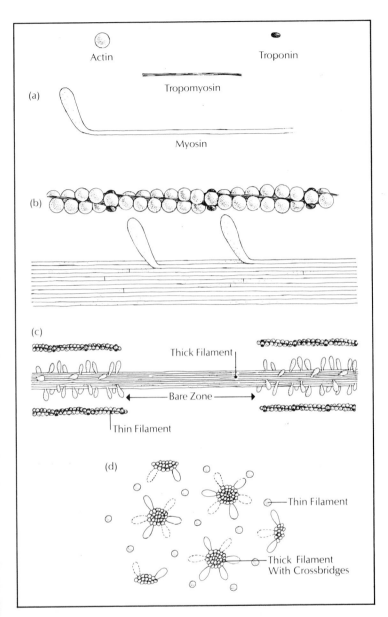

Figure 26.17 *The probable organization of proteins within the contractile unit of muscle. (a) Approximate relative sizes and shapes of the four protein components. (b) A closeup view showing the probable organization of the components. The myosin molecules are packed in the thick filament in such a way that the shafts overlap one another and the heads project to form "crossbridges" to the thin filaments. The actin molecules are aligned to form a long double helix that forms the bulk of the thin filaments. There is one fibrous tropomyosin molecule for every seven actin molecules; it appears that the tropomyosin lies near the grooves between adjacent actin helices. There is one troponin for each tropomyosin. (c) A lower power view of the structures shown in (b). Myosin molecules at opposite ends of the thick filament are oriented in opposite directions, with their shafts pointing away from the ends of the filament. As a result, there is a bare zone in the middle of the filament in which shafts from both ends overlap, but no crossbridges (heads) project. In the region in which crossbridges do project they occur in threes; each threesome forms an equilateral triangle, but alternate threesomes are out of phase by 60°. (d) An end view, showing the side-to-side organization of thick and thin filaments. Adjacent thick filaments are arranged in regular hexagons. Thus, each thick filament interacts with six thin filaments, while each thin filament interacts with three thick filaments. At any one level, however, a thick filament has crossbridges to only three of the six adjacent thin filaments (solid crossbridges); at a different level in the fiber it has bridges to the other three (dotted bridges). Other models for arrangement of crossbridges have been suggested that differ only slightly from those shown in this figure.*
(From John M. Murray and Annemarie Weber, "The Cooperative Action of Muscle Proteins," copyright © 1974 by Scientific American, Inc. All rights reserved.)

filament to form *crossbridges* between thick and thin filaments. The thin filament is predominantly a double helix formed by association of many molecules of the globular protein **actin.** But, in addition, the thin filament contains lesser amounts of the proteins **tropomyosin** and **troponin.** A diagram of one probable arrangement of these proteins within the thick and thin filaments is provided in Figure 26.17.

Contraction of a muscle requires two components in addition to the four proteins just listed: calcium ions (Ca^{++}) and ATP. The ATP is hydrolyzed during the contraction process, and it is this hydrolysis that provides the energy that somehow results in motion. The head of the myosin molecule contains an enzymatic site capable of binding

ATP, but unless the myosin interacts with actin the ATP is not split. And myosin and actin cannot interact in the presence of troponin and tropomyosin unless Ca^{++} ions are present. One of the aspects of this process that puzzled researchers for a long time was that ATP is required not only for contraction but also for relaxation. (This fact explains rigor mortis: As ATP disappears after death, the muscles lose the capacity to either contract *or* relax; they become locked in position and the entire body becomes stiff.) All of these observations have now been fitted together in a comprehensive scheme, which is outlined in Figure 26.18. The important points of this scheme are the following: *Sliding of the filaments relative to one another occurs when ATP is hydrolyzed, causing the myosin cross-*

(text continues on page 602)

Figure 26.18   One model for the contraction-relaxation process. Other models differ in certain minor details, but all agree on the importance of calcium in activating the contraction process and the role of ATP hydrolysis in causing some shape change in the myosin crossbridges that results in sliding of the filaments.

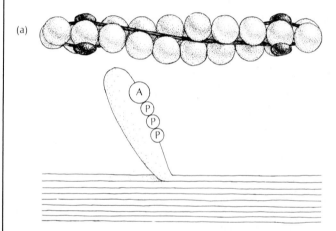

(a)

Step 1. ATP is bound to the myosin crossbridge (head). The position of the troponin-tropomyosin complex is such that contact between actin and myosin is prevented.

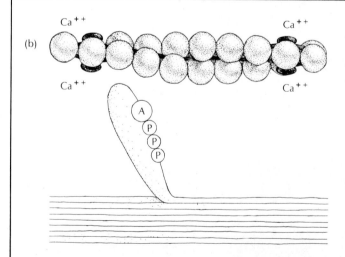

(b)

Step 2. When calcium (Ca ++) ions become available, they bind to the troponin, causing it and the tropomyosin to withdraw into a groove of the actin double helix.

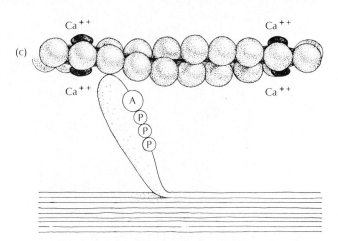

(c)

Step 3. Now the myosin-ATP complex attaches to the actin. This activates the enzymatic side of the myosin.

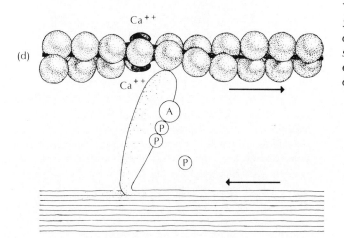

(d)

Step 4. The ATP is split to ADP plus P_i. This causes a change in the shape of the myosin molecule. This shape change causes the filaments to slide with reference to one another. In this form the actin-myosin complex is stable.

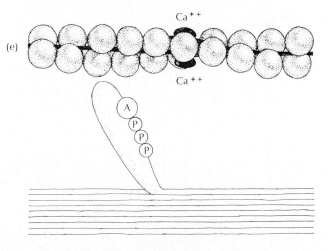

(e)

Step 5. Only when a new ATP molecule attaches to the myosin, displacing the ADP and P_i, does the actin-myosin complex break down and the crossbridge swivel back to its original shape. If calcium is still present, the contraction cycle will be repeated 50 to 100 times per second, resulting in a ratchetlike movement of the filaments past one another. But once Ca^{++} ions are withdrawn, no further attachment of crossbridges occurs and the muscle relaxes.

bridge to bend. This hydrolysis occurs only when the myosin-ATP complex interacts with actin. However, the troponin-tropomyosin complex prevents such interaction in the absence of calcium. *Thus, addition of calcium ions leads to contraction by causing the troponin-tropomyosin complex to withdraw so that actin and myosin are free to interact.* Once the ATP is split, the actin-myosin complex is stable until the myosin binds a new ATP molecule. Thus both contraction and relaxation require ATP; *ATP is bound during the relaxation phase of the cycle and is split during the contraction phase.*

The key to controlling contraction, then, is the control of calcium ion concentration within the sarcomere. How is this control achieved in a functioning muscle? The answer resides in the **sarcoplasmic reticulum,** a complex reticular structure that wraps around each bundle of contractile filaments (Figure 26.19). These membranous sacs act as the reservoir for Ca^{++} ions. At each Z line the sarcoplasmic reticulum of adjacent sarcomeres makes intimate contact with a series of long, thin tubules called the **transverse tubules,** which are actually infoldings of the cell membrane. The way in which this system works is the following.

An action potential entering the muscle in motor neuron causes release of neurotransmitter at the specialized synapses known as **neuromuscular junctions.** As a result of the neurotransmitter action, the muscle membrane becomes depolarized and fires an action potential that sweeps over the surface of the cell. This firing results in a depolarization of the membrane of the transverse tubules throughout the cell, and as the transverse tubules depolarize, they cause the adjacent sarcoplasmic reticulum to increase in permeability. Thus Ca^{++} ions flow out of the sarcoplasmic reticulum into the sarcomere, triggering a contraction. As long as the neural impulses continue to arrive at the muscle the transverse tubules remain depolarized, the sarcoplasmic reticulum remains permeable to Ca^{++}, and contraction continues. But once the neural impulses stop, membranes repolarize and the Ca^{++} pores in the sarcoplasmic reticulum close. Now an ATP-requiring active transport enzyme in the membrane of the sarcoplasmic reticulum quickly pumps Ca^{++} ions back out of the sarcomere and into the sarcoplasmic reticulum. The muscle relaxes.

Clearly, if an organism is to match its responses to a wide variety of situations, muscles must be capable of graded responses, not an all-or-none type of contraction. Different animals achieve such a gradation of response by different mechanisms. In vertebrates, each individual muscle cell responds in an all-or-none manner but the muscle as a whole does not. By controlling how many motor neurons carry action potentials at once, the central nervous system controls how many cells within the muscle contract at once: the more cells that contract, the more forceful the movement.

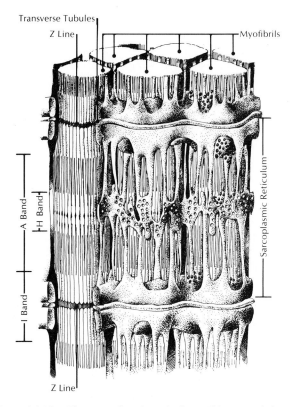

Figure 26.19 The sarcoplasmic reticulum. This network is intimately associated with the contractile elements of the muscle cell and with the transverse tubules that penetrate from the cell membrane to the deepest reaches of the muscle cell. The sarcoplasmic reticulum acts as the reservoir of calcium ions required to intiate contraction.

Furthermore, the response can be graded by modifying the rate at which action potentials are sent down the motor neurons. If they arrive at high speed, the muscle has no opportunity to relax between contraction cycles, and successive contractions become additive. In some invertebrates, however, the strength of muscular contraction is regulated by inhibitory neurons as well as excitatory neurons; the strength of contraction depends on the balance between the two kinds of inputs. Yet other invertebrates produce no action potential in the muscle membrane. Thus input from a single motor neuron causes only one region of a muscle cell to contract, and input from many neurons on different parts of the cell is required to cause all sarcomeres to contract at once. This results in a slow and graded muscular contraction.

PERSPECTIVE

The sensory input and motor output systems discussed in this chapter are, in most cases, more complex than their descriptions have indicated. This greater complexity lies both in structural considerations and in the process of neural coding. In the vertebrate visual system, for example, the pathway from rods and cones to bipolar and horizontal cells, and then from bipolar cells to ganglion and amacrine cells, is relatively easy to visualize as long as we restrict our considerations to just a few members of each cell type. However, as soon as we expand our view to ask how a specific ganglion cell comes to produce just the sequence of action potentials it does, we have to deal with a large number of subtle effects produced by interaction with adjacent retinal regions. Beyond this, how is the coded information from the retina fed into the visual cortex in such a way as to generate the appropriate orientation, movement, and shape characteristics recorded there? The codes must become successively more intricate and the placement of synapses vastly more complex.

The output system represents the same sort of difficulty. The instructions to the muscles in the hands of a pianist must be trivially simple when compared to the interactions in the motor areas of the brain necessary to produce them. Feedback from the skin and muscle receptors must be integrated precisely so that the next set of instructions produces just the right movement.

Between the inputs and the outputs lies the most perplexing and fascinating system of all—the conscious brain. The reason this system has not been discussed is quite simple: There is almost nothing known about the neural bases of volition, thought, and ideation. With an understanding of these processes as the ultimate goal, the neurosciences have taken two routes. One group of workers, the neurophysiologists, is struggling to reconstruct the functioning nervous system from knowledge gained about neurons and their interactions. Another group, the behavioral biologists, is attempting to dissect behavior into its fundamental elements in the hope that these units will yield basic insights into the functioning of the brain. It is as though two teams of workers are digging from opposite sides of a mountain to build a tunnel. It seems that both teams are making progress, but no one has any idea how deep the mountain is or whether the workers will ever meet in the middle.

SUGGESTED READINGS

BENTLEY, DAVID, and RONALD R. HOY. "The Neurobiology of Cricket Song," *Scientific American*, 231 (August 1974), 34–44. A combination of careful neurophysiology, behavioral analysis, and genetics has permitted these authors to present the first clear-cut evidence for a genetically determined complex behavior.

CASE, JAMES. *Sensory Mechanisms*. New York: Macmillan, 1966. Many helpful diagrams and extensive references to original research findings are used to illustrate the most important features of sensory processes in a variety of organisms.

MERTON, P. A. "How We Control the Contraction of Our Muscles," *Scientific American*, 226 (May 1972), 30–37. Merton describes the muscle spindle system of sensory and motor control. It is this tiny system of specialized muscles, sensory neurons, and motor neurons that allows us to move as we choose.

Section VI
Biological Behavior

Even though it is useful to think of an organism as a separate physical and chemical being, at some point in our study of life we must come to realize that an organism cannot be fully understood in isolation from its environment. It is linked in time and space to its habitat and to other organisms with which it comes into contact—by chance or by choice. An organism's behavior in its environment is controlled by its genetic endowment and is subject to the same evolutionary pressures as reproduction, respiration, and heart rate. But supplementing the predetermined patterns of inherited behavior is a capacity to learn from experience and to give new responses to repeated stimuli—in other words, to give responses that become more and more adaptive with time and individual history.

The point is that behavior is not a thing apart from other biological adaptations. The capacity to learn is as much a result of genetic change and natural selection as the capacity to produce enzymes only when they are needed. It is the appearance of learned behavior and its concurrent "unpredictable" responses that make the analysis of behavior and the attempt to draw generalizations from that analysis difficult. Even so, behavior is most understandable as a series of evolutionary adaptations—not as a series of random curious events.

Chapter 27

Innate and Learned Behavior

Can a nation brought up on goodhearted anthropomorphism in its nature stories come to look at animals as they really are, and not as we imagine them to be?

Most of us, at one time or another, have been fascinated or amused by the behavior of the animals around us. Depending on the extent of our interest, we might idly muse about what it is we see, or we might explore the significance of the behavior in terms of what it means to the way of life of the animal. Consider, for example, the two photographs that open this chapter. Obviously (we might say), the male bird on the right is propositioning the female bird on the left; and, well-bred female that she is, she promptly rejects his dissolute request with dignity and with a few choice words. He, shocked and embarrassed, is left speechless.

Such misguided logic is called **anthropomorphism**—the reading of human motivations, characteristics, and behaviors into (among other things) animals. Now consider what the photographs mean to someone who has been trained in **ethology**—the scientific study of behavior.

Obviously (he would say), the photographs are of Bengalese finches, a species first domesticated in China and then imported to Japan, where it has been bred in captivity for many centuries. The photographs capture part of the courtship display. The male first bows deeply to the female. Then, with bill opening and closing rapidly, head feathers and belly feathers fluffed, and tail open and pointing upward, he sings and sways his body from side to side, bowing intermittently. If the female is receptive, she will invite copulation by quivering her tail rapidly up and down. The ethologist would go on to say that both members of the mated pair will participate in nest building. Unlike most bird species, which usually carry nest materials in bundles at 90-degree angles to the long axis of their bill, the Bengalese finches will carry straws one at a time, almost always by one end of the straw, with the straw pointed forward. Unlike the "open cup" nests of most small birds, these finches will build roofed-over nests, stretching their bodies in a characteristic way to shape the overhead arch.

The female will lay one egg a day until she completes a clutch of four or five. Both parents will take turns incubating the eggs until they hatch, and both will feed the young.

This glimpse into the life history of the Bengalese finch illustrates a number of concepts. One of the most important is the idea of **innate behavior**—the heritable disposition to perform certain behaviors. In other words, some behavioral traits may be inherited even as anatomical and morphological traits are inherited. *Behavior patterns therefore may be subject to natural selection in the wild and to artificial selection in captivity.*

Although innate behavior is widespread in nature, there are also many cases of **learned behavior**—altered behavioral response as a result of experience. For example, the zebra finch, a native of Australia and a relative of the Bengalese finch, has an entirely different display from the Bengalese. In the laboratory, zebra finch foster parents will hatch the eggs of Bengalese, and they will raise the chicks to maturity. Now, among these fostered birds, the courtship dance of the males will be typically Bengalese—which demonstrates that the dance is inherited. Moreover, simple vocalizations in their repertoire (alarm calls, contact calls) will also be found to be inherited. But the song the male birds sing will be the song of the zebra finch foster father—it will be a learned behavior. In this chapter and in the chapters to follow, you will see that with many animals, *dispositions to perform some behavior patterns may be innate, others may be learned, and still others may be a mixture of both.*

As interwoven as these sources of behavior may be, it is one goal of ethologists to sort them out for study. To do this, they often begin their investigations by observing an animal—ideally under natural conditions but also in captivity—with the least possible disturbance. They attempt to catalog its entire behavioral repertoire—not only what the animal *can* do, but also what it *does* do in a given circumstance. Such a cataloging is called an **ethogram.**

Often, experimental manipulation is done in order to shed light on some of the questions that may be implied in an ethogram. What, for example, causes the male Bengalese finch to sing? Is it the male hormone testosterone? To find the answer, an ethologist may first surgically remove the gonads (the source of testosterone) from a male bird. Then, if the bird stops singing, the bird can be given an injection of the hormone to determine whether or not testosterone restores singing. The ethologist may then ask: Does the rate and amount of singing change in the presence or absence of a female? To find the answer, the song rates for paired and isolated birds may be compared. The experimenter thus explores the *causation* of a behavior pattern—whether it is affected by internal factors, external factors, or both.

An ethogram also permits analysis of the phylogenetic origins of a behavior pattern. Consider the fact that during courtship, the Bengalese finch fluffs up a good part of its feathers. From what ancestral behavior pattern is it derived? Feather fluffing normally functions in thermoregulation; it holds a layer of warm air around a bird's body, serving as an effective insulator in cold weather. But during courtship, this behavior is emancipated from its original function. In this case it is a form of **ritualization**—a behavior that typically occurs in members of a given species in a highly stereotyped fashion and without any direct physiological need. Another example will show how variations on a behavioral pattern have come to exist among related species. During courtship, the spice finch not only bows like its close relative, the Bengalese finch, it also occasionally wipes its bill on the perch. The bows appear to be incomplete bill-wiping movements. (A behavior that does not complete its original intention is called a **ritualized intention movement.**) In the related zebra finch, bill-wiping is prominent and bowing is absent. In still another species, the chestnut-breasted finch, the bow has been reduced to a nod. This sort of gradation of traits in a behavior pattern exhibited by several related species is called an **ethocline.**

Analysis may also be made of the adaptive value of behavior patterns. Fluffing, for example, occurs during the courtship displays of many bird species. It apparently is used in communication; it has **signal value.** It tends to make the courting male look larger and more conspicuous to females. If females are to select mates on the basis of appearance, and if the fluffing display is a mode of attracting a female's attention, then this stereotyped component of the display should have survival value for the species.

So far, we have looked at only a sampling of the questions that our opening photographs might evoke. Because each aspect of behavior in a complex animal has implication for the survival of its species, it is important to determine how a behavior is acquired, and how it might change in time and space.

INNATE AND LEARNED BEHAVIOR ARE NOT ENTIRELY SEPARABLE THINGS

Innate behavior (once called "instinctive" behavior) is an automatic and species-specific response to a given stimulus. It can be elicited even when an animal has been raised without any contact with other members of its species. Many complex patterns of mating and nesting (such as those already described for Bengalese finches) are considered innate, for they are performed in a precise manner by animals that have been reared in isolation. The head-bobbing and push-ups of some lizards, which are displays used in courtship and territorial behavior, develop normally in individuals that have been hatched and raised in isolation. In a sense, such innate behaviors represent the "phylogenetic learning" of a species—its individual members have the appropriate behavior to survive and reproduce. Through evolution, many genetically determined behaviors that are appropriate to new situations gradually accumulate.

When an innate behavior first appears during the life of an individual, it does not require practice to become perfected. It is part of a stereotyped pattern of behavioral acts, or a **fixed action pattern,** that is emitted by an organism in an essentially identical fashion whenever the appropriate stimuli are present. Such sequences include many directed activities related to food-getting, courtship, and the preparation of or search for shelter. A fixed action pattern may be little more than a simple response to a single stimulus (Figure 27.2), or it may be a complex response to a broad spectrum of stimuli and circumstances. The specific stimuli that trigger the performance of fixed action patterns may be chemical, visual, auditory, or tactile in nature; all are called **behavioral releasers.** But even fixed action patterns may be modified, depending on the physiological state of the animal, on environmental conditions, and on the animal's past experiences. In short, particularly in the case of complex animals, stereotyped behavior may have learned as well as innate components.

Part of the learning process involves **memory**—the internalization of information about stimuli and the responses made to them. As information is received and processed through sensory systems, it is sent on to the brain (Chapter 25). There it is stored in some form that permits it to be used to modify the response to the same stimuli in new situations. This kind of stored information can accumulate progressively and become modified by further experience, and the animal thereby is capable of adaptive responses as situations change (Figure 27.3). Another way of saying this is that the *capacity* to learn is to some extent determined genetically. Therefore, it, too, is subject to natural selection. When environmental conditions change rapidly, and if the change can be best accomplished only through a behavioral response, then the individuals capable of that

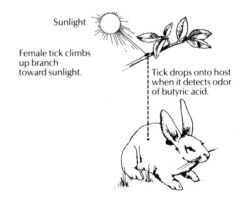

Figure 27.2 Example of a fixed action pattern in a mature female tick. In response to sunlight on its photosensitive body surface, a female tick climbs up a branch toward sunlight, where it waits (sometimes for years) until a mammal passes by. Only then does the tick release its grip on the branch, falling (if successful) on the warm body of a potential host. Once there, the tick responds to the body heat by inserting its proboscis into the skin in order to engorge on blood.

This fixed action pattern depends on three stimuli: sunlight, the odor of butyric acid, and warmth. A mature female tick will let go of its perch for anything that gives off the odor of butyric acid; it will sink its proboscis into any warm body (including a balloon filled with warm water). The taste of blood means nothing to the tick.

response will be the ones to survive. Thus their capacity for rapid learning will be passed on to the next generation.

There is an interplay, then, between learned and innate behavior, particularly in the more complex animals, and these two types of behavior are not entirely separable. To the extent that attention has recently been focused on alteration of behavior as a result of learning—as opposed to a focus merely on "mechanistic" responses of animals to stimuli—the distinction has been useful.

FORMS OF LEARNED BEHAVIOR

Imprinting: Whither Thou Goest I Will Go

One form of learning occurs in highly social species, such as birds. In **imprinting,** a series of responses apparently serve to establish social associations during a very early stage in an animal's life—associations that will play a crucial role in its subsequent interactions with other members of the species. This type of early social learning was first reported in 1911 by Oskar Heinroth, who reared geese in isolation from the time they were hatched. He found that the birds followed him everywhere as if he were their parent and companion. It was his student Konrad Lorenz who in 1935 formalized the concept of imprinting. Lorenz found that species of birds such as geese and chickens invariably follow the first slowly moving object they see (particularly if it makes sounds) and form a strong attachment to it.

That imprinting is under internal control (hence is preprogrammed genetically) is shown by the fact that such animals respond positively to moving objects they encounter at one specific time phase in their development, whereas they respond negatively to the *same* objects if presented at a later time. It turns out that there are two distinct manifestations of imprinting. The first is the "following reaction," in which the animal adopts a child-parent relationship to any slowly moving object of about the right size and shape. A second and much later manifestation of imprinting concerns the species of animal toward which the imprinted animal will direct its sexual activity.

Our current concept of imprinting may be illustrated with examples from Klaus Immelmann's work with zebra finches that were hatched and raised either in isolation or by Bengalese finches.

1. Imprinting takes place during a genetically programmed **sensitive period.** Such periods vary in length from one species to the next.

2. Imprinting is irreversible. In Immelmann's study, some mis-imprinted male zebra finches that had been raised with Bengalese finches were placed with females of their own species in isolated chambers. These birds mated and raised

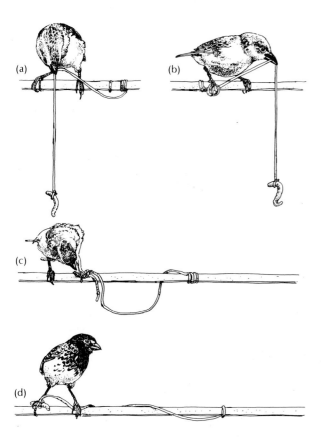

Figure 27.3 Examples of the genetic component of the capacity to learn among tool-using bird species. Some species of birds use their feet to clamp food against a perch; other species seldom do. The species that use their feet are better performers when it comes to learning how to pull up a string with food tied to the other end. In (a) and (b), two species of Galápagos finches show a basically similar neuromuscular coordination of bill and feet in string-pulling behavior. The plain titmouse of the United States and the Galápagos finch (c and d) are ecological and behavioral equivalents. Here, both birds are shown after they have sidled along their perch. Both have obtained a worm by string-pulling and both hold the worm with one foot during feeding.

(a)

(b)

(c)

(d)

Figure 27.4 (left) Konrad Lorenz and friends.

Figure 27.5 (below) Effect of imprinting on the courtship behavior of zebra finches. Raised by Bengalese finch foster parents from the time it was hatched, this fluffed-up male shows a preference for Bengalese females over the females of his own species. In other studies, hand-reared zebra finch males sang courtship songs at the sight of the experimenter and attempted to mate with his fingertips and ear lobes.

young. But anywhere from nine months to seven years later, when the mis-imprinted males were given their choice between Bengalese and zebra finch females, they preferred the Bengalese (Figure 27.5).

3. Imprinting gives rise to behaviors that will be directed toward more than one individual of a species. Thus, the imprinted male zebra finches courted any female belonging to the species of their foster mother. The ethologist would say that the effects of imprinting are *supra-individual*.

4. Imprinting itself is completed before the correlative behaviors emerge. Thus, the courtship preferences of the male zebra finches were not evident until the appropriate stage of maturity had been reached, long after the imprinting had been completed.

Thus we see that imprinting involves both innate and learned behavior. Genetic factors control both the capacity to become imprinted at specific times and the behavioral patterns released in the imprinted individual. But the object or objects toward which these stereotyped behavior patterns are to be directed may be learned as a result of early experience.

Why is it that behaviors as fundamental as species identification and mate selection are left to learning rather than being genetically predetermined? One possibility is that the imprinting mechanism carries with it a potential for rapid evolutionary change. If species identity were rigidly predetermined, the young would tend to reject individuals with adaptive modifications similar to those possessed by their natural parents, and they would preferentially associate with, and mate with, individuals retaining the ancestral traits. Thus, genetic predetermination of species identity would tend to be a conservative mechanism impeding evolutionary adaptation of a population.

Habituation: Learning *Not* To Respond

If you were to move from a quiet neighborhood to a place near a railroad line, you would probably become startled every time you heard a train pass by—at least for awhile. In time, you would come to realize the sound was neither relevant nor cause for concern, and you would probably become so used to the noise that you would not even be aware of it. Any bird or mammal usually will react to a loud noise of this sort, becoming startled, turning its head in the direction of the sound, and undergoing various changes in physiological function, such as an increase in heart rate. But if that same noise is repeated at regular intervals, the response will invariably taper off. Often it will disappear entirely. This phenomenon is not restricted to the response of vertebrates to auditory stimuli. If, for example, the gill of a nudibranch (a gastropod) is touched with a bristle, the gill is rapidly retracted as the result of a simple reflex arc. But with regular repetition of the stimulus, the response becomes more and more sluggish and eventually ceases to occur at all.

This form of learning is called **habituation**—an animal ceases to respond to repeated visual, auditory, chemical, or tactile stimulation that turns out not to be significant or to have harmful effects. Habituation is an important and long-lasting process. If an animal were not able to screen out all the trivia from its surroundings, its ability to respond to stimuli of real consequence (a predator, for example) would be gravely impaired.

Habituation is often difficult to distinguish from the related phenomenon of sensory adaptation, such as occurs when rapid repetition of identical stimuli leads to temporary loss of sensitivity in the receptor (Chapter 26). For exam-

ple, when you place your hand in warm water, you rapidly lose any perception of warmth as the temperature-sensitive nerve endings in your hand adapt to the stimulus. But this is a temporary phenomenon. When you now briefly immerse the same hand in ice water and then return it to the warm water, you will once again perceive its warmth.

Even though habituation is sometimes regarded as a basic characteristic of animals, it does not occur when the animal is repeatedly confronted with a potentially *harmful* stimulus (such as a predator). Underlying the responses to harmful stimuli seems to be an inherited resistance to habituation, which has great survival value, to say the least.

Interestingly, if a new stimulus is interjected into a monotonous sequence of stimuli to which an animal has become habituated, the next time the old stimulus is repeated it will evoke a response once more. If a monotonous stimulus suddenly disappears and is kept away for some time, the same thing will happen when the stimulus is presented for a second time. This phenomenon is called **dishabituation.**

Conditioning and Extinction: Acquiring and Blotting Out a Response to a Reinforcing Stimulus

An animal's response to a given stimulus may be modified by the presence or absence of another stimulus that comes to be associated with it. For example, it is possible to modify the triggering of a fixed action pattern so that it becomes associated with a reinforcing stimulus that is not normally associated with the response. Subsequently, the reinforcing stimulus alone may become sufficient to release the fixed action pattern in the absence of the behavioral releaser. This form of learning, called **conditioning,** was first studied by the Russian physiologist Ivan Pavlov.

Pavlov was originally interested in the factors controlling the secretion of digestive juices in response to eating. In his experiments with dogs, he first observed that saliva was secreted almost at once when he placed an extract of meat in the animal's mouth. He deduced that this was a simple reflex response. Pavlov then began a series of experiments in which he rang a bell just before placing the meat extract in the dog's mouth. Gradually, the dog began to salivate at the sound of the bell—the response had been transferred from one stimulus to another that was regularly associated with it (Figure 27.6*a*).

Now, after the conditioned response had been established, if Pavlov repeatedly rang the bell but did *not* follow up the stimulus with food, the amount of saliva produced in the dog's mouth began to decrease, and eventually the response disappeared (Figure 27.6*b*). The acquired response had been blotted out—a process Pavlov called **extinction.**

Conditioning is a widespread form of learning. Interestingly, human autonomic reflexes, which we tend to think cannot be consciously controlled, can often be conditioned. Heart rate, for instance, can be speeded up or slowed down with the appearance of a given cue. For example, an expert marksman regularly (and quite unconsciously) slows his heartbeat as he prepares to pull the rifle trigger. Such a person cannot stop himself from giving the conditioned response unless it is gradually extinguished.

Trial-and-Error Learning: A Special Case of Conditioning

Pavlov observed another kind of conditioned learning in his dogs. For example, when he consistently lifted a dog's paw just before putting meat powder in its mouth, the dog eventually began to lift the paw itself when it was hungry.

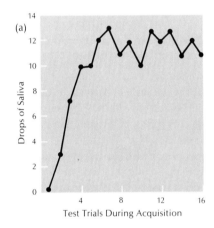

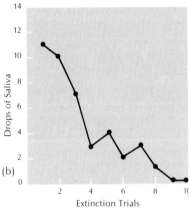

Figure 27.6 Results from Pavlov's experiment with the saliva-secretion conditioned stimulus in dogs. (a) An increase occurred in the response to a stimulus that immediately preceded the presentation of food; (b) there was gradual loss of the response when the stimulus was not followed by the appearance of food.

In this case, the dog had learned after several trials to repeat a response because it was followed by a reward. (If the result had not been rewarding after several trials, the dog would not have learned the response.) In such **trial-and-error learning,** responses followed by rewards are likely to be repeated, whereas responses followed by punishments are not likely to be repeated. Thus, any normal behavior may become more or less likely to recur, depending on its consequences. New behavior patterns or alterations in existing stimulus-response relationships can be brought about in this way.

Trial-and-error learning has been extensively studied by B. F. Skinner, his students, and his associates. Skinner's training box (Figure 27.7) has become the basic piece of equipment for the study of the conditioning and learning of such behavior not only with animals but also with human beings. (This kind of learning is also called **instrumental conditioning,** or **operant conditioning,** because the reinforcing stimulus occurs only after the animal performs—or fails to perform—some specific operation.)

Through reinforcement in trial-and-error learning, animals can be trained to *discriminate* between various stimuli. In fact, complex behavior patterns can be *shaped* by reinforcing ever closer approximations to the behavior that is desired. For example, a porpoise may first be given reinforcement (a fish) simply for jumping out of the water whenever a particular stimulus is presented. Later, the reinforcement may be made only when the porpoise jumps in a particular section of the pool and, still later, only when it throws its tail somewhat forward as it reenters the water. By gradually narrowing the range of behaviors that will produce the reward, a trainer can teach the porpoise to do a somersault above the water at a particular spot in the pool—a shaped behavior that the porpoise might never have performed as a result of random behaviors.

From reinforcement experiments, it has been found that animals also possess the ability to *generalize* stimuli—to perceive similarities among stimuli by learning only the most characteristic cues and ignoring the others. For example, Irenäus Eibl-Eibesfeldt, in training toads to avoid inedible prey models, found that at first they reacted specifically to negative models that were in a certain location and that moved in a certain way. Later the toads began to generalize their responses to the models in other situations. Eibl-Eibesfeldt found that some toads generalized on the basis of color, and they avoided different models that were not marked with that color. After a few such sessions, some toads learned to avoid *everything* but mealworms. One female toad learned to distinguish between prey pulled on a string and prey moving on its own. Eventually this female avoided even mealworms that were pulled on a string.

In the natural environment, the reinforcement associated

(a)

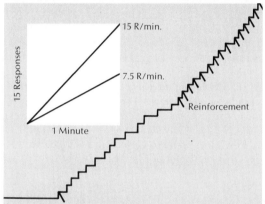

(b)

Figure 27.7 (left) The Skinner box (a), used in the study of trial-and-error learning. A Skinner box contains a lever (or key) that an animal presses in order to give a response to a stimulus. The box is outfitted in such a way that various stimuli (lights, sounds, and so forth) can be presented to the animal. It also contains a mechanism that presents food to the animal—by some automatic timing device or when the animal manipulates the lever. If the animal is hungry, the food acts as a reward for the behavior of lever-pressing. Similarly, shaved rats placed in a refrigerator can learn to press a lever in order to turn on a heat lamp; the raising of environmental temperature serves as a reinforcement. The result of this reinforcement is that the lever-pressing increases in frequency, and this behavior persists—the animal presses the lever again and again.

(b) A typical record of a training session. This graph is a cumulative record of the number of lever presses as a function of the time elapsed after a rat was placed in the box. Each reinforcement is shown by a diagonal mark. After the first lever-pressing was reinforced, the rat continued to operate the lever some thirteen times without further reinforcement, although the rate of lever-pressing began to decline somewhat. Reinforcement of each lever pressing during the last part of the training session caused a continuing high frequency of the behavior.

Figure 27.8 (below) Moments in the life of a captive porpoise and a captive killer whale, whose behaviors are being shaped to elicit favorable responses from human audiences.

with trial-and-error learning takes on added significance, particularly in mating and in the search for food. Birds, for example, soon learn to avoid the monarch butterfly, which first appears as a positive stimulus (food) and then turns out to be a negative stimulus (having eaten a butterfly, which contains a toxin, a bird becomes nauseated). They learn to avoid a species of stinging wasp for much the same sort of reason.

Because predators have a tendency to generalize the conditioning stimulus, it is possible for other species to *mimic* the conditioning species and thereby avoid predation. (The best known example of mimicry is the viceroy butterfly, which so resembles the monarch butterfly that it fools the predators that have learned to shun the latter.)

Even such trial-and-error learning has its genetic aspects. Clifford Henty showed that each new generation of European song thrushes must learn how to smash a snail on a rock in order to break the shell and have access to the food it houses. Learning the technique by observing adult birds is not required; they gradually improve their technique by trial and error. But it has never been possible to teach birds of related species (for example, the European blackbird) to break snails in the manner of the European song thrush—even though they readily eat pre-shelled snails. Even if snails that are almost completely freed are presented to them, these related species apparently lack the capacity to learn the operations involved in smashing the shell.

In the long run, effective behaviors are selected for because they are successful and are passed down to progeny through a combination of direct inheritance and learning. Selection is a necessary part of the adaptive process, whether genetic or learned.

Exploratory Behavior: Learning Through Play and Curiosity

Play is an essential part of the early stages of the life cycle of many animals—particularly mammals and some birds—for it is through play that they learn many of the vital strategies for survival. Juvenile monkeys, for example, run about together, engaging in mock fighting and fleeing. The period of play, and the kind of practice it provides, sharpens their agility, which may later save their life. In addition, through their play these animals form close associations that help bind the group together when they mature.

Harry Harlow at the University of Wisconsin raised several groups of macaque monkeys from birth without giving them any opportunity to play with their peers. All these infants developed into disturbed animals. Some sat dumbly in their cages, staring blankly. Others rocked and swayed compulsively, hour after hour, sucking at their thumbs and fingers and pinching at their skin. When Harlow brought these macaques into contact with one another, they were unable to establish normal relationships.

Figure 27.9 Play behavior. In young carnivores, such as the tiger cubs seen here, play behavior is thought to be essential for the maturation of reflexes that will later be required for success in hunting. But in some mammalian species—most notably otters—play behavior is seen throughout the adult life and serves no apparent physiological role.

They fought with each other; the males and females were unable to copulate.

Harlow then raised another group of infant macaques, isolating each animal in its own cage but allowing it to play with the others for twenty minutes a day. After a short period of uncertainty, the infants played together vigorously. In less than a year, the males and females began to take on their normal roles in the social group. These experiments confirmed what field observations of monkeys would suggest: that mingling with peers is essential for proper development.

In some species, play behavior does not necessarily cease once an animal reaches maturity. There are many instances of play behavior during the stages of life when animals are fully capable of serious activity—not only in domesticated varieties such as dogs and cats but in such wild creatures as river otters, which seem to get great satisfaction out of "skiing" down snowy slopes on their bellies in winter.

Underlying play behavior is a more general form of exploratory behavior, called curiosity. Curiosity not only involves interactions with other members of a species, it also involves interactions with the environment that lead to knowledge about its physical characteristics and arrangements. When an animal comes across a new object in its environment, or when it finds itself in new surroundings, it shows ambivalence in wanting to explore and wanting to withdraw. As it overcomes its hesitancy, it begins to probe. Foxes and raccoons may sniff about, mice may gnaw at new objects and try to hoard them, birds may peck at a new object, a chimpanzee may pick up an unfamiliar object and inspect and manipulate it.

Unlike conditioned behavior, exploratory behavior is not associated with any immediate reward. There does not appear to be any particular or immediate motivation regularly associated with this form of learning. But it may be that the information being acquired will turn out to be useful at some time in the future—knowing the location of a hollow log in which to hide, for example, may someday mean the difference between life and death for an animal being pursued by a predator. Thus curiosity may have its own selective advantage in the generalized preparation it gives the animal for dealing with the unexpected at some later time.

Insight Learning: Implicit Manipulation of Experience

An advanced form of learning involves the ability to put together mentally a number of isolated experiences, the outcome being an entirely different response to a situation. Many animals learn by trial and error, but animals that display **insight learning** find the correct response much more rapidly, possibly through "internalized" trials (Figure 27.10). Such insight learning is probably restricted to the more complex animals, such as apes and human beings. It was a key factor in the process of human evolution, as the recorded bits of cultural evolution would imply (Chapter 33). But because of its apparent absence in most species and its rudimentary nature in those nonhuman species in which it exists, virtually all extensive studies of the phenomenon have been performed with human subjects. Consequently, extensive generalization is not yet possible. (Nonhuman animals have less occasion to use insight learning in their natural habitats because innate behavior, conditioning, and so forth are adequate to cope with most everyday situations. On the other hand, humans have had to depend on insight learning to survive for most of their existence.)

THE MECHANISM OF LEARNING

What mechanism underlies all the various learning processes just described? That mechanism must be explained in

Figure 27.10 Photographs illustrating Wolfgang Kohler's findings of insight learning in chimpanzees. In this experiment, Kohler hung bananas from the ceiling, out of reach of the chimpanzees, and then he put boxes of various sizes inside the room. When the bananas were suspended low enough so that they could be reached simply by standing on one box, the animals quickly found the solution without the need for trial-and-error learning. When two boxes were needed to reach the bananas, the chimpanzees would first try one, then step back and eye the situation, then suddenly run to another box, put it on top of the first one, and climb up to reach the bananas. (In one case, the chimpanzee led the experimenter by the hand so that he was right below the bananas, and then the animal leaped on his shoulders and grabbed the fruit.)

terms of the basic structure of the nervous system. Somehow, experience produces changes within the nervous system so that a repetition of the stimulus elicits a new pattern of motor outputs and, hence, a new form of behavior. These changes in neural output represent a sort of record of the experience—in other words, a memory, or memory trace.

But what is the nature of the change that occurs when a memory is stored? How does a given sensory input produce a given memory? How does the same stimulus pattern now call for playback of a learned behavior? Where is a memory stored?

There are some indications of localization of learning processes in the brain. For example, destruction of the rear part of the cortex in a rat impairs the ability to discriminate between different stimuli—but it does not impair the ability to learn certain sequences of responses to a single stimulus. In contrast, destruction of the front part of the rat's cortex impairs performance in sequence learning—but it does not interfere with sensory discriminations. Similarly, damage to certain areas of a monkey cortex somehow interferes with learning tasks that involve different senses or different kinds of problems. But it is not clear from these experiments whether the brain damage is affecting the ability to process sensory information, the ability to perform certain kinds of associations, the ability to store and retrieve memories, or the ability to organize motor outputs.

Although the associative areas of the cortex do appear to be involved in learning and in memory, it has been impossible to assign a specific function to any localized region in these areas. Most evidence is consistent with the idea that storage of memory involves changes occurring over a wide region of the cortex, and probably in other parts of the brain as well. This diffuse storage of information is one of the key puzzles that must be explained by any theory or model of memory and learning.

A Structural Model for the Learning Process

John Eccles has argued for a simple structural model of learning processes. He suggested that *use* of a neural pathway facilitates later transmissions along it, whereas *disuse* makes later transmissions more difficult. Certain experiments support this model. For example, if the part of a spinal nerve that is peripheral to the dorsal root (sensory) ganglion is cut off, the input of sensory impulses through that nerve is prevented. The lack of input causes the corresponding motor nerves leading from the spinal cord to shrink in size. Therefore, the strength of the reflex arc that can be evoked by electrical stimulation of the stub of the dorsal root diminishes with time. In many cases, the number of synaptic terminals at the axonal ending of dorsal root neurons diminish as a result of the cutting.

Similarly, use or disuse of a neural pathway may cause alterations in cerebral cortex tissue. Each dendrite of a cortical neuron is covered with hundreds or thousands of minute spines upon which axons from other neurons synapse. The number of these spines may decrease when input to that area of the cortex is reduced. Conversely, an increase of activity leads to an increase in the number of spines. Spine growth could aid further transmission of impulses along that pathway. Various kinds of anatomical alterations of the nervous system do result from various kinds of experience. However, no alteration has yet been definitely associated with the storage of a memory.

A fascinating study shows how important it is to use neural circuits if their normal function is to be maintained. Consider a newborn cat, whose eyes have just opened. This animal has neurons in its visual cortex that are sensitive to certain complex shapes of visual stimuli. Many of the neurons are sensitive to input from either eye. If the cat is raised with one eye shut for a few critical months, it loses most of the binocular neurons in its visual cortex (*Interleaf 26.2*). The cells are still present—but they are driven by only one eye. Animals deprived of complex visual stimuli for a few months after they open their eyes appear to lose most of the cortical neurons that are sensitive to complex shapes or motions. Thus it would seem that complex neural circuits cannot be maintained unless they receive normal stimulation of some type, at least in one critical period of life. Whether this finding can be extrapolated to account for formation of new synapses remains to be seen. If it can, then it will be a basis for a memory storage hypothesis.

Chemical Theories of Learning

In chemical theories of learning, memory is said to result from the manufacture of specific new molecules or of

Figure 27.11 Hypothetical structural changes in learning. These diagrams show several possible but unproven ways in which learning could be mediated by anatomical changes in the processes or synapses of neurons. In cases 1 and 2, the increased use of a pathway enhances the efficiency with which its synapses function—the vital involvement of glial cells may or may not be necessary. Case 3 illustrates that some branches of a single axon may be strengthened, whereas others may be weakened as a result of the action at two different synapses. Cases 4 and 5 show structural changes that could account for conditioning. At first, both a conditioned stimulus (1) and an unconditioned stimulus (2) are required in order to fire an unconditioned response (3). If the two stimuli are paired, the synapses of neuron 1 are strengthened so that the conditioned stimulus (1) alone elicits the firing of 3 (which is now the conditioned response). In case 5, the pairing of two stimuli leads to the formation of a new synapse, so that neuron 1 comes to fire both output neurons.

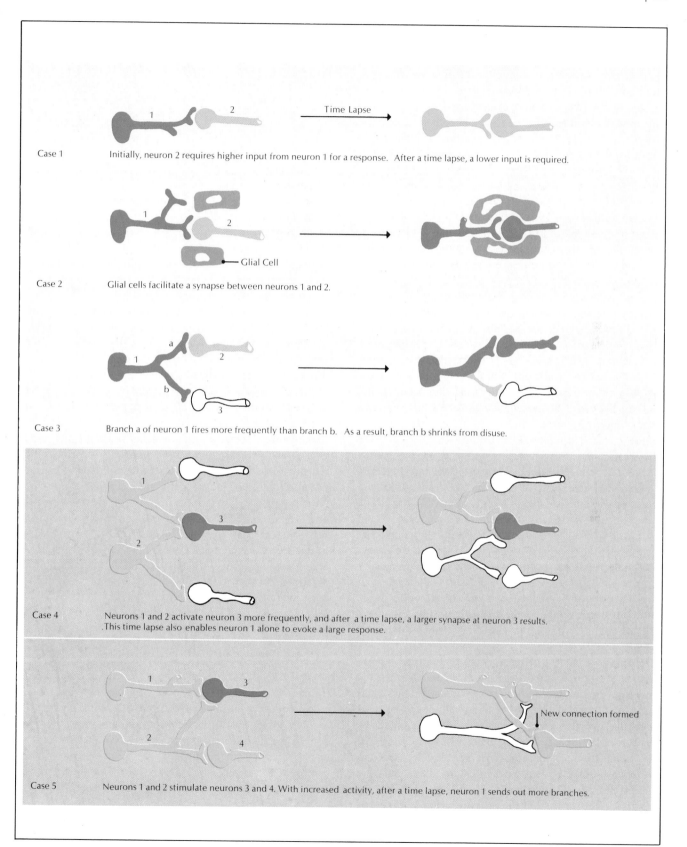

Case 1   Initially, neuron 2 requires higher input from neuron 1 for a response. After a time lapse, a lower input is required.

Case 2   Glial cells facilitate a synapse between neurons 1 and 2.

Case 3   Branch a of neuron 1 fires more frequently than branch b. As a result, branch b shrinks from disuse.

Case 4   Neurons 1 and 2 activate neuron 3 more frequently, and after a time lapse, a larger synapse at neuron 3 results. This time lapse also enables neuron 1 alone to evoke a large response.

Case 5   Neurons 1 and 2 stimulate neurons 3 and 4. With increased activity, after a time lapse, neuron 1 sends out more branches.

alterations in the concentration, location, or availability of existing molecules. Any measurable chemical changes that accompany learning or any chemicals that can be shown to alter learning are thought to imply that molecules must play an important role in memory.

Among the first and most controversial experiments in this area were those that presumably demonstrated the transfer of learning in planarians. If a trained planarian is cut in half, the head section regenerates a new tail, the tail section regenerates a new head, and—according to the early reports—both of the new individuals show some higher-than-expected ability to relearn the same task. It has been reported further that if trained worms are cut in several pieces, all the regenerated sections are better at relearning. The intriguing thing about these experiments is that all but the head sections must grow an entirely new head ganglion, or "brain."

Could it be that memories might be stored in chemical changes in cells throughout the worm's body? Planarians were trained, cut up, and fed to untrained, cannibalistic planarians. The cannibals were subsequently trained on the same task as that learned by the worms they had eaten. Planarians fed on "educated" worms were said to learn the task faster than did control animals fed on untrained worms! Because RNA is an abundant macromolecule that is known to be involved in major cellular alterations through protein synthesis, the researchers suspected that RNA might be the "memory molecule." To test this theory, they extracted RNA from trained worms and injected it into untrained worms. They reported that the injected worms performed better at learning than did worms injected with RNA extracted from untrained worms. However, more recent research suggests that a similar effect occurs when planarians are fed with untrained worms that have been stimulated in a manner that has nothing to do with the learning task being studied, or when they are injected with RNA from similarly stimulated worms, or even by providing RNA extracted from yeast! Moreover, subsequent tests have failed to confirm the results of the early "memory transfer" experiments.

Most recent studies of memory transfer have used extracts of the brain of trained and untrained animals. For the most part, the results have been rather equivocal. Some sort of memory transfer has now been reported in many experiments that appear to be well controlled; the magnitude of the differences between the performance of rats injected with extracts from brains of trained and untrained rats was greater than could be explained by chance alone. In some cases, a nonspecific stimulation of learning ability appears to be ruled out, because enhanced learning did not seem to occur with regard to stimuli or responses other than those used in conditioning the donor animals. Indeed, in at least one experiment, the two populations of rats used as a source

Figure 27.12 The effect of the protein-inhibiting drug puromycin on long-term memory. (a) Three groups of rats were trained to perform a simple task. One minute after the training period one group (C) received an injection of puromycin, the second group (B) received an injection of salt solution, and the third group (A) received no injection. At first there were no significant differences between the tested performances of the puromycin-injected rats and the controls, but after several hours the puromycin-treated rats performed more and more poorly. Apparently, protein synthesis is required to convert short-term memory to long-term memory. (b) If puromycin injection was delayed ninety minutes or more after training, the drug did not seem to interfere with memory.

of brain extract were conditioned in different ways. Each of these extracts *appeared* to transfer the corresponding responses to the differently trained recipients.

Those who look at such experiments with a critical eye invariably find weaknesses in the experimental design—if not in the behavior, then in the chemistry or the statistics. (Indeed, one thing that makes biologists leery of accepting this kind of report is the absence of any consistency in the chemical extraction and purification procedures used by different research groups.) For obvious reasons, feelings run high on this issue. Many scientists who would view research in any other area quite objectively tend to be either overly critical and conservative or overly uncritical and receptive in evaluating these experiments. It now appears that the number of independent reports of successful transfer is so large, yet the number of difficulties in experimental design and analysis so great, that the only conclusion warranted is that final judgment must be suspended.

In studies of the effects of drugs on memory retention, it has in fact been shown that drugs interfering with protein synthesis have no effect on short-term memory—but that they prevent long-term memory storage (Figure 27.12). However, studies with drugs that interfere with RNA synthesis failed to suggest a role for RNA in memory storage. In these latter studies, memory was not impaired even when RNA synthesis was reduced to 4 percent of its normal level. Unfortunately, the doses used in these studies caused the animals to die within twenty-four hours after injection, so it is not possible to determine how RNA synthesis might act in long-term memory storage. Another line of research has supported the concept that after training, a change can be detected in the composition of an animal's nerve cell RNA. But once again, there is controversy over the proper interpretation of these findings.

In summary, it appears that long-term memory storage probably involves changes in the RNA content and in protein synthesis within neurons. But the relationship of these changes to memory mechanisms is not known.

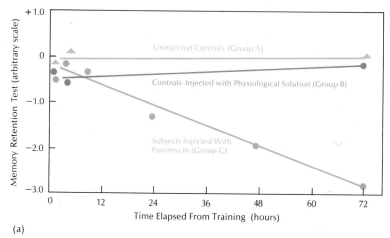

(a)

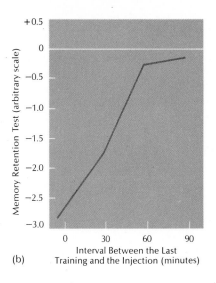

(b)

Fundamentally, the questions are these: Does memory involve synthesis of rather generalized molecules in specific neurons? Or does it involve the synthesis of very specific molecules that in a sense encode the memory? Is it the molecules themselves, or the cells in which the new molecules are accumulated, that determine the nature of the memory storage that has occurred? The whole history of neurobiology—with its emphasis on precise interconnections and pathways from stimulus to response—would seem to suggest it should be the neuronal pathways that provide specificity. But the fact that certain kinds of memory banks cannot be localized in defined regions of the cerebral cortex is seen by some researchers as supporting what the memory transfer experiments suggest—that memory is not so much the enhancement of a specific pathway as it is a specific chemical state of the cerebral cortex.

PERSPECTIVE

The behavioral patterns of animals, like all the other physiological and morphological adaptations seen in living organisms, are designs for survival that have been worked out over evolutionary time. Some are more complex than others because selective pressures have existed that have made them so. If complex behaviors were not called for, the animal and all the generations following retained a simple behavioral repertoire, consisting of stereotyped responses to fairly predictable stimuli. As long as conditions remained the same, even such limited responses would be effective for survival.

All this sounds plausible enough, given what we know of the evolutionary record. However, the actual roads leading to complex forms of behavior will never be known. They must have paralleled the course of ever-increasing complexity of design seen in fossil forms. But evolving forms of behavior cannot be fossilized. Behavior is a response to a stimulus—an act that is a moment in time, leaving only tantalizing echoes in existing behaviors.

Today we try to examine the "phylogenetic learning" of

an animal—its innate behaviors that are inherited just as other characteristics of its species are inherited. And we also try to sort through the layerings of learned behavior—the changes in response as a result of experience. Although little is left to learning in many simple animals, such as the female tick locked in her genetically programmed ambush of a mammalian passerby, in complex animals the interplay among behaviors has to be astounding. So much is variable: the nature, timing, duration, and intensity of any experience, as well as the genetically determined capacity of a given animal to learn from it. The little we do know about the learning process has been sketched out in this chapter. In the subsequent chapters of this section, we will turn to the level at which most has been observed—the level of the whole animal and its behavioral relationship with its environment.

SUGGESTED READINGS

HINDE, R. A. *Biological Bases of Human Social Behavior*. New York: McGraw-Hill, 1974. An important work bringing together much of the recent literature.

LORENZ, KONRAD. *King Solomon's Ring*. New York: Crowell, 1961. If you haven't as yet been turned on to animal behavior, you will be after reading this book.

MCGILL, T. E. *Readings in Animal Behavior*. New York: Holt, Rinehart and Winston, 1965. An excellent collection of some of the important recent advances in the field.

MAIER, N. R., and T. C. SCHNIERLA. *Principles of Animal Psychology*. Rev. ed. New York: Dover, 1964. This reprint of the 1935 classic includes updating supplementary articles.

MARLER, PETER, and W. J. HAMILTON. *Mechanisms of Animal Behavior*. New York: Wiley, 1966. A very good general reference in animal behavior.

TINBERGEN, NIKO. *The Study of Instinct*. New York: Oxford, 1951. A classic in animal behavior.

Chapter 28

Orientation in Time and Space

Success in the game of life demands that an animal be able to respond rapidly to changes in the physical environment that affect its ability to function optimally. Here we see a horned lizard doing just that. It is using overt behavior to do what mammals do physiologically: control body temperature. But in many cases, success demands more than the capacity to respond—it demands the capacity to predict changes before they occur: to predict the coming of daylight and to be where prey is when the prey appears, to predict the coming of tides or seasonal changes and respond in advance. What are the mechanisms by which such orientations in time and space are achieved?

With the beginning of a new day, a horned lizard emerges from its desert sleeping site to begin its daily cycle of food-getting and other activities. In the early morning light, its legs hold the body off the cool ground, chest muscles expand its rib cage to enlarge the body surface, and most of the time the body is held at right angles to the sun. Together these behaviors tend to maximize the amount of heat the lizard gains from the sun and minimize the amount being lost to the cool morning sand. But as the day progresses, the rib cage tends to collapse somewhat and the body is held closer to the ground and more nearly parallel to the sun's rays, which decreases the amount of solar heat being gained. As the desert temperature rises to its peak, the lizard darts in and out of the shade cast by a cactus, burrowing for a period in the sand and, at times, panting and secreting fluids from its cloaca. By this combination of orientational changes to relevant parts of its environment, this so-called "cold-blooded" lizard maintains a relatively constant body temperature throughout a day in which the temperature of the surrounding air varies by as much as twenty or thirty degrees!

If any animal is to survive in this world, its behavior must be closely correlated with the physical conditions in its environment. Through its sensory organs and internal control mechanisms, an animal seeks favorable conditions and avoids unfavorable ones. Such responses are forms of orientation. In **spatial orientation**, animals adjust their positions in space by movements in response to such stimuli as light, touch, and gravity. They may orient to various stimuli—for example, visually (as a frog does when it lines itself up with a target fly), acoustically (as bats do), and chemically (as ants do). In **temporal orientation**, animals respond to regularly recurring events—the alternation of day and night, high and low tides, the changing of seasons. Spatial and temporal orientation collectively account for much of the activity we call animal behavior.

SHORT-RANGE ORIENTATION IN SPACE: TAXES AND KINESES

In simple life forms, two different mechanisms may lead to orientation. In one case, organisms perceive inequalities of light, heat, chemicals, gravity, and so forth through their sensory receptors, and they respond by making directed movements toward or away from the source of the stimulus. Such directed movement along an environmental gradient is called a **taxis** (plural, **taxes**). In the other case, organisms orient spatially by becoming relatively immotile as they enter regions that are best suited to their physiological "needs." Thus they tend to linger where favorable conditions exist. But if they should wander out of the area, their rate of movement and/or turning speeds up. This behavior,

combined with the random nature of their turning, assures a more rapid return to a favorable location. Such orientation achieved by differential rates of movement or turning is called **kinesis.**

A simple series of experiments can demonstrate not only the role of taxes in orientation but also how taxes are subject to modification by the whole complex of environmental conditions under which relevant stimuli are presented. *Polychaerous carmelensis* is a simple flatworm that resides in tide pools on the California coast. If we capture one of these worms and place it in a test tube that is completely filled with sea water and then capped, the worm will climb up the wall of the tube. If the tube is then inverted, the worm turns at once and heads upward again. As often as the tube is inverted, the worm turns and heads upward, demonstrating a **negative geotaxis** (movement directed away from the center of the earth).

If we remove some of the water from the tube, a large air bubble will brush past the worm every time the tube is inverted. As the worm crawls toward the top and the air bubble brushes past, the worm does not turn and head upward, as it did before. Now the worm continues to crawl downward. And a second inversion of the tube causes the worm to turn at once and head downward again! Thus, when the water is turbulent, signaled by the presence of air bubbles, *Polychaerous* demonstrates **positive geotaxis** rather than the negative geotaxis seen in still water.

If we now place the worm in a flat dish and shine a bright light on one spot, the worm immediately turns and heads toward the brightest part of the water, demonstrating **positive phototaxis.** But if we rock the dish as we shine the light, the worm turns *away* from the light, demonstrating **negative phototaxis** in turbulent water.

What is the adaptive significance of all this to the worm? When the water in its tide pool is quiet (when the tide is out), the worm responds negatively to gravity and positively to light, crawling up out of the crevices between the rocks and into the light to graze in its algal pastures. But as the tide rises and the first wave splashes into the pool, it responds negatively to light and positively to gravity, crawling to the safety of a deep crevice and escaping injury from the battering of the surf. Thus, much of the behavior of this simple organism can be explained on the basis of two simple taxes and an environmental modifier.

It was once assumed that the behavioral orientations of more complex organisms could be explained on such simple bases, even though the number of interacting stimuli was expected to be high. But today there is better appreciation of the roles of learning and choice in orientation and day-to-day life in the environment. For example, honeybees, when exposed to smoke, normally enter their hive and engorge with honey—in apparent preparation to abscond with it in the event of fire. Although this behavior has been described as innate and has been explained in ''simple'' mechanistic terms, more recent research indicates that it is modifiable. When bees are deliberately conditioned to associate the odor of smoke with the presence of food at an experimental feeder, they readily learn to leave their hive and fly *to* the food dish whenever they are exposed to smoke.

HOMING BEHAVIOR OFTEN INVOLVES COMPLEX ORIENTATION MECHANISMS

Animals with a nest site must be able to return to it after foraging, gathering nest materials, or escaping from predators. This kind of orientation is called **homing behavior.** It occurs in a wide variety of animals, and most often it can be explained by invoking the concept of memorization of landmarks. An animal somehow memorizes the location of distinctive objects and thereby find its way back home (Figure 28.2).

Homing pigeons and a few other animals often return to nesting sites after being displaced for great distances and then released in unfamiliar territory. There are cases in which pigeons released almost 1,000 kilometers (about 600 miles) from their home have returned within a single day! It appears that such long-range homing is a three-stage operation. Birds released in an unfamiliar territory initially circle in ever-widening arcs, next they travel in relatively straight lines on as-yet ill-defined cues, and then they change course and fly home rather directly once they have sighted familiar landmarks. It is the second stage of the search that is the most puzzling. It has been suggested that birds might orient themselves by means of odors drifting downwind. But this explanation would restrict homing capacity to upwind directions—which is not supported by field observations. Some researchers have suggested a magnetic orientation, some an orientation by means of variations in the apparent position of the sun overhead, and others an orientation by means of turbulences in air masses (as are characteristic of coastlines). But because homing behavior is not restricted to movement parallel to magnetic lines of force, to sunny days, or to coastlines, these suggestions are inadequate to explain all cases. Whatever the process, long-range homing behavior indicates the ability of animals to orient themselves spatially and to maintain this orientation over long distances. The most dramatic examples of this ability are found in the movements of migratory animals.

MASS MOVEMENT AND MIGRATION

At certain times, thousands of animals can be seen traveling in the same direction. In many cases they are merely moving with or against the wind or a water current. Sometimes they are briefly moving away from a disturbance or toward a food supply. Movements may also persist for days on end with no clear relationship to wind speed or direction. It is also possible that relatively *few* members of a population may travel great distances, even though most of the population remains in one area. All these mass movements involve forms of orientation. But each may represent something quite different from the others in terms of its biological significance. How can we be certain that actual migration is occurring?

Consider the populations of painted lady butterflies in southern California. It is not unusual to see thousands of these insects travel by in the same direction for several days in a row. Clearly, they all are orienting to the same

Figure 28.2 Spatial orientation of a female digger wasp. The ethologist Niko Tinbergen perceived that the wasp must distinguish arrangements of objects around its burrow so that it can find its way back from foraging expeditions. Tinbergen trained the wasp to recognize a circle of pine cones around a burrow (a). Then, when the wasp was away foraging, he moved the cones slightly away from the burrow—which nevertheless was still in plain view (b). In such experiments the wasp could not find the burrow.

To test whether differentiation was made according to the forms themselves or to the arrangement of forms, Tinbergen offered the wasp a choice between a circle of pebbles (c) and a triangle of pine cones (d). The wasp responded to the pebbles, which indicated that the arrangement of objects in the environment—not the objects themselves—is used in orientation.

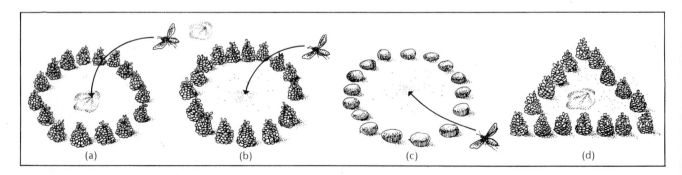

(a)   (b)   (c)   (d)

environmental stimulus, and we can call it a mass movement. But is it also a migration? The answer is not yet known. Another example of mass movement is the huge locust swarms in North Africa and the Middle East. But such swarmings are not goal-directed migrations. The best evidence available suggests that when locusts are short of food, they move out en masse, flying against light winds but being carried by strong winds. By knowing enough about prevailing winds and local weather, it is possible to estimate the ultimate "destination" of a swarm of locusts.

In contrast to these puzzling cases of mass movement, there are many species of animals that characteristically travel long distances and return home again. Some golden plovers make an annual trip from their breeding grounds in northeastern Canada to South America and back—a round trip covering almost 26,000 kilometers (about 16,000 miles). Amazingly, the time it takes a golden plover to travel the nonstop, open-ocean part of the journey from Nova Scotia to northern Brazil—a distance of nearly 5,000 kilometers (about 3,000 miles)—is a mere 48 hours! Similarly, the western population of plovers makes its nonstop flight from Alaska to Hawaii in 35 hours! This is a prodigious feat, considering the small size of these birds.

These examples enable us to make a distinction between mass movement and migration. If virtually all animals of a population move in a given direction at a certain time of the year, if they have apparent goal orientation and thereby end up in predictable locations year after year, and if the same animals make round trips, a true **migration** exists.

What are the mechanisms that guide migrating species unerringly to their destination? It has been suggested that some animals might use prominent landmarks to find their way south in the fall and north in the spring. For example, the most common routes of migration that birds use in the Western Hemisphere are river courses such as the Mississippi Valley in the Midwest, the long Central Valley in California, the predominantly north-south mountain ranges of the eastern and western states, and the coastlines. The use of landmarks appears to be particularly important in the relatively short-range movements of migratory mammals such as American elk, which move into mountainous country in spring and back down onto the plains in the winter. Similarly, caribou migrate seasonally in the arctic tundra, and some African mammals move seasonally with changing rainfall. There is no reason to believe that landmark-cued migration involves anything other than learning by the young, which—while accompanying the adults—learn both the seasonal cues and the routes of migration that have proved to be of adaptive value to the species in the past.

But the use of landmarks alone cannot explain all migratory movements. Every three or four years, green turtles migrate from Brazil to a tiny island in the South Atlantic Ocean, traveling through the high seas for more than 1,000 kilometers and yet invariably homing in on a bit of land 8 kilometers (5 miles) across. Are there cues in the currents of wind and water? In the earth's magnetic field? In the sun and stars? The answers to these questions are not yet known. Part of the problem lies in the fact that more than one possible orientational cue exists in each case, and we are probably not yet aware of the nature of all the cues that are used.

For example, once salmon hatch in mountain streams, they soon begin a journey that takes them to the rich feeding grounds of the open sea, hundreds of miles away. After a

Atlantic Golden Plover Breeding Range

Pacific Golden Plover Breeding Range

Winter Ranges

Figure 28.3 Distribution and migration of the golden plover. Adults of the eastern form migrate across northeastern Canada and then by a nonstop flight reach South America. In spring they return by way of the Mississippi Valley. Their entire route is therefore in the form of a great ellipse with a major axis of about 13,000 kilometers (8,000 miles) and a minor axis of more than 3,000 kilometers (about 2,000 miles). The Pacific golden plover, which breeds in Alaska, apparently makes a nonstop flight across the ocean to Hawaii, the Marquesas Islands, and the Low Archipelago, returning in spring over the same route.

(a)

(b)

(c)

Figure 28.4   A moment in the mass movements of (a) monarch butterflies, (b) Canadian geese, and (c) whales.

The monarch butterfly (Danaus plexippus) *has been thought to be the only species of butterfly that performs a seasonal migration. Each winter monarchs congregate in enormous populations on specific groves of trees in the south (most notably in California and Mexico), where they spend many weeks in relative dormancy. Some individuals marked in the north have been recovered in the Southern aggregations. But some recent research casts doubt on the concept that the bulk of the individuals found in the winter aggregations make such an extensive round trip. Rather, it has been suggested, they may be predominantly southern-born individuals that serve as a reservoir for northward movement in the spring.*

Canadian geese have summer breeding ranges from northern California and the north central United States to the Arctic. But winter finds them in the southernmost parts of the United States and in Mexico.

Each year, as the ice pack begins to form in the Bering Sea, gray whales stop feeding to begin their migration southward along the Pacific Coast of North America. Eventually they reach the warm lagoons of Baja California and the Sonora-Sinaloa coast of Mexico, where calving takes place. In spring, the journey is reversed and the whales spend the summer feeding in northern seas. The round trip is 14,000 miles, or about 22,500 kilometers.

few years, they unerringly return to the same stream in which they were hatched—no matter how far their ocean wanderings have carried them away from the estuary that marks the gateway home, no matter how many different streams feed into the same river system, no matter how much the course bends and twists and climbs past foaming rapids. Through the studies of Arthur Hasler, we know that salmon have particularly sensitive chemoreceptors. When Hasler plugged the noses of homing salmon with cotton, the fish could not locate their spawning grounds. Thus salmon rely extensively on the detection of chemical characteristics of water in different ocean currents and fresh-water streams to help guide them back to their spawning grounds. But is their sense of smell the only orientational factor? Possibly landmarks, temperature gradients, turbulence associated with ocean currents, and sounds (made by waterfalls along the homeward route, for example, and by rapids) also act as cues. But even though it may be possible to identify the cues themselves, how is it that salmon remember *all* the cues along a one-time round trip that may be thousands of miles long?

The astonishing migrations of certain birds are even more puzzling. The golden plovers mentioned earlier have no obvious landmarks to follow. Studies of European storks, which migrate in the winter to Africa, show that even birds that travel primarily over land may orient themselves by maintaining a particular compass direction rather than by following landmarks. In these studies, young storks isolated from their flock before their first migration were moved a considerable distance east or west. When they were released, they did not head directly toward the normal destination. Instead, they followed the precise *compass direction* characteristic of the migration of their species at that time of year. Apparently, because they were starting from the wrong location, their flight path correspondingly carried them to a wrong destination. Similar results have been obtained with other bird species.

Such compass-oriented flight requires a finely tuned navigational sense. Studies of day-flying birds indicate that they use the sun as a directional indicator. In the 1940s, the German ornithologist Gustav Kramer noticed that starlings kept in an outdoor aviary flew about randomly most of the year, but in spring and fall their flutterings were highly directional, corresponding to the migratory orientations of their species. In other words, these birds were showing what is known as **migratory restlessness.** When the starlings were placed in a covered circular cage that had several narrow windows, they oriented themselves in a certain compass direction on sunny days. On heavily overcast days, no such orientation occurred. Both of these behaviors suggested that starlings were using visual cues with respect to sun position. Further evidence came when the visual cues were distorted. Mirrors were placed outside all of the windows, so that the view from each window was displaced 90 degrees in a clockwise direction. (For example, in looking out the west window, the birds saw instead the view to the north.) In this experiment the birds were still able to orient themselves on sunny days—but their orientation was displaced by 90 degrees from the usual compass direction!

Even at night, some night-flying birds show the same sort of migratory restlessness displayed in the daytime by starlings—provided that the stars are visible. If there is a bright moon (which causes stars to be less visible), the birds may become disoriented.

Two German zoologists, F. Sauer and E. Sauer, tested the theory of celestial navigation by experimenting with warblers under the artificial sky of a planetarium. They used both experienced birds and birds that had been raised in the laboratory without seeing either the daytime or nighttime sky. When the stars and constellations appeared, *both* groups tried to fly in the direction of the migration route characteristic of their species.

In another planetarium study, this time with indigo buntings, Stephen Emlen first demonstrated that these birds can navigate by the stars. They oriented themselves according to the way the *stars* were projected overhead, not according to true south. Emlen went on to demonstrate the existence of internal mechanisms that help determine responses to directional cues. He kept birds under artificial lighting conditions and altered the length of time the lights were on each day, thereby creating the illusion of natural seasonal changes. One group of birds was exposed to increasingly shorter periods of light and longer periods of darkness; thus it was led to respond as if it were time for the autumn (southward) migration. Another group was exposed to lengthening periods of light as if the time for the spring (northward) migration was approaching. When Emlen tested both groups at once under an artificial spring sky in the planetarium, the groups gave entirely different responses! The birds on an autumnlike light cycle tried to fly south; the other birds oriented themselves in the opposite direction.

The use of sun or stars in navigation requires an incredibly precise time sense. Not only does the apparent angle of the sun in the sky vary from minute to minute during the day, it varies from day to day during the year. At any given point on our planet, the compass direction defined by the sun one hour after dawn depends on the day of the year. And with each passing hour, the sun appears to move 15 degrees from east to west and a variable amount from north to south or from south to north. In order for a human being to use the sun as a compass, then, it is necessary to know the day of the year, the hour of the day, and the latitude from which the sun is being viewed. If a migratory bird is to use the sun as a compass, it must continuously compensate not only for the sun's apparent east-west and north-south movement but also for its own north-south movement! The stars, too, show the same apparent seasonal and hourly displacements, which must be taken into account by night-flying birds. What are the internal mechanisms that enable animals to synchronize their behavior with such complex rhythmic changes of the environment?

RHYTHMS AND BIOLOGICAL CLOCKS: ORIENTATION IN TIME

Rhythmic events occur throughout the world. The sun rises and sets, the moon moves through its monthly cycle, the tides and seasons repeat their inexorable rhythms. Temperature, light, humidity, weather, and other factors in the environment vary accordingly with each cyclic change.

Organisms adapt behaviorally as well as physiologically to these rhythms of nature, thus enhancing the likelihood of getting enough food and of producing offspring. These rhythmic adaptations occur at the levels of cells and organs as well as at the level of the whole organism; they affect metabolism, physiology, and behavior. Thus, animals not only can exploit the most favorable aspects of the day (or month, or season, or tide), they can even anticipate them.

Circadian Rhythms Are Approximately One-Day Cycles

Behavioral activities that are correlated with a one-day cycle under fairly constant conditions are called **circadian rhythms**. Both **diurnal** and **nocturnal** organisms (those normally active in the daytime and in the nighttime, respectively) exhibit circadian rhythms that are tied to the daily light cycle.

As an example of a circadian rhythm in a simple life form, consider the ascomycete *Daldinia concentrica*, whose black, spherical fruiting body is found on dead trees. The outside of this fungus is pitted with numerous cavities, each lined with many sacs that ripen and periodically discharge spores at night for a period of several weeks. Under natural conditions, a single fungus may release as many as 100 million spores in a single night. This circadian rhythm was studied in a rather unusual manner. Detached, ripe fruiting bodies were mounted on a model-railroad flatcar and covered with a transparent top with a narrow opening (Figure 28.5*a*). The loaded flatcar was pulled very slowly along a short length of track at a uniform rate by a clock motor and pulley system. Twelve glass slides were attached on a framework above the rack so that the car passed beneath a new slide every two hours. As the sticky spores were discharged through the opening in the covering, they became stuck to the glass slides. Later they were washed off and counted. In this manner, the rate of spore discharge was continuously monitored during the daily reproductive cycle of the fruiting body. Spore discharge was found to be confined primarily to the dark period of the 24-hour cycle (Figure 28.5*b*).

Circadian rhythms also control events that occur only once in an individual's life. A well-studied example is the emergence rhythm of *Drosophila pseudoobscura*. A population of this species of fruit fly was maintained at constant temperature in an environment where 12 hours of light alternated with 12 hours of darkness. On the seventeenth day of their twenty-five-day life cycle, emergence of adults

from puparia began near the onset of the light period. Within a few hours, emergence stopped, but another peak of activity occurred exactly 24 hours after the first one. As Figure 28.6*a* shows, the amplitude of the 24-hour rhythm gradually decreased from day to day until all flies had emerged (by the sixth day). If the larvae were never exposed to light-dark cycles, no such rhythm was observed (Figure 28.6*b*). Under natural conditions, this species of *Drosophila* emerges from the pupal cases a few hours after dawn—a time when humidity tends to be high. This timing is critical for the emerging fly, for its cuticle is still hardening and its delicate wings are still unfurling. If it emerged later, the drier air would cause the wings to dry before they had unfurled. If it emerged earlier, the drying and hardening of the wings and body would be delayed and the fly would be exposed to the danger of predation, because it would be unable to escape by flight.

Circadian rhythms are widespread and their control is complex. But before examining this problem in more detail,

Figure 28.5 (a) Apparatus used to measure spore discharge of the asocomycete Daldinia concentrica *during 24-hour periods for eleven days (see text). (b) Periodicity of spore discharge in* Daldinia concentrica. *The rate of spore discharge can be correlated with time and conditions of illumination. Day-night periods are indicated by the horizontal strip below the bar graphs. Spore discharge is highly rhythmic within the 24-hour period and is confined chiefly to the dark period.*

Notice that when day length was modified on July 8, the spore release cycle was modified accordingly: two peaks of release occurred on days with two light and two dark periods. But when the organism was plunged into total darkness, spore release reverted to a circadian pattern, which—although less synchronous—peaked around midnight or early morning. Taken together, these results suggest two things: Spore release can be triggered in other than a circadian pattern by alternating periods of light and dark, but in the absence of light and stimuli, it maintains a circadian rhythm.

(a)

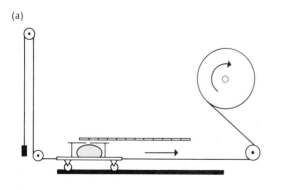

(b)

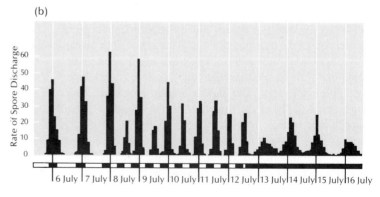

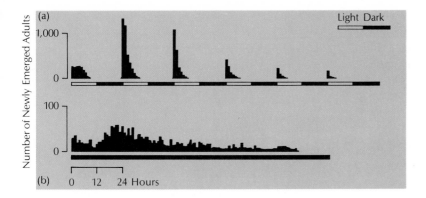

let us look briefly at certain other natural rhythms of greater duration, for the control of all such rhythms shares common features.

Tidal Rhythms Are Linked With Certain Ecological Niches

At certain times of the year along the California coast, on foaming breakers of the particularly high tides that occur on nights of the full moon and of the new moon, thousands of the fish called grunion come ashore to lay eggs. In correlating their spawning behavior with high tide, the grunion are able to reach a position on the beach where they can bury their eggs in the sand near the highest water line, out of reach of the daily wave action that would wash the eggs away. The buried eggs incubate in the sand and do not hatch until two weeks later. The tiny grunion emerge just in time for the next high tide, to be carried out to sea by the retreating waters.

Clearly the spawning behavior of this species is linked to both the 12.4-hour daily rhythm of the tides and the monthly cycle of the moon's rotation about the earth. Other animals, such as molluscs, synchronize their feeding behavior with the tides; still others scurry to shelter before and during the time when the water recedes from the shore. Consider the fiddler crab, which lives in the intertidal zone. This crab changes color as the pigment in its epidermal chromatophore cells moves in synchrony with the changing of day into night. This rhythm is not only circadian, it also is tidal: the pigment is darkest at the time of low tide. Crabs captured on the beach and then kept completely away from both light and tides become their darkest at nearly the same time every fifteen days, which coincides with the interval required for peaks of the 24-hour light-dark cycle and the 12.4-hour tidal cycle to occur together! Experiments with artificial light cycles suggest that both the circadian rhythm and the tidal rhythms of these crabs can be phase-shifted by light stimuli that occur in other than a 24-hour repeat. Thus,

Figure 28.6   The role of light in establishing a circadian rhythm in emergence of Drosophila pseudoobscura *adults from their pupal cases. A population of pupae was placed in an automated device that collected newly emerged adults every half-hour. (a) When the pupae were exposed to alternate 12-hour periods of light and dark, the emergence of adults was highly synchronized and reached its peak immediately after the lights came on. (b) In continuous darkness, no such circadian rhythm is detectable. But when larvae and pupae are maintained in constant darkness except for a brief flash of light once every twenty-four hours, the emergence of the adults is synchronous, just as it is in the normal alternating light-dark cycle.*

*Figure 28.7   The fiddler crab (*Uca minax*). These intertidal animals exhibit rhythmic changes in coloration that can be correlated with light-dark and tidal cycles.*

as with the fungus discussed earlier, in the absence of visual cues the crabs seem to maintain an internal clock that runs on a 24-hour basis and predicts both light cycles and tide cycles. But this clock can be reset daily by the cyclic appearance of alternating periods of light or dark. This, as we will see, appears to be a rather generalized phenomenon: an ''internal'' clock that can be reset daily by appropriate environmental stimuli.

Photoperiodic Events in Annual and Seasonal Rhythms

Many seasonal and annual biological rhythms are **photoperiodic events;** in other words, certain critical aspects of the daily light-dark periods (such as seasonal changes in day length) trigger changes in physiology and behavior. Among the events under photoperiodic control are the flowering of certain plants, the germination of some seeds, the hibernation of some vertebrates, the metamorphosis in the life cycle of some insects, the initiation of reproductive cycles in many species, and the migration of birds and mammals.

In many such cases, it has been shown that it is not how much light the organisms are actually exposed to that regulates photoperiodic events. Rather, it is the *apparent* length of day and night that is important. Many experiments show that two brief light periods separated by a brief dark period will often be summed by an organism to yield an effect identical to that of a long period of continuous light.

A case in point is the behavior of the male white-crowned sparrow. In these sparrows, as in many bird species, the testes of the male enlarge in spring in preparation for the annual reproductive cycle. In the laboratory, this enlargement can be achieved by exposing the birds to light periods of 10 hours or more per day. But if the birds are given only 8 hours of light per day in two periods separated by a short dark period, they behave as if the lights had been on continuously during this period and they undergo sexual development (Figure 28.8).

The common house finch of western North America may be used to illustrate further the nature of photoperiodicity and the interaction between light-dark periods and the circadian rhythm. The testes of these finches also become enlarged in response to long days (10 to 12 hours of light per day or more).

During the early 1960s, William Hamner explored the nature of the biological clock in these birds. First, control finches were kept in an environment with a light-dark cycle of 6 hours of light and 18 hours of darkness. As Hamner expected, these birds showed no signs of testicular enlargement, even at the time of year when this phenomenon normally occurs in wild birds. Next, separate groups of

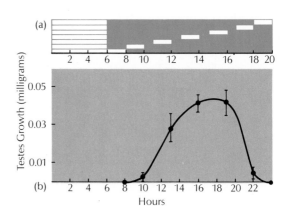

Figure 28.8   Testicular enlargement in male white-crowned sparrows as a function of apparent day length. (a) The light-dark cycles to which each group of birds was exposed. All received 6 hours of continuous light. The subsequent 18 hours of darkness was interrupted each day by a 2-hour light period, which occurred at a different time for each group. Thus each group experienced a total of 8 hours of light per day, but the duration of their dark periods varied. (b) The growth response of the testes in the various groups. Apparently, the birds tended to include in their light period the shorter of the two dark intervals to which they were exposed, treating only the longer dark interval as the night. Thus, if one longer dark period was less than 14 hours, the birds reacted as if they were on a ''long day'' (10 hours of light or more) and underwent testicular enlargement typical of the lengthening days of spring.

Figure 28.9   The effect of variable dark periods on testicular enlargement in male finches exposed to light for 6 hours at a time. If the dark period was such that the second light period began in the first quarter of the day (18, 42, or 66 hours later) the birds acted as though they were exposed to short days, and no testicular development occurred. (This is indicated by negative signs to the right.) But if the dark interval (6, 30, or 54 hours) was such that the second light period fell in the third quarter of the day, the birds acted as though they were on long days and testicular development ensued. (Positive signs to right.) Thus birds receiving illumination only 6 hours every two and one-half days acted as though they were on long days! The simplest interpretation is that the birds bear some record of when prior periods of illumination occurred in their circadian cycle and that they sum real and remembered periods of illumination to obtain a measure of apparent day length.

experimental birds were exposed to 6-hour light periods interspersed with dark periods of 6, 18, 30, 42, 54, or 66 hours. Those birds exposed to 6-, 30-, or 54-hour dark periods underwent testicular enlargement as would be expected if they perceived that they were on a long day. But those experiencing 18-, 42-, or 66-hour dark periods showed no testicular enlargement! How can we explain such results? It is *as if* the birds bear some record of the period during their circadian cycle when light was last present. Then, when a new light period does occur, the two are summed to yield an apparent day length (Figure 28.9).

Many additional experiments reinforce this interpretation that birds exposed to prolonged darkness do, by some mechanism, recall the duration of light to which they were previously exposed. Thus, birds exposed to long days for a sufficient number of cycles and then plunged into continuous darkness continue to develop as though the long days were continuing. (In contrast, if a similar series of long days is followed by a series of short days, sexual development is reversed.) Such long-day reactivity in the dark can be prolonged and intensified by presenting brief flashes of light at the hours the lights came on and went off during the last long day.

Similar phenomena have been described by the German physiologist Erwin Bünning, especially in arctic plants, many of which require 13 hours of daylight to initiate flowering. Alteration of the photoperiod is employed by many commercial florists to produce flowers out of season.

WHAT EXPLAINS PERSISTENT BIOLOGICAL RHYTHMS IN CONTROLLED ENVIRONMENTS?

It is clear from the preceding discussion that direct stimulation by environmental rhythms is not the only factor governing the rhythmicity of animal behavior. When animals are removed from their natural habitat and placed in a controlled environment in which light intensity, temperature, pressure, humidity, and chemical composition are held constant, they may continue to exhibit rhythmic fluctuations.

Theories concerning this persistence of behavioral rhythms fall into two categories. According to the theory of **exogenous periodicity,** there are always subtle periodic changes in the planet itself (such as changes in the magnetic field) that influence even laboratory-isolated animals. These geophysical factors vary cyclically and are said to *entrain*

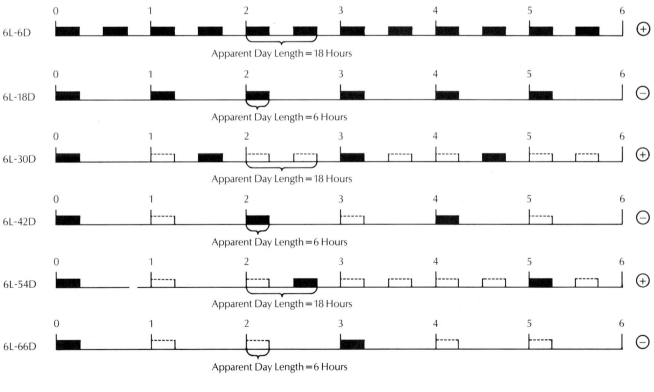

Period of Actual Illumination   Period of "Remembered" Illumination

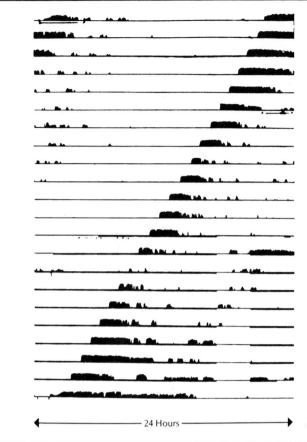

Figure 28.10   Twenty-two-day record of the running activity of a small mammal kept in a laboratory darkroom without the daily light-dark cycle. The chart records of each day, placed below one another, show that the activity began earlier each day.

← 24 Hours →

(or synchronize) the organism's behavior. According to the theory of **endogenous periodicity,** animals have *internal biological clocks* that determine the timing of changes in physiological and behavioral state. Stimuli from the outside world are said to reset this clock only periodically so that it does not get out of step with the physical world.

We can get an inkling of the complexity of the problem of rhythm persistence by observing what happens when an animal is placed in an environment that is free of the usual external rhythmic stimuli. The **free-running behavioral cycles** that emerge in such a controlled environment are usually a bit different from the 24-hour rhythms seen in nature, and they differ slightly from one individual of the species to the next. For example, Figure 28.10 shows the rate of running activity of a small mammal kept in constant darkness in the laboratory. The period of activity drifted relative to real day and night, and more importantly, it drifted *differently* in different litter mates. Such variations, then, would seem not to be correlated with geophysical factors.

Furthermore, the period of a free-running circadian rhythm shows a slight temperature dependence, for room

temperature changes of 10°C may speed up or slow down the rhythm by about 10 percent. It is difficult to reconcile this change with geophysical factors. On the other hand, chemical reactions, which are usually thought to be the basis for internal clocks, are altered to some extent by temperature changes.

If an animal exhibiting a free-running rhythm is exposed to brief periods of certain stimuli at certain times within its activity cycle, the phase of the free-running rhythm may be altered. Such alteration is presumably the mechanism by which internal clocks are normally kept synchronized to the changes in the external world.

For example, consider the findings of Jürgen Aschoff and his colleagues at the Max Planck Institute in Germany, who studied human circadian rhythms under constant environmental conditions. In this case, the "controlled environment" was a series of underground bunkers in which male human subjects could live in complete isolation for a few weeks. In these experiments, each subject established his own cycle of events—when he would pick up mail and food left in a small room adjacent to the bunker, when he would collect a urine sample, and so forth. The subject was asked

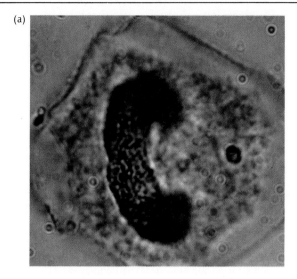

(a)

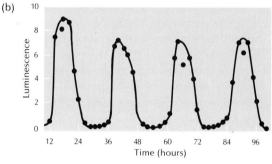

(b)

Figure 28.11   (a) The dinoflagellate Gonyaulax polyedra, *an organism that is responsible for "red tides" (Chapter 4 and 5). This organism shows circadian rhythms in photosynthesis as well as in luminescence. The rhythm of luminescence shown in (b) indicates entrainment to the 12-hour light-dark period on which the population was maintained.*

to lead a "regular" life—for example, to eat three meals a day—but not to nap after lunch. Except for doing a few tests, he was free to study, read, or listen to music.

After several days, each individual taking part in the test was out of phase with the external world. In most cases there was a 1- or 2-hour shift from the normal 24-hour day. For instance, one male kept in isolation for 19.5 days perceived 18 "days" of physiological activity. In other words, at the end of the experiment he was about 12 hours out of phase and had "lost" a day because he had maintained a circadian cycle of about 26 hours. Although the subjects seemed to become quickly entrained to the normal light-dark cycle once it was restored, it was actually several days before all their rhythmic physiological functions became fully reentrained to the natural cycle.

Experiments of this sort have implications for the planning of human environmental conditions. In modern societies, people are subjected to artificial cycles of activity and rest. If you have ever traveled by jet across several time zones, you know that a shift in a natural cycle can be an uncomfortable experience, with effects that may persist for several days. Similarly, normal circadian rhythms affect

worker efficiency, accident rates, and error rates, although little is yet known about the underlying mechanisms involved.

SEARCHING FOR THE BIOCHEMICAL CLOCK

Is it possible that a single master "clock" controls all the different behavioral and physiological rhythms of the sort described in this chapter? Or are there separate clocks underlying each one? In either case, how are these rhythms synchronized and reset?

Single-celled organisms such as *Gonyaulax*, a dinoflagellate that exhibits circadian rhythms in luminescence and photosynthesis (Figure 28.11), have been used to study the chemical basis of biological clocks. It has been found that various metabolic poisons can affect some but not all of the circadian rhythms of *Gonyaulax*. For example, the luminescence rhythm can be interrupted with no effect on the photosynthetic rhythm. To date, no master control system has been identified in this organism.

Richard Wurtman and Julius Axelrod, among others, found that many mammalian organs and glands exhibit circadian rhythms in isolation from the animal. Attention has been focused on neuroendocrine organs, such as the adrenal glands and the pituitary system. Hamster adrenal glands, if maintained *in vitro*, show some metabolic cycles that can be entrained by light-dark cycles. In the intact animal, a hormone secreted with a circadian rhythm from the adrenal gland apparently controls many body rhythms, such as glycogen metabolism in the liver and epidermal mitotic activity. These cycles stop if the adrenal glands are removed, but the hamster's activity rhythm continues —indicating that the adrenal glands are *not* the site of the master biochemical clock. Investigators have, in fact, begun to suspect that there may be several clocks that are synchronized in healthy animals, clocks that may be capable of running quite independently of one another.

PERSPECTIVE

All animals have complex adaptive patterns of spatial and temporal orientation. This capacity for orientation is essential to survival, and for that reason orientation is among the most significant consequences of the evolutionary process. Reflect once more on the behavior called migration—the mass movement of animals in a goal-oriented direction that may extend for many thousands of miles in space and for rhythmic seasonal periods in time. How could such long-range migration patterns and the navigational senses they require have evolved?

Undoubtedly, the first migrations spanned lesser distances. Perhaps they had their origins in homing behaviors, those short-range movements we see today in many species. A flock of birds might find one site well endowed with nesting materials and free of predators; it might locate still another site with abundant food. Thus, there might have been frequent, rather short-term mass movement of the sort displayed by starlings that spend each night in the city and each day in the fields of the surrounding countryside.

Now, as seasonal variations in climate became more pronounced in modern times (Chapters 9 and 31), such short-range, daily mass movements might readily have been transformed into more extensive north-south seasonal movements that were fundamentally of the same nature—adaptation to one locale for seasonal feeding and another for nesting and reproduction—but that covered greater distances and time spans. Once this pattern began to develop and the magnitude of the displacements increased, the channeling effect of natural selection would undoubtedly have been potent. Individuals failing to respond to the same seasonal cues and to the same directional stimuli as other members of the population would simply fail to appear at the feeding or nesting grounds at the appropriate time, would therefore fail to leave offspring, and their genes

would be lost from the species gene pool. It is indeed difficult to imagine a more effective mechanism for channeling a population than long-range migration.

But because the selective pressure probably has always been simply to follow the same environmental cues as other members of one's own species, and because many potential cues exist, it would indeed appear unlikely that all migratory species place precisely the same emphasis on all the environmental variables that may be used either to initiate or to direct migration. Therefore, it is not unlikely that many of the controversies that have occurred concerning how long-range navigation is accomplished may be attributed to species-specific differences between various organisms that investigators have chosen to study. Each species may turn out to represent a special case, to some extent.

We might now ask, Why is it that southward-migrating birds either stop their fall journey before they reach the tropics (as in the case of Canadian geese, which migrate to the southern extremes of the temperate zone) or pass over the tropics entirely to reach the temperate region of the Southern Hemisphere (as in the case of the golden plovers)? Why are the rich resources of the tropics not exploited by migratory birds? The answers are straightforward. Rich and constant as the productivity of the tropics may appear to be, all the ecological niches are filled. Furthermore, should a migratory species ever find an available habitat in the tropics, the relative constancy of the tropical environment would be expected to act to prevent a return to the migratory habit—just as migratory birds that chance upon a zoo lagoon, where food is continuously abundant, often tend to take up year-around residence.

Orientation in space has clearly not been the only solution for survival. By orienting their activities to different times of day and night, to tides, and to seasons, for example, different animals have come to fill different ecological niches in the same location. If you were to spend a day at the ocean's edge, from dawn to dusk, and were then to watch the shore by moonlight, you would see an appearance and disappearance of birds and crabs, fishes and sandhoppers that is synchronized with patterns of light and tides—an ebbing and flowing of life as timeless as the rhythms of the physical world. If you were to find yourself in the prairies of the Midwest, the same sort of rhythms would be revealed in the activity of owls and rodents, coyotes and snakes. The rhythms extend into plant and microbial communities. Wherever you look in the natural world, you will see movements in time and space that are in one sense unique to a given animal. But in the broader sense, there is an underlying unity in these movements: the search for sustenance, for shelter, for protection, for a mate—in short, the search to assure survival of one's kind.

SUGGESTED READINGS

BROWN, FRANK A., J. W. HASTINGS, and J. D. PALMER. *The Biological Clock: Two Views.* New York: Academic Press, 1970. This book is especially interesting because it presents two contrasting possible mechanisms for the·regulation of biological rhythms.

FRAENKEL, GOTTFRIED S., and DONALD L. DUNN. *The Orientation of Animals.* New York: Dover, 1961. A reprint of a classic first published in 1940. It tends toward mechanistic explanations but is a very comprehensive discussion of the earlier works in animal orientation. Many of the experiments described can be repeated by students.

ORR, ROBERT T. *Animals in Migration.* New York: Macmillan, 1970. This book has been called ''a brilliant account of the movements—great and small and often tragic—that stir the populations of the animal kingdom.'' We agree.

STORM, ROBERT (ed.). *Animal Orientation and Navigation.* Corvallis: Oregon State University Press, 1967. Each year Oregon State University hosts a colloquium on a biological subject of general interest; publication of the papers presented gives access to the thinking of experts in the field. The 1967 volume on animal orientation includes contributions by Arthur Hasler, Denzel Ferguson, Archie Carr, William Hamilton III, Frank Bellrose, and Kenneth Norns.

Chapter 29

Behavioral Interactions Within and Among Animal Species

To understand behavior, one must understand both the sensory experience by which an animal judges its world—sight, sound, smell, touch—and the action that changes in its world provokes.

It does not matter, Alfred Wallace once said, how large and handsomely constructed an animal is if it cannot regularly find enough food to sustain itself. And it is of little long-term significance, said Charles Darwin, how well adapted an animal is to its environment if it cannot mate and thereby pass on its complex of adaptive traits to future generations. Both of these scientists perceived the importance of the physical environment in the life of every organism, but both also perceived that the ways organisms interact with others within and beyond their species boundaries is equally significant. In this chapter, we will survey the kinds of interactions in nature that underlie these intraspecific and interspecific relationships.

SIMPLE SIGNALS MAY RELEASE COMPLEX BEHAVIOR PATTERNS

If you were to observe for the first time the mock battle and chase that erupts when one male stickleback fish wanders into the established territory of another male stickleback, it would be very easy to assume that the interaction represents specific strategies devised on the spot to deal with the moment's challenge. But if you were to take an analytical approach to the meaning of this behavior, you would come to an entirely different conclusion. First of all, a simplified situation would have to be created so that the behavior could be dissected into its component parts. Perhaps this would entail carving various models of a male stickleback to see which one triggers a response from a test fish that duplicates the observed behavior. If you were to do this, you would find that no matter how lifelike the model appears to be, and no matter how it is moved in the water, the test fish will not attack it—unless the belly of the model is painted red. The amazing thing is that the response to the red-bellied model will be nearly as complex and extensive as it is in a normal encounter! Through further analysis, you would find that it is the color itself, not any particular colored shape, that elicits the whole pattern of complex behavior (Figure 29.2).

This now-classic experiment was first devised by Niko Tinbergen, and it illustrates two key characteristics of animal behavior. First, many complex behavioral displays are **fixed action patterns:** they are sequences of movements performed in a manner characteristic of the males and/or females of a species. Second, complex fixed action patterns often may be triggered by relatively simple stimuli, or **behavioral releasers.**

This second characteristic, incidentally, reaffirms a point made by the medieval scholar William of Occam: Entities, he said, should not be multiplied beyond necessity. In other words, *try simple explanations first.* In modern times his perception has been dubbed the ''law of parsimony,'' or ''Occam's razor.'' When Occam's razor has been applied to the analysis of animal behavior, it frequently has turned out

that many complex behavioral interactions are fixed action patterns triggered by simple behavioral releasers. However, such innate connections between releasers and fixed action patterns should not be taken to mean that all such patterns have no learned components. Although it is true that both the production of the releaser and the response to it often appear to be genetically predetermined, in many other cases the ability to produce a releaser appears to be learned. Furthermore, in many cases the significance of the releaser must be learned. And finally, the fixed action pattern itself may be learned and subject to extensive modification through experience.

The reaction evoked by the red-belly model of the male stickleback is an example of **aggression,** which is defined as behavior of one animal that implies intent to do injury to another. There are countless other examples of complex aggressive behavior that can be triggered by simple releasers. To give one more example, a male European robin (*Erithacus rubecula*) is unmoved by the sight of a robin model of proper shape but neutral coloration. But confront

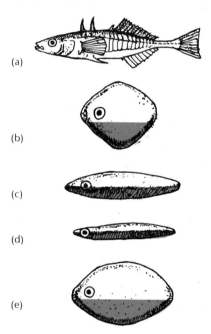

Figure 29.2 The importance of color and position as visual releasers in the behavior of a male stickleback fish. A male stickleback may ignore the uncolored model (a), which to us looks the most like the stickleback, and yet readily attack any of the four ''painted-belly'' models (b through e). In this case the position of the red patch is important. If any of the models (b) through (e) is turned upside down, a response is no longer elicited.

Once a male stickleback stakes out a territory, its belly turns red—becoming, in effect, a flag for aggressive behavior by other male sticklebacks; hence the response to these models.

him with a simple ball of red feathers similar in color to the chest feathers of a male robin, and his entire aggressive behavior pattern is released just as it would be by a real male robin wandering into his territory in spring.

Behavioral releasers are not restricted to aggressive interactions. They have in many cases been identified as agents that elicit sexual behavior. One example comes from the work of D. Magnus, who was interested in the causative factors underlying pursuit of the female fritillary butterfly (*Argynnis paphia*) during courtship. What was it that signaled the male—was it the shape of the female, her coloration, or how she fluttered her wings? Magnus constructed various models and counted the number of times each model elicited pursuit behavior in the male. In this case, shape was unimportant. An efficient releaser turned out to be a cylindrical drum painted with alternating black and red-orange stripes, rotated to produce a flicker of color reminiscent of the flickering color of the female's wings. The larger the colored cylinder, the better. Moreover, when the cylinder was rotated at high speed and the male was offered the choice between it and a slower model that more closely approximated the flickering wings of the female, he chose the more rapidly flickering one. Only when the rotating cylinder flickered at an extremely high rate did the male begin to lose interest.

A remarkable finding is that artificial releasers of this sort often appear to be more compelling than natural ones! Exaggerated artificial releasers are called **supernormal stimuli.** Oystercatchers and gulls, to give another example, will attempt to brood a model egg several times larger than their own eggs—even if the model is so large that the bird cannot assume a normal brooding position (Figure 29.3). Supernormal stimuli have also been identified in studies of the feeding response of young herring gulls. The parental

birds hold food in their beaks when they present it to the young, which peck at the beak in order to signal that they are ready to receive the food. Analysis shows that it is the characteristic red spot on the beak that functions as the releaser. A model that exaggerates this pattern acts as a supernormal stimulus (Figure 29.4). Thus, *quantitative as well as qualitative aspects of a releaser appear to be important in eliciting a given response.*

But behavioral releasers are by no means restricted to visual stimuli. Chemical, auditory, and tactile releasers are also widely employed. **Pheromones,** for example, are chemicals that act as species-specific behavioral releasers. Several of these chemical releasers were discussed in Chapter 26, such as the sexual attractant produced by certain female moths that interacts specifically with receptors on the antennae of the male of the same species. As few as 100 molecules of the pheromone are adequate to release searching behavior in the male moth. The male is also sensitive to changes in concentrations of the attractant and therefore is able to fly along the concentration gradient to find the female.

In social insects such as ants and termites, the use of pheromones figures prominently in the release of several different behavior patterns. Food-seeking behavior is released by a *trail pheromone* (Figure 29.5), defensive behavior is released by an *alarm pheromone*, and so on. In mammals, pheromones are commonly used to release avoidance behavior. An individual marks the boundaries of its territory with its personal scent. Prospective intruders of the same species detect the scent and, in most cases, turn away. Similarly, in some species, such as the social mongooses, females are marked by their mates with their personal scent as a warning for other males to keep away.

Auditory releasers are also widespread. Some of these

Figure 29.3 A herring gull attempting to brood a model egg that is several times larger than its own egg. The bird's preference for this supernormal visual releaser remains steadfast, even though the bird cannot assume a normal brooding position.

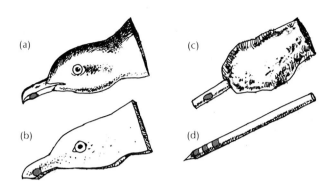

Figure 29.4 *Testing the visual releasers that trigger the feeding response of young herring gulls. The model that most resembles the head and beak of the parent (a) releases feeding behavior, provided that the characteristic red spot is present (as it is on the parent's beak). Details of the model's shape are unimportant; (b) and (c) are as effective as the first. But the most effective releaser of all is a striped pencil (d) in which the color pattern in exaggerated. This pencil is an example of a supernormal releaser.*

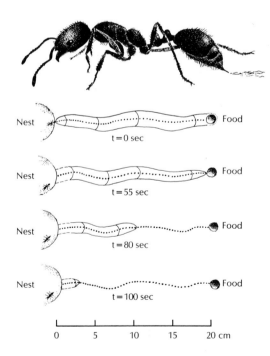

Figure 29.5 *Fire ant worker establishing an odor trail with its extended stinger, and the history of a representative odor space of the trail pheromone. The pheromone odor fades with time unless other ants restore it as they move along the trail from the food. Thus as long as the food source persists, the trail will continue to be reinforced. But once the food supply is exhausted, the trail vanishes rapidly.*

stimuli will be discussed later in the chapter, but one type—the calling song of male crickets—will be discussed here because it clearly portrays how a releaser and the behavior it elicits are tied together as a result of natural selection. In some parts of the United States, it is possible to hear as many as twenty species of crickets "singing" at once. This auditory releaser is produced when crickets rub a "scraper" on one wing against a "file" on the other wing in a rasping motion, a process called *stridulation*. Although different sound patterns can be produced to release different kinds of intraspecific behavior, the dominant sound contributing to the din of a summer's evening is the male calling song. This signal releases searching behavior in the female, who moves toward the source of the sound. But how does she distinguish males of her own species if males of nineteen other species are rasping away at the same time? It turns out that, although the songs of different species vary in pitch and in various other qualities, the female is most sensitive to the *rate* at which the song characteristic of her species is repeated.

Now, the repeat rate in the song of each cricket species is a function of temperature. As the evening cools, all songs have a lower repeat rate. This variation would seem to pose a problem for the female. But in fact, *her* perception of rate changes as a function of temperature in parallel with the sending system of the male! Thus, she responds to a higher repeat frequency at higher temperature and a lower frequency at lower temperature; in this way she is always locked in on the sending frequency of the male of her species.

The most dramatic evidence for genetic coupling of such sending and receiving systems came from a recent laboratory experiment. Two species of crickets that never interbreed in nature were experimentally caused to do so. As a result, the hybrid male offspring produced a novel song that carried certain features of each parental species. (It was not, however, a simple intermediate song.) When hybrid females were given their choice of males of either the parental type or the hybrid type, they moved toward the source of the hybrid song!

It is in this context, then, that animal behaviors are properly viewed. They are not curious random events; *many behaviors are mechanisms that have been selected for in evolution because they aid in the adaptation, isolation, and perpetuation of the species.* Let us now turn to how some of these behavioral patterns and their releasers act to structure the distribution and interactions of animals in the wild.

INTRASPECIFIC BEHAVIOR GIVES STRUCTURE TO THE BREEDING POPULATION

The patterns in which individuals of a breeding population are grouped vary tremendously. Large carnivores often spend most of their lives isolated from others of their species; other carnivores hunt in small family groups. There are fish that swim in enormous schools of equally spaced individuals, and insects such as termites that live in highly structured and functionally subdivided societies. But underlying the spectrum of organizational plans we find a common pattern of opposed behavioral forces that determine the spacing pattern of the individuals. First of all, there normally is a capacity for some degree of mutual recognition between members of the same species. In some cases (as discussed in Chapter 27), this capacity for recognition is learned through imprinting, but in many cases it appears to be innate. Having recognized another individual as being of the same species, there are characteristically two opposing kinds of behavioral traits that an individual will display: **approach** and **avoidance.** *It is largely through variations in the intensity and form of the approach and avoidance behavior released when two members of a species encounter each other that the spatial patterns and social organizations of species are distributed.* In what follows, then, we will attempt to examine some of these patterns and to discern how such interactions result in very different population structures. *It is clear that in each species, the balance between approach and avoidance behavior causes individuals to be distributed in a way that permits the best use to be made of whatever resources limit the success of the species.*

The Balance Between Approach and Avoidance Establishes the Boundaries of Individual Distance

When two human beings of Western society are introduced for the first time in a social context, there tends to be a stereotyped behavior pattern. After making momentary contact through a handshake, they tend to stand at a relatively fixed distance from each other. If the distance is too great, there commonly are vague feelings of anxiety due, perhaps, to a sense of rejection. In contrast, if the two are not quite far enough apart, there may be an even greater feeling of apprehension. (To verify this statement, try talking to a stranger with your head six inches from his and see what reaction you elicit!) In the latter case, something you value highly but are seldom conscious of has been violated: your personal space, or **individual distance.** The boundaries of individual distance may be somewhat variable, depending on the individual, but in all cases it is a sphere that, if violated, evokes a greater or lesser sense of uneasiness. Individual distance is not strictly a human construct, for it is common throughout the animal kingdom. It is clearly seen in many species of birds that travel or feed in flocks (Figure 29.6); it also occurs among schooling fish and herding mammals.

Individual distance appears to be controlled by homeo-

Figure 29.6 Distance boundaries in gulls. The regular spacing often seen in such aggregations is no mere result of chance. Rather, it results from interactions among individuals in which a balance is struck between the opposing tendencies of approach and avoidance.

static negative feedback mechanisms. How close one animal may come to another depends largely on prevailing environmental conditions (temperature, for example) and on such essential motivations as the need to reproduce. If the approach is too close under existing circumstances, the intruder is repelled, either passively or actively. Consider what happens in a line-up of equally spaced gulls that are waiting for a feeding opportunity to present itself. If one gull moves too close to its neighbor, the second gull may respond in one of two ways. It may—particularly if it is at the end of the line—simply move away a corresponding distance. Or it may—particularly if to move away would bring it closer to another individual—perform an aggressive display by flapping its wings and lurching toward the violator with beak open and making ritualized pecking motions. Such ritualized intention movements (Chapter 27) figure prominently in the spacing of animals in nature.

Strong Avoidance Reactions May Lead to the Establishment of Individual Territories

When the avoidance reaction of individuals within a species is sufficiently strong, adult individuals of the same sex tend to be separated by distances that are relatively great in comparison to their body size. In such cases, the individual distances carved out are known as **territories.** The existence of territories is exceptionally widespread, and they are defended vigorously with aggressive displays directed against intruders of the same species. *Such territorial behavior leads to an optimum distribution of limited resources among a maximum number of individuals of a species.*

A male dragonfly will establish a territory surrounding a fencepost and will leave his perch on the post to attack any other male of the same species that intrudes or to mate with any female that happens to fly within its boundaries. Similarly, a male song sparrow establishes his territory each spring and moves from fencepost to fencepost and bushtop to bushtop around its boundaries, singing to announce the limits of his domain to other males of the same species. He is warning them, in effect, that if they cross the boundary they will have him to deal with. Mammals, on the other hand, tend to mark territorial boundaries with personal scents deposited in the form of urine or secretions from specialized scent glands. Some fish as well as some insects tend to delineate the boundaries of their territories by continual patrolling and ritualized aggressive displays directed toward potential intruders.

Although the details of the behavioral interactions that occur between individuals protecting and invading a territory vary widely from species to species, they share many similar features. First of all, *territorial interactions rarely involve a struggle to the death.* The existence of such death struggles upon each chance encounter would be of low survival advantage for the species. Usually the interaction terminates with the voluntary retreat of one individual.

Second, territorial interactions tend to involve a series of highly stereotyped, species-specific movements, threats, and aggressive displays. Taken together, *territorial interactions constitute a pattern of ritualized intention movements characteristic of the species* (Figure 29.7).

Third, in the majority of cases the outcome of an aggressive interaction is predictable. Particularly when the territory is well established, the defender is usually successful in driving away an invader irrespective of differences in size, strength, development of specialized structures important in the aggressive display, and so forth. This is most clearly seen in the case of two individuals with adjacent territories. Here, each individual is usually successful in defending its own territory yet unsuccessful in attempts to encroach on its neighbor's domain. *In every interaction, each individual appears to be driven by two opposing tendencies: fight and flight.* The closer to the center of its own territory an individual is, the greater appears to be its motivation to fight. But the farther it is from the center of its home territory, the greater appears to be the tendency for flight. The boundaries between adjacent territories, then,

delineate the points at which the two individuals normally exhibit a conflict behavior between these two opposing drives. It appears, in fact, that *most aggressive interactions have the function of establishing the location of boundaries between territories.*

Finally, we can generalize that once territorial boundaries are firmly established, they tend to be respected. This appears to be the case, at least, in most species that have been carefully studied. Hence *continual aggressive interactions generally do not persist throughout the life cycle of an animal.*

From what has been said to this point, you may have concluded that the territories established by members of a species might be variable in size. This is often the case. When the density of **conspecific individuals** (members of the same species) is *high* in an area, each territory tends to be immediately adjacent to several others and there is competition for space. Attempts to enlarge a territory will lead an individual into someone else's domain, and the challenger will be rebuffed. Hence territorial size will fall to some relatively low value. In contrast, when density of conspecifics is *low*, territorial size tends to rise. Thus external factors work to *regulate* the absolute size of the territory an individual may establish.

But it is innate factors that appear to establish the upper and lower *limits* of territorial size. Thus, song sparrows never establish territories much greater than 4,000 square meters (1 acre) in size, even in the absence of competition from conspecifics. Apparently this is all the territory that innate mechanisms permit an individual to patrol. The corollary is that song sparrow territories seldom fall below about 2,000 square meters regardless of the density of individuals and thus of the extent of competition for space. Under such conditions, there is a fixed limit beyond which invaders will not be tolerated, regardless of the frequency of aggressive encounters required to maintain boundaries. Inevitably, when density is high some juveniles will be "squeezed out" and forced to emigrate to find suitable territory elsewhere. Such forced emigration as a result of

Figure 29.7 Two male impalas in ritualized territorial combat. The territory in question is a courtship arena in which females will be courted and in which mating will take place. Participants in these aggressive displays are rarely injured, and the loser withdraws from the territory. Similarly, an orynx antelope never uses its twin horns to gore its opponent during highly ritualized combat—and yet it has been known to stab lions with them. And the giraffe, with its formidable legs and hoofs, uses instead its stubby horns in territorial combat.

crowding has been clearly demonstrated in muskrat populations, to give one example.

In many vertebrates, one result of crowding, and of the subsequent increase in frequency of aggressive encounters, is continual stimulation of the adrenal gland by a combination of neurological and hormonal mechanisms (Chapters 22 and 25). In several species, the ensuing increase in adrenal size and function has now been shown to lead to decreased fertility. Hence, we see once again the existence of a homeostatic feedback loop that constitutes one of the mechanisms regulating the size of a population. High reproductive success leads to overcrowding. Overcrowding leads to increased frequency of aggressive interaction. This in turn leads to hormonal changes and lower reproductive success, thereby diminishing the population density in the next generation.

When the space available to conspecifics is not enough to establish territories of the normal minimum dimensions, and if flight is impossible, behavioral aberrations may occur. For example, in one experiment two male sticklebacks were placed in an aquarium that simply lacked sufficient space for them to establish separate territories of the minimum size set by innate factors. At first, both attempted to establish territories. But as soon as each left the center of its own range, it found itself so close to the center of the other's range that it would normally be dominated by the flight reaction. Thus, each position in the tank elicited two simultaneous but opposing drives (fight and flight), each sufficient in magnitude to have normally dominated their behavior. As a result, both fish abandoned normal territorial behavior and spent almost all their time digging holes in the sand on the bottom of the tank, which soon became strewn with pits. Such inappropriate or apparently misdirected activity in an organism experiencing two irreconcilable drives or whose normal behavior has been frustrated is called **displacement activity.**

Different Species Establish Territories to Guard Different Resources

One of the fundamental aspects of territoriality that should be understood (but is often neglected) is the fact that not all territories are defended to maintain control of the same resource. In some species, such as song sparrows, the territory is a feeding domain; the male isolates and defends an area with enough food resources to supply himself, his mate, and their brood. But in other cases, the territory is established predominantly to provide and to protect a nesting site. Swifts, for example, feed on high-flying insects, and they cannot define or protect a region of sky. Hence aggressive encounters over food are not observed among swifts. But they do actively compete with one another for nesting sites, thereby establishing small nesting

territories. In general, *resources that cannot be protected are not the focus of aggressive interactions.* Thus many species defend feeding territories from intrusion by conspecifics, for example, but share a common watering hole.

The nature of the territory and its resources determine, to a large extent, the way in which it is defended. If the territory is predominantly or exclusively a nesting site, it is commonly defended by the male against intrusion by conspecific males. But if it is also a feeding territory, it is not uncommon for conspecific intruders to be thwarted by both male and female.

Is defense of territories directed solely toward other members of the same species? Not in all cases. Although territorial animals will ignore members of most other species within the territory, they will often defend it vigorously against species that represent a threat to the resource being protected. For example, aggressive displays are commonplace against predators that pose a real or potential threat to the young. A cat that wanders into the territory in which mockingbirds are nesting will often be attacked furiously for prolonged periods until it moves out of the birds' domain. Similarly, animals defending a feeding territory will ignore members of other species except for those with similar feeding preferences. In that case they often will challenge the intruders as vigorously as they would conspecifics.

Social Organisms Also Demonstrate Territorial Behavior

In some animal species, the intraspecific avoidance reaction is so strong that individuals are solitary. But in most species, of course, contact is required during the breeding season, at the very least. In some cases, pairs that become established break up as soon as the mating act is completed. In others, they remain together through the birth and development of the young before going their separate ways. In yet other cases, the pair remain associated over long periods, producing many offspring that leave the parents when they mature. Among carnivores such as wolves and lions, an entire family group may form the basis of the functional unit—the *pack,* or *pride.* And in many primate species, several family lineages may be combined in one large *troop.* The extreme in this progression of family-based units is seen in the matriarchal societies of insects such as bees, ants, and termites in which a large, highly ordered society is produced from the young of a single mating.

Whatever the degree of association, the members of these social groups are held together and in fact are defined by specific behavioral interactions. Such interactions also distinguish animal social groups from **aggregations,** in which many individuals of a species are found in a single place merely because of favorable environmental conditions.

(The collection of sowbugs you may see if you turn over decaying vegetation represents such an aggregation, not a society.)

Although it is possible to make a general distinction between solitary and social species, clear-cut boundaries do not exist. There is instead a spectrum of intraspecific relationships. From the solitary extreme to complex social groupings, there is a progressive decrease in the strength of avoidance reactions between members of a group. There is also a decrease in the extent of **competition** for resources and an increase in the extent of **cooperation** against predators (Figures 29.8 and 29.9) and in the guarding and harvesting of resources. *But the decrease in avoidance reaction and the increase in cooperative behavior usually is extended only to members of the immediate social group—it is not extended equally to all members of the species.*

Consider, for example, the aggregations (or colonies) formed by marine mammals such as sea lions during the breeding season. The basic social unit here is not the entire colony but the *harem*—a large adult male and the collection of females with whom he has been able to establish mating relationships. Each harem occupies a distinct territory determined by aggressive interactions between males at the beginning of the breeding season. Territories of adjacent harems usually are separated by undisputed corridors leading to the sea. Adjacent harems coexist peacefully only as long as territorial boundaries are respected. There is a distinction, then, between members of the in-group and members of the out-group. It is not a permanent condition among these animals, however. Sea lions establish territories only during the breeding season and only for breeding purposes. And among other species, such as social primates, territories are defended as a group, with aggressive behavior directed against rival troops of the same species that attempt to intrude.

Thus we see that social species differ from solitary individuals not by an absence of intraspecific avoidance and aggressive behavior but because of the existence of double standards. A series of behavioral modifications work to *minimize* aggressive behavior within the group, and at the same time a series of behavioral responses function to *increase* the strength of approach behavior. Let us now turn to some of these behaviors and explore how they facilitate the formation and maintenance of social groups.

Courtship Often Involves Modified Aggressive Display

Among species whose reproductive cycle involves internal fertilization of eggs, the male and female must break the barriers surrounding individual distance. Some arthropod species carry this requirement to extremes. For example, the male praying mantis is preprogrammed for copulatory activity, but throughout most of his life this behavior is under continual inhibition by impulses generated in the brain that trigger avoidance of the somewhat indiscriminately voracious female. When the female mantis is prepared for sex, however, she nevertheless finds a suitable male and simply decapitates him with a bite. His inhibi-

Figure 29.8 Cooperative behavior in social groups. When the pronghorn antelope detects danger, the hairs of the white rump patch are erected, producing a conspicuous white patch visible for miles on the open plains. When one such animal dashes away, the flashing white signal alerts the others even if the herd is widely scattered. Such protective devices greatly increase the security of the herd.

Figure 29.9 The defensive formation of a herd of musk oxen on sighting their only natural enemy, the wolf. (Attempts are being made to domesticate these animals, which are prized for their fur. One person established a small herd on the Olympic Peninsula in Washington. Eventually they came to accept him as part of their group—to the extent that, when a neighbor's dog came bounding toward them in a field, they formed a protective ring around their "vulnerable" keeper. The keeper didn't know whether to feel flattered or insulted.)

tions now lost, the male ends his life in a flurry of copulatory activity. In some spiders, the male attempts to distract the female by presenting her with a tidbit he has wrapped in the threads he secretes. If he is lucky, the female spider is sufficiently distracted by the offering that he is able to enter her personal space and mate. If she is insufficiently distracted, he becomes the meal instead of the gift-wrapped fly. Female spiders of other species are more uniformly receptive at the appropriate stage, but many consume their mates following copulation anyway.

But in most species the sexual act is not so all-consuming. Usually the barrier to approach is circumvented as the result of a **courtship display,** a complex pattern of behavior that functions (when successful) to release approach behavior and ultimately to permit prospective mates to make contact. Courtship often involves the most elaborate and colorful displays in the repertoire of the species.

In many cases, the same morphological features and behaviors used by males in aggressive displays are involved in attracting the female. For example, the male frigate bird (Figure 29.10) has a large, inflatable, brilliantly colored throat pouch that acts to release aggressive behavior in other males and approach behavior in females. The courtship dance of the male stickleback contains many features common to its aggressive display; it also has many unique features released only by the sight of a female stickleback with a swollen abdomen (Figure 29.11). As soon as the female has been induced to lay her eggs, however, aggressive display becomes dominant behavior once again and the female is driven from the territory.

Often the courtship display includes some distinguishable structural or behavioral element that serves to diminish the

Figure 29.10   Representative courtship display. The great frigate bird at a Galápagos Islands hatchery extends his red gular pouch, which, when inflated, catches the attention of the female. The pouch also serves as an aggressive display in confrontations with conspecific males.

Figure 29.11   Sequential stages in the courtship and mating of the three-spined stickleback fish. The male is attracted by the female's swollen abdomen. He maneuvers her into the nest he has prepared and induces her to lay eggs. He follows her through the nest, fertilizing the eggs, and then chases her out of his territory.

female's avoidance reaction while intensifying her approach reaction. Male terns present the female with a fish, the bowerbird builds an elaborately ornamented display ground, and the male chimpanzee reassures his uncertain mate by extending the hand, palm upward. Although the details vary, the pattern is generally the same: *Aggressive behavior can be reduced to lead to the establishment of a social relationship.* Similar reduction of aggressive behavior among members of the same sex can occur and thereby establish other kinds of social bonds.

Dominance Hierarchies Minimize Aggression Within a Social Group

In any social grouping there is a certain amount of differentiation of roles based on biological differences, with offspring, juveniles, adult females, and adult males participating in different ways. But if the group is based on more than one breeding pair of adults, each of these categories will contain several or many members. And although the existence of the social grouping implies a lessening of competition and aggressive interactions between equivalent individuals, it does not imply that they are completely absent. Usually, competition for shared resources—food, mates, nesting sites—still exists. And structural and behavioral releasers of aggressive displays also persist.

The way in which many animal societies prevent such competition and aggressive behavior from destroying the integrity of the group is by the formation of a **dominance hierarchy**—a system in which each adult has an established social ranking relative to every other adult of the same sex.

The first studied and most widely recognized dominance relationship is the *pecking order* that exists in domestic hens. The hierarchy established among hens is particularly simple. As a result of initial aggressive interactions, a linear order is produced in which each hen achieves a rank that can be symbolized by numbers from 1 to *n,* where *n* is the number of hens in the flock. Number 1 can peck with impunity at any other hen but is not itself pecked at. Number 2 can peck at any individual *except* number 1, and so on down to scruffy number *n,* who is much pecked at and who has nothing to peck at but the ground (Table 29.1).

Seldom are the relationships of dominance and submission so simple. In other species, each individual may attack all others and the dominance hierarchy defines only the relative *frequencies* with which various attacks occur. In other cases, circular relationships may be established such that individual *Z* is dominant over *X,* despite the fact that *X* is dominant over *Y* and *Y* is dominant over *Z.* Also, rank is often subject to change. As a young animal matures, it may move up the dominance hierarchy as it becomes more aggressive. Or a low-ranking individual that mates with one of higher rank may be automatically elevated in stature.

Table 29.1
Dominance Hierarchy in a Flock of Hens

Hen 1 pecks	2	3	4	5	6	7	8	9	10	11	12	13
Hen 2 pecks		3	4	5	6	7	8	9	10	11	12	13
Hen 3 pecks			4	5	6	7	8	9	10	11	12	13
Hen 4 pecks				5	6	7	8	9	10	11	12	13
Hen 5 pecks					6	7	8	9	10	11	12	13
Hen 6 pecks						7	8	9	10	11	12	13
Hen 7 pecks							8	9	10	11	12	13
Hen 8 pecks								9		11	12	13
Hen 9 pecks									10	11	12	13
Hen 10 pecks							8			11	12	13
Hen 11 pecks											12	13
Hen 12 pecks												13
Hen 13 pecks	0											

Source: Adapted from W. C. Allee, *The Social Life of Animals* (New York: Norton, 1938).

Dominance hierarchies have been studied primarily among captive animals, and they are less readily discerned in the same species in the wild. For that reason, it was once thought that such hierarchies might be artifacts of confinement. But many cases of similar hierarchies have now been observed for social groups in the natural environment. It does appear, however, that hierarchical behavior is intensified under crowded conditions or when resources become scarce.

How are hierarchies formed in the first place, and how are they maintained? When a group of similar individuals—such as a flock of hens or a pack of wolves—is created artificially by bringing together unrelated individuals, aggressive interactions are widespread. As with aggressive behavior in solitary species, these interactions often are highly ritualized, consisting more of intention movements than of outright fighting. But it differs in many cases from aggression in nonsocial animals in that it is terminated not by flight of one individual but by a behavior known as an **appeasement action**—a behavior that signals submission and thereby effectively stops aggression. For example, a wolf that is losing a fight with another wolf may suddenly turn and stretch its neck, exposing its most vulnerable area—the jugular vein. Presented with this opportunity to finish off its opponent with one bite, the victor instead ceases aggressive activity. The battle is over, but the dominance-subordinance relationship is established. Now, whenever these two wolves encounter each other, the relationship is regularly reinforced by a system of stereotyped greeting postures. When they meet, the dominant wolf holds head, ears, and tail erect; the submissive wolf holds its head down, folds its ears back, and tucks its tail between his legs. Both thereby recognize the nature of their relationship in the absence of further aggressive displays.

Similar dominance-subordinance gestures exist in many social species.

What are the consequences of a dominance hierarchy for the individual and for the group? For the individual, dominance assures priority in the choice of food, nesting sites, mates, and the like. And such advantages in turn assure that the dominant individual has the best opportunity for survival and reproductive success. For the group, dominance assures stability. Once the hierarchical order has been established, aggression over resources and mates is kept to a minimum. In one study, the investigator deliberately kept disrupting the dominance relationships in a flock of hens. The outcome was that the hens fought more, ate less, gained less weight, and suffered more serious injuries than the control flock in which the dominance relationship was stable. In an interesting study of urban rats, dominant males were trapped in one city block and released in another, thus modifying the structure of the population in the receiving block. The fighting that resulted during this experiment was reported to far more drastically reduce the rat population than could possibly have been achieved by simply killing trapped rats. (Unfortunately, the experiment was terminated when the city fathers were told that somebody was releasing wild rats in the city.)

And what is the effect of a dominance relationship on the evolution of the species? Because the most dominant male gets first choice of mates, he can be expected to contribute disproportionately to the gene pool of the next generation. To the extent that aggressive behavior is genetically determined, this will tend to favor aggressiveness in subsequent generations and suggests a strong survival advantage for aggressive dominance. However, dominant females tend to be more difficult to court in most species. Hence submissive females are often selected preferentially, and their genetic contributions tend to lower the average aggressive behavior in the next generation. Also, in many cases it has been observed that the most dominant male is incapable of mating—females release his aggressive reactions rather than courting reactions. In such cases, subordinate males tend to do most of the mating with subordinate females. *Thus hyperaggressiveness carries the seeds of its own disappearance; there is a tendency toward a homeostatic situation in which aggressive behavior remains near the optimum for reproductive success of the group.*

Having looked at role relationships established in a social group and at the advantages they offer, you might ask why it is that all species have not evolved in this direction. One reason might be that before such groups can be established, there must be enough food to maintain the high population density a social group represents. Because food resources are not universally abundant, there has not been equally strong pressure on all species to form groups. Some species

survive only because of the continuance of individual territoriality that distributes the population uniformly in correspondence with available resources.

Complex Communication Systems Develop in Many Social Groups

Solitary species require relatively simple means of intraspecific communication. They need little more than a system to declare territorial boundaries, one to release avoidance behavior, and one to break down avoidance behavior at the time of mating. But in a social species, the selective pressure to develop a more complex communication system would inevitably be strong. How else could the potential for cooperation in food-getting and defense be realized unless the individuals were capable of communicating the source of available food or the presence of a threat?

Consider the elaborate systems of vocal and visual communication that have evolved among many primates. The arboreal spider monkeys of tropical forests in South America, when disturbed, will erupt as a group into a vocal and visual display replete with growling, shrill barking, a great deal of leaping about, and a frenzied scratching of arms. This aggressive display lasts until the more vulnerable members of the group (females and juveniles) have fled from the scene. Primate vocal signals generally consist of various kinds of roars, grunts, barks, growls, screeches, and screams. Certain sounds apparently have particular meanings, but most represent steps along a continuum. For example, in studying the vocalizations of rhesus monkeys, Thelma Rowell distinguished nine sounds, but all fell along a continuum between a roar and a squeak.

In some primate species, however, more complex signals exist. For example, vervet monkeys use thirty-six or more distinct auditory signals. All these sounds are uttered in a social context, and each occurs only in certain situations. Those situations and the behavior they apparently elicit provided a basis for assigning "meanings" to each sound. A striking example of signal use among vervets is their five distinct *alarm calls,* of which at least three are correlated with specific events. Whenever a ground-dwelling predator is sighted, adult females utter a "chirp" (abrupt, loud, low-frequency calls with higher overtones), which sends the group fleeing to the trees. A predatory bird evokes, in addition to the chirping, a "raup" call. Members of the group flee not to the branches but to the shelter of undergrowth when they hear it. Another distinct alarm call is a "chutter," consisting of repeated sounds with low frequencies. This call is given by females and juveniles when a cobra or a puff adder is sighted. On hearing this signal, nearby monkeys gather together to observe the snake and to follow it with continual chuttering until it is far enough from their territory to no longer pose a significant threat.

Such signals obviously are part of an elaborate communicative system—but is that system "language"? In the human language each word has a denotation, and different words may be combined in different ways to convey complex and often subtle distinctions and new concepts. The rules by which individual signals or symbols can be combined into longer messages are the **syntax** of language. But even among the "higher" apes, whose communicative potential might be expected to be most similar to our own, attempts to find a "language" have been markedly unsuccessful. (Some birds are said to have a semblance of syntax. Sounds they utter at one stage of their life to mean one thing are combined at a later stage to mean something quite different. But at both stages the meanings are rather rigidly defined and predetermined. Hence this is not true syntax as the term is usually defined.)

Attempts to teach young chimpanzees to speak have failed almost completely, with the animals mastering only a few simple words and showing no awareness of syntax. However, ethological field studies by Jane van Lawick–Goodall (and others before her) show that chimpanzees have a rich repertoire of visual signals, in which the hands often figure prominently. With this in mind, Allen and Beatrice Gardner raised a young female chimpanzee, attempting to duplicate as closely as possible the conditions under which a human child normally learns language. From about ten months of age the chimpanzee shared their living quarters. They reasoned that the absence of a spoken language in chimps might reflect inadequate adaptations of the vocal apparatus rather than an absence of the neural processes required to develop syntactical ability. Therefore all conversations in the chimpanzee's presence were conducted in American Sign Language. She had the opportunity to learn the sign language both in special training sessions and by observing people communicating among themselves. Figure 29.12 depicts some of the results. It is difficult to avoid the impression that a primitive syntax was emerging—*although it is possible that the chimpanzee imitated not only signs but sequences used by others, rather than creating new and meaningful combinations of her own.*

Experiments by David Premack and his colleagues at the University of California at Santa Barbara may be more telling. Premack's group began working in 1968 with a five-year-old chimpanzee named Sarah. They used small plastic objects of varying shapes and colors as signals. These objects had metal backing and were arranged in vertical columns so that they could be moved on a magnetized slate to form sentences. Sarah seemed quite proficient at the use of syntax. For example, when an experimenter placed on the slate the words "red on green," Sarah put a

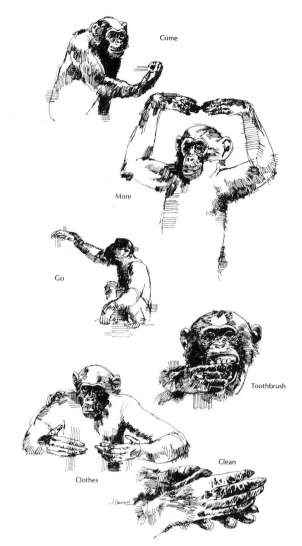

Figure 29.12 *Hand signs used by the Gardners' chimpanzee Washoe within twenty-two months of the beginning of training. Signs are presented in order of their original appearance in her repertoire.*

At the age of three and one-half, Washoe responded appropriately to several hundred signs. She also showed readiness to generalize not only among objects of a given class but to photographs of them. The Gardners have motion picture films of Washoe sitting before a picture book and giving appropriate signals as the pages are turned: "flower," "baby," "dog," "cat," and so on.

Washoe not only used signs independently but combined them in sequences that suggest some capacity to employ a meaningful syntax. The most common combinations involved combining signals the Gardners called emphasizers (signals for "please," "come-gimme," "hurry," and "more"), with one other signal. She also used sequences of more than two signs involving names or pronouns, such as "you go gimme," "Roger you tickle," or "please Roger come."

red card on top of a green one. If the experimenter wrote "green on red," Sarah responded appropriately. She learned to carry out such complex instructions as "Sarah insert banana pail apple dish" by putting a banana in a pail and an apple in a dish. She presumably recognized such abstract words as "shape," "color," "size," "same," "different," and "name." She responded appropriately to a symbol representing a question mark. It would seem, then, that the chimpanzee appears to have the *ability* to master certain syntactical aspects of human speech.

But does language per se exist in the natural state? The most compelling evidence in support of a possible language in nonhuman animals was that gathered by Karl von Frisch,

the Austrian zoologist. Von Frisch noticed, as others had before him, that repeated visits of a single bee at a feeding dish were usually followed by the arrival of other worker bees from the same hive. By placing food dishes at various distances from hives and carefully observing the behavior of returning foragers, he discovered the now well-known "waggle dance" of bees (Figure 29.13). He showed that the dance in fact contains information concerning direction and distance to the food site. (A trained human observer with a stopwatch is able to determine not only the direction but also the approximate flying time to the food by watching the dance.) Foragers apparently recruited hive mates, and these hive mates preferentially ended up in the field at or

Figure 29.13   The waggle dance of bees. Forager bees that discover a rich food source return to the hive and perform a dance on the vertical face of the comb. Other workers within the hive cluster about the dancers, then leave the hive to seek out the food source. The dancing bees move in a figure-eight pattern, with a straight "waggle run" in the center of the pattern. The angle between the waggle run and the vertical is the same as the angle between the direction toward the sun and the direction toward the food source.

The rate of dancing varies with the distance to the food; a slower dance corresponds to a more distant source. In (a), for example, this round dance is performed only when the nectar is close at hand. The figure eight (b) is traced at about a 120-degree angle to the sun; the abdomen is wagged rapidly, indicating a relatively close location. In (c) the figure eight is traced at a 60-degree angle; the abdomen is wagged slowly, indicating a more distant location.

It appears, then, that each feature of the dance carries a message about the external environment with respect to direction and distance.

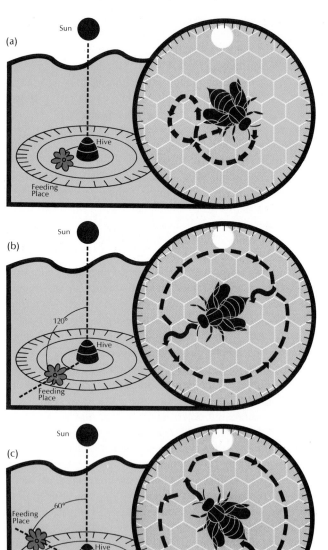

near the same site originally visited by the forager bee. Von Frisch concluded in 1946 that the successful recruits had used quantitative information obtained from the foragers during the waggle dance contact in the hive to locate the food source. It did indeed look as if bees had meaningful and symbolic communication.

Twenty years later, however, von Frisch's hypothesis was challenged when Adrian Wenner, Patrick Wells, and their students found anomalies in the behavior of searching bees. They found that recruits were often unsuccessful and took too long searching for the food source to have gone "directly out" as specified by the language hypothesis. Furthermore, Wenner and Wells suggested that the von Frisch experiments did not provide controls against odors, such as those drifting downwind from the established flight line of foragers and from the locality itself (Figure 29.14). They have demonstrated that bees can use odor to locate food sources under many conditions and can locate food sources on the basis of odor in the absence of a waggle dance. But they have not as yet proven that all bees are incapable of using the information contained in the waggle dance to locate food sources. And that demonstration is what is needed before we can conclude that the waggle dance does not constitute a form of language. Thus on this intriguing question, as on so many others in biology, judgment must be suspended until further evidence is in.

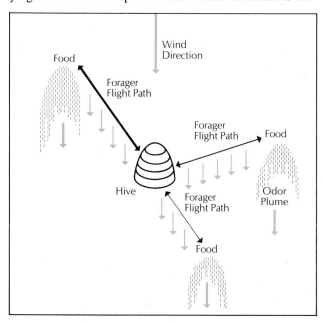

Figure 29.14 Alternative theory to the von Frisch theory of language in bees. Instead of using "language" information, it is conceivable that recruited honeybees could use environmental odors. Odors drifting downwind from the hive, from food sources, and perhaps from the flight lines for foragers could provide orientation cues for searching bees.

INTERSPECIFIC BEHAVIOR

So far in this chapter we have focused primarily on the behavioral interactions among members of the same species. Equally important in the evolution of animals has been the behavioral adaptations to animals of other species—whether they be predator or prey, symbiont or competitor.

Predatory Behavior: The Procurement of Food

In the sea, on land, and in the air, animals are in continuous hot pursuit of other animals as quarry. Most often we think of this behavior as being released by visual cues, as when a cheetah runs down an antelope on the African plains, or when a bird chases an evasive butterfly. But forms of pursuit can rely on other signals as well. For example, predators such as bats, porpoises, and sea lions emit sounds in their search for food, and oil birds echolocate to find their roosting place in dark caves. Because these frequencies correspond to very short wavelengths, the sounds diffuse very little, and when they strike an object and echo back from it, they permit the precise location of prey. Such behavior is called **echolocation.** It has been studied extensively in bats, following the pioneering work of Donald Griffin and his colleagues. Through echolocation, bats can avoid a maze of extremely fine wires strung across a dark laboratory and can locate tiny flying insects without the use of sight (Figure 29.15).

Interestingly enough, whirligig beetles of the family Gyrinidae seek out food not by reflections of sound waves but by reflection of water waves. The waves they generate as they swim are reflected off objects at the surface of the water. The beetles swim intermittently, and presumably their pauses in swimming enable them to sense their environment as surface waves strike prey, are thereby distorted, and are sent back to them. Furthermore, movement of a potential prey creates waves that reveal its location to the searching beetle.

Even more incredible are the electric fish that have evolved independently in Africa and South America. They send out an electrical signal and analyze distortions of the electric field to develop a picture of their surroundings. They use this system not only for communication with others of their own species but also to detect, locate, and pursue prey.

Whereas such animals openly seek their prey, others wait in ambush. The archer fish lurks just below the water's surface, spraying a jet of water at insects that are unfortunate enough to find themselves on leaves at the water's edge. A host of assassin bugs—about 2,500 species in all—have short yet powerful curved beaks adapted for sucking the juices out of insects, and all have a form of adhesive padding on their legs for latching onto prey. They lie in wait in dense foliage, capturing bees, ants, and other

Figure 29.15 A fish-eating bat that searches for prey by echolocation. (In this photograph, a trained bat approaches a wire that marks a piece of fish.)

Similarly, as a result of conditioned learning, insect-eating bats can come to discriminate between intact insect larvae and larvae whose tiny bristles have been shaved. This is a signal that the bristleless larvae are inedible (having been injected with a substance that makes them taste bitter). At random times, both kinds of larvae are propelled into a totally darkened room. They remain suspended only for an instant, but in that brief interval the bats can avoid the form they have learned will be bitter and catch the other!

insects of various sorts. Some coat their legs with resinous ooze from conifers and hold them aloft as traps; some secrete a nectarlike substance to attract the ants. (A few species, of course, are not above the fairly straightforward behavior of running down their prey and pouncing on it.) Spiders, too, practice deceptive behavior, building nests in the ground beneath trap doors, ready to spring on an edible passerby. One remarkable species, the lasso spider, throws a thread with a sticky ball attached at insects!

And some organisms have adapted behaviorally and morphologically to imitate specific releasing stimuli that trigger behavior patterns in organisms of other species. In other words, they falsify signals. Consider the alligator snapping turtle, which lurks in river bottoms. In its dark-colored mouth is an equally dark-colored tongue, but at the tip of the tongue are two thin, bright red processes. These processes are wiggled in the water, looking for all intents and purposes like small worms. Fish are attracted by the visual cue and begin to nibble away at the potential meal, but suddenly unsuspecting predator becomes prey. The angler fish employs a similar lure in its predatory fishing.

Various behaviors have also evolved around food that is finally procured. Raccoons usually wash their meal in a stream or pond. The California sea otter floats on its back with a rock on its stomach, against which it smashes

shellfish until they open. Squirrels gather nuts and seeds, storing them in their burrows.

Behavioral Responses of the Hunted

Among the most important aspects of an animal's behavior are the responses that protect it when it is threatened with danger. In most cases, getting out of the way takes precedence over other possible behaviors. But in some cases the first response is **cryptic behavior:** remaining motionless and perhaps thereby avoiding detection. It is the success or failure of this strategy that has provided the selective force by which so many animals have developed **cryptic coloration**—colors and patterns that tend to blend into the predominant background. Certain molluscs, fish, and reptiles are capable of changing color and pattern to blend into the background (Figure 29.16). Many insects resemble leaves or twigs so closely that it is possible to be looking at them from a few inches away and to not detect their presence until they move.

But if cryptic behavior fails and the prey is detected anyway, flight may become essential. One of the key determinants of survival in prey is being able to determine whether they have been detected and how close a predator may be allowed to approach before initiating flight. Young rabbits are not highly skillful at such discrimination and may lurch out of the undergrowth practically as one's foot is about to fall on them. Not surprisingly, most rabbits die in the first few weeks of life. The direction of fleeing behaviors is often quite specific. A sudden dimming of illumination—as might be caused by the shadow of an approaching predator—elicits a sudden and rapid withdrawal of annelid worms such as *Sabella* into their tubes. A pursued moth may fold its wings and drop toward the earth when it detects an echolocating bat. A normally sedentary scallop that is touched by a predatory starfish may rapidly open and close its shell (ejecting a stream of water on each closure) and swim away by jet propulsion. A squirrel takes to the trees, a rabbit to its burrow, a frog to the bottom of the pond. Each of these avoidance responses is elicited by a stimulus that has been associated with possible danger to an organism during its development or during the evolution of a species. Such a response has obvious strong survival value for the individual and for the species.

Often, avoidance responses are erratic, making the behavior less predictable to the predator. Such is the response of a school of fish, which explodes in all directions at the approach of a predator; similarly, a rabbit will twist and turn in its flight. But what happens if there is no alternative but confrontation? The puffer fish may assume an extremely formidable posture (Figure 29.17); the squid may try to lose itself in a cloud of ink. Many organisms, if no other choice is possible, will turn and display aggressive behav-

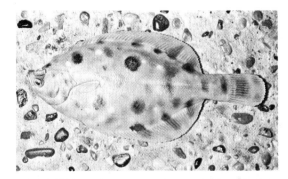

Figure 29.16   (left) An example of cryptic coloration. The flounder can change its color pattern to blend in with its background.

Figure 29.17   (below) The puffer fish, or blowfish, with normal body contour (insert at upper right). The same fish is shown in a defensive pose with body inflated and spines erect. Such a defense mechanism is most effective in discouraging predators.

ior—despite apparently overwhelming odds. Depending on the nature and state of hunger of the predator, this may be an amazingly successful defense!

The behavior of some animals has made their world relatively secure. Few predators will attack a skunk or porcupine twice, for example. And the bombardier beetle, which can aim a most noxious spray of chemicals toward its disturber, can send ants into paroxysms and frogs in the other direction (Figure 29.18). Many organisms that possess noxious defense mechanisms announce this fact to potential predators with **warning coloration:** bright colors or unmistakable markings. Monarch butterflies (Figure 28.4) are resistant to the cardiac glycosides found in their main food plants, and they may accumulate large quantities of these compounds in their body. Most birds and mammals find these compounds nauseating and highly toxic. The bright orange-and-black pattern of the butterfly warns those who have made the mistake once or twice what they are in for if they try again. Most experienced birds will refuse to eat monarch butterflies despite prolonged hunger.

Symbiosis: Living Together for Better or for Worse

Interactions between organisms of different species are by no means restricted to predator-prey relationships. Countless cases of **symbiosis** exist: relationships in which organisms of two different species live together in intimate, long-term contact. *Indeed, it is doubtful whether there is an animal alive that does not have a symbiotic relationship with at least one other life form.*

In many cases, one or both of the animals has an absolute dependence on the other. A prime example of this *obligate symbiosis* is the relationship between termites and the flagellated protistans living in their gut (and nowhere else in nature). The termite cannot digest its normal foodstuff—wood—in the absence of its internal guests, which are capable of breaking down the wood into digestible molecules. Because both host and resident gain significant advantage from this relationship, it is also an example of the form of symbiosis known as **mutualism.** (We have a

Figure 29.18   A successful adaptation for survival. The bombardier beetle shown here secretes three chemicals—hydrogen peroxide and two hydroquinone compounds. When under attack, the beetle can blast a noxious spray of these chemicals in all directions with a high degree of accuracy. The effectiveness of this deterrent is illustrated here by this indiscriminate frog, which is gagging on a well-aimed shot down its gullet.

(a) (b)

Figure 29.19 Examples of protective coloration that involve falsification of signals. Large eyes that appear suddenly seem to elicit widespread avoidance responses. Many organisms successfully avoid predators because they have tuned in to this response. (a) This Io moth flashes false eyes on its wings. (b) The spicebush larva, too, has false eyes that elicit avoidance behavior in its predators.

Figure 29.20 Symbiosis. On first approaching an anemone with which it will take up residence, the clownfish makes a series of progressively closer passes until its body accumulates a coating of the mucous film by which the anemone's tentacles recognize one another as "self." At this point the fish can settle down unnoticed in the lethal jungle. In exchange for this impenetrable defense, the anemone receives occasional scrap of food that falls from the fish's mouth. Thus, this symbiotic relationship is of the type called commensalism.

similar, although less dramatic, relationship to the *Escherichia coli* in our gut—providing it with a warm home and rich food supply in exchange for vitamins and protection against far more hazardous potential inhabitants of our digestive tract.)

In other cases, a symbiotic relationship exists between organisms that are in fact capable of getting along without the other. This relationship is called *facultative symbiosis*. Consider the rhinoceros and the tickbird. The tickbird feeds on mites and ticks it finds embedded in the skin of the rhinoceros; the rhinoceros is not only relieved of a certain amount of itching and blood loss as a result of the tickbird's diet, it is alerted to impending danger by the alarm call of

the tickbird, whose visual acuity far exceeds that of its nearsighted host. But each *can* get along without the other.

Similarly, the worm *Urechis caupo* (a member of a small phylum known as the echiuroid worms) has derived its common name from its symbiosis with many other organisms. This creature is about an inch in diameter and six inches long, and it digs a twisting U-shaped burrow about as wide as its body in rich coastal mudflats. Sitting in its underground home, it extracts food and oxygen from the water it continuously draws through the tube by a pumping action of its muscular body. If you carefully excavate a *Urechis* burrow at low tide, you may find it occupied by a ménage of fish, molluscs, annelids, arthropods, and so on.

Although all these organisms are capable of independent life elsewhere, they all reside in the tube, enjoying its protection and feeding on whatever *Urechis* brings in but does not use. Because of its neighborliness, *Urechis caupo* is commonly known as "the innkeeper." Thus, every organism in the burrow derives positive benefit from the symbiosis except the innkeeper. Such a relationship is called **commensalism.** This is a relationship in which the host is neither helped nor harmed by the symbiosis.

Living in prolonged association with a host, a commensal individual achieves a significant survival advantage relative to its conspecifics if it develops a mechanism for tapping the resources that the larger host represents. Thus we see that certain of the barnacles attached to whales produce outgrowths of tissue that penetrate the skin of the whale, digest away bits of flesh, and absorb the nutrients. These barnacles are less dependent than their ancestors were on the vagaries of the environments in which the whale swims—if food is lacking on the outside it can tap some from the inside. We can readily visualize where this tendency is headed evolutionarily.

Commensal relationships are relatively widespread in nature. Barnacles swim through the sea attached to the backs of whales, skimming the waters for food as they go. Anemones ride about on mollusc shells that are occupied by hermit crabs, and fruit flies feed and breed in our garbage cans. But commensalism is usually facultative and therefore is probably the least stable of symbiotic relationships in evolutionary terms. In order to become an obligate—hence stable—relationship, there is strong evolutionary pressure favoring the development of either a mutualistic relationship or the exact opposite: **parasitism,** in which the resident is detrimental to the host to a greater or lesser extent. Some parasites, such as fleas and ticks, merely penetrate the body while remaining on the outside. They are called **ectoparasites.** Their adaptations to parasitism are usually behavioral and structural. But many parasites move inside the host and become **endoparasites.** Their adaptations are usually biochemical.

BEHAVIORAL INTERACTIONS WITH THE ENVIRONMENT

In emphasizing animal-animal interactions in this chapter we have drawn a picture of a world composed largely or exclusively of animals. Although it is true that many significant features of animal behavior are directed toward other animals, it is of course in the nature of the mobile way of life that all aspects of the animal life cycle involve behavior.

As you read in Chapter 28, interaction with the physical environment involves many behavioral adaptations. Many additional examples could be cited. In the continuous night

of the Antarctic winter, emperor penguins not only survive winds as high as 140 kilometers per hour and temperatures below −60°C, they manage to court, mate, and incubate their eggs. It is in their social behavior that they find the means to survive the rigors of winter: the penguins huddle in V formations that serve to break the wind and to maintain their body temperature at about 35.7°C. Individuals that become isolated from the group during storms have been known to have a body temperature perilously lower than that. The spectacular termite towers of Kenya are another example of how social behavior moderates the environment. Worker termites build the hard, thick walls of their termitaria with a mixture of saliva and clay. The high mound has ridges that are used for ventilation and air ducts that move air vertically through the tower. Air temperature is regulated by narrowing or widening these ducts. Bees, too, air-condition their homes.

But if we are to understand fully the unity and diversity of life, we cannot neglect the behavioral interactions of animals with plants. The animal's way of life absolutely depends on the plants in its surroundings—whether or not it eats them. Why does the giraffe restrict its browsing to leaves far above the ground? Why does the gerenuk stand on its hindlegs to browse, thereby ignoring lower leaves on the same bush? The answers to such questions come with understanding the structure of plant-animal-decomposer communities and the relative value, in terms of evolutionary survival, of specialization and generalization in feeding behavior.

In the next section of this book, we will see how all these factors interrelate and how the behavior of an animal may play a key role in structuring the community of life forms in which it finds itself. We will see that many of our concepts of animal-animal interactions—mutualism, parasitism, predator-prey, facultative and obligate relationships, and so forth—apply equally well to animal-plant interactions and yield great insight into the coevolution of the members of the living community, and the stability that the community possesses.

PERSPECTIVE

Convinced as we are of the fundamental unity of life, we must look continuously for generalizations that simplify the task of understanding the diversity we see about us and, not incidentally, of relating those generalizations to our own lives. In many cases we are successful. For example, we find that most of what we learn about the details of protein synthesis in the liver cells of a rat can be extrapolated to protein synthesis in our own cells. But when it comes to interactions among animals, are generalizations that encompass human interactions as valid?

In one respect, yes. Animal communication everywhere

involves one party sending a signal and another party receiving it—whether that communication involves a fire ant laying out a chemical trail for other foragers of its social group; or a predatory bat sending out signals and a moth that would choose not to receive them, or a courting tern presenting a freshly caught fish to a prospective mate; or a male cricket breaking the silence of the night with chirping that leads the female to him; or one human holding out his hand to another. And throughout nature, these and myriad other activities seem to be influenced to greater or lesser degrees by opposing tendencies—approach and avoidance, fight and flight, aggression and appeasement, competition and cooperation.

In another respect, however, we must remember that the details of behavioral interactions vary from one group to another, from one individual to another, and from one moment to another as the strengths of these opposing tendencies become modified. Territoriality, for example, is widespread throughout the animal kingdom, and territories are defended with aggressive displays. Our primate relatives, the baboons, defend their territories vigorously. But does that mean that we are justified in concluding (as many popular writers have done) that we, too, are inherently bound by our primate heritage to aggressive defense of territory? Are we the "killer ape"? To accept this notion is to ignore the complex shifts in the balance between opposed behaviors that have evolved in every species even as the species themselves have evolved. The point is that competition and therefore aggressive behavior exist at every level of animal life; they have throughout most of evolutionary time. But aggression is only one part of an evolutionarily complex picture for humans as well as for all other organisms. Many behavioral strategies have evolved to assure an enduring supply of resources, of mates, of conspecifics—and cooperation is one of them. It is a counterpoint to aggression in the baboon social group; it is a counterpoint to our episodic wars against ourselves. And we, more than any other species, have the capacity to set our own balance point between competition and cooperation.

But there is yet a broader framework within which animal behavior can be viewed. If, in studying the myriad forms of animal interactions, we concentrate on the question, "What has been the evolutionary consequence of the complex of behavior patterns that we see in every group?" we derive perhaps the most important generalization of all. The measure of evolutionary success of any behavioral complex has been whether it led to a pattern of resource consumption that could be maintained indefinitely. Species in which behavior did not lead to conservation of the resources essential for the life of the species are extinct. Is the present complex of behavior patterns in *our* species one that ensures the continued existence of the precious resources upon which our survival depends?

SUGGESTED READINGS

EVANS, WILLIAM F. *Communication in the Animal World.* New York: T. Y. Crowell, 1968. This paperback provides an excellent introduction to communication among animals and techniques of study.

FRINGS, HUBERT, and MABLE FRINGS. *Animal Communication.* New York: Blaisdell Publication Company, 1964. An excellent introduction to animal communication.

HALL, EDWARD T. *The Hidden Dimension.* Garden City, N.Y.: Doubleday, 1966. A noted anthropologist examines the concept of personal space in animals and goes on to probe the role individual distance plays in human interaction, overcrowding, and architecture.

SEBEOK, THOMAS A. (ed.). *Animal Communication: Techniques of Study and Results of Research.* Bloomington: Indiana University Press, 1968. A collection of chapters, each written by an authority in his or her field, on communication and techniques of study in various groups of animals. For a more meaty coverage of the field.

WENNER, ADRIAN. *The Bee Language Controversy: An Experience in Science.* Boulder, Col.: Educational Programs Improvement Corp., 1971. This book is as much about the scientific process as it is about the controversial topic.

Section VII

Populations, Communities, and Natural Selection

Here we find ourselves returning to the question asked in Section II: Why are there so many kinds of organisms in the world? Now that we have some idea of how organisms are constructed at the molecular and cellular levels and of how they function as whole individuals, we may better understand how they behave as populations and communities of populations. It is at this level that the pieces begin to fall into place, for the true unit of evolution is the population—not the individual. It is at the population level that selection acts and that species change over time.

Chapter 30

Interactions in Natural Communities

Why are organisms found where they are in nature? We might wonder why this Andira *tree came to be in the first place, towering as it does above the surrounding vegetation. We might ask whether the animals associated with this tree are there by chance or are interacting with it in some way. By careful observation and analysis, we can begin to perceive patterns to the locations of organisms here as well as in all other places on our planet.*

Throughout this book, we have been able to apply the principle of emergent properties to the examination of the hierarchy of atoms, molecules, macromolecules, organelles, cells, and tissue systems that provide the building blocks for individual organisms. At each of these levels, we have encountered emergent properties that result from an ordering of components from lower levels in the hierarchy. When we finally turn to the level of the whole organism, it might seem logical that new properties will now cease to emerge. But this is not the case. *Individual organisms are themselves part of larger natural systems, and the order that is characteristic of these systems also generates emergent properties.* As in the other levels of organization, ordering gives rise to properties that not only favor the retention of order but actually create conditions favorable to the evolution of new patterns of order—and thus to still newer properties.

In exploring the structure and function of systems composed of organisms, we enter the realm of **ecology**—the study of the interaction of organisms with their environment. This "environment" is not simply a matter of temperature, rainfall, and a variety of other abiotic factors; it includes the total biological array that the organism must contend with in a given unit of time and space. If we attempted to analyze patterns of interaction at the planetary level, the complexity of the problem would be overwhelming. To make any sort of sense out of ecological interactions, smaller systems must be examined. The basic unit of ecological classification is the biotic **community,** a definable array of interacting organisms. Communities can be recognized in all sizes and varieties. Depending on the scope or goals of a given study, the examination might be limited to the small aquatic community present in the water-filled cavity of a tree stump; or it may encompass the forest community of which the tree stump is but a single part. Although increasingly larger communities could be considered, the point would soon be reached where the units would be so large that they would become unwieldy and difficult to define. In practice, the best community concepts involve units of biological interaction that are, to some extent, self-contained. Should the need arise to consider still larger units, the ecologist defines more complex **ecosystems,** composed of a variety of individual communities. In this and the following two chapters, we will be concerned with the derivation of principles and mechanisms involved in the structure, function, and evolution of biological communities.

INTERACTIONS AMONG ORGANISMS IN A COMMUNITY: A CASE STUDY

A survey of the organisms to be found at any one place at any particular time reveals a sample in time and space of the biotic community. The sample can be described in terms of numbers of individuals and species, distribution in time and space of the individuals and populations, and observed activities and interactions. The characteristics of the sample can be explained in terms of interactions among populations and among individuals within populations.

As an example, consider a sample of a tropical forest community, taken on one morning during the dry season. Some characteristics of the sample can be explained in terms of the present interactions among organisms. For example, the sample includes an unusually large number of solitary bees—3,482 individuals of thirty-one different species. The bees are found on the flowers of a large adult tree, *Andira inermis,* in the sample area. Each morning during its month-long flowering period, this tree produces about 10,000 new flowers. Like most other tropical trees, *Andira* grows during the rainy season and flowers during the dry season. The female bees gather nectar for food and for provisioning their nest cells; the male bees collect nectar for "fuel" to keep themselves alive while they search for female bees.

The characteristics of the sample can be explained further through a consideration of events in the recent past—within a few life spans of the longest-lived individuals in the community. The *Andira* tree has such a large crop of flowers because it has spread its canopy to the maximum possible size—shading out its competing neighbors rather than being shaded out by them. Its extensive growth was possible because during the last rainy season it used all of its energy reserves for growth of branches and leaves rather than flowering a second time. When the growing season began with the first rains, it was prepared with an extensive canopy to take maximum advantage of the photosynthetic energy available for further growth. Furthermore, although its neighbors may have been hampered in their growth by attacks of plant-eating insects, the *Andira* tree remained relatively free of such pests. Part of the reason for its freedom from insect pests is the great distance of this tree from other *Andira* trees. The caterpillars and leafhoppers that feed upon new *Andira* leaves did not travel the great distance from infected *Andira* trees to this lone individual.

This *Andira* tree happens to be far from other individuals of its species because long ago a bat carried an *Andira* fruit far from the parent tree before eating the fruit and dropping its seed. This tree has not become surrounded by its own offspring because most of every seed crop has been destroyed by the weevils that maintain a local population under each *Andira* tree.

There are so many bees because last year the *Andira* and its neighbors of other species flowered at this time, allowing the female solitary bees to build and provision the maximum possible number of nest cells. During the past year, however, many of the old flowering trees in the vicinity were cut down by a lumbering operation, greatly reducing the number of food sources for bees and thus increasing the number of bees feeding on each tree, including the *Andira*. Still another reason for the large number of bees is that the previous dry season was unusually severe. It is likely that few of the parasites that normally infest the bees' nests survived the long, hot search between individual nests, and the mortality due to parasites among this year's crop of young bees was consequently quite low.

These examples are only a few of the interactions among organisms in the present and the recent past that have produced the characteristics of the community sample. The list could be extended almost indefinitely, involving interactions among all the species present and the nonliving environment. Still another level of explanation can be reached by considering interactions stretching over the distant past—a perspective often termed an evolutionary time scale. In effect, these evolutionary explanations represent the summation over a long time of many interactions of the sort described above.

The behavior of the bees and the *Andira* tree in any interaction is greatly influenced by their genetic programming, the result of natural selection acting over many generations, influenced largely by the multitude of ecological interactions that confronted the ancestral populations of bees and *Andira* trees. The relationship between present-day phenotype and those past interactions can only be inferred, for no human observer was present to record what happened. However, an examination of the present and recent past events in the context of the entire community can lend support to these inferences.

The *Andira* tree flowers in the dry season because individuals of past *Andira* populations that flowered during the rainy (growth) season probably were shaded out by individuals that devoted all their resources to rapid growth of leaves and branches. These individuals did not produce as many seeds as did the individuals that flowered during the dry season, when no species was expanding its canopy. Furthermore, the trees that did not produce a large number of flowers per day were visited less frequently by bees. Their flowers were less likely to be pollinated, particularly by pollen grains carried from other trees. Thus, the individuals that flowered out of phase with the other trees of the forest or that produced small numbers of flowers for any reason became genetically isolated from the general population and, because of their selective disadvantage, these genotypes were eventually eliminated.

The isolated *Andira* tree of this sample suffered little insect damage primarily because most leaf-eating insects in the tropical forest community are relatively host-specific. In their evolutionary past, the insects have become specialized

to overcome the biochemical, morphological, and behavioral defenses of particular tree species. Insects that have become adapted to overcome the defenses of some other tree species are a minor threat to *Andira* trees. On the other hand, the *Andira* population has survived because it has been able to change its biochemical, morphological, and behavioral genotype sufficiently to keep one step ahead of the insects that are adapting specifically to attack it.

The ability of the *Andira* population to make these changes of genotype depends heavily on the extensive genetic recombination occurring during cross-pollination. Self-pollination contributes little to the evolutionary change of the population gene pool. (Although self-pollination is technically a sexual process because it involves meiosis and fusion of gametes, it is essentially equivalent to a sexual reproduction in that genes are not exchanged between individuals in the population.) In this light, the roles of the bees, the large flower crop, and the time of flowering take on added significance.

Andira trees with large seeds enjoyed a selective advantage because the greater supply of nutrients enhanced the likelihood that its seedlings would survive. The larger fruits were more attractive to bats and thus were more likely to be transported far enough from the parent tree to minimize competition between parent and offspring for light and nutrients and to minimize intertree exchange of pest populations.

The evolution of bee populations has been influenced strongly by interactions with the tree populations. Some bees responded to cues in the physical environment that were synchronized closely with the cues used by *Andira* and other trees to time their flowering. These bees emerged from their underground nest cells a year after the construction of the cells and found an ample supply of food. Those bees responding to other cues emerged at times when flowers were scarce or unavailable and produced few offspring. Female bees that concentrated their foraging on the few large trees in full bloom were able to produce a large number of nest cells in the short time that these trees bloomed. Thus, these females produced more offspring than females that expended flying time and energy searching for less conspicuous and smaller food sources during this blooming season. On the other hand, bees with the searching behavior pattern were able to specialize in feeding on other species of plants with less conspicuous flowers and longer flowering periods and thus were able to avoid competition with the bees specializing in trees such as *Andira*. Female bees that nested in isolated patches of ground produced offspring with a lower rate of mortality due to nest parasites than did bees that nested in large aggregations.

The listing of population interactions over evolutionary

time scales could also be expanded indefinitely. Such inferences can lead to an incredible set of fairy tales about the possible significance of this or that interaction between pairs of populations. The nearly infinite complexity produces a range of possible speculation that has led many biologists to throw up their hands in despair, abandoning hope of finding any general and reliable principles of evolutionary interaction and concentrating instead on the mechanisms of interaction that can be observed and experimentally studied within short time spans. Such principles can be generated, but they must be based on close observation and experimentation with existing systems. Pure description of interactions in natural systems—no matter how fascinating and complex (and therefore seemingly intellectually sophisticated)—is of little use unless it makes possible the development of some general statements or principles that can be used to predict the characteristics of new systems.

The general principles that will be discussed in this chapter have already been suggested by the brief examination of the interactions among *Andira inermis* and the other populations in its community. Many other general principles will undoubtedly be discovered as further research is done in the relatively new area of population and community ecology.

The most basic feature of any community is the struggle to obtain and to retain energy and the basic building blocks that allow an organism to obtain and to retain energy. The success of this manipulation of energy is ultimately evaluated by the success of the organism in having its genotype represented among the members of future generations. This success is not necessarily proportional to the energy harvested, retained, or expended. The expenditure of a small amount of energy to place a toxic compound in a small number of seeds and thus permit all of the seeds to survive without predator damage may be just as successful evolutionarily as an immense amount of energy expended on seed production (so that seed numbers are great enough to satiate seed predators and ensure survival of a few seeds). In a habitat where large amounts of energy are needed for other life processes, survival may require the development of a means of seed production that uses little energy. On the other hand, in a habitat where abundant energy is available for seed production, there may be some advantage in the production and dispersal of a large number of seeds even though few survive. The competition for energy underlies each of the general principles that will be explored through various examples in the following sections.

CONSPECIFIC SEPARATION IN SPACE AND TIME

The distance in time and space between individual organisms of the same species (**conspecific individuals**) is determined both by interactions among the individuals of this species and by interactions with other populations. Consideration of extreme examples will help to clarify the kinds of interactions involved.

Suppose that a tree seed is carried a long distance by water, wind, or bird and happens to land on an oceanic island unpopulated by its species. A consideration of its fate reveals the importance of interactions within the tree population of the mainland community. The isolated individual has left far behind the entire complex of host-specific predators and parasites that caused high mortality among each generation of new members in the tree population. Evolutionary pressures have resulted in a genotype that produces a large number of seeds in each crop in order to ensure survival of a few seedlings. On the island, many thousands of seeds in a viable condition may be dispersed by the single tree.

For example, *Leucaena glauca,* a small and shrubby legume of the Central American mainland, became established on the island of Puerto Rico but left behind at least three species of pea weevils, or bruchid beetles, that destroy more than 90 percent of each seed crop on the mainland. Although this plant is relatively rare on the mainland, it is extremely common in Puerto Rico, partly because each island plant disperses as many as 100 times more viable seeds than does each mainland plant.

The plant that immigrates to an island also leaves behind an array of species that carry pollen from one plant to another or that help to disperse its seeds. Most of these species subsist in part or in whole on the flowers and fruits of the mainland population. The single island plant must produce its first generation of offspring through self-pollination. If this species has evolved mechanisms to reduce self-pollination, the production of viable seeds may be so small that the island population is unable to get started, even in the absence of host-specific predators. Even as the population density of reproductive adults begins to increase, the absence of species that serve as pollinators on the mainland may lead to a heavy reliance on self-pollination. In addition to the lack of genetic variability, because all individuals are descended from the single migrant individual, the limitation of sexual recombination can lead to a low rate of adaptation in the island population for the first several generations.

The lack of species that disperse fruits or seeds on the mainland may also hamper the spread of the island tree population. Most fruit-eating vertebrates utilize a wide variety of different kinds of fruits, but such animals are rare on most islands, probably because they cannot survive without fruit-bearing trees. But fruit-bearing trees may not become well established without the animals to disperse their seeds. Thus, the nearly simultaneous arrival of immigrants from both populations may be necessary for the establishment of a stable community.

In the first few generations of the island tree population, each individual will have little competition from other members of the same species. Because of the absence of dispersal agents, a seed is more likely to germinate beneath its parent and near its siblings than is the case in mainland communities. A similar proximity of conspecific individuals is found in populations that rely on wind or other inanimate agents for seed dispersal, as is common among the tree species of temperate forests.

At the other extreme, close proximity of conspecific adults has important consequences of a quite different sort for the interactions within the population. For example, wind pollination is a highly effective out-crossing mechanism over the short intertree distances in coniferous forests but is very ineffective in tropical forests, where conspecific individuals are widely spaced. In the spring season of temperate zones, wind pollination can occur much earlier and more reliably than can pollination that relies on insects. Conspecific individuals are so closely spaced that the tree of the temperate zone can bear male flowers at a different time than female flowers. The tree thus avoids self-pollination, but there is a high probability that some nearby tree will be producing opposite-sex flowers at the appropriate time.

But proximity of conspecific adults can also be disadvantageous to the population because it maximizes the ease of movement from plant to plant of host-specific seed predators and parasites. In the case of wind-carried diseases, even wide spacing between conspecific individuals provides little protection. The evolution of mechanisms for resisting attack is the only hope for survival of the host species. However, natural selection will tend to eliminate parasite species that are too successful in destroying their host populations, so that evolutionary trends in both the parasite and host populations tend toward a balance in which a number of host individuals are able to survive parasite attack. In the case of diseases carried by insects—such as the Dutch elm disease, which is caused by a fungus carried from tree to tree by a bark beetle—moderate spacing of conspecific adults may slow or stop the spread of infection sufficiently that the death of diseased adults will be matched by production of new adults. The population density of adults will decrease after the introduction of such a disease until this moderate spacing is attained or a mechanism of resistance to infection is evolved. The latter situation has been observed in a number of crop plants.

Separation of conspecific individuals in time or in space may have an advantage in reducing the damage caused by less mobile or less lethal predators and parasites. For example, an acorn buried by a squirrel escapes in space from an immense population of insects (dominated by acorn weevils of the genus *Curculio*). This escape is accomplished close to the parent tree and by a movement of only a few inches downward. Predation by squirrels is the price that the adult tree pays for protection of new nuts buried before insects can find them.

In the coniferous forests of the Pacific Northwest, escape from predators and parasites is accomplished by separation in time. Many trees of the temperate zone share the trait of producing seeds only during years of a **mast crop,** a crop that follows several years of nearly sterile vegetative growth. Populations of insects and squirrels that feed on the seeds decline during the "off years," despite the high density of adult trees in the area. When the mast crop is produced, the small populations of predators are soon saturated with food and many seeds escape to germinate. In the Pacific Northwest, as many as six species of conifers in the community may synchronize the timing of their mast crops. This synchronization allows a much greater proximity in space of conspecific adult trees for a given amount of seed predation, because the trees have escaped the predators by spacing their reproductive activities in time.

A high density of conspecific individuals in space may be accomplished despite high predation if there is enough separation in time. An extreme example is provided by the periodic cicadas, which spend a period of thirteen to seventeen years underground as larvae. After this long larval period, the entire population of highly predator-susceptible adults emerges simultaneously. This sudden appearance of large numbers of insects is not anticipated by the predator populations. The stomachs of all the local vertebrate predators are soon stuffed, and most of the female cicadas oviposit successfully. The few cicadas that emerge in years before and after the general emergence stand little chance of survival because they lack the usual predator-avoidance behavior patterns of cicada species that emerge annually. Thus, natural selection in this population tends to maintain the extreme synchrony of emergence.

If conspecific adults are closely packed in both space and time, they usually have effective morphological defenses (such as the hard shells of oysters and barnacles) or chemical defenses against predators and parasites. Among the few exceptions to this generalization are populations on islands that have not developed or cannot sustain predator populations.

One of the best examples of chemical defense in dense populations is seen in mangrove swamp communities found along rivers throughout the world's tropics. Such communities have one to five tree species, and although most of the species of mangrove trees have evolved from different families, they are all characterized by high tannin content in their bark and foliage. Their wood is so insect resistant that it is eagerly sought for fence posts, and these trees supplied the raw material of the tannin industry for many years. When an insect eats the foliage, the high concentration of tannin makes it almost impossible for the insect to utilize any of the proteins in the leaf. This same effect apparently protects the mangrove seeds from insect damage, and the trees produce great numbers of seeds nearly all year around.

In a similar fashion, conifers are protected from insect attack by systems of oleoresin ducts, which not only produce chemicals that discourage insect feeding but also drown or mechanically push out bark beetles that attempt to bore into the living tree. When, for some reason (such as drought stress or senescence), the oleoresin pressure of the tree decreases, the increased success of insect attack often leads to a population explosion among the tree's parasites. The large number of insects attacking healthy trees may then cause the failure of the oleoresin defense system in much of the tree population.

Cases of intermediate proximity of conspecific adults are found in the tropics, where virtually any combination of the defense mechanisms mentioned in this section may be found within a single forest. A single plant species may employ mast crops, chemical defenses, and a relatively low conspecific density. One such plant, *Hymenaea courbaril*, is common in the deciduous forests of Central America. It is most famous for its production of the resin that, when fossilized, forms much of the New World amber. The adult plants, usually spaced at distances of 50 to many hundreds of meters, produce fruit only at intervals of three to five years. Because the individual trees are not synchronized in fruit production, the fruit crop is only one-third to one-fifth as dense for the seed-eating weevil *(Rhinochenus stigma)* as might be thought from a simple count of the adult trees. The weevil must move between the relatively widely spaced trees, and it will find relatively few of those trees to be suitable hosts for the next year. In northern Central America and in Puerto Rico, where this weevil is not present, trees of this species bear fruit every year.

Among vertebrates, a high conspecific density is commonly accompanied by some form of intraspecific territorial behavior. As the probability increases that one member of the species will find the resource that another member is seeking, there is greater value in expending time and energy to expel that other member from the area. This kind of interaction has been demonstrated in the case of blackbirds nesting on marshes, where the size of nesting territories is directly related to the productivity of the marsh plants. Similarly, meadow mice (voles) show a dramatic increase in the intensity of territorial defense as the density of the mouse population rises. In fact, the mice may become so aggressive that they never mate!

The spacing of conspecific individuals is influenced by many kinds of interactions, both within the population and with other populations in the community. Whereas a high population density provides advantages for maximal use of resources and ease of mating, other factors, such as intraspecific competition and predation, tend to give an advantage to populations of low density. The balance reached in any particular case can be explained only by a thorough examination of the interactions experienced by the population on both the evolutionary and ecological time scales.

INTERSPECIFIC SEPARATION IN SPACE AND TIME

The separation in space and time between organisms of different species is affected by all of the interspecific interactions within the community. The population densities of other species greatly influence the distance that an organism will maintain from its neighbors of other species.

Between a simple community made up of a few populations (for example, the community of an arctic, alpine, desert, or seashore splash-zone region) and a complex community of a lowland wet tropical forest, there is an increase in the number of close relationships between pairs of species—mutualisms, parasitisms, predations, and so on. For each species in the complex community, population density is likely to depend heavily on the densities of a number of other populations, as well as on the weather and other parameters of the physical environment. Some of these interdependencies have been illustrated in preceding sections, but a few more examples will help to underscore their importance in the community structure.

Mutualism

Numerous cases of **mutualism** (a relationship between two species that is beneficial to both) between plants and pollinators or dispersal agents exist in most communities. The frequency of such mutualisms increases as the daily and seasonal fluctuations of the physical environment become more regular and as the availability of sunlight and water becomes greater. Two species can become dependent on one another for various resources only if both species have been present in the habitat at the necessary times in the necessary numbers and in the necessary age classes over the evolutionary time scale.

Along a north-south line from the Arctic to Panama, the number of species of mammals per unit area increases regularly. However, the great increase in the number of mammal species from southern Mexico to Panama is accounted for primarily by an increase in bat species. If bats are excluded from the sample, the increase in species density stops in southern Mexico, and the diversity of mammals is approximately constant from there south to the Equator. Furthermore, the number of insect-eating bat species is about the same from California to Panama; the increase is in bat species that feed on fruits, flowers, fish,

Figure 30.2   Bat pollinating a flower. The body of the bat is pressed tightly against the inflorescence, and in this way the pollen is picked up and later carried to another inflorescence.

Figure 30.3   Male Eulaema *orchid bees pollinating a* Catasetum *orchid. The relationship of these bees to the orchids has evolved into a form of mutualism that is obligatory for both parties.*

birds, small mammals, and other bats. The greatest increase is among the bats that visit fruits and flowers (Figure 30.2). There are many bat-pollinated flowers (such as *Hymenaea courbaril)* and bat-dispersed fruits (such as *Andira inermis*) that begin to appear in plant communities in lowland southern Mexico, and their numbers rise steadily toward the Equator. The key to this relationship lies in the fact that fruits and flowers are relatively nutrient-poor food sources, particularly for reproduction and for the storage of winter or dry-season fat reserves. A bat specialized on fruits and flowers must have them available throughout the year.

Several closer mutualisms are immediately apparent to any researcher working on tropical community structure. Botanists investigating the extreme diversity of tropical orchids have described a number of the intricate inter-specific relationships that support this diversity (Chapter 5). One of the most complex mutualisms is that between male "orchid bees" (*Euglossa, Euplusia, Eulaema*) and orchids such as *Catasetum, Gongora,* and others that are pollinated only by these bees (Figure 30.3). The male bees appear to require highly volatile chemicals that are produced by the flowers. The bees collect the compounds from modified parts of the plants with small brushes on the front feet and then transfer the material to special grooves in the hind legs, where the substance is absorbed into the bee's body. At times, the bee gets enough of these chemicals to alter his flight behavior dramatically. In the process of obtaining the compound, the bee is guided by a series of complex floral structures to a position where the pollinia (a pair of sacs containing pollen) are glued to some predictable part of his body. Upon entering a female flower at a later date, the bee is again guided by peculiar flower morphology to a position where the pollinia are removed by the stigma of the female

flower. The bees cannot survive without the chemicals produced by the orchids, and the orchids can be pollinated only by bees with these specific behavior patterns.

The coevolutionary steps leading to the development of this obligatory mutualism are a subject of speculation. Further coevolution of the two species produced the highly specialized behaviors and morphologies observed in the modern populations. Both the orchid bees and the orchids they pollinate are absent from most Caribbean islands—an emphatic example of the difficulty of simultaneously establishing two populations that are extremely dependent upon each other. Because the male bees cannot survive without the orchids and the bee population cannot survive without males, most of the large number of plant species pollinated by females of these bee species on the Central American mainland are also missing from the islands.

Another close mutualism is displayed by dry- and moist-habitat shrubs of the genus *Acacia*, which appear in early stages of succession in the plant communities of Central America. Ants of the genus *Pseudomyrmex* live in the swollen thorns of the plant, gain their sugar from nectaries on the leaves, feed their larvae with modified leaflet tips that are rich in proteins and steroids, and have a nearly continuous food supply because these species of *Acacia* remain green during the dry season (in contrast to other *Acacia* species not associated with ants). The ants, in turn, drive away plant-eating insects and prune back vines and shrubbery that might crowd out the *Acacia*. This activity is of immediate benefit to the ants because it keeps the *Acacia* strong and healthy and ensures a more continuous and abundant food supply. The larger the ant colony, the more effective the continuous protection that it provides for the plant; thus, both ants and *Acacia* can maximize their growth through this close mutualism. The coevolution of this interaction has continued to a point that the leaves and shoot tips of these *Acacia* species lack the insect-repelling compounds found in most plant leaves.

In drier or cooler habitats, tropical ant-plant interactions disappear from the community. In areas with long dry seasons, the *Acacia* cannot hold its leaves throughout the year, and the ant colony cannot survive through the dry season to protect the plant during following rainy seasons. In cooler regions, the ants spend more and more time inactive inside the thorns and less and less time protecting the leaves of the host. In both cases, the interspecific interaction disappears from the community (leading to a simpler community) because environmental conditions make the interaction impossible, although the conditions are not directly harmful to either participating population.

On the other hand, the ant-*Acacia* interaction has enabled this mutualistic pair to invade much wetter (and more complex) communities than have other *Acacia* species. The interaction enables the ants to avoid almost all direct competition with other ant species. The mutualism, which is possible only in the tropical habitat, allows the "stacking" of more species into the community than is possible in less favorable environments where ants and plants must be more generalized in their life styles and hence engage in greater competition with other species.

Predator-Prey Relationships

Predator-prey interactions have effects opposite those of mutualism. For maximal survival, the prey must maximize the distance in time and space between himself and the predators, whereas the predator must minimize this distance. Each time that a predator is successful in capturing a prey individual, he slightly increases the average distance between predator and prey and thus improves the survival chances of the remaining prey. As a result, predator-prey interactions are extremely "density-dependent." The success (or failure) of the predator is dependent on the density of the prey population and vice versa. The percentage of the remaining prey population that will be captured by predators declines as the predators are successful in reducing the prey population. Thus, it becomes increasingly profitable for the predator to switch over to hunting some other prey population, a situation that may even cause effective immunity from predation until a prey population can build itself back up again. A homeostatic balance tends to exist in which both predator and prey populations fluctuate around an equilibrium density.

The community, then, can be viewed as a collection of populations, some of which are declining and some of which are rising at any given instant. The rates of rise and decline depend on such factors as the efficiency of the

predators in using energy and materials from the prey to reproduce, the reproduction rate of predators and prey, the ability of the predator to shift from one prey species to another, the costs to the predator in energy and materials of maintaining generalized metabolism and behavior patterns that enable it to utilize several prey species, the number of secondary predators feeding on the primary predators, the amount of resources available to the prey, and so on.

One of the most important effects of predator-prey interactions is the reduction of competition between prey species that share a common predator. For example, the sea star *Pisaster* is a major predator on sedentary molluscs and barnacles of the intertidal zone. If the sea star is excluded from the community, one or two of the sedentary species soon crowd or starve out the other sedentary species because of their competitive advantage in feeding and reproduction. However, if the sea star is allowed access to the simplified community, it removes many individuals in these successful sedentary populations, leaving space for immigration of individuals of several other species. In other words, the addition of a single predator species can lead to an increase in the total number of prey species.

The same principle applies to forest trees. As in the intertidal zone, members of the prey species compete for space, which represents the opportunity to gather energy (sunlight) and nutrients (inorganic ions from the soil). The predator species include a large array of generalist and host-specific insects, fungi, and vertebrates that eat seeds and seedlings. Beginning with predation on the developing embryo in the green seed pod, the predators cause a steady attrition of the plant population in each generation up through dispersal and germination of the seed. In the absence of such predators, one tree species would tend to dominate any particular habitat. The predator's ability to depress the density of any one tree species to a point that it does not competitively displace the other tree species is primarily a function of how effectively the predators on juvenile plants can move across space and time between successive crops of seeds and seedlings. In habitats where an occasional late spring frost kills most members of a major seed predator population, there is a large population of tree seedlings that year. Which species of tree will be represented among the new adult trees produced from these seedlings in later years is determined by the outcome of competition among the seedlings of various species. Even if it is a relatively poor seedling competitor in a predator-free environment, the species that has the most effective defenses against predation will most likely come to dominate the community.

Along the gradient from temperate zone habitats to wet lowland tropical habitats, the probability declines that any one species of tree will escape predators either through sudden environmental fluctuations or through weather con-

(text continues on page 662)

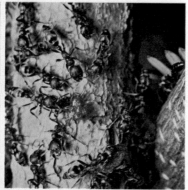

Figure 30.4   Ants and acacias: a classic study in mutualism. Many species of thorny acacias in the tropics have coevolved in symbiotic relationship with particular ant species similar to those depicted here. (1) A mature Acacia collinsii *tree, 2 meters tall; this tree was host to 19,000 worker ants at the time the photo was taken. (2) A branch of A.* cornigera *showing the pattern of foliage growth. (3) A close-up showing the enlarged thorns that form the residence for the ants. (4) The culmination of the acacia-ant mating flight; the queen holds on to the tree trunk while the much smaller male, holding on only by its genitalia, deposits sperm. (5) A queen swollen with eggs; the smaller white bodies are newly laid eggs. (6) The entrance hole to a thorn. The first entrance is cut by the queen; all subsequent ones are cut by worker ants. (7) A pair of thorns broken open to show the population of ants at various developmental stages contained within. (8) The tip of a leaf showing the bright orange structures known as Beltian bodies. The only known function for these food bodies is as a source of proteins, fats, and vitamins for the ants. (9) A view of the second specialized structure the ants use as a source of nutrients: the extrafloral nectaries, found at the base of the leaves. The drop of nectar welling up has taken about twenty-four hours to be produced. (10) Another view of the nectaries; these serve primarily as a source of calories (sugar) for the ants. A guard ant looks on from the thorn entrance. (11) An ant drinking from the nectar. (12) In exchange for thorns to live in and the food supply of the Beltian bodies and nectaries, the ants keep the acacia free of other insects. This picture shows the density of patroling ants that may be seen on the surface of an undisturbed tree. (13 and 14) A battle between two ant species for rights to an Acacia tree. Such a battle occurs when the branches of two ant acacias grow into contact. The largest ant colony usually wins. (15, 16, and 17) In addition to freeing the acacia from insect predators, the ants also protect it from competition from other plants. Frame 15 shows an acacia that harbors an ant colony, while frame 16 shows an equivalent plant nearby that has been deprived of ants for about a year. The latter tree is so overgrown with vines and so ravaged by insects that it will soon be dead. Frame 17 shows the circular clearing that is maintained by the ants around the base of the acacia, preventing overgrowth by other plant species and competition for light. (18) The acacia in turn does its part by remaining green when other foliage turns brown in the dry season, thus providing the ants with a hospitable year-round home.*

1	2	3	4	5	
	6		7	8	9
10	11		12	13	14
15	16	17		18	

ditions that are generally harmful to the predator. The result is a situation that has been recognized for many years: Tropical lowland wet forests are characterized by a large number of species of trees, each present in a population density much lower than those of the relatively few tree species found in temperate zone communities.

The same phenomenon of density-dependent mortality stated previously in general terms applies to the populations of trees and their predators. As predation on juveniles of a particular tree species increases, the probability of an embryo surviving to form an adult tree decreases. As the population of this tree species declines, the predators have to move farther between host seed crops, fewer predators reproduce, and fewer juvenile plants are destroyed. As fewer juvenile plants are destroyed, the population of the tree species begins to rise and the entire cycle repeats itself. Thus, the density of adult trees of each species tends to approach some equilibrium value, and the actual number of trees—if observed over a long period of time—fluctuates around this value. Any factor that decreases the efficiency of the predators will lead to an increase in the equilibrium density of tree populations, but the number of species and/or the density of other species in the habitat must decline (because there is only a finite amount of space in the habitat for the tree crowns).

PROXIMATE AND ULTIMATE FACTORS

For any given trait of an individual, a population, or a community, two kinds of explanatory causes may be distinguished: immediate physiological stimuli (the **proximate factors**) and long-range selective pressures (the **ultimate factors**).

When the physical environment undergoes regular and major fluctuations, many species in the habitat show periodic changes in behavior correlated with those environmental cycles. For example, in some relatively dry tropical habitats, many tree species flower shortly after the end of the rainy season. This regular time of flowering is of great importance to the large complex of bee species that emerge at this time to harvest pollen and nectar from these trees. The fruits that are produced from these flowers during the dry season may be of special importance to many mammals and birds because fewer leaves and insects are available as food than during the rainy season.

In such a case, it is possible to search for the direct physiological stimuli that cause each tree to become reproductive and to explore the physiological mechanisms by which these stimuli lead to changes in the physiology and morphology of the trees. Such an investigation leads to one kind of explanation for the flowering of many trees at a particular time of the year, an explanation in terms of proximate factors.

In general, it is more profitable to explore the benefits that accrue to a tree flowering at this time. The assumption can then be made that this characteristic has provided a selective advantage over the evolutionary time scale and that selection has developed some physiological mechanism that enables the tree to flower regularly at the appropriate time. From this point of view, the important causes of the synchronized flowering are the ultimate factors that provide a selective advantage for trees flowering at this time. It is not surprising that different species have evolved different mechanisms responding to different environmental cues for advantageous timing.

A number of selective pressures may lead to the flowering of many trees during the early part of the dry season. First, and probably most important, the tree that uses all available energy for vegetative growth during the growing season is most likely to maintain an optimal location in the general vegetative canopy. It can then store any excess energy obtained throughout the growing season and use these reserves for reproduction after dry-season leaf-fall when, for the most part, no vegetative competition is occurring. The reserves can always be used for vegetative growth if an emergency does arise during the growing season. Second, a tree that flowers out of phase with the remainder of the population will have to rely on generalist pollinators (because the specialized pollinators of the species are not present or are not engaging in pollinating behaviors) and on self-pollination. If the tree is not capable of self-pollination, it will not contribute to the gene pool of succeeding generations, and the tendency to flower out of phase will be eliminated from the population. This effect is increased as more and more of the trees in the population become better and better synchronized, because the bees coevolve a peak in emergence to match the cycle of the plants. Third, flowering during the rainy season may lead to rain damage of the flowers and pollen, which makes it more difficult for bees to arrive at the plant at a regular time of day to find newly opened flowers. Fourth, by maturing its fruits before the end of the dry season, the tree maximizes the probability that new seeds will be on the ground at the beginning of the next rainy season.

In short, any new genotype that is able to utilize an environmental cue and flower at the beginning of the dry season is likely to have a selective advantage. As such genotypes become more common in the population and as bee populations coevolve matching cycles of emergence, the selective advantage of flowering at this time increases.

In some cases, the tree may not respond to the environmental cue until it has stored up enough energy to produce a full crop of fruits and flowers. This is probably the case with the *Hymenaea courbaril* trees, which set fruit only every three to five years.

As is often the case, however, there are organisms in the community that have evolved radically different strategies to handle very similar problems. For example, in the tropical forests there are some tree populations such as figs

(*Ficus*) in which some individual trees are setting fruit at any time of the year. The small seeds are dispersed by bats and birds and are dropped along watercourses, where germination can occur throughout the year (removing one of the selective advantages of seasonal flowering). Because their roots are in wet soil along the river and they remain evergreen in most habitats, figs are in vegetative competition with other trees nearly all year (removing another selective advantage of seasonal flowering). Because the fig flowers are pollinated by tiny, highly host-specific gall wasps and are not damaged by rainfall, the other selective advantages of seasonal flowering have little effect on the fig population. In addition, there is a strong selective advantage in this population for continuous fruiting. Because the wasps can develop only within the figs of a particular host species and because they die very soon after emerging from the fig, there must be another fig tree with fruits ready for pollination nearby at the time the fig wasps emerge, or the population of these wasps will decline and disappear. Because the fig trees are pollinated only by the wasps, the fig population will also disappear if the distance between fruiting trees becomes very great.

In view of the small distances between conspecific individuals in the fig populations, with the resulting risk of high predation, it is not surprising that *Ficus* species are noted for copious quantities of milky latex that contains toxic compounds, probably an effective defense against many insects. The direct physiological stimuli that cause a particular tree to begin fruiting at a particular time are only a minor part of the data needed to understand the *Ficus* population as a part of the interactions of the community.

ENERGY COMPETITION WITHIN THE ORGANISM

Each organism must carry out at least three major functions with the finite amount of energy and materials that it can obtain from the habitat per unit time: *maintenance, reproduction, and defense.* The allotment among these three activities is a function both of the physical environment and of the traits of the other organisms in the habitat.

It is apparent from the study of physiology and biochemistry that there are many opportunities for competition between different cells, tissues, and organ systems for the finite amount of energy and materials taken in by an individual plant or animal. A given environmental challenge may strongly influence the balance among these competing systems and therefore influence the allotment of resources among the functions of maintenance, reproduction, and defense. Often, the environmental challenge takes the form of an interaction with some other species in the habitat.

For example, the "secondary substances" produced by plants have long been regarded as waste products. These substances include terpenes, alkaloids, free amino acids, cyanogenic glycosides, resins, and a variety of other

(a)

(b)

*Figure 30.5 (a) Foliage and fruit of wild fig (*Ficus*) trees of Central America; the host-specific gall wasp enters through the small pore at the distal end of the fruit. (b) Split wild fig fruits with fruitlets lining the inner cavity.*

chemicals. But for the most part, the molecules found among the secondary substances of a given species are unique to that species and closely related species. In fact, the secondary substances often provide a "chemical fingerprint" that permits unambiguous species identification. It is no coincidence, however, that these substances are also generally or specifically toxic to an immense array of insects, fungi, and vertebrates, many of which are potential predators or parasites of the plant. A growing body of evidence indicates that the substances present in a plant species (or in a part of each plant) are a coevolved result of the presence of certain animal species in the community and the resources available to the plant. For example, plants of the bean family (Leguminosae) have root nodules that bear nitrogen-fixing bacteria. These plants use primarily nitrogen-rich defensive compounds (alkaloids and free amino acids, such as canavanine and L-dopa). Depending on the extent of predator and parasite threat, a bean plant may devote more or less of its metabolic resources to the production of defensive compounds. Normally, a bean plant produces compounds that require the least expenditure of energy and materials. It tolerates a certain amount of damage in order to minimize the resources devoted to defense and to maximize the resources available for other activities.

THE IMPORTANCE OF ENERGY IN COMMUNITY STRUCTURE

Because the flow of energy through the community is obviously a major component of the community structure, it has been traditional to think of those organisms that store or process large amounts of energy as the most significant members of the community. The deceptiveness of this assumption can be appreciated by noting the effects of the disappearance of some inconspicuous insect populations.

When the herbaceous weed St. John's wort (*Hypericum*) was accidentally introduced into pastures of the west coast of the United States, it quickly spread and became one of the most common members of the plant community. A small and inconspicuous leaf beetle (*Chrysolina geminata*) was introduced from Australia and quickly caused near-extinction of the plant. The beetle browses on the leaf rosettes at the base of the plant until the plant is so weakened that it loses out in competition for light and space with other plant species. In the sunny parts of pastures, where the beetle grows rapidly, the plant is now locally extinct. It survives, however, in the shade of fence rows, where the beetle does poorly. Both beetle and plant are now rare in the pasture community. Even at the peak of its population growth, the direct contribution of the beetle to the total energy flow of the community was trivial, yet these beetles in effect limited the reproductive potential of a plant that otherwise would have dominated the communities in which it was found.

A very small daily drain on the resources of an organism may have a very large cumulative effect. A caterpillar eating 1 centimeter from the tip of a growing tree branch removes only an insignificant fraction of the tree's stored energy. However, the loss of the growing apex means the loss of a number of mature leaves that would have appeared later and would have carried out a great deal of photosynthetic activity for the plant. Not only does the delayed leaf production mean loss of energy gathered, it may also mean loss in height or status within the canopy. By the time a new axillary shoot has elongated to replace the original branch end, the branches of neighboring plants may have grown considerably higher.

Similarly, a few ounces of succulent plant matter can make the difference between survival and death for a deer in the late winter, when fat reserves are low and the threat of predation or starvation is high. Those few ounces, however, are a very trivial part of the deer's annual intake.

In short, the temporal and spatial distribution of resources can be as important as their nutritive value. A few calories invested in production of nectar may lead to extensive cross-pollination by bees with a subsequent heavy seed set; the same amount of energy put into a few more seeds might have a much smaller impact on later representation of the parental genotype in later tree populations. Natural selection provides the test in which the value of various energy allocations is judged by their success in reproduction.

PREDATORS DO NOT EAT LATIN BINOMIALS

In thinking about community structure, it is easy to fall into the trap of regarding species as natural units made up of individuals with uniform morphological and behavioral characteristics. The name of an organism is no more than a convenient pigeon-holing device; predators do not select their prey on the basis of its Latin binomial label. The members of a species come in many ages, sexes, behaviors, sizes, and so on.

If a species of lygaeid bug is observed to feed on many kinds of seeds, dead insects, fecal matter, and leaf parts, it is tempting to regard this species as polyphagous—able to eat many kinds of food. Such a classification, however, tends to obscure the fact that the female bug can obtain the nutrients and other materials necessary for egg production only from one or two of the seed species. The other foods are adequate only for fuel to keep the female going until she locates the appropriate seeds and can reproduce.

Many caterpillars feed freely on new foliage of their host plants, but they cannot feed on matured leaves, which contain various toxic secondary substances. Thus, the insect may be sitting in the middle of a pure stand of its "host plant" and yet be starving to death. Tropical trees produce new leaves in periodic bursts of activity, separated by long periods when no new leaves are produced, thus separating leaf crops in time and helping to keep the caterpillar population low. Selection strongly favors such genotypes in relatively warm climates of moderate rainfall, where plant-eating insects would otherwise thrive.

It is often noted that the bigger the animal, the longer the list of plant species on which it can feed. There are two components of this observation that are of interest in the study of community structure. First, these plants generally can be arrayed in a rough order of preference, which is probably determined by such things as content of toxic substances, ease of finding, speed of digestion, energy content, work to process, and exposure to predators in finding and feeding. For larger animals, many of these factors are not very important. Second, the mere presence of all of these plants in the habitat does not ensure survival and reproduction. For example, it is commonly noted that big game animals eat small amounts of many species of plants. It is tempting to speculate that if the animal were forced to feed on only a single plant species, it might die of poisoning from the secondary substances of the leaves. In short, in addition to passing its food through the processing of the stomach acids and of the bacterial culture in the intestines, the large browsing mammal also dilutes the

Figure 30.6 Moth caterpillars feeding on a leaf. Many such caterpillars feed on the new foliage of their host plants but cannot feed on mature leaves that may contain higher levels of secondary toxic substances. Thus, certain plants may regulate both the quality and quantity of the toll exacted by their insect enemies.

secondary substances from one plant species with those of many others. Thus, it avoids ingesting a harmful amount of any one toxic substance. In a system such as this one, the animal could starve if half its potential food species disappeared from the habitat, even though each of those remaining became twice as common.

Although an acorn and its parent oak tree are both individuals of the species *Quercus alba*, the removal of one by a predator has a very different effect on the community from the removal of the other. Similarly, if ants of the species *Solenopsis geminata* are consistently found in the gut of a bird, it makes a great difference to the eventual structure of the community whether they are queen, male, or worker ants. A bird eating several worker ants would have little effect on an established colony, but every queen consumed would destroy the potential for the establishment of an entire colony.

PERSPECTIVE

The composition and structure of a biotic community is the result of a long series of events culminating in the present array of organisms that occupy the site. The present structure can be described by an accurate survey of the numbers and kinds of different organisms present, but determining *why* the community has a certain structure is much more complex. The answers to such questions involve not only a careful assessment of how and to what extent various species utilize community resources, but also a careful analysis of the varied roles played by each species throughout its life cycle. Given the complexity of even the simplest communities, we have a long way to go before we acquire a thorough understanding of even a small number of the biological interactions in the world around us. Data collected from observation of communities can be used to derive inferences on some of the factors operating within the community, and both the data and the inferences can be incorporated into generalized models that can have predictive value in the analysis of still other systems. Continual modification of the models is required as some inferences are shown to be in error and other data become available. Although biologists are making only tentative inroads into the problems involved in constructing predictive models, such models are an absolute requirement for minimizing the impact of human activities on the natural world.

As humanity increases in both numbers and technological capability, it becomes ever more critical to be able to provide an accurate assessment of how certain projects might affect the "environment"—in practical terms, usually one or more biotic communities. These concerns have led to the development of the "environmental impact statement," which is essentially a prediction of the effects of a particular technological project. Our understandable desire for such statements presently outstrips our ability to provide adequate data on which to base them. Ecologists are understandably cautious, for in virtually all cases examined so far, the actual factors maintaining community integrity are far more subtle than was initially supposed. Active support by society as a whole of basic investigations of community structure and function will not only provide useful insights into biological principles; they can be expected to be of material use in optimizing humanity's interaction with the rest of the natural world.

SUGGESTED READINGS

JANZEN, D. H. "Coevolution of Mutualism Between Ants and Acacias in Central America," *Evolution,* 20 (1966), 249–275. A detailed account of ant-acacia interactions with an analysis of some of the probable selective pressures involved in initiating and maintaining the mutualism.

MacARTHUR, ROBERT H., and EDWARD O. WILSON. *The Theory of Island Biogeography.* Monographs in Population Biology. Princeton, N.J.: Princeton University Press, 1967. Case studies and analysis of the factors and strategies found in island populations. A highly desirable reference for anyone interested in evolution and ecology.

VAN DER PIJL, L. *Principles of Dispersal in Higher Plants.* 2nd ed. New York: Springer-Verlag, 1972. Evolution of dispersal mechanisms and strategies in flowering plants.

Chapter 31

Ecology: The House We Live In

For uncounted millenia, voracious predators have roamed the earth, living at the expense of other life forms. And yet the prey abound. Why have the world's great herbivores not stripped the earth of its vegetation? And where in the continuing cycles of predator and prey are the controls that lead to balance in their numbers?

Why are there so many kinds of organisms in the world? Why haven't a handful of "most fit" species become predominant? Why are the species grouped so differently in different places? Why do we tend to find plants of the same species clustered in the temperate zones but spread widely from one another in the tropics? Why are there so many more kinds of plants and animals in most tropical forests than in most temperate forests? And why is it not possible to farm successfully in the tropics, given the rich plant and animal populations the land supports?

These are the kinds of problems that the field of ecology attempts to deal with. **Ecology,** translated literally, means the "study of the house." It attempts to explain organisms in terms of the complex of physical and biological features that form the environment in which the organism lives.

When we seek to explain why a species succeeds or fails in a given environment, we quickly come to realize that we must focus our attention on the *population* of individual species members, not just on the individuals themselves. Because individuals are inevitably lost through death, the critical question is whether the population can continuously produce new individuals fast enough to replace those that are lost. Our search therefore must begin with the factors that control whether a population will rise, decline, or remain the same in size.

But in analyzing population growth, we soon come to realize that availability of resources for growth and reproduction is often the critical consideration. Therefore, we must inevitably focus our attention on the place of the population within the *community* of populations in which it finds itself. Which other populations will provide the resources, and how successful will they be? Which other populations will be competing for resources, and what will determine the outcome of that competition? What other populations will be using the population we are interested in as a resource? And how successful will they be?

The answer to these additional questions requires that we first understand the physical aspects of the environment—the availability of water, minerals, sunlight, heat, and so forth. Thus our attention is drawn to considerations of still broader scope—to the *ecosystem* in which our community interacts with other communities and with the physical environment of the surrounding areas. And the physical features are so characteristic of certain regions of the earth's surface and yet so different between others that we find it useful to subdivide the earth's surface into *biomes,* where key features of geography tend to give rise to unique kinds of solutions to the survival equation. But when we try to set boundaries on these biomes that at first appear so different, we find them shading into one another and

interacting, thus revealing once again the fundamental unity and interdependence of all life in our *biosphere.*

We see, then, that the task of deriving the answer to our simple question, "Why does a species succeed in one place and not another?" is not an easy one. Yet at each level of analysis, many key insights have been derived. This chapter will explore a few of them.

SOME CHARACTERISTICS OF POPULATION GROWTH

One of the most astonishing features of living things is the rate at which they are capable of reproducing. Consider the fact that under suitable conditions some bacterial cells are capable of dividing once every twenty minutes. If we were to allow a single bacterium to grow and divide in a large culture dish containing appropriate nutrients, we could expect to see a maximum rate of population increase of the sort given in Table 31.1. Within the six-hour time span of this experiment, the culture vessel would contain more than 250,000 individuals. If this rate of growth could be maintained for two days, the mass of the bacteria so produced would exceed the mass of the earth! The growth rate in this theoretical system is **exponential:** Each reproductive episode doubles the effective breeding population. *All organisms, regardless of their reproductive rates, show exponential growth under ideal conditions.* The only variable is the time it takes to reach extreme population size. Charles Darwin pointed out that even elephants—notoriously slow

Table 31.1
Growth of Hypothetical Bacterial Population*

Time (minutes)	Population Size (number of individuals)	Natural Logarithm of Population Size
0	1	0.00
20	2	0.69
40	4	1.39
60	8	2.08
80	16	2.77
100	32	3.47
120	64	4.16
140	128	4.85
160	256	5.55
180	512	6.24
200	1,024	6.93
220	2,048	7.63
240	4,096	8.32
260	8,192	9.01
280	16,384	9.70
300	32,768	10.40
320	65,536	11.09
340	131,072	11.78
360	262,144	12.47

*It is assumed that each individual divides at 20-minute intervals to give rise to two daughter cells and that no individuals are lost from the population through death.

breeders that they are—possess the same potential for explosive population growth. In his calculations, he assumed that all elephants would live to an age of 100; that the females would breed between the ages of 30 and 90; and that the average number of offspring produced by each female would be six. He concluded that, from the original pair of elephants, there would be 19 million elephants alive in a mere 750 years!

These two hypothetical cases describe the maximum possible reproductive rate, or the **intrinsic rate of increase** of the two species. Obviously, however, we are not neck deep in bacteria and we are not living shoulder-to-shoulder with elephants, so we may surmise that the intrinsic rate of increase is rarely achieved in actual populations. Figure 31.2 relates the intrinsic rate of increase (solid line) to the kind of growth normally seen in a real population (yeast, in this example). Although the other two curves initially approximate the intrinsic rate of increase, certain factors apparently intervene to reduce the actual growth rate. The dotted curve is typical of a population in a small, closed culture dish containing limited medium. The population increases at the intrinsic rate for a short time (often called a *logarithmic growth phase*), but the rate of increase gradually falls off, finally reaching zero. Now population size remains constant for a time; this is called the *plateau phase*. But eventually the number of live cells in the culture begins to fall until finally there are no more live cells.

From observations on populations such as the yeast culture, we may derive some obvious but important generalizations regarding the relationship of birth and death to population size. First, if the birth rate exceeds the death rate, population size increases. Second, if the birth and death rates are equal, population size remains static. And third, if the death rate exceeds the birth rate, population size declines.

What sort of factors cause birth rates and death rates to change? Consider the yeast cells just described. These cells obtain energy by breaking down sugars to form alcohol and carbon dioxide (Chapter 14). It seems likely that the cells might simply be running out of the sugar they need as an energy source. We could test this assumption by periodically adding sugar to the culture. Under such conditions, the growth cuve would follow the logarithmic rate for a slightly longer period and the population size would become somewhat larger, as shown by the dashed curve in Figure 31.2. It would thus appear that a shortage in some essential resource (in this case, sugar) can limit both the rate of growth and the size of a population. Ecologists refer to this factor as the **law of the minimum:** *Of all the various resources needed by a population, the resource that is present in the smallest quantity in relation to the needs of the population acts as a limiting factor on maximum population size.*

Interestingly enough, even if we were to continue adding sugar to the culture, the population of yeast cells would *not* maintain its maximum size; eventually it would actually decline sooner than if we had not added more sugar! If we were dealing with a natural population, we might be tempted to look for various sorts of other limiting factors; and indeed, if we were to observe even this controlled population for any length of time, we would discover that other resources become limiting factors once sugar is available in adequate amounts. But even if we were to supply all essential nutrients in extremely abundant amounts, we would not be able to keep the yeast population growing indefinitely. We would be able to achieve a certain maximum population and no more. And this time the population would begin to die out even faster than before! Why is this so? Is something other than the availability of resources capable of setting the limit on population size?

We might speculate that something is accumulating in the culture medium that is killing the cells. To test this hypothesis, we can try a new experiment. Instead of merely adding sugar to the culture, let us try removing some of the old medium at regular intervals and replacing it with new medium. The result of such an experiment is shown in Figure 31.3. We see that renewing the medium has two

Figure 31.2 Theoretical growth curves for yeast cells grown in the closed culture system with a sugar water medium. The solid curve is the population growth rate at the intrinsic rate of increase. The dotted curve is the population growth in a closed system, and the dashed curve is the population growth in a closed system with the periodic addition of more sugar. The breaks in the curve indicate a period of variable duration during which population size is constant.

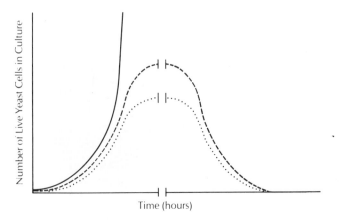

Number of Live Yeast Cells in Culture

Time (hours)

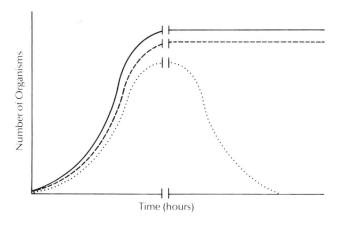

Figure 31.3 Effect of renewing medium on growth of a yeast culture. The dotted line shows the population curve when the medium is not changed. If some of the old medium is removed and replaced with new medium at regular intervals, the maximum population size achieved is greater and the population is maintained rather than dying out (dashed line). If the medium is changed more frequently, the maximum population size is increased further (solid line).

effects. First, it increases maximum population size. But, more importantly, it prevents the decline in population size that occurs in unrenewed medium. Now the population of live cells is maintained at a relatively high, stable value. What accounts for the difference?

If we perform chemical analysis on the medium, we find that as sugar molecules are broken down by yeast, the acidity of the medium increases because some carbon dioxide remains in solution; furthermore, the amount of alcohol increases as sugar is consumed. If these metabolic by-products are allowed to accumulate, the medium becomes increasingly toxic to the yeast cells—which results in ever-increasing deaths and, eventually, the decline of the population. But if we replace some of the medium regularly, we prevent these toxic compounds from accumulating in as great amounts. The death rate does not become as great and the population size is therefore maintained at higher levels.

Thus maximum population size can also be affected by tolerance to environmental factors (in this case, the metabolites of the cells themselves). This concept is often expressed as the **law of tolerance:** *Where and to what extent a population can grow is limited by its tolerance to environmental factors, and any single factor that approaches the tolerance limit of the species will impose a limit on maximum population size.*

Environment Controls Population Size by Affecting Birth and Death Rates

In order to understand how tolerance to environmental factors and availability of resources regulate population size under natural conditions, it is necessary to discuss the concepts of natality and mortality. **Natality** refers to the rate at which individuals in a population reproduce in a given unit of time. **Mortality** refers to the rate at which death removes individuals from the population in a given unit of time. If we were to examine small samples of the population of yeast cells periodically, we would find that during the logarithmic growth phase natality approaches the intrinsic

rate of increase, with reproduction occurring rapidly in all cells. But soon we would begin to see a decrease in natality, with each cell requiring more time between reproductive episodes. In addition, dead cells would begin to appear. Such increasing mortality coupled with decreasing natality causes the population curve to level off. At maximum population density, natality and mortality rates would be in balance for a time. Eventually, however, mortality in the culture with unchanged medium would exceed natality, and the population would begin to decline. But in the culture in which the medium was changed regularly, this large increase in mortality would not occur. Rather, natality and mortality would remain in balance, resulting in a stable population size.

In organisms that reproduce sexually, natality is much more complex than in microorganisms that reproduce by binary fission. The maximum natality that a species can achieve is determined by several factors related to the biology of the organism. Among the most important are the sex ratio in the population, the time required for a female to reach sexual maturity, the number of young produced per reproductive cycle, the frequency of reproductive cycles, and the length of time over which the female remains reproductively active. Because all these factors are variable from species to species, each species will have a characteristic maximum natality rate. But maximum natality is not commonly achieved by natural populations. Limited resources and/or environmental parameters that are near the tolerance limits of the species tend to affect nearly all these parameters in such a way as to *lower natality*. (In other words, such factors delay the onset of sexual maturity, decrease the number of young per cycle, and so on.) Thus, for each natural situation we see that what biologists call the *realized natality* of the population is lower than the *maximum natality* of the species by an amount that is determined by environmental parameters.

The mortality rate for a species is commonly represented by a life table of the sort shown in Table 31.2, which tabulates the average life expectancy for a specific population of cottontail rabbits at age intervals up to thirty-nine months. But different species show quite different patterns with respect to the age dependence of the mortality rate. Thus, the pattern of mortality is as much a species characteristic as the natality rate.

From data such as those in Table 31.2, it is possible to graph the percentage of individuals that survive to any given age. Such graphs are called **survivorship curves.** They tend to follow one of three general shapes (Figure 31.4), although intermediates between the three are also known.

Table 31.2
Life Table for 10,000 Cottontail Rabbits

Age Interval (months)	Number Living at Beginning of Interval	Number Dying During Interval	Mortality Rate*	Life Expectancy†
0–4	10,000	7,440	0.74	6.5
4–5	2,560	282	0.11	6.6
5–6	2,278	228	0.10	6.5
6–7	2,050	246	0.12	6.5
7–8	1,804	307	0.17	6.4
8–9	1,497	150	0.10	6.4
9–10	1,347	175	0.13	6.3
10–11	1,172	164	0.14	6.3
11–12	1,008	212	0.21	6.3
12–13	796	143	0.18	6.3
13–14	653	98	0.15	6.2
14–15	555	55	0.10	6.0
15–16	500	65	0.13	5.8
16–17	435	31	0.07	5.6
17–18	404	24	0.06	5.3
18–19	380	49	0.13	5.0
19–20	331	36	0.11	4.9
20–21	295	47	0.16	4.6
21–22	248	20	0.08	4.4
22–23	228	39	0.17	4.2
23–24	189	32	0.17	4.0
24–25	157	13	0.08	3.7
25–26	144	7	0.05	3.4
26–27	137	30	0.22	3.1
27–28	107	12	0.11	2.9
28–29	95	13	0.14	2.6
29–30	82	32	0.39	2.4
30–31	50	7	0.14	2.3
31–32	43	9	0.21	2.1
32–33	34	11	0.33	1.9
33–34	23	16	0.70	1.9
34–35	7	3	0.35	2.3
35–36	4	0	0.00	2.0
36–37	4	0	0.00	1.5
37–38	4	0	0.00	1.0
38–39	4	4	1.00	0.5

*Fraction of those alive at the beginning of this interval that die during the interval.
†Average number of months of life remaining at beginning of age interval.
Source: R. D. Lord Jr., "Mortality Rates of Cottontail Rabbits," *Journal of Wildlife Management,* 25(1961), 33–40.

Among cottontail rabbits, nearly three-fourths die within the first four months of life; the average life span for the survivors is about 10.6 months, but some individuals live more than three years. Thus the survivorship curve drops rapidly just after birth and then decreases slowly. Similar curves are typical for many small mammals, fishes, and invertebrates. At the other extreme, many large mammals tend to have rather low infant mortality; most individuals live for a relatively long time, but then there is a sudden drop in survivorship. The intermediate case—found among hydra, mice, and many birds—is one in which mortality is roughly constant regardless of age over most of the life span of the species.

Now, although the shape of the survivorship curve for a species tends to be relatively constant under constant environmental conditions, it, like natality, can be affected drastically by changes in environmental parameters. The mortality curve for the human population in many developing nations would look very different from the curve in Figure 31.4, which was plotted for members of an affluent society. And the high infant mortality of cottontail rabbits is strongly dependent on climatic conditions and the density of predators in the environment. In short, limiting environmental factors tend to raise the mortality rate.

Control by Density-Dependent Factors Yields a Sigmoid Growth Curve

Many of the environmental parameters that affect natality and mortality rates in a population exert a stronger effect as the density of individuals in the environment increases; these are called **density-dependent factors.** In our yeast

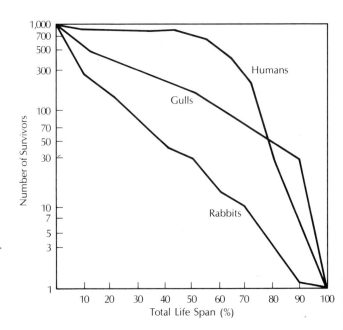

experiment, the amount of sugar in the culture medium was a density-dependent factor: It did not exert an effect on growth rate of the yeast population until the number of cells in the culture dish reached a certain critical point. *Limiting resources usually affect population growth in a density-dependent manner.* (But other factors are density dependent, too, as you will read shortly.)

What are the growth characteristics of a population limited by density-dependent factors? When the population size is low, density-dependent factors will exert little effect on natality and mortality, and population size will increase rapidly for a time. But as the density increases, the density-dependent factors increasingly come into play, and the growth rate of the population falls. If the environment remains relatively constant, a homeostatic process now sets in that maintains population size at a fixed level. The reason is that if the size of the population falls, the effect of the density-dependent factors on birth and death decreases and the population grows more rapidly again. This intensifies the effect of the density-dependent factors, and growth rate falls again. *Thus, as long as the environment is constant and the population is controlled by density-dependent factors, population size will oscillate around some constant value.* This value is called the **carrying capacity** of a given environment for a given species. The carrying capacity is neither an intrinsic property of the environment nor an intrinsic property of the species; it is a result of their interaction. If either changes, the carrying capacity may change.

Returning to the yeast cultures once again, let us apply the concepts just developed. When the medium was re-

Figure 31.4   Three typical shapes of survivorship curves. The life spans for humans, gulls, and rabbits are taken to be 103, 10 and 3.3 years respectively. The average length of life in these cases is 70 years, 2.4 years, and 3 months.

newed at regular intervals, the effect was one of maintaining a constant environment; the level of sugar oscillated slightly between changes but had some constant average value. This average sugar concentration acted as a density-dependent regulator and established the carrying capacity of the environment. When the medium was renewed more frequently, a higher average sugar concentration, and thus a higher carrying capacity, was established. This was reflected in a higher population density in the culture.

The result of density-dependent regulation of population size is always an **S-shaped curve,** or **sigmoid growth curve.** In sigmoid growth, a newly introduced species grows exponentially until it approaches the carrying capacity of the environment, whereupon growth rate drops to zero and population size is constant.

Such a sigmoid curve can be described by a simple mathematical equation:

$$\frac{dN}{dt} = rN\left(\frac{K - N}{K}\right)$$

where

N equals the number of individuals in the population

$\frac{dN}{dt}$ represents the change in N as a function of time (t); in other words, the growth rate of the population

r is the reproductive potential of each individual (thus rN equals the intrinsic rate of increase or maximum growth rate for the population)

K is the carrying capacity of the environment for that species

This equation is known as the **logistic growth equation.** Because it generates a sigmoid growth curve, such a curve is sometimes called a *logistic growth curve.* The meaning of this equation is straightforward. When N is very small relative to K (in other words, when the population density is low relative to the carrying capacity), $K - N/K$ is nearly equal to one. Therefore, the population grows almost at its maximum rate: rN. But as N approaches K in size (in other words, as the population size approaches the carrying capacity of the environment), the value $K - N/K$ falls to a small fractional number. Hence the growth rate falls to a small fraction of the maximum possible growth rate. When $N = K$ (when the population size equals the carrying capacity of the environment), $K - N/K$ equals zero and the growth rate equals zero—the population is stable. But if N exceeds K for a brief period, $K - N/K$ becomes a negative value. Therefore, the population experiences negative growth—it decreases in size.

Figure 31.5 shows the growth curve for a population of sheep introduced into one region of Australia. Although the

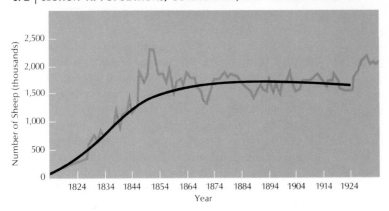

Figure 31.5   Changes in size of population of sheep following their introduction to one region of Australia in 1814. The smooth line gives the theoretical growth curve calculated from the logistic equation. The initial overshoot of the population past the carrying capacity of the area probably can be attributed to the fact that prior to the introduction of the sheep, the vegetation (the density-dependent limiting factor) had achieved a density higher than could be maintained with sheep present. Possible causes for subsequent variations in sheep population are discussed in the text.

general shape of the growth curve is sigmoidal, the curve is far from the smooth curve obtained for yeast grown in the laboratory. Population size oscillates above and below the carrying capacity. This is characteristic of sigmoid growth curves obtained with such populations in the wild. Of the several possible reasons for such irregularities, three are worth mentioning here. First, part of the reason for the irregularity is the biological difference between yeast and sheep. Sheep, for one thing, live much longer and reproduce more slowly than yeast. Hence, a change in natality or mortality takes a far longer time to express itself in terms of a change in population size, and once it does it exerts its effect for a much longer time. When a new yeast cell is formed, it immediately plays a role equivalent to that of the other cells in the population in terms of consumption of resources and reproductive potential. The same is not true with respect to a newborn lamb. Thus populations of large, slowly developing organisms tend to exaggerate and therefore to display more clearly the kind of oscillation about a mean value that is intrinsic to a homeostatic feedback system.

A second factor that enters into a determination of the degree of oscillation of a population is its uniformity in space. A population of live yeast cells in a culture dish tends to be rather uniformly distributed in the environment, and limiting resources tend to be uniformly distributed as well. Neither of these statements is true of grazing sheep. Thus, localized population densities at any one time may deviate significantly from the average value, and so may localized resource availability. As a result, density-dependent factors may exert a nonuniform effect.

The third factor, and perhaps the most important one, is that the environment under natural conditions is never as constant as it is usually kept under laboratory conditions. And fluctuations in environmental conditions may exert effects that are independent of population density and lead

to deviations from logistic growth. Let us now consider what some of these factors are that affect population size independent of population density and what kind of effect they have on population growth.

Density-Independent Factors May Lead to a J-Shaped Growth Curve

Let us return once more to consideration of the yeast culture, this time following the course of the population when the medium was not renewed. Initially the population grew in the usual sigmoidal manner and plateaued at the carrying capacity of the environment. But the environment did not remain constant. One important environmental parameter changed continuously: the concentration of alcohol. And when the concentration of alcohol exceeded the tolerance of the species, cells began to be killed in a density-independent manner. Even when the density of the population had fallen to very low levels, the effect of the alcohol was not diminished: The same fraction of the population died in each interval of time regardless of the absolute number of live individuals still remaining. *When an environmental parameter exceeds the average tolerance of the species, it tends to affect each organism on an individual basis.*

Density-independent factors are most apparent in environments that fluctuate markedly over time. For example, in some species of desert insects, only the eggs are able to survive the prolonged dry season. But when the torrential rains of spring appear and vegetation begins to grow rapidly, the eggs hatch and the insect population grows explosively—at or near the intrinsic rate of increase for the species. But with the return of the searing dry season, the entire population of adults disappears once more—until the next seasonal episode of growth (Figure 31.6). This kind of growth curve, in which the population rises exponentially but then falls abruptly, is called a **J-shaped**

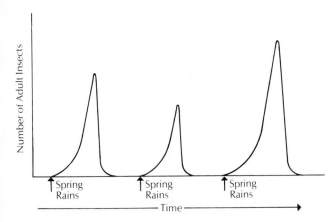

Figure 31.6   Fluctuation in population size among desert insects in three successive years. This kind of population profile is called a J-shaped growth curve.

growth curve. (The terminology is misleading in that the curve really resembles an inverted V more than it does a J.) Similar growth patterns are often exhibited by algae in polluted ponds and lakes. As the water warms in early summer, the population enters exponential growth (an algal ''bloom''), which is followed by a population collapse in autumn.

Density-Dependent and Density-Independent Factors Interact in Controlling Population Size

Although the shape of the peaks in Figure 31.6 can be attributed largely to the intervention of density-independent factors, the height of successive peaks depends on a combination of density-dependent and density-independent factors: the number of live eggs present at the beginning of the rainy season and the length of the rainy season. And the number of live eggs present at the beginning of spring is also determined by a combination of density-dependent and density-independent factors: the number of reproducing adults during the previous wet season and the severity of the intervening dry season.

Similarly, the severity of the winter weather affects survival of a deer population in a somewhat density-independent manner. But the effect is intensified if the population competing for the available food is high, and it is minimized if the population is low. Thus it is seldom possible to identify situations in nature in which populations are controlled strictly by density-dependent or density-independent factors.

Returning to the growth curve for Australian sheep shown in Figure 31.5, we can imagine that both kinds of factors were operating to cause the oscillations about the carrying capacity of the environment. Extremely cold or wet weather during the lambing season could act as a density-independent factor that would have a drastic effect on survival of the young. But the severity of the effect in any particular year would greatly depend on the average nutritional status of the ewes, which would clearly be density-dependent.

Social Behavior in Animals Functions as a Homeostatic Control of Population Size

The intraspecific behavioral interactions discussed in Chapter 29 function as a homeostatic feedback system to control the size of animal populations in a density-dependent manner. Among solitary animals that occupy individual territories, when density rises some individuals are unable to obtain a suitable feeding or nesting territory. Those individuals will be reproductively unsuccessful. Similarly, the dominance hierarchy of social animals assures the most aggressive members of the population first choice of food, mates, and nesting sites within the group. Thus if density rises above the carrying capacity of the environment, only the dominant members will be reproductively successful. In both cases, natality will be adjusted by the group to match the carrying capacity of the environment.

As was also mentioned in Chapter 29, behavioral interactions in times of overcrowding may act on vertebrate populations by hormonal means. In experiments with rats, mice, and voles, definite physiological changes accompanied increases in population density. An increase in the size of a population confined to a constant space led to an increase in the weight of adrenal glands and a decrease in the weight of thymus and reproductive glands. The degree of the effect was inversely related to social rank. Dominant individuals were affected little if at all; subordinate individuals were strongly affected. These changes were accompanied by decreases in reproduction and increases in death among affected individuals.

Similar effects seem to occur in natural populations of several animals when population density rises—apparently as a result of increased frequency and severity of aggressive interactions. During peaks of the population cycle in snowshoe hares, many individuals die from "shock disease," a condition of severe physiological stress characterized by low levels of blood sugar and liver glycogen such as occurs following prolonged adrenal stimulation.

A Simple Predator-Prey Interaction Can Lead to Oscillating Populations

In all the examples discussed so far a crucial density-dependent factor has been the availability of resources—the energy and materials all living systems need in order to function. Because food resources are largely living things, predator-prey systems are effective regulators of population size. That effectiveness, however, is directly related to the complexity of the system itself. To illustrate this point, let us first take a look at the populations of snowshoe hares and lynxes in the Canadian Arctic. Compared with other habitats, the environment of these animals is exceptionally harsh, and the number of species present is accordingly quite small: The snowshoe hare is a herbivore that feeds on sedges and lichens as its primary food source; the lynx is a carnivore that feeds largely on the snowshoe hare. Thus, limited biotic diversity has shaped a very simple predator-prey system.

As Figure 31.7 shows, the populations of the two animals in this predator-prey system undergo large periodic fluctuations that are closely correlated to each other. Does this correlation in the peaks and valleys of population size mean that the relative proportions of predator and prey remain roughly constant? In other words, does the same relative predation pressure exist at low population levels as it does at higher levels? Recall an important concept that was introduced in Chapter 30: *Even if the proportions of predator and prey populations are constant relative to each other, the predator's effectiveness declines when both the hunter and the hunted are present in small numbers.*

Small predator and prey populations mean more distance between individuals; each predator must cover increasingly larger distances and exert greater effort to obtain prey. Now, snowshoe hares (like most rabbits) have a high intrinsic rate of increase. During years when their large numbers of young are not subject to heavy predation, the numbers of hares build up rapidly. When that begins to happen, individual lynxes capture prey more easily, but the number of lynxes is not great enough to affect the explosive hare population growth. Gradually, however, its success at hunting assures the lynx of ample food reserves for optimum reproduction. It is then that the lynx population begins to swell.

Because the hare population grows so fast, the prey tend to be concentrated. And soon, increasing numbers of lynxes tend to concentrate their activity within this smaller area. Competition for food and pressure from predators exert progressively greater stress on the hare population, which eventually plummets. The lynx population in its turn becomes progressively stressed as hunting activities systematically reduce the food source, and adult animals who now exceed the carrying capacity of the environment begin to starve. The number of lynxes declines—which begins the cycle once more. Thus the mainspring of this interrelated variability is the absolute dependence of one population on the other. Any factor that alters the population level of one affects the other.

Increased Species Diversity Yields Increased Population Stability

Under certain conditions, population variability in a system involving *two* prey species and a single predator can be dramatically decreased. The first of the two prey species may be the focus of the predator until its numbers begin to decline. Then the predator, faced with diminishing success in its foragings, shifts its attention to the second species. In doing so, it reduces pressure on the first species, thereby permitting the population to recover. By the time the second prey population begins to decline, the first is recovering and the predator shifts again. This type of system is intrinsically

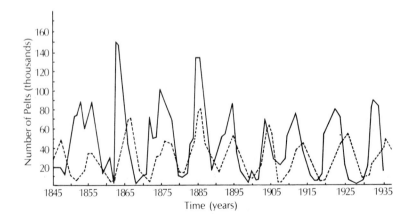

Figure 31.7 Cyclic oscillation in the density of the snowshoe hare and lynx populations. (What is actually plotted is the number of pelts turned in at the Hudson's Bay Company, but that is generally believed to give a rough estimate of the population sizes.)

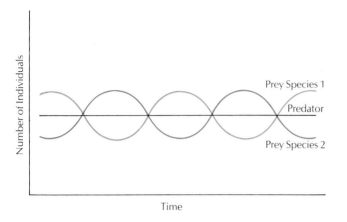

Figure 31.8 Population dynamics of a system involving two prey species and a single predator.

less variable than the one-predator/one-prey interaction in that predator population levels remain somewhat constant and neither prey species undergoes massive oscillations in population size (Figure 31.8). The predator in such a multiple prey system must respond to a so-called "switching response" and change its predation patterns in response to the relative size of the prey populations. Such switching responses have been identified in a number of natural communities.

Generally speaking, *the greater the number of possible links or interrelationships in the structure of a community, the less variability will be encountered in the population levels of the component species.* This concept has been expanded by many ecologists, and although it has never been proven, it is now generally accepted that in most cases *the greater the biotic diversity of a community, the greater its inherent stability.* As you will read later, the diversity of biotic communities also appears to affect the efficiency with which energy and resources are processed.

MANY FACTORS COMBINE TO CONTROL THE DISTRIBUTION OF POPULATIONS

If populations are grown under controlled laboratory conditions, the response of a species to a range of environmental conditions can be determined and charted as shown in Figure 31.9. But charting those responses is only the beginning of the search for variables that dictate the actual geographic distribution, or range, of members of a particular species under natural conditions. For one thing, the reproduction and growth of entire populations must be dealt with, because tolerance to any given factor may vary at different times during the life cycle. For example, it is quite common for juvenile forms to be more demanding in their environmental needs than adults of the species. Consider how many ornamental plants, such as magnolia trees, are grown in areas that are far colder than their natural environment. Although the adult forms can persist under cultivation, very often the formation and functioning of the

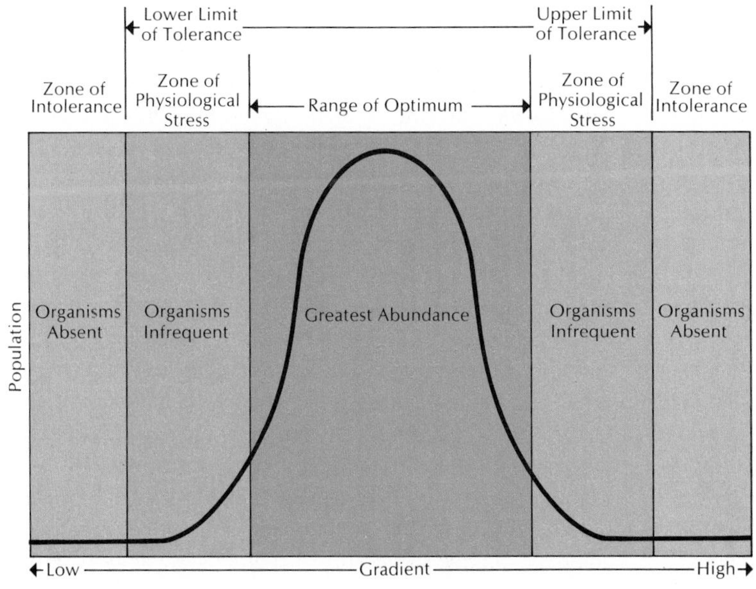

Figure 31.9 Growth response of a population under various conditions of a specific environmental factor such as temperature. This kind of graph shows the range of tolerance of an organism to a given environmental factor in terms of how it correlates with population size.

reproductive structures or the development of the young seedlings cannot occur because at a critical time of the year the environment exceeds the low temperature tolerance of those stages of the life cycle. And immobile organisms such as plants obviously cannot maintain viable populations in a given locale unless all stages of the life cycle can be completed.

On the other hand, organisms do live in many regions where the conditions at some time of the year are outside their tolerance range. Such distribution patterns are made possible by a variety of adaptations that permit organisms to withstand seasonal extremes. Desert annual plants complete their life cycle during the wet season and spend the dry season as resistant seeds. Many desert perennials lose their leaves during the dry season and get a new crop in the next wet season, just as deciduous forest trees of temperate regions lose their leaves in the fall and produce a new crop each spring.

Many desert animals have underground burrows that are essentially microenvironments in which they can spend the day protected from the extremes of desert heat. Burrowing animals often forage actively during the evening when conditions on the surface are within their tolerance range. Some animals—particularly birds—have developed a most effective way of avoiding environmental extremes: They simply leave an area when conditions become inhospitable. As you read in Chapter 28, many waterfowl have their breeding grounds in high arctic latitudes during the summer months, and then they fly to warmer climates for the winter; many mammals hibernate.

Biological Interactions Modify Distribution Patterns

In many species, the **habitat** (the environmental situation in which a species is characteristically found) does not correspond with optimum conditions for the species. Often this is the result of interaction with another life form. For example, the giant saguaro cactus can be grown under laboratory conditions to determine the optimum environmental conditions (such as temperature, moisture, and soil type) for its growth. When natural areas having such conditions are identified, some large saguaro will be found growing under the predicted conditions—but their numbers will be small. The population will show the greatest number of plants in areas that are *marginal* in terms of tolerance to environmental extremes. This paradox appears to have been brought about by a biotic factor. The young saguaro plants are preyed upon by a number of desert rats and mice. These rodents are numerous in areas where saguaro growth should be optimum, and they take a heavy toll of young seedlings. The rare seedling that survives this predation fares well, but few escape the predators. But few predators survive in the marginal growth areas; the extreme conditions generally

exceed *their* tolerance limits. *In short, although we largely define habitats in terms of such abiotic factors as light, temperature, and water availability, biotic factors—an organism's interactions with other members of the community—are also important.*

Interspecific Competition Leads to Niche Isolation

Interspecific interactions other than predator-prey relationships affect distribution of two species. Chief among them is **competition.** Competition arises whenever two species must contend with each other in obtaining the same limiting resource (light, food, water, and so on). What impact does competition have on the population sizes of two different species? As long as the resource is plentiful, neither species will be limited by its relative abundance and both will tend to grow. But as the combined populations begin to reach the carrying capacity of the environment, the effects of competition emerge. Now the *slightest difference* in the capacity of the two species to obtain the resource in question will be telling. The species that is even slightly less effective will begin to feel the effect first. And it will feel it as a drop in natality, an increase in mortality, or both. Hence, its population size will stop increasing first as the other population continues to increase for a time. This will exaggerate the difference, for now there will be proportionally greater numbers of the more efficient species and they will take a larger share of the disputed resource. This will leave less of the resource for the less efficient species, which will mean a further reduction in natality and/or increase in mortality—resulting in a decrease in population size. Hence the difference between the success of the two populations will progress in a self-intensifying manner until the less efficient species is extinguished!

This is the principle of **competitive exclusion:** *Two species limited by the same resource cannot coexist in the same environment indefinitely.* This concept was first derived mathematically, and *it is a logically necessary corollary to the logistic growth equation.* The competitive exclusion principle was verified experimentally by G. F. Gause and is often called "Gause's principle." One of his classic experiments is shown in Figure 31.10. (Similar results have now been obtained for many species pairs.) Now, the critical point is this: Although the outcome of the experiment shown in Figure 31.10 was the same for every trial under one set of conditions, Gause found other growth conditions under which the outcome was reversed.

We can visualize a situation in which environmental factors are heterogeneous—for example, an environment with spatial variations in temperature, moisture, and light. We can further visualize that there are two species that are limited by the same resources and that each species alone could be highly successful throughout the region. If one

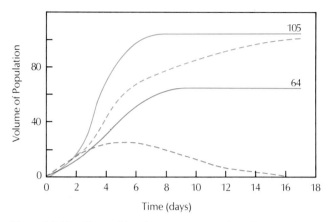

Figure 31.10   Competition between two species of Paramecium, P. caudatum *(red) and* P. aurelia *(blue). When either species is grown alone in culture (solid curves) with a constant food supply, both organisms show typical sigmoid growth curves. When the two organisms are introduced into the same culture system (dashed curves),* P. aurelia *excludes* P. caudatum. *Under different growth conditions not shown here,* P. caudatum *is capable of excluding* P. aurelia.

species has a competitive advantage under the combination of conditions in one region of the environment and the second has an advantage in a different region, *each species will become established where it has the competitive edge and will exclude the other.* They will have developed what we call different **niches.** A niche indicates both the position *and* the role of an organism in a community: where it lives, what it eats, what eats it, what limits its population size, and so on. We can now modify the competitive exclusion hypothesis as follows: *Two species cannot coexist in the same niche indefinitely.* It follows that if two species coexist with stable population sizes, they must occupy separate niches. In other words, different factors must limit their population size. It further follows that there must be at least as many niches in a natural community as there are species.

Two species that have totally nonoverlapping niches do not compete. But if two niches overlap in part, there will be some competition for resources. And the more similar the niches are, the more competition there will be. It follows, then, that *the fiercest competition in the community is intraspecific.* The reason is that equivalent members of the same species share an identical niche, by definition. It is the competition within a species for the resources limiting population growth that leads to survival of the "fittest." It is the driving force of evolution.

The need for each species to secure a discrete niche has consequences for the diversity in community structure. In order to survive under harsh conditions, where resource availability is uniformly low (for example, in the arctic tundra), the species must be flexible enough in their life styles to take advantage of whatever opportunities come their way. But to do so they must have broad niches—they must be generalists. The occurrence of broad niches within such environments means that comparatively few species will be present, for niches can overlap only so far before competitive exclusion begins to operate. Such factors undoubtedly underlie the limited biotic diversity of such harsh environments as the Arctic. Under more hospitable environments, such as the tropical forests discussed in Chapter 30, organisms can become much more specialized. And the more specialized the niche, the less likely it will overlap that of another species. As a result, more species can live within the same community and biotic diversity will be high. *When environmental conditions are favorable for development of a large community, natural selection acts to favor the development of highly specialized niches, thereby reducing interspecific competition and permitting greater biotic diversity.* Let us now turn our attention to some of the ways in which these diverse life forms interact in natural communities.

ENERGY FLOW THROUGH ORGANISMS DICTATES COMMUNITY STRUCTURE

In natural environments, one species rarely exists by itself. Almost always, a group of populations occupy the same area, interchanging materials and energy and thereby forming a **biotic community.** Members of the community can be producers, decomposers, or consumers of various sorts. Taken together they represent a system through which energy flows; in other words, a **food chain.** *Producer organisms*—photosynthetic and chemosynthetic bacteria as well as algae and plants—use energy from the nonliving environment to build organic substances. (For a few communities, such as those in caves or deep in the ocean, the main source of energy and organic molecules may be the by-products or debris from other communities, and producers may be rare or absent.)

In the cycling of energy and matter through biotic communities, the producers must have a constant supply of nitrogen, phosphorus, and other crucial elements. These substances are made available by the *decomposers*—the bacteria and fungi—that reclaim them from dead organisms. Carbon, oxygen, and hydrogen are available in the water and in the atmosphere, but even these materials must be recycled. Only in an environment with a constant influx of inorganic nutrients and a constant removal of organic debris by nonbiological means would it be possible for a community to exist indefinitely without decomposers.

The number of consumers in the community depends on the amount of organic material the producers make available. Although theoretically it would be possible to have a community without consumers, it is a rare community in which some organisms have not taken advantage of the ready food supply represented by the producers. *Primary consumers,* or herbivores, obtain organic nutrients from tissues of the producers. *Secondary consumers,* or carnivores, feed on the tissues of primary consumers. In communities with dense producer populations, there may even be *tertiary consumers,* or second-level carnivores, that feed mainly on the secondary consumers.

Matter recycles, but energy flows one way through these various levels of nourishment, or **trophic levels** (Chapter 12). The amount of energy stored in the organic substances of each trophic level is called the **biomass;** the term refers to the total dry weight of the organisms making up a trophic level. Normally, less than 10 percent of the biomass consumed by organisms in a food chain is actually stored as biomass. Most is used as a source of energy and is eventually lost as waste products and heat. New biomass enters the trophic level of producer organisms by photosynthesis. The new biomass that is thus created is called *primary productivity.* The primary producers immediately use some of this biomass as a source of energy to carry out metabolic processes. How much they require varies from as little as 10 percent in some rapidly growing algae to more than 50 percent in many higher plants. The rest is available to sustain the consumers in the community and is called *net primary productivity.*

As Table 31.3 shows, primary productivity varies greatly from one community to the next, depending on the availability of resources other than light that are required to support plant growth. Deserts and grasslands are limited by the availability of water; other areas may have infertile soil. Paradoxically, the open oceans (which many people erroneously look to as the future breadbasket of humankind) are lacking in nutrients. The surface waters over most deep ocean regions are low in productivity because of a lack of essential minerals! Marine organisms from these regions drift downward after death to become part of the abyssal sediment and take their essential minerals with them! Decomposition proceeds slowly at the near-freezing temperature of the ocean floor, and few nutrients are liberated that are of use to the overlying ocean ecosystem. Only where vertical currents (*upwellings*) bring this rich store of nutrients to the surface do marine productivity rates reach relatively high levels. Arctic and Antarctic seas are highly productive as a result of seasonal upwellings, but most of the earth's oceans show negligible rates of primary production.

The biotic diversity of the producers in a community can also affect productivity rates. Figure 31.11 shows two extremes in diversity. In the first case, the forest consists of a single tree species. Regardless of how efficient the tree species may be in processing solar energy, a certain amount

Table 31.3

Net Primary Production of Major Ecosystems and of the Earth's Surface

Type of Ecosystem	Area (millions of square kilometers)*	Net Primary Productivity per Unit Area (dry grams per square meter per year†) Normal Range	Average	World Net Primary Production (billions of dry tons per year)
Lake and Stream	2	100–1,500	500	1.0
Swamp and Marsh	2	800–4,000	2,000	4.0
Tropical Forest	20	1,000–5,000	2,000	40.0
Temperate Forest	18	600–3,000	1,300	23.4
Boreal Forest	12	400–2,000	800	9.6
Woodland and Shrubland	7	200–1,200	600	4.2
Savanna	15	200–2,000	700	10.5
Temperate Grassland	9	150–1,500	500	4.5
Tundra and Alpine	8	10–400	140	1.1
Desert Scrub	18	10–250	70	1.3
Extreme Desert, Rock, and Ice	24	0–10	3	0.07
Agricultural Land	14	100–4,000	650	9.1
Total for Land	149		730	109.0
Open Ocean	332	2–400	125	41.5
Continental Shelf	27	200–600	350	9.5
Attached Algae and Estuaries	2	500–4,000	2,000	4.0
Total for Ocean	361		155	55.0
Total for Earth	510		320	164.0

*One square kilometer is equal to about 0.39 square mile.
†One gram per square meter is equal to about 0.0033 ounce per square foot.
Source: Robert H. Whittaker, *Communities and Ecosystems* (New York: Macmillan, 1970).

of the incident sunlight passes through the tree canopy. This sunlight represents a portion of the incoming energy that is not used by the producers in the community. In the second case, the forest is composed of a canopy species, subcanopy trees that grow under the main canopy, numerous species of shrubs, and a layer of herbaceous plants growing near the soil surface. The trees, shrubs, and herbaceous plants growing beneath the canopy must function in the filtered light created by the taller species, but a community that has such plants uses more of the incident solar energy and thus has a higher rate of productivity.

Figure 31.12 summarizes the energy flow through a fresh-water spring community. Below the energy flow diagram in this figure are two pyramids that correspond to the structure of the community. The **energy pyramid** depicts the directional flow of usable energy through the community. Because some energy is used within each trophic level, the base of the pyramid (the producers) is the largest, and each succeeding trophic level is considerably smaller.

Such energy flow data are difficult to obtain, and for that

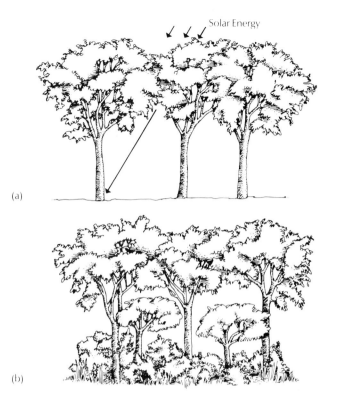

(a)

(b)

Figure 31.11 (a) A forest system with low biotic diversity: a single tree species. Sunlight that penetrates the canopy is "wasted," in that it does not result in primary production. (b) A forest system with high diversity, with a number of understory trees, shrubs, and herbaceous plants. A much greater percentage of the incident light is utilized in this case, resulting in a higher rate of primary production.

Figure 31.12 (below) Energy flow through various trophic levels in a fresh-water spring in Florida. Of the 410,000 kilocalories of energy that flow through the primary producers, only about 2 percent is available for use in other trophic levels. Of this net primary productivity, nearly 60 percent flows directly to the decomposers in the form of dead plants. The remaining 40 percent or so flows through the herbivore-carnivore chain. Only about 10 percent of the energy entering the herbivore and carnivore levels is available to the next trophic level in the form of biomass. Most of the remainder leaves the spring in one form or another—insects that fly away after having developed in the spring, fish that swim downstream, and so on.

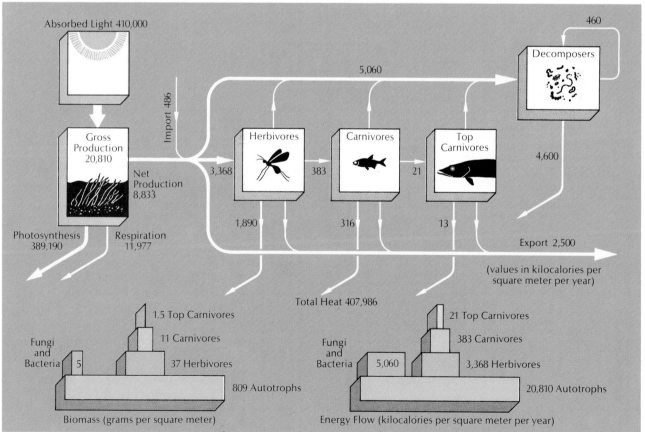

reason ecologists often summarize community structure with a **pyramid of biomass,** which simply requires weighing the members of the various trophic levels. For most communities, the general form of the biomass pyramid parallels that of the energy pyramid, as is the case in Figure 31.12. But by no means is such a biomass pyramid any kind of quantitative representation of the importance of the various levels in terms of energy flow. There may be a real disproportion between these two parameters, particularly where microorganisms are involved. In the community shown in Figure 31.12, the decomposers at any one time represent about 0.5 percent of the biomass of the community but they process 17 percent of the energy that flows through the spring each year! The decomposers have metabolic turnover rates that are extremely high compared to other members of the community. Thus they handle quantities of energy that are far greater than their biomass would imply. A similar situation occurs in many marine communities, where the producers consist of microscopic algae, or phytoplankton.

Figure 31.13 shows biomass and energy pyramids from a marine community in Long Island Sound. The biomass pyramid for this community is actually inverted, with the consumers (small zooplankton and bottom fauna) outweighing the producers (planktonic algae) by a factor of 2 to 1. In contrast, the energy pyramid has the structure normally associated with decreasing energy availability to higher trophic levels. The biomass pyramid is inverted for two main reasons. The microscopic algae have a very high metabolic efficiency, partly because they do not need much energy to develop their simple body forms. Their metabolic efficiency permits them to process relatively large quantities of energy per unit of biomass. In addition, the algae have a high reproductive potential that enables a rather large zooplankton population to subsist on a small "standing crop" of available algae. Because new cells are replaced as fast as others are consumed, the algae population can support a large number of herbivores despite its apparent

small size. Thus, despite the inverted biomass pyramid associated with many planktonic communities, the form of energy utilization within the community structure is identical with that of communities in which the biomass pyramids are proportional to energy utilization.

In most communities relationships between trophic levels become very complex. Although diagrams such as Figure 31.12 can summarize the basic pattern of energy flow, they cannot describe the complex food relationships within a community. Predators in complex communities not only have alternative choices of prey species, they may also function on several trophic levels. For example, omnivorous animals can eat both plant and animal material, depending on the nutritional needs of the omnivore and the relative availability of different types of food. Although certain carnivores may restrict themselves to herbivorous species (thus functioning as simple carnivores), there is little to prevent occasional predation on smaller carnivores or on the young of even larger carnivores. Thus the food relationships within a community are probably best expressed as a **food web** rather than a food chain. It is the very complexity of such relationships that provides a measure of community stability, for few of the species involved in the web depend entirely on one other species. For that reason, large fluctuations in population size do not occur.

RESOURCE CYCLING IN COMMUNITIES

The pulse of life on our planet depends on continuous energy from the sun; should that flow cease, life eventually would come to a halt as the energy stored in organic molecules gradually radiated away. In the case of material resources, however, the flow is not one-directional—elements must be recycled through the community.

In a sense, natural communities are areas of concentration of resources. By using energy, individual living cells can accumulate materials against concentration gradients, so that even though critical elements may be present in low concentrations in the environment, living things can acquire

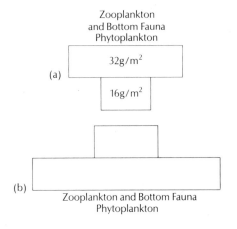

Figure 31.13 Biomass (a) and relative energy (b) pyramids for open-water communities in Long Island Sound. The biomass pyramid is "inverted," in that the consumers have a greater mass than the producers, whereas the energy pyramid has the more typical form. Such inverted biomass pyramids are characteristic of aquatic communities where the producers consist largely of algae.

and hold them. Each living cell or whole organism can be looked on as a storehouse of relatively rare but necessary chemical elements. A community of organisms acts much like a sponge in the way it concentrates these resources. If you were to pour liquid fertilizer on bare earth, much of the valuable nitrates and phosphates would leach away through the soil. The same fertilizer, poured onto a forest plot, stands little chance of getting away. The multitude of increasingly deeper root systems would absorb the essential materials, lodging them within their own tissues. These elements could then circulate among the various trophic levels of the community until they were eventually liberated into the soil by the action of the decomposers. Once in the soil, the minerals could be reabsorbed by other plants.

The role of living things in the acquisition and concentration of resources is rarely appreciated at first glance. If mineral levels are monitored in streams leading out of a forest that is being cut down, a great pulse of minerals will be noted following destruction of the community—minerals that were acquired and hoarded by the natural community at the cost of a continuous expenditure of energy. Once the community dies, these materials diffuse into the environment, becoming less and less concentrated.

In our search for agricultural land, the sites of the world's lush tropical forests appear at first glance to be ideal for cultivation. But if the forests are cut and removed, the land is productive only for a few seasons. The reason is that virtually all the key mineral resources are concentrated in the standing crop—the plants and animals—of the forest community. The extremely rapid metabolic turnover in such diverse communities means that materials are recycled into other living things as fast as biomass is made available. *Removal of the forest represents removal of virtually all the resources of the site!* Even burning the forest, which returns the minerals to the soil in the form of ash, is ineffective, because our simple agricultural communities lack the diversity to reacquire the nutrients before they leach away in the heavy seasonal rainfall of the tropics. *Efficiency of resource utilization is intimately linked to biotic diversity.*

COMPETITION LEADS TO SUCCESSIONAL CHANGE IN BIOTIC COMMUNITIES

As the various organisms that make up certain communities reproduce, the overall quantitative and qualitative structure of the community remains the same with the passage of time. Such stable systems are called *climax communities.*

In some parts of eastern North America, climax vegetation typically is a forest of deciduous trees. Oak and hickory trees often are the dominant forms of the community. Other tree species are present, particularly as understory trees (below the canopy of hickory and oaks), where they are associated with numerous species of shrubs and herbaceous

plants. And living in stable association with the plants are countless species of animals: squirrels, deer, mice, foxes, owls, and songbirds and insects by the thousands—to name but a few.

How does such a stable community develop? As is often the case, an unsuccessful human experiment gives us some insights. During colonization of the United States, settlers cleared large tracts of such forest for farming purposes. But later, when it was found that farming was much more profitable on the prairies of the Midwest, many farms in the East were deserted and eventually returned to something quite close to their original state. Such a developmental sequence leading to a stable climax community is called **ecological succession.** Although the details of succession vary from spot to spot, the progression shown in Figure 31.14 is generally applicable in many oak-hickory climax areas. It is instructive to examine how this proceeded.

Even while a field was being cultivated, a large number of annual herbaceous plants (weeds) could be found growing along with the cultivated crop. These annual "weed" species were not at all typical of the forest vegetation that had previously existed in the area, but they became established in the plowed fields, where they were able to compete effectively. When the fields were abandoned, these weeds temporarily became dominant and created structurally simple communities.

The plants of such communities tend to be widely spaced and diversity of herbivores is low. As a result, biomass is created that is not used as a food source. Decomposer arrays of such pioneer communities are rudimentary and much of the biomass accumulates on the site. The plant species may appear to be quite hardy, for they can germinate on bare soil surfaces and withstand the environmental extremes characteristic of their exposed position in the field. However, all these species have adapted to conditions found only in bare or disturbed areas and, as a consequence, they are not highly suited to competition in more crowded biotic communities. The very existence of the pioneer plants in the field spells their doom, for they change the environment in such a way that species that previously were unable to grow in the field can now become established. Plant debris accumulates, and the additional shelter provided by the pioneer plants encourages seed germination and the growth of various perennial grasses and shrubs. Broomsedge, a perennial grass, soon begins to crowd out the pioneer species and dominates the community for several years. But during this period, the slower growing shrubs begin to overtop the broomsedge. Although the broomsedge has been able to eliminate or outcompete the pioneer weed species, it is not highly tolerant to shade, and increasing development of the shrubs begins to limit its success. Animals such as birds that prefer the broomsedge communi-

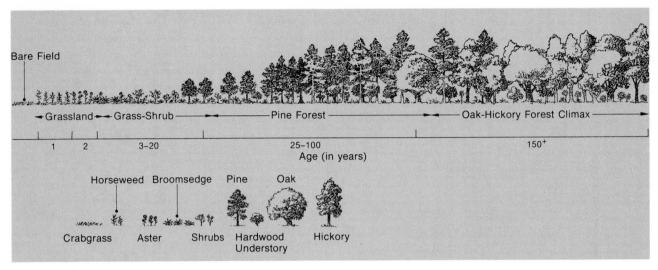

Bare Field

◄Grassland►◄ Grass-Shrub ───────── Pine Forest ──────── ◄───── Oak-Hickory Forest Climax ─────►

1   2   3–20   25–100   150⁺
Age (in years)

Horseweed Broomsedge   Pine   Oak

Crabgrass   Aster   Shrubs Hardwood   Hickory
                               Understory

Figure 31.14   Oak-hickory climax community. This diagram illustrates a typical plant succession from open land to a midlatitude deciduous forest. In the initial stages of the succession, low, fast-growing grasses and shrubs dominate. Each stage alters the soil and microclimate of the land, enabling other species to establish themselves and become dominant. The final stage consists of high trees that overshade and force out some of the low shrubs of earlier stages.

ties for food or shelter now give way to an animal complex adapted for life in the developing shrub community.

The shrub phase may persist for as much as a decade, but as more leaves and plant litter accumulate and as decomposers become more active, soil conditions improve. The taller shrubs also provide greater protection, resulting in a small **microclimate** in which temperature and humidity variations are far less extreme than was the case in the earlier broomsedge community. In this protected environment, several tree species—particularly pine—become established. The pines eventually grow above the shrubs and begin to shade them out. Although the shrubs could grow in the light shade of the broomsedge, they cannot compete in the heavier shade of the developing pines and they gradually fade out. The microclimate of the pine forest is even more insulated from environmental extremes than was the shrub stage, and more animals and plants become established. Increasing plant diversity improves community productivity, and increased consumer and decomposer diversity increases the efficiency with which the community resources are utilized.

In early stages of the successional sequence, production levels exceed the total community respiration, resulting in an accumulation of biomass. As the community matures and becomes more complex, metabolic turnover becomes more complete, and community respiration begins to ap-

proach the rate of production. Thus the community begins to stabilize. The successional process in Figure 31.14 continues until a plant community is derived that can reproduce itself under the conditions it creates. The pine stage in the sequence is unstable, because although these trees provide the conditions necessary for growth of young oaks and hickories, they themselves cannot reproduce in the shade that results when the oak and hickory trees mature. The oak-hickory complex *is* stable and will reproduce successfully without being replaced. Development of such a climax forest may require more than 200 years following the abandonment of the original cultivated field.

The entire process can be viewed as a series of shifting logistic growth equations and competitive exclusions. Until the climax conditions are reached, at each stage we find plant populations expanding to fill the carrying capacity of the environment and thereby modifying the environment in a way that modifies the growth equation of another species, which then expands and outcompetes its benefactor.

Such successional processes are not restricted to abandoned fields. Most of the lakes and ponds that we see in the Northern Hemisphere were carved out by the advancing glaciers of the last ice age. They are all in the process of successional change. Sediments accumulate in the basins, and plants gradually encroach on the water's edge. The muds and organic sediments give rise to wet meadows or bogs, ultimately developing into a climax forest characteristic of the area. This successional sequence has been completed in many small postglacial lakes and ponds and is well advanced in many lakes of moderate size. As clear, deep waters give way to shallow, weed-choked waters, the types of fish and other aquatic life change, much as the animal components of land communities change with alterations in the plants. Lakes in the early stages of development are generally the most desirable from a recreation standpoint, so many people have a vested interest in slowing or stopping this form of succession. Extreme steps such as dredging and poisoning of aquatic plants are often required to slow the otherwise inevitable progress of succession. Pollution that introduces high levels of nutrients into lakes speeds up the successional sequence in a process called **eutrophication.** Polluted lakes are even more difficult to manage successfully.

Many processes can intervene in a successional sequence to halt the process before the ''normal'' climax is reached. Certain soils may be unfavorable for the more common progression of vegetation, and succession may terminate in a complex that is unique to a particular area. Thus we often find natural glades and glens within a climax forest. Periodic fires can arrest the successional sequence, resulting in small grassland areas within a predominantly forested region. Small differences in slope exposure and drainage may also lead to variations. Although it is convenient to refer to ''climax communities,'' most areas consist of a mosaic of vegetation and animal types.

Several generalizations concerning succession apply to a variety of situations:

1. There is a gradual increase in biotic diversity throughout a successional sequence, which increases the efficiency of energy and resource utilization.

2. The species found in early successional stages devote considerable energy reserves to reproduction, whereas species in late successional stages devote less energy to reproduction and more to strategies involving energy and nutrient procurement.

3. Early succession species tend to have wide tolerances to environmental extremes but are relatively intolerant to biotic competition. Species of late succession or climax communities are capable of maintaining themselves in a complex biotic community. Because of their more limited environmental tolerances, they require such complex communities in order to survive.

4. Because productivity exceeds community energy utilization in early stages of succession, biomass accumulates progressively. Community energy utilization in a climax community generally balances community productivity so that the biomass of the community complex remains relatively constant.

5. Although climax communities may vary widely in terms of diversity and relative productivity in different geographical regions, each apparently represents optimum energy and resource utilization under existing conditions.

GLOBAL DISTRIBUTION OF VEGETATION

As mentioned earlier, the main factor governing the nature of climax communities appears to be climate—essentially, the interaction of temperature and available rainfall. Figure

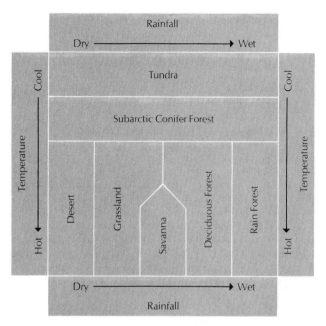

Figure 31.15   Generalized relationship between rainfall and temperature and the occurrence of major vegetation types.

31.15 shows a general relationship between temperature, rainfall, and the development of seven major climax vegetation types. Specific types of vegetation and the animals they support constitute what ecologists refer to as **biomes.** Figure 31.16, which outlines the global distribution of vegetation types, indicates as well the distribution of biomes throughout the continents of the world.

The **tundra** (Figure 31.17) is a vast expanse of vegetation that develops best south of the permanent northern polar caps. In tundra, trees are absent because of extremely low average temperatures and a growing season of only two months or less. The vegetation consists of lichens, grasses, sedges, and a few species of dwarf shrubs such as willow, which are confined to flat mats on the soil surface. The low temperatures of the growing season limit transpiration so that relative water availability does not have a major effect in governing the distribution of tundra plants. Most of the land area occupied by tundra is relatively flat because it is repeatedly scoured by polar ice. Low, water-filled depressions are common during the summer months. Mammals such as reindeer (Europe and Asia), caribou (North America), musk ox, arctic hare, lemming, and arctic fox, and birds such as the snowy owl and ptarmigan are active throughout the year. During the short summer season, the tundra supports large insect populations and numerous species of migratory birds that use it as a breeding area.

Increasing activity directed toward exploitation of arctic oil deposits can be expected to have considerable impact on

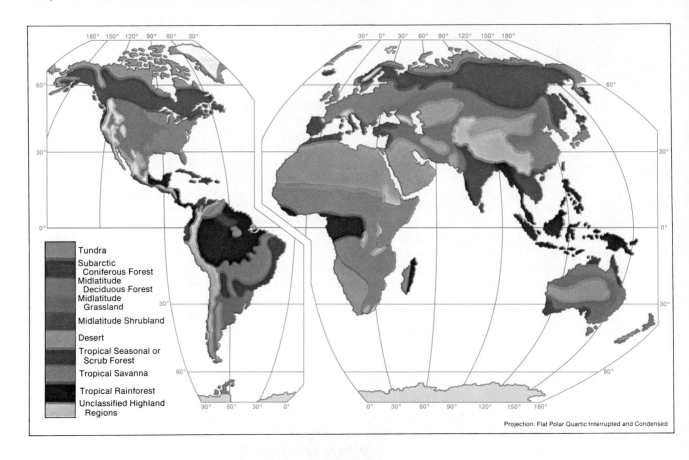

Figure 31.16 Distribution of major vegetation types. Climate, soils, and vegetation are strongly interacting systems, and their global distributions bear marked similarities.

Figure 31.17 Tundra vegetation in Norway.

tundra communities. The low biotic diversity of tundra ecosystems makes them particularly vulnerable to disturbance. The short growing season and slow growth rate of tundra vegetation result in slow recovery when damage occurs.

South of the tundra in North America and Eurasia is a broad belt of **subarctic coniferous forest,** often referred to as the *boreal forest,* or *taiga.* This evergreen forest is composed largely of spruce, fir, and pine (Figure 31.18), which can tolerate the short growing season and low winter temperatures. Despite rigorous environmental conditions, productivity in the boreal forests can be moderately high because the evergreen trees can begin photosynthesis whenever temperatures rise above freezing. The high resin content of conifer needles makes them generally unsuitable as a food source for larger herbivores; insects are the main predators on the dominant trees. Herbivores such as moose, snowshoe hare, and numerous birds depend on angiosperms such as aspens and shrubs in successional areas and along the forest borders and also depend on the grasses, sedges, and water plants near the numerous lakes that dot the glaciated landscape. The lynx, fox, bear, and wolf are the main large mammalian predators, with owls functioning in the same role.

Deserts are found throughout the world wherever moisture is severely limited. Generally, desert vegetation is subdivided into two types. The cold deserts of the Northern Hemisphere may exhibit annual temperature extremes but typically are quite cold in the winter season. Warm deserts (Figure 31.19) are characteristically warm or hot throughout much of the year. Various species of cactus are among the most important components of North and South American warm deserts, along with various seasonal shrubs, trees, and annual plants. Warm deserts in Africa and Australia have cactuslike plants, but they are not closely related to the true cacti of the Western Hemisphere. The harsh conditions of desert environments have produced remarkable examples of convergence in growth form and strategies in desert plants and animals throughout the world. Reptiles such as snakes and lizards and a large number of small mammals (particularly rodents) are characteristic of many deserts. Larger mammals in North American warm deserts include deer, peccary (wild pig), fox, and puma (mountain lion).

Where additional rainfall is available, various grasses and herbaceous plants come to dominate extensive areas. The great prairies of central North America represent **grasslands** of this type (Figure 31.20). Prairie dogs, mule deer, pronghorn antelope, and bison are the main mammals. Virtually all the major grasslands of the world are heavily utilized for agricultural purposes. Where rainfall is limited, they are used for grazing of sheep and cattle; where more moisture is available, they have been plowed for the cultivation of grain crops. The major wheat-producing areas in North America are former grasslands. Extensive exploitation of grasslands has resulted in the widespread destruction of natural prairies, particularly in North America. Lands that once supported teeming herds of bison have been overgrazed and subjected to poor range management to the point that they barely support cattle. A growing awareness of the need for proper range management may eventually restore much of the agricultural productivity of this land even if the natural communities it once supported are largely a thing of the past.

As indicated in Figure 31.15, grasslands in cooler regions tend to an even transition with deciduous forest where additional rainfall is available, but in warmer regions another vegetation type, the **savanna,** is widespread. A savanna is essentially a grassland with isolated trees and shrubs scattered across the landscape (Figure 31.21). Savannas can be quite productive and often support a variety of grazing herbivores and associated predators. Grazing animals such as the zebra, various wild cattle, many species of antelope, rhinoceros, giraffe, and baboon, and predators such as the hyena, lion, leopard, and cheetah are typical African

Figure 31.18   A lake margin in the boreal forest (taiga) of North America.

Figure 31.19   A warm desert in Baja California, Mexico.

Figure 31.20   A grassland (prairie) in the Wichita Mountain Game Reserve in Oklahoma.

Figure 31.22   A Michigan deciduous forest in winter.

Figure 31.21   A savanna in Amboseli Park in Kenya (Africa).

Figure 31.23   A rain forest.

savanna species. Humans, too, are an evolutionary product of the fierce struggle for survival played out on the African plains. Rising populations are placing increasing agricultural pressure on savanna communities, and much of the unique wildlife is in danger of extinction. The solutions to such problems of wildlife preservation are not at all simple. It is easy for people in developed countries to demand the preservation of wildlife in underdeveloped areas, but each of us might have a different outlook if we had elephants trampling our small subsistence plots. Many excellent game preserves exist in Africa, but few of the governments of the newly independent countries have the resources to completely eliminate exploitation of such parks.

Sometimes there is enough moisture to support forest vegetation, but there may be seasonal extremes in either temperature or water availability. Under these conditions deciduous forests tend to develop. **Deciduous forests** are composed of trees that lose their leaves for part of the growing season, an adaptation that enables the plants to withstand unfavorable environmental conditions. The temperate deciduous forests of eastern North America (Figure 31.22), western Europe, and eastern Asia are similar in composition. In areas where environmental conditions are particularly favorable (such as the southern Appalachians), these forests are highly diverse and productive. Virgin stands of deciduous forest are quite rare in the more developed parts of the eastern United States, where second-growth communities have arisen in cut-over forests or former agricultural lands. Subtropical and tropical decid-

uous forests are common, but the loss of leaves in such communities is related to the occurrence of pronounced dry seasons rather than the seasonal low temperatures encountered in temperate deciduous communities. The diverse animal life of temperate deciduous forests includes insects, reptiles, and numerous mammals such as shrews, mice, several different species of squirrels, rabbits, deer, bear, wild boar, bobcat, and mountain lion.

Where ample moisture and consistently warm temperatures exist throughout the year, complex forest communities develop. The **rain forests** of the world's tropics (Figure 31.23) probably represent something close to the optimum conditions for the development of diverse terrestrial ecosystems. Here, species diversity at all trophic levels is high and niches are extremely specialized. Some of the most intricate mutualisms between organisms have developed, and many of the factors discussed in Chapter 30 apply with particular force. The physical structure of rain forest communities is quite complex. Isolated trees extend above the canopy in many places, and the canopy itself often consists of many distinct layers. Vines and epiphytes (plants that grow on other plants) are extremely common, each of these groups using other plants for support and thus growing high in the canopy without the need for massive supporting trunks of their own. Many insects, reptiles, birds, and mammals are confined to distinct levels in the forest structure, never venturing away from their limited microenvironment. Because of their high diversity, rain forests, particularly in the tropics, may be quite productive. But as you read earlier,

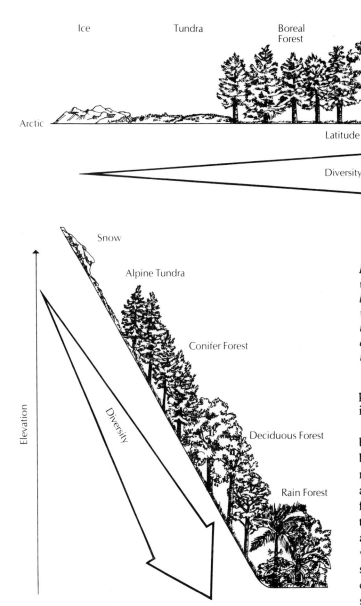

Ice   Tundra   Boreal Forest   Deciduous Forest   Rain Forest

Arctic   Latitude   Tropics

Diversity

Snow

Alpine Tundra

Conifer Forest

Deciduous Forest

Rain Forest

Elevation

Diversity

Figure 31.24 Relationship of latitude and elevation on vegetation distribution and community diversity. Increasing latitude or elevation results in a shift to cooler vegetation types with a decrease in community diversity. Climbing 15,000 feet up a tropical mountain will reveal shifts in communities analogous to what could be observed in a trip from the tropics to the pole.

probably causing extinctions faster than many of the organisms can be discovered and described.

Because temperature plays such a determining role in biome development, there tends to be a regular relationship between biome and latitude. If we could sample a series of regions from the equator to the Arctic under conditions of adequate moisture availability, we would pass from rain forest at the equator to deciduous forest at middle latitudes, to coniferous or boreal forest still farther north, finally arriving at tundra communities. An increase in elevation, with the drop in temperature that results, can cause a similar sequence (Figure 31.24). A high mountain on the equator could have a rain forest at its base, a deciduous forest several thousand feet up the mountain, a coniferous forest at still higher elevations, and, if the mountain is high enough, alpine tundra just below the snow line. Relatively modest mountains in New England may have a deciduous forest at the base, a coniferous forest on the high slopes, and tundra vegetation on the highest peaks. The distribution of vegetation is controlled largely by the temperature and available rainfall, and wherever the conditions for a given vegetation type occur, regardless of geographic position, that particular type can develop.

Because communities are composed of individual species, each with similar but not identical limits of tolerance, the transition from one community to another and even between biomes occurs on a gradual continuum. If you were to travel to an area in the northern United States or southern Canada that is shown on the map in Figure 31.16, you

the rapid turnover rate at all levels in the community tends to concentrate available resources within the community structure.

Because tropical rain forests are the only sources for a number of exotic woods such as ebony, mahogany, and balsa, many of these forests have been severely disrupted by lumbering activities. There is little hope that this situation will improve, for many of these timber crops are presently uneconomical to grow in plantations. These complex natural communities are quite stable in an undisturbed state, but many species of plants and animals that live there are entirely dependent on the integrity of the community structure. There is little doubt that human disturbance is would find that there is no clear boundary between the deciduous and coniferous forest biomes. The vegetation on any particular site would be a result of the complex of environmental variables on that site and not a function of precise geographic location. The north slope of a hill (which would be somewhat cooler than the south slope) might support a coniferous forest; the south slope might be cloaked with a deciduous forest. Slightly cooler sites farther south of the transition area might support conifers, and yet deciduous trees could still be found in protected areas to the north. Similar variations in the distribution of specific community types within a biome could also be seen. Given the time required to develop climax communities and the delicate interaction between communities and the prevailing environment, it is probable that most major units of vegetation in the Northern Hemisphere have not yet reached equilibrium following the climatic fluctuations of the Pleistocene (Chapter 9) but are still in the process of gradual change.

PERSPECTIVE

The factors controlling the distribution and structure of communities are at all levels quite complex. Individual organisms and the communities of which they are a part respond not only to the major aspects of the environment, such as climate, but also to a number of feedback systems that derive from the nature of the organisms themselves. The biotic interrelationships within a community are crucial in regulating population structures. Induced changes in a community that serve to alter one or more biotic components of the system can have far-reaching consequences that are not entirely predictable. Our brief analysis has highlighted numerous examples in which human activities have altered or in some cases almost completely destroyed large-scale biotic arrays. The pressure of human activities on natural systems is due in part to two factors: a steadily increasing human population with its expanding sphere of activities, and the increasing rate of utilization of various resources by those populations.

Aesthetic considerations have historically proved to be powerful forces in the preservation of natural communities. People, particularly in industrialized countries, appreciate unspoiled natural areas, but they also expect access to such areas for recreational purposes. Goals involving the preservation of wilderness areas and those involving the use of such areas often come into conflict. Heavy visitation in national parks is causing severe pressure on park facilities with an ever-increasing potential for deterioration of the site. The influx of visitors to such parks creates pressure on administrators to provide additional roads and visitor facilities. Obviously, realization of such objectives is not consistent with the prime mission of such parks—the maintenance

of natural areas in the best approximation of an undisturbed state.

We also occasionally err in our efforts to "preserve" some natural areas. The groves of Big Trees (*Sequoiadendron giganteum*) in the Sierra Nevada are a good case in point. In the past, the groves of these giant redwood trees apparently were maintained in part by periodic natural fires, which removed many competitive tree species but did not ever reach temperatures hot enough to penetrate the thick bark. Once the groves became protected, the fires were reduced, other tree species entered the area, and brush and litter accumulated. When widely separated fires now occur (almost a certainty because of the number of visitors to such areas, as well as the unpredictable nature of lightning), the fires have so much fuel to burn that they become hot enough to damage the Big Trees.

Obviously we cannot preserve a community if we fail to understand the factors that have interacted in the past to cause the community to exist in the form that it does today. Any effort to preserve a community with unique requirements may demand specific management practices to maintain the community in the absence of normal controls. Fortunately, as knowledge accumulates it is sometimes possible to modify our practices before it is too late. The park and forestry services of the United States once saw it as their responsibility to prevent forest fires whenever possible. But recently a program of controlled burning (setting fires) is being practiced in certain areas.

In developing countries, where few of the needs of the population can be met, it is far more difficult to generate a sense of urgency regarding preservation of natural areas. Aesthetics is hardly sufficient compensation if exploitation of an area might result in a higher standard of living. If aesthetics, measured against human problems, fails to provide sufficient justification for maintaining natural communities, why do biologists continue to emphasize the need for protection? Although the argument is not nearly as easy to perceive as that for aesthetics, the answer to the question is survival! Every natural community represents a composite answer to a realistic survival equation. Stresses encountered by human communities are engendered in part by three factors: lack of stabilized populations, an increasing per capita utilization of energy and materials, and a resource strategy that emphasizes acquisition and minimizes recycling. Natural communities are stable because they operate on a balanced energy budget and devote a large percentage of their energy resources to the management and recycling of material resources. Each type of natural community represents a biotic accommodation to a specific set of environmental conditions. In a sense, each community represents a storehouse of biological information (the total genetic complement of the members of the community), which, taken together, results in long-term survival. The genetic endowment of a single species is insufficient for survival, because any single species (and we are no exception) is inherently destructive of the very resources upon which its survival depends! *Only when a species is integrated with others in a complex community of organisms is there any chance of long-term stability.* We, as a species, attempt to survive under conditions of limited biotic diversity—our domestic animals and crops. Because these organisms have not been coadapted and in no way constitute a biological community, maintenance of these systems (not to mention "creature comfort" activities) demands tremendous quantities of energy and resources in the form of fossil fuels, fertilizers, pesticides, and so on.

Natural communities, if they were nothing more than models, would still provide us with valuable insight into how to alter our own systems to make them more stable with less energy input. In fact, solutions to present and future human problems may well involve the application of specific kinds of ecological information. Because we cannot predict what will be useful to us under future circumstances, we should try to preserve as much as possible of the biotic diversity that remains. Such preservation is not without cost. But measured against the potential for survival it may provide, it is a task worthy of the greatest effort.

SUGGESTED READINGS

FLANAGAN, DENNIS (ed.). *The Biosphere.* San Francisco: W. H. Freeman, 1970. A collection of eleven articles reprinted from *Scientific American,* covering the subjects of energy flow, recycling in natural systems, and the impact of human activities on the biosphere.

GOOD, RONALD. *The Geography of the Flowering Plants.* 3rd ed. New York: Wiley, 1964. A detailed account of the geographic distribution of the earth's vegetation with an analysis of the factors governing distribution.

MCLAREN, IAN A. (ed.). *Natural Regulation of Animal Populations.* New York: Atherton Press, 1971. A collection of articles on the various mechanisms that regulate animal population sizes.

ODUM, EUGENE P. *Fundamentals of Ecology.* 3rd ed. Philadelphia: Saunders, 1971. A standard introductory text.

Chapter 32

Mechanisms of Evolution

The ultimate motive force of evolution is selection. Selection operates upon the genetic variation that exists in natural populations. This scanning electron micrograph shows three abnormal red blood cells that are an outward manifestation of the sickling gene. Sickle-cell anemia is one example of genetically different types which are maintained in some populations by the action of natural selection.

The individual organisms of any species are the ephemeral vessels that briefly carry the hereditary material of life in its complex path through time. As diverse as they may be, all the representatives of life today share a single (monophyletic) origin. Thus if we could retrace the path of human evolution, we would come to those junctures where lines leading to human, chimpanzee, and gorilla first went their separate ways; much further on we would pass the point where mammals diverged from reptiles; and ultimately, descending through more than 3 billion years of evolutionary history, we would come to a single thread of nucleic acid that was the primeval source of all the fantastic diversity of life on earth. The conclusions we could draw from this journey are threefold. *First*, the genetic messages of the hereditary material have been gradually transformed through time. *Second*, from time to time, lines of hereditary continuity split and thereafter diverge from one another. And *third*, because the individuals are transient, the process of change occurs at a level of organization beyond that of single organisms.

Let us begin with the third point. It is crucial, for it defines the appropriate unit of study: the population. Here we are referring not to just any collection of living organisms, but to *a population of interbreeding individuals*. Why is the distinction so important? In interbreeding, the hereditary material of the individuals is recombined and passed on from generation to generation, which means that interbreeding populations have a genetic continuity. These populations (also called **Mendelian populations**) are said to share a common **gene pool:** their collective genetic resources are considered to be passed on as a unit. The gene pool concept is an abstraction that sweeps away consideration of individuals and focuses on the essential features of genetic continuity and change.

Identifying Mendelian populations, however, is not always an easy thing to do. The stand of Big Trees (*Sequoiadendron giganteum*) near Angels Camp, California, appears to be one clear example of such a population. But consider the difficulty you would have if you were asked to define a population of human beings—knowing (for instance) that people from New York City may mate with people from Poughkeepsie, whereas various groups within the city may never intermate. What is the Mendelian population in this case? Even though there are practical problems in applying the population concept there is no denying that it is a powerful theoretical tool, for it defines a new level of biological organization. Recall that in Chapter 1, emphasis was placed on the emergent properties that become manifest at each new level of organization. The emergent property of Mendelian populations is that they evolve. *Evolution is not an individual property; only populations evolve.*

Taking the population as the appropriate level of organization for our discussion, let us turn now to the mechanisms responsible for evolutionary change. There are two phases of evolution, and we will be dealing with the mechanisms for both: changes in gene frequencies and the phenomenon of speciation.

WHAT IS EVOLUTION?

It was the genius of Charles Darwin and Alfred Wallace to propose the central mechanism of evolution—natural selection—which accounts for the elaboration of structures that better adapt organisms to their environment. It is useful in this context to recall the three points of the Darwin-Wallace theory listed in Chapter 3. In a reordered and slightly restated form, these points are the following:

1. The individuals of any population have a vastly greater reproductive potential than is realized. Because a population's size is limited by environmental carrying capacity, excess individuals either die early or fail to reproduce (Chapter 31).

2. Individual members of species differ from one another, and some of these differences are genetically determined.

3. It follows that individuals with variations that best suit them to their environment will have a better chance of surviving and reproducing. And herein lies the core of the theory of evolution by natural selection: *Individuals with heritable variations that render them more successful in survival and reproduction will contribute their hereditary material to the next generation to a degree that is disproportionate to their representation in the present generation.*

The Darwin-Wallace theory is remarkably elegant and simple. Yet at the time it was advanced, it had one glaring weakness: no one knew *how* heritable variations were manifested among individuals or *how* they were transmitted from one generation to the next. To see what an important problem this was, consider a theory of inheritance that Darwin himself accepted for a time. According to the "blending theory of inheritance," hereditary material was a fluid (like blood, perhaps); at conception the new individual received equal portions of this fluid from each parent. The fluids then completely intermingled, as would dye in water, and the offspring had the average of its two parents' genetic endowments. The heredity fluid produced by the offspring of such a union was now intermediate between the parental fluids, and this consolidation was repeated in every generation. The outcome of such a scheme is that the differences between parents would be halved in every generation. After one generation, only one-half the original hereditary variation would remain in the population; after two generations, the amount of heritable variation would be quartered; and after ten generations, the amount of heritable variation would be virtually nonexistent—a mere 1/1024 of the original amount!

Such a scheme of inheritance is clearly fatal to evolution by natural selection because favorable variations would disappear faster than they could be selected for. Consequently, a system of inheritance that *conserves* variation is essential for evolution by natural selection. As you read in Chapters 16 and 17, the particulate inheritance of DNA has precisely this conservative property.

The unit of change in the evolutionary process occurs when a single gene takes the place of another gene in a population. This sequence of events is initiated when a new form of the gene arises due to a base change in the DNA message (Chapter 17). The new form of the gene may then increase in frequency until the original gene is replaced entirely. Therefore, *evolution may be defined as a change in gene frequency in a population.* A fundamental tenet of modern biology is that this process of evolution can be explained through a set of simple principles and that these principles are enough to account for the diversity of life.

CONSERVATION OF GENETIC VARIANCE: THE HARDY-WEINBERG LAW

How are the genetic resources of the gene pool distributed among the individuals in a population? An answer to this question will tell us how effective natural selection can be in changing gene frequencies. After some thought, it will become evident that the question really amounts to a query about how two genes at a given locus are drawn from the gene pool of one generation to form a new genotype in the next.

Many rules for drawing genes from the gene pool can be imagined. For instance, we could have a rule that if the first gene drawn was of type *A*, then the second one chosen must also be of the same type. Or the converse could be specified, where a draw of *A* means that the second gene must be other than *A*. In the real world, however, individuals get one copy of a gene from the male parent and one from the female parent, so our rules about drawing genes really amount to specifications about the pattern of mating among genotypes. In most animal populations, mating is *nearly* random with respect to genotype.

If we assume for the moment that random mating occurs, we can develop simple mathematical formulas to describe the distribution of genes among individuals in a population and to predict whether such distributions should change from generation to generation. To proceed, we need to adopt a method of measuring the relative amount of each kind of gene in the gene pool.

Suppose there are N individuals in a population. Then there are 2N genes at any given locus, because each individual carries two complete pairs of chromosome sets.

(Sex chromosomes are an obvious exception here, but we will ignore that complication for the moment.) Now, consider a locus with two different alleles, which we will call A_1 and A_2. (Recall from Chapter 16 that an **allele** is one of two or more alternative forms of a gene at a given chromosomal locus.) This means that, through sexual reproduction, there are three possible genotypic combinations at that locus: A_1A_1, A_1A_2, or A_2A_2. The number of individuals with the A_1A_1 genotype can be designated $N_{1,1}$. Similarly, the other two genotypes can be designated $N_{1,2}$ and $N_{2,2}$. Because there are only three genotypes (of the *A* locus) in our population of N individuals, it follows that

$$N = N_{1,1} + N_{1,2} + N_{2,2}$$

How many genes of type A_1 are there in the group? For every A_1A_1 individual, there are two; for every A_1A_2 individual, there is one; and for every A_2A_2 individual, there are none. Therefore, the total number of A_1 genes is

$$(2 \times N_{1,1}) + (1 \times N_{1,2}) + (0 \times N_{2,2})$$

Next we may ask: What fraction of the genes at the *A* locus are of the A_1 allelic type? The fraction of all the genes at one locus that are of one allelic type is called the **relative gene frequency** of that allele in the population. The relative gene frequencies of all the alleles at a locus therefore add up to 1. For convenience, let us use the letter *p* to stand for the relative gene frequency of the A_1 allele. To calculate the value of *p*, we need to divide the number of A_1 genes by the total number of genes at this locus:

$$p = \frac{2N_{1,1} + N_{1,2}}{2N}$$

Now let us use the letter *q* to represent the relative gene frequency of the A_2 allele. Because *p* plus *q* must equal 1, there are two ways we can calculate *q*, as shown below:

$$q = 1 - p = \frac{2N_{2,2} + N_{1,2}}{2N}$$

The concept of the relative gene frequency of an allele is useful for analyzing the behavior of the allele between generations. The reason is that it represents the *probability* that if we were to pick genes randomly at this locus, we would come up with this particular allele. Thus the probability of gene A_1 being drawn in random matings within our population is *p*, and the probability of gene A_2 being drawn is *q*. If the chance of drawing A_1 is *p*, then the chance of randomly drawing two A_1 genes in a row (to yield an individual with the genotype A_1A_1) is $p \times p = p^2$.

The way this works can be shown by using the Punnett square (Chapter 16). First, consider the possible genotypes that arise by randomly combining sperm and eggs:

Sperm

	A_1	A_2
A_1	A_1A_1	A_1A_2
A_2	A_1A_2	A_2A_2

Eggs

Now if, in such a Punnett square, we substitute the frequencies of the two alleles in our population for the alleles themselves, we can determine the frequencies of the three genotypes produced:

Sperm

	p	q
p	$p \times p = p^2$	$p \times q = pq$
q	$q \times p = pq$	$q \times q = q^2$

Eggs

From this we can see that the frequency of the genotype A_1A_1 is p^2, that of A_1A_2 is $2pq$, and that of A_2A_2 is q^2. What, then, are the relative gene frequencies of the two alleles in this new generation? By simple algebra, we can compute that the relative frequency of allele A_1 in the second generation is p and the relative frequency of allele A_2 is q. The gene frequencies have remained constant! If we were to repeat the process of randomly drawing sperm and eggs from the gene pool for a second generation, we would also discover that the genotypic frequencies have remained constant in the proportions $p^2(A_1A_1)$, $2pq(A_1A_2)$, and $q^2(A_2A_2)$. This result yields one of the fundamental principles of population genetics: In the absence of selection or other disturbing forces, *the frequency of genotypes in a population remains constant as long as mating in the population is random.* In other words, for any pair of alleles of relative gene frequencies p and q, the ratio of genotypes will remain fixed at p^2, $2pq$, and q^2 as long as mating is random. This is the **Hardy-Weinberg law,** named after the English mathematician G. H. Hardy and the German physician W. Weinberg, who derived it independently in 1908. It is sometimes called **Hardy-Weinberg equilibrium** in order to indicate the property of invariance in genotype frequency that it implies.

There are two important consequences of the Hardy-Weinberg law. The first is that—in contrast to the blending system of inheritance widely accepted in Darwin's time—*Mendelian inheritance preserves the distribution of genetic variability in a random-breeding population.* The second important consequence amounts to a mathematical convenience: *The genetic structure of random breeding populations can be represented solely in terms of gene frequencies.*

DEVIATIONS FROM HARDY-WEINBERG BEHAVIOR RESULT IN GENETIC DIVERSITY

The equilibrium defined by the Hardy-Weinberg law suggests that, *under the conditions defined,* a population remains genetically static indefinitely—it cannot evolve. Obviously, if all populations of organisms had followed such behavior for all time, there would be no genetic diversity and, hence, no diversity of organisms. Thus, if organisms do change, there must be deviations from Hardy-Weinberg behavior. The paradox is that if all populations had always been in Hardy-Weinberg equilibrium, there would not even be the kind of genetic variability that the equilibrium protects! Hardy and Weinberg did not attempt to deal with the question of how variability arose; they simply took it as given that variability existed, based on the rapid accumulation of breeding information in the first decade of this century. But in attempting to analyze how populations change, we must first explore the ultimate source of genetic variability.

Mutation Changes Genetic Structure of a Population by Introducing New Alleles

We now know that the source of all genetic variability is mutation (Chapters 16 and 17). A **mutation** is defined as a sudden, permanent change in the genetic material; it occurs by some change in a DNA molecule. Although such changes commonly occur as a result of errors in the duplication of DNA molecules, the frequency of such errors is extremely low. Thus DNA possesses the two essential requisites of a molecule capable of mediating evolution: constancy and change.

Several kinds of large mutational changes are known to occur: *deletions* of stretches of DNA, *duplications* of genetic regions of variable size, *translocation* of genetic material within or between chromosomes, and so on. But the most common form of mutation in nature (and the one we will focus on here) is now known to be a change in a nucleotide base pair at a specific point in a DNA molecule: a **point mutation.** Several mechanisms are now known to exist whereby one base pair can mutate to a different one (Chapter 11). This will change the nucleotide sequence of the gene and, about two times out of three, it will therefore change the amino acid that is called for by the nucleotide triplet that has been changed. This results in a gene product—a protein—of modified amino acid sequence that may therefore have sufficiently modified properties to cause a change in function of the protein. In short, a new allele is introduced into the population. Because a mutation occurs in a single individual, its initial frequency in the population is low.

What is the frequency with which mutations occur in a population? Direct analysis of several kinds of organisms has been attempted. This analysis leads to estimates that vary somewhat, but they tend to fall in the range from 10^{-5} to 10^{-6}. This means that each gene will tend to mutate about once for every 100,000 to 1,000,000 times it is duplicated. Considering that there are about 600 nucleotide pairs in an average gene that must be matched up precisely every time the gene is duplicated, this suggests that an error is introduced only about once every hundred million times a nucleotide is being added to a growing DNA chain! Nevertheless, mistakes do occur and they tend to accumulate. And although the incidence of mutation in any one gene is low, the number of genes in any one cell numbers in the thousands (it is much higher in complex eukaryotes than in prokaryotes). Therefore, the probability of any one cell possessing a mutant gene is far from negligible. Because most mutations are deleterious, in that they cause some degree of functional deficiency, there is justifiable concern over technological "advances" that are causing a progressive build-up of environmental factors—radiation and certain chemical pollutants—that raise the level of mutation.

Can mutation, acting alone, lead to a replacement of one allele by another? To answer this question, we must first consider the vast range of mutational states to which any gene can mutate. Suppose there are 600 nucleotide pairs in gene A (an average value). There are then 4^{600} possible nucleotide orderings and therefore 4^{600} possible mutational states, a number so large as to be considered effectively infinite. Now if we think about all possible mutations that involve only a single nucleotide change, we see that there are still 1,800 such changes (three possible erroneous substitutions for each existing nucleotide pair in the original A_1 gene). Evidently, almost every new mutation will be to a unique state. Suppose gene A_1 mutates to any of these other forms with a frequency of 10^{-5}. How fast will A_1 disappear from the population? There is a simple mathematical formula that gives us the answer. If p_o is the relative gene frequency of A_1 at the outset, at the end of some time t (measured in generations), the relative gene frequency will be reduced by the factor $(1 - \mu)^t$, where μ is the mutation rate, to yield a new frequency p_t. Thus

$$p_t = p_o (1 - \mu)^t$$

Fitting the above assumptions into this equation, we find that at the end of 10,000 generations (about 200,000 years in the case of *Homo sapiens*), the relative gene frequency of the original allele would be

$$p_{10^4 \text{ generations}} = (1) (1 - 10^{-5})^{10^4}$$
$$= (0.99999)^{10^4}$$
$$= 0.9048$$

Thus, in an organism with a generation time like that of humans, in 200,000 years mutation would be expected to

reduce the frequency of a common gene by only 10 percent!

Although the frequency of A_1 might diminish by 10 percent in 200,000 years, many of the mutations would be expected to be different. Therefore, we can conclude that *although mutation is important as a source of genetic variability in a population, it changes gene frequency very slowly and is not regarded as a significant force in effecting evolutionary change.*

Are mutations directed or random? Some mutations bestow a distinct survival advantage upon the organisms in which they occur when those organisms encounter specific environmental conditions. It is fundamentally important, if we are to understand how evolutionary changes occur, that we know whether these environmental conditions specifically increase the frequency of occurrence of mutations that are beneficial in that environment. For example, does heat *preferentially* increase the frequency with which genes mutate to yield heat resistance (relative to the rate at which other kinds of mutations occur under conditions of heat)? Does penicillin *preferentially* increase the frequency of mutations that confer penicillin resistance? And so on.

If we slowly raise the level of the environmental factor in question, we find a progressive increase in the percentage of individuals in the population that are genetically resistant to the parameter involved. But does that mean that the environment *caused* the mutations to a drug resistance (or heat resistance, or whatever) in a directed manner? Or did the mutations *preexist* in some individuals and confer a survival advantage on those individuals? If environment can act to elicit genetic changes that are specifically of survival advantage in that environment, then we would have a very simple explanation for the process of organic evolution. The question then becomes, is mutation **preadaptive**? Does it occur on a random basis and confer survival advantage to some environment the organism may or may not ever experience? Or is it **postadaptive**—does it occur in a directed manner in response to the existing environment?

It is true that some environmental changes *can* increase the rate of mutation and thereby increase the number of individuals that are genetically resistant to a given environmental parameter. For example, irradiation increases the rate at which organisms mutate to a radiation-resistant state. But further analysis shows that, at the same time, the irradiation increases the rate with which a vast array of other mutations occur. It is not selective in stimulating mutation to radiation resistance.

One of the most clear-cut demonstrations that mutation is preadaptive came from a now-classic experiment on the evolution of penicillin resistance in *Escherichia coli*. A population of bacteria was grown on the surface of an agar-filled petri dish that contained no antibiotic. (In such a culture situation, individuals that are related by descent tend to stay adjacent to each other on the plate.) Next, a piece of sterile velvet was cut in the shape of the petri dish, to transfer individuals from the first plate to a series of other plates that did contain penicillin. Because the orientation of the velvet was kept constant, all plates had similar spatial distributions of related cells. The results were that the cells capable of growth in the presence of antibiotic were found in the same position on all plates. This was clear evidence that the mutations had occurred prior to exposure to penicillin and were not induced by it. *Mutation was preadaptive, not postadaptive.*

Although few other organisms lend themselves as well to such an analysis, studies of a parallel nature have been performed on a variety of plants, animals, and other microorganisms. As a result of such studies, most biologists would now conclude that *mutations occur under all conditions in a random rather than in a directed manner; environmental influences that increase mutation rate increase the frequency of all classes of mutations more or less equally.*

How, then, do we account for the many observations that the frequency of resistant individuals usually increases with the time of exposure to an environmental variable? The answer is straightforward: Prolonged exposure of a population to any environmental extreme will increase the frequency of individuals in the population that are resistant to the extreme—not as a result of differential mutation, but as a result of differential survival! This is the process of natural selection in action. As we will see shortly, selection is the main force acting to change relative gene frequency within populations. But first let us explore some other forces that do not involve selection and yet act to modify the frequency of genes and genotypes within the population.

Genetic Drift May Alter Gene Frequencies by a Random Process

The Hardy-Weinberg law states that the frequency of two alleles in a population will remain constant as long as breeding is random. But this assumes that the population is so large that in each generation the genes forming the next generation are a representative sample of all the genes in the pool. *But the probability that genes drawn from a pool will reflect precisely the composition of that pool varies with the number of genes drawn in each generation.*

To see what this principle means, imagine an extremely large barrel containing an equal number of gold and silver balls that have been tumbled about until they are randomly distributed. Now suppose you were blindfolded and you drew one million balls at random from the barrel, two at a time, with an observer tabulating the color of the balls in each draw. You would undoubtedly find that over the course of the experiment, you drew very close to the

theoretical half gold and half silver; you had maintained a Hardy-Weinberg equilibrium. But if you now looked back at the record of individual draws, you would find that *about half the times you drew two balls, they were both of one color or the other.* You would probably find that somewhere along the line, you drew many successive balls (perhaps as many as 100!) of one color. The only reason the final average came out close to one-to-one was that you made so many draws, and inequalities in one direction were eventually balanced out by inequalities in the other. If you used a computer to analyze the data, you would find that the probability that a group of draws would yield a one-to-one ratio depends directly on the size of the sample taken. The smaller the size of the sample (number of draws), the greater the probable deviation between the color ratio of the chosen balls from the color ratio existing in the barrel at the outset!

Translated to the drawing of genes from a gene pool, the results of this experiment have important implications, for they suggest that the probability that relative gene frequencies will remain constant between generations is directly proportional to the size of the breeding population. The corollary is the following: *The smaller a breeding population is, the greater is the probability that deviations from the Hardy-Weinberg equilibrium will occur due to chance alone.* This is the principle of **genetic drift.** As the term "drift" implies, the deviation from Hardy-Weinberg equilibrium may occur in either direction in each generation; a given allele may fall in relative frequency in one generation and rise in the next. But in fact, having fallen in one generation, it is *just as likely* to fall as to rise in the second generation! (Similarly, if you flip a coin and obtain fifty heads in a row, your chances of getting a tail on the fifty-first flip are only one in two—just as they were on the first flip!)

As a result, if the population is small enough, the probability becomes high that eventually one of two *functionally equivalent* alleles will be lost from a population during some generation. And once lost, it remains lost unless it happens to reappear through mutation. Thus it is possible for one allele to become **fixed** (the only allele present in a population) by genetic drift. This process is illustrated in Figure 32.2. But two equivalent populations (noninterbreeding) that both start out with two alleles in the same frequency might fix opposite alleles.

An extreme case of genetic drift is seen in the **founder effect.** If, for example, a pregnant female insect is blown to a newly produced volcanic island and sets up housekeeping, she will carry with her an extremely small sample of the variability that existed in her home population. The new population she establishes almost invariably will have a different structure from that of the population from which

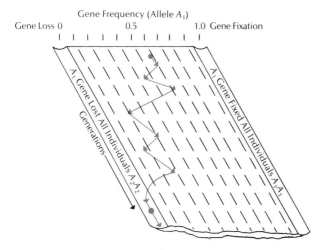

Gene Frequency (Allele A_1)

Gene Loss 0   0.5   1.0 Gene Fixation

Figure 32.2   A model illustrating genetic drift. The relative gene frequency of an allele is pictured as a ball rolling down a bowling alley. As long as the ball remains on the alley, it is free to wander about. But once the ball reaches the gutter, its route is determined. Said another way, as long as both alleles are present in the population, genetic drift occurs. But once one allele is lost altogether in one generation, the remaining gene is fixed.

she came. In short, *sizable shifts in gene and genotypic frequencies of a population can occur by chance alone if the size of the breeding population is low or if a long period of time is considered.*

Inbreeding May Shift Genotype Frequencies Without Changing Gene Frequencies

The Hardy-Weinberg law assumes the existence of a local population in which all individuals have an equal probability of mating with each other. Such a breeding pattern is called **panmixis** and a population breeding in this manner is said to be **panmictic.** We might now ask: What will be the change in the genetic structure of the population if all individuals breed with equal frequency, but if mate selection is not random? Suppose, for example, that each individual has a higher probability of mating with a close relative than it does of mating with an unrelated member of the population. Such a mating pattern is called **inbreeding.** The most extreme case of inbreeding is *self-breeding*, or *selfing.* It occurs in some plants that are capable of self-fertilization and in some animals, such as nematodes, that are capable of self-fertilization. It constitutes one extreme exception to the assumption of panmixis.

The effect of self-breeding, as shown in Figure 32.3, is to subdivide the population into several separate subpopulations, which tend increasingly to "breed true." But it does this without affecting the frequency of the various alleles within the population. *Thus, inbreeding tends to increase*

(a)   First Generation

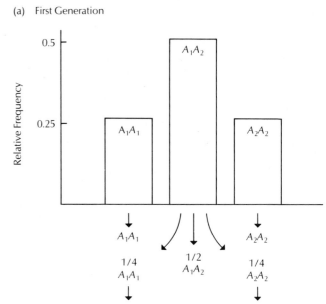

(b)   Second Generation

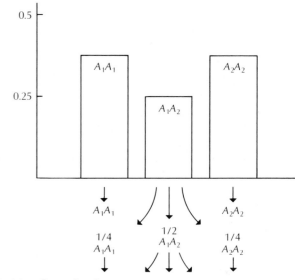

(c)   Many Generations Later

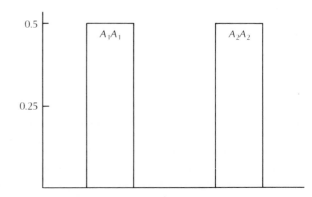

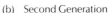

Figure 32.3   The effect of self-fertilization on genotype frequencies. If we start with a population in which heterozygotes are predominant, we see that they decrease proportionately in each generation, because one-half their progeny are homozygotes. Thus, after several generations of self-fertilization, we tend to end up with separate, pure-breeding lines. But this change occurs without any change in relative gene frequencies in the population as a whole. The A_1 and A_2 genes are as abundant at the end of the process as at the beginning. But they have been segregated into different lines.

genetic disparity between individuals without affecting the amount of genetic variability in the population as a whole. If we combine the effects of inbreeding and genetic drift, we see that any force acting to subdivide a breeding population will tend to increase genetic disparity between the breeding groups; the more extensive and complete the fragmentation, the greater the effect.

Migration Serves to Link Two or More Populations and to Lower Their Genetic Disparity

Fragmentation of one breeding population into two or more tends to raise the level of genetic disparity between them. The corollary is that factors tending to link two or more breeding populations into one tend to lower the level of genetic disparity between them. The main force acting to link two or more populations is **migration.**

Migration is just what the name implies: the exchange of genes between separate populations. The effect of migration is to equalize gene frequencies between the communicating populations. To see why gene frequencies are equalized, try another simple experiment. Put a collection of red balls in one jar and a collection of white balls in a second jar. Once every minute, select a ball from the red jar with your eyes closed and place the ball into the white jar and shake the container. Next, take a ball from the white jar, also with eyes closed, and put it in the red jar, again shaking the container. After a time, you will discover that the frequency of red balls and of white balls has become more and more similar in the two jars. This experiment illustrates how migration causes the equalization of gene frequencies between populations. From an evolutionary perspective, however, the migrant must contribute its genes to the gene pool of the recipient population; if not, then the migrant is of no consequence. This emphasis on the migration of *genes* makes migration the most difficult evolutionary force to study experimentally. The reasons are that the physical presence of a migrant individual in an observed population is not enough, and it is often very difficult to verify whether migrants reproduce successfully and, if so, how often. The rate at which populations exchange genes plays a key role in the theory of speciation, and consequently the practical difficulties associated with the measurement of migration rates have constituted a serious impediment to quantifying evolutionary phenomena. In any case, it is obvious that migration, when it does occur, can be quite effective in preventing the deviation in gene frequency that might otherwise develop between populations as a result of drift.

The Principal Force Acting to Modify Gene Frequencies Is Selection

The fundamental assumption of the Hardy-Weinberg law is the existence of random mating within the population. This assumes that all individuals have equal probabilities of survival and reproduction—whatever their genetic constitution. Similarly, the earlier discussion of the role of mutation in changing gene frequencies carried the implicit assumption that individuals bearing mutant genes had the same probability of reproductive success as individuals lacking them. And the discussion of genetic drift was based on the assumption that genetic variants exist that are functionally equivalent. Although all of these concepts appear valid when the underlying assumption of equivalence of two allelic genes is met, in many cases the two alleles are *not* equivalent. It has now been clearly shown that *the probability of reproductive success often depends on the genotypes of the individuals involved.* The result of this genetically determined differential reproductive success is what we call **natural selection.**

There can be many bases for differential reproductive success. Clearly a mutation that blocked the production of eggs or sperm would interfere with reproductive success in a rather direct and absolute way. So could a mutation leading to modified mating behavior. But such effects are *not* restricted to genes that affect the mating process. *Any mutation that lowers the capacity of the individual to survive in the existing environment can act to decrease reproductive success.* Failure to survive long enough to mate is just as effective a block to reproductive success as sterility. Let us examine one well-documented case of such natural selection.

Industrial Melanism: An Example of Directional Selection

In the mid-1840s, during the burgeoning of the industrial revolution in England, a change began to occur in the countryside surrounding newly industrialized cities. The tree trunks, which had previously been covered with lichens, became coated with black soot from the chimneys of the new factories. The soot deposits totally altered the background against which the peppered moth (*Biston betularia*) rests (Figure 32.4*a*). A look at Figure 32.4*b* shows the moth on a lichen-covered tree trunk and also shows how

(a)

(b)

Figure 32.4 The selective advantage of protective mimicry. In (a), a Biston betularia *and a* B. betularia carbonaria *are shown on a soot-covered tree trunk. In (b), they are shown on a lichen-covered tree trunk. Other examples of protective mimicry are given in Chapter 29. Actual field studies of the rate of moth consumption by birds has confirmed that birds are three times as likely to eat a mottled moth as a black one in industrialized areas, where the trees have the appearance shown in (a); and the reverse is true in nonindustrialized areas.*

well camouflaged the moth is on the background to which it had become morphologically adapted. The camouflage is especially important to the peppered moth because exposed individuals are likely to be devoured by birds. In 1848 in Manchester, England, collectors came across a new type of *B. betularia* that was totally black. Because the new black form was naturally camouflaged on the sooty tree trunks, it suffered less predation in polluted areas than the original peppered type. As a result, by the turn of the century the frequency of the black morphological type had reached 90 percent in populations around Manchester! A similar process of evolution to darker forms in industrial areas has been

identified in several species. The process is known as *industrial melanization* (melanin is a dark pigment).

Studies of the inheritance of the black morphological type (called *carbonaria*) show that the trait is due to a dominant gene at a single locus. Mutations to the black form are known to occur at a very low frequency. On lichen-covered trees, new *carbonaria* mutants would be immediately seen and eaten by birds. But when the environment changed, those variants with darker coloration suddenly became advantageous. Because they escaped predation more often than the form that was adapted to an aspect of the environment that no longer existed, the gene for dark coloration increased in frequency in every generation. This kind of process, whereby one gene replaces another in a population, is called **directional selection.**

This example of industrial melanism underscores two points. First, it provides documentary evidence that selection works to change gene frequencies. Second, it shows that the selective value of a genotype depends on the environment—and that changes in the environment alter the existing selective regime.

How does selection change relative gene frequencies and lead to departures from the Hardy-Weinberg equilibrium? In order to visualize this, we need to define a theoretical parameter known as the relative fitness. **Relative fitness** is defined as the probability that individuals of one genotype will survive relative to the probability of survival of individuals with some arbitrarily chosen standard genotype at that locus. Relative fitness is usually symbolized by W. It is sometimes convenient to define $W = 1$ for the most fit genotype at a locus. Other combinations of alleles at that locus must therefore have W between 1 and 0. (Zero implies no survival potential; in other words, a lethal gene.) An alternative form of fitness that is more useful in assessing the course of selection is the **selection coefficient,** symbolized as s and calculated as $s = 1 - W$. The selection coefficient can be defined as the probability of reproductive failure for the genotype in question relative to the most fit genotype. Thus, s varies inversely with W. *The most fit genotype at any locus has a selection coefficient of 0; a lethal genotype has a selection coefficient of 1.* (The latter is *bound* to be reproductively unsuccessful.)

In each generation, the frequency of individuals of any one genotype can be determined by multiplying the expected frequency of that genotype (if there were no selection) by the relative fitness of the genotype (W, or $1 - s$). How does this apply to the case of the peppered moth? The dominant gene (which results in dark color) may be called A_1, and its relative gene frequency, p; the recessive gene may be called A_2, and its frequency, q. If there had been no selection, the frequencies of the various expected genotypes would have been those listed in the third column of Table

Table 32.1
Frequency of Expected Genotypes in the Peppered Moth

Phenotype	Genotype	Frequency Without Selection	Fitness (W)	Frequency After One Generation of Selection
Black	A_1A_1	p^2	1.0	$(p^2)(W_{1,1}) = (p^2)(1)$
Black	A_1A_2	$2pq$	1.0	$(2pq)(W_{1,2}) = (2pq)(1)$
Mottled	A_2A_2	q^2	0.5	$(q^2)(W_{2,2}) = (q^2)(0.5)$

32.1. But on soot-blackened tree trunks, the mottled individual has reduced fitness. (Actual estimate placed its fitness—which we will call $W_{2,2}$—at about 0.5; it was only half as likely to survive and reproduce as a black moth.) Because the homozygous A_1A_1 individuals and the heterozygotes were equally inconspicuous, they both had fitness values of 1 ($W_{1,1} = W_{1,2} = 1$). After one generation of selection, the frequency of A_2A_2 (mottled) individuals was reduced by half (Table 32.1). This process would continue in each generation as long as the relative fitness values remain unchanged. *Interleaf 32.1* develops the algebra required to make quantitative predictions concerning the rate of change of relative gene frequencies, given the relative fitness values of the alleles.

Using such an approach, it is possible to represent graphically the expected course of selection, as in Figure 32.5 for the peppered moth. When such a curve is prepared, it immediately becomes apparent that *selection may act extremely rapidly once the favored gene is reasonably abundant,* but that it is a slow process at first. Similarly, when the recessive gene of lower fitness falls below 0.1 in frequency, selection slows rapidly. The reason is that selection acts only upon *homozygous* recessive individuals, and when the frequency of the recessive allele falls to low

levels, most of the recessive genes are carried by heterozygous individuals who do not show the phenotype that is being selected against. For example, when 10 percent of the alleles in the population are recessive, only 1 percent of the offspring will be homozygous recessive and 18 percent will be heterozygotes, on the average.

The fate of selected genes depends on the pattern of relative fitness values as well as the strength of selection. Figure 32.6 compares the course of gene frequency change for a number of different choices of selective values. Notice that a dominant lethal gene (curve A) can be removed from the population in a single generation, whereas the frequency of a recessive lethal gene (curve H) only approaches zero but never becomes exactly zero.

One consequence of the failure of selection to remove rare recessive genes is that they remain in the population as a reservoir of genetic variability that may be selected for in future generations if conditions change. *The fitness value associated with a given gene is not an intrinsic property of the gene: it is dependent upon the environment in which the fitness is tested.* A case in point: In recent years, concern over air pollution in England has led to increasing use of fuels that produce less soot. Tree trunks in many areas are returning to their earlier condition. Selection *against* the mottled moth variety has been relaxed and their numbers are on the increase. We can readily predict that if this pattern continues, mottled moths will once again predominate in industrial areas, as they always have in nonindustrial areas. But if the "energy crisis" forces a return to soot-rich fuels, the process will be reversed once again.

Sickle-Cell Anemia: An Example Of Balanced Polymorphism

Industrial melanism exemplifies directional selection in which the tendency is to replace one allele almost entirely with another. But not all selection takes this form. For example, in many cases selection acts to retain two or more different alleles in relatively high frequency. The existence

(text continues on page 702)

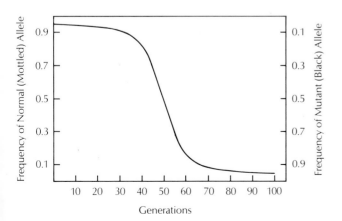

Figure 32.5 Probable course of selection in the industrial melanization of the peppered moth. This curve assumes a constant difference in fitness between the two alleles: that measured when the trees were fully blackened with soot. In fact, the early course of selection was probably slower than shown here, because the difference in fitness developed progressively with the darkening of the tree trunks. Despite the large differences in fitness, selection acts very slowly when one of the alleles is rare (relative gene frequency less than 0.1).

Interleaf 32.1

Calculating the Effect of Selection on Relative Gene Frequencies

How rapidly will relative gene frequencies change in a population as a result of selection? The answer is that the rate of change depends on the initial relative gene frequencies, the strength of selection, and the difference in fitness of the three genotypes in question.

As an example, let us consider two alleles, A_1 and A_2, that differ in their functional effectiveness within the organism and therefore affect the fitness of the individual with respect to the environment. Let us call the fitness of individuals of the A_1A_1 genotype $W_{1,1}$, that of the A_1A_2 genotype $W_{1,2}$, and that of the A_2A_2 genotype $W_{2,2}$. If in the first generation we examine this population, the relative frequency of the A_1 allele is p and that of the A_2 allele is q, and if mating is random, zygotes of the A_1A_1, A_1A_2, and A_2A_2 genotypes will be produced in relative frequencies p^2, $2pq$, and q^2, respectively. If the total number of zygotes produced is N, then the numbers of individuals of each genotype will be obtained by simply multiplying relative frequency of each genotype by N. Thus

$$N = Np^2 + N2pq + Nq^2$$

But before the next cycle of breeding can begin, the numbers of individuals of various genotypes will

be altered in proportion to the fitnesses of the genotypes. Thus, to determine the numbers of each genotype remaining after selection, we simply multiply the above values by the appropriate fitness values. Thus

$$N\overline{W} = Np^2W_{1,1} + N2pqW_{1,2} + Nq^2W_{2,2}$$

or

$$N\overline{W} = N(p^2W_{1,1} + 2pqW_{1,2} + q^2W_{2,2}).$$

The value $\overline{W}$ is called the *weighted average fitness* of the population. It can be seen from the second form of the equation that the mean fitness is equal to the sum of the fitnesses of the individual genotypes times their relative frequencies. The number of individuals left in the population after selection is equal to N—the number of individuals present initially, times $\overline{W}$, the mean fitness.

How has one generation of selection affected relative gene frequencies? Following the logic developed in the text for computing gene frequencies, we can see that the new frequency of the A_1 allele (which we shall call p', to distinguish it from p) will be equal to twice the number of the A_1 homozygotes plus the number of heterozygotes divided by twice the total

number of individuals in the population (two alleles per individual in a diploid organism). Thus

$$p' = \frac{2(Np^2W_{1,1}) + N2pqW_{1,2}}{2N\overline{W}}$$

Dividing numerator and denominator by 2N, we obtain

$$p' = \frac{p^2W_{1,1} + pqW_{1,2}}{\overline{W}}$$

To what extent has the frequency of the A_1 allele been changed by one generation of selection? If we define the rate of change in gene frequency, Δp, as $p' - p$ (the increase in relative gene frequency following selection), then it follows that

$$\Delta p = \frac{p^2W_{1,1} + pqW_{1,2}}{\overline{W}} - p$$

or

$$\Delta p = \frac{p^2W_{1,1} + pqW_{1,2} - p\overline{W}}{\overline{W}}$$

or

$$\Delta p = \frac{p(pW_{1,1} + qW_{1,2} - \overline{W})}{\overline{W}}$$

Now, in order to get the equation into a more useful form, let us modify the numerator of the Δp expression by replacing $\overline{W}$ with its equivalent as defined above, and then make some simple algebraic rearrangements:

$p(pW_{1,1} + qW_{1,2} - \overline{W})$

$\qquad = p(pW_{1,1} + qW_{1,2} - p^2W_{1,1}$

$\qquad\quad - 2pqW_{1,2} - q^2W_{2,2})$

$\qquad = p[(pW_{1,1} - p^2W_{1,1}) + (qW_{1,2}$

$\qquad\quad - pqW_{1,2}) - pqW_{1,2} - q^2W_{2,2}]$

$\qquad = p[pW_{1,1}(1-p) + qW_{1,2}(1-p)$

$\qquad\quad - pqW_{1,2} - q^2W_{2,2}]$

Now, recalling that $q = 1 - p$, we can further modify this expression to

$p[pW_{1,1}q + qW_{1,2}q - pqW_{1,2} - q^2W_{2,2}]$

and moving q outside the brackets we obtain

$pq(pW_{1,1} + qW_{1,2} - pW_{1,2} - qW_{2,2})$

By further rearrangement of terms, we can transform this to

$pq[p(W_{1,1} - W_{1,2}) + q(W_{1,2} - W_{2,2})]$

Now, reinserting this expression in the formula for Δp we obtain

$$\Delta p = \frac{pq[p(W_{1,1} - W_{1,2}) + q(W_{1,2} - W_{2,2})]}{\overline{W}}$$

This equation tells us that Δp, the rate of change of frequency of the A_1 allele, is a function of—among other things—the relative frequency of the two alleles in question. Whatever the fitness values, the rate of selection will be greatest when p and q are both significantly different from zero. As

either p or q approaches zero, the numerator of the fraction becomes very small and the frequency of the A_1 allele changes only very slowly. This relationship is reflected in the S-shape of the selection curves in Figures 32.5 and 32.6 (which are derived from the above equation). Once either p or q reaches zero, then Δp must also become zero. This restates the obvious: Once one of the alleles is lost from the population, there will be no further change in relative gene frequency due to selection.

But is there any condition under which both p and q have values between 0 and 1 and yet Δp equals zero? The answer is yes. There are two cases. If $W_{1,1} = W_{1,2} = W_{2,2}$ (if all genotypes have equal fitness), Δp will be equal to zero. All this says is that if there is no difference in fitness between genotypes, there will be no selection—another statement of the obvious. But the remaining case is less obvious and less trivial. Referring back to the last equation, we can see that the value of Δp will be zero and there will be no change in genotype frequency due to selection whenever

$p(W_{1,1} - W_{1,2}) + q(W_{1,2} - W_{2,2}) = 0$

In order to examine the equilibrium relationships, we shall again use the fact that $q = 1 - p$ and then make some of the algebraic rearrangements in this expression:

$p(W_{1,1} - W_{1,2}) + (1 - p)(W_{1,2} - W_{2,2})$

$\qquad = p(W_{1,1} - W_{1,2}) + (W_{1,2} - W_{2,2})$

$\qquad\quad - p(W_{1,2} - W_{2,2})$

$\qquad = p[(W_{1,1} - W_{1,2}) - (W_{1,2} - W_{2,2})]$

$\qquad\quad + (W_{1,2} - W_{2,2})$

$\qquad = 0$

or

$$p = \frac{W_{2,2} - W_{1,2}}{(W_{1,1} - W_{1,2}) - (W_{1,2} - W_{2,2})}$$

Now for p to lie between zero and one, both the numerator and denominator must be of the same sign. If $W_{1,2}$ is greater than $W_{1,1}$ and $W_{2,2}$, then p will always lie between zero and one. (This is just the situation we observed for sickle-cell anemia.) There is a second case. When $W_{1,2}$ is less than $W_{1,1}$ and $W_{2,2}$, p also lies between zero and one; but this second case produces an unstable equilibrium: if the frequency is disturbed from this equilibrium point, it will move to $p = 0$ or $p = 1$ (depending on the direction of disturbance), rather than returning to the equilibrium point. Hence only the stable situation ($W_{1,2}$ greater than $W_{1,1}$ and $W_{2,2}$) is of biological interest.

Rephrased, this means that *whenever the heterozygote has a higher fitness than either homozygote, natural selection will lead to the establishment of a particular set of relative gene frequencies that will remain stable as long as selective pressures are unchanged.* The equilibrium so established is a *balanced polymorphism.* The force maintaining it is the *heterozygote advantage.* By knowing the fitness values for the genotypes it is possible to predict the relative gene frequencies at which equilibrium will be established.

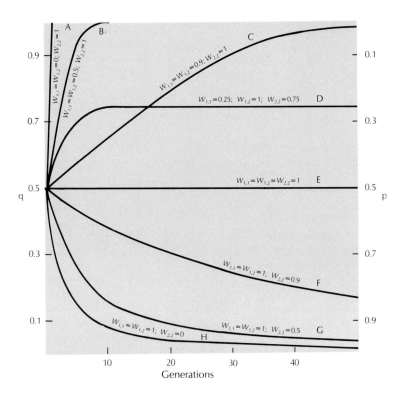

Figure 32.6 Selection curves given as a function of fitness value. For simplicity all genes are shown starting at a relative gene frequency of 50 percent. Here, p and q are the frequencies of dominant and recessive alleles, respectively. A, B, C: Selection against dominant alleles with fitnesses of 0 (lethal), 0.5, and 0.9 respectively. The lower the fitness, the more rapid the elimination of the gene. F, G, H: Selection against recessive genes with fitnesses of 0.9, 0.5, and 0.0 respectively. The difference in rate of selection against dominant and recessive genes is most clearly shown by comparing A with H (although the same trend is seen by comparing B with G and C with F). Although a dominant lethal gene (A) will be eliminated in one generation, a recessive lethal gene (H) can never be completely eliminated by selection. D: The path of selection when the homozygous recessive has a higher fitness than the homozygous dominant, but the heterozygote is more fit than either homozygote; this is called heterozygote advantage and is discussed in the text. E: When all fitness values are equal, there is no selection and the population maintains Hardy-Weinberg equilibrium.

of two or more distinct phenotypes in a population in frequencies higher than would be expected on the basis of mutation alone is known as **polymorphism** (differences between life stages or the sexes are excluded, however). When natural selection acts to maintain such multiple phenotypes, the result is known as *balanced polymorphism*. And balanced polymorphism is one kind of result of what is known as *stabilizing selection*. As the name implies, stabilizing selection differs from directional selection in that it acts to maintain a certain intermediate range of relative gene frequencies rather than leading toward one extreme or the other.

The human disease **sickle-cell anemia** represents one of the clearest cases of a balanced polymorphism. The gene involved is that coding for one of the two polypeptide chains of human hemoglobin: the so-called beta chain. The hemoglobin molecule consists of four polypeptide chains, two of the alpha type and two of the beta type. The capacity of hemoglobin to carry oxygen in the blood and release it to the tissues depends on the detailed interactions between the alpha and beta chains. As oxygen is picked up and released, the chains undergo subtle shifts in shape and their relationships to one another change (Chapter 21).

Individuals with sickle-cell anemia have an aberrant beta chain. As the result of a point mutation, their beta chains contain the amino acid valine as the sixth amino acid in the sequence, where the common form of human beta chains have a glutamic acid group. Hemoglobin containing this aberrant beta chain is called hemoglobin S (HbS) to distinguish it from the normal type, called hemoglobin A (HbA). When the red blood cell is loaded with oxygen, HbS causes no major problem. But as the HbS molecules lose their oxygen, they tend to interact with one another in a way that HbA molecules never do. They stack end-to-end and form long chains that distort the cell; they can even punch holes in the red blood cell membrane (Figure 32.7). Such sickle-shaped cells create log jams in the blood vessels, stopping the flow of blood; thus they deprive the affected tissues of oxygen, leading to tissue damage, pain, and often death. In early stages, the destruction of cells caused by the sickling leads to low levels of red blood cells in the circulation, which is the basis for the anemia.

For purposes of discussion, we will call the allele coding for the aberrant beta chain "*S*" and that coding for the normal gene "*A*"; thus a heterozygote will have the genotype *AS*. Because sickle-cell anemia is often fatal in early childhood, the *S* allele can be considered a recessive lethal gene. Yet in large areas of the world, it is far more common than you would expect a recessive lethal to be if it were being selected against. The reason for this distribution can be seen by comparing Figure 32.8 to Figure 32.9, which shows the distribution for the malaria parasite. Malaria has long been one of the leading causes of death in many parts of the world. Now, it happens that *individuals heterozygous for the S gene (AS genotype) lack symptoms of sickle-cell anemia, but they are resistant to malaria.* The

Figure 32.7   Deformed red blood cells from a human being with the sickle-cell gene. The grim disease of sickle-cell anemia represents evolution in progress among humans today and is the prime case of a genetic condition now understood in chemical detail.

malaria parasite takes up residence in red blood cells (Chapter 4). As it uses up the oxygen carried by the cell, it apparently causes the *AS* cells (which normally sickle only at high altitudes, where oxygen is inadequate) to sickle. When phagocytic cells of the body then destroy the sickled cell, they destroy its resident parasite at the same time, thereby interrupting the disease process!

In areas where malaria is prevalent, then, individuals lacking the *S* gene (*AA* genotype) have a high probability of death from malaria. Those homozygous for the *S* gene (*SS* genotype) will suffer from sickle-cell anemia. Heterozygotes (*AS*) suffer neither fatal anemia nor fatal malaria. This constitutes what is called *heterozygote advantage*.

In Africa, if the relative gene frequency of the *S* gene falls, the number of *AA* individuals rises and they are selected against by malaria, which lowers the relative frequency of the *A* gene in the next generation. But if the frequency of *S* rises, the number of *SS* individuals rises also; they are selected against, which lowers the frequency of the *S* gene in the next generation. Thus an equilibrium is achieved in which the disadvantage of the *A* gene is balanced by the disadvantage of the *S* gene. This balance is maintained as long as both selective pressures remain the same. (Americans of African ancestry have been undergoing a decline in frequency of the *S* gene, owing to the absence of malaria as a selecting agent in this country.) Because death from sickle-cell anemia has a higher probability in *SS* individuals than death from malaria does in *AA* individuals, the balance that is struck in this polymorphism is not 50-50. The *S* gene seldom is found to be present at a frequency of more than 0.2, in which case 4 percent of the population would be expected to be born with the *SS* genotype and 32 percent with the *AS* genotype.

How common is heterozygote advantage? This is one of the major controversies of modern population genetics. When population geneticists began in the 1960s to examine a large number of proteins in natural populations of various organisms, they found themselves faced with a totally unanticipated richness of genetic diversity. Although the values varied from species to species, it was found that in most cases about one-third of all genes examined were polymorphic. In other words, in population after population it has been found that two or more variants are present—in reasonably high frequency—in fully one-third of the body proteins. Are these polymorphisms the result of selection? Or do they represent functionally equivalent alleles that have no effect on phenotype and, hence, are "selectively neutral"?

One mechanism that allows the maintenance of two or more alleles in a population is heterozygote advantage. And that, of course, implies a homozygote disadvantage. Some mathematical calculations show that, with one-third of all genes involved, if even a tiny homozygote disadvantage accrues at each locus (fitnesses deviating from unity only slightly), most individuals are bound to be homozygous at many loci and will suffer a disadvantage of some major consequence. The cumulative effect of many homozygous disadvantages has been termed the **genetic load** the species must carry in order to maintain these polymorphisms. Some believe that no species could survive such a genetic load (loss of most individuals because of homozygosity at various loci) and that most polymorphisms must therefore be selectively neutral. Others point out that patterns of polymorphism observed are far from random on an ecological, biochemical, or physiological basis and appear to show the clear imprint of selection. So far this controversy has not been resolved to the satisfaction of all. But it has stimulated much active research into the kinds of genetic variations that do exist in nature and the strength of selective forces that are at work.

We can pause at this point to review what we have read so far concerning changes in gene frequency within populations: The *Hardy-Weinberg equilibrium* tells us that populations have genetic inertia. In the absence of other forces, the *Mendelian system of inheritance* tends to keep gene frequencies static between generations. *Mutation* acts to introduce new variability but it changes gene frequencies very slowly. *Genetic drift* can cause large changes in

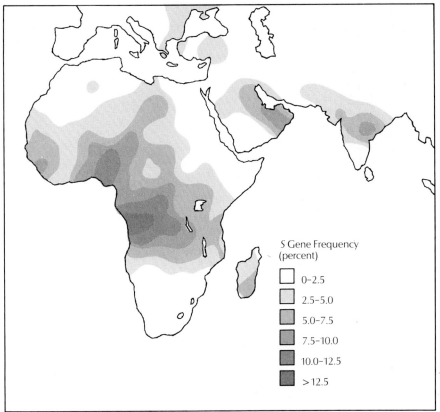

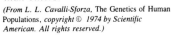

Figure 32.8 Distribution of the sickle-cell gene in Africa, the Middle East, and India. Sickle-cell gene is commonest in populations of tropical Africa; in Zaire, for example, the S gene frequency is about 18 percent, which means that some 30 percent of the population carry the AS trait.
The sickle-cell gene is also found in the Mediterranean, particularly in Greece and Turkey, and in northwestern Africa, southern Arabia, Pakistan, India, and Bangladesh. Individuals who carry the AS trait are more resistant to malaria than others.

(From L. L. Cavalli-Sforza, The Genetics of Human Populations, *copyright © 1974 by Scientific American. All rights reserved.)*

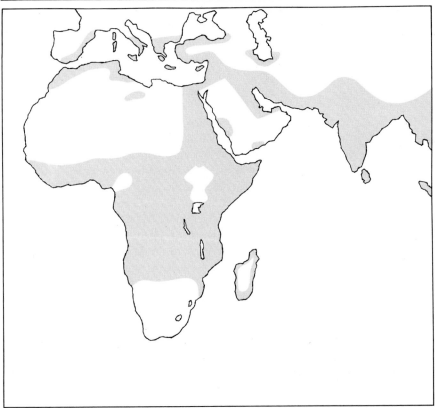

Figure 32.9 Distribution of malignant malarias caused by the parasite Plasmodium falciparum. *Malaria was common in the 1920s in the parts of the Old World indicated on this map. Overlap with sickle-cell gene distribution is extensive, as seen in Figure 32.8. In many regions where malaria is prevalent but HbS is not, other mutant hemoglobins are commonly found.*

frequency and the loss of alleles due to chance alone; its importance increases as population size falls. Any factor such as inbreeding that tends to subdivide a population into separate breeding units tends to increase genetic disparity between individuals without necessarily changing overall gene frequencies. Successful *migration* of individuals between separate breeding populations tends to reduce genetic disparity between them. But the most potent force acting to change gene frequencies is *selection*.

Let us now move on to the question of how those factors may act to give rise to distinct species.

SPECIATION

The problem of the origin of species is an old one. The 1859 title of Darwin's great treatise is *On the Origin of Species by Means of Natural Selection,* and yet a fully satisfactory theory for the origin of species is *still* in the process of being developed. Darwin and Wallace explained how species could be altered through time; they could not explain how **speciation** (the derivation of two distinct species from one) might occur. The current view is that speciation involves the divergence of different populations within a system of populations. (In contrast to this interpopulational view, the Darwin-Wallace theory of natural selection focuses on how a single population changes through time.) *No new evolutionary forces are postulated to account for speciation, but a new level of biological organization is necessary to explain this process.* This new level of organization is called the biological species and, like the Mendelian population, it has a careful definition. In the **biological species concept,** populations belong to the *same* species if their members can interbreed; they belong to *different* species if their members are prevented from interbreeding (exchanging genes) by any of a number of isolating barriers. This is what is meant when we say that humans and chimpanzees belong to different species; we recognize not only that they differ morphologically but also that they do not interbreed. *It is the absence of interbreeding that prevents gene migration and that therefore preserves morphological differences.*

How much genetic variability occurs in any species? How is this variability distributed among the geographically separated populations of the species? And how much genetic differentiation accompanies speciation? Answers to these questions are incomplete and have only recently begun to come together as a result of a new technique, called *gel electrophoresis,* which permits detection of certain kinds of amino acid substitutions in proteins. The technique is based on the separation of protein molecules that differ in charge. Recall that in HbS, valine replaces the glutamic acid found in the beta chain of HbA. The side chain of glutamic acid carries a negative charge, whereas

the side chain of valine has no charged group. The result is that the abnormal beta chain has one less negative charge than the normal chain, and when the two are placed in an electric field, they migrate at different rates and can therefore be separated. Electrophoresis has been applied to many of the proteins of a wide variety of organisms. It is on the basis of such electrophoretic analysis that we now know that in many species fully a third of all proteins may be polymorphic.

Consider the research being done on a group of *Drosophila* species known as the *Drosophila willistoni* complex. These species are found throughout much of Central and South America. The complex is composed of several *sibling species* (species that are nearly indistinguishable morphologically) and of several morphologically recognizable species. Sibling species are assumed to be very closely related because of their morphological identity; the morphologically distinguishable species are assumed to be less closely related. The simplest parameter to use to make comparisons is one called *genetic identity* (I), which simply compares the extent to which gene frequencies are similar between two populations. An I value of 1 implies that the two groups not only have the same alleles, they have exactly the same relative gene frequencies at the locus in question. An I value of 0, in contrast, means the populations do not share any alleles at the locus.

Application of the electrophoretic technique to geographically different populations from within and between species reveals (1) that even widely separated populations from *within a species* are very similar in their pattern of gene frequency, and (2) that different species differ markedly in their gene frequency distribution. *The average values of I between populations within species exceed 0.95, which means that individuals from the same species, even if they come from widely separated populations, are genetically very similar.* But as Figure 32.10 shows, the relationship is very different when one compares populations of different species. This figure shows us that sibling species are indeed more genetically similar than are morphologically recognizable species. *But nearly 35 percent of the gene loci have completely different alleles between the sibling species.* This degree of differentiation, if extrapolated to the whole genome, suggests that more than a thousand loci have undergone gene substitution during the course of the evolution of these sibling species! We can therefore conclude that *major genetic changes accompany the process of speciation.*

What accounts for the similarity of populations within species? There are probably two forces that tend to maintain similar gene frequencies: migration and balancing selection (similar to the heterozygote advantage observed for sickle-cell anemia). These are not mutually exclusive forces and

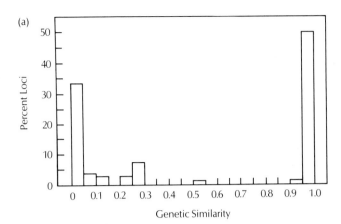

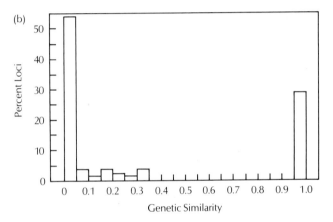

Figure 32.10 Histograms showing the distribution of loci with respect to genetic similarity, I, when pairs of sibling species are compared (a) and when pairs of nonsibling species are compared (b). Even sibling species (which cannot be distinguished morphologically) have no shared alleles (genetic similarity index of 0) at 35 percent of their loci. In morphologically distinguishable species, more than 50 percent of the loci have no shared alleles.

undoubtedly both are to some degree responsible for the pattern observed.

What about subspecific categories, such as **races** and **varieties**—how do they differ? Studies of the amount of genetic differentiation between human populations suggest that on the average, there is very little difference. Only about 12 percent of the genetic variation in the human gene pool is not held in common among various geographically distributed groups. The amount of genetic variation between Caucasian, black, and Japanese populations is about the same as between local populations of the common house mouse. These similarities reflect the arbitrary nature of racial groupings. The human species shares a common gene pool; there is relatively free genetic exchange between populations, and consequently the genetic differences among races are minor. In fact, there is no valid biological

criterion to distinguish subspecific categories; they are inventions that vary widely from one authority to the next.

What accounts for the high level of differentiation observed between even very similar species? The most widely accepted theory of animal speciation is based on two postulates. First, geographically different populations of a species are said to become separated by extrinsic isolating barriers, such as a mountain range, a river, or a glacier, which stop gene exchange. And second, during a long course of time, these isolated populations are seen as accumulating gene differences due to drift and to different patterns of directional selection dictated by the different environments in which the populations find themselves. Such selection in opposite directions in two populations living in two environments is called **disruptive selection**. Whereas stabilizing selection acts to keep relative gene frequencies fixed at some intermediate level throughout the species, disruptive selection tends to drive relative gene frequencies apart in the two populations concerned. This process has been seen in the peppered moths discussed earlier. At the point in time when the black form of the moth came to constitute 95 percent of the population in the heavily industrialized areas of England, populations in nonindustrialized areas had 95 percent mottled individuals, because of different selective pressures.

Now as long as two populations remain part of the same species—as long as there is gene migration between the populations—neither population will lose the genotype that is being selected against. If it is lost by genetic drift in one generation, it will take very little migration to reintroduce it in the next generation. But once gene flow stops between the populations—for any reason—the alleles that had been undergoing disruptive selection may now readily become *fixed* in their respective populations (each population comes to possess only one of the two alleles). Thus we see the key role that may be played by migration in knitting populations together. Once such gene migration is interrupted by any form of barrier, two populations may undergo divergence at one or more gene loci. And as one gene-controlled function changes, it often creates new *internal* selective pressures. Because the functioning of all intracellular enzymes is so tightly linked in the multiple pathways of the cell, a change in one favors compensatory changes in others. Thus, adaptive processes tend to evolve not by isolated changes of one gene here and one there, but in subtle shifts of many blocks of genes. The result is the formation of **adaptive complexes**—groups of genes co-selected not only for their ability to meet the challenge of the external environment but also to meet the challenge of cooperating smoothly in the internal environment. As a result, when the populations are again able to come into contact, they have accumulated so many gene differences that, as a by-product of differentia-

(b)

(a)

Figure 32.11   *(a)* Drosophila cyrtoloma *from Waikamoi, Maui, compared with (b)* Drosophila melanogaster.

tion, they are no longer able to successfully interbreed. This is the theory of **geographic speciation.**

A remarkable illustration of the theory of geographic speciation can be found among the *Drosophila* species of the Hawaiian archipelago. According to plate tectonic theory, the great plate of the Pacific basin has been slowly moving west into the Philippine trench. During its progress, the plate has crossed a relatively stationary hot spot, which has periodically caused volcanic eruptions through the ocean floor. The eruptions have resulted in a series of volcanic islands beginning with Kure and Midway islands to the northwest and culminating with the island of Hawaii in the southeast. The older islands have been so severely eroded during the 40 million or more years of their existence that today they amount to nothing more than low reefs. The most recent island (Hawaii) is only about 700,000 years old and is characterized by high volcanic mountains and a diversity of climatic and vegetational zones. The southeast islands have produced more than 700 species of *Drosophila* in their several-million-year history. This is certainly the greatest episode of concentrated speciation known to contemporary biologists.

The story of this creative adventure has been worked out in some detail. When the archipelago first began to appear, a single pregnant female fly was blown from the Asian continent or Japan and by chance arrived on one of the new islands. A population was founded, subsisting on the vegetation and associated fungi that had already colonized the island (also by chance immigration). As each new island appeared to the southeast, chance colonizing events oc-

curred. Meanwhile, the older islands were gradually planed away by erosion and their populations became extinct.

The arrival of a single pregnant female *Drosophila* on a new island constitutes an extreme example of the founder effect. The new population so formed begins with some genetic differentiation relative to its parental population, and with a reduced level of genetic variability. The chance of interisland migration is so small that the new population is also genetically isolated. A recently colonized island presents a great variety of habitats. As the population occupies these relatively empty habitats, it comes under the strong directional selection unique to each new environment. The process of populations moving into empty environments, and then undergoing rapid evolutionary divergence as they adapt to these unexploited habitats, is known as **adaptive radiation.** These kinds of episodes produce rapid speciation and facilitate the emergence of major groups.

The colonization of the Hawaiian Islands produced such outbursts of speciation among the *Drosophila*. Other factors facilitated the speciation. For instance, islands of vegetation within an island are often created by the vagaries of lava flow. These vegetational outposts in the lava fields, called *kipukas*, are initially isolated from other patches of vegetation—as are their insect fauna. The geographic isolation prevents gene exchange and therefore helps give rise to speciation. Yet another source of new species has been the occasional reverse migration of a derived species to an older island. These species are highly differentiated from their ancestral species, and when they migrate to an older island they establish populations of their own in unoccupied habitats. Thus speciation can occur in many ways. The essential thing is for the gene pool of an emerging species to be able to maintain its own genetic integrity. This usually requires geographic isolation to prevent gene exchange.

It is therefore apparent that the central issue in speciation is reproductive isolation. Most animal evolutionists doubt that two geographically contiguous populations can achieve species status, because gene exchange would swamp selective differentiation. This viewpoint accounts for the present emphasis on geographic separation and its attendant extrinsic reproductive isolation. But this emphasis raises another very different practical problem. When have geographically separated populations become different species? How do we know whether these populations would be prevented from interbreeding if brought into contact? Usually, a definitive answer to these questions is not possible, so one infers reproductive isolation by such criteria as morphological differentiation, behavioral differences (particularly as they relate to reproductive behavior), and different ecological preferences.

Ultimately studies of speciation come to focus on two kinds of **reproductive isolating barriers.** The first is *postmating* barriers—mechanisms that prevent gene exchange only after mating has occurred. For instance, gametic mortality, where the gametes of one sex (male) do not survive in the reproductive tract of the second sex to effect fertilization, is one such barrier. Gametic mortality may be particularly common in plants where the pollen tube is prevented from normal growth in the style of a second species. Another example is zygote mortality. Here, fertilization is successfully accomplished, but genetic incompatibilities cause embryonic death. Still another postmating barrier occurs when the zygote survives but is either sterile or has very low viability.

The second category of reproductive isolating barriers is *premating* barriers. Among the ways that mating may be prevented entirely is seasonal or habitat isolation, in which potential mates simply do not meet because they breed at different times or in different localities. The time of flowering varies widely among plant populations, and a shift in flowering time between two populations can effectively create reproductive isolation. An important premating barrier in many animal populations is behavioral, or ethological, isolation. In *Drosophila*, for example, males go through a complex and carefully orchestrated sequence of behaviors in order to bring the female to a level of stimulation that makes her receptive. Any change in the sequence or timing of these behavioral events destroys the recognition pattern that the behaviors represent, and the female is not aroused. Mechanical isolation, which prevents the transfer of sperm, also qualifies as a premating barrier.

Mechanical isolation may be particularly common among many insects, where the genital armatures of these species are presumed to act rather like a lock and key. If the complicated structures of the male genitalia are not exactly right, then successful copulation may be prevented.

We have deliberately concentrated on the theory of geographic speciation because it is believed to be the most important mechanism for the production of new species. There are, however, other mechanisms of speciation. We will describe just one, polyploidy (Chapter 16), because of its great contrast with geographic speciation. Polyploidy is important in plant speciation. Of all angiosperms, between 30 percent and 35 percent are polyploid; this figure rises to 75 percent for the grasses. *Allopolyploidy* (the doubling of the chromosomal complement of an interspecific hybrid) is far more important in plant speciation than is *autopolyploidy* (the doubling of the chromosomal complement of a normal individual to produce multiples of the normal state of diploidy).

How does polyploidy work? Let us symbolize the haploid genome of species 1 as A, and the haploid genome of species 2 as B. An interspecific hybrid will therefore have the diploid constitution AB. Now, if A and B are dissimilar, normal chromosomal pairing will not occur at meiosis and functional gametes will not be produced; thus the hybrid AB will be sterile. Occasionally, the chromosomal complement becomes doubled, and when this happens, the hybrid will be tetraploid—with genomic constitution $AABB$. Normal pairing is now possible, for there are two of each chromosomal type and the tetraploid is fertile. However, the new tetraploid will produce gametes of constitution AB. If a cross occurs with one of the parents, say A, an individual of constitution AAB (triploid) results. Triploids also have meiotic difficulties and are highly sterile. Thus the new species is isolated from its parental species and has arisen at a single step without geographic separation. This is one example of **sympatric** (''same country'') as opposed to **allopatric** (''other country'') speciation. *Although sympatric speciation has played an important role in plant evolution, most animal evolution probably has occurred by geographic isolation and hence is allopatric.*

The evolution of bread wheat is a classic example of sympatric speciation through allopolyploidy. Modern bread wheat (*Triticum aestivum*) is a hexaploid whose genomic constitution can be denoted $AABBDD$. An intergeneric cross occurred between diploid wheat (*Triticum monococcum*) and goat grass (*Aegilops speltoides*) to produce *Triticum dicoccum* with $AABB$ genomes. Later, a second intergeneric cross between *Triticum dicoccum* and *Aegilops squarrosa*, which contributed the D genome, occurred to produce modern bread wheat. The sequence of these events is illustrated in Figure 32.12.

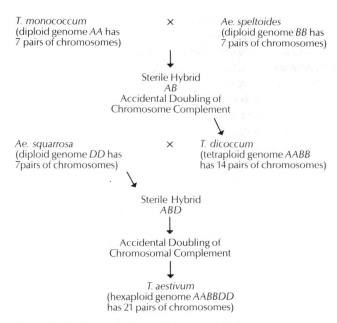

T. monococcum (diploid genome *AA* has 7 pairs of chromosomes)	×	Ae. speltoides (diploid genome *BB* has 7 pairs of chromosomes)

Sterile Hybrid
AB
Accidental Doubling of
Chromosome Complement

Ae. squarrosa (diploid genome *DD* has 7 pairs of chromosomes)	×	T. dicoccum (tetraploid genome *AABB* has 14 pairs of chromosomes)

Sterile Hybrid
ABD

Accidental Doubling of
Chromosomal Complement

T. aestivum
(hexaploid genome *AABBDD*
has 21 pairs of chromosomes)

Figure 32.12 Events in the evolution of bread wheat.

This concludes the discussion of speciation, the phenomenon responsible for the forks in evolutionary trees. Speciation accounts for the diversity of the biological world, and it is one of the major creative forces bringing about evolutionary change. There are many ways that speciation can be brought about; we have discussed two of the most important mechanisms. There remain many unsolved problems in speciation theory and there is much active research in this area.

PERSPECTIVE

Born of mistakes, genetic variability underlies all the diversity of life forms that we see about us. Carried along by the inertia of the Mendelian system of inheritance, such mutations lie quietly in the gene pool of the population. Even if they are deleterious they are seldom lost from the gene pool completely, unless the population is small and another chance event, called genetic drift, intervenes. Carried by migrants from population to population, these mutations spread through the species but remain at a low level. But then, if conditions change, what was once a harmless error—or perhaps even a negative attribute—may become a positive asset determining survival chances in an important way. Those possessing this mutation may now live longer, eat better, escape predation more successfully, or in some other way manage to leave more and healthier offspring. Slowly at first, and then with ever accelerating speed, the trait that was once of no importance becomes a dominant adaptive feature of the population. And as one trait changes under the drive of selection, other traits change

in parallel, to build adaptive complexes of genes all selected for their capacity to cooperate successfully in the new environment. And as long as populations are in breeding contact, these changes will tend to flow back and forth between populations. But if two populations are isolated from each other for sufficient periods and are subjected to different selective pressures, they may have gone so far down separate roads of adaptation that when brought together they can no longer interbreed successfully. Speciation has occurred.

As these slow but inexorable processes have been occurring over eons of past time, so are they occurring today. As one species, *Homo sapiens*, continuously changes the environment of population after population, the pace of the process quickens—perhaps even faster than it was when ice sheets grew and shrank, when supercontinents splintered and drifted apart. What changes will occur we cannot now predict, but given the plasticity of the gene and the living cell, we can predict that change itself is inevitable.

SUGGESTED READINGS

CALDER, NIGEL. *The Life Game.* New York: Viking Press, 1974. A readable, popular account of the exciting research issues in contemporary evolutionary biology.

CAVALLI-SFORZA, L. L. ''The Genetics of Human Populations,'' *Scientific American*, 231 (September 1974), 80–89. An excellent article on human population genetics, in a special issue of the magazine that is devoted entirely to the subject.

CROW, JAMES F., and MOTO KIMURA. *An Introduction to Population Genetics Theory.* New York: Harper & Row, 1970. The basic treatise for those students who wish to explore the mathematics of the field.

GRANT, VERNE. *Plant Speciation.* New York: Columbia University Press, 1971.
MAYR, ERNST. *Populations, Species, and Evolution.* Cambridge, Mass.: Belknap Press, 1970.
Two more specialized books, the first on plant speciation, and the second on animal behavior.

SHEPPARD, PHILIP M. *Natural Selection and Heredity.* 3rd ed. London: Hutchinson University, 1967.
STEBBINS, G. L. *Processes of Organic Evolution.* 2nd ed. Englewood Cliffs, N.J.: Prentice-Hall, 1971.
Two good, basic books that expand on the material in this chapter.

SIMPSON, G. G. *The Major Features of Evolution.* New York: Simon and Schuster, 1953. A classic perspective on paleontology.

Section VIII
Human Biology

For centuries, we have considered ourselves apart from nature—different from all other life forms in being somehow central to variously defined grand schemes in the universe. In a sense, we *are* unique in our extraordinary ability to contemplate past and present and, from that, to shape the future more to our liking. But in our self-congratulations, we sometimes lose sight of a scheme far more eloquent than that of our imaginings—the scheme of evolution. In that greater story, we are one form of countless millions of forms that have flowed through the biosphere, one transient guardian of the properties of life in its movement through time and space. In this book we have seen how some life forms have risen to dominance, only to be replaced as the conditions which favored their survival gradually changed. In this section we will turn to the human organism and its place in the evolution of life—to the manners in which it has, like other organisms in times past, altered its environment. We will also consider, from the biological perspective, what the long-term consequences of those alterations inevitably must be.

Chapter 33

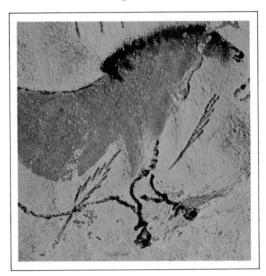

Origin and Evolution of the Human Species

The human animal is a maker, a giver of form—not as a termite, which builds as it must by the dictates of its genes, but as a learner who re-creates and invents the shapes of its dreams and imaginings. The human is a Midas, transforming nature into artifact at every touch until all that surrounds it is increasingly artificial. Is there yet time for it to be reminded by its hunger that it remains a part of nature?

What is a human being? Beneath this seemingly simple question lies the history of a turbulent search for evidence of human origins and debate over what is acceptable as evidence. Indeed, in the past there were differing perceptions among early travelers concerning which creatures among their contemporaries were human. In encountering people living in distant places and having appearances, costumes, and life styles different from their own, these travelers sometimes decided that they were observing not humans but some lower or (at times) higher animals. Europeans seemed to vacillate between labeling other humans as "noble savages" or "dirty savages." There were also "factual" reports of monstrous human creatures (orangutans and other apes) in remote regions of the world.

It is a matter of major consequence in human history that some people have not always awarded the category "human" to other people. In some languages and cultures, this category meant people speaking one's own language and following one's own life style. Those who were disqualified from the human status often had physical appearances—skin color, facial features, hair type—different from those of the group applying the labels. We are speaking here of **ethnocentrism,** a tendency to see the world from the point of view of one's own group, and of its biological counterpart **racism,** which is a tendency to view human differences as if humankind were composed of a multitude of different species. The shock of the Darwinian viewpoint was not simply in the idea of evolution of species but in its implicit attack on the more pervasive mode of human thinking that divided what was a single species into as many pseudospecies as there were differences to be perceived. Evolution is a record of common origins and divergence, of unity and diversity. It gave humans a set of relatives they had been anxious to disown.

But the Darwinian revolution, for all of the resistance it encountered, has had pervasive effects. There has been a broadening of human self-conception. Considering the fact that populations of human beings are spread all over the earth, in environments that range from tropical forests to deserts to polar regions, one of the most extraordinary things about all human beings is that they constitute a single species, which is the sole member of the genus *Homo* and the sole surviving member of the (sub)family Hominidae.

THE PRIMATE HERITAGE

Homo sapiens, or modern man, is a member of the order **Primates,** along with the prosimians, monkeys, and apes (Table 33.1). Primates are a varied lot, but they generally share certain traits. As Figure 33.2 suggests, primates have

Table 33.1
A Classification Scheme for the Order Primates

Suborder	Superfamily	Family	Living Representative Forms
Prosimii (prosimians)	Tupaioidea		Tupaia Tree shrew (?)*
	Lemuroidea	Lemuridae Indridae Lorisidae	Lemur Indri Loris Galago
	Tarsiodea	Tarsiidae	Tarsier
Anthropoidea (anthropoids)	Ceboidea (New World monkeys)	Callithricidae Cebidae	Marmoset Cebus monkey Spider monkey Howler monkey
	Cercopithecoidea (Old World monkeys)	Cercopithecidae	Macaque Baboon Colobus Langur
	Hominoidea (apes and humans)	Hylobatidae Pongidae Hominidae	Gibbon Orangutan Chimpanzee Gorilla Humans

*The tree shrew is placed in a separate order in some taxonomic schemes.

forward-facing and highly developed eyes. They also have collarbones and flexible shoulder joints that permit a wide range of arm movements. All primates have functional digits and flattened nails, and the thumb and usually the big toe are set in apposition to the other digits. Primates also have a variety of teeth that are of at least three functional types—incisors, canines, and molars—and that can be used on an assortment of foodstuffs through cutting, piercing, tearing, crushing, and grinding actions. Other traits common to primates are an enlarged cerebral cortex and the production (generally) of only one offspring at a time.

Given these shared characteristics, what can we say about the common ancestral form that gave rise to the separate primate lines? *Much of primate evolution must have taken place in the trees.* However, in the beginning, life in the trees did not mean swinging from branch to branch, hand over hand, as modern apes do. Rather, it meant cautiously climbing along branches, clinging to them with four limbs and perhaps the tail. Such was the probable existence of the ancestral quadruped that gave rise to the primates—a tiny insect-eater that is thought to have resembled the modern

Figure 33.2   Representative primates. (a) A tarsier. Its forward-directed eyes, grasping digits, and flat nails represent the arboreal adaptations of primates. (b) A spider monkey. The prehensile tail is a specialized adaptation of New World monkeys. (c) This gibbon is brachiating (swinging by the arms), a mode of locomotion quite unlike the quadrupedal running on branches used by most lower primates. The chimpanzee and gorilla are brachiators but spend much of their time on the ground in quadrupedal knuckle-walking. (d) A male baboon threat display. (e) A tree shrew. Although its status as a primate is debatable because of such primitive traits as clawed digits, its generalized form and some skeletal features suggest the tree shrew may resemble the ancient link between insectivores and the first primates.

tree shrew (Figure 33.2). Perhaps this quadruped first took to the trees to avoid predation and competition for food on the ground.

When the earliest primates moved toward life in the trees, they were confronted with the challenges of an entirely different habitat. Limbs designed for running along the ground became subject to an entirely new set of selective pressures: They had to become modified for climbing and grasping, clinging and swinging. Digits would become modified for grasping branches; claws that at first were useful for digging into bark during climbing would flatten into nails as sensitive tactile pads developed on the digits. On the ground, where danger could come from any direction, eyes on the sides of the head provided vision over a large field; but in the trees, forward-directed, three-dimensional vision would be essential if an animal was to leap from one branch to another and not crash to the forest floor. Moreover, there would be strong evolutionary pressure to limit the number of offspring with each pregnancy (imagine leaping through the trees with a litter clinging to your body). In all this activity there would most certainly have been continual selection for fine neural and muscular coordination—which must have been a factor in the early expansion of the primate brain.

The arboreal habitat, then, was the point of origin for the radiation of primates. From an insect-eating quadruped that lived between 75 and 60 million years ago, evolutionary lines diverged that would lead eventually to present-day prosimians, to Old World and New World monkeys, to apes, and to the **hominids**—the family of primates of which modern human beings are the only living members.

The questions that come to mind at this juncture are these: Where and when did our ancestors diverge in primate evolution from the lines leading to other apes? Why did they evolve the special characteristics that led to humaniza-

tion? These questions are biologically significant, for the answers speak not only of the evolutionary process but of changes in the evolutionary process itself. In the hominids we see the emergence of the biological capacity for culture, which enables humans to be many things without being many species. *Through their cultural inventions, humans mitigate the direct selective pressures of their environment, interposing cultural adaptations where survival might otherwise have required direct biological adaptation.*

EVIDENCE IN SUPPORT OF VARIOUS THEORIES OF HUMAN EVOLUTION

In following the course of hominid evolution, we are talking about events that took place many millions of years ago, and most of the evidence we have comes from the fossil record. Some relatively intact fossils have been literally scratched out of rock with dental picks and brushes. But some of the most important fossils have accidentally turned up in fragments, blasted apart in quarry operations. Reconstructing the whole specimen from such fragments calls for a good deal of skill, to say the least.

Problems in Interpreting the Fossil Record

What can such fragments tell us about creatures that lived so long ago? Lines and ridges on bones indicate areas of muscle attachment. The thickness of bone walls tells something of the stresses, strains, and shearing forces to which the bones were subjected. The pattern of teeth may differentiate between a hominid and an ape. Through the pattern of tooth eruption and wear, the age of the owner and its diet may be inferred. Limb bones give evidence about posture or locomotion as well as the possible manipulative abilities of hands and feet.

But there is a problem of statistical inference when such remains are interpreted. We are acutely aware from the study of living organisms that traits are variable within a population, and the ways they combine into coherent clusters of traits are also variable. Therefore, any single fossil may represent an unusually rugged or thin-boned member of a population—or a larger or smaller or diseased and deformed one. Even more difficult is the problem of determining the sex of the fossilized individual, for humans (like other animals) exhibit a considerable degree of sexual dimorphism, and many secondary sexual characteristics depend on soft tissues that are not reliably reconstructed from fossils. Thus, every description of a fossil is a hypothesis about a population, and that hypothesis can be strengthened only as the sampling of that population is extended through the discovery of more fossils that can be definitely associated with it in time and space.

Furthermore, there is a real problem with taxonomy when it comes to the fossil record of hominids. More than a

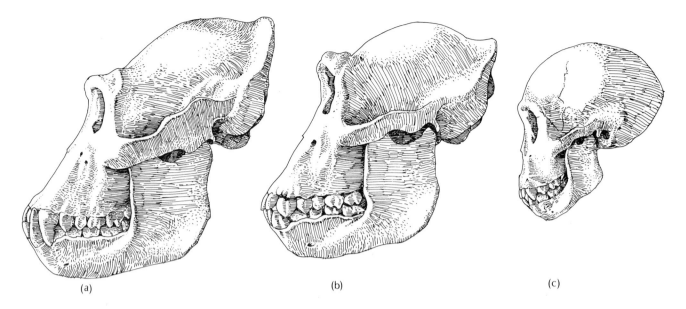

(a)　　　　　　　　　　　　　　　(b)　　　　　　　　　　　　　　　(c)

hundred species and twenty-two genera have been proposed! In the sections to follow, this plethora of names has been reduced to three possible genera—and there are some who believe the number should be reduced even further to two, or one. The vexing problem of taxonomy may always be with us because in the case of extinct forms, we cannot use the idealized criteria for setting species boundaries that are described in Chapters 3 and 32. In other words, we cannot determine from the fossil record whether gene flow might have been possible between two quite different appearing hominids. Species names are assigned to fossils on the basis of morphology, and morphology alone can be misleading. For example, who would suspect, on the basis of morphology, that a Great Dane and a Pekingese are cross-fertile members of the same species?

Chronology: Assigning Fossils in Time and Space

The history of the hominids is not an orderly, unilineal sequence. It is replete with side branches and persistences, as well as anticipations represented among contemporary populations. Therefore, we cannot in a particular case decide that a given fossil is earlier than another because it looks more "primitive," even though there is an overall correlation between morphology and chronology. For that reason, we must depend on methods of **relative dating** (chronological correlations between fossils and deposits at a given site, or from one site to another) and **absolute dating** (the dating of fossil material based on the known decay rates of associated radioactive material).

Many of the places where ancestral primates lived have been gradually covered by deposits from the flooding of rivers, lakes, or seas, or by layers of volcanic ash. Occasionally, fossils are encased in the dense mineral deposits formed on the floor of a cave. Fossils found in successive layers of such natural deposits can be assigned a relative chronological order with little difficulty. Moreover, it is often possible to correlate the sequence in one locality with that in another. Much of hominid history took place during the Pleistocene, when great ice sheets spread over a large part of the Northern Hemisphere (Chapter 9). So much water became locked in ice that the level of the oceans dropped hundreds of feet, and droughts occurred in areas that were not directly affected by the ice itself. Thus the glacial epochs of the European Pleistocene show correlation with periods of low rainfall in Africa—the geographic region where much of the fossil record has been pieced together. Chronological correlations between different sites may also be established through plant and animal remains associated with them. As hominids were evolving, so were other animals—the remains of which are often found in the same sediments or in the refuse heaps of areas where hominids butchered or consumed prey.

How can we be sure that all fossils at a given site are from the same time period? For example, some of the bones may have been washed into or out of their area of original deposition. Human skeletons may be buried in a stratum unrelated to the surface on which they lived. In such cases, fluorine content estimations and related techniques can be used for relative dating. If the bones at a site have a comparable fluorine content, it is one indication that they have been buried under the same conditions for roughly the same amount of time. (This method works only within a given site, however, for the rate of fluorine accumulation may differ from one site to the next.)

For the relatively recent past (some 40,000 years), the radioactive isotope ^{14}C, serves as an *absolute* clock. As you

Figure 33.3   Comparison of the skulls of (a) an adult male gorilla, (b) an adult female gorilla, and (c) a juvenile gorilla. These skulls illustrate the degree of variation that can exist among members of a single species and, by implication, the difficulties in analyzing relationships among fossils from the same period.

read in Chapter 10, this isotope of carbon decays at a precise, measurable rate. Therefore, the less ^{14}C there is in organic remains, the greater the elapsed time since the death of the organism. But hominid evolution began much earlier than 40,000 years ago, and for the distant past another radioactive isotope is used as the clock. In potassium/argon dating, the measurement is based on the age of volcanic or other igneous material that may have been deposited below or above a given fossil. The method is useful for dating fossils within the entire range of life on earth. It has been particularly useful in areas such as East Africa, where there was frequent volcanic activity during the Pleistocene. Volcanic deposits have also been dated by the fission track technique, which measures the number of tracks caused by spontaneous fission of uranium-238. Still other absolute dating techniques are based on correlating fossils with known reversals in the earth's magnetic field and on the study of changes in the amino acid content of fossils.

The Evidence of Evolving Tool Use

Another kind of evidence for their evolution was produced by the hominids themselves. Marking the advent of culture are stone tools. At times they are found by the thousands. These persistent artifacts reflect degrees of cultural advancement as well as the development of human skills; their shapes hint at possible uses to which they were put. For example, we may conclude that some early tools were used for butchering, for skinning, and possibly for scraping hides. Some may have been used as shaft sharpeners and would be of particular interest in the progression from tool use to toolmaking to the higher conceptual level of making tools for making tools. Because it is possible to compare sites in terms of the kinds and proportions of tools found there, we know (for example) that Pleistocene hominid cultures were highly stable over long periods of time. However, even though there is generally a correlation between fossil types and tool types, there is an element of unreliability in making this correlation. The reason is that the invention of a tool or a hunting strategy can be communicated from one group to another, independently of any genetic relationship between the groups.

Comparative Studies Among Living Primates

Comparative anatomy was initially crucial to the argument for the evolution of man and his relation to the other primates. It is still useful in attempts to trace the probable transformations of structure that led from one form to another. A comparative anatomist working with existing species has the advantage of observing intact, functioning organisms. The skeletal remains can be interpreted only to the extent that we know the functional relations of bone to muscle, viscera, nerves, and blood supply. It is also the comparative anatomist who is able to postulate what changes in brain size might mean in terms of the structure and organization of the brain. The early hominids had brains no larger than those of living apes, and yet they may have had greater cultural capacities. This would imply that organizational changes in the brain—and not merely increases in size—have been important.

A vital source of evidence for the process of becoming human is the comparative study of primate behavior. Such studies have given us insights into behaviors associated with structures of the early hominids, and they have narrowed the seeming evolutionary gap between humans and the living apes. For example, Jane van Lawick–Goodall, who has spent many years observing chimpanzees in the wild, has pointed out that these primates use tools regularly. They shape grass stems for "fishing" termites from termite hills. Occasionally they use branches and stones in aggressive displays. These animals, like all other modern apes, are **brachiators**—their limbs are adapted for swinging through trees by hanging from the branches. They spend most of their waking hours on the ground as knuckle-walkers. Yet, under certain circumstances, they walk upright on two legs—awkwardly, but on two legs nevertheless. The gorilla, too, uses the bipedal stance in aggressive display and charging. Furthermore, the apes and other primates eat meat when they can get it through scavenging and occasional hunting, although the chimpanzee depends basically on fruit and the gorilla on fibrous plants. The baboon also has displayed what seems to be purposive and cooperative hunting behavior.

Evidence From Molecular Biology

Within the past decade, molecular biology has had considerable impact on the understanding of hominid evolution. It is possible now to demonstrate the degree of similarity or difference in a considerable number of molecules for any two species. So far, comparative studies on a steadily increasing number of proteins found in humans, the primates, and other mammals consistently point to an extremely close relationship between humans and the higher apes. In their DNA, hemoglobin, transferrin, and albumin molecules, the chimpanzee and the gorilla have proved to be almost indistinguishable from human beings.

In *On the Origin of Species,* Charles Darwin argued for the transmutation of species in the evolutionary process, but he sidestepped the implications his theory held for the evolution of human beings. However, soon after Darwin had published this work, Thomas Huxley addressed the issue. In *Evidence as to Man's Place in Nature,* he argued on the basis of comparative anatomy and comparative behavior that our closest living relatives are the chimpanzee and the gorilla. Darwin later supported Huxley; in *The Descent of Man,* he presented further evidence for our anthropoid ancestry. One hundred years later, biochemical studies would provide additional evidence to support their assertions. In 1971, Bill Hoyer, David Kohne, and others compared the similarity of DNA from different species by using DNA-DNA hybridization experiments, which measure the degree of similarity in nucleotide sequence between the DNA molecules of two species (Chapter 17). They found a mere 2.5 percent difference between the DNA of chimpanzees and the DNA of humans. Between humans and the monkeys that were studied, the correspondence was less complete: there was a difference of about 10 percent. These findings have been used to construct a tree of relationships between certain primates (Figure 33.4).

In other lines of research, comparisons were made of the actual sequences of amino acids in various protein molecules from different animal species. Even though a close relationship had been suspected since the time of Darwin, it was nevertheless startling to learn that the hemoglobin of humans and of chimpanzees shows absolutely no difference in the sequencing of the 141 amino acids of the α chain and the 146 of the β chain! Between humans and gorillas, only 2 differences out of 287 exist. Between a human and a monkey there are 12 differences, whereas between humans and horses there are 43 differences. In a comparison of the fibrinopeptide molecules, again there was no difference between humans and chimpanzees, whereas 7 differences were found to exist between a human and a monkey. Many such sequences have been worked out and compared. The results are remarkably consistent: In terms of their proteins, *humans are very closely related to the chimpanzee and only slightly less closely related to the gorilla.* Attempts have been made to use such data to ask the question: When did the line leading to the humans diverge from the line leading to modern apes?

WHEN AND HOW DID THE HOMINID LINE DIVERGE?

In a traditional view, humans and the modern apes share a common apelike ancestor. Some biochemical data appear to support the view that such an ancestor existed a mere 2 million to 5 million years ago (*Interleaf 33.1*). But consider the implications of this estimate.

The anthropologist Sherwood Washburn argues that the divergence leading eventually to humans and apes must have occurred after the development of the brachiating mode of locomotion. According to this theory, human beings still share brachiating traits with the apes—a broad trunk, flexible arms, a strong collarbone. Washburn suggests that terrestrial adaptation was occurring in this period of common ancestry. The later hominid mode of moving about on two legs may have been preceded by a stage of knuckle-walking. In this view, the period following divergence would call for an extremely rapid transformation from apelike to human form under the evolutionary stimulus of adaptation to open-country hunting, tool use, and

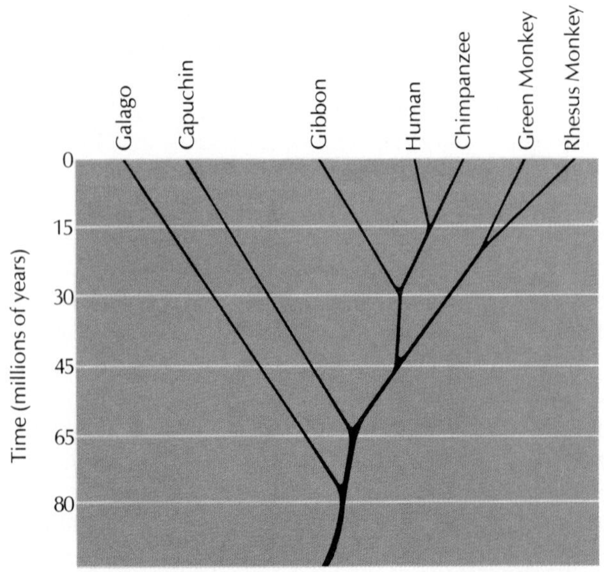

Figure 33.4 Phylogenetic tree for various primates, showing proposed times of divergence based on DNA-DNA hybridization experiments.

culture. Is such a transformation likely in a span of a few million years? And is it morphologically plausible? To explore the implications of this question, let us turn now to the fossil record and to the behavioral and morphological events it suggests.

To go from an apelike form (even if less specialized than the modern apes) to the human form required several major changes. The arms and trunk may already have been similar in proportion, but the hand would have to be transformed before it would become the manipulative human hand with a fully apposable thumb. More striking, perhaps, would be the development of relatively long hindlimbs for two-legged walking. (In comparison, a brachiating ape has relatively short hindlimbs.) Also, a foot such as that seen in the chimpanzee or gorilla would have to develop a "landing platform" type of heel, a compact and double-arched foot, and shortened toes; and the main axis of the foot would have to shift toward the line of the big toe. Furthermore, teeth such as those of modern apes (which are similar to teeth of a number of Miocene fossil apes) are very different from human teeth. The transformation would require a drastic reduction in the size of the anthropoid canine teeth, which probably functioned in threat display and in piercing and holding during combat. It would require a shift in emphasis from the anterior teeth used for cutting and tearing to the cheek teeth, as well as a change in the architecture of the jaws, palate, and dental arch.

If we were to look for our earliest hominid ancestor among the fossil primates, there would be a number of candidates. Some have argued for an early point of hominid divergence, mainly on the ground that an apelike ancestor would be too specialized to give rise to the more generalized structure of humans. Following the lead of the French anatomist Marcellin Boule, they see our hominid ancestor as a generalized monkeylike creature. (F. Wood Jones even proposed a very early tarsierlike prosimian ancestor on the ground that it would be easier in theory to derive humans from a small-toothed, generalized form than to have to explain a reduction in the size of teeth.) But others have suggested that the **dryopithecines**—apes of the Miocene period that were not specialized brachiators—are suitable common ancestors for ape and human. However, some have argued that the dryopithecines may have already diverged into lines leading toward modern apes and humans by the Miocene. If so, the last common ancestor of ape and human may lie still further in the past—perhaps in a transitional form such as the Oligocene *Aegyptopithecus,* which shows many traits intermediate between monkey and ape. Going back still further to the lower Oligocene, a generalized, small-toothed form known as *Propliopithecus* has been suggested as the point of departure.

The first definite hominid is generally thought to be **Ramapithecus.** The remains of this creature have been found from India to Africa. In fact, by the late Miocene it was so widely distributed that the radiation of hominids may have started considerably earlier. *Ramapithecus* shows traits that are difficult to visualize in the line leading to the modern ape. Its upper teeth look distinctly hominid, and the tooth area of the face does not protrude as much as it does in the apes. There are as yet no discoveries of bones of the arms or legs or pelvis, which would establish whether or not *Ramapithecus* moved in an upright position. But there are some indications that the earlier dryopithecines, its likely predecessors, were at least capable of upright posture; thus it is reasonable to assume that *Ramapithecus,* too, could have moved in this way.

What brought about such changes? According to one theory, bipedalism and changes in dentition began to evolve because of extreme changes in the habitat of the prehominids. The theory is that during the late Tertiary (Chapter 9), periods of drought led to the reduction of forests, and clear spaces and grasslands formed between forested regions. It was then that the forest-adapted prehominids may have begun to venture into open country. In the new habitat, a bipedal gait was selected for, because an animal with an upright stance could better survey the bounties and dangers of the terrain. In this view, the emergence of bipedalism freed the forelimbs for using tools and weapons, which in turn caused a reduction of the anterior teeth because they were no longer needed as much in feeding and defense. Bipedalism may have developed further because it offered advantages to tool carriers.

Even though this theory has been around for some time, it does not explain why other primates became terrestrialized *without* developing bipedalism. They either remained quadrupeds (like the baboon) or near-quadrupeds (like the knuckle-walking chimpanzee and gorilla). Furthermore, there is a counterargument that tool use did not have much to do with evolution of upright posture, the reduction of anterior teeth, and at least the initial major expansion of the cortex.

The fact that modern apes hunt, occasionally eat meat, and occasionally make crude tools has sometimes been cited as evidence for the prehominid status of these traits as factors in hominidization. But Clifford Jolly argues that "it is illogical to invoke the behavior of living apes to explain the origin of something they themselves have not developed"—in other words, bipedalism and dental reduction. Such behaviors were not necessarily the impetus behind the transformations that occurred. And as you will soon read, bipedal locomotion and smaller, humanlike teeth were already established hominid traits *before* the advent of characteristically human toolmaking and *before* the hominid brain had surpassed that of the higher apes in size.

Some time ago, John Robinson suggested that if the early hominids were vegetarians, their diet might have led to a

(text continues on page 721)

Interleaf 33.1

How Recently Did Human and Ape Lines Diverge? A Molecular Approach to the Question

It has traditionally been held that *Homo sapiens* probably shared a common ancestor with the great apes (chimpanzee and gorilla) as recently as 5 million years ago. This view has been brought into question in recent years (as the text points out) by discovery of one ancient hominid after another, reaching back to *Ramapithecus,* which apparently was widespread well over 20 million years ago and which already shows clear signs of the divergence of the hominid line from lines leading to the great apes.

Recently, attempts have been made to bring molecular analysis to bear upon this controversy. One of the most interesting of these studies was performed by Vincent Sarich and co-workers, studying the differences in serum albumin molecules among modern primates. They used time-honored immunological techniques. Antibodies directed toward the serum albumin of one primate species were obtained, and then a series of other primate serum albumins were tested for their cross-reactivity (Chapter 24). The greater the degree of chemical similarity between the albumins of two species, the greater the extent of cross-reactivity observed when antibodies to the serum albumin of one are reacted with the serum albumin of the other. The methods employed had been previously shown to be capable of distinguishing two proteins that differed by as little as one amino acid somewhere in the sequence.

Using these techniques, Sarich obtained results that generally confirm the pattern of relationships among the primates suggested by traditional methods and other molecular comparisons. But Sarich further proposes that there seems to be a *steady rate of change* in the primate serum albumin molecule. For example, human, chimpanzee, gorilla, and gibbon albumin all show about the same degree of dissimilarity from the albumin of the rhesus monkey. In other words, after the hominoids and the Old World monkeys diverged, the albumin of these "higher apes" changed at about the same rate relative to the rhesus monkey. Researchers studying other proteins have concluded that although the rate of change for different molecules is different, each molecule seems to show a characteristic but constant rate of change. So far, this has been said to apply to cytochrome c, insulin, the hemoglobins and several other proteins. If this is true, the degree of difference in amino acid sequence of a protein between two species might be translatable into their times of divergence. This is the assumption upon which Sarich's conclusions are based (Figure *a*).

Sarich estimates that in the albumin molecule there has been one amino acid substitution per million years per lineage from a time of divergence between the prosimians and the anthropoids (assumed to be about 65 million years). But if his calculations and assumptions are correct, then—based on the observed differences in their albumins—a common ancestor to humans, chimpanzees, and gorillas would have existed as recently as 2 to 5 million years ago! This estimate conflicts with the recent reading of the fossil record by some authorities.

What are the sources of error, if any, in Sarich's estimate? At least two can be identified. First, is the rate of change of any protein really constant over time? If this assumption is invalid, the argument falls. Second, assuming for the moment that this assumption is correct, how accurately has the rate of change been determined in this case?

If we assume that the rate of protein change is constant, then to translate degree of difference into time of separation all we need is to know the rate at which changes occurred. To determine the rate, we must have two clearly demarcated points on the scale—two points of divergence that are established on other grounds. Unfortunately, every point of divergence

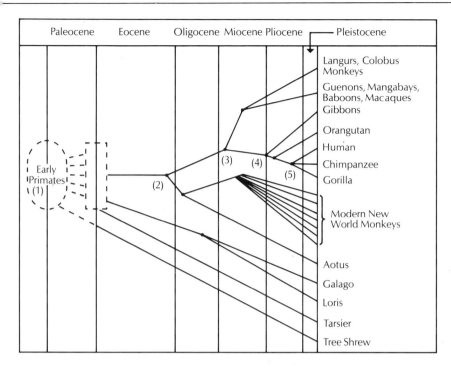

Figure (a) *Primate evolution, as proposed on the basis of immunological study of primate albumin molecules. The time axis is drawn to scale, with the beginning of the Paleocene taken to be 65 million years ago. At that time the prosimian and the anthropoid lines diverged (1). Between 33 and 39 million years ago (2), the lines of the Old World monkeys are said to have diverged; between 20 and 24 million years ago (3), the hominoids are seen as separating from the cercopithecoid line. Between 6 and 8 million years ago (4), the lines leading to the pongids (orangutan, chimpanzee, gorilla, and human) separated from that leading to modern gibbons. Based on these observations, it would appear that the divergence of the gorillas, chimpanzees, and hominids occurred between 2 and 5 million years ago.*

plotted on Figure (a) is subject to the same kind of uncertainty and controversy as the one on which Sarich is seeking to shed light—the time of divergence of human and ape lines. Thus Figure (a) uses a series of uncertainties in trying to establish one point with certainty.

But the other question is of far greater fundamental importance: Is the method valid? Is it true that the rate of change of amino acid sequence of any protein is constant throughout time and in all lines of evolutionary descent?

If it could be rigorously demonstrated that the rate of change of a given protein is constant in all evolutionary lines, throughout time, this would lead to one of two important conclusions: Either changes in protein sequence do not occur as the result of natural selection, or the intensity of natural selection is identical under all environmental conditions, in all lines of evolutionary descent, and at all times. Now, few would accept the latter point of view. It is simply impossible to interpret the evolu-

tionary record as revealing a constant rate of change in all lines of descent at all times. The habitats to which different organisms are adapted clearly show different degrees of stability over prolonged periods, and the organisms within those habitats show different rates of visible evolutionary change. For example, some marine invertebrates (such as the horseshoe crab) have shown very little change over the last 200 million years, whereas at least 700 species of the fruit fly (genus *Drosophila*) have evolved in the brief period since the Hawaiian Islands arose from the sea by volcanic action and were invaded by an Asian fruit fly (Chapter 32). Because of this demonstrable unevenness of selection in time and space, those who believe that protein sequences change at a constant rate generally assume that such changes are not the result of natural selection at all but rather are random changes that are *selectively neutral*—that neither enhance nor diminish the prospects for survival—and that accumulate

in the course of time through chance processes. Such a viewpoint leaves unanswered the question of how selection could act at the level of visible features if it does not act at the level of the primary gene products, the proteins. The concept of selective neutrality has generated much debate and controversy. But rather than reiterate that controversy here, let us examine how well the data actually fit the concept of a uniform rate of change.

First it should be pointed out that different proteins clearly show different rates of sequence change. If Sarich's estimates of the rate of serum albumin evolution are correct, then it has been changing only about one-fifth as fast as the molecules known as fibrinopeptides; but it has been changing slightly faster than hemoglobin, four times faster than cytochrome c, and over one hundred times faster than histone! It is incomprehensible that such differences in rates of evolutionary change should be due to chance alone.

Table 33.A
Estimation of Time of Divergence From Cytochrome c Sequences[*]

Comparison	Average Number of Amino Acid Differences	Time Since Divergence, Estimated From Cytochrome c Data (millions of years)[†]	Time Since Divergence, Estimated From All Other Data (millions of years)
Primates[‡] vs. other mammals[§]	10	200	100
Primates vs. birds[‖]	12	240	290
Other mammals vs. birds	9	180	290
Rattlesnake vs. primates	14	280	310
Rattlesnake vs. snapping turtle	22	440	?
Snapping turtle vs. birds	8	160	250

[*]All numbers have been rounded for purposes of clarity.
[†]Based on the average rate of one amino acid substitution per 20 million years.
[‡]Human, chimpanzee, and rhesus monkey.
[§]Dog, rabbit, horse, donkey, cow, whale, and kangaroo.
[‖]Pigeon, chicken, and duck.

They almost certainly reflect different intensities of selective pressures acting on different molecules. Proteins that interact closely with other complex molecules in a specific manner and play a rigorously defined role in the cell—as histones and cytochrome c do—will undoubtedly fall under the conservative influences of selection because most changes in structure will interfere with function and will be strongly selected against. On the other hand, proteins with less precisely defined roles would be expected to be less strongly conserved—more change could be tolerated. (Serum albumin functions mainly to regulate the osmotic properties of blood, and the fibrinopeptides are the pieces cut off and discarded when the blood-clotting protein, fibrin, is activated; neither of these roles is highly demanding chemically.) Thus it is not surprising that different molecules show different *average* rates of change. But it is a long step from saying a protein has shown a certain *average* rate of change to saying that it has shown a rate of change so constant that it can be used as a stopwatch to time evolutionary events.

Just how uniform is the rate of change of amino acid sequence in a given protein? To answer that question let us examine the best-studied case: cytochrome c. The complete amino acid sequences of the cytochrome c molecules of more than twenty species of animals (as well as several species of plants and fungi) have been determined. In several cases the complete three-dimensional structure has been established as well.

Taken together, the data on cytochrome c indicate that there has been a *tendency* for a rather uniform rate of change in amino acid sequence. *On the average* there has been about one amino acid changed every 20 million years in each line of descent. But what do we find if we attempt to use these data to time individual points of divergence precisely? Table 33.A is a list of amino acid differences selected from the existing data specifically because of the anomalies they point out. These data suggest that the nonprimate mammals are at least as closely related to birds as they are to primates, that the rattlesnake is more closely related to primates and the turtle more closely related to birds than either is to the other! The message of this table is clear: *Because of demonstrable unevenness in the rate of evolutionary change in the amino acid sequence of a protein among different lines of descent, such changes in a single protein cannot possibly be relied upon to give an accurate estimate of the time at which any two lines diverged.* It is difficult to avoid the corollary conclusion that, because the changes are clearly non-random, they reflect the action of natural selection, not random events.

deemphasis of the front teeth and canines and an emphasis on the grinding action of the molars. Jolly has developed this idea by suggesting that a much wider range of hominid traits can be explained if in fact the early hominids ate not only roots and shoots (and occasionally meat) but the seeds of wild grasses. Today there are seed-eating baboons that live in open country. For example, the Gelada baboons feed by picking up grass and seeds between thumb and forefinger. They have developed a number of adaptations in parallel with those of the hominids: a shortening and increased apposition of the thumb and digits; compaction of the foot; and reduction of some digits of the foot, with some loss of gripping power. But these are adaptations for terrestrialism, not bipedalism. The Gelada baboons have remained quadrupeds even though they do much of their feeding in a squatting position. Like bipedalism, this position also frees the forelimbs for manipulation.

In these baboons the temporal muscle that runs from the jaw to the temporal bone in the skull is adapted to powerful crushing and grinding of small objects. The use of the front teeth is deemphasized. Various features of the jaw, teeth, and palate resemble those of the hominids. Jolly sees the development of the rounded palate as making room for a larger tongue, which functions to keep returning the seeds to the chewing platform. Although such traits may have been derived from seed eating, they are preadaptive to speech.

Where did all these transformations take place? According to the seed-eating theory, the transformation into hominids took place in grasslands that were subject to periodic or seasonal flooding. Fossils of early Pleistocene hominids are in fact often found in such seasonal deposits on the flood plains of rivers and lakes. The seasonal nature of seed crops may have led to periodic movement or to adjustments in diet. Hands adapted to picking and gathering seeds could have become less useful for assisting locomotion. Climatic change at a later stage leading to an intensification of seasonality could have precipitated the shift to increased hunting.

Given the theories just presented, how might we summarize the picture of hominid origins? It is likely that the point of origin lies farther in the past than the first approximations to a biomolecular clock would indicate. There is the possibility that the ancestral form from which human and ape diverged was more generalized in structure than either evolutionary product. It may have had relatively unspecialized primitive teeth and limbs; its mode of moving about may have ranged from swinging through the trees to climbing along branches and walking on the ground. Perhaps it was able to feed and to visually scan the horizon with at least an upright trunk; perhaps it could resort to occasional bipedalism when needed for full display or in the search for predators or prey above the grass in seasonally flooded areas or in open stretches between woodlands. We may assume that they had considerable abilities to grasp and manipulate and that at times they may have used sticks, bones, and stones as tools. They may have wielded a bludgeon, leaving behind some of the cracked bones and skulls found in the company of early hominids. They were probably already a part of a small band of males, females, and offspring exhibiting some organization and division of labor in defense, and perhaps in occasional hunting and scavenging.

The alternative to such an unspecialized ancestor would be one that was quite apelike but, as a result of dietary specialization or the transfer of some of the functions of the mouth and teeth to the hands (and tools), underwent rapid change in tooth and mouth structure and developed a bipedal gait. That diet would have been a factor in such changes seems persuasive. That tool use was a factor in these early stages seems more dubious, although it undoubtedly played a major role in the humanization process.

In either case, *there is general agreement that the onset of intensive hunting of large game was the stimulus for humanization.* In this life style, the hunting male would be able to cover a wider territorial radius if the female remained closer to a home base with the young. Such sexual division of labor would be compatible with the sexual division of reproductive function. Much of the food would have to be brought back to camp from some distance. This would be easier to do if it were butchered on the spot, which would explain the possible function of some of the earliest tools. At the same time, the female could gather seeds and other edible plant parts, presumably using some kind of container as one of the first artifacts to bring her yield back to camp for food preparation. *The hunting and gathering adaptation stimulated artifact production as well as the beginning of the long process of increasing social complexity through production, exchange, and sharing.*

If we accept *Ramapithecus* as an early but perhaps not the earliest hominid, then the place of origin is uncertain, considering the wide range over which *Ramapithecus* and the Oligocene and Miocene ape fossils are to be found. But the earliest *Ramapithecus* is East African. C. Loring Brace and J. S. Weiner, among others, argue convincingly that humans bear the marks of tropical adaptation that must have occurred very close to the point of origin. Hominids manifest the traits of tropicalization: the loss of body hair, the development of a profusion of sweat glands over the entire body, protective pigmentation and the capacity to increase it through tanning, and a relatively high body temperature below which the shivering reaction sets in.

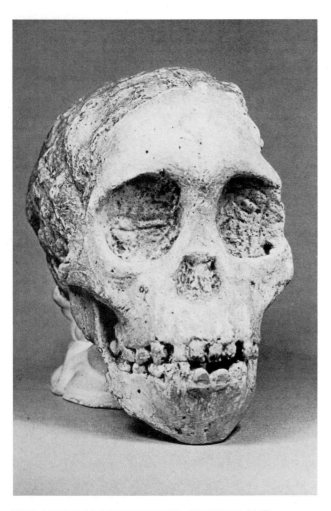

Figure 33.5 Cast of an immature specimen of Australopithecus *from Taungs, the first of this kind of hominid fossil to be excavated.*

Figure 33.6 (right) Comparison between (a) an Australopithecus *skull from Sterkfontein and (b) a* Paranthropus *skull from Swartkrans.* Paranthropus *is distinguished from* Australopithecus *primarily on the basis of the teeth and jaws, which broadly resemble the earlier form of* Ramapithecus. *Although* Australopithecus *shows reduced canines and incisors, this reduction has gone farther in* Paranthropus, *where there seems to have been a shift in importance from the front teeth to the back teeth. As in many earlier hominids there is a sagittal crest (a bony crest that runs along the center of the top of the skull), which, in* Paranthropus, *has shifted to a more forward area of attachment of the temporal muscle, thereby imparting force to the grinding surfaces of the back teeth.*

THE AUSTRALOPITHECINES: VARIETY AND TAXONOMIC PUZZLES

The **australopithecines** ("southern ape-men") are the first undisputed hominids. The first specimen was discovered in 1924 by Raymond Dart, who excavated the skull of a child from Taungs in South Africa (Figure 33.5). More specimens soon began turning up under the assiduous search of Robert Broom. The average brain size of these specimens was about 440 cubic centimeters—no larger than that of a chimpanzee and smaller than that of some gorillas. And yet there were signs that this creature had a body much like that of modern humans and that it walked upright on limbs that differed little from our own. After a long search, the remains of some australopithecines were found in association with tools. The teeth of some forms were much larger than those of modern humans, yet they were not the teeth of apes. The canines were reduced, the incisors were quite small, and the overall conformation of the dental arch looked quite modern.

Other fossils turned up farther north in Olduvai Gorge, which is part of the rift valley cutting through the Serengetti Plain of northern Tanzania. Their discoverers, Louis and

Mary Leakey, searched for twenty-nine years before they found their first hominid skull, a rugged australopithecine. Many more were found at Olduvai and recently in the East African area of Lake Rudolf, in research led by Richard Leakey, and in the Omo River Valley, in work led by F. Clark Howell and others. By now, some 200 to 300 australopithecine individuals are represented in the various fragmentary remains of skulls, teeth, and postcranial bones. There is also tentative evidence that the australopithecines and related forms or concurrent species and genera were distributed beyond Africa into Asia, perhaps into China.

There has been an excessive tendency to assign generic and specific names to these (and other) fossil finds. As mentioned earlier, the problems of taxonomy of fossils cannot be resolved on morphological grounds. But we have to keep in mind that when we make taxonomic distinctions, our choices may bear little correspondence to biological species (between which genetic flow could not exist). Therefore, the taxonomy given here is an attempt to perceive order and progression in an increasingly complex fossil record. Bernard Campbell calls attention to the arbitrariness of boundaries that are drawn between sequen-

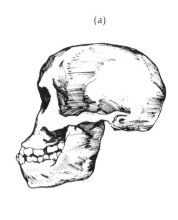

(a)

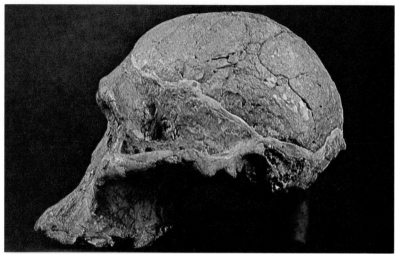

(b)

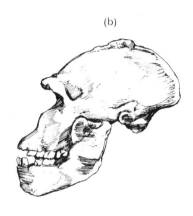

tial hominid species; he adopts a strategy for defining broad periods of varied but coexisting forms. Accordingly, the terms ''australopithecine'' and ''pithecanthropine'' used here are convenient labels for such periods that may contain phylogenetically heterogeneous forms.

The two descriptive terms used most frequently in reference not only to australopithecines but to later forms leading into modern man are **gracile** (relatively small, light-boned, less rugged forms) and **robust** (large, heavy-boned, more rugged forms with ridges or crests of bone at muscle attachments). Between ''gracile'' and ''robust,'' however, there is every degree of gradation. There are also differences among the australopithecines in terms of brain size as well as in cultural associations. Are all these fossils of a single genus with two, three, or four species? Or had the australopithecines already differentiated into two or three genera, reflecting differing lines of adaptation as far back as the late Pliocene? This latter view was proposed by Broom, who differentiated between a genus ***Australopithecus*** and a genus ***Paranthropus.*** This view is rejected by those who would prefer to group all the South and East African finds of this period into various species or sub-

species of australopithecines. But the distinctions remain, whether defended at the generic level or at a lower taxonomic level.

Australopithecus seems to have been a smaller, gracile, and less specialized form than *Paranthropus.* Its more generalized dentition presumably was adapted to an omnivorous diet. *Australopithecus africanus,* as represented at Sterkfontein in South Africa (Figure 33.6a), precedes *Paranthropus* in the fossil record. But it appears that the two forms were living in the same regions at the same time; they are found in association in a number of sites in East Africa. This living together over a long period of time indicates a complementarity of adaptation that prevented direct competition for the same foodstuffs. *Paranthropus* (Figure 33.6b) may have followed the route suggested by Robinson and Jolly, perhaps continuous from *Ramapithecus* as a seed-eater of some sort. The possibility of speciation between *Paranthropus* and *Australopithecus* on the basis of dietary specialization implies only a minimal level of cultural development; in fact, William Howells suggests that it may have been the last time in hominid history in which direct biological speciation would occur.

Paranthropus seems to have been an evolutionary dead end after well over a million years of existence. Its extinction possibly was brought about by the emergence of human competition. Oddly enough, there are tools found in a number of *Paranthropus* sites, yet there are none definitely established in association with the more gracile (albeit equally small-brained) *Australopithecus africanus.* But what would an herbivore and seed-eater need with tools that could well have served to butcher animals? Detailed examination of australopithecine sites seems to suggest that neither *Paranthropus* nor *Australopithecus africanus* was a maker of stone tools. Who, then, were the toolmakers, the first practitioners of a tangible human culture?

At Olduvai, the Leakeys discovered a fossil hominid of the gracile variety with a relatively smooth, well-domed skull and a brain size in the range of 600 to 700 cubic centimeters, which is substantially larger than that of the South African *Australopithecus africanus.* They believed this specimen should be assigned to the genus *Homo* even if it was about 1.8 million years old and even if it was a contemporary of the more robust forms. So impressed was Louis Leakey with its potential modernity that he called it *Homo habilis,* which he believed to be in the direct line of modern man, by-passing the later forms called *Homo erectus.* Further exposure of a number of occupation sites seems to link the pebble tools (Figure 33.7) with *Homo habilis,* not *Paranthropus.* At these sites were signs of the construction of shelter and of hunting. There were large piles of bones, many split or broken, from rhinoceros, giraffes, horses, antelopes, wart hogs, baboons, and small reptiles—and eggshells.

Whether or not the term *Homo habilis* is taxonomically appropriate, the evolutionary implications of hunting, stable camp sites, and toolmaking would apply. There perhaps was a sexual division of labor and a further division based on age, with very few older individuals in the population. A South African study based mainly on dental eruption and wear shows that more than a third of the known *Australopithecus africanus* forms died before reaching adulthood, and that of the robust forms, more than 50 percent of the remains are of children and preadults. Given the probable demographic situation, small bands were probably knit together with others over an extensive area by the need to secure mates outside of the group. Such a need would stem from the erratic sexual ratio to be expected of such small groups.

We do not know whether the australopithecines or *Homo habilis* communicated with a spoken language structured like modern languages. The other indications of culture might imply the use of language, yet it is possible that coordination of hunting groups could be conducted without articulate speech by relying on visual signals and relatively

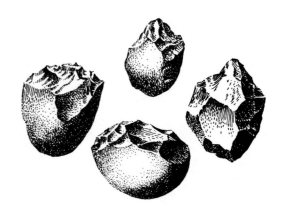

Figure 33.7 Pebble tools. The most common tool in Oldowan assemblages are crude choppers, made by removing flakes along one side of a pebble to form an irregular cutting edge.

simple audible sounds, communicating little more than states of feeling.

The pebble tool industry seems to extend back at least 3 million years, and it persisted with little change over a very long span of time. If culture was evolving and accumulating during that time, it was not doing so in any material way that we can detect. The slow rate of change may indicate that during the Olduwan tool period, the transmission of toolmaking techniques may have been largely imitative and relatively non-innovative. There may have been some experimentation and variation transmitted by example, but not the play of combinations and forms that characterizes the language and cognition of modern man.

The overall picture of the early Pleistocene hominids is changing rapidly as dozens of new specimens are brought to light each year. For example, in 1972 Richard Leakey found a remarkable fossil cranium in an area east of Lake Rudolf. This cranium has a capacity of more than 800 cubic centimeters—nearly double that of *Australopithecus africanus* and substantially larger than the average for *Homo habilis.* Yet this specimen (ER 1470) was found beneath a layer of volcanic ash dated to 2.6 million years—perhaps a million years older than *Homo habilis* from Olduvai! Anthropologists are startled and some are dubious of the date. And yet this reaction is typical of the response to each new find that upsets the pattern into which the previous fossil record seemed finally to settle. Richard Leakey's find would carry the genus *Homo* back to the time of relatively early australopithecines. If it derives from these forms—as it probably does along with *Homo habilis*—the branching point for the genus *Homo* from the general line of hominid evolution is certainly much earlier than previously suspected. If the dating and classification of this fossil continue to hold up, they will imply the presence of three genera of fossil hominids in the period between 3 and 2 million years ago: *Australopithecus, Paranthropus*—and *Homo*.

THE PITHECANTHROPINES: ON THE THRESHOLD OF HUMANNESS

What lies between the australopithecines and modern human beings? Fossils of the type **Homo erectus** have been found that date from 800,000 to 300,000 years ago. As in the case of the australopithecines, however, the name *Homo erectus* does not refer to just one morphological type. Diverse specimens have been found at sites that range from Olduvai Gorge in Africa to Java, China, Algeria, Hungary, and Germany. To indicate the existence of a spectrum of diverse characteristics, the populations of this period are collectively called the **pithecanthropines.**

By the end of the early Pleistocene, the australopithecines had become widely dispersed in numerous small populations that were adapted to various habitats. Some populations may have developed in the direction of *Homo habilis* and some toward *Homo erectus.* Others may have already arrived at the point of extinction. Still others may have persisted to become the contemporaries—and perhaps the victims—of their more advanced descendants, the pithecanthropines.

The pithecanthropines were larger in stature than the australopithecines. Their brain size ranged from 750 to about 1,200 cubic centimeters—a size that overlaps the range of modern humans. The skull of these hominids tended to be quite broad at the base, with a rugged but relatively flattened vault; above the eyes was a heavy torus (a protruding bar of bone).

Fossils include pelvic and long bones that point to a bipedal gait and a posture as upright as our own. A *Homo erectus* specimen characteristically has a pronounced occipital torus, which is a bar for the attachment of powerful neck muscles. In comparison with the robust forms of australopithecines, the teeth of a *Homo erectus* specimen indicate a further reduction in size, especially in the molars. The incisors are broad and in some ways larger than those of the gracile australopithecines. The overall dentition reflects an omnivorous rather than a specialized diet.

What do we know of the pithecanthropine life style? At Choukoutien in northern China, numerous bones were found of many large animals, including deer, elephants, and rhinoceros. Many of these bones had been split or broken for their marrow. There are deposits of ash and burnt bone that seem almost certainly to be the remains of hearths, so it is probable that human beings had by that time become users of fire. The fact that food was being cooked could account for the remaining reduction of hominid teeth and jaws that has continued to the present. Equally significant are signs of cave dwelling, the construction of shelters, and the probable use of animal skins. Such cultural adaptations could carry human beings out of the tropics.

We have spoken of the tropicalization of the early hominids. We may now speak of their "detropicalization" through culture. Even with their handful of cultural adaptations, human beings migrated throughout the world. This migration related to the pursuit of game, and the tendency was clearly established by the time of *Homo erectus.* Cultural adaptations to temperate and cold climates and to the hunting of large migratory animals must have been a stimulus for the rapid development of modern human types and the accelerated growth of human culture. Such ecological conditions raised the premium on technological and organizational innovation and, correspondingly, the selective advantage for further biological adaptation for cultural capacity.

Among the bones in the refuse heap at Choukoutien were those of humans, which would strongly suggest cannibalism. It would be surprising if cannibalism were not widely practiced by premodern hominids, as it was part of so many cultures of *Homo sapiens* until quite recently. Among the selective pressures for cultural and social development must have been that of struggles with other human groups.

Also at Choukoutien were hand axes, chopping tools, flakes, points, cleavers, and perhaps scrapers as well as bone tools used for hunting and butchering. Signs of organized predation are also found at open-air sites in Europe. For example, at Ambrona, Spain, F. Clark Howell has been uncovering the evidence of *Homo erectus* as being a big-game hunter. An enormous number of elephants, rhinoceros, horses, and wild oxen bones are concentrated in a small area. There are signs that the animals were butchered there and part of them carried away. Similarly, herds may have been driven into a swamp in the steep-sided valley of Torralba, Spain, and there killed and butchered. Cooking hearths, stone tools, and the remains of some wooden tools are found in these sites, which are about 300,000 years old. An extraordinarily large and systematic excavation at the Terra Amata site in southern France, dated to the middle Pleistocene, turned up a great number of cultural objects. Evidently the site was a camp for seasonal hunting. There are remains of a number of oval huts, ranging from twenty-six to forty-nine feet in length. Each contained a hearth and a shallow pit (sometimes paved with pebbles), and some had a small stone wall at one end that may have served as a wind screen.

From such evidence, it would seem that the larger brain of *Homo erectus* was associated with a far more complex culture. This culture greatly advanced the human process of creating its own artificial environment through sheltered spaces, in which meat and perhaps grains were cooked and in which the body, cloaked in animal skins, was kept warm.

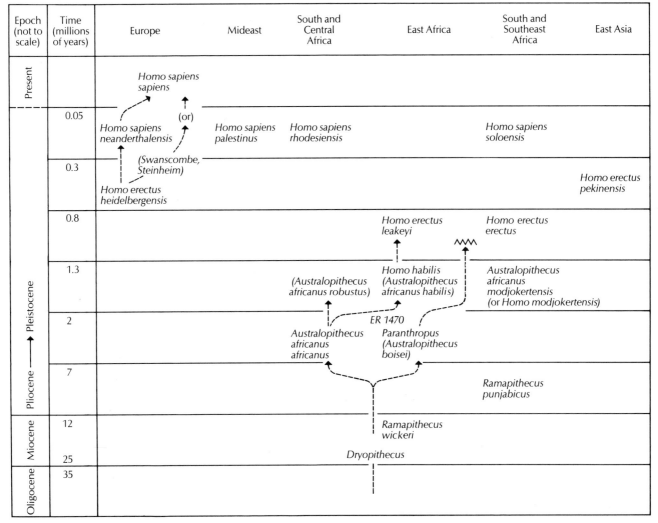

Figure 33.8 Array of hominid fossil types. Although the hominid fossils under study number in the hundreds, the complex array of types is not easily placed in a phylogenetic tree of relationships. Resemblances point in various directions. No positive test of speciation is possible, and we can only infer subspecies, species, and generic differences from how similar or different the fossils look to us. Boundary lines between successive species such as Homo erectus *and* Homo sapiens *(if, in fact, they are different species) can only be arbitrary. The boundaries suggested here (after B. G. Campbell) are intended to suggest only transitions between the most widely recognized fossil types. The fossil types of the same period in the same or different regions may be subspecies represented by differing local populations or they may be phylogenetically more diverse.*

Some alternative derivations discussed in the text are indicated. Paranthropus may be regarded as a separate genus or may be subsumed under the genus Australopithecus. Similarly, Homo habilis may be considered a charter member of the genus Homo—or an advanced form of Australopithecus africanus.

Richard Leakey's find (ER 1470) is indicated in that possible line, although its 800 cubic centimeter brain and 2.6 million year date may seem out of place in many conceptions of the hominid tree. Similarly, the Swanscombe and Steinheim fossils are either advanced and late forms of Homo erectus or early forms of Homo sapiens, little different from modern human beings.

In view of the phylogenetic and taxonomic ambiguity and the seeming parallelisms in evolutionary trends, a lattice of genetic relationships among widespread but intercommunicating populations of a single genus (and perhaps of a single species) may be more appropriate than a tree diagram.

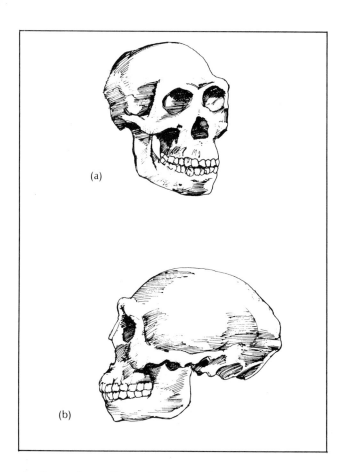

Figure 33.9   Representative specimens of Homo erectus *known as Java man (a) and Peking man (b). The crania of Javanese* Homo erectus *skulls indicate an average volume of about 860 cubic centimeters. The skulls themselves are heavy, not so much in overall thickness as in the density and thickness of the outer and inner bone tables. The brow ridges are prominent, heavy, and almost solid bone, with only very small frontal sinuses. The front teeth are larger and more prominent than those of modern humans. The molars show further reduction, a trend that seems continuous through the hominid record.*

Peking man was found in northern China. This population is represented by numerous skull, jaw, and postcranial bone fragments deposited in a large limestone cavern near Choukoutien. They date from about 300,000 years ago. The main difference from earlier pithecanthropines seems to be in brain size: the Choukoutien skulls average about 1,043 cubic centimeters.

A site such as Terra Amata speaks clearly of a more complex social organization. Hundreds of human beings were divided in some way, perhaps as extended families or lineages, into residential groups. We cannot tell at what point the characteristic human family occurred, in which a male was attached, more or less, to one or more maternal units consisting of a female and her offspring. The disappearance of **estrus** (spaced periods of sexual receptivity in the female) somewhere during the course of hominid evolution resulted in potentially continuous sexual access to the female; this has been cited as a factor in the binding of the male to the family. We may with greater confidence cite the sexual division of labor. As hunting and gathering became increasingly specialized, the family became stabilized, perhaps around the hearth, cooking, more complex food preparation, and shelter—all of which enhanced, not incidentally, survival of offspring.

Thus began a process that differed considerably from the adaptive processes that had gone before in the evolution of other species: *Human beings were adapting to the environment by the use of nongenetic, cultural inventions.* No longer would the survival of humans be determined strictly by the biological features with which they were born.

Increasingly, their survival would be determined by the nature of their inventions.

THE EMERGENCE OF *HOMO SAPIENS*

Where and when did modern *Homo sapiens* originate? Some authorities once argued that in each of the major regions of the Old World, there was a parallel progression from a type such as *Homo erectus* to various intermediate forms associated with the Neanderthal type and then to the current varieties of living humans. Today, neither this scheme nor a simple unilineal succession is considered valid. Such a parallelism leading from one species to another single species in separate lines seems most improbable in terms of evolutionary theory.

Thus we must entertain the hypothesis (which in any case we cannot refute) that from the australopithecines onward, *we may be dealing with the diverse populations of a single evolving species.* This would mean there was no absolute interruption of potential gene flow between successive and contemporaneous populations. We cannot even know whether gene flow might not have been possible between australopithecines and modern human beings. At any given time, more than one of these populations may have been undergoing the process of modernization, especially marked by encephalization, dental reduction, and gracility. At times, seemingly more advanced forms coexisted with a continuing potential for gene flow with other populations in which some ancestral traits persisted. Populations may have been more or less geographically isolated, undergoing some local biological adaptation but not to the extent that there was complete interruption of potential gene flow.

In short, the current taxonomic labels that are suggestive of genera and species are useful in providing access to the literature and as a way of bringing some conceptual order to a diversity of hominid populations. But they do not refer to a well-founded sequence of levels implying genetic discontinuity.

The rather confusing picture of the late Middle and early Upper Pleistocene supports such an interpretation. There are only a relatively small number of good fossils from this period; nevertheless, a number of relatively modern transitional fossils have been found that date from about 250,000 years ago. Two of the most well known and important are the Swanscombe and Steinheim fossils.

The Swanscombe individual was probably a female in her early twenties. Brain size and all the structural features of the skull seem thoroughly modern. It differs only in being thicker boned (which is true of all of the fossil remains of hominids until quite recently). Cranial capacity was between 1,100 and 1,200 cubic centimeters. In fact, the fossil could represent *Homo sapiens* of an archaic sort or a highly advanced *Homo erectus.* However, tools associated with the fossil are of the type of hand ax widely used by *Homo erectus.*

Swanscombe seems quite similar in type to the Steinheim skull, which was found near Stuttgart in West Germany. Steinheim has "puffy" brow ridges and a relatively low forehead, but they are not as pronounced as in *Homo erectus.* Its face protrudes somewhat more than that of modern man but is relatively straight and tucked in under the brain case in comparison with *Homo erectus.* The incisors may have been rather large but the back teeth are modern. The back of the skull was well rounded, unlike that of *Homo erectus,* which tended to form an angle.

In a current view, Swanscombe and Steinheim are accepted as *Homo sapiens* in transition from *Homo erectus,* for the fossils still show some primitive traits. This assignment would carry the emergence of *Homo sapiens* back to about 250,000 years ago. In Fontéchevade in France, two skulls have been found that may also be classified with *Homo sapiens,* and they date from a period between 150,000 and 70,000 years ago. The tools associated with them are of the sort generally found with *Homo erectus.* Again, in spite of a general robustness, they lack projecting brow ridges and are otherwise modern. From this same period, however, there are perhaps the first recognizable Neanderthal forms—one from East Germany and two well-preserved skulls from Italy.

THE "NEANDERTHAL PROBLEM"

Many writers on human evolution speak of the "Neanderthal problem." Some defend the notion that modern humans everywhere had Neanderthaloid ancestors. According to this view, a rapid transition began about 40,000 years ago—a reduction of robustness that is still going on. It has been suggested that to hold any other view is antievolutionary. What is at question, however, is not the theory of human evolution; it is simply how that evolution is reconstructed.

By the Pliocene, hominids had spread over an enormous area into varied habitats, and even within the same habitat they had probably assumed somewhat differing adaptations. We now know that some of the main factors leading to humanization did not suddenly appear 100,000 years ago with the emergence of the Neanderthals and their varied contemporaries. It seems reasonable, therefore, to accept the view of classic Neanderthal as a regional subspecies—*Homo sapiens neanderthalensis*—coexisting with many other regionally differentiated populations.

Early portrayals of the Neanderthals overemphasized the somewhat primitive morphological traits suggested by the fossils. For example, the Neanderthal skull is capacious but it is lower than that of modern Homo sapiens, bulging at the sides and to the rear. The rear of the skull is somewhat bulbous at the area of muscle attachment, where there is often a bun-shaped protrusion. The brow ridge is continuous, and it projects outward. The face is high and prominent; the nose was probably large and forward-projecting. The mouth and teeth were set well forward, which probably made the chin appear to recede.

As a consequence of such traits, Neanderthals were pictured as brutish, apelike creatures walking in a bent shuffle—as a kind of powerful gnome. They were contrasted to the Cro-Magnons—their tall, noble, clean-limbed, clear-browed successors. Today they are both seen as subspecies of *Homo sapiens.* The morphological differences may reflect their distinctive adaptation to the rigors of the glacial European tundras.

Howells and others have suggested that the classic Neanderthal may have been isolated by the ice sheets of northern Europe and the Alps and by large stretches of tundra. Therefore, communication and gene flow with populations to the east were prevented, except for a path along the Mediterranean coast. At the time, the climate of western Europe and southern France was probably cold, windy, snowy, and damp. Carleton Coon suggested that the Neanderthal face was adapted to cold, its prominence selected in response to the need for moistening and warming inhaled air. This adaptation would protect the lungs. Perhaps more essentially, the forward projection of the nose and face and the increased size of sinuses in the cheekbones would put greater distance between the exposed face and the arteries carrying blood to the brain.

Albert Steegmann has tested the response of facial skin surfaces to low temperatures. There seem to be indications that faces prominent in the middle, relatively long, and with slanting, nonprominent cheekbones are more resistant to frostbite. However, the theory of cold adaptation to frostbite damage has its problems. The earliest Neanderthal fossils from the interglacial period preceding the last glaciation, as well as a number of the Near Eastern Neanderthals, show the same facial configuration. One would have to say, then, that the cold adaptation occurred in the preceding glaciation and that the Near Eastern forms originated to the north.

By 30,000 years ago there were probably representatives of the modern aboriginal populations of Australia and the older population of Melanesia. A number of varied and locally distinctive Upper Pleistocene forms have been found in Rhodesia and South Africa; they are sometimes referred to as *Homo rhodesiensis*. These forms have a heavy brow ridge like that of *Homo erectus;* a high, prominent face like that of Neanderthal; and a sinus structure all their own.

In short, *on the verge of modern humans, we find a situation comparable to each preceding period: there were quite varied regional populations with local combinations of modern and more ancient traits.*

Many Neanderthal sites are suggestive of big-game hunting. Some populations may have been seasonally migratory, traveling north into the glacial tundra in summer and south in winter. Others seem to have occupied particular territories over long periods. Combe Grenal, a site near Les Eyzies, France, was probably occupied continuously for more than 10,000 years. It took Francois Bordes eleven years to excavate it. From it he collected some 19,000 artifacts, including weapons, butchering tools, woodworking and boneworking tools, and tools for food preparation. Here, also, were burials. At Combe Grenal and a number of other Neanderthal sites, bodies seem to have been buried with care, with ritual, with concern for positioning, and sometimes with evidence of grave offerings. At the Shanidar site in Iraq, there are signs in one grave that the body had been buried on a bower of flowers. It is not unreasonable to see this concern with the dead as representing religious and magical belief in the existence and survival of a soul. It in fact reflects a level of cognitive development like that of modern *Homo sapiens.*

There is further evidence of the attempt at magical control over the environment. A number of sites yield evidence of a Cave Bear cult. The huge cave bear of the time was both predator and prey that had to be displaced if the Neanderthals were to occupy the best caves. At a site in Switzerland, a number of skulls of cave bears were found stacked in a pit that is neatly lined with stone. Other such elaborately prepared and oriented crypts have been found in Austria and France—an indication of a culture that transcended the practice of local groups. There is no reason why we should not infer the presence of the rest of culture: language, myth, some systematization of knowledge and morals, taxonomies of kin and of natural objects and phenomena. How far back we may extend these aspects of nonmaterial culture cannot be resolved on the basis of the fossils themselves. However, it is not likely that they appeared instantaneously with the emergence of *Homo sapiens.*

CRO-MAGNON FORMS OF THE UPPER PALEOLITHIC

In the late Pleistocene, classic Neanderthal probably represented only one of the many locally differentiated populations of *Homo sapiens.* But between 30,000 and 40,000 years ago, populations virtually identical with the modern populations of Europe appear in the locales where Neanderthal was formerly found—and was suddenly found no more.

What happened to the Neanderthal populations? It is possible that other groups evolved into modern forms in areas to the east and south and then, as the climate became milder at the end of the glacial period, they began to move into Western Europe. They may have been a more developed culture with which Neanderthal could not compete. (For example, a more developed culture might have a population and social structure that could mobilize larger fighting groups.) In replacing Neanderthal, there was probably some merger of gene pools rather than a total termination of the Neanderthal gene pool. There may have been a situation of cultural and social domination, such as that which has occurred so often in human history. The newcomers are sometimes called **Cro-Magnon** after the site in France where they were first discovered.

There is a cultural discontinuity from Neanderthal to Cro-Magnon. The Cro-Magnon stone tools reflect a decidedly higher level of skill, with much more use of blades and flakes struck off from larger cores (Figure 33.10). We see a continuation of magic practices that had already been established in Neanderthal times. But there is something

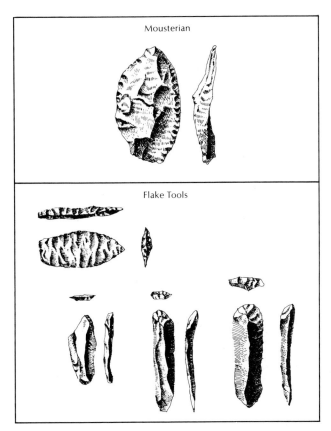

Figure 33.10   Comparison of a Neanderthal (Mousterian) stone tool with some stone tools typical of Cro-Magnon (Aurignacian).

more in the aesthetic, graphic embodiment of these imaginative ideas in cave art (Figure 33.1), sculptures, and decorations of objects. These remarkable works are sometimes read as a sign of Cro-Magnon's superior cultural capacity. But superior capacity cannot be read simply from a comparison of cultures or even from their differential survival. Relatively "primitive" cultures have existed contemporaneously with "modern" ones to the present time. Such great cultural variation is not to be explained biologically and is radically alterable from one generation to the next. Thus, in New Guinea there are some peoples famous for their sculpture and decorative arts, and others who have decorated scarcely anything at all, who have done little with stone, and who have subsisted quite well with artifacts largely derived from wood and fibers. There are others with elaborate ritual and mythology; and yet their neighbors seem little concerned with such matters and concentrate instead on the elaboration of highly varied fishing technology. Some produce local music of great tonal complexity while their neighbors practice dirges with an invariant

simple tonal pattern and direct all their attention to the verbal content. *The point is that these are cultural specializations, which are subject to drastic change; they should not be confused with biological, genetic differences.* This knowledge should caution us against inferring a biological revolution taking place in Europe between Neanderthal and Cro-Magnon, although it does not rule out the possibility of some further increment in the biological basis for cultural capacity.

HUMAN UNITY AND DIVERSITY

During the Upper Paleolithic and shortly thereafter, human beings came to occupy every continent and an incredible number of islands. Much of this movement was accomplished by people still living as hunters and gatherers, following the game herds. Some crossed over from Asia to the New World on a large land bridge that existed more than 40,000 years ago (Chapter 9). At the end of the last glaciation, hunters and gatherers in many places became sedentary (although there is evidence of relatively stable populations before that). Selective gathering of wild seeds and plants, and perhaps the transplantation of them to more convenient locations, gradually led to the domestication of plants. Domestication of animals may have begun with the intermittent association of animals whose food supply was supplemented by the refuse of human occupation sites. To natural selection was added human selection in the modification of those plants and animals over very long periods and many generations. In other areas, hunting and gathering persisted. Where the environment was ungenerous, people limited their population through the spacing of births and through infanticide, a practice known to have been widespread in hunting and gathering bands.

In spreading throughout an enormous geographic area, humans developed stabilized cultural adaptations ranging from tropical horticulture to almost total dependence on hunting in the case of circumpolar peoples. They became distributed in a large number of relatively small local populations. And yet, *Homo sapiens* remained a single species. At the same time it was a polytypic species, manifesting many superficial variations of skin, hair, and facial conformation.

The major geographic subspecies, or **races,** are semi-isolated breeding populations. Such superficial variations as exist among them may represent relatively early climatological adaptations. Consider, for example, variations in skin color. The skin of tropical peoples is protected from ultraviolet radiation by the pigment melanin. In accordance with the theory of tropical origins, it is not unlikely that the early hominids (and perhaps all human beings until recently) were dark-skinned. Such an adaptation may have been related as well to the heat economy of the body, as well as to hairlessness and the abundance of sweat glands with their excretory and evaporative cooling functions. Although a dark body may absorb more radiation than a lighter one, it also is more efficient at radiating it.

The reduction of pigmentation in northern populations may seem more difficult to explain than an increase of pigmentation. Once selective pressures have been mitigated or nullified through cultural intervention—such as the use of animal skins to cover the body—what remains is mutation pressure. As Brace has argued, such pressure more often leads to the reduction rather than to the intensification of a given structure or process.

However, there are several possible adaptive functions that could explain selection for reduced pigmentation. According to one line of reasoning, normal mammalian skin divested of its fur is susceptible to damage from the ultraviolet rays of sunlight; prolonged exposure can lead to the development of skin cancer. The adaptive response to this pressure is melanin, which blocks penetration of ultraviolet radiation. At the same time, ultraviolet radiation takes part in the synthesis of the essential D vitamins, which are sterols activated in the upper layers of skin. In northern climates, pigmentation would have to be reduced in order to *admit* ultraviolet radiation. (You might ask why, then, do the Eskimo of the Arctic have dark skin if this is true? Interestingly enough, the Eskimo diet has been one in which fish is a staple—and the animal fats in fish are high in vitamin D content.) According to still another line of reasoning, lightly pigmented skin is less susceptible to frostbite than darkly pigmented skin. Such a theory would make sense if our evolutionary history began in the tropics, which the fossil record suggests did happen.

Human variation—overlapping, indefinitely bounded and intergrading as it is for any given trait—reflects an incipient biological response to adaptation in different ecological niches. If humans had followed the normal course of organic evolution, this incipient divergence might have led to speciation. Incipient speciation was aborted by the intervention of culture, which has guaranteed the continuing single-species status of mankind. It was not only that cultural inventions facilitated the restless mobility of human populations, thereby leading to ever shifting patterns of gene flow that interrupted semi-isolation. Even where a period of isolation led to some local biological adaptation, cultural inventions intervened to lessen the selective pressures that might otherwise have carried such adaptations further.

Recently Napoleon Chagnon and James Neel did a cultural and biogenetic study of small hunting and gathering bands from three Amazonian Indian cultures. They found that within a particular linguistic group even the nearby small communities differed from one another in a series of selected blood factors. The difference was as much as that between widely separated Indian tribes. This degree of genetic variation among local populations is taken as typical of the material upon which evolution operated in the course of hominid development. Much of this variation may have depended on chance in the small samples represented by these very small populations. This effect would be heightened by the tendency of such societies to fission along lineage lines, so that migrants would be more closely related and less representative than a random sample of the parent group would be. Some part of the variation is based on the cultural patterning of gene flow and still another part is probably based on selection that affects differential reproductive success. The practice of polygyny in these Amazonian cultures and in many other cultures acts to amplify differences in the contribution that individual males make to future generations. In contrast, in many societies and increasingly as a modern trend, inequality of reproduction is greatly reduced and all males and females contribute about equally to the next generation. This trend tends to nullify selective processes operating to translate behavioral differentials into reproductive differentials.

There have been two opposed tendencies in human evolution. On the one hand, there has been a trend toward division and differentiation; on the other, there has been a trend preventing such division from creating truly isolated subspecies with a potential for speciation. Given the amount of genetic intergradation and overlap among human populations, what people have perceived as "races" or "species" or "subspecies" or as "people of different blood" are largely cultural constructs. One speaks with some confidence of the traditional broad geographic racial divisions. But as soon as there is any attempt to draw boundaries based on morphology, or even on chemically derived gene frequencies, it becomes apparent that precisely bounded "races" on any scale are cultural artifacts. The important thing about race is what human beings have made of it: a basis for self-exhaltation—and contempt, domination, and even genocide. Such cultural definitions are highly motivated, but they frequently have little relation to biological fact. Neither do such facts provide support for *invariant* group behavioral differences. Although mankind potentially constitutes a single gene pool and potentially approaches a state of panmixia, in fact the perception of difference of nationality, of religion, of class, of race and the use of these perceptions as a basis for assortative mating remain extremely strong and persistent traits of human cultures. They have a powerful effect in channeling gene flow. It would be misleading to say that their effect is diminishing.

At the same time, no human population is a complete breeding isolate. There has always been considerable gene flow that has continued to knit the human tree into a cross-lacing lattice. For example, gene flow has often occurred under conditions of dominance. No matter how disparaged the subject population, under conditions of cultural dominance the dominant males exploit sexual access to the subject females. The harshest sanctions are imposed to prevent backflow. Gene flow of considerable proportions takes place even at the same time that a common humanity may be denied. In short, our definitional boundaries have turned out to be permeable, and the human species has remained one.

PERSPECTIVE

The unity of the human species derives from the effect of culture on the evolutionary process. In the course of hominid evolution, culture—consisting of learning embodied in behavior and of artifacts—was interposed between humans and the environment. Biological adaptation was increasingly supplemented by cultural adaptations. This is not to say that changes in gene frequencies are not possible or that there is no longer any basis for differential reproductive contributions to future generations. The point is that such biological trends may no longer be relevant or in close relationship to the trends that gave rise to the human cultural capacity. For example, beginning with our hominid ancestors, there has been a tripling of brain size, an exponential increase. But this process of encephalization has perhaps now come to an end, at least for the foreseeable future. It has even been suggested that *Homo sapiens neanderthalensis* had reached an average cranial capacity somewhat larger than that of modern *Homo sapiens* and that there has been not only a leveling off but a slight regression. We may speculate that human beings became just ''brainy'' enough to develop a cultural capacity sufficient to interrupt the development of their brain by mitigating the very selective pressures that had produced it. Like all other major evolutionary developments, growth of the brain was a self-limiting process. Aside from the mitigation of environmental selective forces by such artifacts as hearths or medicines, cultural innovations may diffuse their adaptive advantage widely, both within and between societies (populations) rather than exclusively promoting the reproductive advantage of its innovators and their progeny. Cultural evolution, then, is the common arena within which humankind shares a common fate.

The development of culture includes the capacity to represent reality, to manipulate it internally, to store it, to embody it in artifacts such as stone tools, books, or magnetic tapes. It is productive, in that it includes the possibility of creating new combinations, new syntheses. Human thought and invention include tremendous capacities for error, yet these same capacities enable us to imagine that which does not yet exist. Our thoughts become images

of a future that we may attempt to construct or to avoid.

Culture may be seen as the basic mode of human adaptation. It did not appear suddenly. It is the culmination of processes that have been traced throughout this book—from the simple irritability of living matter to the steady increase in the repertoire of behaviors. We may see these processes in the development of organs for the acquisition and storage of information, and for the utilization of experience. Long before we reach even the mammals, we may see the intervention of learning superimposed on innate behavioral mechanisms. We may trace, in the evolution of neural mechanisms, the development of the capacity for delay of action. Delayed action allows for an increased number of intervening variables between stimulus and response—a space that becomes increasingly occupied by intelligence.

We may follow the lineage of humankind through the more generalized representatives of each preceding type of animal that kept its options open, leading to specialists in versatility. We may see in tool use the beginnings of an enormously rapid process of developing cultural rather than organic extensions of ourselves. Artifacts have extended sight, speed, memory, the capacity to store and retrieve experience, and the ability to survive in environments far different from the tropics.

Culture *is* human nature. The natural environment for human beings is the artificial environment. Yet this process, too, has its limits and could be self-aborting. Man remains an animal. All that we have learned of life continues to apply. And yet we are only now beginning to question the extent to which we can continue to exist in an increasingly artificial environment and to question the extent to which culture is transforming the earth itself. For in terms of evolutionary time, culture is a spectacularly rapid process which, through communication, can spread like wildfire. Unlike the slow process of biological evolution through natural selection, the process of cultural evolution can be directed. The problem arises because such direction is based on human-centered value systems, not on a system that has, over time, brought about long-term stability for and survival of life itself.

SUGGESTED READINGS

CAMPBELL, BERNARD. *Human Evolution: An Introduction to Man's Adaptations.* 2nd ed. Chicago: Aldine, 1974. Comparative analysis of hominid form and function, written with authority and flair.

HOWELLS, W. *Evolution of the Genus Homo.* Reading, Mass.: Addison-Wesley, 1973. A careful survey of the fossil record of human evolution. (Contrast the views presented here with those of Washburn and Moore.)

JOLLY, CLIFFORD. "The Seed-Eaters: A New Model of Hominid Differentiation Based on a Baboon Analogy," *Man*, 5 (March 1970), 5. For more detail on an ingenious but still controversial theory concerning hominidization.

POURIER, F. *In Search of Ourselves*. Minneapolis: Burgess, 1974. A textbook that gives an overview of current thinking on human evolution and variation.

WASHBURN, S., and P. J. DOLHINOW (eds.). *Perspectives on Human Evolution*, vol. 1. New York: Holt, Rinehart and Winston, 1972. (See also vol. 2.) Selected articles on human evolutionary biology; includes the views of Sarich and Howell as briefly discussed in the chapter.

WASHBURN, SHERWOOD, and RUTH MOORE. *Ape Into Man: A Study of Human Evolution*. Boston: Little, Brown, 1974. Explores the evolutionary possibilities of a relatively recent divergence of humans and the "higher" apes.

Chapter 34

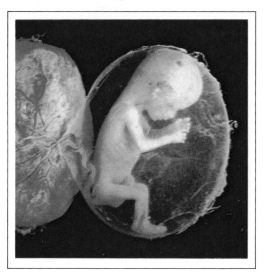

Human Reproduction and Development

In our sexual behavior, we express one of the strongest of our evolutionary heritages. Today, as a result of cultural as well as biological evolution, we have the capacity to shape not only future generations but also our own psychological health and that of our sexual partner. One of the great advances of our age has been the realization that we are more likely to deal responsibly with the biological and psychological aspects of sexual activity if we act with knowledge rather than out of ignorance, shame, or fear.

Sexual reproduction arose in simple organisms as an alternative to various methods of asexual reproduction—fission, budding, and so forth. But this strategy turned out to be more than just another way of reproducing. Through the twin processes of meiosis and syngamy, it gave rise to an enormous increase in genetic diversity. And with greater genetic diversity, new mutations were tested in combination with older ones and were selected for much more rapidly. With sexual reproduction, then, came a rapid formation of new complexes of genes adapted to unique conditions and, hence, an explosive radiation of new species throughout the biosphere.

The entire life style of animals is based on early determination of the numbers and positions of body parts, so that they may be properly wired into the nervous system that will integrate their functioning. As a result of early determination, all cells in the body except the germ cells lose the capacity for producing a new individual very early in the life cycle (Chapter 18). Consider the fact that human development from conception to birth takes an average of 266 days. Before this period is one-tenth of the way over, about a hundred cells are set aside to play no role in the functioning of the body other than as potential reproductive cells. It is from the progeny of these germ cells that all the gametes (eggs or sperm) of the individual will develop. And it is to these cells that the future of the species is entrusted.

Yet despite the central role of sexual reproduction in the biology of the species, no other area of human behavior has been so fraught with ignorance, superstition, and psychological complexity. The notion that human sexual behavior is somehow a thing apart from biology has been prevalent. Mating behavior in lower life forms has been observed with great interest, but until rather recently sexual activity in our own species has been considered somehow inappropriate for basic biological investigations.

In view of the many serious problems that face the human species if sexual reproduction proceeds at maximal rate (Chapters 36 and 37), this point of view has become untenable. Many decisions regarding sex clearly face each of us, both as individuals and as members of our society and of our species. Shall I reproduce? If so, how often and under what conditions? If I do choose to reproduce, are there critical stages at which development of my child can be affected by my life style? When does new life actually begin? Should society place limits on who should reproduce, or how frequently? Should abortion be an individual prerogative, or should it be condemned? If we are to make rational decisions in these matters, we must begin by placing human reproduction in the biological context it deserves.

THE FEMALE REPRODUCTIVE SYSTEM

The reproductive system of the human female consists of the ovaries, fallopian tubes (oviducts), uterus, vagina, and external genitals (Figure 34.2). The **ovaries** are ovoid glands located at the sides of the pelvic cavity; they are attached by ligaments to the uterus and the fallopian tubes. The **fallopian tubes** extend from the ovaries to the uterus, thus forming a passageway for the ova (female gametes or egg cells). The ovarian end of the tube expands into a funnellike structure with a fringed border. The tube is lined with cilia that move the ovum toward the uterus, where the tube ends in a small opening in the uterine wall.

The **uterus,** or womb, is a pear-shaped organ lying between the bladder and the rectum. The fallopian tubes open into the upper portion of the uterus, which in its turn opens into the vagina. Ligaments attach the ovaries, fallopian tubes, and uterus to the walls of the pelvic cavity. The thick uterine walls are made of smooth muscle. The inner lining, or *endometrium,* consists of glandular tissue and a supporting framework. Normally the uterine cavity is almost closed, but during pregnancy it expands enormously. The lower part of the uterus, projecting into the vagina, is called the *cervix.*

The vagina is a dilatable, muscular tube, about $7^1/_2$ to 10 centimeters (3 to 4 inches) long, that lies almost at right angles to the uterus. The vaginal muscle layers are much thinner than those of the uterus, and the interior of the vagina is lined with a thin layer of nonglandular epithelial cells. From the muscular rim of the cervix, which extends into the tube, the vagina leads to the exterior genitals.

The external genitals, or **vulva,** include a number of structures. The *mons veneris* is a mound of fatty tissue over the pubic bone at the front of the genitals; it becomes covered with hair at puberty. The *labia majora* are thick, prominent folds of skin and fatty tissue lying on the sides of the genitals and covered with pubic hair on their outer surfaces. The *labia minora* are smaller folds of skin and fatty tissue lying inside the labia majora and forming the rim of a depression called the *vestibule.* Where the labia minora meet at the top of the vestibule is a small erectile organ, the *clitoris,* that corresponds to the penis of the male. It is composed of spongy tissues that are expanded and stiffened by blood engorgement during sexual excitement.

It is within the vestibule that the openings of the urethra (urinary tube) as well as the vagina are found. Stretched across the front of the vaginal opening is a fold of mucous membrane called the *hymen.* In the young female, the hymen commonly exists as a partial closure of the vaginal opening and is usually torn during childhood or during the first sexual intercourse. The *glands of Bartholin* are located on either side of the vagina, just beneath the skin surface. They open through small ducts into the vestibule, in the grooves between the hymen and the labia minora. It is the fluid from these glands that lubricates the vaginal opening during intercourse.

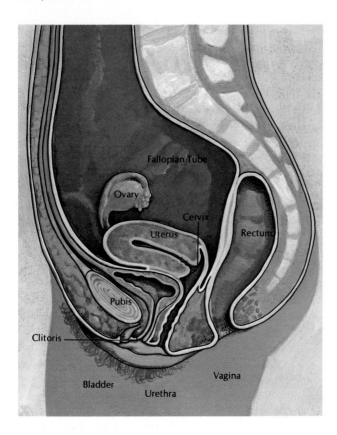

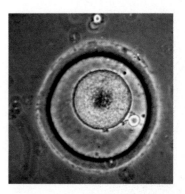

Figure 34.2   The female reproductive system.

Figure 34.3   A living human ovum. The human egg is approximately the size of one of the periods on this page. Germ cells do not divide in the mammalian ovary after birth. Of the 2 million oocytes present in the ovary of a newborn human female, fewer than 500 ever mature, and usually fewer than a dozen are ever fertilized. Like other mammalian ova, the human egg lacks significant amounts of yolk; the embryo depends on nourishment from the mother's blood via the placenta. (From Rugh and Shettles, From Conception to Birth: The Drama of Life's Beginnings, *Harper & Row, 1971)*

During the menstrual cycle, the female reproductive system undergoes various changes (Chapter 22). As hormones flow from the anterior pituitary gland and the ovary, the wall of the uterus becomes thickened and its blood supply becomes more highly developed in preparation for receiving a fertilized egg. The uterus reaches its peak of development about midway between menstrual periods. At this time, a single egg (but sometimes two or more) is released from the ovary in the process called **ovulation.** A day or two before ovulation, there is usually an increase in body temperature of no more than one degree.

Ovulation defines the period of fertility; *conception* (a successful union of egg and sperm) usually results if intercourse occurs within the two days preceding or the day following release of the egg from the ovary. The life of the human ovum is between 12 and 24 hours. Sperm, however, can live in the female genital tract for 4 to 5 days. *On the average,* ovulation occurs 14 to 16 days before onset of menstruation, but the actual point of ovulation is extremely variable from one female to the next. By making appropriate measurements of body temperature, of the chemical composition of vaginal fluids, and so forth, it is often possible to determine the time of ovulation during a menstrual cycle with a fair degree of precision. Nevertheless, there is also extensive variation from cycle to cycle in some individuals.

If conception does not occur, the pattern of hormone flow changes. As a result, much of the tissue in the uterine wall that has been prepared to receive the embryo is now sloughed off in the process of **menstruation** (Chapter 22).

THE MALE REPRODUCTIVE SYSTEM

The reproductive system of the human male consists of the testes, scrotum, seminal ducts, epididymis, seminal vesicles, ejaculatory ducts, accessory glands, and the penis (Figure 34.4). The **testes** are the glandular organs in which male gametes (sperm cells) are produced. Before birth, the testes move from the abdominal cavity down into the **scrotum,** a pouch of skin near the base of the penis. Each testis is an oval organ containing interstitial (or supporting) cells and the hundreds of coiled tubules within which sperm cells are formed. The testis is covered by several layers of membrane as well as by the thin muscle and skin layers of the scrotum.

All the tubules within the testis lead into about a dozen small ducts, which leave the upper surface of the testis and drain into the epididymis. The **epididymis** is a single, thin tube about 6 meters (20 feet) long, but it is coiled and closely packed on the top and back of the testis, where it is held in place by some of the surrounding membranes.

The epididymis functions in several ways to help move sperm from the testis toward the penis. The muscle and

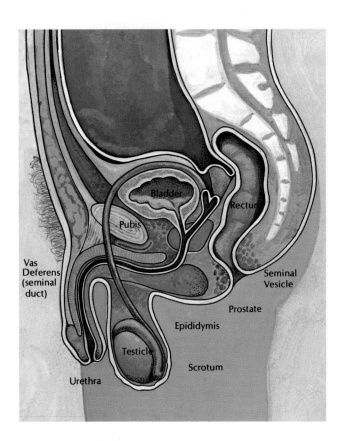

Figure 34.4   The male reproductive system.

ciliated cells of the duct system propel the sperm along their way. The sperm enter the epididymis against considerable pressure. Tubules within the epididymis remove fluids, cell debris, and pigment accompanying the sperm—and the sperm, too, if they are produced in greater numbers than needed. The epididymis also serves to increase the effectiveness of the male gametes, for sperm removed from the ducts near the testis have poorer fertilizing ability than those taken from the other end of the epididymis.

Near the lower portion of the testis, the duct of the epididymis connects with a **seminal duct,** or **vas deferens.** This duct travels up the side of the testis next to the epididymis as part of the spermatic cord, up to a canal passing through the abdominal wall above the pubic bone, across the pelvic cavity beside the bladder, over the ureter, and down to the back of the bladder, where it meets the seminal duct from the other testis. Alongside the end of the duct between the bladder and the rectum is an oblong pouch, called the **seminal vesicle,** which contains a single tube packed in close coils. The seminal vesicles convert glucose into fructose, which is present in the semen in concentrations about three or four times as great as glucose concentration in the blood. This sugar apparently acts as an energy source for the sperm cells.

The seminal duct and the tube from the seminal vesicle join to form the **ejaculatory ducts.** These ducts lie side by side and open into the urethra just below the bladder. The urethra, which extends from the bladder to the tip of the penis, carries both urine and seminal fluid to the exterior. Surrounding the urethra, just below the bladder, is the **prostate gland,** which is an organ composed of both glandular and muscular tissue. Most of the seminal fluid is secreted from this gland. Fluid from the prostate gland and seminal vesicles is involved in the maintenance and activity of the sperm cells. The fluid from the prostate enters the urethra through a small opening between the openings of the ejaculatory ducts. Near the base of the penis, two small glands empty into the urethra. These **bulbourethral glands** (or Cowper's glands) also contribute to the seminal fluid.

The **penis** is a cylindrical organ composed of three long bodies of spongy tissue, bound together with fibrous tissue. During sexual excitation, blood is pumped into the spongy tissues, making the entire structure larger and rigid. Two of the spongy bodies (also called cavernous bodies) are attached to the pubic bone at the sides of the opening in the lower part of the pelvis. They run along the sides of the penis and are fused together to form the main part of the penis shaft. Within the groove between these two bodies on the lower region of the penis is another cavernous body that surrounds the urethra. This body is expanded at the base of the penis to form a bulblike structure beneath the bulbourethral glands. It also expands at the tip of the penis to form a caplike structure, the *glans penis,* that is wrapped around the end of the penis. The urethra ends in a slitlike opening at the tip of the glans. The entire penis is covered by a thin, loosely attached layer of skin that is continuous with the scrotum and with the skin surrounding the genitals. Near the tip of the penis, the skin is folded back on itself to form the *foreskin.* This fold of skin may be removed soon after birth by circumcision. Unlike other primates, humans have no bone or cartilage within the penis.

As in other mammals, human **spermatogenesis**—the division of male germ cells and their differentiation (from spermatocyte to the spermatid to spermatozoan)—normally is continuous throughout the male's lifetime. Sperm cells are continually being formed in normal testes, although some decrease of mitotic activity in old age may slow the further differentiation of primary spermatocytes. This is in marked contrast to the female of the species, who is born with all the egg cells she will possess as an adult. But whereas the human female normally produces no more than 400 eggs capable of being fertilized during her lifetime, the

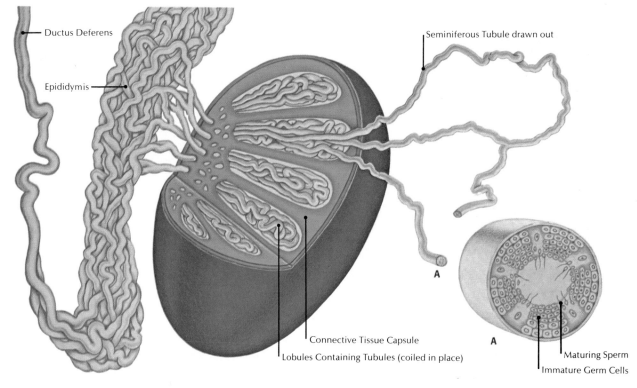

Ductus Deferens

Epididymis

Seminiferous Tubule drawn out

A

Maturing Sperm

Immature Germ Cells

Connective Tissue Capsule

Lobules Containing Tubules (coiled in place)

Figure 34.5 A cutaway, diagrammatic view of the human testis. The numerous seminiferous tubules contain the primordial germ cells and are the sites of sperm formation. The germ cells of the male, in contrast to those of the female, divide mitotically throughout the reproductive lifetime of the individual. Thus the number of sperm that can be formed is extremely great.

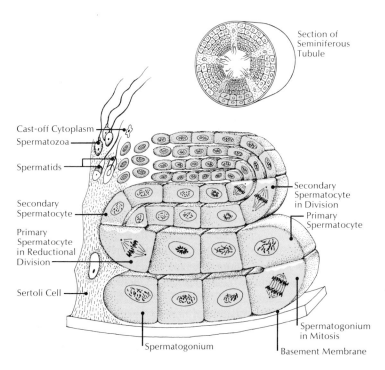

Section of Seminiferous Tubule

Cast-off Cytoplasm
Spermatozoa

Spermatids

Secondary Spermatocyte

Primary Spermatocyte in Reductional Division

Sertoli Cell

Secondary Spermatocyte in Division

Primary Spermatocyte

Spermatogonium in Mitosis

Basement Membrane

Spermatogonium

Figure 34.6 A highly schematic diagram showing the steps involved in spermatogenesis within the seminiferous tubules of an adult male. The primary germ cells, or spermatogonia, divide mitotically. The cells that remain near the basement membrane continue to grow and divide throughout the reproductive life of the individual. But the spermatogonia that are displaced toward the lumen become primary spermatocytes. They undergo the usual two meiotic divisions.

male releases on the average more than a quarter of a *billion* sperm during each ejaculation!

Both spermatogenesis and the secretion of the testicular hormone **testosterone** (Chapter 22) are regulated by the peptide hormones secreted by the pituitary. Follicle-stimulating hormone (FSH) affects some critical steps in the development of the primary spermatocyte, and it appears that the maturation of early spermatids into mature spermatozoa also depends on FSH. Spermatogenesis up to the primary spermatocyte stage apparently occurs automatically, without the influence of pituitary hormones.

During the prepubertal period, interstitial cells of the testes are differentiated from certain interstitial connective tissue cells. Spermatogenic activity begins at the same time, but complete development of the interstitial cells lags behind that of germ cells. The development of the interstitial cells depends on luteinizing hormone (LH), which is also known as *interstitial cell stimulating hormone* (ICSH). ICSH stimulates growth of interstitial cells as well as mitotic activity among spermatogonia (Figure 34.6). FSH and ICSH stimulate spermatid formation. The testosterone secreted by the interstitial cells maintains a favorable environment within the tubules for sperm cell development.

The hormones produced by the interstitial cells also affect the accessory reproductive organs. They stimulate the prostate gland and the seminal vesicles to produce most of the seminal fluid, or **semen.** Testosterone inhibits spermatogenesis by suppressing the release of FSH from the pituitary. Thus, the male has a complex interbalancing

system of sexual hormones but not a prominent cycle of hormone variation.

THE PHYSIOLOGY OF COITUS

During sexual intercourse, both the male and the female experience similar response patterns, which have been identified by William Masters and Virginia Johnson. These response patterns are grouped together in four sequential phases: excitement, plateau, orgasmic, and resolution. In this section the physiological responses of the male will be described first and then the responses of the female.

Physiological Responses in the Male

As a result of sexual stimulation, the male body undergoes extragenital responses such as increased heart rate and blood pressure. Elevated tension (myotonia) in both voluntary and involuntary muscles appears early in the *excitement phase*. Early genital reactions also are visible. The penis becomes erect as primarily arterial blood collects in the three cavernous bodies that run the length of the organ. (Such a concentration of blood is called **vasocongestion.**) In this way, the penis acquires the rigidity needed to enter the vagina of the female. The scrotal sac, too, becomes elevated through vasocongestion and through a thickening of the scrotal skin. Testicular lifting occurs as the spermatic cord shortens by an involuntary contraction of adjacent muscles.

The penis reaches full erection during the excitement phase and then shows a slight increase in circumference during the *plateau phase*. This late development is restricted to the glans penis. As testicular elevation progresses, an increase in testicular size becomes apparent. Testes show about 50 percent size increase, and if plateau levels of sexual tension are prolonged, up to 100 percent increase may occur.

As the culmination of the sexual act (*orgasm*) is approached, a preejaculatory fluid originating in Cowper's gland may exude from the glans penis. Frequently the fluid contains active sperm. Orgasmic approach may occasionally be accompanied by a sex flush (a superficial vasocongestive reaction) that affects the chest, neck, face, forehead, and sometimes shoulders and thighs. Impending ejaculation is also signaled by increases in heart rate, breathing rate, and blood pressure, and by myotonia. In the *orgasmic phase,* semen is ejected forcefully from the urethra in the process called **ejaculation.** The ejaculatory process occurs in two stages. The first involves contractions of the entire genital tract—from epididymis through seminal ducts to seminal vesicles. As seminal fluid collects in the urethra, the urethral bulb at the base of the penis involuntarily expands to twice or three times its normal size, in prepara-

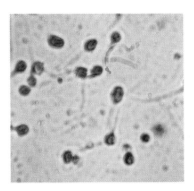

Figure 34.7 Living, active human sperm highly magnified. Although human sperm and egg differ 85,000-fold in volume, their genetic contributions to the embryo are equal. (From Rugh and Shettles, 1971)

tion for the second stage of ejaculation. As the ejaculatory process begins, the sphincter (muscle ring) at the bladder closes, which prevents seminal fluid from being forced back into the bladder and at the same time prevents urine from being forced into the seminal fluid.

The second stage of ejaculation begins with a relaxation of the urethral sphincter at the base of the prostate, allowing the seminal fluid to flow into the distended urethral bulb and penile urethra. Contractions of muscles in the perineum (the region between testicles and anus) and the penis propel the fluid along the penile urethra. Regular contractions of the urethral bulb also aid in propulsion. The first one-third of the seminal fluid that is expelled contains about 75 percent of the sperm. The remainder of the emission consists largely of fluids from the seminal vesicles and prostate gland.

Following orgasm, there is a *resolution phase* in which the return to the unstimulated state is usually quite rapid. The sex flush fades, and perspiration sometimes occurs. Detumescence (loss of swelling) of the penis occurs with the abatement of localized vasocongestion. This loss also leads to the descent of the testes into the relaxed scrotum. There is a general decrease in muscle tension, usually no more than 5 minutes after the beginning of this phase.

Physiological Responses in the Female

Many parts of the female body in addition to the genitalia respond to sexual stimulation. Heart rate and blood pressure elevation begin in the *excitement phase.* The breasts show nipple erection and a slight increase in size as a result of vasocongestion. Vasocongestion occurs in other body parts as well, including the labia minora and the clitoris. It is instrumental in the development of the sex flush, which commonly appears late in this phase and spreads from the breasts over the lower abdomen and shoulders as sexual tension increases. Myotonia is another generalized sexual response involving both voluntary and involuntary muscles. Coital position has a role in determining which muscle groups will exhibit this reaction during a particular sexual response cycle.

Genital changes during the excitement phase include clitoral gland expansion and vaginal lubrication. The swelling of the gland is a result of vasocongestion and always accompanies sexual tension. Vaginal lubrication is not a result of glandular activity in the vagina, for there are no glands in the vaginal walls. The lubricating fluid passes through the pores of the vaginal tissue, like sweat, in response to significant dilation of a number of blood vessels and to the consequent massive vasocongestive condition. Like lubrication, vaginal expansion is involuntary.

In the female, the first part of the *plateau phase* is mainly a continuation of reactions that originated during the preceding phase. If effective sexual stimulation is maintained,

Figure 34.8   Graphs summarizing three patterns of the female sexual response cycle (a) and two patterns of the male sexual response cycle (b).

the sex flush spreads, myotonia and vasocongestion increase, and breast expansion advances. The clitoral gland and shaft now withdraw.

The expansion that affected the inner two-thirds of the vagina during the excitement phase now extends to the outer one-third. This tissue, even more than the inner area, becomes engorged with venous blood. Both the outer third of the vagina and the labia minora are involved in this major vasocongestive reaction. Together they form the anatomical basis for the physiological expression of orgasm and therefore are called the **orgasmic platform.**

The uterus showed partial elevation in the preceding phase; it now attains complete elevation and moves backward toward the spine. It remains in that position until the onset of the resolution phase. As sexual tensions increase and orgasm becomes imminent, further increases in respiration, heartbeat, and blood pressure are seen.

The physiological onset of the *orgasmic phase* is indicated by contraction in certain organs. First the orgasmic platform contracts for 2 to 4 seconds, then it undergoes a series of shorter contractions less than a second apart. The factors that initiate this response may be neural, hormonal, muscular, or some combination; the answer is not known. The platform contractions are accompanied by uterine contractions of a less definite pattern and often by contractions of the external rectal sphincter. As indicated in Figure 34.8, some women experience several orgasms in a relatively short period of time.

The *resolution phase* is characterized by a fairly rapid return to a precoital condition. The average time is about 5 to 10 minutes. Myotonia, sex flush, and the orgasmic platform subside; the clitoris regains normal size and position. Changes resulting from vasocongestion disappear

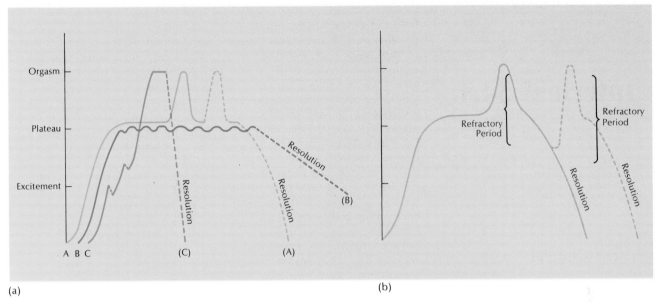

(a)

(b)

throughout the body in an irregular flow of abatement. This process is much slower if plateau levels of tension were reached but orgasm did not occur. In this case, 30 minutes or more may be required. Complete restoration does not occur between cycles if more than one orgasm is attained.

MOVEMENT OF SPERM THROUGH THE FEMALE TRACT FOLLOWING COITUS

Within minutes after ejaculation, sperm ascending the cervical canal can reach the uterus. Because sperm swim at only about 0.5 centimeter per minute, forces other than their own motility must transport them through the female genital tract. After the sperm have entered the cervix, a complex system of contractions, fluid currents, ciliary action, and "anatomical barriers" help to influence the rate at which sperm move toward the site of fertilization. Some evidence now suggests that substances in the seminal fluid cause relaxation of the uterine walls, aiding the flow of cervical secretions and sperm into the cavity of the uterus.

Normal fertility depends on various anatomical, physical, and chemical changes in the cervix and in the mucus that it secretes. Cervical mucus, which is normally alkaline, reaches a peak of alkalinity at the time of ovulation. This alkalinity helps to overcome or minimize the detrimental effects that the slightly acidic vaginal mucus has on sperm motility and survival. If cervical mucus is plentiful, sperm may be able to move directly from the alkaline semen into the alkaline cervical mucus and thus avoid the unfavorable vaginal acidity.

There is a heavy loss of sperm within the female tract. Secretions from female organs, unfavorable conditions of acidity or alkalinity, and phagocytosis by leucocytes—as well as physiological changes in the sperm cells themselves—contribute to their depletion.

CONCEPTION

One mystery not yet solved is the question of how the tiny sperm, swimming at random through the relatively huge passages of the fallopian tubes, find the egg at all. A mechanism of chemotaxis has been suggested, but evidence to support this suggestion is lacking. A flow of fluid in the tubes toward the ovary, vigorous contractility of the muscles at the ovarian end of the tubes, and the relatively large size of the egg and its attached cells may be sufficient to account for the high probability of sperm meeting egg.

If active sperm cells are in the female genital tract within the period from 48 hours before ovulation to about 12 hours after ovulation, fertilization is very likely to occur. Within seconds after the head of the sperm touches the egg, the fertilized egg reacts with violent undulating movements that bring the sperm and egg nuclei close together, thus restoring the full diploid set of twenty-three chromosome pairs.

In most mammalian species, including the human species, several sperm contact each egg. But normally only one penetrates the innermost layer, the *vitelline membrane,* and fertilizes the egg. The nature of this block to multiple fertilization is being studied chemically and ultramicroscopically, but the underlying mechanism is not yet known.

Every mature egg carries one X chromosome, but half the sperm carry X chromosomes and half carry Y chromosomes. If an X-bearing sperm fertilizes the egg, an XX zygote results, and the zygote normally will develop into a female. If a Y-bearing sperm fertilizes the egg, an XY zygote results and normally will develop into a male. *Sex*

Interleaf 34.1

Birth Control

Evolution has produced both a strong drive toward sexual activity and a relatively foolproof means of guaranteeing fertilization; these adaptations have ensured the survival of the human species for millions of years. And although attempts to enjoy coitus without fertilization have been made throughout human history, no method yet devised for circumventing this efficient system has proved to be completely effective.

Probably the most effective means of contraception is surgical sterilization—vasectomy in the male and tubal ligation or vaginal hysterectomy in the female. A vasectomy, in which the seminal ducts are severed and tied off, can be performed in a doctor's office under local anesthetic within a few minutes. Tubal ligation for a woman is a slightly more complex procedure in which the fallopian tubes are cut and tied so that ova cannot be released into the uterus. The operation must be performed in the hospital, requiring about a two-day stay. In both vasectomy and tubal ligation there is a very slight (less than 1 percent) chance that a sperm may somehow manage to reach an ovum despite the elimination of the normal paths.

Next to sterilization, the two most effective means of birth control in use today are the intrauterine device (IUD) and various forms of birth control pills. IUDs are made of soft, flexible plastic, molded into various shapes. It takes only a few minutes for a doctor to insert one of these devices into the uterus. The woman commonly experiences uterine contractions (cramps) for a few hours after the IUD is inserted, and her next few menstrual periods may be irregular, but otherwise the IUD is generally unnoticed by the woman who wears it. Its obvious advantages include the simplicity and the absence of any need to prepare for coitus. However, some women are unable to use the IUD. The device may be expelled spontaneously from the uterus, or symptoms such as bleeding and continued cramps may require the doctor to remove it.

No one yet knows quite how the IUD works, but it seems to interfere with implantation of the developing embryo in the uterine wall. The pregnancy rate for women who use the IUD is 3 to 4 per 100 woman-years. That is, three or four pregnancies will occur each year for every 100 couples who use the IUD as their sole method of birth control. Newer IUDs, such as the Cu-7, are reported to have an even lower pregnancy rate.

Even more effective than the IUD is the birth control pill, or oral contraceptive. The Pill introduces into the body synthetic equivalents of estrogen and progesterone that serve to prevent ovulation. Different brands contain different amounts and proportions of hormones, but the most widely used types have a pregnancy rate of 0 to 0.3 per 100 woman-years.

A major flaw in the Pill is the fact that it is to be taken daily with no omissions for three weeks and then omitted for seven days while the woman menstruates. If the user forgets three or more pills, and sometimes even two or one, the contraceptive effect may be lost for the month, and pregnancy may occur.

The present formulations of the Pill depend highly on estrogen. This hormone has been implicated in a possible side effect of current oral contraceptives—an increased incidence of diseases involving blood clots in the veins. These clots may impair the circulation of the legs and could cause death if they travel to lungs, heart, or brain. The danger of this complication, though, is twenty times less than the risk of similar complications during or following normal pregnancy. Hormones in the Pill are also believed in rare instances to elevate the blood pressure of susceptible women and possibly to alter the metabolism of fats in the body. The new "minipill," which contains no estrogen, has fewer side effects and complications but a slightly higher pregnancy rate.

Until development of the IUD and oral contraceptives, the most common birth control devices were the condom and the diaphragm. In fact, the condom is still the leading mechanical method of conception control throughout the world (coitus interruptus is first of all methods). The condom, or rubber, is simply a thin, balloonlike rubber sheath that fits over the penis and traps the semen. Its disadvantages include a tendency to develop leaks or tears (particularly if lubricated with petroleum jelly, which dissolves the rubber), a dulling of pleasurable sensations for both partners, and the need to stop foreplay to put on the device after erection is achieved. The average pregnancy rate with condom use is 15 per 100 woman-years.

The diaphragm is a dome-shaped membrane of rubber with a metal ring around the edge, shaped to fit over the cervix and thereby block the passage of sperm. A spermicidal jelly is used to block any leaks around the diaphragm and to help hold it in place. The pregnancy rate with use of a diaphragm is 10 to 12 per 100 woman-years. Improper insertion and forgetfulness probably account for most pregnancies with this method.

Other methods of contraception are rather ineffective but are probably slightly better than nothing (Table 34.A). Spermicidal suppositories or aerosol foams may be inserted into the vagina before coitus, or the couple may use the rhythm method, which is based on abstinence during the period when ovulation is most likely to occur. Unfortunately, ovulation can occur at any time during the menstrual cycle (even during menstruation) on some occasions, so that the rhythm method usually proves little better than luck. Withdrawal just before ejaculation (coitus interruptus) is often used to avoid conception but is also very unreliable. Not only does it require good timing and strong willpower, but many active sperm may be released in drops of fluid that ooze from the penis long before ejaculation.

Many new methods of birth control are now under experimental study, including a pill that can be taken after fertilization that prevents implantation (the "morning-after" pill), a form of hormonal contraceptive that can be implanted under the skin and will remain effective for months or years, an injection of a synthetic progesterone given every 3 to 6 months, and various forms of semipermanent but reversible sterilization. A number of forms of male contraceptives are also being developed. However, it will probably be several years before any of these new methods will be made generally available.

Table 34.A
Comparison of Various Birth Control Methods

Method or Device	Way It Works	Average Pregnancy Rate (per 100 woman-years)
Sterilization	Permanently blocks egg or sperm passage	0.003
Oral contraceptive (combination type)	Prevents ovulation	0–1
Intrauterine device (IUD)	Thought to prevent implantation of egg	3–4
Diaphragm with chemical	Barrier to sperm	10–12
Condom	Prevents sperm from entering vagina	15
Rhythm	Abstinence during fertile period	14–16
Withdrawal	Ejaculation outside of vagina	16
Foams and jellies	Barrier to sperm; spermicidal	20–22

Sterilization

Oral Contraceptive

IUD

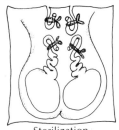

Diaphragm

Condom

Rhythm

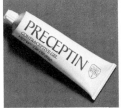

Vaginal Jelly

Douche

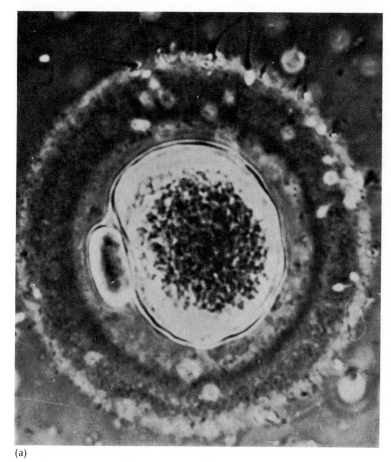

(a)

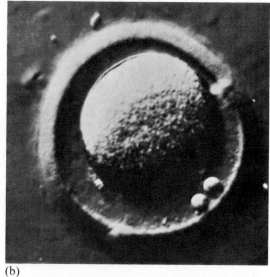

(b)

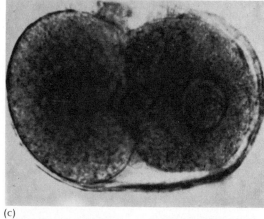

(c)

Figure 34.9   Early stages in human development.

(a)   Photomicrograph of a living human egg at the instant of fertilization. The presence of only one polar body (left) indicates that the egg still has one more meiotic division to complete. Clearly visible are numerous sperm in contact with the egg; only one sperm will penetrate the egg.

(b)   A human zygote, 12 hours after fertilization. The discarded polar bodies have been produced during meiotic division of the egg nucleus. The first cleavage of the egg typically takes place 30 hours after fertilization. (From Rugh and Shettles, 1971)

(c)   A human embryo at the two-cell stage. (Courtesy Carnegie Institution of Washington)

(d)   A human embryo after four divisions, which result in sixteen cells. Differentiation has not yet begun. (Courtesy Dr. L. B. Shettles)

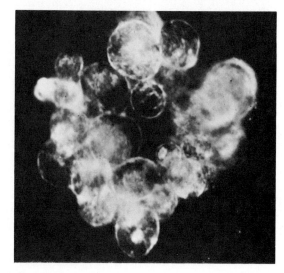

(d)

therefore is determined genetically at the moment of fertilization, depending on which of the two types of sperm reaches the egg first. For some reason—possibly a minute difference in weight or activity favoring the Y-bearing sperm—there are 106 boys for every 100 girls born in the overall population.

THE FIRST TRIMESTER OF EMBRYONIC DEVELOPMENT

The 9 months, or 266 days, of pregnancy are conveniently divided into trimesters, each consisting of 3 months. The first trimester involves basic organization from an apparently unorganized zygote into a fetus with recognizably human features. It is during this period of organ formation that drugs, viral diseases, or radiation may cause **congenital anomalies** (defects that are not heritable). These defects are brought about by certain traumatic events, including alcoholism, excess smoking, German measles, influenza, polio, and other diseases, or direct exposure of the developing embryo to excessive radiation.

There is a growing tendency to eliminate drug prescriptions for the pregnant woman because the drugs most often prescribed are tranquilizers, sedatives, and so on, all of which can affect the embryo. Recent experience with the tranquilizer thalidomide (which causes such grotesque fetal anomalies as shortening or loss of limbs, mental retardation, and so on) has greatly increased awareness of dangers in taking any drugs during pregnancy. Alcohol, in contrast to most other drugs, has its greatest effect during the third trimester, when alcohol concentrations are ten times as great in the fetus as in the mother, especially in the fetal brain and liver. After the organs have formed, they cannot be damaged so readily, but more subtle and functional defects can be caused in the second and third trimesters, affecting behavior and intelligence.

During the first month, the embryo reaches a total length of about 0.32 centimeter, or about 0.13 inch. During the first month, the embryo increases its weight about 500 times, a greater change than in any later month. Some 30 hours after fertilization, the zygote divides into two equal cells, and 10 hours later into four cells. By 70 hours, there are sixteen cells—each identical in size and appearance to the original zygote. With each cleavage, the cells become smaller and smaller. They are enclosed in a translucent membrane (the **zona pellucida**), which holds them together like parts of a mulberry. This stage is called the **morula.** While cleavages are occurring, the embryo is propelled downward through the oviduct toward the uterus, largely by means of hairlike cilia lining these cavities, but also by muscular contractions in their walls.

During the next 3 days, the morula is free within the uterine cavity, but then it finds a place to implant, usually in the posterior uterine wall. At the time of implantation, the embryo is a hollow sphere. One side of the sphere (the **trophoblast**) is thin and will give rise to the membranes that surround the embryo. The other side of the sphere is thick with cells that make up the embryo proper. The total fluid-filled sphere is called the **blastocyst.** The zona pellucida disappears, and then the trophoblast secretes an enzyme that helps it to invade and penetrate the lining of the uterus. As it does so, the blastocyst digests away some of the blood vessels in its path, so that the embryo comes to lie in a minute pool of the mother's blood. By day 12, after fertilization, implantation is completed with the aid of the uterine tissues, and the endometrium closes over the injured surface of the uterus.

Outgrowths from the trophoblast, known as **chorionic villi,** penetrate the maternal tissues and begin formation of the **placenta,** an organ mutually formed by the embryo and mother. The placenta is a transfer area for wastes and carbon dioxide from the embryo and for nutrients and oxygen from the mother to the embryo. It forms a rich network of small blood vessels from the embryonic circulatory system. These vessels penetrate the endometrial tissues and blood vessels, which then break down to form a spongy, blood-filled tissue around the placental vessels. Thus, the fetal blood is separated from maternal blood only by the walls of the fetal capillaries, and exchange of substances between the two circulatory systems is rapid and efficient. (The placenta at birth weighs about 450 grams, or about 1 pound, and is discarded, along with the umbilical cord, as the *afterbirth*.)

The human embryo makes great progress in basic development before the end of the first month. It forms a **primitive streak,** which is its main body axis, and the trophoblast begins to form membranes that enclose the embryo and protect it physically. Of the various systems, the nervous system is the first to start development. It appears as a neural plate, a neural fold, and the neural tube (day 24), which will become the brain and spinal cord and will give rise to many of the cranial and spinal nerves. The forward part of the neural tube wall thickens and the tube expands, soon (day 26) to be pinched to form four primary brain vesicles, each of which will form a specific part of the brain. Only the germ cells take precedence over brain and nervous system development. Associated with the brain are the sense organs—eyes, nose, and ears—which begin to appear at this time. Even the lens and retina of the eyes start to form.

On each side of this neural axis the embryo acquires, during this first month, thirty-two pairs of muscle blocks, or **somites,** which will give rise to most of the voluntary muscles of the body, much of the skeleton, and the skin. By day 28, there are three pairs of visceral arches on each side of the pharynx. These arches are vestiges of distant ancestry, when they were related to functioning gills. The human embryo, however, never develops gills. A membrane over the mouth ruptures in the first month, even though the organism will not take in any food for a long time.

Elements of the lower jaw appear, followed shortly by those of the upper jaw. The lung primordia (day 27), and the beginnings of trachea and bronchi (day 31) are formed. Blood cells appear in the yolk sac and in the chorionic membrane, and simultaneously (day 21) the tubular heart appears. By day 24, the heart begins to pulsate, even before it is completely developed. Its first beats are irregular and slow, but they increase over a period of weeks until they may occur as rapidly as 180 per minute. By day 27, the embryo forms a pair of primitive kidneys. Budlike thickenings develop (day 28) that will become arms. The primordia of the important endocrine organs, such as the thyroid, anterior pituitary, and pancreas all make their appearance just before the end of the first month.

The events of the second month become vastly more complex. By the end of the second month, the growing organism measures about 3 centimeters (about 1 $1/4$ inches) in total length and has small but definite limbs, a body with a distinct head, recognizable ears and nose, open but lidless eyes, and open mouth. It is entirely enclosed in a watery **amniotic sac,** which affords some physical protection against contusions, adhesions, and temperature changes. The amniotic fluid is gradually increased but is kept clean by constant exchange with the mother's circulatory system so that it is completely replaced about every 3 hours. The embryo can swallow or inhale this liquid without harm. The **umbilical cord** is now evident and joins the circulatory system of the embryo to the placenta.

During the second month, somites are added to make a total of forty-nine pairs. The germ cells reach the fetal kidney region. Arm and leg buds are distinct by day 35. The vestigial tail of earlier stages begins to be resorbed. The eyes are forming with lens and retina, the ear canals arise, and jaws develop. By day 46, the reproductive organs begin to form ovaries or testes. Before the end of the second month, fingers and toes are distinguishable on the webbed paddlelike appendages. Ossification centers appear in the jaws and clavicle region, indicating the beginning of skeletal formation. The first 3 months are generally considered to be the period of the embryo. By the end of this period, the growing organism resembles a miniature human and is called a **fetus.**

By the end of the third month, the organism is about 7 $1/2$ centimeters (3 inches) in body length (half of that length is

head) and weighs about 14 grams (about $1/2$ ounce). Its thumb and forefinger are opposed to each other, an evolutionary advantage over other vertebrates. The muscles and their nervous connections are so much better developed that the breathing, eating, and general body movements become more purposeful. Variations between fetuses begin to appear—behavior becomes individualized, particularly with regard to facial expressions. Numerous taste buds have developed—theoretically, the fetus has a keener sense of taste than it will at any future time, because many of these buds are lost during later development. Probably the most pronounced changes are seen in the reproductive and excretory systems, which arise in close proximity to each other and retain some mutual functions throughout life. X-rays show that many of the cartilage centers are changing into bone; the skeleton is forming extensively.

The third month completes the first trimester of pregnancy, and the human fetus has acquired all of its major organ systems. Although it is a functioning organism, it is still unable to survive if removed from the mother. During the second trimester, there will be refinements in all newly developing systems.

THE SECOND TRIMESTER

Although the brain starts to form at an early stage, the rest of the body grows faster than the head after the first trimester. Eventually, the head will be only 10 percent of the total body length. By the end of the fourth month, the fetus weighs 115 to 170 grams (about 4 to 6 ounces) and is 18 to 20 centimeters (7 to 8 inches) long. Its back becomes straight as the internal viscera enlarge and are enclosed by the abdominal wall, and it can hold its head erect. The skin is so well formed that the palms of the hands and soles of the feet have distinct patterns of lines that distinguish this fetus from all other humans. The fetus reacts to stimuli at first with total body response and then gradually with typical reflexes. It spontaneously stretches its arms and legs, movements that the mother may be able to feel. Its heart now pumps regularly, some 25 quarts of fluid per day (mostly recirculated blood), and this pumping can be heard with a stethoscope.

The brain is beginning to form convolutions to add to its surface area and complexity. The eyes are beginning to be light-sensitive, but the ears are not yet sensitive to sound. The placenta is now disk-shaped and covers a large portion of the inner surface of the uterus.

By the end of the fifth month, the fetus is 23 to 28 centimeters (approximately 9 to 11 inches) long and weighs about 225 grams, or half a pound. It is now freely mobile within its amniotic sac, surrounded by a quart of amniotic fluid, which is changed at the rate of about 23 liters (6

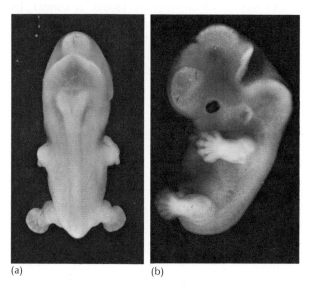

(a)   (b)

Figure 34.10 A human embryo 40 days old. Notice the paddlelike feet, the spinal cord, and the brain (a). In lateral view (b), it is possible to observe the deep cleft (isthmus) in the brain that separates the midbrain from the hindbrain. By the sixth week, finger buds have formed. (From Rugh and Shettles, 1971)

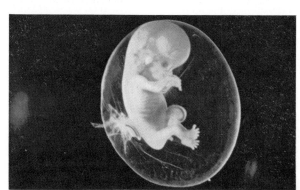

Figure 34.11 A human fetus at three months with placenta attached. By the end of the third month, the fetus is about 3 inches; the head continues to be relatively large, with a high prominent forehead, a prominent nose, external ears level with the lower jaw, and eyelids that are sealed shut. (From Rugh and Shettles, 1971)

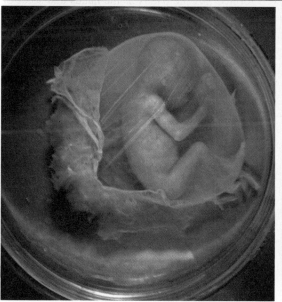

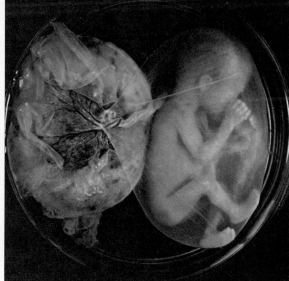

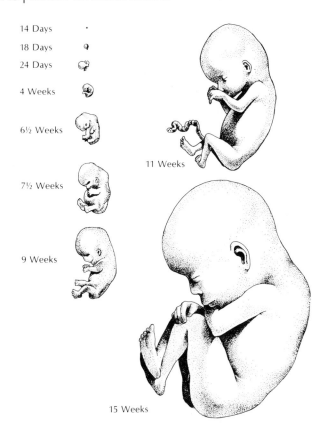

14 Days
18 Days
24 Days
4 Weeks
6½ Weeks
11 Weeks
7½ Weeks
9 Weeks
15 Weeks

Figure 34.12   A size chart comparing embryos of varying ages. It is clear that by the end of the first trimester features of the developing fetus are distinctly human in appearance.

gallons) per day. Although the 5-month fetus would appear to be fully formed, if severed from the placenta, it would be unable to survive outside the uterus. The youngest known surviving premature infant was born at 25 weeks, weighed 650 grams (about 23 ounces), and required almost complete artificial sustenance by temperature regulation, intravenous feeding, oxygen supplementation, and so on. The fetus does have complete lungs, but the alveoli are not yet functional, even though amniotic fluid is taken into the lungs. The fetus' skin is covered by a pastelike substance composed of loose cells and secretions from the sebaceous (oil) and sweat glands. This substance is protective, but the skin is not ready for the colder atmosphere. The digestive organs are well formed but are not ready to take in and digest food.

Fingernails and toenails begin to form—often, the nails must be cut at birth to keep babies from scratching themselves. Up to this time, growth and expansion have been the most prominent changes, but now some organs (particularly the skin) begin to slough off outer layers of cells and replace them with new cells.

Most exciting for the parents is the fact that kicking and turning of the fetus become almost constant during the fifth month, except during periods when it is known to be sleeping. Occasionally, the fetus will hiccough every few seconds, but such spells do not last long. Some mothers schedule their periods of sleep and rest to coincide with those of the fetus to avoid interruption of their own sleep. There is an increasing burden on the mother's lungs, heart, and kidneys as she deals with increasing loads of fetal oxygen, nutrients, and waste products.

About the sixth month (end of the second trimester), the fetus measures about 30 to 35 centimeters (12 to 14 inches) and weighs about 680 grams (1 ½ pounds). Now the fetus is a well-proportioned miniature human being and may be able to survive if delivered prematurely by Caesarean section. Its skin is red and wrinkled, and it looks rather like an old person.

While the skeleton has been developing, some of the 222 bones develop directly, without going through a cartilage phase. Skeletal formation is very active during the sixth month, and the mother must take in more calcium than she needs for herself in order to provide adequately for the mineralization of the fetal skeleton. The fetal bones are only 12 percent calcified, but this amount will increase to 90 percent in the adult.

THE THIRD TRIMESTER

The third trimester is the hardest for the pregnant woman because of the added weight of the fetus, the increased pressure on her own body organs, and the increased demands the fast-growing baby makes on her system. She must breathe, digest, excrete, and circulate blood for two individuals. The mother's blood volume at 7 months is 30 percent greater than normal, and her blood pressure and circulatory rate also are above normal. About 16 percent of the mother's blood is in her uterus and the placenta. The fetal heart beats vigorously now, but the mother's heart words harder than ever to keep her circulation and that of the placenta flowing. Breathing may become somewhat difficult because of pressure against the lungs, until the process of ''lightening'' occurs several weeks before delivery. This process involves a change of position by the fetus, moving head downward and low in the pelvis. Lightening is a great relief to the mother, particularly through relaxation of pressure on her diaphragm.

The third-trimester fetus may survive outside the uterus if it is removed by Caesarean section or by premature birth. Although only 10 percent of those delivered during the seventh month survive, the survival probability increases to 70 percent in the eighth month and 95 percent in the ninth month. In the last trimester, the fetus must obtain large amounts of calcium, iron, and nitrogen through the foods that the mother eats. During this period, 84 percent of the calcium that the mother consumes goes into the fetal skeleton. About 85 percent of the iron that she takes in goes into the hemoglobin of the fetal bloodstream. Nitrogen is needed as a major constituent of the many proteins being synthesized as the fetal nervous system and brain complete the final, rapid stages of their growth. The great importance of a proper maternal diet during the final trimester has been recognized only recently. It now appears that the tendency of persons of low socioeconomic status to have lower-than-average scores on various kinds of intelligence tests may be more closely related to maternal diet during the final trimester of pregnancy than to either genetic inheritance or postnatal education (Chapters 35 and 36).

Antibodies of the immune systems can be transmitted through the placenta between the maternal and fetal blood systems during the last trimester. Almost any infection or disease contracted by the mother—measles, mumps, whooping cough, scarlet fever, colds, or influenza—will cause her to develop antibodies against the toxins of the disease. The antibodies pass to the fetal bloodstream, giving the child the same immunity to those diseases for about 6 months after birth. But in rare cases this exchange of antibodies can have undesirable effects. If the mother has Rh⁻ blood and her husband has Rh⁺ blood, the baby can inherit the Rh⁺ factor from his father. Some of the Rh⁺ antigens may enter the mother's bloodstream during birth (they normally cannot get across the placenta during pregnancy). The mother then may form antibodies against the Rh⁺ factor. If later fetuses have Rh⁺ blood, the antibodies from the maternal bloodstream may enter the fetal bloodstream and begin to immobilize the red blood cells of the fetus, causing erythroblastosis fetalis (hemolytic disease of the newborn). Thus, second or later children of such a union have been stillborn in about 35 percent of the cases. A recently developed technique for transfusing blood of a certain type into the fetus during weeks 30 through 37 has saved most of the "Rh babies" that would otherwise have died. An even more recent discovery is a drug called Rhogam, which contains anti-Rh antibodies.

During the ninth month, the fetus often seems less active than in earlier months, because its own growth has caused it to become confined in a space that permits very little movement. By this time, the uterus may have stretched to sixty times its original size, reaching a volume of about 4 liters. Yet the smooth muscles of the uterus wall, after the baby is born, are able to contract and to return the uterus to its prepregnancy volume, about the size of an orange.

LABOR AND DELIVERY

It is possible that the placenta has a major role in determining the date of final delivery of the child. As early as the seventh month, the placenta begins to check its growth and activity. Before birth, it shows areas of degeneration and breakdown of its circulatory bed. These changes seem to force the child to seek a new environment, usually between

256 and 276 days from the time of conception, or about 280 days from the beginning of the last menstrual period. Although 75 percent of babies are born within this period, prematurity is not abnormal, particularly for third or later births. In a first-born, prematurity may be related to alcoholism, smoking, or failure of the cervix to retain the baby in the uterus.

During the ninth month, the rate of growth and development of the fetus slows. If the early growth rate continued after birth, the child would weigh 200 pounds at his first birthday. Fortunately, there is a regulating mechanism that limits growth to certain heights and weights.

The birth of the child is anticipated by certain events collectively known as labor and delivery. This is probably the single most critical period in the life of the child, emerging as it does from a warm and watery chamber into a cold, airy, and unlimited environment.

Labor is divided into three steps. *Dilatation* (lasting 2 to 16 hours) begins with the onset of labor contractions and ends with the full expansion of the cervical canal. The contractions usually last for 25 to 30 seconds and come at intervals of about 15 to 20 minutes. Toward the end of this stage is the period of "crowning," when the baby's head makes its appearance through the cervix and vaginal opening. The second or *expulsive stage* lasts from 2 to 60 minutes. Contractions at this stage last 50 to 90 seconds and may occur at 1- or 2-minute intervals. Almost immediately after the head emerges, the shoulders follow, then the whole child. The placenta, already degenerating, is disconnected when the umbilical cord is cut, and the resultant build-up of carbon dioxide in the baby's blood stimulates the respiratory center of its brain; the newborn child expands its lungs, takes its first breath, and issues its first cry—heralding its safe arrival into the external world. Occasionally, a baby may delay a bit in this response, and the obstetrician may rub its back or spank its feet, stimulating the baby to cry and thus to breathe. Almost immediately, a nurse and/or pediatrician takes the child and cleans and examines it while the obstetrician cares for the mother. The child is given the Apgar test, which evaluates its respiratory effort, muscle tone, reflex irritability, and heart rate. The pediatrician then examines the baby's heart and lungs with a special stethoscope; checks its skin, evidence of herniation, descent of testes if it is a boy, and its reflexes; and takes certain measurements. The nurse takes its footprints and on the same card usually places the mother's fingerprint so that no mixup will follow. Silver nitrate is put into the baby's eyes to prevent infections, and vitamin K is injected to regulate the blood clotting time.

The third phase is known as the *placental stage*, which involves contractions of the uterus and expulsion of fluid, blood, and the placenta, or afterbirth, from the uterus and vagina. Recovery for the mother usually is so rapid that she

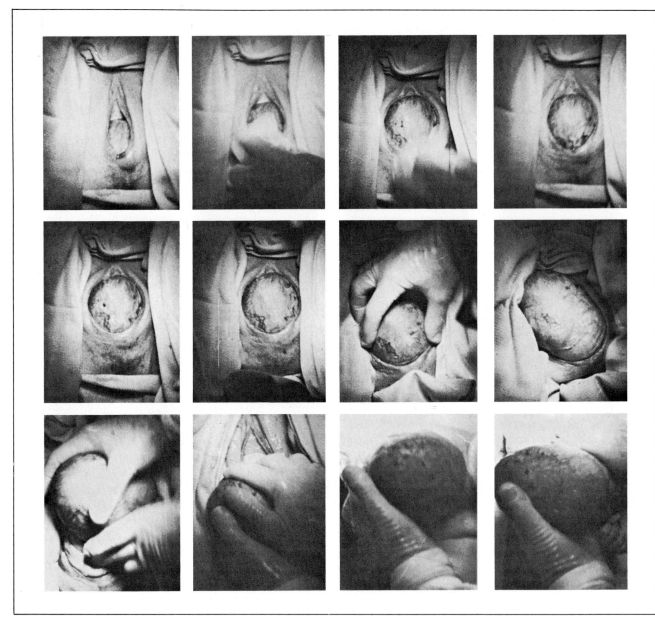

Figure 34.13   The birth of a child. (From Rugh and Shettles, 1971)

may wish to hold and even try to nurse her baby almost immediately. She often is exhilarated, forgetting almost completely the discomfort she has just experienced.

As Sigmund Freud and other psychologists have stressed, the moment of birth may be traumatic for the baby. All the systems so intricately developed over the preceding 9 months are suddenly shifted into full operational status. Without pause, the newborn child embarks on a lifelong stage of development and change, both physical and behavioral, that will terminate only with death.

MISCARRIAGE AND ABORTION

In most cases, the fertilization of an egg sets into operation the entire sequence of events described above, culminating 9 months later in the birth of a child. Occasionally, something goes wrong somewhere in the process, and the embryo or fetus is expelled from the uterus, which terminates the pregnancy. Anything that terminates a pregnancy before the child is able to survive independently is called an **abortion.** If it occurs accidentally, it is called a spontaneous abortion, or a **miscarriage.** A miscarriage can occur—often without the mother even knowing that she was pregnant—if the trophoblast invades the maternal blood vessels prematurely. Other things can go wrong with the establishment of the vital circulatory link between the embryo and the mother. If this connection is not established properly, the embryo will be rejected sooner or later because it fails to develop normally. The mother's body often seems able to recognize an embryo that is developing abnormally because of genetic or other defects, for about half of all miscarriages involve embryos with serious defects in structure or physiology. Some miscarriages in later stages of pregnancy occur because the cervix is unable to hold the fetus within the uterus. A weak cervix can now be detected long before problems occur and can be corrected surgically. There is approximately one miscarriage for each four live births in the United States.

Therapeutic abortions are performed in cases in which the fetus is believed to be abnormal or in which the birth of a child is believed to represent a serious risk to the health—mental or physical—of the mother. Laws specifying conditions under which therapeutic abortions can be performed vary from country to country. Judicial decisions in the United States have facilitated the use of abortion as an acceptable medical technique. This has led to a dramatic decline in deaths and injuries resulting from illegal and self-inflicted abortions.

Most therapeutic abortions are performed during the first trimester. A surgical procedure is employed that is normally used to obtain samples of the uterine lining or to remove unwanted substances or growths from the uterus. The cervix is distended (dilated) by using a series of metal instruments with increasing diameter. The interior of the uterus is then scraped with an instrument called a *curette*—a wide, smooth loop of steel attached to a special handle. One method gaining favor for use in very early stages of pregnancy involves a mild vacuum or suction device to pull the early embryo from the uterus.

If the operation is done by a skilled surgeon under sterile conditions, complications develop in fewer than 1 out of every 100 patients. With suitable pain-killing drugs, there is little discomfort associated with the operation. Bleeding soon stops, and the woman recovers completely within a few days. In illegal abortions, however, there is a serious risk of complications and of death. The abortionist may not be a skilled surgeon, the equipment used may be inappropriate, and conditions may be unsanitary. In such cases, the uterus may be punctured or infected, and serious injury or death is not uncommon.

PERSPECTIVE

When does a human life begin? Philosophers, theologians, doctors, and biologists have argued this question for centuries. Some say life begins at fertilization; others say it begins when implantation occurs, when the embryonic heart begins beating, or when the embryo becomes a fetus with recognizably human characteristics. Many have argued that life begins with the first independent kicks or squirms of the fetus, but others claim that life does not begin until the newborn takes its first breath and becomes relatively independent of its mother's physiological systems. To most modern biologists—particularly to embryologists—these arguments are irrelevant. *Life began only once, billions of years ago, and every modern living thing has a direct connection to that primitive life and to all of life.* Sperm and egg are every bit as much alive as the zygote that results from their fusion. But if an egg is not fertilized by a sperm within a few hours of its release from the ovary, its life is ended. Are chastity, birth control, and abortion all forms of manslaughter, then? These are questions that have no clear biological answer, but an understanding of the biological realities involved can aid individuals in forming their own personal decision. Because the answers *are* personal, one question of great social importance is the extent to which one individual's decision should be permitted to regulate another individual's right to make a different decision. This is an issue that will be addressed in Chapter 36.

SUGGESTED READINGS

MCCARY, JAMES LESLIE. *Human Sexuality.* 2nd ed. New York: D. Van Nostrand, 1973. The author explores the psychological and sociological factors of human sexuality as well as the physiological. Interesting reading.

MASTERS, WILLIAM H., and VIRGINIA E. JOHNSON. *Human Sexual Response.* Boston: Little, Brown, 1966. This classic work in the anatomy and physiology of sexual response details the processes of sexual expression in clinical terms.

RUGH, ROBERTS, and LANDRUM B. SHETTLES. *From Conception to Birth: The Drama of Life's Beginnings.* New York: Harper & Row, 1971. A detailed account of embryonic and fetal development, including more than a dozen remarkable color photographs of the developing human fetus.

Chapter 35

Human Health and Disease

These fourteenth-century portrayals of one patient being given a physical examination and another about to undergo brain surgery remind us that our capacity to deal with illness and to maintain health is a relatively recent phenomenon. But is this capacity equally available to all on the basis of need alone? And, understanding the need for maintaining health, do we all act as if our health is the prized possession we claim it to be? Or have we reached the point that many of us are our own greatest menace to our health?

For most of the several million years that human beings have walked the earth, life has centered on elementary pursuits essential for survival. Finding food, avoiding predation, and weathering the elements have been all-consuming tasks for most of human history. When disease struck, little could be done other than to endure it passively or to succumb to it. But slowly, as culture and technology accumulated, humanity turned its skills to the challenge of alleviating physical suffering. By trial and error, certain plants were found to be useful in alleviating various maladies. Edward Jenner scratched the skin of human beings with a needle dipped in the exudate of a cowpox pustule and gave humankind the means to eradicate the scourge of smallpox. Louis Pasteur, Robert Koch, and others found first one and then another disease to be associated with specific bacteria; Joseph Lister developed aseptic techniques for surgery. Slowly the tide of battle against disease began to turn.

But more progress in combating disease has been made since the start of this century than occurred in all the tens of thousands of centuries that went before. Progress has been so rapid that in Western society we now take a different approach to defining health itself. No longer are we satisfied with the negative definition of the past, in which health was considered to be the absence of incapacitating and life-threatening disease. Rather, most would now prefer to define health as the World Health Organization has suggested: a state of complete physical, mental, and social well-being.

In this chapter, we will touch briefly on some of the factors that tend to promote health, as well as on those that tend to decrease it. We will see that health is a phenotypic trait that, like any other phenotypic trait, involves an interaction between genotype and environment. We will focus on the environmental parameters that affect various aspects of this phenotypic trait. In pursuing this topic, we will encounter a series of profound paradoxes: As great as the contributions of modern technology have been in alleviating diseases, technology and the search for a better life have combined to introduce and exacerbate a new spectrum of health problems. As great as our concern for well-being may be, many of our contempory health problems are self-inflicted. Even as we have developed the capacity to prevent and cure heritable diseases, that capacity carries with it the virtual certainty of increased incidence of heritable disease. Even though one of the major public health problems of contemporary Western society is venereal disease—a disease that has ceased to be feared because it is known to be curable—it often goes uncured. And finally, the very factors that have lowered death rates around the world now threaten humanity with a potential health problem far greater in magnitude than any ever seen before—a population exploding beyond the capacity of the biosphere to maintain it.

What is the reason for these paradoxical situations? Is it that we have lost sight of the fundamental nature of life? Is it that we as a society have come to think that because we have the *capacity* to modify momentary conditions in our environment, we also have the power to escape the fundamental properties of energy and matter? Perhaps the major challenge of the future is to restore a greater measure of biological perspective to our use of technology, realizing that the search for "the good life" can be successful in the long run only to the extent that it takes into account the basic realities of the universe.

MODERN MEDICINE HAS HAD MAJOR IMPACT ON RATES AND CAUSES OF DEATH

Although human health cannot be defined merely as the absence of life-threatening disease, the causes of death and the ages at which deaths occur in a population are measures of the major disease problems within the population. For example, the death rate in the United States has undergone a continuous downward trend since the beginning of this century. Today, it is only about one-third what it was a mere seventy-five years ago. Partial insight into the reasons for this trend may be gained by examining the causes of death over this period. As Figure 35.3 shows, in 1900 infectious diseases (tuberculosis, pneumonia, diarrhea, diphtheria, and so on) accounted for 60 percent of all deaths. In contrast, by 1969 the same diseases accounted for only 6 percent of deaths. This sweeping change was brought about largely by improvements in sanitation, greater resistance to infection as a result of improved nutrition, programs of

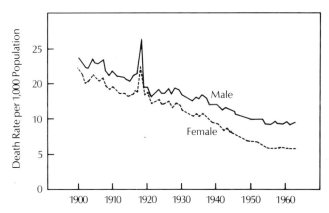

Figure 35.2 Age-adjusted death rates in the United States between 1900 and 1963. The peak occurring in 1918 was due to a severe influenza epidemic. It can be seen that even though both males and females have experienced progressively lower death rates, the trend has been much more pronounced in the case of women. Presently the death rate among females is only about two-thirds that of males.

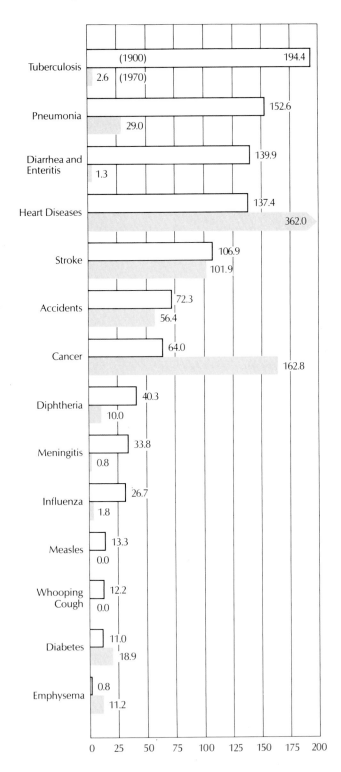

Figure 35.3   Leading causes of death in the United States, 1900 and 1970. The figures shown represent deaths per 100,000 individuals from each of the diseases. Notice the drastic decline in deaths due to infectious diseases and the rise in death rates due to cancer and heart disease.

mass immunization, and improved medical care of infected individuals. The introduction of antibiotics in the 1940s was influential in controlling bacterial diseases such as pneumonia, but their role in lowering the death rate can be greatly overstated. Significantly, several infectious diseases that were major causes of death in 1900 (tuberculosis, meningitis, and influenza) are no longer cause for widespread concern, despite the fact that they cannot be cured by antibiotics.

But even as the frequency of deaths from such diseases follows a downward trend, the frequency of deaths from afflictions of a different sort is rising to take their place. Equally evident from Figure 35.3 is the fact that two categories of disease—heart disease and cancer—have now risen to prominence as major causes of death.

Many important changes in patterns of health and disease cannot be understood from merely examining death tables. For example, such tables do not reflect the fact that in the United States in this century, average height at maturity has increased by two inches; neither do they show that many incapacitating but nonlethal nutritional diseases such as rickets, scurvy, and pellagra have all but vanished, or that tooth decay has diminished greatly. But the pattern is clear nevertheless: Medical technology has had dramatic effects on the nature of the health problems facing the members of the society.

RESULTS OF MEDICAL ADVANCES ARE NOT EQUALLY AVAILABLE TO ALL HUMAN BEINGS

The lowering of death rates in this century has had a marked effect on **life expectancy** (the number of years that an individual can be expected to live, on the average). Over the past fifty years, average life expectancy in the United States has risen by nearly seventeen years (Figure 35.4). Similar life expectancies are now seen in most of the developed nations (Table 35.1). But it has not increased equally for all members of society. First of all, life expectancy has risen much more dramatically for women than it has for men. This difference is due largely to a higher and earlier incidence of heart disease and related diseases in males (a subject to which we will return later.) It is equally obvious that there is a difference in life expectancy between black and white members of society. Although the percentage increase in life expectancy has been greater for blacks than for whites over the past fifty years, it is still true that blacks of either sex can be expected to die five to six years sooner than their white counterparts.

What is the reason for this discrepancy? Insight into the question comes from analysis of causes of deaths in the two groups. The diseases that have declined so sharply in the overall population (Figure 35.3) take a higher toll of black individuals. Tuberculosis is three times as common as a

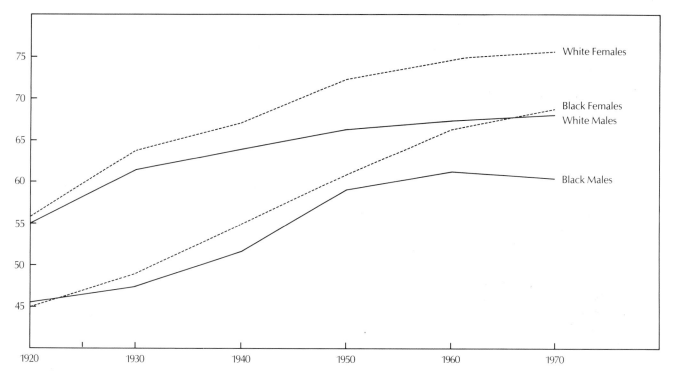

Figure 35.4   Changes in life expectancy at birth by sex and race in the United States, 1920–1970.

cause of death in blacks as it is in whites. Influenza and pneumonia are more than half again as common, and infectious childhood diseases claim two and a half times as large a percentage of black infants as they do white infants of the same age. Because these diseases have been shown to be manageable under appropriate environmental conditions and with adequate medical care, the conclusion seems inescapable: Living in a society with technical skills does not ensure an individual access to those skills. Access to health historically has been proportional to wealth.

This picture becomes more clear when we compare statistics from different countries. For example, Figure 35.5 compares the relative frequencies of deaths from five causes in the United States and in Mexico. It can be seen that the pattern of mortality in Mexico at present resembles that of the United States many years ago. This pattern becomes even more exaggerated when we examine death rates in less highly developed countries. From such observations, we can draw the following conclusion: *The major causes of death in the world population are those that we already know how to prevent or cure.* Thus, on a world-wide basis, the major human health problems relate to nonuniform delivery of existing health care practices—not to the development of new medical skills.

Export of medical technology from the highly developed countries has been under way for some time. As a result,

Table 35.1

Life Expectancy for Men and Women in Seventeen Western Countries (1968)

Country	Life Expectancy (years)	
	Men	Women
Australia	67.1	72.4
Canada	68.4	74.2
Czechoslovakia	67.2	72.8
Denmark	70.4	73.8
England	68.0	73.9
France	67.2	74.1
Iceland	70.7	75.0
Israel	70.9	73.0
Japan	67.2	72.1
The Netherlands	71.4	74.8
New Zealand	68.2	72.8
Norway	71.1	74.7
Puerto Rico	67.3	72.1
Sweden	71.3	75.4
Switzerland	69.5	74.8
United States	66.6	73.4
West Germany	66.9	72.3

Source: Public Health Service.

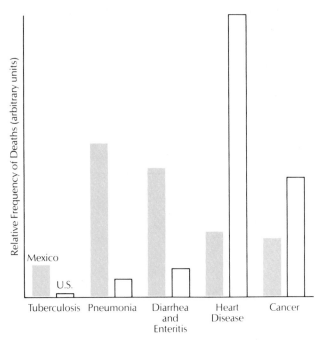

Figure 35.5   Relative frequency of deaths from five categories of disease in Mexico and the United States. The average life expectancy in Mexico is sixty-one years; in the United States it is seventy-one years.

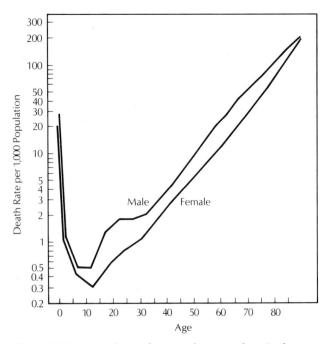

Figure 35.6   Annual mortality rates by age and sex in the United States, 1963. The vertical scale in this figure is logarithmic.

death rates have fallen and life expectancies have risen appreciably around the globe. This has already led to explosive rates of increase in population size in country after country. Simple calculations demonstrate that if death control is achieved everywhere to the extent that it has been in the countries listed in Table 35.1, humanity must soon come to grips with a problem of major dimensions: finding enough food to feed the world population. This must not be interpreted to mean that such medical aid should be withheld. It means that we must recognize the nature of the problem in advance in order to find a solution that is ethically as well as biologically right. This topic is treated in greater depth in Chapters 36 and 37.

So far, we have talked only about death rates averaged for individuals of all ages. But a look at Figure 35.6 shows clearly that death rates vary strongly with age, as do the causes of death and the severity of a variety of nonfatal health problems. Therefore, let us move on to an analysis of the major health problems encountered during various periods of life, starting with birth.

INFECTION, NUTRITION, AND HEREDITY DETERMINE THE HEALTH OF THE NEWBORN

As Figure 35.6 shows, even today in highly developed nations death claims many children before their first birthday. In fact, not again until the individual reaches the age of sixty-five does the probability of dying within the year become as high as it is at birth. Even so, the death rate in newborns has dropped more dramatically than the death rate for any other age group in the last three generations (Figure 35.7). Indeed, this decline in infant mortality is the major reason that death rates have fallen and life expectancy has risen for the population as a whole. (Once again, infant mortality is 50 percent higher in black Americans than it is in white Americans. And in most of Latin America, Africa, and Asia, infant mortality is presently as high as it was in the United States forty or fifty years ago.)

About 70 percent of all infant deaths occur in the first month of life. Many are the result of developmental abnormalities that cannot be remedied. But **asphyxia** (inadequate oxygen supply) just before or during birth and complications resulting from low birth weight account for most of the others.

Asphyxia not only is a major source of infant mortality, it is a major cause of mental retardation and cerebral palsy. It may result from inadequate blood supply to the uterus, from inadequate exchange of oxygen between maternal and fetal blood, or from compression of the umbilical cord during the birth process. The occurrence of such a disorder can be detected by careful monitoring during labor (Chapter 34), and if the infant is delivered immediately and is provided with oxygen, the symptoms can be prevented.

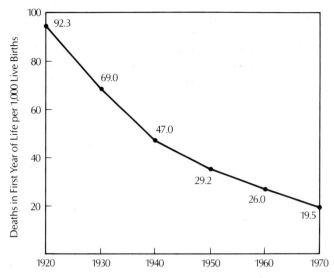

Figure 35.7   Changes in infant death rates in the United States, 1920–1970.

The average birth weight in the United States at present is 3,250 grams. Babies weighing less than 2,500 grams are said to be *at hazard,* which means that the likelihood of serious postnatal problems is increased. The causes of low birth weight are many. The most obvious is **prematurity** (birth appreciably before the usual period of about 280 days after conception). But **dysmaturity** (inadequate intrauterine development) is also important. Mothers who are under nineteen years of age, smoke cigarettes, use drugs, or are undernourished during pregnancy are much more likely to give birth to smaller babies. Abnormalities of the fetus or of the placenta are other common causes of dysmaturity. One of the most common difficulties of premature infants is hyaline membrane disease, which causes severe respiratory difficulties. Babies born with this disorder require careful observation and support if they are to survive. A major decrease in infant mortality has been accomplished by developing procedures for dealing with the spectrum of problems that follow immediately after birth.

The remainder of the reduction in infant mortality has been achieved largely by control of otherwise fatal infectious diseases. Yet infectious disease is still the prime threat to the health and well-being of the infant, particularly after the first few weeks. Among the most important killers in the first years of life are whooping cough, measles, pneumonia, and meningitis (an infection of the linings around brain and spinal column).

The Newborn Infant Is Immunologically Immature

Thrust from the womb into the outside world, the newborn child is incompletely prepared to meet the challenges of an environment teeming with potential parasitic microorgan-

isms. The capacity to make antibodies against disease organisms, and thus to develop immunity, is not fully developed, nor will it be for some weeks or months. Thus the newborn is dependent upon two sources of protection derived from the mother. During life in the uterus, antibodies from the mother's bloodstream pass the placenta and are accumulated in the infant's blood. If the child is suckled rather than being bottle-fed, the antibodies gained in intrauterine life are supplemented. The secretion of the mammary glands for the first two to four days is very different from the milk that eventually replaces it. Called **colostrum**, it is rich in proteins and, most notably, in antibodies that provide protection against intestinal diseases leading to diarrhea.

Together these antibodies provide critical protection for the infant. It has been shown in experimental animals deprived of both sources of maternal antibodies that even *Escherichia coli*—which would otherwise become a peaceful resident of the gut—uniformly becomes a fatal disease-causing organism that the body has no capacity to resist. (The protective action of colostrum is but one reason that many physicians are now reversing earlier trends and are strongly recommending breast-feeding.) Maternal antibodies begin to break down and disappear well before the infant's own immune system is mature. It is in this critical transition period that infections of all kinds may be life-threatening and must be quickly recognized and treated medically if the infant is to reach the first birthday. And it is in availability of this kind of continuing diagnosis and treatment that major differences are seen in different socioeconomic groups.

Bacterial residents can cause disease by three major routes. In some cases, such as pneumonia, the bacterial invaders and their products accumulate in such mass that they interfere physically with the performance of vitally important bodily functions (breathing, in the case of pneumonia). In other cases, such as tetanus, the disease organisms produce and release products known as **toxins** that adversely affect functioning of vital organs. In the immunologically mature individual, protective antibodies are made against both the bacteria and the toxins; in the immature infant, neither are made in sufficient quantities to prevent illness. Finally, there is another class of disease, typified by tuberculosis, in which most of the disease symptoms are created as a by-product of the immune system trying in vain to destroy an invader that has effective defense mechanisms of its own. (The waxy coat of the tubercle bacillus shields it from effective destruction by antibodies and immune cells.) Such disease symptoms do not develop prior to development of the immune system, even though the disease organism may be present and growing. Most of these bacterial diseases can be brought under control by medical means, using antibiotics and other chemotherapeutic drugs. (Even so, antibiotics serve as a potent selective force and have led to the evolution of resistant strains that are causing ever greater medical difficulties.)

But another class of infectious agents—the **viruses**—is outside the reach of antibiotics. Bacteria are autonomous. They possess the full range of machinery required for reproduction. And many of their life processes are sufficiently different from the host's life processes that they can be selectively blocked. But viruses are not autonomous—they are obligate intracellular parasites that use the host cell's own machinery to reproduce (Chapter 4). Hence the approach used to attack bacterial parasites is ineffective against viruses.

Penicillin kills bacteria because it blocks cell wall synthesis—a process many bacteria require but animal cells do not. Streptomycin, another antibiotic, disrupts normal protein synthesis in bacteria without affecting the host's cells because of the differences between bacterial ribosomes and mammalian ribosomes. But the ribosomes the virus uses for protein synthesis are those of the host. To block their functioning would kill the host. Thus viral diseases are a major threat to the infant.

Although vaccination has brought many formerly devastating viral diseases such as smallpox and poliomyelitis under control, it is of no use to attempt vaccination in the infant before the immune system is achieving maturity. But once it has matured, a program of vaccination against diphtheria, whooping cough, tetanus, and poliomyelitis can be initiated in the third month of life and will be of vital importance to the child.

As the acute problems presented by birth trauma and infection are brought more and more under control, attention is focusing to an increasing extent on diseases of intrinsic, rather than extrinsic origin: heritable or genetic diseases.

Inborn Errors of Metabolism Pose a Threat to Many Infants

As was pointed out in Chapter 16, the concept that genes control the nature of specific enzymes was first developed by Archibald Garrod, who worked with hospitalized children suffering from heritable diseases. It is now estimated that one-tenth of all the children admitted to hospitals in the United States each year are victims of disorders with a genetic basis. More than 1,800 human diseases have been described that appear to be genetically determined. We can do no more here than give a brief overview of some of the more common types and the steps that are being taken to diagnose, treat, or prevent them.

Genetic disorders are known that fall into several of the categories of mutations discussed in Chapter 16: *dominant*

traits, *recessive traits*, *sex-linked traits*, and *traits due to imbalance in chromosome number*. (Examples of certain of these diseases are described in Chapter 16.) But perhaps the most frequently seen is the recessive type, in which both parents are disease-free, apparently normal heterozygous carriers, and only their homozygous offspring suffer disease symptoms.

One example of a disease with a recessive genetic basis is **phenylketonuria**, which causes severe symptoms if undiagnosed but virtually none if properly diagnosed and treated early. The gene involved in this disease codes for the enzyme *phenylalanine hydroxylase,* which catalyzes one step in the breakdown of the amino acid phenylalanine. About one person in a hundred bears a mutant gene at this locus, which codes for a nonfunctional enzyme. In the presence of a normal gene, the mutant gene does not express itself (the enzyme produced by the normal gene is sufficient to meet body needs). But as a result of random mating (see the discussion of the Hardy-Weinberg equilibrium, Chapter 32), about 1 child in every 40,000 born has two mutant genes (is homozygous). In the absence of functional phenylalanine hydroxylase, and in the absence of specific treatment, excess phenylalanine and alternate metabolic products build up in the body to toxic levels, despite the excretion of phenylketones in the urine (which is the basis for the term "phenylketonuria"). Other metabolic pathways are affected in turn, resulting in progressive, severe brain damage and irreversible mental retardation. But the infant bearing the disease can be readily detected very early in life by either measuring the level of phenylalanine in the blood or checking the urine for the presence of phenylketones. And if the disease is detected, treatment is simple and fully effective. If the infant's diet simply provides only as much phenylalanine as the body requires—and no excess—few or no disease symptoms develop! Because the symptoms are so devastating if untreated and yet so easily prevented, most states now require testing of all newborns for phenylketonuria.

Galactosemia is a genetic disease in which one of the enzymes required to metabolize the galactose derived from milk sugar is missing. It resembles phenylketonuria in that it is treatable by diet. The blindness and widespread tissue damage that occur in an untreated infant can be completely prevented if the child homozygous for the mutant genes is identified and provided a dietary substitute for milk. Certain genetic diseases, such as diabetes, can be treated by supplying the deficient gene product (insulin in this case). Others can be treated with specific drugs of one sort or another.

Unfortunately, most genetic diseases are not subject to such simple manipulation of the environment to prevent phenotypic expression of the genotype. For example, in sickle-cell anemia (discussed in some detail in Chapter 32), the children bearing the disease can be readily identified, but no phenotypic cure for the disease exists. By adopting a protected childhood and thereby avoiding exposure to cold, infections, or the vigorous exercise or accidental injury that might trigger a painful episode of severe sickling and subsequent tissue damage, the victim can minimize some of the disease symptoms. But the afflicted individual is by no means likely to become free of the symptoms of the disease.

Research is under way to find phenotypic cures for many of the as-yet-uncurable genetic diseases. But meanwhile, much effort is being directed toward aiding known carriers of certain mutations in efforts to avoid bearing a homozygous offspring with the disease symptoms. One recent advance involves early detection (in the uterus) of fetuses bearing certain devastating genetic defects. When both parents are known to be carriers of a particular mutation, this procedure can be used to distinguish normal or heterozygous fetuses from those homozygous for one mutant gene, thereby giving the parents a better basis on which to decide whether the fetus should be permitted to complete development and be born. The technique employed is called **amniocentesis** (Figure 35.8). In amniocentesis, cells derived from the fetus are removed from the uterus by withdrawing a sample of the fluid in which the fetus is floating. These cells are then grown in culture dishes. In many cases, the chromosomal abnormality or biochemical defect that is associated with specific disease symptoms can be detected in the cultured cells. If the disease is one with devastating symptoms that cannot be relieved medically, more and more parents are finding abortion (Chapter 34) an acceptable alternative. But if the disease is less severe or, occasionally, is subject to therapy, the decision becomes more difficult. The ethical aspects of this and other forms of genetic counseling are dealt with more thoroughly in Chapter 36.

One irony, of course, is that the more proficient we become at curing and selectively avoiding genetic defects, the more prevalent they will become. It is obvious that if children who would once have died of a genetic disease before reproducing are rescued medically and are provided a normal life, they will contribute genes to the future gene pool in greater proportions. What is perhaps less clear is that such processes as selective abortion of homozygous individuals will also tend to increase the frequency of the corresponding genes in the pool. Experience has already shown that in many cases parents who had previously avoided bearing children for fear of producing a defective child will establish more typical reproductive aspirations and produce somewhat greater numbers of heterozygous carriers if they can be assured that they will not give birth to a homozygous, diseased child. Now, the rate of such

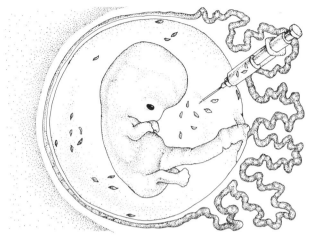

Figure 35.8   Amniocentesis. A sterile needle is inserted through the body wall and uterine wall into the amniotic cavity surrounding the fetus, taking care to avoid the placenta. A small sample of fluid is withdrawn, which invariably contains a few suspended cells derived from the skin and lungs of the fetus. These cells can then be grown in the laboratory and studied to determine whether they possess the biochemical abnormalities associated with any particular genetic disease.

increases can be shown to be extremely slow in all cases (see selection curves for rare genes, Figure 32.6), but the increases will surely occur and the frequency of genetically determined problems will slowly but surely rise.

NUTRITION AND ENVIRONMENT OF THE NEWBORN HAVE LONG-LASTING IMPLICATIONS

The milk of a well-nourished, healthy mother provides a nearly perfect diet for the newborn child. Always available, fresh, free of bacterial contaminants, and at body temperature, it provides nearly all the essential nutrients the child requires in proper proportions. (Only vitamins C and D and iron may be required from some supplemental source.) But the nourishment of the mother during the lactation (nursing) period may play a role of major consequence in the life of the child.

Controlled studies of experimental animals have shown that those borne by mothers or suckled by mothers whose diet was deficient in protein have failed to undergo normal brain development after birth. Not only was brain size permanently reduced (relative to body size), capacity for learned behavior was irreversibly diminished relative to the capacity of genetically identical animals whose mothers were given adequate protein. No amount of training could bring the performance level of the deprived animals up to that of their normal relatives.

Such controlled experimentation on genetically identical humans obviously is not possible. But several lines of evidence suggest that a similar dependence of mental development on maternal nutrition probably exists. The human brain shows two bursts of cell division and one continuous period of growth. The production of glial cells and much of the increase in brain size occur after birth. During the first six months after birth, the brain increases by about 50 percent in size. But it is not simply in size that the brain is developing in the first two years of life: There is normally an extensive increase in the number of synaptic connections being made, and conduction rates of neurons increase greatly. Severe malnutrition during this period can be catastrophic, but less severe malnutrition probably has the same sort of prolonged effects upon brain performances seen in laboratory animals.

Nutrition is by no means the only determinant of the rate and extent of neurological development in the newborn. Studies with several species of experimental animals have shown that sensory stimulation during critical periods of neonatal life is essential to the development of brain function. Animals raised in uniformly gray environments are unable to distinguish shapes as adults; those raised with only horizontal stripes are unable as adults to learn behavioral tasks that require recognition of vertical patterns *(Interleaf 26.2)*.

Field studies on human children clearly demonstrate a similar relationship between early stimulation and later mental performance. In one set of studies, a large number of economically deprived urban families with newborn infants were divided into two carefully matched groups. The infants in the experimental group were visited once a week over a period of some months during the first two years of life. They were held and were exposed to music, colorful picture books, and so on for merely one hour per visit. The control group was unaware of its involvement in the experiment and was left to its own family patterns. Then the performance of the children from both groups was followed when they entered school, years later. There was a clearly significant difference in performance of the two groups, as judged by several different criteria. Those whose early sensory stimulation had been supplemented performed at considerably higher levels by all criteria. But the amazing thing is that the major effects of stimulation during the first two years of life were not seen until adolescence, when there is normally additional physiological maturation of the brain induced by the sex hormones. Parallel studies showed that no amount of intervention after two years of age had the equivalent effect. The conclusion drawn from these studies is that the first two years of life (perhaps less) constitute a critical period in which important brain connections that will be completed only much later are initiated. If such development does not occur in this time period, it cannot occur later.

Finally, there is one other aspect of childhood that has far-reaching implications in terms of future health. Recent research has shown that it is during childhood that the body determines the number of fat cells, or adipocytes, that will be present throughout life. The child who overeats develops many more adipocytes than the child who eats only enough to maintain normal rates of growth. In later life, these adipocytes act as continuous reservoirs for dietary energy, lowering blood levels of nutrients and thereby stimulating appetite. The result is obesity. And, as we will see, obesity is one of the major determinants of health in the adult.

Feeding patterns during childhood establish qualitative as well as quantitative aspects of future food consumption. Strong food preferences or dislikes are readily established during childhood, and they are likely to have long-lasting influences. It has been shown that individuals with strong inflexible food prejudices are less likely to choose a balanced diet spontaneously than those lacking such prejudices.

VENEREAL DISEASE AND DRUG ABUSE ARE GROWING SOCIAL PROBLEMS

In an era and in a country in which infectious bacterial diseases have been abolished as major causes of death, it is somewhat incredible to find easily curable bacterial diseases—the venereal diseases—a major public health problem. But that is the situation in the United States today. And in an era when drugs have been responsible for the abolition of so much human suffering, it is ironic to find drugs—that is, drug abuse—as one of the major sources of human suffering. But that is the situation in America today.

Venereal diseases are infectious diseases that are primarily transmitted during sexual intercourse, homosexual relations, and other sexual activity. Syphilis and gonorrhea are by far the two most common and fearsome diseases of this category in Western society. Although other types of genital infections are known, it is for these two that the common use of the term "venereal disease," or VD, is reserved.

The New and Current Epidemic of Gonorrhea

In the late 1950s, after a decade of encouraging control of venereal disease through antibiotics, the venereal disease **gonorrhea** began showing dramatic increases until it has now reached epidemic proportions. In most communities, gonorrhea cases alone outnumber all other reportable infectious diseases combined. There will be more than 2 million new cases of venereal disease in the United States this year, and the rate of increase of cases among persons fifteen to nineteen years of age will be greater than for all other age groups. Currently, one of every fifty teenagers contracts gonorrhea.

The organism causing gonorrhea is the gonococcus, or *Niesseria gonorrhoeae*. In smears taken from the urinary tract of an infected individual, it is found within white blood cells. There the organisms are typically grouped as pairs, or diplococci, looking like coffee beans set side to side. The infection is transmitted through homosexual as well as heterosexual contacts. The organism usually finds its entry in the mucous membranes of the urethra, the cervix of the uterus, or the rectum. The cunjunctivae of the eyes and the lining membranes of the pharynx are occasionally the sites of primary infection. The organism is unable to penetrate intact, normal skin. In men, first symptoms occur after an incubation period of from two to five days. These symptoms typically are pain upon urination and the development of a profuse yellow discharge from the penis. The infection spreads into adjoining tissues through lymphatic channels and the bloodstream. Often the prostate and epididymis are involved. Scarring caused by the disease in the epididymis may lead to sterility.

The discomfort of the first manifestations of the disease in males causes them to seek treatment early. In the female, however, the situation is quite different. The large majority of women will have no complaints. Only rarely is there increased frequency of urination, pain, or vaginal discharge due to gonorrhea. As a result, many women with the infection are not treated and continue to spread the organism by infecting their sexual partners. It is therefore very important for women who have had exposure to infected male or female partners to be tested for presence of the disease. A major reason for the continuing epidemic proportions of the disease lies in the fact that many women (lacking symptoms) go untreated.

Gonorrheal infection in the female not infrequently spreads through lymphatic channels in the uterus to the fallopian tubes, producing a localized infection called *salpingitis*. The result of untreated infection at this site is partial or complete obstruction of the tubes—a defect responsible for sterility or enhanced likelihood of tubal pregnancy (development of the fetus in the fallopian tubes rather than in the uterus). Pregnant women with gonorrhea have unusually high rates of spontaneous abortion, prematurity, and stillbirth.

In both sexes, gonococcal infection may spread to other organs and sites. Such infection occurring on joint surfaces causes a form of arthritis that may be painful and destructive. Less frequently, the organism produces infections of the heart valves (endocarditis) and of the lining membranes

of the spinal canal (meningitis). A particularly dreaded and unfortunate event in the past was infection of the membranes of the eyes of newborn babies, produced during the birth process in women with pelvic infection. Blindness resulted in many children. A nineteenth-century German physician, Karl Crede, first proposed that a dilute solution of silver nitrate be put into the eyes of newborns, a procedure that even today affords effective protection against gonococcal conjunctivitis and the resultant blindness.

Unfortunately, gonorrhea produces little if any immunity to subsequent reinfection. Repeated attacks are common, particularly in sexually active younger persons.

Treatment of this disease was unsatisfactory and relatively ineffective prior to the beginning of the antibiotic era. Today the physician is able, by appropriate choice of antibiotic, to provide prompt relief of symptoms and eradication of infection. Nevertheless, therapeutic management is sometimes complicated by the fact that antibiotic-resistant organisms have evolved.

Syphilis: A Multistage Disease

Although the frequency of the venereal disease **syphilis** is less than one-tenth as great as that of gonorrhea, its severe disease symptoms make it a source of considerable concern. The spiral-shaped bacterium (spirochete) that causes syphilis is called *Treponema pallidum*. It does not long survive the drying effects of air, but it will grow profusely in the warm, moist tissues of the body. The mucous membranes of the genital tract, the rectum, and the mouth are ideal breeding grounds for the organism. The disease begins when a spirochete enters the mucous membrane or a tiny break in the skin. The infected person may show no sign of the disease for ten to ninety days. When he does, the sign is in the form of a *chancre*, an open lump or swelling about the size of a dime or smaller, teeming with spirochetes. The sore often appears at the site of infection, usually in the genital region—on the shaft of the penis or on the vulva. Unfortunately, it can also develop out of sight: deep in the recesses of the vagina, the rectum, or the male urethra, and never be noticed. Thus many infected persons—women in particular—never know they have the disease during the initial phase. But visible or hidden, the chancre is dangerously infectious and readily transmits the organism from person to person.

At this stage, a diagnosis can easily be made by a doctor and the disease can then be treated. Even without treatment, the chancre disappears within several weeks, thereby giving the infected person a false sense of security. But, in fact, the infection has entered the bloodstream and the spirochetes are being carried to all parts of the body. The primary stage of syphilis has ended, and the secondary stage has begun.

Secondary-stage symptoms (perhaps a skin rash, small

lesions, low-grade fever, whitish patches in the mouth and throat, and loss of hair) appear anywhere from a few weeks to several months and occasionally even a year after the appearance of the chancre. The symptoms vary greatly in intensity. Many people show no symptoms at all; others become disabled. The symptoms may last only a few days or may persist for several months. If lesions develop, they may heal and leave no scars even without treatment, again lulling the afflicted person into concluding the disease has passed.

During the secondary stage, the disease is more contagious than at any other phase of its development. All the lesions are filled with spirochetes; hence any contact with open lesions—even without sexual intercourse—can transmit the disease.

The third stage of syphilis is called the latent period because all signs and symptoms of the disease disappear. Nevertheless, the spirochetes are actively invading various organs, including the heart and the brain. This phase of the disease usually lasts only a few months, but it can also last for twenty years or until the end of life. In this stage, the infected individual appears disease-free and is usually not infectious, with one important exception: a pregnant woman can pass the infection to her unborn child. Although there are no symptoms, a blood test during this stage will reveal syphilis.

The late stage of syphilis generally begins ten to twenty years after the beginning of the latent phase, but it can occasionally occur much earlier. For the infected person, it is the most dangerous stage of the disease. The disabling effects of late syphilis depend on which organ or organs the spirochetes settle into during the latent period. In late syphilis, 23 out of every 100 untreated patients become incapacitated. They develop serious cardiovascular diseases or progressive brain or spinal cord damage that leads to blindness, insanity, or crippling.

Syphilis is easily cured with antibiotics when treatment is begun in the first two stages or even in the latent phase. Unfortunately, an individual can be infected with this disease over and over again—syphilis confers no immunity to succeeding infections, and there are no preventive vaccines.

Drug Abuse: A Self-Inflicted Problem of Increasing Seriousness

The word **drug** refers to any biologically active substance that is foreign to the body and that is deliberately introduced to affect its functioning. The development of specific drugs to cure diseases to relieve symptoms has contributed importantly to the improved health of human beings around the world. But an offshoot has been the production of a drug-conscious culture that—contrary to frequently expressed opinions—knows no generation gap. Got a headache? Pop an aspirin! Got an upset stomach from eating foods your system can barely tolerate? Pop an antacid! Got a big test coming up? Pop a dexie! But any drug (or any other substance) can be harmful to the human body if taken in large enough doses, too often, or in an impure form. Those drugs now considered to be a particular health problem are the ones that primarily affect the mind. On being taken into the body, they can temporarily change a person's perceptions, mood, or behavior. These are the so-called *psychoactive drugs.*

The major drugs in the psychoactive category are alcohol, nicotine, caffeine, barbiturates, tranquilizers, amphetamines, cocaine, marijuana, narcotics (opium, morphine, heroin), LSD and other psychedelics, and antidepressants. Such miscellaneous substances as glue, gasoline, antihistamines, morning glory seeds, nutmeg, and others also have exhibited psychoactive properties. In recent years, psychoactive drugs are being used increasingly in the United States. Accompanying this rise has been a noticeable increase in drug abuse. **Drug abuse** is excessive use of any drug to the point that it measurably damages health or impairs social or vocational adjustment.

One of the major hazards involved in using durgs to alter perception, mood, or behavior is that a stage may be reached where the individual is compelled to continue using the drug in order to maintain the state of well-being it produces. At this point, the user is said to be psychologically dependent on the drug, or **habituated** to it. When deprived of the drug, the habituated person becomes restless, irritable, uneasy, or anxious. Another characteristic of persistent drug use is that the user often develops drug **tolerance:** The body becomes adapted to it from daily use of large and increasing amounts, and the individual requires ever increasing doses to create the same responses that a smaller dose once elicited. Tolerance also means that the individual can withstand larger and larger doses without the acutely damaging effects. For example, the long-term heroin or alcohol addict can tolerate dosages that would be fatal to the new or moderate user.

Tolerance may develop with drugs that bring psychological dependence, but it always occurs with **addiction,** or physical dependence. Physical dependence takes roughly six or more weeks and results from an alteration in the physiological state of the user. The body now requires continual administration of the drug in order to prevent an extremely painful syndrome known as withdrawal illness, or abstinence syndrome. **Withdrawal** is a temporary physical illness that occurs when someone who is physically dependent on a drug no longer receives it or has a sharp reduction in the amount the body has chosen to tolerate. The delirium tremens (DTs) attack of the alcoholic represents his withdrawal syndrome: hallucinations, nausea, vomiting, tremors, and convulsions are some of the main symptoms. In some cases, death follows.

Fortunately, although almost anything can produce psychological dependence, physical dependence can occur only with central nervous system depressants: alcohol, opium and related narcotics, and sedatives such as barbiturates. The narcotics carry with them the greatest risk of addiction, followed by alcohol and barbiturates.

The physiological effects of psychoactive drugs are relatively unexplored. It is believed that psychoactive drugs affect behavior by somehow blocking, altering, or replacing neurotransmitters. Amphetamines, for example, have a chemical structure closely resembling that of norepinephrine. Thus, it is probable that they act as analogs to the neurotransmitter either by performing the same task—"energizing" the same neural centers and neural networks—or by keeping the transmitter-destroying substance so busy that the natural transmitter is protected and thus made more effective. Conversely, drugs such as tranquilizers may act to deplete the neurotransmitter and thus to "slow things down."

Alcoholism: Legal Drug Abuse

By far the largest drug abuse problem in the United States today is alcoholism. It is estimated that there are between 9 million and 10 million people whose drinking is associated with serious problems.

When used in moderation, alcohol can reduce anxiety and tension while providing feelings of relaxation and well-being. These effects help explain why alcohol has been accepted in so many cultures. Nevertheless, few societies have been able to enjoy the benefits of alcohol without complications that are inherent in its intoxicating properties. Alcohol is a systemic drug, carried by the bloodstream to act on the central nervous system with both psychological and physiological consequences. Pharmacologically alcohol is a tranquilizer, a depressant, and an anesthetic. It may seem at times that the drug is a stimulant because it can spark conversation and activity in a social setting. But in fact, such mood changes are induced because alcohol depresses the part of the brain that suppresses impulsive behavior and is involved in judgment and memory. It also depresses the motor control centers in the cortex and medulla, resulting in impairment of motor coordination.

Besides its effects on the nervous system, even moderate doses of alcohol can affect the cardiovascular system by increasing the heart rate and dilating blood vessels near the skin. This vasodilation gives the drinker an illusion of feeling warmer, although he is actually losing heat more rapidly from his body. Alcohol has no direct effect on coronary circulation, but cardiovascular abnormalities do occur in chronic heavy drinkers, largely as a secondary result of malnutrition and vitamin deficiency.

Because alcohol supplies calories, it is often used in place of food and has a tendency to depress the appetite. But it does not supply essential vitamins and amino acids. As a result, a variety of disorders and illnesses are frequently associated with chronic drinking, including vitamin deficiencies, fatty deposits throughout the body, and a degenerative disease of the liver known as cirrhosis.

Smoking: The Man-made Epidemic

Since cigarette smoking became a national habit about sixty years ago, lung cancer has grown from a relatively rare disease to the killer of more than 55,000 Americans in 1969. Bronchitis, emphysema, heart disease, and cancer of the kidney, pancreas, and bladder also have been on the rise, thanks in part to tobacco smoking.

Studies in which selected groups of people (including physicians, war veterans, and industrial workers) were observed for as long as ten years dramatically revealed the body-damaging, life-shortening effects of excessive cigarette smoking (Figure 35.9). Cigarette smokers were found to have a 30 to 80 percent greater overall mortality rate than nonsmokers, all death causes considered, and the rate differences depended on how much or how long the subjects had been smoking.

This excessive mortality rate was caused by a variety of diseases, but 80 percent of the increase was tied to lung cancer, chronic bronchitis, emphysema, other respiratory ailments, plus heart disease. Lung cancer incidence was eleven times greater, death from pulmonary diseases six times more frequent, and coronary artery disease almost two times more numerous than for nonsmoking subjects. From the increased mortality rate ascribed to smoking, it is clear that smokers are their own worst enemy. Recent data also indicate that harmful effects occur in the unborn child of the smoking woman. Smoking mothers have twice as many stillbirths and spontaneous abortions and more premature babies than nonsmokers. Furthermore, babies born to women who smoke during pregnancy are on the average 100 to 250 grams lighter than babies born to nonsmoking mothers. How tobacco affects the fetus is not known. It has been suggested that the oxygen supply to the fetus may be reduced by carbon monoxide (one of the gases found in cigarette smoke) poisoning the red blood cells, or by nicotine constricting the arteries and reducing placental blood flow.

Nicotine is the psychoactive component of cigarette

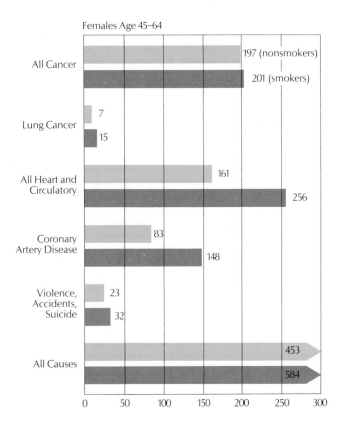

Females Age 45–64

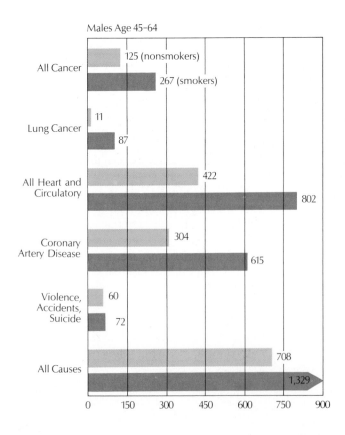

Males Age 45–64

Figure 35.9 *Mortality rates of cigarette smokers versus nonsmokers by selected diseases related to smoking (rates per 100,000 person-years).*

smoke. Like other psychoactive drugs, it produces habituation and tolerance but—unlike depressant drugs—no physical addiction. It is known that nicotine mimics some of the effects of the neurotransmitter acetylcholine, enhancing transmission when applied at low doses and blocking it at the higher dose range. Although it is likely that many of the effects of smoking on heart and vascular tissues may be attributed to nicotine, it is not yet clear what component(s) of cigarette smoke is responsible for the induction of lung cancer and emphysema.

CANCER KNOWS NO AGE BOUNDARIES

It is commonly believed that cancer is a disease of the aged. Although it is true that cancer strikes fatally in persons of advanced age with greater frequency than it does in persons in their youth, it is by no means restricted to the elderly. *Cancer is the principal cause of "natural" death among schoolchildren.* It ranks second only to accidents as a cause of death in this age group.

A cancer usually begins as a tumor, a swelling or mass that is formed when cells that normally cooperate in performing a useful function no longer act in concert but instead begin to multiply independently, often rapidly, taking nourishment from normal cells and no longer contributing to the functional activity of the tissue or organ. Such a group of cells, growing in an uncontrolled fashion, is called a **neoplasm.**

A cancer is a tumor, but not all tumors are cancers. Tumors that are not cancers are termed **benign,** and they generally grow slowly, are surrounded by a capsule so they remain localized in the tissue that generated them, and do not recur once they are removed. The fact that they are benign does not mean that they do no damage. They can cause pressure and subsequent harm to surrounding structures, and they can rob normal tissues of their blood supply.

Malignant tumors, on the other hand, *are* cancers. Multiplying rapidly, free from the restraints of any capsule, they compress, invade, and ultimately destroy surrounding tissues. Cancer cells also invade neighboring blood vessels and lymphatic channels, from which they can be swept into the bloodstream or the lymph fluid and then carried to distant parts of the body. There they settle, again multiplying rapidly and unrestrictedly, forming another tumor that invades and destroys neighboring tissues (Figure 35.11).

Such secondary tumors, which may be of considerable distance from the original site, are called **metastases.** The process by which secondary growth is produced is called **metastatic growth.** Each metastasis, and the original

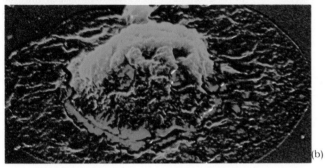

Figure 35.10 (a) A benign tumor. (b) A malignant tumor.

Figure 35.11 (below) The generalized process of cancer growth in lung tissue. Basal cells that underlie the bronchial lining become irritated and begin to increase in number. This is followed by loss of the ciliated respiratory epithelial cells that function to keep harmful materials out of the lungs. The remaining cells flatten out and enlarge to take on the characteristic ''squamous'' structure found in patients with lung cancer. The cancerous cells themselves vary in size and shape, proliferating into a localized cancer that may break through to a lymph vessel or blood vessel and spread to other sites.

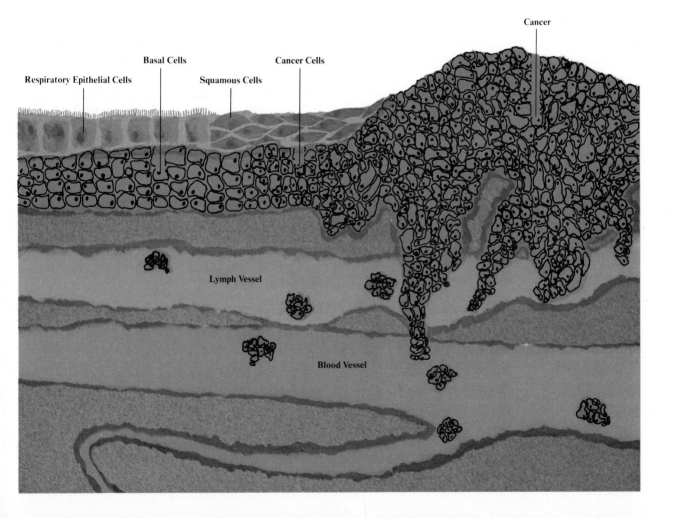

cancer itself, is capable of seeding more sites. In this way, the entire body can become literally riddled with cancer.

The cure for cancer involves the complete removal or destruction of *every* malignant cell. Once the metastatic state is reached, it becomes difficult to remove all the cancer from the body. Because there generally is a time lag before the metastatic state is reached, early diagnosis and treatment can eradicate the cancer before it has had a chance to spread.

A variety of factors have been found to promote cancer in man and in experimental animals. Among such established **carcinogens** are hundreds of chemicals, tobacco smoke, dusts from uranium and other radioactive ores, and x-rays and other types of radiation. A great deal of research is being done to try to discover the mechanism by which these agents are able to transform normal, regulated cells into wildly growing parasites that destroy surrounding tissues, metastasize, and finally kill their host.

Patterns of living and changing environment have been shown to be important determinants of developing cancer at various sites in the body. A prime example is the rapid increase in mortality from lung cancer in American men: From 1930 to 1965 lung cancer death rates increased by a factor of more than 15. Currently, this is the chief cause of cancer deaths in men, accounting for nearly one-fifth of all cancer mortality. Cigarette smoking has contributed to this epidemic. In contrast, deaths due to cancer of the stomach have decreased by two-thirds in the last four decades in both men and women living in the United States. Yet Japan and Chile are confronted with mortality from cancer of the stomach that is six or seven times the rate seen in the United States. The factors determining these differences and changes have not been identified, but it is likely that diets and food practices play a significant role.

Do viruses cause cancer? In experimental animals they clearly do. Viruses isolated from cancer cells can be injected into animals and can be shown to cause the development of a malignancy identical to the one from which they were isolated. They are called **RNA tumor viruses,** and several different types are now known that cause a specific type of tumor in specific species of animals. Each RNA tumor virus contains not only its own RNA genome but also a unique enzyme known as *reverse transcriptase*. When a virus particle infects a cell, the reverse transcriptase makes several DNA copies of the viral RNA, by reverse of the usual transcription process. These

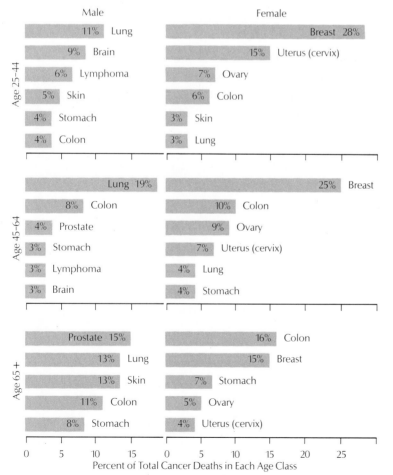

Figure 35.12 *Relative frequencies of various types of fatal cancer as a function of age and sex. Patterns of age and sex dependence of the various sites for cancer development are clear. Lung cancer, which is a major killer in males, is low in frequency in females. Prostate cancer becomes increasingly prevalent in males with advancing age, as does cancer of the colon in both sexes.*

DNA molecules then become incorporated into the chromosomes of the cell in many places and somehow transform the cell into a rapidly growing malignant cell.

Do viruses cause human cancer? Particles very similar to the particles known to cause cancer in animals and containing RNA and reverse transciptase have been isolated from some human cancers. They are not found in noncancerous cells of the same tissue type. Furthermore, DNA sequences homologous to the viruslike RNA of the isolated particles have been found in the nuclei of the cancer cells—but the identical sequences are not found in normal cells of the same tissue type. Although the critical test of transferability has not been performed (for obvious reasons), the conclusion is becoming inescapable: Some human cancers are caused by viruses.

But there are probably one or more other causes as well. Some evidence has been found in support of the suggestion that all human cells may contain viruslike cancer-causing genes that have become part of the hereditary material of the species, being permanently integrated into human chromosomes. These **oncogenes,** as they have been called, are viewed as being normally silent until derepressed by some environmental stimulus (a carcinogen). Thereupon the products of these oncogenes are viewed as transforming the cell to the cancerous state. This theory is still highly controversial.

Whatever the causes of cancer, evidence is increasing that failure of the immune system to destroy the cancerous cells is an important consideration in the establishment of the tumor as a life-threatening force. It appears that most cancers are probably rapidly destroyed by the immune system; in this view only the rare malignant tumor escapes detection and becomes a threat to the host (Chapter 22). Thus, much current research is directed toward analysis of the factors determining whether a tumor is or is not recognized as foreign and is destroyed by immune cells.

CARDIOVASCULAR DISEASE HAS BECOME THE MAJOR CAUSE OF DEATH IN WESTERN SOCIETY

As the data in Figure 35.2 demonstrated, cardiovascular diseases (mainly heart disease and stroke) were far and away the leading causes of death in the United States in 1969, accounting for nearly three times as many deaths as cancer (the second most common fatal disease) and eight times as many deaths as accidents. In individuals over sixty-five years of age, diseases of the circulatory system account for nearly two-thirds of all deaths (five times as many deaths as are caused by cancer in the same age group).

The fundamental problem in most cardiovascular disease is **atherosclerosis**: the thickening and hardening of the walls of arteries caused by the buildup of fatty deposits (Figure 35.13). This decreases the elasticity of the arteries

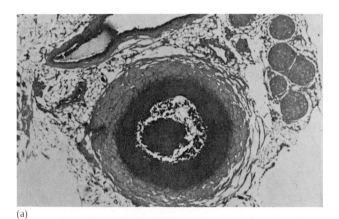

(a)

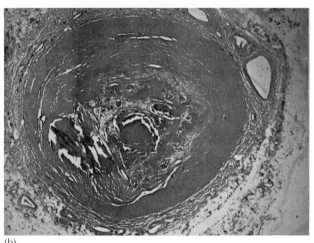

(b)

Figure 35.13   Cross sections of a normal artery and an atherosclerotic artery. The wall of the normal artery (a) is uniform in thickness, providing a smooth central lumen for the flow of blood. In the atherosclerotic artery (b) the wall has become so thickened and distorted by fatty deposits that the lumen is a tortuously distorted slit. Such deposits decrease the volume and elasticity of the vessel, thereby leading to high blood pressure. In addition, they act as a stimulus for the formation of blood clots and as a trap for such clots once they have been formed.

Table 35.2
Recommended Daily Dietary Allowances* (revised 1974)

Category	Age (years)	Weight (kg)	Weight (lb.)	Height (cm)	Height (in.)	Energy (kcal)	Protein (g)	Fat-Soluble Vitamins Vita-min A (IU)	Vita-min D (IU)	Vita-min E Activity (IU)
Infants	0.0–0.5	6	14	60	24	kg × 117	kg × 2.2	1,400	400	4
	0.5–1.0	9	20	71	28	kg × 108	kg × 2.0	2,000	400	5
Children	1–3	13	28	86	34	1,300	23	2,000	400	7
	4–6	20	44	110	44	1,800	30	2,500	400	9
	7–10	30	66	135	54	2,400	36	3,300	400	10
Males	11–14	44	97	158	63	2,800	44	5,000	400	12
	15–18	61	134	172	69	3,000	54	5,000	400	15
	19–22	67	147	172	69	3,000	54	5,000	400	15
	23–50	70	154	172	69	2,700	56	5,000		15
	51+	70	154	172	69	2,400	56	5,000		15
Females	11–14	44	97	155	62	2,400	44	4,000	400	12
	15–18	54	119	162	65	2,100	48	4,000	400	12
	19–22	58	128	162	65	2,100	46	4,000	400	12
	23–50	58	128	162	65	2,000	46	4,000		12
	51+	58	128	162	65	1,800	46	4,000		12
Pregnant						+300	+30	5,000	400	15
Lactating						+500	+20	6,000	400	15

*The allowances are intended to provide for individual variations among most normal persons as they live in the United States under usual environmental stresses. Diets should be based on a variety of common foods in order to provide other nutrients for which human requirements have been less well defined.

Source: Food and Nutrition Board, National Academy of Sciences–National Research Council.

and is one of several factors contributing to development of **hypertension**: elevated blood pressure. Hardening of the arteries and elevated blood pressure together create the situation in which **heart disease** and **stroke** (damage to the brain due to loss of blood supply in a local region) become prevalent.

The cardiovascular disease causing more deaths than any other is **coronary artery disease**; it accounts for approximately 700,000 deaths in the United States each year. In young to middle-aged individuals it is five to ten times as common in males as in females and therefore accounts for most of the difference in mortality rate and life expectancy between the two groups. The cause of death is a *myocardial infarction*—a heart attack. Arteries supplying the heart wall become choked by atherosclerotic plaques, a vessel becomes completely occluded, and the flow of blood stops. The region of heart muscle served by that vessel becomes starved for oxygen; the heart may stop entirely, it may falter in its rhythm, or it may beat so weakly that an inadequate supply of blood is pumped to the rest of the body. Often a heart attack is initiated by a small blood clot becoming trapped in the clogged vessels and blocking flow; this is known as a *coronary thrombosis*. (A similar clot, or thrombus, in the brain can result in stroke.)

Three characteristics have been clearly identified as risk factors of primary importance for coronary artery disease: hypertension, elevated blood cholesterol level, and cigarette smoking. They work in additive fashion to increase the risk of this disorder. Recognition and correction of these characteristics may reduce the risk accordingly.

Fortunately, modern drugs permit control of high blood pressure. Stopping smoking decreases the risk of heart attack, but the individual needs sufficient understanding of the health significance of smoking to generate the personal motivation to quit. Serum cholesterol levels greater than 250 milligrams are associated with high risk. Modification of the diet can effectively reduce serum cholesterol levels despite the fact that this sterol is synthesized in the body. Diet can be modified by reducing the proportion of animal or saturated fat and substituting vegetable oils or polyunsaturated fat and by restricting daily cholesterol intake to less than 300 milligrams (most Americans consume about 600 milligrams or more cholesterol per day). Such dietary modifications are likely to be most effective before atherosclerotic changes have been produced in the coronary vessels. Therefore, it is advisable to begin them early in adult life, for atherosclerotic buildup probably begins in the teens in most cases.

Water-Soluble Vitamins							Minerals					
Ascorbic Acid (mg)	Folacin (μg)	Niacin (mg)	Riboflavin (mg)	Thiamin (mg)	Vitamin B_6 (mg)	Vitamin B_{12} (μg)	Calcium (mg)	Phosphorus (mg)	Iodine (μg)	Iron (mg)	Magnesium (mg)	Zinc (mg)
35	50	5	0.4	0.3	0.3	0.3	360	240	35	10	60	3
35	50	8	0.6	0.5	0.4	0.3	540	400	45	15	70	5
40	100	9	0.8	0.7	0.6	1.0	800	800	60	15	150	10
40	200	12	1.1	0.9	0.9	1.5	800	800	80	10	200	10
40	300	16	1.2	1.2	1.2	2.0	800	800	110	10	250	10
45	400	18	1.5	1.4	1.6	3.0	1,200	1,200	130	18	350	15
45	400	20	1.8	1.5	2.0	3.0	1,200	1,200	150	18	400	15
45	400	20	1.8	1.5	2.0	3.0	800	800	140	10	350	15
45	400	18	1.6	1.4	2.0	3.0	800	800	130	10	350	15
45	400	16	1.5	1.2	2.0	3.0	800	800	110	10	350	15
45	400	16	1.3	1.2	1.6	3.0	1,200	1,200	115	18	300	15
45	400	14	1.4	1.1	2.0	3.0	1,200	1,200	115	18	300	15
45	400	14	1.4	1.1	2.0	3.0	800	800	100	18	300	15
45	400	13	1.2	1.0	2.0	3.0	800	800	100	18	300	15
45	400	12	1.1	1.0	2.0	3.0	800	800	80	10	300	15
60	800	+2	+0.3	+0.3	2.5	4.0	1,200	1,200	125	18+	450	20
80	600	+4	+0.5	+0.3	2.5	4.0	1,200	1,200	150	18	450	25

There are several other factors that seem to be important in reducing the risk of coronary artery disease and that are under control of the individual. Among these are regular physical activity and exercise, which help to increase heart capacity, to oxidize fats, and to relieve the effects of psychological stress (a major "cause" of hypertension). Keeping one's weight at a normal level and temperate use of alcohol also keep down the risk. Nevertheless, other, less controllable factors contribute to the risk of heart disease. Diabetes and hereditary disorders, which produce elevation in the quantity of cholesterol and triglycerides in the blood, are responsible for development of more rapid and extensive atherosclerotic change.

PROPER DIET AND PHYSICAL FITNESS PROVIDE INSURANCE AGAINST MANY DISEASES

All living things have certain well-defined nutritional requirements. The primary energy necessary to human life is provided by the carbohydrates, proteins, and fats in foods. In addition, the diet must provide materials necessary for growth, development, and normal function. Such necessary materials, which cannot be synthesized by the human body, are the *essential* nutrients, which include certain amino acids, a fatty acid (linoleic acid), vitamins, minerals, and trace elements (Table 35.2).

Health problems develop when the diet has an excess or a deficiency of one or more nutrients. The starving millions of the world suffer and die prematurely because their diets do not provide adequate amounts of energy or the right kind of protein. Such diets are also frequently deficient in vitamins and minerals. Even in a highly developed country such as the United States, where hunger and starvation are not major problems, nutritional deficiencies are widespread. People who do not consume a variety of foods may be lacking the balance of nutrients their body requires. For example, because of the differences in amino acid composition between most plant and animal proteins, it is difficult—although not impossible—to establish a completely vegetarian diet that provides all the essential amino acids in the proportions in which they are required.

The energy supplied in food is measured in kilocalories. Caloric content, or value, of a given food is the heat energy produced by a specified amount of it when it is eaten and "burned" by the metabolic processes in the body (Chapter 14). Humans differ widely in their caloric requirements, depending on size, age, sex, occupation, and so on. The twenty-five- to thirty-five-year-old male of average height needs about 2,700 kilocalories a day, a woman of similar description needs about 2,000, and a twelve- to fifteen-year-old girl or boy requires from 2,400 to 2,800. If an individual takes in more calories than he burns (as too many Americans do), the extra calories are converted to fat, and the person gains weight. However, if one does not take in enough calories to sustain his daily activities, his body begins to convert its own tissue into the calories it needs, and he loses weight.

Every person has an ideal weight based on height, sex, and bone structure (Table 35.3). The term ''overweight'' is used when an individual exceeds his ideal weight by 10 to 20 percent. If the individual is more than 20 percent over his ideal weight, he is categorized as **obese.** Obesity enhances the likelihood of a variety of disorders, including high blood pressure, stroke, diabetes, arthritis, gall bladder disease, and kidney disease. Most importantly, obesity can aggravate heart disease because it places a greater work load on an organ that is already operating below peak efficiency.

The obese person may also be confronted with psychological problems that develop from a negative self-image and lack of social acceptance. And even when the individual is highly motivated to lose weight, he may lack the understanding that weight reduction can be achieved *only* by maintaining calorie deficits, so that stores of body fat are burned to meet energy requirements. Despite frequent claims for fad diets, *the most appropriate and long-lasting approach is a permanent change in eating habits: eating less, maintaining a varied and balanced diet, and avoiding high-calorie foods.* It is not glamorous, it takes a long time to show results, and there's no end to it—but it works. Fad diets, on the other hand, tend to work only in the short run, and the individual regains the lost pounds soon after returning to his ''regular'' diet. Under any circumstance, diets providing less than 1,200 kilocalories daily are likely to be deficient in some essential nutrients, particularly iron and thiamin.

Overweight and obesity develop from a combination of excess food calories and lack of physical activity to burn those calories. The physical demands of modern life are few compared to those of our ancestors who had to move about in order to survive: obtaining food, seeking shelter, escaping from danger. But even in his more sedentary life, present-day man is equipped with a body that needs to move for other purposes. The efficient fat-storage mechanism in man might have assured his survival in his history of starvation and deprivation, but in times of overnutrition and underactivity this same mechanism conspires against his health and survival.

Regular exercise and planned physical activity are a boon to health and to physical conditioning as well as being a means for control of body weight. **Endurance exercise training,** which involves continuous rhythmic cardiovascular-respiratory overload, has been shown to be particularly valuable in human health. Important changes in cardiovascular function occur with such training. The resting heart rates of trained persons are less than those of untrained individuals. The stroke volume and maximal cardiac output are both increased, producing enhanced work capacity and supply of oxygen to muscle. In addition, endurance training increases the capacity of skeletal muscle to oxidize fatty acids, resulting in a reduction of total body fat stores. Other adaptations occur in pulmonary function with increase in *vital capacity* (maximal volume of air expired from full inspiration) and in *maximum breathing capacity* (maximum volume of air that can be exchanged in the lungs per minute). As noted earlier, some of these effects of endurance training provide a certain degree of protection against coronary artery disease and heart attacks. More immediately, endurance exercise imparts to the individual a feeling of well-being and improved self-image.

PERSPECTIVE

In the past three-quarters of a century, medical advances of major proportions have been made. These advances have had sweeping effects on the rather small segment of the world's population that they have touched. No longer is

Table 35.3
Desirable Weights for Men and Women*

Group	Height (with shoes on)	Small Frame	Medium Frame	Large Frame
Men	5′ 2″	112–120	118–129	126–141
(1-inch	5′ 3″	115–123	121–133	129–144
heels)	5′ 4″	118–126	124–136	132–148
	5′ 5″	121–129	127–139	135–152
	5′ 6″	124–133	130–143	138–156
	5′ 7″	128–137	134–147	142–161
	5′ 8″	132–141	138–152	147–166
	5′ 9″	136–145	142–156	151–170
	5′10″	140–150	146–160	155–174
	5′11″	144–154	150–165	159–179
	6′ 0″	148–158	154–170	164–184
	6′ 1″	152–162	158–175	168–189
	6′ 2″	156–167	162–180	173–194
	6′ 3″	160–171	167–185	178–199
	6′ 4″	164–175	172–190	182–204
Women†	4′10″	92– 98	96–107	104–119
(2-inch	4′11″	94–101	98–110	106–122
heels)	5′ 0″	96–104	101–113	109–125
	5′ 1″	99–107	104–116	112–128
	5′ 2″	102–110	107–119	115–131
	5′ 3″	105–113	110–122	118–134
	5′ 4″	108–116	113–116	121–138
	5′ 5″	111–119	116–130	125–142
	5′ 6″	114–123	120–135	129–146
	5′ 7″	118–127	124–139	133–150
	5′ 8″	122–131	128–143	137–154
	5′ 9″	126–135	132–147	141–158
	5′10″	130–140	136–151	145–163
	5′11″	134–144	140–155	149–168
	6′ 0″	138–148	144–159	153–173

*Weight in pounds according to frame (in indoor clothing).
†For girls between 18 and 25, subtract one pound for each year under 25.
Source: Metropolitan Life Insurance Company, 1959.

every human life necessarily subject to the ravages of the disease-causing organisms that have taken such a heavy toll in human lives in past eras. As a result, the young born into privileged sectors of human society have a life expectancy that is at least sixteen years greater than it would have been a mere fifty years ago. Continued research into the causes, prevention, and cures of the two remaining great killers of Western society—cardiovascular disease and cancer—hold out the hope of adding still more years to the average human life span.

But access to these modern life-extending procedures is not equally available to all. The application of modern knowledge concerning diagnosis, treatment, and prevention of disease has, by its very complexity, demanded a whole new approach to medical care. The obstetrician cares for the woman during pregnancy and during the delivery of her infant. The pediatrician assumes responsibility after birth and cares for the child until adolescence, after which the internist is in charge, calling upon the services of surgical specialists and medical subspecialists when needed. Assisting in the process are paramedical personnel—nurses, laboratory technicians, x-ray technicians, inhalation therapists, occupational therapists, physical therapists, speech therapists, social workers, and, more recently, physician assistants and pediatric nurse assistants. Integral with this medical attention is an array of highly sophisticated equipment and facilities. All of this has not only resulted in the escalation of cost of treatment, it has tended to restrict availability of the advantages of modern medicine to a relatively small number of human beings. How can we find methods of providing broader access to this complex system of medical care? How might we broadly apply the procedures of preventive medicine to assist in avoiding or delaying the onset of disease throughout our own country as well as in countries the world over? These are questions of the first magnitude, not only from the humanitarian point of view or even from the standpoint of simple economics; these questions relate also to the whole question of biological ethics in terms of our health and well-being as a species, as defined in Chapter 37.

SUGGESTED READINGS

BOWER, W. W. (ed.). *Today's Health Guide.* New York: American Medical Association, 1965. A richly illustrated manual intended to give the individual the opportunity to make the best and most economical use of available health information and medical care.

DUBOS, RENÉ. *Man Adapting.* New Haven, Conn.: Yale University Press, 1965. Dubos considers health and disease to be expressions of an organism's success or failure to adapt to a changing environment.

MAYER, JEAN. *Overweight: Causes, Cost, and Control.* Englewood Cliffs, N.J.: Prentice-Hall, 1968. Mayer attempts to dispel misconceptions about obesity and explains the physiological causes and effects of this condition. He provides useful information on weight control and on the variety of medical treatments currently in use.

ROUECHÈ, BERTON. *Annals of Epidemiology.* Boston: Little, Brown, 1967. A series of fourteen investigations into puzzling outbreaks of disease.

SHIMKIN, MICHAEL B. *Science and Cancer.* Rev. ed. Washington, D.C.: U.S. Government Printing Office, 1973. This illustrated Public Health Service publication was written to inform the general public about the medical and biological aspects of cancer. It also discusses some recent research developments in the causes and treatment of cancer.

STARE, FREDERICK J. *Eating for Good Health.* Rev. ed. New York: Cornerstone, 1969. A no-nonsense, readable book on selection of food to meet health needs.

U.S. DEPARTMENT OF HEALTH, EDUCATION AND WELFARE. *The Health Consequences of Smoking.* Washington, D.C.: U.S. Government Printing Office, 1972. A supplement to the original Surgeon General's report that presents the results of 2,000 additional studies into the health significance of smoking.

Chapter 36

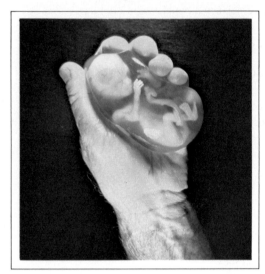

Social Implications of Biological Research

In a very real sense, we hold the future of our species in our hands. As knowledge increases, we progressively gain the capacity to determine how many shall be born and how many shall live, who they shall be and under what conditions they shall live and die. For much of recent human history, the dominant theme has been Progress: Whatever can be done, should be done. Biological research has followed much the same course. But are we reaching the point at which the consequences of the things we have the capacity to undertake might spell disaster for our species? Perhaps we have reached the point, finally, when we must say instead: Whatever should be done, can be done.

Science can benefit life. Science can also be used as an instrument of death and oppression, to help people kill each other physically in war and emotionally in a myriad of ways. What can we do to enhance science's benefits and eliminate its misuses? As a start, we must face the problems honestly, learn about them, and endeavor to deal with them. We must also realize that a consistent use of science to benefit life requires, ultimately, a society dedicated to a better life for all—not to wealth, power, and prestige for a few. The problems of science are not separable from those of society.

Most biological research is not done for military or political purposes. Much of biological research is motivated by humanitarian goals or by a desire for basic knowledge of biological mechanisms. However, the technical and political problems that impede the use of research to benefit humanity are enormous. The basic theme is the same: How can available knowledge be used and new knowledge be developed for the benefit of all? What can prevent the misuse of this knowledge for political control or personal glorification?

The problems to be discussed in this chapter are complex and have no simple solutions. In reading about these problems, we urge you, the reader, to develop your own perspectives and to act with regard to the pressing social issues of our times. Although this discussion must necessarily be brief, the references at the end of the chapter can be used to explore the subjects further.

PROBLEMS IN CONTROLLING GENETIC DISEASE IN HUMANS

At least 10 percent of all pediatric admissions to hospitals result from genetically derived disorders; clearly genetic disease is a major medical problem (Chapter 35). What are the possible solutions? First, people likely to have children with genetic disease can decide not to have children. Second, there can be "selective abortion" of only those fetuses likely or certain to have genetic disease. Third, there can be an attempt at a "phenotypic cure"—an alleviation of the symptoms of genetic disease by drugs, diet, or a change in environment. Fourth, there may soon be the possibility of a "genotypic cure"—the replacement of defective genes either by transplanting a nondefective organ or by introducing new genetic material into individual cells by processes analogous to bacterial transduction or transformation. At the present time, only the first three possible solutions are at a stage of real applicability, and for many genetic diseases, only the first is a "choice."

Genetic Counseling and the Decision Whether to Have a Child

The first two approaches listed above depend on medical diagnosis and advice, usually termed genetic counseling. Stated somewhat simplistically, the diagnostic problem is to determine whether there is a substantial likelihood that a mating will result in a child with a serious genetic defect. "Substantial" and "serious" are catch-words considered further below. The advising problem concerns what (if any) action should be taken if the likelihood of genetic disease does exist. Prospective parents who have been found likely to encounter such a problem are typically in desperate need of information. For most genetic diseases, the information that the counselor can supply is limited to three crucial but inconclusive bits of data: the probability that the child will have the genetic defect, the nature and course of the disease, and the available treatments and their likelihood of success. The ultimate decision becomes particularly agonizing because a true phenotypic cure is seldom (if ever) achieved, and the degree of success differs in individual cases involving the same disease.

For some genetic diseases, more information can be obtained through a diagnosis of the fetus itself at an early stage of development. This is done by sampling the amniotic fluid that surrounds the developing embryo. Amniotic fluid contains skin and respiratory cells of the fetus, which can be subjected to biochemical assays or to chromosome analyses in cell culture (Figure 35.8). Thus, in some cases, embryos certain to have a particular genetic disease can be detected and selectively aborted if the parents so desire. In this way, a man and woman may have a child with the knowledge that their infant will be free of the feared genetic disease that they carry. For example, in the case of one of the most severe genetic disorders, Tay-Sachs disease, a healthy but heterozygous individual can be identified by a biochemical test; because a fetal diagnosis by amniocentesis is also possible, the likelihood of two known carrier parents giving birth to a pre-doomed child can be shifted from one in four to essentially zero—provided that abortion is an acceptable solution for them.

The Problems of Genetic Counseling: Information, Privacy, and Individual Freedom

Most of the problems associated with the counseling approach to genetic disease are obvious; the solutions are not. One major problem is that of genetic information: How is it to be obtained? Who is to have it? Another is that of decision: Who is to decide which approach should be adopted, given the potential of genetic disease in a specific case? (For a many-sided and extensive discussion of these questions, the reader should refer to the collection of papers in *Ethical Issues in Human Genetics*.)

Perhaps the best way to perceive the difficulties is to begin with an example that is least controversial: individuals with a family background of a defined genetic disease.

Presumably, such individuals would want to have information about the nature of the disease and its inheritance as a guide to their life style and reproductive decisions. However, information about the presence of or potential for genetic disease may do more harm than good if it is not fully understood by the individual and if its confidentiality is not protected, as the following paragraphs will point out.

From the limited surveys done to date, even individual counseling typically does not communicate a real understanding of genetic disease and its inheritance. This problem is likely to be acute in the case of a heterozygous carrier, for two reasons. First, heterozygotes often think that they themselves have a "genetic disease" even if there are no known symptoms in the heterozygous state. For example, the heterozygous sickle-cell trait is often confused with the homozygous sickle-cell disease (Chapter 32). Second, heterozygotes often do not understand that transmission of the true homozygous disease to a child depends on the generally low probability of mating with another heterozygote. And even in such matings between two carriers, the probability is only one in four that a child will have the disease. Thus, limited understanding of genetic information can communicate an unwarranted sense of inferiority to the person bearing the gene.

The problem of incomplete communication obviously becomes even more acute when mass screening programs are established for "high-risk" racial populations, for whom individual consultation is not available (for example, the mass screening of blacks for the sickle-cell trait and of Ashkenazic Jews for the Tay-Sachs trait). The ultimate goal is certainly valid in the case of a severe disease such as Tay-Sachs, for which fetal diagnosis is possible. But it is essential that the impersonality of such programs not be permitted to lead to a further increase in a stereotyped sense of racial inferiority through incomplete communication of information.

The concept of mass screening for genetic information brings up two additional problems. First, what do we consider a genetic disease? We can easily foresee a shift from efforts to prevent the most devastating illnesses toward the establishment of criteria for birth based on some scorecard of "desirable" and "undesirable" traits. Second, in a given situation, is mass screening the best allocation of scarce scientific resources? A major program of sickle-cell screening might predict most of the one-in-a-hundred cases in which matings within the high-risk populations give a one-in-four probability of a sick child. But what if the same amount of money and people were devoted to efforts to find a phenotypic cure for the sickle-cell disease? The disease might cease to be a problem.

So far, only one type of informational problem has been considered: understanding by the concerned individual or prospective parents. What of the problem of giving out information to others? Who should have access to information about the presence or potential for genetic disease in an individual? Relatives, employers, medical and life insurance companies? The stereotype of "genetic disease" can cast a long shadow. If a disease can on occasion be associated with mental retardation or has a purported link to "antisocial behavior" (as it does for individuals with an extra Y chromosome), the attitude of a typical prospective employer is easily predictable. Thus privacy of genetic information is an important issue. The problem of release of information becomes particularly complex in the case of near relatives who may be unknowing heterozygous "carriers" or in the case of investigators who wish to study the disease for humanitarian reasons and who need a population of individuals with the disease for their research.

Let us turn to the problem of decision making once the possibility of a genetic disease has been established. Should the man and woman involved try to avoid conceiving a child? Because conception may occur despite their efforts, should sterilization be considered? If amniocentesis is a possibility, should it be done and the option of selective abortion be exercised? Should the prospective parents gamble on the odds for a partial phenotypic cure? Clearly there are no simple generalities as to what is the "best" decision. More pertinent for general discussion is the question of who should make the decision: the prospective parents, the genetic counselor, or a government committee with a numerical scorecard? Traditionally, and we believe properly, the prospective parents have made the decision. However, the presentation of adequate information by the counselor and its thorough understanding by the counselees is crucial in this process. If the "decision" is to be truly made by the prospective parents, the counselor must go out of his way to see that they are thoroughly informed despite his personal prejudices. He must explain amniocentesis thoroughly, even if he is personally opposed to abortion; make completely clear the limitations of phenotypic cures, even if he is a strong believer in a traditional medical treatment approach; and avoid minimizing the potential for treatment because of his personal concern over accumulation of "bad genes."

Prospects and Problems for Genotypic Cures

At the beginning of this section we noted two general possibilities for what we have termed genotypic cures: transplantation of a normal organ or tissue capable of alleviating the genetic defect and introduction of normal DNA into the genome of individual cells. An example of the first approach is transplantation of a normal kidney to replace a defective one. Although potentially available now, this approach to genetic disease is inherently limited to those cases in which a genetic defect is limited in its effect to one organ; it is also limited technically by problems of immune rejection (Chapter 24) and the availability of organs to transplant.

The ethical problems of transplants have been widely discussed, and they will be touched on only briefly here because it is unlikely that transplant operations will ever become a major approach to genetic disease. However, the problems are important to consider because they confront us with the concept of ethical limits in a present-day context. For example, there is probably general agreement that an operation should be done only if it is likely to help a patient, not solely to explore a new technology. But who will speak for the recipient patient with the terminal illness (the traditional experimental animal)? Also, in the scarce world of donor organs, how do we protect the grievously injured person from premature "donation," and how do we decide who of many potential recipients is to receive that which is donated? Wealth and "value" to society are not adequate criteria. Finally, there is an ultimate ethical limit that transcends technology, exemplified most cogently by a brain transplant, were that ever to become technically feasible.

Genetic modification of individual cells to restore a normal genotype is a general approach of great theoretical promise. But it is separated from practical reality by our lack of understanding of how to do it. For example, in the case of single gene defects that are treatable after birth, one can conceive of direct therapy of a limited number of cells, particularly through a viral transduction (Chapter 17). Alternatively, cells might be removed from the infant, genetically transduced or transformed under defined conditions, and then reimplanted.

There is a fundamental problem in this area: How can we acquire the technology and still protect the rights of the human beings who are the experimental animals on whom the technology is perfected? Are there ethical limits to which a technique—even in principle—should be put?

Turning to the technical problems of cellular genotypic alteration, the immediate concern is the enormous public health problem. We know a great deal about transfer and regulation of genes in microbial systems. We also know how to prepare and reproduce segments of the eukaryotic genome by joining eukaryotic DNA fragments to a bacterial plasmid, which can then be replicated in large quantity in bacterial cells. These eukaryotic DNA fragments can also be inserted into an animal virus. Thus the preparation of human genes and their introduction into human cells is within range. However, we know essentially nothing about regulation of eukaryotic genes and differences between normal and abnormal expression. There is great danger that too rapid a leap will lead to the introduction of genetic material that is not susceptible to control because of its location in the genome or because of its association with a virus. In other words, malignant growth (cancer) or other aberrant types of gene expression may be produced. Therefore, efforts to develop a technology that is designed in principle to benefit life may have the opposite effect if concern is not shown in the early stages of research.

In the long-range view, cellular genotypic alteration will presumably be added as a fourth general approach to the problem of genetic disease. The available choices will be broader. But only for some diseases will the decisions be simpler, because this new technology will clearly not be a universal cure for all genetic defects.

"Genetic Engineering"

The term "genetic engineering" refers generally to deliberate genetic change in human cells, although it might apply to deliberate genetic change in any cells. Cellular transduction or transformation is thus an example of genetic engineering. As noted above, one example of such an approach involves removal of cells, genotypic alteration in culture, and reimplantation.

As the nature of the genotypic alteration becomes more profound, the question of ethical limits becomes involved. For example, we can consider the somewhat more complex situation in which the genotypic alteration is carried out on an egg cell. But why stop with addition of one gene? Other genes might be added for characteristics that are deemed desirable. Or the preexisting nucleus might be replaced with a nucleus from a "desirable" person in order to produce a new person with an identical genotype—a clonee. From there, it would be a short step to the production of many identical individuals with some set of supposedly desirable characteristics. Obviously all these stages are far off. But it is not too early to ask the question: Is there an ethical limit?

Should There Be Legal Rights and Ethical Limits?

So far, many questions have been raised but few general conclusions have been drawn. In fact, in matters of childbearing, no general rules are possible to guide a "best" decision. However, there should be some general rules with regard to the use of genetic information and the process of decision making.

First, individuals should have the right of access to complete information from a genetic counselor. Second, parents should have the right to make decisions with respect to the birth of a child. Third, individuals should have the right to privacy of genetic information; there should be *no* disclosure without consent. These must be legal rights, even though arguments against every one of them could be made on behalf of "medicine" or "society." Such protection of individual rights is essential in the light of recurring efforts to define "superior" racial and social classes and recurring expressions that genetics must be used to produce a "better" person, as will be discussed in the next section. In the final analysis, there must be faith in the capacity of a truly informed individual to make decisions of ultimate benefit to society.

Let us return briefly to the problems of ethical limits. Such limits are broadly defined by those acts that attempt to alter in a major way the hereditary information of an individual or its unique expression. Within this context, a genotypic cure of a defined genetic disease is clearly within the limit; cloning, massive genetic alteration, and brain transplants are not. Lacking the wisdom and sensitivity to solve our present problems, it is not likely that we can somehow engineer ourselves into a "higher" state. Those who wish to produce their concept of a perfect person should do it with a computer, some sheet metal, and a riveting machine.

DYSGENICS AND EUGENICS

Dear Madam:

. . . our records show that Ruby Lee Jackson, who was admitted to this hospital from Richmond, Va., on Feb. 14, 1940, was eugenically sterilized. . . . I hope you have been getting along nicely since you left.

(Letter from superintendent of Central State Hospital, Petersburg, Va., to Ruby Lee Jackson with regard to her sterilization at age fifteen.)

As phenotypic alleviation of the most disastrous effects of genetic disease becomes more and more successful, the number of individuals in the population with serious genetic lesions will increase. This trend has led to expressions of concern about "dysgenic trends" in the population: deterioration of the human race due to accumulation of genetic defects. It is a concern with a considerable history in the field of genetics, beginning with the Eugenics Movement for "race improvement" of the early twentieth century ("eugenic" and "dysgenic" are words constructed to signify "well-born" and "bad-born").

With regard to inherited disease, the geneticist James Crow has noted that changes in the overall frequencies of rare deleterious genes are likely to be slow whatever policies are adopted. We are talking about a few percent in ten generations. Thus the dysgenic argument seems to be exceedingly weak with regard to a decision whether or not to have children in this generation.

However, the concepts of dysgenics and eugenics are at the center of another area in which genetics and society interact: the controversy over heredity, intelligence, and the purported existence of a *genetic* class structure in which the poor and black have lower status in our society because they are genetic have-nots.

Political Influence of the Eugenics Movement

The Eugenics Movement was a strong political force in the first half of this century. Although much of the original interest in the concept of eugenics derived from utopian ideas for correcting genetic deficiency, the political impact of the Eugenics Movement was undeniably to support racism and social oppression. Unfounded theories of race improvement were used as a "scientific" basis for sterilization laws in thirty-one states and for miscegenation laws prohibiting racial intermarriage. ("Miscegenation" means the interbreeding of what are purported to be distinct human races.) Thousands of people have been sterilized within the legal and philosophical framework engendered by the excesses of the Eugenics Movement. This framework exists even today; sterilization operations are still performed in the absence of informed consent.

One of the major political activities of members of the Eugenics Movement was in the field of immigration legislation. This has been particularly well documented in Kenneth Ludmerer's book *Genetics and American Society.* The Immigration Restriction Act of 1924 was notable not only for the imposition of quotas but for the choice of quotas based on immigration patterns determined by the census of 1890 rather than that of 1920. This entailed severe limitation of immigration from southern and eastern Europe—the major sources of immigrants between 1890 and 1920. The intent was to favor the so-called "better" races of Europe—the Nordic and Anglo-Saxon.

Scientific "authority" for this legislation and for the sterilization and miscegenation laws was provided by testimony from many of the leading eugenicists of the period. For example, Harry Laughlin, a member of the Carnegie Institution of Washington, secretary of the Eugenics Research Association, superintendent of its Eugenics Record Office at Cold Spring Harbor, and editor of its journal *Eugenic News,* testified frequently before Congress as its appointed "expert eugenics agent." He strongly supported the sterilization and immigration bills.

Many popular books appeared during this time on various aspects of race supremacy and the dangers of dysgenic trends. One line of supporting "evidence" for these claims was the results of IQ tests (tests for "intelligence") given to arriving immigrants on Ellis Island and to World War I draftees. These results were analyzed in detail by Carl Brigham in his book *A Study of American Intelligence,* which was frequently cited throughout the Congressional hearings on the immigration law. Brigham's analysis showed a strong correlation between performance on IQ tests and years of residence in the United States. He drew the remarkable conclusion that the basis for this result was the ethnic background of the new immigrants—Jews, Italians, Poles, and Russians—*rather than any bias of the test in favor of those acclimated to an English-speaking culture.* He argued that the "decline in intelligence" paralleled the decline in "Nordic blood" and proclaimed that "we are incorporating the negro into our racial stock, while all of Europe is comparatively free from this taint. . . . revision of the immigration and naturalization laws will only afford a slight relief . . . the really important steps are those looking toward the prevention of the continued propagation of defective strains in the present population."

The political history of the Eugenics Movement was one of sweeping social and political conclusions drawn from limited or nonexistent data. The failure of responsible scientists to point this out at an early time is clearly a tragedy. By the middle 1920s, public statements of repudiation began to appear, but in the meantime a generation had been exposed to the concept of race supremacy as something founded on "scientific fact." We have seen the extremes to which these ideas were later put when Nazi Germany translated the concept of racial supremacy into mass genocide.

The New Hereditarian Movement

In recent years, there has been a resurgence in claims of a genetic basis for race and class supremacy. Although the scientific analysis is more sophisticated, this New Hereditarian Movement seems to be following essentially the same path as its predecessor. Sweeping social and political conclusions are drawn from limited or nonexistent data. The battleground is now mainly the field of education and social legislation, but the political message is the same: "There is a genetic class structure in which the poor will remain poor because of their inherited inferiority." The social consequences of this message are enormous: Poverty and unemployment are not to be blamed on an unjust social structure and inadequate educational structure—they are inevitable. Because of the social importance of the conclusions of the New Hereditarian Movement, we believe that everyone should familiarize himself with the nature of the arguments for and against the New Hereditarian position and take a stand on this issue.

HEREDITY, INTELLIGENCE, AND IQ

Nature has color-coded groups of individuals so that statistically reliable predictions of their adaptability to intellectually rewarding and effective lives can easily be made and profitably be used by the pragmatic man in the street.
William Shockley

The problem of Negro-White inequality in educability is thus essentially the problem of Negro-White differences in intelligence.
Arthur Jensen

. . . the tendency to be unemployed may run in the genes of a family about as certainly as bad teeth do now.
Richard Herrnstein

The central theme of the New Hereditarian Movement is that there are substantial differences in intelligence between races and social classes and that these differences are inherited and determine potential for achievement in our society. Arthur Jensen and William Shockley have concentrated on differences between blacks and whites. The starting point for their analysis is the observation that the mean IQ scores of groups of black children are approximately 15 points below the mean scores of white children. Their subsequent analysis involves three assumptions: first, that IQ scores are adequate measures of intelligence; second, that IQ is largely an inherited trait; third, that racial differences in IQ are also inherited. Richard Herrnstein has applied the same sort of analysis to develop a theory for a hereditary class structure (or "meritocracy"). Let us examine each of these assumptions.

Intelligence and IQ

What is intelligence? Can it be measured, and does the IQ test measure it? Even attempting a definition of intelligence is a complicated thing. Perhaps we cannot even define intelligence without introducing an enormous cultural bias, because we believe that we are intelligent and therefore intelligence must somehow describe us. One definition that indicates some of these problems is the following: Intelligence is cognitive ability, expressed through environmental experience subjectively viewed from the standpoint of a given culture at a given time. If we admit that intelligence is subjectively viewed by a given culture at a given time, it is clear that no person can produce an intelligence test that is free of cultural bias.

Alfred Binet designed the first IQ test in 1905 to predict the success or failure of largely middle-class children in the French school system and to identify children who required "special classes" because they were "slow." *Questions that gave results in accordance with teachers' estimates of their pupils' abilities were retained; others were dropped.* In the American version of the IQ test, the Stanford-Binet test of 1916, girls scored higher than boys; in the 1937 revision of the test, *questions were added or dropped in order to equalize the means between sexes.* However, *no efforts have been made to change the test from the substantially white middle-class cultural background on which it was originally normalized.* This is notable, because as the Stanford-Binet test has been moved from one country to another, large changes have been required in the test to produce the same mean score!

The IQ Test and What It Measures

How much cultural bias is there in the Stanford-Binet test? A major section of the test is a vocabulary list, primarily of words that a child would rarely come across except by reading English literature. Other questions are clear tests of background and attitude: a picture, and a question: "Which woman is prettier?" "What's the thing for you to do when you have broken something that belongs to someone else?" (The correct answer must include an offer to *pay* for it as well as an apology. "Feel sorry" and "Tell them I did it" are wrong answers.) In addition to the attitudes required for correct answers on the test, we must also consider the attitude of the child taking the test. The child who wants to please his teacher will clearly do much better in such a test than one who does not. Jane Mercer has described how many black and Chicano children have been unjustly tracked into programs for the mentally retarded on the basis of IQ tests.

IQ and Heredity

What of the claim that IQ is largely an inherited trait? A complex, continuously variable characteristic such as IQ is usually influenced by both genetic and environmental factors. In order to ascribe differences in this characteristic to genetic differences, comparison must be made of two groups maintained at the same time under identical or properly randomized environmental conditions. The heritability of a given trait is defined as the fraction of the variation between individuals that is determined by genetic differences. The arguments for a high heritability of IQ are based primarily on two types of studies that attempt to separate the genetic and environmental components of IQ: those of monozygotic ("identical") twins reared in separate homes and those of adopted children or of children reared in foster homes.

For the case of monozygotic twins, the genotypes are identical. Therefore, any differences in a measured trait are presumed to derive from environmental influences. If the twins are placed in separate, *random* environments, then a high correlation in IQ scores implies that there is little influence of environmental factors on IQ—in other words, that IQ has a high heritability. Several reports have stated that IQ test scores of separated twins are very similar; Jensen concludes from his analysis of these reports that the heritability of IQ is 0.7 to 0.8.

The validity of this conclusion has been challenged by several people. A detailed study of the original papers (for example, *The Science and Politics of IQ* by Leon Kamin) indicates that the twins were not reared in random environments. Usually they were carefully placed in homes of the same social and economic class—often in the homes of relatives or friends. In addition, most of the studies did not take into account differences in age from one set of twins to the next—a factor with a large effect on IQ test scores. Kamin has shown that age effects alone can account for the correlation of twins' IQ scores in two studies used in Jensen's analysis. In at least two of the four principal studies upon which Jensen's conclusion is based, the problem of experimental bias becomes apparent. When James Shields, the author of one study, administered the test to both members of a pair of twins, the average difference in "total intelligence score" was 4.9. However, when Shields tested one twin and his associate tested the other, the average difference was 13.2, about the same as for the population as a whole! The raw data for the largest of the twin studies, that of Cyril Burt, no longer exist. But the published accounts of how the data were collected and analyzed contain numerous inconsistencies, which raise serious doubts about the objectivity of the investigator. Burt's analysis did not even use IQ scores; instead it relied on "final assessments" of test scores (by Burt) based upon "criticism or correction" by teachers or on "personal interviews." Arthur Jensen, who cited Burt's analysis repeatedly in his earlier publications, has recently agreed with the criticism of this work and has admitted that Burt's correlations are useless for hypothesis testing.

A second approach to the heritability of IQ is to test adopted children in foster homes and to try to correlate the children's IQ with that of their natural mother or with their race. These studies are nearly impossible to control adequately. Kamin has pointed out that the parents in adoptive families were often older and had higher average incomes and educational levels and fewer children than the control "natural" families. Kamin has also noted that in one study in which the IQ of the adopted child correlates poorly with that of the parent, the IQ of a natural child correlates just as poorly.

Another approach that has not been widely used is to analyze IQ scores of children of different races who have been reared together in a group situation that might approach a common environment. Barbara Tizard has made an interesting preliminary analysis of children reared in residential nurseries judged to be relatively free of racial bias. Her analysis indicates that there is no significant difference between the IQ scores of white, black, and mixed-race children.

In an extensive genetic analysis of the available data, David Layzer concludes: "Published analyses of IQ data provide no support whatever for Jensen's thesis that inequalities in cognitive performance are due largely to genetic differences."

Differences in IQ Between Races and Social Classes

What is the significance of differences in IQ between races and social classes? Even if IQ had been shown to have a high heritability within one relatively homogeneous group, it does not follow from genetic theory that there is a similar high heritability within another group subjected to a different environment. Nor does it follow that differences in IQ between groups maintained in different environments are genetic in origin. The differences between black and white skin and between wealth and poverty clearly constitute enormous environmental factors in our society. The inheritance laws that confer wealth upon children of the wealthy are scarcely genotypic in origin. An interesting demonstration that environment *can* greatly affect IQ has been provided by the work of Rick F. Heber and his associates in Wisconsin. They exposed black infants from poor backgrounds to an enriched environment and found that after five years the infants' IQ scores were some 30 points higher than those of a control group!

In summary, the evidence for inherited differences in intelligence between racial and social classes is a pyramid of hypotheses, resting on assumptions that lack scientific validity and conclusive data. No one can question the freedom of individuals to do research in this area. However, those who treat these theories as fact and draw sweeping social conclusions should and must be challenged by the scientific community before another generation is indoctrinated with a "scientific" concept of race and class supremacy.

PLANT GENETICS AND CROP IMPROVEMENT

I have heard here this morning that people may become dependent upon us for food. I know that was not supposed to be good news. To me, that is good news, because before people will do anything they have got to eat. And if you are really looking for a way to get people to lean on you and to be dependent upon you, in terms of their cooperation with you, it seems that food dependence would be terrific.

Hubert Humphrey, 1957

The problem of world hunger and malnutrition is often attributed to the rapid growth rate of the population relative to the rate of increase in the food supply. This is certainly part of the problem. However, the political and social structure that determines how the food will be distributed is also very important. Geneticists and agriculturists have attempted to solve the first problem by selecting for genetic strains that have the potential to double or even quadruple the yield per acre of certain crops relative to local strains of the same crop. High-yield varieties (HYV) theoretically can be selected for any crop. But the cases in which this approach has been the most successful are "hybrid" corn, "wonder" wheat, and "miracle" rice. The application of these HYV crops to food production and agricultural development has been called the "green revolution."

As a basis for an analysis of the green revolution, it is extremely important to realize that HYV strains have been selected to produce higher yields under what amounts to "laboratory conditions" of optimum (high) amounts of chemical fertilizers, pesticides, and irrigation water (Chapter 37). In addition, experimental farms are usually large plots of level land located in temperate zones. These facts carry with them obvious social and political implications when the laboratory crop is introduced into underdeveloped (and often tropical) countries. In many such countries, 70 to 90 percent of the farmers cultivate small plots of land with no irrigation. For most of these small farmers, it is a struggle to produce the food needed by their own families; little if any is left over to sell. Therefore, they do not have the cash necessary for the purchase of HYV seeds, fertilizers, and pesticides. As a consequence, one of the major effects of the introduction of HYV crops has been to increase the difference in wealth between the owners of large farms, who have the money to invest in new techniques, and the peasant farmers.

In the sections to follow, we will discuss some of the major problems with the past programs of selection and widespread application of a limited number of strains of a major food crop. We will then point out, with a few specific examples, some of the reasons for recent failures of the green revolution. Finally, we will ask how the application of HYV crops has affected the standard of living in regions where it has been the most "successful."

Problems of "Monocultural" Crops

One of the most obvious dangers of planting most of a given area with a single variety of food crop is the risk of total disaster if pathogens infect the plants. The classic example of this type of catastrophe is the potato famine that took place in Ireland in the 1830s. An estimated 2 million people died in that decade and another 2 million emigrated, leaving behind only 4 million people, many in extreme poverty.

This disaster was the result of a previously unknown fungus to which the few varieties of potato imported from South America proved highly susceptible.

A more recent example of this type of epidemic disease, which actually destroyed a far greater amount of food than the potato rust, is the corn blight that spread across the southern United States in 1970 and 1971. Prior to the appearance of this new fungus, *Helminthosporium maydis* (southern corn blight), 80 to 85 percent of the hybrid seed corn in the United States carried the marker Tcms (Texas cytoplasmic male sterility), which confers male sterility on the plant. This enables the production of hybrid corn without the laborious tasks of hand-pollination or detasseling the corn plants. Unfortunately, for reasons that are still unknown, this same marker rendered the plant hypersensitive to the new fungus. The total financial losses were estimated to be $1 billion. In many of the southern states, 50 percent of the 1970 corn crop was lost. If the blight had taken place in a country such as Guatemala—where people receive half their caloric intake from corn—famine would have been widespread.

Numerous other examples of such epidemics could be cited. The "miracle" rice in the Philippines has turned out to be very sensitive to the tungro virus, and the HYV wheat in northern India and Pakistan is especially susceptible to a new strain of yellow rust. The latter case is especially discouraging because one of the characteristics selected by Norman Borlaug when he developed these varieties of wheat in Mexico was resistance to rust! Thus, *it is essential to maintain a diversity of genetic strains in order to minimize the effects of epidemics.* In addition, *it is important to preserve a large variety of native strains from which to select new strains.* As H. Garrison Wilkes and Susan Wilkes point out, there have been recent proposals to establish world crop banks for this purpose.

Failure to Consider Local Needs

Other crucial considerations in designing a selection program for higher yield plant varieties are the desires of the community the strains are supposed to help. Such desires may seem obvious, but they frequently have been ignored. For example, the Rockefeller Foundation has devoted an extremely small fraction of its agricultural research in Mexico toward the improvement of bean crops, the principle source of protein for most of the people in that country. In fact, the bean program was essentially dropped in 1960 because of slow progress. Instead, the Foundation has focused its efforts on wheat, largely a "cash" crop in northern Mexico, and on hybrid corn.

Although hybrid corn has been available in Mexico for nineteen years, only 10 percent of the corn acreage is planted in the new varieties. Farmers dislike it because it is more sensitive to weevils, it is not adaptable to the wide variety of terrain and water supplies throughout Mexico, and new seeds must be purchased each year. The farmers with large areas to cultivate use the hybrid corn for two reasons: the seed size is more uniform and hence more adaptable to mechanical processing; and for a corn farmer to obtain a government loan, he must plant hybrid corn.

In Asian countries where "miracle" rice strains have been introduced, the problem of neglecting the small farmer's needs has also arisen. The HYV rice strains are dwarf varieties that have shorter, tougher stalks than local varieties. These characteristics were selected because they make the rice more resistant to winds and the stalk capable of supporting heavier heads of grains. Unfortunately, these short, tough stalks are distasteful to cattle and unsuitable for roof thatching—two important side products of the rice crop. Moreover, because the stalks are short, the rice is more susceptible to the flooding that usually accompanies the high winds of seasonal typhoons. In addition, these varieties mature about forty days earlier than the native varieties during the *kharif* season (summer and early fall)—which means that they are ready to be harvested during the monsoons. Only farmers with mechanical dryers can prevent their rice from rotting. Ironically, these same strains have a longer maturation time than the local varieties when planted in the *rabi* season (winter and early spring), which is very dry; the result is an absolute requirement for irrigation.

As noted earlier, the heavy requirements of the HYV rice and wheat for fertilizer and irrigation ensure that only the more wealthy farmers can use them—unless some direct assistance is given to the small farmer. There has been a dearth of local assistance of this type, however, and outside help has most often been allied with the goals of large American corporations and American foreign policy. In the Philippines, Esso established 400 agricultural stores with what an AID (Agency for International Development) report called "a sales staff of agent-representative-entrepreneurs" who were given the task of converting the peasants to the new HYV rice. They worked closely with AID officials throughout the country. It is no coincidence that these Esso Standard Fertilizer Company stores sell the chemicals required by these crops.

In theory, government low-interest loans could make improvements more accessible for the small farmers. In practice, these loans have generally been feasible only for farmers with large holdings. Often the small farmer—when he can obtain a loan—is unable to sustain even a single year of crop failure without forfeiting his loan and losing his land. In India, in regions where government-financed irrigation canals exist, agriculture has flourished. Elsewhere it has remained unchanged. Extensive studies have shown that even within the small areas affected by the green-revolution crops, it is only the farmer with more than 10 acres who has actually increased his yield per acre with the HYV rice and wheat. This excludes 90 percent of the cultivating families.

As you will read in Chapter 37, another serious problem with the application of modern technology to agricultural development that has become extreme in the past few years is the rising costs and diminished quantities of available fertilizers, chemical pesticides, and machinery as well as gasoline to run it. The results of inflation and the "energy crisis" have paralleled a *decline* in the world market price for many of the crops produced by "developing" countries. Thus, many African, Latin American, and Asian countries cannot recover even their "input" costs of producing high-yield crops.

Secondary Problems From Irrigation and Pesticide Programs

In northern India and Pakistan, where numerous government and privately financed wells have been drilled, the water table has been lowered. As a result, wells must be sunk deeper every year in some areas. Not only is this drilling expensive, it may have disastrous long-range ecological effects. Another undesirable effect of massive irrigation projects in many areas has been the increasing salinity and alkalinity of the soil as a result of the rapid evaporation characteristic of semiarid regions. Elizabeth Whitcombe has described the situation in Uttar Pradesh, a state in northern India, *where intensive irrigation practices have rendered 7 million acres unfit for cultivation.*

The use of pesticides to stem crop disease epidemics brings with it a host of problems that have been well publicized and will not be discussed in detail here. Briefly, in addition to the vast ecological damage often rendered by such pesticides, small farmers cannot afford them, and many pests are very quick to mutate to a resistant form, which renders the pesticides useless in any event. In 1969 and 1970, Indonesia contracted private corporations (among which CIBA was the largest) to implement the green revolution. Marvin Harris has described this program, in which the insecticide Demicon 100 was sprayed from the air over vast, densely populated areas of Java, whether farmers wanted their land sprayed or not. The result was that large numbers of fish—the main source of protein in this area—were killed. Claims have been made that children and water buffalo were also killed; CIBA denies that Demicon 100 was responsible. The entire program was later dropped by the government because the rice was costing almost three times the world market rate to produce.

How Successful Is the Green Revolution?

Have HYV rice, wheat, and corn really been responsible for increased production of these crops in any countries? In the United States, mechanized farming techniques, large farms, and increased fertilization have converted food production into a big business. But what about countries in which the population density is high, the poverty is extreme, and the weather and land conditions are far from ideal? In such countries one cannot find an example of increased production due solely or even primarily to HYV crops. Many claims by government and foundation officials have been made, however. In every case in which an increase in production has been attributed to HYV crops (wheat in Mexico, Pakistan, and India; rice in the Philippines) there have also been increases in the numbers of acres planted, in the application of fertilizer, in the use of irrigation, and in the crucial support of government-subsidized prices. In the past few years the outlook has been even worse—the absolute yields of rice in the Philippines and India and of wheat in Pakistan and India have been decreasing. The HYV strains are less productive in their third, fourth, and fifth years—partly because the plants develop large root systems that deplete the soil of nutrients and water and therefore require increased fertilization and irrigation.

Finally, we can ask whether there have been improvements in the quality of life as a result of these programs. Data are of course very difficult to obtain, but the outlook is depressing (Chapter 37). Statistics gathered in India indicate that the percentage of people below the "minimum level of living" increased in almost every state in the period between 1960 and 1968. The average increase is 40 to 50 percent, whereas in some states where the green revolution has had the most impact, such as Punjab, it has almost tripled! In many regions, farmers and tenants have migrated to the cities after losing their land to large landowners who now find farming profitable. This migration serves to increase the enormous unemployment rates. The reason is that industrialization typically is not yet sufficient to provide jobs for all those who have been displaced from the land by mechanization and by the conversion of many small tenant plots into larger ones. In India, agricultural development sponsored by the government has followed the pattern of an initial program piloted and funded by the Ford Foundation. In this scheme, certain promising areas are singled out for "intensive" development—areas where the holdings are large, the soil is good, the water supply is adequate, and so forth. This leaves the farmers in marginal areas—who most need help—with no government aid.

Can genetics and agricultural science provide the world with more food? The answer does not have to be no. Proper care can be taken to select and develop strains that can satisfy the needs of the people who will use them. Agricultural development can be made available to the majority of farmers (those who cultivate small plots of land). Extensive land reform and redistribution programs can be carried out rather than blocked by landowner-politicians and government officials. And large farms can be owned collectively, so that those who work the land receive a fair share of the food produced from them. Only then can tremendous gains in the quality of life be made. For these reasons, it is important that scientists consider both the direction and the application of their research programs in terms of the people they are supposed to benefit.

THE SOCIAL STRUCTURE OF SCIENCE

The preceding discussion has focused on some of the problems that arise when the results of basic research are applied to the problems of society. Obviously, the technical and political problems of translating a laboratory experiment into the real world are enormous. But as we stated at the outset, the problems of biological science are not separable from those of society.

The basic elements of scientific endeavor are creativity and communication: the original research and the transmission of the knowledge acquired to others. The usual form of communication is through publication in a scientific journal as an individual publication from the research worker. This is pure science as presented by most textbooks: the creative search for knowledge by a community of scholars. However, the practical business of carrying out this research has led to the evolution of a more complex social structure for science than for any form of activity.

Research requires money, facilities, and time. In biological research, the money is typically derived from federal grants; facilities and time to do research are attained through a position on the faculty of a university or a research institute. These necessities of research life are obtained through units of currency—and the individual publication is the primary unit of scientific currency. The resultant social structure of science has become a highly competitive individual entrepreneurship. As such it is characterized not only by creativity but by many of the promotional features of any commercial enterprise. (For an illuminating personal exposition of creative, competitive, and promotional aspects of biological science, the reader should refer to James Watson's *The Double Helix*.)

This social structure is in many respects undesirable, both for science and for the individuals who do science. Most persons who become scientists are initially attracted to the field for a varying mixture of two rather idealistic motivations: the desires to benefit life and to be creative. But often the scientist can become enmeshed in an atmosphere that is far different: a struggle for personal power and self-

glorification that is marked by great determination but little joy, creative or otherwise. A drive for priority in publication is a major symptom in this atmosphere; secrecy, jealousy, exploitation, and a loss of real creativity can be the costs.

To place the discussion on more familiar ground, the student should consider the effect of a highly competitive academic situation on his or her own attitudes or on those of associates. Does intense competition for grades for medical school increase a person's interest in creative thinking along new lines? Does it enhance one's motivation to help one's fellow students as a prelude to a career devoted to the benefit of life?

Are there problems arising from the social structure even if science is viewed simply in terms of its productivity or yield of new knowledge? Consider what happens if a number of research groups do exactly the same thing because they are afraid to exchange information, or because they all want to share the credit for something that is obviously important and obviously needs to be done. Scientific progress will certainly occur at a lower rate than if those research groups had communicated freely and set off on perhaps overlapping but distinctly different paths. One of the most exciting and most productive aspects of science is the free exchange of ideas at an even earlier stage, before research on a subject has begun. Yet it is at this stage that the scientist in a competitive world is often even more reluctant to discuss his new ideas on which he has not actually even begun to work.

Data on this subject are obviously difficult to find. One study in another field was carried out by Jerry Gaston, who interviewed nearly all the high-energy nuclear physicists in England concerning their attitudes about secrecy. Gaston found that 63 percent of these scientists admitted that they would not discuss an idea with others before actually starting experimental work on it.

As long as it is structured to maximize the reward for individual achievement, there will be two other major problems for science. In a highly individualistic and competitive society lacking in real community, it is very difficult for scientists to act together to point out misuses and abuses of their work in a larger society. It is also difficult to reverse the tendency for concentration of an increasing fraction of the financial resources for science under the direct control of a small number of persons through large grants and contract research, in which a single individual may control the disbursement of millions of dollars (see, for example, Nicholas Wade's account of the cancer virus program).

In earlier chapters you read how the really impressive thing about the field of science is the communal nature of scientific progress. Each "great advance" is nearly always a small brick on top of a large communal structure built by the prior achievement of many individuals. The myth of the scientific superman contributes to the gulf in understanding between science and the rest of society: the "mystification" of science in which the scientist appears as a practitioner of a complex art—good or evil, depending on one's point of view—that is incomprehensible to the rest of humanity.

PERSPECTIVE

In this chapter we have noted that the use of biological science in a consistent and effective way to improve the human condition is limited by the social and political context in which the research work is done and applied. What can be done to improve the situation? At a "local" level within science, there should be an acceptance of the communal nature of scientific progress as something to be embraced rather than hidden in the quest for individual recognition. There should be efforts to organize a true scientific community that could not only create a better world within science but serve as a model for other areas of human endeavor. There should be more effective communication of the nature of scientific progress to the society at large, coupled with real efforts toward public understanding of the prospects and perils of research—a "demystification" of science. The nonscientist in turn should demand complete information about research, its applications, and its funding. But the typical scientist and nonscientist alike must also become more directly involved with the social and political world. Biology will truly be an instrument for life only in a society dedicated to the benefit of life.

SUGGESTED READINGS

BRIGHAM, C. C. *A Study of American Intelligence.* Princeton, N.J.: Princeton University Press, 1923. An analysis of IQ scores from tests given to 2 million World War I draftees.

FRANKEL, FRANCINE R. *India's Green Revolution: Political Costs of Economic Growth.* Princeton, N.J.: Princeton University Press, 1971. A detailed account of the impact of the green revolution on the five states in India where it has been most intensely applied.

GASTON, J. "Secretiveness and Competition for Priority of Discovery in Physics," *Minerva,* 9 (1971), 472. A discussion of attitudes toward competition and its consequences among British high-energy physicists.

HARRIS, M. "How Green the Revolution?" and "The Withering Green Revolution," *Natural History,* June 1972, p. 29, and March 1973, p. 20. Brief critical discussions of some of the problems of the green revolution.

HERRNSTEIN, RICHARD J. "IQ," *Atlantic Monthly,* 228 (September 1971), 43. A discussion of Herrnstein's thesis that a "meritocracy" exists in the United States in which people are either rich or poor because of their high or low IQ.

HILTON, B., D. CALLAHAN, M. HARRIS, L. CONDLIFFE, and B. BERKLEY (eds.). *Ethical Issues in Human Genetics.* New York: Plenum Press, 1973. A collection of articles on many aspects of human genetics, with emphasis on genetic counseling.

JENSEN, ARTHUR R. *Educability and Group Differences.* New York: Harper & Row, 1973. Recent summary of Jensen's arguments that the difference between the mean IQ score of black and white children is largely due to genetic differences in intelligence.

KAMIN, L. *The Science and Politics of IQ.* Potomac, Md.: Erlbaum Associates, 1974. A detailed critical analysis of the data used to argue that IQ has a high heritability and an account of the history of the IQ test and its role in the Eugenics Movement.

LAYZER, D., "Heritability Analysis of IQ Scores: Science or Numerology?" *Science,* 183 (1974), 1259. A critical analysis of the assumptions and calculations required to determine the heritability of IQ.

LUDMERER, KENNETH M. *Genetics and American Society.* Baltimore: Johns Hopkins, 1972. A historical account of the Eugenics Movement and its political role.

MERCER, JANE R. "IQ: The Lethal Label," *Psychology Today,* 6 (September 1972), 44.

PADDOCK, WILLIAM, and ELIZABETH PADDOCK. *We Don't Know How.* Ames: Iowa State University Press, 1973. A detailed description of the ineffectiveness of United States foreign aid programs, especially in agriculture, to Mexico and Central America.

SHOCKLEY, WILLIAM. "The Apple-of-God's-Eye Obsession," *Humanist,* 32 (January-February 1972), 16–17. A presentation of Shockley's ideas on dysgenics, including his "bonus sterilization plan" to encourage sterilization of persons with low IQ.

WADE, N. "Special Virus Cancer Program: Travails of a Biological Moonshot," *Science,* 174 (1971), 1306. A discussion of contract research at the National Institutes of Health.

WHITCOMBE, E. "The New Agricultural Strategy in Uttar Pradesh, India, 1968–70: Technical Problems," in R. T. Shand (ed.), *Technical Change in Asian Agriculture.* Canberra: Australian National University Press, 1973. A discussion of the problems in Uttar Pradesh that have resulted from short-sighted agricultural development schemes, especially irrigation projects.

WILKES, H. G., and S. WILKES. "The Green Revolution," *Environment,* 14 (October 1972), 32. A discussion of the dangers inherent in "monocultural" programs of agricultural development.

Chapter 37

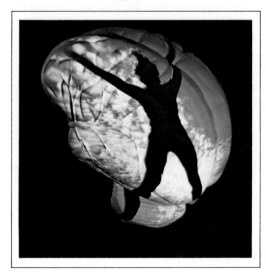

Bioethics: Toward Ecological Engineering

Freedom is mine
Food is mine
Shelter and space are mine
Thought 3 billion people in the world

There is, in the nature of ecological processes, a control of human destiny—a control that demands obedience and, perhaps, reverence. For many, this controlling power is an unseen but all-knowing divinity; for others, it resides not in a superior being but in the inherent nature of life. There are those who would argue that some kind of principle underlies this control, guiding us all to a predetermined (or at least progressively defined) end. And there are others who would argue that the outcome is entirely a matter of randomness and chance. Regardless of viewpoint, the central issue remains the same: *The nature of ecological processes controls human destiny along with the destiny of other living and nonliving components of the biosphere.*

Within the context of this issue, control is not entirely one-way. At the same time an organism is controlled by the living and nonliving forces in its environment, it is influencing and thereby controlling some part of those forces. We, the human organism, are an extreme case: the control we exert over ecological processes is unparalleled in the world of living things. But what are the *effects* of our controls? To what extent are they disrupting the ecological processes that have for billions of years nurtured life on earth? Increasingly we find ourselves wondering about the repercussions of our activities; increasingly the word "survival" makes us pause uneasily as we leave our imprint on one ecosystem after another. Perhaps it is because we do *not* know the answers that we are beginning to feel a need for a set of rules of ecological conduct. This is one justification for a biological ethic, or **bioethics**—a survival-oriented system of rules governing human behavior.

Now, it would be self-deluding to pretend that our fundamental concern resides outside our own well-being; any ethical system, in the final analysis, is structured not only to preserve itself but to preserve its devotees or practitioners. Thus, a first step toward developing a biological ethic is to recognize that the primary goal is preservation of the human species. What is done to nature must be considered in terms of its real, potential, or even suspected effect on our survival. The bioethical goal must also be global. It must include all humankind, for it is the collective pool of genetic resources and potential that enables a species not only to cope with existing diversity of ecological systems but to adapt to continuously changing ones.

There is, however, an essential qualification to this line of reasoning. We are not just *quantitative* beings. If we were, we would be nothing more than a complex of biophysical and biochemical properties and processes. At our best we are also *qualitative*—conscious, creative, and contemplative beings. Merely to survive is not enough: a rationale for survival must articulate a survival with dignity

and meaning, with quality. And that, in turn, points to the kinds of interpersonal relationships and social structures that must exist.

This plea for a survival ethic is premised on the need for it, and the need for it arises from certain givens, observations, and assumptions. Some of them have been mentioned in passing in earlier chapters in this book, but here they will be reconsidered in the bioethical context.

GIVEN: THE RESOURCES OF THE BIOSPHERE ARE FINITE

The most powerful ecological consideration is the nature of the planet earth—its position and relationship in the solar system, its history, and its constitution. For now and the foreseeable future, there is no other place that can provide us with food and protection, shelter and warmth. What earth has now in the way of pieces and parts is it.

Almost all of the usable energy the earth receives is solar in origin. Receipt may vary from place to place and from season to season, but the sum total is constant and relatively well assured for some billions of years hence. Every minute, about 1 gram calorie per square centimeter of solar energy falls on the earth's surface. This solar input is converted by microscopic and macroscopic plants into calorie-laden organic compounds. According to a number of independent estimates, the world's production from this primary energy source can be increased sixfold or, at most, ninefold. Whatever the precise limit, there is a limit.

Similarly, the total amounts of material resources may not be fully known, but finite amounts do exist and they can be depleted. Over long periods of geologic time the amount of water bound in polar ice or free in the oceans may vary, but the total (about 266×10^{23} kilograms) is relatively constant and limited. The amount of iron or gold or any other mineral is finite. At present rates of consumption, the known supply of natural gas and oil, mercury, tin, tungsten, and helium may well be exhausted by the end of the century; coal may be used up in about 200 years. More crucially, some resources are not only limited in amount, they are nonrenewable. Fossil fuels are a prime example: once used, they cannot be renewed or reused. Other resources, such as those in deep-sea sediments, are presently inaccessible; still others, such as the mineral components of seawater, cannot at present be economically extracted.

Finally, there is a finite amount of terrestrial space—approximately 32 billion acres. Although more or less land may be exposed as polar ice sheets advance and recede, the amount available over several hundred human generations is constant and essentially limited. Further constraints exist because not all land can support human habitation. Antarc-

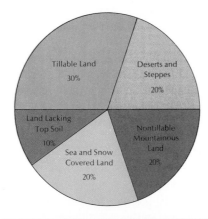

Figure 37.2   Potential farmland on a global scale. The table shows changes in world land utilization between 1882 and 1952. The net addition of tilled acreage amounts to 240 million hectares (1 hectare = 2.471 acres) during a period when the world population grew by almost 2 billion people. Thus the gain was reduced to only 0.5 hectare (1.25 acres) per individual.

	1882	Percent	1952	Percent	CHANGE 1888–1952	Percent
Forest	5.2	45.4	3.3	29.6	−1.9	−36.8
Desert and wasteland	1.1	9.4	2.6	23.3	+1.5	+140.6
Built-on land	0.87	7.7	1.6	14.6	+0.73	+85.8
Pastures	1.5	13.4	2.2	19.5	+0.7	+41.9
Tilled land	0.86	7.6	1.1	9.2	+0.24	+24.5
	9.53	83.5	10.8	96.2	+1.27	+12.9
Area not especially utilized	1.81	16.5	0.27	3.8	−1.54	−79.9
Total	11.34	100	11.07	100	−0.27	−2.4

Changes in Land Utilization 1882–1952
(billion hectares)

tica, for example, represents one-tenth of the world's land surface but is essentially uninhabitable. And there is only so much land that can be used for agricultural and grazing purposes (Figure 37.2). About 16 billion acres are potentially suitable for farming or grazing. But only 3.5 billion acres are now being used for farming, and only 4.5 billion acres for grazing.

Is it possible to use the remaining 8 billion acres of potential agricultural or grazing land? The constraints are severe. First, more than one-third lies in tropical regions, where the soil is subject to extreme and rapid mineral loss or where the soil that is exposed to air hardens to rocklike quality. Second, most of the remaining potential agricultural soil is in desert regions in Spain, Israel, central China, and the Colorado River Basin of the United States. Such soil could be made productive only with an extremely heavy investment in irrigation.

For thousands of years, in successive waves of exploration and of migration, the various peoples of the world came to know and to take what seemed an endless resource—land. But now the land is charted and mapped; the major and most minor configurations on a world map are now set. Space *is* limited. Although we have had trouble accepting the limit on space and adjusting our life styles to it, we are beginning to recognize the limit is there. As yet, we do not seem ready to acknowledge that there is a limit also to other

of earth's resources—minerals, metals, and fuels. That, too, will come. It must.

GIVEN: THE BIOSPHERE IS A COMPLEX OF ECOSYSTEMS

The earth may be considered a single, immense, and complex ecosystem. Like any ecosystem, it has biotic and abiotic components; it has interacting, interdependent processes; it exhibits well-defined or definable phenomena; it is dependent on a continuous flow of energy; and it is characterized by a cycling of matter. Within this ecosystem are many, almost innumerable ecosystems. But the smaller ones differ from the global ecosystem in a significant way: they theoretically can or actually do depend for energy and matter on other ecosystems. In fact, *one of the singular characteristics of ecosystems is not their unique biotic and abiotic structure and function but their interrelatedness to other unique ecosystems* (Figure 37.3). It is this interrelatedness that gives rise to environmental impact often far removed in space and time from the source—the heavy radioactive fallout in Lapland from atomic detonations in the mid-Pacific, for example, and DDT on islands thousands of miles from the continents on which it was used.

Interrelated and even interdependent, this collection of more or less unique ecosystems forms the **biosphere,** the collective but finite ecosystem that is the planet earth. But

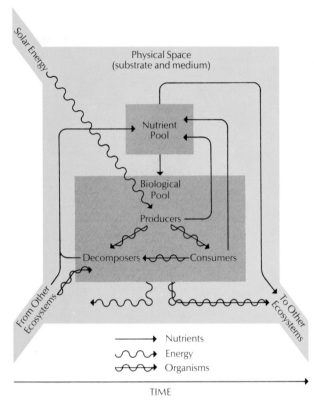

Figure 37.3 *The interrelated and interdependent flow of matter and energy through the ecosystems of the earth.*

the earth is not interrelated with other biospheres—there are none in our solar system. We are alone. Although there are theoretical reasons for assuming life exists on hundreds of thousands of planets outside the solar system, the earth has no relationships such as exist among earthbound ecosystems. For humankind, then, earth is it. From an ecological operating perspective, this isolation is limiting; from an ethical perspective, it is awe-inspiring.

OBSERVATION: EXPLOSIVE POPULATION GROWTH AFFECTS THE QUALITY OF LIFE

Among the many problems justifying the need for a bioethic, three make up much of the case. Those problems deal with the nature of population growth and development, the energy relations within ecosystems, and ecosystem growth and development.

Given an optimum environment, a population—be it of paramecia, peas, or people—appears to grow more or less exponentially and, at least in theory, limitlessly (Chapter 31). But environments and their resources are limiting. As a consequence, a natural population in a natural setting eventually arrives at some kind of equilibrium in which displacement through death is relatively balanced by replacement through birth.

Modifications of the environment are reflected in fluctuations from the equilibrium level. Sometimes modifications

lead even to the extinction of populations. The modification may be the outcome of a natural physical event such as a landslide, or a fire, or a chemical agent that affects the available nutrients. It may also be the outcome of a biological event, such as the advent of a windborne fungus or the range expansion of a predator—or the application of human technology that most decidedly modifies preexisting balances among populations. Some of these maladjustments caused by human activity have in turn wreaked heavier tolls on our own intents and purposes; for example, the inadvertent elimination of natural or biological controls of pest populations. This is an observation, not a judgment of good or bad, right or wrong. It is a statement of our ecological impact on the environment.

However, it is with respect to our own population that our modifications have been and are being increasingly felt. Regardless of the measures that are used—doubling time, actual numbers, density—the growth of the world's human population has been dramatic. Although the magnitude of the numbers may not be readily grasped, the growth pattern itself (Figure 37.4) is startling. It is decidedly exponential: if present trends continue, it will have more than doubled in the years between 1970 and 2000 (Table 37.1). This rate suggests to many that the human population is following a J-shaped curve (Chapter 31) and is headed for collapse.

Birth and death are the most significant control agents in

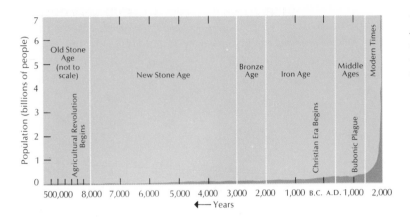

Figure 37.4 Growth rate of the human population for the past 500,000 years. It is only within the very recent past, with the rise of modern technology, that the growth curve has taken on the alarming J-shaped configuration shown here.

Table 37.1
World and Regional Population Projections

Year	Projected Population *(millions of persons)*							
	World	Africa	Asia	North America	Latin America	Europe	Oceania	USSR
Mid-1969	3,551	344	1,990	225	276	456	19	241
2000 (UN estimate based on constant fertility)	7,552	860	4,513	388	756	571	33	402
2000 (UN medium estimate)	6,130	768	3,458	354	638	527	32	353

Source: Population Reference Bureau, *1969 World Population Data Sheet* (Washington, D.C.: Population Reference Bureau, Inc., 1969).

population growth. In countries such as Colombia, the Philippines, Pakistan, and Mexico, there is a high birth rate but a low death rate, and the population grows rapidly (Table 37.2). In countries such as Nigeria, there is a high birth rate and a high death rate, so population growth is not as rapid. In countries such as East Germany, a low birth rate coupled with a high death rate means that the population grows little or even declines. Emigration and immigration might have bearing on population size in a limited area. But if the world-wide population is considered, emigration from one area does not affect the total; it only affects local density.

For human beings, the crucial factor in burgeoning population size has not been an increase in the birth rate but a dramatic reduction in the death rate. In countries such as Ceylon, Taiwan, Malaya, and Japan, the death rate was cut in half in little more than a ten-year period (Figure 37.5). That more people live is the result of better sanitation, better nutrition, and better health care. Pneumonia, an infectious disease that once was the primary killer of human beings, was brought under control by the so-called miracle drugs. Most childhood diseases have been controlled by immunization. Diseases such as malaria and yellow fever are held in check. Such controls over disease have enabled people to live longer. That is the main reason why degenerative conditions of the heart and circulatory system have become so prominent; that is why diseases more characteristic of old age, such as many types of cancer, concern us now (Chapter 35).

An outcome of this burgeoning in human population is that we need more space to live, more space to farm and fish, more minerals and timber to provide shelter and technological accoutrements—more and more of what becomes less and less. Given the finite nature of the earth and the nonrenewable nature of most of its resources, and given the nature of population growth, the end result must be obvious: *the human population cannot grow indefinitely.*

But who is to determine what the limits of growth should be? Such a determination is beset with all sorts of scientific, social, and ethical questions. What are the limits of food production? What is the minimum sufficient diet for humans? What are the limits of mineral and other resources? How recyclable might they be? Whose population is to remain stable—whites, blacks, Asians, Latin Americans?

Table 37.2
Birth, Death, and Growth Rates in Number of Individuals per 1,000 Total Population of Selected Modern Nations (1973)

Nation	Birth Rate	Death Rate*	Growth Rate** (%)	Doubling Time (years)
Colombia	45	11	3.4	21
Ecuador	45	11	3.4	21
Paraguay	45	11	3.4	21
Venezuela	41	8	3.4	21
Philippines	45	12	3.3	21
Pakistan	51	18	3.3	21
Mexico	43	10	3.3	21
Honduras	49	17	3.2	22
United Arab Republic	50	19	3.1	23
Mongolia	42	11	3.1	23
Cambodia	45	16	3.0	23
Zambia	50	21	2.9	24
Indonesia	47	19	2.9	24
Iran	45	17	2.8	25
Brazil	38	10	2.8	25
Albania	35	8	2.7	25
Costa Rica	34	7	2.7	26
Nigeria	50	25	2.6	27
Laos	42	17	2.6	28
India	42	17	2.5	28
Turkey	40	15	2.5	28
Guinea	42	18	2.4	29
Nepal	45	23	2.2	32
WORLD AVERAGE	*33*	*13*	*2.0*	*35*
Australia	21	9	1.9	37
Mainland China	30	13	1.7	41
Chile	26	9	1.7	41
Argentina	22	9	1.5	47
Puerto Rico	25	7	1.4	50
Uruguay	23	9	1.4	50
Japan	19	7	1.2	58
Canada	16	7	1.2	58
Spain	19	8	1.1	63
Portugal	21	11	1.0	70
Switzerland	14	9	1.0	70
Poland	17	8	0.9	77
United States	16	9	0.8	82
Greece	16	8	0.8	82
Norway	17	10	0.7	99
Italy	17	10	0.7	99
France	17	11	0.6	112
Denmark	16	10	0.5	139
Ireland	22	11	0.5	139
Czechoslovakia	17	12	0.5	139
Hungary	15	11	0.4	231
Finland	13	10	0.3	231
Belgium	14	12	0.2	700
West Germany	12	12	0.0	—
East Germany	12	14	−0.2	—

*Low death rates in rapidly growing countries are largely a result of the small proportion of older individuals in those populations.
**Calculated growth rates include allowance for immigration and emigration, which is very significant in some countries.
Source: Population Reference Bureau, *1973 World Population Data Sheet* (Washington, D.C.: Population Reference Bureau, Inc., 1973).

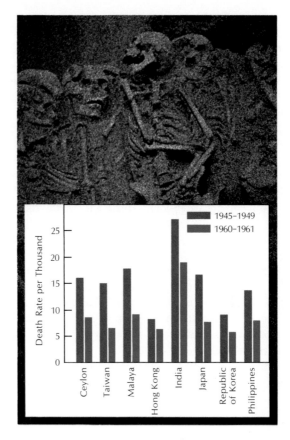

Figure 37.5   Changes in the rate of mortality in a few Asian nations. The average death rates for the period between 1945 and 1949 are compared with those between 1960 and 1961.

Who controls whom? Who decides? The very nature of the questions underscores not only the imperative for a bioethic but the need to work out its precepts.

OBSERVATION: ENERGY TRANSFER IN FOOD CHAINS IS INESCAPABLY INEFFICIENT

Perhaps one of the most sobering ecological observations is that the flow of energy among the biotic components of an ecosystem is relatively inefficient. Because this topic has been considered several times in this book, only a key point—the diminution of energy in ecosystems—will be stressed here. Primary producers capitalize, on the average, less than 1 percent of incident solar radiation. Each subsequent transfer passes on only 10 or at most 15 percent of the energy in the preceding level. Consider, for example, a simple food chain of grass-beef-man. For every 10,000 calories of solar energy, there would be 100 calories of plant, 10 calories of beef, and 1 calorie of man.

The relative inefficiency of energy transfer from one level to the next imposes some natural limits on the effective length of food chains and tells us something of the kinds of food chains that can support the most people. For example, the grain-based societies of the East, which constitute roughly two-thirds of the world's population, represent a two-level pyramid consisting of plant producers and human consumers. An average Chinese individual uses about 400 pounds of grain per year; an average American uses about 2,200 pounds. But, for the American, only about 140 pounds are eaten directly as grain in bread or other cereal products. For the Chinese, 360 of the 400 pounds are eaten as grain. Jean Mayer, a nutritionist at Harvard University, put it another way: "The same amount of food that is feeding 210 million Americans would feed 1.5 billion Chinese on an average Chinese diet."

If the eating habits characteristic of Western society remain the same as the number of people increases, then there must be an increase in primary food production. This can be done by increasing the area or volume for production and/or by increasing the productivity of a given area or volume. But given the limits on fertile land, more emphasis has been placed on increased productivity. In the so-called **green revolution,** crop yields have been increased by deliberate genetic selection for certain traits. The increase, however, has come at the expense of decreased food value, particularly protein content. For example, low-yield corn and wheat have about twice the protein content as their newly developed high-yield counterparts. Put another way, pigs were once raised quite well on low-yield corn, but today protein supplements must be added to their diet—which consists of high-yield crops! The increased dependence of developing areas on these "miracle crops" also decreases the genetic diversity of the crop systems in such areas, thus rendering these crops more susceptible to disease and predation.

Increased productivity has also followed from increased irrigation and from intensive use of fertilizers and pesticides. In the twenty years between 1943 and 1963, the total acreage devoted to crops in the United States dropped 35 percent. However, there was an increase of 38 percent in yield—accomplished in no small measure by a 290 percent increase in the use of fertilizers. Significantly, fertilizers themselves are "energy intensive." Much energy is required to mine, ship, process, transport, market, and distribute them. *In fact, more nonrenewable energy is expended in the production, marketing, and application of fertilizers than "new" energy is produced.* John and Carol Steinhart estimate that industrialized food systems require 5 to 10 calories of energy to get 1 calorie in food. In so-called primitive cultures, each calorie of energy produces 5 to 50 calories of food. In other words, if all countries followed the industrialized pattern, the world would use 80 percent of its annual energy just to produce food! Moreover, the introduction of new crop varieties in underdeveloped areas results in an increasing dependence on energy-intensive fertilizers and cultivation practices, without which the crops of the green revolution will not produce their maximum yields.

OBSERVATION: ECOSYSTEMS UNDERGO DYNAMIC BIOLOGICAL CHANGE

Ecosystems have structure and function. They are dynamic entities of interaction between and among their biotic and abiotic components. They respond to stimuli and stress, they change, they adapt. They interrelate with other ecosystems. Of all the properties of ecosystems, those most pertinent to the argument for a survival ethic are themselves interrelated—maturation and homeostasis.

In the **maturation process,** ecosystems develop from simple structural and functional beginnings into a mature complex of interconnections. A young ecosystem has relatively few kinds and numbers of organisms. Some are simplified to the point that they consist of only a few species of producers and a rudimentary array of decomposers. In extracting resources from the environment and excreting by-products into it, these organisms effect changes in the abiotic environment. *Changes brought about by metabolic activity may turn out to be harmful to the species responsible for them but beneficial to other species that invade an ecosystem.* As a result, succession occurs where new or different combinations of species and connections among both the abiotic and biotic components are established (Chapter 31).

Now, consider the dynamics that accompany these replacements. In a young ecosystem, energy and nutrient turnover is rapid and storage is limited. Algal populations, for example, transform solar energy and use nutrient resources, but the populations are short-lived and their remains are promptly decomposed so that the nutrients are available for the next production cycle. Furthermore, the oxygen needs for the collective respiratory needs of an ecosystem are met by the ecosystem's productivity. There is little if any net accumulation of energy and nutrient as biomass (energy stored as organic compounds). In immature terrestrial systems, energy and nutrient turnover is incomplete because of the general lack of a well-organized decomposer and consumer system. This results in gradual accumulation of biomass, because productivity exceeds total community respiration.

As the community matures, resource utilization becomes more complete as the various components of the community structure become more diverse. A mature and stable community contains a certain amount of stored energy in the form of a stable litter layer and the standing crop of organisms (Chapter 31), but the amount of such biomass is constant, indicating that community respiration equals community productivity. That energy-nutrient biomass may be living (as in the case of a mature hardwood forest) or nonliving (as in the case of peat).

Homeostatic attributes of ecosystems parallel their maturation. Even young ecosystems have a kind of adaptive capacity that enables them to "snap back" to some balanced state. But this capacity is quite limited: environmental constancy and predictability are not characteristic of a young ecosystem. Whatever environmental factor is assessed (for example, oxygen level or pH), it will exhibit considerable fluctuation and variation. Basically, young ecosystems are highly unstable in population size, in composition, and in constancy of physical and chemical properties. Minor environmental perturbations sweep through them as major catastrophes.

As ecosystems develop, stability increases until the mature ecosystem reaches what essentially is a homeostatic state. Biologists recognize this state as dynamic rather than static: there is a kind of fluctuation around a mean, like a vibrating violin string. Minor environmental perturbations elicit little or no response; even major ones, such as a fire, may have only temporal effects. Not surprisingly, there is high correlation between species diversity and this homeostatic state. The more kinds there are, the more variation there is to assure stability under changing conditions.

How do we interrelate with such ecosystem development and stabilization? By and large, we depend on the two developmental extremes in ecosystems—very young ones (for food) and quite mature ones (for "shelter"). Agricultural and maricultural practices are most efficient in young ecosystems, where much of the energy is channeled into reproductive structures, such as seeds. Such energy-rich seeds—corn, cereal grains, sorghum, and rice—form the basis of much of the world's agricultural production. Annual crops are a prime example of this kind of ecosystem output. But these ecosystems are highly vulnerable to environmental perturbations because of their reduced homeostatic properties. In order for such systems to function without disturbance, large investments of energy in the form of cultivation, pesticides, and herbicides are required. In contrast, the homeostasis of the mature forest is attained over time, five human generations not being at all unusual. And such systems are inherently stable. However, once exploited for human purposes (as in clear cutting), the ecosystem reverts to the immature, unstable, vulnerable state. Again, no value judgments are implied here—these are observations on the processes of dynamic biological change that do, however, need to be reckoned with in ascertaining the need for a biological survival ethic.

ASSUMPTION: NEEDS AND EXPECTATIONS ARE NOT NECESSARILY THE SAME THINGS

We can assume that our needs for food, clothing, and shelter—the fundamental prerequisites to survival—will increase exponentially along with the exponential increase in population (Figure 37.6). But somehow this assumption seems a little too abstract, a little too far removed from the world we know, to be met with widespread alarm. To understand what the concept of exponential growth means, envision a pond with one lily pad and imagine that the number of lilies doubles each day. On the second day there are two; on the third day, four; on the fourth day, eight; and so on. Now also imagine that we do nothing about the growth of the lily pads until they fill half of the pond. The daily rate of doubling is such that on the twenty-ninth day the pond is half-filled. Is there enough time to do something before the thirtieth day? For then it will be too late: in only one more day the pond will be filled. That's exponential growth!

More people will mean more food, more clothing, and more habitations. What is not clear, of course, is *how* much more. For example, the United Nations recommends a minimum daily caloric level of 2,200 kilocalories. If we accept that as standard, then we can project caloric food needs at various increased population levels. If we accept as

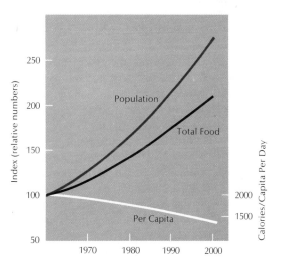

Figure 37.6 Projected world food production contrasted with population. Although food production is rising rapidly throughout the world, it is not rising as rapidly as human numbers.

standard a more enriched diet, the projections will yield a need for higher food levels at any given population level. *The sobering fact is that almost two-thirds of the world's population currently subsists on less than a minimum caloric level and hence is already in the midst of widespread famine* (Figure 37.7).

It is at this juncture that a second assumption, compounding the first, comes to bear: The undernourished two-thirds of the world's population are largely in the undeveloped nations; they will not remain content at minimal subsistence levels. Demands for food, clothing, and shelter will undoubtedly far exceed present levels and will come to approximate the seeming rights of affluent nations. How will we—as conscious, creative, and contemplative beings—meet those demands?

Consider the problem of producing enough food. Most of what is available to the undernourished two-thirds of the population is primary production material—the grains. Most of the food of the well-fed one-third is secondary production material—meat. Because there is about a 90 percent loss of useful energy in "converting" grain into meat, the implications are obvious: *There is no way the world's population can be supported by present agriculture and mariculture at Western caloric levels, let alone at Western levels of meat consumption.*

The situation is even more critical and more imminent than the preceding remarks imply. Most of the people in the world do not get enough protein (Figure 37.7). At least 12 percent of an individual's caloric intake should be protein—and the "improved" grains contain less protein than older varieties. Protein is especially needed in brain development, which is most rapid in the first few years of life. Its deficiency in the diet at such a time is believed to result in permanent brain damage and mental retardation. Furthermore, vitamin deficiencies accompany poorly balanced as well as inadequate diets. In Bangladesh alone, 50,000 people a year become permanently blind from vitamin A deficiency.

Aside from the problem of finding enough food for the present world population (let alone an increased one), consider the parallel increased demands for clothing and shelter. More people means the need for more living space, and more living space means less space for raising crops, growing timber, herding animals, and disposing of biological and technological wastes.

Or consider the problem of sharing the technological way of life. The accoutrements of Western civilization increasingly are being sought after by the rest of the world. The market for Western technological trappings and commercial "conveniences" is burgeoning faster than population itself. These devices and contrivances are largely manufactured of nonrenewable but recyclable materials fabricated with the energy of other nonrenewable but mainly nonrecyclable resources. The implication is again obvious: There cannot be enough, given the finiteness of the earth, to satisfy an infinite demand. Who will be the "haves," and who the "have nots"?

Consider, finally, the positive, optimistic faith that the future will be better. For some, such confidence is based on a belief in God; for others, it is based on belief in humanity per se or in its technology. This optimism is a powerful sustaining force. In its most elemental form, however, there is a kind of fatalism that "things will work out by themselves"—a fatalism that presumes a positive, rewarding end. Humanists more typically take the view that only by direct human intervention will things "work out" to some kind of positive, rewarding end. Only insofar as this divine or humanistic sustaining faith in the future encompasses the realities of the givens, observations, and assumptions can we count on survival. Only insofar as we endeavor to develop and practice a bioethic can we have survival.

THE CHALLENGE: SURVIVAL

By recognizing the finiteness of resources, by acknowledging the growth and development of populations and the thermodynamics in the maturation of ecosystems, and by accepting the nature of human expectations, we can more readily perceive the imbalance of organisms and resources. This imbalance arises from expectations that exceed the capacity to deliver, and from mismanagement of limited resources. The challenge is to bring demand into balance with supply. In the simplest terms, this challenge can be met in one of two ways.

First, population size can be reduced, or the demands from the existing number of people can be reduced. People may be able to learn to live with less, do more with less, be content with less. People may also be able to learn to produce fewer people. They will have to learn to do all of these things.

Second, a balance of supply and demand may also come through a recycling system. Recycling is essential for survival. As we are confronted with increasingly critical shortages, the need will become more evident. Glenn Seaborg, a former chairman of the Atomic Energy Commission, recently suggested that in a recycling society, everything "will be labeled in such a way that their use, origin and material can be readily identified; and all will have a regulated trade-in value."

Finiteness of resources and infiniteness of demand can be balanced by resource management and by management of and behavioral changes in demands. Management of resources is a form of engineering task. Interestingly enough, the stem of the word "engineering" derives from the Latin word meaning "to beget by wit"—engineering our resources is to live by our wits. This task will require not only a large financial investment but a more persistent investment of our collective wit to conserve, to find alternatives to nonrenewable resources, and to renew the renewable ones. But to be effective, that collective wit needs to be channeled properly. It will not happen without guidance, manipulation, and even coercion. There are at least two major forces that can steer that course—our cultural system, particularly government and academia, and human behavior. Because this book is used primarily by American students, the context of the following discussion is that of the United States. The portion dealing with human behavior has no such parochial boundaries.

The Role of Government in Ecological Engineering

All three major governmental functions—legislative, executive, and judicial—are agents of ecological salvation. Whatever the record has been in general, recent pressures have prompted acknowledgment of factors critical to our survival. Perhaps the key statement is found in "A National Policy for the Environment," developed in 1968 by leaders of Congress, the executive branch, industry, commerce, academia, and science:

The ultimate responsibility for protecting the human-serving values of our environment rests jointly with the legislative, executive and judicial branches of our Government. The Congress, as a full partner, has the obligation to provide comprehensive oversight of all environment-affecting programs of the executive branch, and also to participate in the overall design of national policy, thus serving both as an architect of environmental management strategy and as the elaborator of goals and principles for guiding future legal actions.

Recognizing the pulls and tugs of the political process, the United States entered the 1970s better equipped by the passage of the National Environmental Policy Act of 1969, which established the Council on Environmental Quality, the "keeper of our environmental conscience." This agency was armed with the authority to demand that "every recommendation or report on proposals for legislation and other major Federal actions significantly affecting the quality of the human environment" must be accompanied by a detailed statement on "the environmental impact of the proposed action." Since then, there has been a cascading effect, with many regional authorities, states, and local municipalities also demanding "environmental impact statements" prior to approving new dams, power plants, condominiums, shopping centers, housing developments, and the like.

There are now at least sixteen major Congressional committees and well over sixty major agencies in the executive branch concerned with environmental matters. The 1970 reorganization of the multiple-agency executive system into the Environmental Protection Agency (EPA) and the National Oceanographic and Atmospheric Administration (NOAA) appears, in general, to have been a step in the right direction. Of course, some agencies have overlapping jurisdictions that would appear to be counterproductive. Nevertheless, even with the labyrinth of agencies, boards, committees, and commissions, the country somehow has moved toward increased environmental protection.

The environmental protection movement has not moved as fast as some would wish, but it has moved too fast and too far for others who have other interests at stake. The political and economic forces of erosion, delay, and deferral are constant. The lack of federal leadership in the 1974 gasoline "crisis" was a singular low mark in environmental responsibility. No sooner was the immediate crisis over than some national leaders again painted rosy pictures about the gasoline supply. It might better have been a time to capitalize on the impact the shortage had on the individual and to undertake a long-term program encouraging mass transportation, research on alternate fuel sources, and the like. The political gain of "solving the crisis" was more powerful than the political loss of advising people to "pull in their belts" for the long haul. This is short-term gain against long-term loss.

In short, if "the people" want a survival environment, it will not come through wishing but, in part at least, by paying attention to the political process, to those politicians whose interests might focus outside the interests of "the people." It is the voter who ultimately controls his representatives, but to control he must be an informed participant in the elective process.

There is little question that the law and the courts will continue to exercise an increasingly influential role in engineering an environment more conducive to human survival. Armed with existing law (including an 1899 Rivers and Harbor Act, which the Army Corps of Engineers had failed to enforce for seventy years), environmentally conscious citizens individually and as groups have employed injunctions and filed suits protesting irresponsible actions against the environment. Some groups see any change as "bad" and might well bear the onus of obstructionists. But the general tenor of court actions has been to give assurance that proper environmental safeguards are incorporated and that, in their absence, the people be compensated for the loss of environmental quality, the damage to their environment and to themselves. The increasing support of the judiciary branch in environmental

Figure 37.7   Distribution of individual caloric and protein intake throughout the world.

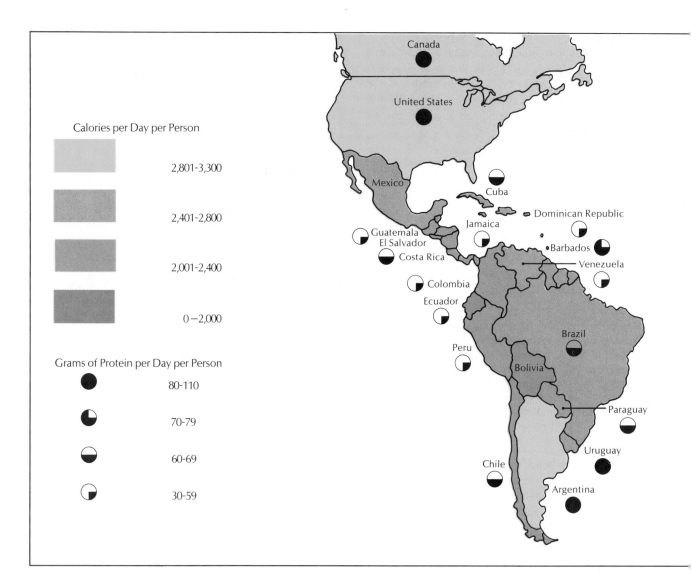

matters shows no signs of abatement; it may become a force perhaps far more pervasive and powerful than either the legislative or executive branches of federal, state, or local governments. Laws do exist to protect that which belongs to all of us, but their existence is worthless if we do not resort to them.

The Role of Academia in Ecological Engineering

Can the educational system meaningfully relate to the issue of survival? Yes, if it becomes not so much a link to the past as a bridge to the future. It must.

Creating a survival environment will require that people be educated to think in terms of ecological engineering—the engineering of the use and alteration of the environment; to consider the effects of technological innovation and application; to examine the manufacture, processing, and use of natural resources with an eye toward total recycling; and to seek ways to maintain and enhance renewable resources. To

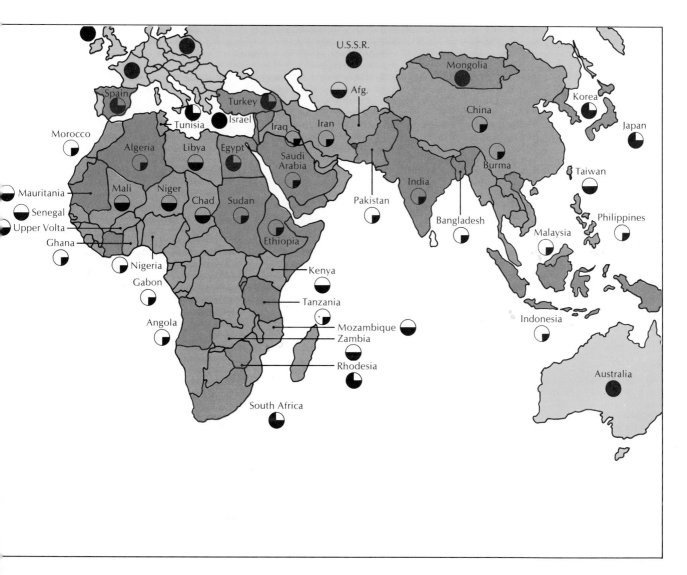

be most effective, this ecological engineering must be done in the context of models of ecological systems, those human approximations of how nature works. Even the simplest of the systems that have been developed are unbelievably intricate in the complexity of interrelationships and channels for feedback, for alternate routes of information storage and retrieval.

Ecologists as yet know little about modeling and ecosystems. And for the most part, what is best known are models of natural lakes, ponds, fields, and forests. But other models urgently needed are those of the environment in which most of mankind lives—cities. In no way has any level of sophistication been reached in systems models of cities. Here one wrestles not only with simple estimates of energy, protein, and vitamin needs but with the economics of transport, sale, and removal; the sociology of groups and enclaves; the behavioral psychology of people; the political lines to other governmental units; and so on. Urban ecology is without question a most urgent area needing study and planning—and one of the most complex.

Another shift that will need to come if the educational system is to contribute to our goal of survival is in its function of transmitting knowledge. There must be a change from emphasis on that which is to be discovered, examined, and preserved to accruing knowledge that leads to a state of wisdom of how to *use* knowledge to develop those values that will work toward both the survival of humankind and improvement in the quality of life.

The philosophical foundation on which the entire curriculum must come to rest is the unity of life. The world is a whole; each individual is a whole. A human being is not of unrelated pieces and parts, of forms merely to function, but rather an entity inextricably entwined and integrated. Science can and will be able to describe, analyze, and predict function from form and form from function; but a human being is more than an intricate complex of bio-physico-chemical relationships. Much more. It is in conveying this holistic synthesis that education's greatest challenge is to be found. Yet because of the explosive expansion of knowledge, the sheer volume of information to be transmitted has led inexorably to the compartmentalization of knowledge and the specialization of the disciplines. The result is a particularization of the knowledge of parts and pieces that limits our view of humanity in total being. More academic energy must be expended in drawing the connections in this highly refined knowledge about the smaller and smaller in order to provide a synthesis about progressively more comprehensive systems.

Those systems—and notably the human system—require that they be looked at as a whole, because that is the nature of things. Disciplines should interact in the way in which their objects of study interact, the focus being not on the object and its particular interactions, but on the total system and its complex of interactions. The examination needs to be timely, to be concerned about contemporary problems. This concern implies a temporal aspect when looking at specific problems and a timeless aspect when looking at others. Sensitivity to the vibrations and dynamic growth processes of the system of human interaction must be accompanied by a flexible educational system capable of rapid response and adaptation, a system that is not cast in stone or mineralized to a fossil state.

This calls not for a particular curriculum program in some kind of applied or engineering environmental science, but for consideration of a curricular attitude that seeks to explore the totality of man in all of his dimensions—his economics, history, sociology, and psychology; his philosophy, aesthetics, and religion; his science, basic and applied. This is man's ecology, the ecology of his survival with quality.

The Goal of Human Behavior

Government and academia working together can do much both to engineer an environment conducive to survival with quality and to help us comprehend our role as an integral and integrated part of that environment. Insofar as each individual is part of the two great processes of government and academia, each person contributes and gains. But there seems to be a gap that deals with the role of the individual as a daily functioning individual, one whose code of behavior reflects a common value system, one whose end goal is survival with quality. This is to be seen as an obligation not so much to oneself and one's contemporaries but to those yet unborn, to all future generations. That a unification of the world community in a common ecological ethic is needed may be argued as a must; *but the start must be with the individual.*

It is you as an individual who must come to grips with and determine an individual course of response and action. It is you who decides whether to walk or to use a bicycle for short trips, or to work toward increased and more efficient group mass transportation for longer ones. It is you who decides about contributing your share to population growth or about working toward population control. It is you who decides whether to eat more than you need each day or to work toward more equitable world-wide distribution of food. It is you who decides to buy a product that is of a nonrenewable resource or to practice conservation of resources by recycling or insisting on alternatives. *Choices are still made largely by the individual—but they are dependent on value judgments, and value judgments are made within a given ethical system.*

Biological science, dealing as it does with life and death, with organization and interaction, with homeostasis and adaptation, with randomness and order, can have much to say in the development of those value judgments that bear on survival. Belief in the value of mankind and his survival must be accompanied by courses of action that enhance those beliefs. The believer is not passive but is actively committed to converting belief into action, rhetoric into reality. Are you willing to believe in the worthwhileness of the future of humankind, and to work to ensure its future?

SUGGESTED READINGS

HARDIN, G. "The Tragedy of the Commons," *Science*, 162 (1968), 1243–1248. A succinct, sobering account of man's misconception and misuse of common resources.

MEADOWS, DONELLA H., *et al. Limits to Growth.* New York: Universe Books, 1972. A provocative conjecture of possible consequences of human population growth based on systems analysis of interaction of various factors in the human environment.

POTTER, VAN R. *Bioethics: Bridge to the Future.* Englewood Cliffs, N.J.: Prentice-Hall, 1971. A thoughtful and challenging discussion of man's need to consider those yet unborn—the future of the species—by developing a code of conduct conducive to survival.

SARGENT, F. (ed.). *Human Ecology.* Amsterdam: North-Holland Publishing Co., 1974. Various experts consider a wide range of topics bearing on human ecology from human biology and behavior to the use and management of resources and the development of policies and plans for environment.

Appendix: A Basic Scheme for Plant and Animal Classification

This appendix provides a basic scheme of classification that encompasses the living world. The scope of any such attempt to present an overview of the diversity of life results in some compromises, however, for phylogenetic classification is both subjective and artificial. If a particular group of organisms has been studied in detail, most specialists will more or less agree on the major subgroupings of organisms within the complex. Unfortunately, those same specialists will probably disagree over the level in the formal hierarchy in which the various subgroups ought to be placed. One taxonomist might be of the opinion that, say, three groups of organisms represent three separate phyla; another might feel those very same organisms are three classes within a single phylum. Increase the number of people specializing in the study of that group of organisms and eventually all permutations and combinations of possible groupings will emerge. Such conceptual difficulties are compounded by the fact that the *criteria* for grouping organisms into the larger units of classification, such as phylum and kingdom, are not the same from one unit to the next. These two problems combine to make schemes of classification somewhat plastic, to say the least.

The fluid nature of the classification process undoubtedly causes many students to question the validity of learning any single scheme of classification. If becoming familiar with the classification of organisms meant the rote memorization of a hierarchy of names, their point would be well taken. But the goal of any student of biology should be one of becoming familiar with the diverse nature of life on our planet, and in this sense classification is a useful tool. It is not an end in itself. You, as a student, should not be dismayed to find that a group considered as a phylum in this book is considered as a class in someone else's book, and vice versa. It is *the organisms themselves* that are significant, and their relative promotion or demotion in the taxonomic hierarchy of one book as opposed to another is merely symptomatic of continuing attempts to assess patterns of relationship within the living world.

We have attempted to make the system that follows as uniform as the groups of organisms themselves permit. Each phylum is subdivided to the level of class whenever possible, and an attempt has been made to assign common names to the organisms within these classes or phyla whenever possible. Text references are also provided to enable you to relate the hierarchy to your text readings.

Kingdom	Subkingdom	Phylum	Subphylum	Class	Representative Kinds (Common Name)

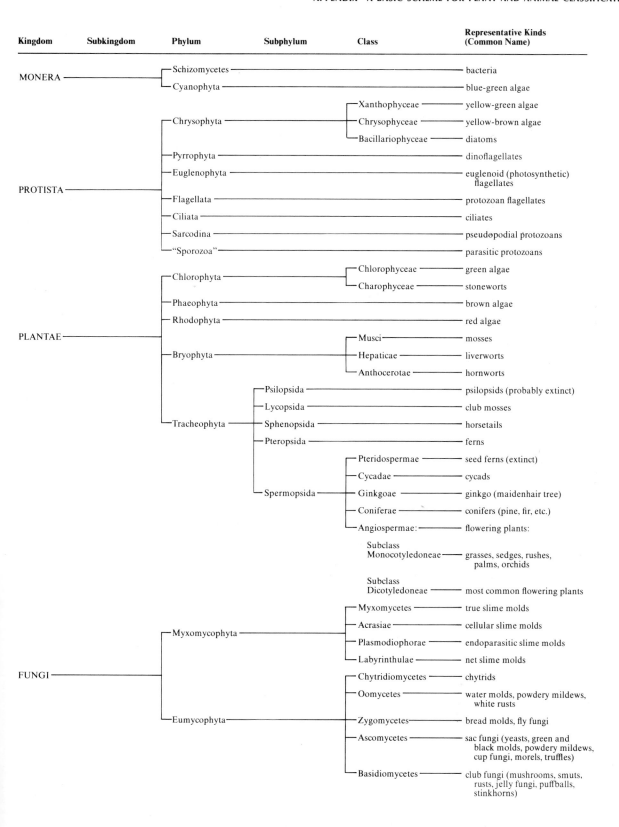

MONERA — Schizomycetes — bacteria
— Cyanophyta — blue-green algae

Chrysophyta — Xanthophyceae — yellow-green algae
— Chrysophyceae — yellow-brown algae
— Bacillariophyceae — diatoms

PROTISTA — Pyrrophyta — dinoflagellates
— Euglenophyta — euglenoid (photosynthetic) flagellates
— Flagellata — protozoan flagellates
— Ciliata — ciliates
— Sarcodina — pseudopodial protozoans
— "Sporozoa" — parasitic protozoans

PLANTAE — Chlorophyta — Chlorophyceae — green algae
— Charophyceae — stoneworts
— Phaeophyta — brown algae
— Rhodophyta — red algae
— Bryophyta — Musci — mosses
— Hepaticae — liverworts
— Anthocerotae — hornworts
— Tracheophyta — Psilopsida — psilopsids (probably extinct)
— Lycopsida — club mosses
— Sphenopsida — horsetails
— Pteropsida — ferns
— Spermopsida — Pteridospermae — seed ferns (extinct)
— Cycadae — cycads
— Ginkgoae — ginkgo (maidenhair tree)
— Coniferae — conifers (pine, fir, etc.)
— Angiospermae: — flowering plants:

Subclass Monocotyledoneae — grasses, sedges, rushes, palms, orchids

Subclass Dicotyledoneae — most common flowering plants

FUNGI — Myxomycophyta — Myxomycetes — true slime molds
— Acrasiae — cellular slime molds
— Plasmodiophorae — endoparasitic slime molds
— Labyrinthulae — net slime molds
— Eumycophyta — Chytridiomycetes — chytrids
— Oomycetes — water molds, powdery mildews, white rusts
— Zygomycetes — bread molds, fly fungi
— Ascomycetes — sac fungi (yeasts, green and black molds, powdery mildews, cup fungi, morels, truffles)
— Basidiomycetes — club fungi (mushrooms, smuts, rusts, jelly fungi, puffballs, stinkhorns)

Kingdom	Subkingdom	Phylum	Subphylum	Class	Representative Kinds (Common Name)

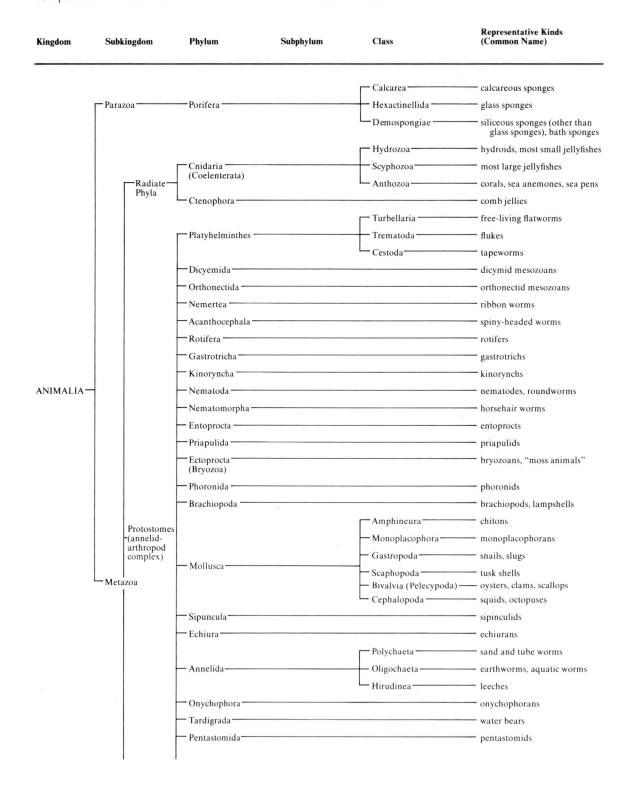

ANIMALIA

Parazoa — Porifera
- Calcarea — calcareous sponges
- Hexactinellida — glass sponges
- Demospongiae — siliceous sponges (other than glass sponges), bath sponges

Metazoa

Radiate Phyla
- Cnidaria (Coelenterata)
  - Hydrozoa — hydroids, most small jellyfishes
  - Scyphozoa — most large jellyfishes
  - Anthozoa — corals, sea anemones, sea pens
- Ctenophora — comb jellies

Protostomes (annelid-arthropod complex)
- Platyhelminthes
  - Turbellaria — free-living flatworms
  - Trematoda — flukes
  - Cestoda — tapeworms
- Dicyemida — dicymid mesozoans
- Orthonectida — orthonectid mesozoans
- Nemertea — ribbon worms
- Acanthocephala — spiny-headed worms
- Rotifera — rotifers
- Gastrotricha — gastrotrichs
- Kinoryncha — kinorynchs
- Nematoda — nematodes, roundworms
- Nematomorpha — horsehair worms
- Entoprocta — entoprocts
- Priapulida — priapulids
- Ectoprocta (Bryozoa) — bryozoans, "moss animals"
- Phoronida — phoronids
- Brachiopoda — brachiopods, lampshells
- Mollusca
  - Amphineura — chitons
  - Monoplacophora — monoplacophorans
  - Gastropoda — snails, slugs
  - Scaphopoda — tusk shells
  - Bivalvia (Pelecypoda) — oysters, clams, scallops
  - Cephalopoda — squids, octopuses
- Sipuncula — sipinculids
- Echiura — echiurans
- Annelida
  - Polychaeta — sand and tube worms
  - Oligochaeta — earthworms, aquatic worms
  - Hirudinea — leeches
- Onychophora — onychophorans
- Tardigrada — water bears
- Pentastomida — pentastomids

Kingdom	Subkingdom	Phylum	Subphylum	Class	Representative Kinds (Common Name)

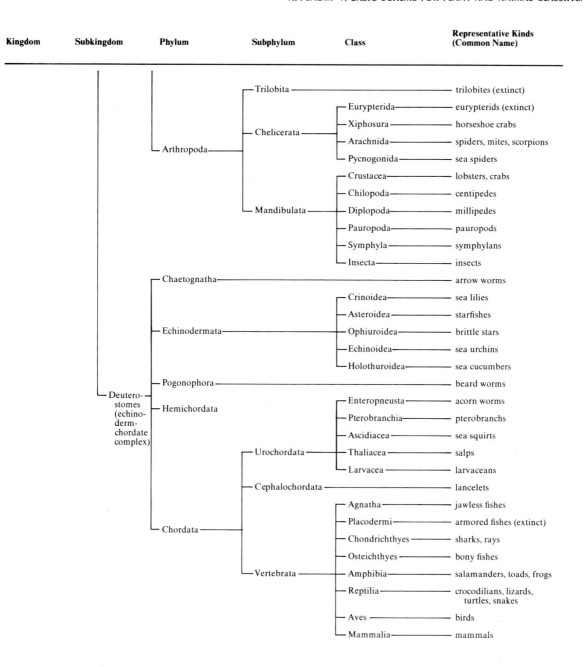

Arthropoda

Trilobita — trilobites (extinct)

Chelicerata
- Eurypterida — eurypterids (extinct)
- Xiphosura — horseshoe crabs
- Arachnida — spiders, mites, scorpions
- Pycnogonida — sea spiders

Mandibulata
- Crustacea — lobsters, crabs
- Chilopoda — centipedes
- Diplopoda — millipedes
- Pauropoda — pauropods
- Symphyla — symphylans
- Insecta — insects

Deutero-stomes (echino-derm-chordate complex)

Chaetognatha — arrow worms

Echinodermata
- Crinoidea — sea lilies
- Asteroidea — starfishes
- Ophiuroidea — brittle stars
- Echinoidea — sea urchins
- Holothuroidea — sea cucumbers

Pogonophora — beard worms

Hemichordata
- Enteropneusta — acorn worms
- Pterobranchia — pterobranchs

Chordata

Urochordata
- Ascidiacea — sea squirts
- Thaliacea — salps
- Larvacea — larvaceans

Cephalochordata — lancelets

Vertebrata
- Agnatha — jawless fishes
- Placodermi — armored fishes (extinct)
- Chondrichthyes — sharks, rays
- Osteichthyes — bony fishes
- Amphibia — salamanders, toads, frogs
- Reptilia — crocodilians, lizards, turtles, snakes
- Aves — birds
- Mammalia — mammals

Contributing Consultants

David L. Kirk, professor of biology at Washington University, received his doctorate in biochemistry from the University of Wisconsin. He previously was an associate professor at the University of Chicago. His research interests center on the molecular basis of embryonic determination: the process whereby cells become restricted to a single developmental potential. At present he is examining the problem in *Volvox*. He is a member of the editorial board of *Physiological Zoology*, and a member of the Society of Developmental Biologists and the American Association for the Advancement of Science.

Dr. Kirk is the person who put this book together. In a weak moment (he has since said that all book builders are mad), he agreed to help draw up a blueprint for the second edition of *Biology Today* and to act as overall academic adviser during its development. Somewhere along the line, he ended up writing Chapters 1, 3, 4, 10 through 15, 17, 18, 20, 22, and 29, and coauthoring Chapters 16, 21, 26, 27, and 28. He also was academic editor for the rest of the book, working to ensure conceptual integration from one chapter to the next. He additionally advised on the entire art program for the book and developed many of the illustrations and many of the interleaves.

Dr. Kirk writes the way he teaches—with intelligence, with insight, and with a reverence for life. Having taught biology for twelve years, he has acquired a knowledge of the kinds of questions students ask and, therefore, of the kinds of conceptual stumbling blocks they run up against. Perhaps part of his commitment to students derives from one of his own experiences as an undergraduate. He had a professor, he told us, who was once asked why something was the way it was. "Do not

ask WHY!" boomed his professor. "Ask what! And ask how! BUT DO NOT ASK WHY!"

It is to all biology students who have ever had a WHY suppressed that Dr. Kirk dedicates this book.

Donald P. Abbott, professor of biological sciences at Stanford University and associate director of Hopkins Marine Station of Stanford, received his doctorate from the University of California, Berkeley. He is a fellow of the American Association for the Advancement of Science and the California Academy of Sciences. His current research is concerned with the behavior and food of tropical sea urchins, the biology of ascidians, and the problem of the origin of the mulluscs. He has coauthored two books and has published over forty papers in marine biology. Dr. Abbott served as the unit adviser for Section II of *Biology Today*.

Isabella A. Abbott received her PhD from the University of California, Berkeley, and is currently professor of biology at Stanford University in Palo Alto, California. Her research activities have been focused on the study of marine algae. Dr. Abbott has served as treasurer of the International Phycological Society and secretary of the Western Society of Naturalists and is currently a member of both those societies and the Phycological Society of America. She is the senior author (with G. J. Hollenberg) of *Marine Algae of California*. Dr. Abbott reviewed Section II of this text.

Preston Adams received his doctorate from Harvard University in 1959 and is now professor of botany at DePauw University. He has published several research papers on the taxonomy of flowering plants based on field study in the southeastern United States, Cuba, Mexico, and Central America. In his teaching, he seeks to merge plant morphology with paleobotany into an inquiry concerning the evolutionary development of plants. He is currently interested in the ecological approach to plant science. Dr. Adams is coauthor of the textbook *The Study of Botany*. Chapter 19 of *Biology Today* is based in part on his original manuscript.

Stephen W. Arch, assistant professor of biology at Reed College in Portland, Oregon, was awarded his doctorate from

the University of Chicago. His principal research interest is in the biochemical and electrophysiological regulation of neurons, with a view toward the understanding of the complex processes associated with "higher" brain function. His recent research has been concerned with the regulatory physiology of a neuroendocrine cell population in the marine mollusc *Aplysia californica*. Dr. Arch authored the research-oriented interleaves for Chapters 25 and 26 and was the academic editor and adviser for those chapters. He also reviewed the section on behavior.

Stuart Bamforth was awarded his doctorate from the University of Pennsylvania in 1957 and is currently professor of biology at Newcomb College of Tulane University. In 1974 he was the recipient of the Student Mortar Board Outstanding Teacher Award. Dr. Bamforth's research interests, which have centered on the study of protozoan ecology, have led him to develop concepts of the role of microhabitats in protistan ecology, and the relationship of soil protozoa to vegetation and moisture gradients. Dr. Bamforth was an overall reviewer for this text.

Luis F. Baptista, whose areas of specialization are ornithology and ethology, teaches in the biology department at Occidental College in Los Angeles, where he also curates the Moore Laboratory Research Collection of Birds (the thirteenth largest collection in the United States and Canada). Dr. Baptista received his PhD from the University of California, Berkeley, and before joining the faculty at Occidental, did research at the Zoologisches Institut, Universität Braunschweig, and the Max Planck Institut Für Verhaltensphysiologie in Germany. His published works include scientific papers on various aspects of orthniology. Dr. Baptista is a contributor to the section on behavior in this text.

James M. Barrett, associate professor of biology at Marquette University in Milwaukee, Wisconsin, received his doctorate in zoology, with minors in biochemistry and physiology, from the University of Illinois. He has been a member of the American Association for the Advancement of Science and the New York Academy of Science and is currently a member of the American Society of Zoologists and the American

Institute for Biological Sciences. His principal research has been in cell biology, especially of protozoa and invertebrates. Dr. Barrett was an overall reviewer for this text.

Wayne M. Becker was awarded his doctorate in biochemistry from the University of Wisconsin, Madison. After spending two postdoctoral years at the Beacon Institute for Cancer Research in Glasgow, Scotland, he returned to the University of Wisconsin, where he is currently associate professor of botany. His recent research has been concerned with the biochemistry of seed germination and with regulation of transcription during eukaryotic development. Dr. Becker was a major reviewer for Sections III, IV, and V of this text.

Thomas Peter Bennett is professor and chairman of biological sciences at Florida State University. He received his PhD from Rockefeller University, where he studied under Fritz Lipmann. His research interests include basic biochemical studies, the biochemical basis of cellular control, and the regulation of protein synthesis. He is the author of two textbooks in biochemistry and many teaching articles in biology and biochemistry, including *Elements of Protein Synthesis,* an instructional model and text for teaching protein synthesis. Dr. Bennett contributed resource material for Chapter 13.

Richard K. Boohar received his doctorate from the University of Wisconsin, Madison. He is currently associate professor of life sciences and coordinator of biology at the University of Nebraska, Lincoln, where he has developed a program of investigative laboratories for mass enrollment general biology sections. Dr. Boohar is a member of the American Society of Zoologists, Sigma Xi, the American Institute of Biological Sciences, and other professional societies. In 1971 he was the recipient of a Teaching Council Summer Faculty Fellowship. His publications include a *Developmental Biology Laboratory Manual,* a *Manual for Investigative Laboratories in General Biology,* and articles in the *Journal of College Science Teaching.* Dr. Boohar was an overall reviewer for this text.

Frank Macfarlane Burnet completed his medical course at Melbourne University,

and his research on agglutinin reactions in typhoid fever began in 1923. He was Director of the Hall Institute of Melbourne Hospital from 1944 to 1965. Dr. Burnet's interest in immunology dates from his early work on staphylococcal toxin and antitoxin. In 1960 he shared the Nobel Prize for Physiology and Medicine with Dr. Peter Medawar for "the discovery of immunological tolerance." He was president of the Australian Academy of Science and chairman of the Commonwealth Foundation. Dr. Burnet was knighted in 1951, received the Order of Merit in 1958, and became a Knight Commander of the British Empire in 1969. His manuscript formed the basis for Chapter 24.

Michael T. Clegg was awarded his doctorate in genetics from the University of California, Davis, in 1972. He is currently assistant professor of biology at Brown University. Dr. Clegg's research is concerned with the distribution of enzymatic variation in plant and animal populations. He has pursued these interests through the study of organisms as diverse as barley, wild oats, and the fruit fly *Drosophila melanogaster.* In addition to experimental work, he has also been engaged in the development of estimation models for detecting components of selection and the mathematical analyses of the effects of selection and mutation within and between various inbred lines. His teaching interests include evolutionary genetics and population biology. Dr. Clegg has coauthored and published several papers on population genetics. He is the author of "Mechanisms of Evolution" in this text.

Elizabeth Cutter, now with the Cryptogamic Botany Laboratories at the University of Manchester, received the Doctor of Science degree from the University of St. Andrews in Scotland. In 1964 she earned her PhD from the University of Manchester and later became professor of botany at the University of California, Davis. Her research interests center on plant morphogenesis and anatomy, with emphasis on the study of cell and organ differentiation in plants, and experiments on the growth and development of ferns and flowering plants. In addition to numerous research papers, she is the

author of *Plant Anatomy: Experiment and Interpretation* and the editor of *Trends in Plant Morphogenesis.* Chapter 19 is based in part on Dr. Cutter's original manuscript.

John Eccles, professor of physiology and biophysics at the State University of New York at Buffalo, received his PhD from Oxford University. He was awarded the Nobel Prize in Physiology and Medicine in 1963 and was knighted in 1958. He has taught at universities in Australia, New Zealand, England, and the United States. Dr. Eccles has served as President of the Australian Academy of Science and he is a foreign associate of the National Academy of Sciences. His expertise in neurophysiology is reflected in his publications, which include *Physiology of Nerve Cells, The Physiology of Synapses, Brain and Conscious Experience, The Cerebellum as a Neuronal Machine, Facing Reality,* and *The Understanding of the Brain.* Dr. Eccles contributed resource material for Chapter 25.

Harrison Echols, who was awarded his doctorate in physics from the University of Wisconsin, developed an interest in biological phenomena at the molecular level while doing postdoctoral work at MIT. He is now a professor in the Department of Molecular Biology at the University of California, Berkeley. His current research interests are focused on gene regulation and genetic recombination using bacteriophage λ as the principal object of study. His memberships include the Genetics Society of America and the American Society of Biological Chemists. Dr. Echols is the coauthor of "Social Implications of Biological Research."

Leland Edmunds Jr. is an associate professor of biology at the State University of New York at Stony Brook. After obtaining his PhD from Princeton University in 1964, he spent a summer at the University of Costa Rica. His research interests include biological clocks, cell biology, and control of the cell cycle. Dr. Edmunds belongs to several professional organizations, including the American Society for Microbiology and the American Society of Plant Physiologists. Dr. Edmunds contributed resource manuscript for Chapter 28.

J. S. Finlayson is a research chemist at the National Institutes of Health, where since 1958 he has been engaged in studying the biochemistry of fibrinogen and other proteins of the blood plasma. He holds MS and PhD degrees from the University of Wisconsin and teaches introductory biochemistry and mathematical preparation for biochemistry at the Foundation for Advanced Education in the Sciences, Bethesda, Maryland. Dr. Finlayson contributed resource material to Chapters 10, 11, and 12.

Lesley Hallick received her doctorate in molecular biology from the University of Wisconsin. She is presently completing her postdoctoral work at the University of California, Berkeley, in the Department of Chemistry. She is studying the mechanism of DNA replication in eukaryotes, using cells in culture and isolated nuclei. Dr. Hallick is a member of the American Society for Cell Biology and the American Chemical Society. She is the coauthor of the chapter titled ''Social Implications of Biological Research.''

Terrell H. Hamilton is a professor of zoology at the University of Texas. He was awarded his PhD from Harvard University in 1960 and was a recipient of the Guggenheim Fellowship in biochemistry in 1964. His research interests include the areas of evolution theory, hormonal and reproductive physiology, and adaptive aspects of sexual dimorphism and species-area phenomena. Dr. Hamilton contributed resource material on population genetics.

Peter Hartline received his BA degree in physics from Swarthmore College. He later pursued his interests in animal behavior through an MA at Harvard University. Because he considered the base of behavior to be the nervous system, he did his doctoral work in the field of neuroscience and received his PhD from the University of California, San Diego, in 1969. His main research interests are in the processing of information in sensory systems and its relation to the perception and behavior of animals. Dr. Hartline contributed to the sections on nervous systems and behavior.

J. Woodland Hastings, professor of biology at Harvard University, is engaged in studies on the molecular mechanism of

bioluminescence and its biological role in energy metabolism. He received his PhD from Princeton University in 1951. Dr. Hastings has served as managing editor of the *Journal of General Physiology* and he has held memberships in the Commission on Undergraduate Education in the Biological Sciences, the National Science Foundation's Panel on Molecular Biology, and the Space Biology Subcommittee. He is currently on advisory committees for the National Science Foundation, the Red Sea Marine Research Station, and the Marine Biological Laboratory at Woods Hole, Massachusetts. Dr. Hastings contributed resource material for Chapter 28.

M. Jonathan Hodge received his doctorate in the history of science from Harvard University in 1970. He has taught at the University of Toronto and has been a visiting professor at the University of California, Berkeley. He is now teaching at the University of Leeds. A historian of biology and philosophy, he has been especially concerned with the origins of the Darwinian theory. He has written papers on Jean Lamarck and Robert Chambers and is working on a book analyzing different traditions in the treatment of the origins of species, from Plato and Aristotle to the present. Dr. Hodge, coauthor of Chapter 16, contributed the manuscript on Gregor Mendel and his work.

John Holland, professor of biology at the University of California, San Diego, received his PhD from the University of California, Los Angeles, in 1957. He worked at the University of Washington, at the University of California, Irvine, and was a visiting scientist at the Institute of Molecular Biology at the University of Geneva in Switzerland. His current research focuses on the biochemistry of animal and human viral infections, and he has published numerous papers in this field. Dr. Holland contributed resource material on viruses for Chapters 4 and 17.

Yasuo Hotta received his PhD in biology from Nagoya University in Japan. He was a postdoctoral fellow at the Plant Research Institute of the Canadian Department of Agriculture and a research associate at the University of Illinois. Currently, Dr. Hotta is a research biologist at the University of California, San Diego. His interest in the chemistry

of nucleic acids is reflected in his numerous publications. Dr. Hotta provided the resource manuscript on the subject of meiosis.

Tom D. Humphreys II earned his PhD in zoology at the University of Chicago in 1962. Before taking his present position as professor of biology at the Pacific Biomedical Research Center, University of Hawaii, Dr. Humphreys taught at the University of California at San Diego, at the Massachusetts Institute of Technology, and at the Marine Biological Laboratory. In addition to his research activities in the biochemistry of specific cell association and the molecular biology of development, he is a member of the Planning Committee for the University Community. Dr. Humphreys contributed resource material for Chapter 20.

Daniel Janzen, professor of biology at the University of Michigan, is well known for his studies in population and community ecology of plants and animals in natural habitats. After receiving his PhD from the University of California, Berkeley, Dr. Janzen taught at the University of Kansas and at the Smithsonian Institution's Summer Institute in Systematics. He later was associate professor of biology at the University of Chicago. Dr. Janzen is the author of numerous publications and is on the editorial committee of the *Annual Review of Ecology and Systematics.* He is the author of Chapter 30.

William A. Jensen, chairman of the Botany Department at the University of California at Berkeley, received both his MS and his PhD from the University of Chicago. He has done considerable research abroad, and his primary botanical interests lie in the areas of histochemistry, cytology, and cell development. Dr. Jensen contributed resource material on plant growth and development.

Marilyn Kirk received her doctorate in biochemistry and nutrition from the University of Wisconsin. At present she is collaborating with Dr. David Kirk at Washington University in research on the molecular basis of embryonic determination. Throughout the development of the second edition of *Biology Today,* Dr. Kirk worked to develop a comprehensive glossary and a workable index—two components of a textbook that are essential for the student but that are too often lacking in the kind of attention to detail that Dr. Kirk has given them.

Robert W. Kistner received his MD degree from the University of Cincinnati, where he also completed his internship and a residency in obstetrics. He received his training in gynecology at Johns Hopkins Hospital, Baltimore, Kings County Hospital, Brooklyn, and the Boston Hospital for Women. He is now associate chief of staff at the Boston Hospital for Women. He has written more than 150 articles in the medical literature and is the author of *Principles and Practice of Gynecology, Progress in Infertility, The Pill—Fact and Fallacy,* and *An Atlas of Infertility Surgery.*

Edward J. Kormondy, member of the faculty and vice president and provost of the Evergreen State College in Olympia, Washington, received his PhD in zoology from the University of Michigan. He has taught at the University of Michigan, at the University of Pittsburgh, and at Oberlin College. He has been director of both the Commission on Undergraduate Education in the Biological Sciences and the Office of the Biological Education of the American Institute of Biological Sciences. His research activities have been focused on three areas: energy relations in ecological succession; the biogeochemistry of zinc; and the ecology of Odonata. Dr. Kormondy is a member of the American Association for the Advancement of Science, the Ecological Society of America, the American Society of Limnology and Oceanography, the National Association of Biology Teachers, and the Society of the Sigma Xi. His many professional activities have included membership on the Education Committee of Ecological Society, the Review Committee of Ecological Society for second editions of BSCS textbooks, and the editorial board for the *Journal of Biological Education.* He has authored or coauthored a number of books on genetics, biology, and ecology and has published more than thirty distinguished research papers and essays. Dr. Kormondy is the author of "Bioethics: Toward Ecological Engineering" in this text.

Eugene N. Kozloff, born in Teheran, Iran, was awarded his doctorate in zoology from the University of California, Berkeley. He was a Guggenheim Fellow in 1953–1954 and is currently professor of zoology at the University of Washington, Seattle. Dr. Kozloff specializes in the biology of several groups of lower invertebrates. His publications include *Seashore Life of Puget Sound, the Strait of Georgia, and the San Juan Archipelago* and a manual for identification of marine invertebrates of Puget Sound and adjacent areas. He has also coauthored a book on microscopic techniques. Dr. Kozloff is the author of Chapters 7 and 8 of this text.

William F. Loomis Jr., who received his PhD from the Massachusetts Institute of Technology, is an assistant professor of biology at the University of California at San Diego. His main research interests lie in the chemical basis of the control of gene activity, and his is studying this phenomenon in the cellular slime mold *Dictyostelium discoideum.* Dr. Loomis contributed resource material for the interleaf in Chapter 6.

Vincent T. Marchesi received his PhD from Oxford University in 1961 and his MD from Yale University in 1963. After an internship and residency in pathology at Washington University, Dr. Marchesi was a research associate at Rockefeller University. He is presently chief of the Section on Chemical Pathology at the National Institute of Arthritis and Metabolic Diseases. His research interests include cell interactions in inflammatory reactions, the chemistry and structure of cell membranes, and the properties of tumor cells. Dr. Marchesi contributed resource material for Chapter 13.

Stanley L. Miller received his early training in chemistry and his PhD at the University of California. Now professor of chemistry at the University of California, San Diego, he focuses his research on the origin of life, enzyme mechanisms, and mechanisms of general anesthesia. Dr. Miller contributed resource material for Chapter 1 and for the interleaf in Chapter 9.

David M. Phillips is an assistant professor of biology at Rockefeller University. He received his PhD in zoology from the University of Chicago and was a postdoctorate fellow at Harvard Medical School. His research interests include the mechanisms of cellular motility and some aspects of cellular nucleic acid metabolism. His studies on motility involve cinematographic analysis of the swimming movement of spermatozoa from various species of insects and mammals and the correlation of these swimming movements with differences in structure. Dr. Phillips contributed resource material for Chapter 13.

David M. Prescott, who has been an exchange scientist to the USSR for a one-month lecture tour, is a professor in the Department of Molecular, Cellular, and Developmental Biology at the University of Colorado. After receiving his PhD from the University of California at Berkeley, Dr. Prescott was an American Cancer Society Fellow at Carlsberg Laboratory in Copenhagen and a Markle Scholar in Medical Science. His research focuses on mechanisms of chromosome replication and function, chromatid exchanges during the cell cycle, exchange of proteins between the nucleus and cytoplasm, and the factors regulating the initial synthesis of DNA during cellular reproduction. Dr. Prescott contributed resource material on the structure and function of the gene.

Roberts Rugh has taught and conducted research in embryology for forty-four years. He received his PhD from Columbia University, where, until his recent retirement, he was professor of radiology in the College of Physicians and Surgeons. His research has focused on the effects of radiation on the embryo and fetus. He has more than 220 publications and 6 books to his credit in the field of embryonic development. Dr. Rugh's most recent publication, *From Conception to Birth: The Drama of Life's Beginnings,* which he coauthored with L. B. Shettles, is illustrated with color photographs he has taken of human fetuses. Dr. Rugh contributed material to Chapter 34.

Theodore Schwartz, professor of anthropology at the University of California, San Diego, received his PhD from the University of Pennsylvania. Although he began work in physical anthropology, he turned to the study of behavioral evolution and of psychological and cultural change. Dr. Schwartz' studies span the past twenty years, including more than eight years in the field in Mexico and Melanesia. His current research is in cross-cultural psychological testing and in cognitive acculturation. He has taught at the University of Michigan, the University of Chicago, and the University of California, Los Angeles. He was a research fellow at the American Museum of Natural History, a postdoctoral fellow of NIMH at the University of Paris, and a senior specialist at the East-West Center, Hawaii. Dr. Schwartz wrote Chapter 33.

Robert E. Shank is the Danforth professor of preventive medicine and head of the department at Washington University School of Medicine in St. Louis, Missouri, where he earned his MD in 1939. He is a fellow of the American Public Health Association and holds memberships in Sigma Xi, the American Association for the Advancement of Science, the Association of American Physicians, the American Board of Nutrition, and other professional societies. He is chairman of the Nutrition Committee of the American Heart Association and has served on the Food and Nutrition Board for the National Research Council and the Committee on Preventive Medicine of the National Board of Medical Examiners. Dr. Shank has been on the editorial board of *Nutrition Today* since 1966 and has authored or coauthored more than sixty medical papers and articles for publication. He is the author of ''Human Health and Disease'' in this text.

Ralph E. Taggart was awarded his doctorate in botany from Michigan State University in 1971. He is currently assistant professor in the Department of Botany and Plant Pathology at that institution and a lecturer in the biological science program. Dr. Taggart's research interests lie in the field of paleobotany and palynology, with emphasis on late Teritary vegetation in western North America. He is also interested in undergraduate education, particularly with

respect to conveying the importance of plants in the evolution of the biosphere. Dr. Taggart was a principal adviser throughout the development of this text. In addition, he was academic editor for Chapters 19 and 23, author of Chapters 5, 6, 9, and 31, and author of the appendix on biological classifications.

J. Herbert Taylor received his PhD from the University of Virginia. He has been a consultant for the Oak Ridge National Laboratories and the Brookhaven National Laboratory. Dr. Taylor has taught biology at Columbia University, the University of Tennessee, and the University of Oklahoma. He is now a professor of biological sciences at the Institute of Molecular Biophysics at Florida State University. Dr. Taylor's research interests include chromosome structure and behavior, DNA replication, autoradiographic studies of macromolecular synthesis in cells, and characterization of the molecular units of chromosomes. He contributed resource material for Chapter 17.

Kenneth Thimann, professor of biology and provost of Crown College, University of California at Santa Cruz, received his PhD from Imperial College, University of London. He holds an honorary doctorate from Universität Basel, Switzerland. Dr. Thimann has served on advisory committees for the President's Medal for Science and the NASA Council on Biosciences for Manned Orbiting Missions. He is a fellow of the American Academy of Arts and Sciences and the National Academy of Sciences. Dr. Thimann has also served on the editorial boards of *American Naturalist, Annual Review of Plant Physiology,* and *Biological Abstracts,* and on the governing board for the American Association for the Advancement of Science. His main research interest is in plant physiology and biochemistry. Dr. Thimann is the author of Chapter 23.

Gordon Tomkins received his MD from Harvard and his PhD from the University of California, Berkeley. Before becoming a professor of biochemistry at the University of California, San Francisco, Dr. Tomkins was chief of the Laboratory of Molecular Biology at the National Institute of Arthritis and Metabolic Diseases. He was awarded the 1967 Prize in Molecular Biology from the Washington Academy of Sciences and

has held the Mider lectureship at the National Institutes of Health and the Jesup lectureship at Columbia University. He has published more than 120 research papers. Dr. Tomkins contributed resource manuscript for Chapter 22.

Harold C. Urey was awarded his PhD from the University of California at Berkeley and went on to do postdoctorate work as an American-Scandinavian Foundation Fellow at the Niels Bohr Institute for Theoretical Physics in Copenhagen. He was awarded the Nobel Prize in chemistry in 1934. In addition to being professor emeritus at Chicago University and university professor emeritus at the University of California at San Diego, his is a consultant to NASA and an advisory member of the Space Science Board of the National Academy of Sciences. His fields of interest include the entropy of gases, chemical problems of the origin of the solar system, the origin of life, the separation of isotopes, and the temperatures of the ancient seas of the world. Dr. Urey contributed resource material for Chapter 9.

Patrick H. Wells, chairman of the biology department at Occidental College in Los Angeles, received his doctorate from Stanford University. His special research interest lies in honeybee environmental physiology and the natural history and physiology of the monarch butterfly in California. Dr. Wells is a member of the American Association for the Advancement of Science, the American Society of Zoologists, the Bee Research Association, Sigma Xi, and other professional societies. He was the director of a National Science Foundation Summer Institute in Biology for high school teachers and is the coauthor of a general textbook in biology. Dr. Wells served as a principal adviser for this text, and he was the author of Chapter 2 and the coauthor of Chapter 21.

Adrian M. Wenner was awarded his doctorate from the University of Michigan in Ann Arbor and is currently professor of biology at the University of California, Santa Barbara, where he has served on the faculty since 1960. Dr. Wenner has published in many professional journals and holds memberships in the American Association for the Advancement of Science, the American Society of Zoologists, Sigma Xi, and The Scientific Research Society

of North America. His research, which
includes studies of bee communication
and the ecology of beach organisms, has
received widespread notice. Dr. Wenner
is a contributor to the behavior chapters
in this text.

We would like also to acknowledge the
assistance of the following individuals in
the development of the second edition of
Biology Today:

Clifford Brunk, University of California, Los Angeles
John Frola, University of Akron
Robert Grey, University of California, Davis
Ralph Quatrano, Oregon State University
Stuart Sell, University of California, San Diego
Stewart Swihart, University of South Florida
Doris Wilson, University of California, Davis
Wilfred Wilson, San Diego State University

Glossary

a

abscission: in plants, the normal separation and dropping of flowers, fruit, and leaves. Separation occurs in a specialized layer of cells called the abscission layer.

absolute dating: assigning absolute ages or dates to rock samples or other materials using methods based on the rate of decay of various radioactive isotopes.

acetylcholine (as′ e til kō′ lēn): a neurotransmitter substance released at the synaptic endings of many neurons of both the central and peripheral nervous systems, including all motor endplates on skeletal muscle and all terminal synapses of the parasympathetic nervous system.

acid: any substance capable of donating a hydrogen ion.

ACTH: see adrenocorticotropic hormone.

actin: one of the four proteins within the contractile unit of muscle; the major protein of the thin filaments of muscle.

action potential: the self-propagating cycle of depolarization and repolarization of the cell membrane that travels along a neural process and constitutes the neural impulse.

activation energy: the energy required to form an activated complex before a chemical reaction can proceed.

active transport: the energy-requiring movement of ions or molecules from areas of low concentration to areas of high concentration; this movement is mediated by membrane-bound enzymes.

adaptive complex: a group of gene variants that complement one another and function together adaptively in a given environment. They are therefore co-selected in the course of evolution.

adaptive enzyme: an enzyme that is present in the cell only under conditions in which it is of clear adaptive value.

adaptive radiation: the process by which an ancestral form gives rise to many different species, each adapted to a different set of environmental conditions.

addiction: a true physical dependence on any drug, as opposed to psychological dependence. It occurs with central nervous system depressants, such as alcohol, opium, and barbiturates.

adenine (ad′ e·nēn): a purine base. It plays an important role not only as a constituent of nucleic acids but also in a variety of essential coenzymes such as ATP, ADP, cAMP, NAD, and NADP.

adenosine diphosphate (ah den′ ō sēn dī′ fos fāt): see ADP.

adenosine monophosphate (a den′ o sēn mo′ nō fos fāt): see AMP.

adenosine triphosphate (ah den′ o sēn trī′ fos fāt): see ATP.

adenyl cyclase (ad′ e nēl sī′ klās): an enzyme that acts to form cAMP from ATP (releasing inorganic pyrophosphate as the other product).

ADH: antidiuretic hormone; see vasopressin.

adipose tissue: the fatty tissue of the body.

ADP: adenosine diphosphate; a product formed in the hydrolysis of ATP with the concurrent release of inorganic phosphate and energy. It is identical to ATP in structure except for the absence of the third (terminal) phosphate.

adrenalin: see epinephrine.

adrenocorticotropic hormone (ACTH): an animal hormone produced and secreted by the pituitary gland; it functions to cause synthesis and release of hydrocortisone from the adrenal cortex.

aerobe: an organism that uses oxygen in its energy metabolism.

agglutination: the aggregation or clumping together of suspended particles, cells, or molecules.

aggression: behavior of one animal that implies intent to do injury to another.

aleurone (al′ yah rōn): a layer of specialized cells surrounding the endosperm of some monocots.

alga, algae: (al′ ga, al′ jē): any photoautotrophic organism lacking complex reproductive structures; includes members of seven phyla in three different kingdoms.

allele (ah lēl′): one of two or more alternative forms of a gene for a single trait at the same locus on a chromosome.

allopolyploidy (al′ o pol ē ploy′ dē): the doubling of the chromosomal complement of an interspecific hybrid, resulting in formation of a new species.

allosteric regulation: the modification of enzyme activity caused by a change in shape of the active site when a regulator molecule binds to a site other than the active site of the enzyme.

alpha helix: a structure found in certain regions of many proteins in which the polypeptide chain is coiled into a spiral structure of fixed dimensions and held together by hydrogen bonding.

alternation of generations: in plant life cycles, the alternation of the haploid gametophyte phase with the dyploid sporophyte phase.

alveolus, alveoli (al vē′ ō lus): a small, saclike dilation or cavity, such as the microscopic air pouches that occur in lung tissue.

amino acid: one of twenty or more different carboxylic acids containing the amino group—NH_2: a constituent of all proteins, which are amino acid polymers.

amniocentesis (am′ nē o sen tē′ sis): removal of a small quantity of amniotic fluid from the uterus during pregnancy; examination of the embryonic cells suspended in the fluid often permits a determination of whether the embryo possesses certain genetic diseases.

amniotic sac: a fluid-filled sac that encloses and protects the embryo in birds, reptiles, and mammals.

AMP: adenosine monophosphate; similar to ADP except that only a single phosphate group is present. It can be phosphorylated by most cells to produce ADP.

amylose: a complex polymer of glucose found in plants; a starch.

anabolism (an ab′ ō lizm): synthetic metabolism; any process in which simpler substances are combined to form more complex molecules in living cells.

anaerobe: an organism that does not require oxygen but makes use of processes such as fermentation and glycolysis to obtain its energy.

anaerobic glycolysis: the metabolic process whereby sugar molecules are split, in the absence of oxygen, to form small organic acids, thereby releasing some of the chemical energy contained in the sugar molecules and producing a small amount of ATP.

anaphase: the stage of mitosis in which the centromeres joining the chromatids break and sister chromatids move to opposite poles.

aneuploidy (an′ ū ploy′ dē): the general term for the absence or duplication of part of the normal diploid chromosome complement.

angiosperm: a member of the class Angiospermae; the flowering plants. Angiosperms are characterized by the occurrence of flowers and by the development of the seed within an ovary.

anisogamy (an ī sog′ a mē): the fusion of two distinguishably different haploid cells in the reproductive cycles of certain plants.

annelid: a member of the phylum Annelida; the earthworms, polychaetes, and leeches.

annulis, annuli: a circular structure or pore occurring at regular intervals over the surface of the nuclear membrane. It regulates the two-way flow of materials between the nucleus and the cytoplasm.

anterior: of or toward the front end; the opposite of posterior.

anther: the structure in a flower in which meiosis occurs, producing microspores with a subsequent development of pollen grains.

antheridium, antheridia: a multicellular reproductive structure producing male gametes in bryophytes and ferns.

anthropomorphism (an′ thrō pō morf′ izm): the reading of human motivations, characteristics, and behaviors into (among other things) the behavior of animals.

antibiotic: any substance produced by one organism that inhibits the growth of or kills another organism.

antibody: one of a related group of proteins (immunoglobulins) capable of specifically interacting with an antigen.

anticodon: a set of three nucleotides in a tRNA molecule that is complementary to a particular codon in mRNA.

antigen: a substance that is capable of interacting with an antibody in a specific manner and, under appropriate conditions, of inducing specific antibody formation.

antigen binding site: a pattern of chemical groups on one particular region of the surface of an antibody that is specifically complementary to chemical groupings on the surface of the antigen.

antigenic determinant: the chemical groupings on the surface of an antigen that react specifically with the antigen-binding site on the antibody.

anus (ā′ nus): the opening through which the solid refuse of digestion is excreted.

aorta: the main arterial trunk of the circulatory system; it conveys blood from the heart to all the arteries.

apical dome: a dome-shaped structure at the very tip of the shoot apex where leaf development is initiated.

apical dominance: the inhibition or prevention of axillary bud growth (hence, branching) by hormones produced in the apex of the main shoot of a vascular plant.

archegonium, archegonia (ar′ kah gō′ nē um): a multicellular female reproductive structure containing an egg; found in bryophytes and ferns.

arthropod (ar′ thrō pod): a member of the phylum Arthropoda; the crustaceans (crabs, lobsters), the arachnids (spiders, scorpions), and the insects.

ascocarp: the fruiting structure in cup fungi (ascomycetes).

ascomycete (as kō mī sēt′): a member of the class Ascomycetes, which includes the yeasts, certain molds, and mildews as well as the cup fungi, morels, and truffles.

ascospore: a spore formed by the meiotic division of the zygote within the ascus of certain fungi, the ascomycetes.

ascus, asci: an elongated, saclike cell in which sexual fusion and meiotic division occur in ascomycete fungi.

asphyxia: inadequate oxygen supply.

atherosclerosis (ath′ er ō skler ō′ sis): a hardening and thickening of the arteries, accompanied by loss of elasticity, as a result of the build-up of fatty, cholesterol-rich deposits.

atom: the smallest unit of an element that still retains the chemical properties of the element.

atomic number: the number of protons in the nucleus of an atom of a particular element; also equal to the number of electrons around the nucleus.

atomic weight: the weight of a representative atom of an element relative to the weight of an atom of the most abundant natural isotope of carbon, which is assigned a weight of exactly 12.

ATP: adenosine triphosphate; a compound occurring in all cells and serving as a source of energy for many physiological processes. Each ATP molecule contains one molecule of the base adenine and one molecule of the sugar ribose to which three phosphate groups are attached in series.

atrioventricular valve (ā′ trē ō ven trik′ ū lar): a valve that separates an atrium and ventricle in the vertebrate heart, thus preventing the backflow of blood.

atrium, atria (ā′ trē um): the chamber of the heart that receives blood from the body and pumps it into a ventricle, from which it returns to body circulation.

australopithecine (os′ tra lō pith′ e sēn): a term (with rather arbitrary boundaries) for the first undisputed hominids in the evolution of man.

autoimmune disease: one of an increasing number of diseases thought to be a result of the breakdown of natural tolerance to self antigens and the consequent production of antibodies that react with self cells and tissues.

autonomic nervous system: the elements of the vertebrate nervous system involved in regulating the functioning of internal organs such as heart, blood vessels, intestinal tract, and others over which there is little voluntary control.

autopolyploidy (aw′ tō pol ē ploy′ dē): the doubling of the chromosomal complement of a normal individual to produce multiples of the normal state of diploidy.

autosome: any chromosome that is not involved in sex determination.

autotroph: an organism that uses an external source of energy to produce organic nutrients from simple inorganic chemicals.

auxin (awk′ sin): one of a group of closely related natural or synthetic plant hormones that are involved in regulating plant growth, especially the control of cell elongation and regulation of primordial development.

Avogadro's number: the number of atoms (6.02×10^{23}) always present in an amount of an element that is equivalent to its atomic weight in grams; also, the number of molecules present in the amount of a compound that is equal to its molecular weight in grams.

axillary bud: a lateral bud in vascular plants that usually develops into a branch in most flowering plants.

axon: a process or extension of a nerve cell that carries impulses *away* from the nerve cell body; an efferent nerve fiber.

axoplasm: the cytoplasm within the axon of a neuron.

axopod: a relatively permanent, immobile extension from the cell body; otherwise similar to a filopod.

b

bacillus, bacilli: a rod-shaped bacterium.

back mutation: the process whereby a gene, having once undergone a point mutation, undergoes a second mutation that restores the original nucleotide sequence.

bacteriophage (bak ter′ i ō fahj): a virus that infects bacteria; frequently simplified to "phage."

bacterium, bacteria: any prokaryotic organism capable of existence outside other cells but lacking chlorophyll *a* and incapable of photosynthesis of the sort that produces oxygen as a by-product.

balanced polymorphism: a situation in which an equilibrium ratio of alternative phenotypes is maintained within a population.

basal body: an organelle located at the base of each cilium and flagellum; identical in structure to a centriole.

basal cell: the larger, less dense of the two cells formed in the first division of an angiosperm zygote; gives rise to the suspensor.

base: any substance capable of accepting and combining chemically with a hydrogen ion.

base pairing: the formation of specific hydrogen bonds between complementary nucleotides (such as guanine and cytosine or adenine and thymine) on two different nucleic acid molecules.

basidiocarp: the complex fruiting structure of club fungi (basidiomycetes).

basidiomycete (ba sid′ ē ō mī sēt′): a member of the fungal class Basidiomycetes; the toadstools and mushrooms.

basidium, basidia: in club fungi (basidiomycetes), a club-shaped structure with sites for haploid spore production.

B-cells: a population of lymphocytes derived from bone marrow lymphocytes and essential for antibody production.

behavioral releaser: a specific stimulus that triggers the performance of a fixed action pattern.

benign tumor: an abnormal growth of cells that is not cancerous. Such tumors usually grow slowly, are surrounded by a capsule, remain localized, and do not recur once removed.

benthic: pertaining to aquatic organisms that live attached to or associated with the bottom of any body of water.

bilateral symmetry: the property of having only one plane of symmetry, which separates two sides that are more or less perfect mirror images of one another. Bilaterally symmetric organisms (such as a fish) have anterior and posterior ends and top and bottom surfaces that are clearly distinguishable.

binary fission: a form of asexual reproduction in prokaryotes in which the cell simply grows larger for a time, then divides into two equal daughter cells.

bioethics: a survival-oriented system of rules governing human behavior.

biomass: the total weight (or volume) of all living organisms or of a specific group of living organisms in a designated area.

biome: the specific vegetation type—and the array of animals such vegetation supports—that is characteristically found in a particular climatic region (for example, tundra or tropical rain forest). All the communities and ecosystems found under a given set of climatic conditions, taken together, constitute a biome.

biosphere: the part of the earth's crust, water, and atmosphere that can support life, and the organisms within it.

biotic community: a definable array of interacting organisms.

bivalve: a member of the molluscan class Bivalvia; the clams, oysters, scallops, and mussels.

blastocyst: a mammalian blastula.

blastomere: one of the cells produced by cleavage of an animal zygote.

blastopore: in animal development the point at which cells of the blastula migrate inward to form the primitive gut during the process of gastrulation; the first opening to be formed between the gut and the exterior.

blastula (blas′ chew la): a stage in early embryonic development in which the cells form a sphere with a fluid-filled cavity in the center.

brachiator: a primate with limbs adapted for hanging from branches and moving through trees by swinging from branch to branch.

branch-point enzyme: the first enzyme in a biosynthetic pathway that branches off the main metabolic pathways of the cell; often subject to feedback inhibition by the end product of the pathway.

bronchiole (bronk′ ē ōl): one of the smaller air passages located in the lungs of mammals.

bronchus, bronchi (bronk′ us): the air passage(s) leading from the trachea to the lung(s).

bryophyte (brī′ ō fīt): a member of the phylum Bryophyta; the liverworts and mosses.

budding: a form of asexual reproduction in some prokaryotes in which a small protuberance appears on the parent cell, enlarges, and breaks off, forming a daughter cell.

buffer: a compound that minimizes the change in pH of a solution by removing hydrogen ions from the solution as the hydrogen ion concentration rises or by contributing hydrogen ions to a solution as the hydrogen ion concentration falls.

C

calorie: a unit of heat; the amount required to raise the temperature of one gram of water 1℃. In the context of nutrition, the term ''Calorie'' is used to refer to 1,000 calories, or 1 kilocalorie.

Calvin-Benson cycle: the dark reactions of photosynthesis in which new sugar molecules are produced for use or storage and the sugar phosphates required of CO_2 fixation are regenerated.

cambium (kam′ bē um): *see* vascular cambium.

Cambrian (kām′ brē an): a geologic period in the Paleozoic era extending from about 600 million to 500 million years ago.

cAMP: cyclic-3′,5′-adenosine monophosphate. cAMP is produced in a wide variety of cell types in response to chemical signals from the extracellular environment; it functions to modify the metabolism of the cell in an adaptive manner.

cancer: in vertebrates, an invasive, malignant tumor resulting from the abnormal and uncontrolled growth of cells.

capillary: a very small or fine tube; especially the network of fine blood vessels through which the blood moves from the arteries to the veins.

carbohydrase: an enzyme that breaks down a complex carbohydrate into smaller units such as simple sugars.

carbohydrate: a sugar or a polymer of sugar, such as starch, glycogen, or cellulose.

carbon dioxide (CO_2) fixation: the incorporation of carbon dioxide into a nongaseous, organic compound; the first of the dark reactions of photosynthesis.

carbonic acid: the acid formed by the combination of a molecule of water and a molecule of carbon dioxide (H_2CO_3).

carcinogen: any factor known to cause or promote cancer in man or in experimental animals.

cardiac muscle: the unique muscular tissue of the heart.

cardiac output: the volume of blood pumped per minute.

carnivore: a flesh-eating animal or an insect-eating plant.

carotene: the orange pigment that gives carrots their characteristic color; one of a family of related pigments called carotenoids that are involved in photosynthesis as accessory pigments.

carrying capacity: in ecology, the largest population of animals of a given species that a given stable environment can maintain indefinitely.

cartilage: a tough, specialized connective tissue composed of protein (collagen), polysaccharides, and widely separated cells.

catabolism (ka tab′ ō lizm): the metabolic degradation of more complex organic compounds to simpler ones, accompanied by a release of usable energy.

catabolite repression: the process whereby the synthesis of enzymes involved in other catabolic (energy-yielding) pathways is prevented as long as sufficient glucose is present to serve as an adequate energy source for the cell.

catalyst: a substance that lowers activation energy and thereby accelerates a chemical reaction but is not itself consumed in the reaction.

cell plate: a collection of membranous vesicles that forms during telophase in plant cell mitosis. Eventually the vesicles fuse to form the new cell membrane that cuts the parent cell into two daughter cells.

cellular immune response: the immune reaction in which the blood contains specifically armed cells that directly attack the foreign material.

cellulose: a complex, usually indigestible, polymer of glucose found principally as a structural element in the cell walls of plants.

Cenozoic (sēn′ ō zō ik): a geologic era extending from about 62 million years ago to the present.

central nervous system (CNS): one of the two traditional divisions of the vertebrate nervous system; includes the neural structures (interneurons) encased in the skull and in the vertebral column; the brain and spinal cord.

centriole: an organelle located at each pole of the mitotic spindle of animal and certain protistan cells. It is composed of microtubules in a characteristic array of nine triplets. Usually found in pairs with the newly formed daughter centriole lying at right angles to one end of the parent centriole from which it arose.

centromere: the point on a chromosome at which sister chromatids are attached after DNA duplication and before separation in mitosis. The spindle fibers attach to structures at the centromere during mitosis and meiosis.

cephalization (sef a lī zā′ shun): in the evolutionary development of animals, a trend toward the accumulation of sense organs and their associated nerve connections near the mouth, in the anterior end of the body; resulted in the formation of the head and brain.

cephalopod (sef′ a lō pod): a member of the class Cephalopoda; the squids and octopuses.

cerebellum: a two-layered lobed region of the vertebrate brain; it lies above the pons and is involved in the coordination of body movements and the maintenance of equilibrium.

cerebral cortex: the external layer of neural cells or gray matter of the cerebrum; it functions in sensory and motor coordination, learning, and memory and is highly developed in the human.

cerebral hemisphere: one of the two halves into which the cerebral cortex is subdivided.

cerebrum (se rē′ brum): the most anterior portion of the vertebrate brain; it integrates sensory information, controls voluntary movements, and coordinates mental activities.

cervix: the lower and narrower section of the uterus opening into the vagina.

chemoreceptor: a neuron specialized so that it is responsive to a specific chemical or chemicals.

chiasma, chiasmata (kī az′ ma): an X-shaped connection between paired homologous chromosomes at meiosis; the point at which crossing over and genetic recombination are occurring.

chitin (kī′ tin): a nitrogen-containing polysaccharide that is an important component in the exoskeleton of insects and other arthropods and in the cell walls of some fungi.

chlorophyll: any of several green, light-absorbing pigments essential as electron donors in photosynthesis. There are several chlorophylls (*a*, *b*, *c*, and so on) with slightly different structures.

chlorophyte: a member of the phylum Chlorophyta, the green algae.

chloroplast: a chlorophyll-containing plastid; an organelle, bounded by a double membrane and containing the enzymes of photosynthesis.

cholesterol (kō les′ ter ōl): a steroid important as a component of animal cell membranes and as a precursor for many hormones. Excessive levels of cholesterol in the blood are a contributing factor in the development of hardening of the arteries and thus in heart disease and stroke.

chordate (kor′ dāt): a member of the phylum Chordata, characterized by a notochord at some stage in the life cycle; includes the vertebrates.

chromatid: one of two coiled fibers making up a chromosome that has recently replicated. These two fibers separate in mitosis, each going to a different pole of the dividing cell. Thus each chromosome consists of a single chromatid except in the period between DNA replication and cell division.

chromatin: the characteristically staining material of the nucleus that becomes visible as specific chromosomal shapes in cell division; contains DNA, RNA, histones, and nonhistones.

chromoplast: any pigment-producing plastid.

chromosome: one of the structures in the nucleus of a eukaryotic cell that bear the genes. Chromosomes contain DNA, a variety of proteins, and RNA. They are normally visible as discrete structures only during the process of mitosis or meiosis.

chromosome puff: in certain insect cells, a swollen region at a particular site on a polytene chromosome that can be shown to be a site of active RNA synthesis.

cilium, cilia (si′ lē um): a structure similar to a flagellum, but shorter. It is composed of a similar 9 + 2 array of microtubules and is used for locomotion or for moving water and mucus.

circadian rhythm (sir kā′ dē an): pertaining to biological cycles and behavioral activities recurring at approximately 24-hour intervals even under fairly constant conditions.

class: a group of related orders; a major subdivision of a phylum.

cleavage: the series of rapid cell divisions in the absence of growth that characteristically occur early in animal development.

cleavage furrow: the constriction in the surface of a dividing animal cell where the process of cytokinesis is initiated.

climax community: the characteristic stable constellation of plant, animal, and microbial species that is found in a given geological and climatic region once ecological succession is complete and the community has reached an equilibrium with the environment.

cloaca (klō ā′ ka): a common cavity into which the intestinal, urinary, and reproductive ducts open in many vertebrates.

clone: a line of cells or organisms derived by common descent from a single ancestral cell.

cnidarian (nī dar′ ē an): a member of the phylum Cnidaria; the polyps and jellyfishes.

CNS: *see* central nervous system.

coccus, cocci (kok′ us, kok′ sī): a spherical bacterium.

cochlea (kōk′ lē a): the fluid-filled chamber of the inner ear.

codominance: incomplete dominance of genes, in which both alleles are expressed more or less equally in a heterozygote.

codon: a set of three nucleotides in mRNA that specifies one amino acid in the sequence of a protein chain; or the corresponding three nucleotides in the DNA from which the mRNA is made.

coelom (sē′ lōm): in higher metazoans, a fluid-filled body cavity that is lined by epithelium and separates the gut from the body wall.

coenzyme: a small organic molecule that attaches to an enzyme and plays an essential role in the catalytic activity of the enzyme. Often the coenzyme accepts or donates electrons and/or atoms involved in the reaction. Many vitamins function as coenzymes.

cofactor: a small inorganic or organic substance necessary to the functioning of an enzyme; organic cofactors are called coenzymes.

coitus (kō ēt′ us): sexual intercourse.

coleoptile (kō lē op′ til): a sheathlike structure covering the first shoot of grass seedlings. It is a part of the cotyledon.

colinearity: the concept that the linear sequence of bases in DNA determines the linear sequence of amino acids in a protein.

collenchyma (kō leng′ ki mah): elongated plant cells with thickened walls, frequently present as flexible supporting tissue.

colon (kō′ lon): the major part of the large intestine; it removes excess water from undigested material.

colostrum: the secretion of the mammary glands for the first few days after having given birth; it is rich in proteins and antibodies.

commensalism: a form of symbiosis between members of two species in which one is benefited and the other is neither benefited nor harmed by the association.

community: an assemblage of individual populations interacting within a limited geographic area. The limits of a community are usually defined by its name (lake, forest, near-shore) and include all the organisms interacting in the area.

competition: the struggle among organisms to obtain limited, essential resources such as space, food, light, and so forth; competition can occur between members of different species but is most intense among members of the same species.

competitive exclusion: the principle that two species limited by the same resource cannot co-exist indefinitely in the same environment; one always excludes the other.

competitive inhibition: the process whereby a compound, similar in structure to the natural substrate of an enzyme, combines with the active site on the enzyme and thereby lowers the capacity of the enzyme to bind and modify the substrate.

complement: the collective term for a series of nine or more blood proteins that, when activated, act serially to lyse a foreign or invader cell, thus leading to its destruction.

compound: a defined chemical substance composed of atoms of two or more elements chemically bonded to one another in fixed proportions.

conception: a successful union of egg and sperm.

conditioned response: the triggering of a fixed action pattern by a reinforcing stimulus that is not normally associated with the response.

conditioning: a form of learning in which a response, such as a fixed action pattern or an autonomic reflex, becomes associated with and elicited by a stimulus with which it is not normally associated.

cone: in vertebrates, one of the two types of photoreceptors in the retina of the eye. There are three kinds of cones in the human eye, each with a different visual pigment. Cones function primarily in bright light.

conformation: in chemistry, the detailed three-dimensional structure of a molecule.

conifer: a member of the class Coniferae; the pine, fir, spruce, and so on.

conjugation: a form of reproduction in some bacteria and protistans in which genetic material is passed from one cell to the other through a cytoplasmic bridge that is formed between them.

conspecific: pertaining to members of the same species.

constitutive enzyme: an enzyme that is always present in the cell regardless of growth conditions.

contractile vacuole: a small cavity seen in certain one-celled organisms living in fresh water. It gradually increases in size, then contracts to expel excess water from the cell through a pore in the cell membrane.

contralateral: of the opposite side; for example, the right cerebral hemisphere exerts contralateral control over the left half of the body in vertebrates.

control gene: a gene that determines when and at what rate a structural gene is transcribed.

copulation (kop ū lā′ shun): sexual union in which the male injects sperm into the body of the female.

corepression: the process whereby a small molecule called a corepressor (the end product of a biosynthetic pathway) combines with a specific repressor protein, making it capable of binding to an operator gene. The result is cessation of synthesis of the enzymes required to synthesize the corepressor.

coronary artery disease: a disease resulting from thickening and hardening of the arteries that nourish the heart.

coronary thrombosis: the condition in which a blood clot is trapped in the blood vessels that feed the heart muscle, thereby cutting off the oxygen and nutrient supply to that portion of the heart, causing it to become inactive.

corpus callosum (kor′ pus kal ō′ sum): the principle structure through which the two hemispheres of the cerebral cortex communicate continuously.

corpus luteum (kor′ pus lū′ tē um): the structure in the ovary that is derived from a follicle after the egg has been ovulated; it is the site of progesterone production and secretion.

cortex: in single cells, such as certain ciliates and the eggs of animals, the outer layer consisting of the cell membrane and intimately associated structures; thought to play an important role in spatial organization during development. In animals, the outer layer of an organ such as the kidney or brain. In plants, the layer of parenchymal cells lying just beneath the epidermis of roots and stems.

cortical granule: a small, membrane-enclosed vesicle found beneath the surface membrane of an ovum before fertilization.

corticotropin releasing factor (CRF): an animal hormone produced and secreted by the hypothalamus; it functions to cause release of ACTH from the anterior pituitary.

co-transduction map: a map of the order of genes within a bacterial genome based on the observed frequencies with which they are co-transduced (transferred from one cell to another) by a single bacteriophage.

cotyledon (kot i lē′ don): a seed leaf formed as part of the embryo in angiosperm development.

coupling: the metabolic process whereby free energy released in electron transport is used to phosphorylate ADP.

courtship display: a complex pattern of behavior that functions (when successful) to release approach behavior and ultimately to permit prospective mates to make contact.

covalent bond: a chemical bond formed by the sharing of electrons by two atoms.

CRF: *see* corticotropin releasing factor.

cristae (kris′ tē): the foldings of the inner membrane of the mitochondrion, in which the enzymes of oxidative phosphorylation are embedded.

crossing over: the process in which chromatids of homologous chromosomes undergo chiasmal formation and exchange more or less equivalent parts during meiosis. If the participating chromatids differ in alleles on opposite sides of the chiasma, chromosomes bearing new combinations of alleles result.

CRP: *see* cyclic AMP receptor protein.

cryptic behavior: behavior patterns that serve to maximize concealment of an organism. Such behavior patterns are well developed in organisms with cryptic coloration.

cryptic coloration: animal colors and patterns developed through selection that tend to blend into the predominant background.

ctene (tēn): a comblike plate, consisting of large cilia; found in eight rows on a comb jelly (ctenophore).

ctenophore (tēn′ ō for): a member of the phylum Ctenophora, the comb jellies.

cuticle: a more or less impervious layer of material covering the outermost cells of many complex organisms.

cutin: a transparent, waxy substance that coats the outer surface of terrestrial plants to reduce water loss.

cyclic adenosine monophosphate: *see* cAMP.

cyclic AMP receptor protein (CRP): in bacteria, a protein that forms a complex with cAMP and then interacts with RNA polymerase to permit transcription of enzymes involved in specific catabolic pathways.

cytochrome (sī′ tō krōm): one of a series of related iron-containing proteins that function in the transport of electrons in respiration and photosynthesis.

cytokinesis (sī tō kin ē′ sis): the process in which the cell divides by the production of a new membrane surface that passes through the plane occupied earlier by the equator of the mitotic spindle at metaphase.

cytokinin (sī tō kī′ nin): one of a class of plant hormones that promotes cell division, among other effects.

cytological map: a chromosome map based on cytology (the microscopic examination of cells).

cytoplasm (sī′ tō plazm): all the nonparticulate matter in a cell, exclusive of the nucleus.

cytosine (sī′ tō sēn): a pyrimidine base found in all nucleic acids.

d

dark reactions of photosynthesis: the formation of sugar from carbon dioxide, utilizing the products of the light reactions of photosynthesis (ATP and reduced NADP).

deamination (dē am i nā′ shun): the enzymatic removal of the amino group from an amino acid.

dehydration synthesis: the formation (synthesis) of larger molecules by the hooking together of small molecules, with a concurrent removal of water molecules (dehydration).

deletion: in genetics, the loss of a block of genetic material involving one or more genes.

denaturation: the loss of active protein structure and properties by any of several means, such as heat, mechanical agitation, or exposure to certain chemicals.

dendrite: a cytoplasmic process or extension of a nerve cell that receives inputs at synapses with other nerve cells and carries them toward the cell body; an afferent nerve fiber.

density-dependent factor: a factor that limits the size of a population of organisms and becomes more intense as the population becomes larger.

deoxyribonucleic acid (dē ok sē rī′ bō nū klā′ ic): *see* DNA.

depolarization: in neurons and other excitable cells, the abolition and reversal of the usual polarity of the membrane such that the interior of the cell (which is normally negative with respect to the exterior) becomes positive with respect to the exterior.

derepression: the process whereby a small molecule (such as lactose) combines with a specific repressor molecule and causes it to dissociate from the corresponding operator gene. The result is initiation of synthesis of the enzymes required to break down the derepressor molecule.

deuterostome (dū′ ter ō stōm′): an animal such as an echinoderm or chordate in which the first opening between gut and exterior (the blastopore) becomes the anus and the mouth develops as a second opening.

diaphragm (dī′ a fram): a sheet of muscle that separates the chest cavity from the abdominal cavity in mammals.

diastole (dī as′ tō lē): the relaxed filling period of the heart while blood flows into the atria and on into the ventricles.

dicot (dī′ kot): a member of the subclass of angiosperms that produces two seed leaves or cotyledons; most familiar flowering plants (other than the grasses, orchids, and palms) are dicots.

dictyosome (dik′ tē ō sōm): a particular kind of golgi complex characteristic of higher plant cells but also found in certain animal cells that secrete large quantities of carbohydrate.

differentiation: the process whereby one cell gives rise to cells different from itself and from one another.

diffusion: a random, thermally induced movement of ions and molecules through a medium from a region of high concentration to one of low concentration.

dihybrid cross: a cross-fertilization between parents that differ in two genetic traits.

dimer (dī′ mer): a compound or complex formed by joining two monomers together.

diploid (dip′ loyd): having two full sets of chromosomes, one set derived from each parent.

directional selection: the process whereby the relative gene frequency of two alleles in a population changes regularly and progressively as a result of natural selection; the gene of lower adaptive value is progressively replaced by the one of greater adaptive value.

disruptive selection: the process whereby directional selection occurs in opposite directions in two populations of a species subjected to two different sets of environmental conditions; it results in populations with very different relative gene frequencies.

diurnal cycle (dī ern′ al): behavioral activities that are synchronized with the period of daylight.

divergence: a concept attributing the differences among species to evolution by natural selection in which gradual changes have accumulated in the many separate lines of descent from a common ancestor.

DNA: deoxyribonucleic acid; a polymer of deoxyribose-containing nucleotides; the genetic material in all organisms except certain viruses in which RNA plays that role.

DNA polymerase (pō lim′ er āse): the enzyme that catalyzes the formation of DNA by polymerization of nucleotides.

dominance hierarchy: a system or set of relationships within a group of social animals in which the more dominant animals control the less dominant ones by threat and aggressive actions.

dominant: pertaining to a gene that is expressed in a diploid cell to the same extent whether present in the homozygous or heterozygous condition.

dorsal: of or toward the upper or back surface; the opposite of ventral.

double helix: the structure in which DNA normally exists in cells: two strands are twisted about each other to form a helix and are held in a fixed relationship by hydrogen bonds between complementary bases.

drug: any biologically active substance that is foreign to the body and that is deliberately introduced to affect its functioning.

duodenum (doo od′ e num): the short segment of the small intestine closest to the stomach into which secretions from the pancreas and liver enter.

e

echinoderm (ē kīn′ ō derm): a member of the phylum Echinodermata; spiny-skinned animals such as sea stars, sea urchins, sea cucumbers, and brittle stars.

echolocation: a technique for determining the size and distance of external objects by the emission of short sound bursts and timing their return after reflection. Echolocation mechanisms are particularly well developed in bats and marine animals such as whales and porpoises.

ecological succession: the sequence of changes in the species composition of a community as it proceeds through several temporary intermediate stages until a stable climax community is formed.

ecology: the study of the interaction of organisms with both the living and nonliving components of their environment.

ecosystem: a system formed by the interaction of an entire community of organisms with each other and with their environment.

ecto-: a prefix, pertaining to the outer region or layers of a structure or organism.

ectoderm (ek′ tō derm): the outermost of the three discrete layers of cells formed during gastrulation of an animal embryo; gives rise to the nervous system, skin, and skin appendages.

egg: a mature reproductive cell of a female; an ovum.

electron: an elementary particle that is a fundamental constituent of matter, has a negative charge, and exists outside the nucleus of an atom.

electron transport: the process by which electrons of relatively high energy are transferred from one electron acceptor to another, falling progressively in their energy level. The energy lost is utilized for the phosphorylation of ADP. In respiration the electrons are derived from food molecules such as glucose and are carried to the electron transport chain by reduced coenzymes. In photosynthesis the electrons are obtained from water and are raised to a high energy level by the effect of light on chlorophyll.

element: a substance that cannot be broken down into simpler substances by any known chemical reaction.

Embden-Meyerhof pathway: the major pathway of glycolysis.

embryo: the early or developing stage of any multicellular organism; the developing product of a fertilized egg.

embryonic development: the period of development in which the embryo lives off the nutrients provided by its female parent.

embryonic regulation: compensation for missing or excess parts in a developing embryo.

emergence: the principle that at each level of increasing complexity of organization new properties emerge that are the result of the precise way in which the parts are arranged; the whole is greater than the sum of its parts.

endergonic: a chemical reaction that will proceed in a reverse direction (as written) starting from standard conditions. Such a reaction has a positive $\Delta G^{\circ\prime}$ (standard free energy).

endo-: a prefix indicating the interior region of a structure or organism.

endocrine gland: an organ containing clusters of cells specialized for the production of one or more hormones.

endocrine system: a series of specialized cells that produce chemical messengers (hormones) and secrete them into the circulatory system to be used at various places in the body. Usually the cells are clustered into discrete organs called endocrine glands.

endocytosis: the process by which an organism or cell takes into itself solids or liquids by surrounding or engulfing them; includes pinocytosis (liquids) and phagocytosis (solids).

endoderm: the innermost of the three discrete layers of cells formed during gastrulation of an animal embryo; gives rise to the gut and associated digestive organs.

endometrium (en dō mē′ trē um): the glandular epithelial lining of the uterus; the tissue on which the embryo lodges and develops.

endoplasmic reticulum: membrane sheets folded through the cytoplasm to form a complex system of tubules, vesicles, and sacs. Some regions are heavily studded with ribosomes.

endoskeleton: an internal skeleton; that is, a series of internal hard parts to which muscles are attached and that functions in support and movement.

endosperm: a multicellular, triploid tissue surrounding the embryo of a developing angiosperm seed and serving as a source of nutrients for the embryo.

entrophy: a measure of the extent of disorganization of energy in a system; that portion of the energy of a system or substance not available for the performance of useful work. Designated by the symbol S.

enzyme: a protein molecule that functions as a catalyst for (speeds up) a specific reaction.

epidermis: the outermost layer of cells in plants or animals.

epididymis (ep i did′ i mis): a long tubelike structure at the top and back of the testes in which sperm are stored and from which they are moved to the penis.

epinephrine (ep i nef′ rin): an animal hormone produced and secreted by the medulla of the adrenal gland. It acts to stimulate the heart, to constrict certain blood vessels, and to stimulate gluconeogenesis and lypolysis. Also called adrenalin.

epithelium (ep i thē′ lē um): a layer of cells covering or lining any free body surface, internal or external; the cells are tightly packed and have little intercellular space.

EPSP: *see* excitatory postsynaptic potential.

equilibrium: in general, a condition in which opposing forces, of any sort, exactly counterbalance each other; a state of balance. In chemistry, the state in which forward and reverse reaction rates are exactly counterbalancing each other.

equilibrium constant: the ratio of concentrations of products to reactants that will exist when a reaction has reached equilibrium. Equilibrium is achieved when the rates of the forward and back reactions become equal and there is no further net change in reactant concentrations. Designated as K_{eq}.

esophagus: the muscular tube that transports food from the mouth to the stomach.

estrogen: an animal hormone produced and secreted by the follicle cells of the ovary; it functions to stimulate development of female secondary sex characteristics and, in mammals, to initiate development of the uterine endometrium in preparation for pregnancy.

estrus: spaced periods of sexual receptivity in the mammalian female.

ethogram: a catalog of the entire behavioral repertoire of an animal, including both actual and potential behavior in a given set of circumstances.

ethology: the scientific study of animal behavior in natural environments.

eukaryote (ū kar′ ē ōt): an organism whose cells contain a membrane-bound nucleus.

eutrophication: refers to the successional process leading from an aquatic system with low productivity through increasingly greater productivity to the gradual development of a terrestrial system on the same site. The term is usually used in the context of a speeding up of the successional sequence in lakes, ponds, or streams because of pollution or other side effects of human activity.

evolution: a change in gene frequencies in a population through succeeding generations (as a consequence of mutation and natural selection) that results in the continuous genetic adaption of the population to the environment.

exchange diffusion: a process in which a particular molecule is permitted to pass out through a membrane only if a compensating molecule is available to be simultaneously brought in to take its place.

excitation energy: energy gained by the electrons of a molecule through the absorption of the vibrational energy of photons of particular wavelengths.

excitatory postsynaptic potential (EPSP): a shift in membrane potential toward the threshhold required to fire an action potential in a postsynaptic cell; a partial depolarization of the postsynaptic cell.

exergonic (ex er gon′ ic): a chemical reaction that will proceed in a forward direction (as written) starting from standard conditions. Such a reaction has a negative $\Delta G°′$ (standard free energy).

exocytosis (ex ō sī tō′ sis): the process by which vesicles formed in the endoplasmic reticulum and the Golgi complex fuse with the plasma membrane and release their contents; the reverse of endocytosis.

exoskeleton: a hard, protective body covering.

exothermic reaction: a chemical reaction in which heat is released.

exponential growth: a process in which each reproductive unit reproduces at a maximal rate; as a result the rate of growth of the population is a direct function of the population size, and the larger the population becomes the faster it grows.

extracellular: outside of cells.

f

facultative: having the capacity to live under more than one set of environmental conditions; for example, facultative anerobes can live and grow in either the presence or absense of oxygen. The opposite of obligate.

FAD: flavin adenine dinucleotide; one of the coenzymes that functions in the Krebs cycle and oxidative phosphorylation. In the electron transport chain it is tightly bound to a protein to form "flavoprotein."

fallopian tube: the oviduct; a tapering duct connecting the ovary and uterus in mammals and forming a passageway for the ova (female gametes, or egg cells).

family: a group of related genera; a major subdivision of an order.

fatty acid: a class of weak organic acids containing an acid group at one end of a hydrocarbon chain; present as glycerides in all animal and vegetable fats.

feedback inhibition: a process whereby the end product of a metabolic pathway controls its own production by inhibiting the activity of the first enzyme in the pathway.

fertilization: the union of male and female gametes, the sperm and ova.

fetus (fē′ tus): in mammals, the unborn young in the uterus, especially at later stages of development. For example, the human young is usually called an embryo for the first three months of uterine life and a fetus thereafter.

filopod: a slender, threadlike pseudopod or projection of a cell.

fixed action pattern: a stereotyped pattern of behavior that tends to emerge more or less unchanged at appropriate times in the life of an individual. It may be a simple response to a specific stimulus or a complex response to a broad spectrum of stimuli and circumstances.

flagellum, flagella: in eukaryotes, a membrane-covered appendage containing eleven microtubular fibers in a characteristic 9 + 2 array and used for locomotion. In prokaryotes, an appendage consisting of a single naked fiber that protrudes from the cell wall and provides motility.

flatworm: a member of the phylum Platyhelminthes.

flavin adenine dinucleotide: *see* FAD.

follicle-stimulating hormone (FSH): one of the gonadotropins; an animal hormone produced and secreted by the anterior pituitary gland that functions to stimulate development of and estrogen secretion by follicle cells in the ovary of the female. Also functions to stimulate spermatogenesis in the male.

food chain: a linear array of organisms related on the basic patterns of predation and trophic level. Because such arrays of organisms are rarely linear except in the simplest communities, it is often more convenient and more accurate to describe a *food web*, involving predation relationships in two or three dimensions.

food web: *see* food chain.

fovea (fō′ vē a): the point of maximal visual acuity in the retina.

free energy: energy available to do useful work; designated by the symbol G. *See also* standard free energy.

FSH: *see* follicle-stimulating hormone.

fungus, fungi (fun′ gus, fun′ jī): a member of the kingdom Fungi; a heterotrophic, eukaryotic organism that obtains nutrients by means of absorption through the cell wall.

g

gametangium, gametangia (gam i tan′ jē um): in plants and fungi, any cell or organ in which gametes are formed.

gamete: a mature haploid cell, male or female, that functions directly as a sexual reproductive cell (sperm or egg, for example).

gametophyte (gam ēt′ ō fīt): the haploid generation of a plant that produces gametes. It alternates with a diploid sporophyte generation.

ganglion, ganglia: a concentration of nerve cell bodies located outside the central nervous system.

gastrodermis: the epithelial layer lining the gut cavity of cnidarians.

gastrointestinal tract: the gut of a vertebrate.

gastropod: a member of the molluscan class Gastropoda; the snails, slugs, and nudibranchs.

gastrula: a stage in embryonic development of animals, following the blastula, in which some cells have moved to the interior, forming the three characteristic cell layers (ectoderm, mesoderm, and endoderm) and a primitive gut.

gene: in classical genetics, a unit of inheritance; in molecular genetics, a unit of nucleic acid function (for example, the unit of DNA coding for a particular polypeptide).

gene amplification: preferential replication of one specific genetic region to expand the number of copies of that region relative to all other regions of the genome.

gene pool: the total aggregate of allelic forms of all genes that exist in a population of interbreeding organisms.

genetic code: the system that determines which amino acid will be incorporated into a growing protein in response to a particular sequence of three nucleotides in an mRNA molecule. The genetic code determines what amino acid sequence will be called for by any particular nucleotide sequence in a structural gene.

genetic drift: the process whereby the relative frequency of two functionally equivalent genes changes randomly from generation to generation as a result of the small size of a breeding population and the sampling error this introduces.

genitals: the organs concerned with reproduction, especially the external ones.

genome: a complete set of hereditary blueprints.

genotype: the sum total of all the genes present in an organism, some of which may be expressed, others of which may not.

genus, genera: a group of related species; a major subdivision of a family.

geotaxis: directed movement of an animal toward or away from the center of the earth.

geotropism: directed plant growth in response to gravity.

germination: the resumption of growth and development following a period of dormancy; may be applied to the seeds of higher plants as well as to the spores of bacteria, fungi, algae, and nonseed plants.

germ plasm: localized cytoplasmic inclusions in the fertilized eggs of many animal species that will eventually cause the development of germ cells (eggs or sperm) in the adult.

gibberellin (jib er el′ in): one of a group of plant hormones chiefly affecting stem elongation.

gill: in aquatic animals, any structure specialized for the exchange of gases between body fluids and the surrounding water.

glial cell: one of the small but numerous cells that fill the spaces between nerve cells.

glomerulus, glomeruli: a cluster such as the cluster of capillaries within the cup of Bowman's capsule in the kidney.

glucagon: an animal hormone, produced and secreted by the α islet cells of the pancreas. It acts antagonistically to insulin.

gluconeogenesis: the synthesis of new glucose molecules from fats and amino acids.

glucose: a six-carbon sugar occurring in many fruits, animal tissues, and fluids; the principal source of metabolic energy.

glycogen (gli′ cō jen): a complex polymer of glucose. It is the chief carbohydrate storage material in animals.

glycogenolysis: the enzymatic splitting of glycogen to form glucose.

glycolysis: the enzymatic breakdown of sugars into simpler compounds with the concomitant release of energy.

Golgi complex (gōl′ jē): an organelle in the cytoplasm of eukaryotic cells composed of layers of membranous sacs; involved in the polymerization and secretion of carbohydrates.

gonad: an organ that produces gametes in metazoans; the ovary in females, the testes in males.

gonadotropin: one of the hormones produced and secreted either by the pituitary gland or placenta that acts as a stimulator of the gonads, or reproductive organs.

gonorrhea: the most common veneral disease; caused by the gonococcus *Niesseria gonorhaeae.*

granum, grana: a structure in a chloroplast (formed by the complex folding and stacking of the inner membrane) in which the light reactions of photosynthesis occur; one granum contains many thylakoid disks and is connected to other grana by the stroma lamellae.

gray matter: the regions of vertebrate brain and spinal cord rich in nerve cell bodies and synapses.

green revolution: a phrase used to refer to programs involving the breeding of new high-yield varieties of food crops in order to increase world food production.

guanine (gwa′ nēn): a purine base. It plays an essential role not only in nucleic acids but also in the coenzyme GTP (guanosine triphosphate), which is essential for protein synthesis.

guard cell: one of two specialized epidermal cells surrounding each stoma of a leaf and regulating the movement of gases into and out of the plant.

gustatory: pertaining to the detection of and response to chemical stimuli associated with the food an animal eats; relating to the sense of taste.

gut: the entire digestive system.

guttation: the exudation of water from leaves.

gymnosperm (jim′ nō sperm): a naked seed plant, such as a pine, in which seeds are borne on the surface of cone scales without protective tissue.

h

habitat: the environmental situation in which an organism or a species is characteristically found.

habituation: a simple form of learning in which the magnitude of an organism's response decreases to zero as it grows accustomed to a particular repeated stimulus that carries with it neither harmful nor beneficial consequences.

haploid: having a single set of chromosomes per individual or cell, as in gametes (*see* diploid).

hapten: an antigenic substance that can react with a specific antibody but cannot induce its formation unless coupled with a high molecular weight carrier.

Hardy-Weinberg law: a basic generalization of population genetics which states that as long as breeding within the population is random, the relative frequencies of alleles and genotypes at *all* gene loci remain constant from generation to generation.

haustorium, haustoria (hos tō′ rē um): a suckerlike extension of a hypha in parasitic fungi; used for obtaining nutrients from host cells.

helix: a geometric shape similar to the curve of a screw thread. Many large biological molecules assume the shape of a helix as a result of hydrogen bonding between repeating groups.

heme: the iron-containing, nonprotein component of hemoglobin.

hemoglobin: the reddish iron-containing protein of the red blood cells. It binds oxygen for transport to the tissues.

herbivore: an animal that feeds on plants.

heterochromatin: a subfraction of the chromatin in a eukaryotic cell that appears to differ in several respects from the bulk of the chromatin. It is highly condensed in the interphase cell, replicates later than other chromatin, and appears to be largely or totally inactive in RNA synthesis.

heteropolymer: a chain of nonidentical monomers linked together covalently to form a large molecule.

heterospory: a condition in which the diploid stage of a plant life cycle produces two types of haploid spores: large spores (megaspores), which will develop into female gametophytes, and small spores (microspores), which will develop into male gametophytes.

heterotroph: an organism that depends on an external source of organic substances for its food and energy.

heterozygous: having different forms (alleles) of a particular gene at the same locus on homologous chromosomes.

histone: one of a group of basic proteins closely associated with DNA in the chromosomes of eukaryotic cells.

holism (hōl′ izm): a theory that the properties of a living system cannot be explained by analysis of its component parts because the parts do not possess the properties of the whole.

holography (hō log′ ra fē): a technique by which laser beams are used to create an interference pattern on a photographic plate that, when viewed by laser light, re-creates a precise, three-dimensional image of the object.

homeostasis: the maintenance of relative stability and constancy in the internal environment of an organism or in the relationship between an organism and its environment.

homing behavior: a type of behavior involving complex orientation mechanisms that enables animals to return to their nest or home, sometimes from great distances and unfamiliar territory.

hominid: a member of the family Hominidae of which modern man is the only living representative; includes man's immediate ancestors and some related forms.

hominoid: a member of the superfamily Hominoidea, which includes the hominids (humans) and the apes.

homogenate (hō moj′ i nāt): a relatively uniform suspension of cellular components formed by mechanical disruption of the cells.

homologue (hō′ mō log): in evolution, a structure that bears detailed resemblance to another structure in both form and development as a result of common derivation from a shared ancestor. For example, the bird wing is a homologue of the mammalian foreleg but not of the insect wing. In genetics, one of a pair of similar chromosomes in a diploid cell; in bisexual organisms, one homologue is inherited from the male parent and one from the female parent.

homopolymer: a chain of identical monomers linked together covalently to form a large molecule.

homospory: a condition in which the diploid stage of a plant life cycle produces only a single type of haploid spore (a homospore). Such spores develop into gametophytes bearing both male and female sex organs.

homozygous: having two identical forms (alleles) of a particular gene at the same locus on homologous chromosomes.

hormone: a substance formed in one part of an organism and transported to another part where it functions. In plants, hormones are produced by cells that are specialized to perform another function; these hormones have widespread effects on growth and development throughout the plant. In contrast, animal hormones are produced in cells highly specialized for hormone production, and the hormones act on specific target cells to effect quite specific changes in metabolism.

humoral immune response: the immune reaction that results in the production of specific, soluble proteins (antibodies) that are released into the body fluids and that interact specifically with the foreign material.

hybrid: in genetics, the offspring of two parents that differ in regard to one or more heritable traits; in biochemistry, a complex formed between two molecules of similar types but dissimilar origins.

hydrocarbon: an organic compound that contains only carbon and hydrogen.

hydrocortisone: an animal hormone produced and secreted by the adrenal cortex; it has many functions, including the stimulation of gluconeogenesis in liver cells.

hydrogen bond: a chemical bond in which a hydrogen atom is shared by two adjacent molecules.

hydrolysis: the breaking of a chemical bond with the addition of H^+ and OH^- ions to the cleaved ends.

hydrophilic: having an attraction for water; polar substances.

hydrophobic: repellent to or having no attraction for water; nonpolar substances.

hydrophobic interaction: the bond formed by mutual attraction between two nonpolar molecules or regions of molecules in a watery environment.

hyperpolarization: in neurons and other excitable cells, an increase in polarization beyond the normal resting potential of the cell.

hypertension: elevated blood pressure.

hypha, hyphae (hī′ fa): a slender, cellular filament in fungi. Collectively, the hyphae make up the mycelium.

hypothalamus (hī pō thal′ a mus): a small area of the vertebrate forebrain, lying in front of the thalamus; it regulates many critical processes in the life-support system of the animal, such as body temperature, heart rate, and hunger.

i

IAA: *see* indole acetic acid.

immune suppression: a variety of procedures used in an attempt to prevent graft rejection by inactivation of the body's normal immune response.

immunity: in general, the capacity of a living organism to resist or overcome an infection. In vertebrates, the capacity to produce antibodies or specific killer cells in response to foreign substances or cells.

immunogen (i mun′ ō jen): any substance that elicits an immune response in a given animal.

immunoglobulin (im′ ū nō glob′ ū lin): one of a related group of proteins that compose all specific antibodies.

imprinting: a form of learning at a very early stage in an animal's life that results in a rigid, irreversible behavior pattern attached to specific stimuli.

indole acetic acid (IAA): a naturally occurring plant hormone; one of the auxins.

induction: in bacteria, a process whereby the synthesis of a group of enzymes is elicited by the molecule those enzymes are designed to metabolize. In embryology, the process whereby one group of developing cells elicits a specific pathway of development in a neighboring group of cells, either by contact or by release of a chemical signal.

inhibitory postsynaptic potential (IPSP): a shift in membrane potential away from the threshold required to fire an action potential in a postsynaptic cell; a hyperpolarization of the postsynaptic cell.

innate behavior: behavioral responses characteristic of a species that emerge in the absence of prior experience and that can be shown to be genetically predetermined.

inorganic: pertaining to chemical substances that do not contain carbon. (Carbon dioxide, carbonic acid, and salts of carbonic acid are the exceptions; they are generally considered inorganic compounds).

insulin: an animal hormone, produced and secreted by the β islet cells of the pancreas. It exerts regulatory effects on the liver, skeletal muscle, and adipose tissue, resulting in a lowering of blood glucose and fat and an increased storage of glycogen.

intercellular: between cells.

intercostal muscle: one of the muscles between the ribs of vertebrates.

internode: the portion of a plant stem between two leaf nodes.

interphase: the interval during which a cell is not dividing and the chromatin material is dispersed. The chromosomes replicate during interphase in preparation for division.

interrupted mating map: a map of the order of genes within a bacterial genome based on the time required after conjugation has been initiated before given genes will be found in the recipient cells; the procedure is based on the fact that genes are duplicated and passed to the recipient cell in a linear order from some genetically determined starting place.

interstitial fluid (in ter sti′ shal): a thin film of fluid lying between the blood vessels and the cells, penetrating all the spaces between cells and bathing and lubricating them.

intracellular: within cells.

invertebrate: an animal without a backbone.

ion: an electrically charged atom or group of atoms formed by the loss or gain of one or more electrons.

ionic bond: a bond formed by the electrical attraction between a positive ion of one element and a negative ion of another.

IPSP: *see* inhibitory postsynaptic potential.

iris: the pigmented muscular structure in the vertebrate eye that constricts and dilates to regulate the amount of light entering the eye.

islets of Langerhans: specialized secretory cells in the pancreas that produce insulin (from the β islet cells) and glucagon (from the α islet cells).

isogamy (ī sog′ a mē): the fusion of two haploid cells that are not distinguishably different, as occurs in the reproductive cycles of some protistans, green algae, and fungi.

isomer: a compound of identical composition but different structure from another compound.

isotope: any of two or more forms of a chemical element having the same number of protons in the nucleus but a different number of neutrons. Isotopes may be stable or unstable (radioactive).

j

J-shaped growth curve: a curve relating the size of a population to time, in which the population grows at a near-maximum rate until some environmental parameter exceeds the tolerance of the species and leads to a rapid collapse of the population.

junctional complex: a specialization of the membranes at the point of contact of two adjacent cells; many kinds are known. They appear to regulate the flow of materials between and among cells in addition to holding the cells together.

k

kinesis (ki nē′ sis): orientation of an organism in the most favorable part of the environment achieved by differential rates of movement and random turning.

kinetechore (ki net′ ō kor): a crescent-shaped granule found at the centromere of each chromosome and to which spindle fibers attach during mitosis and meiosis.

kinetic energy: energy of motion. The kinetic energy of molecules rises with the temperature.

kingdom: the largest and most inclusive category into which organisms are usually classified. In the scheme used in this book five kingdoms are recognized: Monera, Protista, Plantae, Fungi, and Animalia.

Krebs cycle: a biochemical reaction sequence in aerobic organisms in which the pyruvate produced as the end product of glycolysis is enzymatically degraded to carbon dioxide and water, producing reduced coenzymes that can be used for the formation of ATP through oxidative phosphorylation.

l

lamella, lamellae: a flattened membranous sac, sometimes closely stacked in parallel arrangement with other such sacs. In chloroplasts two kinds of lamellae exist, stroma lamellae and grana lamellae. Together they are the site of the light reactions of photosynthesis.

larva, larvae: an immature form in the life cycle of some animals that undergoes radical transformation into the adult form.

lateral: to the side; of the side.

learned behavior: a change in a behavioral response as a result of experience.

leucoplast (loo′ kō plast): a colorless plastid of plant cells; site of conversion of glucose into polysaccharides, lipids, or protein and their storage.

LH: see luteinizing hormone.

lichen (lī′ ken): a product of the close symbiotic association between an alga (usually a blue-green or green alga) and a fungus (usually an ascomycete).

light reactions of photosynthesis: the sequence of reactions in which light energy is used to excite electrons released by the splitting of water; passage of these excited electrons along the electron transport chains is coupled to the production of molecules of ATP and reduced NADP used in the dark reactions.

linkage group: in genetics, a group of genes that fail to assort randomly and thus are inferred to occur on the same physical unit (chromosome).

linkage map: a chromosome map based only on the degree of linkage between gene pairs.

lipase (lī′ pās): an enzyme that breaks down fat molecules into simpler units such as free fatty acids and glycerol.

lipid (lī′ pid): any of a group of fatty organic compounds, such as fats, waxes, steroids, and phospholipids. All are soluble in organic solvents and insoluble in water.

lipolysis (lī pol′ i sis): the enzymatic breakdown of fat to fatty acids and glycerin.

locus, loci (lō′ cus, lō′ sī): in genetics, the location or position of a particular gene on a chromosome.

logarithmic growth: see exponential growth.

luteinizing hormone (LH): one of the gonadotropins, an animal hormone produced and secreted by the anterior pituitary gland that functions to stimulate development of and progesterone secretion by the corpus luteum in the ovary of the female. It also stimulates production and secretion of testosterone by cells in the testis of the male.

lycopod (lī′ cō pod): a member of the tracheophyte subphylum Lycopsida; all have true roots, stems, and leaves.

lymph: in vertebrates, a clear, yellowish fluid containing lymphocytes that is derived from tissue fluids, transported by lymphatic vessels through lymph nodes (where it is filtered), and then returned to the bloodstream.

lymph node: one of many lymphocyte-rich structures located widely throughout the lymphatic system of the body.

lymphocyte: one of a variety of small white blood cells derived from the thymus, bone marrow, or lymph glands.

lysis (lī′ sis): destruction of a cell that occurs when the cell membrane is broken down by physical, chemical, or viral agents.

lysosome: a sac of hydrolytic enzymes isolated from the cytoplasm by a single unit membrane; acts as the disposal unit of cytoplasm.

m

macrophage (mak′ rō faj): a large phagocytic cell (a cell that eats other cells) found either free in the body fluids or localized in various tissues of the body.

malignant tumor: a cancer; a group of rapidly multiplying cells, unrestrained by a capsule, that compress, invade, and ultimately destroy surrounding tissue.

mantle: in molluscs, the body wall covering the visceral mass; secretes substances needed to build the protective shell.

mechanoreceptor: a pressure-sensitive sensory neuron.

medulla (me dul′ a): in general terms, the inner part of an organ such as the adrenal gland or kidney; with specific reference to the nervous system, a region of the vertebrate hindbrain that is like the spinal cord in structure and function. It controls many important automatic activities, such as those of respiration and circulation.

megaspore: a haploid plant spore that develops into a female gametophyte.

meiosis (mī ō′ sis): the process involving two cell divisions by which a diploid cell gives rise to four haploid cells; these haploid cells function as or give rise to sexual reproductive cells.

membrane mosaic: a contemporary modification of the unit membrane concept in which the cellular membranes are visualized less as a continuous film and more as a complex structure studded with patches of specialized proteins that penetrate the lipid layers of the membrane and spread out over both interior and exterior surfaces in highly specific ways.

membrane potential: the potential difference, or voltage, across the plasma membrane that results from the asymmetrical distribution of ions across the membrane.

Mendelian inheritance: a process whereby each heritable unitary trait of a diploid individual is determined by two factors (genes), one inherited from each parent.

menstrual cycle: a cyclic event in the human female, the function of which is to prepare the endometrium, once each month, to receive an embryo. If a fertilized egg is not received, much of the endometrium is sloughed off and the cycle starts again.

menstruation: the periodic discharge of blood and mucosal tissue from the uterine wall (in humans and certain other primates) when conception does not occur.

meristem: the undifferentiated cells in a growing plant that continue to divide mitotically and give rise to new structures throughout the life cycle; it may occur at the growing tips of shoots and roots (apical meristem) or around the circumference of shoots and roots (lateral meristem).

mesenchyme (mes′ en kīm): a tissue derived from the middle (mesodermal) layer of an animal embryo.

mesoderm: the middle layer of the three discrete layers of cells formed during gastrulation of an animal embryo; gives rise to a variety of internal organs such as skeleton, muscle, blood vessels, and heart.

Mesozoic (mes a zō′ ik): a geologic era extending from about 230 million to about 62 million years ago.

metabolism: all the chemical processes in an organism by which substances are produced, maintained, and destroyed and by which energy is made available for cellular functions.

metamorphosis: a drastic transformation in basic shape or structure such as occurs in the development of some insects and amphibians between the larval and the adult stage.

metaphase: an intermediate stage of mitosis during which the chromosomes condense, line up on the equator of the mitotic spindle, and attach to a spindle fiber running to the poles.

metastasis, metastases: a secondary tumor; caused by cancer cells from an original malignant site that have traveled through the bloodstream or lymphatic system to another part of the body, where they form a new tumor.

metazoan: a multicellular animal.

meter: a unit of measurement equal to 39.37 inches; the basic unit of length in the metric system.

microfilament: a minute supportive and shape-directing fiber in the cytoplasm of some cells.

micrometer (mīk′ rō mēt′ er): a unit of measurement equal to one millionth of a meter (10^{-6} meters).

microspore: a haploid plant spore that develops into a male gametophyte.

microtubule: a microscopic tubular or cylindrical structure found in cilia, flagella, centrioles, spindle apparatus, and various other organelles in the cytoplasm of eukaryotic cells.

microvillus, microvilli: fingerlike projections on the surface of some cells. They increase surface area and absorptive capacity of the cell; seen abundantly on cells lining the intestinal villi.

migration: the movement of virtually all animals of a species in a given direction at a certain time of year to a predictable destination, followed by a return trip at another time of year.

minute respiratory volume: the volume of air exchanged in the lungs per minute; a product of the tidal volume and the respiratory rate per minute.

Miocene (mī′ ō sēn′): a geologic period in the Cenozoic era extending from about 22 million to about 7 million years ago.

mitochondrion, mitochondria (mī′ tō kon′ drē on): an organelle in the cytoplasm of eukaryotic cells, bounded by a double membrane and responsible for the reactions of respiratory metabolism, among other things.

mitosis (mī tō′ sis): the process of separation of the hereditary material (chromosomes) during cell division in eukaryotes.

mitotic spindle: (mī tot′ ik): the complex array of microtubules formed in dividing eukaryotic cells and involved in moving sister chromatids to opposite ends of the cell.

molarity: the number of moles of a solute in 1 liter of solution.

mole: an amount of a compound equivalent to the molecular weight of that compound in grams; 1 gram molecular weight.

molecular weight: the sum of the atomic weights of the elements that have combined to form a chemical compound.

molecule: a unit of matter composed of two or more atoms held together by chemical bonds.

mollusc: a member of the phylum Mollusca; includes snails, clams, squid, and so on.

moneran (mō ner′ an): a member of the kingdom Monera; a bacterium or blue-green alga. All monerans are prokaryotic.

monocot: a member of the subclass Angiospermae (flowering plants). Monocots produce a single cotyledon, or seed leaf. Grasses, cereal grains, orchids, and palms are common monocots.

monohybrid cross: a cross-fertilization between parents that differ in only one genetic trait.

monomer: a single molecule that is joined with others to form a larger complex or compound; may be used either to refer to small molecules that are coupled covalently to form a polymer or to macromolecules that are associated by noncovalent bonds to form a larger functional unit.

monophyletic: refers to a group of organisms whose members are related by divergent evolutionary descent from a common ancestor.

monosomy: the absence of one chromosome from the complement of an otherwise diploid cell.

monosynaptic reflex arc: a reflex circuit that incorporates only one synapse between the sensory input and the motor output.

morphogenesis: the development of form.

morphogenetic movement: the active movement and rearrangement of parts in an embryo in such a way as to give rise to specific form.

mortality: the rate at which members are removed from a population of organisms by death.

morula (mor′ ū la): in mammals, a solid membrane-enclosed mass of dividing cells resulting from cleavage of the ovum; it develops into the blastocyst.

mutation: a sudden and permanent change in a unit of heredity. The term is sometimes used synonomously with point mutation, but in other cases it is used to include larger changes in chromosomes (such as deletions) that affect more than one gene.

mutualism: a form of symbiosis between members of two species in which both are benefited.

mycelium, mycelia (mī cē′ lē a): a fungal body, composed of a mass of filaments or hyphae.

mycoplasma: the smallest known cellular life form.

myelin sheath: the many-layered wrapping around some nerve fibers; composed of Schwann cells.

myeloma: a form of cancer arising from a single antibody-forming cell that divides endlessly to form a large clone. The myeloma proteins (each is an immunoglobulin of identical sequence) have been invaluable in elucidating immunoglobulin structure.

myocardial infarction: a heart attack resulting from a stoppage of the blood flow to some part of the heart wall musculature.

myosin: a large protein of muscle, shaped somewhat like a golf club with a long, straight, shaftlike portion and a swollen ''head'' extending from one end at an angle; interaction of the head of the myosin molecule with actin generates the contractile force.

myotube: a long, multinucleate cell formed by fusion of many mononucleate cells as a first step in the formation of muscle.

myxomycete (mix′ ō mī sēt′): a member of the class Myxomycetes, the true slime molds.

n

NAD: nicotinamide adenine dinucleotide, one of the coenzymes that functions in cellular oxidation reduction reactions. NAD serves as the major intermediate linking glycolysis and the Krebs cycle to the process of oxidative phosphorylation.

NADP: nicotinamide adenine dinucleotide phosphate; a coenzyme that functions in electron transfer in several metabolic pathways. Perhaps its most important function is in photosynthesis, in which it is reduced in the light reactions and is used to reduce CO_2 in the dark reactions. NADP differs from NAD by the presence of one additional phosphate group.

nanometer (nan′ ō mēt′ er): a unit of measurement equal to 10^{-9} meters.

natality: the rate at which members are added to a population of organisms by birth.

natural selection: the process whereby the frequency of heritable variations that better adapt members of a population to the environment increases from generation to generation, as a result of increased reproductive success of the individuals possessing these variants.

negative feedback: any process in which an entity acts as the signal controlling the rate of its own production or removal so that a relatively constant level is maintained despite fluctuating conditions.

nematocyst (nē mat′ ō sist): a minute stinging structure that certain cnidarians use to paralyze and capture prey; also used in defense against potential predators.

nematode (nē′ ma tōd): a member of the phylum Nematoda; the roundworms.

nephridium, nephridia: in certain animals, a funnel-shaped organ, lined with cilia, through which body fluid is drawn, passed down a duct, and excreted to the exterior.

nephron: one of the many microscopic units that make up the mammalian kidney; consists of a network of blood capillaries and a renal tubule.

neural integration: the summation of positive and negative increments of membrane potential resulting from excitatory and inhibitory postsynaptic potentials.

neurofibril: one of the delicate threads, or microtubules, running through the cytoplasm of a nerve cell; in ciliates, a system of fibers analogous to the nerve network in higher animals.

neurofilament: a microtubule of nerve processes.

neuron: a nerve cell; the structural unit of the nervous system.

neurosecretory cells: a cell, nervelike in origin, structure, and function, that secretes its effector substance into the circulatory system rather than into synaptic contact with the target cells.

neurotransmitter: a chemical substance known to be released from presynaptic cells and to cause changes in the membrane potential of postsynaptic cells.

neutron: an elementary particle that is a fundamental constituent of the nucleus in all atoms except hydrogen. It has nearly the same mass as the proton but carries no electrical charge.

niche (nitch): in ecology, the position and role a species occupies in a community; includes where it lives, what it feeds on, what its predators are, and what factor limits the growth of its population.

nicotinamide adenine dinucleotide: *see* NAD.

nicotinamide adenine dinucleotide phosphate: *see* NADP.

nocturnal cycle: behavioral activities that are synchronized with the period of night or darkness.

node of Ranvier (rahn vē ā′): a gap occurring between successive Schwann cells on the axon of a myelinated neuron.

nonpolar compound: a compound composed of molecules whose atoms are joined by nonpolar covalent bonds and that therefore lacks asymmetrical distribution of charges in the molecules.

nonpolar covalent bond: a covalent bond in which electrons are shared essentially equally between the two atoms involved.

norepinephrine (nor′ ep i nef′ rin): a neurotransmitter released at the synaptic endings of many neurons of both the central and peripheral nervous systems, including all cells of the parasympathetic nervous system. Norepinephrine is also produced by the adrenal medulla, but in lesser amounts than epinephrine (from which it differs only slightly in structure and function).

notochord: a rodlike cord of cartilage cells forming the first skeletal structure of the chordate body; it lies under the nerve cord and above the gut. It may disappear in later development or may be replaced by the bony vertebral column in vertebrates.

nuclear envelope: the double layer of membrane and associated annuli that characteristically enclose the hereditary material of a eukaryotic cell.

nuclease: an enzyme that digests nucleic acids to simpler units such as nucleotides.

nucleic acid: a polymer of nucleotides. The two major kinds are DNA and RNA.

nucleolus (nū klē ō′ lus): the organelle within the nucleus where ribosomes are made.

nucleoplasm: the complex mixture of substances and structures found in the cell nucleus.

nucleoprotein: a complex formed by association of nucleic acids with protein.

nucleoside: a molecule consisting of a 5-carbon sugar and a purine or pyrimidine base. Addition of a phosphate group converts a nucleoside to a nucleotide.

nucleotide: a molecule consisting of phosphate, a 5-carbon sugar, and a purine or pyrimidine base.

nucleus: in chemistry, the positively charged mass at the center of each atom that contains the neutrons and protons of that atom. In biology, the membrane-bound organelle of a eukaryotic cell that contains the chromosomes and associated material.

o

obesity: the condition in which a person is more than 20 percent over his ideal weight. This condition enhances the likelihood of a variety of serious disorders.

obligate (ob′ li git): restricted to a particular condition of life; for example, obligate parasites can live only in association with certain specific host organisms. The opposite of facultative.

olfactory: pertaining to the detection of and response to chemical stimuli carried in the water or air in which an animal lives; relating to the sense of smell.

olfactory bulb: the region of the cerebrum concerned with processing inputs from the organs responsible for the sense of smell.

oligomer (ō lig′ a mer): a compound or complex formed by joining a relatively small number of monomers together.

omnivore: an animal that eats both plants and other animals.

oncogene: a gene(s), postulated to be present in all cells of an organism, that is capable of inducing the cancerous state but that is normally inactive. Cancer is thus viewed by some as an activation of these normally silent genes.

oocyte (ō′ o sīt): in animals, a female germ cell that is in the process of developing into a mature egg.

oogamy (ō og′ a mē): the fusion of a motile reproductive cell (sperm) from a male parent with a nonmotile reproductive cell (egg) from a female parent.

oogenesis (ō′ o jen′ i sis): the process of egg formation from undifferentiated sex cells in plants or animals.

oogonium, oogonia (ō′ o gōn′ ē um): in animals, an undifferentiated female germ cell that divides to give rise to the cells from which eggs develop; in certain algae and fungi, the unicellular female reproductive organ containing one or more eggs.

oomycete (ō′ o mī sēt′): a member of the class Oomycetes—the water molds, downy mildews, and certain plant rusts.

operant conditioning: a form of learning in which the conditioning stimulus (the reward or punishment) occurs only *after* the animal performs (or fails to perform) some specific operation; also called instrumental conditioning.

operator gene: a gene that determines whether or not an operon can be transcribed; acts as a binding site for a repressor.

operon: a coordinated group of genes (usually located adjacent to one another on a single stretch of DNA) that operates as a single unit; contains one or more control genes, in addition to the two or more structural genes.

orbital: the volume of space surrounding the nucleus of an atom in which a particular electron could be expected to be located 90 percent of the time.

order: a group of related families; a major subdivision of a class.

organelle: an organized structure having a definite function within a cell, such as a mitochondrion or a chloroplast.

organic: pertaining to carbon-containing substances or compounds, other than carbon dioxide, carbonic acid, and salts of carbonic acid.

organ of Corti (cor′ tē): the organ of hearing that contains specialized mechanoreceptors, called hair cells.

osmoregulation: the maintenance of a relatively constant osmotic pressure in body fluids, in spite of changes in the osmotic pressure of the external environment.

osmosis: the movement of water across a semipermeable membrane. When the concentration of solutes is greater on one side of the membrane than the other, the *net* movement of water will be from the region of lesser to the region of greater concentration of solutes.

osmotic pressure: a measure of the tendency of water to move from an area of high concentration to an area of lower concentration across a semipermeable membrane; it is related to the difference in concentration of dissolved substances that are unable to pass through the membrane.

ovary: in animals, the female sexual organ in which the ova (eggs) are formed and by which the female sex hormones are produced. In plants, the enlarged basal portion of a carpel, or of fused carpels, that becomes the fruit after fertilization.

ovulation: the release of a mature egg from the ovary.

ovule: in plants, the structure within which the female gametophyte (including the egg cell) is located; when mature the ovule becomes the seed.

oxidative phosphorylation: a series of metabolic reactions in which reduced coenzymes, formed during the series of reactions in the Krebs cycle, pass their electrons to an assembly of electron acceptors called the electron transport chain. As the electrons travel down this chain some of the energy they release is coupled to the phosphorylation of ADP.

oxygen tension: the partial pressure of free oxygen with which the oxygen dissolved in a fluid (such as plasma) is in equilibrium.

oxytocin (ok sē tō′ sin): an animal hormone produced in the hypothalamus and secreted by the posterior pituitary gland; it functions to regulate uterine contractions.

p

pacemaker: a small region of muscular tissue that initiates the contraction of the heart and therefore controls the rate of beating of the heart as a whole. Also refers to an artificial device, implanted by surgery, that maintains normal heart rhythm.

Pacinian corpuscle (pa sin′ ē an): a type of mechanoreceptor found in the deep layers of skin; a single sensory neuron process wrapped in many layers of connective tissue and highly sensitive to pressure.

Paleozoic (pā lē ō zō′ ik): a geologic era extending from about 600 million to about 230 million years ago.

palisade layer: in the leaves of flowering plants, a layer of densely packed, vertically aligned cells lying directly beneath the upper epidermis; the palisade cells contain numerous chloroplasts and constitute the most active site of photosynthesis in the plant.

pancreas (pan′ krē us): in vertebrates, a gland, located near the stomach, that secretes a variety of digestive enzymes and the hormones insulin and glucagon.

panmixis: the property of a population in which mating is completely random. Populations having such a breeding pattern are said to be panmictic.

paradigm (pair′ a dīm): (as applied to the history of science by Thomas Kuhn) a set of laws, theories, ideas, and techniques to which there is a shared commitment by a community of scientists and that serve to define the legitimate problems and methods of a research field.

parasite: an organism that lives on or in another organism, called the host. It benefits at the expense of the host, but contributes nothing useful in return.

parasympathetic nervous system: the subdivision of the autonomic nervous system that acts to conserve energy by slowing many body processes and promoting digestion.

parenchyma (pa renk′ i ma): in plants, living, unspecialized, thin-walled cells with large vacuoles; they serve to store water and nutrients and to support the body of nonwoody plants.

parthenogenesis (par then ō gen′ e sis): a form of asexual reproduction involving the development of an egg that has not been fertilized by a sperm.

penis: the male sex organ through which sperm are deposited in the female reproductive tract during copulation.

peptide bond: a covalent bond in which the nitrogen in the amino group of one amino acid is attached directly to the carbon in the carboxyl group of another amino acid by dehydration synthesis.

periodic table: a chart on which the elements are listed in order of increasing atomic number and arranged in a form so that each vertical column includes elements of similar chemical properties.

peripheral nervous system (PNS) (pa rif′ er al): one of the two traditional divisions of the vertebrate nervous system; includes all nerve processes and neurons outside the central nervous system.

peristalsis (per i stal′ sis): rhythmic contractions of muscles in the walls of the gut; causes movement of food through the digestive tract.

peroxisome: a sac of enzymes isolated from the cytoplasm by a membrane; contains one or more enzymes that produces hydrogen peroxide as a by-product of its catalytic role in certain metabolic pathways and an enzyme that destroys hydrogen peroxide.

pH: a measure of the concentration of hydrogen ions in a water-based solution. pH is the negative log of the hydrogen ion concentration. Thus the pH rises as the hydrogen ion concentration falls. Solutions of pH 7 are neutral, those below pH 7 are acidic, and those above pH 7 are basic.

pH optimum: the hydrogen ion concentration at which an enzyme exerts its maximum catalytic effectiveness.

phaeophyte (fā′ ō fit): a member of the phylum Phaeophyta, the brown algae.

phagocytosis (fag′ ō sī tō′ sis): the process by which solid particles are engulfed and taken into a cell; "cellular eating."

pharynx: the muscular part of the gut between the oral cavity and the esophagus.

phenotype: the structural and functional appearance of an organism that results from the interaction of genes with one another and with the environment; certain genes (particularly recessive ones) may be present in the genotype but not expressed in the phenotype.

pheromone: any substance released by an organism that stimulates a physiological or behavioral response in another individual of the same species.

phloem (flō′ um): one of the vascular tissues in plants; consists of living sieve tubes and companion cells and uses cellular energy to transport the products of photosynthesis from the leaves throughout the rest of the plant.

phosphodiesterase (fos′ fō dī es′ ter ās): an enzyme that acts to destroy cAMP, forming AMP as the product.

phospholipid: a lipid containing phosphorus in addition to fatty acids, glycerin, and a nitrogenous base; an important constituent of cellular membranes.

phosphorylase: an enzyme that catalyzes glycogen breakdown, producing glucose phosphate.

phosphorylation: the covalent coupling of a phosphate group to an organic molecule.

photoautotrophic: capable of using light energy to produce all the organic molecules required for metabolism; for example, plants.

photolysis (fō tol′ i sis): a light-dependent enzymatic process by which electrons are removed from water during photosynthesis.

photon: a unit of radiant energy (principally light). The energy of a photon varies inversely with its wavelength.

photoperiodic event: a biological activity such as migration in animals or flowering in plants that is triggered by seasonal changes in the length of the period of daylight.

photophosphorylation: the process in certain bacteria and all plants whereby phosphorylation of ADP is coupled to the transport of electrons produced by pigments that have been excited by the absorption of light energy.

photoreceptor cell: a sensory neuron specialized to convert light into a membrane potential change by virtue of a photoreceptor pigment in the membrane.

photosynthesis: the metabolic processes by which plants transform carbon dioxide and water into carbohydrates by using solar energy absorbed by chlorophyll.

phototaxis: directed movement of an animal toward or away from a source of light.

phototropism: directed plant growth in response to light; results in bending or turning of the plant toward the source of the light.

phycocyanin (fī kō sī′ a nin): a blue pigment found in blue-green algae that, with chlorophyll *a*, contributes to the process of photosynthesis.

phycoerythrin (fī kō a rēth′ rin): a red accessory pigment in plants that can absorb light of wavelengths that chlorophyll does not absorb and can pass this excitation energy on to neighboring chlorophyll molecules.

phylogenetic classification: a classification of organisms based on the presumed evolutionary relationships among them.

phylum: the major subdivision of a kingdom; a group of organisms, all of which are built on the same basic body plan.

pinocytosis (pin′ ō sī tō′ sis): the process by which droplets of liquids are engulfed and taken into a cell; "cellular drinking."

pistil: the female component of a flower, usually structurally differentiated into a stigma (a pollen receptacle), a style (a supporting column), and an ovary.

pituitary gland (pi too′ i tear ē): a vertebrate endocrine gland attached to the base of the brain; it secretes a large number of hormones that affect body growth, regulation, and development.

placenta: an organ, formed by intimate contact between the tissues of a developing embryo and the reproductive tract of the mother, through which nutrients, waste products, and gases are exchanged between maternal and embryonic bloodstreams; found in most mammals, some sharks, and certain invertebrates.

plankton: a collective term for the organisms, large or microscopic, that float or drift at random in a body of water.

planktonic: pertaining to aquatic organisms that live suspended in open water rather than associated with the bottom.

planula: an elongated, ciliated larva, found in the life cycle of most cnidarians.

plasma: the noncellular portion of blood.

plasma cell: a large, distinctively staining white blood cell, derived from a lymphocyte, that participates in the immune response by actively synthesizing and secreting antibodies.

plasma membrane: the outer layer or surface membrane of a cell. It has the ability to regulate the passage of substances into and out of the cell.

plasmodesma, plasmodesmata: a cytoplasmic connection between two adjacent plant cells permitting large molecules and even some cellular organelles to move from cell to cell.

plasmodium, plasmodia: in myxomycetes (true slime molds), a multinucleate mass of cytoplasm with no cellular crosswalls; characteristic of the diploid phase of the life cycle.

plasmotomy (plas mot′ ō mē): an asexual form of reproduction in which some organisms with multiple nuclei pinch apart into two or more pieces that become separate individuals.

plastid: a specialized membranous organelle in plant cells; involved in photosynthetic energy conversions, storage of nutrients, or determination of coloration.

Pleistocene (plīs′ tō sēn): a geologic period in the Cenozoic era extending from about 2.5 million years ago to the present. Some geologists call the period since the retreat of the last ice age (10,000 years ago) to the present the Recent period rather than a part of the Pleistocene.

Pliocene (plī′ ō sēn): a geologic period in the Cenozoic era extending from about 7 million to about 2.5 million years ago.

pluripotent: with regard to nuclei and cells of a developing embryo, retaining many, but not all, developmental capacities.

PNS: *see* peripheral nervous system.

pO₂: partial pressure of oxygen; the amount of pressure due exclusively to the oxygen in a mixture of gases.

point mutation: a change in the hereditary material that is restricted to one point in a single gene.

polar compound: a compound composed of molecules whose atoms are held together by covalent bonds in which unequal sharing of electrons leads to asymmetric distribution of electrical charge in each molecule.

polar covalent bond: a covalent bond in which electrons are shared unequally by the two atoms involved. The result is an unequal distribution of electric charge between the atoms.

polarized: possessed of two opposite poles; with respect to the membrane of a neuron (or other excitable cell), the term refers to the existence of an excess of negative charge on the interior and an excess of positive charge on the exterior during the resting state.

pollen: the male gametophytes of seed plants at the stage at which they are shed.

pollination: the transfer of pollen from where it was formed (the anther) to a receptive surface (usually the stigma) of plants.

polymer: a compound formed by the covalent linking of simpler molecules or monomers.

polymorphism: in genetics, the existence of two or more distinct phenotypes in a population. (Phenotypic differences due to differences in developmental state or sex are not included.)

polypeptide: a polymer of amino acids linked by peptide bonds.

polyploidy: the presence of one or more complete sets of chromosomes beyond the usual diploid number.

polyribosome: a row, cluster, or rosette of ribosomes in the cytoplasm held together in such configurations by a single molecule of mRNA; often shortened to polysome.

polysaccharide (pol ē sak′ a rīd): a complex carbohydrate molecule; a polymer of simple sugars; includes starches, glycogen, and cellulose.

polysome: *see* polyribosome.

pons: an extension of the portion of the brain known as the medulla; it contains neurons involved in hearing, respiration, chewing, salivation, and other functions.

population: a group of interacting individuals of the same species within a limited geographic area.

posterior: of or toward the hind end; the opposite of anterior.

pre-Cambrian: *see* Proterozoic.

predator: in the narrow sense, an animal that eats another live animal. In the broadest sense, any organism that gains its nutrient at the expense of another living organism.

primary immune response: the production by a vertebrate of antibodies and/or immune cells in response to a first exposure to a foreign cell or substance.

primate: a member of the order Primates, which includes man, apes, monkeys, and lemurs.

primordial: of, or constituting, the beginning or origin. Often used in an evolutionary context to refer to the first life forms arising out of the abiotic sea or to that sea itself. Used in embryology to refer to the first discernible stage in development of a structure.

primordium, primordia: in plants and animals, the first detectable stage in the development of an organ.

proboscis (prō bos′ kus): an extensible, elongated, often tubelike structure near the mouth that is involved in bringing food to the mouth from some distance; well developed in nemerteans, certain insects, and elephants.

procambium, procambia: the primary meristem, formed near a growing tip, from which the vascular tissues of the plant subsequently develop.

progesterone (prō jes′ ter ōn): an animal hormone produced and secreted by the corpus luteum of the ovary of the mammalian female. One of its functions is to stimulate development of and glandular secretion by the uterine endometrium in preparation for pregnancy.

prokaryote: an organism that lacks a membrane-bound nucleus.

prolactin: an animal hormone produced and secreted by the anterior pituitary that functions to initiate milk production by cells in the mammary gland of the mammalian female.

promotor gene: the genetic site at which RNA polymerase attaches to begin transcription of an operon; the promotor determines how fast an operon will be transcribed when it is active.

prophase: the first stage of mitosis during which the chromatin strands coil up into visible chromosomes, the nucleolus disappears, and the nuclear envelope is breaking down.

prostate gland: a glandular and muscular organ surrounding the urethra just below the bladder in the male mammal. It secretes most of the seminal fluid.

protease: an enzyme that digests proteins.

protein: a complex macromolecule consisting of one or more polypeptide chains in which amino acids are linked to one another covalently by peptide bonds.

protein kinase: one of the group of enzymes that couples phosphate groups to specific proteins; many protein kinases are activated by cAMP.

Proterozoic (prō′ ter ō zō′ ik): a geologic era extending from the origin of the earth to about 600 million years ago; often termed the "pre-Cambrian" period.

protistan: a member of the kingdom Protista, which includes all organisms not considered to be plants, animals, fungi, or monerans. It is a varied group of distantly related organisms, all of which are eukaryotic and most of which are unicellular.

proton: an elementary particle that is a fundamental constituent of all atomic nuclei. It has a positive charge equal in magnitude to that of the negative electron.

protostome (prō′ tō stōm): an animal, such as a nemertean, annelid, arthropod, or mollusc, in which the mouth is derived from the blastopore (the first opening between the gut and the exterior).

pseudoplasmodium, pseudoplasmodia (soo′ dō plas mō′ dē um): a structure formed in the life cycle of cellular slime molds as a result of the clustering of the individual amoeboid cells.

pseudopod (soo′ dō pod): a temporary projection of the membrane and cytoplasm of a cell. It functions in both feeding and amoeboid motion.

psychoactive drug: a drug that can temporarily change a person's perceptions, mood, or behavior. For example: alcohol, barbiturates, marijuana.

pupa, pupae (pū′ pa): an intermediate stage of development between the larva and the adult in insects that undergo complete metamorphosis.

purine (pūr′ ēn): a type of nitrogenous base composed of two rings, such as adenine or guanine.

pylorus (pī lor′ us): the muscular ring (sphincter) at the juncture between the stomach and intestine.

pyrimidine (pi rim′ i dēn): a type of nitrogenous base composed of a single ring, such as cytosine or uracil.

pyruvate (pī′ roo vāt): a salt or ester of pyruvic acid, an intermediate product in the glycolysis of sugars.

q

quantum, quanta: a fundamental unit of radiant energy as defined by quantum theory.

r

radial symmetry: the property of having many planes of symmetry, all of which pass through a single axis. It is only along this axis that the structure or organism demonstrates asymmetry. Example: a pear.

radioactive decay: the process whereby nuclei of unstable isotopes break down, releasing radiation in the form of x-rays, electrons, or alpha particles.

radioactive tracer: a chemical compound containing one or more radioactive isotopes that is administered to an organism as an aid in analyzing metabolism; by determining the subsequent fate of the radioactive atoms, it is possible to infer the metabolic pathways through which the compound was passed.

radula (radj′ ū la): a band of toothlike or rasplike devices in the mouth of many molluscs; used for scraping food from rocks, tearing plants, and drilling holes in shells.

recessive: pertaining to a gene that is expressed in a diploid cell only when present in the homozygous condition.

recombination: in genetics, the processes occurring during meiosis and syngamy that lead to the production of young possessing combinations of genes different from the combinations possessed by the parents.

rectum: a short section at the end of the large intestine where waste material is stored prior to elimination.

reductionism: a theory that the phenomena of life can be understood on the basis of the chemistry and physics of its smallest component parts.

regulator gene: a gene that makes a chemical mediator capable of regulating the transcription of a specific operon; in some cases the product of the regulator gene acts as a repressor of transcription, while in other cases it acts as an activator of transcription.

relative dating: assignment of a relative age to rock units or to fossils within such rocks based on the position of the units within a series. A rock sequence that has not been disturbed has the oldest rock units at its base with relatively younger rocks higher in the sequence.

relative fitness: the probability that an individual of a given genotype will survive and reproduce, relative to the probability that individuals with the most fit (best-adapted) genotype will survive and reproduce. Symbolized by W.

relative gene frequency: in an interbreeding population the fraction of all genes at one gene locus that are of given allelic type.

renal: pertaining to the kidney.

replication: the process by which the hereditary material (DNA) is duplicated prior to cell division.

replicon: a unit of replication in eukaryotic DNA, lying between a specific initiation point and either one or two termination points.

repolarization: in neurons and other excitable cells, the reestablishment of the normal charge distribution following a depolarization.

repression: the process whereby a repressor protein combines with an operator gene and thereby blocks transcription of adjacent structural genes.

repressor protein: a regulator gene product that is capable (under certain conditions) of binding to a specific operator gene, thereby blocking transcription of the adjacent structural genes.

respiration: in whole animals the process of taking in oxygen and releasing carbon dioxide. In cells, the liberation of metabolically useful energy (ATP) from food molecules through the Krebs cycle and oxidative phosphorylation.

respiratory center: the region of the medulla that is concerned with the coordination of muscular activity in breathing.

resting membrane potential: the voltage measured across the membrane of an inactive neuron or other excitable cell; it results from asymmetrical distribution of ions between the interior and exterior of the cell.

retina: the layer of neurons lining the inner surface of the eye; includes the photosensitive rods and cones and the various associated nerve cells that integrate the impulses arising from the rods and cones and generate the nerve impulses that leave the eye via the optic nerve.

rhizoid (rī′ zoyd): a threadlike, nonphotosynthetic cell that attaches certain plants to their substrate.

rhizome (rī′ zōm): a rootlike stem that runs horizontally at or below the soil surface.

rhodophyte: a member of the phylum Rhodophyta, the red algae.

ribonucleic acid: *see* RNA.

ribosome: a small organelle composed of RNA and protein that serves as the site for protein synthesis.

ritualization: a behavior that occurs typically in members of a given species in a highly stereotyped fashion and quite independent of any direct physiological significance.

RNA: ribonucleic acid; a polymer of ribose-containing nucleotides. Three classes of RNA molecules participate in protein synthesis: messenger RNA (mRNA), transfer RNA (tRNA), and ribosomal RNA (rRNA).

RNA polymerase: one of the enzymes that catalyzes transcription of the genetic code from DNA to RNA.

rod: one of the two types of photoreceptors in the retina of the vertebrate eye. Rods contain the visual pigment rhodopsin and function in light of low intensity.

S

sagittal (saj′ i tal): in a plane parallel to the long axis of an organism or structure.

saltatory propagation: the mechanism of neural impulse transmission in myelinated axons. The impulse jumps from one node of Ranvier to the next.

saprophytic (sap rō fit′ ic): pertaining to a heterotrophic organism that feeds on non-living organic material.

sarcomere (sar′ cō mēr): the repeating functional unit of muscle contractions; the region between successive Z lines of a striated muscle cell.

sarcoplasmic reticulum (sar cō plas′ mik re tik′ ū lum): a series of complex vesicles that wrap around each bundle of contractile filaments of a striated muscle and act as a reservoir for calcium ions, thereby playing an important role in regulating contraction.

satiated (sā′ shē āt ed): supplied with anything to a satisfactory or excessive level.

Schwann cell: a flattened accessory cell that wraps many times around certain vertebrate axons and forms a sheath; the Schwann cell wrapping forms the myelin sheath.

scrotum: the pouch of skin near the base of the penis that contains the testes.

secondary growth: in plants, growth initiated by lateral meristematic tissue that results in increased diameter of roots and stems.

secondary immune response: the heightened and prolonged production of antibodies and/or immune cells that occurs in an animal exposed to a foreign cell or substance toward which it has executed a primary immune response at an earlier time; the secondary response is a reflection of specific immunological memory.

sedimentation coefficient: the rate of movement of a molecule or particle in response to a defined centrifugal force; a measure of size and shape of the substance; measured in Svedberg units, symbolized S.

segmentation: a characteristic feature of several animal groups (such as annelids, arthropods, and vertebrates) in which part or all of the body is composed of serially repeating units of similar structure.

semen: the thick, whitish, sperm-bearing secretion of the male reproductive organs of mammals; also called seminal fluid.

semiconservative replication: the process whereby each of the strands of a DNA double helix serves as the template upon which a new, complementary strand is formed; as a result half the parent molecule is conserved in each daughter molecule—hence the name.

semilunar valve: a valve that separates the aorta or the pulmonary artery from the left or right ventrical, respectively, thus preventing the backflow of blood.

seminal duct: the passage for conveyance of semen and sperm from the epididymis to the ejaculatory duct; also called the vas deferens.

seminal vesicle: the portion of the male reproductive duct in which sperm are stored prior to copulation.

senescence (se nes′ ence): the gradual deterioration of structure and function caused by aging.

sensory adaptation: a temporary loss of sensitivity in a receptor cell caused by rapid repetition of identical stimuli.

sepal (sē′ pal): a specialized leaf forming one of the outermost structures of a flower; usually green, but may resemble the petals in form or in coloration.

sex: the fusion of two cells derived from different individuals; the specializations in structure and behavior that facilitate the occurrence of such a fusion.

sickle-cell anemia: a hereditary disease caused by a mutant form of hemoglobin and characterized by sickle-shaped red blood cells.

sigmoid growth curve: a curve relating the size of a population to time, in which the population grows at a near maximum rate until some environmental resource becomes limiting, whereupon the growth rate of the population falls to zero and a relatively stable population size is maintained.

skeletal muscle: striated muscle that is attached to skeletal elements and is subject to voluntary control of contraction, resulting in body movement.

smooth muscle: muscle lacking the regularized arrangement of contractile proteins characteristic of striated muscle; found in blood vessel walls, the gut, and other internal organs and usually not subject to voluntary control of contraction (hence often called involuntary muscle).

soma: body; in animals, all the tissues of the body except the germ cells; in neurons, the main part of the cell body, exclusive of axons and dendrites.

somatic: "of the body," not participating directly in sexual reproduction.

somatic nervous system: the elements of the vertebrate nervous system involved in integrating processes that are under voluntary control.

somite: one of the segments formed during vertebrate development by condensation of the mesoderm alongside the neural tube. Each somite will form a vertebra and associated muscles.

sorus, sori: aggregations of sporangia on the surface of fern leaves, usually with specific structural adaptations to facilitate spore dispersal.

spatial orientation: a type of response in which animals adjust their behavior to maintain a certain position and movement with respect to various directional stimuli from the environment.

speciation: the derivation of two distinct species from one as a result of reproductive isolation between two previously interbreeding populations. (In plants sometimes the process is essentially reversed; a new species is produced by hybridization of, and subsequent reproductive isolation from, two parental species.)

species: a group of related individuals that are actually or potentially capable of interbreeding; a group of organisms constituting a single gene pool.

sperm: a mature, motile reproductive cell of a male; a spermatozoan. Also used to refer to many spermatozoa collectively.

spermatogenesis: the process of sperm formation.

sphincter (sfingk′ ter): a ringlike band of muscle that opens and closes a passage.

spinal cord: the dorsal nerve cord of a chordate. In vertebrates the spinal cord is enclosed in the vertebral column.

spindle apparatus: the structure composed of microtubules to which chromosomes attach during mitosis or meiosis and by which equivalent sets of chromosomes are drawn to opposite sides of the cell in preparation for cell division.

spirillum, spirilla: a corkscrew-shaped bacterium.

spongy mesophyll: a layer of loosely arranged cells between the palisade layer and the lower epidermis of a leaf; concerned principally with gas exchange, although some photosynthesis occurs here.

sporangium, sporangia (spor an′ gē um): a spore-producing structure in plants and fungi.

spore: in certain prokaryotes and simple eukaryotes, a dormant cell that is resistant to heat, drying, and absence of nutrients; produced under unfavorable growth conditions. In certain protistans, plants, and fungi, the haploid cells produced by meiosis.

sporophyte: the diploid generation of a plant that produces spores. It alternates with a haploid gametophyte generation.

stamen: the pollen-bearing or male organ of a flower, usually consisting of a supporting filament and an anther.

standard free energy: the change in free energy per mole of reactant as carried out under standard laboratory conditions of one molar concentrations of all reactants and products and a pH of 7. Designated by the symbol $\Delta G^{\circ\prime}$.

statocyst: a sensory organ concerned with orientation of an animal with respect to gravity.

statolith: a dense ball or knoblike structure in a statocyst that tends to be drawn down toward the center of gravity and stimulates different nerve endings, leading to righting behavior in the organism.

stereoisomer: one of a pair of isomers in which one of the structures is a mirror image of the other.

steroid: a lipid molecule with a characteristic four-ring structure.

stoma, stomata: a small pore or opening in the epidermis of a leaf that permits exchange of gases (CO_2, oxygen, and water vapor) between internal and external environments; each stoma is bounded by a pair of guard cells that act to regulate the dimensions of the opening.

striated muscle: muscle fibers in which the contractile proteins are organized into regular repeating units called sarcomeres, thus giving a striped (striated) appearance to the tissue when examined microscopically.

stroke: damage to the brain due to the loss of the blood supply in a local region. Usually caused by a combination of atherosclerosis, hypertension, and/or a blood clot trapped in a blood vessel.

stroke volume: the volume of blood pumped from the heart per contraction.

stroma: in chloroplasts, the complex, nonmembranous matrix containing (among other things) the enzymes involved in the dark reactions of photosynthesis.

stroma membrane: in chloroplasts the membranous sheets running through the stroma and connecting the inner membrane of the chloroplast to the grana and the grana to one another.

structural gene: a gene that codes for the structure of a specific protein.

surface tension: a cohesion of molecules on the surface of a liquid that gives it high resistance to penetration.

suspensor: the filament by which the developing angiosperm embryo becomes suspended in the seed.

symbiosis (sim bī ō′ sis): the close association or living together of two organisms of different species for their mutual or one-sided benefit.

sympathetic nervous system: the subdivision of the autonomic nervous system that promotes energy expenditure by mobilizing the body's resources for action and suppressing digestion.

synapse (sin′ aps): a specialized structure through which neural signals pass from one neuron to another or between a neuron and an effector cell. The communication may be electrical or chemical.

synaptic vesicle (sin ap′ tik): a small organelle in a presynaptic nerve terminal containing neurotransmitters (chemical substances known to cause changes in the membrane potential of the postsynaptic cell).

syncytium (sin sish′ um): a multinucleate structure formed either by the fusion of many cells and the loss of membranes separating them or by extensive nuclear division without concomitant cell division.

syngamy (sin′ ga mē): the fusion of haploid cells during sexual reproduction.

syphilis: a venereal disease caused by the spirochete bacterium *Treponema palladum.*

systole (sis′ tō lē): the contraction period of the heart during which more blood is forced from the atria into the ventricles and from the ventricles out to the lungs or body.

t

taxa: groupings, such as classes and orders, in a classification system.

taxis, taxes: behavior in which organisms respond to inequalities of light, heat, chemicals, gravity, and so forth by making directed movements toward or away from the source of the stimulus.

taxonomy: any system of classification of organisms.

T-cells: a population of lymphocytes derived from thymus lymphocytes, dependent on a thymus hormone for their maintenance and function and essential for cellular immunity as well as for some aspects of antibody formation.

telophase (tē′ lō fāz): the final stage of mitosis in which the chromosomes reorganize to form daughter nuclei and the cytoplasm divides to form two complete daughter cells.

template: a pattern or mold; for example, the model of coded information stored in the DNA molecule from which other DNA or RNA molecules are synthesized.

temporal orientation: a type of behavior in which animals respond to regularly recurring events such as day and night, high and low tide, and the changing of seasons.

terminal cell: the smaller and denser of two cells formed in the first division of an angiosperm zygote; the cell that differentiates into the embryo.

territorial behavior: the tendency of some animals or groups of animals to establish an area relatively great in comparison to their body size and to defend this area vigorously from trespassing by other individuals or groups of the same species.

testis, testes: the male gonad; the glandular organ in which male gametes (sperm cells) and male sex hormones are produced.

testosterone (tes tos′ ter ōn): the hormone produced by the testes. It maintains a favorable environment within the testes for sperm cell development and stimulates development of male secondary sex characteristics.

tetraploid: pertaining to cells with four complete sets of chromosomes.

thalamus (thal′ a mus): a region of the vertebrate brain involved in the receipt, integration, and transmission of impulses from and to many diverse sources. The great relay station of the brain.

thallus: the body of a plant.

thoracic cavity: the chest cavity.

thorax: in insects, the body region between the head and abdomen and bearing the legs and wings; in mammals, the anterior part of the body, containing the heart and lungs.

threshold potential: the characteristic potential at which the gradual depolarization of a given nerve cell is replaced by explosive depolarization.

thylakoid disk (thī′ la koyd): one of the sacs of a granum (and its enclosed material) formed from the inner membrane of the chloroplast.

thymine (thī′ mēn): a pyrimidine base found in DNA.

thymus (thī′ mus): a lymphocyte-rich organ located in the chest, behind the top of the breast bone; important in the production and maintenance of immune cells.

thymus-dependent antigen: an antigen that cannot elicit antibody formation unless T-cells are present in addition to B-cells.

thymus-independent antigen: an antigen that elicits antibody formation in the absence of T-cells.

thyroid-stimulating hormone (TSH): an animal hormone produced and secreted by the anterior pituitary gland that functions to cause release of thyroxin from the thyroid gland.

thyrotropin releasing factor (TRF): an animal hormone produced and secreted by the hypothalamus that functions to cause secretion of thyroid stimulating hormone by cells of the anterior pituitary.

thyroxin: an animal hormone produced and secreted by the thyroid gland that functions to regulate the level of cellular respiration in a wide variety of cell types.

tidal volume: the amount of air moved in and out of the lungs per breath.

tolerance: in immunology, natural tolerance is the failure to respond immunologically to self antigens; induced tolerance is the state of immunological nonresponsiveness that occurs when a foreign substance is introduced in such a way that the body reacts to it as if it were a self antigen. In physiology, drug tolerance is the condition in which the body becomes adapted to regular use of a drug, thereby requiring ever-increasing doses to produce a constant response.

totipotent (tō tē pō′ tent): with regard to nuclei and cells of a developing embryo, retaining all developmental capacities; capable of directing or undergoing all phases of development.

toxin: a substance produced and released by a microorganism that adversely affects the functioning of another organism and causes disease symptoms.

trachea, tracheae (trā ′ kē a): a breathing tube. In arthropods tracheae branch and carry air directly to all cells; in vertebrates the tracheae carry air to the bronchi of the lungs.

tracheid (trā′ kē id): an elongated, tapering xylem cell adapted for conduction and support.

tracheophyte (trā′ kē ō fit): a member of the phylum Tracheophyta, the vascular plants.

transcription: the enzymatic process by which the base sequence of DNA is used to form an RNA molecule of complementary base sequence.

transcriptional regulation: regulation of expression of a gene by controlling synthesis of the corresponding RNA.

transduction: in genetics, the transfer, by means of a bacteriophage, of genetic information (DNA) from one bacterium to another.

translation: the biosynthetic process by which amino acid sequences in proteins are determined by base sequences in the mRNA template on the ribosome.

translocation: in genetics, a rare event resulting in the exchange of parts between nonhomologous chromosomes.

transpiration: the loss of water (in the form of water vapor) from the stomata (pores) in the surface of a leaf.

trematode (trem′ a tōd): a parasitic flatworm of the class Trematoda; a fluke.

TRF: *see* thyrotropin releasing factor.

trichoblast (trik′ ō blast): a densely cytoplasmic cell that occurs in the epidermal layer of some plant roots and develops into a single-celled extension called a root hair.

trichocyst (trik′ ō cist): an effector organelle embedded in the body surface of ciliated protozoa and containing a fine, hairlike filament that can be ejected into potential prey or predators or into a surface to serve as an anchor for the organism.

triploid: pertaining to cells with three complete sets of chromosomes.

trisomy (trī′ sō mē): the presence of an extra chromosome of one type in an otherwise diploid cell.

trochophore (trōk′ ō for): a free-swimming, short-lived larva of some molluscs and annelids.

trophic level: the nutritional role a set of organisms plays in a community: producers, consumers, and decomposers represent three different trophic levels.

trophoblast: in mammals, the thin-walled side of a blastocyst that gives rise to the placenta and the membranes that surround the embryo.

TSH: *see* thyroid-stimulating hormone.

u

umbilical cord: in mammals, the cord through which blood vessels run between the fetus and the placenta.

uniformitarianism: a theory stating that while many conditions in the world have changed with time, the laws governing natural events have not; thus ''the present is a guide to the past.''

unit membrane: a structure originally conceived to be the basic membranous component of cells, composed of a continuous double layer of lipid sandwiched between the layers of protein and modified to form the various specialized membrane systems of the cell. *See also* membrane mosaic.

uracil: a pyrimidine base found in RNA in the locations where thymine would be found in DNA; also plays an essential role in the structure of several coenzymes.

urea: one of the nitrogenous waste products of mammals and some other vertebrates, formed by a multistep reaction from ammonia and carbon dioxide.

urethra (ū rēth′ ra): the tube through which urine is carried from the bladder and discharged from the body.

uterus: the womb; the organ in which the embryo is contained and nourished in female mammals.

v

vaccination: inoculation with a modified virus to induce a state of immunity to a related, unmodified, disease-causing virus.

vacuole: a membrane-bound, liquid-filled chamber or cavity in a cell.

vagina (va jīn′ a): the canal in the mammalian female reproductive tract that receives the penis in copulation.

valence: the number of electrons an atom of a given element may gain, lose, or share in the formation of chemical bonds.

vascular bundle: a linear aggregation of conducting tissue that extends through the stem of a vascular plant. A typical vascular bundle includes both xylem and phloem tissue and may include cambial cells as well.

vascular cambium: a cylindrical, meristematic tissue that produces secondary phloem and secondary xylem.

vas deferens: *see* seminal duct.

vasopressin (vā zō pres′ in): an annual hormone produced in the hypothalamus and secreted by the posterior pituitary gland; also called antidiuretic hormone (ADH). Its principal function is in regulating absorption of water (by kidneys, gills, or skin) to maintain a constant osmotic pressure in the blood.

vegetative: not related to or involving sexual reproduction.

venereal disease: an infectious disease, such as syphilis or gonorrhea, that is transmitted primarily during sexual intercourse, homosexual relationships, or other sexual activities.

ventral: of or toward the underside or belly surface; the opposite of dorsal.

ventricle: the chamber of the heart that receives blood from the atrium and pumps it out to the body.

vertebrate: an animal whose nerve cord is located inside a backbone—a column of bony segments called vertebrae.

vesicle: a membrane-bound sac.

villus, villi (vil′ us): a small protrusion such as that caused by the extensive outfolding of the inner walls of the intestine.

virus: a submicroscopic, noncellular infectious particle capable of reproduction only inside a living cell, using the enzymatic machinery of that cell.

vital capacity: the maximum amount of gas that can be expelled from the lungs following a maximal inhalation (maximum exchangeable volume).

vitalism: a theory that the unique properties of living things derive from a ''vital force'' that can be imparted to matter only by another living thing.

vitreous humor: the transparent gelatinous substance filling the main chamber of the eye that keeps the eyeball distended.

vulva: all the external genitals of the mammalian female.

w

white matter: the regions of vertebrate brain and spinal cord that are rich in myelinated nerve fibers.

X

X chromosome: the term given to the more abundant of the two sex-determining chromosomes in any species. In humans and many other species, females normally possess two X chromosomes while males possess only one, but in some species it is the male that possesses two Xs and the female that possesses only one.

xylem (zī′ lum): one of the vascular tissues in plants; consists of the cell walls of dead cells and conducts water and minerals from the roots upward by purely physical processes.

y

Y chromosome: the term given to the less abundant of the two sex-determining chromosomes in any species. In humans and many other species only the male normally possesses a Y chromosome.

z

zoospore (zō′ ō spor): a small, flagellated, motile stage in the life cycles of certain algae and fungi that is capable of giving rise to an entire multicellular organism by mitosis. In some cases zoospores are produced by meiosis; in other cases they are derived by differentiation of either haploid or diploid cells.

zygomycete (zī′ gō mī sēt′): a member of the class Zygomycetes, the bread molds and fly fungi.

zygospore: a thick-walled diploid resting spore produced by members of the fungal class Zygomycetes.

zygote (zī′ gōt): a fertilized ovum in plants or animals; the diploid cell resulting from fusion of male and female gametes.

index

(italic numbers refer to illustrations; boldface numbers refer to definitions)

Credits and Acknowledgments

Special thanks are extended to the following persons for their assistance in the preparation of *Biology Today Second Edition*: Cynthia Davidson (publishing coordination); John Odam and Julie Hernly (design); Tralelia Robinson (copy-editing); Gary Sawade (research); Sherida Bush and Ruth Wilson (typing); Mary Bess Holloway, Kari Johnson, Margaret Kassner, Virginia Roos, Lois Huettner, Laura Szalwinski, Teri Marshall, and Jane Wilkins (editorial services).

Chapter 1

2—David MacDermott; 3—(*left*) The Bettmann Archive, Inc., (*right*) John Dawson; 6—The Bettmann Archive, Inc.; 7—The Granger Collection; 8—The Bettmann Archive, Inc.

Chapter 2

12—David Cavagnaro from *This Living Earth*, © 1972 American West Publishing Company; 13–16—Louis Neiheisel; 19—Allan Roberts.

Chapter 3

22—Karl Nicholason; 24—Doug Armstrong after Charles Singer, *A History of Biology*, Abelard-Schuman; 25—The Bettmann Archive, Inc.; 26—(*left*) The Granger Collection, (*right*) The Bettmann Archive, Inc.; 27—John Dawson after J. M. Savage, *Evolution*, Holt, Rinehart and Winston, 1969; 29—(*left*) The Granger Collection; 30—(*left*) The National Maritime Museum, England, (*top right*) Doug Armstrong, (*bottom right*) George Harrison/Grant Heilman; 31—John Dawson, 32—The Granger Collection; 35—(*top*) Courtesy of Laboratory of Tree-Ring Research, University of Arizona, (*bottom*) John Dawson; 36–37—John Dawson and Doug Armstrong.

Chapter 4

38—Dr. Gary Grimes, Hofstra University; 40—(*left*) Fisher Scientific Co., Educational Materials Division, Chicago; 41—(*top left*) Fisher Scientific Co., Educational Materials Division, Chicago, (*bottom right*) John Dawson; 42—Glenn L. Decker; 43—(*left*) Dr. George Chapman, (*right*) T. F. Anderson, E. L. Wollman, and F. Jacob; 44—William T. Hall, Electro-Nucleonics Laboratories, Inc.; 45—(*top*) John Dawson, (*top center*) Lynwood M. Chace/National Audubon Society, (*bottom*) M. Woodbridge Williams; 46—John Dawson; 47—(*top*) Dr. A. K. Kleinschmidt, (*center*) Dr. Robley C. Williams, (*bottom*) Lee D. Simon; 49—(*left*) P. L. Walne and J. H. Arnott, *Planta* 77:325–354, 1967, (*right*)·Julie Hernly; 50–52—John Dawson; 54—Doug Armstrong; 55—Dr. David Kirk; 60—John Dawson; 62—John Dawson after David Kirk; 63—(*left*) John Dawson after David Kirk; 64—(*top left*) John Dawson, (*center*) Carl Zeiss, Inc., New York; 65—Julie Hernly after Schiller, *Rabenhorst*, Akademische Verlagsgesellschaft, Geest and Portig, K.-G., Leipzig; 66—(*top left*) Barbara Hoopes, (*top right, center left*) Julie Hernly, (*bottom left*) Dr. Lewis G. Tilney; 67—Werner Wetzel; 69—G. Adrian Horridge; 70, 71—John Dawson.

Chapter 5

74—Dennis Brokaw; 76—Doug Armstrong; 78—(*bottom*) John Dawson; 79—(*top*) Gabrielle Wunderlich, (*bottom*) John Dawson; 80—(*top*) Ward's Natural Science Establishment, (*bottom*) John Dawson; 81—Chuck Nicklin; 82—Douglas P. Wilson; 83—(*bottom*) John Dawson; 84—Grant Haist; 85—John Dawson; 86—(*top*) Grant Haist, (*bottom*) John Dawson; 87—Grant Haist; 88—(*top*) Philip Hyde, (*center*) Dennis Brokaw, (*bottom left*) Grant Haist, (*bottom right*) Dr. A. T. Cross, Michigan State University; 89—John Dawson; 90—(*top, center*) William H. Amos, (*bottom*) Dr. David Kirk; 91—(*top*) Bill Call, (*bottom*) John Dawson; 92—John Dawson; 95—(*top*) John Dawson, (*bottom*) Douglas Ray; 96—John Dawson; 98–99—(#13) John H. Beaman, (#14) Allan Roberts, all other photographs by Dr. Ralph Taggart; 100—Hermann Eisenbeiss/Photo Researchers.

Chapter 6

102—Werner Kalber/Busco Nester; 104—(*top*) Hugh Spencer/National Audubon Society, Inc., (*center*) Hugh Spencer, (*bottom*) John Dawson; 106—J. T. Bonner; 108—drawings by John Dawson; 110—John Dawson after P. H. Raven and H. Curtis, *Biology of Plants*, © 1970 by Worth Publishers; 111—(*bottom*) John Dawson; 112—(*top*) Dr. David R. Stadler; 113—(*left*) Stanley L. Flegler, Michigan State University, (*right*) Ward's Natural Science Establishment; 114—(*top*) S. Rannels/Grant Heilman, (*bottom*) John Dawson; 115—(*top*) John Running, (*bottom*) Grant Haist; 116—(*top left*) Allan Roberts, (*top right*) USDA Photo, (*center*) Grant Haist, (*bottom*) Dennis Brokaw.

Chapter 7

118—William H. Amos; 120–122—John Dawson; 123—(*top*) John Dawson, (*bottom*) James Endicott; 124—(*top left*) John Dawson, (*top right, bottom*) James Dutcher; 125, 126—John Dawson; 127—(*top, bottom left*) John Dawson after I. W. Sherman and V. G. Sherman, *The Invertebrates: Function and Form*, Macmillan Publishing Co., 1970, (*bottom right*) John Dawson after Ralph Buchsbaum, *Animals Without Backbones: An Introduction to the Invertebrates*, University of Chicago Press, 1948; 128—(*left*) John Dawson, (*right*) John Dawson after Parker and Haswell, *A Textbook of Zoology*, 6th ed., Macmillan Publishing Co., 1940; 129—John Dawson after Ralph Buchsbaum, *Animals Without Backbones: An Introduction to the Invertebrates*, University of Chicago Press, 1948; 130—(*top*) John Dawson, (*bottom*) Paul K. Dayton; 131—(*top left*) John Dawson after Ralph Buchsbaum, *Animals Without Backbones: An Introduction to the Invertebrates*, University of Chicago Press, 1948, (*top right*) James Dutcher, (*bottom left*) Grant Heilman, (*bottom right*) M. Woodbridge Williams; 132, 134—John Dawson; 135—John Dawson after Paul A. Meglitsch, *Invertebrate Zoology*, 2nd ed., Oxford University Press, 1972; 136–138—John Dawson; 139—John Dawson after Bayer and Owre, *Free-Living Lower Invertebrates*, Macmillan Publishing Co., 1968; 140—Dr. Eugene Kozloff.

Chapter 8

142—B. K. Filshie and C. D. Beaton, CSIRO Division of Entomology, Canberra, Australia; 143—John Dawson; 144—Louis Neiheisel; 145—John Dawson after T. I. Storer, *General Zoology*, 3rd ed., © 1957 by McGraw-Hill, Inc. Used with permission of McGraw–Hill Book Company; 146—(*left*) Allan Roberts, (*center*) Eugene N. Kozloff, (*top right*) James Dutcher; 147—(*top*) Eugene N. Kozloff, (*bottom*) John Dawson; 148—Louis Neiheisel; 149—(*top*) Courtesy of the American Museum of Natural History, (*center left*) Dennis Brokaw, (*center right, bottom*) Eugene N. Kozloff; 150—(*top center*) Grant Heilman, (*top right, bottom right*) James Dutcher, (*bottom left*) courtesy of Fisher Scientific Co., Educational Materials Division, Chicago; 151—Allan Roberts; 152—(*top left*) Bio Photography: Richard Trump, (*top right, bottom left, center right*) Grant Haist, (*center left, bottom right*) Eugene N. Kozloff, (*center*) Jack Dermid; 153, 154—John Dawson; 155—(*top left, center right*) Grant Heilman, (*top right*) James Dutcher, (*bottom center*) Douglas P. Wilson, (*bottom right*) Allan Roberts, 156—(*left*) Courtesy of the American Museum of Natural History, (*right*) General Electric Medical Systems Division; 157—(*left*) John Dawson after Ralph Buchsbaum, *Animals Without Backbones: An Introduction to the Invertebrates*, University of Chicago Press, 1948, (*right*) John Dawson; 158—(*left*) John Dawson, (*right*) Julie Hernly; 159—John Dawson; 160—(*top left*) Douglas P. Wilson, (*center left*) M. Woodbridge Williams, (*bottom left*) William H. Amos, (*center right*) Gordon Robilliard, (*top right, bottom right*) Eugene N. Kozloff; 161, 162—John Dawson; 163—(*top*) Grant

Heilman, (*bottom*) James Dutcher; 164—(*top left, bottom left*) Jack Dermid, (*top center, center right*) Grant Heilman, (*top right, center top left*) Ron Garrison and F. D. Schmidt/San Diego Zoo, (*center left*) Corson Hirschfeld, (*bottom right*) Dr. Franklin Kosdon; 165, 166—John Dawson; 167—(*top left and right, bottom right*) Ron Garrison and F. D. Schmidt/San Diego Zoo, (*top center*) James Dutcher, (*bottom left*) G. R. Roberts, Nelson, New Zealand; 168—(*top right*) Leonard Lee Rue III, (*top center right, bottom left, center*) Ron Garrison and F. D. Schmidt/San Diego Zoo, (*center left*) Jack Dermid, (*bottom center*) James Dutcher, (*bottom right*) Irven DeVore/Anthto-Photo.

Chapter 9

170—NASA; 172–173—Calvin Woo; 175—John Dawson after Robert Jastrow, *Red Giants and White Dwarfs*, Harper & Row, 1971; 176—Courtesy of S. W. Fox, Institute for Molecular and Cellular Evolution, University of Miami; 178—J. William Schopf, University of California, Los Angeles; 180—Barbara Hoopes; 181—(*top*) Herb Orth, painting by James Lewicki, Time-Life Picture Agency, © Time, Inc., (*bottom*) John Dawson; 182–183—Painting by James Lewicki, Time-Life Picture Agency, © Time, Inc.; 184—Courtesy of Her Majesty's Geological Survey, British Crown copyright; 185—Courtesy of the American Museum of Natural History; 186–187—Painting by R. Zallinger, Time-Life Picture Agency, © Time, Inc.; 197—(*bottom*) Werner Wetzel/PPS; 188, 190–193—Painting by R. Zallinger, Time-Life Picture Agency, © Time, Inc.

Chapter 10

196—Jon Brenneis; 197—Fisher Scientific Company; 200—Louis Neiheisel; 201—John Dawson; 202—Louis Neiheisel; 203—Doug Armstrong; 204—Louis Neiheisel; 205—Doug Armstrong; 206—Louis Neiheisel; 207—Julie Hernly; 208—Calvin Woo; 212—Louis Neiheisel.

Chapter 11

214—F. D. Schmidt/San Diego Zoo; 216—John Dawson; 218—Barbara Hoopes; 219—Doug Armstrong; 221—Calvin Woo; 223—Louis Neiheisel; 225—Doug Armstrong; 228—John Dawson; 231, 233—Doug Armstrong; 235—John Dawson; 240–242—Doug Armstrong.

Chapter 12

244—Hale Observatories; 247—Calvin Woo; 248, 249—Doug Armstrong; 250—The Granger Collection; 251, 252, 254, 255, 258—Doug Armstrong.

Chapter 13

262—Dr. Jean Paul Revel, California Institute of Technology; 263—(*top left, bottom*) The Bettmann Archive, Inc., (*top right*) The Granger Collection; 264—Photograph courtesy of Dr. J. Rhodin, from Rhodin, *Histology*, Oxford University Press, 1974, drawings by John Dawson; 265—Photograph courtesy of Dr. William A. Jensen, drawings by John

Dawson; 266—Doug Armstrong; 267—John Dawson; 268–269—(*top*) Doug Armstrong; 268—(*bottom*) Dr. Edward J. Reith; 269—(*bottom left*) Courtesy of Dr. J. Rhodin, from Rhodin, *Histology*, Oxford University Press, 1974, (*bottom right*) courtesy of Dr. E. deHarven and Miss N. Lampen, Sloan-Kettering Institute for Cancer Research; 271—Tom Lewis; 272—(*left*) Tom Lewis, (*right*) Vincent T. Marchesi; 273—(*top, bottom right*) John Dawson, (*bottom left*) Vincent T. Marchesi; 274 and 276—John Dawson adapted from S. J. Singer and G. L. Nicholson, "The Fluid Mosaic Model of the Structure of Cell Membranes," *Science*, vol. 175, pp. 720–731, February 18, 1972. Copyright © 1972 by the American Association for the Advancement of Science; 275 and 278—Doug Armstrong; 279—(*top*) Vincent T. Marchesi, (*bottom*) Barbara Hoopes; 280—Keith R. Porter; 281—(*top*) Dr. William A. Jensen, (*bottom*) G. F. Leedale, J. D. Meeuse, and E. G. Pringsheim in *Arch Mikrobiology*, vol. 50, 1965; 282—Keith R. Porter; 283—David M. Phillips; 284—(*top*) Keith R. Porter, (*bottom*) Barbara Hoopes; 285—Dr. Donald Fawcett, Harvard Medical School; 287—(*top*) James Herbert Taylor, Florida State University, Tallahassee, (*bottom*) John Dawson; 288—John Dawson; 289—Doug Armstrong; 290—(*left, top right*) John Dawson, (*bottom right*) photo courtesy of Fisher Scientific Company, Education Materials Division, Chicago; 291—(*top left*) David M. Phillips, (*top right*) Doug Armstrong, (*bottom*) J. B. Rattner and K. Phillips, *Journal of Cell Biology*, vol. 57, 1973; 293—William A. Jensen; 294—(*top, top center*) Dr. Elliott Robbins. (*center bottom*) David M. Phillips, (*bottom left*) Dr. Lewis G. Tilney, (*bottom center*) Myron C. Ledbetter, Brookhaven National Laboratory, (*bottom right*) John Dawson; 295—(*top*) J. B. Rattner, (*center*) E. R. Lewis and D. E. Hillman, University of California, Berkeley, (*bottom*) Dr. Goran Bredberg, Department of Otolaryngology, University of Uppsala, Sweden; 296—Keith R. Porter; 297—Myron C. Ledbetter, Brookhaven National Laboratory; 298—(*top left*) Courtesy of Sherwood W. Wise, Florida State University, (*top center*) Mick Church, (*top right*) Dr. S. Bartnicki-Garcia, University of California, Riverside, (*center left*) B. K. Filshie and C. D. Beaton, CSIRO Division of Entomology, Canberra, Australia, (*center right*) Amoco Production Research Corp., Tulsa, Oklahoma, George Massey and Aureal T. Cross, (*bottom left*) Dr. Jerome Gross, (*bottom right*) The Bettmann Archive, Inc.

Chapter 14

300—Construction by Joyce Fitzgerald, Photography by Werner Kalber, Busco Nestor Studios; 302—Doug Armstrong; 303, 304—Louis Neiheisel; 305—(*top*) Doug Armstrong, (*bottom*) Louis Neiheisel; 311 — Louis Neiheisel; 312— Doug Armstrong; 313—Louis Neiheisel; 314—Calvin Woo; 316—Louis Neiheisel; 317—Doug Armstrong; 318—(*left*) K. R. Porter, (*right*) Rob-

ert Kinyon/Millsap and Kinyon; 319—Robert Kinyon/Millsap and Kinyon; 320—Dr. H. Fernandez-Moran, University of Chicago; 321—Robert Kinyon/Millsap & Kinyon; 323, 324—Louis Neiheisel; 325—C. R. Hackenbrock, *Journal of Cell Biology*, 37:345, 1968; 326—Louis Neiheisel; 328—Doug Armstrong.

Chapter 15

330—Jack Dermid; 332—(*top*) Dr. William Jensen, (*center*) John Dawson, (*bottom left*) Myron C. Ledbetter/Brookhaven National Laboratory, (*bottom center*) Garth Nicholson, (*bottom right*) R. B. Park; 333—Doug Armstrong; 335—The Art Works; 337—Doug Armstrong; 338—(*left*) Dr. R. S. Wolfe, (*right*) Doug Armstrong; 339, 340—Doug Armstrong; 342—John Dawson; 343—Louis Neiheisel; 345, 346—Doug Armstrong.

Chapter 16

348—Grant Heilman; 351, 352—Louis Neiheisel; 353—The Granger Collection; 356—Barbara Hoopes; 357—Calvin Woo; 358—(*top*) John Pierce, (*bottom left and right*) The Nobel Foundation, (*bottom center right*) Wide World Photos; 359, 360—John Dawson; 361—(*top*) Tom Lewis after William Keeton, *Biological Science*, W. W. Norton & Co., 1967, (*bottom*) Dr. James Kezer, Department of Biology, University of Oregon; 364—Dr. Ulrich Clever; 365—From C. B. Bridges, "Correspondences Between Linkage Maps and Salivary Chromosome Structure, as Illustrated in the Tip of Chromosome 2R of *Drosophila melanogaster*," *Cytologia*, Fujii Jubilee Volume, 1937, p. 750, fig. 1; 366—Dr. William D. Loughman, University of California, Berkeley; 368—The Nobel Foundation; 369—(*top*) Douglas Roy, (*center*) Gabrielle Wunderlich.

Chapter 17

372—O. L. Miller, B. A. Hamkalo, and C. A. Thomas Jr., *Science*, vol. 169, 1970; 374—Louis Neiheisel; 375—(*left*) Tom Lewis after William Keeton, *Biological Science*, W. W. Norton & Co., 1967, (*top right*) courtesy Cold Spring Harbor Laboratory, (*center, bottom right*) The Nobel Foundation; 376—Tom Lewis after Payson Stevens; 377—(*top*) John Dawson, (*bottom*) courtesy of H. Fernandez-Moran, University of Chicago; 378, 379—Doug Armstrong; 380—The Nobel Foundation; 381—(*left*) Doug Armstrong, (*right*) Tom Lewis; 382—(*top*) John Cairns, (*bottom*) Julie Hernly after Prescott, *Proceedings of the National Academy of Sciences*, vol. 69, 1972; 384, 387—Louis Neiheisel; 388—Doug Armstrong; 389—Louis Neiheisel; 391–393—Doug Armstrong; 394—Calvin Woo adapted from S. H. Kim *et al.*, "Three-Dimensional Tertiary Structure of Yeast Phenylalanine Transfer RNA," *Science*, vol. 185, pp. 435–440, fig. 1, August 2, 1974; 396, 398—Calvin Woo; 400—(*top*) Doug Armstrong, (*bottom left*) courtesy of Alexander Rich, (*bottom right*) courtesy of Dr. Henry S. Slayter, Harvard Medical School.

Chapter 18

402—Allan Roberts; 405—(*top*) Mia Tegner, Scripps Institution of Oceanography, (*bottom*) Everett Anderson, *Journal of Cell Biology*, vol. 37, 1974; 406—(*bottom*) Terry Lamb; 408—Barbara Hoopes; 409—Photographs courtesy George Watchmaker and Hector Timourian, University of California, Lawrence Livermore Laboratory, under the auspices of the U.S.A.E.C., drawing by Julie Hernly; 410—Ward's Natural Science Establishment; 411—Terry Lamb; 412—Julie Hernly after Perry Karfunkel, "The Mechanisms of Neural Tube Formation," *International Review of Cytology*, Academic Press, 1974; 413—Julie Hernly, (*left*) after Perry Karfunkel, "The Mechanisms of Neural Tube Formation," *International Review of Cytology*, Academic Press, 1974; 414—Barbara Hoopes; 415—Terry Lamb; 417—Doug Armstrong; 418—(*top*) Joseph Gall, Yale University, (*bottom*) O. L. Miller Jr., Barbara R. Beatty, and Barbara A. Hamkalo, "Nuclear Structure and Function During Amphibian Oogenesis," *Oogenesis*, Biggers and Schultz (eds.), University Park Press, 1972; 419—(*top*) Dr. David Brown, Carnegie Institution, (*bottom*) Oscar Miller, Oak Ridge National Laboratory; 420—Terry Lamb after Hans Spemann, *Embryonic Development and Induction*, Hafner Publishing Co., 1962. By permission of Macmillan Publishing Co.; 421—Terry Lamb; 422—Terry Lamb after Hans Spemann, *Embryonic Development and Induction*, Hafner Publishing Co., 1962. By permission of Macmillan Publishing Co.

Chapter 19

426—Dr. E. G. Cutter from *Plant Anatomy*, Part 2, Addison-Wesley and Edward Arnold (Publishers) Ltd.; 428—Dr. E. G. Cutter; 429—John Dawson, Barbara Hoopes; 431—Dr. R. H. Falk; 432—(*top*) Dr. E. G. Cutter from *Phytomorphology*, vol. 17, 1967, p. 440, (*bottom*) John Dawson; 433—(*left*) John Dawson, (*right*) Grant Heilman; 434—(*top*) Dr. E. G. Cutter; 435—Joe Garcia; 436—(*right*) John Dawson; 437—John Dawson; 439—Dr. E. G. Cutter, from *Plant Anatomy: Experiment and Interpretation*, Part 1, Addison-Wesley and Edward Arnold (Publishers) Ltd.; 440—(*right*) Barbara Hoopes.

Chapter 20

442—Dr. Jack Griffith; 444—Barbara Hoopes; 445, 448–450—Doug Armstrong; 452—The Nobel Foundation; 453—Calvin Woo; 455—Doug Armstrong; 456—Calvin Woo after Payson Stevens; 457—Doug Armstrong; 458—Calvin Woo after Payson Stevens; 459—François Jacob; 460—Barbara Hoopes; 461—Dr. Ulrich Clever; 463—Barbara Hoopes; 466—Calvin Woo.

Chapter 21

470—V-Dia/Scala; 471–473—Doug Armstrong; 474—Millsap and Kinyon; 475—(*top*) John Dawson after Arthur C. Guyton, *Textbook of Medical Physiology*, 4th ed., Philadel-phia, W. B. Saunders Company, 1971, (*bottom*) Barbara Hoopes; 476—Dick Oden; 477—John Dawson after Warren R. Guild, Robert E. Fuisz, and Samuel Bojar, *The Science of Health*, © 1969; by permission of Prentice-Hall, Inc., Englewood Cliffs, N.J.; 478—Barbara Hoopes; 479—Ray Bravo; 481—Doug Armstrong after Arthur C. Guyton, *Textbook of Medical Physiology*, 4th ed., Philadelphia, W. B. Saunders Company, 1971; 482—From R. E. Dickerson and I. Geis, *The Structure and Action of Proteins*, W. A. Benjamin, Inc., Menlo Park, California. Copyright © 1969 by Dickerson and Geis; 483, 484—Doug Armstrong; 486—Millsap and Kinyon; 487—Doug Armstrong; 488—(*top*) John Dawson, (*bottom*) Doug Armstrong; 490—Kwo-Yih Yeh; 492—John Dawson.

Chapter 22

494—William Vandivert; 496—Barbara Hoopes; 499—(*top*) Doug Armstrong, (*bottom*) Barbara Hoopes; 501—Barbara Hoopes; 502—(*top*) Barbara Hoopes, (*bottom*) Doug Armstrong; 504, 505—Doug Armstrong; 507—John Dawson; 509—Barbara Hoopes; 510—Doug Armstrong; 511—John Dawson; 512—Doug Armstrong.

Chapter 23

514—John Launois/Black Star; 515—Tom Lewis after William Keeton, *Biological Science*, W. W. Norton & Company, 1967; 516—Tom Lewis; 518—Bernard Phinney; 520—John D. Goeschl; 521—Terry Lamb; 522—(*top*) S. H. Wittwer, Michigan Agricultural Experiment Station, (*bottom*) Neill Cate after P. W. Brian and H. G. Hemming, 1955, with permission of Physiologia Planturum (Scandinavian Society for Plant Physiology); 524—Tom Lewis after William Keeton, *Biological Science*, W. W. Norton & Company, 1967; 525—(*center, bottom*) A. H. Westing.

Chapter 24

528—Construction by Suzan Anson, Photography by Busco Nestor Studios; 529—The Granger Collection; 530—Doug Armstrong; 531, 534—Calvin Woo; 536—John Dawson; 537—Ron Estrine; 538—John Dawson; 539—Tom Lewis after Payson Stevens; 540—Francis V. Chisari, M.D., Department of Molecular Immunology, Scripps Clinic and Research Foundation, La Jolla, California; 542—Calvin Woo; 543—Doug Armstrong.

Chapter 25

546—E. R. Lewis; 548—(*top right*) Doug Armstrong, (*center*) Terry Lamb after D. Aidley, *The Physiology of Excitable Cells*, © 1971 by Cambridge University Press, (*bottom*) Lester V. Bergman; 549—(*top*) Sir John Eccles, (*bottom*) Doug Armstrong; 551—Doug Armstrong; 552—Doug Armstrong after John C. Eccles, *The Physiology of Nerve Cells*, fig. 8, © 1957 by The Johns Hopkins Press; 553—Barbara Hoopes; 554—Julie Hernly; 555—(*top*) Calvin Woo; 556—Lester V. Bergman; 557—(*left*) Doug Armstrong, (*right*) S. L. Palay; 558—(*left*) Barbara Hoopes, (*right*) Doug Armstrong after John C. Eccles, "Modes of Transmission Within Nerve Cells and Between Nerve Cells," *Nova Acta Leopoldina*, vol. 28, 1964; 559—Doug Armstrong; 561—Julie Hernly; 563—Calvin Woo after Willows, Dorsett, and Hoyle, *Journal of Neurobiology*, vol. 4, p. 255–285, © 1973 by John Wiley & Sons. Reprinted with permission; 564—Tom Lewis; 566, 567—Terry Lamb; 568—Terry Lamb after D. Aidley, *The Physiology of Excitable Cells*, © 1971 by Cambridge University Press; 570—(*top*) Douglas Roy, (*bottom*) Terry Lamb; 571—Dick Oden; 572—John Dawson; 573—Millsap and Kinyon.

Chapter 26

578—Andreas Feininger; 581—Dick Oden; 582—John Pierce; 583—(*right*) John Dawson; 586—John Dawson; 587—Doug Armstrong; 588—John Dawson; 589—Doug Armstrong; 590—The Art Works; 591—John Dawson; 593—Doug Armstrong; 596—John Dawson; 597—Tom Lewis; 598—Courtesy of Hugh E. Huxley; 599–602—John Dawson.

Chapter 27

604—From Desmond Morris, *Proceedings of the Zoological Society*, London, vol. 131, © 1958 by The Zoological Society of London; 606—Barbara Hoopes; 607—John Dawson; 608—(*left*) Thomas McAvoy/Time-Life Picture Agency, © Time, Inc., (*right*) John Dawson; 610—Doug Armstrong; 611—(*top, bottom*) Steve McCarroll, (*center*) Doug Armstrong; 612—San Diego Zoo; 613—John Dawson; 615—Doug Armstrong; 617—Neill Cate.

Chapter 28

618—Ron Garrison/San Diego Zoo; 620—John Dawson from N. Tinbergen, *Animal Behaviour*, © 1965 by Time, Inc.; 621—Barbara Hoopes adapted from F. C. Lincoln, U.S. Government Printing Office, 1950; 622—(*left*) Roy Pinney/National Audubon Society, (*top right*) John H. Gerard/National Audubon Society, (*bottom right*) George Leavens; 624—(*left*) Doug Armstrong, (*right*) Doug Armstrong after Ingold and Cox, *Annals of Botany*, Oxford University Press, 1959; 625—(*top*) Doug Armstrong, (*bottom*) Frank A. Brown Jr.; 626—Doug Armstrong; 627—Calvin Woo; 628—K. S. Rawson from *Photoperiodism and Related Phenomena in Plants and Animals*, #55. Copyright 1959 by the American Association for the Advancement of Science; 629—(*top*) J. Woodland Hastings, (*bottom*) Doug Armstrong.

Chapter 29

632—Tom Lewis; 633—John Dawson after N. Tinbergen, 1951; 634—Thomas McAvoy/Time-Life Picture Agency, © Time, Inc.; 635—John Dawson (*top*) after N. Tinbergen, 1951; 636—David Plowden/Photo Researchers; 637—Grant Heilman; 639—(*top*) Buddy Mays/Photo Researchers, (*bottom*) Carleton Ray/Photo Researchers; 640—(*left*) Grant

Haist, (*right*) John Dawson; 643—John Dawson; 644—Tom Lewis; 645—Doug Armstrong; 646—Roderick A. Suthers, Indiana University; 647—(*top*) Allan Roberts, (*bottom*) James Dutcher; 648—Thomas Eisner, Cornell University; 649—(*top*) Lynwood M. Chace, (*bottom*) Jen and Des Bartlett/Photo Researchers.

Chapter 30

652—Daniel H. Janzen; 658—(*left*) Photograph by H. G. Baker and B. J. Harris, *Evolution*, II:499–460, 1957, (*right*) Daniel H. Janzen; 660–661, 663—Daniel H. Janzen; 665—Treat Davidson/National Audubon Society.

Chapter 31

666—The Smithsonian Institution; 668, 669—Barbara Hoopes; 670, 672—Doug Armstrong; 673—Barbara Hoopes; 674—Barbara Hoopes adapted from E. Odum, *Fundamentals of Ecology*, 3rd ed., W. B. Saunders Company, 1971; 675—(*top*) Barbara Hoopes after Wilson and Bossert, *Primer of Population Biology*, Sinauer Associates, 1971, p. 140, (*bottom*) Doug Armstrong; 677—Calvin Woo adapted from G. F. Gause, *The Struggle for Existence*, ⓒ 1934 Williams & Wilkins Co., Baltimore; 679—(*top*) Barbara Hoopes, (*bottom*) Tom O'Mary after H. Odum, *Ecological Monographs*, 1957, and E. P. Odum, *Fundamentals of Ecology*, 3rd ed., ⓒ 1971 W. B. Saunders Co.; 682—John Dawson after E. P. Odum, *Fundamentals of Ecology*, 3rd ed., ⓒ 1971 W. B. Saunders Co.; 683—Calvin Woo; 684—(*top*) John Odam and Andy Lucas after Vernon C. Finch and Glenn T. Trewartha, *Physical Elements of Geography*, ⓒ 1949 McGraw-Hill Book Company, (*bottom*) Brain Hawkes/Carl Ostman Agency; 685—(*top*) Peter Murphy, Michigan State University, (*center*) Christopher Cross, (*bottom*) Ralph Taggart; 686—(*left*) John Lewis Stage/Photo Researchers, (*right*) Peter Murphy, Michigan State University; 687—Barbara Hoopes.

Chapter 32

690—Dr. Robert Hochmuth, Department of Biomedical Engineering, Washington University; 696—(*left*) Doug Armstrong after R. Ehrlich and R. W. Holm, *The Process of Evolution*, McGraw-Hill Book Company, 1963, (*right*) Calvin Woo; 698—Dr. H. B. D. Kettlewell; 699—Calvin Woo; 702—Neill Cate; 703—Dr. Robert Hochmuth, Department of Biomedical Engineering, Washington University; 704—Doug Armstrong (*bottom*) after M. F. Boyd (ed.), *Malariology*, W. B. Saunders Company, Philadelphia, 1949; 706—Calvin Woo adapted from F. Ayala and Tracy, *Proceedings of the National Academy of Science*, vol. 71, 1974; 707—(*left*) Hamptom L. Carson, (*right*) Dr. Harrison D. Stalker.

Chapter 33

710—European Art Color, Peter Adelberg, N.Y.; 712—(*top left, bottom right*) Ron Garrison and F. D. Schmidt/San Diego Zoo, (*top right*) Dorothy and Lewis Klein, (*bottom left*) George Holton/Photo Researchers, (*bottom center*) Irven DeVore/Anthro-Photo; 714—John Dawson; 716—Barbara Hoopes; 719—Doug Armstrong after Vincent M. Sarich, "The Origin of Hominids; An Immunological Approach," *Perspectives on Human Evolution*, S. L. Washburn and Phyllis Jay (eds.). Copyright ⓒ 1968 by Holt, Rinehart and Winston Publishers. Reprinted with permission; 722—John T. Robinson; 723—(*left*) Karl Nicholason, (*right*) John T. Robinson; 724—John Dawson; 726—Calvin Woo; 727—Karl Nicholason; 730—John Dawson.

Chapter 34

734—From R. Rugh and L. B. Shettles, *From Conception to Birth: The Drama of Life's Beginnings*, Harper & Row, 1971; 736—(*left*) John Dawson; 737—John Dawson; 738—Ray Bravo; 741—The Art Works after Masters and Johnson, *Human Sexual Response*, Little, Brown and Co., 1966; 743—Drawings by Tom Lewis, Photographs by Werner Kalber/PPS; 744—(*top left, bottom right*) From L. B. Shettles, *Ovum Humanum*, Urban and Schwarzenberg, 1960; 748—John Dawson.

Chapter 35

752—Photographie Giraudon; 753—Calvin Woo adapted from National Center for Health Statistics; 754—Calvin Woo adapted from Department of Health, Education and Welfare; 755—Calvin Woo adapted from U. S. Public Health Service, Vital Statistics of the United States; 756—(*top*) Calvin Woo, (*bottom*) Doug Armstrong adapted from National Center for Health Statistics; 757—Doug Armstrong adapted from U. S. Public Health Service, Vital Statistics of the United States; 759—(*top*) John Dawson, (*bottom*) from Department of Neurosciences, University of California, San Diego; 764—Doug Armstrong adapted from U. S. Public Health Service; 765—(*top*) Dr. Max E. Elliott, University of California, San Diego, (*center*) Patrick Thurston/Transworld Feature Syndicate, Inc., (*bottom*) Tom Lewis; 766—Doug Armstrong adapted from World Health Organization, 1970; 767—Julius Weber.

Chapter 36

772—From R. Rugh and L. B. Shettles, *From Conception to Birth: The Drama of Life's Beginnings*, Harper & Row, 1971.

Chapter 37

784—Werner Kalber/PPS, William MacDonald; 786—(*bottom*) Neill Cate after R. R. Doane, *World Balance Sheet*, Harper & Row, 1957; 787—Calvin Woo after E. J. Kormondy, "Natural and Human Ecosystems," *Human Ecology*, F. Sargent (ed.), 1974; 788—Neill Cate after *Population Bulletin*, vol. 18, no. 1. Courtesy Population Reference Bureau, Inc., Washington, D.C.; 789—Photograph by Dan Morrill, Graph by Doug Armstrong; 791—Doug Armstrong after J. Bonner, *The Next 90 Years*, R. P. Schuster (ed.), California Institute of Technology; 794–795—Doug Armstrong after NEA. Reprinted by permission of Newspaper Enterprise Association.